Vorträge des X. Internationalen Leibniz-Kongresses · VI

„Für unser Glück oder das Glück anderer"
Vorträge des X. Internationalen Leibniz-Kongresses
Hannover, 18. – 23. Juli 2016

Veranstalter:

Gottfried-Wilhelm-Leibniz-Gesellschaft e.V.
Leibniz-Stiftungsprofessur der Leibniz Universität Hannover

in Verbindung mit:

Leibniz Society of North America
Sociedad Española Leibniz
Societas Leibnitiana Japonica
Sodalitas Leibnitiana
Société d'études leibniziennes de langue française
Association Leibniz Israel
Red Iberoamericana Leibniz
Centre d'Études Leibniziennes
Societatea Leibniz din România
Sino-German Leibniz Research Centre

Georg Olms Verlag
Hildesheim · Zürich · New York
2017

„Für unser Glück oder das Glück anderer"
Vorträge des X. Internationalen Leibniz-Kongresses
Hannover, 18. – 23. Juli 2016

Herausgegeben von
Wenchao Li

in Verbindung mit
Ute Beckmann, Sven Erdner, Esther-Maria Errulat,
Jürgen Herbst, Helena Iwasinski und Simona Noreik

Band VI

Georg Olms Verlag
Hildesheim · Zürich · New York
2017

Das Bild auf dem Umschlag wurde entnommen aus:
Johann August Eberhard, Gottfried Wilhelm Freyherr von Leibnitz. Chemnitz 1795,
Nachdruck Hildesheim 1982, zwischen S. 176 und 177 („Leibnitz stirbt").

Das Werk ist urheberrechtlich geschützt. Jede Verwertung
außerhalb der engen Grenzen des Urheberrechtsgesetzes ist ohne Zustimmung
des Verlages unzulässig. Das gilt insbesondere für Vervielfältigungen,
Übersetzungen, Mikroverfilmungen und die Einspeicherung und
Verarbeitung in elektronischen Systemen.

Die Deutsche Bibliothek verzeichnet diese Publikation
in der Deutschen Nationalbibliografie; detaillierte bibliografische Daten
sind im Internet über http://dnb.ddb.de abrufbar

ISO 9706
Gedruckt auf säurefreiem und alterungsbeständigem Papier
Umschlaggestaltung: Inga Günther, 31134 Hildesheim
Satz: Simona Noreik, 38300 Wolfenbüttel
Herstellung: Hubert & Co, 37079 Göttingen
Printed in Germany
© Georg Olms Verlag AG, Hildesheim 2017
Alle Rechte vorbehalten
www.olms.de
ISBN 978-3-487-15439-8

Inhaltsverzeichnis

Abkürzungsverzeichnis 11

Vorwort 13

Eröffnungsansprache und Grussworte

Eröffnungsansprache
Prof. Dr.-Ing. Erich Barke, Präsident der Gottfried-Wilhelm-Leibniz-Gesellschaft 17

Grußwort zur Kongresseröffnung
Thomas Herrmann, Bürgermeister der Landeshauptstadt Hannover 21

Grußwort zum Empfang der Teilnehmerinnen und Teilnehmer
im Neuen Rathaus
Thomas Herrmann, Bürgermeister der Landeshauptstadt Hannover 27

Eröffnungsvorträge

Leibniz on War and Peace and the Common Good
Catherine Wilson (York) 33

On the Grain of Sand and Heaven's Infinity
Herbert Breger (Hanover) 63

Plenarvorträge

Pragmatism and Idealism in Leibniz's Ways of Distinguishing Real
from Imaginary Phenomena
Robert Merrihew Adams (Princeton, NJ) 83

Leibniz's Mirrors: Reflecting the Past
Pauline Phemister (Edinburgh) 93

Les étapes de la dynamique leibnizienne: de la réforme à la fondation
Michel Fichant (Paris) 109

„[…] daß die Nachwelt von seinen Meriten und großen Capazität nicht viel mehr als ein blosses Andencken von seiner Gelehrsamkeit aufweisen kan". Zur frühen Leibnizrezeption nach 1716
Nora Gädeke (Hannover) 129

Why Leibniz Was Not an Eclectic Philosopher
Ursula Goldenbaum (Atlanta, GA) 153

Leibniz's Mereology in the Essays on Logical Calculus of 1686–90
Massimo Mugnai (Pisa) 175

Thinking in the Age of the Learned Journal: Leibniz's Modular Philosophy
Daniel Garber (Princeton, NJ) 195

ÖFFENTLICHER ABENDVORTRAG

Individualität bei Leibniz
Volker Gerhardt (Berlin/Hamburg) 207

FESTVORTRAG ZUR VERLEIHUNG DER VGH-PREISE

Leibniz' unverstandene, aber wohl zu verstehende Metaphysik
Heinrich Schepers (Münster) 227

BERICHTE DER LEIBNIZ-EDITIONSSTELLEN

Leibniz-Edition Berlin
Harald Siebert 245

Leibniz-Forschungsstelle Hannover / Leibniz-Archiv
Michael Kempe 251

Leibniz-Forschungsstelle Münster
Stephan Meier-Oeser 267

Leibniz-Edition Potsdam
Friedrich Beiderbeck / Stephan Waldhoff 273

Einführung in die Benutzung der Akademie-Ausgabe
Herma Kliege-Biller (Münster) 281

SEKTIONSVORTRÄGE

The Role of aequitas in Leibniz's Legal Philosophy – a Formal Reconstruction
Matthias Armgardt (Konstanz) 305

Leibniz and Mortalism
Aderemi Artis (Flint) 315

Leibniz, Marx und der Marxismus. Theoretische Grundlagen und konkrete Beispiele einer komplexen Beziehungsgeschichte
Luca Basso (Padua) 325

Geschichte und Methode – Leibniz' Beitrag zur Geschichtswissenschaft
Annette von Boetticher (Hannover) 337

La critique leibnizienne de la définition cartésienne du mouvement
Laurence Bouquiaux (Liège) 353

The Material Perspective in Leibniz through the *Sympnoia panta*
Manuel Higueras Cabrera (Granada) 367

Spinoza and Leibniz on Chimaeras and Other Unthinkable Things
J. Thomas Cook (Winter Park, FL) 375

On the Leibnizian Principle of Continuity
Sorin Costreie (Bucharest) 389

Perspectivisme et Monadologie
Martine de Gaudemar (Paris) 399

Can We Unify Theories of the Origin of Finite Things in Leibniz's
De Summa Rerum?
Shohei Edamura (Kanazawa) 415

Leibniz on Compossibility and the Unity of Space and Time
Michael Futch (Tulsa, OK) 429

Leibniz in Early Twentieth-Century Spanish Philosophy: d'Ors,
Ortega y Gasset, and Zubiri
Mattia Geretto (Venice) 441

Gottfried Wilhelm Leibniz' Naturrecht im Kontext der frühneuzeitlichen
Autonomisierung der Ethik
Holger Glinka (Berlin) 455

Leibniz on Time and Duration
Geoffrey Gorham (Saint Paul, MN) 473

Calculus Ratiocinator: Aspects of Leibniz' Contribution to the Origins
of Symbolic Logic
Natascha Gruver (Berkeley/Vienna) 487

Ad felicitatem publicam: Leibniz' „Scientia Generalis" – Momente einer
Wissenschaftskonzeption und deren gegenwärtige Relevanz
Natascha Gruver / Cornelius Zehetner (Wien) 499

Leibniz's View on Time in the Light of His General Views on the Nature
of Mathematics. Reading Emily Grosholz's "Leibniz's Mathematical and
Philosophical Analysis of Time"
Julia Jankowska (Warsaw) 513

The Problem of Scientific Demonstration in Early Writings of Leibniz
(1667–1672)
Ryoko Konno (Paris) 525

The End of Melancholy. Deleuze and Benjamin on Leibniz
and the Baroque
Mogens Lærke (Lyon) 539

Leibniz' Diskussion mit Baudelot über den Pariser Nautenpfeiler oder
Wie weit trägt die Sprache als Quelle der Geschichtsschreibung?
Stefan Luckscheiter (Potsdam) 553

Leibniz's Language Tools, Practices, and Strategies: Notes on
De Docendis Linguis
Cristina Marras (Rome) 567

The Role of 'ius strictum' in the Legal Philosophy of Leibniz
Stephan Meder (Hannover) 581

Raummetaphorik in Sprache, Denken und Realität. Leibniz über
Präpositionen
Stephan Meier-Oeser (Münster) 617

Von der „Cité de Dieu" zum „weltbürgerlichen Ganzen".
Zu Glückseligkeit, Kulturarbeit und Moral bei Leibniz und Kant
Anselm Model (Freiburg im Breisgau) 631

Das andere „Beste". Leibniz und das allgemeine Wohl
Keisuke Nagatsuna (Tokio) 639

Leibniz and the Political Theology of the Chinese
Eric S. Nelson (Hong Kong) 647

The Language of the Last Leibniz: *Monadologie* vs. *Principes*
Roberto Palaia (Rome) 665

Leibniz in Rom
Roberto Palaia (Rom) 673

Francesco Bianchini und die römische Kalenderkongregation
Margherita Palumbo (Rom) 685

Leibniz and minutiae
Enrico Pasini (Turin) 697

Malebranche dans le *Discours de métaphysique* : à propos des notions de Dieu et de perfection
Paul Rateau (Paris) 707

"La place d'autruy". Perspectivism and Justice in Leibniz
Mariangela Priarolo (Siena) 721

Leibniz' Akademiepläne als europäisches Projekt
Hartmut Rudolph (Hannover) 737

Leibniz' Begriff der „Justitia". Mit Schwerpunkt auf der „aequitas"
Kiyoshi Sakai (Tokio) 747

Erudition, Rhetoric and Scientific Hypothesis. Some Remarks on the Structure of Leibniz's *Protogaea*
Federico Silvestri (Milan) 761

The Pharmaceutical Preparations in Leibniz' Manuscripts: Presentation and Comments
Sebastian W. Stork (Berlin) 773

Natürliche Theologie und Philosophia perennis. Leibniz' Interpretation der alten und modernen chinesischen Philosophie in der Abhandlung Niccolò Longobardis S.J.
Rita Widmaier (Essen) 781

Sartres und Leibnizens Sicht auf Freiheit und Faktizität
Rainer E. Zimmermann (München/Cambridge) 807

Leibnizforschung im Spiegel von zehn Leibniz-Kongressen
Hans Poser (Berlin) 823

Corrigenda 829

Alphabetisches Verzeichnis der Autorinnen und Autoren (Bd. I–V) 831

Abkürzungsverzeichnis

A Gottfried Wilhelm Leibniz: *Sämtliche Schriften und Briefe*, hrsg. v. d. Preußischen (später: Berlin-Brandenburgischen und Göttinger) Akademie der Wissenschaften zu Berlin, Darmstadt (später: Leipzig, zuletzt: Berlin) 1923 ff. (Akademie-Ausgabe).

C *Opuscules et fragments inédits de Leibniz. Extraits des manuscrits* […] par Louis Couturat, Paris 1903 (Nachdruck: Hildesheim 1961 und 1966).

Dutens Gottfried Wilhelm Leibniz: *Opera omnia, nunc primum collecta* […] *studio Ludovici Dutens*, T. 1–6, Genevae 1768.

GM Gottfried Wilhelm Leibniz: *Leibnizens mathematische Schriften*, Bd. 1–7, hrsg. v. C. I. Gerhardt. Berlin (später: Halle) 1849–1863 (Neudruck: Hildesheim 1962).

GP Gottfried Wilhelm Leibniz: *Die philosophischen Schriften von Leibniz*, Bd. 1–7, hrsg. v. Carl Immanuel Gerhardt, Berlin 1875–1890 (Neudruck: Hildesheim 1960–1961).

Grua Gottfried Wilhelm Leibniz: *Textes inédits d'après les manuscrits de la Bibliothèque provinciale de Hanovre*, vol. 1–2, publ. et ann. par Gaston Grua, Paris 1948.

Klopp Gottfried Wilhelm Leibniz: *Die Werke von Leibniz*, Reihe I, Bd. 1–11, hrsg. v. Onno Klopp, Hannover 1864–1884.

LBr Nieders. Landesbibliothek Hannover, Leibniz-Briefwechsel.

LH Nieders. Landesbibliothek Hannover, Leibniz-Handschriften.

VE Vorausedition der Akademie-Ausgabe.

Vorwort

Mit dem vorliegenden VI. Band wird die schriftliche Dokumentation des X. Internationalen Leibniz-Kongresses abgeschlossen.

In den Band aufgenommen wurden die Eröffnungsansprache von Prof. Erich Barke, Präsident der Gottfried-Wilhelm-Leibniz-Gesellschaft, das Grußwort von Thomas Herrmann, Bürgermeister der Landeshauptstadt Hannover, die Eröffnungsvorträge von Catherine Wilson und Herbert Breger, sowie weitere Plenarvorträge einschließlich der öffentliche Abendvortrag von Volker Gerhardt am 20. Juli im Lichthof des Welfenschlosses und der Festvortrag von Heinrich Schepers am 21. Juli auf der Verleihung der VGH-Preise für hervorragende Leibniz-Dissertationen.

Am 19. Juli fand, wie auch während vorangegangener Kongresse, ein Empfang der Landeshauptstadt Hannover für alle Teilnehmerinnen und Teilnehmer statt. Mit der Aufnahme des Grußwortes des Bürgermeisters Thomas Herrmann wurde erstmals auch diese Veranstaltung dokumentiert.

Einen weiteren Themenschwerpunkt bilden die Berichte der vier Leibniz-Editionsstellen in Berlin, Hannover, Potsdam und Münster. Frau Dr. Herma Kliege-Biller (Münster) war freundlich bereit, auf dem Kongress erstmals einen Workshop zur Benutzung der Akademieausgabe durchzuführen. Auf Wunsch zahlreicher Kolleginnen und Kollegen hat sie ihre Einführung schriftlich ausgearbeitet, die wir in Anschluss an die Editionsberichte drucken.

Bis auf einige wenige Texte handelt es sich bei den übrigen Beiträgen um Texte, die den Herausgeber erst nach dem Kongress erreicht haben. Sie werden hier in alphabetischer Reihenfolge veröffentlicht; eine Zuweisung in die thematischen Zusammenhänge, wie es in den ersten fünf Bänden der Fall war, wurde nicht vorgenommen.

Der Beitrag von Mogens Lærke wurde in Band II unvollständig wiedergegeben; mit dem vorliegenden Druck soll die dortige Wiedergabe ersetzt werden. Verwiesen sei auf die Corrigendaliste, die allerdings alles andere als vollständig ist.

Hans Poser hat seine Anmoderation der Abschlussveranstaltung schriftlich festgehalten und überarbeitet. Mit seinem Rückblick auf die bisherigen Kongresse schließen wir die Dokumentation.

Allen Teilnehmerinnen und Teilnehmern, allen Mitarbeiterinnen und Mitarbeitern, allen Journalistinnen und Journalisten, allen Förderinstitutionen und ihren Vertreterinnen und Vertretern sei nochmals herzlich gedankt!

Wenchao Li
Hannover/Berlin/Potsdam, im Dezember 2016

Eröffnungsansprache und Grussworte

Eröffnungsansprache

Prof. Dr.-Ing. Erich Barke, Präsident der Gottfried-Wilhelm-Leibniz-Gesellschaft

Sehr geehrte Damen und Herren Landtagsabgeordnete,
sehr geehrte Frau Ministerin Heinen-Kljajić,
sehr geehrte Ratsmitglieder und Abgeordnete der Regionsversammlung,
lieber Herr Bürgermeister Herrmann,
lieber Herr Krull,
lieber Herr Professor Li,
sehr geehrte Kongressteilnehmerinnen und Kongressteilnehmer – und jetzt muss ich wirklich mal zeigen, wie international dieser Kongress ist, denn die Teilnehmerinnen und Teilnehmer stammen aus Argentinien, Brasilien, Belgien, Bulgarien, China, Chile, Costa Rica, Deutschland, England, Estland, Finnland, Frankreich, Indien, Israel, Italien, Japan, Kanada, Kolumbien, Litauen, Mexiko, Nepal, Österreich, Polen, Portugal, Rumänien, Russland, der Schweiz, Spanien, Tschechien, Tunesien, Ungarn, Ukraine, den USA. Toll!

Verehrte Gäste, sehr verehrte Damen, sehr geehrte Herren,

ich begrüße Sie zur Eröffnungsveranstaltung des diesjährigen internationalen Leibniz-Kongresses.
    Zur Einstimmung hörten wir soeben Ausschnitte aus den Opern *Orlando Generoso* und *Servio Tullio* von Agostino Steffani. Bevor wir später mit den Eröffnungsvorträgen fortfahren, werden wir etwas aus Georg Philipp Telemanns Concerto G-Dur für Streicher und Basso continuo hören und vor dem Empfang durch die VolkswagenStiftung schließlich Ausschnitte aus Georg Friedrich Händels Oper *Agrippina* sowie die Aria con saggio tuo consilio.
    Es spielt das Ensemble des Instituts für Alte Musik der Hochschule für Musik, Theater und Medien Hannover unter der Leitung von Prof. Bernward Lohr und ich finde, sie machen das großartig. Vielen Dank.

Meine Damen und Herren,

dies ist der X. Internationale Leibniz-Kongress, den die Gottfried-Wilhelm Leibniz-Gesellschaft, diesmal in enger Zusammenarbeit mit der Leibniz-Stiftungsprofessur der Leibniz Universität Hannover, ausrichtet. Der erste Kongress fand im Gründungsjahr der Leibniz-Gesellschaft vor 50 Jahren, also 1966 statt, unter anderem auf Initiative des damaligen Leitenden Direktors der

Niedersächsischen Landesbibliothek Prof. Wilhelm Totok, der heute unter uns ist; lieber Herr Totok, herzlich willkommen.

Der heutige ist natürlich in vieler Hinsicht ein besonderer Kongress, denn er fällt in ein besonderes Jahr hinein: Wir gedenken des 300. Todestages von Leibniz, wir feiern seinen 370. Geburtstag. Die Leibniz Universität feiert ihr zehnjähriges Jubiläum, unsere Gesellschaft wird 50! Dementsprechend groß war das Interesse. Wir haben, wie Sie bereits aus der Presse erfahren konnten, den bisher größten Kongress organisieren dürfen: Angemeldet haben sich 444 Teilnehmerinnen und Teilnehmer, es sollen 334 Sektionsvorträge und 7 Plenarvorträge auf Deutsch, Englisch bzw. Französisch gehalten werden; hinzu kommen Workshops, Führungen durch Leibniz-Ausstellungen, Exkursionen zu Leibniz' Wirkungsstätten, ein öffentlicher Abendvortrag; ein Empfang durch die Stadt Hannover und den Verlag Walter de Gruyter und schließlich wird erstmals auf dem Kongress ein von der VGH Versicherungen gestifteter Preis für hervorragende Leibniz-Dissertationen verliehen werden.

Der Kongress steht unter dem Motto „Für unser Glück oder das Glück anderer". Es stammt aus einer Schrift von Leibniz aus dem Jahr 1678. Mit der Auswahl gerade dieses Mottos wollen wir zum einen die Kontinuität des Leibniz'schen Denkens unterstreichen und zum anderen eines seiner zentralen Anliegen hervorheben: Das Allgemeinwohl! Oder eben anders gesagt: das Glück anderer! Zu diesem Leibniz'schen Gedanken und zu weiteren Themen wie Geschichte, Naturwissenschaften und ihre Theorien, politische Philosophie, Erkenntnistheorie, Logik, Rechtsphilosophie, Kultur und Technik, Theologie und Ökumene, Wissenschaftsverständnis und Wissensgeschichte, interkultureller Austausch, Leibniz Rezeption und die gegenwärtigen Herausforderungen werden wir interessante und inspirierende Beiträge hören.

Kaum eine andere Forschung ist so eng mit der Edition sämtlicher Werke des Beforschten verknüpft wie die Leibniz-Forschung. Seit dem letzten Leibniz-Kongress sind beachtliche 9 Bände der Akademie-Ausgabe erschienen, so dass wieder mehrere tausend Seiten bisher unveröffentlichter Texte aus dem Leibniz-Nachlass kritisch erschlossen der Forschung vorliegen. Diese neuen Texte werden in vielen Kongress-Referaten ihre Auswertung finden. Erstmals wird auch ein Workshop zu Benutzung der Leibniz-Edition angeboten.

Ein Mammutprogramm bedeutet auch organisatorisch eine Mammutaufgabe; schon jetzt möchte ich die Gelegenheit nutzen, Herrn Li, dem Inhaber der Leibniz-Stiftungsprofessur und Schriftführer der Leibniz-Gesellschaft, und seinem großartigen Team für die vielfältige Organisationsarbeit zu danken; danken möchte ich auch den Leibniz-Gesellschaften in China, Japan, Israel, Italien, Rumänien, Frankreich, Spanien, der Vereinigung französischsprachiger Leibniz-Forschung und dem Ibero-amerikanischen Leibniz-Netzwerk für die gute Zusammenarbeit.

Wir haben dankenswerterweise vielfältige ideelle Unterstützung und finanzielle Förderungen für den Kongress bekommen, genannt sei neben der Deutschen Forschungsgemeinschaft und der VolkswagenStiftung insbesondere das Land Niedersachen. Herr Ministerpräsident Stephan Weil war freundlicherweise bereit, die Schirmherrschaft zu übernehmen, die Landeshauptstadt Hannover und das Niedersächsische Ministerium für Wissenschaft und Kultur unterstützen uns in vielfältiger Weise.

Vielen Dank, dass Sie mir zugehört haben.

Grußwort zur Kongresseröffnung

Thomas Herrmann, Bürgermeister der Landeshauptstadt Hannover

Sehr geehrte Frau Ministerin Heinen-Kljajić,
sehr geehrte Präsidenten Prof. Barke und Prof. Epping,
sehr geehrter Herr Prof. Li,
verehrte Kongressteilnehmer/innen und Mitglieder der Leibniz Gesellschaft,
meine Damen und Herren,

es ist mir eine außerordentliche Freude, den X. Leibniz-Kongress der Gottfried-Wilhelm-Leibniz-Gesellschaft inmitten unseres gemeinsamen Leibniz-Jahres eröffnen zu können.

Ich darf Ihnen die herzlichsten Grüße von Oberbürgermeister Stefan Schostok ausrichten, der heute leider nicht hier sein kann.

Herr Schostok wünscht dem Kongress einen erfolgreichen Verlauf und bedankt sich bei allen, die sich bei der umfangreichen Vorbereitung engagiert haben – allen voran natürlich bei der Gottfried-Wilhelm-Leibniz-Gesellschaft sowie bei Prof. Li und seinem Team.

Sie haben hervorragende Arbeit geleistet!

Meine Damen und Herren,

mittlerweile ist es eine gute Tradition, dass der Leibniz-Kongress auch von städtischer Seite mit eröffnet wird.

Als ich vor wenigen Tagen das umfangreiche Programm zum X. Leibniz-Kongress das erste Mal in den Händen hielt, war ich sehr beeindruckt. Die Fülle der Vorträge und die parallelen Sessions erinnern mich ein wenig an evangelische Kirchentage (oder Soziologen- und Politologentage).

Das gilt – im übertragenen Sinne – auch für die Breite der interessanten Themen: von Marx über Monadologie und Metaphysik bis hin zur Musik.

Und wie bei diesen großen, mehrtägigen Kirchentagen oder Wissenschaftskongressen haben die Besucherinnen und Besucher die sprichwörtliche Qual der Wahl.

Die Qual der Wahl hatte Gottfried Wilhelm Leibniz nach eigener Aussage auch schon damals. Seine vielen Gedanken, die er frühmorgens schon im Bette hatte, auch am selben Tage noch niederzuschreiben.

Französisch-Kenntnisse, meine Damen und Herren, scheinen bei Ihrem Kongress auch von Vorteil zu sein. Vor allem wenn man sich für die interessante Forscherin Émilie du Châtelet und ihre Beziehung zu Leibniz' Werk interessiert.

Da im 18. Jahrhundert Frauen so gut wie keine Möglichkeit hatten, sich wissenschaftlich zu betätigen, wurde ich an dieser Stelle neugierig.

Ich habe mal ganz unwissenschaftlich – bitte verzeihen Sie dies einem Bürgermeister, auch wenn er von der Ausbildung her Sozialwissenschaftler ist – bei Wikipedia nachgeschaut.

Und ich fand ein Zitat von Émilie du Châtelet, das auch zum Titel dieses Kongresses passt:

„Wer *vernünftig* sagt, meint *glücklich*".

Höchste Tugend ist für sie, etwas zum Wohl der Gemeinschaft beizutragen. Und diese Tugend erzeugt individuelles Glück.

Die Parallele zu Leibniz:

„Es ist eine meiner Überzeugungen, dass man für das Gemeinwohl arbeiten muss, und dass man sich im selben Maße, in dem man dazu beigetragen hat, glücklich fühlen wird."

Ein Motto, das heute immer noch zeitgemäß zu Wissenschaft und Forschung passt.

Oberbürgermeister Stefan Schostok hat es bereits bei der Feier anlässlich des 10. Jahrestages der Umbenennung der Universität Hannover in die *Leibniz Universität* gesagt:

Gottfried Wilhelm Leibniz ist ein Glücksfall für unsere Stadt. Denn Leibniz steht für viele Dinge, die heute nicht nur die Universität, sondern auch unsere Stadt attraktiv machen (die drei „I"):

— Interdisziplinarität,
— Innovation und
— Internationalität und Weltoffenheit.

Besonders beeindruckend ist es, wie Leibniz die Forschertätigkeit mit seiner bürgerlichen und politischen Existenz verbunden hat.

Für Leibniz gehörten Wissenschaft und Gesellschaft untrennbar zusammen.

Und wir könnten nicht gleichzeitig für die Hochschul- und Wissenschaftsstadt Hannover werben, ohne Leibniz zu erwähnen.

Vor diesem Hintergrund hatte der Rat der Stadt Hannover, dem ich vorsitze, im Jahr 2010 beschlossen, gemeinsam mit der Leibniz Universität eine Stiftungsprofessur ins Leben zu rufen.

Als Stadt haben wir die Leibniz-Stiftungsprofessur sechs Jahre lang mit jährlich 100.000 Euro unterstützt. Dies ist in Zeiten von Haushaltskonsolidierung übrigens eine beträchtliche Summe.

Ziel der Stiftungsprofessur sollte es sein, Leben und Werk dieses wirklich vielseitigen Mannes, dieses Universalgenies in der Stadt sichtbar zu machen.

Mit Prof. Wenchao Li haben wir einen versierten Leibniz-Kenner gewinnen können, der nun auch hier in Hannover die Forschung zu Leibniz weit voran gebracht hat.

In den letzten Jahren gab es daher viele Veröffentlichungen, internationale Tagungen – und nun den X. Leibniz-Kongress.

Heute können wir mit Überzeugung sagen: Alle Investitionen in die Marke „Leibniz" haben sich in vielerlei Hinsicht gelohnt.

Und Leibniz würde sich heute bestimmt nicht wieder so despektierlich über Hannover äußern wie damals, als er die Stadt langweilig fand, als weit im Abseits liegende Provinz jenseits der Weltzentren Paris, London oder Wien, weil ihm hier die kongenialen Gesprächspartner fehlten.

Ganz im Gegenteil: Heute wäre er sicher begeistert darüber, wie sich sein Hannover zu einem international anerkannten Kultur-, Wissenschafts- und Hochschulstandort entwickelt hat.

Leibniz hat zahlreiche Spuren in Hannover hinterlassen.

Historische, wie die Pläne zur großen Fontaine hier im Großen Garten von Herrenhausen oder das Leibnizhaus.

Und *ideelle*, wie die Namen zahlreicher Einrichtungen in unserer Stadt, die sich der leibnizschen Forschung oder Tradition verpflichtet fühlen.

Und manche meinen, auch der Keks mit den 52 Zähnen zählte zu seinen Erfindungen…

Dieser Leibniz-Kongress markiert auch die *Halbzeit im Leibnizjahr 2016*.

Ich finde, wir haben allen Grund, auf das umfangreiche und vielfältige Programm zum Leibnizjahr stolz zu sein:

Mehr als 100 Angebote sind das Ergebnis intensiver und kreativer Zusammenarbeit von vielen engagierten Partnern in Hannover und darüber hinaus.

Zahlreiche Veranstaltungen rund um das Wirken und Leben liegen bereits hinter uns.

Zur Halbzeit können wir feststellen, dass wir es im Sinne von Leibniz mit einer spannenden „Vielfalt in der Einheit" zu tun haben.

- Es gab zahlreiche wissenschaftlich hochkarätige Vorträge für ein kundiges Publikum.
- Mehrere tausend Menschen haben im Neuen Rathaus die Ausstellung „Leibniz in bester Gesellschaft" besucht und die Filme auf dem Multimediaportal der „Initiative Wissenschaft Hannover" angeschaut.
- Viele Menschen werden in den nächsten Monaten die neu eröffnete Gottfried Wilhelm Leibniz Bibliothek erkunden und sich mit dem letzten Lebensjahr von Leibniz beschäftigen.
- Gleichzeitig haben sich hunderte junger Menschen in diesem Leibnizjahr das erste Mal mit dem Universalgelehrten beschäftigt.

Und darum müssen Sie sich als Teilnehmerinnen und Teilnehmer des 10. Leibniz-Kongresses um den Nachwuchs keine Sorgen machen.

350 Schülerinnen und Schüler aus fünfzehn niedersächsischen Schulen haben sich im Unterricht mehrere Monate mit dem „Leben in der besten aller möglichen Welten" interessiert und kritisch auseinander gesetzt.

Das Themenspektrum war dabei ähnlich breit, wie hier auf dem Kongress, wenn auch mit deutlich aktuellerem Bezug.

Die Schülerinnen und Schüler beschäftigte vor allem, wie sich die aktuelle Gewalt, Ausbeutung, Ungerechtigkeit und Umweltzerstörung mit der Vorstellung von Leibnizens „besten aller möglichen Welten" verbinden lässt.

Die Ernsthaftigkeit der Diskussionen, aber auch der Optimismus der jungen Menschen, hierauf aktiv Einfluss nehmen zu können, war beeindruckend.

Auch in der zweiten Halbzeit des Leibniz-Jahres bleibt es spannend.

Und wer sich eher spielerisch – wenn auch ebenso anspruchsvoll – Leibniz nähern will, kann dies mit unserer Leibniz-Geocaching-Tour machen.

14 sogenannte Caches führen zu Leibniz-Orten und vermitteln sein Leben und Werk. Die Tour wird übrigens in der weltweiten Community hoch gelobt.

Meine Damen und Herren,

lassen Sie mich abschließend noch einmal auf das Kongress-Programm zurückkommen.

Fünf Tage Vorträge von morgens bis abends liegen vor Ihnen. Fast müsste ich Sie bedauern angesichts so viel notwendigen Sitzfleisches.

Wenn es nicht Prof. Li gäbe:

Er hat in seiner bekannten Umtriebigkeit für jeden Abend auch einen schönen Empfang organisiert. Das Feiern ist also mit inbegriffen und erleichtert so die Rezeption neuer Gedanken und den Austausch in der Leibniz-Community.

Und damit ich morgen noch etwas Stoff für mein Grußwort beim Empfang im Neuen Rathaus habe, schließe ich jetzt hier.

Ich wünsche Ihnen in den nächsten Tagen gute Gespräche, viele neue Anregungen und Anstöße.

Und genießen Sie auch unsere Stadt. Lassen Sie sich von den Herrenhäuser Gärten inspirieren, nutzen Sie diese räumliche Nähe, um auch mal „auszureißen." Vielleicht ergeht es Ihnen dann wie Gottfried Wilhelm Leibniz und Sie bekommen beim Spazieren eine Eingebung, die ihren weiteren wissenschaftlichen Lebensweg maßgeblich beeinflusst.

Wir freuen uns auf jeden Fall, Sie alle in Leibniz-Stadt mal wieder begrüßen zu dürfen.

Grußwort zum Empfang der Teilnehmerinnen und Teilnehmer im Neuen Rathaus

Thomas Herrmann, Bürgermeister der Landeshauptstadt Hannover

Sehr geehrter Prof. Wenchao Li,
sehr geehrter Präsident Prof. Barke,
verehrte Kongressteilnehmer/innen,
verehrte Mitglieder der Leibniz-Gesellschaft,
meine Damen und Herren,

es ist mir eine außerordentliche Freude, den X. Leibniz-Kongress der Gottfried-Wilhelm-Leibniz-Gesellschaft hier im Neuen Rathaus begrüßen zu dürfen.

Sie haben bereits einige Grußworte zur Bedeutung von Leibniz für die Wissenschaft gehört und weitere werden folgen in den nächsten Tagen.

Daher möchte ich diese Gelegenheit nutzen, um Ihnen zu erläutern, wie stark Leibniz in den letzten Jahren Teil der städtischen Kultur geworden ist.

Sie wissen es bereits: Leibniz hat zahlreiche Spuren in Hannover hinterlassen.

Für uns als Stadt und Stadtgesellschaft wiederum ist der Hochschul- und Wissenschaftsstandort untrennbar mit Leibniz verbunden.

Wie bereits in meiner gestrigen Eröffnungsrede erwähnt, haben wir im Jahr 2010 gemeinsam mit der Leibniz Universität eine Stiftungsprofessur ins Leben gerufen, die wir auch trotz der angespannten kommunalen Haushaltslage gerne finanziell unterstützt haben.

Mit Prof. Wenchao Li haben wir nicht nur einen engagierten Leibniz Kenner für die Stiftungsprofessur gewonnen, sondern gleichzeitig auch einen wertvollen Vermittler in Richtung China.

Da der Rat der Stadt Hannover und die Verwaltung in den letzten Jahren die Beziehungen zur Volksrepublik China erheblich ausgebaut haben, ist dies von unschätzbarem Wert gewesen:
— So war ein Highlight des China-Tages im Neuen Rathaus ein Vortrag von Prof. Li zu Leibniz und seinen Beziehungen zu China.
— Während einer mehrtägigen Reise der Vorsitzenden der Ratsfraktionen nach China im letzten Jahr stellte Oberbürgermeister Schostok eine Leibniz-Büste in Shanghai auf. Auch hier konnten wir auf die Vermittlung und Unterstützung des Chinesischen Zentrums, des Konfuzius Instituts und der Leibniz-Stiftungsprofessur zählen.

- Und wann immer wir im Neuen Rathaus oder auf der Messe eine Delegation aus China begrüßt haben, gab es diese wunderbaren Aha-Momente, wenn wir stolz verrieten, dass der hannoversche Leibniz-Kenner aus China kommt.

Gottfried Wilhelm Leibniz ist längst zum außerordentlichen Botschafter für die Stadt Hannover geworden.
- Viele internationale Persönlichkeiten, aber auch hannoversche Bürgerinnen und Bürger, wurden in den letzten Jahren mit einer Leibniz-Büste im Rathaus geehrt.
- Vor kurzem erhielten übrigens die Gravitationswissenschaftler der Leibniz-Universität im Team von Prof. Danzmann die wertvolle, kleine Porzellanbüste. Die Forscherinnen und Forscher hatten Anfang des Jahres zusammen mit internationalen Kolleginnen und Kollegen Albert Einsteins Gravitationswellen nachweisen können.
- Aber es gibt auch jüngere Menschen, die für ihr Engagement – z. B. als Leselotsen – belohnt werden. In dem Fall wird als Auszeichnung das Buch *Leibniz für Kinder* von den hannoverschen Wissenschaftlerinnen Annette von Boetticher und Annette Antoine überreicht.

Wie es sich für eine Leibniz-Stadt gehört, orientieren sich auch die Tourismus- und Marketing-Aktivitäten Hannovers an dem Universalgenie.
- So gibt es seit Jahren informative Stadtführungen mit Leibniz (und der damaligen Kurfürstin – und man möchte fast sagen – kongenialen Gesprächspartnerin – Sophie). An ausgewählten Tagen können kleine Gruppen den Raum in den Herrenhäuser Gärten besuchen, wo Leibniz an den Papieren zur Gründung der Wissenschaftlichen Sozietät gearbeitet hat.
- Die Hannover Marketing und Tourismus Gesellschaft wirbt im In- und Ausland mit Leibniz als Gesicht für den Hochschul- und Wissenschaftsstandort.
- Im Museum vom Schloss Herrenhausen steht natürlich die Original-Leibniz-Büste.
- Mehrere kulturelle und wissenschaftliche Einrichtungen veranstalten einen Leibniz Sommer.
- Bei den großen wissenschaftlichen Events in Hannover sind Vorträge oder Schülertage zu Leibniz selbstverständlich. Auch beim 5. November der Wissenschaft, bei dem in diesem Jahr wieder 40.000 Menschen bei über 200 Veranstaltungen erwartet werden, hat Leibniz seinen angestammten Platz.

Besonders gewürdigt wird das Vermächtnis von Leibniz aber jedes Jahr am 14. November, seinem Todestag.

Dann veranstaltet die Gottfried-Wilhelm-Leibniz-Gesellschaft mit anderen städtischen Partnern die alljährliche Ehrung an seinem Grab in der Neustädter Hof- und Stadtkirche.

Um das Leben und Wirken von Leibniz in die Stadt und Welt hinauszutragen, braucht es viele Menschen und Ideen.

Vor allem muss es gelingen, das Interesse an Leibniz noch stärker bei jüngeren Menschen zu wecken.

Dafür ist manchmal etwas Mut und Experimentiergeist notwendig. Also Eigenschaften, die sehr gut zu Leibniz passen.

Wir haben als Stadt im Rahmen des Leibnizjahres 2016 neue Formate und Kooperationen ausprobiert. Und dies mit großem Erfolg!

Da gab es im Juni den ersten Leibnizschülertag im Pavillon, der von Oberbürgermeister Schostok eröffnet und von dem bekannten Hip-Hop Sänger Spax begleitet wurde.

– Wir haben bei der Organisation von philosophischen Schülersessions sehr gute Erfahrungen in der Zusammenarbeit mit dem Seminar für angehende Philosophielehrerinnen und –lehrer sowie mit dem Forschungsinstitut für Philosophie gemacht.
– Sehr großen internationalen Erfolg hat unsere Geo-Cachingtour Leibniz Ge(o)heimnisse. Mehrere tausendmal wurden diese sogenannten „Schätze" bereits seit Mai gehoben.
Die Tour ist innovativ und anspruchsvoll, denn es wurden dafür völlig neue technische Rätsel und Lösungen entwickelt.
Wer fit in Mathe ist und den Binärcode beherrscht, ist übrigens eindeutig im Vorteil. Ansonsten kann die Geo-Cachingtour ganz einfach mit dem Smartphone gemacht werden.

Die Tour startet übrigens hier im Rathaus am Tourismus-Counter. Dort finden Sie auch den Info-Flyer.

Meine Damen und Herren,

beim Betreten des Rathauses ist Ihnen vielleicht der große Leibniz-Kopf im Eingangsbereich aufgefallen. Dieses Kunstwerk des Künstlers Tobias Schreiber ist Teil der Ausstellung „Leibniz in bester Gesellschaft."

Sechs Monate lang haben wir das Leben und Werk von Leibniz anhand seiner Korrespondenzen mit Persönlichkeiten wie Isaac Newton, Kurfürstin Sophie und Zar Peter dem Großen gezeigt.

Die Texte entstanden in Zusammenarbeit mit der Gottfried Wilhelm Leibniz-Gesellschaft und Prof. Kempe.

Gleichzeitig haben wir das ganze medial ergänzt:
- mehrere kurze Filme wurden produziert.
- Ein Schauspieler erweckt anhand ausgewählter Korrespondenzen Leibniz zum Leben.
- Und das Rattern der nachgebauten Leibniz-Rechenmaschine war beeindruckend.

Dieses publikumsnahe Konzept inmitten des Rathauses ging auf.

Mehr als 10.000 Besucherinnen und Besucher wurden gezählt.

Alle Filme und auch die Hördateien mit den Leibniz-Briefen finden Sie auf dem Multimediaportal der Initiative Wissenschaft Hannover.

Merken Sie sich einfach wissen.hannover.de.

Für Sie, als fachkundiges Publikum, ist der Leibniz Kongress sicher ein Höhepunkt im Jahr 2016.

Für die Hannoveranerinnen und Hannover folgen noch viele weitere Veranstaltungen.

Und bei einigen Formaten steht bereits heute fest, dass sie, wie das Geo-Caching, auch über das Leibnizjahr hinaus fortgeführt werden.

In diesem Sinne freue ich mich auf künftige Projekte im und außerhalb des Leibnizjahres.

Als Landeshauptstadt Hannover würden wir uns sehr darüber freuen, wenn die Kontakte in der internationalen Leibniz Community fortgesetzt und weiter entwickelt werden.

Ich schließe mit einem Zitat von Leibniz, mit dem wir gerne die Aktivitäten der Initiative Wissenschaft Hannover beschreiben:

„Es lohnt sich, die Entdeckungen anderer zu studieren, da für uns selbst eine neue Quelle für Ideen entspringt."

Eröffnungsvorträge

Leibniz on War and Peace and the Common Good

Catherine Wilson (York)

> There is a book by Dicaearchus on *The Destruction of Human Life*. He was a famous and eloquent Peripatetic, and he gathered together all the other causes of destruction – floods, epidemics, famines, and sudden incursions of wild animals in myriads, by whose assaults, he informs us, whole tribes of men have been wiped out. And then he proceeds to show by way of comparison how many more men have been destroyed by the assaults of men – that is, by wars or revolutions – than by any and all other sorts of calamity.[1]

1. Human Destruction and the Common Good

The concept of the common good that is the theme of this Congress resonates widely with us in a period in which hostilities between nations, civil war, and terrorism once again dominate in the news.

Leibniz presents us with some challenges in this regard. Metaphysically, the Leibniz-world consists of living, sensing, appetitive individuals that perceive and respond to everything that happens to create a condition of universal harmony. Their characteristics and efforts are thought to realise – to bring into phenomenal reality – the world that is the best possible. Everything that happens in the phenomenal world flows from this metaphysical perfection, as time takes us towards greater and greater improvement in the transformation of chaos and disorder into order and beauty.

> "Who does not see that these disorders have served to bring things to the point where they now are, that we owe to them our riches and our comforts, and that through their agency, this globe became fit for cultivation by us […]."[2]

Leibniz regarded the metaphysical image as a bulwark against moral and political pessimism, as furnishing an incentive to make things better than they

---

[1] Marcus Tullius Cicero: *De Officiis* (*On Duties*) II: 5 transl. by Walter Miller, Cambridge, MA 1913; XXI: 185.
[2] Gottfried Wilhelm Leibniz: *Théodicée*, § 247, in: *Theodicy: Essays on the Goodness of God, the Freedom of Man, and the Origins of Evil*, ed. by August Farrer, transl. by E. M. Huggard, La Salle 1985; . GP VI, 263f.

were, and his vision has long been regarded as a kind of guiding model or template for a pacific and generous world, in which individuals are unimpeded by pressures from other individuals, in which all forms of life are valued, and plenitude and diversity are welcomed.[3] At the same time, every student of Leibniz is aware of the mixed reaction to his optimism, which appeared to other philosophers an absurd and even pernicious delusion. Natural disasters such as earthquakes and failed harvests might be regarded as inevitable given by the laws of nature, so friendly to humanity in other respects, but even the wider cultivation of the globe and the spread of commerce did not establish that our species was on an upward trajectory. Pierre Bayle famously described history as "no other than a collection of the crimes and misfortunes of mankind", suggesting that good and evil will alternate forever as the Manichaeans taught.[4] The evils occurring on a regular basis in Voltaire's satire *Candide* (1759) are not hail, frost, and the misbegotten, but human slaughter, which Voltaire described graphically.[5]

---

[3] See representatively: Gaston Grua: *La Justice humaine selon Leibniz*, Paris 1956; Peter Hanns Reill: *The German Enlightenment and the Rise of Historicism*, Berkeley/Los Angeles 1975, esp. pp. 6f., pp. 33–55; Hans Heinz Holz: "Leibniz und das commune bonum", in: *Sitzungsbericht der Leibniz-Soziataet* 13 (1996), pp. 5–25; Jean Seidengart: "Cassirer: Reader, Publisher, and Interpreter of Leibniz's Philosophy", in: *New Essays on Leibniz Reception*, ed. by Ralph Krömer/Yannick Chin-Drian, Basel 2012, pp. 129–142; more recently, Franklin Perkins: "Virtue, Reason, and Cultural Exchange: Leibniz's Praise of Chinese Morality", in: *Journal of the History of Ideas* 63 (2002), pp. 447–464; Justin Smith: *Nature, Human Nature and Human Difference: Race in Early Modern Philosophy*, Princeton 2015, esp. pp. 160–182; Pauline Phemister: *Leibniz and the Environment*, Abingdon 2016, esp. pp. 130–154; Christoph Sebastian Widdau: *Cassirer's Leibniz und die Begründung der Menschenrechte*, Basel 2016.

[4] Pierre Bayle: Art. "Manichaeans", in: *General Dictionary, Historical and Critical*, vol. VII., London 1734–41, p. 400, footnote (D).

[5] While the rival kings are giving their thanks to God, Candide wanders over the scorched earth of their battlefield, where all has been conducted "agreeably to the laws of war." Here lay a number of old men covered with wounds, who beheld their wives dying with their throats cut, and hugging their children to their breasts, all stained with blood. There several young virgins, whose bodies had been ripped open, after they had satisfied the natural necessities of the Bulgarian heroes, breathed their last; while others, half-burned in the flames, begged to be dispatched out of the world. The ground about them was covered with the brains, arms, and legs of dead men." François-Marie Arouet (Voltaire): *Candide*, in: *The Works of Voltaire. A Contemporary Version,* vol. I, transl. by T. Smollett, rev. William F. Fleming, New York 1901, pp. 68f.; cf. The *Philosophical Dictionary* (1764) article 'War,' it is "doubtless a very fine art […] which desolates countries, destroys habitations, and in a common year causes the death of from forty to a hundred thousand men. […] Each marches gaily to crimes, under the banner of his saint."

Leibniz rejected the view that human-made evils should be regarded differently than natural evils.

> "M. Bayle will say that there is a difference between [...] disorder in inanimate things, which is purely metaphysics, and a disorder in rational creatures, which is composed of crime and suffering. He is right in making a distinction between them, and I am right in combining them."[6]

It seems to follow that for any horror or sadness of human making you consider, whether it involves genocide, or exploitation, or any form of immiseration, the implication is, had all this not happened, the world would be less perfect than it is, and this thought is not acceptable to the contemporary observer any more than it was to Bayle.

But are we really being fair to Leibniz, you will rightly protest, in bringing forward such old accusations against his *Theodicy*? What about Leibniz's passionate wish to reunify the churches, to put an end forever to the religious divisions that spawned or at least fuelled and sustained such horrific conflicts as the Thirty Years' War? What about his passionate desire to bring peace and stability to Europe by promoting a theology Protestants and Catholics could agree on, and by arresting the depredations of Louis XIV.? We cannot imagine Leibniz approving of such goings on as Voltaire invents in his fable. His bitter and emotional essay, *Mars Christianissimus,* refers to

> "the thousands immolated by iron, by hunger and by miseries, only so that they have some cause to write on the gates of Paris the name of Louis the Great in letters of gold."

What greater crime, Leibniz asks in this connection,

> "can one conceive than to be responsible for all the evils of Christendom, for so much innocent blood spilled, for outrageous actions, for the curses of the miserable, for the moans of the dying, and lastly for the tears of widows and of orphans which rise to pierce heaven, and which will move God sooner or later to vengeance."[7]

Recent scholarship has, moreover, revealed to us the benevolent aspects of Leibniz's applied philosophy. We have been made increasingly aware of his utilitarian projects, his desire for natural and social scientific investigation to

---

[6] Leibniz: *Théodicée*, § 247.
[7] Gottfried Wilhelm Leibniz: *Mars Christianissimus*, in: Leibniz: *Political Writings*, trans. and ed. by Patrick Riley, Cambridge 1988, p. 141; A IV, 2, 98.

be applied to inventions and discoveries for the good of all. Following his recent biographer, we could mention Leibniz's hopes and plans for the reform of the imperial constitution, the reorganization of the legal system, state supported schools, vocational training, poverty-reduction, health improvement, pensions, and life insurance.[8] The universal language, the reform of jurisprudence, and the advancement of pure and applied science and mathematics, were to have as their beneficiaries specifically those deprived of resources, opportunities, and justice.[9]

> "One must", Leibniz said, "furnish the poor with the means of earning their livelihood, not only by using charity and charitable foundations to this end, but also by taking an interest in agriculture, buy furnishing to artisans materials and a market, by educating them to make their productions better, and finally by putting an end to idleness and abusive practice in manufactures and in commerce."[10]

In metaethics, Leibniz argues that justice requires not only that one forebear from harming others or giving them cause for complaint; justice requires helping them by seeking their good and preventing evil when doing so is not too difficult.[11] This is the principle that Schopenhauer describes as "the fundamental proposition concerning whose purport all teachers of ethics are *really* in agreement: *neminem laede, imo omnes, quantum potes, juva.*" [Injure no one; on the contrary, help everyone as much as you can.] Leibniz may be said to have anticipated the universalist insights of Kant, Pareto, and Rawls in replacing the injunction to do unto others as you would have them do unto you with the injunction to "Put yourself in the place of another, and you will have the true point of view for judging what is just or not." By this Leibniz meant: Imagine that all who would be affected by your proposal are "well-informed and enlightened," and ask yourself, will they approve it or not? Although it is "impossible to act so that the whole world is content," the affected ones can be made as content as possible."[12] Leibniz's statement in the letter to Peter the Great of Russia,

---

[8] Maria Rosa Antognazza: *Leibniz: An Intellectual Biography*, Cambridge 2011, p. 196.
[9] Ibid., p. 210.
[10] Ibid., p. 106.
[11] Gottfried Wilhelm Leibniz: "Meditations sur la notion commune de la justice", in: Gustl Mollat: *Mitteilingen aus Leibnizens ungedruckten Schriften*, Leipzig 1893, pp. 53–56; Leibniz: *Political Writings*, pp. 53–55.
[12] Ibid., 58f.; p. 56f.

> "I am not one of those impassioned patriots of one country alone, but I work for the well-being of the whole of mankind, for I consider heaven as my country and cultivated men as my compatriots"[13]

seems to capture the impartiality and generosity that lie at the heart of true morality.

In his concrete, applied thinking, however, Leibniz was not a believer in the fundamental equality of human beings, in the sense of valuing all human ways of life, or taking servitude to be an unnatural and fundamentally wrong arrangement. Nor was he averse to harming people by killing them if the common good could be thereby advanced. We should not be too surprised by this because the fundamental ethical principle *neminem laede*, even if we take *neminem* literally, as applying only to individual members of the species *homo sapiens*, not to animals, landscapes, languages, and so on, has almost always been regard as subject to three main categories of exceptions. First, the extension of the terms 'people' or 'persons' is determined by the cultural context and the beliefs of those who use the term. Outsiders, 'barbarians,' and slaves are human beings who, in many contexts, are not considered people, and it was long considered permissible to hurt them, along with children and wives thought to require discipline. Second, punitive actions such as the persecution of heretics, or in our time, imprisonment under harsh conditions, have been permitted or demanded on the grounds that they are for the victim's own good. Third, it is generally accepted that we may harm one person or some people in order to bring about a better overall situation for others.

Arguments in favour of so-called just or legal warfare have traditionally appealed, tacitly or explicitly to each of these categories of exceptions. The people we are allowed to hurt or kill may be seen as having never had or as having lost their entitlement to be called human; it is thought that they or their village and cities may be destroyed allegedly in order to prevent them carrying out further damnable acts; and their sacrifice may be said to be entailed by some argument proceeding from the notion of the greater good – making the world safe, halting atrocities, or just facilitating commerce or profit making or ideological control. In all such cases it is said either that what looks like harm is not really harm or that it is justified.

---

[13] Gottfried Wilhelm Leibniz, Letter to Peter the Great, in: Id.: *Selections*, ed. and transl. by Philip P. Wiener, New York 1951, pp. 596f.

Leibniz employed versions of all these exceptions to the *neminem laede* principle, and although we can all agree that there must be some such exceptions, his understanding of the well-being of the whole of mankind was different to the range of views we would consider presentable – even if contentious – today. In what follows I regret to have to summarize for you a number of his less sympathetic views. This will be painful for his most devoted admirers, but I must ask them to bear with me until the end, for there are important conclusions to be drawn from this cheerless exercise. We cannot change what we do not understand, and the present state of conflict calls for understanding and change. My paper is accordingly directed, on one hand, to understanding a positive vision we can no longer share with Leibniz, and, on the other to exploring a positive vision we can share with him and that we also need to understand better. The vision we cannot share with him is that of a fully Christianised world, improved by being cleansed of 'barbarians' and pacified by military means. The vision we can share with him is one in which educational resources, above and beyond economic help, are furnished to those who lack them, and in which scientific knowledge is applied principally to the reduction of harm and deprivation, only secondarily to create, stimulate and satisfy desires; and where the motive of charity rather than the motive of profit furnishes the principal incentive. The world we live in today is not a Leibniz-world.

2. Ancient Greek and Judaeo-Christian War Theory

Before going on to discuss Leibniz's views on war and peace, subordination and equality, I want to provide some background on the philosophical and religious traditions of Western philosophy with its mixed Judaeo-Christian and Greek heritage.

The ambivalence with which human beings have always regarded kingship and warfare is evident in certain biblical passages. In 1 *Samuel* 8, God is reluctant to let Samuel cede to the demand of the Israelites for a king, predicting that they will not like it. God tells him to communicate to them that their sons will be pressed into running before the king's chariots, their daughters into producing luxuries, and they themselves into slavery, and that a king will choose favorites and despoil others to reward them. But the Israelites insist that they want to "be like all the other nations, with a king to lead us and to go out before us and fight our battles," and they get their wish. The same skeptical God who warns against the military state commands slaughter and predation, such as the massacre of the adult Midianites, men and women, for their impiety, preserving only the virgin girls for sex slavery. "[T]hey burnt all their cities wherein they dwelt, and all their goodly castles, with fire." [14]

The 'cult of frightfulness' was widespread in ancient civilisations, and it did occasion protest.[15] The fifth century BCE Greek historian Herodotus described the atrocities he supposed to have been perpetrated by the Persian king Cambyses with evident horror, and Thucydides lamented warfare and the destruction of the Athenian civil order. The connection between war and luxury was noted.[16] The ancients recognized that wars are often irrational or proceed from small provocations, a recognition expressed in archaic literature by making the personal rivalries of the Gods, anthropomorphically conceived, triggers of war, which they bring about by manipulating human emotions. The fact that victory is determined 'by luck, or superiority of numbers, or strength or resources, or by advantage of position, or excellence of allies, or skill on the part of a general' – by everything but the moral superiority of the cause – is suavely noted by Aristotle,[17] but nothing is made of this glaring *reductio ad absurdum* of the moral usefulness of warfare in determining whose cause is just. The preeminent Greek philosophical position is based on a number of premises that seem to us moderns remarkably complacent.

The two ancient philosophers most esteemed and studied in later periods – Plato and Aristotle – took war for granted as an inevitable fact of human social existence. In their texts, there is a remarkable discrepancy between strife as it is conceptualised for the private domain and as it is conceptualised in relation to territory. Plato mentions the word or words translated as 'love' 753 times in his *Complete Works,* but 'hate' and 'strife' only 86 times. Aristotle mentions 'love' 178 times, and 'hate' and 'strife' 50. On the territorial scale, however, the proportions are dramatically reversed. There are 454 references to 'war' in Plato vs. 174 to 'peace'; 137 references to 'war' in Aristotle

---

[14] Numbers 31:10.
[15] "No one ever speaks of 'terrible wealth' or 'terrible peace', or 'terrible well being', but we do hear of 'terrible disease', 'a terrible war', 'terrible poverty'". Plato: *Protagoras* 341a-b; in: *Complete Works*, ed. by John Cooper/Douglas S. Hutchinson, Indianapolis 1997, p. 773. The dialogue, on the standards of good and evil, nevertheless praises war as 'honourable.'
[16] Thus Plato: "Then the city must be further enlarged, and not just by a small number, wither, but by a whole army, which will do battle with the invaders in defense of the city's substantial wealth and all the other things we mentioned." Plato: *Republic* 373e–374a; in: *Complete Works*, p. 1012.
[17] Aristotle: *Rhetoric to Alexander* 1424b, 21–25, in: *Complete Works*, ed. by Jonathan Barnes, Princeton 1984, II: 2278.

vs. 31 to 'peace.' In personal relations, human affection is the more salient phenomenon to the philosophers; in relations with strangers, enmity dominates. This observation is in accord with what ethnologists tell us. In the absence of special ethical teaching, human beings are mostly kind and accommodating to friends and relatives, but fearful of and hostile towards strangers and foreigners.[18] Or at least, they can be trained to hate the outside more easily than they can be trained to love him.

For Plato, in the ideal Republic, young children are to be

> "led into war on horseback as observers and [...] wherever it is safe to do so, they should be brought close and taste blood, like puppies."

Those who enjoy war and do well at it, he continues, "are to be subscribed on a list" for future training.[19] The conventions of war do not prescribe mercy to captives any more than the Old Testament requires for its human prey. "Shouldn't anyone who is captured alive be left to his captors as a gift to do with as they wish?" "Absolutely."[20] For ancient authors, soldiering is a just one more occupation. A city needs shoemakers, confectioners, and also soldiers.

> "Of the common people," says Aristotle, who also recognizes piracy and brigandage as occupations, "one class are farmers, another artisans; another traders, who are employed in buying and selling; another are the sea-faring class, whether engaged in war or in trade, as ferrymen or as fishermen."[21]

A community must have soldiers "if the country is not to be the slave of every invader."[22] The scientific and the social are linked, in that warfare are the necessary conditions of the contemplative, scientific life, which is the opposite of slavery.

---

[18] For evolutionary explanations of this disposition, see Johan M. G. van der Dennen: "Ethnocentrism and In-group/Out-group Differentiation. A Review and Interpretation of the Literature", in: *The Sociobiology of Ethnocentrism: Evolutionary Dimensions of Xenophobia, Discrimination, Racism and Nationalism*, ed. by Vernon Reynolds/Vincent Falger/Ian Vine, North Holland 1986, pp. 1–47.
[19] Plato: *Republic* 537a, in: *Complete Works*, p. 1152.
[20] Plato: *Republic* 468a-b, in: *Complete Works*, p. 1095.
[21] Aristotle: *Politics* 1291b 19–21. II: 2050.
[22] Ibid., 1291a, 7–9; II: 2049.

In the *History of Animals* Book IX, Aristotle describes the wars between various species of animals, such as snakes and roosters, establishing the omnipresence of such hostilities in nature. Where humans are concerned, because nature makes nothing in vain,

> "[T]he art of war is a natural art of acquisition, for the art of acquisition includes hunting, an art which we ought to practise against wild beasts, and against men who, though intended by nature to be governed, will not submit; for war of such a kind is naturally just."[23]

The purpose of small scale war is the capture of those who deserve to be slaves, and the acquisition of empire is "for the good of the governed."[24] In his *Rhetoric to Alexander*, Aristotle addresses the important topic of persuasion, in a way that makes disturbingly clear the problem of the relationship between rhetoric and reasoned argument. He lists a set of standard arguments for rousing emotions and persuading a group either to go to war or not to go to war, depending on the outcome the speaker desires.

> "If […] you collect from amongst all these and similar arguments those which are most applicable to the circumstances", he says, "you will have no lack of material for speaking about peace and war."[25]

Yet, Aristotle confesses to some philosophical bemusement. In the *Politics*, he condemns the Spartans for being able to do no more than fight and for mismanaging the revenues of their state and impoverishing it.[26] The *Nicomachean Ethics* describes the function of war as the promotion of peace, apparently denying that anybody enjoys it.

> "We are busy that we may have leisure, and make war that we may live in peace. The activity of the practical excellences is exhibited in political or military affairs, but the actions concerned with these seem to be unleisurely. Warlike actions are completely so (for no one chooses to be at war, or provokes war, for the sake of being at war; any one would seem absolutely murderous if he were to make enemies of his friends in order to bring about battle and slaughter)."[27]

---

[23] Ibid., 1256b, 21–5; II: 1994.
[24] Ibid., 1333b, 392–1334b5; II: 2116.
[25] Id.: *Rhetoric to Alexander* 1425b, 16–9; II: 2278.
[26] Id.: *Politics* 1271b, 1–19.
[27] Id.: *Nicomachean Ethics*, Bk X, Ch 7, 1177b5–12.

> "Facts, as well as arguments, prove that the legislator should direct all his military and other measures to the provision of leisure and the establishment of peace."[28]

Western philosophy beginning with the Greeks has accordingly taken the following positions on warfare. First, preparation for and participation in war is a normal and needful human occupation. Second, it is glorious and virtuous, affording opportunities for the display of manliness, strength, courage, and self-sacrifice. As Aristotle says, "political and military actions are distinguished by nobility and greatness."[29] Third, it can enrich the wealth and prestige of the nation and can be good for the conquered. Fourth, even if you were to dispute the truth or moral relevance of those propositions, war is absolutely inevitable since, as Thucydides ruefully pointed out

> "the nature of man [...] is wont even against law to do evil' and the horrors of war 'have been before and shall be as long as human nature is the same."[30]

Fifth, nevertheless, there is much that seems wrong about war.

How could Christianity have absorbed the pagan ideology? Passivity and endurance in the face of aggression, the reinvention of monotheism as irrelevant to geopolitical concerns, and the absolute rejection of Old Testament militarism are, one might point out, the chief moral lessons the New Testament sought to inculcate. It has been argued that it was only with the rise of the Byzantine empire headed by the convert Constantine that

> "the essentially subversive quality of Christian pacifism became an embarrassment [...]. From St Augustine of Hippo to the present, Christian thinkers have sought a way to balance the dictates of their faith with the realities of a coercive and violent world, distilled surprisingly early in just-war theology."[31]

---

[28] Id.: *Politics* 1333b, 392–1334b5; II: 2116.

[29] Id.: *Nicomachean Ethics*, Bk X, Ch 7, 1177b, in: *Basic Works*, transl. by W. D. Ross and ed. by Richard McKeon, New York 1941, p. 1105.

[30] Thucydides: *The Peloponnesian War*, in: Book III, § 82, transl. by Thomas Hobbes and ed. by David Grene, Chicago 1989, pp. 204f.

[31] N. N.: Article: "Pacifism", in: *The Oxford Companion to Military History*, Oxford 2003, p. 689. There is scant evidence for pacifism, as opposed to a distaste for heathen military glory and its trappings, amongst the Fathers of the Early Church.[31] According to the great historian of warfare, Michael Howard, "the medieval order, as it developed in Europe between the eighth and the eighteenth centuries, was largely a matter of a successful symbiosis between the ruling warrior class that provided order and the clerisy that legitimized it." Michael Howard: *The Invention of Peace: Reflections on War and the International Order*, New Haven 2000, p. 6.

Despite his equation of empire with brigandage,[32] Augustine was compelled to fit war into a providential framework:

> "God's providence", he states, "constantly uses war to correct and chasten the corrupt morals of mankind, as it also uses such afflictions to train men in a righteous and laudable way of life, removing to a better state those whose life is approved, or else keeping them in this world for further service."[33]

From a secular point of view, the proposition that Christians could serve in war and make war seemed to follow from the notion of goodness and justice itself, as some of Aristotle's remarks indicated. As the natural lawyer Francisco de Vitoria argued, one of many proofs of the legality of warfare

> "[...] comes from the end and aim and good of the whole world. For there would be no condition of happiness for the world, nay, its condition would be one of utter misery, if oppressors and robbers and plunderers could with impunity commit their crimes and oppress the good and innocent, and these latter could not in turn retaliate on them."[34]

Hugo Grotius's answer to the question "Whether it is ever lawful to wage war", posed in Chapter II, Section I of his *Laws of War and Peace*, presents arguments for the positive case from nature, history, the *consensus omnium*, and scripture. He is momentarily held up by Christ's command to forget the *lex talionis* and to 'Resist not him that is evil.'

> "From this some infer", Grotius observes, "that no injury ought to be warded off, or made the subject of a demand for requital, whether as a public or a private matter. And yet", he continues, "that is not the meaning of the words [...].

---

[32] Augustine: *City of God*, IV: 4 in: Augustine: *Political Writings*, ed. and trans. by M. W. Tkacz/Douglas Kries, Indianapolis 1994.
[33] Ibid., I,1, p. 6, p. 9. "Eventually", says Howard, "critics emerged from within that clerisy who denied the essential legitimacy of their rulers on the grounds that war was not a necessary part of the natural or divine order, but a derogation of it. It was then that peace, the visualization of a social order from which war had been abolished, could be said to have been invented; an order, that is, resulting not from some millennial divine intervention [...] but from the forethought of rational human beings who had taken matters into their own hands." Howard: *Invention of Peace*, p. 6.
[34] Francisco de Vitoria: *De Indis, De Jure Belli*, Pt. III, § 1 ed. by Ernest Nys, transl. by John Pawley Bate, Washington, D. C. 2017.

> Christ [...] is not treating of injuries in general but of a specific sort of injury, such as a slap on the cheek."[35]

His aim, like that of all just war theorists, is not to abolish warfare, but to control its excesses.

> "I have seen a wantonness in warfare among Christians which would be shameful even among barbarians; I have seen men run to arms for frivolous or nonexistent reasons, and having taken them up, who have no reverence for divine or human law, as if at a world their fury had been unleashed and they were capable of any crime."[36]

3. Leibniz and the Early Moderns on Slaves, 'Barbarians', and Conquest

There appears to be no direct expression in Leibniz's writings of the view that peace is enervating, or warfare sublime, or that warfare is an aspect of the drive towards perfection, sentiments that can be found in later writers such as Johann Valentin Embser,[37] Immanuel Kant,[38] and G. F. Hegel,[39] who promulgated a secularised version of the concept of redemptive warfare. Nevertheless, as courtier, lawyer, and theist, Leibniz had no doctrinal or personal basis of resistance to the understanding of warfare as inevitable and, when directed against the infidel or 'barbarian,' as 'just.'

Leibniz rejected Grotius's dictum that the laws of war and peace

> "would be relevant even if we were to suppose what we cannot suppose without the greatest wickedness that there is no God, or that human affairs are of no concern to him."[40]

---

[35] Hugo Grotius: *The Laws of War and Peace* (*De Jure Belli ac Pacis Libri Tres*) (1625), transl. by Francis W. Kelsey, London/New York/Oceana 1964, Book I, Ch. II, § I, p. 71f.
[36] Grotius: *Laws*, Prolegomena, III: 1753.
[37] Johann Valentin Embser: *Widerlegung des ewigen Friedens*, Mannheim 1797; id.: *Die Abgoetterei unseres philosophischen Jahrhunderts*, Mannheim 1779, repr. München 1990–1994.
[38] Immanuel Kant: *Critique of Judgement*, Gesammelte Schriften, vol. V., ed. by Akademie der Wissenschaften, Berlin 1902, p. 262f. and p. 432f.
[39] Georg Friedrich Wilhelm Hegel: "Introduction", in: *Reason in History*, transl. by Robert S. Hartman, New York 1953, pp. 18–13; see Yves-Jean Harder: "La philosophie de l'histoire est elle la veritable theodicée?", in: *L'idée de théodicée de Leibniz à Kant: héritage, transformations, critiques*, éd. par Paul Rateau (= Studia Leibnitiana Sonderhefte 36), Stuttgart 2009, pp. 207–219.
[40] Hugo Grotius: *The Rights of War and Peace*, vol. III, ed. by Richard Tuck, Indianapolis 2005, 1748.

Nor did he accept Pufendorf's claim that, despite the yearning of the human heart for immortality, and despite the widespread conviction, supported by revelation alone, that life is eternal and that punishment and reward follow in the afterlife,

> "the scope of the discipline of natural law is confined within the orbit of this life, and [...] forms man on the assumption that he is to lead this life in society with others."[41]

The secularisation of legal theory, Leibniz says, would mean "cutting off the best part of the science [of law], and suppressing many duties as well."[42] Like John Locke, he doubted that any internal motivation such as the love of virtue for its own sake could reliably produce good conduct. External motivators like the Hobbesian sovereign were insupportable alternatives, usurping the function of God, who alone deserves our absolute obedience, and destroying the balance of powers that Leibniz considered the real source of political stability.

For Leibniz, the good and the right are acknowledged and commanded by God and cannot be extrapolated from empirical observation of human society and reflection thereupon. By contrast, on the approach of Grotius and Pufendorf, we are impelled into society by our shared needs and our common natural sociability, and the law recruits this sentiment and makes co-existence easier.[43] "Human nature itself is the mother of natural law."[44] For Hobbes, who stands the sociability argument on its head, it is still human nature that makes the law; we are impelled by the fearsome natural right of appropriation amongst equals in the state of nature; the law recruits our fear and protects us.

Hierarchy and domination, rather than contracts between equals, are built in to Leibniz's metaphysics, with the superiority and inferiority of individuals determined along a number of parameters. Clarity of perception, associated with the possession of sensory organs, differentiates sentient beings

---

[41] Samuel Pufendorf: "Preface", in: *On the Duty of Man and Citizen According to Natural Law*, ed. by James Tully, transl. by Michael Silverstone, Cambridge 1991, p. 8.
[42] Gottfried Wilhelm Leibniz: "Opinion on the Principles of Pufendorf", in: Leibniz: *Political Writings*, p. 67. See the discussion of Ian Hunter of Leibniz's rebellion against the desacralisation of politics in his *Rival Enlightenments: Civil and Metaphysical Philosophy in Early Modern Germany*, Cambridge 2001, pp. 95–147.
[43] "Amongst the Things peculiar to Man is his Desire of Society, that is, a certain Inclination to live together with those of his own Kind, not in any Manner but peaceably [...]." Hugo Grotius: *Preliminary Discourse. The Rights of War and Peace*, vol. 1, ed. by Richard Tuck, Indianapolis 2005, pp. 79–81.
[44] Grotius: *Rights*, ed. Tully, vol. 3, 1749.

from slumbering monads, and there are infinite gradations between human perception, cognition, and agency and that of God, at least in other possible worlds, if not actually. The soul is described as a 'dominant monad,' responsible for the co-operation of the bodily organs to sustain life.[45] It has been vigorously argued that the metaphysical concepts of hierarchy and domination are compatible with a commitment to human equality in Leibniz, insofar as he recognises that all people are descended from a common stock and are rational and to some extent educable.[46] However, the positive assertion of fundamental equality to be found in Hobbes and Pufendorf[47] is conspicuously lacking in Leibniz, and there are numerous positive assertions to the contrary.[48] As Carl Friedrich rightly remarks, Leibniz was a "believer in a natural aristocracy of the talented,"[49] though his dislike for the common man "is really a dislike for the common in man."[50]

It is important not to caricature and to give moral credit where it is due. While Pufendorf appears to treat the relationship of wife to husband as comparable to that of slave and master, child and parent, relationships that in his view imply mutual if tacit consent for mutual benefit, Leibniz more appealingly describes the society of man and wife as one of "unlimited equality," like that between "true friends" or between parents and grown children.[51] But

---

[45] For explication, see Brandon Look: "On Monadic Domination in Leibniz's Metaphysics", in: *British Journal for the History of Philosophy* 10/3 (2002), pp. 379–399.

[46] Justin Smith: *Nature, Human Nature, and Human Difference*, Princeton 2015, pp. 160–182.

[47] Samuel Pufendorf: *On the Duty of Man and Citizen*, transl. by Michael Silverstone and ed. by James Tully, Cambridge 1991, p. 61. Pufendorf is however thinking of human beings as 'adult men'. Like Hobbes, he begins from the observation that where their physical strength is not equal, the weak can overpower the strong though arms or cunning. On Hobbes's sociopolitical egalitarianism see Baruch Baumrin: "Hobbes's Egalitarianism: The Laws of Natural Equality", in: Michel Malherbe (ed.): *Actes Du Colloque de Nantes*, Paris 1989, pp. 119–127.

[48] "If therefore one were to ask me what really is the common man, I do not know how to describe him except by saying that he comprises those whose mind is preoccupied with questions about their sustenance, who never rise to the point of imagining what might be the passion to know or spiritual pleasure (*Gemuetslust*) any more than a deaf-born man can judge a marvelous concert. These people are without enthusiasm or excitement; it seems they are made of Adam's earth, but the spirit of life was not blown into them. They live day by day and move on like cattle", quoted in: Carl J. Friedrich: "Philosophical Reflections of Leibniz on Law, Politics and the State", in: *Natural Law* Forum 1 (1966), pp. 79–91, here p. 90.

[49] Ibid., p. 90. Friedrich indicates contractualist sentiments in Leibniz, but gives little textual support; the observations on Pufendorf emphasize rather the need for a transcendental guarantor of justice and agreements.

[50] Ibid., p. 91.

[51] Leibniz: "On Natural Law", in: Leibniz: *Political Writings*, p.79.

on the question of slavery he rejects the contractualist re-analysis of Pufendorf in favour of the traditional Aristotelian account. For Pufendorf, legal slavery must imply a contract in which mutual needs are satisfied; the slave, recognising his poverty or lack of intelligence, commits his labour to the master, who in turn promises him lifelong sustenance – this presumably even when the slave is too old to work. The slave cannot be sold against his will to anyone else or abused in any way.[52]

Leibniz, for his part, expresses some reserve over theory of natural slavery. He insists that it cannot be right to say that there are natural slaves, who exist solely for the sake of the master. It is only cattle who can be thought to fall into this category, beings existing solely for our use. And, unlike Philo and St. Paul who asserted that slavery was permissible because only the body of the slave was subordinated, while the mind remained free (and enslaved only by its own vices and passions),[53] Leibniz insisted that both souls and bodies belong to God, not to the temporal master. This puts limits on what one can do to a slave; perfect servitude, as in late Roman law, in which the master possessed all rights over the slave's body, including sexual usage and any form of punishment and torture,[54] is impossible, and slavery "in all its sharpness" is wrong. One may not make a slave "bad or unhappy." Further, all humans, even those who appear to lack understanding and initiative, are capable of acquiring understanding and happiness – and perhaps, the suggestion is, they will, "especially because" souls are immortal.[55] Slavery is contingent and temporary, but only because life is eternal. And even if the servitude of the dumb, uneducable animals does not apply to humans, "there is still something which is similar and comes close to it, which is sometimes conformable to nature."[56]

The common good was accordingly widely agreed in the 17th century to be compatible with natural or contractual slavery. In addition, it justified the brutal handling of the 'barbarian' world outside of Christian Europe. The Chinese were excepted because they were in Leibniz's view civilised and ethical, and they did not pose a threat to Europe.[57] Although as Ian Almond has

---

[52] Pufendorf: *On the Duty of Man and Citizen*, pp. 129–131.
[53] Catherine Hezer: *Jewish Slavery in Antiquity*, Oxford 2006, pp. 59f.
[54] Kyle Harper: *Slavery in the Late Roman World*, Cambridge 2016, pp. 275–425.
[55] Leibniz: "On Natural Law", in: Leibniz: *Political Writings*, p. 78.
[56] Ibid.
[57] On Leibniz's respect and admiration for Chinese culture, Franklin Perkins: "Virtue, Reason, and Cultural Exchange: Leibniz's Praise of Chinese Morality", in: *Journal of the History of*

shown, Leibniz's attitude to the Muslim world incorporated moments of real scientific and philological curiosity and became less panicked after the end of the war between the Ottomans and the Holy League of Austria, Poland and Venice in 1699, in his prime he maintained a crusading and conquistadorial outlook.[58] Not only did the threat of an Ottoman takeover of Europe have to be met, but the infidel had to be converted and the barbarian civilised, and this meant invasion, not conciliation. If Leibniz had hoped that his metaphysics could bring peace by bridging the divisions between Protestants and Catholics, there was no such hope in the case of Christianity and Islam, or Europeans and native people, whose barbarism made this impossible. They could however be used. In an alarming note,

> "A Method for Instituting a New, Invincible Militia That Can Subjugate the Entire Earth, Easily Seize Control over Egypt, or Establish American Colonies," the youthful Leibniz of 1671 proposed ejecting the population from "certain island of Africa, such as Madagascar."

> "To this island slaves captured from all over the barbarian world will be brought, and from all of the wild coastal regions of Africa, Arabia, New Guinea, etc. To this end Ethiopians, Nigritians, Angolans, Caribbeans, Canadians, and Hurons fit the bill, without discrimination. What a lovely bunch of semi-beasts! But so that this mass of men may be shaped in any way desired, it is useful only to take boys up to around the age of twelve, as this is better than [attempting to] transform girls and adults."[59]

In this scenario, they are put through rigorous physical training enabling them to topple even European fortifications and then set loose on the world.

The theme of the *Mars Christianissimus* of 1683 is that the slaughter of Christians by Christians is unacceptable and that French aggression would be better directed towards the 'Turk.' The 'Egyptian Plan' of a decade earlier, to which Leibniz hoped to persuade Louis XIV. had a similar aim. Thus the first principle of exception to *neminem laede*: the others are not altogether human, is invoked along with the third principle of the general good. Wars, Leibniz says,

---

Ideas 63 (2002), pp. 447–64 and id.: *Leibniz and China: A Commerce of Light*, Cambridge 2004.

[58] Ian Almond: "Leibniz, Historicism, and the 'Plague of Islam'", in: *Eighteenth-Century Studies* 39/4 (2006), pp. 463–483.

[59] A IV, 1, 408–410; transl. by Justin Smith. http://www.jehsmith.com/philosophy/2009/01/a-method-for-instituting-a-new-invinvible-militia.html#more.

> "should not be waged on men but on beasts (that is, barbarians)" to tame them [...]. "If the most rigid censor of inner conscience should pass judgement he would not only approve but even order [a holy] war."[60]

For Bacon has shown that "a war (having the greatest efficacy) for promoting culture and religion among barbarians is just." Its aim should not be extermination or servitude but "wisdom and happiness and the emendation of human kind." The success of the Egyptian Plan would be the first step towards

> "expansion without limit, towards expansion on the scale of Alexander the great; thus the Gospel would be carried to the most distant region with happiness filling the whole earth."

Austria would then dominate the East, France the West.[61] The holy war undertaken by a unified Christian Europe would not only put an end to barbarism and save souls. It would effectively strike at Dutch commercial dominance and achieve control of the Mediterranean for France.[62]

Leibniz's *Caesarinus Fuerstenerius* of 1677 invokes a scheme combining theocracy, directed inwards to European conciliation and outwards towards barbarian elimination, with autonomy for individual princes, whose hands, he thinks, must not be tied in administering domestic affairs. According to this scheme, there is a supreme commander, a Caesar,

> "the born leader of the Christians against the infidels: it is mainly for him to destroy schisms [...] to maintain good order, in short to act through the authority of his position to that the Church and the Republic and Christendom suffer no harm."[63]

Over and over, then, we encounter in Leibniz's early writings the view that the unification of the Christian churches is an enabling condition of waging war effectively against the threat of Islam.

---

[60] Translation Perkins: *Leibniz and China*, p. 111.
[61] A IV, 1, 386; tr. Almond: "Plague of Islam", p. 472.
[62] Ivo Budil: "Gottfried Wilhelm Leibniz and the Idea of Conquest of Egypt in the Context of the Emergence of the World Economy", in: *Prague Papers on the History of International Relations* (2009), pp. 65–86.
[63] Leibniz: "Caesarinus Fuerstenerius", Amsterdam, 1677; A IV, 2, N. 1, transl. in: Leibniz: *Political Writings*, p. 111.

To summarise, Leibniz's value system in the realm of real politics is elitist, nationalistic,[64] and decentralised, and, at the same time, charitable and aspirational. His views on distributive justice correspond in many respects to Grotius's: we should reward the "more intelligent" over than the "less intelligent," value our neighbours over strangers, and assist the poor and needy.[65]

4. The 'System of War' and its Critics

Opposition to warfare in general, as a survey of ancient political philosophy indicates, and to holy war in particular, is scarce and sporadic in Western philosophical and theological writings. Erasmus is one of the very rare pre-modern critics of warfare, seeing it as an institution detrimental to the common good as disruptive, expensive, and encouraging of the worst human tendencies.[66] His *Querela Pacis* is an indictment of the irrationality, expense, and futility of warfare; he regards kings as ordinary humans, petty, vindictive, and spoiling for a fight, rather than as God's chosen agents.[67] The Turk, Erasmus says, is "our brother," and better allured by

> "gentle, kind, and friendly treatment […] than by attacking him with the drawn sword, as if he were a savage brute, without a heart to feel, or a reasoning faculty

---

[64] See Almond's discussion of the "Ermahnung an den Deutschen" and "Plague of Islam", p. 11f.
[65] "As a result, it behooves us when distributing resources responsibly to individuals or groups to ensure that we give more weight to the intelligent than to the less intelligent, more to a neighbour than to a stranger. And more to the poor than to the rich, as their conduct and the nature of the case requires." Hugo Grotius: *Laws of War and Peace*, transl. by Kelsey, III: 1748.
[66] "You have exhausted your treasury," he declares to royalty, "You have fleeced your people, you have loaded peaceable good subjects with unnecessary burdens, and you have encouraged the wicked unprincipled adventurers in acts of rapine and violence […]. The taste for science, arts, and letters, languishes a long while. Trade and commerce continue shackled and impeded." Erasmus: *The Complaint of Peace. Translated from the Querela Pacis* (A.D. 1521) transl. by Thomas Paynell, Chicago 1917, repr. Indianapolis 2001. (Online Library of Philosophy), p. 67.
[67] "[…][If] war is so unhallowed that it becomes the deadliest bane of piety and religion; if there is nothing more calamitous to mortals, and more detestable to heaven, I ask, how in the name of God, can I believe those beings to be rational creatures; how can I believe them to be otherwise than stark mad; who, with such a waste of treasure, with so ardent a zeal, with so great an effort, with so many arts, so much anxiety, and so much danger, endeavour to drive me away from them, and purchase endless misery and mischief at a price so high? God made man unarmed." Erasmus: *The Complaint of Peace*, p. 2f.; José A. Fernández: "Erasmus on the Just War", in: *Journal of the History of Ideas* 34/2 (1973) pp. 209–226; Fred R. Dallmayr: "A War Against the Turks? Erasmus on War and Peace", in: *Asian Journal of Social Science* 34/1 (2006), pp. 67–85.

to be persuaded,' and only peace can open 'universal intercourse among mankind."[68]

However, Erasmus, like Leibniz, was most dismayed by the warfare of Christians with Christians.

> "If we must of necessity go to war [...]. It is certainly a lesser evil to contend with an infidel, than that Christians should mutually harass and destroy their own fraternity."[69]

Erasmus's works landed on the Index of prohibited books, and new moral-theological justifications for military conquest outside of Europe were added in the era and the Spanish conquest of the New World. These drew on philosophical-theological sources, including the Old Testament story of the invitees who refused the King's invitation to his son's wedding and murdered his emissaries, and who were justly destroyed along with their city in retaliation;[70] Christ's declaration that he came not to bring peace but a sword and division;[71] and Aristotle's theories of war and slavery. Yet, within the just war philosophical tradition, 'holy war' was a contested concept. In the argument between Bartolemeo de las Casas and Bishop Sepulveda in 1550–51, the latter invoked the notion of natural superiority and the "for their own good" argument, describing the inhabitants of the New World as barbaric, illiterate, ignorant, unreasoning, vicious, cruel and impious, while las Casas defended their intelligence, culture, and rationality. The latter did however refer to "Turks and Moors" as the "truly barbaric scum of the nations."[72]

Scholars are divided over whether the natural lawyers of the early modern period were more concerned to consolidate European identity and to legitimate warfare and empire or to hold the actions of princes to standards of religious and moral accountability.[73] The emphasis varies from one author to

---

[68] Erasmus: *The Complaint of Peace*, p. 56.
[69] Ibid.
[70] Matthew 42, 1–10.
[71] Luke 12, 51.
[72] Bartolemeo de las Casas: *In Defense of the Indians*, ed. and trans. by Stafford Poole, DeKalb IL 1992, p. 47. See Nina Berman: "Imperial Violence and the Limits of Tolerance: Reading Luther with las Casas", in: Florian Kläger/Gerd Bayer (eds.): *Early Modern Constructions of Europe: Literature, Culture, History*, Routledge 2016.
[73] On the former interpretation, see Richard Waswo: "The Formation of Natural Law to Justify Colonialism, 1539–1689", in: *New Literary History* 27/4 (1996) pp. 743–759; Robert Williams: *The American Indian in Western Legal Thought*, Oxford 1992. For a more balanced view,

another, but the lawyers are concerned to enunciate the exceptions they believe appropriate to the tacitly accepted principle of *neminem laede*, discouraging excesses, and emphasising the priority of the universal natural law over the limited religious authority of the Pope and the temporal authority of rulers. So Francisco de Vitoria argued in lectures published as *De Indis De Jure Bellis* of 1557, and known to Leibniz, that Christians had no right to invade, dispossess and enslave non Christians in America on the grounds that they were heretics, atheists or idolaters, or on account of their sexual practices. He defended only the right of foreigners to travel in their lands without being molested, to trade, and to carry off gold and silver. They were allowed to preach the Gospel and to make everyone listen, though not to force its acceptance.[74] The natives could be justly killed if they refused to offer hospitality in this regard.

The purpose of civil society, said Leibniz's most famous follower, Christian Wolff, nearly two centuries later in his *Jus gentium* (1749) is "to give mutual assistance in perfecting itself and its condition, consequently the promotion of the common good by its combined powers."[75] Although Leibniz would surely have subscribed to this formula, Wolff's departures from Leibnizian political theory were significant. Wolff regarded nations as "free individual persons living in a state of nature,"[76] and so as morally required by the law of nature to assist one another in promoting the good universally. He insisted that Christ's injunction to love your enemies was to be taken seriously as the "best interpreter of law of nature" and as corrective of the earlier "absurd belief" that, he says, "has obsessed so many that we should love our friends and pursue our enemies with hatred."[77] War must be waged without hatred; otherwise war would not be allowable, for love and affection to others is an "absolutely unchangeable" natural obligation. Love of enemies may be rare, he concedes, – it is not a doctrine for the crowd – but it should be taught insofar as "some may at least perform their duties if they know them."[78] Thus,

---

Georg Cavallar: *Imperfect Cosmopolis: Studies in the History of International Legal Theory and Cosmopolitan Ideas*, Cardiff 2011; Sankar Muthu: *Enlightenment against Empire*, Princeton 2009.

[74] Francisco de Vitoria: *De Indis*, Id. Part II, §III.

[75] Christian Wolff: *The Law of Nations Treated According to a Scientific Method* (*Jus gentium methodo scientifica pertractatum*), transl. by Joseph H. Drake, Oxford 1934, Prolegomena § 8, p. 11.

[76] Ibid., §2, p. 5 and p. 9.

[77] Ibid., §156, p. 84.

[78] Ibid., §177, pp. 92f.

"every nation ought to love and cherish every other nation as itself, even though it be an enemy. [...] Every nation ought to have the fixed and lasting desire to promote the happiness of other nations and to do all it can to make them happy and avoid making them unhappy."[79]

Holy war was incompatible with that duty.

Foreign nations, Wolff thought, may not be punished for wickedness, violations of the laws of nature, or offences against God.[80] Evil is not punishable by itself, and atheism, deism and idolatry are not just causes for war; certain things, he says, must just be endured.[81] For Wolff, a learned and cultivated people have an obligation to improve the others – but not by coercion: "barbarism and uncultivated manners give you no right against [another] nation."[82] He denies that utility is a legal justification for war, excluding as just causes or rationales "increase in power, desire for fame, passion of vengeance, and display of strength."[83] Fear of a neighbour is not a just cause, nor is their building of fortifications or their preparing for war.[84] Only injury, occurrent or predicted on the basis of strong evidence, by another nation, is a justifying reason.[85]

The condition of waging war with your beloved enemy puts considerable strain on Wolff's purportedly mathematically rigorous treatment of the law of peoples, insofar as love does not preclude assassinating the enemy's leaders, burning their crops, fields, houses and orchards, poisoning them (though not their springs), or pillaging their cities and villages to recoup damages, though not raping their women.[86] Throughout the text, we witness Wolff's well-meaning attempts to balance his belief in the superiority of Christian nations with a tolerance for 'barbarism' and to balance his ideals of universal sociability and mutual aid with the need to react with effective force against aggressors.

Although Hobbes is not usually seen as Erasmus's pacifist successor, this issue deserves to be rethought, for he strongly promoted the advantages

---

[79] Ibid., §161–162, pp. 86f.
[80] Ibid., § 637, p. 326.
[81] Ibid., § 638, p. 327.
[82] Ibid., §168–169, p. 89.
[83] Ibid., § 645, p. 331.
[84] Ibid., § 641, p. 329
[85] Ibid., § 617, p. 314.
[86] Ibid., §876–882, pp. 449–452.

of the peace dividend, the possibility of living "securely, happily, elegantly."[87] He seems to have derived his notion of the "war of all against all," not primarily from his observation of individual behaviour, but from his knowledge of group vs. group belligerence: the reported conduct of the "savages" in North America, of the Athenians according to Thucydides; of early humans as imagined by Lucretius; and from the civil wars in Britain and the disturbances of the continent. Hobbes notes that there is constant readiness for international warfare, producing some degree of hostility and anxiety, but he observes that as long as it does not interfere with and may even encourage "the Industry of their Subjects," it does not necessarily render life nasty, brutish, and short or drive people everywhere to unite for their own preservation under a transnational sovereign.[88]

Sixty years later, however, the notion that a transfer of power from fractious nation-states to an overarching authority was the key to peaceful economic and cultural development was taken up by the Abbé de St. Pierre in his *Projet pour rendre la Paix Perpetuelle en Europe* first published in 1713, a remarkable and little studied document for whose central proposal Kant seems to receive most of the credit. The Abbé begins from a starting position of concern for the "conflagrations, atrocities, and cruelties" suffered on the frontiers and "all the evils caused to the sovereigns of Europe and their people" by European warfare.

> "[S]ensibly moved by all the evils which War causes the sovereigns of Europe and their subjects, I resolved to penetrate to the original sources of the evil and to seek through my own reflections whether this evil was so attached to the nature of sovereignty and sovereigns that it was absolutely without remedy [...] The nature of man himself seemed an obstacle [...]."[89]

---

[87] Thomas Hobbes: *De Homine* § 3, in: *Man and Citizen*, ed. by Bernard Gert and transl. by Charles T. Wood/Thomas S. K. Scott-Craig/Bernard Gert, Indianapolis 1991, p. 40.
[88] "Though there had never been any time, wherein particular men were in a condition of warre one against another; yet in all times, Kings and Persons of Soveraigne authority, because of their Independency, are in continual jealousies, and in the state and posture of Gladiators; having their weapons pointing and their eyes fixed on one another. [...] But because they uphold thereby, the Industry of their Subjects; there does not follow from it, that misery, which accompanies the Liberty of particular men." Thomas Hobbes: *Leviathan*, ed. by Richard Tuck, Cambridge 1996, p. 90.
[89] Charles-Irénée Castel/Abbé de St. Pierre: *Projet pour rendre la Paix Perpetuelle en Europe*, Paris 1986, pp. 9f.

The sovereigns of Europe, he thinks, resemble those of the barbarians of Africa and America. Their rivalries and strivings produce a "perpetual restlessness," and up to now no method of resolving differences except war has ever been tried. The balance of power between France and Austria, he reflects, does not prevent foreign wars or civil disturbances.[90] Equilibria of power are by nature fragile and readily disturbed by any sovereign who is ambitious and impatient.[91] The remedy is to appoint arbiters more powerful than the arbitrated and motivated to arbitrate.[92] The Abbé does not envision an imperium headed by a Hobbesian autocrat but a consort of nations, a union of the existing eighteen sovereignties of Europe. A tribunal is to be established in Utrecht, and deputies will be assigned from each country to resolve disputes amongst them. Demobbed officers of national armies and others negatively affected by pacification are to receive compensation. There will be a standing army for defence of the Union against non-Union aggressors, but the Abbé foresees, in the short run the incorporation of the Turks and the Moscovites, and eventually all of Africa and Asia into the Union.[93]

To defend his proposal, the Abbé compares what he calls the "system of war" with "system of peace" on a number of counts. The system of war implies revolutions and upsets, seizure of territory and aggrandisement, whereas the system of peace preserves individual nations and their boundaries intact.[94] In the system of war, chance largely determines who wins or loses and who is killed. In the system of peace, everyone is less vulnerable to chance and so freer and more independent because others cannot aggress with impunity. Peace allows for progress in education, law and other institutions; the Abbé favours even the education of women in village schools.[95] War promotes barbarism; for the arts and sciences flourish and progress when the talented are not drawn off into the military.[96] Peace preserves the enduring monuments

---

[90] Ibid., p. 11.
[91] Ibid., p. 38.
[92] Ibid., p. 29.
[93] Tomaz Mastnak in an otherwise valuable essay cites D'Alembert's report that the the Abbé sought "l'anéantissement futur du mahométisme", as evidence of his participation in the syndrome of Christian unification for the destruction of Islam. But the context of the phrase makes clear that the anéantissement was meant to occur through enlightenment, not conquest. Abbé de Saint-Pierre: "European Union and the Turk", in: *History of Political Thought* 19/4 (1998), p. 575. Cf. Jean Le Rond d' Alembert: *Eloges*, vol. III., Paris/Berlin 1821, p. 278.
[94] Castel/St. Pierre: *Projet*, p. 98.
[95] Ibid., p. 127.
[96] Ibid., p. 128.

of civilization: academies, colleges, libraries canals, aqueducts, hospitals palaces, temples, ports, bridges, sculpture, architecture, records. Commerce, "universal, free, open and equal," can flourish uninterrupted; the rural population can devote itself to agricultural production, enhancing tax revenues; and there are vast savings in the expenses for navies and foot soldiers.

There are other moral advantages to peace, the Abbé finds. The honour of sovereigns and their glorious ambitions, would be praiseworthy if they didn't cause such misery to so many millions, but the sovereign cannot reasonably wish his reputation to be based on the burning of villages, the massacre of inhabitants, and the ruin of families. With peace, he can choose his own occupations. Rather than making his aim the acquisition of territory; the sovereign required to respect national boundaries will concentrate instead on internal affairs.[97] Further, because foreign powers are typically involved in civil insurrections, which occur when people lose confidence in their own sovereign, peace should eliminate civil conflict and the assassinations and poisonings undertaken for policy ends. A pacified union need not be secretive, fearing and plotting against its neighbours. Finally, the Belgian, Swiss, German, and Netherlandish unions of provinces show that it is not impossible to form them.[98] The renunciation of conquest by Henry IV., the most powerful monarch in Europe of his time, shows that great princes can undergo conversion by reason.[99] After laying out the advantages of peace, the bulk of the *Projet* was taken up with citing and responding to objections, practical, theoretical and theological, including the objection that his book was too long and that "princes do not read."

Leibniz was initially unpersuaded. To Hobbes's argument that lethal conflict and fear of death made peace the chief political and moral imperative, Leibniz replied that Hobbes's "fallacy" was that "he thinks things which can entail inconvenience should not be borne at all."[100] Certain geographical and historical situations entail that a prince must fight continuously, he remarks in the *Codex Juris Gentium* of 1693, and peace can only offer a "breathing space" between wars.[101] Both Hobbes's scheme and the Abbé's ran up against Leibniz's longstanding preferences for regional autonomy, distributed authority

---

[97] Ibid., p. 32.
[98] Ibid., p. 52.
[99] Ibid., p. 264.
[100] Leibniz: "Caesarinus Fürstenerius", in: Leibniz: *Leibniz. Political Writings*, p. 119.
[101] Leibniz: *Codex Juris Gentium*, Hannover 1693, Preface; A IV, 5, N. 7; transl. in Leibniz: *Political Writings*, p. 166.

and balance of power in worldly matters involving Europe and for submission to a centralised authority only as members of the virtual kingdom of God and – perhaps – under a single spiritual-military leader of the Christian world.

In June 1712, Leibniz wrote to the historian and savant Jean-Léonor Le Gallois de Grimarest that he had seen "something" of the project of M. de St. Pierre for maintaining a perpetual peace in Europe. "I am reminded," he said "of a device in a cemetery, with the words: *Pax perpetua;* for the dead do not fight any longer; but the living are of another humor; and the most powerful do not respect tribunals at all."[102] The *Projet* is, he says, a "romance" – though Leibniz goes on to suggest, fancifully, that the Pope might be called upon to serve as the president of a peace-enforcing tribunal in which case

> "it would be necessary at the same time that the ecclesiastics resume their old authority, and that an interdiction and excommunication make kings and kingdoms tremble."[103]

The *Projet*, with its careful treatment of contingencies and objections, had not yet been published, so Leibniz's reaction was not well considered. His last remarks, dated 1715, the year before his death, indicate that the book had only just reached him, sent by the Abbé himself. Leibniz was no longer dismissive. In writing up his "Observations," on the book, he says that he is persuaded that the project of perpetual peace is "on the whole, feasible, and that its execution would be one of the most useful things in the world."[104] And he wrote to the Abbé that "It is always good to tell the public about [such schemes] [...] someone may be moved by them when one least expects it." Although no minister would risk offending a prince by recommending them during his tenure, he thinks the project might be worth proposing "at the point of death, particularly if family interests did not oblige him to continue his policies in the tomb and beyond."[105] And in a letter of the same year to Rémond de Montmort, he describes war, plague, and hunger as the three greatest evils besetting the human race and voices the opinion that human beings could free them-

---

[102] Leibniz, Letter to Grimarest, Dutens V, 65f; transl. in: Leibniz: *Political Writings*, p. 183.
[103] Ibid., p. 184.
[104] Leibniz: "Observations on the Abbé de St. Pierre's Projet", in: Dutens V, 56–60; transl. in: Leibniz: *Political Writings*, p. 178.
[105] Leibniz, Letter to the Abbé de St. Pierre, Dutens V, 61f.; transl. in: Leibniz: *Political Writings*, p. 177.

selves from all of them, but that the first two are within the power of individuals; the latter requires the co-operation of sovereigns which is difficult to obtain.[106]

5. Leibniz's 'Memoir' and the 'System of Peace'

There are several possible apologetic responses to the identification of reprehensible views in a philosopher valued and admired on other grounds. One response is to try to show why the field of intellectually available positions was far narrower in the philosopher's own time then than it is today and why the social context and the philosopher's own livelihood favoured some positions over others. Another strategy is to search for qualifications to seemingly straightforward assertions, and to locate misgivings, ambivalences, and changes of opinion with age and experience. I have employed each of these strategies in the preceding sections. Anti-militarism was and remains an eccentric doctrine outside of mainstream political philosophy; Leibniz was a jurist employed by princes; and, just at the end of his life when it was no longer necessary to please his masters, he may have undergone a significant change of heart.

A fourth response takes the position that we contemporary readers must and may choose from the writings of the past what we think is valuable and what we prefer to ignore. We are interested, after all, in what was *innovative* in our philosophers, not in the 'prejudices of their times' or the positions to which their temperaments and circumstances disposed them. We may attend to the letter, not the spirit, developing it to suit our own times and indeed our own temperaments and circumstances. And so I turn to the positive aspect of Leibniz's conception of the common good.

As noted at the start, Leibniz was a 'projector' – a very great projector. He argued as a member of the political and scientific elite with the ear, if not the full attention of princes, and he argued for an important goal. The goal was the redirection of national revenues and the redirection of human effort and ingenuity to scientific projects that were neither conquistadorial, nor aimed at gratifying the vanity and curiosity of patrons in intervals of peace, but at erasing the deprivations and increasing the happiness and security of the badly off.

---

[106] Leibniz, Letter to Rémond de Montmort, Dutens V, 20f.; quoted in Antonio Tryuyol Serra: "Die Lehre vom gerechten Krieg bei Grotius und Leibniz und ihre Bedeutung für die Gegenwart", in: *Studia Leibnitiana* 16 (1984), pp. 60–72, p. 69.

In this connection, Leibniz asserts that human health and happiness will be furthered by our inquiring into "the nature of bodies in the universe [...] to notice the respects in which they can be useful to our preservation and even to our greater perfection." And he says that it is "important to know human history, and the arts and sciences which depend on it," including literary history, which teaches us about the progress of knowledge, also history of laws and of conflicts and revolutions, and the history of religion.[107] What he calls "the torrent of general corruption" can only be staunched, by addressing "the want of attention or of application, and the want of intelligence or of information."[108]

To a large extent, the redirection of national revenues towards the acquisition of useful knowledge has happened. Resources unthinkable in the 17th and 18th century are devoted to research in the natural and social sciences, and it can be assumed that virtually all appeals to financing bodies cite humanitarian applications for the discoveries the applicants hope to make: life shall be longer, healthier, more fun, more secure, more productive through the harvesting of the fruits of the natural and social sciences. On the domestic side we have evidence that this system of knowledge production and transfer, directed and funded by governments and other patrons, works for some aspects of the public good, with regard to medicine and technology, and to some extent for transportation and energy. The flow of resources has been less successful with respect to the problems of poverty and deprivation, and, with regard to the problems of international conflict, warfare and readiness for warfare, its results are tragically mixed.

We are still here, but we live in what St. Pierre called the "system of war." The commitment to military preparedness and the struggle for military superiority underwrites jobs, including academic jobs, manual labour, and employment and research funding in the technology sectors. Scientists, manufacturers and vendors and their taxing regimes profit from military inventions and from arms sales, the effects of which in fomenting conflict are well established.[109] Allegedly, militarism keeps us safe, though we are beginning to feel,

---

[107] Gottfried Wilhelm Leibniz: "Memoire pour des Personnes éclaireée et de bonne intention" (c.1692); A IV, 4, 616; transl. in: Leibniz: *Political Writings*, pp. 103–110.
[108] Ibid., p. 103.
[109] Arms transfer, whether in the form of 'foreign aid' or direct weapons sales, appears to predict and so to be likely a cause of warfare to a far greater extent than such factors as repression and colonial legacy. See Cassady Craft/Joseph P. Smaldone: "The Arms Trade and the Incidence of Political Violence in Sub-Saharan Africa, 1967–97", in: *Journal of Peace Research* 39/6 (2002), pp. 693–710.

and to be very unsafe in places we used to feel safe. The outgoings on the system of war are massive – in the USA amounting reportedly to 54% of discretionary spending of tax revenues – while governments plead their inability to finance health care, or to support and incentivise protection of the environment and repair of infrastructure. All this is not conducive to the common good. So why, with all the intelligence and organisational power of humanity, do we remain, in international politics in the Hobbesian state of nature? Must just war theory in the hands of philosophers forever remain focussed on the question: What are the exceptions to *neminem laede*? Which ones may I hurt, and how may I hurt them? With drones but not with germs?

One answer to this question is that the world presents us with an insoluble prisoner's dilemma. No one can downscale or disarm unless all do. But how could such a general agreement ever come into force, especially when so many nations are ruled by bullies, tyrants, and madmen? So, it seems, we will interminably run up against the problems of incentives, motivations, risks, strategies and payoffs, and contemporary discussions of the problem of perpetual peace will continue to circulate around the problem of how to achieve co-operation and how much co-operation vs. autonomy is desirable or possible.[110]

Although for Leibniz improvements in the arts of war were amongst the foreseen benefits of the increase of knowledge, so too were improvements in the arts of peace.[111] There are actions a nation can undertake unilaterally without having solved the problems of co-operation and sovereignty. But the knowledge regarding the art of peace that we need not take the form of theories about the justified exceptions to *neminem laede*; rather, we need to know how to make ourselves so that others do not want to hurt us and how to dissuade them from hurting us or other people. We need knowledge of how to react so as to prevent escalation when they do hurt us or hurt others.

We have a head start on the problem, insofar as we know far more about the causes of warfare than about the causes of cancer, which as involving an array of molecular phenomena embedded in complex biological systems is still relatively poorly understood. By contrast, since the first days of historiography, our political theorists have revealed the causes of warfare to us. International politics is the realm of blackmail, hostage-holding, psychopathic charisma and pathological obedience, and these are well-studied phenomena.

---

[110] See the essays in James Bohman/Matthias Lutz-Bachmann (eds.): *Perpetual Peace: Essays on Kant's Cosmopolitanism*, Cambridge MA 1997.
[111] Gottfried Wilhelm Leibniz: "Memoir", in: Leibniz: *Leibniz. Political Writings*, p. 108.

The causes of war include: the need of expanding populations for natural resources; the desire for personal and national glory; the satisfaction taken in the exhibition of valour and self-sacrifice, retaliation for old injuries; the moralistic aggression aroused by disgust at other people's practices; and susceptibility to the charisma of leaders. Add to them the love of technology and technological innovation, appreciation for beautiful and powerful – or at least nowadays powerful – weaponry, the excitement of mass mobilisations, and the satisfaction to be taken in the teamwork and co-ordination involved in recruitment, mobilisation, and logistics, and you have a formula for conflict without end, or at least until someone impulsively presses a button.

The claim that warfare is rooted in human nature means that these motives and incentives weigh heavily with human beings and survive in a range of economic and social systems, not that they cannot be redirected or moderated. If we cannot, or in some cases should not suppress them, we must divert them, and to less harmful ends, which need not be a version of the Egyptian Plan. The humanistic and social science disciplines cited by Leibniz have an important role to play because their object of study is 'human nature.' They are in the best position to understand why people want to hurt one another, how their delusions get a grip on them, and how they deceive themselves in formulating their nefarious plans. Our sociologists and anthropologists of religion,[112] and our historians and philosophers who have long studied the dark and the bright moments of intellectual and political history, can contribute meaningfully. We will need to develop models for successful international policing that are based on the important concept of 'non-offensive defense.'[113]

For Leibniz, not only inadequate attention, application, and financing, but also despair of succeeding in the pursuit of useful knowledge was a major obstacle to progress. In his 'Memoir,' he presented his metaphysical vision of the virtual commonwealth of souls as "true unities," unassailable by external forces and harmoniously co-existing, thereby assigning the visible world with its bloody strife and sometimes fragmented people and objects to the realm of well-founded phenomena, at the same time remaining alert to signs of concrete social progress. Even if, for most of us, the metaphysical image of the monad-

---

[112] Scott Atran: *Talking to the Enemy: Faith, Brotherhood, and the (un) Making of Terrorists*, New York 2010.
[113] Najib Mahmood: 'Non-Offensive Defense and Nonviolence Response to Terrorism,' U.S. Army War College, Carlisle Barracks, PA, 2008. Approved for public release. www.dtic.mil/cgi-bin/GetTRDoc?AD=ADA479791

world will not provide a motive for political effort, and critics who see metaphysics as a distraction from and as offering excuses for what Bayle called the "crimes and misfortunes of mankind" have a point. But a solid Leibnizian moral that might be drawn is that, for "enlightened persons of good intention," a commitment to the growth of knowledge in the service of the common good will require imagination and moral concern of a fundamentally different quality from that that guides our everyday *Realpolitk*.

On the Grain of Sand and Heaven's Infinity[*]

Herbert Breger (Hanover)

1. A Quarrel in Paris

In 1702 Leibniz received a letter from Pierre Varignon in Paris.[1] Varignon was working with the new infinitesimal calculus and for this he was criticised by some Parisian scholars, in particular by Gallois and Rolle, who considered the infinitesimal calculus to be faulty. As of late these opponents of infinitesimal calculus were referring to an essay by Leibniz in the *Journal de Trévoux*,[2] which they saw as confirmation of their criticism. This had put Varignon on the spot, and he asked Leibniz for a clear and unmistakeable statement in order to be able to show this to the opponents of the infinitesimal calculus.

In the essay in question, Leibniz had reacted to a critical observation on infinitesimal calculus by the editor of the *Journal de Trévoux*. With this method of calculation one was attempting to penetrate into infinity, and not only that: one was also attempting to grasp the infinite of the infinite, even an infinity of infinities.[3] Since the journal was published by the Jesuits, this critique had clear theological and philosophical references. Leibniz wrote to his correspondence partner Pinsson, and the latter passed on the text of the reply to this critique to be printed in the *Journal de Trévoux*. So Leibniz was writing here for philosophically and theologically educated readers as well, who were familiar with the very elaborated medieval discussions on various types of the infinite and who possessed a rather superficial knowledge of mathematics. How could one explain to such readers infinitely small magnitudes, which were nevertheless supposed to be infinitely large in relation to the differentials

---

[*] My kind thanks to Dr. Catherine Atkinson for the translation.
[1] A III, 8, 798–801. The letter dates from 28 November 1701; Leibniz received it late.
[2] A I, 20, 492–494 (letter to Pinsson from the end of September 1701); *Journal de Trévoux* = *Mémoires pour l'histoire des sciences et des beaux arts*, November/December 1701, pp. 270f.; reprint: *Journal de Trévoux ou Mémoires pour l'histoire des sciences et des arts*, vol. I, 1701, pp. 270–272. The *Journal de Trévoux* had already printed a letter from Leibniz to Pinsson in January/February 1701; thus one can assume that Leibniz wrote to Pinsson about infinitesimal calculus so that the latter would hand on the text for publication in the *Journal de Trévoux*.
[3] *Journal de Trévoux* = *Mémoires pour l'histoire des sciences*, May/June 1701, p. 223.

of the second order? Leibniz sought to find a way of answering this conveniently without getting tangled up uselessly in metaphysical unpleasantness.[4] In the essay in question in the *Journal de Trévoux,* he first mentioned the success of the new method of calculating and as regards mathematical rigour referred to the book by L'Hôpital. To placate the experts in medieval philosophy, Leibniz added that one did not need anything infinite or infinitely small in the strict sense of the word. In optics one also speaks of the sun's rays entering parallel – just as if the sun were infinitely far away. One regards the earth as a point in relation to the distance of the fixed stars. And as regards the existence of infinitesimals of the second order, then one can continue the illustrative comparison: In relation to the earth's radius, a small ball in our hand or a grain of sand can be seen as a point.[5] This would be sufficient; the infinitely small magnitudes are not really needed. It is not surprising that the opponents of infinitesimal calculus triumphed and Varignon felt uneasy.

In his answer to Varignon on 2 February 1702, Leibniz explains why he chose his examples; it was his intention "pour rendre le raisonnement sensible à tout le monde."[6] But this should not be judged as an admission of a mistake, since he repeats his comments on fixed stars, the earth and the grain of sand and he certainly does not make the impression of having been caught making a false statement or even just clumsy wording. However, he supplies further explanations, speaking among other things of the fact that the earth's diameter is incomparably small in relation to the distance of the fixed stars and that a grain of sand is incomparably small in relation to the earth's diameter, and he refers to his comments on the incomparably small magnitudes in the *Acta eruditorum.*[7] Varignon is clearly satisfied with the explanations; he

---

[4] GM III, 692: "Literis ejus respondeo, ut vides, nec video qua alia commodiore ratione possim, ne tricis metaphysicis frustra implicemur." Accompanied by these words Leibniz sent his reply to Varignon on 3 February 1702 to be forwarded to Bernoulli. Cf. also GM III, 836 and ibid. IV, 91: Leibniz wanted to avoid "des controverses metaphysiques" and "ces subtilités".
[5] In A I, 20, 493 and in the *Journal de Trévoux,* Nov./Dec. 1701, p. 271 there is only talk of a small ball or sphere. Varignon speaks of a grain of sand in his letter to Leibniz on 28 November 1701 (A III, 8, 799, 800). In his reply to Varignon of 2 February 1702 Leibniz then speaks also of a grain of sand (GM IV, 91f.). – In the essay in the *Acta eruditorum* (Ibid. VI, 150f., 168), Leibniz had attempted to make the possibility of infinitesimals of the second order seem plausible with a different argument; however, this argument would have been too complicated for the *Journal de Trévoux.*
[6] Ibid. IV, 91–95.
[7] *Acta eruditorum,* February 1689, pp. 85f.; ibid. VI, 150f., 168.

gives Leibniz's letter to the *Journal des Savants* to be published.[8] When Varignon reports to Leibniz that Gouye, the editor of the *Journal de Trévoux,* sees a change in Leibniz's point of view compared with his letter to Varignon of 2 February 1702,[9] Leibniz answers that he had said more in his letter to Varignon than in the article in *Journal de Trévoux*, but nothing contrary to that.[10]

2. The Criticism of Leibniz.

But that was by no means the end of the matter. L'Hôpital (and others) asked Leibniz not to repeat his comments on the fixed stars, the earth and the grain of sand, and Leibniz clearly complied for a long time; but after L'Hôpital's death he does mention the matter in an essay in the *Acta eruditorum* in 1712 and again in a letter to d'Angicourt in 1716.[11] This is interesting because it again demonstrates that Leibniz was not conscious of any faulty wording.

The only author I know of who has dealt with the matter and agrees with Leibniz is Christian Wolff.[12] Wolff speaks of the fact that the height of a mountain does not change when the wind blows away a grain of sand from the mountain peak. The diameter of the earth can also be seen as a point in relation to the distance of the fixed stars. Whether Wolff understood Leibniz correctly in every respect will be discussed later.

When presenting his theory of differentials as zeros, Leonhard Euler perhaps did not have Leibniz directly in mind, but presumably Christian Wolff's rendering.[13] The infinitely small magnitudes are equal to zero; if one considers them like grains of sand compared to a mountain or the earth, then one deviates from geometric rigour. The names of Wolff and Leibniz are not mentioned. Abraham Kästner is probably also referring to Leibniz and Wolff when he talks of propositions that "appear to offend against the first principles

---

[8] *Journal des Savants*, 20 March 1702, pp. 183–186.
[9] Cf. GM IV, 97.
[10] Ibid., 98.
[11] Ibid. V, 389; Dutens III, 500f.
[12] Christian Wolff: *Elementa Matheseos Universae*, vol. 1, Halle 1713, pp. 452f.; id.: *Elementa Matheseos Universae*, vol. 1, Geneva 1743, p. 418.
[13] Leonhard Euler: *Institutiones calculi differentialis*, St. Petersburg 1755, pp. XI–XIV; German translation: Leonhard Euler: *Vollständige Anleitung zur Differenzial-Rechnung*, ed. by Johann Andreas Christian Michelsen, vol. 1, Berlin/Libau 1790, pp. LXIII–LXXI.

of all human knowledge" and names as an example among other things: "infinitely large things that are nothing in comparison with others, and infinitely small things that are infinitely large in comparison with others."[14]

In the secondary literature, Leibniz's remark on fixed stars, the earth and the grain of sand constituted the standard example to demonstrate that infinitesimal calculus rested on insecure foundations and that Leibniz's own thinking was less than clear in this respect. In 1883 the Neo-Kantian Hermann Cohen wrote:

> "for Leibniz had professed to *relativizing* the infinitesimally small, in fact he did this repeatedly in an inadequate comparison; it was like a grain of sand compared to the earth", and he recognised in Leibniz "a constant vacillation in this respect."[15]

Oskar Becker saw "in Leibniz a leaning towards giving occasionally popular and thus inexact accounts of his discoveries."[16] "Inexact" here is really a polite paraphrase; if the accusations are correct, then Leibniz's explanations are simply false. Carl Benjamin Boyer reports:

> "In a somewhat less critical vein he said that the differential of a quantity can be thought of as bearing to the quantity itself a relationship analogous to that of a point to the earth or of the radius of the earth to that of the heavens. In another place he said that as the earth is infinite with respect to a ball held in the hand, so the distance of the fixed stars is doubly infinite with respect to the ball; and this analogy he repeated later, substituting a grain of sand for the ball."[17]

And Rupert Hall observes:

---

[14] Abraham Gotthelf Kästner: *Anfangsgründe der Analysis des Unendlichen* (= *Mathematische Anfangsgründe* III, 2), Göttingen ³1799, p. III.
[15] Hermann Cohen: *Das Prinzip der Infinitesimalmethode*, Frankfurt /Main 1968, p. 111: "Leibniz hatte sich nämlich, und zwar zu wiederholten Malen in einem unzulänglichen Vergleiche zu einer *Relativierung* des Unendlichkleinen verstanden; es sei wie ein Sandkorn zur Erde"; "fortwährendes Schwanken in dieser Beziehung."
[16] Oskar Becker: *Grundlagen der Mathematik in geschichtlicher Entwicklung*, Frankfurt a. M. 1975, p. 164: "Neigung Leibnizens zur gelegentlichen populären und daher ungenauen Darstellung seiner Entdeckungen".
[17] Carl B. Boyer: *The History of the Calculus and its Conceptual Development*, New York 1959, p. 212.

> "Leibniz took refuge in analogies, likening the infinitesimal to a grain of sand infinitely little in comparison to the Earth, and yet infinitely smaller in comparison with the whole universe. For long the greatest achievement of mathematics rested on a shaky foundation."[18]

It would be easy to add further quotations; the criticism of Leibniz's comments on fixed stars, the earth and the grain of sand can be found continuously right up to the present day. I would like to confront this with two arguments – one from the perspective of literary history, the other a terminological one – that have hitherto not really been taken into consideration or indeed not considered at all.

3. The Earth as a Point

By describing the earth as a point in relation to the distance of the fixed stars from the earth, Leibniz is consciously reverting to a centuries-old tradition. As early as the *Almagest*, in the heading of the sixth chapter of the first book, Ptolemy speaks of the fact that the earth is like a point in relation to the heaven.[19] As proof of this he states the fact that during all observations the distances of the stars to each other had been found to be the same. In other words: the fixed stars do not show any parallax. As a further argument, Ptolemy states that the level of the horizon halves the celestial sphere. If the earth were of an appreciable size in relation to the starry sky, then only a level laid through the centre of the earth could halve the celestial sphere. Instead of saying that within measuring accuracy the earth acts like a point in relation to the vault of the sky, one can also say that the distance of the fixed stars is so great that it is not distinguishable from an infinite distance. Similarly, one can say (as Leibniz did in the *Acta eruditorum*)[20] that the earth's diameter is infinitely small in relation to the distance of the fixed stars.

In 525 Boethius wrote *De consolatione philosophiae* in his death cell. To set forth the inanity of striving for fame, Boethius explains that the earth is only a point in space, that only a small part of the earth is inhabited and that

---

[18] Rupert Hall: *From Galileo to Newton*, New York 1981, p. 98.
[19] Ptolemy: *Almagest*, Venice 1515, p. 4; id.: *Opera omnia*, Basle 1541, p. 6; id.: *Syntaxis mathematica*, ed. by Johann Ludwig Heiberg, vol. 1, Leipzig 1898, pp. 20–21. Cf. also Árpád Szabó: *Das geozentrische Weltbild*, Munich 1992, pp. 67–69.
[20] GM VI, 151, 168.

to be held in esteem by other humans was not so important.[21] Boethius' book was a classic in the Middle Ages and later; Leibniz could have been thinking of this passage when he wrote to Tschirnhaus in 1694 about striving for fame that even the wisest only relinquish this at the end.[22]

In Sacrobosco's work, an astronomical classic of the Middle Ages, one also finds the phrasing that the earth is like a point in relation to the firmament.[23]

In *De revolutionibus orbium coelestium* Copernicus remarks that, according to our sensory perception, the earth relates to the heavens like a point relates to a body or like something finite relates to an infinite thing.[24]

For the theory of Copernicus, the lack of a fixed star parallax has very considerable consequences. As yet we have only looked at observations made at various places on the earth; if Copernicus' theory was correct, then constant observations of the fixed stars should lead to annual rhythms. The basis of the parallax measurements was no longer two places on the static earth, it was now a complete diameter of the earth's orbit around the sun. But since the fixed stars showed no parallax, then they had to lie at a really incredible distance from the earth; this is why the lack of the fixed star parallax was an important astronomical argument against the heliocentric theory.[25] Copernicus was aware of this problem; so he expressed himself accordingly in Axiom 4 of the *Commentariolus* that the relationship of the sun-earth distance to the distance of the fixed stars was imperceptible.[26]

From the 16th century one might also mention the mathematician Maurolyco; in 1543 he wrote that the earth was like a point in relation to the firmament or rather that the radius of the earth was meaningless ("nullius esse momenti") in relation to the radius of the heavens.[27]

---

[21] Manlius Boethius: *De consolatione philosophiae*, Strasbourg 1515, II, 7, fol. D II verso.
[22] A III, 6, 43. We know that Leibniz knew *De consolatio philosophiae* from, among other things, A VI, 4, 1952, 2674, 2719 and A IV, 3, 824.
[23] Johannes de Sacrobosco: *Sphaera mundi*, Bologna 1480, no page numbers, page 8; id.: *Libellus de Sphaera*, with a foreword by Melanchthon, Wittenberg 1568, fol. C 1 verso.
[24] Nicolaus Copernicus: *De revolutionibus*, Basle 1566, I, 6, fol. a 4 recto/verso; cf. also I, 10, fol. c II recto. – Also Lorenzo Valla: *De expetendis et fugiendis rebus*, [Venice 1501], XXIII, cap. V, states that the earth behaves almost like a point in relation to the heavens.
[25] Ernst Zinner: *Entstehung und Ausbreitung der copernicanischen Lehre*, Munich ²1988, pp. 303, 305. On attempts to measure the parallax, cf. ibid., pp. 320f., 366f., 381, 398.
[26] Nicolaus Copernicus: *Das neue Weltbild*, Hamburg 2006, pp. 6f.
[27] Francesco Maurolyco: *Cosmographia*, Venice 1543, p. 11, cf. also p. 13. Cf. also id: *Opuscula mathematica*, Venice 1575, p. 8.

In 1632, in the *Dialogo,* Galilei explained that the size of the earth was almost imperceptible in relation to the distance of the fixed stars; the distance of the fixed stars can be regarded as infinitely large in relation to the small size of the earth.[28] In his *De corpore*, Hobbes refers to an existing common parlance: "Eo sensu quo Terra *punctum* [...] vocari solet."[29]

According to Otto von Guericke our planetary system is only a point in relation to the fixed star heavens, in this respect our earth is even less than that.[30]

In 1838 Friedrich Wilhelm Bessel succeeded in measuring the parallax of a fixed star for the first time. Thus the distances of at least a few fixed stars became distinguishable from an infinitely great distance.

4. What Does "Incomparable" Mean?

I now turn to my second argument. Leibniz had written to Varignon:

> "Il suffisoit d'expliquer icy l'infini par l'incomparable, c'est à dire de concevoir des quantités incomparablement plus grandes ou plus petits que les nostres."[31]

What do "incomparable" and "incomparablement" mean? Is this a rhetorical turn of phrase or is incomparability meant seriously?

In fact, in a number of authors one does find a use of *comparare* in a mathematical context. For present purposes it is not necessary to investigate the mathematical usage of comparare comprehensively; it will suffice to provide a few examples that place Leibniz's use of comparare in mathematics in a historical context.

In his *Physics,* Aristotle discusses the question of whether every change is comparable (συμβλητὴ) with every other change, in particular whether there

---

[28] Galileo Galilei: *Le Opere*, Edizione Nazionale, vol. 7, Florence 1897, "Third Day", pp. 310, 311.
[29] Thomas Hobbes: *Elementorum philosophiae sectio prima de corpore*, vol. 2, London 1655, caput VIII, § 12, p. 68.
[30] Otto von Guericke: *Experimenta nova (ut vocantur) Magdeburgica de vacuo spatio,* Amsterdam 1672, p. 153. Elsewhere Guericke remarks that the distances between the earth and sun, moon and planets are not comparable with the distance of the earth from the fixed stars (ibid., p. 26); on comparare used here, cf. further below. However, one should note that Guericke also states that the earth's diameter is incomparabilis with the diameter of Saturn's orbit (ibid., p. 27).
[31] GM IV, 91.

is a particular quantitative ratio between a circular motion and a straight one.[32] If that were the case – Aristotle reasons – then one can conclude that a straight line and a curve segment can be equal. But a straight line and a curve segment cannot be compared with one another; as a consequence, the two movements cannot either. And two pages further on Aristotle explains that the straight line and the curve segment are of a different kind.[33]

Euclid had defined the ratio of two magnitudes to each other when the two quantities are of the same kind: Magnitudes are said to have a ratio to one another which are capable, when multiplied, of exceeding one another.[34]

Theon of Smyrna explains Euclid's definition: only magnitudes of the same kind can be in a ratio to one another. White and sweetness or warmth cannot be compared with one another (ἀσύγκριτα καὶ ἀσύμβλητα). But one can compare magnitudes of the same kind, for example lengths can be in a certain ratio to lengths, areas to areas, volumes to volumes, numbers to numbers, time to time.[35]

The Latin word comparare does not only mean to compare. It can also mean "to place together in a corresponding position", "to match, couple, unite, pair", "to treat (one person or thing) as equal to another, put in the same class with, regard as comparable."[36] Even if in the following text comparare is always translated with "compare", one has to think of the other nuances of meaning as well.

In his *Consolatio philosophiae*, Boethius explains that a comparison between the finite and the infinite is not possible; the finite is not small in comparison with the infinite, it is nothing ("nulla").[37] Copernicus remarks on

---

[32] Aristoteles: *Physikvorlesung*, Darmstadt ⁴1983, 248 a 10–248 b 1, pp. 205–208, p. 661.
[33] Ibid., 249 a 1, p. 208.
[34] Euclid: *Elementa*, Book V, Definitions 3 and 4; Thomas Heath: *A History of Greek Mathematics*, vol. 1, New York 1981, p. 384.
[35] Theon von Smyrna: *Expositio rerum mathematicarum ad legendum Platonem utilium*, ed. by Eduard Hiller, Leipzig 1878, pp. 73f. Theon von Smyrna: *ΤΩΝ ΚΑΤΑ ΤΟ ΜΑΘΗΜΑΤΙΚΟΝ ΧΡΗΣΙΜΩΝ ΕΙΣ ΤΗΝ ΠΛΑΤΩΝΟΣ ΑΝΑΓΝΩΣΙΝ. Exposition des connaissances mathématiques utiles pour la lecture de Platon*, ed. by Jean Dupuis, Paris 1892, pp. 118–121; François Viète: *Einführung in die Neue Algebra*, Munich 1973, pp. 24f. Theon gives an account of Adrastos' opinion.
[36] *Oxford Latin Dictionary*, vol. 1, Oxford ²2012, p. 409. Cf. also *Thesaurus linguae latinae*, vol. 3, Leipzig 1907, cols. 2017–2021; Karl Ernst Georges: *Lateinisch-Deutsches Handwörterbuch*, vol. 1, Leipzig ⁹1843, cols. 824f.
[37] Boethius: *De consolatione philosophiae*, II, 7, fol. D III verso.

the distance of the earth from the fixed stars that it is "incomparabilem adhuc."[38]

The Euclid edition by François de Foix-Candale of 1566 is interesting. If two magnitudes are of a different kind, then they are not in ratio to one another; sound and movement, time and weight, line and surface cannot be compared with one another.[39] Magnitudes are of the same kind and are in a certain ratio to one another if they can exceed each other when multiplied.[40] In a commentary on Euclid III, 16, Foix-Candale remarks that the horn angle is of a different kind from a rectilinear angle; a comparatio between these angles of a different kind is not admissible. One cannot state as a counter-argument that a horn angle is smaller than every rectilinear angle, for the largest gnat is smaller than the smallest camel.[41]

François Viète refers back to the passage quoted from Theon of Smyrna when he formulates his law of homogeneity in 1591: "Homogenea homogeneis comparari."[42] The law is supposed to be valid for equations and proportions; it requires that only magnitudes of the same kind should be added together or subtracted from one another or be in a ratio to, or equated with, one another. A length cannot be added to an area and a volume cannot be in a certain ratio to a length. Incidentally, for his calculations using letters of the alphabet, Viète defines the equation as a comparatio between an indefinite and a definite magnitude.[43]

The Jesuit Christoph Clavius writes in the explanations to his edition of Euclid that the ratio is a type of comparatio.[44]

Almost half a century later, Descartes abolishes the law of homogeneity.[45] Descartes does still adhere to the Aristotelian thesis of the qualitative difference of a straight line from a curve segment,[46] but soon after, thinking in

---

[38] Copernicus: *Das neue Weltbild*, Hamburg 2006, p. 108 (= Copernicus: *De revolutionibus*, I, 6). Cf. also Copernicus: *Das neue Weltbild*, p. 104, p. 138 (= Copernicus: *De revolutionibus*, I, 6 and I, 10) and Euclid: *Opera omnia*, vol. 7, ed. by Johann Ludwig Heiberg, Leipzig 1895, pp. 156–159.
[39] Euclid: *Elementa*, ed. by Franciscus Flussates Candalla, Paris 1566, fol. 38 verso.
[40] Ibid., fol. 39 recto. Comparatio is also used at ibid., fol. 39 verso.
[41] Moritz Cantor: *Vorlesungen zur Geschichte der Mathematik*, vol. 2, Leipzig 1913, p. 554; Euclid: *Elementa*, ed. by François de Foix-Candale, Paris 1566, fol. 24 verso–25 recto.
[42] François Viète: *Opera Mathematica*, Leiden 1646, p. 2.
[43] Ibid., p. 11.
[44] Christoph Clavius: *Euclidis Elementorum Libri XV*, Frankfurt 1607, p. 353, cf. also p. 351.
[45] René Descartes: *Œuvres*, vol. 6, Paris 1982, pp. 369–372.
[46] Ibid., p. 412.

terms of qualitative difference was to be replaced or abolished.[47] The fact that one can also compare straight and curved line segments with one another was already asserted by Fermat in the title of his treatise on rectification: *De linearum curvarum cum lineis rectis comparatione dissertatio geometrica.*[48]

The Jesuit Richard employs comparare and comparatio in his edition of Euclid in the familiar way;[49] between the finite and infinite as well as between points and lines there is no comparatio.[50] The Jesuit Aynscom explains Euclid's definition of ratio: there can only be a ratio between magnitudes of the same kind, magnitudes of a different kind cannot be compared with one another.[51] Aynscom also remarks: the fact that a ratio exists between two magnitudes and that these two magnitudes can be compared according to their quantity is the same thing.[52] This observation is quoted by Wallis.[53] According to Wallis there is no ratio between the finite and the infinite.[54] The comparatio of numbers and homogeneous magnitudes is mentioned by Wallis.[55]

Even Euler still uses comparare and comparatio as the terms for setting up a ratio.[56] Zedler's *Lexicon* explains comparatio as "equality, comparison" and *proportio* as the comparison of magnitudes.[57] But by and large the mathematical use of comparare appears to decline from about the middle of the 17th century; the specific meaning of the word gradually falls into obscurity. This may also be due to the decreasing importance assigned at the time to thinking in proportions. Proportions are also understood less stringently. If one once said "at constant speed the paths behave in the same way as the corresponding times" (thus, one is comparing like with like), one was able to say later (and today) "at constant speed the ratios of the paths to the times are constant".

---

[47] Herbert Breger: *Kontinuum, Analysis, Informales – Beiträge zur Mathematik und Philosophie von Leibniz*, ed. by Wenchao Li, Berlin/Heidelberg 2016, pp. 62–64, pp. 68–71.
[48] Published as an appendix to Antoine de la Loubère: *Veterum geometria promota*, Toulouse 1660; Pierre de Fermat: *Œuvres*, vol. 1, Paris 1891, pp. 211–254.
[49] Euclid: *Elementa*, ed by Richard, Antwerp 1645, p. 111, p. 113.
[50] Ibid., p. 114.
[51] François Xavier Aynscom: *Expositio ac deductio geometrica*, Antwerp 1656, p. 1.
[52] Ibid., p. 11.
[53] John Wallis: *Opera*, vol. 2, Oxford 1693, p. 640.
[54] Ibid., p. 614.
[55] Id.: *Opera*, vol. 1, Oxford 1695, p. 134.
[56] Euler: *Institutiones*, p. 13.
[57] Johann Heinrich Zedler: *Grosses vollständiges Universal-Lexicon*, vol. 6, Leipzig 1733, col. 861, vol. 29, Leipzig 1741, cols. 889–890.

Let us now turn to the meaning of comparare in Leibniz. Of course, the word often occurs in Leibniz's mathematical texts with a different meaning, for example in the method of comparing coefficients[58] or with a non-mathematical meaning. However, the word is also used in the meaning already known to us in connection with the law of homogeneity[59] and in connection with rectification.[60]

Leibniz even gives an explicit definition of comparare: to compare two things according to their quantity means to seek a way and means of determining the quantity of one thing from that of another thing.[61] At first sight this definition appears to be more general than the hitherto common parlance. But this first impression is deceptive. The definition is to be found under the heading *De ratione et proportione* and both earlier and later ratio is called "forma comparationis."[62] In fact, a more general definition of comparare was not supposed to be given, the reason why precisely the ratio is the forma comparationis was supposed to be deduced. Leibniz first discusses the question of whether, according to this definition, the sum or the difference could not also be viewed as a suitable means of comparison. He then continues by finding the largest common divisor of two (initially: commensurable) magnitudes in the familiar way;[63] the result is the ratio of the two magnitudes. In notes written in 1715[64] he denoted two magnitudes that are incommensurable with one another as homogeneous and comparable.

Leibniz's use of incomparabilis fits well to this use of comparare. As early as 1689 Leibniz had explained in an essay in the *Acta eruditorum* that instead of infinitesimals, incomparably small magnitudes could also be used; one even finds there the idea of the earth as a point in relation to the distance of the fixed stars.[65] Leibniz has often referred to this observation on incomparable magnitudes ("lemma incomparabilium").[66] In a letter to L'Hôpital of 1695, Leibniz gives an explicit definition of incomparable magnitudes: two

---

[58] Cf. for example A VII, 3, 531.
[59] A VII, 4, 135, 347; GM VII, 65, 87.
[60] A VII, 4, 657, 326.
[61] GM VII, 40. Dating according to catalogue of the Leibniz Edition: ca. 1680.
[62] GM VII, 40, 41, 42, 42f., 44, 45 ("formam comparationis sive rationem").
[63] Euclid: *Elementa*, VII, 1–2.
[64] GM VII, 32. Dating according to catalogue of the Leibniz edition.
[65] Ibid. VI, 150f. Cf. also ibid., 168.
[66] Ibid. V, 275, 323; ibid. VII, 40; A III, 5, 149; Ibid., 6, 416; ibid., 7, 235, 576, 618, 857f.; Ibid., 8, 91. – Contrary to today's mathematics, here "lemma" means "assumption", cf. Thomas Heath: *History of Greek Mathematics*, vol. 1, New York 1981, p. 373.

magnitudes are called incomparable if the one cannot exceed the other by means of multiplication with an arbitrary (finite) number, and he expressly points to Definition 5 of the fifth book of Euclid quoted above.[67] So two magnitudes are incomparable when no ratio exists between them. From this one can immediately deduce a conclusion for calculating with incomparable magnitudes. In real (standard) analysis, two numbers are equal if the absolute value of their difference is smaller than any positive real number. Since every real number can be in a ratio to every other real number and since this is not true of an incomparably small number, it follows that an incomparable small number is smaller than every positive real number. Consequently Leibniz emphasized, contradicting Nieuwentijd, that two real magnitudes are equal if their difference is incomparably small,[68] for then their difference is also smaller than any positive real magnitude. By way of example Leibniz comments that the addition of a point to a line does not change the length of the line, since line and point are incomparable.[69]

We can state as the result that "incomparablement petit" is the term for a small magnitude of another quality, namely a small magnitude that is not in ratio to a normal (i.e. real) magnitude. The secondary literature has understood incomparably small magnitudes as extraordinarily small normal magnitudes. In that case Leibniz's comments would appear to be wrong, but only then.

I do not propose to look into Leibniz's use of the word incomparable in physics.[70] It can remain open whether incomparable is only used there in rhetorical phrases or whether the existence of ever smaller particles or of ever greater velocities is meant.

5. What Are Incomparably Small Magnitudes?

To be sure, it is not yet clear what exactly Leibniz meant by contrasting the earth with a grain of sand. Without doubt, 12 713 000 000 mm (diameter of the earth from pole to pole) and 0.2 mm (diameter of a grain of sand) are comparable magnitudes. In the first attempt at an interpretation, a hypothesis will be discussed that the earth and a grain of sand are not comparable. How could Leibniz have justified this hypothesis?

---

[67] A III, 6, 416f.
[68] Ibid., 412; GM V, 322.
[69] Ibid.
[70] Ibid. IV, 91 and the Papin correspondence in A III, 7.

On the earth there are mountains and valleys, and the sea level can also vary by several meters as a result of meteorological phenomena such as El Niño. Without designating a norm, the earth's diameter cannot be determined exactly. After Richer's measurement of the seconds pendulum in Cayenne, it was possible, in principle, for the earth's flattening to become a topic of debate, although a wider discussion only began after Leibniz's death.[71] Newton had already published his justification for asserting a flattening of the earth at the poles,[72] and Leibniz knew that an oval shape of the earth was also being discussed.[73]

After Eratosthenes, al-Ma'mun and others, Jean Picard was actually conducting a measurement of the earth during Leibniz's lifetime;[74] Leibniz knew of this.[75] Picard's measurements only deviate less than 0.02% from the result that, according to Lalande in 1771, was considered the best and that according to Lalande had likewise only made a mistake of less than 0.02%.[76] Rosenberger has called Picard's measurement a very exact result due to a fortunate compensation of mistakes.[77] If we accept Lalande's estimate of mistakes, then we have a mistake of ca. 2.5 km for the earth's diameter at the poles. Considering the complexity of the measurements, Leibniz could hardly have expected it to be possible to determine the earth's diameter more precisely (quite apart from the necessary standardisations; the result depends for example – as Picard knew – on the height above sea level).

One could attempt the following interpretation: magnitude A is characterised by an irresolvable indeterminacy a; for another magnitude B, one can say that $B<<a$; then B is incomparably smaller than A. So it does not depend on the difference in size of the earth and the grain of sand, but rather on the difference in size between the grain of sand and the indeterminacy of the earth's diameter. So one could deduce from this that $A+B=A$ and $B\not\equiv 0$, whereby B is of a different kind from A; the normal calculation rules do not

---

[71] Jean Richer: *Observations astronomiques et physiques*, Paris 1679, p. 66; A III, 4, 112; John W. Olmstedt: "The Scientific Expedition of Jean Richer to Cayenne (1672–1673)", in: *Isis* 34 (1942), pp. 117–128, in particular footnotes 6 and 97.
[72] Isaac Newton: *Principia mathematica*, London 1687, liber III, prop. XX, pp. 424–426.
[73] A III, 5, 242, 270; A I, 7, 346.
[74] Jean Picard: *Mesure de la terre*, Paris 1671. Cf. also Rudolf Wolf: *Handbuch der Astronomie*, vol. 2, Zurich 1892, pp. 166–177.
[75] A III, 3, 626; ibid., 4, 112; ibid. II, 3, 664.
[76] Joseph Jérôme de Lalande: *Astronomie*, vol. 3, Paris 1771, p. 87.
[77] Ferdinand Rosenberger: *Die Geschichte der Physik*, vol. 2, Hildesheim 1965 (1st ed. Braunschweig 1884), p. 184.

apply or rather have to be redefined, if this is at all possible. This interpretation would at any rate have the advantage of being able to explain the property postulated by Leibniz and L'Hôpital: *x+dx=x* and *dx≠0*.[78] But there is no indication in the text that Leibniz was thinking of this interpretation. In fact, this interpretation must contradict Leibniz's observation in the text refuting Nieuwentijd,[79] for one can multiply the diameter of the grain of sand with a number so that the product is larger than the earth's diameter. So one has to regard this interpretation as wrong.

Christian Wolff's opinion was only partially discussed above and now needs to be addressed again. Wolff uses comparare and comparatio as the terms for establishing a ratio.[80] He calls an infinitesimal "incomparabilis"[81] or smaller than every specifiable magnitude. He deduces from this that if one views an infinitesimal as zero, then one thereby produces a mistake that is smaller than every specifiable magnitude, in other words is equal to zero. Finally, Wolff emphasises that the infinitesimals are not real.[82] Wolff's account does, however, have its weaknesses. He always talks of infinitely small magnitudes, while Leibniz distinguishes between infinitely small magnitudes (which of course are also incomparable) and incomparable magnitudes (which are not necessarily infinitely small). When Wolff, as quoted above, talks of a grain of sand on a mountain, then this grain of sand is neither infinitely small nor incomparably small, since a number can be specified so that the product of this number and the diameter of the grain of sand exceeds the height of the mountain.

Let us try a second interpretation in order to understand what Leibniz meant by referring to the grain of sand. To be sure, he only speaks of the grain of sand in the singular, but then he continues in such a way that one has to think of smaller and smaller grains of sand. In the essay in the *Journal de Trévoux,* one reads that instead of the infinitely small one uses such small magnitudes that the mistake is smaller than a given (positive) magnitude.[83] In

---

[78] Cf. GM VI, 130; GP VI, 321; Guillaume François Antoine de L'Hôpital: *Analyse des infiniment petits*, Paris 1696, pp. 2f.
[79] GM V, 322; cf. also A III, 6, 416–417.
[80] Christian Wolff: *Elementa Matheseos Universae*, vol. 1, Halle 1713, pp. 46 (twice), 47; id.: *Elementa Matheseos Universae*, vol. 1, Geneva 1743, pp. 43 (twice), 44.
[81] Id.: *Elementa Matheseos Universae*, vol. 1, Halle 1713, p. 452; id.: *Elementa Matheseos Universae*, vol. 1, Geneva 1743, p. 417.
[82] Id.: *Elementa Matheseos Universae*, vol. 1, Halle 1713, p. 453; id.: *Elementa Matheseos Universae*, vol. 1, Geneva 1743, p. 418.
[83] A I, 20, 494; *Journal de Trévoux*, Nov./Dec. 1701, p. 271.

a letter to Varignon, he stresses that the incomparably small magnitudes are certainly not "fixes ou determinés"; they can be chosen as small as one wants; the resultant mistake will be smaller than any given magnitude.[84] In the 1689 essay in the *Acta eruditorum,* one reads that one can use such small magnitudes as one considers sufficient, so that the mistake will be smaller than the given magnitude.[85] In his 1712 essay in the *Acta eruditorum,* Leibniz speaks of the distance of the fixed stars, the earth's diameter and the diameter of a grain of sand, however, expressly in such a way that every one of the magnitudes can be chosen arbitrarily larger or smaller.[86] Leibniz expresses himself similarly in a letter to d'Angiecourt.[87] In a letter to des Bosses from 1706, referring to Gouye, Leibniz also explains that one can take arbitrarily small magnitudes instead of infinitely small magnitudes, so that the mistake is smaller than any given magnitude and thus equal to zero.[88] Incomparable magnitudes or indefinite magnitudes are the same thing; one can also refer directly to the principle of continuity; the mistake will be smaller than any given magnitude.[89] When determining a volume, too, one can base this on incomparable parts; the mistake will be smaller than any given magnitude.[90]

According to the definition of "incomparable"[91], infinitely small magnitudes are likewise incomparable magnitudes. But Leibniz speaks here of incomparable magnitudes that are not infinitely small. In the passages mentioned here, he says again and again that smaller and even smaller real magnitudes can always be chosen as incomparable magnitudes; he speaks of a mistake that is smaller than every given magnitude (and thus zero) and he refers to the apagogical proofs of Archimedes. The simplest interpretation of these quotes seems to be the following. The incomparable magnitudes can be understood as placeholders for normal (real) positive magnitudes; so one can

---

[84] GM IV, 92. In GM IV, 98 Leibniz remarks likewise that he was not speaking of a fixed and particular quantity.
[85] Ibid. VI, 151, cf. also ibid. VI, 168.
[86] GM V, 389: "sed ita ut quodvis horum in suo genere quantumvis majus aut minus concipi posse intelligatur."
[87] Dutens III, 501: "Et plus on faisoit la proportion ou l'intervalle grand entre ces degrés, plus on aprochoit de l'exactitude, et plus on pouvoit rendre l'erreur petite et même la retrancher tout d'un coup par la fiction d'un intervalle infini, qui pouvoit toujours être réalisée à la façon de démontrer d'Archimède."
[88] GP II, 305. Cf. also A III, 5, 149.
[89] GM III, 836.
[90] Ibid. VII, 40.
[91] A III, 6, 416f.; GM V, 322. Cf. also ibid. IV, 92: One can understand incomparable magnitudes as one likes, whether as infinitely small or otherwise.

calculate with normal magnitudes instead of incomparable magnitudes, however always on the condition that the calculation can always be repeated or corrected (or rather: ought to be) with smaller and smaller normal magnitudes. An example can illustrate this: if $y=x^2$ is a parabola; then it follows that $y+\eta=(x+\xi)^2$ with the incomparable magnitudes ξ,η. Further, it follows that $\eta=2x\xi+\xi^2$ or $\eta/\xi = 2x + \xi$. Now, if for ξ (and thus also for η) smaller and smaller normal magnitudes are employed, the left side differs from the slope of the tangent to the parabola by an arbitrarily small amount and the right side differs by an arbitrarily small amount from $2x$. One can prove this (and thus the identity of the slope of the tangent and $2x$) with the method of proof used by Archimedes with traditional rigour. But one does not need to do so – rather like a mathematician today would immediately conclude from the equation $2x^2+5=55$ that $x=5$, without producing a very long-winded proof derived from the Peano axioms. Such a train of thought seems to be what Leibniz regarded as a "raw proof."[92] The experienced mathematician "sees" the proof without producing it. In this sense, Leibniz also speaks of the fact that this method carries its proof in itself.[93]

For an understanding of calculating with incomparable magnitudes, it is of course not sufficient to be able to calculate $y+dy=(x+dx)^2$. In today's discussions from the perspective of philosophy and the history of mathematics, maybe one does not always appreciate how much previous knowledge, how much mathematical experience and how much know-how about dealing with the continuum are indispensable preconditions for understanding incomparably small magnitudes (including infinitesimals).

This interpretation of incomparable magnitudes corresponds to the practice in the second half of the 17th century. Even Huygens, who later had difficulties with understanding the calculus of infinitesimals, used infinitely small magnitudes as an abbreviation for epsilontic arguments.[94] The fact that the infinitely small (and the incomparably small) magnitudes derived their justification from epsilontics was simply self-evident. Leibniz did not consider it necessary to explain this in any depth.

---

[92] Cf. Breger: *Kontinuum, Analysis, Informales*, p. 144.
[93] GM V, 322; A III, 8, 92.
[94] Cf. Breger: *Kontinuum, Analysis, Informales*, pp. 150–153.

"In order to prove our calculations with infinitesimals rigorously," Leibniz wrote to Bodenhausen in 1697,[95]

> "one only needs to look at my lemmata incomparabilium, which I once published in the *Acta eruditorum*. One uses normal geometry,[96] whereby one leaves out the incomparably small. One can prove, namely, always following Archimedes, that whatever one leaves out is smaller than an arbitrarily given positive magnitude."

Incomparable magnitudes are of course (just like infinitely small magnitudes) fictions. They are of a different kind from normal magnitudes. One can calculate with the incomparably small differentials dx just as well as one can calculate with infinitely small differentials. Leibniz set up rules for what to leave out.[97] Perhaps these rules are not complete or not unequivocal. But that is not a serious problem. As yet no-one has set up a general and complete system of rules for the cases in which a mathematician may say "as one can easily see". Mathematics happens to be something that one cannot understand without knowledge and experience of the theory concerned. We know in any case that Leibniz understood his infinitesimal calculus as an analysis, so the question of proof was secondary anyway.[98]

---

[95] A III, 7, 576; cf. also GM IV, 92.
[96] I.e. without infinitesimals.
[97] A III, 8, 91f.
[98] Breger: *Kontinuum, Analysis, Informales*, pp. 132–134, pp. 167–170.

PLENARVORTRÄGE

Pragmatism and Idealism in Leibniz's Ways of Distinguishing Real from Imaginary Phenomena

Robert Merrihew Adams (Princeton, NJ)

I will focus, in this half hour, on a short paper, written by Leibniz in the timeframe 1683–86. He gave it the title, *De modo distinguendi phenomena realia ab imaginariis*/On the Way to Distinguish Real from Imaginary Phenomena [hereafter, *De Modo*, for short]. Many if not all of us are familiar with it. I will focus primarily on a single passage in the paper, just two sentences long.

It is preceded by Leibniz's answer to the question, "by what evidence, or what indications [*quibus indiciis*] we come to know which phenomena are real."[1] I take that to be a straightforwardly epistemological question. I, and not I alone, have sought in *De Modo* indications of Leibniz's views on profoundly metaphysical issues. But that is not how the little essay begins. In the question that I quoted just now Leibniz is merely asking how we can tell, correctly, which phenomena are real and which are merely imaginary.

He replies by listing marks or indications that he counts as evidence that phenomena that have them are real. The list is not particularly original; it's a pretty typical early modern list of marks that indicate the reality of bodies that we seem to perceive. Leibniz mentions the "vividness" of the phenomenon's apparent qualities, and its having "qualities that are varied and useful for setting up many tests and new observations," as well as "the parts of the phenomenon [having] the same position, order, and outcome that similar phenomena have had." He says,

> "the most powerful indication of the reality of phenomena, which is even sufficient by itself, is success in predicting future phenomena from past and present ones, if that prediction is based on a reason or hypothesis that has been sustained thus far, or on the normal behavior [*consuetudo*] of things as thus far observed."[2]

This "most powerful indication" is very similar to the principal criterion offered for the reality of bodies at the end of Descartes's sixth Meditation.[3] And

---

[1] A VI, 4 B, 1500.
[2] Ibid., 1500f.
[3] *Oeuvres de Descartes*, ed. by C. Adam and P. Tannery, Paris, 1897–1913, vol. VII, 89f. (= AT, cited by volume and page).

Leibniz's list, as a whole, overlaps even more extensively with the answer that Berkeley, three decades later, would offer in response to a similar question.[4]

The two sentences that particularly engage my attention here come next. They raise a question that goes beyond epistemology, and give it an answer that contains much food for thought. "Nay more," Leibniz says,

> "Even if this whole life were said to be nothing but a dream, and the visible world nothing but a phantasm, I would call this dream or phantasm real enough, if we were never deceived by it when making good use of reason. And just as we learn from these indications which phenomena ought to be seen as real, so, conversely, we count as merely apparent whatever phenomena conflict with those that we judge to be real, and likewise those whose deceptiveness we can explain from their causes."[5]

Those are the two sentences that I propose to examine more closely.

Much of the great interest of this pair of sentences hangs on the phrase 'real enough' ['*satis reale*']. It seems to suggest – and I believe is meant to suggest – that some things are *more real* than just real enough. Leibniz does not exactly leave us to *guess* whether that is what he means. For just over a paragraph further on, he says that the "marks of real phenomena" that he has listed, "even taken all together," do not yield demonstrative or metaphysical certainty, so that

> "it cannot be absolutely demonstrated by any argument that there are bodies, nor that anything prevents some well ordered dreams from being objects of our minds which would be judged by us to be true and would be equivalent [*aequivaleant*] to true ones as far as usefulness is concerned [*quoad usum*], because of their agreement with each other."[6]

And he goes on to suggest that "our nature" might not be "capable of [experiencing] real phenomena."[7]

Indeed, as the passage I just now quoted suggests, the thought that Leibniz expresses using the expression 'real enough', *arises* from his finding that he can also think, but cannot "absolutely demonstrate" the thought of something being *real*, or *true*, in a sense that is much *heavier metaphysically* than the sense in which he has used 'real enough'. – Not that what Leibniz says in

---

[4] *The Works of George Berkeley*, ed. by Arthur Aston Luce and T. E. Jessup, vol. 2, London 1949, p. 235.
[5] A VI, 4 B, 1502.
[6] Ibid.
[7] Ibid.

such a "heavier" sense was meant more seriously or more emphatically than what he says using the metaphysically lighter expression 'real enough'. On the contrary, I suspect that what is said using 'real enough' is the most serious thing said in *De Modo*.

It was certainly not a passing fancy. It appears, in a much briefer discussion, in a more celebrated text, in §14 of the *Discourse on Metaphysics*. There Leibniz says,

> "these phenomena [that we perceive] keep to a certain order ... which enables us to make observations that are useful for regulating our conduct, [so that] we are often able to judge of the future by the past without making mistakes. [And] that suffices for us to say that these phenomena are true [*veritables*], without troubling ourselves as to whether they are outside us, and whether other [people] perceive them too."[8]

And the idea gets a fuller development in an earlier document, from about 1679–1680, where Leibniz says,

> "The states of the World are different at different times. But one of them is born from another, according to certain Laws, which it is the physicist's [job] to teach, so that we may gather past and future [facts] from present ones, for use in living [*in usum vitae*]. ... Therefore the objections that the Skeptics raise against observations are inane. They may certainly doubt about the truth of things, and if they will they may call the things that happen to us dreams. But it suffices that these dreams agree with each other, and preserve certain laws, and in that way leave room for human prudence and predictions. If that is granted, there is merely a question of name, for we call appearances of this sort true; and I do not see how truer ones can be given or hoped for."[9]

This earlier passage shares two important points with what I have quoted from *De Modo*.

1. In both the question is raised, what we could say, and what we would say, because we have reason to say, if we accepted the skeptical view that our experiences of physical objects and events are nothing more than dreams – or, as I might have preferred to put it, somewhat anachronistically – that they are nothing more than internal intentional objects of our conscious states. In what I have quoted from *De Modo* the pivotal predicate whose application to apparent physical things is in question is 'real'; whereas in

---

[8] Ibid., 1550.
[9] Ibid., 1397f.

what I have quoted from the earlier document (and from the *Discourse on Metaphysics*) it is 'true'. That difference strikes me as unimportant. 'Real' and 'true' have often been used interchangeably in philosophical contexts. Indeed I have already quoted a passage in *De Modo* in which Leibniz seems to use 'true' with much the same meaning as 'real' has in his use of 'real enough'. For he speaks of the possibility of "well ordered dreams" that we would judge to be "true", and that "would be equivalent to true [objects] as far as usefulness is concerned."[10]

2. In the earlier piece as well as in *De Modo*, the *reason* most plainly suggested for saying that the well ordered "dream" events and objects (if such they be) are "real enough", or as "true" as can be hoped for, is a *pragmatic* or *practical* reason. It is that by taking them seriously we are able to "gather past and future [facts] from present ones, for use in living [*in usum vitae*]", as Leibniz puts it in the earlier document.

The pragmatic or practical character of the argument is further underlined in *De Modo* by the way in which Leibniz rejects Descartes's argument that God would be a deceiver if bodies did not have a metaphysically heavy existence outside our minds. "For what if our nature were not capable of [perceiving] real phenomena?" Leibniz asks, using what is obviously a metaphysically heavy sense of 'real'. And he answers:

> "Assuredly we should not blame God, but thank him, since by bringing it about that since those phenomena could not be real, they would at least agree with each other, he has provided us with what *aequipolleret* [what would work the same] as real phenomena for every use in living."[11]

Underlying this argument is surely the thought that it is reasonable to characterize with the same predicate (in this case 'real') phenomena that "work the same for every use in living," without worrying about whether they differ in deep metaphysical characteristics of which we have no proof.

Much the same reasoning recurs approximately two decades later, in Leibniz's *Nouveaux Essais*, in response to similar views expressed by John Locke. In Book IV, ch. ii, §14 of his *Essay concerning Human Understanding*, Locke is discussing "*Perception* of the Mind, employ'd about *the particular existence of finite beings without us*" (that is, outside the mind). He imagines

---

[10] Ibid., 1502.
[11] Ibid.

a skeptic who holds that we merely dream such things. Locke responds with the obviously pragmatic argument,

> "That we certainly finding, that Pleasure or Pain follows upon the application of certain objects to us, whose Existence we perceive, or dream that we perceive, by our Senses, this certainty is as great as our Happiness or Misery, beyond which we have no concernment to know, or to be."[12]

Responding to that chapter of Locke, Leibniz quotes, accurately enough, the passage that I have just quoted from it. He states that "the truth of sensible things consists only in the interconnection of the phenomena", and comments, much as he had in *De Modo*, that

> "provided the phenomena are linked together, it doesn't matter whether we call them dreams or not, since experience shows that we do not go wrong in the steps that we take on the basis of the phenomena, so long as we take them in accordance with the truths of reason."[13]

Thus far I have been documenting the occurrence of a particular thought in Leibniz's writings – the thought that is expressed by the sentence,

> "Even if this whole life were said to be nothing but a dream, and the visible world nothing but a phantasm, I would call this dream or phantasm real enough, if we were never deceived by it when making good use of reason."

It is time now to try to place this thought in a larger context, and first of all in the context of Leibniz's more general views about the role that practical reason should have in our lives.

It is clear, in many places in his writings, that Leibniz assigns a much wider range of topics and propositions to the province of practical reason than many philosophers would. Not that the scope of his pragmatism (if such we call it) is as all-embracing as the scope of William James's pragmatism. James declared that

---

[12] John Locke: *An Essay concerning Human Understanding*, critical edition by Peter H. Nidditch, Oxford 1975, p. 537.
[13] A VI, 4 A, 375. I have only slightly emended, in a more literal direction, the felicitous translation of Peter Remnant and Jonathan Bennett in: Gottfried Wilhelm Leibniz: *New Essays on Human Understanding*, Cambridge 1981.

> "'The true' [...] is only the expedient in the way of our thinking, just as 'the right' is only the expedient in the way of our behaving. Expedient in almost any fashion; and expedient in the long run and on the whole of course [...]."[14]

James admitted no exception to that thesis, but Leibniz assigns a rather sharp boundary to the province of practical reason.

A particularly full and explicit drawing of the boundary is found in a letter written in 1697 to the Scottish gentleman intellectual and amateur diplomat Thomas Burnett of Kemnay. Leibniz tells Burnett that

> "Philosophy has two parts, the theoretical and the practical. Theoretical Philosophy is founded on the true analysis, of which the Mathematicians give examples, but which ought also to be applied to Metaphysics and to natural theology, in giving good definitions and solid axioms. But practical Philosophy is founded [...] on the art of estimating the degrees of proofs."[15]

Similarly, in the same paragraph, he divides truths into "two species". He says the first species, presumably including the truths of theoretical philosophy, "could be demonstrated absolutely with metaphysical necessity and in an incontestable way." "The others," the second species, that is, the ones that cannot be demonstrated with metaphysical necessity, "can be demonstrated morally – that is to say, in a way that yields what is called moral certainty," and is presumably founded, as practical philosophy is, "on the art of estimating the degrees of proofs," or weighing probabilities.[16]

Why did Leibniz assign the drawing of conclusions from probable reasoning to the realm of practical reason? His repeated association of probable reasoning with *moral* certainty may be a clue. The morally certain, it is commonly said, is what has enough certainty to be an acceptable basis for action. About any proposition whose truth is not absolutely necessary, logically or mathematically or metaphysically, we may ask under what circumstances, if any, it would pass that test of acceptability. And that is a question for *practical* reason, as the circumstances to be considered involve not only questions about degrees of probability, but also (for example) questions about the *values* of what may be at stake when one acts.

---

[14] William James: *Pragmatism*, New York 1955; first published 1907, p. 145.
[15] GP III, 193;A I, 13, 554. My translation differs in minor ways from the rendering in the complete translation of the letter in: Gottfried Wilhelm Leibniz: *The Art of Controversies*, trans. and ed. by Marcelo Dascal with Quintín Racionero and Adelino Cardoso, Dordrecht 2006, pp. 365f.
[16] Ibid.

The two disciplines with regard to which, in writing to Burnett, Leibniz most emphasizes the role of practical reason are jurisprudence and theology. I will leave it to others to comment on specific features of Leibniz's philosophy of law, but it is obvious enough why one would think that practical reason should have a large role in the theory and practice of law. One might be more surprised, however, to see theology, and its reasoning about God, or much it, located in the realm of practical rather than theoretical reason.

In fact, debate about the question, whether theology is a theoretical or a practical science goes back at least as far as the thirteenth century. St. Thomas Aquinas argued that theology is primarily a theoretical science. St. Bonaventure, however, argued that it is primarily a practical science, on the ground that its principal end is "that we should become good," and particularly that we should be moved to love God.[17]

Leibniz largely shared Bonaventure's view on that (whether or not he knew it was Bonaventure's). In an outline of the ends or proper purposes of various disciplines, sketched on the back of a letter in 1693, Leibniz suggests that "the end of theology is blessedness," and that "theology shows the way to attain perpetual happiness, through the divine will or grace."[18] And that way, as Leibniz insists in many writings, from the early 1670s to the end of his life, is by loving God, purely and above all things, for God's own sake. Leibniz also presents, in many of his writings, a theory of the nature of love, from which it follows that such love of God is intrinsically beatific, as he explains in 1714 in §16 of "The Principles of Nature and of Grace":

> "since God is the most perfect and the happiest, and consequently the most lovable, of substances, and since *true, pure Love* consists in the state that makes one taste pleasure in the perfections and in the happiness of that which one loves, this Love must give us the greatest pleasure of which one can be capable when, God is its object."[19]

For that reason Leibniz identified "the love of God above all things" as "the principle of true religion."[20]

---

[17] St. Thomas Aquinas: *Summa Theologiae*, I, q. 1, a. 4; St. Bonaventure: In: *Primum Librum Sententiarum*, Prœmii qu. 3.
[18] Grua, 240.
[19] Gottfried Wilhelm Leibniz: *Principes de la nature et de la grace*, ed., with Leibniz's *Monadologie*, by André Robinet, Paris 1954, p. 59.
[20] In 1677, Grua, 161.

From that fundamental principle Leibniz derives more detailed practical principles that are to play a part in governing what we say about God. For instance,

> "It is contrary to the practice of virtue to attribute to God anything akin to tyranny and cruelty, which subverts the notions of goodness and justice."[21]

Some such principle as that drives a great deal of the argument of Leibniz's Theodicy, as he makes clear in his preface to the Theodicy.[22] And Leibniz's copious writings connected with projects of reunion of churches are liberally seasoned with such practical principles, and practical arguments based on them.

I find it interesting that although the texts of Leibniz's correspondence and his controversies contain evidence of people disagreeing with many of his *conclusions*, I don't recall reading of anyone calling him out for using practical or pragmatic *arguments* in theology. I believe in fact that the use of such arguments was commonplace in his intellectual and religious environment.

It is clear, however, that Leibniz was over-simplifying, on the back of that letter in 1693, when he mentioned only blessedness as "the end of theology," whereas the end he assigned to philosophy was more theoretical, namely, "science, that is [*seu*] cognition that requires reasoning."[23] In his considerably fuller discussion for Burnett, however, Leibniz divided the domains of both theology and philosophy into theoretical and practical parts. I have already quoted his contrast of theoretical and practical philosophy. As for theology, Leibniz says that

> "Theological truths and inferences are of two species: one species have metaphysical certainty, and the others have moral certainty. The former presuppose definitions, axioms, and theorems, taken from the true Philosophy and from natural Theology. The latter presuppose, in part, History and facts, and in part the interpretation of texts."[24]

Here what is commonly called "revealed theology," which presupposes certain historical facts, and depends on interpretation of texts, finds itself on practical reason's side of the dividing line, while important parts, at least, of "natural theology" are assigned a place in theoretical reason's territory. The opening

---

[21] Ibid., 477; Leibniz: *The Art of Controversies*, p. 413.
[22] GP VI, 25–29.
[23] Grua, 240.
[24] GP III, 193; A I, 13, 554. My translation differs in minor ways from that of Dascal et al. in: Leibniz: *The Art of Controversies*, pp. 365f.

sections of the *Theodicy*'s "Preliminary Discourse on the Conformity of Faith with Reason" also make clear that that was indeed Leibniz's view.

Leibniz says much less to Burnett about the role of practical reason in *philosophy* than about its role in *theology*, and about the value and importance of *jurisprudence* for an understanding of practical reason. It is of interest for my project in this talk, however, that the very first example Leibniz gives Burnett of something we can know, but only with *moral* certainty, not with metaphysical necessity, is

> "that we are not dreaming now, when we read and write this letter, even though it would be possible for God to make everything appear to us in a dream the same way it appears to us now."[25]

It's time to return to my topic sentence from *De Modo*:

> "Even if this whole life were said to be nothing but a dream, and the visible world nothing but a phantasm, I would call this dream or phantasm real enough, if we were never deceived by it when making good use of reason."

What is the philosophical import of saying that? And what is the role of practical reason in saying it? It is *not* guiding us in this context to a way of becoming more virtuous morally or loving God more purely. The behavior it seeks to govern is, in the first place, *linguistic*. As Leibniz said in the earliest document that I quoted earlier as parallel to *De Modo* on this point, "there is merely a question of name, for we call appearances of this sort true."[26] In other words, what practical reason is directing us to do is to use the word 'true', or the word 'real', in a certain way, or sense. And if we do use the word 'real' in that way or sense, we will say, and *it will be true*, that the world as it appears to us in sense experience, and is explained in our physical science, *is real*, so long (and only so long) as the predictions we make on that basis are successful enough to satisfy the demands of our practical reason – because we won't be saying anything more than that when we say that it is real.

One more historical comparison may be illuminating at this point. According to Immanuel Kant's second postulate of empirical thinking in general, "What coheres with the material conditions of experience (of sensation) is actual [*wirklich*]."[27] Here too we are offered a necessary and sufficient condition

---

[25] Ibid.
[26] A VI, 4 B, 1398.
[27] Immanuel Kant: *Critique of Pure Reason* (A218/B265).

for a sort of reality of the world as we experience it. Here too that is not seen as the metaphysically deepest sort of reality; Kant famously holds that we do not experience anything as it is in itself. Famously also, he holds that believing certain metaphysical propositions, regarding human free will, life after death, and the existence of God, is justified, and indeed required, by practical reason.

But there are very significant differences between Leibniz and Kant regarding the role of practical reason. (1) Kant does not treat his actuality postulate as depending on an exercise of practical reason. He argues on theoretical grounds that it must be satisfied in any experience that is possible for us at all. (2) Kant does not allow practical reason to shape assent to propositions having theoretical content, except insofar as such assent can be seen as necessary for our compliance with the strictly moral or ethical demands of practical reason.

I suggest that the root of these differences is that Kant's principles of justification, in the use of practical as well as theoretical reason, are much more austere than Leibniz's, with the result that the scope allowed for broadly pragmatic considerations is much narrower in Kant's philosophy than in Leibniz's. In that respect Leibniz's approach seems to me more plausible than Kant's.

Leibniz's Mirrors: Reflecting the Past

Pauline Phemister (Edinburgh)

My aim in this paper is to explore Leibniz's intriguing description of the monad as a living mirror of the universe.[1] I begin with a few brief observations on the status of mirrors in seventeenth century France, before embarking on a more detailed examination of the metaphor itself that focuses in particular on the ways in which mirrors represent space and time, the varying degrees of clarity and distinctness of their representations, and the ways in which mirrors reflect themselves. After arguing that all reflections are reflections upon the past and that self-reflection rests in part on the ability to perceive others different from the self, I turn finally to the question of how self-reflecting moral beings might best reflect the lives of others, and conclude by suggesting that self-reflecting beings have a moral imperative to love other self-reflecting beings, be they in the past, the present or the future, and to mirror the beauty of the world and its creator God as best they can.[2]

---

[1] In references, I employ the standard abbreviations: AG = Gottfried Wilhelm Leibniz: *Philosophical Essays*, ed. and transl. by Roger Ariew/Daniel Garber, Indianapolis 1989; DSR = Id.: *De Summa Rerum: Metaphysical Papers, 1675-1676*, transl. by G. H. R. Parkinson, New Haven/London, 1992; L = Id.: *Philosophical Papers and Letters*, ed. and transl. by L. E. Loemker, Dordrecht ²1969; LA = Gottfried Wilhelm Leibniz/Antoine Arnauld: *The Leibniz-Arnauld Correspondence*, ed. and transl. by H. T. Mason, Manchester 1967; LTS = G. W. Leibniz: *Leibniz and the Two Sophies: The Philosophical Correspondence*, ed. and transl. by Lloyd Strickland, Toronto 2011; LV = Gottfried Wilhelm Leibniz/Burchard De Volder: *The Leibniz-De Volder Correspondence*, ed. and transl. by Paul Lodge, New Haven/London 2013; RB = Gottfried Wilhelm Leibniz: *New Essays on Human Understanding*, ed. and transl. by Peter Remnant/Jonathan Bennett, Cambridge 1981.

[2] On Leibniz's use of metaphors more generally, the following studies are invaluable: Marcelo Dascal: *Leibniz. Language, Signs and Thought: a collection of essays*, Amsterdam/Philadelphia 1987; Cristina Marras: *On the Metaphorical Network of Leibniz's Philosophy*, PhD Dissertation, Tel Aviv University 2003; Id.: "Leibniz and his metaphorical labyrinths: the manneristic and the unicursale", in: Dominique Berlioz/Frédéric Nef (eds.): *Leibniz et les puissances du langage,* Paris 2005, pp. 285–300; Id.: "The role of metaphor in Leibniz's epistemology", in: Marcelo Dascal (ed.): *Leibniz: What Kind of Rationalist?*, Dordrecht 2008, pp. 199–212; and Donald Rutherford: "Metaphor and the Language of Philosophy", in: Berlioz/Nef (eds.): *Leibniz et les puissances*, pp. 271–284.

1. Seventeenth Century Mirrors

Michel Foucault's critique of signs in the French classical period may have given rise to the modern characterization of the period as the 'age of representation,'[3] but Molière scholar Larry Norman suggests that the age might equally and perhaps more appropriately be labeled, the "age of the mirror."[4] Of course, as Sabine Melchior-Bonnet observed in her groundbreaking history of the mirror,

> "Man has been interested in his own image since prehistoric times, using all sorts of expedients – from dark and shiny stones to pools of water – in order to catch his reflection."[5]

But even the standing or handheld, highly polished gold, silver or bronze metal mirrors of ancient Egyptian, Greek and Roman civilizations were as nothing in comparison to the glass mirrors produced in the early modern age. During the Renaissance, Venetian masters had developed techniques that vastly improved the production and quality of glass mirrors. They guarded the secrets of their success very closely, but in the seventeenth century, France broke into this monopolized market, founding the Royal Company of Glass and Mirrors and eventually succeeding in producing mirrors of reasonable quality at lower cost than their higher quality Venetian counterparts.[6] The net result of this industrious activity was that by the middle of the seventeenth century, mirrors were no longer luxuries of only the royals and aristocratic nobility. The lower prices and increased availability enabled the bourgeoisie and the mercantile classes to indulge in the craze for the new glass reflective surfaces. Mirrors by this time had become fashionable symbols of success and increasingly common in everyday life, no longer relegated to boudoirs and dressing rooms, but found above mantle-pieces in drawing rooms, between doorways and windows, as well as on jewelry, belts, and buttons. And so it was that when Leibniz visited Paris in the 1670s, he entered into a veritable 'age of the mirror'.

---

[3] Michel Foucault: *The Order of Things: Archaeology of the Human Sciences*, London 1970. Originally published *as Les Mots et les Choses: une archéologie des sciences humaines*, Paris 1966.
[4] Larry Norman: *The Public Mirror: Molière and the social commerce of depiction*, Chicago 1999, p. 2.
[5] Sabine Melchior-Bonnet: *The Mirror: A History*, transl. by Katharine H. Jewett, London 2001, p. 9. First published as *Histoire du Miroir,* Paris 1994.
[6] Melchior-Bonnet: *The Mirror*, ch. 2.

Mixing in the circles that he did, he would have found mirrors practically everywhere he turned.

2. Monads as Mirrors

Reflections on the surfaces of the mirror are images or representations of the world outside of the mirror. It is this feature of the mirror that is uppermost in Leibniz's mind when he introduces the mirror as a simile for the individual substance in the text of section 9 of the 1686 *Discourse on Metaphysics*. Like mirrors, each finite perceiving substance is a representative being, albeit one whose reflections mirror not only the whole universe, but also its creator, God: "every substance is like a complete world and like a mirror of God or of the whole universe."[7] In later texts we find Leibniz abandoning the mirror as a mere simile in favour of the mirror as a metaphor. Repeatedly in letters to Remond, to Des Billettes, and to the Electress Sophie, he makes the point that "each simple substance is a mirror of the same universe";[8] "[e]very soul is a mirror of the entire world;"[9] "a perpetual mirror" of the universe and as durable as the universe itself;[10] and each a mirror of the universe "in its way"[11] or "according to its point of view."[12] The metaphor is retained in writings from Leibniz's final years, making its way into both the *Monadology*[13] and the *Principles of Nature and Grace*. In these texts, Leibniz is keen to emphasize the differences between ordinary souls and those capable of rational thought. Accordingly, in contrast to the opinion he expressed in the earlier *Discourse on Metaphysics* that every substance is "like a mirror of God", in later writings, being "an image of the divinity" is presented as a feature that distinguishes reasonable souls from those that mirror only the works of God.[14]

With the shift from simile to metaphor in the 1690s, substances are no longer merely *like* mirrors: they have *become* mirrors. The introduction of the

---

[7] A VI, 4 B, 1542; AG 42.
[8] Leibniz to Remond, July 1714; GP III, 623.
[9] Leibniz to Des Billettes, 4./14. December 1696; GP VII, 452; L 473.
[10] Leibniz to Sophie, 4. November 1696; GP VII, 542; LTS 151–152.
[11] Leibniz to Sophie, 6. February 1706; GP VII, 567; LTS 347. See also *Monadology* § 63; GP VI, 618.
[12] To Des Billettes, 4./14. December 1696; GP VII, 452; L 473.
[13] For instance: *Monadology* § 63; GP VI, 618.
[14] *Principles of Nature and Grace* §14; GP VI, 604/ AG 211. See also *Monadology* § 83; GP VI, 621.

stronger mirror metaphor coincides with Leibniz's increasing use of the term 'monad' to describe the foundational substances of the Leibnizian universe. As primitive forces, monads are inherently active beings and Leibniz modifies his mirror metaphor to accommodate this. Souls or monads are *living* mirrors. Each simple substance is "a perpetual, living mirror of the universe,"[15] each one "endowed with internal action."[16]

As *living* mirrors, monads differ from ordinary mirrors in significant ways. Monads are naturally indestructible unities, lacking component parts into which they could be broken.[17] Self-contained, non-interacting and independent, with their own internal life forces, they bring forth the images contained in their own essences. Not depending upon any other mirrors, their perceptions arise spontaneously and would still occur even if no other mirror existed. "[E]ach substance is like a world apart, independent of all other things."[18] Even their reflections of themselves are entirely internal affairs, something ordinary mirrors can have only with the assistance of other mirrors. However, more significant are the respects in which living mirrors agree with their ordinary lifeless mirror counterparts. We turn now to consider some of those shared features, beginning with the spatio-temporal characters of their representations of the world.[19]

3. Space and Time

Italian Renaissance masters, such as Filippo Brunelleschi and Paulo Uccello, perfected the art of perspective by making lines in the two-dimensional painting draw the viewer's eye towards one or more infinitesimal vanishing points, thereby creating the illusion of a three-dimensional spatial image on a two-dimensional canvas. Mirrors played no small part in the development of the

---

[15] *Monadology* § 56; GP VI, 616; AG 220. See also, for instance, Leibniz's unpublished remarks on the extract from the Bayle's *Critical Dictionary*, article Rorarius, comment L; GP IV, 532 and Leibniz's Fifth Letter to Clarke; GP VII, 411.
[16] Principles of Nature and Grace §3; GP VI, 599; AG 207.
[17] *Monadology* §77; GP VI, 620. See also, Leibniz to Sophie, 6. February 1706; GP VII, 567.
[18] *Discourse on Metaphysics* § 14; A VI, 4 B 1550; AG 47. See also *New System of the Nature of Substances and their Communication*; GP IV, 484.
[19] Living mirror monads – and ordinary mirrors too – contain infinity. I do not enter here into the complexities of mirrors' infinite natures, but the infinity of the living mirror is addressed in Ohad Nachtomy: *Living Mirrors: Infinity, Unity, and Life in Leibniz's Philosophy*, forthcoming, ch. 7.

technique. When one looks in a mirror, one sees not a flat two-dimensional image, but an image with spatial depth that seems to exist in the space behind the mirror. Looking at the mirror, one may feel, like Lewis Carroll's Alice,[20] as though if one could only walk into the mirror, one would enter a world whose contents and spatial dimensions, although reversed, are the same as those in the real world that the mirror reflects. Such imaginary outings must remain, however, in the realm of fiction. In the actual world, one cannot walk into the mirror: beyond its glass remains a closed space, enclosed within the mirror itself, a *private* image of a *public* world.

In this regard, Leibniz's mirror-metaphor is strikingly apt. Monads' perceptual representations of the world – their mirror images – also represent the external world as a world of bodies with length, breadth and depth situated in a three-dimensional space, a world that appears as one into which an external being could enter, but from which it is forever barred. The three-dimensional space of the mirror monad is private to that monad alone, internal to the monad that has no windows through which anything can enter or depart and whose representations of the external world cannot be transgressed by anything from outside. We can no more walk into the three-dimensional world of another monad than we can walk into the three-dimensional world of the glass mirror.

Both the artist's perspectival paintings and the glass-worker's mirrors produce representations of three-dimensional space. However, there is one crucial difference between the artist's reproduction of a three-dimensional space and the image in the mirror. On completion, the scenes represented in the painting remain static. Barring any later modifications, portraits, still-life studies, and landscape paintings do not change: they simply capture in perpetuity a moment in time now past. As a consequence of the passage of time in which the light passes from the external object to the mirror itself, the images in the mirror similarly capture moments in time now past. However, unlike the unchanging images in a finished painting, the images in the mirror are in constant flux, keeping pace with the changing nature of the things outside that they reflect.

In this regard too, the appropriateness of Leibniz's mirror-monad is evident. The monad's images also change as the world it represents changes, never the same from one moment to the next. Monads' perceptions or representations keep track with the world outside. Moreover, as in ordinary mirrors

---

[20] Lewis Carroll: *Through the Looking-Glass, and What Alice Found There*, London 1871.

and paintings alike, there is a lapse of time between the event happening in the world and its representation in the living monad. Monads represent the world through the medium of their own bodies, each one perceiving the changes external bodies have made on its organic body.[21] Just as it takes time for the light from an object to travel to the mirror, so too it takes time, however short, for the light to travel to the perceiver's eye. In his *New Essays on Human Understanding*, Leibniz makes the point that our present perceptions of paintings are always perceptions of the painting, not as it exists now, but as it existed a moment before. Although we might believe that "we immediately see the thing that causes the image", in fact:

> "we see only the image, and are affected only by rays of light. Since rays of light need time – however little – to reach us, it is possible that the object should be destroyed during the interval and no longer exist when the light reaches the eye; and something which no longer exists cannot be the present object of our sight."[22]

It is not only in the viewing of paintings that time-lapses intervene. Inanimate objects and living bodies alike, perceived through any organ of sense, might no longer exist by the time their presence has been registered in a perception in the soul. Nor are images in ordinary mirrors or sensory images in living mirrors excepted: they too register *not* the present state of the world, but rather its immediately preceding state.

A monad's present images represent the immediately preceding past, but of course, as we know, Leibniz holds that the whole of the past and the whole of the future are also represented in each present image, although always less distinctly than its present perception of the immediate past. Each passing present reflection is an effect of all the prior causes that have led up to the events now reflected in the monad-mirror. In this sense, the monad-mirror's images stretch backwards in time, even into deep geological time. As Leibniz tells Arnauld, "the indications [*les traces*] of the past are preserved for ever in each thing."[23] So too, pointing forwards, one perception paves the way for the next, and for the one after that, and for the one after that, and so

---

[21] As Leibniz explains in a letter to Arnauld, 9. October 1687; A II, 2, 242; LA 145: "since we perceive other bodies only through their relationship to ours, I was right to say that the soul expresses better what pertains to our body; therefore, the satellites of Saturn or Jupiter are known only in consequence of a movement which occurs in our eyes."
[22] A VI, 6, 135; RB 135.
[23] Leibniz to Arnauld, 30. April 1687; A II, 2, 188; LA 123.

forth. Hence, the present image not only retains "the indications of the past" but also already contains the "lineaments [*les traits*] of the future."[24]

Leibniz's causal explanation of the monad's mirroring of the past and the future would seem to apply equally to ordinary mirrors. Their present images too reflect objects with causal histories and future consequences and these past causes and future effects might be regarded as in some way also contained in mirrors' images. All mirrors, living and nonliving, can be said to embrace the past, the present and the future in each of their fleeting images or perceptions. As the following discussion will highlight, however, they do so with varying degrees of clarity or distinctness.

4. Degrees of Representation

Each monad is a living mirror of the whole universe, reflecting each and every one of the infinitely many, mutually reflecting, living monad-mirrors that comprise Leibniz's universe. Insofar as they all represent the same universe, the representational content of each of their perceptions is the same. This means that it is not possible to differentiate one monad from another by reference only to the content of their perceptions. However, they can be differentiated by the differing ways in which that content is exhibited. Leibniz addressed the issue in a draft letter to Nicolas Remond:

> "each simple substance is a mirror of the same universe, as lasting and as ample as it, although these perceptions of created beings can only be distinct with respect to a few things at once and they are differentiated by the relations or, so to speak, by the points of view of the mirrors, which make it that the same universe is multiplied in an infinity of ways by as many living mirrors, each representing it in its own way."[25]

Each perception "can only be distinct with respect to a few things at once." Among the "few things" that each monad perceives relatively more distinctly is its own organic body. We've already had reason to note how although the soul perceives everything in the universe, it does so from the perspectival view afforded by its perceptions of its own body. The soul perceives external bodies only through their relationship to its own. What Leibniz infers from this is that,

---

[24] Ibid.
[25] Leibniz to Remond, July 1714; GP III, 623 / Donald Rutherford, http://philosophyfaculty.ucsd.edu/faculty/rutherford/Leibniz/translations/RemondVII1714.pdf

although it mirrors the whole universe, each soul perceives most distinctly what is closest to it, namely, the organic body to which it is attached and within this organic body, those parts that are in more immediate contact with the external bodies are perceived most distinctly of all. Hence, the nerves are:

> "more sensitive parts for us than others, and it is perhaps only through them that we apperceive others, which apparently occurs because the movements of the nerves or of the liquids belonging to them imitate impressions better and confuse them less."[26]

Ordinary mirrors too represent their surroundings with different degrees of clarity and distinctness. Some have surfaces that are blurred or damaged and can represent things only confusedly; others have surfaces that are cleaner and brighter and their images are correspondingly sharper and more distinct. Equally, just as living monads mirror the universe through the prism of their own immediately present and more distinctly perceived bodies, nonliving mirrors too represent most distinctly the things in their immediate environs. Similarly capable of distinctly representing only "a few things at once", they reflect most distinctly what is closest to them, less distinctly whatever is further away in space and in time.[27]

Although all monads perceive their own bodies more distinctly than they perceive the rest of the world, rational monads can also distinctly perceive their own perceiving selves. In the following section, we consider how self-reflections arise in monad-mirrors and contrast this with the conditions that allow ordinary mirrors to contain reflections of themselves.

5. Self-Reflecting Mirrors

At *Monadology* § 30, Leibniz states that it is:

> "through the knowledge of necessary truths and through their abstractions that we rise to *reflective acts*, which enable us to think of that which is called 'I' and enable us to consider that this or that is in us."[28]

---

[26] Leibniz to Arnauld, 30. April 1687; A II, 2, 175f.; LA 113f. See also, Leibniz to Arnauld, 9. October 1687; A II, 2, 241f.
[27] Neither the finite monad mirror nor the ordinary physical mirror, we may add, reflects its surroundings with absolute clarity and distinctness.
[28] GP VI, 612; AG 217. Cf. *Discourse on Metaphysics* § 34; A VI, 4 B, 1583.

Being able to think in abstract terms, the self-conscious rational being is able to conceive distinctly the 'I' (a thing that, a we shall see, by its very nature thinks about many things) and to distinguish this perceiving 'I' from the things in the world at large that it perceives. This means that self-conscious minds or rational souls "have incomparably greater perfection than the forms thrust into matter."[29] Nevertheless, although the (substantial) forms "thrust into matter" do not consciously know themselves as perceivers, it is conceivable that they, albeit obscurely, perceive their own perceptions. While in Paris, Leibniz had written a short piece known as *On Reminiscence and on the Mind's Self-reflection.* The piece is an account of Leibniz's own forays into the spiral of thoughts generated by his thinking of his thinking, then thinking of his thinking of his thinking, and so on. Being aware of the recursive nature of the procedure and of the temporal internal between each reflection upon a past reflection – an awareness of the "intervals of these beats" – allows Leibniz to conclude that each:

> "reflection of a reflection – in the mind a little before [...] already existed before, and so the perception of a perception to infinity is perpetually in the mind."[30]

In *On Reminiscence and on the Mind's Self-reflection,* Leibniz is concerned only with those reflections of reflections of which he is consciously aware. However, if the reflections of reflections are already in the mind, then prior to their being consciously perceived, they must be in the mind as obscure rather than distinct perceptions of perceptions. Indeed, we may presume that there is an infinity of obscurely perceived perceptions of perceptions in the mind. And this in turn opens up the possibility that even though the lowest, most obscurely perceiving monads have no distinct awareness of themselves as perceiving beings, perceptions of perceptions might nevertheless occur *ad infinitum* in them too.

Whether perception of their perceptions to infinity occurs in all monads will not be further investigated here. It is sufficient for our purposes to note that bare monads' perceptions of their perceptions, if such they have, and minds' reflections of themselves arise entirely from within the monads themselves. None has any windows through which anything can enter or depart.[31]

---

[29] *New System*; GP IV, 478; AG 140.
[30] DSR 74f.
[31] *Monadology* § 7; GP VI, 607.

All of a monad's perceptions, including any self-perceptions, arise, not through the action of anything external, but solely through the activity of the monad's own internal force.

As concentrated worlds,[32] complete in themselves, living mirrors reflections of themselves or their perceptions of their perceptions occur independently of, and irrespective of, the existence or non-existence of other living mirrors. Ordinary, nonliving mirrors, on the other hand, contain reflections of themselves and reflections of their own images only in the presence of other existing mirrors. Only when nonliving mirrors are placed directly in front of each other does the image of the one reflected in the other find its way back to the first as a reflection of the reflected image. Admittedly, when nonliving mirrors reflect each other in this way, the reflections in each facing mirror multiply *ad infinitum*. Like the mind's "perception of a perception to infinity" described by Leibniz in his Paris Notes, each mirror's image of itself is reproduced endlessly over and over again. Still, it remains the case that an ordinary lifeless mirror can only 'see' itself, as it were, by reflecting the image of itself as it appears in the other. Whether mirrors' self-reflections do or do not depend upon the existence of other mirrors would therefore appear to mark a fundamental point of difference between living and nonliving mirrors: ordinary mirrors' self-reflections occur only if other mirrors exist, but monads' self-reflections occur regardless of whether any other monad-mirrors exist.

All metaphors eventually reach a point of collapse and we might consider this to be that point. However, although undoubtedly the issues exposes tension in the metaphor, I do not believe we have yet reached the metaphor's final breaking point. The metaphor has yet more to reveal, for although it is the truth that the indivisible unity and independence of the monad means that the actual existence of other mirrors is not essential to the monad's ability to reflect upon itself, the monad's self-reflection, like self-reflection in nonliving mirrors, is dependent upon the mirror's ability to contain in itself images of external things.

We began this section with a quotation from the *Monadology* in which Leibniz describes the mind's "*reflective acts*" as acts that "enable us to think of that which is called 'I' and enable us to consider that this or that is in us" and in which he claims that these acts of self-reflection are made possible "through our knowledge of necessary truths and through their abstractions."[33]

---

[32] Leibniz to De Volder, 20. June 1703; LV 262f.
[33] *Monadology* § 30; GP VI, 612; AG 217.

The omission of any reference to the soul's sensory perceptions of others encourages the view that Leibniz regarded sense perceptions of external things as irrelevant to the mind's ability to reflect upon itself. His highlighting of knowledge of necessary truths and abstractions gives the impression that he believes that the only things that the self-reflecting mind needs to consider as being in it are its abstract and necessary innate ideas. This impression is reinforced by some remarks of Leibniz in the Preface to the *New Essays*:

> "reflection is nothing but attention to what is within us, and the senses do not give us what we carry with us already. In view of this, can it be denied that there is a great deal that is innate in our minds, since we are innate to ourselves, so to speak, and since we include Being, Unity, Substance, Duration, Change, Action, Perception, Pleasure, and hosts of other objects of our intellectual ideas?"[34]

However, as Leibniz had already observed in the *Discourse on Metaphysics*, the distinction between ideas that are innate and ideas that are derived from the senses, although useful, is not in metaphysical strictness, defensible.[35] Everything that is 'in us' is innate. Technically, the senses do not give us anything at all. The point is made even in the opening chapter of the *New Essays*, where Leibniz confesses his belief that "all the thoughts and actions of our soul come from its own depths and could not be given to it by the senses."[36] Leibniz reiterates the point a few years later in a letter to Coste:

> "I have also shown that when we take things in a certain metaphysical sense, we are always in a state of perfect spontaneity, and that what we attribute to the impressions of external things arises only from confused perceptions in us corresponding to them."[37]

There are 'in us' not only those ideas we call 'innate', but also numerous confused perceptions and even "at every moment there is an infinity of perceptions unaccompanied by awareness or reflection."[38] When, therefore, the mind reflects upon itself and considers "this or that" to be in it, should not the "this or that" include at least the mind's sensory perceptions as well as its more

---

[34] A VI, 6, 51; RB 51. See also, *Discourse on Metaphysics* § 27; A VI, 4 B, 1571f. and Letter to Queen Sophie Charlotte of Prussia: *On What is Independent of Sense and Matter*; GP VI, 501f.
[35] *Discourse on Metaphysics* § 27; A VI, 4 B, 1571f.
[36] A VI, 6, 74; RB 74.
[37] Leibniz to Coste, 19. December 1707; GP III, 403; AG 195.
[38] *New Essays* Preface; A VI, 6, 53; RB 53.

abstract thoughts? After all, "this nature that pertains to the soul is representative of the universe in a very exact manner (though more or less distinctly)."[39] When self-consciously reflecting upon its own representative nature as a mirror of a universe populated by an infinity of other mirrors, should not the mind take into account not only its general abstract idea of itself as a perceiving substance, but also its particular perceptions of these other mirrors, as seen from its own unique perspective?

If so, the self-reflections of rational living mirrors are not so far removed from the self-reflections ordinary nonliving mirrors as first it seemed. The nonliving mirror can only contain images of itself by reflecting the image of itself that is contained in another. Effectively, it needs to have an image of the other mirror if it is to reflect itself. Of course, the windowless living mirror self-reflects by turning inwards to perceive its own substantial self and its perceptions, but its own nature dictates that within itself are contained perceptions or images of mirrors outside of itself. Effectively, it too needs to have images of other mirrors if it is to self-consciously reflect on its reflections. It would appear, then, that for both the living and the nonliving mirror, self-reflection involves the having of images of mirrors other than itself.

In the next and final section, our discussion turns to morals. Throughout history, ordinary mirrors have been regarded as having instrumental value and significance for the moral improvement of human beings.[40] However, they are obviously not themselves moral agents. I will therefore put aside discussion of the ordinary mirror in order to explore, albeit with a broad brush, the moral nature of rational self-reflecting minds and why it is important ethically that the mind's images of other mirrors are as distinct or perfect as it is possible for them to be.

6. Moral Mirrors

On account of their rationality and knowledge of the eternal truths – the facilitating grounds of their self-reflective acts – minds are able not only to consciously appreciate the perfection of God's works, but also to self-consciously imitate God's works in their own productions and activities, basing their choices and deliberations on considerations of what is good and what is for

---

[39] *New System*; GP IV, 485; AG 144.
[40] See, for instance: Bonnet: *The Mirror*, pp. 105–115.

the best for themselves and for others. For these reasons, each mind is said to be "an image of the divinity"[41] and is a member of the moral City of God where God, ruling as both monarch[42] and legislator,[43] ensures that "there will be no good action that is unrewarded, no bad action that goes unpunished."[44]

As rational images of the divine, it is incumbent upon us to perfect our own natures so that we may reflect the glory of God to the very best of our abilities. The perfecting of our own natures consists in making our perceptions as distinct as we can: "the soul itself knows the things it perceives only so far as it has distinct and heightened [*revelées*] perceptions; and it has perfection to the extent that it has distinct perceptions."[45] To perfect our souls is to polish our mirror, so that it reflects the universe without blemish or contortion. Mirroring the best possible world distinctly exposes its perfection: its harmony, beauty, and goodness. Leibniz defines beauty in terms of the pleasurable feelings we derive from contemplating beautiful things[46] and he conceives benevolent love in terms of the disposition to derive pleasure from "the perfection, well-being or happiness" of those beings who are themselves capable of pleasure or happiness.[47] We wish well those whom we love, assist them in their endeavours, and, when they flourish, we are pleased for their sakes, not for our own.

Mirrors, as we found earlier, reflect the past, present and future of the universe. This prompts the question whether the love we feel towards beings capable of happiness is possible only in relation to those who are present to us today or can (and perhaps should) it be extended to those in the past and in the future? How could this be so, one might ask? Surely those who existed in the past cannot be objects of love for they no longer exist and are no longer capable of happiness. Equally, those who might exist in the future cannot be the objects of our love for they do not yet exist and indeed they might never come into existence. Currently, they are only vague possibilities and possibilities are not capable of pleasure and happiness. But no such response is available to

---

[41] *Principles of Nature and Grace* § 14; GP VI, 604; AG 211. See also *Monadology* § 83; GP VI, 621.
[42] *Monadology* § 87; GP VI, 622.
[43] *Monadology* § 89; GP VI, 622.
[44] *Monadology* § 90; GP VI, 622; AG 224.
[45] *Principles of Nature and Grace* § 13; GP VI, 604; AG 211.
[46] *Elements of Natural Law*; A VI, 1, 464; L 137: "We seek beautiful things because they are pleasant, for I define beauty as that, the contemplation of which is pleasant".
[47] *New Essays*; A VI, 6, 163; RB 163.

Leibniz. The indestructibility of the monads entails that everything created in the first moment of time still exists in some form now and will continue to exist in some form in the future, while pre-established harmony ensures that the futures of all living things are not mere possibilities, but are already mapped out with certainty.

"[D]eath", considers Leibniz, "is nothing but the contraction of an animal, just as generation is nothing but its unfolding."[48] Death is neither the end of existence nor the end of perception, but merely the falling into unconsciousness, as if into a deep sleep, where all perceptions are insensible and indistinct.[49] For nonhuman animals, Leibniz theorizes, death consists in a diminution of their being that causes them to "reenter the recesses of a world of minute creatures", from which they may at some point in the future emerge.[50] Rational minds, however, enjoy a different fate. They do not find themselves exiled to the depths of the material world.[51] Nor is their citizenship of the City of God revoked: the "republic can never lose any of its members"[52] and it is because of this, that minds "must always keep their moral qualities and their memory."[53] Whether Leibniz considered minds might self-consciously retain their memories in death is not clear. When, for instance, in the preface to the *New Essays*, he writes that "death can only be a sleep, and not a lasting one at that", he confines his remark to the animals, declining to "discuss the case of man, who must in this regard have special prerogatives for safeguarding his personhood."[54]

Whatever the precise nature of their post-death states, it is clearly Leibniz's view that rational souls – and indeed all souls – continue to exist as substances after death and that each continues to mirror, however obscurely, the universe from its own point of view. If rational beings retain their personalities and their memories even after death, then either they remain self-conscious in their death states or they will one day awaken from their deep slumbers. In either case, might we not assume that they are still capable of happiness and perfection, and therefore still possible objects of love – love, as we recall,

---

[48] To Johann Bernoulli, 18. November 1698; GM III, 553; AG 169. See also *Principles of Nature and Grace* § 6; GP VI, 601f.
[49] *New Essays* Preface; A VI, 6, 55: RB 55.
[50] Leibniz to Arnauld, 30. April 1687; A II, 2, 189; AG 88.
[51] Ibid.
[52] Ibid.; A II, 2, 189f.
[53] Ibid.; A II, 2 189.
[54] A VI, 6, 55; RB 55.

being the disposition to be pleased by the other's "perfection, well-being or happiness?"[55]

Our own perfectibility, as was have seen, lies in the making more distinct our perceptions of the world, so that we may more distinctly perceive the perfection, beauty and goodness of the world and each of its constituents, and through this come to love not only God, the most perfect being, but also all rational beings capable of happiness that God has created. And insofar as we are rational living mirrors of the universe whose perceptions extend backwards into the past and forwards into the future, do we not have a moral responsibility to seek the good throughout the whole, not just in that little part of the mirror that represents the present (or more precisely the near past), and to love to the best of our abilities *all* the rational beings we find there?

Leibniz is one such rational being. In this tercentenary year of his death, we commemorate his mirrored perspective on the world. And when we reflect on the perceptions that are in each of us, let us find among them reflections of Leibniz that distinctly highlight the beauty and perfection of his mirror of the best possible world, reflections that dispose us to love Leibniz and to derive pleasure from the thought of his present or future happiness and well-being.

---

[55] *New Essays*; A VI, 6, 163; RB 163.

Les étapes de la dynamique leibnizienne: de la réforme à la fondation

Michel Fichant (Paris)

Je suis intervenu pour la première fois à Hanovre devant un Leibniz-Kongress voici 44 ans, en 1972. C'était le deuxième Congrès. Le titre de ma communication était « La réforme leibnizienne de la dynamique d'après des textes inédits. »[1]

Il s'agissait principalement de la première présentation des manuscrits répartis et numérotés en 10 liasses sous le titre de *De corporum concursu*,[2] et soigneusement datés par Leibniz de janvier 1678. L'édition annoncée de ces textes alors entièrement inédits, même si leur existence avait été mentionnée, occasionnellement et rarement,[3] dut attendre assez longtemps, puisqu'elle n'est parue qu'en 1994.[4] Je rappellerai dans un moment pourquoi on peut y voir l'acte de naissance de la dynamique leibnizienne.

En cette année 2016, nous allons prochainement, grâce aux soins d'Andrea Costa et d'Enrico Pasini et à mon plus modeste concours, disposer de la première édition critique de la *Dynamica de potentia et legibus naturae corporeae* de 1690, avec tous les états des manuscrits et non plus seulement ce que nous connaissions par le volume VI des *Mathematischen Schriften*, où Gerhardt a reproduit la copie que Leibniz avait fait réaliser en vue d'une publication à laquelle il renonça finalement.

En cet état, et si maîtrisée et ordonnée que soit la composition du texte de la *Dynamica*, il s'agit d'un ouvrage encore inachevé, auquel il manque au moins un chapitre ainsi que des annexes que Leibniz se proposait d'y adjoindre. C'est donc de façon contingente que le dernier morceau de la *Dynamica* qui en est de fait la fin sans en être l'achèvement est aussi intitulé *De concursu corporum*. Pour l'historien qui n'a à tenir compte que de la réalité des textes tels qu'ils sont, édités ou non, achevés ou non, tout se passe donc

---

[1] « La < réforme > leibnizienne de la Dynamique d'après des textes inédits », in : *Akten des Internationalen Leibniz-Kongresses*, tome 2, Stuttgart 1974. – Étude prolongée par les « Neue Einblicke in Leibniz' Reform seiner Dynamik », in : *Studia Leibnitiana,* 22/1 (1990), pp. 48–68.
[2] La dixième liasse (*scheda decima*) porte la date de janvier-février 1678 et a pour titre *De concursu corporum.*
[3] Erich Hochstetteer: « Von der wahren Wirklichkeit bei Leibniz », in: *Zeitschrift für philosophischen Forschung* 20 (1966), p. 428; Leonard J. Russell: Art: « Leibniz », in : *The Encyclopedia of Philosophy*, vol. 4, ed. par Paul Edwards, London 1967 [Repr. 1972], pp. 425sq.
[4] Gottfried Wilhelm Leibniz : *La Réforme de la Dynamique. De Corporum concursu (1678), et autres textes inédits*, edition, présentation, traductions et commentaires par Michel Fichant, Paris 1994.

comme si, de 1678 à 1690, Leibniz avait parcouru une boucle, d'un *De corporum concursu* à un *De concursu corporum* : le traité de la *Dynamica* se termine de fait par où tout avait commencé, l'établissement des lois du choc des corps. C'est la configuration de cette boucle que nous pouvons aujourd'hui mieux voir, en discernant quelles sont les impulsions qui en ont déterminé le point de départ et les orientations de son tracé, jusqu'à un point d'arrivée encore provisoire.

Mais les plus récentes recherches associées à la préparation de l'édition de la *Dynamica* ont conduit à s'intéresser de plus près à la structure discursive de cette œuvre, à laquelle Leibniz a attaché beaucoup d'importance dans les phases de sa rédaction. Ainsi s'est posée la question du sens de la distinction entre deux parties, l'une traitant des *Dynamica simplicia seu a rebus abstracta*, et l'autre des *Dynamica concreta circa ea quae in systemate rerum contingunt*.[5] Or, en 1678, le *De corporum concursu* avait mis fin à une période où les recherches de Leibniz sur les lois du mouvement s'étaient inscrites précédemment dans la dualité de méthodes et de niveaux d'intelligibilité qu'avaient établie les deux ouvrages complémentaires de 1671, *Theoria motus abstracti* et *Theoria motus concreti seu Hypothesis physica nova*. Comment faut-il comprendre qu'en 1690, Leibniz accorde de nouveau à une dualité formulée en termes apparemment semblables une fonction architectonique relativement à la science des lois de la nature, du mouvement et de la nature corporelle ? Comme si la précédente boucle s'inscrivait dans une autre qui ramènerait à une distinction dont l'instauration de la dynamique en janvier 1678 avait signifié l'abandon ?

1.

Quoique le nom de « dynamique » ait été inventé par Leibniz en 1690 au cours même de la rédaction de son traité, il est d'usage constant et légitime de l'appliquer à une partie des travaux antérieurs : en tout cas, on peut dire qu'il y a déjà, sans l'appellation, une dynamique dans l'ensemble du corpus doctrinal constitué autour de la définition de la force ou puissance par le produit mv^2, avec la formule qui en résulte d'un principe de conservation de la somme des forces absolues contre le principe cartésien de la conservation de la quantité brute de mouvement, et avec aussi les deux équations complémentaires de la

---

[5] GM VI, 285. On remarquera qu'ici, comme assez souvent dans ses premiers emplois, le terme de « *dynamica* » est un neutre pluriel. L'emploi au féminin singulier finira par s'imposer.

conservation de la direction totale ou force directive et de la conservation de la vitesse relative des corps concourants ou force respective. En ce sens, la dynamique est acquise lorsque, au début du huitième feuillet (*scheda octava*) du *De corporum concursu* de janvier 1678, Leibniz, dans une note ajoutée *a posteriori*, résume le résultat acquis en ces termes :

> « Calculus ex his tribus principiis : virium servatarum, servatae directionis in summa, et servatarum apparentiarum. »[6]

Je rappelle que l'ensemble du manuscrit du *De corporum concursu* est consacré à la recherche par le calcul associé à la figuration schématique d'une solution générale au problème du choc direct de deux corps, auquel Leibniz s'était appliqué intensément tout au long de l'année 1677 comme l'attestent de très nombreux brouillons datées ou aisément datables de cette période. Sur les sept premières liasses du dossier de janvier 1678, Leibniz tente d'obtenir la solution en continuant d'adhérer à la formule cartésienne de la conservation de la quantité absolue de mouvement. Les premières lignes du huitième cahier opèrent ce que Leibniz lui-même a qualifié de « *reformatio* », avec la reconnaissance du facteur mv^2 comme définition de la force. À cet égard la comparaison des premières lignes du feuillet 1 et de celles du feuillet 8 est saisissante : dans les deux cas la force (*vis*) est nominalement définie de la même manière comme *quantitas effectus*. Mais au feuillet 1, cette définition associée à la proposition générale « In omni motu eadem semper vis servatur », conduit à la définition réelle :

> « Vis est quantitas effectus, sive quod hinc sequitur factum ex quantitate corporis ducta in quantitatem velocitatis. »[7]

Au feuillet 8 nous lisons d'emblée :

> « Vis est quantitas effectus. Hinc vis corporis in motu existentis aestimari debet ex altitudine ad quam ascendere potest. »[8]

Dans un premier temps, la quantité de l'effet est la quantité de mouvement, et donc l'effet est le mouvement, caractérisé sans autre détermination par sa seule vitesse. Une fois de plus, les tentatives de Leibniz d'établir par le calcul

---

[6] Leibniz : *La Réforme de la Dynamique*, p. 152.
[7] Ibid., p. 71.
[8] Ibid., p. 153.

un ensemble cohérent de règles échouent. La « *reformatio* » consiste en ce que, dans un second départ, l'effet est déterminé comme la hauteur d'ascension du corps en mouvement. Le raisonnement classique qui s'impose définitivement, permet, en référence aux formules de Galilée, de mesurer cette hauteur et donc la force par le carré de la vitesse.

Il n'y a pas à revenir ici sur l'analyse détaillée des motifs qui ont conduit Leibniz à cette découverte, ou plutôt à cette redécouverte. J'ai pu suggérer que le recours à l'expérimentation, dont il est important de remarquer que Leibniz *l'a effectivement réalisée* en consignant les résultats sur des tableaux chiffrés, avait pu jouer un rôle décisif, non pas par ces résultats eux-mêmes, mais par la schématisation du module du dispositif expérimental, directement emprunté du reste à Mariotte[9]: ce dispositif consiste en deux boules de bois suspendues à des fils de même longueur ; on écarte une ou deux des boules de la verticale et on la ou les laisse retomber jusqu'à ce qu'elles se heurtent et rejaillissent l'une sur l'autre en remontant à une hauteur déterminée par l'effet du choc[10]. Le module du dispositif fournit une schématisation ou expression simple et directe du principe, établi en toute généralité depuis 1676 comme fondement de la mesure de la puissance, le principe de l'égalité de la cause pleine et de l'effet entier, d'où résulte que cause et effet ont même puissance.[11] Ici, la cause pleine est de façon manifeste identifiable à la hauteur à laquelle les corps sont élevés et d'où ils acquièrent la vitesse qui intervient dans le choc ; l'effet est la hauteur à laquelle ils montent selon la vitesse résultante du choc. La force invariante qui est identiquement celle de la cause pleine et de l'effet entier sera donc mesurable par la considération de ces hauteurs :

> « Nempe vis in corpore non aestimanda est a celeritate et magnitudine corporis, sed ab altitudine ex qua decidit. Sunt autem altitudines ex quibus corpora deciderunt, ut quadrata quaesitarum celeritatum. Ergo et vires, corporibus positis iisdem. Generaliter autem vires sunt in composita ratione ex simplici corporum, et duplicata celeritatum. »[12]

---

[9] Edme Mariotte : *Traitte de la percussion ou du chocq des corps*, Paris 1673, pp. 8–22.
[10] Leibniz : *La Réforme de la Dynamique*, p. 131.
[11] Publié par Heinz-Jürgen Hess : « Die unveröffentlichten naturwissenschaftlichen und technischen Arbeiten von G. W. Leibniz aus der Zeit seines Parisaufenthaltes », in : *Leibniz à Paris (1672–1676)*, Tome 1 : *Les Sciences* (= *Studia Leibnitiana, Supplementa* XVII), Wiesbaden 1978, pp. 202–205.
[12] Leibniz : *La Réforme de la Dynamique*, p. 134.

Ce point acquis, Leibniz s'engage sur une voie dégagée, ses calculs s'ordonnent aisément, et il peut conclure l'étape franchie sur le huitième feuillet par un satisfecit : « Atque ita ex solo calculo cuncta absolvimus. »[13]

Mais il y a plus. La « *reformatio* » de 1678 consiste en fait à habiliter comme véritables lois du mouvement les règles du choc telles qu'elles avaient été établies par Huygens, Wren, puis exposée par Mariotte. Leibniz a lu dès sa parution en 1669 le mémoire de Huygens publié par les *Philosophical Transactions* ;[14] il a lu de près et annoté à Paris fin 1673-début 1674 le *Traitte de la percussion ou du chocq des corps* de Mariotte.[15] En 1669, Leibniz avait renvoyé les règles de Huygens et de Wren au plan des « phénomènes » présentés par les corps tels qu'ils apparaissent dans le monde sensible, pour y opposer les véritables raisons du mouvement indépendantes des sens. En effet :

> « Motus dupliciter tractari potest ratione et sensu, et sensus rationi praejudicare non potest, ratio tamen sensui. »[16]

C'est là l'origine de la dissociation qui sera déployée par les deux théories de 1671, dont les titres complets sont : *Theoria motus abstracti seu Rationes Motuum universales, à sensu & Phænomenis independentes*, et *Hypothesis physica nova, Quâ Phænomenorum Naturæ plerorumque causæ ab unico quodam universali motu, in globo nostro supposito, neque Tychonicis, neque Copernicanis aspernando, repetuntur*. Les règles de Huygens et de Wren, en dépit de leur forme mathématique, seront désignées comme des phénomènes, en ce que qu'elles présupposent dans les corps l'élasticité et la gravité, qui sont des propriétés relevant de la perception sensible ; on ne peut rendre compte de ces propriétés que par une Hypothèse générale sur la constitution du «système» formé par le monde visible ; cette hypothèse est celle du mouvement universel unique de circulation d'un éther omniprésent qui est le véhicule de la transmission de la lumière.

Or sur ce plan, le *De corporum concursu* est formel : les nouvelles équations du mouvement établissent l'intelligibilité de ce que Leibniz désigne comme le «système», alors que le fondement axiomatique de l'égalité de la

---

[13] Ibid., p. 158.
[14] A VI, 2, 336–340.
[15] Cf. Michel Fichant : « Leibniz, lecteur de Mariotte », avec la publication des notes de lecture inédites, in : *Revue d'Histoire des Sciences* XLVI/4 (1993).
[16] A VI, 2, 159.

cause pleine et de l'effet entier permet de faire l'économie de toute hypothèse. Ainsi la formule citée du feuillet 1, – la force ou quantité d'effet mesurée par le produit de la grandeur du corps par la vitesse – est-elle accompagnée après coup (*post reformationem*) de la remarque :

> « Error : id hinc non sequitur in nostro systemate. »[17]

La vraie mesure mathématique de la force est donc déterminée par la structure du système et par les lois physiques qui y sont réalisées, notamment la loi de la chute des graves selon la formule de Galilée :

> « In nostro systemate necesse est momenta esse quadrata celeritatum ; quia effectus est ascensus ad quem corpus ascendendo pervenire potest ; ascensus autem sunt ut quadrata celeritatum. In alio forte systemate Mundi, ubi celeritates aliam habent relationem ad altitudines, etiam alia facienda esset virium aestimatio. »[18]

Cette référence au « système » a dans le contexte de la « *Reformatio* » une signification qui doit être comprise à partir de la distinction de 1671 entre une *Theoria motus abstracti* et une *Hypothesis physica nova seu theoria motus concreti* : selon les qualifications que Leibniz lui-même en donnera plus tard, la première traite le mouvement « hors du système comme si c'était une chose purement mathématique », la seconde se trouvant caractérisée comme « l'*Hypothèse du mouvement concret et systématique*, tel qu'il se rencontre effectivement dans la nature. »[19] Le rapport au système est ainsi le point de dissociation de l'abstrait et du concret. D'un côté, les

---

[17] Leibniz : *La Réforme de la Dynamique*, p. 71.
[18] Ibid., p. 134.
[19] Lettre à Foucher de fin juin 1693, GP I, 415 et A II, 2, 712. De façon similaire dans le *Phoranomus seu de Potentia et Legibus naturae*, l'évocation des anciennes théories oppose « les Lois des mouvements abstraites de la matière sensible » à « la constitution du système» (édition, avec traduction italienne, par Gianfranco Mormino dans: Gottfried Wilhelm Leibniz: *Dialoghi filosofici e scientifici*, a cura di Francesco Piro, in collaborazione con Gianfranco Mormino e Enrico Pasini, Milano 2007, pp. 872sq.), ou encore « l'état brut et naturel des corps » à leur « état systématique » (ibid., p. 782) – Et dans Le *Specimen dynamicum*: « Mihi adhuc juveni […] excidit libellus *Hypotheseos physicae* titulo, quo Theoriam motus pariter a systemate abstractam, et systemati concretam exposui » (GM VI, 240).

« Fundamenta motuum », relevant d'une « doctrina de abstracta motuum ratione » d'où les expériences doivent être écartées comme elles le sont des raisonnements géométriques, – « talia enim non ex facto et sensu, sed terminorum definitionibus demonstrantur. »[20]

Selon ces définitions, le corps n'est autre chose, du point de vue rationnel ou abstrait, que « id quod est in spatio, Res spatio coextensum »[21], qui ne connaît pas d'autre action ou passion que le mouvement, défini comme « mutatio spatii. » Enfin la théorie abstraite complétement développée met en jeu le concept géométrisé de *conatus*, qui est au mouvement ce que le point est à l'espace, ou encore « initium finisque motus. »[22] D'un autre côté, on observe aussi que les lois ainsi obtenues divergent de ce que l'expérience du monde physique rend manifeste. La *Theoria motus concreii* est ainsi en charge de réduire la contrariété en faisant intervenir les propriétés physiques de la gravité et de l'élasticité requises par les « phénomènes hugeno-wrenniens (*Hugeno-Wrenniania phaenomena*). »[23]

En janvier 1693, Leibniz rendra compte de cet état antérieur de sa pensée, en rappelant le paradoxe principal auquel buttait les règles abstraites du choc :

« Au commencement de mes études mathematiques je me fis une theorie du mouvement absolu, où supposant qu'il n'y avoit rien dans le corps que l'étendue et l'impenetrabilité, je fis des règles du mouvement absolu que je croyois veritables, et j'esperois de les pouvoir concilier avec les phenomenes par le moyen du systeme des choses […] Suivant cette theorie, il se feroit seulement une composition de l'effort (*conatus*) que le corps a déja, avec celuy qu'un autre tache de luy imprimer de plus, en sorte que chaque effort se conserve, mais deux efforts égaux contraires dans un même sujet degenerent en repos. Les choses deuvroient aller ainsi, si les corps n'estoient que ce qu'on s'en imagine. »[24]

---

[20] A VI, 2, 160.
[21] Leibniz : *La Réforme de la Dynamique*, p. 167.
[22] Ibid. – Que ce soient là les trois concepts fondamentaux de la théorie est relevé par le rappel figurant dans la première rédaction du début du second Dialogue du *Phoranomus*: « Corpus scilicet definiebam quod spatium implet et Motum spatii mutationem ; et *conatum* […] considerabam ut motus extremum, nempe initium vel finem, seu ut *statum* ejus quod in motu momentaneum est. » *Phoranomus*, dans *Dialoghi filosofici e scientifici*, p. 874).
[23] A VI, 2, 231 et cf. aussi A VI, 2, 228 : « Hugenii Wrennique experimenta » pour désigner les lois du choc publiées en 1669. La plus centrale est la « permutatio viarum et celeritatum Hugenio-Wrenniana » (ibid., 231), ou permutation des vitesses et des directions dans le choc direct de deux corps parfaitement élastiques.
[24] À Malebranche, fin janvier 1693, GP I, 350sq. A II, 2, 659sq. Formulations semblables dans la lettre à Bodenhausen du 17 novembre 1690 (GM VII, 354 et A III, 4, 653) et dans la lettre à Jean Bernoulli du 12/22 juillet 1698 (GM III, 515, 521).

À s'en tenir à ce que les deux théories de 1671 présentent comme leur rapport de complémentarité, la supériorité du point de vue de la science semblerait se trouver du côté de la théorie abstraite, enchaînement de propositions démontrées avec toute la rigueur géométrique, alors que la théorie concrète resterait prise entre d'une part l'observation des faits sensibles et d'autre part une construction hypothétique du système du monde, faisant appel à l'imagination, confirmée il est vrai par les phénomènes. Mais notre attention doit être retenue par le fait que la distinction entre l'abstrait, « hors du système », et le concret, « dans le système », est exposée selon une métaphore tirée du droit et de la politique comme la différence entre un état de nature des corps et une sorte d'état civil. Dès 1669, les raisons des mouvements considéraient ceux-ci « tels qu'ils sont dans le pur état de nature (*qualia sunt in puro naturae statu*). »[25] L'*Hypothesis physica nova* identifie « *in abstracto* » et « *in statu libero seu naturali* », qui est aussi l'état premier des corps et des mouvements. Le paradoxe crucial de la communication des *conatus* dans l'abstrait peut donc être formulé :

> « Cum in statu libero seu naturali, quantacunque a quantuliscunque facile moveantur, in statu praesenti systematico, atque, ut sic dicam, civili, non nisi proportionata ad sensum a proportionatis. »[26]

Les travaux ultérieurs où Leibniz a entrepris de remanier et de perfectionner les théories de 1671 montrent comment cette métaphorisation a guidé sa pensée vers un primat croissant de la systématique sur l'abstrait. Dans cette évolution se dessinent les conditions de la critique ultérieure d'une physique purement géométrique, qui ne connaîtrait des corps que ce que la figuration mathématique permet d'en concevoir. Au cours de ces travaux, Leibniz oppose

> « deux genres de mouvements dans le monde, les uns purs ou privés, les autres publics ou affectés par le système », ou encore « diversement concrets (*varie concretos*). »[27]

Pour les premiers, il est fait abstraction de l'intervention du milieu, pour les seconds le milieu ambiant, sa structure physique et ses mouvements propres constituent le facteur de liaison qui détourne les corps du simple déploiement

---

[25] A VI, 2, 160.
[26] Ibid., 227.
[27] « Sciendum est duo esse genera motuum in mundo, alios puros seu privatos, alios publicos seu a systemate affectos. » (A VI, 2, 314).

libre et sans obstacle de leurs *conatus* propres. Mais du coup l'instance d'intelligibilité supérieure passe *du côté du système* et des « lois systématiques », et non plus de celui de l'abstrait, et de sa nécessité brute :

> « In statu naturae puro (ut in intermundiis Epicuri) omnia sunt bruta[,] conatuum compositione determinantur, in statu systematico omnia videntur intelligentia quadam fieri, miraque ratione ad harmoniae sapientiae et justitiae leges exigi, […] philosophi officium est, quo modo Combinatione purorum seu brutorum motuum Leges systematis tam admirandae, tam ad vitam necessariae sint enatae. »[28]

Ainsi, l'état systématique réalise l'intention d'une physique vraiment rationnelle, telle qu'elle avait déjà été annoncée dès 1670 à Thomasius, quand Leibniz, sous l'invocation, qui restera constante, du célèbre passage du *Phédon* de Platon contre Anaxagore, en appelait à l'application dans la physique d'« une sorte de science politique » :

> « Opus est igitur philosophis naturalibus, qui non geometriam tantum inferant physicis (geometria enim caret caussa finali), sed et quandam civilem scientiam in naturali exhibeant. Ipse enim mundus grandis quaedam respublica est. »[29]

Les exposés autobiographiques ultérieurs qu'on trouve dans le *Phoranomus* et dans le *Specimen dynamicum* reprennent explicitement les métaphores anciennes. Par exemple, dans le second Dialogue du *Phoranomus*, en mettant en avant une inertie naturelle des corps, confirmée par les expériences,[30] Leibniz observe :

> « Sed experimenta haec fiunt in corporibus gravibus, et in statu corporum systematico, atque ut ita dicam civili, quando velut in Rempublicam coiere. »[31]

---

[28] Ibid., 315.
[29] 19/29 décembre 1670, A II, 1, 119.
[30] Phoranolmus, dans Dialoghi *filosofici e scientifici*, p. 782.
[31] La première rédaction du début du second Dialogue procédait un peu différemment : il résulte de ce qui précède qu'un corps B double de A, pour une même vitesse, a une puissance double. Leibniz enchaîne alors : « Ego olim […] in alia eram sententia, et credebam secundum abstractas a sensibili materia motuum Leges corpus magnum et parvum modo eandem haberent velocitatem, ejusdem quoque potentiae fore; contrarium autem ex constitrutione systematis velut in quadam corporum Republica, statu naturali in civilem mutato evenire .» Suit alors le résumé des théories de 1671 (*Phoranomus*, dans *Dialoghi filosofici e scientifici*, p. 872sqq.).

Leibniz opère alors un retour en arrière et rappelle les conceptions de la *Theoria motus abstracti*. Il revient sur les règles paradoxales de la communication du mouvement résultant de la conception selon laquelle il n'y a rien d'autre dans la matière que l'étendue et l'impénétrabilité, et que le mouvement n'est que changement d'espace. La mise en doute de cette notion du mouvement conduit à reconnaître que

> « ce qu'il y a de réel et absolu dans le mouvement ne consiste pas en ce qui est purement mathématique […], mais dans la puissance motrice même. »[32]

Et il conclut :

> « Ut igitur ex illo Labyrintho me tandem expedirem, non aliud filum Ariadnaeum reperi, quam aestimationem potentiarum assumendo Principium hoc Metaphysicum *Quod Effectus integer sit semper aequalis causae suae plenae*. Id vero cum experimentis perfecte consentire et […] eo magis confirmatus sum in ea quam dixi sententia, causas rerum non esse surdas ut ita dicam et pure Mathematicas, ut sunt concursus Atomorum aut caeca quaedam vis naturae, sed ab intelligentia quadam proficisci, quae metaphysicis rationibus uteretur. »[33]

La mesure des puissances ainsi désignée a pris son effet, comme nous le savons, en janvier 1678, avec l'intégration de la mesure de la force par mv^2, et par elle, de ce que le *Specimen dynamicum* appelle

> « l'explication systématique des choses (*systematica rerum explicatio*) » par les « les règles mêmes du mouvement que j'ai appelées systématiques (*ipsae regulae motus, quas systematicas appellaram*). »[34]

Le *De corporum concursu* de janvier 1678 marque ainsi le moment où le point de vue du système a définitivement prévalu. A la fin de son étude, Leibniz pouvait s'accorder une déclaration de victoire :

> « Conclusimus inquisitionem de regulis motus, et satisfecimus tandem nobis, »[35]

---

[32] « Quod in motu reale et absolutum est non consistere in eo quod est pure mathematicum, qualis est mutatio viciniae sive situs, sed in ipsa potentia motrice » (*Phoranomus*, dans *Dialoghi filosofici e scientifici*, p. 800).
[33] Leibniz : *La Réforme de la Dynamique*, p. 802.
[34] GM VI, 241.
[35] Leibniz : *La Réforme de la Dynamique*, p. 165.

de sorte que cet achèvement rendait caduque la théorie abstraite et par là-même vide de sens la dualité de l'abstrait et du concret qui structurait la dualité des théories de 1671.

Les mois suivants en verront venir les conséquences métaphysiques : l'éviction de la notion purement mathématique du corps ouvre la voie à la réhabilitation des formes substantielles (automne 1679). Dans les échanges postérieurs, et notamment dans les polémiques publiques ouvertes par la *Brevis demonstratio erroris mirabilis Cartesii* de 1686, la base constante sur laquelle s'édifient les arguments de ce qui ne s'appelle pas encore « dynamique » restera : primauté de l'axiome d'égalité de la cause et de l'effet (qui justifie l'argument par l'impossibilité du mouvement perpétuel mécanique), conjonction des trois équations de conservation (force absolue, direction totale, vitesse relative), prouvées *a posteriori* par la mesure d'un effet où la force est intégralement épuisée, avec enfin pour conclusion cette « remarque de conséquence pour la métaphysique » que l'essence du corps ne consiste pas dans l'étendue.[36]

2.

Que se passe-t-il avec la *Dynamica* de 1690 ? En tant que « Nouvelle science », la dynamique au sens strict de l'usage terminologique leibnizien, se caractérise d'abord par la *dualité conceptuelle* qui sépare puissance et action. Elle n'est plus seulement une science de la puissance ou force, elle est science *de Potentia et Actione*.[37]

Le concept d'action a été introduit par Leibniz entre autres motifs pour répondre à la critique des cartésiens qui lui reprochaient de n'avoir pas tenu compte du temps dans la mesure de la force. Comme la force ou puissance, l'action sera mesurée à partir d'un effet, mais un effet dans lequel la force

---

[36] Cf. « J'adjouteray une remarque de consequence pour la Metaphysique. J'ay monstré que la force ne se doit pas estimer par la composition de la vistesse et de la grandeur, mais par l'effect futur. Cependant il semble que la force ou puissance est quelque chose de reel dès à present, et l'effect futur ne l'est pas. D'où il s'ensuit, qu'il faudra admettre dans les corps quelque chose de different de la grandeur et de la vistesse, à moins qu'on veuille refuser aux corps toute la puissance d'agir. » (GP III, 48, texte envoyé à Bayle et publié dans les *Nouvelles de la République des Lettres* de février 1687.)

[37] Cf. Michel Fichant : « De la puissance à l'action: la singularité stylistique de la Dynamique », *Revue de Métaphysique et de Morale* 100/1 (1995). Repris dans *Science et Métaphysique dans Descartes et Leibniz*, Paris 1998.

n'est pas dépensée : effet formel ou essentiel du mouvement, « mouvement absolument libre, lequel est uniforme, horizontal, dans milieu non résistant, »[38] et dont la quantité est mesurée par la translation d'un corps sur une longueur déterminée, en un temps quelconque : quel que soit le temps qu'on y emploie, c'est toujours le même effet de parcourir d'un mouvement uniforme 10 mètres. L'action ajoute à cet effet la considération du temps ou de la vitesse : c'est une action double d'accomplir le même effet (le même déplacement) en un temps moitié moindre ou à une vitesse double.

Ce nouveau concept est une innovation qui se constitue dans les brouillons préparatoires de la *Dynamica*, et qui était encore absente, quelques semaines auparavant, du *Phoranomus*. Leibniz justifie la transposition d'un terme emprunté à la métaphysique et doté d'une métrique nouvelle par la commodité et l'absence d'ambiguïté :

> « Si quis autem vocabulum Metaphysicum aegrius fert in re mathematica, cogitet non aliud commodius suppetiisse, et assignata definitione omnem ambiguitatem esse sublatam. »[39]

La métrique de l'action permet en outre d'établir une démonstration *a priori*, qui fait l'économie de toute considération de la structure du système du monde, des lois particulières de la nature et des propriétés physiques des corps, « suivant les raisons du mouvement abstraites de la matière sensible (*ex abstractis a materia sensibili motuum rationibus*) »: la proposition démontrée est que « l'action de faire le double en un temps est quadruple de l'action de faire le simple en un temps simple, »[40] autrement dit que pour un même mobile (ou des corps égaux) se déplaçant uniformément, une vitesse double représente une action double. De façon générale, pour des quantités de matière égales et en des temps égaux, « les actions formelles des mouvements seront en raison double des vitesses. »[41]

Mais il y a plus : la construction *a priori* de l'action permet maintenant de construire tout autant *a priori* le concept de la force ou puissance, dite ici « *potentia absoluta* » : cette puissance est

---

[38] « Haec autem semper intelligantur de Motu liberrimo, qualis est uniformis, horizontalis, in medio non resistente » (GM VI, 291).
[39] Ibid., 346.
[40] « Actio faciens duplum tempore simplo est quadrupla actionis facientis simplo seu eodem » (ibid., 291).
[41] « Si aequales sint materiae quantitates, et tempora actionum aequalia, actiones motuum formales erunt in duplicata ratione velocitatum vel longitudinum motus » (ibid., 357).

« proportionnelle à la quantité d'action formelle que le mobile exercerait si le mouvement continuait uniformément dans un temps d'une grandeur déterminée. »[42]

La conséquence en est immédiatement qu'en des temps égaux et pour des actions formelles uniformes, « les puissances motrices absolues sont comme les actions formelles (*potentiae motrices absolutae sunt ut actiones formales*). » D'où résulte aussi que :

« Si des mobiles contiennent une quantité de matière égale, les puissances motrices absolues sont en raison doublée des vitesses ou comme les carrés des vitesses. »[43]

C'est bien retrouver la proposition établie depuis 1678, mais redécouverte comme un corollaire de la seule définition de la puissance mesurée

« par l'action résultante *per se* (donc uniformément) de cette même puissance s'exerçant dans un temps de grandeur déterminée. »[44]

Le rapport dual entre puissance et action peut être définitivement établi sans aucune ambiguïté. D'une part, la puissance est à l'action comme le momentané est à la diffusion ou extension dans le temps :

« Nempe in potentia momentaneum est, quod in actione succedente per tempus uniformiter est diffusum. »[45]

Et d'autre part, ce qui en est la réciproque :

« Potentiis existentibus aequalibus, actiones sunt ut tempora quibus exercentur. »[46]

---

[42] « Potentia absoluta ejus quod movetur est affectio ejus, proportionalis quantitati actionis […] quantitati actionis formalis, quam exerceret mobile, si motum per datae magnitudinis tempus uniformiter continuaret. » (ibid., 359).
[43] « Si mobilia æqualem contineant materiæ quantitatem, potentiæ motrices absolute sunt in ratione duplicata velocitatum seu ut velocitatum quadrata. » (ibid., 362).
[44] « […] per positam definitionem potentiæ, quam actione ex ipsa per se consequente (adeoque uniformi) intra datæ magnitudinis tempus exercenda, æstimamus. » (ibid., 364).
[45] Ibid., 364.
[46] Ibid., 366.

Plus simplement encore, on retrouve une proposition métaphysique usuelle, désormais traduite en langue mathématique : l'action est l'exercice de la puissance dans le temps, $A=pt$, c'est-à-dire aussi $A=mv^2 t$. Comme on voit, l'originalité et l'apport de la *Dynamica* ne consistent pas seulement à dédoubler la doctrine de la puissance ou force précédemment établie *a posteriori* par une doctrine de l'action démontrée *a priori* : le traitement de la puissance est lui-même dédoublé en étant intégré au développement *a priori* de la dynamique, via l'équivalence qu'exprime la résolution de l'action comme produit de la puissance par le temps.

À un moment terminal de la rédaction de la *Dynamica*, ce résultat trouve sa traduction dans l'organisation que Leibniz décide de donner à son traité : sa structure comportera une division en deux parties qui est formulée dans le *Conspectus operis*, envoyé par Leibniz à Bodenhausen de Venise le 18 mars 1690.[47] C'est alors qu'intervient la formule déjà citée, selon laquelle l'œuvre peut être divisée en deux parties : « *Dynamica simplicia seu a rebus abstracta, et Dynamica concreta circa ea quae in systemate rerum contingunt.* »[48]

Le plan détaillé montre en effet que la deuxième partie (concrète) synthétise et ordonne dans un exposé démonstratif les acquis de la période antérieure et met en forme l'établissement *a posteriori* des lois de la nature ; en l'état de sa rédaction incomplète, elle s'achève par où tout avait commencé, c'est-à-dire par un nouveau *De concursu corporum*.[49] La première partie (abstraite) isole tout ce qui relève de la nouvelle voie *a priori* ouverte par l'innovation du concept d'action.

On doit donc s'arrêter ici à la remarque, qu'il faut prendre en considération, de Martial Gueroult :

> « En se laissant entraîner à la suite des Cartésiens à vouloir […] démontrer toute la physique de façon absolument *a priori*, Leibniz était de nouveau induit par le mirage de sa jeunesse, celui de la *phoronomia elementalis*. »[50]

---

[47] A III, 483sq.
[48] GM VI, 285.
[49] Sectio tertia de la Pars II, GM VI, 488sq. D'après le *Conspoectus operis*, l'ouvrage aurait du comporter une Sectio 4 *De applicatione virium seu de Machinis*.
[50] M. Gueroult : *Dynamique et métaphysique leibniziennes*, Paris 1934 ; deuxième édition sous le titre: *Leibniz – Dynamique et métaphysique*, Paris 1967, p. 153.

Ce mirage est évidemment celui de la *Theoria motus abstracti* de 1671, où figure bien l'appellation de « phoronomia elementalis. »[51] Que faut-il penser de ce qui est ici une critique implicite, puisqu'aussi bien la découverte par la voie *a posteriori* de la mesure mv^2 de la puissance avait permis en 1678 de surmonter l'échec des premières théories ? y a-t-il un retour en arrière à des conceptions qui auraient dû rester dépassées ?

3.

Au vu de la réussite réalisée à partir de janvier 1678, dont la satisfaction intellectuelle est célébrée par les exposés autobiographiques, comment comprendre la résurgence, dans la structure des *Dynamica* de 1690, de la distinction entre une partie « abstraite des choses », où peut se déployer la démontration *a priori* de l'action et de la puissance absolue, à partir des seuls concepts mathématiques de l'espace et du temps, et une partie concrète portant sur « ce qui arrive dans le système des choses, » ordonnant les acquis des années précédentes ?

La reprise verbale des formulations de vingt ans antérieures n'est ici, en réalité, qu'apparente.

De façon superficielle, on pourrait penser qu'une analyse du mouvement en termes mathématiques d'espace et de temps reconduise à la conception du corps mathématique de la théorie abstraite de 1671. L'action reconnue au corps en état de translation horizontale uniforme sans rencontrer de résistance reviendrait au mouvement dit jadis « à l'état de nature », « libre » ou « privé. » Une différence de taille apparaît toutefois ; le concept de *conatus* de 1671 et les règles de la composition géométrique des *conatus* ne donnaient lieu à aucune métrique précise, alors que le concept dynamique d'action est précisément constitué pour exprimer une métrique du mouvement. En outre, les règles de la composition des *conatus* étaient manifestement contraires aux lois qui rendent compte de la communication des mouvements dans le système. En 1690, la métrique de l'action établie *a priori* s'accorde à celle de la puissance, telle qu'elle avait été prouvée *a posteriori* avant de devenir à son tour susceptible d'une validation *a priori*. Dès lors les deux parties du Traité des dynamiques, la partie abstraite et celle qui tient compte du système des

---

[51] A VI, 2, 275. Dans un fragment postérieur « Phoronomia universalis seu pura », dont les démonstrations sont « non moins que la Géométrie indépendantes de la sensibilité (*a sensu non minus quam Geometria, independentis*) » (ibid., p. 314, cf. p. 336).

choses, se rejoignent et leurs formules coïncident sans qu'il soit besoin de passer par la construction de l'hypothèse physique qui était requise pour raccorder indirectement les «phénomènes hugeno-wrenniens» au formes abstraites.

Cette conjonction trouve une expression unique dans la structure discursive du Traité de 1690. On pourrait en reconnaître l'originalité en la comparant à la manière dont Leibniz procède dans d'autres exposés, tels l'*Essay de dynamique* de 1692, le *Specimen dynamicum* de 1695 et l'autre *Essay de dynamique* lus tardif (*circa* 1700). Je renvoie et examen à un autre travail.

Dans le cadre de cet exposé, je me limiterai à examiner les tâtonnements par lesquels Leibniz s'est approché du concept d'action, sans l'atteindre encore, dans le *Phoranomus*. Au début du Deuxième Dialogue est rappelée l'équivalence selon laquelle, si deux corps A et B se déplacent à la même vitesse et si la grandeur de A est double de celle de B, sa puissance aussi est double, puisqu'elle doit surmonter une double inertie. Mais, demande-t-on alors, peut-on dire symétriquement selon quel rapport, pour un même corps, le doublement de la vitesse entraîne un accroissement de la puissance ? la puissance est-elle en ce cas aussi doublée ?[52]

C'est pour répondre à cette question que Leibniz va donner une nouvelle interprétation à la définition de la puissance par la quantité d'effet : l'innovation du *Phoranomus* est de reconnaître comme effet de la puissance le simple mouvement uniforme, reconnu comme étant le mouvement propre au corps considéré *per se*, et antérieur à l'accélération et au mouvement des graves. Cet effet est déterminé par la composition de deux réquisits, l'espace parcouru et la vitesse. Autrement dit, ce qui est appelé en ce sens dans le *Phoranomus « Effectus »* équivaut à ce qui sera ensuite dans les *Dynamica* désigné comme *« Actio »*, sous la condition que l'effet soit alors réduit au seul déplacement séparé de la vitesse. Dans le *Phoranomus*, l'effet comme mouvement uniforme à une vitesse déterminée est rapporté directement à la puissance sans qu'intervienne le dédoublement de la puissance et de l'action. Par une série de raisonnements, Leibniz aboutit à la formule selon laquelle le doublement de la vitesse quadruple la puissance mesurée par son effet dans le mouvement uniforme. On rejoint ainsi par une *ratio a priori* une conclusion dont la suite du dialogue va bientôt confirmer ce que l'on savait déjà, à savoir qu'elle est

---

[52] *Phoranomus*, dans *Dialoghi filosofici e scientifici*, p. 804.

attestée par des « démonstrations *a posteriori* invincibles. »[53] L'interlocuteur de Leibniz-Luninianus dans le dialogue peut alors avouer son admiration devant ce résultat:

> « In stuporem me dedisti Lubiniane, tot inexpectatis et tam admirabilibus *novae de potentia et effectu scientiae* decretis, quibus ipsi universo leges praescribuntur. »[54]

Nous trouvons donc dans le *Phoranomus* une situation logique où la légitimation de la voie *a priori* repose entièrement sur la possession préalable de la preuve *a posteriori*. C'est la conséquence du fait qu'ici l'effet du mouvement uniforme est posé directement comme expression de la puissance. Mais il en résulte aussi une équivoque, puisque le même mot de « puissance » se trouve impliqué dans deux modes de quantification différent, l'un où la puissance croît ou décroît en fonction d'une hauteur de chute ou d'ascension, l'autre où elle est mesurée à partir du mouvement uniforme. La dissociation de la puissance et de l'action dans la de chute ou d'ascension, l'autre à partir du mouvement uniforme. La dissociation de la puissance et de l'action dans la *Dynamica* mettre fin à cette confusion. Dès lors l'estime de l'action pourra être établie entièrement *a priori*, et déterminer en retour celle de la puissance, elle-même définie comme on l'a vu à partir de l'action (comme exercice de la puissance dans le temps).

La Ia Pars des *Dynamica* se construit donc comme une doctrine de la mesure : sont successivement formés les concepts métriques de la quantité de matière, du mouvement uniforme et de la vitesse, de l'action et de la puissance, du mouvement varié ou difforme, de la quantité de mouvement et de la quantité de translation. L'ensemble est encadré par une présentation générale de la mesure (*de rerum aestimatione in universum,* chap. 1 de la Section 1) et un échantillon de l'application du calcul infinitésimal à la dynamique (*Specimen calculi analytici pro phorometria dynamica*, chap. 4 de la Section 5). C'est là que sont obtenues *a priori* la métrique de l'action formelle et de la

---

[53] « Et cum mox invictis a posteriori demonstrationibus veram esse conclusionem appariturum sit; non puto aliam in natura dari rationem a priori, quam quae hic allata est. » (*Phoranomus,* dans *Dialoghi filosofici e scientifici,* p. 814sqq.).
[54] *Phoranomus,* dans *Dialoghi filosofici e scientifici,* p. 824. Cette science nouvelle ne s'appelle pas encore « dynamique » : pour obtenir la définition de la Dynalque, il faudra remplacer « effectu » par « actione. »

puissance absolue et prouvée l'entière équivalence de leurs rapports aux accroissements de vitesse, toujours sous la condition que

> « corpora consideramus ut in medio liberrimo translata et gravitate exuta, vel si gravitatem ipsis relinquamus, ut mota in horizonte. »[55]

Cette partie abstraite ne formule pas encore de principe de conservation, puisqu'un tel principe, qu'il s'agisse de la puissance ou de l'action, est relatif à la structure du monde ou au système des choses, et relève donc de la seconde Partie de l'œuvre.

Il revient à cette seconde Partie d'appliquer au système du monde la métrique établie abstraitement dans la Ière. Elle le fait en définissant d'emblée la puissance dite active relativement aux propriétés physiques de la gravité et du ressort et, avec elles, de la résistance au mouvement par l'inertie de la matière. Un effet est dit actif quand il produit un changement que d'elle-même la matière inerte ne produirait pas. C'est par rapport à un tel effet qu'est reformulé le principe de l'équivalence de la cause pleine avec l'effet entier où elle est entièrement absorbée.[56] Il est ici désigné comme un Axiome ou une

> « proposition de la Métaphysique la plus élevée, qui ne se paie pas de mots vides mais qui traite des attributs universels des choses » :

sans cette loi, il ne resterait aucun moyen de mesurer les puissances ou d'établir la grandeur des effets à partir des causes.[57] On parviendra ainsi aux propositions 7 : la même puissance se conserve toujours dans un système isolé de corps et 8 : il y a toujours la même puissance dans l'univers, d'où l'on montre facilement qu'il se conserve la même quantité d'action dans l'Univers en des temps égaux.[58] Il ne reste qu'à confirmer à leur lieu fixé par la rigueur démonstratives les résultats des contestations antérieures en montrant que dans les interactions des corps, ce n'est pas la même quantité de mouvement, mais la même quantité de puissance absolue qui se conserve,[59] et que deux corps ayant la même quantité de mouvement n'ont pas pour autant la même puissance.[60] D'où cette section se conclut par ces mots :

---

[55] GM VI, 366.
[56] *Sectio 1, De causa et ezffectu activis*, ibid., 435sqq.
[57] Ibid., 437.
[58] Ibid., 440sq.
[59] Prop. 40, GM VI, 460.
[60] Prop. 41 et 42.

> « Atque ita fontes Scientiae Dynamicae de natura potentiae et actionis hactenus non satis exploratos aperuisse mihi videor, sublatis ambiguitatibus et simplicissimo generalissimoque principio aequalitatis inter causam et effectum constituto. »[61]

Telle est, douze ans après la «réforme» initiale, la fondation de la dynamique dans la mise en forme la plus rigoureuse de son exposé intégral.

On voit mieux alors comment cette mise en forme permet la conjonction directe des deux parties des *Dynamica*, sans que s'y interpose le hiatus qui séparait en 1671 la théorie abstraite de la théorie concrète, quand l'intelligibilité du système relevait d'une hypothèse. En 1690, la partie abstraite établit avec tout un luxe de détails et de distinctions conceptuelles les relations mathématiques d'une métrique du mouvement qui trouve son centre dans la quantification de l'action formelle et de la puissance absolue. Les concepts mathématiques ainsi obtenus fournissent les instruments d'intelligibilité applicables au «système des choses» dont la structure est ordonnée, sans hypothèse, par l'axiome métaphysique de l'égalité ou équivalence de la cause pleine et de l'effet entier. Ainsi est obtenue la «conformité» entre la raison *a priori* et la preuve *a posteriori*, la conjonction harmonieuse de l'abstrait (la nomenclature des rapports quantifiables) et du concret (la légalité du système de la nature). La dynamique abstraite fournit en quelque sorte l'organon formel de la dynamique concrète ou systématique.

On opposera donc à Gueroult, qu'il n'y a pas retour aux impasses de l'ancienne « *phoronomia elementalis* ,» mais création d'un dispositif entièrement nouveau derrière la similitude apparente du vocabulaire de l'abstrait et du concret. De cette façon, les équations de la dynamique offrent bien « un echantillon de quelque chose de Mathematique dans la Metaphysique, »[62] par le moyen des quantifications qui transposent au mouvement le concept, de provenance métaphysique, d'action. On pourrait encore en cela trouver une illustration à une formule de Leibniz qui, dans un autre contexte, soutient que « le reel ne laisse pas de se gouverner parfaitement par l'ideal et l'abstrait. »[63] Ainsi, la Dynamique, par sa composition et son architectonique met en évidence la correspondance des idéalités mathématiques avec l'ordre des phénomènes.

---

[61] GM VI, 464.
[62] À Bourguet, 23 mars 1714, GP III, 569.
[63] GM IV, 93. Lettre à Varignon du 2 février 1702. Il s'agit ici des concepts et des opérations du calcul de l'infini, mais on peut reconnaître à la formule une portée générale.

Comme le dira encore Leibniz : « Il y a là un beau mélange de Metaphysique, de Geometrie et de Physique. »[64]

Mais nous savons qu'un mélange de ce genre était aussi pour Leibniz un des moyens de parvenir, par le progrès de la science et le perfectionnement de l'esprit, à ce qu'indique le titre de ce dixième Congrès : « *ad felicitatem nostram alienamve.* »

---

[64] À Pellisson-Fontanier, juillet 1691, A I, 6, 227 et A II, 2, 435.

"[...] daß die Nachwelt von seinen Meriten und großen Capazität nicht viel mehr als ein blosses Andencken von seiner Gelehrsamkeit aufweisen kan". Zur frühen Leibnizrezeption nach 1716[*]

Nora Gädeke (Hannover)

Die Tätigkeit von uns Editoren (auch wenn sie sich keinesfalls in Transkription und Textpräsentation erschöpft) gilt traditionell eher als Grundlagenarbeit denn als Forschung im eigentlichen Sinn: Wir liefern den Stoff. Und im Mittelpunkt steht für uns nicht der Leibniz-Diskurs, sondern die Leibniz-Überlieferung. Damit beschäftigt sich auch mein Beitrag. Zugleich und in enger Verbindung damit widmet er sich einer bestimmten, außerordentlichen Phase der Leibnizrezeption – den Jahren unmittelbar nach 1716.

Edition spiegelt, so hat Stefan Lorenz es einmal formuliert, immer auch Rezeption.[1] Über den Druck hinaus kann man das ausgeweitet sehen auf die Vorstufen: die Sammlung und Konservierung des Materials. Das erschließt sich zum Teil aus Metadaten der Edition, den Bibliotheksorten, aber auch, und in nicht geringem Maße, aus jenen Vorgängen begleitenden Briefwechseln. Vor zwei Jahren ist das auf einer Tagung in Hannover unter dem Dach der Leibniz-Stiftungsprofessur bereits thematisiert worden, unter dem Titel *Leibniz in Latenz. Überlieferungsbildung als Rezeption (1716–1740)*; der Band dazu soll in wenigen Monaten erscheinen.[2] Daran schließe ich jetzt an, wenn ich folgende Fragen in den Raum stelle: Was konnte man in den Jahren un-

---

[*] Den Veranstaltern des Leibniz-Kongresses danke ich für die Ehre, die mir mit diesem Vortrag gewährt wurde. Den Kolleginnen und Kollegen in Hannover und Potsdam Sabine Sellschopp, Malte-Ludolf Babin, Herbert Breger, Siegmund Probst und ganz besonders Stephan Waldhoff danke ich für ihre kritische, hilfreiche Lektüre meines Textes, für Hinweise und Korrekturen; ebenso habe ich Martin Mattmüller (Basel) für Hinweise zu danken. Der Universitätsbibliothek Kiel, der Kongeligen Bibliotek Kopenhagen, dem RGADA Moskau und dem Germanischen Nationalmuseum Nürnberg danke ich für die Bereitstellung von Scans. Anja Fleck, Elea Rüstig und Marc Schaefer (GWLB Hannover) waren bei technischen Problemen mit den Bilddateien eine große Hilfe.
[1] Stefan Lorenz: „‚Auferstehung eines Leibes dessen Glieder wunderbahrlich herum zerstreuet sind': Leibniz-Renaissancen und ihre editorischen Reflexe", in: Annette Sell (Hrsg.): *Editionen – Wandel und Wirkung* (= Editio Beihefte 25), Tübingen 2007, S. 65–92.
[2] Nora Gädeke/ Wenchao Li/ (Hrsg.): *Leibniz in Latenz. Überlieferungsbildung als Rezeption (1716–1740)* (= *Studia Leibnitiana*, Sonderhefte 50, im Druck).

mittelbar nach 1716 eigentlich über Leibniz und sein Werk überhaupt wissen?[3] Von welchen Quellen wurde dieses Wissen genährt? Wie wurde es am Leben gehalten, wie nahm es seinen Lauf – stetig und zunehmend fließend, oder gab es retardierende Momente, Stillstand, Versickerung? Das sind Fragen, die ich hier schlaglichtartig, an einzelnen Beispielen, behandeln möchte.[4]

Wer heute mit der Leibniz-Überlieferung arbeitet, hat den sogenannten Ritter- oder Arbeitskatalog zur Verfügung, zentrales Arbeitsinstrument (nicht nur) der Edition, Wegweiser seit ihren Anfängen.[5] Die (insbesondere für die Briefe sehr weit fortgeschrittene) Katalogisierung bietet, inzwischen digitalisiert und online,[6] einen detaillierten, systematischen Überblick über das Material und erlaubt Orientierung zu den einzelnen Stücken und den Korrespondenzen. Erst die Katalogisierung hat es möglich gemacht, den Umfang von Leibniz' auf uns gekommenem Œuvre einigermaßen abzuschätzen. Ergänzend liegen auch für die von der inzwischen weit vorangeschrittenen Akademie-Ausgabe noch nicht erfassten Materialien und Zeiträume weitere Hilfsmittel und Wegweiser vor.[7]

Das muss man sich vor Augen halten, wenn man versucht, sich die Situation von vor 300 Jahren vorzustellen. Unmittelbar nach 1716 muss noch viel lebendiges Wissen über Leibniz vorhanden gewesen sein, das heute verloren ist; Bruchstücke davon finden sich in zeitgenössischen Korrespondenzen,

---

[3] Als repräsentativ für das, was dem Lesepublikum unmittelbar nach Leibniz' Tod biobibliographisch an Kenntnis vorlag, könnte man wohl den Nachruf Christian Wolffs nehmen: „Elogium Godofredi Guilielmi Leibnitii", in: *Acta Eruditorum* (Juli 1717), S. 322–336.

[4] Exemplarisch für einen derartigen Ansatz (und sehr viel facettenreicher als hier möglich) ist die Untersuchung von Detlef Döring: *Die Philosophie Gottfried Wilhelm Leibniz' und die Leipziger Aufklärung in der ersten Hälfte des 18. Jahrhunderts* (= *Abhandlungen der Sächsischen Akademie der Wissenschaften zu Leipzig, Phil.-Hist. Kl.*, Bd. 75, H. 4), Stuttgart/Leipzig 1999.

[5] Zum Ritter-Katalog Hans Poser: „Die Frühphase der Leibniz-Edition", in: Wenchao Li (Hrsg.): *Komma und Kathedrale. Tradition, Bedeutung und Herausforderung der Leibniz-Edition,* Berlin 2012, S. 23–35, hier S. 28–32.

[6] http://mdb.lsp.uni-hannover.de/ (eingesehen am 8. Oktober 2016).

[7] Neben den zahlreichen Teileditionen etwa Kurt Müller/Gisela Krönert: *Leben und Werk von Gottfried Wilhelm Leibniz. Eine Chronik* (= *Veröffentlichungen des Leibniz-Archivs* 2), Frankfurt a. M. 1969; die Bibliographie der Leibniz-Drucke von Emile Ravier: *Bibliographie des œuvres de Leibniz*, Paris 1937 (Nachdruck Hildesheim 1966) und die kontinuierlich aktualisierte Leibniz-Bibliographie, inzwischen online: www.leibniz-bibliographie.de (eingesehen am 8. Oktober 2016). Hinzu kommt der im Aufbau befindliche digitale Transkriptionspool des Leibniz-Archivs Hannover mit Transkriptionen der (insbesondere für Reihe I vorgesehenen) Briefe, in rückläufiger Folge von 1716 ausgehend. (http://www.gwlb.de/Leibniz/Leibnizarchiv/Veroeffentlichungen/Transkriptionen.htm; eingesehen am: 9. Oktober 2016).

wie etwa der zwischen Christian Wolff und Ernst Christoph Graf Manteuffel.[8] Aber Leibniz' Œuvre, für das bereits erste Editionspläne aufkamen, allein schon die materielle Überlieferung, das muss wie von einem dichten Nebel umgeben gewesen sein, in dem Ausdehnung und Grenzen nicht sichtbar waren, und in dem sich nur schwer ein Weg finden ließ.

Aufschlussreich dafür ist das Zitat im Titel meines Beitrags. Es stammt von 1718, aus einem Leipziger Journal, den *Neuen Zeitungen von Gelehrten Sachen,* herausgegeben von Johann Gottlieb Krause;[9] vor etwa 20 Jahren wurde es ausgegraben – wie so vieles andere – von Detlef Döring.[10] Es steht in einer Besprechung von Joachim Friedrichs Fellers *Otium Hanoveranum*; diese Ausgabe von Auszügen vor allem aus Leibniz' Korrespondenzen wird vorgestellt mit den Worten:[11]

> „Sie enthält nur wenig Jahre von des gelehrten Hn. Leibnitzens Leben, und kan man daraus schlüssen, was vor ein schöner Vorrath von merckwürdigen Nachrichten in den Briefen dieses berühmten Mannes müssen verborgen seyn, welcher wohl den grösten Theil seines Lebens mit Correspondentzen und Reysen zugebracht, dadurch aber verhindert worden, daß die Nachwelt von seinen Meriten und grossen Capacität nicht viel mehr als ein blosses Andencken von seiner Gelehrsamkeit aufweisen kann."

Diese Beurteilung, die mit einer schon zu Leibniz' Lebzeiten verbreiteten Topik arbeitet,[12] dürfte signifikant für die zeitgenössische Einschätzung des

---

[8] Vgl. *Der Briefwechsel zwischen Christian Wolff und Ernst Christoph von Manteuffel 1738 bis 1748.* Transkriptionen aus dem Handschriftenbestand der Universitätsbibliothek Leipzig (Signaturen MS 0345, MS 0346, MS 0347). Open Access-Publikation des DFG-Projekts Historisch-kritische Edition des Briefwechsels zwischen Christian Wolff und Ernst Christoph Graf von Manteuffel (http://www.qucosa.de/recherche/frontdoor/?tx_slubopus4frontend[id]=10647) (eingesehen am 2. November 2016).
[9] Dazu Rüdiger Otto: „Johann Gottlieb Krause und die ‚Neuen Zeitungen von gelehrten Sachen'", in: Detlef Döring/Hanspeter Marti (Hrsg.): *Die Universität Leipzig und ihr gelehrtes Umfeld 1680–1780*, Basel 2004, S. 215–328, v.a. S. 273–310.
[10] Detlef Döring: „Leibniz-Editionen in Leipzig. Der Druck der Schriften und Briefe von G. W. Leibniz in der ersten Hälfte des 18. Jahrhunderts", in: *Leipziger Kalender*, Leipzig 1998, S. 69–95, hier S. 69, sowie Ders.: *Philosophie*, S. 29f.
[11] Neue Zeitungen von Gelehrten Sachen, auf das Jahr MDCCXVIII, Leipzig 1718, S. 62.
[12] Die zentrale (und zeitraubende) Rolle der Korrespondenz in Leibniz' Leben wird öfters thematisiert. Im Brief an Joachim Bouvet vom 15. Februar 1701 (A I, 19 N. 202, 411) etwa zählt er selbst zu den „mille occupations", die ihn an der Beschäftigung mit seinen eigentlichen Interessengebieten, der Metaphysik und der Naturphilosophie, hinderten, auch das Briefeschreiben. Kurfürstin Sophie äußert sich am 20. September 1704 (A I, 23 N. 524) skeptisch zu Leibniz' Ambitionen auf das Vizekanzler-Amt zu Hannover: Eher als die damit verbundenen Pflichten dürfe ihm das „corespondre jusqu' aus Indes" liegen. Aus Leibniz' unmittelbaren häuslichen

Œuvre sein (wenngleich es auch andere Stimmen gab). Um Detlef Döring selbst zu zitieren: „Aufgrund der relativ geringen Zahl an Publikationen galt Leibniz unter seinen Zeitgenossen nicht unbedingt als ein besonders produktiver Autor."[13]

Wir wissen es heute natürlich besser. Leibniz war, im Gegenteil, außerordentlich produktiv; nur weniger für den Buchmarkt als vielmehr für Teilöffentlichkeiten wie die Korrespondenten,[14] die Höfe, ad hominem – oder ‚für die Schublade'.[15] Nicht alles ist auf uns gekommen; in den ersten Jahrzehnten nach Leibniz' Tod muss die Materialfülle insbesondere bei seinen Briefen noch größer gewesen sein. Für den jetzigen Überlieferungsstand hat Hartmut Rudolph einmal durchgerechnet, wie lange wohl jemand brauchen würde, der sich durch die gesamte Leibniz-Hinterlassenschaft durchläse: er kam auf über 20 Jahre (unter heutigen arbeitsrechtlichen Bestimmungen noch viel mehr).[16] Dass die Überlieferung in dieser Reichhaltigkeit vorliegt, und das größtenteils in der prekären Form Handschrift, ist, wie immer wieder betont wird, ein Glücksfall, der doch in enger Verbindung mit Leibniz' Lebenssituation zu sehen ist: Mit seiner dienstlichen Funktion am Hofe zu Hannover, aus der die Versiegelung seiner Arbeitsräume resultierte.[17] Mit der Überführung des Nachlasses in institutionelle Verwahrung lag eine Voraussetzung für dessen hervorragende Konservierung bereits Anfang 1717 vor.[18] Leibniz selbst mag

---

Umfeld stammt die Charakterisierung: „Seine Correspondance war sehr groß, und benahm ihm die meiste Zeit" (J. G. von Eckhart: „Lebensbeschreibung des Freyherrn von Leibnitz. Ex Autographo", in: Christoph Gottlieb von Murr: *Journal zur Kunstgeschichte und zur allgemeinen Litteratur*, 7. Theil, Nürnberg 1779, S. 123–231 [Nachdruck in: Johann August Eberhard, Johann Georg Eckhart: *Leibniz-Biographien*, Hildesheim/Zürich/New York 2003], S. 199). Zum Topos der „Verzettelung" durch die ausgedehnten Reisen und Korrespondenzen vgl. Döring: *Philosophie*, S. 29f.
[13] Döring: „Leibniz-Editionen", S. 69.
[14] Es genügt ein Hinweis auf Leibniz' vielzitiertes Diktum, er „pflege mehr in Brifen, als in offentlichen Schriften zusagen"; indirekt als Zitat überliefert in A I, 10 N. 391.
[15] Heinrich Schepers: „Zur Geschichte und Situation der Akademie-Ausgabe von Gottfried Wilhelm Leibniz", in: Kurt Nowak/Heinrich Schepers (Hrsg.): *Wissenschaft und Weltgestaltung. Internationales Symposion zum 350. Geburtstag von Gottfried Wilhelm Leibniz vom 9. bis 11. April 1996 in Leipzig*, Hildesheim/Zürich/New York 1999, S. 291–298, hier S. 291, betont, Leibniz habe seine Arbeiten „gehortet", um sein Scientia generalis-Projekt nicht durch eine öffentliche Diskussion seiner Schriften zu gefährden.
[16] Mündliche Mitteilung, bestätigt per E-Mail vom 11. Juli 2016.
[17] So etwa Schepers: „Akademie-Ausgabe", S. 291.
[18] Dazu Günter Scheel: „Leibniz als Historiker des Welfenhauses", in: Wilhelm Totok/Carl Haase (Hrsg*.): Leibniz. Sein Leben – sein Wirken – seine Welt*, Hannover 1966, S. 227–276, hier S. 228f.

wenig für die Nachhaltigkeit seines Werkes getan haben – aber der fragile Status leicht zu zerstreuender handschriftlicher Überlieferung in privaten Händen, das Los vieler Gelehrtennachlässe, war damit, so scheint es, in einer ersten Stufe überwunden.

Hier ist allerdings zu relativieren. Markus Friedrich hat (am Beispiel Archiv, aber auf Bibliotheken übertragbar) kürzlich festgestellt, ein institutioneller Speicher von Quellenmaterial sei nicht per se ein Wissensort, sondern erst dann, wenn er entsprechend aktiviert werde, und auch dann nicht unbedingt verfügbar.[19] Und: Archivalische Überlieferung impliziert noch nicht Dauerhaftigkeit. So lassen denn auch die Beiträge von Sabine Sellschopp und Charlotte Wahl zum Latenz-Band erkennen, dass zumindest im 18. Jahrhundert institutionelle Aufbewahrung nicht immer Sicherung garantierte.[20]

In den ersten Jahrzehnten nach 1716 tritt der Nachlass in Hannover praktisch nicht in Erscheinung. Er ist mehrfach verschlossen; nicht nur hoheitlich, durch die Hannover'sche Regierung. Denn zusätzlich sitzt vor diesem Schatz ein Drache: Leibniz' Nachfolger Johann Georg Eckhart. Aufschluss- und detailreich sind dessen eigene Briefe an einen potentiellen Nutzer, den Kieler Professor für Dichtkunst und für Moral Sebastian Kortholt.[21] Dieser war bereits 1717 beschäftigt mit der Sammlung von Leibnitiana. Das damit

---

[19] Markus Friedrich: *Die Geburt des Archivs. Eine Wissensgeschichte*, München 2013, hier S. 15–17 und passim.
[20] Sabine Sellschopp: „Versprengte Überlieferung von Leibnitiana. Ein Überblick auf der Basis des Arbeitskatalogs der Leibniz-Edition" mit dem Fazit: „Aufbewahrung in einer hoheitlichen Einrichtung bot keine Gewähr für ungestörte Überlieferung." Charlotte Wahl: „Zur Provenienz der Gothaer Leibnitiana Chart. A 448–449 und zum umstrittenen Leibnizbrief" gibt ein drastisches Beispiel für die Fluktuation von Handschriften aus dem Besitz der Königlichen Bibliothek Hannover in der Mitte des 18. Jahrhunderts. Beide Aufsätze werden erscheinen in: Gädeke/Li (Hrsg.): *Leibniz in Latenz* (im Druck). Eine – im dargestellten Fall nur potentielle, aber prinzipiell vorhandene – Gefahr für die Bewahrung des Nachlasses dürfte das Wirken von Leibniz' Nachfolger Johann Georg Eckhart dargestellt haben; ein instruktives Beispiel dafür bei Stephan Waldhoff: „Leibniz' sprachwissenschaftliche und polyhistorisch-antiquarische Forschungen im Rahmen seines *Opus Historicum*. Mit einem Blick auf die *Collectanea Etymologica*", in: Wenchao Li (Hrsg.): *Einheit der Vernunft und Vielfalt der Sprachen. Beiträge zu Leibniz' Sprachforschung und Zeichentheorie* (= Studia Leibnitiana, Supplementa 38), Stuttgart 2014, S. 269–311, hier S. 275 u. S. 305f.
[21] Biogramm im Kieler Gelehrtenverzeichnis (http://www.gelehrtenverzeichnis.de/person/25f335f2-9e99-9452-259a-4d9c737f7d92?lang=de; eingesehen am 6. 10. 2016). Vgl. auch Gabriel Wilhelm Götten: *Das jetztlebende gelehrte Europa*, Bd. 1, Braunschweig 1735, S. 203–210.

verbundene Editionsvorhaben wird im Latenz-Band behandelt.[22] Hier werde ich, auf erweiterter Quellenbasis, erneut darauf eingehen.

Mit einer Frage nach Leibniz' „großen" Korrespondenzen und der Bitte um Material wandte Korthold sich wohl erst einmal nach Hannover – und wurde enttäuscht. Denn von Eckhart kamen zwar ein paar Korrespondentennamen, nämlich die von 14 Fürsten und Fürstinnen, mit dem pauschalen Zusatz „und sonst vielen grossen Leuten" und eine verheißungsvolle Bemerkung über die zu erwartende Fülle an „gelehrten Geheimnissen" – aber vor allem Erklärungen, weshalb er nicht in der Lage sei, Kortholts Bitte zu entsprechen.[23] So wird dessen erster Brief bereits mit Verzögerung beantwortet, mit dem Hinweis auf vielfältige eigene Okkupationen in Sachen Leibniz. In einem späteren Brief bringt Eckhart fehlende Überlieferung ins Spiel („Der seel. Leibnitz ließ wenig Briefe abcopiren, als nur die etwas lang, und von wichtigen Materien waren").[24] Das – auch später wiederholte – Hauptargument aber ist, er habe selbst noch keinen vollen Zugang zum Material.[25] Aber er stellt etwas in Aussicht,[26] und vereinzelt gibt er dann doch Stücke heraus – so zwei Briefe Bouvets und Le Gobiens[27] und den *Discours sur la Theologie naturelle des Chinois*,[28] der Eile wegen im Original.[29] Diese Transaktion hat Wenchao Li auf dem Leibniz-Kongress 2006 behandelt.[30] Eine andere Sendung, von Eckhart bezeichnet als „artigen Dialogue de Mr. Leibnitz […] über seine Théodicee,"[31] scheint verloren gegangen zu sein, auch die beiden Briefe der

---

[22] Nora Gädeke: „Edition im Netzwerk – Christian Kortholts *Godefridi Guil. Leibnitii Epistolae ad diversos* und die Sammlung seines Vaters Sebastian Kortholt", in: Gädeke/Li (Hrsg.): *Leibniz in Latenz*. Die im Folgenden im Mittelpunkt stehende Edition *Viri illustris Godefridi Guil. Leibnitii Epistolae ad diversos* […] erschien, hrsg von Christian Kortholt, Bd. 1–4, Leipzig 1734–1742. Bd. 4 enthält (S. 116–130) einige Briefe Eckharts an Sebastian Kortholt aus diesem Kontext.
[23] Eckhart an Sebastian Kortholt, 6. April 1717 (gedr.: *Epistolae*, 4, S. 116–118).
[24] Brief vom 20. Mai 1718 (Zitat: *Epistolae*, 4, S. 122).
[25] Vgl. Gädeke: „Kortholt", mit Anm. 93 u. 94.
[26] Eckhart an Sebastian Kortholt, 29. November 1718 bzw. 3. Januar 1719 (*Epistolae*, 4, S. 122–126, hier S. 124 u. S. 126).
[27] Eckhart an Sebastian Kortholt, 31. Dezember 1720 (*Epistolae*, 4, S. 129f. hier S. 130).
[28] Eckhart an Sebastian Kortholt, 20. Mai 1718 (*Epistolae*, 4, S. 121f.).
[29] Die beiden Briefe (A I, 20 N. 328 u. N. 329) sind nur noch durch den Erstdruck überliefert: Christian Kortholt: *Recueil des diverses Pieces sur la Philosophie, les Mathematiques, l'Histoire etc. par M. de Leibniz,* Hamburg 1734, S. 68–77 (und danach in den *Epistolae*, 3, S. 3–14).
[30] Wenchao Li: „Christian Kortholts Edition des *Discours* von Leibniz", in: Herbert Breger/Jürgen Herbst/Sven Erdner (Hrsg.): *Einheit in der Vielheit. VIII. Internationaler Leibniz-Kongress.* Vorträge 1. Teil, Hannover 2006, S. 457–466.
[31] Eckhart an Sebastian Kortholt, 16. Juni 1719 (*Epistolae*, 4, S. 126f., hier S. 127).

China-Missionare liegen nur noch im Druck vor – in der Frühzeit war die hoheitliche Verwahrung der Leibnitiana eben noch kein Garant für Sicherung.

Dass Leibniz' Nachfolger in Hannover – durchaus auch in amtlichem Auftrag – über dessen Nachlass von großen Ausmaßen verfüge, muss sich bald herumgesprochen haben. Sein Plan einer Briefedition war bereits 1717 durch Christian Wolffs Nachruf auf Leibniz in den *Acta Eruditorum* bekannt gemacht worden.[32] 1720 äußert der Helmstedter Theologe Justus Christoph Böhmer, Eckhart habe dem Vernehmen nach riesige Mengen von Leibniz' Kollektaneen „in potestate sua."[33] Freilich wäre es falsch, hier nur zu personalisieren. Noch in den 1730er Jahren, bald 10 Jahre nach Eckharts Flucht nach Würzburg, wird ein anderer Sammler von Leibnitiana, Louis Bourguet, die Leibnizhandschriften in Hannover als „ensevelis" bezeichnen.[34] Und noch einmal 10 Jahre später wird Sebastian Kortholts Sohn Christian klagen, es sei völlig unklar, ob die Briefe seines Vaters an Leibniz wie an Eckhart überhaupt noch vorhanden seien:[35] Die Hannover'schen Bestände lagen immer noch wie im Nebel. Bald sollten sich die Benutzungsmöglichkeiten diametral ändern; für eine Reihe von Jahren werden aus verschlossenen Türen offene Scheunentore, wird der Zugang mehr als freizügig.[36]

Eckhart begrüßt Kortholts Vorhaben durchaus („indem ich sehr begierig bin, ein so schönes Denckmahl, als sie meinem seel. grossen Freunde bereiten, befördern zu helfen").[37] Aber er, der sich in seiner kleinen Leibniz-Vita (die zwar erst gegen Ende des 18. Jahrhunderts im Druck erscheinen, aber

---

[32] Wolff: „Elogium", S. 336.
[33] Böhmer an Sebastian Kortholt, 15. Oktober 1720 (Kiel Universitätsbibliothek Cod. ms. SH 406 B1 Nr. 17): „Eccardus omnes, quantum ex aliis audivi, in potestate sua habet, vastumque insuper collectaneorum Leibnitianorum et incomparabile opus; id quod ipse non uno specimine, post obitum summi viri evulgato, palam fecit. An autem quid [-] eorum Tecum communicaturus sit, scio iuxta cum ignarissimis."
[34] Louis Bourguet an Gabriel Seigneux de Correvon von 1731: „Malheuresement, le Bibliothécaire de Hannovre n'est apparement pas capable de donner au public un Recueil des Ecrits de Leibniz. Peut-être qu' à cause des Anglois, grands admirateurs de Mr. Newton, on laissera, par politique, tous ces écrits ensevelis parmi les manuscripts de la Bibliothèque Electorale"; zitiert bei Ravier: *Bibliographie*, S. 164, Anm. 3. Den Hinweis auf dieses Zitat verdanke ich Stephan Waldhoff.
[35] In der Praefatio zu *Epistolae*, 4, S. 55.
[36] Vgl. dazu Wahl: „Gothaer Leibnitiana." Ähnliches geht hervor aus der Praefatio zu Johann Ludwig Uhl: *Sylloge nova epistolarum varii argumenti*, Bd. 1, Nürnberg 1760, Bl. 3[a] v f., der den vom Hannover'schen Minister Gerlach Adolph von Münchhausen beförderten liberalen Zugang zu den Handschriftenbeständen der Königlichen Bibliothek schildert, gipfelnd in der Aussage „magnaque eiusdem pars ab illustri eius praefecto, Scheidio […] iamiam sit transmissus."
[37] Eckhart an Sebastian Kortholt, 6. April 1717 (Zitat *Epistolae*, 4, S. 116f.).

bereits lang zuvor ein blühendes Eigenleben entwickeln sollte[38]) in der Sorge um das Begräbnis als den eigentlichen Erben von Leibniz darstellt,[39] muss hier auch einen Konkurrenten erblickt haben.

Dafür spricht die Aufzählung eigener Leibniz-Aktivitäten:[40] Die in Arbeit befindliche Vita im Auftrag der Herzogin Elisabeth Charlotte von Orléans als Basis für Fontenelles Eloge, eine ausführlichere Lebensbeschreibung „aus seinen Schrifften und Correspondentzen von Jahr zu Jahr", die Drucklegung der *Collectanea Etymologica*, die Vollendung der *Annales Imperii* – und eine geplante Edition von Leibniz' Werken, der zweite der geplanten drei Bände solle auch „nach den Materien rangierte Excerpte seiner Correspondentzen" enthalten.[41] Dass Kortholt dennoch ein paar Stücke zugingen, kann man auch als Befolgung der Verhaltensnormen der Gelehrtenrepublik, als Akt gelehrter *générosité* werten – und als Erfüllung ungeschriebener Verpflichtungen in einem Gabentausch;[42] denn durch Kortholt hatte Eckhart umgekehrt hochkarätiges Material für seine sprachwissenschaftlichen Forschungen erhalten.[43]

---

[38] Eckhart: *Lebensbeschreibung*. Dieser Text, der erst 1779 in Druck ging, war für Herzogin Elisabeth Charlotte von Orléans verfasst worden als Grundlage für Bernard Le Bovier de Fontenelle: „Eloge de M. Leibnitz", in: *Histoire de l'Académie Royale des sciences Année 1716* (1718), S. 94–128, lag aber wohl auch Christian Wolff für dessen Leibniz-Nachruf in den *Acta Eruditorum* vor; vgl. dessen Aussage „qui nobiscum liberali manu communicavit ad Elogium Leibnitii profutura" (Wolff: „Elogium", S. 333). Von dort aus fanden viele von Eckharts Aussagen weitere Verbreitung.

[39] Eckhart: *Lebensbeschreibung*, S. 191f. Traditionsbildend war hier insbesondere die Aussage, Eckhart sei als einziger bei Leibniz' Begräbnis zugegen gewesen. Dagegen heißt es bei Wolff: „Elogium", S. 336: „Ut honeste sepeliretur, nihil omisit haeres unicus Loeflerus".

[40] Im Brief vom 6. April 1717.

[41] Zitate *Epistolae*, 4, S. 117.

[42] Saskia Stegeman: *Patronage and Services in the Republic of Letters. The Network of Theodorus Janssonius van Almeloveen (1657–1712)*, Amsterdam/Utrecht 2005, hier v. a. S. 170–174.

[43] Seine bereits in diesem ersten Brief geäußerte Anfrage nach dem dänischen Handschriftensammler Frederik Rostgaard und „einer Communication seiner Manuscriptorum Theodicorum und Glossarium" (*Epistolae*, 4, S. 118) und die durch Kortholt geweckte Hoffnung auf die Übermittlung von Rostgaards Kollation der damals in Rom befindlichen zentralen Handschrift des Evangelienbuchs Otfrieds von Weißenburg (heute Heidelberg Universitätsbibliothek Cod. Pal. lat. 52) durchzieht mehrere Briefe der Korrespondenz, bis am 3. Januar 1719 Eckharts Dank an Rostgaard erfolgt für „die mir gethan[e] Communication seiner schoenen Lectionum Variarum Ottfridinarum" (*Epistolae*, 4, S. 125), verbunden mit Überlegungen zu deren Veröffentlichung (die er später verwirklichte). Eckhart erwähnt die Übersendung am 25. Dezember 1718 auch gegenüber einem seiner zentralen Korrespondenten zur Historie, dem Melker Konventualen Bernhard Pez, jedoch ohne Hinweis auf Kortholts Vermittlerdienste. Angesprochen sind diese in Bezug auf eine andere Handschriftentransaktion (Werke des Zisterziensers Hermann von Soest). Edition dieses Briefes in: Thomas Stockinger/Thomas Wallnig u. a. (Hrsg.): *Die gelehrte Korrespondenz der Brüder Pez. Text, Regesten, Kommentare* (= *Quelleneditionen*

Hannover erwies sich also als ziemlich unergiebig. Das brachte Kortholt aber nicht von seinen Sammelaktivitäten ab. Er, der Leibniz persönlich gekannt hatte und mit ihm durch einen umfangreichen, über anderthalb Jahrzehnte bis in dessen letzte Lebenswochen geführten Briefwechsel verbunden war,[44] muss sich in der Tat berufen gesehen haben, diesem ein Denkmal zu setzen. An seiner heimischen Universität trug er eine Eloge vor, die auch im Druck erschien,[45] darüber hinaus skizziert er den Plan einer Vita, woraus bald (mitunter alternierend) der einer Briefedition wird.[46] Diese sollte nicht nur seine eigene Korrespondenz mit Leibniz enthalten (wie es fast gleichzeitig andere, etwa Driesch oder Leeuwenhoek, unternahmen[47]), sondern darüber hinaus weitere Korrespondenzen. Nach diesen begab er sich als alsbald auf die Suche – und diese Suche war mühsam.

Kortholt gehört zu einer Reihe von Personen, die – wieder ist Detlef Döring zu zitieren – „schon kurz nach Leibniz' Tod ein großes Engagement im Zusammentragen von Handschriften von Leibniz, vor allem aber seiner Briefe, entfalteten."[48] Man fragt sich: Woher wussten diese frühen Sammler von Leibnitiana eigentlich, wohin und an wen sie sich auf ihrer Suche wenden sollten?

Konstitutiv für Leibniz' Bild war bereits zu seinen Lebzeiten die ungeheuer große, weit ausgedehnte Korrespondenz.[49] Aber wer wusste schon, mit wem konkret er Briefe wechselte?[50] Er selbst hielt Briefschaften unter Verschluss, ziemlich abgeneigt, etwas davon in die Öffentlichkeit kommen zu lassen (erst in den

---

des Instituts für Österreichische Geschichtsforschung) Bd. 2: 1716–1718, 2. Halbband, Wien 2015, Nr. 1032, S. 1108–1112.

[44] Dazu Gädeke: „Kortholt", mit Anm. 82.

[45] Sebastian Kortholt: *Ad auditionem orationis academicae de Vita Leibnitiana invitatio*, Kilonii 1718.

[46] Den Plan einer Vita muss Kortholt auch gegenüber Böhmer, Johann Fabricius, La Croze und Rudolf Christian Wagner geäußert haben.

[47] Vgl. z. B. Ravier: *Bibliographie*, Nr. 334, Nr. 339, Nr. 345.

[48] Döring: „Leibniz-Editionen", S. 71.

[49] Hinweis auf Zeugnisse bei Nora Gädeke: „Au-delà de la philosophie. L'Édition de la correspondance générale, politique et historique de Leibniz", in: Michel Fichant/Arnaud Pelletier (Hrsg.): *Leibniz en 1716: Comment (ne pas) être Leibnizien? Les Études Philosophiques* (2016), S. 578–595, hier S. 579, Anm. 15.

[50] Das spiegelt die Auflistung von Leibniz' Korrespondenten bei Carl Günther Ludovici: *Ausführlicher Entwurff einer vollständigen Historie der Leibnitzischen Philosophie*. Thl. [1.] 2 Leipzig 1737, hier 2, S. 99–212 (§112–304). In diesem Werk, in dem der biobibliographische Kenntnisstand der damaligen Zeit umfassend und minutiös dokumentiert ist (bereits auf den Ergebnissen von Kortholts Sammelbemühungen basierend), sind knapp 190 Korrespondenten (d. h. ca. 15% der heute angenommenen Anzahl) aufgelistet.

letzten Lebensjahren sollte sich das etwas ändern),[51] und er hat kein Verzeichnis seines *commercium epistolicum* hinterlassen, wie es für manch anderen Gelehrten vorliegt. Wohl wurden viele seiner Briefe nicht nur vom Adressaten gelesen, sondern kursierten – aber vor allem in einigermaßen abgegrenzten Clustern; die freie Weitergabe seiner Briefe konnte Leibniz scharf kritisieren.[52]

Wenn Kortholt sich also auf die Suche nach Leibnizbriefen außerhalb Hannovers begeben wollte, musste davor erst einmal die nach Korrespondenten stehen. An wen konnte er sich wenden? Natürlich an sein eigenes universitäres Umfeld, die Familien mehrerer (größtenteils bereits verstorbener) Kieler Professoren, mit denen Leibniz korrespondiert hatte.[53] Und vereinzelt waren Briefe dann doch bereits gedruckt.[54] Vor allem gab es die Publikationen Joachim Friedrich Fellers, insbesondere das *Otium Hanoveranum* mit Exzerpten aus etwa 50 Briefwechseln.[55] Sie gehen allerdings nicht über 1698 hinaus, und die Korrespondenten bleiben mitunter namenlos. Zudem gerieten Fellers Druckwerke im Kreise von Leibniz' Anhängern schon bald in die Kritik[56] – für Sebastian Kortholt dürfte das keine Basis für sein Denkmal gewesen sein.

Hier kommt nun ein Netzwerk zum Einsatz, zu dem ich erst einmal einen Exkurs einschalten muss. In den ersten Jahren nach seinem Tode ist Leibniz auf dem Buchmarkt sehr präsent; es erscheinen Leuchttürme wie die *Collectanea Etymologica* und der Clarke-Dialog,[57] die Eloge Fontenelles,[58] der Nachruf Christian Wolffs in den *Acta Eruditorum*,[59] die *Theodicee*-Übersetzungen, die Monadologie-Übersetzung, der *Recueil* Des Maizeaux'.[60] Aber man

---

[51] Beispiele etwa wären der Dialog mit Samuel Clarke und die *Collectanea Etymologica*.
[52] An einem Beispiel Herma Kliege-Biller: „Neuigkeiten – Netzwerke – Nachrichten: Claude Nicaise und Leibniz", in: Li (Hrsg.): *Komma und Kathedrale*, S. 301–314, hier S. 309.
[53] In den *Epistolae* vertreten sind Schelhammer, Tiede, Reyher (*Epistolae*, 1, S. 172–189 bzw. S. 213–229); hinzu kommt der Kieler Schulrektor Franz Theodor Kohl (*Epistolae*, 4, S. 239f.). Vor allem Schelhammer war häufig Thema in Leibniz' Korrespondenz mit Sebastian Kortholt gewesen.
[54] Dazu Gädeke: „Kortholt", mit Anm. 71–75.
[55] Hierzu demnächst Stefan Luckscheiter: „Joachim Friedrich Feller (1673–1726) als Leibniz-Herausgeber", in: Gädeke/Li (Hrsg.): *Leibniz in Latenz*.
[56] Etwa (nach anfänglicher Begrüßung) in den *Neuen Zeitungen von Gelehrten Sachen*; dazu demnächst Luckscheiter: „Feller". Aufschlussreich ist auch die brieflich geäußerte Befürchtung Michael Gottlieb Hanschs gegenüber Christian Goldbach vom 14. August 1718 (Moskau RGADA Bestand 181 Verzeichnis 16 Aktenstück 1413 Teil 1 Bl. 184), Leibniz' Andenken werde durch diese Publikation verdunkelt.
[57] Ravier: *Bibliographie*, Nr. 328 bzw. Nr. 327.
[58] Fontenelle: „Eloge" mit der Übersetzung Ravier: *Bibliographie*, Nr. 349.
[59] Wolff: „Elogium".
[60] Ravier: *Bibliographie*, Nr. 344, Nr, 349, Nr. 352, Nr. 354.

findet auch eher unspektakuläre Verlautbarungen, in kleineren Publikationen – oder unterhalb der Ebene des Buchmarkts. Leibnizrezeption in den ersten Jahren nach 1716 nimmt anfangs auch die Form von säkularer Memoria ein, durch Personen, die sich ihm verbunden fühlten, die seinen Namen hochhielten. Bei den im Folgenden zu behandelnden Äußerungen handelt es sich nicht nur um vereinzelte Stimmen; sie spiegeln vielmehr ein Netzwerk von Leibnizianern.

Das zeigen Nachrufe: neben der schon erwähnten Eloge Kortholts aus Kiel, neben dem Epitaph Christians Grundmanns aus dem Umfeld des Zeitzer Hofes[61] vor allem die in den *Neuen Zeitungen von Gelehrten Sachen*. Sie bringen bereits im Januar 1717, neben der abwertenden Erwähnung eines Pasquills, eine Eloge auf Leibniz von Christian Goldbach,[62] im Februar („[i]n Erwartung mehrer Umstände vom Lebens des Herrn von Leibnitz") vorab eine Beschreibung der emblematischen Ausgestaltung des Sarges,[63] im Juni schließlich einen Nachruf.[64] Zudem werden weitere Nachrufe aufgeführt.[65] Der Band zu 1716 (zum Zeitpunkt des Drucks war Leibniz bereits verstorben[66]) enthielt eine auf mündlicher Unterrichtung basierende Wiedergabe von dessen Kommentaren zur Vorjahresausgabe des Journals.[67] Auch in den Jahren danach war er hier präsent; das zeigt bereits ein Blick in die Bandregister. Der Herausgeber Krause, dessen Wirken detailliert von Rüdiger Otto untersucht worden ist, hatte selbst mit Leibniz korrespondiert.[68] Für eine frühere

---

[61] Christian Grundmann: Ossa et cineres quorundam in Republica Orbis Europaei tum Civili, tum imprimis Literaria, A. O. R. MDCCXVI defunctorum, pio studio collecta, urnis literariis reverenter recondita, Francofurti 1717, S. 16–23. Bereits in der Praefatio (Bl. 5[c]) dieser Sammlung von (zumeist knappen) Nekrologen auf Verstorbene aus der Welt der Höfe und der Gelehrten wird Leibniz' Name genannt, zusammen mit einigen anderen prominenten Gelehrten. Der Verfasser, Pfarrer und Literarhistoriker aus Heuckewalde, hatte mit Leibniz wohl über den Zeitzer Hof in Verbindung gestanden und auch kurzzeitig korrespondiert. Mit den Neuen Zeitungen von Gelehrten Sachen scheint er in lockerer Verbindung gestanden zu haben.
[62] „In obitum G. G. Leibnitii", in: *Neue Zeitungen von Gelehrten Sachen auf das Jahr 1717* (30. Januar 1717), S. 69f. Diese Verse (einleitend vorgestellt als die „eines der geschicktesten Lateinischen Poeten unserer Zeit") erfuhren messbare Resonanz. In der Eloge auf Leibniz in den *Nouvelles Litteraires* (14. August 1717), S. 97–128, hier S. 111, sind neben zahlreichen nur pauschal genannten Versen auf Leibniz' Tod speziell sie angesprochen; bei Ludovici: *Entwurff*, 1, S. 251–253, sind sie erneut abgedruckt.
[63] *Neue Zeitungen von Gelehrten Sachen* (24. Februar 1717), S. 125f.
[64] *Neue Zeitungen von Gelehrten Sachen* (9. Juni 1717), S. 369–376.
[65] Ebd. S. 504 und S. 769f.
[66] Dies geht aus einer Notiz *a. a. O.* (1716), S. 371, hervor.
[67] „Herrn Gottfried Wilhelm Leibnitzens Gedancken über einige Stellen in denen gelehrten Zeitungen des Jahres 1715 aus seinem Munde aufgezeichnet", in: ebd., S. 545–552.
[68] Otto: „Krause", S. 229.

Publikation, den *Neuen Bücher-Saal,* hatte er (vergeblich) auf dessen Mitarbeit gehofft. Dieses Journal hatte sich gleich mit dem ersten Jahrgang, 1710, zu Leibniz bekannt: Als Titelkupfer zeigt es sein Portrait.[69] Man wird Johann Gottlieb Krause als Leibniz-affin bezeichnen können.

Aber nicht nur das: Er gehörte einem Kreis von Leibniz-Anhängern an. In einer (wohl nicht vollständigen) Liste seiner Korrespondenten[70] finden sich mehrere Personen, die jeweils miteinander in Verbindung stehend, ebenfalls Leibniz-affin waren. So etwa der königliche Bibliothekar und Sprachforscher in Berlin, Mathurin Vezière de La Croze, der mit Leibniz in Berlin oft zusammengetroffen war und einen umfangreichen Briefwechsel geführt hatte.[71] An ihn wendet Krause sich nach Bekanntwerden von Leibniz' Tod mit der Bitte um Material für seinen Nachruf.[72] Kurz zuvor hatte La Croze Krause einen jungen Gelehrten aus Königsberg anempfohlen, Theophil (Gottlieb) Siegfried Bayer, später Mitglied der Akademie der Wissenschaften zu St. Petersburg, Pionier der Sinologie.[73] Dieser wäre auch beinahe Korrespondent und Mitarbeiter von Leibniz geworden: Ein einziger Brief an diesen vom Herbst 1716, La Croze zur empfehlenden Weiterleitung übergeben, blieb dort zunächst liegen – und dann war Leibniz tot.[74] Im umfangreichen Briefwechsel zwischen La Croze und Bayer ist er (insbesondere mit Sinica) sehr präsent, und Bayer

---

[69] Ebd., S. 228.
[70] Ebd., S. 313f. sowie S. 286 mit Anm. 410.
[71] Vgl. Malte-Ludolf Babin: „Armenisch, Albanisch, Hokkien […] Zum sprachwissenschaftlichen Teil von Leibniz' Korrespondenz mit Mathurin Veyssière La Croze (1704–1716)" in: Li (Hrsg.): *Einheit der Vernunft und Vielfalt der Sprachen*, S. 207–218. Zu La Crozes' Biographie und seinen gelehrten Kontakten Martin Mulsow: *Die drei Ringe. Toleranz und clandestine Gelehrsamkeit bei Mathurin Veyssière La Croze (1661–1739)*, Tübingen 2001. Die im Folgenden angesprochenen La Croze-Korrespondenzen sind zitiert nach: J. L. Uhl (Hrsg.): *Thesaurus epistolicus Lacrozianus*, Bd. 1–3, Lipsiae 1742–1746; online vorliegend unter http://www.uni-mannheim.de/mateo/cera/autoren/lacroze_cera.html (eingesehen am 16. Oktober 2016).
[72] Krause an La Croze, 20. Dezember 1716 (Uhl: *Thesaurus*, 1, S. 229f.), hier S. 230: „in vita eius conscribenda nunc versor; quare si Tibi Vignolioque […] annotata quaedam de summis eius in rempublicam literariam meritis fuerint, maxim0 me beneficio affectum reputabo, si uti iis pace vestra mihi licuerit."
[73] Zu seiner Vita vgl. Knud Lundbaek: *T. S. Bayer (1694–1738). Pioneer Sinologist* (= *Scandinavian Institute of Asian Studies. Monograph Series* 54), London/Malmö 1986; zur Empfehlung an Krause Otto: „Krause", S. 223.
[74] La Croze an Bayer, 14. Oktober 1716 (Uhl: *Thesaurus*, 3, S. 9f.), Bayer an La Croze, 16. Oktober 1716 (Uhl: *Thesaurus*, 1, S. 7); La Croze an Bayer, 30. November 1716 (Uhl: *Thesaurus*, 3, S. 14–16); La Croze an Bayer, 14. Januar 1717 (ebd., S. 17f.).

hat sich aktiv um Leibniz' Gedenken bemüht: Auch er verfasste ein Epigramm,[75] durch ihn gelangte die Eloge Goldbachs an Krause und damit in den Druck.[76] Goldbach wiederum zählte ebenfalls zu Bayers Freundeskreis. Von diesem erhielt er die Nachricht von Leibniz' Tod,[77] über ihn kam auch er mit La Croze in Verbindung.[78]

Christian Goldbach kommt im Folgenden eine zentrale Rolle zu. Auch er stammte aus Königsberg, hatte nach einem Jura-Studium mehr als ein Jahrzehnt auf Reisen verbracht und dabei viele Verbindungen zu Gelehrten in ganz Europa aufgebaut; auch er kam in den 1720er Jahren nach St. Petersburg, wo er als Prinzenerzieher und als Konferenzsekretär der Akademie wirkte.[79] Heute ist er vor allem als Zahlentheoretiker bekannt;[80] damals galt er insbesondere als exzellenter Stilist.[81] Mit Leibniz, den er mehrmals aufsuchte, führte er einen kleinen Briefwechsel vor allem zu musiktheoretischen Fragen.[82] Leibniz muss auch ein zentrales Thema seiner Korrespondenz gewesen sein, die weitgespannt und umfangreich war und nicht wenige Personen umfasste, die selbst mit Leibniz korrespondierten hatten.[83] Adolf P. Juškevič stellt in seiner Goldbach-Biographie fest:

---

[75] Bayer an La Croze, 5. Dezember 1716 (Uhl: *Thesaurus*, 1, S. 7–9) mit dem Epigramm.
[76] Eine Abschrift der Eloge findet sich unter den Briefen Bayers an Krause (Halle Universitäts- und Landesbibliothek Sachsen-Anhalt Misc. 2 8); vgl. Otto: „Krause", S. 313.
[77] Dies geht hervor aus Goldbachs Antwort an Bayer vom 8. Dezember 1716 (Nürnberg Germanisches Nationalmuseum Autographen Allgemeine Sammlung: K33 Goldbach Christianus). Hier bringt er den besonderen Verlust für Bayer zur Sprache: „[…] quod tibi tanto acerbius fuisse puto, quo propius in Summi Viri benevolentiam eras admissus" – und seine eigene Bereitschaft, eine Eloge auf Leibniz zu verfassen.
[78] Vgl. etwa La Crozes Briefe an Bayer vom 26. April 1717 u. vom 10. Mai 1717 sowie seinen Brief an Goldbach vom 17. Januar 1718 (Uhl: *Thesaurus*, 3, S. 25–27, S. 27–30 u. S. 138).
[79] Zu Goldbachs Biographie Adolf P. Juškevič/Judith Kh. Kopelevič: *Christian Goldbach 1690–1764*, Basel 1994 [Übersetzung der russischen Ausgabe Moskau 1983].
[80] Ebd., S. 109–118. Als Mathematiker tritt Goldbach vor allem in Erscheinung in seinem Briefwechsel mit Leonhard Euler, vgl. Franz Lemmermeyer/Martin Mattmüller (Hrsg.): *Leonhardi Euleri Commercium Epistolicum cum Christiano Goldbach* (= *Leonhardi Euleri Opera Omnia* 4), Basel 2015, mit der biographischen Einführung in Bd. 1, S. 3–31.
[81] Zu Goldbachs stilistischen Fähigkeiten vgl. die bei Paul Heinrich Fuss: *Correspondance mathématique et physique de quelques célèbres géomètres du XVIIIième siècle*, Bd. 1, St. Petersburg 1843, S. XXXI u. S. XXXIII zitierten Aussagen sowie das Zitat oben in Anm. 62.
[82] Gedruckt in: Adolf P. Juškevič: „La correspondance de Leibniz avec Goldbach", in: *Studia Leibnitiana* 20 (1988), S. 175–189.
[83] Dazu Gädeke: „Kortholt" mit Anm. 111. Zu Goldbachs Korrespondenz vgl. den Überblick bei Juškevič/Kopelevič: *Goldbach*, S. 192–195 (auf der Basis von Beständen in Moskau und St. Petersburg), sowie die Gesamtbeurteilung bei Adolf P. Juškevič/Eduard Winter (Hrsg.): *Leonhard Euler und Christian Goldbach. Briefwechsel 1729–1764* (= *Abhandlungen der Deutschen*

„Bei aller Vielfalt der Gegenstände, die Goldbachs Korrespondenz während der Jahre in Königsberg [gemeint ist die Zeit von Ende 1714 bis Anfang 1718 NG] berührt werden, gibt es doch ein Thema, das viele Briefe durchzieht. Dieses Thema ist Leibniz."[84]

Dieser Kreis – zu dem auch Michael Gottlieb Hansch[85] und Johann Jacob Mascov gehörten[86] – sollte sich in den Jahren nach Leibniz' Tod als eine Gemeinschaft erweisen, in der Leibniz' Gedächtnis gepflegt wurde; weniger in großen Akten und Monumenten als auf einer nicht-öffentlichen Ebene, gespiegelt vor allem im brieflichen Austausch. Am Ende sollte dann aber doch ein Monument stehen: *Godefridi Guil. Leibnitii Epistolae ad diversos*, auf Sebastian Kortholts Sammlungen beruhend, in vier Bänden 1734–1742 in Leipzig herausgebracht – aber nicht von ihm, sondern von seinem Sohn Christian.[87] Zum Zustandekommen hat der Kreis um Goldbach nicht unwesentlich beigetragen.

Diesem selbst wird von Christian Kortholt in besonderem Maße Dank abgestattet.[88] Aber eigentlich war bald der Eindruck in der Welt, die Materialsammlung habe sich quasi wie von selbst ergeben:

Akademie der Wissenschaften zu Berlin. Klasse für Philosophie, Geschichte, Staats- Rechts-, und Wirtschaftswissenschaften 1965, 1), Berlin 1965, S. 2.

[84] Juškevič/Kopelevič: *Goldbach*, S. 29.

[85] Zu seiner Leibniz-Verbindung mit Krause (als Rezensent der *Theodicee* in dessen *Neuen Bücher-Saal*, 1712, Die XIIX. Oeffung, S. 377–394, Die XX. Oeffung, S. 529–552) vgl. Stefan Lorenz: *De Mundo Optimo. Studien zu Leibniz' Theodizee und ihrer Rezeption in Deutschland (1710–1791)* (= *Studia Leibnitiana, Supplementa* 31), Stuttgart 1997, S. 128–133, sowie Döring: *Philosophie*, S. 22f. Zu seiner freundschaftlichen Verbindung zu Goldbach vgl. Juškevič/Kopelevič: *Goldbach*, S. 18–20 u. passim. Die in Moskau bzw. St. Petersburg von 1710 bis 1748 überlieferte Korrespondenz beläuft sich auf über 50 Briefe (ebd., S. 193).

[86] Mascov, der mindestens zwei Jahrzehnte lang brieflich mit Kortholt in Verbindung stand (und auch mit Bayer, La Croze, Goldbach und Krause gut bekannt war) äußert sich in seinen in der Universitätsbibliothek Kiel überlieferten Briefen (Cod. ms. SH 406 B7) an jenen nur zweimal zu Leibniz, hier aber substantiell: Am 14. Januar 1722 (Brief Nr. 23) bietet er an, für die geplante Edition Briefe von Freunden zu beschaffen („potero sane copiam nonnullarum ab amicis Tibi procurare"), mit der Einschränkung, nur solches Material schicken zu wollen, „quae ad rei literariae [...] aliquid faciant". Am 26. Mai 1727 (Brief Nr. 26) fragt er nachdrücklich nach, wie es denn nun mit dem Projekt stehe („Quid de Leibnitii epistolis tandem statueris scire vehementer cupio").

[87] Im Folgenden zitiert als: *Epistolae*. Zu Christian Kortholt (nicht zu verwechseln mit seinem gleichnamigen Großvater, dem Kieler Theologen) vgl. den biographischen Abriss bei K. Hamann: *Universitätsgottesdienst und Aufklärungspredigt. Die Göttinger Universitätskirche im 18. Jahrhundert und ihr Ort in der Geschichte des Universitätsgottesdienstes im deutschen Protestantismus*, Tübingen 2000, S. 222–234.

[88] Kortholt: *Recueil,* Preface, S. VI.

„so bald dieser gelehrte und berühmte Mann sein Vorhaben bekannt gemachet hatte, erachteten sich diejenigen Gelehrten, welche mit dem Hrn. Leibnitz Brief gewechselt hatten, vor verpflichtet die Leibnitzischen Brieffe hierzu an ihn einzusenden";

so steht es in Carl Günther Ludovicis *Entwurff einer vollständigen Historie der Leibnizischen Philosophie* von 1737.[89] Das ist eine pointierende Übersetzung von Kortholts Praefatio: „Eruditi viri, ad quos datae sunt litterae, eo consilio illas cum Parente meo officiose communicarunt."[90] Damit wäre die oben gestellte Frage, wie Sebastian Kortholt zu Korrespondenten und Briefen gekommen sei, eigentlich geklärt. Es gibt aber Zeugnisse, die seine Sammeltätigkeit ganz direkt spiegeln, und sie sprechen zum Teil eine andere Sprache. In erster Linie stammen sie aus seinem Briefnachlass, überliefert in der Universitätsbibliothek Kiel.[91] Auch wenn dieses Material vorerst nur selektiv aufgearbeitet werden konnte, ergibt sich bereits ein nuancenreiches Bild – das Kortholts und Ludovicis Narrativ nur teilweise bestätigt.

Es gibt in der Tat Korrespondenten, die sehr aktiv bei der Materialbeschaffung mitwirken, an erster Stelle eben Goldbach, der 1720, auf einer seiner Reisen, mit Sebastian Kortholt zusammengetroffen war. Bereits damals muss der Editionsplan zur Sprache gekommen sein, im anschließenden Briefwechsel ist er häufig Thema.[92] Goldbach macht an verschiedenen Orten Leibnizkorrespondenten und -briefe ausfindig; etwa in Nürnberg, Wien (unter anderem mit Hinweis auf Des Bosses[93]), Basel,[94] St. Petersburg.[95] Nicht immer

---

[89] Ludovici: *Entwurff*, 1, § 267, S. 300.
[90] *Epistolae*, 1, Praefatio Bl.)(5r. Eine ähnliche Aussage findet sich in Kortholt: *Recueil*, Preface, S. VI.
[91] Kiel Universitätsbibliothek Cod. ms. SH 406 B. Das mir zum Zeitpunkt des Vortrags selektiv, nach den Angaben des Arbeitskatalogs der Akademie-Ausgabe, vorliegende Material ist jetzt vollständig online zugänglich. Den Hinweis darauf verdanke ich Siegmund Probst (http://dibiki.ub.uni-kiel.de/viewer/!metadata/PPN789396114/0/LOG_0000/).
[92] Gädeke: „Kortholt", mit Anm. 113–118.
[93] Goldbach an Sebastian Kortholt, 16. September 1724 (Kiel Universitätsbibliothek Cod. ms. SH 406 B4 Nr. 4): „Narravit mihi Vindobonae Drieschius permagnum cumulum epistolarum Leibnitii ad Bossium (seu des Bosses) Jesuitam Coloniae Agrippinae superesse."
[94] Goldbach an Sebastian Kortholt, 28. August 1721 (Kiel Universitätsbibliothek Cod. ms. SH 406 B4 Nr. 2): „A Nicolao Bernoullio Johannis filio audivi ingentem copiam epistolarum Leibnitii ad Parentem superesse sed quae describi vix possint nisi ab homine calculi Differentialis perito."
[95] Zum Folgenden Gädeke: „Kortholt", mit Anm. 116–120. Die weiteren Hinweise beziehen sich auf den Astronomen Wurzelbaur; die beiden kaiserlichen Leibärzte (Vater und Sohn) Garelli, den kaiserlichen Hofbibliothekar Gentilotti, den kaiserlichen Hofantiquar Heraeus; Heinrich Huyssen.

führt das zur Erweiterung der Sammlung. So werden unter anderem Briefe des kaiserlichen Hofbibliothekars Gentilotti aussortiert, da ihr Inhalt unbedeutend erscheint; auch muss Material verloren gegangen sein, etwa eine Sendung Huyssens. Aber etliche Briefe, und nicht nur seine eigenen, muss Goldbach laut den Vorworten direkt beschafft haben.[96] Zudem sind einige Korrespondenzen in den *Epistolae* vertreten, für die Übermittlung durch ihn nicht bezeugt ist, bei denen aber sein Netzwerk zum Einsatz gekommen sein könnte[97] – das gilt vor allem für Hansch; seine Korrespondenz mit Leibniz bildet einen der größten Bestände der *Epistolae*.[98]

Auch ein weiteres großes Kontingent stammt aus diesem Kreis: die Briefe an La Croze.[99] Kortholts erste vorsichtige Anfrage datiert bereits vor seiner Bekanntschaft mit Goldbach. Anfang 1719 wendet er sich an den königlichen Bibliothekar zu Berlin: Er habe gehört, in dessen Händen seien Leibnizbriefe an Spanheim, Rabener, Ancillon, Des Vignoles; der Nachsatz „sed haud scio, an firmus sit rumor" illustriert das tastende Vorgehen.[100] La Croze wird, nach einigem Zögern und unter Vorsichtsmaßnahmen, dann zwar nicht diese Korrespondenzen aus dem Umfeld der Berliner Sozietät, aber eigene Leibnizbriefe in größerer Zahl (nicht alle) liefern: „ob incomparabilis viri memoriam."[101]

---

[96] Neben Goldbachs eigenen Leibnizbriefen ist die Lieferung eines Briefes an Huyssen wahrscheinlich, bezeugt ist die eines Briefes an Buddeus sowie mehrerer an Heraeus.
[97] Etwa im Falle des Wiener Hofmathematikers Marinoni oder von Driesch; vgl. Gädeke: „Kortholt", mit Anm. 121 bzw. Anm. 123. Marinoni stand auch mit Hansch in Verbindung; vgl. Götten: *Das jetztlebende Europa*, 3, S. 465f.
[98] Etwa 30 Briefe (*Epistolae*, 3, Nr. S. 64–96 und 4, Nr. S. 111–115) sowie ein Brief Hanschs an Goldbach (vom 30. Juli 1712). Laut Götten: *Das jetztlebende Europa*, 3, S. 458, hatte Kortholt diese Briefe direkt von Hansch erhalten. Zu diesen Briefen sind in *Epistolae*, 4, S. 111–115 angefügt: *Addenda ad Epistolas G. G. Leibnitii ad M. G. Hanschium ex G. G. L. Principiis Philosophiae more geometrico a M. G. H. demonstratis Excerpta.*
[99] Kiel Universitätsbibliothek Cod. ms. SH 406 B2. Die Korrespondenz zwischen Kortholt und La Croze ist (mit Auslassungen und Kürzungen) gedruckt bei Uhl: *Thesaurus*, 1, Nr. 182–189, S. 214–229, und 3, Nr. 105–110, S. 191–200. 3. Mai 1719 (im Druck ausgelassen).
[100] Sebastian Kortholt an La Croze, 11. Januar 1719 (Uhl: *Thesaurus*, 1, S. 214f.).
[101] Zitat aus dem Brief La Croze an Sebastian Kortholt, 3. Mai 1719 (Kiel Universitätsbibliothek Cod. ms. SH 406 B2 Nr. 26, nicht gedruckt). Details dazu bei Gädeke: „Kortholt", mit Anm. 134–136.

Die bei weitem größte Briefmenge (weit über 100 Stück) stammt von dem Helmstedter Theologen Fabricius, der zu den intensivsten Leibnizkorrespondenten gehört hatte.[102] Er hat nun wirklich bereitwillig auf eine Anfrage Kortholts von 1720 reagiert, der ihm wohl eine ähnliche Brokerfunktion wie Goldbach zugedachte hatte.[103] Damit steht er ziemlich allein unter den Helmstedter Professoren, von denen viele Leibniz' Protektion genossen und mit ihm korrespondiert hatten.[104] Fabricius erklärt die Ablehnung der meisten damit, sie seien eben „difficiles et morosos"; seinen und Leibniz' langjährigen Vertrauten, den Theologen Schmidt, ebenfalls einer der Hauptkorrespondenten, entschuldigt er mit schwerer gesundheitlicher Beeinträchtigung.[105] So ist die in Leibniz' Korrespondenz stark vertretene Academia Julia in den *Epistolae* außer in Fabricius nur in wenigen Korrespondenten und Briefen präsent. Dazu gehört Rudolf Christian Wagner, Leibniz' Adlatus und ebenfalls einer der Hauptkorrespondenten, der sich, von Kortholt selbst angeschrieben, mit vielen Worten und unterschiedlichen Begründungen entschuldigt (unter anderem wird angeführt, die Briefe, oft Alltäglichem gewidmet, seien nicht interessant genug);[106] mit der Lieferung eines Briefes (über die Seele der Tiere) kommt es zumindest zu einer symbolischen Geste.[107] Zu denen, die sich, direkt angeschrieben, ganz verweigern, gehört auch der Helmstedter Theologe Böhmer, der Neffe eines weiteren großen Leibnizkorrespondenten; er meldet

---

[102] Dazu die Tabelle bei Nora Gädeke: „Leibniz' Korrespondenz im letzten Lebensjahr – Gerber reconsidered", in: Michael Kempe (Hrsg.): *1716 – Leibniz' letztes Lebensjahr. Unbekanntes zu einem bekannten Universalgelehrten*, Hannover 2016, S. 83–109, hier S. 108f.
[103] Sebastian Kortholt an Fabricius, 29. April 1720 (Kopenhagen Kongelige Bibliotek Ms. Thott 1228): „Impetres mihi quaeso ab amicis Tuis epistolas Leibnitianas, Tuarumque etiam facias copiam, si forte illustris scriptoris litterae ad Te quoque commearunt". In seiner Antwort an Kortholt, 6. Mai 1720 (Kiel Universitätsbibliothek Cod, ms. SH 406 B3 Nr. 2) kündigt Fabricius an, 131 Leibnizbriefe an ihn zur Verfügung zu stellen, äußert sich aber skeptisch über das Helmstedter Umfeld (vgl. Gädeke: „Kortholt", mit Anm. 131).
[104] Dazu Nora Gädeke: „Leibniz' Korrespondenz mit Professoren der Universität Helmstedt", in: Herbert Breger/Jürgen Herbst/Sven Erdner (Hrsg.): *Natur und Subjekt: IX. Internationaler Leibniz-Kongress 26. September bis 1. Oktober 2011*, Bd. 1, Hannover 2011, S. 368–377.
[105] Brief vom 6. Mai 1720. Schmidts hier angesprochene Halbseitenlähmung bestand in der Tat seit Jahren.
[106] Wagner an Sebastian Kortholt, 18. Oktober 1720 (Kiel Universitätsbibliothek Cod. ms SH 406 B11 Nr. 20): „Es hätte längstens geschehen sollen, wenn nur mit einer feinen serie seiner brieffe hätte aufwarten können. So aber ist es lauter unvollkommen werck, und die meisten seiner brieffe betreffen des Seel. Manns Rechenmaschine.
[107] Wagner an Sebastian Kortholt, 20 Januar 1721 (Kiel Universitätsbibliothek Cod. ms SH 406 B11 Nr. 21) „Ich will [...] wenigstens derowegen egebenst aufwarten und deroselben einen ausbündig schönen Brief communiciren, den Er [...] de anima an mich geschrieben."

nicht nur für seine eigene Korrespondenz mit Leibniz Fehlanzeige, sondern auch für die seines Onkels, des Loccumer Abtes Molanus: Durch die räumliche Nähe habe es da kaum Briefaustausch gegeben.[108]

Es lohnt sich, noch einen Augenblick bei solchen Verweigerungen zu verweilen. Denn die Sammlung, insbesondere in Verbindung mit einem Publikationsvorhaben, war nicht ohne heikle Aspekte. Briefsammlungen illustrer Gelehrter waren nicht unüblich.[109] In einer Veröffentlichung mochten die Zeitgenossen aber auch etwas Zwiespältiges sehen. So sieht sich Christian Kortholt noch 1734 zu einer etwas sophistischen Erläuterung berufen, weshalb es erlaubt und geradezu angeraten sei, Briefe, die Leibniz selbst nur für einen kleinen Kreis bestimmt habe, jetzt an die Öffentlichkeit zu bringen.[110] Und seinem Vater hatte anderthalb Jahrzehnte früher La Croze sein Material nur mit der Auflage überlassen, bei zur Sprache kommenden Personen Diskretion walten zu lassen.[111] In der Tat muss das, was in den *Epistolae* vorliegt, das Ergebnis kräftiger Kürzungen sein; das zeigen Vergleiche mit noch vorhandenen Abfertigungen.[112] Aber auch so wurde die Diskretion nicht immer gewahrt, etwa im Fall des Literärhistorikers Jakob Friedrich Reimmann.[113] Auch er war Leibniz' Korrespondent,[114] von diesem sehr geschätzt; das spiegeln dessen Bestrebungen, Reimmann aus der abgeschiedenen Pfarrei Ermsleben an den Wolfenbütteler Hof zu ziehen. Das hatte damals, 1706, Eingang

---

[108] Böhmer an Sebastian Kortholt, 15. Oktober 1720 (Kiel Universitätsbibliothek Cod. ms. SH 406 B1 Nr. 17): „Ad me ille scripsit quam rarissime: et vix duas, aut tres ab eo, accepi litteras, breviores omnes, quaeque nonnisi de rebus agunt familiaribus: neque avunculus meus Gerardus, Abbas Luccensis multas possidet, quippe quem, in eadem secum urbe commorantem, coram adire solebat, si quid eum vellet." Tatsächlich gehört der Molanus-Briefwechsel mit fast 300 überlieferten Briefen aus 40 Jahren ebenfalls zu Leibniz' umfangreichsten Korrespondenzen.
[109] Döring: „Leibniz-Editionen", S. 70f.
[110] *Epistolae*, 1, Praefatio, Bl. [ ](6)v: „Id quod me obligat, ut respondeam quaerendo investigaturis, quis mihi potestatem concesserit, ut illa arcana ante omnium oculos exponam". Die Antwort ist (ebd. Bl. [ ](7)r): Leibniz habe für den (konkret angesprochenen) irenischen Dialog zwar keine Publikation zu Lebzeiten gewünscht, wohl aber eine in späterer Zeit. Vgl. Gädeke: „Kortholt", mit Anm. 58–61.
[111] La Croze an Sebastian Kortholt, 3. Mai 1719 (Kiel Universitätsbibliothek Cod. ms. SH 406 B2 Nr. 26; nicht gedruckt): „in quibus si qua erunt, quae alicuius famam laedant operam te daturum puto, ut ea quam cautissime tractentur."
[112] Dazu Gädeke: „Kortholt", mit Anm. 56.
[113] Zu ihm vgl. den Sammelband Martin Mulsow/Helmut Zedelmaier (Hrsg.): *Skepsis, Providenz, Polyhistorie: Jakob Friedrich Reimmann (1668–1743)*, Tübingen 1998.
[114] Seit 1703 (beginnend mit A I, 22 N. 424).

gefunden in Briefe an Fabricius[115] – und aus deren Veröffentlichung im ersten Kortholt-Band, also sozusagen aus der Zeitung, will Reimmann von diesen Bemühungen, die (ohnehin ergebnislos) ihm selbst anscheinend verborgen geblieben waren, erfahren haben; so jedenfalls steht es in seiner Autobiographie.[116]

Aber zurück zum Hauptthema. Die umfangreiche Kortholt-Edition, in der sich zwar auch Stücke finden, die auf bereits gedruckte Vorlagen zurückgehen, und in die auch ein paar Akquisitionen Christians eingegangen sind,[117] basiert weitgehend auf dem, was sein Vater Sebastian in den ersten Jahren nach Leibniz' Tod zusammentragen konnte – mit beträchtlichem Aufwand und nicht ohne Fehlschläge. Warum brachte nicht er selbst den Druck zum Abschluss, sondern erst sein Sohn, Jahre später? Dieser nennt den Vater als Urheber der Sammlung, die wegen dessen Arbeitsüberlastung dann ihm übergeben worden sei.[118] Das lässt sich natürlich nicht mehr nachprüfen.[119] Die Überlassung von Material findet sich auch andernorts im Rahmen gelehrter *générosité*; mit einer solchen Edition mochte der Vater dem Sohn zudem eine Eintrittskarte in die Gelehrtenrepublik verschaffen. Es sei aber auch auf das Phänomen des „Edieren-Lassens" hingewiesen: Eine aus irgendeinem Grund riskante Edition wird einem anderen überlassen.[120]

---

[115] Insbesondere Leibniz an Fabricius vom 18. Mai bzw. vom 31. August 1706 (gedr.: Kortholt: *Epistolae*, 1, S. 113f. bzw. S. 115f.; für A I, 26 bearbeitet und online zugänglich unter http://www.gwlb.de/Leibniz/Leibnizarchiv/Veroeffentlichungen/I26.pdf; eingesehen am 12. Oktober 2016).
[116] Postum erschienen als: Jakob Friedrich Reimmann: *Eigene Lebens-Beschreibung oder Historische Nachricht von sich selbst*, Braunschweig 1745, hier S. 44f: „Ich würde auch von dieser seiner Absicht nicht das geringste gewust und erfahren haben, wenn ich seine Briefe nicht gelesen, die er an den Abt zu Helmstädt Joh. Fabricium meinetwegen geschrieben […]. Diese Briefe sind in den lateinischen Epistolis Leibnitianis mit befindlich, die Herr Kortholt im Jahre 1734 erst publiciret". In einer Fußnote gibt der Herausgeber Friedrich Heinrich Theune einen Überblick über die weitere Verbreitung dieser Nachricht in Druckwerken.
[117] Dazu Gädeke: „Kortholt", mit Anm. 179–181.
[118] *Epistolae*, 1, Bl.)(5r f.: „Thesaurum hunc litterarium collegit Parens meus […] Sebastianus Kortholtus. […] Is vero compluribus negotiis Academicis, et scriptorum quorumdam suorum elaboratione impeditus, ipse sibi sumere non potuit editoris partes".
[119] Auch wenn diese Begründung im Folgenden in Frage gestellt wird, ist nicht außer Acht zu lassen, dass sich das Editionsprojekt in der Tat als zeitraubend für Sebastian Kortholt herausgestellt haben muss; gegenüber Johann Fabricius entschuldigt er die verzögerte Rücksendung des zur Verfügung gestellten Materials mit Überlastung.
[120] So erhielt Leibniz von Jean Mabillon eine Abschrift des *Liber de anima* des Ratramnus von Corbie zur Edition (vgl. A I, 18 N. 422 u. A I, 19 N. 72), von einem Korrespondenten ironisch kommentiert „Sans doute, il y a quelque chose qui sent le fagot, et qui auroit pu faire tort à celuy qui l'auroit divulgué en France" (A I, 19 N. 109). Zur Edition durch Leibniz, nach der Mabillon sich noch Jahre später erkundigen sollte, kam es nicht.

Was konnte riskant sein an einer Edition von Leibniz' Briefen? Stefan Lorenz hat in seinen Überblick über frühe Leibnizeditionen und -editionsprojekte den Ausdruck „engagierte Edition" eingebracht,[121] dem lassen sich auch die *Epistolae ad diversos* subsumieren.[122] Deren vierter Band beginnt mit einem Text aus Christians eigener Feder, einer *Disputatio de philosophia Leibnitii Christianae Religioni haud perniciosa*.[123] Diese Leibniz-Apologie von 1742 nimmt direkt Bezug auf die große Affaire um Christian Wolff: In diesem, der sich derselben „philosophandi ratione et via" wie Leibniz bedient und mehrere von dessen Hypothesen in sein System integriert habe, sieht Kortholt den „Schuldigen" dafür, dass Leibniz' Philosophie als gefahrvoll für die christliche Religion angesehen werden konnte:

> „Forte Leibnitiana philosophia in tot controversias adducta non fuisset, nisi lites ob philosophiam celeberrimi Christiani Wolfii ortae occasionem dedissent."[124]

1742 war Wolff längst wieder in allen Ehren nach Halle zurückgekehrt.[125] 1740 war eine vom preußischen König Friedrich II. veranlasste Leibniz-Vita erschienen:[126] Ein öffentliches Bekenntnis zu Leibniz war nicht sehr riskant. In den beiden Jahrzehnten davor war das anders; das zeigen die Untersuchungen Detlef Dörings und Rüdiger Ottos zur frühen Leibnizrezeption in Leipzig.[127] Und das spiegeln auch Briefe im Nachlass Sebastian Kortholts in Kiel.

---

[121] Lorenz: „Leibniz-Renaissancen", S. 74–76.
[122] Hier ist auch hinzuweisen auf die Feststellung Paul Schreckers: „G. W. Leibniz Lettres et fragments inédits", in: *Revue philosophique* 108 (1934), S. 5–134, hier S. 13–15, Christian Kortholt habe von den Briefen, die er von Leibniz' Neffen Löffler erhalten habe, diejenigen nicht gedruckt, die Leibniz aus der Perspektive der lutherischen Orthodoxie als unkritisch gegenüber dem Calvinismus erscheinen lassen mochten. Diesen Hinweis verdanke ich Stefan Lorenz.
[123] *Epistolae*, 4, S. 3–56, mit gesonderter Paginierung.
[124] Ebd., S. 8.
[125] Vgl. Carl Hinrichs: *Preußentum und Pietismus. Der Pietismus in Brandenburg-Preußen als religiös-soziale Reformbewegung*, Göttingen 1971, S. 441.
[126] Jakob Friedrich Lamprecht: *Leben des Freyherrn Gottfried Wilhelm von Leibnitz. An das Licht gestellet*, Berlin 1740.
[127] Döring: *Philosophie*; Rüdiger Otto: „Gottscheds Leibniz", in: Friedrich Beiderbeck/Stephan Waldhoff (Hrsg.): *Pluralität der Perspektiven und Einheit der Wahrheit im Werk von G. W. Leibniz. Beiträge zu seinem philosophischen, theologischen und politischen Denken*, Berlin 2011, S. 191–263, hier S. 211–217.

Zu dessen langjährigen Korrespondenten gehörte der Magdeburger Generalsuperintendent Johann Justus Breithaupt, einer der Protagonisten des halleschen Pietismus.[128] Er war einst Schüler gewesen von Sebastians Vater, dem „großen Kortholt", noch immer dessen Familie sehr verbunden – und er war Mentor von Wolffs Haupt-Antagonisten Joachim Lange. Dem väterlichen Freund[129] muss Sebastian Kortholt schon früh von dem Editionsplan berichtet haben. Und der reagierte besorgt. Ein erster Brief, von Ende 1720, antwortet auf ein Schreiben Sebastians, das Breithaupt Anlass gibt, ihn eindrücklich zu ermahnen, sich nicht der Weltweisheit und ihren Argumentationen zuzuwenden und diese der Theologie vorzuziehen.[130] Und auch vor Leibniz warnt er:

„Weil Leibnitius durch diese enge Pforte nicht gangen noch sie erkannt; so fürchte ich sehr, es dürffte unter deßen scriptis vieles so unlauter seyn, das Sie hermahlen bereuen müßten edirt zu haben."

Der nächste Brief, vom 29. April 1723, wird deutlicher.[131] Anfangs wird noch differenziert: „Nemo pejor est talis Wolfio, [...] Leibnitzii haerede et defensore: quanquam nescio, an Leibn. aeque malus fuerit". Aber dann folgt eine heftige Verurteilung der *Theodicee* („ein boden alles bösen") als einer Verführung zum Atheismus, und Kortholt wird beschworen, von jeder Beschäftigung mit Leibniz abzulassen: „so gebe zu bedencken, ob es zurathen, mit solchen Dingen sich zu beschmutzen. Wolte man gleich ein und anders refutiren, würde es doch keinen effect haben [...]. Das gipfelt in dem Satz: „was ich des refutirens wehrt achte, das publicire ich nicht, sondern laße es lieber nicht ans Licht kommen". Schließlich wird Wolffs Rektoratsrede von 1721 mit ihren Folgen direkt angesprochen:[132]

---

[128] Kurzvita im Artikel von Kurt Aland: „Breithaupt, Joachim Justus", in: *Neue Deutsche Biographie*, Bd. 2, Berlin 1955, S. 576; kurze Charakterisierung seiner theologischen Position bei Johannes Wallmann: *Der Pietismus*, Göttingen 2005, S. 124–126.
[129] Korrespondenz ist bereits seit 1695 überliefert.
[130] Breithaupt an Sebastian Kortholt, 29. Dezember 1720 (Kiel Universitätsbibliothek Cod. ms. SH 406 B2 Nr. 13).
[131] Breithaupt an Sebastian Kortholt, 29. April 1723 (Ebd. Nr. 15).
[132] Zur Rektoratsrede Albrecht Beutel: „Caussa Wolffiana. Die Vertreibung Christian Wolffs aus Preußen 1723 als Kulminationspunkt des theologisch-politischen Konflikts zwischen halleschem Pietismus und Aufklärungsphilosophie", in: Ulrich Köpf (Hrsg.): *Wissenschaftliche Theologie und Kirchenleitung. Beiträge zur Geschichte einer spannungsreichen Beziehung für Rolf Schäfer zum 70. Geburtstag*, Tübingen 2001, S. 159–202; wiederabgedr. in: Albrecht Beutel: *Reflektierte Religion. Beiträge zur Geschichte des Protestantismus*, Tübingen 2007, S. 125–169, hier S. 134–159; zur Rolle Breithaupts S. 136.

> „Vorm Jahr hielt obgedachter Wolfius, bey Ablegung des Prorectorats, eine sehr anstößliche Orationem de Philosophia Sinica (welche nicht anders ausfiel, als daß dagegen des Christenthumbs nicht nöhtig wäre, so alles verbis naturalibus, könte erreichet werden). Dawider ich u. andere sofort geprediget haben, das Ärgerniß zutilgen. Wie denn auch von Hoffe remedirung erfolgete."

Nun eine ganz direkte Warnung:

> „Solte nun auff der Universität Kiel de Philosophia Sinica disputirt oder geschrieben werden, und zwar secundum Leibnitii ductum, quid vides, an non dicerent, Te Wolfianum asseclam Leibnitii? Facilior, maculam vitare, quam delere. Nihil periculosior hodie, quam suspicionem eam contrahere."

Der erste Brief hatte Sebastian Kortholt nicht vom Editionsplan abbringen können; das zeigt seine weitere Korrespondenz.[133] Aber die Wirkung des zweiten ist unverkennbar. Gegenüber La Croze erwähnt er im August 1724 Breithaupts Brief, auch die Übersendung von Langes *Entdeckung der schädlichen Wolffianischen Philosophie*; ein Rückzieher von geplanten „observationes" zur Leibnizschen Philosophie wird angedeutet (sie seien noch nicht druckfertig).[134] Wenn man darin eine Distanzierung sehen will, so war sie indirekt und verklausuliert. Aber direkt und ganz deutlich geht sie hervor aus einem weiteren Brief Breithaupts vom Frühjahr 1725 mit dem freudigen Ausruf: „Ach, wie lieb ist es mir, quod non edideris Tua Leibniziana!".[135] Das Editionsprojekt war erst einmal zum Erliegen gekommen, für fast 10 Jahre.

Der *Epistolae*-Edition, die ab 1734 dann doch in Leipzig ans Licht kam,[136] hatte Christian Kortholt unmittelbar zuvor eine andere Kollektion von Leibnitiana vorausgeschickt, den *Recueil des diverses Pieces sur la Philosophie, les Mathematiques, l'Histoire etc.*, in Hamburg, ebenfalls 1734, gedruckt. Damit konnte der Herausgeber sich wohl auf unsicherem Terrain Rückendeckung verschaffen: Er hatte das Werk der britischen Königin Caroline gewidmet, die im Vorwort als Leibniz' große Mäzenin angesprochen ist, und

---

[133] Etwa mit La Croze, Goldbach und Mascow.
[134] Sebastian Kortholt an La Croze, 19. August 1724 (Uhl: *Thesaurus*, 1, S. 229): „Dissertationem Leibnitianam de Philosophia Sinica tecum communicare nondum possum. Neque enim prelo paratae sunt observationes, quibus obloquor dogmatis quibusdam Leibnitianis".
[135] Breithaupt an Sebastian Kortholt, 27. April 1725 (Kiel Universitätsbibliothek Cod. ms. SH 406 B2 Nr. 16).
[136] In ihr sind etliche Briefe konserviert, für die es inzwischen keine handschriftliche Grundlage mehr gibt, etwa an Jakob Thomasius oder Fogel.

erhielt Gelegenheit, es ihr persönlich zu überreichen.[137] Bald muss der kleine Band vergriffen gewesen sein; die meisten Stücke daraus sind in den *Epistolae* erneut gedruckt.[138] Diese wurden zum Meilenstein; in dieser Frühzeit trugen sie wesentlich zur Erweiterung dessen bei, was man von Leibniz und seinem Werk wusste. Das spiegelt Ludovicis *Entwurff*, insbesondere in den Kapiteln zur Biographie und zu den Korrespondenten; das zeigt sich an Dutens' *Opera*, die in hohem Maße auf den *Epistolae* basieren.[139]

Das kam mit Verspätung: eigentlich hätten die *Epistolae* neben anderen frühen Monumenten aus den ersten Jahren nach 1716 stehen sollen. Das öffentliche Bekenntnis zu Leibniz, das in der Edition gelegen hätte, erschien dann aber doch zunächst wohl als zu riskant. Aber der Öffentlichkeit verborgen gingen auch in dieser Zeit Sammlungen von Leibnitiana weiter, etwa im Umfeld von La Croze: durch seinen Zögling Jordan und seinen Korrespondenten Bourguet.[140] Doch das ist eine andere Geschichte.

---

[137] Götten: *Das jetztlebende Europa*, 3, S. 163. Vgl. auch Gädeke: „Kortholt", mit Anm. 6–10.
[138] Dazu *Epistolae*, 3, Praefatio, Bl. [a6].
[139] Gädeke: „Kortholt", mit Anm. 16 bzw. 14.
[140] Dazu Jens Häseler: *Ein Wanderer zwischen den Welten. Charles Etienne Jordan (1700–1745)*, Sigmaringen 1993, v. a. S. 91–94; Ders.: „Leibniz' Briefe als Sammelgegenstand – Aspekte seiner Wirkung im früheren 18. Jahrhundert", in: Herbert Breger/Jürgen Herbst (Hrsg.): *Leibniz und Europa. VI. Internationaler Leibniz-Kongreß*, Vorträge 1, Hannover 1994, S. 301–308; Fritz Nagel: „Schweizer Beiträge zu Leibniz-Editionen des 18. Jahrhunderts. Die Leibniz-Handschriften von Johann Bernoulli und Jacob Hermann in den Briefwechseln von Bourguet, König, Kortholt und Cramer", in: Ebd., S. 525–533; Nora Gädeke: „Der Unmut der Königin über die Krönung. Zugleich eine Miszelle zur Leibniz-Überlieferung", in: Beiderbeck/Waldhoff (Hrsg.): *Pluralität der Perspektiven*, S. 175–188, v.a. S. 183–188; jüngst Ursula Goldenbaum: *Ein gefälschter Leibnizbrief? Plädoyer für seine Authentizität* (= Hefte der Leibniz-Stiftungsprofessur 6), Hannover 2016, S. 37–39.

Why Leibniz Was Not an Eclectic Philosopher

Ursula Goldenbaum (Atlanta, GA)

Calling Leibniz an eclectic or his philosophical method eclectic, is very common in Leibniz literature and beyond, beginning in the 19th century and continuing into our own time.[1] Often, such talk about Leibnizian eclecticism is a rather loose expression, pointing to the philosopher's conciliatory attitude or his intense reception of so many other significant philosophers. But sometimes it is more pointed, ascribing an explanatory significance to eclecticism as needed to understand Leibniz's philosophy. It is the aim of my paper to question both views because I don't see Leibniz as an eclectic in either way. Rather, I find it surprising that one of the most systematic thinkers in modern philosophy could ever cause such a misunderstanding.

In a first section, I will clarify the actual meaning of the term "eclectic" in common language, at least for the languages that were and are relevant for Leibniz research. This will already show why we should never apply the term to Leibniz if we don't mean precisely what this term associates. In a second section, I will shed some light to the occurrence of the term in the history of philosophy. Fortunately, I can use some recent research in Germany about the rise of a new school of eclecticism in the last decades of the 17th century in Germany, just during Leibniz' life time. Only then I will discuss the arguments of three distinguished Leibniz scholars of our time who use 'eclecticism' to support their respective interpretations of Leibniz – Marcelo Dascal, Christia Mercer, and Patrick Riley.[2]

---

[1] Since 1983, we got a wave of research on modern eclecticism in Germany, above all the big monograph: Michael Albrecht: *Eklektik: Eine Begriffsgeschichte mit Hinweisen auf die Philosophie- und Wissenschaftsgeschichte*, Stuttgart/Bad Cannstatt 1994. Albrecht mentions Foucher de Careil, Kanthack, Gouhier, Schmalenbach, Mahnke, Nourisson, Loemker, Moll, and Heinekamp as authors who falsely ascribe eclecticism to Leibniz. Ulrich Johannes Schneider discusses the positions of three Leibniz scholars more extensively – Nourisson, Mahnke, and Schmalenbach – who interpreted Leibniz as an eclectic philosopher, that Leibniz was not an eclectic. See Ulrich Johannes Schneider: "Leibniz und Eklektizismus", in: *Neuzeitliches Denken. Festschrift für Hans Poser zum 65. Geburtstag*, ed. by Günter Abel/Hans-Jürgen Engfer/Christoph Hubig, Berlin/New York 2002, pp. 233–250.

[2] This is not my first criticism of these three interpretations. In case of Patrick Riley this is clear from his own reference to our exchange in the early 1990s. See Patrick Riley: *Leibniz's Universal Jurisprudence: Justice as the Charity of the Wise*, Harvard 1996, pp. 270, 322, and fn. 46 on p. 330. In case of Christia Mercer's book (*Leibniz's Metaphysics: Its Origins and Development*, Cambridge 2007), I sent her my comments before its publication and we had further

1. What the Dictionnaries Tell Us about 'Eclectic'

While I agree that Leibniz had a remarkable conciliatory attitude and always tried to find the true aspects in any philosophy, I can't see how this makes Leibniz an eclectic. These two terms – conciliatory and eclectic – are not synonymous. While there is no question that 'conciliatory' points to peaceful behavior – reaching out, being friendly, acting according to the principle of charity – the term 'eclectic' seems to be less clear and is sometimes used interchangeably with 'conciliatory'. What does 'eclectic' actually mean? In all the dictionnaries I consulted, there is an overwhelming agreement about the common use of this term in everyday (non-philosophical) language: an eclectic is imitating without creativity and simply collects or composes something from already existing sources.

The *Digital Dictionary of German Language*, run by the *Berlin-Brandenburg Academie* provides three groups of synonyms in German language for "eclectic":

1. Auswählend, eklektisch, elektiv, selektiv
2. Eklektisch (high language style), epigonal, epigonenhaft, in der Manier von, nachahmend, nicht eigenständig, nicht kreativ, schon dagewesen (colloquial), unschöpferisch.
3. Collagiert, eklektisch, zusammengestückelt, zusammenmontiert

I doubt that any serious Leibniz scholar would want to apply such a description to Leibniz' philosophizing.[3]

---

discussions since. I also published my critique on her rejection of any Leibnizian Spinoza reception in my article "Why shouldn't Leibniz have studied Spinoza? The Rise of the Claim of Continuity in Leibniz' Philosophy out of the Ideological Rejection of Spinoza's Impact on Leibniz" (in: *The Leibniz Review*, December 2007, pp. 107–138). In case of Marcelo Dascal's attempt to interpret Leibniz as following to different kinds of reason, – hard or radical and soft reason – I uttered my criticism already during the Q&A period of his first presentation at the Leibniz Congress in Berlin in 2001 (Marcelo Dascal: "Nihil sine ratione → Blandior ratio", in: *Nihil sine ratione. Mensch, Natur und Technik im Wirken von G.W. Leibniz. Vorträge des VII. Internationalen Leibniz-Kongresses*, 3 vols., ed. by Hans Poser in connection with Christoph Asmuth, Ursula Goldenbaum and Wencho Li, Berlin 2001, pp. 276–280). I published my systematic criticism of his interpretation in: Ursula Goldenbaum: "'Reason light'? – Kritische Anmerkungen zu einer neuen Leibnizinterpretation", in: *Studia Leibnitiana* 36 (2004), pp. 2–21. I mention these earlier discussions to emphasize that my criticism concerns mutually recognized disagreements *in re* in our interpretations of Leibniz notwithstanding my great respect for the work of all three authors.

[3] See DWDS (Das Wortauskunftssystem zur deutschen Sprache in Geschichte und Gegenwart): https://www.dwds.de/wb/eklektisch#wb-1, checked on Nov. 13, 2016.

The French dictionnaire *LaRousse* labels somebody as "eclectique" who is interested in or has knowledge about a great variety of things or areas without any outstanding interest in any of them in particular: "Caractère de quelqu'un qui s'intéresse à choses ou des êtres très divers, qui a des connaissances en des domaines très variés sans manifester aucune exclusive."[4] In addition, it names a tendency in the fine arts that builds on the exploitation and conciliation of styles of the past, especially in Western culture of the 19th century. I dare to add, that the Hearst Castle from the 20th century is an extreme example of such a tendency in architecture. It has the roof of an old German Peasant house covering the entrance of the churchlike main building of the Castle,[5] its library has lamps whose screens are made from medieval manuscripts,[6] and its Greek swimming pool has Angels' wings as grab handles at the ladders.[7]

The Italian Dictionary *Repubblica* and the *Diccionario de la lengua espagnola* are – in all points – similar to these definitions of the *LaRousse*. In the Spanish *Diccionario* though, the first point – referring to 'eclectic' as indicating a mere variety – is nicely illustrated by the existence of a *Café Eclectico* on Teneriffa promising a great variety of food.[8]

The English use of the word is similar too. Merriam-Webster has "selecting what appears to be best in various doctrines, methods, or styles" and "composed of elements drawn from various sources."[9] But it also refers to "heterogeneous" and lists the following sentence as an example: "The museum's eclectic collection has everything from a giraffe skeleton to medieval musical instruments." The Oxford Dictionary has for 'eclectic': "Deriving Ideas, style, or taste from a broad and diverse range of sources" and provides the following example: "universities offer an eclectic mix of courses."[10]

---

[4] See *Dictionnaires de françaises*: http://www.larousse.fr/dictionnaires/francais/%C3%A9-clectique/27569#7RbdX5UzlPUWgVEI.99, checked on Nov 13, 2016.
[5] http://www.sanluisobispo.com/news/local/community/cambrian/sk7n87/picture54473545/ALTERNATES/FREE_640/hearst%20castle, checked on Nov 13, 2016.
[6] See http://andresalvador.smugmug.com/ARCHITECTURE-PHOTOS/HEARST-CASTLE-SAN-SIMEON/i-K7HHX57/0/L/DSC4467-Hearst-Castle-web-L.jpg, checked on Nov 13, 2016.
[7] See http://www.randrews4.com/6209002222661.jpg, checked on Nov 13, 2016.
[8] See http://assets1.domestika.org/project-items/000/637/231/944528_311747888955865_401345088_n-big.jpg?1405961228, checked on Nov 13, 2016.
[9] See Merriam-Webster: http://www.merriam-webster.com/dictionary/eclectic, checked on Nov 13, 2016.
[10] See Oxford Dictionary: https://en.oxforddictionaries.com/definition/eclectic, checked on Nov 13, 2016.

To summarize, the different languages – and I mentioned only the most important in Leibniz research past and present – deviate only slightly in their definitions of the term. The German understanding of it seems to be the most dismissive although the meaning of a sheer variety of different things, styles, or features has a slightly pejorative meaning in all languages. This is nicely illustrated by the mention of the coffee shop *Eclectico* but also by a Romanian internet portal for artwork named "Eclectico" – it offers indeed all kinds of artwork from all periods and styles.

I doubt that anybody would want to characterize Leibniz's philosophy as a loose collection of ideas of great variety without creating something new or as imitator of other philosophers. However, the frequent labeling of Leibniz to be a Platonist, an Aristotelian, a Hobbesian or more rarely a Spinozist, a semi-Augustinian or a semi-Platonist seems to reduce Leibniz's philosophy into a mere collection of such varieties. At least, I do not know of any other philosopher of Leibniz's rank who has been labeled after other philosophers. Aristotle a Platonist? Kant a Humean? Hegel a Kantian? Locke a Hobbesian, or perhaps a semi-Hobbesian? The fact that they created their own, particular philosophy would hinder us to call them after those philosophers to whom they owed great insights before they worked out their own philosophy. The same ought to be granted to Leibniz.

2. 'Eclecticism' in the History of Philosophy

The above mentioned dictionaries *DWDS* and *LaRousse* refer also to a *philosophical* meaning of 'Eclecticism', pointing to an ancient eclectic philosophical sect in Greece.[11] This sect is supposed to have been founded by Potamon; the very little facts we know about him came down to us through Diogenes Laertius and Suedas who don't perfectly agree about his life time.[12] This ancient eclectic sect is said to have intended to choose the best from a variety of

---

[11] See DWDS: https://www.dwds.de/wb/Eklektiker, checked on Nov 13, 2016, and LaRousse: http://www.larousse.fr/dictionnaires/francais/%C3%A9clectisme/27570, checked on Nov 13, 2016.

[12] Cf. Edmund Zeller: *A History of Eclecticism in Greek Philosophy*, transl. by Sarah Frances Alleyne, London 1883, pp. 109–111. For a more recent monograph see Myrto Hatzimichali: *Potamo of Alexandria and the Emergence of Eclecticism in Late Hellenistic Philosophy*, Cambridge UK/New York 2011, especially p. 5, and pp. 68–72.

philosophical sects without holding a philosophical system on its own.[13] The French *LaRousse* adds two references to modern forms of philosophical eclecticism, Diderot's articles for the Encyclopedia about "eclecticism" and "eclectics" and the modern eclecticism of Victor Cousin. The German *DWDS* points to a philosophical school of eclecticism in the late 17th century, that is during the life time of Leibniz.

Interestingly, this philosophical school in Germany has attracted new attention over the last three decades and the systematic research has produced some new insights about a largely forgotten and remarkable revival of philosophical eclecticism in German and Dutch philosophy, rising in the last third of the 17th and declining over the first third of the 18th century. Michael Albrecht published an entire book on this German eclecticism but in addition, we got a great variety of highly interesting articles. According to Ulrich Johannes Schneider, the eclectic avalanche of the 17th century had first been triggered through the editions of Diogenes Laertius by Gerhard Johannes Vossius and Justus Lipsius.[14] Both editors explicitly expressed their deep sympathy for the ancient sect of eclectics – namely for their anti-sectarian gist. In Germany, this move had been taken up by the influential author of the first systematic history of philosophy, Johann Jacob Brucker,[15] and to some extent by the influential enlightened Lutheran theologian Johann Lorenz von Mosheim.[16] While they did not have to provide much information about the

---

[13] Helmut Holzhey was the first who took an interest in the revival of eclectic philosophy in early modern time ("Philosophie als Eklektik," in: *Studia Leibnitiana* 15 [1983], pp. 19–29). He sees the Dutch scholars Lipsius and Vossius as inaugurators of modern eclecticism: when editing Diogenus Laertius and Suedas (apparently only sources of our knowledge of Potamo as the founder of the ancient sect of eclecticism), they expressed their symphathy with his anti-sectarian gist. Besides the already mentioned monograph of Albrecht, Horst Dreitzel also gave an extensive and instructive survey about the surprizing renewal of this ancient sect in early modern time in "Zur Entwicklung und Eigenart der 'eklektischen' Philosophie", in: *Zeitschrift für historische Forschung* 18 (1991), pp. 281–343. For Vossius and Lipsius see pp. 282–84.

[14] Ulrich Johannes Schneider: "Eclecticism and the History of Philosophy", in: Donald R. Kelley (ed.): *History and the Disciplines. The Reclassification of Knowledge in Early Modern Europe*, Rochester 1997, pp. 82–101, here p. 85.

[15] Johann Jakob Brucker: *History of Philosophy*, printed for J. Johnson: London 1791; see also Michael Albrecht: "Brucker und die Eklektik," in: *Mitteilungen. Zeitschrift des Instituts für Europäische Kulturgeschichte der Universität Augsburg* 15 (2005), pp. 31–46.

[16] See Ulrich Johannes Schneider: "Das Eklektizismus-Problem in der Philosophiegeschichte", in: Wilhelm Schmidt-Biggemann/Theo Stammen (eds.): *Jacob Brucker (1696-1770). Philosoph und Historiker der europäischen Aufklärung* (= *Colloquia Augustana, Institut für Europäische Kulturgeschichte der Universität Augsburg* 7), Berlin 1998, pp. 135–158, here pp. 140–142.

sect, they both – just as Vossius and Lipsius before, emphasized their anti-sectarian gist with great sympathy.

Given that Diderot widely used Brucker's history of philosophy for his *Encyclopedia*, his respective articles on "eclectic" and "eclecticism" may well have been inspired by Brucker.[17] And Diderot's articles may have been the source for Victor Cousin who would develop his own eclectic philosophy.[18] Both philosophers had their particular reasons for such an adoption.

In Germany and the Netherlands at the end of the 17th century though, the rising eclectic philosophy with its call against sectarianism and in favor of reconciliation was closely associated with the call for peace among Christians and in particular among Protestants. The German historian Horst Dreitzel sees the widest spread of philosophical eclecticism in the decades around 1700 at *Protestant* universities where it competed with Aristotelianism on the one hand and Cartesianism or Wolffianism on the other.[19] Indeed, Lipsius and Vossius in the Netherlands just as then Brucker and Mosheim in Germany had been engaged in and suffered from the many theological controversies among Christian denominations, above all between Reformed and Lutheran theology. In these controversies, attempts of reconciliation were blamed as syncretism by orthodox theologians.[20] In contrast, ecumenically inclined theologians who argued in favor of reconciliation praised eclecticism (thereby avoiding the bad term syncretism) – and wanted to choose the best from all positions respecting them all. Thus the discussion about eclecticism in German philosophy during the six decades around 1700 should not be approached as a mere philosophical discussion but as driven by theological as well as philosophical intentions.

---

[17] See Rainer Jehl: "Jacob Brucker und die 'Encyclopédie'", in: Ibid., pp. 239–261. See also Albrecht: *Eklektik*, pp. 562–566.

[18] About Victor Cousin's philosophical eclecticism see Patrice Vermeren: *Victor Cousin. Le Jeu de la Philosophie et de l'Etat*, Paris 1995 (Collection "La philosophie en commun"). See also Albrecht: *Eklektik*, pp. 610–622.

[19] See Dreitzel: "Zur Entwicklung und Eigenart", p. 292. Eclecticism could be used to attack either modern or scholastic philosophy as sectarian, and thus either to reject Descartes and other moderns as just as sectarian as scholastic Aristotelians or to hide one's inclination to modern, anti-Aristotelian philosophy. Protestant philosophers were cautious to fully embrace Aristotelian philosophy because of some views incompatible with Christian dogma, but they had concerns about the moderns as well.

[20] We know that even the young Leibniz has been under such suspicion of syncretism when he as a Lutheran studied Reformed authors like Biesterfeld. See Paul Schrecker's "Introduction" to Gottfried Wilhelm Leibniz: *Lettres et fragments inédits sur les problèmes philosophiques, théologiques, politiques de la réconciliation des doctrines protestantes (1669–1704)*, ed. by Paul Schrecker, Paris 1934, pp. 19–34.

Protestantism had shielded itself against Catholicism with a deep suspicion against any kind of metaphysics or philosophical systems. Luther saw metaphysics as one cause of the destruction of true religion through the Roman church – with their philosophical system teinted by ancient pagan philosophers like Aristotle and Plato. For him the human soul was corrupt through the fall and human reason could not find the right way without the Scripture. Besides such Lutheran distrust against reason there was however the Melanchthon tradition of metaphysics in the gist of Aristotle. And in the middle of the 17th century, Aristotelianism had already become the prevailing philosophy at Protestant universities although with a clear awareness of its insufficiencies due to its pagan roots. It was first Aristotelian logic that has been adopted but then also moral philosophy, less so metaphysics and physics.[21] While it obtained increasing acceptance, justifications to hold Aristotelian views in spite of his Pagan character are frequent. Even a strong Aristotelian as Leibniz's teacher Jakob Thomasius distinguished between the philosophical achievements of the ancient philosopher, worth to be preserved, and his pagan failings, e.g. in the question about the eternity of the world.[22]

The surprising rise of philosophical eclecticism in Germany in the last decades of the 17th century appears to have been a way to walk between Scylla and Charybdis, between rejecting philosophy altogether or embracing the pagan Aristotle. One could adopt certain philosophical positions without any obligation to draw all of its consequences, especially when they threatened a dogma of the respective Christian denomination, be it Reformed or Lutheran. Moderate eclecticism could provide arguments against scepticism.[23] While eclecticism shared the suspicion about human knowledge with modern scepticism, it stopped short of the radical denial of human knowledge with its dangerous consequences. On the other hand, eclectic philosophy built a strong bulwark against modern philosophy such as that of Galileo, Gassendi and Descartes with its threat of necessitarianism.[24] We can see the use of eclectic arguments against Cartesianism in Dutch and German philosophy of the 17th

---

[21] Cf. Peter Petersen: *Geschichte der aristotelischen Philosophie im protestantischen Deutschland*, Leipzig 1921.
[22] See Albrecht: *Eklektik*, p. 297.
[23] Jacob Thomasius, who disagreed with eclectic philosophers, accepted them as tolerable because they stood against scepticism. See Albrecht: *Eklektik*, p. 299; Dreitzel: "Zur Entwicklung und Eigenart", pp. 307f. and p. 317.
[24] Cf. Ursula Goldenbaum: "How Theological Concerns Favor Empiricism over Rationalism", in: Arnaud Pelletier (ed.): *Leibniz's Experimental Philosophy* (= *Studia Leibnitiana*, Sonderhefte 46), Stuttgart 2016, pp. 37–63.

century and then, in the 18th century, against the rising Wolffianism. The suggestion is always that, instead of blindly following a "system", either of the ancient pagan philosophers Aristotle or Plato or of the new sectarians Descartes, Leibniz or Wolff, we should choose the best in all systems without becoming systematic and dogmatic ourselves. The obvious question for eclecticism how to decide what is actually best and thus should be chosen, was answered by theological considerations. The almost exclusive criterium for choosing the best was the compatibility with *their* own theological dogmatics. In this way, Lutheran theologians as Johann Franz Budde and Johann Georg Walch, or the reformed philosopher Arnold Wesenfeld promoted eclectic philosophy.[25]

There were, however, also a few philosophers and indeed scientists who called themselves eclectics. In contrast to their theological colleagues, they used the brand "eclecticism" to justify new ways of doing science and philosophy. They were indeed interested in obtaining *new* knowledge instead of only choosing from old schools. They strongly emphasized self-thinking and the freedom of philosophizing and used the eclectic attitude to justify their criticism of both, theological concerns as well as Aristotelianism. But they also used it against the modern systems of Descartes, Spinoza, Leibniz and Wolff – as systems, while accepting ideas from them. In contrast to the eclectic theologians and moral philosophers who were concerned mostly with Christian dogma, the criterium of these philosophers and scientists for choosing the best from different philosophical positions was not exclusively Christian dogmatics (although that mattered to them as well). But they were above all interested in scientific investigation of nature or politics to obtain new knowledge.

The most famous German eclectic of this kind was Johann Christian Sturm who would publish the first volume of his *Physica electiva sive hypothetica* in Altdorf 1686. He was not only a contemporary of Leibniz but even his correspondent. Of course, as a Lutheran, he was committed to Lutheran religion and also shared the Protestant suspicion against metaphysics and against human knowledge after the fall. But as a scientist and mathematician,

---

[25] The Lutheran theologian and philosopher Johann Franz Budde published his philosophy lectures held at the University at Halle 1694–1705 under the title *Institutiones philosophiae eclecticae*, Halle 1697–1705; the Reformed philosopher Arnold Wesenfeld published *Dissertationes philosophicae quatuor materiae selectioris de philosophia sectaria et elective*, Frankfurt a. d. Oder 1694. Cf. Albrecht: *Eklektik*, on the eclectic philosophers Budde: *Institutiones philosophiae*, pp. 434–450), and Wesenfeld: *Dissertationes philosophicae*, pp. 387–395.

he closely followed modern physics, astronomy and mathematics, that is Galileo, Kepler, Descartes, and Boyle. Therefore, he rejected the officially commended Aristotelianism at Protestant universities. But he did not accept Cartesianist dualism either. His methodological principles ressembled mostly those of Robert Boyle.[26]

Another philosopher who belongs to this second group of eclectic philosophers aiming for freedom of philosophizing and for empirical methods to find new truths was Christian Thomasius, the son of Leibniz's teacher. He was less interested in natural science but aimed for a new approach to law and politics. He picked up on modern ideas for the foundation of law, the political state, sovereignty, but stopped short to fully embrace the modern political philosophy of Hobbes or Spinoza. Rather, he sided with Pufendorf with whom he was in close connection.[27] Pufendorf, established at the court of Brandenbourg (since 1701 Prussia) would also help him to find a position at the new Brandenbourg university at Halle when he fell out with the Lutheran theologians in Saxony.[28] Although Thomasius could and did go a long way together with theological eclectics like Budde or Walch, his emphasis on freedom of philosophizing and in particular on political sovereignty, as independent from the church, caused a deep opposition between them, resulting in Thomasius' departure from Leipzig in Saxony and his move to the new Prussian university at Halle in Brandenbourg.

Leibniz knew all the above mentioned declared eclectic theologians, philosophers, and scientists well enough. Thus what did he think of their positions? To be sure, his encounter with Budde was quite unagreeable. One of Budde's students attacked Leibniz's *Theodicy* as deviating from orthodoxy, obviously not without the support of his teacher, who even sent this thesis to the philosopher; in his response letter to Budde, Leibniz reacted with unusual vigor.[29] Leibniz had also correspondences with Johann Christoph Sturm and

---

[26] About Johann Christoph Sturm see Albrecht: *Eklektik*, pp. 309–357, and Dreitzel: "Zur Entwicklung und Eigenart", pp. 310–319.

[27] About Christian Thomasius, see Albrecht: *Eklektik*, pp. 398–416, and Dreitzel: "Zur Entwicklung und Eigenart", pp. 324–330.

[28] See Frank Grunert: "'Händel mit Herrn Hector Gottfried Masio'. Zur Pragmatik des Streits in den Kontroversen mit dem Kopenhagener Hofprediger", in: Ursula Goldenbaum (ed.): *Appell an das Publikum. Die öffentliche Debatte in der deutschen Aufklärung 1687–1796*, vol. 2, Berlin 2004, pp. 117–174.

[29] For an account of Budde's rejection of Leibniz's Theodicy and thereby his metaphysics and Leibniz's response, see Stefan Lorenz: *De Mundo Optimo. Studien zu Leibniz's Théodicée und*

with Christian Thomasius, both self-declared eclectics. Do Leibniz's letters display any sympathy to their eclectic views? The author of the most recent and most comprehensive work on German eclecticism, Michael Albrecht, summarizes his findings in a clear judgment:

> "Nowhere, Leibniz expresses any sympathy with eclecticism or with the eclectic principle of choosing. Just the opposite! In the year 1694, he rejects every sect and in particular the eclectics. In 1711 he distances himself from the eclectics in a letter to Vierling."[30]

He also points to an explicite statement of Leibniz about a book dedicated to eclectic philosophy, in a letter from 1694 to Gerhard Meier.[31] There Leibniz thanked Meier for recommending to him Arnold Wesenfeld's *Philosophia eclectica*, a major book in favor of eclecticism.[32] He obviously read the book or at least skimmed through. After a polite compliment, however, Leibniz makes a clear statement in favor of methodical thinking in the gist of rationalism, saying:

> "Not that I approve of a peculiar sect as e.g. the eclectics. I believe we should not belong to any sect, following the symbol of the *Royal Society* 'Nullius in verba'. We want to emulate the mathematicians where nobody distinguishes Euclidians, Apollonians, or Archimedians."[33]

While one could argue that he agrees with the original ancients eclectics not to follow any sect, he does not follow their principle to choose the best from all. Instead, he positively lays out the method that alone can free us from such

---

ihrer Rezeption in Deutschland (1710–1791) (= *Studia Leibnitiana, Supplementa* 31), Stuttgart 1997 pp. 107–121.

[30] Albrecht refers to the following passage Leibniz wrote to Vierling on July 7, 1711, to clarify how Leibniz was in no way an eclectic philosopher (Albrecht: *Eklektik*, pp. 294f.): "Cartesiana philosophia jam minus floret, quam ante hos 30 annos, nam ubi experimentis incumbi coepit, apparuit, plurima in prinicipiis ejus tradita stare non posse. Et hodie eo res devenit, ut multa in Philosophia sint extra dubitationis aleam collocata, quae antea agitabantur, sed id paucis exploratum est, cum pauci in interioribus sint versati, praesertim illi, qui Eclectici habentur. Itaque non assentior, quod ais, nullas in rebus Physicis quaerendas demonstrationes (p. 83), nisi hod politico, quem informas, dictum velis. Huic experimenta sufficiunt. Si pergit genus humanum quo cepit gradu, mirabitur aliquando non exspectatas opes" (GP VII, 497).

[31] Leibniz to Meier 1694; A I, 10, N. 403, 592.

[32] About Wesenfeld see footnote 25 above.

[33] See footnote 31 above.

sectarian gist – the method of mathematicians, the geometrical method embraced by Galileo, Hobbes, Spinoza, and Leibniz.[34]

Given Leibniz's awareness of the rising new philosophical eclecticism in Germany and his criticism of it, we should not confuse the rationalist Leibniz with a school he clearly disagreed with. But what about Leibniz's relation to Sturm, the scientist and eclectic philosopher who openly embraced modern ideas? Both philosophers had an exchange about their different philosophical approaches after Sturm's publication of his Philosophia electiva, mediated either by Sturm's son, who taught in Wolfenbüttel, or by Christoph Pfautz, the well-known reviewer of mathematical writings in the *Acta eruditorum* in those years. This controversy concerned their different concepts of nature and of force.[35] While both philosophers agreed that matter is passive, Leibniz insisted on the clear distinction of nature as the world of phenomena and on the necessity of force in any given body although not residing in matter, positions rejected by Sturm.

Moreover, Sturm also defended Christian Thomasius against Leibniz in a controversy that concerned the concept of substance. Thomasius had provoked the philosophers of his time, in particular Aristotelians, by raising the question for a consistent definition of Substance.[36] Leibniz first intended to answer with a letter to Thomasius, then sent a paper to the *Acta eruditorum* but the editors did not want to have a controversy with Thomasius in their journal given the latter's trouble with theologians at that time. Thus Leibniz revised the paper turning it into a non-controversial essay.[37] We owe one of the most famous Leibniz writings – *De primae philosophiae emendatione et de notione substantiae* to this controversy.[38] There was no way that Leibniz

---

[34] Ursula Goldenbaum: "The Necessitarian Threat of the Mathematizing of Nature," in: Geoffrey Gorham/Christopher Hill et al. (eds.): *The Language of Nature. Reassessing the Mathematization of Natural Philosophy in the Seventeenth Century* (= *Minnesota Studies of Science*, Special Issue), pp. 274–307.

[35] For the controversy between Sturm and Leibniz about the concepts of nature and force in the years 1694 and 1695, see A II, 2, N. 277 and 291, and A II, 3, N. 36 and N. 37. Leibniz kept these letters in a special folder to which he later added A II, 3, N. 145, as is reported by the editors.

[36] Christian Thomasius: *Quid sit substantia?*, Halle/Magdeburg 1693.

[37] "De notione Substantiae ad quam edendam V. Cl. Christianus Thomasius Theologos et Philosophos nuper provocavit" (LBr. 724, 26–7). This manuscript, not published by Leibniz although a clean copy exists, has first been published by Gerda Utermöhlen: "Leibniz's Antwort auf Christian Thomasius' Frage", in: *Studia Leibnitiana* 11/1 (1979), pp. 82–91, here 85f. Utermöhlen's article provides a comprehensive and highly interesting presentation of this Leibniz-Thomasius controversy.

[38] *Acta eruditorum*, March 1694, pp. 110–112.

would agree with any of these eclectic philosophers when it was about the foundation of metaphysics, being the foundation of science and to some extent, of theology, for Leibniz.

3. Explaining Leibniz's Philosophy by His Alleged Eclecticism

Besides the rather loose addressing of Leibniz as an eclectic thinker in Leibniz scholarship, some authors see Leibniz as a true eclectic and find this to be helpful to explain the very different or, as they see it, even mutually exclusive aspects of his philosophizing. In their approaches to Leibniz, his alleged eclecticism becomes central for any consistent understanding of Leibniz. While such an eclectic understanding of Leibniz goes back to the 19th century, I will focus on three more recent interpretations of Leibniz by three distinguished Leibniz scholars: Christia Mercer's monograph on the young Leibniz, Patrick Riley's book on Leibniz' philosophy of law, and Marcelo Dascal's presentation of the "other" Leibniz, that is the Leibniz of "soft reason" besides the rationalist.[39]

3.1. On Christia Mercer's Recycling Leibniz

Christia Mercer included an entire chapter on Leibniz's eclecticism in her book. Blaming Leibniz scholarship for ignoring Leibniz's adoptions from a great variety of sources, ancient and modern, Mercer makes some very strong claims: "One of the overlooked aspects of Leibniz' brilliance is his success in building such an original and sublime edifice out of *recycled materials*."[40] Addressing the question what these recycled materials were she writes: "that some of Leibniz's most basic metaphysical beliefs *were taken directly from* the Aristotelian, Platonist, and mechanical philosophies."[41] How Leibniz could still build a *system* from such recycled materials, taken directly from other philosophers, is explained as follows:

---

[39] For their works see footnote 2 above.
[40] Mercer: *Leibniz's Metaphysics*, pp. 52f. (my emphasis U G).
[41] Ibid., p. 58 (my emphasis U G).

> "Leibniz's system is the result of a clever conciliation of these sorts of assumptions [self-sufficiency of substances, creatures as emanations of God's essence, mechanical explanation of corporeal features]. Instead of a set of doctrines that were deduced from first principles, his philosophy is a *brilliant blending of ancient and modern views*."[42]

Thus it is not through deduction or the geometrical method but through "blending" that Leibniz can bring the recycled materials into one system. To be sure, "blending" in philosophy is a mere metaphor taken from fine cuisine or from the production of whiskey and there exist quite precise methods to do such blending. But how is that done in philosophy?

To be sure, Mercer still wants to see Leibniz's philosophy as a *system*, and that should mean, as one consistent theoretical building. But the very idea of building a system is contradictory to the idea of philosophical eclecticism. It was the very pride of the ancient sect of eclectics as well as the new German eclecticism to do away with any system. Notwithstanding of building a system, Leibniz, according to Mercer, did not deduce his set of doctrines from first principles and did not intend to do so. She thereby somehow anticipates Dascal's view that Leibniz was not a "common" rationalist. She writes

> "[…] he was not a rationalist who believed that one arrives at fundamental truths through armchair intuition and then deduces from them other truths. Rather, for Leibniz and his predessessors, the truths are *borrowed* from the great philosophical systems."[43]

Was there ever a rationalist who fits such a description?

I do not deny that Leibniz knew the great philosophical systems and moreover, even the small and hardly known systems. He was clearly one of the most erudite philosophers. Not only knew he mathematics and politics, mechanics and medicine, logic and history, having been the last universal genius; he also studied the history of philosophy, and indeed in order to benefit from it for his own work. But even if Leibniz had "borrowed" the truths of his system from others, the mere gesturing toward the many sources Leibniz studied would not yet explain anything about his choices. Thus if he adopted certain ideas from Aristotle, why these ideas and not others? The explanatory work would not yet been accomplished by pointing to similarities or apparent similarities. This being said, I do not see any idea Leibniz simply "borrowed"

---

[42] Ibid. (my emphasis U G).
[43] Ibid., p. 57 (my emphasis U G).

from Aristotle or any other philosopher and then "recycled". Already the most obvious candidate for such an alleged borrowing of Leibniz from Aristotle, the concept of substance, has little in common with Leibniz's concept of a substance as Jakob Thomasius pointed out to him.[44]

Leibniz did not build his own philosophical system by combining bits and bites of other systems in the way Hearst built his castle from European pieces of architecture and culture of different periods and styles. Instead, Leibniz worked out his philosophy as one piece even if he never finished his system. He turned to metaphysics because he did not find a philosophy that could respond to the challenges of modern science for Christian religion. It was his goal to work out a philosophy that was compatible with and supportive to modern science and at the same time to Christian religion. His metaphysics was meant to lay the ground for all the different sciences, natural sciences including empirical sciences as medicine as well as jurisprudence, history and politics. His epistemology aimed to provide the metaphysical basis from where the coherence of necessary and contingent truths could be stated and explained. While Leibniz could not work out that entire system of sciences based on his metaphysics and epistemology, and while he did not give us a book but instead many pieces and fragments, we can still recognize the grand systematic character of his thinking. The unity of his system is constituted by his methods.

3.2 On Marcelo Dascal's Soft versus Radical Reason in Leibniz

It was at the Leibniz Congress in Berlin in 2001 when Dascal first introduced his idea of the so far unknown *other* Leibniz of soft rationality. I have criticized this view since.[45] In his first paper promoting soft rationality, Dascal based his new interpretation on the term "blandior ratio". I have shown elsewhere that Leibniz does not use this term more than one time (as far as we know the texts), concluding that it is not a technical term of Leibniz and can thus not bear the burden of proof for the new interpretation. I also pointed out that Leibniz used this term precisely in reference to *mathematics*,[46] that is in

---

[44] See Thomasius to Leibniz on Oct 2/12, 1668; A II, 1, N. 10, 12f.
[45] See footnote 2 above.
[46] The single passage where blandior ratio occurs in Leibniz's writings is the following: "This light is *also desired in mathematics*; therefore other sciences have to work through – according

the realm of Dascals's "radical" reason. Leibniz wanted to allow mathematical rigorous demonstrations to become more easily available to human understanding. Instead of cumbersome long chains of deduction, the truth of such demonstrations should be made immediately visible, e.g. by denotation. This has nothing to do with softening the strictness of demonstrations as Dascal seems to believe.

Heinrich Schepers, in his exchange with Dascal, pointed out, how Dascal's efforts to establish *soft* reason as a new and other kind of reason in Leibniz's thinking, come down to the well-known Leibnizian distinction between necessary and contingent truths. He admits: "For Leibniz, the chasm between necessary and contingent truths cannot be bridged."[47] But he then continues:

> "Nevertheless the sudden insight into their structural identity supplied Leibniz with the necessary light (*inexpecta lux*) for later developing his theory of monads. As I made clear only these structural properties are transferred by Leibniz from the necessary to the contingent truths: the inclusion of the predicate in the subject, implying its analyzability in infinitely many steps."[48]

Both kinds of truth are based on Leibniz's containment logic as celebrated by Couturat:

> "Ce principe [de raison suffisante] signifie, exactement, que, dans toute proposition vraie, le prédicat est contenu dans le sujet. [...] Pour ce qui est des vérités contingentes, en particulier, Leibniz affirme leur soumission au principe de raison avec une netteté et une insistance qui ne laissent place à aucun doute. Par suite, les vérités contingentes ne sont pas synthétique, à quelque degré que ce soit, comme on le croit généralement; elles sont tout aussi analytiques que les vérités nécessaires."[49]

Of course, *we* can only accomplish the analysis of abstract concepts. The complete concepts of concrete individuals can be known by God alone because their analysis is infinite. Human beings can grasp them by empirical investigation alone.

---

to the example of mathematics – to reach the certainty such that the roughness of mathematics is to be treated by another *softer reason* and <according to the example of the others> has to be mitigated: that we at the same time snatch the belief from the will as clearly satisfy the sense aiming for causes." (My translation and emphasis U G) (A IV, 4, N. 81, 342; C, 34).

[47] Heinrich Schepers: "Non Alter, sed etiam Leibnitius: Reply to Dascal's Review *Ex pluribus unum?*", in: *The Leibniz Review* 14 (2004), pp. 117–135, p. 126.
[48] Ibid.
[49] Louis Couturat: "Sur la métaphysique de Leibniz", in: *Revue de métaphysique et de morale* 10/1 (1902), pp. 1–25, here pp. 7f. and 10.

Dascal though wants us to see Leibniz as an eclectic who chooses the best from all methods using two absolutely different and independent ways of reasoning, soft and hard (or radical) reasoning. For him, just as for Mercer, Leibniz's alleged eclecticism is more than just a conciliatory attitude, namely the use of different methods in different areas of knowledge, belonging either to *radical* or to *soft* reason which are different in kind: one is heavy with demonstrations, and one comes as *reason light*. These two ways of reasoning are supposed to co-exist because they can never be brought into coherence:

> "It [soft reason] cannot, therefore, be explained away as a derivative of the 'radical reason' picture, and must co-exist side by side with it, in the capacity of a full-fledged independent and different counterpart and partner. It is fully there and fully other, not just there."[50]

Sometimes Dascal even sounds as if there is no area left for a-priori reasoning in Leibniz at all, as if he respected every position equally in their value for truth – being a true eclectic. Dascal states:

> "Leibniz in fact argues against the 'method of exclusion', on the grounds that *every serious doctrine or method, if attentively and charitably examined, contains weaknesses as well as strengths, so that no one can erect itself as the arbiter* of all the others – a true *eclectic* manifesto."[51]

Interestingly, the words emphasized by me are indeed a true eclectic manifesto and could so be found in German eclectic philosophers as Leibniz's contemporaries Christian Thomasius or Arnold Wesenfeld, philosophers Leibniz rejected. Instead of joining them, however, Leibniz asked us to follow the mathematicians and their methods.

While it is true that human beings have no access to complete concepts of concrete things, all truths are – in principle – analyzable. This creates a shared framework for all truth: true propositions are such where the predicate is included in the subject. This statement is valid for contingent as well as for necessary truths even if human beings can't accomplish the analysis far enough to see it. For Leibniz, notwithstanding the admitted limits of human

---

[50] Marcelo Dascal: "Alter et etiam: Rejoinder to Schepers", in: *The Leibniz Review* 14 (2004), pp. 137–151, here p. 144.
[51] Id.: "Ex pluribus unum? Patterns in 522+ Texts of Leibniz's Sämtliche Schriften VI, 4" [Review], in: *The Leibniz Review* 13 (2003), pp. 105–154, p. 120 (my emphasis U G).

understanding, the principle of contradiction is valid in both, contingent and necessary truths and no empirical finding can be held against necessary truths:

> "I acknowledge that we must not deny what we do not understand, but I add that we are *entitled to deny* (within the natural order at least) whatever is absolutely unintelligible and inexplicable. [...] Everything that is in accord with the natural order can be conceived or understood by some creature."[52]

That is what Schepers emphasizes against Dascal: The structural identity of necessary and contingent truths

> "is a rational achievement that can hardly be overestimated, even though we have grown used to it by now. [...] Even if no such complete knowledge is possible for us this theory aims at a metaphysically far-reaching account which cannot be achieved by mere metaphors."[53]

As limited as we are as human beings, knowing this structural identity of contingent and necessary truths together with the validity of the principles of contradiction and sufficient reason provide an enormous support for even our empirical work in finding contingent truths. This approach offers tools to order observations and to make experiments along theoretical hypotheses.

Dascal's emphasis on presumptions as alleged soft reasoning is contradicted by Leibniz's use and explanations of hypotheses which are rationally *demonstrated* although one has to presuppose an undemonstrated assumption and remain aware of that. All of Dascal's talk about the significance of probability as allegedly soft reasoning looses its force when facing Leibniz's efforts to calculate probability, that is to bring necessary truths and contingent truths together. All his gesturing to controversies and debates must ignore Leibniz's strong efforts to formalize just these controversies and debates – to make them capable to be treated by strictly rational procedures. All his emphasis on the *scale* to *weigh* arguments instead of *counting* them is nothing but the well-known principle that it is not the number of arguments but their power that counts when we want to convince somebody.[54]

---

[52] Gottfried Wilhelm Leibniz: *New Essays on Human Understanding*, transl. and ed. by Peter Remnant and Jonathan Bennett, Cambridge/New York 1995, p. 65 (my emphasis U G).
[53] Schepers: "Non Alter", pp. 126f. (my emphasis U G).
[54] I laid out these arguments in more detail and with Leibniz quotes in the above mentioned article Goldenbaum: "Reason light?", see footnote 2.

Leibniz's containment logic that provides the framework for necessary as well as contingent truths, is well established as his *own* creation[55] that he did not achieve by *borrowing and recycling* the best from any authors he read. He arrived at it when trying to find a way to avoid Spinoza's necessitarianism while aiming to maintain the geometrical method of the moderns. In his critical discussion of Spinoza he created his own new concept of 'contingency' that includes causality according to the principle of sufficient reason but points to the non-contradiction of the opposite of contingent things or events. Nothing happens without a reason though. Leibniz famously stated:

> "The predicate or consequent always is in the subject or antecedent, and here the general nature of truth lies, [...] in the connection between the terms of a proposition [...] and this holds for every affirmative truth, universal or singular, necessary or contingent."[56]

This new and genuine Leibnizian approach, using one kind of reasoning, would allow him a coherent epistemological approach to necessary as well as contingent truths and also contribute to his new metaphysics.

3.3 On Patrick Riley's Twofold Modern as Well as Medieval Leibniz

Although Patrick Riley does not use the term 'eclectic' to understand Leibniz's philosophy, in particular his philosophy of law, his view of Leibniz's thinking clearly fulfills the criteria of eclecticism as laid out above, according to common language just as well as to the philosophical school of eclecticism:

> "It was characteristic of Leibniz to try to reconcile apparently conflicting ideas, to take from each kind of thought that which was soundest and to synthetisize it with the seemingly incommensurable truths of other systems; thus he struggled throughout his life to fuse Platonism, Cartesianism, Augustinian voluntarism, Christian charity, Scholasticism, Hobbesian mechanistic materialism, and a number of other doctrines into a plausible whole whose apex would be a rational theology."[57]

---

[55] Stefano di Bella emphasizes: "Leibniz introduces what he himself later will present to Arnauld as the very heart of the matter, and the decisive argument against all objections. I allude to the so-called '*containment theory of truth*'" (Stefano di Bella: *The Science of the Individual: Leibniz's Ontology of Individual Substances*, Dordrecht 2005, p. 4).

[56] A VI, 4, 1644; this translation from the French is taken from Di Bella: *The Science of the Individual*.

[57] Riley: *Leibniz's Universal Jurisprudence*, p. 14.

This is more than stating Leibniz's "desire for reconciliation, for harmony, for synthesis" which Riley emphasizes as well and which I can recognize in Leibniz too.

In the course of his erudite book, Riley identifies only three main sources of Leibniz's philosophy of law – Platonian wisdom, Christian or more specifically Paulenian Love, and Augustinean benevolence.[58] While he gestures to Leibniz's early familiarity with Plato, Augustine and Christian tradition – being beyond any doubt – he nowhere explains *why* Leibniz developed his clearly unique understanding of justice as the love of the wise man and, moreover, why he did so in 1671. He does not explain either how this new concept was the solution of a problem that Leibniz had not seen before. Instead he spends many pages to show the *similarity* of Leibniz's views with those three traditions he wants him to agree with. In contrast, he strongly emphasized Leibniz's alleged absolute rejection of the moderns. I quote:

> "he is hostile to Descartes, Hobbes and Spinoza (as radical voluntarists who deny or destroy Platonic eternal verities), and he is favorable to Plato, St. Paul, and (much of) Augustine."[59]

From his findings about Leibniz's alleged embracing Plato, Augustin, and Paulinian Christianity and allegedly complete rejection of the moderns in the field of law and politics, Riley states a sharp contrast between a modern Leibniz when it comes to mathematics or science and a premodern Leibniz who wants to resist modern political theory and philosophy of law: "indeed unless one recalls Leibniz' prominent place in modern mathematics and science he will look briefly (in the moral sphere) like an ancient chastising modernity."[60] We do not get any explanation though why Leibniz had these likes and dislikes. We do not learn why Leibniz worked so hard to find his new concept of justice during his time in Mainz. And no reason is given why Leibniz was so very proud of this newly found concept of justice in 1671, as can be seen from his letters to Velthuysen and Arnauld.[61] Instead we are assured once and again:

> "In many ways Leibnizian 'wise charity' is the last flowering (or last gasp) of a long and distinguished Graeco-Roman-Christian tradition which was to be

---

[58] Ibid., pp. 266f.
[59] Ibid. Subsuming Spinoza under "voluntarism" is striking given Spinoza's criticism of free will.
[60] Ibid.
[61] A II, 1, N. 51, and N. 87.

definitively overturned by Hume, Rousseau, and Kant no more than a half-century after Leibniz' death. [...] Leibniz epitomized a world view which was on the hedge of extinction."[62]

Leibniz – the most backward moral and political philosopher? The dreamer of Christian love in total ignorance of modern political reality? I could not disagree more and could provide ample evidence of Leibniz's enormous admiration of modern moral and political philosophers such as Hobbes and even Spinoza. It may suffice to point to his first letter to Hobbes and to his letter to Conring about Hobbes giving clear evidence that Leibniz was a great admirer of Hobbes and shared some fundamental ideas with him.[63] Above all, he agreed that philosophy of law has to start with human individuals who strive to persevere and can develop further concepts – as e.g. justice – only from there. His pride of the solution for the problem, to have selfish individuals on the one hand who are to agree to justice on the other, is due to his discovery that love is an affect of human beings that bridges selfish interests of individuals simply because they can enjoy the pleasure of the other as their own pleasure through the affect of love. Thus Leibniz's definition of love has more in common with Hobbes than with Augustine or Plato but it cannot be reduced to Hobbes either. Rather it is the insufficiency of Hobbes' approach as well as of the approaches of Plato, Augustine, and Paulus that made Leibniz work very hard to find his own solution which will be new, unheard of, and very modern.[64]

Leibniz did not divide his thinking between mathematics and science on the one hand and politics, law, and history on the other as Riley suggests, claiming that Leibniz was a modern in the former but a pre-modern in the latter. Rather, the rationalist philosopher distinguished between demonstrated truths that could be found in mathematics, logic, natural law [ius naturale] and natural religion alike, and empirical or contingent truths or truths of fact which

---

[62] Riley: *Leibniz's Universal Jurisprudence*, p. 274.
[63] Leibniz wrote to Conring in May (?) 1671: "Concerning the art of defining, I don't know whether it goes back hundreds of years – except Aristotle, the ancient scholars of law, Julius Cäsar Scaliger and Jacob Cujas – and if it should not rather be attributed to Thomas Hobbes. The latter seems to have demonstrated as many excellent proposition as Aristotle himself and is perhaps the most apodictic [ἀποδεικτικώτατος] among all mortals, besides the mathematicians and ancient scholars of law" (A II, 1, N. 49, 95). Leibniz's enthusiastic letter to Hobbes (who never received it) is from July 13/23, 1670 (A II, 1, N. 25).
[64] See Ursula Goldenbaum: "It's Love! Leibniz' Concepts of Love and Justice as Results of His Struggle With Hobbes' Naturalism", in: Mark Kulstad/Mogens Lærke (eds.): *The Philosophy of the Young Leibniz (= Studia Leibnitiana, Sonderhefte 35)*, Stuttgart 2008, pp. 249–266.

could be found in natural science as well as in positive law, church history and other areas. Nonetheless, all these truths would be conceived in the shared framework of Leibniz's containment logic where true sentences are true because their subject includes the predicate – whether we human beings are capable to see that or not.

4. Conclusion

There has always been a great variety of Leibniz interpretations and I can tolerate most of them because they include great insights inspiring a better understanding of the great thinker Leibniz. Understanding Leibniz as an eclectic, however, especially in the systematic sense of the three authors presented, will lead to a split of his philosophy into different incoherent parts, each ruled by incompatible methods supposed to be different in kind. Such an understanding destroys the very heart of Leibniz's philosophy, I am firmly convinced. To repeat, there is no question that Leibniz was one of the most erudite men in human history, that he read a huge number of philosophers, not to mention all the other authors of other disciplines. He knew the arguments and philosophical solutions provided by other great philosophers very well and used them to sharpen his own approach. But – learning from others is not what we call 'eclectic'; otherwise, the term would be used inflationary to describe all human beings, making it meaningless.

Also, I agree that Leibniz had an extremely conciliatory attitude and followed the principle of charity. But that does not hinder him to express always exclusively his own philosophical position. Gotthold Ephraim Lessing, according to whom Leibniz would not have written any line in vain, explains this very well. He admits that Leibniz had indeed the courtesy to adapt his terminology to other philosophers but insists that he, nonetheless, never ever taught any but his own philosophy – as the truth:

> "Everything that he did from time to time in the interest of *his system* was quite the opposite: he tried to adapt the dominant principles of all parties to *that system*. [...] In his quest for truth, Leibniz never took any notice of accepted opinions; but in the firm belief that no opinion can be accepted unless it is *in a certain respect*, or *in a certain sense* true, he was often so accommodating as to

turn the opinion over and over until he was able to bring *that certain respect* to light, and to make *that certain sense* comprehensible."[65]

In my eyes, this is a perfect way to explain Leibniz's conciliatory attitude without turning this most systematic thinker into someone he explicitly dismissed – an eclectic thinker.

---

[65] Gotthold Ephraim Lessing: "Leibniz on Eternal Punishment", in: Id.: *Philosophical and Theological Writings*, ed. by H. B. Nisbet, Cambridge/New York 2005, p. 46.

Leibniz's Mereology in the Essays on Logical Calculus of 1686–90[*]

Massimo Mugnai (Pisa)

1.

Even though the notions of part and whole play an important role in Leibniz's metaphysics, *Mereology*, the doctrine of the relations of part to whole and of parts to parts, has so far awoken the interest of only a small number of Leibniz scholars. In the period since the publication of the pioneering paper of Hans Burkhardt and Wolfgang Degen (1990), which is entirely devoted to Leibniz's mereology, very few works have been published on the same topic. Moreover, these works tend to consider mereology in the general setting of Leibniz's metaphysics and do not pay due attention to those essays where Leibniz systematically develops a proper mereological calculus.[1]

In the years 1686–1690, indeed, Leibniz wrote a series of essays,[2] which are usually regarded as pertaining to logic, even though their topic belongs more properly to *mereology*. That these essays concern primarily mereology is clearly shown by the simple, linguistic fact that in them Leibniz does not speak of *terms*, but of *things*, of generic *wholes* and parts.

Usually, Leibniz employs the Latin neuter, singular or plural, mainly of pronouns to denote a 'part' or a 'whole', as in the following passage:

> "*si quid alteri inest adiectum ei, non facit aliud ab eo* [if something which is in another thing is added to it, it does not make anything different from that other]".[3]

---

[*] This paper grew out of several discussions with Achille Varzi, to whom I am deeply indebted for his helpful advice on some questions concerning mereology.
[1] Cf. Hans Burkhardt/Wolfgang Degen: "Mereology in Leibniz's Logic and Philosophy", in: *Topoi* 9/1 (1990), pp. 3–13; Roy T. Cook: "The Logic of Leibniz's Mereology", in: *Studia Leibnitiana* 32/1 (2000), pp. 1–20; Paul Lodge: "Leibniz's Notion of an Aggregate", in: *British Journal for the History of Philosophy* 9/3 (2001), pp. 467–486; Glenn A. Hartz: *Leibniz's Final System: Monads, Matter, and Animals*, London et al. 2006, pp. 54–79 in particular.
[2] *Specimen Calculi Coincidentium* (A VI, 4 A, 816–22); *De casibus in quibus componendo nihil novi fieri potest* (A VI, 4 A, 823–28); *Specimen Calculi coincidentium et inexistentium* (A VI, 4 A, 830–45); *Non inelegans Specimen demonstrandi in abstractis* (A VI, 4 A, 845–55); *De Calculo irrepetibilium* (A VI, 4 A, 855–58).
[3] A VI, 4 A, 837.

In translations for the most part, however, the 'quid' (= 'aliquid') of the Latin text has been rendered with an expression equivalent to the English 'term'. Thus, for instance, Parkinson translates the above sentence as:

> "if any term which is in another is added to it, it does not make anything which is different from that other";[4]

and the French translation of the same text has:

> "si un terme est dans un autre et lui est adjouté, il ne vient rien de plus."[5]

As has been remarked by Wolfgang Lenzen, this is not a mistake because Leibniz's calculus, displayed in these essays, can be applied *even* to "terms" (concepts).[6] Leibniz's aim in these essays, however, is more ambitious and corresponds to the attempt to construct a general mereology capable of being applied to a variety of things including concepts and material objects.

This is very much in agreement with an attitude which is constantly present in Leibniz's philosophical works and which can be traced back to the *Dissertation on the Combinatorial Art* (1666). The image of the world that we get from the *Dissertation*, indeed, is analogous to that usually associated with any atomistic point of view: every existing thing is thought of as a whole, which can be decomposed into lesser wholes and these latter, in turn, into lesser wholes again, till the smallest components parts (atoms or molecular aggregates of some sort) are reached. By a simple process of combination of the parts, in the reverse direction, one may then recompose the whole. The same procedure can be applied to non-material things as well like, for example, to concepts, propositions, geometrical figures and numbers. Thus, combinatorics applied to mereology, the doctrine of the whole and parts, becomes in Leibniz's hand a kind of all-purpose tool capable of introducing us to the intimate secrets of nature:

---

[4] G. W. Leibniz: *Logical Papers. A Selection*, transl. and ed. with an introd. by G. H. R. Parkinson, Oxford 1966, p. 135.
[5] Id.: *Recherches générales sur l'analyse des notions et des vérités. 24 thèses métaphysiques at autres textes logiques et métaphysiques*, introductions et notes par Jean Baptiste Rauzy, Paris 1998, p. 416.
[6] Wolfgang Lenzen: "Guilielmi Pacidii Non plus ultra, oder: Eine Rekonstruktion des Leibnizschen Plus-Minus-Kalküls", in: Uwe Meixner/Albert Newen (ed.): *Philosophie der Neuzeit: From Descartes to Kant* (= *Philosophiegeschichte und logische Analyse* 3), Paderborn 2000, pp. 71–118, here 79–82.

"Since all things that exist, or can be conceived in thought, may be said to be made up of parts, either real or at least conceptual, whatever differs in kind must necessarily differ either in parts, and here lie the Applications of Complexions, or by a different situs, hence the application of Dispositions. [...] With these complications, not only can geometry be enriched by an infinite number of new Theorems [...] but we have also (if it is indeed true that great things are made up of little things, whether you call them atoms or molecules) a unique way of penetrating into the arcana of nature."[7]

The system of variations elaborated in the *Dissertation on the Combinatorial Art*, Leibniz observes, "leads the mind that yields to it almost through all infinity, and embraces at once the harmony of the world, the inner workings of things, and the great chain of being."[8] Introducing the seventh specimen, devoted to the application of combinatorics to geometrical figures, Leibniz emphatically writes:

"With these complications, not only can geometry be enriched by an infinite number of new Theorems, as every complication brings into being a new, compound figure, by the contemplation of whose properties we may devise new theorems and new demonstrations; but we have also (if it is indeed true that great things are made up of little things, whether you call them atoms or molecules) a unique way of penetrating into the arcana of nature. This is because the more one has perceived the parts of a thing, the parts of its parts, and their shapes and arrangements, the more perfectly one can be said to know the thing. [...] when you enter upon natural history and the question of being, that is, upon the question of the real constitution of bodies, the vast portals of Physics will stand open, and the character of the elements, the origin and mixture of the qualities, the origin of mixtures, the mixing of those mixtures, and everything that formerly lay hidden in darkness will be revealed."[9]

Later in his life, Leibniz recalls that, for a brief period in his youth, he favored atomism.[10] This is quite in agreement with the parenthetical remark made in the first passage above, which shows no prejudice against atoms as the least components of natural bodies.

In the *Dissertation on the Combinatorial Art* Leibniz's atomism is, however, wedded with a metaphysical doctrine centered on the notion of

---

[7] A VI, 1, 187; ll. 29–33.
[8] A VI, 1, 187.
[9] A VI, 1, 187–88.
[10] On Leibniz's atomism cf. Richard Arthur: "The Enigma of Leibniz's Atomism", in: Daniel Garber (ed.): *Oxford Studies in Early Modern Philosophy*, I, Oxford 2004, pp. 183–227; Daniel Garber: *Leibniz: Body, Substance, Monad*, Oxford 2009, pp. 62–70, 81–82.

immeation or *perichoresis*, according to which everything is related to everything on the basis of the two relations of *similarity* and *dissimilarity*. *Perichoresis* is the transliteration into English of a Greek word meaning 'circle' or the effect of revolving, which was employed in theology "to explain the relation of *coherence* of the three persons of the Trinity".[11] The Latin word *immeatio* was coined to translate *perichoresis* and according to Johann Heinrich Bisterfeld, the main source of Leibniz on this issue, it was meant to designate "the varied concourse, combination and complication of relations".

Thus, in the *Dissertation on the Combinatorial Art*, Leibniz deeply modifies the account of the world which was usually associated with the traditional atomistic doctrines, based on the aggregation and disaggregation of atoms, without any trace of intrinsic finalism and governed by mere chance. To this view he substitutes the picture of a world composed of beings connected by a net of reciprocal relations generating a mutual union and communion, analogous to that of the three persons in the holy Trinity. This picture was clearly meant to avoid the materialistic and atheistic consequences implicit in genuine atomistic theories as, for example, that displayed by Lucretius in his poem *On the Nature of Things*.

It is not difficult to see the existence of a latent conflict between Leibniz's acceptance of atomism on one hand, and his agreement with a metaphysics motivated by religious issues and influenced by a philosophy largely inspired by doctrines of neo-platonic origins.[12] As soon as the conflict came to light, in the years immediately following the edition of the *Dissertation on the Combinatorial Art*, Leibniz decided to abandon the atomistic theory, but in a certain sense he never stopped flirting with it. Thus, when he attempts to explain to his contemporaries his hypothesis of the monads, he uses the expression 'spiritual atom' to characterize what he properly intends to denote with the word 'monad'. As formerly in the *Dissertation*, in his mature thought Leibniz attempts to reconcile an atomistic perspective with an anti-materialistic metaphysics.

---

[11] Maria Rosa Antognazza: "Bisterfeld and 'Immeatio': Origins of a Key Concept in the Early Modern Doctrine of Universal Harmony", in: Martin Mulsow (ed.): *Spätrenaissance-Philosophie in Deutschland 1570–1650: Entwürfe zwischen Humanismus und Konfessionalisierung, okkulten Traditionen und Schulmetaphysik*, Tübingen 2009, pp. 57–83.

[12] On the influence of Neoplatonic ideas on Leibniz's philosophy cf. Christia Mercer: *Leibniz's Metaphysics: Its Origins and Development*, Cambridge 2001.

2.

In the essays we are considering, Leibniz introduces the relation of *containment* as follows:

> "If several things taken together coincide with one, any one of those several things is said 'to be in' or 'to be contained in' that one thing, and the one thing itself is said to be the 'container'. Conversely, if some thing is in another, it will be among several which together coincide with that other thing."[13]

> "That A 'is in' L, or, that L 'contains' A, is the same as that L is assumed to be coincident with several things taken together, among which is A."[14]

According to Leibniz, the relation of *Containment* or *inherence* has the property of being:

(C.1) Reflexive: "A is in A. Anything is in itself."[15]

But it is also

(C.2) Transitive: "A content of a content is a content of the container; i.e. if that thing in which there is another is in a third thing, that which is in it will be in that third thing; or *if A is in B and B is in C, A will also be in C*."[16]

and

(C.3) Antisymmetric: "If A is in B and B is in A, then $A = B$".[17]

Leibniz thinks of the relation of *containment* in very general terms. Given two aggregates, A and B, if all the elements that are in B *are in A*, Leibniz says that *A contains B*, without raising the question of the nature or of the reciprocal connections of the elements of B. This means that the elements of B may be

---

[13] Leibniz: *Logical Papers*, p. 122 (here and in the following quotations from this edition the translation has been slightly modified according to the remarks made at the beginning of the present paper); A VI, 4 A, 846.
[14] Leibniz: *Logical Papers*, p. 132.
[15] Leibniz: *Logical Papers*, p. 133; A VI, 4 A, 835.
[16] Leibniz: *Logical Papers*, p. 126; A VI, 4 A, 850.
[17] Leibniz: *Logical Papers*, p. 136; A VI, 4 A, 839.

heterogeneous not only as regards the elements of A, but even as regards themselves:

> "We say that the concept of the genus is in the concept of the species, the individuals of the species in the individuals of the genus; a part in the whole, and the indivisible in the continuum – such as a point in a line, even though a point is not a part of a line. Thus, the concept of an affection or predicate is in the concept of the subject. In general, this consideration extends very widely. We also say that inexistents are contained in those things in which they are. Nor does it matter here, with regard to this general concept, how those things which are in something are related to each other or to the container."[18]

In a text written five or six years before the essays on *real addition*, Leibniz observes that to compose a whole, it is not necessary that the components of the whole exist all "at the same time or place":

> "If, as soon as several things are put together, we understand that one thing immediately originates, then those things are called *parts* and the latter *whole*. And it is not necessary that they all exist at the same time or place, but it is sufficient that they are considered at the same time. Thus, from all Roman emperors we compose simultaneously one aggregate."[19]

Later on, around 1690, the *composition* becomes even more general and evolves to the *real addition*, which strongly resembles what is now known in contemporary mereology as the "non restricted sum".

Leibniz calls *real* this kind of addition to distinguish it from the arithmetical one, and employs the symbol '$\oplus$' to designate it. Whereas in the case of arithmetical sum we have $A + A = 2A$, the real addition is *idempotent*, i.e. it obeys the law according to which $A \oplus A = A$.[20] Real addition, however, as the arithmetical one, is *commutative* and *associative*. Thus, we may summarize as follows the main properties of real addition:

$A \oplus A = A$ (idempotence);
$A \oplus B = B \oplus A$ (commutativity);
$(A \oplus B) \oplus C = A \oplus (B \oplus C)$ (associativity).

---

[18] Leibniz: *Logical Papers*, p. 141; A VI, 4 A, 832-33.
[19] A VI, 4 A, 627.
[20] On the differences between "real addition" and the arithmetical operation of sum in Leibniz, cf. W. Lenzen: "Arithmetical vs. 'Real' Addition. A Case Study of the Relation Between Logic, Mathematics and Metaphysics in Leibniz", in: N. Rescher (ed.): *Proceedings of the 5th Annual Conference in Philosophy of Science,* Lanham, MD 1989, pp. 149–57.

In Leibniz's words:

> "As general algebra [*speciosa generalis*] is merely the representation and treatment of combinations by signs, and as various laws of combination can be discovered, the result of this is that various methods of computation arise. Here, however, no account is taken of the variation which consists in a change of order alone, and AB is the same for us as BA. Next, no account is taken here of repetition; i.e. AA is the same for us as A. Consequently, whenever these laws are observed, the present calculus can be applied."[21]

Here, Leibniz characterizes "real addition" through the properties of *idempotence* and *commutativity* and is clearly thinking of an uninterpreted calculus susceptible of being applied to any domain of things, in which an operation corresponding to the 'real addition' may be performed and these two properties hold. This explains, for example, why in the essays based on 'real addition' he tends not to mention *terms* or *propositions*, referring, instead, to generic 'things': the letters employed in these essays stand, indeed, for any kinds of things which obey the rules of the calculus. Even though he does not mention explicitly the associative property, he usually employs it, taking its validity for granted.

In the more general calculus based on the relation of containment, the 'real addition' is clearly non-restricted:

> "Any plurality of things, such as A and B, can be taken together to compose one thing, $A \oplus B$, or, L."[22]

Further on, in the same essay, Leibniz emphasizes again the non-restricted nature of *real addition*:

> "[…] our general construction depends upon the second postulate, in which is contained the proposition that any term can be compounded with any term. Thus, God, soul, body, point and heat compose an aggregate of these five things."[23]

Leibniz also proves some theorems linking the operation of sum with the relation of containment. Theorem 5 of the *Not inelegant specimen of abstract*

---

[21] Leibniz: *Logical Papers*, p. 142; A VI, 4 A, 834.
[22] Leibniz: *Logical Papers*, p. 132; A VI, 4 A, 834.
[23] Leibniz: *Logical Papers*, p. 139; A VI, 4 A, 842.

proof, for instance, states that if *x* contains *y* and *x* contains *z*, then *x* contains the sum of *y* and *z*:

(Cxy & Cxz) → Cx(y ⊕ z).²⁴

Theorem 6 of the same work states that if *x* contains *y* and *w* contains *z*, then the real addition of *x* and *w* contains the real addition of *y* and *z*:

(Cxy & Cwz) → C(x ⊕ w)(y ⊕ z).²⁵

Around 1680, Leibniz begins to distinguish quite sharply between the relation of *inherence* or *containment* and the *part-whole* relation. The difference is clearly stated in an essay belonging to the group of essays I referred to at the beginning:

> "Not every inexistent is a part, nor is every container a whole. For example, a square inscribed in a circle and a diameter are in the circle; the square is a part of the circle, but the diameter is not a part of it. Something must therefore be added if the concept of whole and part is to be explained accurately […] Further, those inexistents which are not parts are not only in something, but can also be taken away. For example, the centre can be removed from a circle, in such a way that all the points except the centre remain. This remainder will be the locus of all points within the circle whose distance from the circumference is less than the radius; the difference between this locus and the circle is a point, namely the centre. In the same way you get the locus of all points which are moved if a sphere is moved whilst two separate points on its diameter are unmoved, if you take away from the sphere the axis, i.e. the diameter which goes through the two unmoved points."²⁶

As we read in another text, composed in the same years, to inhere are not only parts, but other things as well. A square inscribed in a circle and the side of the square, for instance, both inhere in the circle, but only the square, not the side, can be properly considered a *part* of the circle.²⁷ In the same text Leibniz remarks that to discriminate a *part* from what we simply inhere we need to take into account the property of *similarity* or that of *congruence*.²⁸

---

[24] Leibniz: *Logical Papers*, p. 126; A VI, 4 A, 850.
[25] Leibniz: *Logical Papers*, p. 126; A VI, 4 A, 851.
[26] Leibniz: *Logical Papers*, pp. 122–23; A VI, 4 A, 846–47.
[27] The circle and the square, indeed, are homogeneous: they have *two* dimensions, whereas the side of the square has only one dimension, and therefore it is not homogeneous with the circle.
[28] A VI, 4 A, 821

Later on, Leibniz considers mainly *homogeneity* as the property best suited to discriminate between simple inherence and parthood. In a text collecting several definitions, for instance, Leibniz writes: "In a more strict sense, the whole is taken as being homogeneous with the parts".[29]

3.

Whereas the relation of *inherence* can subsist even in cases of aggregate of completely heterogeneous things, the part-whole relation can be applied to homogeneous things only. Thus, homogeneity imposes a restriction on the relation of inherence, if we want to have a part-whole relation.

Leibniz's definition of *homogeneity* is quite stable over time and is strongly connected with that of *similarity*. In an essay written in 1687, we find a definition of *similarity* that Leibniz repeats in many other texts:

> "Similar are those things, which have the same attributes, i.e. those, which belong to the same lowest species, i.e. those which, considered in themselves, cannot be distinguished the one from the other."[30]

One of Leibniz's favorite examples to illustrate similarity is that of two circles different only in size. If a circle drawn on paper is presented to us and then another similar to the first differing only by virtue of a small difference in the diameter, it is quite probable that we will think that the same circle has been presented to our eyes twice. We are able, indeed, to discover that the two circles are different, only if we perceive both simultaneously, not successively, the one after the other.

Leibniz defines *homogeneity* by means of *similarity*:

> "*Homogeneous* are those things which are similar or may be made similar through a transformation."[31]

Leibniz here thinks of the *transformation* as analogous to a *continuous geometric* transformation (a translation, for example, of a figure on the Euclidean

---

[29] C, 476.
[30] A VI, 4 A, 872.
[31] GM VII, 30.

plane). The transformation goes in both directions, from homogeneous to similar things and from similar to the homogeneous ones:

> "All homogeneous things may be transformed into similar ones and all similar things may be made homogeneous by means of a transformation."[32]

In a marginal note to an essay written in 1685-86, however, Leibniz alludes to the possibility of expressing the notions of *part* and *homogeneity* without appealing to similitude and transformation, and says that this is exactly what he has done 'somewhere [*alicubi*]', without giving further references. We find an attempt to define homogeneity independently of similarity in a text written very early, probably in the year 1676:

> "*Homogeneous* are those things that agree, even though in different ways, in some form or nature intelligible in itself."[33]

In this case, Leibniz mentions as an example two things, one white and the other black, which agree in terms of some common nature, such as mass or corporeity.[34] In the *New Essays* (1702), homogeneity continues to be associated with the sharing of the same kind or genus:

> "Furthermore, one should distinguish between the *physical* (or rather real) genus and the *logical* (or ideal) genus. Things which are of the same physical genus, or which are 'homogeneous', are so to speak of the same *matter* and can often be transformed from one into the other by changing their modifications – circles and squares for instance."[35]

Agreement is evoked again with regard to homogeneity in the following passage, belonging to the years 1680–84:

> "*Homogeneous* are those things that agree [*conveniunt*] on the same thing on which both, any part of them whatsoever and the whole, agree as well."[36]

---

[32] A VI, 4 A, 418.
[33] A VI, 3, 483.
[34] A VI, 4 A, 483.
[35] A VI, 6, 63.
[36] A VI, 4 A, 418.

Occasionally, Leibniz speaks even of a *basis* for homogeneity: a *basis* in such a case is something that, existing in both, the part and the whole, is the reason of their similarity.[37]

Thus, according to these definitions, we may conclude that, for Leibniz, two 'things' are homogeneous if there is at least a property on which they agree. This condition, however, is too weak: as we have seen from a passage quoted above, Leibniz does not consider the property of being colored shared by three different things as sufficient to determine their homogeneity. Clearly, when considering homogeneity, we must think of some more substantive property, like mass or a specific nature, such as being a mineral, a vegetable or an animal.

Homogeneity is clearly reflexive, transitive and symmetrical:

(H.1) Hxx (every homogeneous thing is homogeneous with itself);

(H.2) $(Hxy \; \& \; Hyz) \rightarrow Hxz$ (if x is homogeneous with y and y is homogeneous with z, then x is homogeneous with z);

(H.3) $Hxy \rightarrow Hyx$ (if x is homogeneous with y, then y is homogeneous with x).

In short: homogeneity determines an *equivalence relation*.

Thus, because the relation of *parthood* arises from that of containment when container and contained are homogeneous, and because homogeneity determines an equivalence relation, it follows that even the relation of parthood is reflexive. Leibniz, however, does not explicitly endorse this claim and when speaking of parthood, he seems to be rather thinking of *proper parthood*. This clearly emerges, for example, from the following passage in the *New Essays*:

> "So it can truthfully be said that the whole theory of syllogism could be demonstrated from the theory 'de continente et contento', of container and contained. The latter is different from that of whole and part, for the whole is always greater than the part [...]."[38]

If Leibniz does not carefully distinguish *parthood* from *proper parthood*, in symmetrical fashion he doesn't put any emphasis on the distinction between *containment* and *proper containment*; he shows not very much interest in proper containment and parthood, but concentrates mainly on containment in

---

[37] A VI, 4 A, 310.
[38] A VI, 6, 486.

general and on the relation of proper parthood. Whereas, according to Leibniz, the relation of containment is *reflexive*, the proper part relation is not; in other words, everything contains itself and nothing is a proper part of itself.

We may conclude then, as one can easily infer from the following text, that the relation of *containment* or *inherence* is more general than that of *parthood*:

> "It is also clear that a part inheres in the whole, or, in other words, that as soon as a whole is given, a part is immediately given as well [...] Yet, there are things that inhere without being parts, as the points in a straight line [...] Therefore, a part must be homogeneous with the whole; and, for this reason, if there are two homogeneous things, A and B and if B inheres in A, A will be the whole and B the part."[39]

We may, therefore, define *Parthood*, and *Proper Parthood*:

(P.1) Pxy (x is Part of y) $=_{df}$ Cxy & Hxy (x contains y and x is homogeneous with y);
(PP.1) $PPxy$ (x is a Proper Part of y) $=_{df}$ Pxy & $\neg(x = y)$;

it follows that Parthood (P) too is reflexive, transitive and antisymmetric — a partial order:

(P.2) Pxx;
(P.3) $(Pxy \& Pyz) \rightarrow Pxz$;
(P.4) $(Pxy \& Pyx) \rightarrow x = y$.

By contrast, *Proper Parthood* (PP), turns out to be a *strict partial order*, as one would expect: that is, it is *not reflexive, transitive* and *asymmetric*:

(PP.2) $\neg PPxx$;
(PP.3) $(PPxy \& PPyz) \rightarrow PPxz$;
(PP.4) $PPxy \rightarrow PPxy$.

As we have Parthood and Proper Parthood, we may have Containment and Proper Containment – that is:

(PC. 1) $PCxy$ (x properly contains y) $=_{df}$ Cxy & $\neg(x = y)$.

---

[39] GM VII, 274.

From this it follows that, if x properly contains y and y is *homogeneous* with x, then *y is a proper part of x* (and vice versa):

(PP. 2) $PPxy \leftrightarrow PCxy \;\&\; Hxy$.

4.

At the beginning of the essays where Leibniz develops his mereological theory, he defines the relation of *sameness* or *coincidence*:

> "*The same* or *coincidents* are those things of which either can be substituted everywhere for the other *salva veritate*."[40]

In a less concise way:

> "Those things are *the same* if one of them can be substituted for the other without loss of truth. Thus, if there are A and B and A enters some true proposition and if on substituting B for A in some place in this proposition we have a new proposition, which is also true; and if this always holds good in the case of any such proposition, then A and B are said to be *the same*. Conversely, if A and B are the same, the substitution which I have mentioned will hold good. The same things are also called *coincident*. Sometimes, however, A and A are called *the same*, whereas A and B, if they are the same, are called *coincident*."[41]

As emerges from this quotation and from other analogous texts, Leibniz carefully distinguishes *identity* or *sameness* in the proper sense from *coincidence*. The sameness of A with itself is a case of identity in the proper sense, whereas if A and B are the same, with the expression $A = B$ Leibniz denotes coincidence.[42] Because Leibniz defines *coincidence* by means of the law of substitutability, we may represent it as follows:

(EQ) $EQxy$ (coincides *x with y*) $=_{\text{def}} \forall \varphi \, (\varphi(x) \leftrightarrow \varphi(y))$.

---

[40] Leibniz: *Logical Papers*, p. A VI, 4 A, 846.
[41] Leibniz: *Logical Papers*, p. 122; A VI, 4 A, 846.
[42] Cf. Raili Kauppi: *Über die Leibnizsche Logik*, Acta Philosophica Fennica, Fasc. XII, Helsinki 1960, pp. 71–76.

Therefore, with (C.1), (C.2), (C3), or alternatively with (C.1), (C.2), (EQ) Leibniz disposes of the basic ingredients sufficient to develop a classical mereology. The same holds for (P.1), (P.2), P.3) (or alternatively for (P.1), (P.2), (EQ)).

Coincidence (EQ) and Containment are connected:

> "*Proposition* 17. If A is in B and B is in A, then $A = B$. Things which contain each other coincide."[43]

Besides the relations of *Containment* and *Proper Parthood*, Leibniz employs in the essays we are considering other mereological relations as, for instance, the relation of *Communicating*, according to which two 'things' x and y are 'communicating' (*Commxy*) if they have something in common:

Commxy $=_{df} \exists z(Czx$ & $Czy)$ ("If some thing, M, is in A, and the same thing is in B, then it will be said to be common to them, and they will be said to be *communicating*").[44]

The relation of *Communicating* is analogous to that of *Overlapping* in contemporary mereology; whereas the following text strongly reminds us of the so-called *principle of supplementation*:

> "If A is in L, and another entity, N, should be produced, in which there remains everything which is in L except what is also in A (of which nothing must remain in N), A will be said to be 'subtracted' or removed from L, and N will be called the 'remainder'."[45]

Another important relation is that of *Disjointness*, (implicit in that of *Communicating*):

> "If some thing, M, is in A, and the same thing is in B, then it will be said to be *common* to them, and they will be said to be *communicantia*. If, however, they have nothing in common [...], they will be called *uncommunicating*."[46]

In other words, two things are *disjoint* if they have no part (proper or improper) in common.

---

[43] Leibniz: *Philosophical Papers*, p. 136; A VI, 4 A, 839.
[44] Leibniz: *Philosophical Papers*, p. 123; A VI, 4 A, 847.
[45] Leibniz: *Logical Papers*, p. 124; A VI, 4 A, 848.
[46] Leibniz: *Logical Papers*, p. 123; A VI, 4 A, 847.

Leibniz thinks of the operation corresponding to the sign '-' as the inverse of the *real addition*. Whereas the real addition denotes "a collection made of several things all taken simultaneously",[47] the sign '-' is employed to designate that something is removed from something else. It properly denotes the operation of *subtraction*:

> "Thus, if $A + B = C$ it will be $A = C - B$ and A is called remainder."[48]

Closely related to the operation of *subtraction* is the notion of *Nothing* that Leibniz introduces in *Axiom 2* of *A not inelegant Specimen*:

> "If the same is added and subtracted, then whatever is constituted in another as a result of this coincides with Nothing. That is, A (however often it is added in the constitution of some thing) - A (however often it is subtracted from the same thing) = *Nothing* [*Nihil*]."[49]

As Leibniz remarks, the *Nothing* does not change the things to which it is added or subtracted: "$A + Nothing = A$".[50] Therefore, we may designate the Leibnizian *Nothing* with the usual symbol '0'.

Now, given the theorem:

> "If something is added to something else, in which it is contained, nothing new is constituted; i.e. if B is in A, then $A + B = A$"[51]

because it also holds '$A + 0 = A$' and from all this it follows that '0' is contained in everything. But this amounts to saying that there exists at least an atom, contrary to what Leibniz firmly believes. Leibniz, however seems to be not aware of these consequences. He never states, for instance, that the 'Nothing' does in fact inhere in every part, even though, as we have seen, this follows from some very natural assumptions of his calculus. Clearly, Leibniz did not consider even the possibility that the *Nothing* could be an atom or something more than... just nothing: he is not interested in the trivial cases of inherence or parthood involving the 'null item'.

---

[47] A VI, 4 A, 819.
[48] Ibid.
[49] Leibniz: *Logical Papers*, p. 124; A VI, 4 A, 848.
[50] A VI, 4 A, 819.
[51] Leibniz: *Logical Papers*, p. 126; A VI, 4 A, 851.

In conclusion, all this shows that Leibniz possesses all the fundamental ingredients constituting what Achille Varzi in the entry *Mereology* of the *Stanford Encyclopedia of Philosophy* calls *core mereology*.[52]

5.

As we have seen, in the *Dissertation on the Combinatorial Art* Leibniz attempts to undermine the materialistic and anti-finalistic tendencies implicit in any classical atomistic account. When he writes the essays on mereology that we are now considering, what he calls 'my hypothesis of the monads' is already defined in its fundamentals. In these essays, Leibniz compares the monad to the geometrical point and the body to a segment; as the point is *in* the segment without being *part* of it, a monad is *in* the body, without being *part* of it. A segment is in a line (or in a bigger segment) and is a part of it, as well. This motivates Leibniz's distinction between the two mereological approaches, the one based on the relation of *Containment* and the other based on *Parthood*.

As Leibniz distinguishes *simple containment* from *parthood*, this distinction is paralleled in his metaphysics by that of *simple aggregates* and *wholes*. An aggregate is the sum of *non-homogeneous* things, while a *whole* is the sum of *homogeneous* things. From this it follows, for instance, that the world we are living in is a mere *aggregate*, not a whole, constituted by individual beings.

Even though Leibniz during his entire life denied the existence of atoms understood as the smallest parcels of matter of 'infinite hardness' and therefore not further divisible into parts, he never stopped flirting with atomism. In a text written during the years 1686-90, for example, he writes:

> "Those people who established the existence of atoms, saw only a part of the truth. They acknowledged, indeed, that we need to reach something that is one and indivisible in itself, as the basis of the multiplicity; but they were mistaken insofar as they sought unity in matter. And they believed it to be possible that a body exists which is truly one and an indivisible substance."[53]

---

[52] Cf. Achille Varzi: "Mereology", in: *The Stanford Encyclopedia of Philosophy* (Winter 2016 Edition), ed. by Edward N. Zalta, forthcoming URL = <https://plato.stanford.edu/archives/win2016/entries/mereology/>.
[53] A VI, 4 A, 1064.

Once Leibniz has converted the atoms of the classical atomistic doctrines into 'spiritual atoms' or 'soul-like' individual substances, he attributes to them the same role that the soul (form of the body) has in the Aristotelian philosophy. It is thus that the idea of a monad dominating a cluster of other monads playing the role of a body originates:

> "Everywhere there are simple substances actually separated from each other by their own actions, which continually change their relations. And each outstanding simple substance or monad which forms the center of a compound substance (such as an animal, for example), and is the principle of its uniqueness, is surrounded by a mass composed of an infinity of other monads which constitute the body belonging to this central monad, corresponding to the affections by which it represents, as in a kind of center, the things which are outside of it. The body is *organic* when it forms a kind of automaton or natural machine not only as a whole but also in its smallest observable parts."[54]

As Leibniz emphasizes on many occasions, matter in itself is devoid of unity. Every existing, material body belonging to our world is the result of an aggregation of soul-like atoms, that is of *monads*. The aggregate of monads, according to Leibniz, generates the corporeal body, but neither the aggregate nor each monad belonging to it, is *part* (proper or improper) of the body, even though the body itself can be part of another body (of 'some mass of matter'):

Clearly, even though an aggregate of these substances [monads] constitutes the body, they don't constitute it as parts, because the part is always homogeneous with the whole, exactly as the points aren't parts of the line. The organic bodies of the substances, however, which are contained in some mass of matter, are parts of this mass.[55]

Monads are simple, spiritual, and therefore indivisible beings. To each monad, God associates an aggregate of other monads, which constitute the *body* of the original monad. Only God, the 'monad of all monads', being a pure spirit, is without a body. Thus, the problem arises as to what is the principle or the main cause responsible for the aggregation of the monads constituting a body. Clearly, if we have to take seriously the analogy between points and monads, the juxtaposition or mere addition of simple monads cannot generate a body (as the addition of a plurality of points does not generate a segment or a line).

---

[54] Nicholas Rescher: *Leibniz's Monadology. An Edition for Students*, Pittsburgh, PA 1991, pp. 227–228.
[55] A VI, 4 B, 1671.

How an aggregate of simple, soul-like and indivisible beings, can produce an extended, material body is a serious problem for Leibniz, who attempts to solve it in ways that traditionally interpreters have found implausible or inconsistent (or both). Consider, for example, that because for Leibniz an absolute space does not exist, the notion itself of an 'aggregate' with its correlated activity of 'aggregating' or 'putting things together' cannot be understood according to its obvious spatial interpretation. Fortunately, the aim of the present paper is to investigate Leibniz's mereological doctrine and we may take for granted the constitution of the bodies out of an aggregate of monads, dispensing ourselves from inquiring about how Leibniz thinks that a given aggregate of simple monads does in fact produce a body.

Thus, let us simply assume the existence of material bodies. As we have seen, Leibniz overtly admits that a body can be part of another. Monads, instead, are not parts of a body, but they *inhere* in the body to whose coming into being they contribute:

> "Therefore, we need not to say that the indivisible substance enters the composition of the body as a part, but rather that it enters as an essential, internal requisite."[56]

Simple, indivisible substances (monads) are situated *in* the body, but they don't have a precise, recognizable location in it. We may only say that the monads constituting a body have a spatial situation by means of the body; they are entirely located where the body is, but we cannot determine in what portion of the body they are. Here, however, the analogy between point and line on one hand and monad and body on the other seems to fail. We are indeed able to find the exact situation of a point in a line, whereas we cannot do the same in the case of a monad in a body.

To briefly recapitulate the basic ingredients of Leibniz's ontology, we have:

1. simple monads;
2. clusters of simple monads;
3. simple monads associated with a cluster of other simple monads.

Leibniz calls *corporeal substances* the items corresponding to (3). As we have pointed out, it is quite puzzling how a concrete, material body emerges from

---

[56] A VI, 4 B, 1669.

an aggregate of simple, soul-like monads, but once we assume that the mysterious transformation has taken place, we may represent as follows the structure of the Leibnizian (existing) world.

Corporeal substances are the building blocks of two main types of aggregates: *simple* and those *with a dominant monad*. Simple aggregates are collections of corporeal substances lacking in unity, like a heap of stones. Of this nature are all inorganic bodies, as for instance a piece of metal, which receives its unity from our perceptions. Aggregates with a dominant monad, instead, are all organic bodies, i.e. all the aggregates possessing a unity in themselves, as in the case of animals and plants. Thus, a blade of a knife, which appears to us as perfectly smooth and without holes and fractures, is an aggregate of an infinity of other aggregates (of corporeal substances), which receives its unity by means of our imagination – a faculty that plays an essential role in our perception of activity. A fish, a man and a tree, instead, receive their unity by means of a monad that dominates their bodies. Therefore, all organic beings are 'animated' and they die – i.e. they cease to be *one* being, breaking down into a multitude of other corporeal substances – when the dominant monad detaches itself from the aggregate subordinate to it.

A peculiar feature of Leibniz's world is that organic bodies are the fundamental constituents of any other body, *inorganic* bodies included. As Leibniz claims on many occasions, if we could investigate the fine-grained structure of a slab of marble with the help of a very powerful microscope, we would discover a 'whole world of creatures':

> "66. From this one sees that there is a whole world of creatures – of organisms, animals, antelechies, and souls – even in the least piece of matter.
> 67. Every bit of matter can be conceived as a garden full of plants or a pond full of fish. But each branch of the plant, each member of the animal, each drop of its bodily fluids, is also such a garden or such a pond."[57]

It follows that 'every bit of matter' is composed of an infinity of items or parts. Therefore, Leibniz's mereology is *atomless*. This, however, seems at odds with the fact that, if we interpret as the *nullset* the *Nothing* of the calculus of 'real addition', we seem to be forced to conclude that the *Nothing* is a mereological atom. I don't think, however, that we are committed to this conclusion: to interpret the Leibnizian *Nothing* as the *null-set* is a mistake. It amounts to attributing to Leibniz ideas and theories of a logician of the 20th century.

---

[57] Rescher: *Leibniz's Monadology*, pp. 227–228.

Because of the presence of an immaterial principle that gives unity to bodies and to the elementary aggregates composing bodies, Leibniz's mereology is evocative of some kind of hylomorphism which probably has its roots in a remote influence of Aristotelian philosophy. From this point of view, Leibniz's mereological account presents some analogies with recent hylomorphic theories in the field of mereology, such as those proposed by Kathrin Koslicki or Thomas Sattig.[58] Leibniz's hylomorphism, however, is quite peculiar; in the last analysis, *matter* and *form*, i.e. the body and the dominant monad, are made of the same ingredients, namely monads. As Leibniz emphasizes on various occasions, simple substances are the only true substances, and everything else (i.e. aggregates) strictly speaking exist only by law.

---

[58] See Kathrin Koslicki: *The Structure of Objects*, Oxford 2008. Thomas Sattig: *The Double Lives of Objects*, Oxford 2015.

Thinking in the Age of the Learned Journal:
Leibniz's Modular Philosophy

Daniel Garber (Princeton, NJ)

Leibniz is not an easy thinker to study, at least for his philosophical and scientific work. Unlike other thinkers of his age, there is no single book or small number books that can be considered as presenting the central elements of his views, no *Meditationes* or *Principia philosophiae*, no *Ethica*, no *Essay* concerning *Human Understanding* or *Principia mathematica philosophiae naturalis* that you can turn to for an authoritative summary of Leibniz's considered thoughts. Instead, as readers of Leibniz, we have a multitude of texts to deal with. For those of us interested in Leibniz's philosophical and scientific projects, there are two books, one published, the *Essais de Théodicée*, and one not, the *Nouveaux Essais*. But neither of these can be accepted as canonical statements of Leibniz's thought. In addition, we have finished essays that appeared in learned journals, finished essays that were never published, unfinished essays, notes that may or may not be early drafts of essays, outlines of books never written, introductions to books never written, short notes written for his own use, thousands of letters written to numerous correspondents, marginal notes in books he was reading, and published reviews of books. Furthermore, these texts are spread over more than fifty years, starting in 1663 and going up until Leibniz's death in 1716.

There are a number of possible reactions to this state of affairs. One is to run quickly in the other direction. A number of my colleagues in the history of philosophy who have done excellent work on figures like Descartes or Spinoza have told me, in confidence, that they could never work on Leibniz: it is just too hard to put it all together, too many small pieces to read, remember and take account of. Spinoza is dense and often enigmatic, but then there are only four volumes of his complete work, something that you can read through many times. Another approach is to designate one or two of the works that Leibniz wrote as central, and use them as the key to interpreting his philosophy. In a way, this is what many of us do when we teach Leibniz's thought through the *Discours de métaphysique* and the *Monadologie*, using these two texts as our guide, and other texts simply as interpretative auxiliaries to these thought-to-be central texts. Another approach still is to try to create the single canonical work that Leibniz himself never wrote. This is Bertrand Russell's project in *A Critical Examination of the Philosophy of Leibniz* (1900 and 1937). Russell wrote:

> "The philosophy of Leibniz, though never presented to the world as a systematic whole, was nevertheless, as a careful examination shows, an unusually complete and coherent system [...] What is first of all required in a commentator is to attempt a reconstruction of the system which Leibniz should have written — to discover what is the beginning, and what the end, of his chains of reasoning, to exhibit the interconnections of his various opinions [...]."[1]

Claiming that Leibniz's thought "would have lent itself far better than Spinoza's philosophy to geometrical deduction from definitions and axioms," Russell presents his book as a kind of *Principia philosophiae leibnitianae more geometrico demonstrata*.

I want to resist all of these temptations. Instead I would like to look at the real Leibniz, as he thought and worked, and try to understand what the curious way in which he developed and made public his thought tells us about his intellectual temperament. I would like to begin by looking at a group of Leibniz's publications, essays and reviews that he published in learned journals. At the moment when Leibniz was just beginning to think and write seriously, in the 1660s, when he was in his late teens and early twenties, learned journals were just beginning to get off the ground: they were the new social media of their day. Much of Leibniz's work, starting in 1675 and going to the end of his life appeared in learned journals. I would like to suggest that this may give us some interesting insight into how Leibniz thought both about presenting his thought, and composing it.

I will begin with some background about the early years of the learned journal, and then turn to Leibniz and suggest some things we can learn by putting his work into this context.

The first learned journals were the *Journal des sçavans*, whose first published issue was 5 January 1665, edited by Denis de Sallo, and the *Philosophical Transactions of the Royal Society*, edited by Henry Oldenburg, Secretary of the Royal Society of London, which first appeared a few months later, on 6 March 1665. A number of years later, Otto Mencke founded the *Acta eruditorum*, which first appeared in Leipzig in 1682.[2]

---

[1] Bertrand Russell: *A Critical Exposition of the Philosophy of Leibniz*, London/New York 1992, pp. 1–2.
[2] On the history of learned journals in the early-modern period, see David Kronick: *History of Scientific and Technical Periodicals*, Metuchen, NJ ²1976; id.: *Scientific and Technical Periodicals of the Seventeenth and Eighteenth Centuries: a Guide*, Metuchen, NJ 1991; Thomas Broman: "Criticism and the Circulation of News: The Scholarly Press in the Late Seventeenth

A glance at the early issues of the *Journal des sçavans* gives an idea of what these early journals were like. The first issue of the *Journal des sçavans* in 1665 begins with a letter from the printer to the reader, outlining the purposes of the journal. The first goal listed is to give "an exact catalogue of the principal books printed in Europe." But the aim was not just a list: the editor wanted to give an account of what they contain, and their utility. In short, the goal was to give what were later to be called reviews of the books. The second goal of the journal was to publish éloges of celebrated scholars, including a bibliography of what they had published. The third was to publish information of scientific interest: physical and chemical observations and experiments, new discoveries, like new machines, as well as observations of the heavens, the earth, and anatomy. Fourthly, the journal sought to inform the reader of legal matters, both secular and ecclesiastical, both in France and outside, as well as the censures coming from universities, both in France and outside. And finally, it sought to contain everything that takes place in Europe worthy of the curiosity of Men of Letters.[3]

The first year of the *Journal des sçavans* was very heavy on the book reviews, which took up the bulk of the *Journal*. (This included a review of the first ""issues of the *Philosophical Transactions of the Royal Society*, which appeared in the very last issue.) But there were ten articles of sorts, including the relation of the birth of a baby with two heads and four arms,[4] some notes on comets,[5] the first part of which is a report on a seminar at the Collège de Clermont in Paris, and éloge to Fermat, who had died in January 1665 (pp. 69–72),[6] and other topics, including a bit of news about the discovery of new writings by Marius Mercator, a theologian who was a contemporary of St. Augustine. A typical form for these sections was a letter or an extract of a letter. The

---

Century", in: *History of Science* 51 (2013), pp. 125-150. For a catalogue of periodicals of the period, see Robert Gascoigne: *A Historical Catalogue of Scientific Periodicals, 1665-1900: with a Survey of their Development*, New York/London 1985. On the *Journal des sçavans* and the *Philosophical Transactions*, see Roger Philip McCutcheon: "The *Journal des Scavans* and the *Philosophical Transactions* of the Royal Society", in: *Studies in Philology* 21 (1924), pp. 626–28; Thomas Broman: "Criticism and the Circulation of News: The Scholarly Press in the Late Seventeenth Century", in: *History of Science* 51 (2013), pp. 125–150. On the *Acta eruditorum*, see Hub. Laeven: *The "Acta Eruditorum" under the Editorship of Otto Mencke (1644–1707). The History of an International Learned Journal between 1682 and 1707*, Amsterdam/Maarssen 1990.

[3] "L'imprimeur au lecteur", in: *Journal des sçavans*, 5 January 1665, unpaginated.
[4] *Ibid.*, pp. 11–12.
[5] *Journal des sçavans*, 26 January 1665, pp. 41-48; *Journal des sçavans*, 2 February 1665, pp. 58–60.
[6] *Journal des sçavans*, 9 February 1665, pp. 69–72.

volume published ten years later, in 1675 looked quite similar, except this time it included twenty-one such pieces that were not book reviews, including Leibniz's first publication in a learned journal. (It is also worth noting that many of the scientific bits are translations from the *Philosophical Transactions*, which, by 1675, was a well-established journal.) The books reviewed in both of these volumes range over a considerable variety of subject matters, including the sciences, history, literature, theology, and horticulture. The book reviews are sometimes serious discussions, but for the most part are simply reports of what the books contain. The *Philosophical Transactions* and the *Acta eruditorum* were different from one another. The *Philosophical Transactions*, for example was more scientific in its orientation than the *Journal des sçavans*. But even so, in many ways their contents were very similar to that of the *Journal*.

The contents of the *Journal des sçavans* shows numerous traces of the literary forms from which it derived. First of all, there is the tradition of the newspaper, which begins in the early seventeenth century. Important here is Théophrast Renaudot's *Gazette*, first published in Paris on 30 May, 1631.[7] The news in the *Journal des sçavans* is more literary than it is political, but even so, it is news, and sees itself reporting to the community, the Republic of Letters, information that is as vital to it as the reports in the newspapers may be to merchants. Another ancestor of the *Journal* are the semi-public letters that circulated in the Republic of Letters through the mediation of figures like Marin Mersenne in Paris and Henry Oldenburg in England. These letters enabled members of learned Europe to find out what others were thinking and doing.[8] It is not accidental that many of the early contributions to the *Journal des sçavans* were published in the form of extracts of letters. One imagines that people recognized that print was a much more efficient way of circulating letters than hand copying them. Another possible model for the *Journal* may have been the *Centuries* published by Renaudot in the 1630s and 1640s. These were collections of reports of the *conférences* Renaudot held at the *Bureau*

---

[7] On the early history of the newspaper, see Andrew Pettegree: *The Invention of News*, New Haven 2014. On Renaudot and his Gazette, see Howard Solomon: *Public Welfare, Science, and Propaganda in Seventeenth Century France. The Innovations of Théophraste Renaudot*, Princeton 1972, chapters IV and V.

[8] On the circulation of learned correspondence, see the excellent project and website, *Cultures of Knowledge: Networking the Republic of Letters, 1550–1750*, directed by Howard Hotson (Oxford), which is attempting to analyze and map the networks of correspondence in the early modern period: http://www.culturesofknowledge.org/.

d'Adresse where both scholars and ordinary people could come and express their opinions on a wide variety of views on subjects ranging from the absurd to the sublime, from scientific to social.[9] And finally, there were a number of published volumes in the period before the *Journal des sçavans* first appeared which were largely collections of recent ideas by a variety of authors, including both letters and short treatises. I have in mind here collections edited by Mersenne, such as the *Cogitata physico-mathematica* (Paris 1644) or the *Chymical, Medicinal and Chyrurgical Addresses Made to Samuel Hartlib, Esquire* (London 1655). What is emerging in these texts and in the journals that they gave rise to is the idea of a journal article.

What does this have to do with Leibniz? Now, Leibniz wrote and sometimes published in a number of formats. He did, of course, publish a number of books. There is, of course, the *Essais de Théodicée* (1710), published toward the end of his life. But there is also the *Dissertatio de arte combinatoria* (1666), the *Nova methodus discendae docendaeque jurisprudentiae* (1667), the *Codex juris gentium diplomaticus* (1693), the *Novissima sinica* (1697), the *Scriptores rerum Germanicum* (1700–1711), and others. (There are also a number of smaller independently published writings, including the *Theoria motus abstracti* (1671) and the *Hypothesis physica nova* (1671), among others, more pamphlets than books.) And among books Leibniz wrote but never published there are, of course, the *Dynamica* and the *Nouveaux essais*. But with the exception of the *Essais de Théodicée*, all of the books he actually succeeded in publishing were in law, history, or politics. In areas like philosophy, natural philosophy, and mathematics, virtually all of the things Leibniz published were essays, and where he published was in learned journals. (In fact, one might argue that even the *Théodicée* itself can be regarded as a collection of shorter pieces, themselves not unlike journal articles.)

When Leibniz was young, and just beginning to write, learned journals were just emerging. He must have been an enthusiastic reader of the journal literature from early on. Leibniz himself began contributing in 1675. His publication started slowly: one article in 1675, two in 1677, two in 1678, one in 1681. But starting in 1682, hardly a year went by without publishing at least one, but often a large number of articles in learned journals. So far as I can see, the only year in which he published nothing is 1688. This is more than made up for by 1692, when he published thirteen articles or 1693 and 1710

---

[9] See, e.g., Solomon: *Public* Welfare, chapter III.

when he published sixteen. In his lifetime, he published a total of almost 200 articles in learned journals.[10] In addition we can identify fifty-six anonymous reviews he wrote and published, almost all in the *Acta eruditorum*.[11]

Leibniz's first publication was in the *Journal des sçavans*, 25 March, 1675, in the "principe de justesse des horloges portatives de son invention." This was followed a month later, on 26 April 1675 by a translation of the same article in the *Philosophical Transactions*. Leibniz would go on to publish only one more piece in the *Philosophical Transactions*, in 1699, despite being a member of the Royal Society. But the *Journal des sçavans* became one of his favorite places to publish, with a total of twenty-eight pieces, plus one more in the *Journal des sçavans, supplement,* two in the Amsterdam edition of the *Journal des sçavans*, and four in the *Nouveau Journal des sçavans*. But far and away the bulk of Leibniz's contributions were published in the *Acta eruditorum*. Starting in the year of its founding in 1682, Leibniz published sixty-nine pieces there, plus two more in the *Deutsche acta eruditorum.* In addition, there were scatterings of pieces in a number of other journals, including the *Miscellanea Berolinensia* (fifteen), the *Mémoires de Trévoux* (twelve), and many others.[12]

Leibniz published some of his most important pieces philosophy and mathematics in journals. In philosophy there are the "Meditationes de cognitione, veritate, et ideais (1684, *Acta eruditorum*), "De primae philosophiae emendatione" (1694, *Acta eruditorum*), the "Système nouveau" (1695, *Journal des sçavans*), "De ipsa natura" (1698, *Acta eruditorum*), the "Considérations sur les principes de vie" (1705, *Histoire des ouvrages des sçavans*), as well as a series of responses to Pierre Bayle's critiques of his philosophy. Among the important technical papers are the "Unicum opticae, catoptricae, et dioptricae principium" (1682, *Acta eruditorum*), the first presentation of the new calculus in the "Nova Methodus" (1684, *Acta eruditorum*), the "Brevis

---

[10] I take my numbers from the chronological index in the marvelous edition, G. W. Leibniz: *Essais scientifiques et philosophiques. Les articles publiés dans les journaux savants*, 3 vols., ed. by Antonio Lamarra and Roberto Palaia, Hildesheim/Zürich/New York 2005, vol. 3, pp. 1319–34.

[11] The reviews are listed in Emile Ravier: *Bibliographie des œuvres de Leibniz*, Hildesheim 1966, pp. 93–107. Though the reviews in the *Acta eruditorum* were published anonymously, the authors can be identified with some confidence due to a small number of copies of the *Acta* that survive with annotations due to the original editors. See Laeven: *The "Acta eruditorum"*, chapter VI. In addition to the 56 reviews Ravier lists, he also notes that Leibniz contributed a few reviews and a number of shorter comments on books (in German) to Eckhardt's *Monatlicher Auszug*. See Ravier: *Bibliographie*, pp. 92, 108–114.

[12] See "Index des journaux", in: Leibniz: *Essais scientifiques et philosophiques*, pp. 1337–50.

demonstratio" (1686, *Acta eruditorum*) and the exchanges that constitute the beginning of the so-called vis viva controversy, the "Tentamen de motuum coelestium causis" (1689, *Acta eruditorum*), and the "Specimen dynamicum" (1695, *Acta eruditorum*). For readers who didn't have the benefit of access to Leibniz's personal correspondence (and that was most readers), these published essays constituted the way in which they had access to Leibniz's thought. But they also represented the limits of people's knowledge of his thought. One of the striking things about Leibniz's publications is that the theory of monads plays almost no role in the published writings: monads are mentioned only rarely, and almost always in such vague terms that it is virtually impossible to infer the central role that they play in his metaphysical thought.[13] Writing to Leibniz on 5 May 1714, Nicolas Remond remarked that a friend of his "spoke rightly when he compared the knowledge we have of your system of monads to that which one would have of the sun by the single rays that escape the clouds that cover it."[14] He was right to complain. The clouds were only lifted in 1620 and 1621, after Leibniz's death, when the "Monadologie," written at least in part in response to Remond's questions, though never sent to him, appeared in print first in German (1720) and then in Latin (1721), both translations of the original French.[15]

What does it mean to publish in this form, as an article in a learned journal? First of all, the articles are reasonably short. And because of that, they can either address a small and well-defined problem, or, if they are outlining a larger project, it must be only in fairly broad and general terms. There is no room for a detailed development of a larger body of material, as there would be in a book. This is the way Henry Oldenburg characterized his hopes for the new *Philosophical Transactions* in his preface to the third year:

---

[13] For an account of discussions of monads as found in Leibniz's published writings, see Daniel Garber: "Monads and the *Theodicy*: Reading Leibniz" in: Larry Jorgensen/Samuel Newlands (eds.): *New Essays in Leibniz's Theodicy*, Oxford 2014, pp. 218–32.
[14] GP III, 616.
[15] On the history of the first publication of the "Monadologie", see Antonio Lamarra/Roberto Palaia/Pietro Pimpinella: *Le prime traduzioni della Monadologie di Leibniz (1720–1721)*, Florence 2001. The original French version did not appear until many years later, in G. W. Leibniz: *Opera Philosophica*, Berlin 1840, vol. 2, pp. 705–712, though a translation of the text into French from one of the earlier translations did appear earlier in Jacques-André Émery: *Esprit de Leibniz, ou, Recueil des pensées choisis, sur la religion, la morale, l'histoire, la philosophie. &c.*, Lyon 1772, vol. 2, pp. 499–535.

> "I think, I may safely assume, that in these *Fragments*, something hath been contributed to sowe such seeds, as may somewhat conduce to the illustration and improvement of Philosophy, and of all Laudable and Useful Arts and Practices."[16]

It is interesting here that Oldenburg characterizes the essays published in the *Philosophical Transactions* as "fragments," incomplete parts of a larger whole.

A second feature of the journal article is the fact that it is relatively self-contained. That is, it is the sort of writing that can be read on its own: in principle, it contains all of the information necessary for a member of the target audience to understand without going outside of the bounds of the essay itself. Now, the reference to the "target audience" is important here: the author of an article on mathematics or physics in the period could assume that the reader would have had an acquaintance with the main lines of contemporary mathematics, or with Descartes' laws of nature, etc. But unlike a chapter in a book, for example, it is generally not assumed that the reader has read the author's other writings, and knows how the essay may fit into the author's larger project in the way in which the reader of a chapter can be expected to have read the previous chapters of the book. Now, it is not entirely true that these articles are completely self-contained. As journal culture developed, there were more and more in the way of exchanges. That is, an essay published could give rise to a response, which may, in turn, give rise to the original author's response to the response, and so on. But even then, the exchange is relatively self-contained in the sense that you don't have to go outside of the journal to follow what is going on.

Both of these characteristics fit Leibniz's intellectual temperament very well. Leibniz's thought is unified and systematic; the different parts of his thought are closely interconnected and make up a systematic whole. But, at the same time, Leibniz tends to develop his thought in a fragmentary way, fragment by fragment. The bulk of his writings, published and unpublished are developments of small and fragmentary parts of the system.

This way of working, I think, derives from at least two features of Leibniz's intellectual temperament. First, I think that Leibniz thought of himself as a "big ideas" person, someone who had the big ideas and left it to others to

---

[16] Henry Oldenburg: "A Preface to the Third Year of These Tracts," in: *Philosophical Transactions*, no. 23, March 11, 1666, pp. 409–15, here p. 409.

work out the details. This is what Fontenelle wrote about Leibniz's mathematical work in his Éloge, a passage the echoes the comments of Oldenburg I quoted earlier:

> "He didn't publish any body of mathematical works, but only a quantity of detached pieces, of which he could have made books, if he had wanted […]. He said that he liked to see the plants for which he had furnished the seeds growing in other people's gardens. These seeds are often more important than the plants themselves […]."[17]

What Fontenelle had in mind is his strategy in publishing the calculus. The mathematical program was first publically announced in the "Nova methodus" in the *Acta eruditorum* in 1684. But what he published there was only a very brief article, which gave only some of the basic rules of his new calculus. The details were only developed later and published by the Bernoulli brothers and by the Marquis de L'Hospital. But it wasn't just the mathematics that Leibniz thought of in that way. In September 1696, Leibniz wrote the following letter to Michelangelo Fardella:

> "I hope that this doctrine can be embellished (*illustrari*) and great illumination added to a variety of my philosophical ideas by you, just as the mathematics or analysis I discovered was wonderfully advanced by the Marquis de L'Hospital and the brothers Bernoulli […]."[18]

This comes at just the moment when we know that Leibniz was beginning to develop his theory of monads, and give up the metaphysics of corporeal substance. What he was asking was for Fardella to help him develop his theory of monads in all its details, in the way in which L'Hospital and the Bernoulli's helped him finish the calculus. Fardella turned him down, and there is reason to believe that Leibniz didn't get around to developing the monadological metaphysics in a systematic way until 1714 with the composition of the "Monadologie" and the "Principes de la nature et de la grâce."

A second feature of Leibniz's intellectual temperament is that it is what might be considered his "modularity". What I mean is this. Even though his philosophy makes up a systematic whole, Leibniz develops it in independent units that can be developed independently of the whole and presented in co-

---

[17] Bernard Le Bouvier de Fontenelle: *Eloges des academiciens avec l'histoire de l'Academie royale des sciences en M. DC. XCIX*, The Hague 1740, tome I, pp. 448–49.
[18] Leibniz to Michaelangelo Fardella, 3/13 September 1696; A II, 3, 193.

herent ways, even when separated from the whole. In this way, Leibniz's system can be considered as a complex machine, a clock, say, where the wheels, the regulator, the spring, etc. can be designed and fabricated independently of one another, yet function together as an interconnected whole. Indeed, Leibniz the clockmaker can make improvements in one part of the complex clockwork, develop a new kind of regulator, say, without having to alter the rest of the machinery. And while all of the pieces of Leibniz's philosophical clockwork are intended to hang together in a coherent whole, at least some of them are explicitly fashioned so that they can be considered independently of the Leibnizian philosophy and adapted to other philosophical contexts. The hypothesis of pre-established harmony, for example, works as well in a Cartesian metaphysical dualism as it does in Leibniz's own system. Similarly, Leibniz's solution of the problem of evil does not require the metaphysical idealism of his later monadological metaphysics, and can be held in the context of a variety of other metaphysical positions. Indeed, the fact that Leibniz was able to publish essays on a wide variety of his metaphysical and physical thought while barely mentioning the theory of monads suggests a philosophy made up of relatively independent moving parts. In this way we can think of Leibniz's philosophy as composed of coherent blocks that can be considered independently of one another, even if they contribute to a larger Leibnizian structure. If this is, indeed, his intellectual strategy, it is not surprising that Leibniz wrote in smaller fragments, or that he was attracted to publishing in the learned journals of his day.

Did the journal culture shape Leibniz's thought? Or was Leibniz attracted to the journal culture because it fit his temperament? Might he have written differently if he had the option to develop ideas through a blog instead? It is impossible to say for sure. But I do think that we can understand Leibniz better if we place his thought in the context of the crucial literary innovation of the early-modern period, the learned journal.

Öffentlicher Abendvortrag

Individualität bei Leibniz

Volker Gerhardt (Berlin/Hamburg)

> „Ich weiß, dass ich ein großes Paradox unternehme, wenn ich versuche, in gewisser Weise die alte Philosophie wieder zu Ehren zu bringen, und die fast verbannten substanziellen Formen wieder in ihr altes Recht zu setzen."[1]

1. Es gehört zu den bereits aus der Antike überlieferten Einsichten der Philosophen und der Ärzte, dass sich Individuelles nicht eindeutig in Begriffe und auch nicht in Diagnosen fassen lässt. *Individuum est ineffabile*[2] ist eine Sentenz, die sich sinngemäß bereits bei Platon und Aristoteles findet und der sowohl mittelalterliche Scholastiker wie auch neuzeitliche Denker eine Wahrheit abgewinnen konnten.

Goethe machte den Ausspruch in seiner heute üblichen lateinischen Fassung populär[3] und Schiller übertrug ihn in die Wendung von der Unaussprechlichkeit der Seele.[4] Einigen Romantikern wurde er zu einer Art Glaubensbekenntnis, das ihnen die Abkehr von den Klassikern erleichterte – Goethe und Schiller eingeschlossen. Und in eben diesem Sinn wurde das Diktum im 20. Jahrhundert zur Abwehr der systematischen Erwartungen des philosophischen Denkens genutzt.

So hat sich Heidegger des Satzes bedient, um damit, wie inzwischen jeder wissen kann, seiner Flucht aus der Philosophie ein rational erscheinendes Motiv zu geben;[5] und Adorno hat darauf seine Abwehr der „Herrschaft" des Begriffs über das „Nicht-Identische" gegründet.[6]

Zum Gestus dieser Abkehr hätte es nicht kommen können, wenn die Philosophie aus dieser von ihr selbst maßgeblich betonten und auch immer wieder begründeten Einsicht, den Schluss gezogen hätte, den ihr Heidegger

---

[1] Gottfried Wilhelm Leibniz: *Discours de Métaphysique*, § 11; A VI, 4 B, 1544.
[2] Sinngemäß: „Das Individuelle ist niemals vollständig zu erfassen."
[3] Brief an Lavater vom 20. September 1780. Dazu: Dirk Kemper: *Ineffabile. Goethe und die Individualitätsproblematik der Moderne,* München 2004.
[4] Im Distichon „Spricht die Seele, so spricht, ach! schon die Seele nicht mehr".
[5] Dazu: Josef Wohlmuth: „Chalkedonische Christologie und Metaphysik", in: Markus Knapp/Theo Kobusch (Hrsg.): Religion-Metaphysik(kritik)-Theologie im Kontext der Moderne/Postmoderne, Berlin/New York 2001, S. 333–354, hier 340.
[6] Theodor W. Adorno: *Negative Dialektik*, Frankfurt a. M. 1966.

und Adorno angeraten haben. Doch sie wusste es besser und hat, bei allem Respekt vor der Einmaligkeit des Einmaligen, das Begreifen nicht aufgegeben. Auch angesichts der Tatsache, dass die Welt voller Individuen ist, wird ihr Geschäft, ihre *Welt* (und keineswegs bloß ihre *Zeit*!) „in Begriffe zu fassen", nicht sinnlos.

Das Begreifen muss auch nicht notwendig zur *Selbstverleugnung* oder zur *Gewalttat* führen. Denn nur im Bewusstsein der Tatsache, dass es Unbegreifliches gibt, kann das Geschäft des Begreifens betrieben werden. Mindestens das können wir von Leibniz lernen, und mir liegt daran, uns vor Augen zu führen, dass dies keine Kleinigkeit ist.

2. Leibniz weiß genau, was mit: *Individuum est ineffabile* zum Ausdruck gebracht wird. Doch indem er die damit bezeichnete Grenze des Begreifens markiert, gibt er an, wie mit der darin liegenden Erkenntnis philosophisch umzugehen ist: In den *Nouveaux Essais* heißt es:

> „So paradox dies auch erscheinen mag": […] „es ist uns unmöglich, von den Individuen eine Erkenntnis zu haben und ein Mittel zu finden, die Individualität einer Sache exakt zu bestimmen, es sein denn, dass man sie selbst bewahre, denn alle Umstände können wiederkehren."[7]

Die als theoretisch denkbar hinzugefügte Kondition der „Bewahrung" des Individuums, bis „alle Umstände wiederkehren", meint nichts anderes als die Leistung der ewigen Wiederkehr des Gleichen, die abzuwarten dem Menschen nicht vergönnt ist – wenn es sie denn überhaupt geben sollte. Also bleibt es unter den endlichen Bedingungen unseres Lebens bei der Einmaligkeit des Auftritts eines jeden Individuums; strenggenommen kann es nur unter diesen Bedingungen als wirklich einzigartig angesehen werden. Die Unmöglichkeit seiner vollständigen Erkenntnis, seine „Unaussprechlichkeit" ist ein unverrückbarer Tatbestand.

Bereits der irreale Zusatz der ewigen Wiederkehr lässt ahnen, dass es eine mit der Natur unseres endlichen Daseins verbundene Bedingung gibt, an der die Unerkennbarkeit des Individuellen hängt: nämlich der Umstand, dass für uns auch die Welt, in der uns Individuen begegnen, *individuell* verfasst ist. Dieser Umstand schließt die für uns selbst nicht unbedeutende Tatsache ein, dass *wir selbst*, wir, denen es um *Erkenntnis* geht, *endlich* und folglich selbst *individuell* – und somit *nicht vollständig erkennbar* – sind!

---

[7] *Nouveaux Essais*, Buch III, Kap. 3, § 6; Deutsch nach der Werkausgabe von Wolf von Engelhardt/Hans Heinz Holz, Darmstadt 2013, Band III/2, 42/43; A VI, 6, 289.

Damit erhält das zunächst so beiläufig, ja, geringfügig erscheinende *epistemische Problem* der stets unvollständig bleibenden Erkenntnis des Individuellen eine *metaphysische Dimension*, die auch ein sich nur auf Gegebenes beschränkender Positivist nicht leugnen kann: Das Individuum kann von einem anderen Individuum, also von *seinesgleichen*, allein schon deshalb nicht vollständig erkannt werden, weil es sich selbst nur unvollständig e*rkennt*. Die Unvollständigkeit seiner *Selbsterkenntnis* aber schließt die Unvollständigkeit seiner *Welterkenntnis* ein.

Wenn wir uns nun mit dieser augenblicklich ins Offene des Daseins gesprengten Perspektive nicht nur auf das zu erkennende *Individuum*, auch nicht nur auf *unsere eigene Individualität als Erkennende*, sondern auch auf die damit bereits eingestandene *Unvollständigkeit unserer Welterkenntnis* einstellen, kann uns die unmittelbar nachfolgende Bemerkung in den *Nouveaux Essais* nicht mehr überraschen:

„Das Bedenkenswerteste ist dabei, dass die Individualität das Unendliche einschließt, und nur derjenige, der fähig ist, sie zu begreifen, könnte die Kenntnis des Prinzips der Individuation für diese oder jene Sache besitzen."[8]

3. Damit ist *jedes Individuum selbst* als der Ausgangspunkt exponiert, den wir zum Verständnis der uns mitunter so fremd, so phantastisch und so überschwänglich erscheinenden Metaphysik dieses nicht nur *universal gebildeten*, sondern auch *umsichtigen, nüchternen, exakten, detailversessenen* sowie stets auch *auf den Nutzen bedachten* Denkers benötigen. Dass wir dabei selbst *konsequent* zu sein haben, sollte sich im wissenschaftlichen Zusammenhang von selbst verstehen. Und um unter dieser Voraussetzung auch den Zugang zu der heute meist verlegen belächelten *metaphysischen Dimension* seines Denkens zu finden, brauchen wir nur, wie es in der *Metaphysischen Abhandlung* heißt, *sincere et serieuse*, nur „weltoffen und ernsthaft" zu sein, so dass wir auch das *Interesse an uns selbst* und an der *Welt* nicht verleugnen müssen,[9] und schon

---

[8] Ebd.
[9] Ich führe hier schon die Bedingungen ein, die ihren über die methodologische Funktion hinausgehenden existenziellen Sinn erst in der Ausgestaltung des Gottesgedanken entfalten kann (*Discours de Métaphysique*, § 36; A VI, 4 B, 1587). Leibniz spricht hier vom Willen des Menschen, wie Gott ihn vom Menschen erwarten kann: Der Wille zum Guten soll „offen und ernsthaft" (sincere et serieuse) sein. Damit wird gefordert, dass er sich weltoffen verhält und sich seiner existenziellen Verantwortung bewusst ist. Hinzu kommt die passionierte Hingabe an das Ganze, also die Liebe (amour) zu Gott. Gegenüber der Welt kann man so wenig gleichgültig sein, wie gegenüber sich selbst. Die Rede von Gott hat den Vorzug, dieser Affektion ein ihr entsprechendes Gegenüber zu geben.

können wir nicht bestreiten, dass die *Unendlichkeit* nicht erst an den Grenzen des Alls oder im infinitesimalen Abstand zwischen mathematischen Größen, sondern bereits *in uns selbst* beginnt.

Die ganze Vermessenheit der Rede von der *Welt*, der *Natur*, der *Gesellschaft* oder von der Existenz oder Nicht-Existenz *Gottes* ist dadurch vorgegeben, dass wir – trotz allem – immerhin sicher sein können, dass wir uns selbst als *Individuum* bezeichnen.

4. So ist es Leibniz selbst, der uns auch mit Blick auf den Kosmos seines Denkens zu der Feststellung nötigt, dass sich zu seinem Werk so viele Zugänge eröffnen, wie es Leser seiner Schriften gibt. Dem sich gern selbst als „modern" begreifenden Leser bietet das Pathos der Individualität, das sich im metaphysischen Denken von Leibniz eine umfassende Perspektive auf die Welt eröffnet, einen besonders naheliegenden Zugang. Und tatsächlich kann nur der *individuelle Ausgangspunkt* verständlich machen, warum es in dieser rationalen Konstruktion, die das Individuum zu seinem Selbst- und Weltverständnis braucht, auch *am Ende* des *Individuums* bedarf, das die Kaskade von Fragen nach dem Sinn mit einer glaubwürdigen Antwort versehen kann. Wenn es das *Individuum* ist, das sich im *Universum* spiegelt, muss ihm im *Ganzen* auch ein Wesen gegenübertreten, in dem es sich, und zwar in seiner *zum Ganzen passenden besten Verfassung*, wiedererkennt – und darin seine Unerkennbarkeit notdürftig kompensiert.

Dazu muss ihm im Ganzen freilich auch die *Gelegenheit* geboten werden. Und dass wir sie tatsächlich geboten bekommen, zeigt sich bereits in der *Tatsache unserer Erkenntnis*, die es uns ermöglicht, in Übereinstimmung mit den von uns verwendeten Dingen, mit unserer Umgebung sowie mit unseresgleichen am Leben zu bleiben und *tätig* zu sein. Da der *epistemisch, kommunikativ* und *praktisch* erschlossene Gesichtskreis eines Individuums nicht in Widerspruch zum Ganzen seines Daseins stehen kann, sollte auch nicht in Zweifel stehen, dass es die Chance zum Leben und zum Erkennen nur in Übereinstimmung mit diesem Ganzen haben kann.

Das Ganze ist eine universale Einheit, die der Mensch nicht gemacht hat und auf die er keinen berechenbaren Einfluss hat. Aber es muss ihm, wie Leibniz immer wieder betont, „*entsprechen*"; ja, in dieser gegenseitigen Entsprechung, auf die jeder bereits in seinem auf die Welt bezogenen Selbstbewusstsein setzt, versteht der Mensch sich selbst, so als „kommuniziere" er nicht nur mit seinesgleichen, sondern auch mit dem Ganzen. Also ist es naheliegend, dieses durch uns selbst und auf uns selbst bezogene Ganze als etwas anzusehen, dass uns zwar unendlich überlegen ist, aber im anspruchsvollen Bewusstsein eines jeden Einzelnen als *gleichartig* empfunden und sogar –

trotz der mit Blick auf beide Seiten bestehenden Erkenntnisgrenzen – als etwas ihm *Nahes* begriffen wird.

Also kann es nicht verwundern, dass Leibniz dieses Ganze mit dem *Namen Gottes* auszeichnet, von dem das ihm zugewandte Individuum Aufschluss über die Fragen erwartet, die sich ihm in der Welt stellen. Jedenfalls erschließt sich in dieser Angewiesenheit des erkennenden Individuums auf das Ganze der Welt,[10] warum es in ihr einen *gnädigen Gott* erkennt, der dem Einzelnen allererst die Möglichkeit gewährt, so zu sein, wie er ist.

5. Bis heute ist die Meinung verbreitet, das Individuum komme erst in der Neuzeit vor. Insbesondere in den Klagen über den Werteverfall, die Partikularisierung und Entsolidarisierung der modernen Gesellschaft wird dem als bindungslos begriffenen Individuum die Schuld am Zerfall der mittelalterlichen Ordnung gegeben, womit dann alles das folgen kann, was viele bis heute irritiert: Die Glaubensgegensätze, die angeblich unaufhaltsame Säkularisierung, der allein auf die Freiheit des Individuums gegründete Liberalismus und der von ihm auf die Welt losgelassene Kapitalismus.

Wäre es so, stünde Leibniz noch ziemlich am Anfang dieser Entwicklung und ihm käme das Verdienst zu, besonders hellhörig für einen Begriff, für etwas zu sein, das am viel beklagten Unglück der Moderne ursächlich beteiligt ist. Also hätte man einen besonderen Grund zu fragen, ob das, was folgte, in seinem Sinne ist.

Doch damit wäre zugleich das Problem aufgeworfen, wie es kommt, dass dieser für die Moderne derart aufgeschlossen Denker offenbar keinen Ehrgeiz hatte, in der *Querelle des Anciens et des Modernes* besonders fortschrittlich zu erscheinen; warum es ihm wichtig ist, der schon damals auf ihre Progessivität bedachten zeitgenössischen Philosophie, in zentralen Fragen zu widersprechen; und man hätte Mühe zu verstehen, warum er so beredt für die Überlegenheit substanztheoretischer Annahmen alter Schule wirbt?

---

[10] Dies könnte der einzige Punkt sein, an dem ich nicht mit Heinrich Schepers meisterhafter Kurzfassung der Metaphysik von G. W. Leibniz übereinstimme. Vgl. Heinrich Schepers: *Die sich selbst und ihre Welt konstituierende Monade*, Deutsch – Englisch – Französisch – Spanisch (= *Hefte der Leibnizstiftungsprofessur* 28), hrsg. v. Wenchao Li, Hannover 2016. Wenn nämlich Schepers sagt: „Denn Welten sind kein Ganzes, sind vielmehr nichts als Gemeinschaften miteinander verträglicher voll ausgebildeter Möglichkeiten" (ebd., S. 11). Vor dem Hintergrund der möglichen Vielfalt von Welten ist Schepers Aussage verständlich. Denn das wahrhaft alles umfassende Ganze muss auch das Insgesamt aller Möglichkeiten einbeziehen. Doch ändert nichts daran, dass auch die von Schepers benannten „Gemeinschaften miteinander verträglicher voll ausgebildeter Möglichkeiten" ein Ganzes ist, das es aus der Perspektive des zugehörigen Individuums notwendig als Einheit zu begreifen ist – ganz so wie das Individuum selbst ein Ganzes ist, obgleich keineswegs alles Reale und auch nicht alles Mögliche zu ihm gehört.

Erklärungsbedürftig wäre dann vor allem, was Leibniz veranlasst hat, ausgerechnet den *Individualitätsbegriff* zum Fundament einer Metaphysik zu machen, die, als sie im Laufe des 18. und des 19. Jahrhunderts bekannt wurde, als so rückständig empfunden wurde, dass sie mit ihrer Konzeption der fensterlosen *Monade* oder ihrer (dem Leid der Menschen anscheinend Hohn sprechenden) *Theodizee* nur Kopfschütteln und Spott ernten konnte?

Doch über die Motive der Verschränkung eines angeblich *modernen Begriffs* mit einer vermeintlich *rückständigen Philosophie* brauchen wir hier nicht zu spekulieren. Denn der *historische Auftritt des Individuums* erfolgt lange vor dem didaktischen Epochenschnitt zwischen *Medivium* und *Moderne*, mit dem sich die Historiker ihre Arbeit erleichtern: Tatsächlich meldet sich das Individuum bereits mit den ersten schriftlichen Aufzeichnungen vor nahezu 5000 Jahren zu Wort – zunächst als das Wesen, von dem in *Urkunden, Katastern, Gerichtsurteilen* und *Handelsdokumenten*, in *Tempel-* und *Grabinschriften* die Rede ist, dann aber auch als das vor vielen anderen ausgezeichnete Individuum, das über die singuläre, Zeit und Raum überbrückende Fähigkeit verfügt, das Geschriebene in Keilschrift in Ton zu ritzen oder in Hieroglyphen in Stein zu meißeln oder auf Papyrus zu malen.[11]

Es sind die über *Schrift* und *Recht*, über *Archive* und *Ahnentafeln*, über *bildende Kunst* und *lehrhafte Religionen* verfügenden *Zivilisationen im afroeurasischen Raum*, in denen Wert darauf gelegt wird, von *Individuen* Zeugnis abzulegen, um sie *öffentlich* in Erinnerung zu halten. Dazu gehören die Berichte vom Erfolg oder Scheitern exemplarischer Menschen.

Besonders bewegend sind die kunstvollen Klagen Einzelner über die Ungunst ihres Schicksals. Hier lässt sich an erster Stelle das *Gilgamesch-Epos* aus der Mitte des dritten vorchristlichen Jahrtausends nennen. Etwas später haben wir aus dem *Mittleren Reich der Ägypter* die ergreifende Beschwerde des von den Steuereintreibern in den Ruin getrieben *Oasenmanns* oder das wie von einem modernen Existenzialisten verfasst Poem eines *Lebensmüden*.

Danach folgen Schübe besonderer Aufmerksamkeit für das Individuum. Etwa in der Blütezeit Athens oder im Rom der Zeitenwende. Die Tragiker bringen mit dem Chor auch das Individuum auf die Bühne; mit Sokrates

---

[11] In kaum einem vollständig erhaltenen Schriftstück verzichtet ein der Keilschrift kundiger Schreiber darauf, sich seiner Kunst zu rühmen und seinen Werdegang – unter Aufzählung seiner gesellschaftlichen Stellung – zu schildern. Um die Individualität des Schreibers zu exponieren, ist immer Platz. Das gilt übrigens auch für die Kunstwerke des frühen Mittelalters, in dem die Individualität angeblich noch gar nicht ausgebildet war.

tritt dann ein Individuum auf den Markt, das dem Philosophieren seinen existenziellen Ernst verleiht; und Platon versteht es, daraus eine neue Literaturgattung zu machen, die dem Individuellen nicht nur in seinen rationalen Erwartungen, sondern auch in seinen Schwächen und Schrullen gerecht zu werden versucht. So werden die auf die individuelle Wahrnehmung, die Korrespondenz von Ich und Du und vor allem auf die eigene Einsicht gegründete Selbst- und Welterkenntnis zum Fundament einer Lehre vom *Wahren*, *Schönen* und *Guten* entwickelt. Sie hat, wie wir wissen, auf Leibniz besonderen Eindruck gemacht.

Ein weiterer historischer Schub erfolgt mit der Ergänzung des Wissens durch den *Glauben* im *Evangelium* des *Neuen Testaments*. Was darin, natürlich nicht ohne den Einfluss des durch die Griechen und Römer kultivierten Denkens, als *Offenbarung* festgehalten ist, verlangt einen dem Wissen nicht entgegenstehenden *Glauben*, der auf einer *intuitiv erfahrenen Wahrheit* beruht, eine *existenzielle Konsequenz* erfordert und mit einem *Gefühl* verbunden ist, deren individuelles Erleben unbestreitbar ist. Dieses Gefühl ist die *Liebe*.

Es kann gar nicht in Frage stehen, dass Leibniz seine Metaphysik in der durch Sokrates und Jesus initiierten, durch Platon und Paulus vermittelten Tradition versteht. Dem gegenüber ist das, was durch die nachfolgende Entwicklung in *Mystik* und *Nominalismus*, durch die *Künste* und *Techniken der Renaissance*, durch die *Kanonisierung des Wissens* im *Humanismus* nichts grundlegend Neues, sondern so, wie wir es Erasmus und Morus, Melanchthon, Montaigne und Lipsius[12] verdanken, eine Verstärkung der Impulse, die er aus Antike und christlicher Botschaft empfangen hat.

Das gilt auch für das auffällig nachwirkende Echo, das die *Gnadenlehre* des Reformators in der Metaphysik von Gottfried Wilhelm Leibniz findet. Es kann gar kein Zweifel sein, dass dieser in der katholischen Welt besonders anerkannte, um ihre Probleme jederzeit kenntnisreich bemühte Gelehrte als ein Paradefall ökumenischer Praxis gelten kann. Und dennoch ist er im Tableau konfessioneller Differenzen ein *Protestant* geblieben. Gleichwohl hat er seine tiefe metaphysische Einsicht in die menschliche Angewiesenheit auf die *Gnade* nicht primär von Luther, sondern vielmehr aus derselben Quelle, aus der auch der Reformator geschöpft hat: Aus dem paulinischen Verständnis des christlichen Evangeliums, das gleich auf doppelte Weise durch exzeptionelle

---

[12] Zu Justus Lipsius siehe: Michael Stolleis: „Lipsius-Rezeption in der politisch-juristischen Literatur des 17. Jahrhunderts in Deutschland", in: Ders.: *Staat und Staatsräson in der frühen Neuzeit. Studien zur Geschichte des öffentlichen Rechts*, Frankfurt a. M. 1990, S. 232–267.

Individuen vermittelt wurde: Durch den Nazarener Jesus und den auf dramatische Weise bekehrten Apostel Paulus, der als der erste gelten kann, der die Individualität der Glaubenserfahrung auf das Niveau einer universellen Verkündigung im Bewusstsein der Toleranz gehoben hat.[13]

6. Das historische Schlaglicht auf die Zivilisationsgeschichte des Individuums gibt keinen Anlass zu der Annahme, dass Leibniz einer – wie auch immer gefassten – „Modernität" der Individualitätskonzeption bedurfte, um das Individuum in den Rang eines Zentralbegriffs seines Philosophierens zu erheben.[14] Er war seiner Zeit verbunden, indem er als *Jurist* und *Diplomat* auf ihre aktuellen Herausforderungen reagierte und – im Anschluss an das im *Westfälischen Frieden* erstmals erprobte Modell juridisch versicherter, multilateraler Verständigung – den *Anteil sachkundiger Mitwirkung* zu erhöhen suchte.

Dass er dabei das *Interesse der Öffentlichkeit* in kluger Dosierung zur Geltung zu bringen vermochte, belegt seine Aufmerksamkeit für die neuen *bürgerlichen Ansprüche* an die Politik, die er jedoch nicht unter die Bedingung unmittelbarer Beteiligung gestellt sehen wollte.[15] Darin war er sogar der gegenwärtigen Politikergeneration überlegen, die dem Irrtum anhängt, eine Entscheidung sei umso besser, je breiter die sogenannte „Basis" ist, die darüber befindet. Von Leibniz' Begriff der Repräsentation wäre heute viel zu lernen.

Die Feststellung, dass Leibniz in seinen *einzelwissenschaftlichen Beiträgen*, vornehmlich zur *Mathematik*, auf der Höhe seiner Zeit gestanden hat, kommt einem nur deshalb nicht leicht über die Lippen, weil nach seinen Beiträgen eigentlich nichts mehr so war wie zuvor. Er hat das disziplinäre Niveau gehoben und damit einen Fortschritt bewirkt, von dem die Wissenschaften bis heute zehren.

Darin kann ihm kein anderer Philosoph das Wasser reichen. Man müsste ihn schon in eine Reihe mit Thales und Pythagoras stellen, um den Rang zu veranschaulichen, der ihm gebührt. Und damit zeigte sich in vollem Umfang, wie lächerlich es wäre, ihn auf das zweifelhafte Podest der *Moderne* stellen zu wollen.

---

[13] Zu Jesus siehe: *Discours de Métaphysique*, § 37; A VI, 4 B, 1588; zu Paulus ebd. § 31; A VI, 4 B, 1580.

[14] In der heutigen Rede von der Moderne schwingt inzwischen immer schon die Erwartung ihres Endes mit. Das trifft auf die Vertreter des Humanismus und der Aufklärung noch nicht zu.

[15] Das habe ich in meiner Betrachtung „Die Öffentlichkeit der Wissenschaft" zu zeigen versucht, in: *Hefte der Leibniz-Stiftungsprofessur*, Bd. 26, Hannover 2013, S. 33–51.

Anders ist es mit seinen ausgedehnten *technischen Interessen*. Mit ihnen repräsentiert er einen neuen Typus des Erkennenden, der die Einsicht auch durch *Erfindungen* voranbringen will. Dafür haben *Ökonomen*, *Architekten*, *bildende Künstler*, *Ärzte* und *weltreisende Naturforscher* seit der Renaissance wiederholt Beispiele gegeben. Ohne Beispiel sind hingegen die sprachwissenschaftlichen Studien, die Leibniz in den Dienst einer globalen Verständigung zu stellen sucht.

In den Zusammenhang von *Lebensleistung*, *experimenteller Technik* und *Wissenschaft* gehört auch, dass Leibniz dem *Nutzenkalkül* eine basale epistemische Funktion zugesteht, die er nicht dadurch abschwächt, dass er im Vorhinein den möglichen *Missbrauch* zum Hindernis erklärt. Hier denkt er wie *Montaigne*, der weiß, dass man nur etwas wirklich Gutes auch effektiv missbrauchen kann.[16] Wer angesichts der Leibniz wohlbekannten Weltlage eine *Theodizee* verfasst, hat sich auf die denkbar gründlichste Weise mit der Technikfolgenabschätzung befasst und deutlich gemacht, dass der endliche menschliche Verstand nachteilige Folgen im Voraus nur in beängstigend engen Grenzen ausmachen kann. Freilich: Wo immer er es zu können glaubt, sollte er den mutmaßlichen Schaden abzuwenden suchen.

7. Also hilft uns auch der Blick auf die großen Leistungen des *Juristen*, *Mathematikers*, *Physikers*, *Ingenieurs* und *Historikers* Gottfried Wilhelm Leibniz wenig, wenn wir klären wollen, warum er in der für ihn vorrangigen philosophischen Disziplin, der *Metaphysik*, dem *Begriff der Individualität* eine derart zentrale Stellung einräumt.

Die Zeitumstände und die aktuelle szientifische Problemlage bieten uns die gewünschte Aufklärung jedenfalls nicht. Und so müssen wir im *Discours de Métaphysique* sowie in den nachfolgenden *philosophischen Schiften* nach einer *systematischen Antwort* suchen, so verdächtig sie den Zeitgenossen des 20. und 21. Jahrhunderts auch sein mag.[17] Tatsächlich fällt sie nicht einfach aus, kann aber dazu beitragen, unser eigenes Selbstverständnis zu fördern.

Um die philosophische Antwort einzuleiten, muss man daran erinnern, dass Leibniz mit dem anfangs auch von ihm favorisierten neuzeitlichen *Er-*

---

[16] Montaigne: *On ne peut abuser que de choses qui sont bonnes* (*Essais* II, VI: De *l'exercitation*).
[17] Ich beschränke mich im Folgenden auf den *Discours de Métaphysique*. Die Parallelen zu *Monadologie* und zu den *Principes de la Nature et la Grace, fondées en Raison* sind offenkundig.

kenntnismodell des Nominalismus nicht zufrieden ist. Er hält es für nicht geeignet, die Eigenart von zu erkennenden *Einheiten* und *Ganzheiten* adäquat zu erfassen.

Leibniz meint vor allem, dass die zu seiner Zeit bereits zum *Sensualismus* gesteigerte nominalistische Prämisse, nach welcher der erkennende Verstand nur das feststellen kann, was ihm *sinnlich gegenwärtig* ist, nicht ausreicht. Denn die Vernunft kann gar nicht umhin, etwas für den Menschen *Wesentliches* zu erkennen, das der allein auf die Wahrnehmung durch die Sinne vertrauende Verstand gar nicht aufzunehmen in der Lage sei. Bei aller unter dem Anspruch der Exaktheit zu beklagenden Unerkennbarkeit enthält unser Begriff von uns selbst und von der Welt wesentlich mehr als ihm durch das Erkenntnismodell des Sensualismus zugestanden werden kann.

Als siebzehnjähriger Student hatte Leibniz bereits 1663 eine Magisterarbeit vorgelegt, in der er unter dem Titel *De Principio Individui* die Schwierigkeiten einer Herleitung von Aussagen über *Individualia* und *Universalia* erörtert.[18] Anlass ist die damals ihren Siegeszug antretende nominalistische Herleitung aller Aussagen aus der sinnlichen Erfahrung.[19] Leibniz kann, was auch der Titelbegriff des *Prinzips der Individuation* anzeigt, der Fundierung aller Erkenntnis auf sinnliche Daten einiges abgewinnen; doch er äußert Zweifel und begründet sie anschaulich durch die niemals allein durch die Sinne verbürgte *Singularität des Sokrates*. Außerdem fragt er, wie es möglich sein soll, die über alle sinnlichen Grenzen hinausgehenden Aussagen der Mathematik allein aus Sinnesdaten abzuleiten.

Er glaubt also nicht, dass man auf die Wirksamkeit von *universalia ante rem* verzichten kann und trifft damit das Problem, auf das der Nominalismus selbst nur dann eine Antwort hat, wenn er auf eine konsequente Anwendung des Primats der Sinne verzichtet.[20]

---

[18] *Disputatio Metaphysica De Principio Individui.* (Disputation unter der Leitung von Jacob Thomasius) Leipzig am 30. Mai 1663; A VI, 1, N. 1. – Das entscheidende Moment findet sich in: § 23; A VI, 1, 17.
[19] Wie gut er sie kennt, führt er dann in den nachgelassenen *Nouveaux Essais* vor. Er lässt die nominalistische Grundposition für die empirischen Wissenschaften gelten, nicht aber für das metaphysische Wissen von der Natur des Lebendigen. Hier bahnt sich eine Unterscheidung an, von der Kant in der Kritik der Urteilskraft Gebrauch macht und die letztlich schon den epistemischen Grund für seine Willenslehre liefert.
[20] Wie wenig ihn der sensualistische Grundsatz: Nihil est in intellectu, quod non ante fuerit in senso überzeugt, legt Leibniz 23 Jahre später in seinem *Discours de Métaphysique* dar. Seine vielfältigen Verpflichtungen als europäischer Wissenschaftsdiplomat erlauben ihm in diesen

Gleichwohl gesteht Leibniz 23 Jahre später, dass er in der Beschäftigung mit physikalischen Problemen und geometrischen Beweisen den Grundannahmen des Nominalismus nahe steht.[21] Dort, wo es lediglich um die Fragen der *Ausdehnung*, der *Gestalt* und der *Bewegung* von Körpern sowie um ihre *exakte Vermessung* geht, da reicht die äußere Betrachtung völlig aus. Hier bietet sie der wissenschaftlichen Erkenntnis sogar eindeutige Vorteile, weil sie die Aufmerksamkeit auf das konzentriert, was für den *technischen Umgang mit den Dingen* und für den *nützlichen Einsatz des Wissens* ausreicht.

In den Fragen der positiven Beschaffenheit natürlicher oder technisch hergestellter Gegenstände, in der Untersuchung ihrer Bewegung in Raum und Zeit, sowie in der Beschreibung und Nutzung der äußeren Natur reicht es somit aus, sie in ihrer *physisch, geometrisch* und *arithmetisch berechenbaren Beschaffenheit* zu erfassen.

Doch der *technische Umgang mit den Kräften der Natur* ist nur das eine. Das andere und philosophisch Entscheidende ist das Verständnis der äußeren Dinge *im Verhältnis zum Verstehenden* selbst. Das beginnt für Leibniz bereits mit dem Begriff der *Kraft*, die er qualitativ von den messbaren und lediglich relativen Größen der Ausdehnung, der Gestalt und der Geschwindigkeit[22] unterscheidet, um ihr einen nicht relativen, einen „realen", oder, wie er auch sagt, einen „realeren" Status zuzuschreiben.[23] Warum? Weil sie eine *echte,* eine *ursprüngliche Wirkungsgröße* sei.

Was damit gemeint ist, wird zumindest im ersten Zugang deutlich, wenn Leibniz diese Wirkungsgröße in anderen Zusammenhängen als „lebendige Kraft" bezeichnet. Das ist eine Kraft, die nicht von außen angestoßen wird, sondern „von innen", zumindest also aus der *internen Organisation lebendiger Wesen* heraus wirkt.[24]

Jahren nicht, den lediglich handschriftlich verbreiteten Text, zu veröffentlichen. In seiner Argumentation aber ist er vollendet und so finden wir hier die Grundlegung für die Auffassung, die ihm später die Abfassung der Schriften über die Monade, die Gnadenlehre und die Theodizee erlauben.

[21] *Discours de Métaphysique*, § 11; A VI, 4 B, 1544.
[22] Vgl. *Discours de Métaphysique*, § 18; A VI, 4 B, 1559.
[23] Ebd., Z. 7: „plus reel".
[24] Was damit gemeint ist, macht der junge Kant deutlich, wenn er sechzig Jahre später eben das Problem erörtert, das Leibniz im *Discours de Métaphysique* zur Veranschaulichung seiner Abkehr vom Alleinvertretungsanspruch des nominalistischen Mechanismus anführt: Auch Kant spricht von „lebendigen Kräften", die in der Massenanziehung und in der Beschleunigung wirken. Ihm ist bewusst, dass er in diesem Punkt dem um ein philosophisches Verständnis der Kraft bemühten Leibniz folgt. Vgl. Immanuel Kant: *Gedanken von der wahren Schätzung der*

Im *Discours* deutet Leibniz diese vielversprechende Eigenart der Kraft nur an.[25] In ihrer inneren Dynamik eröffnet dieses von ihm und später von Kant und Hegel, aber seitdem leider viel zu wenig genutzte Verständnis der Kraft: die Möglichkeit, die *Natur als Ganze* als ein *System lebendiger Kräfte* zu denken.

Das scheint bis heute, trotz der bereits vor einiger Zeit proklamierten „Wende" zu den Lebenswissenschaften, ein befremdlicher Gedanke zu sein. So basiert die aktuelle Verwendung des Begriffs „Naturalismus" unverändert auf einem rein *mechanischen Naturverständnis*, das die größere Zahl der gegenwärtigen Philosophen mit dem guten Gewissen strenger Wissenschaftlichkeit vertritt, und es damit einer kleineren Zahl von Fachvertretern leicht macht, an irgendeiner älteren Spielart eines dualistischen Idealismus festzuhalten.

Beide Fraktionen sollten beachten, dass sie damit nicht mit der Zustimmung von Leibniz rechnen können, der sein Beispiel von der *Kraft* als einer „realen" Wirkungsgröße zu einer entschiedenen Abgrenzung von „den Modernen" nutzt, die uns, wie er sagt, „einreden wollen", dass alles, was sich von Körpern sagen lässt, in der „Ausdehnung und deren Modifikationen" besteht.[26]

Das geht direkt gegen Descartes und macht noch einmal deutlich, wie wenig uns mit einer Herleitung des Begriffs der Individualität aus den Konstellationen der Moderne geholfen ist. Es macht zugleich aber deutlich, dass auch die Individuen sowohl in ihrer Einheit wie auch in ihrer wechselseitigen „Entsprechung" (*s'entrerépondence*) zum Ganzen der Natur gehören.

8. Leibniz geht es also um die *Einheit der Natur* und die *Einheit der in ihr wirkenden natürlichen Wesen*. Und beides kann nur gedacht werden, wenn die *Einheit des Ganzen der Natur* mit der *Einheit der sie ausmachenden Elemente* zusammenstimmt. Das heißt: Sie müssen nach einem jederzeit wirksamen Prinzip zusammenstimmen.

Mit der Berufung auf das Prinzip scheidet ein nur gelegentliches Übereinstimmen, wie es in den kosmischen Umläufen einer *ewigen Wiederkehr* gedacht werden kann, definitiv aus. Deshalb bleibt Leibniz auf die *Gegenwart des Gegebenen* bezogen und gewinnt alle Verbindlichkeit, die sich auch in der

---

lebendigen Kräfte (1747). Die Schrift versucht, die Kraft, im Unterschied zur gemessenen Ausdehnung und zur Geschwindigkeit, als etwas Lebendiges anzusehen. Und in diesem Versuch schließt Kant an die Überlegungen von Leibniz an.
[25] *Discours de Métaphysique*, § 22; A VI, 4 B, 1564–1566.
[26] *Discours de Métaphysique*, § 18; A VI, 4 B, 1559.

sinnlichen Gewissheit definitiv nicht findet, aus der aktualen begrifflichen Entsprechung zwischen dem *Ganzen der Natur* und dem jeweiligen *Ganzen ihrer einzelnen Glieder*.

Den Status eines solchen sich als *Einheit* erweisenden *Gliedes der Natur* haben alle *einzelnen Wesen*, in denen die Kraft als ein *von innen wirkender* Impuls zum Ausdruck kommt. *Sie wirken aus sich selbst* und müssen insofern als *spontan* und *frei* begriffen werden.[27] Also haben wir in ihnen die nicht nur *zur Natur gehörenden*, sondern sie in ihrer Eigenart, ja, sie in ihrer „Verfassung" allererst „konstituierenden",[28] sie systematisch tragenden *Kraftzentren*, die in ihrem lebendigen Zusammenhang das Ganze der Natur nicht nur ergeben, sondern *bewegen* und durchgängig *lebendig* halten.

Diese *sich selbst bestimmenden Zentren sich selbst ausdrückender Kraft* sind die *Individuen*. Ihre Eigenart besteht nicht allein in ihrer *Singularität*, also nicht bloß darin, dass sie sich jeweils an *einem Ort*, zu einer *bestimmten Zeit* und mit einem *spezifischen Quantum an Kraft* befinden.[29] Es ist vielmehr erst ihre *Selbstbezüglichkeit*, in der sie *als Ganze*, also unter konzentrierter Einbindung *aller ihrer Organe* selbst als Einheit wirksam werden. Und darin kann sie mit Gewissheit erkannt werden.

Wie sich das zeigt, führe ich gerade (in meinem Reden und Sprechen) vor: Es mag ja richtig sein, dass in der Präsentation meines mündlichen Vortrags wesentlich meine *Lunge*, meine *Zunge* und meine *Lippen* zum Einsatz kommen; gewiss tragen auch meine *Augen* und *Ohren* und meine gestikulierenden *Hände* ihren Teil dazu bei; und da ich hier stehe, haben auch meine *Beine* ihren Anteil an dem, was ich zum Ausdruck bringe. Freilich: Mit einer alle physischen, physiologischen und psychischen Details einbeziehenden Exaktheit kann ich das nicht erkennen.

Dennoch fühlte ich mich missverstanden, wenn in der Diskussion ein kundiger Arzt aufstehen würde, der die Leistung der primär beteiligten Organe für medizinisch unauffällig erklären und sich dann wieder setzen würde, als sei damit alles Wesentliche zu meinem Vortrag gesagt.

---

[27] *Discours de Métaphysique*, § 32; A VI, 4 B, 1581.
[28] *Discours de Métaphysique*, § 21; A VI, 4 B, 1563.
[29] Diese Kriterien führen lediglich zu einem physischen Verständnis von Identität und Individualität, wie sie im Anschluss an Kants Anschaulichkeitstheorem vielfältig diskutiert worden ist. Als das individualisierende Medium gilt hier die Anschauung, die begrifflich Erfasstes mit einer eindeutigen Raum-Zeit-Stelle versieht und dadurch einmalig macht. Das genügt dem von Leibniz angelegten Maßstab für Individualität ausdrücklich nicht. Individualität verlangt einen reflexiven Selbstbezug, in dem sich die Reflexivität des Ganzen, d.h. sein geistiger Charakter spiegelt.

Es ist vielmehr so, dass ich *selbst* über etwas spreche, das zur Welt gehört und von dem ich hoffe, dass es auch von anderen Individuen verstanden werden kann. Dabei lege ich das ganze Gewicht meiner *Person* in den sachlichen Gehalt und die sprachliche Form meiner Ausführungen. Mit dem Begriff des *Selbst* erhebe ich Anspruch auf eine in meiner Wirksamkeit zum Ausdruck kommende *Einheit*, die der Einheit derer entspricht, die für diesen Ausdruck in dem von mir gemeinten Sinn empfänglich sind. Und mit Blick auf die *Selbsterkenntnis* unter den Konditionen gemeinsamer Weltbewältigung, wie die Vernunft sie uns ermöglicht, genügt das auch.

Es ist somit eine gleichermaßen *korrelative* wie *korresponsive* Totalität, die im unauffällig-beiläufigen Nomen des Selbst auf den Begriff gebracht wird. Das *Selbst* bündelt unterschiedliche Aktivitäten aus dem Ganzen des von ihm, vom Selbst, zwar nicht vollständig erkannten, aber eindeutig repräsentierten organischen *Körpers* und bringt sie zum *einheitlichen Ausdruck*, der aber nur von *seinesgleichen verstanden* und nur unter dieser *kommunikativen Bedingung* in eine *allgemeine Bedeutung* überführt werden kann.

9. *Das Selbst ist das Signum der Individualität.* Das solcherart Umschriebene verweist auf die Einheit, die es Leibniz ermöglicht, von der „Substanz" zu sprechen, und es ihm leicht macht, sie immer wieder auch als *Person* zu bezeichnen. Das muss nicht heißen, dass alle von ihm derart ausgezeichneten und dann als „*Monaden*" benannten individuellen „Substanzen" *ich* sagen und den Anspruch erheben können müssen, als *Personen* respektiert zu werden.

Die Rede vom Selbst gibt lediglich zu erkennen, nach welchem *Modell* die Individuen konzipiert sind und wie wichtig es ist, die nach dem *personalen Selbstverständnis* vorgestellte *spezifische Wirkungsweise* der Monaden zu beachten. Das erleichtert es uns dann auch, den *Monaden*, so wie wir das von menschlichen Individuen hinlänglich kennen, durchaus unterschiedliche *Grade von Bewusstheit* zuzuschreiben.

Schließlich muss auf allen Stufen des Bewusstseins eine Bedingung erfüllt sein, ohne die kein Selbst präsent und wirksam werden kann – eine Bedingung, die im sensualistisch angeleiteten Skeptizismus notorisch vergessen wird, ohne die es jedoch unmöglich wäre, überhaupt vom Selbst zu sprechen:

Zum sinnvollen Gebrauch des Begriffs des Selbst – und somit bereits zu seinem Selbstverständnis – gehört die *Gegenwart von seinesgleichen*. Das Selbst kommt nur im Gegen- und Miteinander mit gleichgearteten (wenn ich so sagen darf) anderen „Selbsten" zur Geltung! Es ist somit ein durch und durch *soziales Modell von der Natur*, nach deren *Einheit* Leibniz sowohl in deren *individuellen Elementen* wie auch in deren alles *umfassender Ganzheit* sucht.

Die implizite Sozialität der Natur wird offenkundig, wenn man auf die Wendungen achtet, in denen Leibniz die Ausdrucks- und Wirkungsformen beschreibt, über welche die Individuen selbsttätig verbunden sind: Sie „entsprechen" sich (*s'entrerépondre*),[30] sie „korrespondieren" (*corréspondre; corréspondance*),[31] handeln in einem sie gemeinsam verbindenden „Sinn" (*bon sens*),[32] und sie „spiegeln" sich (*miroir*)[33] sowohl ineinander wie auch im Ganzen.

Und dieses Ganze wird nicht als physischer Zwangsverband unter der Determination von Ursache und Wirkung, sondern als eine *Personalunion*, als ein auf *Freiheit* gegründetes „Reich" gedacht,[34] das unter einer einsichtigen „Verwaltung" (*l'oeconomie generale*) steht.[35]

Die ist möglich, weil die im sozialen Ganzen der Welt verbundenen Individuen sich wechselseitig bedingen. Sie fordern *und* fördern sich in ihrem Zusammenhang als lebendige Wesen, in dem sie jeweils nur *als Ganze* auf einander reagieren können. Sie „begrenzen" und sie „beeinträchtigen" sich dabei durchaus, und insofern wirken sie auch „aufeinander ein". Sie sind, wie Leibniz sagt, „genötigt [...], sich einander anzupassen" (*s'accommoder entre elles*).[36] Doch die Einheit der beteiligten Ganzheiten bleibt in jedem einzelnen Fall gewahrt, obgleich sich ihr Einfluss und ihre Selbstschätzung ändern können – und dies nicht nur in Korrelation zu den Einwirkungen aus der unmittelbaren Nachbarschaft, sondern auch durch den „Eindruck", den das Ganze selbst, also diese vorgestellte Gesamtheit aller Einheiten im Ganzen auf sie macht.

Darin zeigt sich die von Leibniz als „wunderbar" (*miraculeuse*) bezeichnete Wirkungsweise Gottes, die niemals direkt, niemals schlagartig von außen (oder gar von „oben") auf uns niedergeht, sondern nur als *Eindruck*

---

[30] *Discours de Métaphysique*, § 14; A VI, 4 B, 1550, Z. 17.
[31] Ebd., 1551, Z. 2.
[32] Ebd., Z. 4.
[33] *Discours de Métaphysique*, § 35; A VI, 4 B, 1585, Z. 11.
[34] *Discours de Métaphysique*, § 35; A VI, 4 B, 1584f.
[35] *Discours de Métaphysique*, § 21; A VI, 4 B, 1563, Z. 18.
[36] *Discours de Métaphysique*, §14; A VI, 4 B, 1591, Z. 3f. – Monaden haben zwar keine „Fenster" und „Türen"; sie lassen also weder Licht noch frische Luft noch andere Menschen und Lebensmittel herein. Doch sie verfügen über Bewusstsein und sind über Affekt und Vernunft mit ihresgleichen verbunden. Also ist ihnen eine intelligible Selbstbestimmung ebenso möglich wie eine kommunikative Einflussnahme auf andere Monaden.

wirksam wird, der sich im *Ausdruck* des betroffenen Wesens zeigt. Darauf lässt sich eine Theologie des alle und alles umfassenden Sinns gründen, gegen die Nietzsches Rede vom „Tod Gottes" geradezu naiv und kindlich anmutet.[37] Doch davon kann jetzt nicht mehr die Rede sein.[38]

10. Ich beschränke mich abschließend auf die zusammenfassende These, dass Leibniz' Metaphysik als eine *Theorie universeller Kommunikation* bezeichnet werden kann, die den Zusammenhang der Welt nach Art einer *universellen*, d.h. auch einer *prinzipiell öffentlichen Partizipation* beschreibt, in der jedes aktiv beteiligte Element als selbstbestimmtes Individuum begriffen und in seinem Bestand auf Dauer garantiert ist. Alles ist auf *Gegenseitigkeit* berechnet, alles geschieht im *wechselseitigen Respekt* vor einander und in der Bemühung um eine *zwanglose Koordination im Ganzen*, die den Namen Gottes trägt. Und das *Individuum* ist das unbestreitbar *Eine*, *Ganze* und *Einzigartige*, dass wir mit Sicherheit wissen können, *weil wir es selber sind*. Und dazu genügt, die – wenn auch epistemisch unzulängliche – *Gewissheit unserer Individualität*.

Mag sein, dass die Zeit für ein Verständnis der Metaphysik von Gottfried Wilhelm Leibniz bislang noch nicht günstig war. Vielleicht waren die *Selbsterhaltung des* Individuums und die *Verfahren seiner Weltbewältigung* noch zu stark auf die Techniken der mechanischen Verfügung über die lebendigen Kräfte bestimmt. Doch mit der Einsicht in den *Primat der praktischen Vernunft durch Kant*, durch seine *Theorie des Lebendigen*, durch *Hegels Logik*, den *Pragmatismus* im Anschluss an Peirce und James, durch *Cassirers Philosophie der symbolischen Formen*, durch die Einsichten der *Gestaltpsychologie*, die Entdeckung der *ökologischen Korrelativität der geophysikalischen und biologischen Prozesse* sowie – allerspätestens – mit der *Digitalisierung der weltweiten Kommunikation* ist der Übergang zu einem neuen *Paradigma gleichermaßen individueller wie universeller Verständigung* über die lebendigen Kräfte geschaffen. Nun muss es dem Mensch gelingen, sich selbst auf dem Niveau der von ihm geschaffenen symbolischen und kommunikativen Leistungen zu bewegen.

---

[37] Ich verkenne nicht, dass Nietzsche die Rede zunächst nur einem „tollen Menschen" und dann vornehmlich seinem Zarathustra in den Mund legt. Dann aber scheint er sie doch im wörtlichen Sinn für sich selbst zu übernehmen. Und viele seiner Leser glauben bis heute daran.
[38] Ich verweise auf die individualitätstheoretisch begründete rationale Theologie in meiner Studie: *Der Sinn des Sinns. Versuch über das Göttliche*, München 2014.

Schafft er es, sich mit seinem bereits in sich selbst *sozial verfassten Bewusstsein* in einer *partizipativen Weise* sich im *öffentlichen Netz* eines globaler Verständigung ohne Verlust seiner *individuellen Eigenständigkeit* selbst zu bestimmen, könnte er zum zeitgemäßen Exempel für das werden, was Leibniz in seiner *Monadologie* zu denken versuchte.

Doch wie dem auch sei: Die medial immer dichter vernetzte Lebenssphäre des Menschen lässt uns erkennen, dass die Metaphysik von Gottfried Wilhelm Leibniz kein Rückfall in vormoderne Zeiten ist, sondern ein philosophischer Ausgriff auf die humane Zukunft des eigenständigen Menschen, der von dem Bewusstsein getragen ist, nicht im Widerspruch zu seiner Welt zu leben. Um mit Leibniz genauer zu sein: Es nicht zu können und es folglich auch nicht zu wollen.

Festvortrag zur Verleihung der VGH-Preise

Leibniz' unverstandene, aber wohl zu verstehende Metaphysik

Heinrich Schepers (Münster)

Ceterum censeo: monadas intelligendas esse

Wir alle lieben Leibniz! Lieben heißt, wie Leibniz so trefflich definierte „sich am Glück des Geliebten erfreuen." „– unserem Glück oder dem Glück anderer" ist dieser Kongress gewidmet. Leibniz' eigenes Glück bestand darin, dem allgemeinen Wohl zu dienen, aber wohl auch, verstanden zu werden. Wenn auch die Mathematik, wie zu recht behauptet wurde, „wohl seine genuine geistige Heimat war", so hat er sie nach eigenem Bekunden „der Theologie wegen" betrieben, die er mit seiner vernünftigen Metaphysik so sicher zu begründen trachtete, dass Frieden zwischen den Konfessionen einkehren könnte, ein Frieden, der auch das Zusammenleben der Staaten garantieren sollte.

Den entscheidenden Schritt zu seiner Selbstbestimmung tat der 20-Jährige Leibniz nach Abfassung hervorragender akademischer Schriften und nach einer glänzenden juristischen Promotion, als er eine Professur ausschlug und die Enge der Universität für immer verließ.

> „Daher erwog der Jüngling", erläutert Leibniz, „als er mit sich über die beste Art zu leben, gleichsam über seine private Verfassung zu Rate ging, vor allem anderen, das ihm als Privatmann dasjenige als das Beste erscheinen müsse, was für die Allgemeinheit am fruchtbarsten wäre, was zum Ruhme Gottes gehöre, den zu verwirklichen dem Einzelnen nicht weniger als der Menschheit angelegen sein müßte."[1]

Im Bewusstsein seiner Auserwähltheit notierte er sich:

> „Ich kenne niemanden, der glücklicher ist als ich, dem Gott diese Einsichten gegeben hat. Daher beneide ich auch keinen König. Ich bin sicher, dass Gott mir besondere Sorge zuwendet und meinen Geist, dem er einen so sicheren und leichten Weg zur Glückseligkeit eröffnet, zu mächtigen Freuden bestimmt hat"[2]

---

[1] „Ergo de potissimo Vitae consilio, et velut Ratione status privati deliberans, ante omnia constituebat, id demum optimum privato videri debere quod publice fructuosissimum esset, quod ad gloriam DEi pertineret, quod effici non facientis minus quam generis humani interesset; mediorum autem homini ad praeclara nullum esse homine praestantius." (A VI, 2, 513).
[2] „Ego neminem me feliciorem novi, vel ideo quod mihi hoc intelligere Deus dedit, quare nulli Regum invideo; certusque sum Deum peculiarem gerere curam mei, id est ingentibus gaudiis mentem meam destinasse, cui hanc tam certam et facilem aperuit viam felicitatis" (A VI, 3, 477).

und wenig später: „Die Religion, der ich folge, macht mich sicher, dass die Liebe zu Gott in einem heißen Verlangen besteht, sich um das allgemeine Wohl zu kümmern, und die Vernunft lehrt mich, dass es nichts Vorteilhafteres für das öffentliche Wohl aller Menschen gibt, als zu ihrer Vervollkommnung beizutragen."[3]

Einsatz für das allgemeine Wohl bedeutete für Leibniz nicht, das Beste zu tun an dem Platz, der einem durch Herkunft und Bildung zugemessen wird, sondern nach Positionen zu streben, die ihn, wenn schon nicht an die Macht, so doch in die Nähe der Macht bringen, was nötig war, um seine Bestimmung zu realisieren. Sicherlich zählte er sich zu denjenigen,

„welche mit Verstand ohne Macht von Gott versehen, denen gebühret zu Rathen." Unerschrocken fährt er fort, „gleichwie die, denen die Macht gegeben, gebühret güthig gehör zu geben, gute Vorschläge nicht in Wind zu schlagen", und mahnt: „sondern zu gedenken, dass guthe aber verachtete Rathgeber vor dem allwißenden Richter dermahls eins, auch schweigend, ihnen als Zeugen ihrer Ignoranz oder Bosheit, zum Schrecken stehen werden."[4]

Leibniz charakterisierte sich selbst als Generalantreiber zum öffentlichen Glück[5] und sagte, er wolle nicht aufhören, diejenigen zu fordern, die es nötig hätten.

Er verfasste dazu eine Vielzahl von Entwürfen, einer der frühesten beginnt:

„Weil das Glück in der Zufriedenheit besteht und die ständige Zufriedenheit in der Sicherheit, die wir von der Zukunft besitzen, eine Sicherheit, die im Wissen, das wir von der Natur Gottes und unserer Seele haben, gründet, folgt daraus, dass das Wissen notwendig ist zum wahren Glück."[6]

---

[3] „[…] car la religion que je suis exactement, m'asseure que l'amour de Dieu consiste dans un desir ardent de procurer le bien general, et la raison m'apprend qu'il n'y a rien qui contribue d'avantage au bien general de tous les hommes, que ce qui la perfectionne" (A VI, 4, 7).
[4] A IV, 1, 533.
[5] „[…] j'ay pris le personnage de Solicitor General du bien public et je ne cesse point de pousser et de sommer ceux qui en ont besoin" (GP III, 262).
[6] „Puisque le bonheur consiste dans le contentement, et que le contentement durable depend de l'asseurance que nous avons de l'avenir, fondée sur la science que nous deuvons avoir de la nature de Dieu et de l'ame; de là il s'ensuit, que la science est necessaire au vray bonheur" (A VI, 4, 3).

Im Bewusstsein, was alles dazu noch zu leisten ist und welche Verantwortung er sich mit dieser Aufgabe aufgebürdet hat, träumt er einen Engel, der ihm sagt:

> „Nutze gut die Zeit, die die Vorsehung dir hienieden bestimmt hat und bedenke, dass deine künftigen Vollkommenheiten den Mühen entsprechen werden, die du dir hier gemacht hast, um sie zu erlangen."[7]

Denn die Vernunft, die Gerechtigkeit und das Gewissen brächten es mit sich, dass ein Jeder das Seine in seiner *Sphaera activitatis* tue, dadurch er vor Gott und dem Tribunal seines Gewissens entschuldigt sei. „Wenn wir schon nicht können, was wir wollen, sollten wir doch wollen, was wir können."[8]

Leibniz' Rationalismus ist radikal: er zwingt, immer nach den Wurzeln, nach dem zureichenden Grund zu fragen; ist fundamental: er denkt in Gegensätzen, Sein oder Nichtsein, notwendig oder kontingent, möglich oder unmöglich, wahr oder falsch, tertium non datur; ist universal: wo es bei Unendlichem keinen Sinn macht, irgendwo einen Schnitt zu machen, eine Grenze zu setzen, ist es ihm geboten, von „jedem", „allem", „keinem", „nichts als", „nur" und Entsprechendem zu reden. So gibt es für Leibniz, im Ausgang von der grundlegenden Frage „warum gibt es eher Etwas als Nichts, warum ist es so und nicht anders?" nichts als einfache Substanzen. Was zur Folge hat, dass alles, was es überhaupt gibt, einfache Substanzen sind und dass unsere Welt nichts anderes ist als die Gemeinschaft aller sich miteinander vertragenden einfachen Substanzen.

Diese einfachen Substanzen, die er später Monaden nennen wird, sind unzerstörbar, im echten Sinn Individuen, wie wir alle, aber nicht alle mit Vernunft begabt. Alle handeln spontan bzw. frei, indem sie perzipieren und von Perzeption zu Perzeption streben, was Leibniz *appetitus* nennt. Diese Perzeptionen sind mehr oder weniger dunkel gemäß dem Grad der Vollkommenheit ihrer Perzipienten. Nur Gott perzipiert in vollkommener Klarheit. Handeln heißt Verändern, Verändern nichts anderes als unmittelbar von A zu nicht-A, zum kontradiktorischen Gegenteil überzugehen und damit ein anderes Individuum zu werden. In seinem Streben nach Existenz bleibt das Individuum iden-

---

[7] „Tu ne vivras pas toujours icy bas, il viendra un temps ou tu seras entierement delivré des chaines de ce corps. Use donc bien du temps que la providence te donne icy, et sache que tes perfections à venir seront proportionées au soins que tu donneras icy pour y attendre [...]" (LH IV, 8, Bl. 52).
[8] A IV, 1, 536.

tisch, aber mit stetigem Wandeln mindestens einer seiner Prädikate. Gegenstand einer Perzeption ist der momentane Zustand der Welt, aber nicht als Etwas außerhalb der Substanz, sondern in ihrem Inneren. Da nicht zu begreifen ist, wie einfache Substanzen aufeinander einwirken können, folgert der Rationalist, muss alles aus ihnen selbst stammen und in ihnen selbst bleiben.

Da Sein im strengen Sinn als notwendiges Sein nur Gott zukommt, fließt das Sein der Kreaturen in einem stetigen Schöpfungsprozess aus Gott und bleibt in Gott, wie unsere Gedanken in unserem Geist. Das nennt Leibniz mit Plotin Emanation.[9]

Diesem Schöpfungsprozess geht ein anderer Prozess voran, der sich in Gottes Vernunft abspielt,[10] wenn die unendlich vielen widerspruchsfrei von Gott denkbaren Kombinationen seiner Attribute sich als Possibilien formen[11] und, da sie nicht alle zusammen möglich sind, sich gemäß ihrer Kompatibilität in möglichen Welten zusammenfinden, so dass jedes Possibile, jedes mögliche Individuum, genau einer dieser Welten angehört. Es gibt keine *transworld-identity*.

Diese möglichen Welten realisieren verschiede Grade der Vollkommenheit, so dass Gott sie betrachtend, diejenige wählen kann, die die höchste Vollkommenheit verwirklicht, um sie zur Existenz zu überführen. Leibniz fingiert unter Abwandlung einer Metamorphose von Ovid,[12] zum besseren Verständnis seiner These, eine geniale Apologie: Als Deukalion und Pyrrha, die einzigen Überlebenden der Sintflut, auf Befehl der Götter, Steine hinter sich warfen, entstanden daraus, anders als bei Ovid, nicht sogleich Männer und Frauen, sondern menschenähnliche Statuen. Deukalion gaben die Götter die Macht, nach seinem Belieben Statuen, die auf die gleiche Weise singen, gemeinsam Menschen werden zu lassen. Nacheinander singen alle Chöre – jede Statue gehört genau einem dieser Chöre an – und erzählen dabei, wie ihr künftiges Leben aussehen würde, falls ihnen das Leben gegeben wird. Deukalion

---

[9] „Or il est premierement tres manifeste que les substances crées dependent de Dieu, qui les conserve et même qui les produit continuellement par une maniere d'emanation, comme nous produisons nos pensées." (A VI, 4, 1549, Anfang 1686). Er definierte die causa per emanationem, der Schulmetaphysik folgend, als eine solche, ubi nulla intercedit mutatio neque tempus, als eine „Wirkung bei der weder Änderung noch Zeit statt hat" (A VI, 4 637), oder als eine „Wirkung ohne eigene Veränderung", causa efficiens sine mutatione sui (A VI, 2, 490).
[10] „Itaque Deus eo ipso dum sese intelligit, omnia possibilia mente complectitur. Sciendum est creaturarum essentias nihil aliud esse quam varias divinae perfectionis expressiones, quas nisi intelligeret Deus, nec se ipsum satis intelligeret" (A II, 2, 589).
[11] „nam essentia Dei in eo consistit, ut sit subjectum omnium attributorum compatibilium" (A VI, 3 514.)
[12] Ovid: *Metamorphosen*, I., 311–315.

trifft seine Wahl. Die Zurückgewiesenen protestieren. Jupiter schickt die Waage der Themis, ein Garant für Gerechtigkeit, die nicht die körperlichen Gewichte, sondern die Gründe abwägt. Alle Arten von Statuen stellen sich auf. Über jedem Chor stehen die von den Parzen mit ewigem Diamant auf goldenen Tafeln eingeschriebenen Gesetze, die sich die Singenden selbst gegeben haben. Diese im „Archiv der ewigen Vernunft" aufbewahrten Tafeln über den versammelten Chören, über den möglichen Welten, halten alles fest, auch, was hätte geschehen können. So dass von der ewigen und unendlichen Weisheit erkannt werden konnte, nachdem die unendlich vielen Welten gleichsam abgewogen wurden, dass keine bessere zu finden war, als die von Deukalion gewählte.[13] Damit seine Wahl gerecht ist, muss Gott die volle Geschichte aller Individuen, nachdem sie von ihnen vollzogen wurde, kennen. Dabei nimmt Gott keinen Einfluss auf diese Geschichte, seine Wahl ändert nichts an der Freiheit der handelnden Individuen, er hat die Possibilien nicht geschaffen, sondern findet sie in seiner Vernunft vor.[14]

Das ist realer Konzeptualismus, so wie ihn Ph. Böhner Wilhelm Ockham zugesprochen hat, der den unversöhnlichen Gegensatz von Realismus und Nominalismus überwindet. Der Konzeptualist verlegt den Ort der platonischen Ideen in die Vernunft, um in ihr eine „mentale Sprache" (*nullius linguae*) mit natürlicher Signifikation anzusiedeln, wie sie Ockham im Anschluss an Augustinus entwickelt hat, und wie sie Leibniz mit seiner „lingua rationalis" zu verwirklichen anstrebte. In den *Nouveaux Essais* lesen wir:

> „Das erinnert uns endlich an das letzte Fundament der Wahrheit, nämlich an den höchsten und allgemeinen Geist, der nicht mangeln kann zu existieren, dessen Verstand, um die Wahrheit zu sagen, die Region der ewigen Wahrheiten ist, wie es der Hl. Augustinus erkannt und auf eine recht lebendige Weise erklärt hat." Und wenig später: „Dort ist es, wo ich den Ursprung der Ideen und Wahrheiten finde, die unseren Seelen eingeschrieben sind, nicht wie Propositionen, aber wie Quellen, aus denen die Anwendung und die Gelegenheiten die aktuellen Aussagen gebähren lassen [...]."[15]

---

[13] Am Ende einer publikationsreifen Schrift *De libertate, fato, gratia Dei*; A VI, 4 N. 309, 1595–1610, bes. ab 1608.

[14] „Ideae vel possibilitates in Deo existentes sunt natura priores mundo, ut ars artificis prior est opere. Itaque possibilitates non sunt mente abstractae a mundo constituto, sed potius ex mente prorumpentes in mundum constituendum" (Diskussion mit Gabriel Wagner ; A II, 3, 706, Mitte März 1698).

[15] „Cela nous mene enfin au dernier fondement des veritez, savoir à cet Esprit Supreme et Universel qui ne peut manquer d'exister, dont l'Entendement, à dire vrai, est la Region des veritez eternelles, comme St. Augustin l'a reconnu, et l'exprime d'une maniere assez vive. Et afin qu'on ne

Dass alle möglichen Individuen, alle Possibilien im Geiste Gottes sind, hat Leibniz wohl als Erster so ausgesprochen und verwertet.

Bereits ein Jahrhundert vor Kant forderte Leibniz eine Kopernikanische Wende in unserem Denken, aber das viel radikaler: wir sollen die Welt nicht als Etwas außer uns, sondern als eine von uns und in uns erzeugte begreifen. An seine Vertraute, die Kurfürstin Sophie schrieb er im November 1696, Kopernikus folgend habe er eine wunderbare Ordnung erfunden.[16] Nur wer versteht, dass jede einfache Substanz, jede Monade – und nicht allein die vernunftbegabten – mit ihrem Handeln, mit der Folge ihrer Perzeptionen, diese Erzeugung, mehr oder weniger deutlich, leistet, wird Zugang zu seiner Metaphysik finden.

Wir bringen weitgehend zu wenig Verständnis auf für die tragische Existenz dieses genialen Denkers, dem Zeit und Muße, vielleicht auch Macht und Mut, fehlten, seine unerhört neuen, ja radikalen Gedanken einen abgeschlossenen, mitteilbaren Ausdruck zu verschaffen. Begabt mit einem aufgeschlossenen Geist, erdrückt von guten Einfallen füllte er, um sie nicht zu vergessen, nach und nach Hunderte von Blättern und Zetteln, seine Niederschriften ständig korrigierend.[17]

---

pense pas, qu'il n'est point necessaire d'y recourir, il faut considerer, que ces veritez necessaires contiennent la raison determinante et le principe regulatif des existences mêmes; et en un mot les loix de l'Univers. [...] C'est là où je trouve l'original des idées et des veritez qui sont gravées dans nos ames, non pas en forme de propositions, mais comme des sources dont l'application et les occasions feront naître des enonciations actuelles" (A VI, 6, 447).

[16] „lorsqu'avec Copernic nous nous sommes placés dans le soleil, au moins avec les yeux de l'esprit, nous avons découvert un ordre merveilleux" (GP VII, 543). Etwas früher schrieb er an Morell, wir befänden uns noch nicht auf dem richtigen Standpunkt [...] wären wir in der Sonne hätten wir die schöne Ordnung des Systems vor Augen, die Kopernikus kraft des Denkens erkannte: Nous ne sommes pas encor dans le vrai point de vue [...] C'est à peu pres comme dans l'Astronomie, ou le mouvement des planetes paroist une pure confusion en le regardant de la terre, mais si nous estions dans le soleil nous y trouverions à vue d'oeil cette belle disposition du systeme que Copernic a decouvert à force de raisonner" (Grua, 137f.); an anderer Stelle lesen wir: „Le système nouveau de l'harmonie préétablie donne une toute autre face à l'univers aussi differente à son avantage de celle qu'on luy donnoit auparavant, que le systeme de Copernic est different de celuy qu'on donnoit ordinairement au monde visible" (*Die Leibniz-Handschriften der Königlichen Öffentlichen Bibliothek zu Hannover*, hrsg. v. Eduard Bodemann, Hannover 1889, S. 63, LH IV, 2, 1h).

[17] „Il me vient quelques fois tant de pensées le matin dans une heure pendant que je suis encor au lit, que j'ay besoin d'employer toute la matinée et par fois toute la journee et au delà, pour les mettre distinctement par écrit" (LH XLI, 10, Bl. 2).

Viele Interpreten, die Leibniz ein Stück weit auf dem Weg seiner abstrakten Reflexion begleiten, fühlen sich plötzlich verpflichtet, ihm weiter die Gefolgschaft zu verweigern, indem sie ihm Schwierigkeiten in den Weg legen, die ihrem eigenen Unverständnis entstammen, teils mangels genügender Kenntnisnahme seiner Aussagen, teils wegen unerlaubter Bezugnahme auf andere Autoren und Lagerbildung, teils wegen Nichtbeachtung seines Sprachgebrauches, seiner Umdeutung tradierter Definitionen. Allgemein gesagt, indem sie ihre Vernunft nicht gebrauchen, um die zwingende Rationalität seiner Metaphysik zu erkennen, sondern um sie zu bemängeln. Es sollte doch nicht so schwer sein, sich ohne Vorbehalte auf Leibniz einzulassen.

Vielen ist vorzuwerfen, den Unterschied nicht beachten zu wollen, den Leibniz Arnauld und de Volder klar zu machen versucht hat, der zwischen Allgemein- und Individualbegriffen besteht, zwischen der *ratio generalitatis* und der *ratio possibilitatis*.[18] Während Allgemeinbegriffe zeitlos sind und unterm Gesetz des ausgeschlossenen Widerspruchs in der Logik ihre Behandlung finden, sind Individualbegriffe, mit der nur ihnen entsprechenden Geschichte einer unzerstörbaren und unverwechselbaren Substanz, dem Satz vom zureichende Grunde unterworfen, Gegenstand der Metaphysik. Ihre Wahrheit zu erkennen, erfordert unendlich viele Schritte und ist daher nur Gott bekannt. Wir lesen exemplifizierend:

> „Im vollständigen Begriff des Petrus, der Gott vor Augen ist, ist nicht nur Wesentliches oder Notwendiges, das aus den unvollständigen oder spezifischen Begriffen fließt und daher aus den Begriffen selbst bewiesen werden kann, enthalten, sondern auch Existierendes, so zu sagen, Kontingentes, bis zum Geringsten, andernfalls wäre der Begriff nicht ultimativ und auch nicht von jedem anderen unterscheidbar, denn was sich im Geringsten unterscheidet, entspricht einem verschiedenen Individuum, und ein Begriff, in dem auch nur der kleinste

---

[18] „Quand on considere en Adam une partie de ses predicats, par exemple, qu'il est le premier homme, mis dans un jardin de plaisir, de la coste du quel Dieu tire une femme, et choses semblables conçues sub ratione generalitatis (c'est à dire sans nommer Eve, le paradis et autres circomstances qui achevent l'individualité), et qu'on appelle Adam la personne à qui ces predicats sont attribués, tout cela ne suffit point à determiner l'individu, car il y peut avoir une infinité d'Adams, c'est à dire de personnes possibles à qui cela convient differentes entre elles. [...] il luy faut attribuer une notion si complete, que tout ce qui luy peut estre attribué, en puisse estre deduit; or il n'y a pas lieu de douter que Dieu ne puisse former une telle notion de luy, ou plustost qu'il ne la trouve toute formée dans le pays des possibles, c'est à dire dans son entendement" (A II, 2, 48). Vgl. zu de Volder GP II, 263: „[...] non distinguis inter naturas universales et singulares [...]."

Umstand unbestimmt bleibt, bewirkt kein Letztliches, kann vielmehr zwei verschiedenen Individuen zukommen."[19]

Man muss davon ausgehen, dass diese Kenntnis von Petrus Gott, dem Allwissenden gegenwärtig ist, und zugleich die ganze Geschichte der Individuen und der Welten, denen sie angehören, umfasst. Ein viel diskutierter Unterschied zwischen essentiellen und akzidentellen Prädikaten entbehrt deshalb jeglicher Bedeutung.

„Zwischen der Erscheinung der Körper uns und Gott gegenüber", sagt Leibniz, „besteht ein Unterschied wie zwischen einer Scenographie und einer Ichnographie. Scenographien sind verschieden, gemäß dem Standpunkt des Betrachters, die Ichnographie, die geometrische Darstellung ist einzig; Gott nämlich sieht, wie es sich verhält gemäß der geometrischen Wahrheit, insofern er zugleich sieht, auf welche Weise die Sache jedem anderen erscheint und birgt auf diese Weise, alle anderen Ansichten vortrefflich in sich."[20]

Der Standpunkt einer Substanz ist die Relation des Nach- und Nebeneinanders zu allen mit ihr kompatiblen Substanzen, die ihre Welt ausmachen, die Zeit und Raum überhaupt erst konstituiert.

„Jede Substanz hat etwas Unendliches als ihre Ursache, nämlich Gott. Sie schließt nämlich eine Spur des Allwissens und der Allmacht in sich ein. Denn in ihrem vollständigen Begriff sind alle ihre Prädikate enthalten, sowohl die notwendigen wie die kontingenten, die vergangenen, die gegenwärtigen wie die zukünftigen, eine jede Substanz drückt, insofern alle Übrigen auf sie bezogen sind, das ganze Universum gemäß ihrem Standpunt und ihrer Sicht aus, und

---

[19] „Respondendum est in hac completa Petri possibilis notione quam Deo obversari concedo contineri non tantum essentialia, seu necessaria, quae scilicet ex notionibus incompletis sive specificis fluunt, adeoque ex terminis demonstrantur, ita ut contrarium implicet contradictionem, sed et contineri, existentialia ut ita dicam sive contingentia, quia de natura substantiae individualis est, ut notio ejus sit perfecta atque completa, omnesque circumstantias individuales etiam contingentes ad minima usque contineat, alioqui non ultima esset, nec a quavis alia distingueretur, nam quae vel in minimo differrent, diversa forent individua, et notio vel in minima circumstantia adhuc indeterminata, non foret ultima, sed duobus individuis diversis communis esse posset" (A VI, 4, 1600).
[20] „Et inter corporum apparitionem erga nos et apparitionem erga Deum discrimen est quodammodo, quod inter scenographiam et ichnographiam. Sunt enim scenographiae diversae pro spectatoris situ, ichnographia seu geometrica repraesentatio unica est; nempe Deus exacte res videt quales sunt secundum Geometricam veritatem, quanquam idem etiam scit, quomodo quaeque res cuique alteri appareat, et ita omnes alias apparentias in se continet eminenter [...]" (GP II, 438, (15. Februar 1712).

daher ist es nicht zu vermeiden, dass manche Perzeptionen obgleich sie klar, konfus sind, da sie Unendliches einschließen."[21]

Für Leibniz ist jeder Geist allwissend, wenn auch nur konfus.[22] Darüber hinaus ist

„jede körperliche Substanz konfus allwissend und limitiert allmächtig. Es geschieht nämlich nichts in der ganzen Welt, was sie nicht perzipiert, und sie erstrebt auch nichts, was nicht das Unendliche berührt."[23] Wir lesen auch: „Allein einem Singulären kommt ein vollständiger Begriff zu, daher schließt es auch Veränderungen ein"[24] und an anderer Stelle: „Ein Singulare ist das, aus dessen Verständnis geurteilt werden kann, ob und wann und wo und ob allein oder mit anderen es existiert, kurz über die volle Allgemeinheit der Dinge. Daraus wird ersichtlich, warum es schwierig ist, Singuläre abzuhandeln, weil sie so viele einschließen."[25]

Einen vollständigen Begriff einer Welt, kann es nicht geben, da Welten keine singulären Einheiten, sondern Sammlungen kompatibler einfacher Substanzen sind.

300 Jahre Leibniz-Interpretation: was die Metaphysik betrifft, eine Kette vom Missverständnissen.

Es geht nicht darum, Leibniz' Metaphysik, die für ihn, wie schon für Aristoteles, eine als solche „stets zu suchende" war, als richtig oder gar als falsch zu erweisen. Es gilt zu zeigen, wie, gesetzt man anerkennt, wenigstens provisorisch, die Richtigkeit der von ihm gemachten Voraussetzungen, der rationale Zusammenhang seiner Thesen einleuchtet. Es geht zum Mindesten darum, ihn vor Missverständnissen zu bewahren.

---

[21] „Unaquaeque substantia habet aliquid infiniti quatenus causam suam, Deum; involvit, nempe aliquod omniscientiae et omnipotentiae vestigium; nam in perfecta notione cujusque substantiae individualis continentur omnia ejus praedicata tam necessaria quam contingentia, praeterita praesentia et futura; imo unaquaeque substantia exprimit totum Universum secundum situm atque aspectum suum, quatenus caetera ad ipsum referuntur, et hinc necesse est quasdam perceptiones nostras etiamsi claras, tamen confusas esse, cum infinita involvant" (A VI, 4, 1618).
[22] „Mihi videtur Omnem mentem esse omnisciam, confuse. Et quamlibet Mentem simul percipere quicquid fit in toto mundo" (A VI, 3, 524).
[23] „Est enim omnis anima aut potius omnis substantia corporea omniscia confuse et omnipotens refracte. Nihil enim in toto mundo fit, quod non percipiat, et nihil ipsa conatur, quod non in infinitum pertingat" (A VI, 4, 1466).
[24] „Itaque in singulari tantum notio completa est, adeoque ea et mutationes involvit" (GP II 277).
[25] „Singulare [est] ex cujus intellectu judicari potest, utrum et quando et ubi et an solum existat an cum aliis, breviter de tota rerum universitate. Hinc patet cur difficile sit tractare singularia, quia tam multa involvunt" (A VI, 4 2771).

Oft sind es gerade hoch angesehene Interpreten, die die Forschung, natürlich ohne Absicht, auf Irrwege leiten. Dagegen hilft nur ein ausdrückliches ad fontes! Wohl war es in der Regel der fehlende oder ungenügende Zugang zu den Quellen, der diese Fehlschritte zur Ursache hatte, oft aber auch das aus mangelnder Anerkennung resultierende Wegsehen. Leibniz selbst trägt Schuld daran, insofern er fast alles vor seinen Zeitgenossen geheimgehalten hat, die Königliche Bibliothek in Hannover aber auch, da sie nur zögernd Einblick in den Leibniz-Nachlass gewährte. Das sind Mängel, die mit dem Fortschritt der Akademie-Ausgabe nach und nach behoben werden, die aber die bedauerlicherweise oftmals fehlende Kenntnis der Originalsprachen nicht ersetzen kann.

Wie Leibniz aus Furcht, jemand könnte sein großes Projekt einer *Scientia generalis* mit unzureichenden Mitteln gefährden, alle Vorarbeiten dazu vor seinen Zeitgenossen verborgen hat, hat er erst recht, sein Hauptanliegen, seine revolutionäre Metaphysik aus Furcht vor Unverständnis und dessen Folgen, Verurteilung durch die Kurie in Rom und Schlimmeres, nur Vertrauten und diesen auch nur zögernd bekannt gemacht. Seine lebenslange Maxime lautete: „nicht alles sagen, schon gar nicht allen."[26]

Schon im Mai 1671 schrieb Leibniz gegen Ende eines bis heute missverstandenen Briefes an Magnus Wedderkopf:

> „Aber dies nur für Dich. Ich würde es nämlich gerne tilgen. Denn auch das Richtigste wird nicht von jedem verstanden."[27]

Gegen Ende seines berichtenden Dialogs von 1676 *Pacidius an Philalethes* kann man lesen, dass Leibniz nicht alles gemeinsam Verhandelte darin festgehalten hat. Verschwiegenheit wäre vereinbart worden, weil nicht alle für würdig gehalten werden, alles zu erfahren, sicher aber schienen nur wenige reif und hinreichend genug dafür vorbereitet zu sein.[28] Ähnlich beschied er Simon Foucher:

---

[26] „neque omnia omnibus prostituenda" (A VI, 2, 419).
[27] „Sed haec ad Te: nolim enim eliminari. Nam nec rectissima a quovis intelliguntur" (A II, 1² 187).
[28] „data acceptaque arcani fide (quaedam enim dicta erant ultro citroque quae huc transferri non possunt, quod non omnes iis digni, aut certe pauci maturi atque praeparati videantur)" (A VI, 3, 571; November 1676).

„Betrachtungen dieser Art sind nicht für alle Welt geeignet, und die Ungebildeten werden, bevor ihr Geist nicht entsprechend vorbereitet worden ist, nichts davon verstehen."[29]

An den großen Antoine Arnauld schrieb Leibniz am 8. Dezember 1686 erwartungsvoll:

„Ich zweifle nicht, dass das Argument, das ich von der allgemeinen Natur der Propositionen genommen habe, einigen Eindruck auf Ihren Geist macht, aber ich behaupte auch, dass es nur wenige Leute gibt, die fähig sind, an solch abstrakten Wahrheiten Geschmack zu finden, und dass wohl niemand außer Ihnen so leicht ihre Bedeutung bemerken wird."[30]

Am Schluss eines – dann doch zurückbehaltenen – Briefes an Nicolas Rémond, in dem er seine Monadenlehre ungewohnt offenlegte, ermahnt Leibniz ihn, dass dieser Brief ausschließlich für ihn bestimmt sei. Viele andere würden ihn absurd oder unverständlich finden. Und auch, er solle nicht zu viel auf einmal darüber nachdenken, besser wäre, darauf zurückzukommen.[31] Ein guter Rat für uns alle!

In Leibniz' Selbstverständnis war es die Annahme bloßer, nicht zur Existenz gekommener Möglichkeiten, die ihn davor bewahrte einen absoluten Determinismus zu vertreten, und das spätestens schon im Mai 1671 in seinem Brief an Magnus Wedderkopf. Das ermöglichte ein von ihm eingeführter Begriff der Kontingenz, der im Gegensatz zu dem, was möglich sein könnte, genau das, was ist definiert.[32] Demnach ist kontingent im Unterschied zu dem, was notwendig ist, nur hypothetisch notwendig, wie Leibniz auch sagt *ex suppositione*, das bedeutet, wegen der vorausgesetzten Schöpfung. Von dieser Notwendigkeit kann er schon damals sagen, dass sie nichts der Freiheit raubt, da

---

[29] „mais ces sortes des considerations ne sont pas à propos à estre vues de tout le monde, et le vulgaire n'y sçauroit rien comprendre avant que d'avoir l'esprit preparé" (GP I, 292; 23. Mai 1687).
[30] „Je me doutois bien que l'argument pris de la nature generale des propositions, feroit quelqu'impression sur vostre esprit; mais j'avoue aussi qu'il y a peu de gens capables de gouster des verités si abstraites, et que peut-estre tout autre que vous ne se seroit pas si aisément apperçu sa force" (A II, 2, 117).
[31] „Mais j'ay peur que cette lettre pleine de pensées si abstraites et eloignées des imaginations receues ne vous rebute. Je ne voudrois pas même que vous meditassiés trop à la fois là dessus: il vaut mieux y revenir. J'ay voulu vous marquer cependant, combien je vous estime et vous honnore, en vous écrivant ce que je n'écrirois pas facilement aux autres. Aussi cette lettre ne doit estre que pour vous. Bien d'autres la trouveroient ou absurde ou inintelligibl […]" (GP III, 634; Juli 1714).
[32] „Contingens est quicquid potest non fieri" (A VI, 1, 466.4 u. 481.8, Juli 1671 bis Ende 1671).

Gott erst nach Kenntnisnahme der vollständig abgeschlossenen Geschichte aller Individuen, im Stande ihrer Möglichkeit, beschloss, die beste der möglichen Welten in die Existenz zu überführen.

Der schlimmste Vorwurf den man Leibniz gemacht hat, ist also, ihn einen Deterministen zu nennen, wo er doch das freie, verantwortliche Handeln als generierendes Konstituens zur Grundeigenschaft jeder mit Vernunft ausgestatteten einfachen Substanz oder Monade bestimmt hat. Und wo er gegen Descartes und Spinoza das Vorhandensein bloßer Möglichkeiten gesetzt und im Geiste Gottes lokalisiert hat, um damit nicht nur die möglichen Welten zu erklären, sondern auch entschieden den Determinismus zurückweisen zu können. Die hypothetische Notwendigkeit bietet keinen Beleg für Determinismus, weil trivialerweise mit der Schöpfung alles als bereits Geschehen anzusehen ist und nichts mehr ungeschehen gemacht werden kann. Es ist auch verfehlt, Gott allein das Handeln zuzuschreiben, wo Leibniz immer wieder betont, dass jede einfache Substanz spontan bzw. frei handelt, ein Handeln, in dem er die „Pforte" zur wahren Metaphysik sieht.[33]

Nicht nur alle notwendigen Wahrheiten haben ihren Sitz in der Vernunft Gottes, ebenso alles widerspruchsfrei Denkbare, alle Possibilien, die – da sie aber nicht alle zusammen möglich sind, sind soweit sie es sind gemäß ihrer Kompatibilität auf unendlich viele mögliche Welten so aufgeteilt, dass jedes Possibile einer und genau einer dieser Welten angehört.

Leibniz betont, dass Gott diese Possibilien nicht geschaffen hat, wohl aber sie in seinem Intellekt betrachtet und dabei feststellt, welchen Grad von Perfektion sie realisieren. Possibilien sind einfache, unzerstörbare, spontan handelnde Substanzen, also Individuen, die mit ihrem Handeln ihre Geschichte gestalten. Von dieser Geschichte eines jeden Individuums besitzt Gott einen vollständigen Begriff.[34] Leibniz erwägt weiter:

> „Wenn Gott etwas über noch nicht Betrachtetes urteilen würde, würde er nicht beschließen Adam zu erschaffen, denn alles ist nötig, was die individuelle Natur beschränkt, und was das betrifft, sind alle Dinge damit verbunden, so dass Gott

---

[33] „semper tamen mihi visum est hanc [activitas substantiae] esse portam, per quam transire e re sit ad Metaphysicam veram" (an B. de Volder, 11. September 1699; GP II, 195).
[34] „Ego contra sentio; etsi Deum concederemus de genere aliquo constituere antequam de omnibus conditionibus constituat (quod tamen nec ipsum verum est, quia Deus nihil constituit nisi omnibus consideratis), tamen non posse constituere de individuo condendo nisi perspecta tota indiuidui ejus conditione, seu, ut ego soleo loqui, notione completa prius considereta" (Grua, 345, 1691–95?).

nichts über das Geringste beschließt, bevor er die ganze Reihe der Möglichkeiten betrachtet hat, um endlich zu entscheiden, dieses eher als jenes Universum zu konstituieren. Daher erschafft Gott nicht einen Menschen, sondern zugleich die ganze Reihe der Possibilien, die seine Welt ausmacht."[35]

Wie kann man nur Leibniz vorwerfen, Gedanken späterer Philosophen, von Kant, Hegel, Heidegger etwa, sowie von modernen Logikern nicht gedacht oder zurückgewiesen zu haben? Wie kann man versuchen, ihn von diesen aus besser zu interpretieren?

Bei Bertrand Russell beginnt ein Irrweg. Anstatt Leibniz' Unterscheidung zwischen Vernunft- und Tatsachenwahrheiten zu beachten, sie war ihm wohl nicht bekannt, nimmt er Kants Unterschied zwischen analytischen und synthetischen Wahrheiten zu Hilfe und fragt, ob existieren ein Prädikat ist. Während Leibniz als Tatsache alles begreift, was von einem wirklichen oder auch nur möglichen Individuum ausgesagt werden kann, bestehen Vernunftwahrheiten dagegen nur zwischen Allgemeinbegriffen und nur sie sind in endlich vielen Schritten durch Analyse beweisbar.

Vergeblich hat Leibniz seinen Hauptsatz gegenüber Arnauld zu verteidigen versucht, dass jede einfache Substanz perzipiert und dabei, wenn auch mehr oder weniger deutlich, das ganze Universum seinem Standpunkt gemäß repräsentiert?[36] Ähnlich noch im Entwurf eines Briefes an Hartsoeker am 6. Februar 1711:

„Die Substanz hat eine Perzeption, und weil sie von Natur das ganze Universum gemäß ihrem Standpunkt darstellt, kann sie niemals aufhören darzustellen, wie

---

[35] „Et vero alioqui de nondum perspecta judicaret si decrevit condere aliquem hominem certis quibusdam praeditum qualitatibus, non ideo decrevit condere Adamum, nam opus est restringentibus ad naturam individualem. Et in universum quae de Adamo vult statuere, vel Adamo largiri, cum totius generis humani, imo totius universi rebus connectantur; itaque Deus ne de minima quidem re universi quicquam statuit ante totam seriem possibilium consideratam, ut scilicet decernet tale potius quam aliud constituere universum. Itaque non homo, sed tota series possibilium faciens hoc universum cum omnibus suis statibus praeteritis praesentibus futurisque simul sumtum, divini decreti objectum est. Atque hoc posito deinde consequuntur decreta Dei particularia de producendis singulis, conservandis, juvandis, impediendis [...]" (Grua, 345, 1691–95?).

[36] „Or chaque substance individuelle selon moy exprime tout l'univers suivant une certaine veue, et par consequent elle exprime aussi les dits miracles. Tout cela se doit entendre de l'ordre general, des desseins de Dieu, de la suite de cet univers, de la substance individuelle, et des miracles, soit qu'on les prenne dans l'estat actuel ou qu'on les considere sub ratione possibilitatis" (A II, 2, 47; Juni 1686).

das ganze Universum niemals aufhört zu handeln."[37] „Die verschiedenen endlichen Substanzen sind nichts anderes als verschiedene Ausdrücke desselben Universums gemäß verschiedenen Hinsichten und Beschränkungen einer jeden."[38]

Jede Substanz, behauptet Leibniz, drückt in ihrem Begriff das ganze Universum aus, und Gott in seinen Ideen, darüber hinaus alles, was widerspruchsfrei gedacht werden kann.[39] „Gott ist allwissend, denn er kennt die Möglichkeiten oder Essenzen der Dinge aus der Betrachtung seines Intellekts."[40]

Leibniz mindert für unser Verständnis öfter die Komplexität seiner Thesen, indem er vorübergehend nur die zur Existenz gebrachte Welt ins Spiel bringt. *Cum rigore metaphysico* gilt aber Gleiches für alle Possibilien, für jede der möglichen Substanzen in jeder der möglichen Welten. Denn sie konnten gerechterweise nur als gleichberechtigte und abgeschlossene Individuen in den aus ihnen resultierenden Welten, zur Wahl anstehen, als es darum ging, welche von ihnen existieren sollten.

Die Formulierung, die Perzeption sei der innere Zustand der Monade, der die äußeren Dinge repräsentiert, ist nicht so zu verstehen, als ob es zunächst die äußeren Dinge gäbe und daneben die ihnen entsprechenden inneren Zustände. Vielmehr ist es so, dass die äußeren Dinge die Phänomene sind, die die Monade aktiv in sich erzeugt.[41] Besonders deutlich formuliert Leibniz:

„In der Seele gibt es zweierlei: einen Zustand und die Tendenz zu einem anderen Zustand."[42]

---

[37] „La substance qui a de la perception, estant naturellement representative de tout l'univers suivant son point de veue, ne sauroit jamais cesser de representer, comme l'univers ne cesse jamais d'agir" (GP III, 521).
[38] „Quin imo substantiae finitae multiplices nihil aliud sunt quam diversae expressiones ejusdem Universi secundum diversos respectus et proprias cuique limitationes […]" (A VI, 4, 1618, Fußnote).
[39] „Car la notion de cette particule de matiere dont cette sphere est faite enveloppe tous les changemens qu'elle a subis et subira un jour. Et selon moy chaque substance individuelle contient tousjours des traces de ce qui luy est jamais arrivé et des marques de ce qui luy arrivera à tous jamais" (A II, 2, 46)
[40] „Deus est omniscius. Nam possibilitates sive essentias rerum novit ex consideratione intellectus sui, qui cum sit perfectissimus, omnia utique ideis suis exprimit, quae cogitari possunt" (A VI, 4, 2317; um 1685).
[41] „la Perception qui est l'état interieur de la Monade representant les choses externes […]" (GP VI, 600).
[42] „In anima duo sunt: Status et tendentia ad alium statum" (an Chr. Wolff, nach dem 5. Mai 1706, GBW, 56).

Selbst die Kraft ist für Leibniz noch 1712 „nichts anderes als ein Zustand, aus dem ein anderer Zustand folgt, wenn nichts es hindert."[43] Das nimmt vorweg die deutlichere Rede in der *Monadologie* vom vorübergehenden, momentanen Zustand, den man *perception* nennen sollte.[44]

Gegenstand einer Perzeption ist also nichts weniger als der jeweilige momentane Zustand der ganzen Welt, die das Individuum zusammen mit allen mit ihm verträglichen Individuen bildet, jedes von seinem unverwechselbaren Standpunkt aus, und nicht das, was wir in der phänomenalen Welt wahrnehmen, wie noch viele Interpreten behaupten zu können glauben. Das bedeutet konsequenterweise, dass jedes Individuum sich durch die Folge seiner Perzeptionen zu dem macht, was es ist, und zwar bereits vor der Schöpfung, was besagen soll, dass Gott keinen Einfluss auf seine Genese nimmt.[45]

Zu definieren: „notwendig ist das, was in allen möglichen Welten gilt und kontingent das, was in mindesten einer der möglichen Welten gilt", ist fernab von Leibniz' Intention. Ersteres wäre trivial, da Logik und Freiheit von Widerspruch unser und Gottes Denken gleichermaßen bestimmt und schon daher in allen Welten gilt. Das Zweite ist schlechthin falsch, denn für Leibniz sind und bleiben alle Individuen in den möglichen Welten *per definitionem* nur möglich.

Es geht auch nicht, Leibniz revolutionäre Theorie von Raum und Zeit, von ihm radikal begriffen als Ordnungen des Nach- und Nebeneinanders, als Ordnungen, die konstituiert werden durch das freie Handeln der Substanzen mit der Abfolge ihrer Perzeptionen, beiseite zu lassen, und an ihrer Stelle seine Auseinandersetzung mit Samuel Clarke (indirekt mit Newton) vorzuziehen, in der Leibniz Raum und Zeit zwar nicht als Substanzen gelten lassen kann, aber den metaphysischen Hintergrund seiner eigenen Theorie, wohl weil sie Clarke uns Newton unzumutbar gewesen wäre, verschweigt.

---

[43] „*Par la force que je donne aux substances, je n'entends autre chose qu'un estat duquel suit un autre estat, si rien ne l'empeche.*" (Arnaud Robinet [Hrsg.]: *Malebranche et Leibniz: Relations personnelles; présentées avec les textes complets des auteurs et de leurs correspondants revus, corrigés et* inédits, Paris 1955, S. 420f. Ähnlich schon 1691, LH IV, 3, 4 Bl. 14. Vgl. GP III, 341 u. GM VII, 17ff.)

[44] „L'état passager, qui enveloppe et represente une multitude dans l'unité ou dans la substance simple, n'est autre chose que ce qu'on appelle la perception, qu'on doit distinguer de l'apperception ou de la conscience." (Monadologie, § 14).

[45] H. Schepers: *Die sich selbst und ihre Welt konstituierende Monade. – Deutsch – Englisch – Französisch – Spanisch* (= Hefte der Leibniz-Stiftungs-Professur 28), hrsg. v. W. Li, Hannover 2015.

Aufgabe des Interpreten ist es, sich auf den Standpunkt des Metaphysikers zu stellen und die von Leibniz geforderte Kopernikanische Wende zu vollziehen. Anstatt sich an scheinbaren Dissonanzen zu reiben, gilt es, deutlich werden zu lassen, wie alles zusammenstimmt, wenn man sich auf seine Grundannahmen einlässt.

Liebe Bewerber um den von der VGH, der ältesten, eine Forderung von Leibniz nach Errichtung von Brandkassen, 1750 verwirklichende Feuerversicherung, alle Individuen streben gleichsam in einem Darwin'schen *struggle for life*, nach Existenz, aber – außer dem Sieger – müssen alle im Stande der reinen Möglichkeit verbleiben.[46] Auch Sie haben sich mit Ihren Dissertationen einem Wettbewerb unterzogen. Prämiert wurden nicht unbedingt die besten, sondern nach reiflicher Begutachtung, die für die besten gehaltenen. Das zum Trost für die Unterlegenen, auch Ihnen bleibt die Zukunft offen.

Erlauben Sie mir, als scherz- und ehrenhaft ernannte „Erzmonade", den aufstrebenden Jüngeren zu empfehlen: ad fontes! mehr Originale lesen – dankenswerterweise ist die Akademie-Ausgabe online zugänglich –, in jedem Fall mehr Primärliteratur, anstelle verkürzender Paraphrasen heranziehen. – Gut begründet zu belegen, was man behauptet. – Sich klarmachen, dass es gilt, nicht die eigene Meinung zu schützen, sondern vor allem die des Autors. Versuchen, ihn zu verstehen, statt zu beschimpfen, statt ihm sogar Unseriösität vorzuwerfen. – Angebracht wäre öfter, mehr Respekt vor der geistigen Situation unseres, sich mit guten Gründen vor Unverständnis, Missverständnis und Verfolgung fürchtenden Autors.

Liebe Bewerber, Sie haben sich in den Kreis der Verehrer von Gottfried Wilhelm Leibniz eingereiht, dessen Name schon heute, mehr und mehr bedeutende Institutionen schmückt, dessen Werk in absehbarer Zeit in der wohl Jahrhunderte überdauernden kritischen Akademie-Edition vorliegen wird und gemeinsam mit der wachsenden internationalen Forschung, wie das dieser X. und weitere internationale Kongresse deutlich bezeugen, beitragen wird, dass seine Ideen noch in ferner Zukunft Früchte für das allgemeine Wohl bringen werden.

---

[46] „il y a un combat entre tous les possibles, tous pretendans à l'existence […] tout ce combat […] ne peut être qu'un conflit de raisons dans l'entendement le plus parfait, qui ne peut manquer […] de choisir le mieux" (*Theodizee* I § 201.)

Berichte der
Leibniz-Editionsstellen

Leibniz-Edition Berlin

Harald Siebert

Schon seit Gründung der Reihen III und VII stand fest, dass für die naturwissenschaftlichen, medizinischen und technischen Schriften eine weitere Reihe in der Leibniz-Edition einzuplanen ist. Für diese neu zu schaffende Reihe VIII wurde eine eigene Arbeitsstelle an der Berlin-Brandenburgischen Akademie der Wissenschaften eingerichtet. Die Leibniz-Edition Berlin nahm am 2. Januar 2001 ihre Arbeit auf. Dank der finanziellen Unterstützung durch die Deutsche Forschungsgemeinschaft, die Alfried Krupp von Bohlen und Halbach-Stiftung und die VGH-Stiftung Hannover konnte sie mit einer digitalen Arbeitsgrundlage ausgestattet werden. Hierzu zählen u.a. eine Online-Datenbank des Ritter-Katalogs und mehr als 40.000 hochauflösende Scans von Leibniz-Handschriften. Damit ist derjenige Teil des handschriftlichen Nachlasses, der in Reihe VIII ediert wird, vollständig als Faksimile digitalisiert und auch online zugänglich (http://ritter.bbaw.de/).

1. Stand der Bearbeitung

Im Jahr 2009 erschien der erste Band (xlvi, 680 Seiten) der naturwissenschaftlichen, medizinischen und technischen Schriften von Gottfried Wilhelm Leibniz. Auf 633 Seiten Editionstext enthält VIII,1 Schriften und Marginalien in Form von 71 Stücken, die in den Jahren 1668 bis 1676 und ganz überwiegend in Paris (1672–1676) entstanden sind. In dieser Zeit beschäftigt sich Leibniz intensiv und produktiv mit unterschiedlichen Themen auf verschiedenen Gebieten, entdeckt neue Felder für sich und setzt sich mit Zeitgenossen und dem Forschungsstand seiner Zeit auseinander. Themen des ersten Bandes sind Nautik, Optik, Pneumatik und Technik.

Der im Leibniz-Jahr 2016 erschienene zweite Band (xlviii, 820 Seiten) der Reihe deckt denselben Zeitraum ab. Wie im ersten Band entspricht auch hier die thematische Einteilung nicht unserem heutigen Verständnis von Disziplinen und Fachgrenzen. Sie folgt derjenigen Klassifikation, die Leibniz selbst in seinen *Observata Philosophica* (VIII, 1 N. 1) liefert. Rubriken, die daraus im zweiten Band neu hinzukommen, sind Astronomie (N. 1, N. 2), Magnetismus (N. 3 – N. 6), Mechanik (N. 7 – N. 52), Meteorologie (N. 53, N. 54), Physik (N. 55 – N. 57), Anatomie (N. 58), Botanik (N. 59, N. 60), Chemie (N. 61 – N. 65), Medizin (N. 66 – N. 77) und Miscellanea (N. 78 – N. 81). Der zweite Band umfasst damit erstmals alle drei Teilbereiche der Reihe. Die 99 Stücke auf 771 Seiten Editionstext verteilen sich auf Gebiete der Naturwissenschaften (63 Stücke, 562 S.), der Medizin bzw. Lebenswissenschaften (15 Stücke, 128 S.) sowie der Technik (17 Stücke, 62 Seiten); daneben gehören vier Stücke zur Rubrik Miscellanea. Keine der im zweiten Band herausgegebenen Schriften war zu Leibniz' Lebzeiten erschienen. 85 Stücke werden hier erstmals veröffentlicht; der Text von insgesamt 14 Stücken ist teilweise oder ganz im Zeitraum von 1849 bis 2001 abgedruckt worden.

Schriften zur Mechanik bilden den weitaus größten Anteil im zweiten Band, was sowohl die Anzahl der Stücke (46) als auch den Seitenumfang (374 Seiten) angeht. Leibniz beschäftigt sich hier mit verschiedenen Teilgebieten der Mechanik, die er in seiner Klassifikation von 1673 nicht eigens berücksichtigt. Hierzu zählen die Unterrubriken Allgemeines, Bewegung, Festigkeit, Kraft, Reibung, spezielle Probleme und Stoß. Innerhalb der Mechanik sind es die Stücke zur Reibung (123 Seiten), die mit Abstand den größten Umfang einnehmen, gefolgt von Stücken zu allgemeinen Problemen (80 Seiten); quantitativ folgen hierauf die Stücke zum Stoß (42 Seiten), zum Kraftbegriff (38 Seiten), zur Festigkeit (35 Seiten), zu speziellen Problemen (33 Seiten) und zur Bewegung (23 Seiten).

Die in VIII, 2 edierten Stücke zeigen, dass sich Leibniz in jedem Jahr seiner Pariser Zeit mit Technik und Mechanik beschäftigte. In der Mechanik konzentrierte er sich 1672 auf die Festigkeitslehre, 1674 auf den Kraftbegriff und 1675 auf Reibungsphänomene; letztere behandelt er besonders ausgiebig. Gemessen an dem Umfang seiner in VIII, 2 edierten Schriften setzt sich Leibniz mit dem Stoß ähnlich intensiv auseinander wie mit Festigkeit und Kraft. Seine Beschäftigung damit verläuft jedoch zeitlich gestreckt, wobei aus dem letzten Jahr seines Paris-Aufenthaltes kein Stück zum Stoß stammt. In diesem letzten Jahr überwiegen Themen, die nicht in den Bereich der Technik und Mechanik fallen, sondern den Lebenswissenschaften zuzurechnen sind.

Werden die Bände VIII, 1 und VIII, 2 ihrer chronologischen Einheit entsprechend zusammen betrachtet, lässt sich anhand der edierten Stücke eine Abfolge von Schwerpunkten für die Pariser Jahre erkennen: 1672 arbeitet Leibniz intensiv auf dem Gebiet der Pneumatik, während er die Festigkeitslehre für sich entdeckt; 1673 steht weiter die Pneumatik im Zentrum, daneben beschäftigt er sich mit Optik; 1674 setzt er sich mit dem Kraftbegriff auseinander; 1675 untersucht er Phänomene der Reibung, liefert hierfür eine begriffliche Differenzierung und mathematische Beschreibung; 1676 beschäftigt er sich überwiegend mit Themen, die in die Bereiche Anatomie, Medizin und Botanik fallen.

2. Nachkatalogisierung

Bei Gründung der Arbeitsstelle konnte nur eine vorläufige Planung der Reihe vorgelegt werden, in der ihr Umfang auf acht bis neun Bände geschätzt wurde. Die Konzeption der ersten beiden Bände erfolgte mit Hilfe des von Albert Rivaud erstellten *Catalogue critique* (Paris, 1924), der die Leibniz-Handschriften aus der Pariser Zeit (1672–1676) sehr genau und detailliert verzeichnet. Für die später entstandenen Handschriften stand eine Planung noch aus. Sie musste aus eigenen Mitteln erfolgen und wurde auch seitens der Kommission gefordert, die das Vorhaben 2012 evaluierte. Im Zuge dieser Evaluation wurde gleichfalls festgelegt, dass alle weiteren Bände der Edition nach Modulen, also thematisch geordnet erscheinen sollten. Voraussetzung für eine modularisierte Bandplanung war es damit, den für Reihe VIII bestimmten Anteil des Leibniz-Nachlasses nicht nur quantitativ, sondern auch inhaltlich zu erfassen. Diese Nachkatalogisierung erfolgte anhand der digitalisierten Handschriften; darüber hinaus wurden Drucke und Marginalienexemplare mit einbezogen. Unberücksichtigt blieben Leibnitiana außerhalb der GWLB Hannover sowie die dort noch unerschlossenen Leibniz-Materialien der Signaturengruppe Ms. im Umfang von 12.200 Blatt. Im Zeitraum von September 2013 bis Oktober 2014 wurden insgesamt 9.312 Handschriftenseiten und 277 Seiten Drucke katalogisiert.

Neben der inhaltlichen Erfassung diente die Sichtung der Handschriften dazu, den Seitenumfang unter Ausschluss von Leerseiten und leeren Seitenbereichen quantitativ zu bestimmen. Dieser Textbestand für die gesamte Reihe wurde auf Quarto-Seiten (ca. DIN A5) umgerechnet und belief sich auf einen Umfang von insgesamt 7.063 voll beschriebenen Quarto-Seiten. Für die Reihenplanung entscheidend war es zu wissen, wie viele Seiten Text in edierter Form sich daraus ergeben könnten? Dazu wurden die bereits edierten bzw. gesetzten Stücke der Reihe VIII herangezogen, um ein Verhältnis zwischen den Editionsseiten und den errechneten Handschriftenseiten (Quarto-Seiten) aufzustellen. Mit dieser Ratio (1,59 PDF/Hs) ließ sich der zu erwartende Editionsseitenumfang für alle erfassten Handschriftenseiten, die zur Reihe VIII gehören, ermitteln. In gleicher Weise konnte für die zu edierenden Drucke aus der Leibniz-Zeit eine eigene Ratio (0,88 PDF/Ds) gewonnen werden; der Umfang zu edierender Marginalien (*LiH*) wurde ausgehend von dem errechneten Anteil (6,83%) bestimmt, den die Marginalienstücke am Editionstext der Bände VIII,1 und VIII,2 haben.

Die inhaltlich Erfassung der Stücke erfolgte nach Rubriken, die größtenteils bei der Konzeption der ersten beiden Bände bereits zur Anwendung gekommen waren: Akustik (A), Chemie (B), Biologie (D), Mechanik (E), Medizin (F), Optik (G), allgemeine Physik (H), Pneumatik (I), Technik (K), Geologie (L), Magnetismus (M), Nautik (N), Reiseberichte (Q), Rechenmaschine (R), Verschiedenes (V), Militärwesen (W). Der größte Teil (43 %) entfällt auf das Gebiet der Medizin (darunter auch eine große Zahl an Abschriften wissenschaftlicher Literatur). Hierauf folgen Mechanik (31 %) und mit deutlich geringerem Anteil Technik (8 %), Militärwesen (5 %) sowie Schriften zu vielen weiteren Themen (siehe Kreisdiagramm der thematischen Zusammensetzung).

Thematische Zusammensetzung der in Reihe VIII zu edierenden Handschriften nach Seitenumfang. Quelle: BBAW.

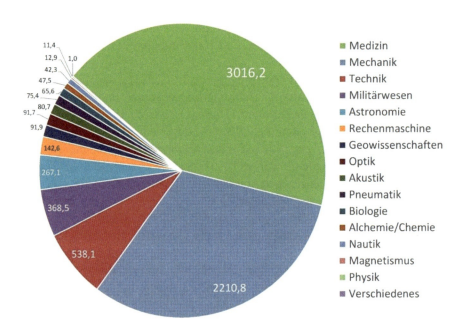

Im Zuge der Nachkatalogisierung wurden 688 Stücke (im Umfang von 3.817 Handschriftenseiten), 53 Drucke (229 Seiten) und 73 Marginalienexemplare entdeckt, die bislang keine Nummer im Ritterkatalog hatten und bei der ursprünglichen Planung der Reihe VIII unberücksichtigt geblieben waren. Dieser hinzukommende Anteil beträgt 42% des neuen Gesamtumfangs. Dementsprechend vergrößerte sich die in Reihe VIII zu edierende Zahl der Bände beträchtlich. Um den gesamten Textbestand zu edieren, der für Reihe VIII katalogisiert wurde, müsste sie sich auf 19 Bände (à 800 Seiten Editionstext) mehr als verdoppeln.

3. Neue Reihenplanung

In Abstimmung mit der Interakademischen Kommission der Leibniz-Edition wurde der Editionsauftrag für Reihe VIII präzisiert, um das Vorhaben in der vorgesehenen Laufzeit zum Abschluss bringen zu können. Ein beträchtlicher Teil der neu katalogisierten Handschriften (umgerechnet 4.473 Editionsseiten) besteht aus fremdhändigen Abschriften fremder Texte. Hierbei handelt es sich ganz überwiegend um Kopien medizinischer Fachliteratur, die Leibniz anfertigen ließ und teils auch mit Anmerkungen versah. Nach den Kommissionsbeschlüssen vom 13. November 2013 und 5. November 2014 soll dieser Teil des Nachlasses nicht in Reihe VIII ediert, sondern in seiner Überlieferung erfasst und dokumentiert werden. Mit diesen Beschlüssen wird die Reihe VIII auch davon entbunden, Leibniz-Marginalien in Handexemplaren zu edieren. Dadurch reduziert sich der Editionsumfang um sieben Bände, so dass die Reihe bis 2055 abgeschlossen werden kann. Die neue Reihenplanung umfasst damit insgesamt 12 Bände, von denen die ersten beiden schon erschienen sind. Nach 2016 werden fünf Bände mit naturwissenschaftlichen Schriften, zwei Bände mit medizinischen und zwei mit technischen Schriften folgen (siehe Tafel mit Überblick über die Reihenplanung). Diese genauere Planung war nur auf Basis der Nachkatalogisierung möglich, die neben der Quantifizierung des Umfangs auch eine inhaltliche Einordnung der Handschriften erlaubte.

Bände der Reihe VIII

Chronologisch (1668-1676)	VIII,1 VIII,2	Naturwissenschaft, Medizin, Technik in Mainz, Paris (London), Hannover
Thematisch (1677-1716)		
Naturwissenschaft	VIII,3 VIII,4 VIII,5 VIII,6	Mechanik (Kinematik, Statik, Stoß, Dynamik, Reibung, Hydromechanik, Akustik, u.a.)
	VIII,7 –	Physik (Optik, Wärme u.a.), Astronomie
	VIII,8 –	Biologie, Chemie, Botanik, Geologie
Medizin	VIII,9 VIII,10	Therapie, Pathologie, Arzneimittel, Diätetik, Kosmetik
Technik	VIII,11 VIII,12	Maschinen, Fuhrwerke, Schiffbau, Militärwesen, Instrumente, Rechenmaschinen

Die Bände der Reihe VIII im Überblick. Im Leibniz-Jahr 2016 ist der zweite Band erschienen. Quelle: BBAW.

Leibniz-Forschungsstelle Hannover / Leibniz-Archiv[*]

Michael Kempe

1. Vorstellung der Arbeitsstelle Hannover und Überblick der seit September 2011 publizierten Bände

Die Leibniz-Edition ist ein von der Akademie der Wissenschaften zu Göttingen und der Berlin-Brandenburgischen Akademie der Wissenschaften gemeinsam betreutes Vorhaben. Ihre Aufgabe ist die Erarbeitung der Ausgabe *Gottfried Wilhelm Leibniz: Sämtliche Schriften und Briefe*. Diese besteht aus acht Reihen und erscheint im Verlag De Gruyter. Die Arbeitsstelle Hannover arbeitet an den Reihen I (*Allgemeiner, politischer und historischer Briefwechsel*), III (*Mathematischer, naturwissenschaftlicher und technischer Briefwechsel*) und VII (*Mathematische Schriften*). Die Editionsarbeit wurde 1962 von der Niedersächsischen Landesbibliothek Hannover, der heutigen Gottfried Wilhelm Leibniz Bibliothek (GWLB), aufgenommen. 1984 hat die Akademie der Wissenschaften zu Göttingen die Betreuung übernommen und die Arbeitsstelle sukzessive in die Förderung des Akademienprogramms überführt. Die Editionsstelle ist weiterhin eng mit der GWLB verbunden und auch dort untergebracht. Alle Bände der Hannoveraner Editionsstelle und weitere Hilfsmittel sind über die Website der Leibniz-Edition zugänglich: www.leibniz-edition.de.

Die Homepage des Leibniz-Archivs findet sich im Internet unter: http://www.gwlb.de/Leibniz/Leibnizarchiv/Einfuehrung/index.html.

Von Reihe I sind vierundzwanzig Bände (plus ein Supplement-Band), von Reihe III sieben Bände und von Reihe VII sechs Bände erschienen. Der erste Band der Reihe I wurde 1923, der erste Band von Reihe III 1976 (2. durchgesehene Auflage 1988) und der erste Band von Reihe VII 1990 publiziert. Der Abschluss von Reihe I ist für 2036 geplant (insgesamt ca. 35 Bände). Der Abschluss von Reihe III ist für 2029 geplant (insgesamt ca. 12 Bände). Der Abschluss von Reihe VII ist für 2053 geplant (insgesamt ca. 30 Bände).

---

[*] Für das Vertrauen und die gute Zusammenarbeit sei der interakademischen Leibniz-Kommission unter der Leitung von Prof. Dr. Jürgen Stolzenberg und seinem Vorgänger Prof. Dr. Wolfgang Künne herzlich gedankt. Ebenso gilt mein Dank allen Mitarbeiterinnen und Mitarbeitern der Hannoveraner Arbeitsstelle sowie der guten kollegialen Zusammenarbeit mit den anderen drei Arbeitsstellen der Leibniz-Edition.

Die Planung für Reihe VII basiert darauf, dass bei Abschluss der Reihe III (2029) und der Reihe I (2036) die jeweils frei werdenden Mitarbeiterstellen zur Aufstockung für die Reihe VII herangezogen werden.

Seit dem letzten Internationalen Leibniz-Kongress (2011) sind folgenden Bände erschienen:

Reihe I: Allgemeiner, politischer und historischer Briefwechsel
— Bd. 21: April bis Dezember 1702, bearbeitet von Malte-Ludolf Babin/ Gerd van den Heuvel/Rita Widmaier (Einleitung: 58 S., Text: 879 S.; publiziert: April 2012)
— Bd. 22: Januar bis Dezember 1703, bearbeitet von Nora Gädeke/Sabine Sellschopp/Regina Stuber/Monika Meier (Einleitung: 95 S., 905 S.; publiziert: November 2011)
— Bd. 23: Januar bis September 1704, bearbeitet von Malte-Ludolf Babin/Gerd van den Heuvel/Regina Stuber (Einleitung: 58 S., Text: 880 S.; publiziert: März 2013)
— Bd. 24: Oktober 1704 bis Juli 1705, bearbeitet von Nora Gädeke/Monika Meier, unter Mitarbeit von Sven Erdner (Einleitung: 94 S., Text: 966 S.; publiziert: November 2015)

Reihe III: Mathematischer, naturwissenschaftlicher und technischer Briefwechsel
— Bd. 7: Juli 1696 bis Dezember 1698, bearbeitet von James G. O'Hara/Charlotte Wahl/Ralf Krömer/Heike Sefrin-Weis (Einleitung: 83 S., Text: 1048 S.; publiziert: Dezember 2011)
— Bd. 8: Januar 1699 bis Dezember 1701, bearbeitet von Charlotte Wahl /James G. O'Hara, unter Mitarbeit von Uwe Mayer (Einleitung: 79 S., Text: 912 S.; publiziert: Oktober 2015)

Reihe VII: Mathematische Schriften
— Bd. 6: Arithmetische Kreisquadratur 1673–1676, bearbeitet von Uwe Mayer und Siegmund Probst (Einleitung: 38 S., Text: 732 S.; publiziert: November 2012). In diesem Zusammenhang ist zu erwähnen, dass Siegmund Probst zwischen 2012 und März 2014 die Nachkatalogisierung des für Reihe VII zu edierenden Materials durchgeführt hat. Damit ist die Grundlage für eine Modularisierung der ca. 22 Bände der Reihe VII mit den mathematischen Schriften der Hannover'schen Zeit (1677–1716) gelegt.

Alle abgeschlossenen Bände sind als PDF im Internet, zugleich ebenfalls die in Bearbeitung befindlichen Bände (i.d.R. wird einmal pro Jahr eine aktuelle Fassung hochgeladen). Aufgeschaltet werden nur Briefe, die bereits gegengelesen sind.

Folgende in Bearbeitung befindlichen Bände sind im Internet zugänglich:

Reihe I: Allgemeiner, politischer und historischer Briefwechsel
- Bd. 25: August 1705 bis April 1706, bearbeitet von Malte-Ludolf Babin/Gerd van den Heuvel/Regina Stuber. Voraussichtlich wird der fertige Band noch Ende des Jahres an den Verlag gehen.
- Bd. 26: Mai 1706 bis (voraussichtlich) Dezember 1706, bearbeitet von Nora Gädeke/Monika Meier.

Reihe III: Mathematischer, naturwissenschaftlicher und technischer Briefwechsel
- Bd. 9: Januar 1702 bis (voraussichtlich) Dezember 1705, bearbeitet von Uwe Mayer/Charlotte Wahl/Michael Kempe.

Reihe VII: Mathematische Schriften
- Bd. 7: Kurven, Constructio aequationum, Méthode de l'universalité, 1673–1676, bearbeitet von Uwe Mayer (bis 30.06.2013)/Siegmund Probst/Achim Trunk (ab 1.11.2013).

Hinzu kommen in der Online-Präsenz Transkriptionen von Briefen noch nicht in Bearbeitung befindlicher Bände. Seit dem letzten Kongress wurde damit begonnen, neben der kontinuierlichen Neuanfertigung von Transkriptionen auch die bisherigen Rohtranskriptionen systematisch zu überarbeiten. Das gilt insbesondere für die späte Leibniz-Zeit, vor allem für 1714 bis 1716. Auf diese Weise arbeitet das Transkriptionsteam (Renate Essi und Malte-Ludolf Babin) der Edition gewissermaßen rückwärtschronologisch entgegen und ermöglicht es der Forschung, auch schon über die letzten Lebensjahre von Leibniz belastbare Aussagen zum Briefwechsel zu machen. Zudem konzentriert sich das Augenmerk der Transkriptionsarbeit, die weitgehend schon den Textstand der künftigen Edition mit Überlieferung (vorbehaltlich späterer Korrekturen und ohne Textapparat) bringt, vorrangig darauf, die nach Katalog ermittelten, bislang in keiner Form gedruckten oder transkribierten Stücke aus dem Jahr 1715 und 1716 vollständig zu erfassen.

2. Exemplarischer Einblick in die Themen und Inhalte der neuen Bände

Was die Leibniz-Korrespondenz insgesamt betrifft, kann man sagen, dass die drei Briefreihen – also neben Reihe I und III auch Reihe II aus Münster – inklusive der im Internet aufgeschalteten in Bearbeitung befindlichen Bände das Jahr 1706 erreicht haben, also damit an der Schwelle zum letzten Lebensjahrzehnt von Leibniz angekommen sind. Nimmt man hinzu, dass mit den Online-Transkriptionen von 1714 bis 1716 ebenso die späte Korrespondenz schon in editorisch einigermaßen zuverlässiger Form vorliegt, dann wird deutlich, dass hinsichtlich der Gesamtkorrespondenz nur noch in den Jahren 1707–1710 der Erkenntnisstand eher dünn ist.

Nun ein kurzer Blick in die Inhalte: Die neuen Bände der Reihe I dokumentieren die ganze Breite der vielfältigen gelehrten und politischen Aktivitäten von Leibniz im fortschreitenden Spanischen Erbfolgekrieg und im Nordischen Krieg. Aus der Vielzahl der Themen und Interessen ragt in Bd. I, 23 eindeutig die fieberhafte Suche nach Materialien für die groß angelegte Welfengeschichte heraus – Leibniz selbst spricht wörtlich von einer Jagd nach alten historischen Manuskripten. In den Zeitraum von Bd. I, 24 fallen der Tod der preußischen Königin Sophie Charlotte, das von den Höfen in Hannover und Celle verfügte „Reiseverbot" für Leibniz und der Beginn der Korrespondenz mit Caroline von Brandenburg-Ansbach.

Zudem sondiert Leibniz die Möglichkeit, in den Dienst des Berliner Hofes zu treten. In den politischen Abschnitten geht es unter anderem um Fortschritte und Gefahren im Konflikt mit den expandierenden Mächten Frankreich und Schweden sowie um die hannoversche Sukzession auf den britischen Thron. Aus den online verfügbaren in Bearbeitung befindlichen Bänden I, 25 und I, 26 seien hier exemplarisch Leibniz' Einmischung in die englische Sukzession und die ins Stocken geratenen Reunionsbemühungen hervorgehoben. Während Leibniz sich in Bd. I, 23 bei seinen Bemühungen um Vorarbeiten für das geplante Werk zur Welfengeschichte vorrangig auf die Zusammenstellung von historischen Quellen konzentriert, steht mit Bd. I, 26 die bevorstehende Drucklegung der „Scriptores rerum Brunsvicensium" im Vordergrund.

Die beiden Bände der Reihe III umfassen ein breites Spektrum an mathematischen, naturwissenschaftlichen und technischen Themen. Eines der zentralen mathematischen Themen von Bd. III, 7 ist das Brachistochronenproblem, d.h. die Frage nach der Bahn, auf der ein Körper im Schwerefeld in kürzester Zeit von einem Punkt zu einem anderen gelangt. Unter den gut drei

Dutzend Korrespondenzen befinden sich so prominente Briefpartner wie Johann und Jacob Bernoulli, de L'Hospital, von Tschirnhaus oder John Wallis.

Vier weitreichende Entwicklungen, das wird vor allem aus Band III, 8 deutlich, prägen die brieflichen Gespräche der Jahre um 1700 und führen zu neuen Themen: die astronomischen, politischen und theologischen Aspekte der protestantischen Kalenderreform 1700; die neugegründete Sozietät der Wissenschaften in Berlin; die Diskussion um Leibniz' Differentialkalkül sowie überdies die Kontroverse mit Denis Papin über die Dynamik. Parallel dazu intensiviert sich die Korrespondenz mit Rudolf Christian Wagner, der in Helmstedt nicht nur die Arbeiten an der Rechenmaschine koordiniert, sondern gleichzeitig ebenso die Umsetzung von Leibniz' Vorhaben, eine schnell schießende Büchse zu entwickeln.

In Reihe VII steht weiterhin die Pariser Zeit im Fokus. Von den etwa 50 Texten des Bandes VII, 6 waren nur fünf bisher ganz oder teilweise im Druck zugänglich, insgesamt etwa ein Drittel des Bandumfangs. Den größten Anteil daran hat die 1993 erstmals von Eberhard Knobloch vollständig kritisch edierte Handschrift der Abhandlung zur arithmetischen Kreisquadratur vom Sommer 1676. Es handelt sich dabei um den umfangreichsten zusammenhängenden mathematischen Text, den Leibniz jemals verfasste. Aus der Exzerpten und Vorstudien von *De quadratura arithmetica circuli* wird der innovative Gedankengang nachvollziehbar, der Leibniz zur Entwicklung seiner universalen demonstrativen Inifinitesimalgeometrie führte.

Der in Bearbeitung befindliche Bd. VII, 7 widmet sich mit diversen mathematischen *Kurven*, mit der *Constructio aequationum* und mit der *Méthode de l'universalité*. Die *Constructio aequationum* ist ein in der zweiten Hälfte des 17. Jahrhunderts bedeutsames, nach 1750 jedoch weitgehend in Vergessenheit geratenes Forschungsgebiet der Mathematik. Es behandelte die Lösung von algebraischen Gleichungen mit Hilfe von geometrischen Konstruktionen. Bei diesen Gleichungen gibt es beispielsweise Fragen nach Abständen zwischen Punkten und Kegelschnitten. Dabei ergaben sich verschiedene, aber doch ähnliche Gleichungen, die sich vor allem in der Vorzeichen („+" oder „-") unterschieden. Um nun alle Fälle in einem einzigen Rechengang zu behandeln, ersann Leibniz in seiner um die Jahresmitte 1674 seine *signa ambigua*, was mit „Doppelvorzeichen" oder „mehrdeutige Vorzeichen" übersetzen werden kann und entwickelte ein systematische Verfahren zur Bildung und gezielten Einsetzung dieser Doppelvorzeichen. Mit Hilfe dieses Verfahrens, das er als *Méthode de l'universalité* bezeichnete und für die Leibniz-Forschung inhaltlich als Teil seiner *characteristica universalis* von Interesse ist, versprach er, verschiedene Fälle, die ohne diese Methode gesondert behandelt werden müssten, in einem einzigen Arbeitsgang zu lösen.

Hingewiesen sei am Schluss dieses exemplarischen Einblicks in die neuen Hannoveraner Editionsergebnisse zum einen auf die jüngsten statistischen Erhebungen von Nora Gädeke zum späten Briefwechsel von Leibniz 1715 und 1716, die offenbaren, dass im Unterschied zur älteren Forschung nicht mit einem Rückgang der Korrespondenztätigkeit von Leibniz zu rechnen ist. Im Gegenteil: mit geschätzten 850 bis 900 Briefen ist sie sogar ähnlich hoch wie bei den Spitzenwerten der Brieffrequenz in den Hochjahren um 1700. Zum anderen hat die Transkriptionsarbeit von Renate Essi und Malte-Ludolf Babin zutage gebracht, dass Leibniz' Kontakte zum Kaiserhof nach Wien nach 1714 nicht abgerissen waren. Gerade der Briefwechsel mit dem Wiener Hofinformanten und Nachrichtenagenten Johann Philipp Schmid, der umfangreichste aus Leibniz' letztem Lebensjahr und zugleich der bislang am wenigsten beachtete, zeigt ein bisher unbekanntes Kapitel seiner intellektuellen Biographie, nämlich Leibniz als Leser geschriebener Zeitungen.[1]

3. Begleitpublikationen der Bände und weitere Forschungsaktivitäten

Neben der Editionsarbeit sind die Mitarbeiterinnen und Mitarbeiter der Forschungsstelle Hannover in vielfacher Hinsicht in der internationalen Leibniz-Forschung aktiv. Verwiesen sei hier pars pro toto auf zwei Aufsatzbände, die 2015 und 2016 erschienen sind:
− Michael Kempe (Hrsg.): *1716 – Leibniz' letztes Lebensjahr. Unbekanntes zu einem bekannten Universalgelehrten*. Bd. 2, Hannover 2016, 416 Seiten mit zahlr. farb. Abbildungen.
− Michael Kempe (Hrsg.): *Der Philosoph im U-Boot. Praktische Wissenschaft und Technik im Kontext von Gottfried Wilhelm Leibniz*, Bd. 1 Hannover 2015, 296 Seiten mit Abbildungen.

---

[1] Siehe auch Malte-Kudolf Babin: „'Vous m'avez déja plusieurs fois questionné sur le poinct des nouvelles' – Johann Philipp Schmids k. k. Nachrichtendienst für Leibniz im Jahre 1716", in: Michael Kempe (Hrsg.): *1716 – Leibniz' letztes Lebensjahr. Unbekanntes zu einem bekannten Universalgelehrten*, Hannover 2016, S. 177–201.

4. Hilfsmittel und IT-Initiativen

An drei Initiativen zur Optimierung der webbasierten Hilfsmittel der Leibniz-Edition ist die Hannoveraner Arbeitsstelle beteiligt:
1. Die Personen- und Korrespondenz-Datenbank der Leibniz-Edition („Leibniz-Connection"). Die Datenbank (u.a. zugänglich über die Hilfsmittelseite unter www.leibniz-edition.de) bietet eine zweifache Recherche-Möglichkeit: Erstens nach Personen, die in den Bänden der Leibniz-Edition erwähnt und in den Personenregistern erfasst sind, sowie zweitens nach Leibniz-Korrespondenten; zusätzlich sind alle bisher im Rahmen der Akademie-Ausgabe gedruckten Briefe verzeichnet und einzeln aufrufbar. Die Datensätze zu den Korrespondenten enthalten größtenteils zusätzlich Kurzbiographien in Form von eigenständigen *Biogrammen* sowie die Nachweise der Fundstellen der einzelnen Briefe in den Bänden der Akademie-Ausgabe. Soweit die Bände der Leibniz-Edition digital vorliegen, führt eine Sprungmarke von dem verlinkten Fundstellennachweis an die entsprechende Position im online verfügbaren Band. Siehe unten, Exkurs I: *Leibniz-Connection*.
2. Im Aufbau befindet sich ein digitales Briefportal Leibniz', mit dem versucht wird, ausgewählte Leibniz-Briefe in einer (HTLM-basierten) Internet-Fassung zu präsentieren. D.h. einzelne Briefwechsel werden bandübergreifend dargestellt und sind Volltext durchsuchbar, der Textapparat ist dabei nach einzelnen Varianten unterschieden anklickbar. Ein erster Testballon soll mit dem bisher vorliegen Briefwechsel von Leibniz mit Johann Bernoulli ausprobiert werden und wird ca. Ende 2016 im Internet zugänglich sein.
3. Gemeinsam mit der Gottfried Wilhelm Leibniz Bibliothek, der Musterfabrik Berlin und dem Fraunhofer Institut für Produktionsanlagen und Konstruktionstechnik IPK führt die Arbeitsstelle Hannover ein von der Klaus-Tschira-Stiftung in Heidelberg gefördertes Projekt zur „Digitalen Rekonstruktion von Textzusammenhängen in den Schriften von Gottfried Wilhelm Leibniz" durch. Es geht am Beispiel der Mathematik-Handschriften der Signaturengruppe LH 35 (GWLB) um ein softwaregestütztes „Zusammenpuzzeln" der von Leibniz zerschnittenen Blattfragmente. Leibniz hatte die Angewohnheit, seine Notizen zu zerschneiden und je nach Thema systematisch zu ordnen. Die überlieferten Bestände an Streifen und Schnipseln sollen nun mithilfe eines digitalen Assistenzsystems wieder zusammengefügt werden, um sie im Rahmen der Leibniz-Akademie-Ausgabe edieren zu können. Einzelheiten zum Projekt siehe unten,

Exkurs II: Michael Kempe / Siegmund Probst: *Digitale Rekonstruktion von Textzusammenhängen in den Schriften von G. W. Leibniz.*

Exkurs I

Leibniz-Connection.
Personen- und Korrespondenz-Datenbank der Leibniz-Edition

Michael Kempe

Die Personen- und Korrespondenz-Datenbank der Leibniz-Edition gehört zu den wichtigen Hilfsmitteln der Leibniz-Gesamtausgabe der Akademie der Wissenschaften zu Göttingen sowie der Berlin-Brandenburgischen Akademie der Wissenschaften. Im Internet ist die Datenbank erreichbar unter dem Pfad: https://leibniz.uni-goettingen.de/. Sie ist zugänglich über die Hilfsmittelwebsite der Leibniz-Edition: www.leibnizedition/de/hilfsmittel.html. Die Datenbank dient den vier Editionsstellen in Berlin, Hannover, Münster und Potsdam als Arbeitsinstrument und wird unter Federführung des Leibniz-Archivs Hannover laufend aktualisiert. Zugleich steht sie der internationalen Leibniz-Forschung und der interessierten Öffentlichkeit zur Verfügung. Konzipiert wurde die Personen- und Korrespondenz-Datenbank der Leibniz-Edition in den Jahren 2013 und 2014 durch das Leibniz-Archiv Hannover in Zusammenarbeit mit der TELOTA-Initiative der Berlin-Brandenburgischen Akademie der Wissenschaften.

Hervorgegangen ist diese Datenbank aus digitalen Kumulationen der Personen- und Korrespondenten-Register der bisher veröffentlichten Bände aller Reihen der Leibniz-Ausgabe. Sie bietet zunächst eine zweifache Recherche-Möglichkeit:

1. nach Personen, die in den Bänden der Leibniz-Edition erwähnt und in den Personenregistern erfasst sind, sowie
2. nach Leibniz-Korrespondenten; zusätzlich sind alle bisher im Rahmen der Akademie-Ausgabe gedruckten Briefe verzeichnet und einzeln aufrufbar.

Im öffentlich zugänglichen Bereich der Datenbank sind derzeit (Stand: 6. Dezember 2016) 6.959 Datensätze zu Personen und Korrespondenten sowie 13.128 Datensätze zu Briefen aufgeschaltet; im editionsinternen (d.h. nur den vier Arbeitsstellen der Leibniz-Edition zugänglichen) Bereich stehen (Stand: 6. Dezember 2016) insgesamt 25.702 Datensätze zu Personen und Korrespondenten sowie 15.237 Datensätze zu Briefen zur Verfügung. Laufend ergänzt wird die Datenbank durch die Nachweise der Personen- und Korrespondentenregister neu erscheinender Bände der Akademieausgabe. Bei älteren Bänden ist es möglich, dass nicht alle Personen-Fundstellen erfasst wurden. Hinweise auf solche Bände mit unvollständig erfassten Fundstellen finden Sie im Feld „Bemerkungen". Die Bände I 4–9, II 1, III 1, IV 1, IV 2, VI 1, VI 2 und VI 6 liegen in der jeweils neuesten Auflage vor.

Die Datenbank bietet für Personen und Korrespondenten die Möglichkeit zu Recherchen u. a. in folgenden Kategorien:

- Namen, Vornamen, ggf. Namensvarianten und Pseudonyme, Namenswechsel oder -erweiterungen durch Heirat oder Standeserhöhungen;
- Lebensdaten;
- Beruf, Funktionen, politische und akademische Titel, Religions- bzw. Ordens-zugehörigkeit, mit der Möglichkeit zur Temporalisierung, d. h. der Zuordnung zu einem bestimmten Zeitraum;
- Fundstellen in der Leibniz-Akademieausgabe, Quellennachweise;
- Beziehungen zur Darstellung des in der Edition abgebildeten Beziehungsgeflechts der betreffenden Person;
- Bei Korrespondenten: Briefdaten und Korrespondenzverläufe

Die Datensätze zu den Korrespondenten enthalten größtenteils zusätzlich Kurzbiographien in Form von eigenständigen *Biogrammen* sowie die Nachweise der Fundstellen der einzelnen Briefe in den Bänden der Akademie-Ausgabe. Soweit die Bände der Leibniz-Edition digital vorliegen, führt eine Sprungmarke von dem verlinkten Fundstellennachweis an die entsprechende Position oder an den Anfang des online verfügbaren Bandes. Verschiedene Filter-Funktionen und kombinierbare Recherchemöglichkeiten stehen für komplexe Suchanfragen zur Verfügung. Personen- und Korrespondenten-Daten sind mit den vorherrschenden Normdatensystemen (national: GND; international: VIAF) durch einen entsprechenden Link verbunden, soweit diese entsprechende Datensätze enthalten. Datensätze können komprimiert ausgedruckt und ins XML-Format exportiert werden. Derzeit wird an einer englischen Fassung der Datenbank gearbeitet.

Exkurs II

Digitale Rekonstruktion von Textzusammenhängen in den Schriften von Gottfried Wilhelm Leibniz*

Michael Kempe / Siegmund Probst

1. Kooperationspartner und Zeitplan

Die *Digitale Rekonstruktion* der Leibniz-Fragmente ist ein gemeinsames Projekt der Leibniz-Forschungsstelle Hannover der Akademie der Wissenschaften zu Göttingen (Leibniz-Archiv) und der Abteilung für Handschriften und alte Drucke der Gottfried Wilhelm Leibniz Bibliothek Hannover (GWLB) zusammen mit der MusterFabrik Berlin (MFB) und dem Fraunhofer-Institut für Produktionsanlagen und Konstruktionstechnik (Fraunhofer IPK) Berlin. Es wird geleitet von Prof. Michael Kempe (Leibniz-Forschungsstelle Hannover) und finanziert durch die Klaus-Tschira-Stiftung (Heidelberg). Der Förderungszusage durch die Klaus-Tschira-Stiftung sind mehrere Projektentwürfe, Vorbereitungen und Anträge bei verschiedenen Institutionen vorausgegangen. Der Erfolg ist vor allem das Verdienst des mehrjährigen, ausdauernden und hartnäckigen Einsatzes aller Beteiligten, insbesondere des unermüdlichen Engagements von Herrn von der Linden (MFB). Die Direktion der GWLB hat das Projekt immer unterstützt, ebenso Prof. Stolzenberg als Vorsitzender der interakademischen Leibniz-Kommission und auf Seiten des Fraunhofer IPK Dr. Nickolay, der Leiter der Abteilung Sicherheitstechnik. Nicht vergessen werden soll, dass am Zustandekommen der Zusammenarbeit mit dem Fraunhofer IPK ursprünglich die Berliner Arbeitsstelle der Leibniz-

---

* Diese Vorstellung des Projekts verwendet Materialien, welche von verschiedenen am Projekt Beteiligten bereitwillig zur Verfügung gestellt wurden. Zu danken haben wir vor allem Patricia Landgraf und Marc von der Linden (MFB), Jan Schneider (Fraunhofer IPK) und Matthias Wehry (GWLB).

Edition wesentlich beteiligt war, besonders Herrn Knobloch und Herrn Hecht ist hier zu danken.

Die erste Projektphase beschränkt sich auf die in der Abteilung LH XXXV des Leibniz-Nachlasses gesammelten Handschriften, hauptsächlich sind dies Mathematica. Das Projekt ist im Herbst 2015 angelaufen und nach einer Reihe von Tests mit verschiedenen Manuskripten, Scantechnik und Rekonstruktionssoftware stehen die Handschriftenscans der Öffentlichkeit bereits seit September 2016 in den „Digitalen Sammlungen" der GWLB zur Verfügung:

http://digitale-sammlungen.gwlb.de/

Abgeschlossen wird das Pilotprojekt im Frühjahr 2017, die Ergebnisse werden der Öffentlichkeit zugänglich gemacht:

http://www.gwlb.de/projekte/digitale-rekonstruktion/

2. Projektziel

Ziel des geplanten Projektes sind die Entwicklung und der Einsatz eines computergestützten Assistenzsystems zur Rekonstruktion von Text- und Blattzusammenhängen im Leibniz-Nachlass. Eine solche Rekonstruktion dient zum einen der Erschließung der Bestände im Nachlass von Leibniz in der GWLB und unterstützt zum anderen den Fortgang der historisch-kritischen Gesamtausgabe. Sie wird sich unserer Ansicht nach als äußerst hilfreich für die Planung zukünftiger Bände erweisen, da beträchtliche Teile des Nachlasses auf Blattfragmenten, losen Zetteln und – allem Anschein nach von Leibniz selbst – zerschnittenen, meist undatierten Papieren überliefert sind. (Für die im Pilotprojekt betroffenen Handschriften aus LH XXXV beträgt die Fragmentierung mindestens 20% bezogen auf eine Blattzahl von 7200, schließt man die Einzelblätter in Oktav- oder Quartformat ein, die mehr oder weniger regelmäßig geformt sind, kommt man auf 35–40%; bezogen auf die Zahl von ca. 4800 Trägereinheiten ergibt sich dann sogar ein Fragmentanteil von fast 70%.).

Gerade für die Schriftenreihen der Leibniz-Edition ist die Rekonstruktion des chronologischen Ablaufs einer der heiklen Punkte. Die Manuskripte sind nur in geringem Maße datiert, da sie zumeist zum eigenen Selbstverständnis niedergeschrieben wurden. Leibniz hat im wörtlichen Sinne eine ‚Zettelwirtschaft' betrieben: Er notierte seine Ideen zu verschiedenen

Themen spontan auf Papierbögen oder Blättern und zerschnitt diese in kleine Zettel. Seine Aufzeichnungen sind daher oft auf Schnipseln oder Blattfragmenten der unterschiedlichsten Art überliefert. Diese Arbeitsweise war vielleicht dadurch verursacht, dass Leibniz in seinen frühen Jahren mit dem teuren Papier sparsam umgehen musste. Auch in den späteren Jahren seit der Übersiedlung nach Hannover behielt Leibniz dieses Verfahren bei, vermutlich auch wegen der häufigen Reisen, auf denen er unterwegs in der Kutsche und in verschiedensten Quartieren Notizen anfertigte. Er selbst äußerte in einem Brief:

> „Mir gefallet des H. Viviani weise sehr wohl, seine gedancken auf schedas dissolutas zu sezen, und hernach einzutheilen, ich thue offt dergleichen, und habe auch ein groß chaos".[2]

Ein weiteres Beispiel – zugleich mit Bezug zum „schreibenden Denken" von Leibniz – ist folgendes:

> „Mir kommen manchmal morgens, während ich noch eine Stunde im Bett liege, so viele Gedanken, dass ich den ganzen Vormittag, ja mitunter den ganzen Tag und länger damit beschäftigt bin, um sie mir durch Aufschreiben klar werden zu lassen."[3]

Da Leibniz' Nachlass mit etwa 100.000 Blatt sehr umfangreich ist, wird die Zugehörigkeit von Blattfragmenten zu einem gemeinsamen Textträger in der Regel nur zufällig oder mit hohem Rechercheaufwand ermittelt. Im Erfolgsfall lassen sich aber gerade daraus häufig wertvolle Rückschlüsse auf zeitliche und inhaltliche Bezüge ableiten. Bei der Bearbeitung der mathematischen Handschriften aus der Zeit des Parisaufenthalts 1672–1676 von Leibniz haben solche Rekonstruktionen wiederholt wertvolle Hinweise geliefert und tun dies auch für den aktuell in Arbeit befindlichen Band A VII, 7.

Eine systematische Rekonstruktion der noch nicht edierten Blattfragmente erfordert aber den Einsatz eines automatisierten Systems. Das Fraunhofer IPK hat in den vergangenen Jahren systematisch solche Methoden zur automatisierten virtuellen Rekonstruktion von beschädigten oder zerstörten

---

[2] Leibniz an Rudolf Christian von Bodenhausen, 26. November (6. Dezember) 1697; A III, 7, N. 162, 652.
[3] LH XLI, 10, Bl. 2r°: „il me vient quelques fois tant de pensées le matin dans une heure, pendant que je suis encor au lit, que j'ay besoin d'employer toute la matinée et par fois toute la journée et au delà, pour les mettre distinctement par ecrit."

Dokumenten entwickelt und erfolgreich umgesetzt. Öffentlich bekannt geworden ist vor allem die virtuelle Rekonstruktion der zerrissenen Stasi-Akten. Diese ist aufgrund der außerordentlichen Vielfalt an Papierfragmenten und der enormen Datenmenge eine schwierige Aufgabe, die lange Zeit als unlösbar galt. Neuartige Bildverarbeitungs- und Mustererkennungsmethoden mussten dafür entwickelt und erprobt werden.[4] Auf den Erfahrungen mit den Stasi-Akten aufbauend, wird in unserem Projekt in Zusammenarbeit zwischen Edition, Bibliothek und MusterFabrik/Fraunhofer IPK eine neue interaktive Software entwickelt, getestet und zum Einsatz gebracht, die in der Lage ist, Leibniz-Handschriften zu rekonstruieren, um damit einen zentralen, innovativen Beitrag für die internationale und interdisziplinäre Leibniz-Forschung zu leisten.

Da die Planungen zur Zusammenarbeit bis ins Jahr 2011/2012 zurückreichen, konnten wichtige Vorarbeiten bereits geleistet werden. Schon vor Beginn der Laufzeit des Projekts waren die ersten Testreihen erfolgreich abgeschlossen worden, so dass die grundsätzliche Funktionsfähigkeit der Technologie für die Fragment-Rekonstruktion gewährleistet werden konnte. Die technische Reife der Entwicklung der Rekonstruktionssoftware war sehr weit fortgeschritten und konnte durch eine zusätzliche Testreihen mit Scans, die seit dem Herbst 2015 angefertigt wurden, weiter erprobt und verbessert werden.

3. Bemerkungen zur verwendeten Technologie

Zum Einsatz kommt ein Hochleistungsscanner, den die GWLB im Dezember 2015 bei der MFB in Auftrag gegeben hat und der nicht aus den Projektmitteln, sondern vom Niedersächsischen Ministerium für Wissenschaft und Kultur (MWK) finanziert wird. Damit sollen in Zukunft weitere Handschriftenbestände der GWLB (und anderer niedersächsischer Institutionen) in höchster Qualität bei Schonung der empfindlichen Papiere und mit möglichst geringem Zeitaufwand digitalisiert werden.

Dieser Scanner erlaubt eine beidseitige, geometrie- und farbtreue Digitalisierung von Dokumenten. Er ist besonders gut geeignet für eine schadensfreie Handhabung von fragilen Dokumenten. Dies wird gewährleistet durch ein berührungsfreies Handling der Fragmente, die in einen Glasrahmen eingelegt werden. Es können mehrere Fragmente oder Blätter auf einmal

---

[4] Weitere laufende Projekte der MFB sind die digitale Rekonstruktion von Beständen des Kölner Stadtarchivs und von Musikalien der Weimarer Herzogin Anna Amalia Bibliothek.

aufgenommen werden. Beim Transport mittels eines Schlittens werden die Handschriften in einem Durchlauf gleichzeitig mit drei Kameras aufgenommen, von oben und unten sowie mit einer Durchlichteinheit. Das Gerät lässt sich bei Bedarf mit weiteren Kameras aufrüsten, z. B. für Infrarot- und Ultraviolettaufnahmen. Der Scanner arbeitet mit einer hohen Durchsatzrate und kann daher große Mengen an Scangut bewältigen.

Die hochwertigen Digitalisate (eine große Rolle spielt dabei auch der technisch manipulierte Hintergrund) werden von der Rekonstruktions-Software verarbeitet: Es ist damit eine pixel-genaue Extraktion von Konturmerkmalen möglich, die für das Puzzeln der Fragmente erforderlich ist. Zusätzlich ermöglichen die Scans auch die Extraktion von Farb-, Textur- und Kontextmerkmalen.

Die Software unterscheidet zunächst (relativ) glatte Außenkanten von unregelmäßiger geformten Schnitt- und Risskanten. Dabei wird die Kontur durch einen Polygonzug approximiert, der durch Hinzufügen weiterer Eckpunkte sukzessive verfeinert werden kann. Umgekehrt kann auch der unregelmäßige Papierrand des handgeschöpften Papiers von geschwungenen aber glatten Schnittkanten unterschieden werden. Damit lässt sich das automatische Verfahren an die spezifischen Eigenschaften der Fragmente anpassen. Da jeder zusätzliche Eckpunkt die erforderliche Rechenleistung erhöht, muss ein Kompromiss zwischen Rechenaufwand und Genauigkeit der Approximation gefunden werden.

4. Ausblick

Das Pilotprojekt lässt in mehrfacher Hinsicht Fortsetzungen und Erweiterungen zu. Der erste naheliegende Schritt ist das Einscannen und Puzzeln des gesamten Leibniz-Nachlasses in der GWLB, was bis 2019 erfolgt sein wird. Erst damit können dann (von Leibniz-Handschriften an anderen Aufbewahrungsorten einmal abgesehen) die bestmöglichen Puzzle-Ergebnisse mittels der Kantenuntersuchung erreicht werden. Andere Möglichkeiten für eine Erweiterung liegen im Heranziehen zusätzlicher Merkmale für das Puzzeln. Beschränkt sich das Pilotprojekt vorerst auf die (unregelmäßigen) Blattkanten der Fragmente, so werden noch Tests mit Linienverläufen durchgeführt, die das Rekonstruieren von ziemlich gerade durchgerissenen oder durchgeschnittenen Blättern bzw. Bögen ermöglichen können. (Auch dafür haben wir bereits einige Beispiele aus der Editionspraxis.) Wieder andere

Merkmale führen aus dem Bereich der Fragmente heraus und führen zu Gruppenbildungen auch kompletter Blätter bzw. Bögen. Dazu können die Durchlichtscans mit der Erfassung der Papierstruktur und der Wasserzeichen dienen. Ebenfalls möglich ist z. B. eine Gruppierung der Handschriften nach Schreiberhänden mittels automatischer Handschriftenerkennung.

Dieses Projekt der digitalen Rekonstruktion kann nur ein Anfang sein, aber – um mit Leibniz zu sprechen – man muss immer mit dem Anfang anfangen: „il faut tousjours commencer par le commencement".[5]

---

[5] Leibniz an Bossuet, 2. (12.) Juli 1694; A I, 10, N. 90, 139.

Leibniz-Forschungsstelle Münster

Stephan Meier-Oeser

In die Zuständigkeit der Leibniz-Forschungsstelle Münster, die gemeinsam von der Akademie der Wissenschaften zu Göttingen und der Universität Münster getragen wird, fällt die Edition der Reihen II (philosophischer Briefwechsel) und VI (philosophische Schriften) der Leibniz Akademie-Ausgabe.

Zum besseren Verständnis der gegenwärtigen Situation der Edition der Reihen II und VI ist Folgendes zu berücksichtigen: Nach dem Erscheinen von Band VI, 4 im Jahr 1999 hat man sich, bedingt durch den Wegfall mehrerer Editorenstellen, entschlossen, die Arbeiten an der Schriftenreihe zunächst einzustellen und sich dafür auf die Bearbeitung der Reihe II zu konzentrieren, da man der begründeten Überzeugung war, die Personalsituation (Editionsleiter und drei Editoren gegenüber sechs Editorenstellen in 1980) lasse die parallele Bearbeitung zweier Reihen nicht zu. Als man sich, wie auf dem vorigen Internationalen Leibniz-Kongress an dieser Stelle berichtet,[1] gegen Ende 2010 entschloss, die Bearbeitung der philosophischen Schriften *zusätzlich zur Weiterführung der Briefreihe* wieder aufzunehmen, waren dafür vor allem zwei Gründe bestimmend – zu denen die Verbesserung der Personalsituation jedoch leider nicht gehörte. Ausschlaggebend war vielmehr zum einen die Einsicht in die schiere Notwendigkeit mit der Edition der philosophischen Schriften irgendwie vorankommen zu müssen, da diese aufgrund ihrer zentralen Bedeutung das Hauptdesiderat der internationalen Leibnizforschung darstellt. Der Grund dafür, dass die Reaktivierung der Reihe VI nicht mit einer zeitweiligen Einstellung der Arbeiten an Reihe II verbunden sein konnte, die Edition also seit 2011 zweigleisig (Schriften *und* Briefe) läuft, war und ist der Umstand, dass die Briefe vielfach wichtige Informationen für die Datierung der von Leibniz zumeist nicht datierten philosophischen Traktate, Skizzen, Notizen und Zettel liefern und in dieser Hinsicht die Bearbeitung der Korrespondenz die notwendige Grundlage für eine Bearbeitung der Schriften bildet.

Nach mehr als fünf Jahren paralleler Arbeit an den Reihen II und VI lässt sich sagen, dass die Entscheidung, dies zu tun nicht nur unvermeidbar, sondern auch richtig war; so hat die Leibniz-Forschungsstelle Münster im Mai

---

[1] Vgl. Stephan Meier-Oeser: „Bericht über die Editionsarbeiten der Leibniz-Forschungsstelle Münster", in: Herbert Breger/Jürgen Herbst/Sven Erdner (Hrsg.): *Natur und Subjekt*, Akten des IX. Internationalen Leibniz-Kongresses, Hannover 26. Sept. bis 1. Okt. 2011, Nachtragsband, S. 322–325.

2015 eine halbe Editorenstelle hinzubekommen, so dass sich zumindest eine positiven Tendenz in der Personalentwicklung abzeichnet. Die parallele Edition der beiden Reihen hat aber natürlich zur Konsequenz, dass durch die damit verbundene Aufteilung der Arbeitskapazität die Bearbeitung jeder der beiden Reihen langsamer vorankommt, als es bei der Konzentrierung auf eine Reihe der Fall wäre.

Es gibt weitere Faktoren, die das nach außen hin wahrnehmbare Tempo des Voranschreitens der Bandproduktion beeinträchtigen. In erster Linie sind dies gleichsam im Hintergrund laufende aber durchaus zeitaufwendig Arbeiten, die primär unsere eigene Dateninfrastruktur betreffen: So etwa 1) die Umstellung unserer TUSTEP-basierten Editionssoftware auf xml-Kompatibilität, durch die nun garantiert ist, dass die im Zuge unserer Editionsarbeiten generierten Daten auch in andere Programmwelten übertragen werden können, 2) der Aufbau einer Bilddatenbank der weit über 3000 bislang nachgewiesenen Wasserzeichen, die dazu beitragen kann, das bei den Schriften oftmals schwierige und mühselige Geschäft der Datierung zu unterstützen, sowie 3) die Digitalisierung und OCR-Bearbeitung der älteren Bände der Akademieausgabe für den Aufbau einer Volltextdatenbank, die es uns ermöglicht, kontextsensitive Abfragen (etwa die Okkurrenz zweier Begriffe in einem Umfeld von beliebig wählbarer Größe) über nahezu alle Bände der Akademie-Ausgabe laufen zu lassen. Das ist für all jene eine große Hilfe, die den kompletten Leibniz noch immer nicht auswendig kennen. Anderes dagegen ist sichtbar, wie etwa 4) die im Downloadbereich unserer Website (http://www.uni-muenster.de/Leibniz) zur Verfügung gestellten Variantenanalysen für alle bisher erschienenen Bände, welche die Lesbarkeit unseres mitunter sehr komplexen Textstufenapparates signifikant verbessert. Aber es kostet natürlich Zeit, so etwas einzurichten.

Gleichwohl schreitet die Bearbeitung beider Reihen voran – langsamer, als wir uns das selber wünschen würden, aber doch so schnell, wie es unter den gegebenen Umständen eben möglich ist. Seit dem letzten internationalen Leibniz-Kongress ist der 2013 in Druck gegangene und im Februar 2014 ausgelieferte Band II, 3 erschienen. Er deckt die Jahre von 1695 bis einschließlich 1700 ab – und damit einen Zeitraum, der für konzeptionelle Ausarbeitung der Leibniz'schen Metaphysik von erheblicher Bedeutung ist.

Mit dem Ende Juni und Anfang Juli 1695 im *Journal des Sçavans* gedruckten präsentiert Leibniz mit seinem *Système nouveau de la nature et de la communication des Substances* erstmals seine Metaphysik (in mehr als nur spärlichen Andeutungen) der Öffentlichkeit. Bereits im Vorfeld hat sich Leibniz seit Anfang des Jahres darum bemüht, seine Korrespondenz mit den prominenten französischen Intellektuellen zu reaktivieren, um mit diesen in eine Diskussion über sein metaphysisches System zu kommen. In dieser Absicht kontaktierte er (mit durchaus unterschiedlichem Erfolg) Malebranche, Foucher und Huet und versucht auch über Basnage de Bauval, Bayle zur Übersendung – oder besser noch: zur Veröffentlichung einer Stellungnahme zu bewegen. Allem Anschein nach war es gerade die anstehende Veröffentlichung seiner in ihren wesentlichen Grundzügen bereits seit längerem vorliegenden Metaphysik, die bei Leibniz, in Antizipation der von ihm selbst immer wieder eingeforderten Einwände und Erwiderungen, zu einem Prozess der vertiefenden Reflexion und begrifflichen Ausgestaltung führte, der sich erst nach der Drucklegung dieser Schrift in terminologisch greifbaren Resultaten konkretisiert hat. Denn erst kurz *nach* dem Erscheinen des *Systeme nouveau* – nämlich in der Zeit von Ende Juli bis Ende September 1695 – prägt Leibniz die für seine Metaphysik zentralen Termini der Monade (*monas*) der „substance simple" und der „harmonie preétablie"; gegen Ende des Jahres wird noch der Begriff der „Theodicaea" hinzukommen.

In einem wichtigen Punkt unterscheidet sich Band II, 3 von den früheren Bänden dieser Reihe: Wie schon im Vorwort von II, 2 angekündigt, enthält er nämlich – wie auch alle späteren Bände (von sehr seltenen und inhaltlich begründeten Ausnahmen abgesehen) – keine sog. „Doppeldrucke" mehr, d. h. es wird auf den Abdruck oder Teilabdruck von Briefen verzichtet, die zwar philosophischen Inhalt aufweisen, aber bereits in einer anderen Reihe veröffentlicht wurden bzw. einer anderen Reihe zur Veröffentlichung zugeordnet sind. Die Gründe dafür sind bereits im letzten Editionsbericht genannt worden sowie in der Einleitung zu II, 3 nachzulesen. Der damit für die Bände der philosophischen Briefreihe zwangsläufig verbundenen Ausfall an Informationen wird dadurch ein Stück weit aufgefangen, dass 1) in der Einleitung gerade auch die inhaltlichen Bezüge von unseren Briefen zu den in anderen Reihen edierten Briefen angesprochen und deutlich gemacht werden und 2) dadurch, dass im Anschluss an die Einleitung ein zweites Inhaltsverzeichnis abgedruckt wird, bei dem in die Liste der in unserem Band edierten Briefe die philosophisch relevanten Briefe der Reihen I und III in chronologischer Folge interpoliert sind. Dabei geben kurze stichwortartige Hinweise Aufschluss über die dort jeweils angesprochene philosophische Thematik.

Der nächste Band, der in Münster fertiggestellt werden wird, ist der nachfolgende Band der philosophischen Briefe, Bd. II, 4, der die Zeit von 1701 bis einschließlich 1706 umfassen wird. Vollständig im Internet stehen daraus gegenwärtig die Korrespondenzen mit Henri Basnage de Beauval,

George Cheyne, Ernst Salomon Cyprian, Friedrich Boguslav Dobrzensky, Pierre-Daniel Huet, Demoiselle Leti, Damaris Lady Masham, Claude Nicaise, William Pulteney (vormals L an Unbekannt), Johann Christian Schulenburg, Giovanni Battista Tolomei sowie mit einem Unbekannten (vormals L an Barbeyrac). Die Erst- und Zweitbearbeitung ist abgeschlossen für die Korrespondenzen mit Pierre Bayle (41 S.) Jaques Bernard (10 S.), sowie für den größten Teil des Briefwechsels mit Burchard de Volder (86 S.). Weitgehend fertig ist die Bearbeitung der Korrespondenz mit Michael Gottlieb Hansch, die sogar schon über die zeitliche Bandgrenze hinausgehend bis zum 16.10.1707 (64 S.) reicht. Diese Briefe werden in jedem Fall noch im laufenden Jahr 2016 im Internet greifbar sein. Band II, 4 wird insgesamt vor Ende nächsten Jahres so weit fertig bearbeitet sein, dass noch 2017 der definitive Text sämtlicher Briefe im Internet stehen wird. Was ferner bedeutet, dass der Band in jedem Fall 2018 in gedruckter Form erscheinen wird.

Erklärungsbedürftig ist wohl der Umstand, dass in II, 4 keine Briefe der bereits 1705 beginnenden Korrespondenz mit Christian Wolff enthalten sein werden. Mit dieser hat es eine besondere Bewandtnis, da wir hier aus inhaltlichen Gründen anders verfahren als sonst üblich. Normalerweise ist jeder Briefwechsel als ganzer einer Reihe zugeordnet. Hier jedoch haben wir uns ausnahmsweise für eine Aufteilung entschieden. Der Briefwechsel ist nämlich zunächst fast ausschließlich auf mathematische Thematik focussiert. Philosophische Themen treten erst später, nämlich im Herbst 1708 deutlich in den Vordergrund. Daher wird die für die mathematische Korrespondenz zuständige Reihe III die Briefe bis zum 1.10.1708 edieren und Reihe II (beginnend mit Band II, 5) alles Spätere.

Neben Band II, 4 ist gegenwärtig Band VI, 5 in Bearbeitung, der – aus Gründen, die im vorigen Bericht der Edition nachzulesen sind – den Zeitraum von Juli 1690 bis 1703 umfassen muss und wird. Der Band deckt damit, genau wie VI, 4, einen Zeitraum von 13 1/2 Jahren. Da die philosophische Aktivität von Leibniz in dieser Zeit nicht geringer geworden ist, kann man also davon ausgehen, dass dieser Band auch vom Umfang her nicht erheblich schmaler ausfallen sollte. Nach dem bisher als einschlägig für VI, 5 ermittelten Material ist jedenfalls von drei Teilbänden auszugehen, die jedoch, anders als im Fall von VI, 4, nicht simultan, d. h. erst nach kompletter Bearbeitung des letzten Teilbandes, erscheinen werden. Vielmehr wird jeder Teilband separat mit allen zugehörigen Registern gedruckt. Da die Aufteilung in Fachgruppen gegenüber Band VI, 4 weitgehend identisch bleibt (A. Scientia generalis, B. Metaphysica, C. Philosophia naturalis, D. Theologia, E. Moralia, F. Jus naturale,

G. Varia), wird also der erste Band die zur Scientia generalis und zur Metaphysik gehörigen Stücke beinhalten.

Auch die Stücke von VI, 5 werden, bevor die Bände im Druck erscheinen, auf der Website der Leibniz-Forschungsstelle als Voraus-Edition im PDF-Format zur Verfügung gestellt. Verschiedenes steht bereits dort. In den nächsten Wochen, d. h. im Herbst 2016, wird eine größere Zahl an Texten hinzukommen, darunter prominente ‚Klassiker' wie das *Système nouveau de la nature et de la communication des Substances* (1. und 2. Konzept), *De rerum originatione radicali*, *Von der wahren theologia mystica* oder die *Animadversiones in partem generalem Principiorum Cartesianorum* – aber auch Texte, die bislang gänzlich unbekannt sind, wie etwa das zwölf engbeschriebene Folioseiten umfassende Stück Aus und zu Henning Huthmanns *Gründlicher Sprachkunst insonderheit auf das Latein eingerichtet* oder Leibniz' recht umfangreiche Marginalien zu Spinozas *more geometrico* Beweis der *Principia Philosophiae* von Descartes (*Renati des Cartes Principiorum philosophiae Pars I, et II, More Geometrico demonstratae per Benedictum de Spinoza*, Amsterdam 1663).

Leibniz-Edition Potsdam

Friedrich Beiderbeck / Stephan Waldhoff

Kurz vor dem letzten Internationalen Leibniz-Kongress (2011) war unser Band 7 in der Bearbeitung durch die Editionsstelle abgeschlossen und an den Verlag gegangen. Er war also noch im Druck und ist gleichzeitig mit zwei weiteren Editionsbänden im Dezember 2011 publiziert worden, trotzdem ist er damals bereits auf dem Kongress vorgestellt worden. Seitdem ist Band 8 im Juni 2015 erschienen. Es ist der erste Band in unserer Reihe, der nicht mehr im jetzt aufgelösten Akademie Verlag erschienen ist, sondern im Verlag Walter de Gruyter (Berlin/Boston). Band IV, 8 behandelt bei einem Umfang von LXX; 788 Seiten die Jahre 1699 und 1700. Der Berichtszeitraum von zwei Jahren (tatsächlich sind es sogar nur knapp zwei Jahre) ist im Blick auf die bisher in Reihe IV erschienenen Bände eher kurz. Das zeigt bereits, dass es um eine politisch stark bewegte Zeit geht, jedenfalls für Leibniz. Im Folgenden sei der Inhalt in seinen Hauptzügen kurz vorgestellt.

Zur biographischen Einordnung muss ein kurzer Blick zurückgeworfen werden: Um die Jahreswende 1697/98 setzte der für Leibniz so folgenreiche Kontakt zu Brandenburg-Preußen ein. Zunächst ging es um kirchenpolitische Fragen, näherhin den Versuch einer Union zwischen Lutheranern (Hannover) und Reformierten (Brandenburg). Einen Höhepunkt der Gespräche bildete die von Leibniz und Gerhard Wolter Molanus gemeinsam verfasste lutherische Unionsschrift unter dem Titel *Unvorgreiffliches Bedencken*, die Leibniz im Februar 1699 in Berlin überreichen konnte. Das *Unvorgreiffliche Bedencken* fällt somit in den Berichtszeitraum des neuen Bandes. Es ist allerdings mit einigen weiteren, ihm eng verbundenen Stücken aus dem Jahr 1699 in Band 7 gedruckt worden.[1] Dadurch sollte zum einen vermieden werden, diese Schrift von ihren Vorarbeiten zu trennen, zum anderen stellt sie eine gewisse Zäsur in den Unionsverhandlungen dar. Jetzt traten von dritter Seite Akteure auf, die aus Leibniz' Sicht eher störten als nützten, weil sie Unruhe und Unübersichtlichkeit in das Gespräch brachten und die konfessionellen Hardliner zur Unzeit aufzuschrecken drohten.[2]

Zeitlich parallel zum Beginn der Verhandlungen mit den Reformierten war das Gespräch mit den Katholiken wieder in Gang gekommen. Der Nach-

---

[1] A IV, 7, N. 76–79, 177.
[2] A IV, 8, N. 60–62.

folger von Leibniz' langjährigem Gesprächspartner Cristobal de Rojas y Spinola als Bischof der Wiener Neustadt, Franz Anton von Buchhaim, hatte im September 1698 mit Molanus und Leibniz in Loccum getagt. Von Ende Oktober bis Mitte Dezember 1700 weilte Leibniz im Gegenzug in Wien und Umgebung. Hier hatte er die Möglichkeit den Nachlass von Rojas einzusehen, sich Exzerpte und Abschriften anzufertigen oder anfertigen zu lassen und konnte sogar eine Reihe von Papieren aus dem Nachlass mit nach Hannover nehmen.[3] Leibniz' Beschäftigung mit Rojas' Hinterlassenschaft weist in zwei Richtungen: Zum einen zurück, in die Sammlung von Dokumenten aus der jahrzehntelangen Wirksamkeit des Bischofs, aus der Leibniz den Versuch einer biographischen Rekonstruktion unternahm,[4] zum anderen voraus unter der Frage, wie sich aus dem Material Ansatzpunkte für zukünftige Verhandlungen gewinnen ließen.[5]

Schließlich sei ein dritter Punkt angesprochen, in dem der neue Band an Früheres anknüpft. Im Jahr 1693 hatte Leibniz eine Sammlung völkerrechtlich relevanter Urkunden aus der Zeit von um 1100 bis 1500 veröffentlicht, den *Codex juris gentium diplomaticus*.[6] Dem ersten, auf das Mittelalter beschränkten Band sollten weitere zum 16. und zum 17. Jahrhundert folgen. Der *Codex* war ein großer Erfolg, und Leibniz erhielt zahlreiche Angebote aus der Gelehrtenrepublik, ihn bei der Fortsetzung des Werkes mit Materiallieferungen zu unterstützen. Zu den beiden Fortsetzungsbänden ist es nie gekommen, aber Ende 1700 erschien ein Supplementband, die *Mantissa codicis juris gentium diplomatici,* die weitere Dokumente aus dem Mittelalter brachte, nun allerdings nicht mehr in chronologischer, sondern in sachlicher Ordnung und ohne sich strikt an das Endjahr 1500 zu halten.[7]

Diese drei Aspekte des neuen Bandes knüpfen an vorangehende Bände der vierten Reihe an. Was begegnet an neuen Themen? Hier sind zwei große Themenfelder zu nennen: zum einen die Akademiegründung in Berlin und zum anderen der Streit um die Spanische Erbfolge. Die Gründung der Akademie oder, wie sie damals hieß, der Sozietät der Wissenschaften zu Berlin ist sicherlich der bekannteste Aspekt des Bandes, auf jeden Fall aber jener, der

---

[3] Ebd., N. 45.
[4] Ebd., N. 51.
[5] Ebd., N. 52–55.
[6] Ebd., 5, N. 1–7, 9.
[7] Ebd., 8, N. 3–5; 7–11; 13f.

am besten erforscht ist. Zum Akademiejubiläum 1900 hat Adolf (von) Harnack im Aktenband seiner Geschichte der Akademie auf mehr als 100 Seiten relevante Briefe und Dokumente abgedruckt[8] und vor gut zwei Jahrzehnten hat Hans-Stephan Brather einen umfangreichen Editionsband über *Leibniz und seine Akademie* vorgelegt.[9] Kann eine Neuedition der entsprechenden Stücke überhaupt noch etwas Neues bringen oder ist sie allein dem Imperativ der Vollständigkeit geschuldet? In der Tat kann unser Band hier Neues bringen – und zwar in dreifacher Hinsicht: quantitativ, qualitativ und mit Blick auf den Kontext.

Quantitativ: Von den 28 Stücken des Bandes, welche die Akademiegründung betreffen,[10] wird ungefähr ein Drittel zum ersten Mal überhaupt gedruckt. Das mag verwundern angesichts der Fülle des bei Harnack und Brather gebotenen Materials. Es handelt sich bei den bisher ungedruckten Stücken nicht um Hauptschriften, eher um peripheres Material. Gleichwohl wird dadurch das Bild der Akademiegründung vervollständigt, nicht zuletzt in biographischer Hinsicht auf Leibniz selbst.

Qualitativ: Erstmals liegen die für die Berliner Akademiegründung relevanten Texte in einer kritischen Edition vor. Weder Harnack noch Brather haben die von ihnen publizierten Texte kritisch ediert. Auch wenn der Letztgenannte zuverlässige Texte bietet, so fehlen ihnen doch die kritischen Apparate. Gerade bei den Texten zur Akademiegründung ist die Textgenese, wie sie im kritischen Apparat der Akademie-Ausgabe rekonstruiert wird, von besonderem Interesse. Leibniz selbst war ja nicht der Gründer der Berliner Akademie – genauso wenig wie später Wilhelm von Humboldt Gründer der Berliner Universität gewesen ist. Die Gründung konnte nur der Herrscher vollziehen. Im Gegensatz zu Humboldt war Leibniz nicht einmal brandenburgisch-preußischer Beamter. Er konnte Ideen ins Spiel bringen, Denkschriften formulieren, Entwürfe für offizielle Schriftstücke aufsetzen. An das, was Rechtskraft erhalten sollte, konnte er nie letzte Hand anlegen. Hier hatten der Fürst und seine Beamten das letzte Wort. Erst die kritische Edition erlaubt in vielen Fällen, Leibniz' Anteil präzise von den Eingriffen der Berliner Beamten abzugrenzen und zu bestimmen. Das stellt, nebenbei bemerkt, die Ausgabe vor

---

[8] Adolf von Harnack: *Geschichte der Königlich Preußischen Akademie der Wissenschaften zu Berlin*, 2. Bd.: *Urkunden und Actenstücke zur Geschichte der Königlich Preußischen Akademie der Wissenschaften*, Berlin 1900, S. 3–128.
[9] Hans-Stephan Brather (Hrsg.): *Leibniz und seine Akademie. Ausgewählte Quellen zur Geschichte der Berliner Sozietät der Wissenschaften 1697–1716*, Berlin 1993.
[10] A IV, 8, N. 72–99.

ein gewisses Problem: An sich dient ihr als Druckvorlage die letzte von Leibniz autorisierte Textfassung. Hier begegnen aber Fälle – etwa die General-Instruktion der Sozietät[11]–, in denen die letzte Fassung in diesem Sinne noch nicht jene ist, die abschließend rechtsgültig und damit historisch wirksam geworden ist. Als Lösung wird in derartigen Fällen zum synoptischen Paralleldruck gegriffen, welcher der Fassung, die Leibniz nach manchen eigenen Eingriffen und Veränderungen aus der Hand gegeben hat, diejenige gegenübergestellt, die schließlich rechtsverbindlich ausgefertigt worden ist.

Mit Blick auf den Kontext: Harnack und Brather haben sich verständlicherweise auf die Akademiegründung konzentriert. In unserem Band – und nicht zuletzt in Verbindung mit den einschlägigen Bänden der Reihe I – tritt ein breiterer Kontext in den Blick. Leibniz hatte der Wissenschaft schon sehr früh die Aufgabe zugewiesen, dem Gemeinwohl zu dienen. Für die von ihm projektierten Akademien als die prominentesten Agenten einer derartig praktisch wirksam werdenden Wissenschaft musste selbstverständlich dasselbe gelten. Gerade in den bisher zumeist unpublizierten To-do-Listen, in denen er sich notiert hat, was in Berlin zu erledigen war, tritt die Einbettung der Akademiegründung in einen breiteren Kontext von ökonomischen und administrativen Reformen hervor, die Leibniz in Berlin propagieren wollte.[12] Da geht es etwa um Brandschutz, Renten und Versicherungen, überhaupt um Fragen der Daseinsvorsorge. Aus dieser Perspektive erklärt sich eine spätere gewisse Verschiebung seiner Berliner Interessen hin zu im engeren Sinne politischen Themen ganz zwanglos.

Das zweite große Thema, das mit dem neuen Band in der Edition der *Politischen Schriften* ans Licht tritt, ist der Streit um die Spanische Erbfolge. Am 1. November 1700, als Leibniz gerade in Wien weilte, war Karl II. von Spanien kinderlos gestorben. Der Tod des spanischen Königs kam freilich nicht unvorbereitet. Im Gegenteil: Ganz Europa hatte ihn seit Jahren erwartet. In der Auseinandersetzung um das Erbe stand Leibniz auf der Seite der Habsburger gegen die Bourbonen, die sich letztlich durchsetzen sollten. Noch in Wien machte er sich an die Arbeit, die habsburgischen Ansprüche publizistisch zu verteidigen. Für eine derartige Arbeit war Leibniz als Jurist und Historiograph des Welfenhauses methodisch gut gerüstet. Bevor er selbst in den publizistischen Streit eingreifen konnte, hieß es zunächst, relevantes Urkundenmaterial zu sammeln, genealogische Beziehungen zu erhellen, sich mit den unterschiedlichen Nachfolgeordnungen der einzelnen Gebiete zu beschäftigen

---

[11] Ebd., N. 80.
[12] Ebd.,, N. 73f.; 76f.; 90.

und die erscheinenden Flugschriften zu beobachten. Vor allem die juristisch-politischen Fragen waren komplex, da das, was in Kastilien galt, in Aragon noch lange nicht gelten musste, und was in Neapel wichtig war, konnte für Mailand irrelevant sein. Auf der Ebene des Sammelns, Recherchierens und Zusammenstellens bewegen sich daher die Aufzeichnungen zur Spanischen Erbfolge, die in Band 8 ediert sind:[13] Vorarbeiten für eine publizistische Intervention. Der Konflikt, der schnell zum Krieg eskalierte, sollte Europa und Leibniz noch mehr als ein Jahrzehnt beschäftigen.

Mit dem Jahr 1701 wird unser neunter, derzeit in Arbeit befindlicher Band eröffnet. Erste, der Öffentlichkeit zugängliche Resultate können als Vorausedition über das den verschiedenen Reihen der Leibniz-Edition gemeinsame Portal abgerufen werden.[14] Eines der großen und Platz greifenden Themen wird auch hier der Spanische Erbfolgestreit sein, der sich 1701 zu einem europäischen Krieg entwickelte. Leibniz stellte seine publizistische Tätigkeit in kaiserliche Dienste: Mit Billigung des Wiener Hofes erschienen im Frühjahr bzw. im Herbst 1701 die beiden Auflagen seiner die habsburgischen Erbrechte verteidigenden Schrift *La justice encouragée*; ein umfangreicher Traktat, mit dem er sich gleichzeitig für den Reichshofratstitel empfahl. Es ist uns gelungen, ein Exemplar der bislang unauffindbaren im Mai 1701 erschienenen 1. Auflage ausfindig zu machen.[15] Diese Erstauflage enthält neben einem *Avertissement de l'imprimeur* zunächst nur die französische Fassung von Leibniz anonym verfasster *Lettre écrite d'Amsterdam*. Leibniz hat diesen unter dem Gesamttitel *La justice encouragée* veröffentlichten Traktat als Antwort auf die Ende 1700 anonym erschiene Flugschrift *Lettre écrite d'Anvers* konzipiert. Die vermutlich aus dem Umkreis des spanischen Diplomaten Francisco Bernardo de Quiros stammende Schrift verteidigt die Entscheidung Ludwigs XIV., das pro-französische Testament Karls II. von Spanien anzunehmen und den Herzog von Anjou als Philipp V. zum neuen König von Spanien auszurufen. Ein Exemplar dieser *Lettre d'Anvers* schickte Leibniz zusammen mit einer handschriftlichen Fassung seiner Replik, der *Lettre écrite d'Amsterdam*, Anfang Februar 1701 an den Wiener Hof. Die günstige Reaktion aus dem kaiserlichen Umfeld ermutigte Leibniz zum Druck der Erstauflage seiner Schrift, die im Mai 1701 unter dem Titel *La justice encouragée contre les chicanes et les menaces d'un partisan des Bourbons* und unter Angabe des fingierten Druckortes Cologne (chez Pierre Marteau) höchstwahrscheinlich in Holland anonym

---

[13] Ebd., N. 19–32.
[14] http://www.leibnizedition.de/baende/reihe-iv-politische-schriften.html.
[15] Eutin, Landesbibl.; Sammlung Adolf Friedrichs, Fürstbischof v. Lübeck.

erschien. Eine kommentierte und ins Deutsche übersetzte Fassung der *Lettre d'Anvers* gab Leibniz schließlich zusammen mit seiner *Lettre d'Amsterdam*, die er dann ebenfalls in deutscher Fassung brachte, in der wohl vor Mitte September 1701 erschienen 2. Auflage der *Justice encouragée* heraus.

Der englischen Sukzession der Welfen widmete sich Leibniz mit großem, persönlichem Einsatz. Vor allem vermöge seiner vertrauten Position bei Kurfürstin Sophie erscheint er als treibende Kraft für das Betreiben des Thronfolgeanspruches. Leibniz hat

> „auf diesem Gebiete die bedeutendste Tätigkeit und Wirksamkeit ausgeübt, die dem sonst weitgehend vom praktischen Handeln ausgeschlossenen Gelehrten im politischen Bereich überhaupt vergönnt war."[16]

Diese Einschätzung scheint durch die Kette der Ereignisse weitgehend bestätigt zu werden: Leibniz drängte über einen längeren Zeitraum die Kurfürstin als präsumtive Thronerbin auf eine entschlossene Verfolgung ihrer in England vor 1700 wenig beachteten Erbansprüche.[17] 1701 kulminierte die Entwicklung in verfassungsrechtlicher Hinsicht: Auf die Initiative Wilhelms III. hin ordnete das englische Parlament mit dem Act of Settlement (22. Juni 1701) die Erbfolge zugunsten Sophies und ihrer Nachkommenschaft. In unserem neunten Band schlägt sich diese Entwicklung in mehreren Stücken nieder: Die Aufarbeitung der Quellen beispielsweise zum Umfeld des sogenannten Celler Conseils (15.–18. Januar 1701) belegt, dass neben den mündlichen Erörterungen, an denen Leibniz beteiligt war, auch seine Aufzeichnungen bzw. Schreiben für fürstliche Willensbildungsprozesse von Bedeutung waren.[18] So bieten wir Leibniz' französische Übertragung einer im Original bisher nicht aufgefundenen englischen Schrift des Schotten Peter Frasier von 1700. Die Übersetzung gehört in den thematischen und zeitlichen Kontext der *Reflexions sur un écrit Anglois*, die auf den 2. Januar 1701 datiert sind und die Leibniz offenbar als Grundlage für ein Gespräch mit Kurfürstin Sophie erstellt hatte.

---

[16] Georg Schnath: *Geschichte Hannovers im Zeitalter der neunten Kur und der englischen Sukzession 1674–1714. Im Anschluß an Adolf Köcher's unvollendete „Geschichte von Hannover und Braunschweig 1648-1714", Band 4: Georg Ludwigs Weg auf den englischen Thron. Die Vorgeschichte der Thronfolge 1698-1714* (= Veröffentlichungen der historischen Kommission für Niedersachsen und Bremen 18), Hildesheim 1982, S. 8.
[17] Z. B. A I, 13, N. 44f.
[18] Vgl., ebd.,19, XXXV–XXXVII.

Mit der Gründung der Sozietät der Wissenschaften in Berlin im Sommer 1700 hatte gleichfalls ein Projekt Gestalt angenommen, das Leibniz dauerhaft umtreiben sollte und das demnach auch im Berichtszeitraum des neunten Bandes einen wichtigen Platz einnimmt. Als Präsident beschäftigte er sich mit dem Vorhaben, unter Betreuung der Sozietät protestantische Missionare nach China zu schicken, wobei Russland als Transitland einmal mehr in den Vordergrund rückte. Nach Leibniz' Vorstellungen sollte die Sozietät sich um die wissenschaftliche Forschung im Zarenreich kümmern und dem kurbrandenburgischen Gesandten Georg Johann von Keyserlingk, der 1701 in das Zarenreich aufbrach, eine entsprechende Begleitung an die Seite geben. Es wurde auch versucht, Elias Kopiewicz als Drucker russischer Bücher für die Sozietät zu gewinnen und ein Privileg auf deren Druckerzeugnisse in Russland zu erhalten. Zusammen mit drei Agendenlisten und einem Vorschlag zur Veranstaltung einer Lotterie sind das neun Stücke, von denen fünf erstmals erscheinen werden. Leibniz entwickelte die Idee, für die Sozietät ein Privileg auf die Produktion von Seide zu erwirken. In diesem Zusammenhang entstanden zahl- und umfangreiche Stücke, die aber möglicherweise erst in Band 10 erscheinen werden.

Die preußische Königskrönung vom 18. Januar 1701 und ihre Rezeption bietet ein Hauptthema, das aufgrund seines Umfanges von gut vier Dutzend Stücken eine eigene Rubrik erhält: ‚Auszug die preussische Crone angehender Schriften' (III.C). Unter diesem Titel hat Leibniz in der Juli- und der August-Ausgabe des *Monathlichen Auszuges* neben zwei Abhandlungen Referate über und Auszüge aus den zu den Krönungsfeierlichkeiten veröffentlichten Schriften vor allem panegyrischen und homiletischen Charakters zusammengestellt.

Hauptstück der Abteilung ‚Kirchenpolitik' (IV.) wird Leibniz' Kommentierung der lateinischen, von dem Berliner reformierten Hofprediger Daniel Ernst Jablonski angefertigten Übersetzung eines englischen Kommentars zum 17. der 39 Artikel der Anglikanischen Kirche sein. Aus Gilbert Burnets Kommentar über die 39 Artikel hatte Jablonski allein die Kommentierung dieses Artikels, welcher der zwischen den protestantischen Konfessionen umstrittenen Frage der Prädestination gewidmet ist, aus irenischer Motivation ausgewählt. Leibniz wollte durch eine Kommentierung des anglikanischen Kommentars aus lutherischer Sicht an diese Motivation anknüpfen. Der von ihm kommentierte Text sollte als 2. Auflage von Jablonskis Werk erscheinen. 1706 scheint das in den Kontext der Unionsverhandlungen zwischen Hannover und Berlin gehörende Projekt zusammen mit den Verhandlungen selbst schließlich abgebrochen worden zu sein.

Zum Komplex ‚Neunte Kur' bieten wir einen sehr umfangreichen, 1702 im *Theatrum Europaeum* gedruckten Bericht über deren Erwerbung.[19] Es handelt sich dabei um eine einzigartige Zusammenstellung wichtiger Dokumente, die das schwierige Ringen um die Neunte Kur für Braunschweig-Lüneburg-Hannover in den Jahren 1692/93 illustrieren. In einem Schreiben von Jobst Christoph Reiche an Leibniz[20] wird ein entsprechendes Vorhaben thematisiert. Weitere Hinweise zu dem Projekt finden sich in den Jahren 1696 und 1699/1700. Wenn nach gegenwärtigem Bearbeitungsstand zumindest davon auszugehen ist, dass Leibniz an der Quellenauswahl entscheidend beteiligt war, so kann nicht ausgeschlossen werden, dass er sich selbst für die Zusammenstellung und die jeweiligen Einleitungspassagen dieses Werkes verantwortlich zeichnete.

Am 19./20. März 1702 wurde Braunschweig-Wolfenbüttel durch Truppen Hannovers und Celles besetzt. Die Erschütterung des welfischen Gesamthauses veranlasste Leibniz dazu, sich mit Vermittlungs- und Versöhnungsvorschlägen zu befassen. In Schreiben an die Geheimen Räte in Hannover vom 24. bzw. 26. März 1702 äußerte Leibniz Bedenken gegen mögliche weitere Gewaltanwendung und empfahl Maßnahmen zugunsten eines innerdynastischen Ausgleiches. Allerdings legte er Hannover auch nahe, von Wolfenbüttel Zugeständnisse in der Frage der Neunten Kur, der Primogenitur und der Vereinigung der Fürstentümer Hannover und Celle zu verlangen. Eine entsprechende, von uns aufgenommene Aufzeichnung müsste denn auch in den Verhandlungs-Zeitraum vor dem Abschluss des inner-welfischen Braunschweiger Vergleiches am 19. April 1702 datiert werden.

Der Tod Wilhelms III. von England, Schottland und Irland am 19. März 1702, der in Personalunion auch als Statthalter der Vereinigten Niederlande fungierte, stellte die Frage nach dem Erbe des oranischen Dynastiebesitzes. Anders als viele – wie auch Leibniz – erwarteten, war nicht König Friedrich I., Sohn von Louise Henriette von Oranien, zum Nachfolger bestimmt worden, sondern Johann Wilhelm Friso von Nassau-Diez. Der Hohenzoller legte Widerspruch ein und Leibniz stellte mit einer Reihe von Denkschriften seine historisch-juristischen Kenntnisse in den Dienst Berlins.

---

[19] *Theatrum Europaeum,* Bd. XIV, Frankfurt a. M. 1702, S. 313–339, 507–509.
[20] Sommer 1696; A I, 13, N. 1.

Einführung in die Benutzung der Akademie-Ausgabe

Herma Kliege-Biller (Münster)

Greift der an Leibniz interessierte Leser zur Akademie-Ausgabe, so sieht er sich im Jahre 2016 knapp 60 umfangreichen Bänden mit mehr als 50.000 Seiten Leibniztexten gegenüber, verteilt auf sieben unterschiedliche Reihen, kritisch ediert mit einem auf den ersten Blick kryptischen Variantenapparat unter dem Text und einem bisweilen nicht viel weniger kryptischen editorischen Bericht im Stückkopf.

In der Edition kann man Autoren in „Kopfarbeiter" oder „Papierarbeiter" einteilen: Leibniz gehört eindeutig zu letzteren. Während der Kopfarbeiter seine Texte lange in Gedanken überlegt und ausformuliert, bevor er sie dann oft wie aus einem Guss und nur mit wenigen Korrektureingriffen niederschreibt, hat Leibniz schreibend gedacht und denkend geschrieben und auf diese Weise an die 50.000 Stücke auf annähernd 200.000 Blatt verfasst sowie gegen 20.000 Briefe mit etwa 1300 Korrespondenten gewechselt (und dies ist nur das Material, das uns heute noch vorliegt). Dieser Prozess spiegelt sich in den zahllosen Eingriffen in den Manuskripten wider, in Streichungen, Ergänzungen, Umformulierungen, Überarbeitungen, manchmal nur ein Wort, eine Phrase oder einen Abschnitt betreffend, oft aber auch so umfangreich, dass eine Niederschrift nicht ausreichte. Ein stark bearbeitetes Konzept, von dem der Schreiber eine Reinschrift anfertigt, die Leibniz erneut überarbeitet, wiederum abschreiben lässt, noch einmal bearbeitet und noch einmal abschreiben lässt, so dass am Ende vier oder fünf aufeinander aufbauende Fassungen vorliegen, sind keine Seltenheit.

75 Prozent des Nachlasses sind nie publiziert worden, und nur die wenigsten Schriften, die außerhalb der Akademie-Ausgabe erschienen sind, liegen in einer kritischen Edition vor, die es ermöglicht, die Entwicklung der Leibniz'schen Gedanken nachzuvollziehen – und nirgendwo wird diese Entwicklung deutlicher als in den Varianten. Leibniz selbst hat zu Lebzeiten nur einen geringen Teil seiner Schriften und Briefe publiziert: „Qui me non nisi editis novit, non novit", schrieb er seinem Hamburger Freund und langjährigen Korrespondenten Vincent Placcius am 2. März 1696 (A II, 3 N. 48, 139): „Wer mich nur aus meinen Veröffentlichungen kennt, der kennt mich nicht wirklich." Erst durch die Akademie-Ausgabe, die den gesamten Nachlass ediert, erschließt sich der Autor Leibniz in allen Lebensbereichen, in seinem Gesamtschaffen, als Philosoph, Mathematiker, Historiker oder Jurist, als Universalgelehrter, im Ringen um inhaltliche und begriffliche Präzision, in allen

Facetten seiner Biographie. Das ist vor allem bei Leibniz wichtig, der zu Lebzeiten nur so wenig von sich preisgegeben hat. Das, was er veröffentlichte, war nur das, was er die Außenstehenden sehen lassen wollte. Sein Innerstes dagegen, seine gesamte schöpferische Persönlichkeit, offenbart sich nur aus dem gesamten Material, und (nicht nur als Editor der Reihen II und VI) bin ich versucht zu sagen: „Wer Leibniz nur ohne Varianten kennt, der kennt ihn nicht wirklich." Daher möchte ich im Folgenden dem an Leibniz interessierten Leser den Zugang zur Akademie-Ausgabe erleichtern, indem ich zum einen die zahlreichen, zumeist bereits online verfügbaren Hilfsmittel zur Erschließung des immensen Nachlasses aufzeige und zum anderen die Darstellungsweise der Edition erläutere. Ein besonderes Gewicht liegt dabei auf dem Variantenapparat, der, wenn man einen zweiten Blick wagt, beileibe kein Hexenwerk ist, sondern dem Leser, der sich darauf einlässt, seine Geheimnisse bereichernd offenbart.[1]

Einführung in die Benutzung der Akademie-Ausgabe

I. Die Akademie-Ausgabe im Internet
I.1.Die gemeinsame Homepage aller Arbeitsstellen: www.leibnizedition.de

Die gemeinsame Homepage aller Arbeitsstellen enthält die Auflistung aller Bände der Akademie-Ausgabe in gedruckter und elektronischer Form, die Links zu bislang 31 zum kostenlosen Download verfügbaren Bänden der Akademie-Ausgabe,[2] zu Transkriptionen und kumulierten Verzeichnissen, online verfügbaren Hilfsmitteln sowie den Homepages der einzelnen Forschungsstellen in

  a) Hannover: www.gwlb.de/Leibniz/Leibnizarchiv/Einfuehrung/index.html
  b) Münster: www.uni-muenster.de/Leibniz
  c) Potsdam: leibniz-potsdam.bbaw.de
  d) Berlin: www.bbaw.de/forschung/leibniz_berlin

---

[1] Das folgende Paper lag dem Workshop „Einführung in die Benutzung der Akademie-Ausgabe" (Hannover, 19. Juli 2016) zugrunde.
[2] Eine weitere Retrodigitalisierung wird angestrebt.

3. Online-Hilfsmittel zur Akademie-Ausgabe

   a) Generelle Übersicht: www.leibnizedition.de/hilfsmittel.html
   b) Ursprüngliche kumulierte Datenbank für Korrespondenten:
      www.gwlb.de/Leibniz/Leibnizarchiv/Veroeffentlichungen/Korrespondentendatenbank/index.php
   c) Ursprüngliche kumulierte Datenbank für Personen:
      www.gwlb.de/Leibniz/Leibnizarchiv/Veroeffentlichungen/Personendatenbank/index.php
   d) Kumuliertes Personen- / Korrespondentenverzeichnis (ab 2015)
      https://leibniz.uni-goettingen.de
   e) Kumuliertes Sachverzeichnis (Index rerum):
      http://telota.bbaw.de/leibniziv/Sachregister/sachreg_start.php
      (zur Online-Recherche)
      http://leibniz-potsdam.bbaw.de/bilder/Sachverzeichnis.pdf
      (als PDF zum Download)
   f) Kumuliertes Schriftenverzeichnis:
      http://www.uni-muenster.de/Leibniz/Schriften/schriften start.html
   g) Kumuliertes Bibelstellenverzeichnis:
      http://leibniz-potsdam.bbaw.de/bilder/Bibelindex.pdf
   h) Umfangreiche Liste für Leibniz nützlicher Links (auch allgemeine Nachschlagewerke, Homepages für Korrespondenten und Zeitgenossen von Leibniz):
      http://www.gwlb.de/Leibniz/Leibnizarchiv/Links/
   i) Konkordanzen (http://www.leibnizedition.de/hilfsmittel.html) zwischen der Akademie-Ausgabe und
   – Leibniz: *Philosophische Schriften* (Hrsg.: Gerhardt)
   – Leibniz: *Mathematische Schriften* (Hrsg.: Gerhardt) sowie Leibniz: *Briefwechsel mit Mathematikern* (Hrsg.: Gerhardt)
   – den von Foucher de Careil herausgegebenen *Œuvres, Lettres et Opuscules, Nouvelles Lettres et Opuscules*
   – Leibniz: *Textes inédits* (Hrsg.: Grua)
   – Leibniz: *Opuscules et fragments inédits* (Hrsg.: Couturat)
   – Leibniz: *Werke* (Hrsg.: Klopp)
   – Leibniz: *Otium Hanoveranum* (Hrsg.: Feller)
   j) Leibniztexte im Netz: www.uni-muenster.de/Leibniz (Unterpunkt: Leibniz im Netz)

k) Lesehilfe für die Varianten der Reihen II und VI: www.uni-muenster.de/Leibniz (im Downloadbereich der jeweiligen Bände s. v. „Variantenanalyse")
l) Filterprogramme von Prof. Schepers zum Auffinden von Begriffen und Begriffskombinationen (Key-Word-In-Context, mit weiterführenden Zusatzinformationen wie Datierung und Druckort) in den philosophischen und politischen Texten (Suchanfragen an schephe@uni-muenster.de)
m) Hauptseite der Gottfried Wilhelm Leibniz Bibliothek / Niedersächsische Landesbibliothek, dort Menüpunkt „Leibniz" mit Verweis auf: Nachlass, Leben und Werk, Bibliographie, Leibniz-Central, Leibniz-Archiv und Leibniz-Gesellschaft: www.nlb-hannover.de

II. Der Leibniz-Nachlass

Der größte Teil des Leibniz-Nachlasses befindet sich in der Gottfried Wilhelm Leibniz Bibliothek (Niedersächsische Landesbibliothek) in Hannover, weitere Konvolute im Niedersächsischen Landesarchiv (Niedersächsischen Hauptstaatsarchiv) in Hannover.

Eine erste Auflistung des Nachlasses erfolgte durch Eduard Bodemann (1867–1906 Bibliothekspräfekt in Hannover) mit der Einteilung in 42 Handschriftengruppen „LH" (Leibniz-Handschriften) und die 1063 Briefnummern in „LBr" (Leibniz Briefwechsel, neue Signatur im Rahmen des Weltdokumentenerbes: „LK-MOW").

– Eduard Bodemann: *Die Leibniz-Handschriften der Königlichen öffentlichen Bibliothek zu Hannover*, mit Ergänzungen u. Register v. Gisela Krönert/Heinrich Lackmann sowie einem Vorwort v. Karl-Heinz Weimann, Hildesheim 1966 (Reprint der Ausgabe Hannover 1895).
– Eduard Bodemann: *Der Briefwechsel des Gottfried Wilhelm Leibniz in der Königlichen öffentlichen Bibliothek zu Hannover*, mit Ergänzungen u. Register v. Gisela Krönert/Heinrich Lackmann sowie einem Vorwort v. Karl-Heinz Weimann, Hildesheim 1966 (Reprint der Ausgabe Hannover 1889).[3]

---

[3] Anmerkung zu den LK-MOW-Signaturen (Leibniz Korrespondenz Memory of the World): LBr 105 Bl. 3 wird zu: LK-MOW Bouvet10 Bl. 3.

– Eduard Bodemann: *Die Handschriften der Königlichen Öffentlichen Bibliothek zu Hannover*, Hannover 1867.

Die 1901 bei der Begründung der Akademie-Ausgabe initiierte, besonders durch Paul Ritter geprägte und bis heute laufend aktualisierte Katalogisierung des Gesamtnachlasses im sog. *Ritter-Katalog*[4] ist online zugänglich als:
– *Arbeitskatalog der Leibniz-Edition*: https://mdb.lsp.uni-hannover.de (Die Suchergebnisse verlinken auf die entsprechenden Seiten der bereits online zugänglichen Bände der Akademie-Ausgabe, auf bereits mehr als 4.000 online zugängliche Manuskriptscans oder auf die Informationen der Personen- und Korrespondentendatenbank.)
– in einer älteren Form als: *Der Online-Ritterkatalog*: ritter.bbaw.de (mit Scan-Galerie für große Teile von LH III, XXXV, XXXVI, XXXVII u. XXXIIX, sowie einigen Beispielen für Scans mit Transkriptionen auf der Eingangsseite).

Darin eingegangen sind:
– Kritischer Katalog der Leibniz-Handschriften: Zur Vorbereitung der interakademischen Leibniz-Ausg., Faszikel 1, bearbeitet v. Paul Ritter, 1908 (handschriftlich und vervielfältigt), Faszikel 2, *Catalogue critique*

Jakob Bernoulli: LBr 56 Bl. 57–58 wird zu: LK-MOW Bernoulli10 Bl. 57–58.
Johann Bernoulli: LBr 57, 1 Bl. 318 wird zu: LK-MOW Bernoulli20 Bl. 318; LBr 57, 2 Bl. 249–250 wird zu LK-MOW Bernoulli 20 Bl. A249–A250.
Nicolas Bernoulli: LBr 58 Bl. 13–14 wird zu LK-MOW Bernoulli 30 Bl. 13–14.
Daraus folgt in der Regel: Die Signatur wird „sprechend" und enthält den Korrespondentennamen: Bouvet, Bernoulli. Gibt es nur einen Namensträger, erhält er den Zusatz 10, bei mehreren Namensträgern 10, 20, 30 etc. Es wird nur der Name umsigniert, nicht aber die Blattangabe. Finden sich Briefe eines Korrespondenten in verschiedenen Konvoluten, oder ist die Korrespondenz wie im Fall von Johann Bernoulli auf zwei Konvolute aufgeteilt (LBr 57, 1 und LBr 57, 2), bekommen sie trotzdem dieselbe Signatur Bernoulli20, vor der Blattangabe jedoch steht für das fremde Konvolut / die fremden Konvolute A249–250, B260–261 etc., da ansonsten dieselbe Seitenzählung doppelt vergeben wäre. Diese A/B/C-Angaben vor der Blattangabe sind bei der Angabe eines Fundortes zu beachten. (In der Datenbank *Leibniz-Central* (s.u.) ist auch weiterhin eine Recherche anhand der LBr-Signaturen und weiterer Angaben wie etwa der Stücknummer nach Ritter oder dem Catalogue critique möglich.)
[4] Der *Ritter-Katalog* ist das wichtigste Erschließungsinstrument für den Nachlass und ermöglicht eine Vielzahl von komplexen Abfrageoptionen, so etwa für Fundorte, Abfassungsdaten, Incipit, Drucke, Korrespondenzzusammenhänge, Bibliotheksbestände, Inhaltsverzeichnisse der einzelnen Reihen und vieles mehr. Er wurde als kontinuierlich zu ergänzendes und zu erweiterndes internes Arbeitsinstrument(!) für die Edition in Form eines Zettelkastenkatalogs konzipiert und nicht als für die Publikation geplante Datenbank. Insofern erhebt er (noch) keinen Anspruch auf Vollständigkeit, elegantes Webdesign, Stolperfreiheit bei der Suche etc.

des manuscrits de Leibniz, Mars 1672–Novembre 1676, hrsg. v. Albert Rivaud, Poitiers 1914–1924.
– Gesamtkatalog (*Ritter-Katalog*) bis zur Digitalisierung nur als Zettelkatalog in den einzelnen Arbeitsstellen vorhanden.

Die Leibniz-Bibliothek in Hannover strebt mit der im Aufbau begriffenen Datenbank *Leibniz Central* (www.leibnizcentral.de) an, alle wichtigen Informationen zu Leibniz und seinem Nachlass zusammenführen (u. a. mit den Datenbanken Central Suche, Leibniz Katalog – MOW (mit hochauflösenden Scans der Briefe), Leibniz-Arbeitsbibliothek, Leibniz-Bibliographie und Handschriften im Umfeld Leibniz).

III. Bibliographien und Nachschlagewerke

Emile Ravier: *Bibliographie des œuvres de Leibniz*, Paris 1937 (Reprint Hildesheim 1966).
 Die *Leibniz-Bibliographie* (www.leibniz-bibliographie.de) umfasst einen laufend aktualisierten Datenbestand von über 30.000 Titeln; darin enthalten auch die gedruckten Vorgängerversionen:
– *Leibniz-Bibliographie*, Bd. 1, begründet v. Kurt Müller, hrsg. v. Albert Heinekamp, Frankfurt a. Main ^{2}1983
– *Leibniz-Bibliographie, Band 2. Die Literatur über Leibniz 1981-1990*, hrsg. v. Albert Heinekamp unter Mitarbeit v. Marlen Mertens, Frankfurt a. Main 1996.

Kurt Müller/Gisela Krönert: *Leben und Werk von Gottfried Wilhelm Leibniz*, Frankfurt a. Main 1969.

Leibniz. Sein Leben – sein Wirken – seine Welt, hrsg. v. Wilhelm Totok und Carl Haase, Hannover 1966.

IV. Ein Stück (Brief) der Akademie-Ausgabe
A. Zum Stückkopf

Jedes Stück (= Schrift oder Brief) ist durch die Angabe: Reihe - Band - Stücknummer innerhalb der Ausgabe eindeutig identifizierbar: „VI, 4 N. 112"; „I, 3 N. 244". Verweise auf die Akademie-Ausgabe finden sich als „A", „AA"

(= Akademie-Ausgabe) oder „LSB" (= Leibniz Schriften und Briefe). Die Stücknummer wird mit „N." angegeben, nicht mit „Nr.". Bei der Vorausedition (auch VE genannt) der einzelnen Reihen ist zu beachten, dass diese Texte bis zur Endbearbeitung noch weitreichende Veränderungen erfahren können. Die Stücknummern der Vorausedition im jeweiligen Band folgen der internen Nummerierung im Gesamtcorpus und sind nicht zitierfähig. Die „ungewöhnlichen" Nummern der Reihen II, IV und VI (wie 1110., 33.380.) bleiben bis zum Ende der Vorausedition für das jeweilige Stück erhalten, die „glatten" Nummern der Reihen I, III, VII und VIII (wie 1., 2., 3.) können sich bei jedem Auffüllen mit weiteren Stücken des Bandes ändern. Nach der Drucklegung der Bände wird die Vorausedition aus dem Netz genommen und durch den endgültigen Band ersetzt. Briefe sind durch Titel, (evtl. Abfassungsort) und Datum (evtl. noch mit Angabe des Fundortes / LH-/LBr-/LK-MOW-Angabe) identifizierbar: „Leibniz an Claude Nicaise, 30. Mai 1701". (Zu den vorläufigen Transkriptionen für die Jahre 1710–1716 ohne konkreten Bandbezug vgl. die Angaben auf www.gwlb.de/Leibniz/Leibnizarchiv/Veroeffentlichungen/Transkriptionen.htm). Für Stücke gelten Titel und Fundort. Leibniz hat sehr vielen Stücken selbst keinen Titel gegeben, so dass dasselbe Stück in verschiedenen Drucken verschieden benannt sein kann. Die Akademie-Ausgabe vergibt für jedes unbetitelte Stück selbst einen Titel und stellt Konkordanzen zur Identifizierung bereit.

Ein Sonderfall ist Band VI, 5 mit 3 Teilbänden und bis zu 3000 Seiten Text. Da die Forschung über einen längeren Zeitraum nur auf diese VE-Texte zurückgreifen kann, bekommen sie eine konstante VE-Nummer und können danach zitiert werden.[5] Im endgültigen Band wird wie in VI, 4 eine Konkordanz den Bezug auf die VE-Nummer sichern.

Jeder Stückkopf enthält:

a) den Titel: von Leibniz selbst (in „Anführungszeichen" im Inhaltsverzeichnis) oder vom Editor vergeben.
b) die Datierung: Angaben in eckigen Klammern wie „[März 1676]" sind vom Editor erschlossen und werden im jeweiligen editorischen Bericht begründet. Angaben ohne Klammern finden sich im Text und gehen auf Leibniz selbst (bzw. seinen Korrespondenten) zurück. In Briefen stehen der Abfassungsort (sofern erschließbar), das Datum

---

[5] Dabei sollte möglichst auf die Angabe von Seitenzahlen verzichtet werden, da diese nach der Bandpublikation nicht mehr zur Verfügung stehen.

sowie bei mehreren Briefen einer Korrespondenz in eckigen Klammern der in diesem Band vorangehende und folgende Brief dieser Korrespondenz. Zu beachten sind bis 1700 (für einige Staaten auch weiterhin) die Angaben für Julianischen (= alter Stil) und Gregorianischen Kalender (= neuer Stil) mit 10 Tagen Differenz. Manchmal gibt Leibniz selbst beide Daten an: „15./25. Oktober 1671", manchmal nur alten Stil: „10. Oktober 1692" (wird zu „10. (20.) Oktober 1692"), selten vor 1700 nur neuen Stil: „5. Juni 1692". Wir ergänzen daher bei Fehlen grundsätzlich die Datumsangabe in neuem Stil in runden Klammern. Eingeordnet, katalogisiert und zitiert werden die Briefe/Schriften immer nach neuem Stil.

c) die handschriftliche Überlieferung: Jeder Überlieferungsträger (Handschrift) bekommt eine Sigle (wie *L*, *l*, *K*) und wird in seiner Funktion charakterisiert (als Konzept, Abfertigung, Abschrift, Auszug, Reinschrift, verbesserte Reinschrift, Aufzeichnung etc.); Fundort, Umfang, Besonderheiten des Manuskripts und der Name des Schreibers (sofern verifizierbar) werden verzeichnet. Die Überlieferung hat die Struktur eines Stemmas, das die Genese des Textes zeigt, beginnend mit dem ersten Entwurf bis hin zur letzten Bearbeitung. Bei mehreren Überlieferungsträgern ist die Druckvorlage für den Edierten Text mit „Unsere Druckvorlage" o. ä. gekennzeichnet.

Abweichungen vom Text der Druckvorlage werden in der Regel im Variantenapparat / Lesartenapparat verzeichnet; bei besonderer Überlieferungslage können dazu auch Fußnoten (*-Noten) dienen (Beispiel: Arnauld-Briefwechsel in Reihe II). Fußnoten sind ein integraler Bestandteil des Edierten Textes. Sie enthalten etwa Anmerkungen von Leibniz zu seinem Text oder zu dem eines Korrespondenten, Randbemerkungen o.ä. Sind die Abweichungen zwischen mehreren Fassungen eines Textes zu groß, um im Variantenapparat gedruckt zu werden, werden die einzelnen Fassungen nacheinander oder im Paralleldruck (Beispiel: „Unvorgreiffliches Bedencken über eine Schrifft genandt Kurtze Vorstellung", A IV, 7 N. 79) wiedergegeben.

Bei Briefen bedienen wir uns des Kunstwortes „Abfertigung". Es handelt sich dabei um den Text, den Leibniz nachweislich an seinen Korrespondenten abgeschickt hat (und der idealerweise in dessen Nachlass zu finden ist und uns dann im Regelfall als Druckvorlage dient). Wenn wir wissen, dass der Korrespondent diese Abfertigung erhalten hat (etwa, weil er im Antwortbrief darauf eingeht), sie aber nicht mehr vorhanden ist, drucken wir häufig nach „dem Konzept der nicht gefundenen Abfertigung" oder sprechen von der

„nicht gefundenen Abfertigung". Wenn Leibniz einen fertig verfassten, mit Abschlussformel, Datum und häufig vollständiger Unterschrift versehenen Brief aber zurückgehalten und nicht abgeschickt hat (oft an einer Bemerkung wie „nicht abgangen" zu erkennen), sprechen wir von einer „verworfenen Abfertigung" oder einer „Reinschrift, ursprünglich zur Abfertigung vorgesehen". Wenn eine Abfertigung im Nachlass in Hannover liegt, kann dies mehrere Gründe haben: sie wurde verworfen; sie ist als unzustellbar zurückgekommen (dann oft Brieffaltung, Siegel(spuren), Aufschrift, Postvermerke als Anhaltspunkt); sie wurde vom Adressaten bzw. von dessen Erben zurückerbeten (dann sind oft mehrere Briefe und Hinweise auf den Vorgang in der Korrespondenz zu finden); sie ist auf bibliothekarischem Weg in den Nachlass zurückgekommen, etwa durch Erwerb bei Auktionen.

Jeder Überlieferungsträger (Handschrift) bekommt eine Sigle, wobei *L* bedeutet, dass Leibniz den Text eigenhändig geschrieben hat, *l* dagegen, dass sich Leibniz eines Schreibers bedient hat. Diese Abschriften entstanden mit Wissen / Einwilligung / im Auftrag von Leibniz und sind daher autorisiert. Nicht von Leibniz veranstaltete und somit nicht autorisierte Abschriften seiner Texte tragen die Sigle *A*. (Entsprechendes gilt für die Korrespondenten oder Mitarbeiter: *K* eigenhändig, *k* von Schreiberhand). Der Schreiber ist als reines Werkzeug zu sehen, als Kopist: seine Schreibfehler werden nicht dokumentiert, sondern nur das, was Leibniz selbst in dieser Kopie verändert. Je nach Reihe lautet dafür die Sigle *Lil* (I, III, IV, VII) oder nur *l* (II, VI). Beispiele für häufig verwendete Siglen:

A	Abschrift, nicht von Leibniz veranlasst
D	Druck
E	Erstdruck
K	Korrespondent oder Mitarbeiter, eigh. (= eigenhändig)
k	Korrespondent oder Mitarbeiter, von der Hand eines Schreibers
L	Leibniz, eigh.
l	Leibniz, von der Hand seines Schreibers
LiH	Leibniz, eigh. Bemerkungen, An- und Unterstreichungen in einem Handexemplar
LiK	Leibniz, eigh. Änderungen, Ergänzungen und Bemerkungen in einem von einem Korrespondenten oder Mitarbeiter verfassten Text
LiL	Leibniz, spätere eigh. Änderungen oder Ergänzungen in einer eigh. Fassung nach einem anderen Textzeugen
Lil	Leibniz, spätere eigh. Änderungen oder Ergänzungen in einer Fassung von Schreiberhand

d) Editionen, die auf direkte Handschriftenbenutzung zurückgehen, mit Angabe ihrer Quelle.

e) weitere Drucke, die ohne Rückgriff auf die Handschriften auf Editionen in d) zurückgehen, mit Angabe ihrer Quelle.
f) Übersetzungen und Teilübersetzungen, mit Angabe ihrer Quelle.
g) einen editorischen Bericht mit Datierungsbegründung, Einordnung eines Briefes in die Korrespondenz (wie: Unser Brief antwortet auf N. 5 …, wird beantwortet durch N. 10 …, wird angeführt / erwähnt in N. 12 u.15 …, war Beischluss zu N. 6 … u. ä.), Begründung für die Wahl einer bestimmten Druckvorlage, Angaben zur Entstehungsgeschichte oder grundlegende Angaben zur Einordnung eines Stücks in einen bestimmten Themenkomplex und seine Beziehung zu anderen Stücken des Bandes (Umfassende Angaben zur Struktur und zu den Inhalten des Bandes liefert die wissenschaftliche Einleitung am Bandanfang).

Wiederholt vorkommende Buchtitel werden abgekürzt. Ihre und weitere Siglen sind den Siglen- und Abkürzungsverzeichnissen der jeweiligen Bände zu entnehmen.

B. Zum edierten Text

Die Textwiedergabe erfolgt, abgesehen von einigen Normalisierungen, vorlagengetreu / diplomatisch. Normalisiert wird etwa u/v (que statt qve), i/j (konsonantisch gesprochenes i, d. h. intervokalisches i (oder i am Wortanfang vor Vokal) wird zu j, hujus statt huius, jam statt iam), Großschreibung am Satzanfang nach Punkt in Leibniztexten. Zum Verständnis notwendige, fehlende Satzzeichen werden ergänzt (stillschweigend am Zeilenende in der Handschrift, ansonsten in eckigen Klammern), Akzente im Lateinischen werden gestrichen, im Französischen bei den Participia Perfecti (esté, obligé), den Substantiva auf -té (facilité) und (um Missverständnisse zu vermeiden) bei à, là und où stillschweigend ergänzt. Unterstrichene oder hervorgehobene Textteile werden gesperrt wiedergegeben. Kursive kennzeichnet wörtliche Zitate, Buchtitel, metasprachlich benutzte Wörter (wie „Sint duo corpora A et B agentia in corpus C, …"), fremdsprachliche Wörter / Wendungen (etwa lateinische Einsprengsel in französischen oder deutschen Texten, verstärkt in frühen Bänden zu finden) oder fremdsprachige Passagen wie eine deutsche Anschrift auf einem lateinischen Brief.

Eingriffe des Editors in den Text werden vermerkt, entweder nur im Apparat (Reihe I, III, VII, VIII) oder zusätzlich noch durch [ ] im Text gekennzeichnet (Reihe II, IV, VI). Worte oder Satzzeichen in [ ] im Text ohne zusätzlichen Vermerk in den Varianten kennzeichnen in allen Reihen Ergänzungen des Editors[,] ferner die Auflösung von Abk[ürzungen]. Kommentare des Editors wie [*bricht ab*] sind kursiv gesetzt.

Wenn Leibniz selbst [ ] eckige Klammern in seinen Texten benutzt, werden sie je nach Funktion zu (: :) aufgelöst oder / und erläutert. Leibniz setzt oft Passagen in [ ], die sein Schreiber bei einer Reinschrift nicht abschreiben soll oder die Leibniz unterdrücken will, ohne sie zu verwerfen / zu streichen. (+ +) kennzeichnen Bemerkungen von Leibniz innerhalb eines fremden Textes, (: :) Bemerkungen von Leibniz meist innerhalb seines eigenen Textes.

Als Marker verwendet Leibniz ferner „N.B." (nota bene) oder das alchemistische Zeichen für distilletur ⚗ im Sinne von „noch zu bedenken".

Weitere Siglen:

[-]: Textlücken, die nicht eindeutig zu ergänzen sind (mehrere Striche weisen auf mehrere ausgefallene Wörter hin).
< - >: Konjektur des Editors für ein nicht entziffertes oder nicht sicher gelesenes Wort (mehrere Striche weisen auf mehrere Wörter hin).
<ita>: nicht sicher gelesenes Wort, Konjektur des Editors ist „ita".
f<a>cit: nicht sicher gelesener Wortteil, Konjektur des Editors ist „facit".
f<->cit: nicht sicher gelesener Wortteil, keine Konjektur des Editors, da keine sichere Entscheidung zwischen „fecit" und „facit" möglich ist.

C. Zu den Apparaten

Als allgemeine, praxisorientierte und gut verständliche Einführung in Editionstechniken ist zu empfehlen: Bodo Plachta: *Editionswissenschaft. Eine Einführung in Methode und Praxis der Edition neuerer Texte*, Stuttgart ²2006 (Reclam Universal-Bibliothek Nr. 17603).

1. Erläuterungen

Die Erläuterungen zu den einzelnen Textteilen dienen etwa der Identifikation von Personen, Schriften, Sachen, Ereignissen und dem Nachweis von Zitaten. Sie verweisen auf Textstellen im vorliegenden Stück oder in anderen Stücken, sofern sie inhaltlich oder formal in Beziehung zum Text stehen. Sie verzichten auf Erklärungen, die in gängigen Nachschlagewerken leicht gefunden werden können, und ihre Formulierung ist möglichst knapp zu halten. Sie geben weder Kommentar noch Wertung ab und bieten nur Voraussetzungen für die Interpretation. Der Erläuterungsapparat ist eng verzahnt mit dem Personen-, Schriften- und Sachregister. Ist etwa eine im Text genannte Person oder Schrift im Register unter demselben Lemma leicht zu finden, wird sie nur dort nachgewiesen und erläutert.

2. Varianten / Lesarten

Der Variantenapparat verzeichnet Leibniz' Korrekturen, Änderungen, Streichungen und Ergänzungen in seinen Texten sowie die Abweichungen zwischen den einzelnen Textzeugen (Entstehungsvarianten). Er berücksichtigt nur autorisierte Texte und Drucke zu Leibniz' Lebzeiten. Abweichungen von nicht autorisierten Abschriften und Drucken, die auf autorisierten Textzeugen beruhen, haben keinen eigenen Quellenwert und werden nicht berücksichtigt (etwa, wenn Gerhardt einen Text nach einer uns vorliegenden Handschrift *L* ediert und eine abweichende (fehlerhafte) Lesung angibt). Nicht autorisierte Abschriften und Drucke werden nur dann für die Textkonstitution herangezogen, wenn sie auf einem autorisierten Text beruhen, der heute nicht mehr erhalten ist, sie also Stellvertreter für diese Handschrift sind, oder wenn sie von einer Handschrift abgeschrieben wurden, die heute zerstörte Partien aufweist (etwa bei Papierverlust, d. h. wenn etwa im Laufe der Zeit der untere Rand eines Blattes zerbröselt ist).

Eine „philosophische" Edition legt in der Regel, anders etwa als eine „germanistische" Edition, den Schwerpunkt auf die Genese des Gedankens. Sie berücksichtigt dabei nicht alle Varianten, wobei es Unterschiede zwischen den einzelnen Reihen gibt. Reihe I etwa selektiert wesentlich stärker als die Reihen II, VI und IV. (Idealfall: Berücksichtigt werden sollten alle Varianten, bei denen eine Sinnrelevanz nicht ausgeschlossen werden kann).

Generell werden Varianten verzeichnet, die

    a)   eine Entwicklung oder eine Veränderung des Gedankens, der Argumentation oder der Technologie erkennen lassen
    b)   für die Entwicklung der Sprache und Terminologie des 17. Jahrhunderts von Interesse sind,

c) Informationen enthalten, die im endgültigen Text nicht enthalten oder nur angedeutet sind (Namen, Fakten),
d) Anhaltspunkte für die Datierung oder die Aufeinanderfolge verschiedener Fassungen bieten,
e) die Konstitution des Textes stützen,
f) Eingriffe des Herausgebers dokumentieren,
g) Hinweise auf die Rezeption des Textes geben.

Nicht verzeichnet werden in der Regel bloß orthographische, grammatische oder stilistische Änderungen und Abweichungen.

Änderungen, die in einer späteren Fassung als in unserer Druckvorlage vorgenommen wurden, werden nicht im Variantenapparat, sondern in den Fußnoten (*-Noten) wiedergegeben.

Im Variantenapparat wird (bis auf den Wegfall der Akzente im Lateinischen) nicht normalisiert und auch bei offensichtlichen Fehlern im Text nicht korrigiert. (Ausnahme: Reihe II/VI führt den u/v- und i/j-Ausgleich auch in den Varianten durch). Der Apparat strebt an, die Genese des Gedankens aufzuzeigen, nicht aber, die Handschrift abzubilden. Wenn Leibniz eine Textpassage am Rand oder über der Schreibzeile ergänzt oder verändert, so ist nur das Faktum der Ergänzung oder Veränderung selbst relevant, nicht aber der Ort, an dem es geschieht – Leibniz ändert eben dort, wo er den Platz für die Niederschrift findet.

Der Apparat steht in Petit unter dem Text, Schriftart recte, beschreibende Hinzufügungen des Herausgebers kursiv. Ist eine gestrichene Passage zu groß oder aber zu stark überarbeitet worden, um sie verständlich in einer Variante wiederzugeben, kann sie als Petittext in den Text hochgezogen werden. Sie wird dann durch eine einleitende Bemerkung des Editors (kursiv) beschrieben, wie der sie umgebende Text normalisiert wiedergegeben, und ihre Korrekturen, Ergänzungen und Streichungen werden wie gewohnt im Apparat verzeichnet. Alternativ kann sie als Paralipomenon hinter dem zugrunde gelegten Text (A IV, 2, 333–338) oder als Paralleldruck in Spalten (A III, 1, 193–201) ediert werden.

Grundlage für den Apparat ist der von dem Germanisten Friedrich Beißner 1943 für die Stuttgarter Hölderlin-Ausgabe entwickelte Treppenapparat (auch Stufen- oder Treppenstufenapparat), der von Sofortkorrekturen während des laufenden Schreibprozesses als Normalfall ausgeht: eine Stufe (*1*) wird vom Autor verworfen / gestrichen und durch den Text der nachfolgenden Stufe (*2*) ersetzt. Leibniz hat seine Texte jedoch immer wieder, auch zu einem späteren Zeitpunkt, verändert, wobei „später" von „noch während er den Satz formulierte", „nach der Fertigstellung des Absatzes", „am nächsten Tag" bis „viele Jahre später" reichen kann. Veränderungen und Korrekturen finden sich auf Wortebene, Satzebene oder auch absatzübergreifend. Um diesen temporalen Aspekt innerhalb der einzelnen Treppenstufen berücksichtigen zu können und um größere Sinneinheiten besser voneinander abgrenzen zu können, hat unsere Ausgabe | | als zusätzliche Marker eingesetzt, um eine Passage als | *Text zu einem späteren Zeitpunkt als der ersten Niederschrift erg.* | oder | *Text zu einem späteren Zeitpunkt als der ersten Niederschrift gestr.* | kennzeichnen zu können. Unser Apparat kann nur eine ideale Entwicklung der Stufen zeigen, da wir meistens nicht wissen können, wann Leibniz welche Korrektur in welcher Abfolge vorgenommen hat, ob er einen bereits geschriebenen Abschnitt zunächst an seinem Ende veränderte, um ihn danach am Anfang ebenfalls umzugestalten, oder ob er vom Anfang zum Ende fortschritt.

Der Variantenapparat wurde erst nach 1943 in der vorliegenden Form in die Edition integriert (Ursprünglich sollte nur der reine Text inkl. Personenverzeichnis ediert werden, weitere Erläuterungen sollten erst nach Beendigung der Textedition in separaten Bänden erfolgen.). Das hatte zur Folge, dass einige Bände nachkommentiert wurden (IV, 1, VI, 1, II, 1) und dass die ersten vier Bände der Reihe I, die vor 1953 erschienen waren, nur den Text mit Personenverzeichnis ohne editorischen Bericht und Apparate enthalten. Ferner bildet Band III, 1 eine Sonderform mit integralem Apparat. Die Akademie-Ausgabe ist ein über mehr als 100 Jahre gewachsenes Editionsprojekt: Entsprechend sind Anpassungen und Abweichungen in der Darstellungsform im Laufe der Zeit unvermeidlich.

Um Sofortkorrekturen im Umfang eines Wortes von späteren Korrekturen unterscheiden zu können, findet sich in den Philosophischen Reihen II und VI die Besonderheit, den zu einem späteren Zeitpunkt ersetzten Text ebenfalls durch ein *erg.* zu kennzeichnen (im Sinne von „A gegen das über der Zeile gesetzte B ersetzt / ausgetauscht, wobei A und B gleichwertig sind und jedes für sich sinnvoll lesbar ist"). Dies geschah in VI, 4 und II, 1 oft noch innerhalb der Variante („ich (*1*) atme (*2*) | lebe *erg.* | *L*"). Der Leser muss also selbst entscheiden, ob es sich um eine „A gegen B Ersetzung" oder um eine „echte Ergänzung" handelt. In den Folgebänden wurde der senkrechte Strich vor die Variantenstufe gezogen. Im Gegensatz zur Sofortkorrektur „ich (*1*) atme (*2*) lebe *L*" ist das Kennzeichen der späteren Ersetzung: „ich (*1*) atme | (*2*) lebe *erg.* | *L*". (Dieses Vorgehen für Einwortersetzungen wurde von Reihe IV nicht übernommen.) Dieses Verfahren kann zur Verdeutlichung auch auf größere Textpartien ausgeweitet werden, etwa um zu zeigen, dass der Inhalt einer Unterstufe (*a*) nachträglich komplett gegen den Bereich (*b*) ausgetauscht worden ist.

Wenn Leibniz zu einem späteren Zeitpunkt in einer zweiten Redaktion Korrekturen in seinem Manuskript vornimmt, die sich durch Kriterien wie Tintenfarbe, Schriftgröße, Federbreite, Schriftführung o. ä. identifizieren lassen, setzen die Reihen II und VI ein verdeutlichendes * vor die Variante bzw. vor die entsprechende Stufe der Variante. Alternativ kann etwa die Sigle *LiL* verwendet werden.

Die Angabe *bricht ab* wird in den Reihen II, VI und IV nur dann verwendet, wenn der Haupttext abbricht, in den anderen Reihen auch, wenn eine Variantenstufe mitten im Wort abbricht.

Im Gegensatz zur temporalen Einbettung einer Variante legen die Reihen I, III, VII und VIII einen semantischen Schwerpunkt: Wenn ein Gedanke, dessen Niederschrift in einer ersten Stufe abgebrochen / gestrichen wurde, in der zweiten Stufe wieder aufgegriffen worden ist, dann wird diese Stufe bis zum Gedankenende fortgeführt, auch wenn es sich dem Befund der Handschrift nach eigentlich um eine Sofortkorrektur handelt. Das Verfahren ist leserfreundlicher, hat aber zur Folge, dass man ohne Handschrifteneinsicht keine Entscheidung über den temporalen Aspekt bzw. die zeitliche Abfolge der Veränderungen mehr treffen kann.

Leibniz schreibt etwa: „que l'un ou l'autre apporte, ~~pour donner raison~~ soit pour plus de clarté, ou même *ex abundanti* pour rendre raison de sa negotation ou distinction."[6]

Sofortkorrektur: apporte, (*1*) pour donner raison (*2*) soit *L*
Semantischer Schwerpunkt: apporte, (*1*) pour donner raison (*2*) soit … raison *L*

Varianten verschiedener Handschriften können miteinander verbunden / verschachtelt werden, solange durch die Hinzufügung der jeweiligen Handschriftensigle (und evtl. | | zur Verdeutlichung) eine klare Trennung der einzelnen Textfassungen erkennbar bleibt.

3. Beispiele für die Gestaltung von Varianten
(Schwerpunkt: Philosophische Schriften und Briefe)

Die Akademie-Ausgabe benutzt einen „positiven Apparat", d. h. jede Variante wird (mindestens) durch ein vorderes und ein hinteres Anschlusswort mit dem

---

[6] Vgl. A III, 8 N. 5, 24.

Edierten Text verknüpft. Die Abfolge der Varianten erfolgt in Stufen und Unterstufen: Der Text in Stufe (*2*) ersetzt den Text aus (*1*), (*b*) ersetzt den Text aus (*a*), (*cc*) ersetzt den Text aus (*bb*) und (*aa*): man steigt sozusagen immer eine Treppenstufe höher und lässt den Inhalt der vorangegangenen Stufe(n) hinter sich. Stufen sind immer mindestens paarig, d. h. sie bestehen aus zwei oder mehr Elementen derselben Gruppe, die Zählung erfolgt in den Hauptstufen (*1*) (*2*) (*3*) etc., danach in Unterstufen (*a*) (*b*) (*c*) etc., (*aa*) (*bb*) etc. bis (*aaaaa*) (*bbbbb*). Je nach Reihe werden die Unterstufen der besseren Lesbarkeit wegen spätestens nach sechs (*aaaaaa*) in griechischen Buchstaben (*α*) (*β*) fortgeführt.

Je nach der Komplexität der Textveränderungen kann die Stufung geschachtelt sein und mit zusätzlichen Angaben in | |, mit *erg.* und *gestr.* kombiniert werden. Auch kann jede Stufe wie (*a*) weitere Unterstufen wie (*aa*), (*bb*), (*aaa*) (*bbb*) (*ccc*) haben, bevor sie mit (*b*) weitergeführt und mitsamt ihren Unterstufen ersetzt wird.

Die jeweils letzte / höchste Stufe / Unterstufe muss identisch mit dem edierten Text sein. Bei komplizierteren Stufungen ist es sehr hilfreich, sich diese vertikal wie eine Treppe mit Einzügen aufzumalen:

```
10–14 (vorderes Anschlusswort)
(1)
(2)
        (a)
                (aa)
                (bb)
        (b)
        (c)
                (aa)
                (bb)
                        (aaa)
                        (bbb)
                        (ccc) (hinteres Anschlusswort)  L
```

Im Edierten Text findet sich entsprechend im Bereich der Zeilen 10–14 der Text der Stufen: (vorderes Anschlusswort) (*2*) (*c*) (*bb*) (*ccc* mit dem hinteren Anschlusswort). Alle anderen Stufen sind von Leibniz verworfen / gestrichen worden.[7]

Bei mehr als drei Worten, die in einer letzten / höchsten Textstufe stehen und die somit identisch sind mit dem Edierten Text, können … gesetzt werden.

---

[7] Für die online verfügbaren Bände VI, 4 und die Reihe II stehen auf der Münsteraner Homepage vollständige, vertikal gesetzte Variantenanalysen zur Verfügung.

Sehr umfangreiche Ergänzungen mit vielen Unterstufen können aus Gründen der Übersichtlichkeit insofern gesplittet werden, als dass zuerst der gesamte ergänzte Bereich in der Form „A ... B *erg. L*" angegeben wird und im Anschluss daran die einzelnen Varianten jeweils separat wiedergegeben werden.

Bei ergänzten Texten kann die Darstellung verkürzt werden. Sie benötigen im Gegensatz zu gestrichenen Partien kein vorderes und hinteres Anschlusswort, weil das erste, letzte oder einzige ergänzte Wort bereits mit dem edierten Text identisch ist.

facile *erg. L* (verkürzt für: id | facile *erg.* | fieri *L*)

quod erat demonstandum *erg.* L^1 u. L^2

par | tout *gestr.* | l'univers L^2

Die folgenden Beispiele sind der abgebildeten Handschrift entnommen, dabei lautet der edierte Text im Bereich der umfangreichen Streichung (A VI, 4 N. 114_2, 451f.):

„Itaque veniam mihi spero ab aequis lectoribus, si cogor de praesenti negotio loqui magnificentius, quam ego de meis rebus sentire soleo, praesertim cum nullam mihi laudem inventoris, sed qualecunque indicis sive praeconis officium tribuam. [...] si quando judicio meo inflammati magni viri, et quod inprimis optandum est, integrae Societates, sibi immortalem confecti operis instauratarum scientiarum gloriam vindicabunt. Factum est scilicet nescio quo fato (nam et in cogitando fortuna est quaedam sive Dei gubernatio), ut mihi pene adhuc puero tenuia licet, foecunda tamen obtigerint initia Artis cujusdam Magnae, cujus, quantum legere vel audire contigit, ne suspicio quidem inter homines fuisse videtur."

„Ich hoffe deshalb, daß die wohlgeneigten Leser mir verzeihen werden, wenn ich gezwungen bin, von dieser Aufgabe großartiger zu sprechen, als wie ich sonst über meine Angelegenheiten zu sprechen pflege, zumal ich mir keineswegs den Ruhm eines Erfinders, sondern nur irgendwie die Rolle eines Verkünders oder Heroldes zurechne. [...] wenn einmal große Männer und, was vor allem zu wünschen ist, ganze Gesellschaften durch meinen Aufruf angefeuert, für sich den unsterblichen Ruhm in Anspruch nehmen werden, das Werk der Neuaufstellung der Wissenschaften zustande gebracht zu haben. Durch irgendein Schicksal – denn auch im Denken gibt es ein Glück oder eine Lenkung Gottes – ist es geschehen, daß mir, als ich fast noch ein Knabe war, zwar noch geringe, aber doch fruchtbare Anfangsgründe einer gewissen großen Kunst zuteil geworden sind, einer Kunst, von der es, soweit ich lesen oder hören konnte, unter den Menschen noch nicht einmal eine Ahnung gegeben zu haben scheint."[8]

---

[8] Wolf von Engelhardt: *Schöpferische Vernunft*, Marburg 1951, S. 209f.

Rem tractare aggressus, cujus vim à multis
agnosci omnium interest, praevaricator essem in causa
publica si quae ad commendationem ejus, atque accendendos
homines necessaria dicta videntur, dissimularem.
itaque veniam mihi spero ab aequis lectoribus, si cogor
de praesenti negotio loqui magnificentius, quam ego
de meis rebus sentire soleo. ~~Quae licet ~~~~
~~verba licet voluerim ejusdem~~ Nomen autem meum
dissimulandum putavi, tum ut ~~abesset~~ vanitatis
~~si~~ suspicio, tum quia usu comperi multa ~~in~~ fructu
caruisse sola erga autores invidia, tum verò maximè
ne Dei beneficium ingenio meo tribuere videar; est
enim et in cogitando fortuna quaedam sive Dei gubernatio
et nonnunquam quae summos viros latuêre, ~~mediocribus~~
etiam infra mediocritatem positis aperiuntur, inter
quos ego me referri facilè patior, quotidie enim
agnosco, quantum à plerisque aliis memoria et
~~carmine vincar~~ id Factum, ~~tamen~~ est nescio quo
fato ~~ut~~ mihi penè adhuc puero ~~ut~~ tenuia ~~obiter~~
~~licet~~ licet, foecunda tamen obtigerint indicia Artis
cujusdam Magnae, cujus ~~ne~~ ~~ex iis~~ quantum mihi legere
vel audire contigit, ne suspicio quidem inter homines
fuisse videtur. Iam postea excolui, quoad licuit
per ~~alias curas~~ distractiones, quibus homines obnoxii
sumus, eoque perveni, ut ~~usum~~ ejus ac potestatem, quae omnibus
incredibilis visa est, modum absolvendae artis, possim
certa demonstratione complecti. Nec ~~in subsidii~~
in generalibus documentis subsiti, sed vim ejus

Die Handschrift[9] (LH IV 7a, Bl. 37 r) bietet den folgenden Befund: Nach „soleo" hat Leibniz zunächst einen Satz geschrieben („Quare ... putavi"). Diesen Satz hat er dann unmittelbar nach seiner Niederschrift gestrichen und in einer 2. Stufe durch den Text von „Nomen ... vincar" ersetzt. Danach schrieb er zunächst mit „Factum est scilicet quo fato ..." weiter, bevor er zurückging und auch diese 2. Stufe strich. Wann genau dies geschah, lässt sich nicht mit Sicherheit sagen, wahrscheinlich aber erst nach der Niederschrift der gesamten Seite, so dass ihm nur noch der freie Rand zur Verfügung stand. Dort schrieb er dann eine endgültige 3. Stufe von „praesertim ... vindicabunt". Da deren Position eindeutig ist, verzichtete er auf ein Einfügungszeichen wie ein + oder ein #, um die Passage mit dem Text zu verknüpfen.

In der Handschrift lassen sich u. a. folgende Korrekturprozesse erkennen:

Sofortkorrektur: Leibniz schreibt, streicht den Text und schreibt unmittelbar danach auf derselben Zeile weiter.

vanitatis (*1*) sp (*2*) suspicio *L*[10]

puero, (*1*) susp (*2*) tenuia (*a*) obtigeri (*b*) licet, (*c*) licet, *L*

cujus, (*1*) ne suspi (*2*) quantum *L*

per (*1*) alias curas (*2*) distractiones *L*

Spätere Ersetzung („ersetzende Ergänzung") eines einzelnen Wortes, häufig über der Zeile (Reihe II, VI):

tantopere (*1*) commendo | (*2*) extollo *erg.* | *L*

inventoris (*1*) vindicem | (*2*) asseram *erg.* | (*3*) ,sed *L*

Ergänzung (bei mehr als drei Worten mit ... für den Mittelteil): Eine mit *erg.* gekennzeichnete Passage ist ein späterer Zusatz zu einem bereits geschriebenen Text. Sie ergänzt den Text, ist aber nicht grammatisch notwendig, d. h. der Text kann sowohl mit als auch ohne die ergänzte Passage sinnvoll und

---

[9] Abdruck mit freundlicher Genehmigung der Gottfried Wilhelm Leibniz Bibliothek / Niedersächsische Landesbibliothek Hannover.
[10] Diese Variante würde (als Einzelvariante) nach den oben genannten Kriterien allerdings im gedruckten Band nicht berücksichtigt werden. Innerhalb einer größeren Variante finden allerdings auch eher marginale Veränderungen Berücksichtigung in den Unterstufen.

sprachlich korrekt gelesen werden. Ist das nicht der Fall, handelt es sich um eine Stufung.

> nam ... gubernatio) *erg. L*

Streichung: Eine als *gestr.* gekennzeichnete Passage ist das Gegenstück zur Ergänzung, d. h. der Text kann sowohl mit als auch ohne die gestrichene Passage sinnvoll und sprachlich korrekt gelesen werden. Ist das nicht der Fall, oder kann man aus inhaltlichen Kriterien nicht erschließen, dass Leibniz die betreffende Passage gezielt nach der Niederschrift des sie umgebenden Textes, also später, gestrichen hat, handelt es sich um eine Stufung. Angenommen, Leibniz hätte die Partie „tum ut abesset vanitatis suspicio" separat gestrichen:

> putavi,| tum ut abesset vanitatis suspicio, *gestr.* | tum *L*[11]

Übergreifende Korrektur: Leibniz schreibt einen Satz (beliebig großen Abschnitt), beendet den Schreibvorgang, geht zurück und korrigiert diesen Satz (Abschnitt) übergreifend. Da die Zeile bereits beschrieben wurde, hat er kaum freien Raum für seine Korrekturen. Er ist daher gezwungen, entweder vorhandenen Text zu überschreiben oder Veränderungen oberhalb und unterhalb der Zeile oder am Rand vorzunehmen. Oft verdeutlicht er diesen Korrekturvorgang durch Einfügungszeichen.

> Factum (*1*) tamen est (*2*) est scilicet *L*

> redditum (*1*) tradere aliis, quam notis infallibilibus ita designare possim (*2*) tradam [...] designem *L*

Für den Bereich der oben analysierten umfangreichen Überarbeitung ergibt sich dabei folgender Befund:

> soleo (*1*) . Quare nomen quoque meum dissimulandum putavi (*2*) . Nomen autem meum dissimulandum putavi, tum ut abesset vanitatis (*a*) sp (*b*) suspicio, tum quia usu comperi multa (*aa*) us (*bb*) fructu caruisse sola erga autores invidia, tum vero maxime ne Dei beneficium ingenio meo tribuere videar; est enim et in cogitando fortuna quaedam sive Dei gubernatio et nonnunquam quae summos viros latuere, (*aaa*) mediocribus (*bbb*) etiam infra mediocritatem positis

---

[11] Um den Bezug zum edierten Text herstellen zu können, ist anders als bei einer Ergänzung ein vorderes und hinteres Anschlusswort notwendig.

aperiuntur, inter quos ego me referri facile patior, quotidie enim agnosco, quantum a plerisque aliis memoria et acumine vincar. *(3)* , praesertim ... vindicabunt. *L*[12]

---

[12] Die Bearbeiter des Bandes A VI, 4 haben sich hier (ausnahmsweise) für eine verkürzte Darstellung der letzten Textstufe *(3)* entschieden, wie sie bei umfangreichen und stark bearbeiteten Ergänzungen genutzt werden kann, und die zahlreichen kleinen Eingriffe dahinter gesondert in Einzelvarianten dargestellt. Ansonsten hätte sich dem Leser wohl das folgende Bild geboten (das bei vertikaler Anordnung mit Einzug der jeweiligen Stufen allerdings viel von seinem Schrecken verloren hätte): *(3)* praesertim ... inventoris *(a)* vindicem | *(b)* asseram *erg.* | *(c)* , sed ... tantopere *(aa)* commendo | *(bb)* extollo *erg.* | non tam *(aaa)* tradere aliis *(bbb)* in potestatem redditum tradere aliis, quam notis infallibilibus ita designare possim *(ccc)* in ... designem, ut a *(aaaa)* majoribus | *(bbbb)* felicioribus *erg.* | ingeniis e latebris suis *(aaaaa)* eru<-> *(bbbbb)* erui ... | enim *erg.* | ... fortunam *(aaaaaa)* simplicem *(bbbbbb)* simplicis ... circumscripsit; *(α)* et gloriam *(β)* et | interea *gestr.* | decus ... qui *(αα)* magna | *(ββ)* summa *erg.* | excitam, ... ita *(ααα)* magnum | *(βββ)* egregium *erg.* | satis operae | meae *gestr.* | pretium consecutus videbor, si *(αααα)* judicio meo excitati *(ββββ)* quando ... sibi *(ααααα)* veram tanti operis laudem immortali gloria vindicent *(βββββ)* immortalem ... gloriam *(αααααα)* as<-> *(ββββββ)* vindicabunt. *L*.

SEKTIONSVORTRÄGE

The Role of *aequitas* in Leibniz's Legal Philosophy – a Formal Reconstruction

Matthias Armgardt (Konstanz)

As Hubertus Busche pointed out,[1] the *Nova Methodus discendae docendaeque jurisprudentiae* written in 1667 presents a three-level-model of the natural law: The *jus strictum* is sometimes corrected by the *aequitas* and the *pietas* but in the most cases supported by them and not changed.[2]

The three levels are harmonized by Leibniz with three legal principles that can be found in an Ulpian quote in the *Corpus Iuris Civilis*[3]:

> Neminem laedere.
> Suum cuique tribuere.
> Honeste vivere.

Busche is right in pointing out the harmonization with the Aristotelian concepts of the *justitia particularis* to which the first two level belong as well as with the Aristotelian concepts of the *justitia universalis* to which the last two levels belong. The *justitia particularis* consists of the *justitia commutativa* and the *justitia distributiva*. The former corresponds to the first level which is the *neminem laedere* or respectively the *jus strictum* while the latter corresponds to the second level known as the *suum cuique tribuere* or the *aequitas*.[4]

Later, Leibniz explores this subject again in his *Méditation sur la notion commune de la justice* (1703).[5] The *Médiation* sees *aequitas* and *pietas* as modes that correct the *jus strictum* when required. We may therefore assume that this three-step basic concept of Leibniz's natural law did not change in the course of his life.

---

[1] Gottfried Wilhelm Leibniz: *Frühe Schriften zum Naturrecht*, Lateinisch–deutsch, ed. by Hubertus, Hamburg 2003, pp. LXVIII ff.
[2] *Nova Methodus*, § 73; A VI, 1, 343.
[3] Ulpian, D 1.1.10.1.
[4] Leibniz: *Frühe Schriften*, pp. LXXI f.
[5] First published in Georg Mollat: *Rechtsphilosophisches aus Leibnizens ungedruckten Schriften*, Leipzig 1885, pp. 41–70; new edition by Stefan Luckscheiter in: Wenchao Li (ed.): *Das Rechte kann nicht ungerecht sein …". Beiträge zu Leibniz' Philosophie der Gerechtigkeit* (= Studia Leibnitiana, Sonderhefte 44), Stuttgart 2015, pp. 137–179.

In the following I want to examine the *aequitas* in more detail and show with the help of some sources how Leibniz struggled with the specification of this term again and again throughout his life.

1. Introduction: Historical Context

The *aequitas* or equity as the corrective of legal solutions is an essential component of legal thinking to this day – not only in civil law but also in common law. This legal concept can previously found in the argumentation of roman classical jurists, as numerous digest fragments prove. Medieval jurists used the *aequitas* as a juridical argument, as well.[6]

Looking at ancient philosophy we find the Aristotelian *epieikeia* in the Nicomachean Ethics. Jan Schröder's ground-breaking study from the year 1997 showed that and how the humanistic jurists took possession of this ancient heritage.[7] According to him the role of *aequitas* changed in the legal thinking of Early Modern jurists: While the *aequitas* was considered to be a legal source on its own in the time between 1550 and 1650 it was afterwards by most jurists regarded as no longer necessary next to the natural law and the positive law.

2. Place and Function of the aequitas in the Nova Methodus, 1667

In the following the *aequitas* shall be analysed in several fragments of Leibniz's work. This shall include a detailed specification of the term and its juridical function. Not only that, but how Leibniz tries to cope with the problem of the indeterminacy of this term shall be examined. One of Leibniz's major goals regarding law was to secure legal certainty which was the title and the content of his revised theory of condition.[8] A blurry, maybe arbitrary *aequitas*-concept would not be compatible with this aim. Thus, it isn't surprising that Leibniz struggled with the clarification of the *aequitas* in his lifetime.

---

[6] Cf., e.g. Norbert Horn: *Aequitas in den Lehren des Baldus*, Graz 1966.
[7] Jan Schröder: "Aequitas und Rechtsquellenlehre in der frühen Neuzeit", in: *Quaderni Fiorentini* 26 (1997), pp. 265–305.
[8] "Specimen certitudinis seu demonstrationum in Jure exhibitum in Doctrina Conditionum"; A VI, 1, 369ff. Cf., Matthias Armgardt: *Das rechtslogische System der Doctrina Conditionum von G. W. Leibniz*, Marburg 2001, pp. 358ff.

I start with the *Nova Methodus discendae docendaeque Jurisprudentiae* (NM) dated 1667 which Leibniz wrote immediately after he finished his dissertation. Here the aequitas is presented as a correction mode of the *jus strictum*:

> §. 73. "[…] Juris Naturae tres sunt gradus: Jus strictum, aequitas, pietas. Quorum sequens antecedente perfectior, eumque confirmat, et in casu pugnantiae ei derogat. Jus strictum seu merum ex terminorum definitione descendit, […]."

In § 74 of the NM Leibniz determines the *aequitas* in more detail:

> §. 74. "*Aequitas* seu aequalitas, id est, duorum pluriumve ratio vel proportio consistit in harmonia seu congruentia. Et coincidit cum Principiis *Aristotelis*, *Grotii* et *Feldeni*: Haec requirit, ut in eum qui me laesit, non bellum internecinum instituam, sed ad restitutionem; arbitros admitti, quod tibi nolis, alteri non faciendum; item ut puniatur non tàm imprudentia, quàm dolus et malitia; item ut infirmentur contractus subtiles, et circumventis subveniatur. De caetero Jus strictum observari ipsa aequitas jubet. […]."

In this fragment we find a rather disordered collection of aspects of equity. It is generally designated as ratio or proportion and traced back to harmony and congruence. The commandment: Do as you would be done by, can also be found at this place. As well as the idea that not the inexperience should be punished but malice and deceitfulness, whereby I do not understand *punire* here in terms of criminal-law but rather of contractual risk diversification. The invalidation of deceitful contracts and avoidances of legal provisions indicate that Leibniz pictured the functions of the *aequitas* to be preventing the abuse of rights and protecting the inexperienced.

Towards the end of § 74 NM Leibniz gives a clue regarding the structure of law which reads as follows:

> §. 74. fin. "[…] Sed aequitas dat solùm Jus laxè dictum, seu *Grotii* stylo aptitudinem uni; alteri verò obligationem plenam, v.g. Aequum est, ut qui dolosis subtilitatibus se à meo debito liberavit, mihi nihilominus teneatur, sed mihi non datur in eum actio persequendi; actio enim vel exceptio, vel quaecunque postulatio ex Jure mero descendit […]."

At this point it becomes clear that the early Leibniz does not consider the *aequitas* to be the base for an action or exception. These only arise from the *jus strictum*. The *aequitas* can, therefore, only lead to a deviating juridical evaluation within an *actio* or *exceptio*.

3. The Aequitas in the Elementa Juris Naturalis

Leibniz devoted himself to the project of the reform of the *Corpus Iuris Civilis* for four years during the Mainz period. In this period the *Elementa Juris Naturalis* (EJN) originated – in which Leibniz developed a deontic logic, amongst others. With the help of the term *vir bonus* he traced this logic back to the alethic modal logic.[9]

We can also find penetrative ideas regarding the *aequitas* within the EJN which, are in my eyes, unique. Here, Leibniz tries to precise this unclear term of the *aequitas* with the help of two concepts from the moral philosophy or respectively the classical Roman law:

The one concept is – as Busche already mentioned – the *innoxia utilitas* (the innoxious utility). The second concept which is not explicitly mentioned by Leibniz in the EJN but mentioned at other points in detail seems to be the *cautio damni infecti* that he combines with the *innoxia utilitas*. The *cautio damni infecti* is about the security a person has to provide for this neighbour if his building or his activity could damage his neighbour's property.

The most important text of the EJN about *aequitas* reads as follows:

> "Ut lucrum meum minus postponam tuo majori […] amicitia exegit. Sed non statim aeqvitas. […] Ut tibi utilitatem mihi non innoxiam vel etiam mihi utilem praestem, à te cogi non possum. Ut necessitatem, possum. Hoc est principium aeqvitatis. Damnum ferre cum recipiendi certitudine seu credere aeqvum est, qvia est utilitas innoxia. Qvin et miseriam aliqvam ferre cum certitudine alterius contra vitandae est utilitatis. Imò fortasse videor me cogi posse ad praestandam innoxiam imò utilem utilitatem, si mihi cavetur de innoxietate."

A first look at the text shows that Leibniz established a border between *amicitia* and *aequitas*:

> "Ut lucrum meum minus postponam tuo majori […] amicitia exegit. Sed non statim aequitas."

Amicitia even demands that I prefer my friend's bigger advantage over my small advantage. On the other hand, I can't legally be forced to grant an item, that is not innoxious or even useful to me, although it may be useful to someone else.

---

[9] A VI, 1, 465.

"Ut tibi utilitatem mihi non innoxiam vel etiam mihi utilem praestem, a te cogi non possum."

Here, the *innoxia utilitas* occurs and I try to give a formal model of the Leibnizean ideas making use of the following abbreviations:

U (x,y) = x is useful for y
N (x,y) = x is necessary for y
I (x, y) = x is innoxious for y
A (x) = x is an action (e.g. to give an object to somebody else)
P (x) = x is an indulgence (e.g. to suffer a damage)
S (x,y,z) = x presents y security for z
O (x, y, z) = x has a claim against y for z

Plain (x) = x is plaintiff
Def (x) = x is defendant

Principle 1:
$\forall x \forall y \forall z \{A(x) \land \text{Plain}(y) \land \text{Def}(z) \land U(x; y) \land [\neg I(x; z) \lor U(\neg x; z)] \to \neg O(y; z; x)\}$

The formula reads as follows:
For all x, y and z the following applies:

If x is an active doing and y is plaintiff and z is defendant and x is useful for y but at the same time x is not innoxious for z or non-x is useful for z, then y won't have an entitlement to x against z.

In contrast, when the other person necessarily needs the item:

"[...] Ut necessitatem, possum. Hoc est principium aequitatis."

Principle 2:
$\forall x \forall y \forall z \{A(x) \land \text{Plain}(y) \land \text{Def}(z) \land N(x; y) \land [\neg I(x; z) \lor U(\neg x; z)] \to O(y; z; x)\}$

The formula reads as follows:
For all x, y and z the following applies:

> If x is an active doing and y is plaintiff and z is defendant and x is necessary for y and x is not innoxious for z or non-x is useful for z, then y will have an entitlement to x against z.

The necessity for the other person is thus predominant over my loss of benefit. Therefore, there is an obligation.

Now a thought comes up, which reminds me of the *cautio damni infecti* being combined with the idea of the *innoxia utilitas*. It deals with the case where I will have to incur a loss if the other one provides a security for its refund. It is therefore about a passive *damnum ferre* resp. *miseriam ferre* instead of an active *praestare*:

> "Damnum ferre *cum recipiendi certitudine* seu credere aequum est, quia est utilitas innoxia. Quin et miseriam aliquam ferre cum certitudine alterius contra vitandae est utilitatis."

Principle 3:

$\forall x \forall y \forall z \{\mathbf{P(x)} \wedge \text{Plain}(y) \wedge \text{Def}(z) \wedge U(x; y) \wedge S[y; z; I(x; z)] \rightarrow O(y; z; x)\}$

For all x, y and z the following applies:

> If x is a sufferance and y is plaintiff and z is defendant and x is useful for y and if y provides a security for x being innoxious for z, y will have an entitlement to x against z.

In other words: There is a passive duty to suffer a loss when there is a security deposit.[10] According to Leibniz this would correspond to the *innoxia utilitas*.

Conclusively Leibniz considers whether this principle can also be transferred to an active *praestare*. However, he has doubts:

> "[…] Imo fortasse videor me cogi posse ad praestandam innoxiam imo utilem utilitatem, si mihi cavetur de innoxietate."

Principle 4?:

$\forall x \forall y \forall z \{\mathbf{A(x)} \wedge \text{Plain}(y) \wedge \text{Def}(z) \wedge U(x; y) \wedge [I(x; z) \vee U(\neg x; z)] \wedge S[y; z; I(x;z)] \rightarrow O(y; z; x)\}$?

---

[10] *Cum recipiendi certitudine* means: with certainty to get it back.

For all x, y and z the following applies:

> If x is an active doing and y is plaintiff and z is defendant and x is useful for y and if y provides a security for x being innoxious for z, then y will have an entitlement to x against z?

Leibniz doubts whether there is a duty to actively grant the *innoxia utilitatis* when a security is provided.

In my opinion, this fragment of the EJN shows that Leibniz wanted to specify the blurry term of the *aequitas* with the help of the concepts of *innoxia utilitas* and *cautio damni infecti*. In the core he works formally, which helps to transfer his thoughts into formulas.

Apart from the fragment I have just mentioned you can find numerous other attempts to define *aequitas* in the EJN. I would like to particularly concentrate on two of them:

> "Aequum est tantum quemque concedere alteri, quantum ab altero posceret sibi. Res difficillime generaliter definiri potest: Aequum est 1) procurare bonum alterius sibi non damnosum, 2) procurare necessarium alteri, tolerabile sibi vel impedire miseriam alterius vitata sua."[11]

This can be interpreted as a summary of the text I just explained.

The following definition is also of interest:

> "Aequum est: procurare felicitatem alterius, salva sua, et impedire miseriam alterius vitata sua. Seu praeferre utilitatem alterius superfluitate suae, et praeferre necessitate alterius utilitati suae."[12]

Expressed in formula:

S (x;y): "x is superfluous for y" (*superfluitas*)
A>B: "A is preferable over B" (*praeferre*)

$U(x; P_i) > S(x; D_i)$
$N(x; P_i) > U(x; D_i)$

There is thus a priority order of *necessitas* to *utilitas* and of *utilitas* to *superfluitas*.

---

[11] A VI, 1, 455 ll. 32ff.
[12] A VI, 1, 456, l. 1f.; Cf. Leibniz: *Frühe Schriften*, p. 38.

4. The aequitas in fragments about extension and reduction of laws

Leibniz deals in numerous fragments with the question of how the *aequitas* and the extension and reduction of laws, are related.

De Jurisprudentia et ejus Capitibus

> "Utrum lex ad eum casum extendi possit, in quo eadem ratio? Videtur cum lex scilicet aequitatem habet. Non ita, cum duram esse constat."[13]

According to Leibniz an extensive interpretation is only possible when the law is not "hard", but corresponds to the *aequitas*.

The following fragment deals with the analogous application of laws or respectively with the teleological reduction of laws:

De Legum Rationibus inquirendis

> "Propositum nobis est in Legum juris civilis rationes inquirere, ut eas interpretari possimus. [...] Nam ex praesumta Legislatoris voluntate legem latam ad similia extendemus [...] Similiter ob praesumtam voluntatem legislatoris legem generalem ex aequitate restringemus, haec enim est natura aequitatis."[14]

The *aequitas* has here the function to justify the reduction of a law that has gone too far regarding the presumed intentions of the legislator.

5. The aequitas in the Méditations

Leibniz's *Méditations* were published in 1703 for his last employer Georg Ludwig who became George I. King of England in 1714. Here Leibniz makes use of the three-stage model of natural law to criticise the legal institution of slavery. The significant passage reads as follows:

> "Je reponds, que quand 'on' accorderoit qu'il y a un droit d'Esclavage parmy les hommes conforme à la raison naturelle, et que selon le jus strictum, les corps des esclaves et de leur enfans sont sous le pouvoir des maistres; il sera tousjours vray 'qu''un autre droit plus fort s'oppose à l'abuse de ce droit. C'est le droit

---

[13] A VI, 4 C, 2753.
[14] Ibid., 2775.

> des ames raisonables qui son naturellement et inalienablement libres; c'est le droit de dieu, qui est le souverain maistre des corps et des ames, et sous qui les maistres sont les concitoyens de leur esclaves; puisque ceuxcy ont dans le Royaume de dieu le droit de Bourgoisie aussi bien qu'eux. On peut donc dire que la proprieté du corps d'un homme est à son Ame, [...]."[15]

Leibniz here discusses the admissibility of slavery. He does not claim at all that the *jus strictum* permits slavery (*accorderoit!*) but examines in what sense a hypothetically allowed *jus strictum* underlies the abuse control. In the course of this discussion Leibniz presents the right of reasonable souls for freedom as natural and inalienable. It is based on a divine law that applies in this kingdom. In my eyes Leibniz here enters the field of the *pietas* which restricts the *jus strictum*. He does, however, not expressly mention this at this stage.

But later Leibniz explicitly works out both correction levels *aequitas* and *pietas*:

> "Mais quand j'accorderois contre la nature des choses, qu'un homme est une proprieté d'un autre homme, le droit du maistre quel qu'il pourroit estre à la rigueur, sera limité par l'Equité, qui veut que l'homme ait soin d'un autre homme, tel qu'il voudroit qu'on eût de luy en pareil cas, et par la charité, qui ordonne qu'on travaille au bonheur d'autruy. Et ces obligatons sont perfectionnées par la pieté, c'est à dire par ce qu'on doit à dieu."[16]

Initially Leibniz concludes that slavery is against the nature of things. But even in the case that such a non-existing right is assumed Leibniz works out a double limitation through *aequitas*:

Firstly, the principle applies that no one may inflict something to another person that he would not want to suffer himself if roles were being reversed. Leibniz takes this up again later in his work *La place d'autruy*[17] as a principle that applies to law, moral and politics.

Secondly, he introduces the Law of Charity (caritas) from the angle of the *aequitas*. According to this, every person is obligated to work for the wellbeing of another person. Therefore, I would also locate the famous definition *justitita est caritas sapientis* as part of the *aequitas*.

Hereafter, Leibniz talks about the *pietas* and refers to God's law, which applies in his kingdom of mercy. The *pietas* thus affects what Leibniz shows

---

[15] Mollat: *Rechtsphilosophisches*, p. 68; Li (ed.): „Das Recht kann nicht ungerecht sein ...", p. 176.
[16] Ibid.
[17] A IV, 3, 903f.

in the end of his Monadology – the relationship between human beings and God.

In my eyes Leibniz defines *aequitas* and *pietas* as follows: The *aequitas* applies to the relationship between human beings among themselves while the *pietas* affects the relationship between human beings and God. Therefore, I think that God is not removable from Leibniz's natural law thinking. However, Leibniz sometimes argues whether his thoughts would also apply when there was no third stage of justice.

The just analysed passage about slavery in the *Méditations* shows that this can also have strong practical consequences.

6. Conclusion

In contrast to the natural law systems of Pufendorf and Thomasius the concept of *aequitas* plays a prominent and important role in Leibniz's legal thinking. It is the second level of the three-level-model of his natural law. *Aequitas* and *pietas* correct the *jus strictum*. Thus we find some sort of defeasible reasoning in Leibniz's Legal Philosophy. In the EJN Leibniz developed a precise concept of *aequitas* by melting the ideas of *innoxia utilitas* and *caution damni infecti*. In the *Méditations* he added the concept of *caritas*.

Leibniz and Mortalism

Aderemi Artis (Flint)

By the time Leibniz was born in 1646, an intense debate had taken place about human immortality and about what happens to us after bodily death, and had been settled broadly along confessional lines. And yet some prominent figures, such as Thomas Hobbes in his 1651 *Leviathan*, had seen fit to reopen old wounds in the controversy. A touchstone to this debate had begun with some questions Martin Luther had raised about purgatory in the Ninety-Five Theses; eventually he came to reject the doctrine entirely. Subsequent debates raged regarding the interim between bodily death and the general resurrection, with Calvin in his *Psychopannychia* (1534) attacking Luther's notion of "soul sleep," while continuing to reject the Catholic doctrine of purgatory. Radical reformers constructed their own views, including the notion of "soul death," that is, that the soul died with the body and was recreated at the resurrection.[1] In the final session of the Council of Trent, the Catholic Church reaffirmed the legitimacy of purgatory, with some cautionary notes. A similar debate had occurred concerning the ultimate fate of the reprobate succeeding the final judgment, with a few radicals rejecting the doctrine of eternal punishment, and with Catholics and magisterial Protestants retaining the belief.[2]

All of these issues were closely connected with the question of natural human immortality, an issue brought to special attention by the Fifth Lateran Council in the wake of Averroistic claims that according to reason alone, human beings are naturally mortal, though we can know by revelation that we are in fact immortal. Again, radicals, such as Fausto Sozzini in *De Statu primi hominis ante lapsum Disputatio* (1610), raised doubts that humans were naturally immortal. Finally, Hobbes stands out for openly arguing simultaneously in favor of natural human mortality, soul death, and the finitude of the punishment of the reprobate in his infamous *Leviathan* (1651). By the mid-1600s, opponents of natural immortality, consciousness between death and the resurrection, or eternal punishment had begun to be associated under a general umbrella which has come to be known as "mortalism," and these are the positions Leibniz frequently contrasts with his own.

---

[1] See Bryan W. Ball: *The Soul Sleepers: Christian Mortalism from Wycliffe to Priestly*, Cambridge 2008, passim, for a survey of such views.
[2] For an overview, see Daniel Pickering Walker: *The Decline of Hell: Seventeenth Century Discussions of Eternal Torment*, Chicago 1964.

What Leibniz's ultimate personal views on mortalism were will likely remain difficult to determine and parse; this is especially true as his motivations for articulating a particular view are at times somewhat opaque. However, he does discuss all three major mortalist issues on various occasions, and lays out, over the course of his career, a number of tantalizing albeit fragmentary and multiform indications of how both mainstream Protestant and Catholic views might be maintained and accommodated after being subjected to critical philosophical scrutiny. It is the thus task of this essay to begin an exploration of Leibniz' positions on natural mortality, the interim between bodily death and the general resurrection, and eternal damnation.

Natural human immortality is a position that Leibniz argues for over the course of his career, but his arguments and grounds for immortality develop and shift somewhat over time; not only that, but so also does his conception of just what it means to be human and to be a person. In the early 1668/69 *Confessio Naturae Contra Atheistas*, he argues that the human mind is immortal, on the grounds that it is, in its activity, essentially without parts and therefore incorruptible:

> "Mens humana est Ens cujus aliqua actio est cogitatio...actio [mentis] est res sine partibus...Omne incorruptibile est immortale... Igitur MENS HUMANA EST IMMORTALIS."[3] Also of note in this early piece is that Leibniz asserts that "Habemus enim imagines in animo etiam quando de iis non cogitamus."[4]

The notion that we can possess mental content that we are in some fashion unaware of is an early foray into the kind of views he will consider later on.

In the 1671 *De Usu et Necessitate Demonstrationum Immortalitatis Animae*, Leibniz not only discusses immortality again, rehearsing a similar argument as that found in the *Confessio Naturae* ("non magis mentem destrui posse, quam punctum. Punctum enim indivisibile est, ergo destrui non potest"[5]), but also suggests that the inquiry into immortality will ultimately give us information, among other things, about "justitia poenarum aeternarum."[6] A year later, in his *Confessio Philosophi*, Leibniz takes up the theme of eternal punishment, and includes two of Leibniz' responses to the notion

---

[3] A VI, 1, 492–493.
[4] Ibid., 493.
[5] A II, 1, 113.
[6] Ibid. For a discussion of the appendix of this work, *De Resurrectione Corporum*, see Lloyd Strickland: "Leibniz, the 'Flower of Substance,' and the Resurrection of the Same Body", in: *The Philosophical Forum* 40/3 (2009), pp. 391–410.

that eternal punishment would be unjust and unfair of God. One response he has is to say that

> "Hoc autem damnationi sufficit. Anima enim cum a mortis momento novis sensibus externis, dum corpus reddatur, non pateat, cogiationibus tantum postremis insistit, unde non mutat, sed auget statum mortis; odium autem Dei, id est felicissimi, sequitur dolor maximus, est enim odium, dolere felicitate (ut amare felicitate amati gaudere)... Dolor maximus est miseria, seu damnatio; unde qui odit Deum moriens, damnat seipsum."[7]

In this passage Leibniz suggests that since the soul loses access to external sensations at bodily death (which access might lead it onto new trains of thought), it continues to think about whatever it was thinking at the moment of death, indeed with even greater intensity. In the case of the damned, they die hating God and this hatred persists into the afterlife, which in turn continually produces their damnation (the opposite would hold for the saved). Along the same lines, he writes later in the dialogue,

> "Qui male contentus moritur, moritur osor Dei: jamque velut in praeceps datus persequitur iter quod ingressus est nec amplius revocantibus externis, occluso sensuum aditu, animam in se reductam, coepto rerum odio atque ipsa illa miseria fastidioque, indignatione, invida, displicentia, magis magisque increscente, pascit. Corpore redunito, reversis etiam sensibus novam perpetuo contemtus, improbationis, irarum materiam invenit, tantoque magis torquetur, quanto minus mutare ac sustinere potest displicentem sibi torrentem rerum."[8]

In this case the hatred of the damned continues after the resurrection, having been twisted beyond repair in the time immediately following bodily death. He also suggests that both sin and damnation contribute to a kind of universal harmony:

> "Harmoniae autem exquisitissimae sit discordantiam turbatissimam in ordinem velut insperato redigi, picturam umbris distingui, harmoniam per dissonantias dissonantiis in consonantiam compensari (quemadmodum ex duobus numeris imparibus par fit) peccata sibi ipsis (quod notandum est) poenas irrogare."[9]

Later in the decade, Leibniz wrote the *Consideratio locorum potissimorum quae pro Purgatorio ex Scriptura Sacra et Sanctis patribus adducuntur* (1677) focusing on surveying and analyzing the opinions of a large number of church

---

[7] A VI, 3, 119.
[8] Ibid., 142.
[9] Ibid., 126.

fathers on the topic of purgatory. One notable feature of this work is that he concludes that some of the fathers did indeed appear to believe in a conception of purgatory that was not very different from the basic notion advocated by the Catholic Church.[10] Over the next decades, Leibniz develops a set of philosophical positions under the rubric of which something like purgatory can be made intelligible as a rational position, while also allowing for the magisterial protestant views and denying that any particular view ought to be held strictly as an article of faith.[11]

By the end of the 1670s Leibniz had shown some interest in the topics of natural (im)mortality, the state of consciousness between bodily death and the resurrection, and the justice of eternal damnation. In the 1680s Leibniz discusses some considerations about the soul and its immortality that do not rely on its indivisibility. For instance, in a short note written sometime between 1683 and 1685, he begins by suggesting a parallel between the beginning and end of the existence of souls:

> "Si animae naturalem haberent originem, etiam naturaliter extingui possent... unum quodque eo modo dissolvi posse ac tolli quo est colligatum et constitutum."[12] He concludes, first, that "animas non nisis creatione id est per miraculum oriri posse, quem [ad] modum immortalitas earum non impedit quo minus annihilatione id est miraculo tolli possent, si Deus vellet."[13]

Second, he lays out the view that souls were created at the same moment as the world itself.[14] Around 1686, Leibniz wrote the *Examen Religionis Christianae*, where he discusses the justification for eternal punishment, echoing the position articulated in the *Confessio Philosophi*:

> "Qui enim ex hac vita discedunt, male affecti erga Deum, hi cum nullis amplius externis sensibus revocentur, videntur prosequi coeptum iter eumque in quo deprehensi sunt animi statum servare, atque eo ipso a Deo separari, unde consequentia quadam in summam animi infelicitatem incidunt ac proinde ut ita dicam damnant semet ipsos."[15]

---

[10] A VI, 4 C, 2127–2144, passim.
[11] For a discussion of these issues see Lloyd Strickland: "Leibniz's Philosophy of Purgatory", in: *American Catholic Philosophical Quarterly* 84/3 (2010), pp. 531–548.
[12] A VI, 4 B, 1494.
[13] Ibid.
[14] Ibid.
[15] A VI, 4 C, 2360.

However, a short note from 1689/90 on *De Cessatione Cogitationum Distinctarum sine extinctione animae* presents a the beginnings of a contrasting view on the state of the soul after bodily death, one without distinct perceptions:

> "Animae extingui non posse facile judicabit, qui meas demonstrationes circa naturam substantiae intelliget, et probe percipiet, quod alibi explicui, cogitationes distinctas (quarum meminisse licet) cessare posse sine ulla extinctione animae, quoties perceptiones ejus sunt multiplices et in aequilibrio, ut non una multo magis quam alia attentionem mentis in se vertat."[16]

Thus, by the 1690s, Leibniz had intimated a number of options about how to think about mortalist themes. He had developed at least two very distinct ways of thinking about immortality, had developed some respect for the doctrine of purgatory, and had suggested at least two explanations for how eternal damnation could be justified. He had also begun to think about consciousness after bodily death offering two different ways of theorizing that state. In an interesting letter to Sophie from 1696, Leibniz discusses, among other things, what happens to us after death, while also introducing yet another reason to believe in immortality. This brief discussion gives us a window into the sort of views Leibniz might have had in mind at the time. In this instance, he argues that since every soul represents the whole universe, like a mirror, each one should last as long as the universe itself:

> "chaque ame est comme un monde à part, represantant le grand monde a sa mode, et suivant son point de veue; et que par consequent, toute ame, depuis qu'elle a commencé une fois d'exister, doit estre aussi durable que le monde même, dont elle est le miroir perpetuel."[17]

He further says that birth and death nothing other than developments and envelopments: "absolument parlant, la naissance et la mort ne sont que des deveopmens et enveloppmens."[18] In light of this remark it is interesting that he continues to say that all sensible perceptions leave some sort of trace that can never be entirely forgotten, so that "les traces des perceptions sensibles...restent toujours et ne s'effacent jamais par un oubly entier."[19]

---

[16] Ibid., 1643.
[17] A I, 13, 90.
[18] Ibid., 92.
[19] Ibid.

Before turning to the triumvirate of the *Nouveaux Essais sur l'entendement humain*, *Essais de Théodicée*, and *La Monadologie*, it is worth turning for a moment to one other letter to Sophie written by Leibniz in 1706. Here, discussing the notion of the soul as a mirror of the universe as well as preformationism, says that death is nothing but a kind of sleep:

> "Il paroist aussi par tout cela que chaque ame estant un miroir de l'univers, doit aller son train comme l'univers même qu'elle represente, sans que ce train reglé d'une Ame soit jamais tout à fait interrompu par la mort, qui n'est qu'un sommeil."[20]

He ends this passage by explaining the nature of sleep, which he says is "un Etat où les perceptions sont plus confuses, et qui dure jusqu'à ce qu'elle se redeveloppent."[21]

In the *Nouveaux Essais*, Leibniz is unsurprisingly, among many other things, concerned with the intersection between immortality and personal identity, as without personal identity it is hard to see exactly how certain forms of reward and punishment can be just. It is partially with this in mind that he remarks that "Un Estre immateriel ou Esprit ne peut estre depouillé de toute perception de son existence passée."[22] On the other hand, he is careful to insist that not all perceptions can be immediately apprehended as distinct: "[des impression] sont le plus souvent trop petits pour estre distinguables."[23] He adds a caveat to this, namely that, concerning even the most indistinct perceptions, "ils pouroient peutestre se developper un jour."[24] This move allows Leibniz to have some leeway in how to conceive of conscious life after death, while also being able to claim that we are responsible for everything we ever think or do. He also puts forward the notion that death is like sleep:

> "la mort ne sauroit estre qu'un sommeil, et même ne sauroit en demeurer un, les perceptions cessant seulement à estre assés distinguées et se reduisant à un estat de confusion dans les animaux qui suspend l'apperception, mais qui ne sauroit durer tousjours, pour ne parler icy de l'homme qui doit avoir en cela des grands privileges pour garder sa personalité."[25]

---

[20] GP VII, 568.
[21] Ibid.
[22] GP V, 222.
[23] Ibid.
[24] Ibid.
[25] Ibid., 48.

In the *Théodicée*, he returns again to the topic of eternal punishment, offering what looks like a variation of the responses he had come up with previously. For instance, he raises an objection to eternal punishment as unjust, that "Il n'y a point de proportion entre une peine infinie et une coulpe finie."[26] To this he responds,

> "la durée de la coulpe causoit la durée de la peine... les damnés demeurant mechans, ils ne pouvoient être tirés de leur misere."[27]

He also suggests that we can make sense of eternal damnation as contributing to a universal harmony, "comme une belle musique ou bien une bonne architecture contente les esprits bien faits."[28] However, there is an interesting moment where, concerning the damned, he writes that although they suffer eternally, their sufferings might undergo a continual lessening, such that

> "La diminution [des peines des damnés] iroit a l'infini quant a la durée: et neantmoins elle auroit un non plus ultra, quant a la grandeur de la diminition; comme il y a des figures asymptotes dans la Geometrie."[29]

The opening passages of *La Monadologie* reiterate a version of the argument for immortality from simplicity:

> "La Monade...n'est autre chose qu'une substance simple... c'est-a-dire sans parties... Il n'y aussi point de dissolution a craindre, et il n'y a aucune maniere concevable par laquelle une substance simple puisse perir naturellement."[30]

For the same reason, he writes, monads cannot come into being naturally, either. Leibniz also repeats the claim that some monads can have perceptions of which they are not aware, that there are "les perception, dont on ne s'apercoit pas."[31] He then connects that claim with the notion that being dead might be like "un long etourdissement."[32] Beginning in section twenty, he goes on to

---

[26] GP VI, 275.
[27] Ibid. He avers elsewhere that the converse is true for the elect: "On peut dire cependant que les damnés s'attirent toujours de nouvelles douleurs par de nouveaux péchés, et que les bienheureux s'attirent toujours de nouvelles joies par de nouveaux progrès dans le bien", ibid., 142.
[28] Ibid., 141.
[29] Ibid., 279.
[30] Ibid., 607.
[31] Ibid., 609.
[32] Ibid.

distinguish mere monads from the kinds of monads that souls are, suggesting that the state of awareness of mere monads is like that of humans who are asleep. Finally, human souls, unlike animal souls, possess reason, reflection, and self-awareness, some of whom are ultimately able to enter the divine commonwealth. After providing a brief summary of preformationism, he writes,

> "j'ay donc jugé que si l'animal ne commence jamais naturellement, il ne finit pas naturellement non plus; et que non seulement il n'y aura point de generation, mais encore point de destruction entiere, ny mort prise à la rigueur."[33]

He then also mentions his argument that since the soul is a mirror of the universe, and the universe is indestructible, the soul must be as well. Interestingly, Leibniz suggests that human souls undergo a kind of development such that prior to natural conception they are merely sensitive, being elevated to reason later on.

Over the course of his career, Leibniz develops, as it were, something for nearly everyone, although not all of them sit comfortably together. He offers at least three distinct grounds for the belief in immortality. One is based on the indivisibility of the soul, one on the "unnaturalness" of death as total annihilation (given the apparent truth of preformationism), and a third on the need for a mirror of the universe to exist for just as long as what it mirrors. On this score, he seems to have accepted versions of all three during the time of the composition of *La Monadologie*. For the time between life and the resurrection, he also offers a number of views. According to the *Confessio Philosophi* and the *Examen Religionis Christianae*, the mind upon death continues to enact the sort of hateful attitude it did during the conclusion of its earthly life, sans bodily sensation, which for the damned is akin to going, so to speak, straight to hell (with the converse holding for the elect). In the *Nouveaux Essais*, the mind goes into a state much like sleep, full of confused, indistinct perceptions. Finally, since the series of developments and envelopments of the soul can happen in an infinite variety of ways, there seems to be room in the Leibnizian corpus for something like purgatory. For instance, the soul might experience some period of time following death having a negative attitude toward God, only to develop and reform itself later on, before the resurrection. As for eternal damnation, he offers at least two accounts, according to one of which the continued damnable thoughts of the reprobate and their hatred of God produce continued suffering. According to the other, damnation comes

---

[33] Ibid., 620.

together with salvation to produce a kind of universal harmony. Finally, he introduces what might be considered a humane element by suggesting that it is possible that the sufferings of the damned will undergo a continual decrease, albeit coming just short of the joys of salvation.

Leibniz, Marx und der Marxismus. Theoretische Grundlagen und konkrete Beispiele einer komplexen Beziehungsgeschichte

Luca Basso (Padua)

Mein Aufsatz betrifft das Verhältnis zwischen Leibniz, Marx und dem Marxismus und demzufolge die Leibniz-Rezeption bei Marx und im Marxismus. Das theoretische und historische Spektrum ist sehr breit, weshalb ich hier nur einige Aspekte in Betracht ziehen kann. Es geht um ein Thema, das sehr wenig erörtert wurde und das neue theoretische und historische Räume öffnen kann. Das bedeutet nicht, eine lineare Verbindung zwischen den gezeigten Elementen in Richtung eines vermeintlichen „Leibniz'schen" Marxismus herzustellen; zu zahlreich sind die Unterschiede, auch in Bezug auf die diversen historischen, politischen und kulturellen Kontexte. Deswegen habe ich im Titel des Textes den Ausdruck eine „komplexe Beziehungsgeschichte" benutzt. Mein Aufsatz ist in drei Teile gegliedert. Der erste, kürzere Teil bildet eine Art Einleitung in das Problem. Der zweite Teil untersucht die Leibniz-Lektüre von Marx und der dritte Teil versucht einige Beispiele innerhalb des Marxismus, insbesondere des sogenannten „westlichen Marxismus", aufzuzeigen. In Bezug auf Marx wurde natürlich der Einfluss der klassischen deutschen Philosophie und insbesondere von Hegel lange betrachtet. Entscheidend in der marxistischen Debatte war die Frage, ob das Marx'sche Denken hegelianisch oder antihegelianisch sei. Und in Bezug auf die Philosophen der Frühneuzeit wurde Spinoza favorisiert. Dagegen wurde das Verhältnis Marx-Leibniz selten untersucht. Aber innerhalb der Frühneuzeit würde ich keinen absoluten Gegensatz zwischen Spinoza und Leibniz sehen. In der Tat scheint die These, dass Marx ein Spinozianer und ein Antileibnizianer war, nicht eindeutig klar (aber auch nicht das Gegenteil). Philologisch kann ich zwei allgemeine Überlegungen anstellen. Erstens werden beide Denker in den Marx'schen Texten zitiert; die Bezüge auf diese Philosophen scheinen also in Kontinuität mit seinem eigenen Denken zu stehen. Die zweite Bemerkung betrifft die Tatsache, dass der junge Marx beiden Denkern Exzerpte gewidmet hat. Es geht um das *Leibniz-Heft* und das *Spinoza-Heft*. Eine ähnliche Situation ergibt sich in diesem Sinne für Leibniz und für Spinoza in der Marxistischen Betrachtung. Der grundlegende Unterschied zwischen den beiden in der Rezeption nach Marx' Tod liegt in der Tatsache, dass das Thema des Verhältnisses zwischen Marx und Spinoza von einigen Strömungen des französischen Marxismus in einer antidialektischen Richtung unterstrichen wurde. Dies kann man hingegen nicht in Bezug auf die Leibniz-Rezeption innerhalb des Marxismus behaupten. Aber es gab (und es gibt) Versuche (wie wir sehen werden), die in eine andere Richtung gehen.

Aber zunächst muss die Bedeutung der Kategorie „Marxismus" erläutert werden. In den Grenzen dieses Aufsatzes beschränke ich mich darauf, zu betonen, dass „Marxismus" im engeren Sinne nach dem Tode von Marx benutzt werden kann. Oft wurde die Marx'sche Behauptung „*je ne suis pas marxiste*" zitiert. So stellt der Marxismus das Ergebnis der Bestrebungen von Engels nach 1883 dar. Mit dem genannten Begriff ist nicht nur eine Philosophie, sondern auch eine politische Aktion in einer engen Verbindung zwischen Theorie und Praxis gemeint. In der ersten Phase kann das marxistische Denken nicht von dem konkreten Handeln der Arbeiterbewegung (zwischen Revolution und Reformen) getrennt werden. Später spielten im 20. Jahrhundert die russische Revolution und die Begründung der Sowjetunion, gefolgt vom chinesischen Weg zum Kommunismus eine erhebliche Rolle für die Definition des Marxismus im Osten, aber auch im Westen. In diesem Aufsatz ist mit „Marxismus" primär das sogenannte „westliche Marxismus" gemeint. Es geht um die vielfältigen Strömungen des kritischen Marxismus im Westen, insbesondere in Deutschland und in Frankreich, wobei aber auch auf die angelsächsische Welt Bezug genommen wird. Es ist nicht so einfach zu entscheiden, ob einige Philosophen (zum Beispiel Deleuze) in engerem Sinne „Marxisten" genannt werden können. Ein gemeinsamer Nenner der Autoren des „westlichen Marxismus" liegt in der philosophischen Basis der Reflexion. Innerhalb dieser komplexen Debatte ist es auch strittig, ob man von „Marxismus" im Singular oder von „Marxismen" im Plural sprechen kann.

Nach diesen einleitenden Bemerkungen konzentriere ich mich im zweiten Teil des Aufsatzes auf das Verhältnis zwischen Marx und Leibniz. In den Marx'schen Texten sind die Bezüge auf Leibniz nicht sehr zahlreich, aber es gibt einige interessante Aspekte und normalerweise eine sehr positive Bewertung. Noch in einem relativ späten Brief an Engels behauptete Marx auf Englisch: „*You know my admiration for Leibniz.*"[1] Marx studierte innerhalb eines hegel'schen – oder posthegel'schen – Milieus und er schrieb die *Dissertatio* über Demokrit und Epikur. Nach der Dissertation in Berlin untersuchte er Leibniz, Hume und Spinoza. Während das *Spinoza-Heft*, insbesondere in

---

[1] Karl Marx an Friedrich Engels, 10.05.1870, in: Karl Marx/Friedrich Engels: *Marx-Engels-Werke, Briefe Januar 1868–Mitte Juli 1870* (= *MEW*), Bd. 32, Berlin 1965, S. 504.

Frankreich und in Italien, Interesse gefunden hat, wurde das *Leibniz-Heft* weniger analysiert. In der Tat hatte Marx ein Heft mit Exzerpten aus der Leibniz'schen Philosophie, und zwar aus der von Dutens besorgten Ausgabe, angelegt, obwohl um 1840 bereits die Erdmannsche Leibniz-Ausgabe in Berlin, wo Marx studierte, erschienen war.[2] Wie bei den anderen Exzerpten fehlt ein Kommentar von Marx und deswegen ist keine gesamtgültige Interpretation von Leibniz vorhanden. In diesem Sinne sollten wir dieses Heft mit einem gewissen Vorbehalt in Betracht ziehen. Aber aus der Wahl und der Ordnung der Leibniz-Zitate lassen sich fruchtbare Elemente ableiten. Zuerst spielt die Frage nach der individuellen Substanz oder der Monade eine erhebliche Rolle. Es ist dazu zu präzisieren, dass Marx sich schon in der *Dissertatio* über Demokrit und Epikur auf Leibniz bezog. Nach einer noch Hegel'schen Lektüre der griechischen Philosophen weist er auf die Grenzen der Betrachtung der Atome bei Epikur hin und favorisiert die Leibniz'schen Monaden als Atome mit einer Form.[3] Hierin zeigt sich die Relevanz von Aristoteles zum Verständnis dieser Marx'schen Position. Im *Leibniz-Heft* spielt der Bezug auf die Monade als Element der Individuation eine bedeutsame Rolle: Das *principium indiscernibilium* ist in diesem Kontext entscheidend. So könnte man behaupten, dass Marx durch die Leibniz'sche Monade die Frage der Individualität vertiefen will. In der *Deutschen Ideologie* zitieren Marx und Engels eine Stelle von Leibniz, „Opus tamen est […] ut quaelibet monas differat ab alia quacunque […]", um die Wichtigkeit des Individuums gegenüber der „Einzigkeit" von Max Stirner zu betonen.[4] Auch in der späteren Kritik der politischen Ökonomie spricht Marx von Individuen, die „in derselben Zeit nicht absolut gleich" sind. In diesem Kontext ist ein Bezug auf Leibniz vorhanden: „[…]

---

[2] Karl Marx: „Exzerpte aus Leibniz' Werken. Philosophie des Leibnitz" (1841), in: Karl Marx/Friedrich Engels: „Exzerpte und Notizen bis 1842", in: *Marx-Engels-Gesamtausgabe* (= *MEGA*), Abt. IV, Bd. 1, Berlin 1976, Text, S. 183–212. Siehe auch den Apparat: „Exzerpte aus Leibniz' Werken", in: *MEGA*, IV, 1, Apparat, S. 751–768. Aus der Edition von Dutens exzerpierte Marx dreißig Texte von Leibniz, unter ihnen *Meditationes de cogitatione, veritate et ideis*, *De primae philosophiae emendatione et de notione substantiae*, Texte aus der Kontroverse mit Clarke, *Réflexions de M. Leibniz sur l'essai de l'entendement humain de Mr. Locke*, *Epistola ad Père des Bosses*, *Principes de la nature et de la grace fondés en Raison*, *Système nouveau de la nature et de la communication des substances*.
[3] Vgl. Karl Marx: „Doktordissertation: Differenz der demokritischen und epikureischen Naturphilosophie im allgemeinen" (1840–1841, post. 1927), in: *MEW*, 40, 1990, S. 288f.
[4] Karl Marx/Friedrich Engels: „Die Deutsche Ideologie. Kritik der neuesten deutschen Philosophie in ihren Repräsentanten Feuerbach, B. Bauer und Stirner, und des deutschen Sozialismus in seinen verschiedenen Propheten" (1845–1846, post. 1932), in: *MEW*, 3, 1958, S. 428.

nicht zwei Blätter, Leibniz [...]."[5] Dazu ist eine Stelle der *Kritik des Gothaer Programms* sehr bedeutsam. Marx betrachtet das Thema des gleichen Rechts und des ungleichen Rechts, wo die Leibniz'sche Frage nach dem zureichenden Grund entsteht. „[...] sie [die Individuen] wären nicht verschiedene Individuen, wenn sie nicht ungleiche wären [...]."[6] Gegen eine weit verbreitete Idee (oder manchmal sogar ein *cliché*) stellt sich Marxens gesamte Laufbahn, meiner Interpretation nach, als Suche nach der Verwirklichung der Individualität dar.[7] Von den ersten bis zu den letzten Werken von Marx wird der Kommunismus als Anerkennung der Individuen konzipiert; hier ist keine „holistische" Perspektive vorhanden. Aber die Tendenz von Marx scheint die Leibniz'schen Monaden sozusagen zu „materialisieren". Bei Marx werden die Monaden als *primae substantiae* nicht im Sinne des Geistes, sondern der empirischen Individuen konzipiert. In dieser Betrachtungsweise treten nicht nur die Kontaktpunkte, sondern auch die Unterschiede zwischen Marx und Leibniz hervor: Die „wirklichen", „bestimmten Individuen" der *Deutschen Ideologie* von Marx und Engels unterscheiden sich von den Leibniz'schen Monaden.

In Bezug auf die Monade sind zwei weitere Aspekte besonders bemerkenswert. Der Eine ist die Verbindung zwischen Monade und Aktion. Wie aus dem von Marx exzerpierten Satz der *Principes de la nature et de la grâce fondés en raison* hervorgeht, „la monade est un être capable d'action."[8] Dies steht unter Hegel'schem Einfluss, aber meiner Ansicht nach spielt das Werk von Ludwig Feuerbach, *Darstellung, Entwicklung und Kritik der Leibniz'schen Philosophie zur neueren Philosophie und ihrer Entwicklung* (1837) in der Marx'schen Rezeption von Leibniz eine erhebliche Rolle.[9] Dieses Werk von Feuerbach ist eine der ersten wichtigen deutschen Monographien über Leibniz. Hier wird einerseits Leibniz als Vorläufer der klassischen deutschen Philosophie, insbesondere in Bezug auf das Verhältnis Subjekt-Handeln interpretiert und aus diesem Grunde herausgehoben, anderseits werden einige „na-

---

[5] Karl Marx: „Ökonomisches Manuskript 1861–1863", Teil I, in: *MEW*, 43, 1990, S. 226.
[6] Ders.: „Kritik des Gothaer Programms" (1875, post. 1890–1891), in: *MEW*, 19, 1962, S. 21.
[7] Vgl. Luca Basso: *Marx and Singularity. From the Early Writings to the ‚Grundrisse'* (2008), aus dem Italienischen von A. Bove, Leiden/Boston 2012; ders.: *Marx and the Common. From ‚Capital' to the Late Writings* (2012), aus dem Italienischen. v. D. Broder, Leiden/Boston 2015.
[8] *Principes de la nature et de la grâce fondés en raison*, 1714, § 1; GP VI, 598. Marx exzerpiert die erwähnte Leibniz-Stelle: vgl. „Exzerpte aus Leibniz' Werken", S. 201.
[9] Vgl. Ludwig Feuerbach: *Darstellung, Entwicklung und Kritik der Leibniz'schen Philosophie zur neueren Philosophie und ihrer Entwicklung (1837)*, Stuttgart/Bad Cannstatt 1959.

turalistische", kartesische Aspekte von Leibniz kritisiert. Es darf nicht vergessen werden, dass die Reflexion des jungen Marx von den jungen Posthegelianern und insbesondere von Feuerbach sehr stark beeinflusst wurde. Die Marx'sche Interpretation (auch in Kontinuität mit der Feuerbach'schen Perspektive) betont den dynamischen Charakter der Monade und deswegen die Funktion von Kraft. Man darf fragen, inwieweit da aristotelische Elemente und inwieweit Aspekte der neuzeitlichen Wissenschaft und Philosophie vorhanden sind. In den Leibniz-Exzerpten gibt es keine Stellen, wo das Thema der Verhältnisse zwischen den Monaden vertieft wird. Aber in der *Kritik des Hegelschen Staatsrechts* benutzt Marx den Leibniz'schen Begriff des *vinculum substantiale* im Streit gegen Hegel.[10] Aber es wäre übertrieben, die These zu vertreten, dass Leibniz mit dem Begriff des *vinculum substantiale* ein Vorläufer des Marx'schen Themas des gesellschaftlichen Verhältnisses sei. Insgesamt könnte man behaupten, dass die Leibniz'sche Monade eine der Quellen (nicht die einzige natürlich und nicht ohne Schwierigkeiten) der Begründung der Individualität bei Marx in ihrer Verbindung mit dem Element des Handelns darstellt. Dazu wurde die Lektüre von Leibniz, ebenso wie die von Spinoza, teils durch die klassische deutsche Philosophie vermittelt, teils gegen diese vorgenommen.

Aber man darf andere bedeutsame Unterschiede zwischen Marx und Leibniz nicht unterschätzen. Zum Beispiel haben Marx und Engels innerhalb einer weiten Betrachtung der neuzeitlichen Philosophie in der *Heiligen Familie* betont, dass der französische Materialismus einen Bruch mit der „Metaphysik" des XVII. Jahrhunderts vorgenommen hat:

> „,Genau und im prosaischen Sinne zu reden', war die französische Aufklärung des 18. Jahrhunderts und namentlich der französische Materialismus nicht nur ein Kampf gegen die Metaphysik des siebzehnten Jahrhunderts und gegen alle Metaphysik, namentlich gegen die des Descartes, Malebranche, Spinoza und Leibniz. Man stellte die Philosophie der Metaphysik gegenüber, wie Feuerbach bei seinem ersten entschiedenen Auftreten wider Hegel der trunkenen Spekulation die nüchterne Philosophie gegenüberstellte."[11]

Es ist bemerkenswert, dass Leibniz und Spinoza als Repräsentanten der „*Metaphysik des siebzehnten Jahrhunderts*" gemeinsam betrachtet werden und ge-

---

[10] Vgl. Karl Marx: „Kritik des Hegel'schen Staatsrechts" (1843, post. 1927), in: *MEW*, 1, 1961, S. 222.
[11] Karl Marx/Friedrich Engels: „Die heilige Familie oder Kritik der kritischen Kritik. Gegen Bruno Bauer und Konsorten" (1845), in: *MEW*, 2, 1957, S. 132.

meinsam kritisiert werden. Auch in diesem Kontext spielt der Bezug auf Feuerbach eine erhebliche Rolle. In den späteren Texten der Kritik der politischen Ökonomie ist ein ironischer Bezug auf die Theodizee und auf den Ausdruck „*le meilleur des mondes possibles*" vorhanden. Die Ironie liegt in der Tatsache, dass die Vertreter der politischen Ökonomie nach Marx zu einer Art von Theodizee des Kapitalismus als „*le meilleur des mondes possibles*" kämen. Hinter diesem scheinbaren Optimismus verbergen sie die Brutalität der gesellschaftlichen Verhältnisse unter der kapitalistischen Produktionsweise. In dieser Hinsicht wird die Leibniz'sche Theodizee durch die Lektüre Voltaires interpretiert. Aber dieses „theologisierende" und christliche Bild von Leibniz wird in einer interessanten Stelle von den Marx'schen *Enthüllungen über den Kommunisten-Prozeß zu Köln* in Frage gestellt:

> „Die preußischen Staatsphilosophen von Leibniz bis Hegel haben an der Absetzung Gottes gearbeitet, und wenn ich Gott absetze, setze ich auch den König von Gottes Gnaden ab."[12]

Hier werden Leibniz und Hegel gemeinsam betrachtet und gemeinsam kritisiert, weil beide „preußische Staatsphilosophen" seien, aber aus einer rationalistischen Perspektive habe schon Leibniz angefangen, Gott abzusetzen.

Ein anderer Bezugspunkt betrifft die wissenschaftliche Methode. Marx und Engels schätzten die logisch-mathematische Seite der Leibniz'schen Reflexion (zum Beispiel in den mathematischen Heften von Marx wird Leibniz betrachtet) und noch mehr die Verbindung zwischen Theorie und Praxis: *theoria cum praxi*. Die Marx'sche Lektüre dieses Verhältnisses geht, anders als bei Leibniz, in eine revolutionäre Richtung. In der Tat behauptet Marx in der Elften (und letzten) *These über Feuerbach*: „Die Philosophen haben die Welt nur verschieden *interpretiert*, es kommt drauf an, sie zu *verändern*."[13] Aber trotz der erheblichen Unterschiede ist es bedeutsam, dass Leibniz zu einer Verbindung zwischen Theorie und Praxis kommt. Der Versuch, die Akademien der Wissenschaften, deren Mitglieder in einem engen Zusammenhang zwischen Theorie und Praxis zusammenwirken, zu begründen, führt zu einer nicht auf die reine Gelehrsamkeit reduzierbaren Konzeption. Der Gelehrte

---

[12] Karl Marx: „Enthüllungen über den Kommunisten-Prozeß zu Köln" (1852) in: *MEW*, 8, 1960, S. 415. Siehe auch Friedrich Engels: „Varia über Deutschland" (1873–1874), in: *MEW*, 18, 1962, S. 590 und 592.
[13] Karl Marx: „Thesen über Feuerbach" (1845), in: *MEW*, 3, S. 7.

kann sich nämlich nicht auf ein enzyklopädisches Wissen beschränken, sondern muss Kultur mit Arbeitsamkeit verknüpfen, weil die Kenntnisse auf die *publica utilitas* zielen. So erscheint die Idee der Wissenschaft als Kommunikation, als Element der Vereinigung zwischen den Individuen mit ihrem politischen Charakter. Erwähnenswert ist, dass die *Nouveaux essais sur l'entendement humain* mit der Suche nach einer „alliance de la Practique et de la Theorie" enden.[14] So ist das Verständnis der Wichtigkeit des „praktischen" im Sinne des angewendeten, operativen Moments in Richtung des *commune bonum* vorhanden. Aus dieser ganzen Betrachtung ergibt sich ein komplexes, nicht lineares Verhältnis zwischen Marx und Leibniz. Im dritten (und letzten) Teil des Aufsatzes werden einige Aspekte der Frage in Bezug auf bedeutsame Themen in der marxistischen Entwicklung nach Marx untersucht.

Noch komplizierter ist die Analyse des Bezugs auf Leibniz innerhalb der Geschichte des Marxismus (oder der Marxismen). Wie am Anfang betont wurde, kann man nur schwerlich eine allgemeine Definition des Marxismus geben. Das Problem liegt in der komplexen Beziehung zwischen Theorie und Praxis. In diesem Kontext kann ich keine analytische Betrachtung anstellen. Ich werde insbesondere von dem sogenannten westlichen Marxismus sprechen, aber es muss betont werden, dass die Rezeption von Leibniz im Osten normalerweise begeistert war. Hierzu hat auch die Marx'sche positive Bewertung von Leibniz, „*You know my admiration for Leibniz*", in erheblichem Maße beigetragen. Ich beschränke mich darauf, vier bedeutsame Fragen aufzuwerfen. Die erste betrifft die Verbindung zwischen Theorie und Praxis, die zweite die Dialektik, die dritte die Monade als Aktion und Kraft und folglich in Bezug auf das Element des Subjektes und die vierte die Lektüre des Kapitalismus. Erstens wurde aus den schon erklärten Gründen die Leibniz'sche *theoria cum praxi* von Marx, Engels und der Geschichte des Marxismus anerkannt. Hier sind Kontaktpunkte, aber auch Unterschiede in Bezug auf diese Frage vorhanden. Das gilt noch mehr für den Marxismus in der Sowjetunion und in den Ländern des sogenannten real existierenden Sozialismus. Aber es ist nicht zu vergessen, dass alle Bände der Leibniz-Ausgabe nach dem zweiten Weltkrieg bis 1989 von der Akademie der Wissenschaften der DDR finanziert und im dortigen Akademie-Verlag erschienen sind. Es ist sehr bedeutsam, dass sich die Akademie der Wissenschaften der DDR an dieser Stelle zum Erbe der preußischen Akademie der Wissenschaften bekannt hat. Zwei Bände der ersten Reihe und zwei Bände der vierten Reihe wurden so fertiggestellt

---

[14] Vgl. *Nouveaux essais sur l'entendement humain* (1703–1705); A VI, 6, 527.

und der Druck des Buches von Hans-Stephan Brather, *Leibniz und seine Akademie,* Berlin 1993, in der Leibniz-Edition vorbereitet.[15]

Zweitens stellt die Dialektik ein entscheidendes Element dar, aber die Betrachtung der Frage ist sehr komplex. Die Mehrdeutigkeit betrifft sowohl die marxistische Lektüre von Marx als auch die marxistische Lektüre von Leibniz. Schon am Anfang der Entwicklung des Marxismus war mit Engels eine dialektische Richtung in Kontinuität mit Hegel vorhanden. In diesem Kontext stellt Leibniz eine Art Vorläufer der klassischen deutschen Philosophie dar. Engels war die Hauptfigur für die „Entstehung" des Marxismus und bei ihm sind zahlreiche Bezüge auf Leibniz vorhanden. Zum Beispiel im *Anti-Dühring* spricht Engels von Leibniz gerade im Verhältnis zu der Dialektik und der Infinitesimalrechnung.[16] Und in der *Dialektik der Natur* bezieht er sich mehrmals auf Leibniz. Insbesondere im Kapitel „Maß der Bewegung – Arbeit" ist eine Auseinandersetzung mit der Leibniz'schen Konzeption von Kraft, Körper, Bewegung vorhanden.[17] Engels hat die Dialektik als Theorie des Gesamtzusammenhangs nicht nur auf den gesellschaftlichen, sondern auch auf den natürlichen Bereich angewendet und in diesem Kontext spielt auch die Physik von Leibniz eine Rolle. Dieses Element ist auch wichtig, um die Entwicklung dieser Fragen im russischen Milieu zu verstehen. Lenin hat diese Frage in der Broschüre *Drei Quellen und drei Bestandteile des Marxismus* dargestellt.[18] Er erkennt folgende drei Wurzeln: den französischen, utopischen Sozialismus, die englische Nationalökonomie und die klassische deutsche Philosophie von Leibniz über Kant bis Hegel. So würde Leibniz zu einer der drei Quellen des historischen Materialismus gehören.

Diese Ansichten wurden im Osten, aber auch im Westen, zum Beispiel in den Arbeiten von Hans Heinz Holz[19] vertreten. Das Werk von Georg Lukács, *Geschichte und Klassenbewußtsein,* war ein Meilenstein für den sogenannten „westlichen Marxismus" und spielte deswegen eine bedeutende dialektische Rolle, mit einem sehr lebendigen und nicht rigiden Charakter.

---

[15] Vgl. A I, 5 (1687–1690), 1990 (zweite durchgesehener Nachdruck, 1. Auflage 1954); A I, 6 (1690–1691), 1990 (zweite durchgesehener Nachdruck, 1. Auflage 1957); A IV, 1 (1667–1676), ³1983; A IV, 2 (1677–1687), Berlin ²1984; Hans-Stephan Brather (Hrsg.): *Leibniz und seine Akademie. Ausgewählte Quellen zur Geschichte der Berliner Sozietät der Wissenschaften*, Berlin 1993.
[16] Vgl. Friedrich Engels: „Anti-Dühring" (1878, ³1894), in: *MEW*, 20, 1962, S. 126.
[17] Vgl. Ders.: „Dialektik der Natur" (1873–1886, post. 1925), in: *MEW*, 20, S. 370–374, 380.
[18] Vgl. Wladimir Iljitsch Lenin: *Drei Quellen und drei Bestandteile des Marxismus* (1913), Berlin 1966.
[19] Vgl. Hans Heinz Holz: *Leibniz in der Rezeption der klassischen deutschen Philosophie,* hrsg. v. Jörg Zimmer, Darmstadt 2015, insbes. Kap. 5, „Von Leibniz über Hegel zu Marx", S. 55–67.

Wenngleich mit erheblichen Unterschieden wurde sicherlich auch die Frankfurter Schule von Lukács beeinflusst. In diesem Kontext ist besonders das Denken von Adorno wichtig, das sich auf die Reflexion von Hegel und Marx (auch mit relevanten Überlegungen zur Leibniz'schen Monadologie) bezieht, aber auch über Hegel und Marx in Richtung einer „negativen Dialektik" bewegt. Die Dialektik, ebenfalls mit Marx'schen Spuren, kann bei den Philosophen des westlichen Marxismus auf die Gesellschaft, aber nicht auf die Natur angewendet werden. In diesem Sinne wurde die Engels'sche Dialektik der Natur nicht akzeptiert. Das gilt nicht nur für die Frankfurter Schule und für Philosophen wie Ernst Bloch, die zum Teil damit verbunden sind. Zum Beispiel kritisierte der französische Philosoph Jean-Paul Sartre, insbesondere in *Questions de méthode* und in der *Critique de la raison dialectique,* jeden Versuch, eine Dialektik der Natur zu konstruieren: diese habe einen deterministischen und positivistischen Charakter. Und ebenfalls in Frankreich interpretierte der anti-dialektische Philosoph Louis Althusser Leibniz in einer dialektischen Weise und kritisierte ihn aus diesem Grund. Seiner Ansicht nach gäbe es die „Linie" Spinoza-Marx gegen die dialektische „Linie" Leibniz-Hegel.

Die dritte, vermutlich interessanteste Frage dazu innerhalb des Marxismus betrifft die Monade in ihrer Verbindung mit der Aktion und der Kraft, wie ich schon im zweiten Teil des Aufsatzes betont hatte. Mehrere Marxisten haben durch die Leibniz'sche Monade und auch durch die aristotelische *dynamis* das Verhältnis zwischen Subjekt und Aktion in einer dynamischen Weise interpretiert. In dieser Perspektive ist der Versuch von Ernst Bloch in mehreren Werken und insbesondere in *Das Prinzip Hoffnung*, Leibniz als einen Denker des Möglichen, zum Teil in Kontinuität mit Aristoteles zu lesen, als fruchtbar anzusehen, da hier das dynamische Moment der Monade anerkannt wird.[20] Entscheidend sind hierbei die *Nouveaux Essais sur l'entendement humain,* die vom Element der *inquiétude,* Unruhe, gekennzeichnet sind. So unterstreicht Gilles Deleuze in der *Falte* mit einer ganz anderen Einstellung das expansive, unruhige Moment der Monade in ihrem aktiven und solidarischen Charakter im Streit gegen jede solipsistische Lektüre der Leibniz'schen Philosophie.[21] Deleuze, der aber nur schwerlich als Marxist definiert werden kann (wenngleich sein letztes Buch, das nicht erschien, den Titel *La grandeur*

---

[20] Vgl. Ernst Bloch: *Das Prinzip Hoffnung*, Frankfurt am Main 1985 (1938–1947, durchgesehen 1953 und 1959), Bd. 2, Kap. 33–42, insbes. S. 1006–1011.
[21] Vgl. Gilles Deleuze: *Le pli. Leibniz et le Baroque*, Paris 1988; aus dem Französ. v. U. J. Schneider übers.: *Die Falte. Leibniz und der Barock*, Frankfurt am Main 1995.

de Marx gehabt hätte), untersucht Leibniz nicht als Vorläufer der Aufklärung, sondern als Philosophen des Barocks zwischen Licht und Schatten. Es ist interessant, dass auch ein Denker mit einer ganz anderen Perspektive wie Jon Elster in seinem Aufsatz *Marx et Leibniz* (1983) die Kontaktpunkte zwischen Marx und Leibniz auch in Bezug auf die Frage des Verhältnisses zwischen Monade und Aktion betont hat.[22] Elster interpretiert in *Making Sense of Marx*, einem der wichtigsten Texte des sogenannten „*analytical marxism*", Marx als einen Individualisten, wobei das Verhältnis zu Leibniz eine erhebliche Rolle spielt.[23] Im Buch von Michel Vadée *Marx penseur du possible* (1988) sind kurze, aber bedeutsame Bezüge auf Leibniz in der Betonung des dynamischen Charakters des Subjektes vorhanden.[24] Auch erweist Jacques d'Hondt in seinem Aufsatz *Le meilleur de mondes de Marx* der expansiven Leibniz'schen Idee, nach der die Gegenwart schwanger mit der Zukunft ist, seine Wertschätzung.[25] Ferner unterstreicht die Arbeit von Hervé Touboul, *Marx, Engels et la question de l'individu*, gerade die erwähnten Elemente durch eine detaillierte Untersuchung der Marx'schen Stellen über Leibniz.[26] In Bezug auf das *Leibniz-Heft* sind der Aufsatz *Marx frühe Leibniz-Exzerpte als Quelle seiner Dialektik* von Hartmut Hecht und das Buch *Marx dalla totalità alla moltitudine (1841–1843)* von Ernesto Screpanti zu erwähnen.[27]

Die vierte (und letzte) Fragerichtung betrifft die gesamte Analyse des Kapitalismus. In diesem Fall werde ich mich auf zwei Versuche beschränken.

---

[22] Vgl. Jon Elster: „Marx et Leibniz", in: *Revue Philosophique de la France et de l'étranger* 2 (1983) S. 167–177: „[…] l'appel au principe des indiscernables pour réfuter toute conception qui gommerait les particularités individuelles est parfaitement délibéré. Il suggère que l'une des racines de la vision marxiste de la société communiste se trouve dans la métaphysique de Leibniz" (S. 177).

[23] Vgl. Ders.: *Making Sense of Marx*, Cambridge 1985.

[24] Vgl. Michel Vadée: *Marx penseur du possible*, Paris 1992, S. 265: „Pour Marx aussi, la force a un côté actif et un côté passif. Il fait partie de ces philosophes qui, comme Leibniz et Hegel chez les modernes, Aristote et Héraclite chez les Anciens, ont rejeté la conception mécaniste de la nature. Comme eux, Marx a une conception dynamiste."

[25] Vgl. Jacques d'Hondt: „Le meilleur des mondes de Marx", in: Albert Heinekamp/André Robinet (Hrsg.): *Leibniz: le meilleur de mondes* (= *Studia Leibnitiana*, Sonderhefte 21) Stuttgart 1992, S. 271–282, hier S. 281.

[26] Vgl. Hervé Touboul: *Marx, Engels et la question de l'individu*, „Actuel Marx Confrontation", Paris 2004, insbes. S. 117 und 126: „Bien sûr, pour Marx point de Dieu, mais l'analogie fonctionne: l'activité matérielle est la force de l'individu et lui donne forme, et elle n'est séparable que par abstraction de sa manifestation […]" (S. 121).

[27] Vgl. Hartmut Hecht: „Marx' frühe Leibniz-Exzerpte als Quelle seiner Dialektik", in: *Berliner Debatte Initial* 4 (2001), S. 27–37; Ernesto Screpanti: *Marx dalla totalità alla moltitudine (1841–1843)*, Pistoia 2013, S. 15–29.

Erstens hat Jon Elster, aber nicht im schon zitierten Werk *Making Sense of Marx,* sondern in *Leibniz et la formation de l'esprit capitaliste* (1975) in einer originellen Weise das Thema der Wirtschaft bei Leibniz zwischen Merkantilismus und Kapitalismus untersucht. Dazu wurde Leibniz zu Marx, aber noch mehr zu Weber und Schumpeter in Beziehung gesetzt.[28] Zweitens hat der marxistische Geograph David Harvey, insbesondere in *Justice, Nature and the Geography of Difference* (1996), auf die Leibniz'sche Theorie der inneren Verhältnisse und auf die Leibniz'sche Konzeption von Zeit und Raum im Streit gegen Newton Bezug genommen. So wurde auch die Perspektive der möglichen Welten in eine emanzipatorische Richtung benutzt, um nach einer räumlichen und zeitlichen Alternative gegenüber dem kapitalistischen Szenario zu streben.[29]

Am Ende dieses komplexen und differenzierten Weges ist eine relevante, aber nicht lineare und unmittelbare Beziehung zwischen Leibniz, Marx und dem Marxismus zu erkennen. So kann dieses zu wenig betrachtete Thema einige neue fruchtbare Freiräume öffnen. Um den expansiven Charakter des Leibniz'schen Denkens zu unterstreichen, ende ich mit den Worten von Ernst Bloch aus seinen *Leipziger Vorlesungen zur Geschichte der Philosophie*:

> „Das Grundton in dieser Philosophie [von Leibniz] ist lebendig; ein Akzent von Tätigkeit […] liegt auf allem […] Diese Tätigkeit ist ein Streben zu etwas hin, eine Tendenz […][30] Der Akzent steht bei Leibniz mehr auf der Vermittlung als auf den Gegensätzen, aber die Gegensätze sind vorhanden: Ruhe und Bewegung, Mensch und Tier, Schlaf und Wachen werden relativiert[31]. So sagt Leibniz auch: Die Zukunft ist nichts anderes als die größere Dimension der auf sie

---

[28] Vgl. Jon Elster: *Leibniz et la formation de l'esprit capitaliste*, Paris 1975, S. 14f.: „[…] le Dieu leibnizien incarne cette rationalité instrumentale, à la différence du Dieu de Descartes ou d'Arnauld […] On verra chez Leibniz une tension constante entre le courant mercantiliste ou statique et le courant capitaliste et dynamique de sa pensée, tension qui apparaît non seulement dans ses écrits proprement économiques, mais aussi et peut-être surtout dans ses travaux les plus métaphysiques […]."
[29] Vgl. David Harvey: *Justice, Nature and the Geography of Difference*, Malden, MA/Oxford/Carlton 1996, S. 255: „Leibniz' findings on multiple possible worlds of space and time are purely logical constructs. But they can be used as a means to look more closely at the differentiation of actual spatial and temporal orderings within and between different modes of production and social formations […] It also permits the exploration of alternative mods of production in terms of the production of different possible worlds of spatio-temporality."
[30] Ernst Bloch: „Neuzeitliche Philosophie I: Von Descartes bis Rousseau", in: Ders.: *Leipziger Vorlesungen zur Geschichte der Philosophie 1950–1956*, Bd. 3, bearbeitet v. U. Opolka, Frankfurt a. M. 1985, S. 126.
[31] Ebd., S. 143.

hin tendierenden Gegenwart selber, sie ist die nach vornhin sich erweitern wollende Gegenwart [...] Hier haben wir echte Zukunft, die etwas Neues enthält, und das Neue ist eben die nach vornhin erweiterte Dimension [...] Tendenz wächst [...] aus der Einengung, aus der Verhinderung. Marx formuliert das einmal so, daß Tendenz die Wirksamkeit eines verhinderten Gesetzes ist [...] Für Leibniz liegt die Tendenz in der Monade [...] Die Monade repräsentiert den künftigen Zustand, zu dem sie auf dem Wege ist [...] In jedem gegenwärtigen Zustand liegt der künftige Zustand als Tendenz."[32]

---

[32] Ebd., S. 149f. Siehe auch ders.: *Subjekt-Objekt. Erläuterungen zu Hegel*, Frankfurt a. M. ²1962, insbes. S. 132f.

Geschichte und Methode – Leibniz' Beitrag zur Geschichtswissenschaft

Annette von Boetticher (Hannover)

> „Es war die große metaphysische Konzeption von Leibniz, die auch Goethe bewundert hat, daß die vielen Spiegel des Universums, die die einzelnen Individuen sind, in ihrer Allheit das eine Universum selbst sind. Das ließe sich zu einem Universum des Gesprächs ausgestalten."
>
> (Hans Georg Gadamer)[1]

1. Geschichte als Wissenschaft

Als Geistes- und Kulturwissenschaft beschäftigt sich *Geschichte* heute mit der Erforschung und Deutung der Vergangenheit, die in der Komplexität ihrer Einzelgeschehnisse und deren Überlieferung die politische, gesellschaftliche, wirtschaftliche und kulturelle Grundlage unserer Gegenwart bildet. Gegenstand der Untersuchung sind in erster Linie Ereignisse, Personen, Strukturen und Dynamiken sozialer Lebensformen[2] sowie politischer oder religiöser Ideologiebildungen und Wertvorstellungen und deren regionale, nationale oder internationale Auswirkungen.

Im 17. und 18. Jahrhundert hatte *Geschichte* noch längst nicht den Rang einer wissenschaftlichen Disziplin, sondern lediglich den Status einer Hilfswissenschaft für Theologie, Philosophie und Jurisprudenz, wenn es darum ging, für Fragen und Probleme der Zeit Begründungen aus der Vergangenheit zu liefern. Die Historiographie, die häufig noch der Poesie[3] zugeordnet wurde, und die Geschichtskunde, d. h. das reine Faktenwissen von vergangenem Geschehen in seinem chronologischen Ablauf, waren terminologisch noch nicht

---

[1] Hans Georg Gadamer: *Hermeneutik II. Wahrheit und Methode* (= *Gesammelte Werke* 2), Tübingen 1999, S. 210.
[2] Annette v. Boetticher: *Wissenschaftliches Arbeiten im Geschichtsseminar. Eine Checkliste*, Hannover 2007, S. 13.
[3] Die wissenschaftliche Zwitterstellung der Geschichte beschrieb Leopold von Ranke, der „Vater" der Geschichtswissenschaft, im Jahre 1837 folgendermaßen: „Die Historie unterscheidet sich dadurch von andern Wissenschaften, daß sie zugleich Kunst ist. Wissenschaft ist sie: indem sie sammelt, findet, durchdringt; Kunst ist sie, indem sie das Gefundene, Erkannte wieder gestaltet, darstellt. Andre Wissenschaften begnügen sich, das Gefundene schlechthin als solches aufzuzeichnen; bei der Historie gehört das Vermögen der Wiederhervorbringung dazu." Zit. nach: Werner Paravicini: *Die Wahrheit der Historiker*, München 2010, S. 4.

klar voneinander getrennt. Seit der Aufklärungszeit ist jedoch eine zunehmende begriffliche Differenzierung festzustellen: Geschichte als Kollektivsingular wird zu einem Prozessbegriff, der sowohl vergangenes als auch künftiges Geschehen und dessen Hintergründe umfasst. Geschichte als Wissenschaft „zielt seitdem auf systematisch und autonom verfasste, in methodischer Ableitung kontrollierte Wahrheitsfindung."[4] Im 19. Jahrhundert etablierte sich die Geschichte neben den Naturwissenschaften und der Philosophie als autonome Wissenschaft auf der Grundlage kritisch-reflektierenden Quellenstudiums. Heuristik, Methodik, Quellen- und Textkritik und Hermeneutik bilden schließlich die Grundlage geschichtswissenschaftlicher Forschung und werden heute unter dem Begriff der Historik zusammengefasst.[5]

2. Leibniz' Auffassung von Geschichte

Für Leibniz hatte die auf Tatsachenwahrheiten beruhende Geschichte mehrere Funktionen: In Verbindung mit seiner Metaphysik diente sie ihm als Teil seines Gottesbeweises, dokumentierte sich doch in der Geschichte letztlich der göttliche Wille. Ziel der Erforschung der Vergangenheit müsse es seiner Auffassung nach sein, die einzelnen Ereignisse oder Teilgeschichten zu einer Universalhistorie zusammenzufügen, um unter Berücksichtigung einer wissenschaftlichen Methodik zu einer weitest gehenden Annäherung an die Wahrheit mit Hilfe der Wahrscheinlichkeitslogik zu gelangen. Zugleich erfüllte Geschichte einen moralisch-didaktischen Zweck, nämlich das Lernen aus der Vergangenheit für die Zukunft, und wäre somit, ganz im Sinne Ciceros, als „magistra vitae" zu bergreifen. Die historischen Kenntnisse eines Faches – Jurisprudenz, Kirchen- oder Rechtsgeschichte – waren für Leibniz unabdingbare Voraussetzungen für ein tieferes Verstehen. Römische Geschichte sollte seiner Auffassung nach der Kenntnis des Zivilrechts, Kirchengeschichte der Kenntnis des Kanonischen Rechts und die Geschichte des Mittelalters der Kenntnis des Lehnrechts dienen.[6] Der Genealogie, und damit der Suche nach der *connexion naturelle des hommes*, galt Leibniz' Interesse, denn letztlich

---

[4] Rüdiger vom Bruch: Art.: „Geschichtswissenschaft", in: Stefan Jordan (Hrsg.): *Geschichtswissenschaft. Hundert Grundbegriffe*, Stuttgart 2002, S. 125.
[5] v. Boetticher: *Wissenschaftliches Arbeiten*, S. 14.
[6] Reinhard Finster/Gerd van den Heuvel: *Gottfried Wilhelm Leibniz mit Selbstzeugnissen und Bilddokumenten*, Reinbek b. Hamburg 1990, S. 93.

war sie der Motor der Geschichte.[7] Den Ursprüngen des Gegenwärtigen in der Vergangenheit der Kausalketten nachzuspüren, reizte ihn von daher in besonderem Maße.[8] Und nicht zuletzt empfand er beim Entziffern alter Urkunden oder Chroniken, eine „Wonne, Konkretes zu erfahren."[9]

Leibniz' historische Arbeiten, seine Veröffentlichungen, Konzepte und Briefe beinhalten eine Bandbreite an Themen, die heute innerhalb der Geschichtswissenschaften wiederum eigene Disziplinen darstellen: neben der allgemeinen politischen Reichs- und Dynastiegeschichte, die Kirchen- und Rechtsgeschichte, Archäologie, Genealogie, Diplomatik, Numismatik und Heraldik.

Als Sammler und Herausgeber historischer Quellen[10] kommt Leibniz das unbestrittene Verdienst zu, auf die Relevanz einer quellenbasierten historischen Forschung hingewiesen zu haben, wobei er gewiss einer der Ersten war, der das Sammeln und Sichten mit empirischer „Vor-Ort-Recherche" verband, was ihn zum „reisenden Historiker"[11] werden ließ. Und auch die erste grundlegende Definition des Berufsbildes des Historikers dürfte von Leibniz stammen. In einem Brief an den Helmstedter Professor Johann Eisenhardt aus dem Jahre 1679, also noch lange bevor sich Leibniz im offiziellen Auftrag mit historischen Forschungen beschäftigte, heißt es dazu:

> „Ein Historiker ist nämlich nichts anderes als ein Zeuge, der sein Zeugnis in schriftlicher Form ablegt, um es der Öffentlichkeit zur Kenntnis zu bringen und der Nachwelt zu überliefern. Es bedarf hier also der Wahrhaftigkeit sowohl des Zeugen als auch der Niederschrift seines Zeugnisses. Dabei ist die Glaubwürdigkeit des Zeugen nach seiner Gesinnung zu beurteilen und den Hilfsmitteln bzw. Hindernissen, die seine Urteilsfindung beeinflusst haben."[12]

Auf der einen Seite erkennt man in diesem Zitat den Juristen Leibniz, der im Sinne einer juristischen Hermeneutik mit dem Begriff des Beweises argumentiert, auf der anderen Seite den Historiker, der diesen Beweis unter Abwägung

---

[7] Werner Conze: „Leibniz als Historiker", in: Erich Hochstetter (Hrsg.): *Leibniz zu seinem 300. Geburtstag 1646–1946*, Berlin 1951, S. 57.
[8] Ebd., S. 58.
[9] Zit. nach Marc Bloch: *Apologie der Geschichtswissenschaft oder Der Beruf des Historikers*, [dt. Ausgabe] Stuttgart 2002, S. 9f.
[10] Nora Gädeke: „Leibniz als Sammler und Herausgeber historischer Quellen", in: *Wolfenbütteler Bibliotheks-Informationen 1–4* (2007/2008), S. 35ff.
[11] Ebd.
[12] Malte-Ludolf Babin/Gerd van den Heuvel (Hrsg.): *Gottfried Wilhelm Leibniz. Schriften und Briefe zur Geschichte* (= *Veröffentlichungen der Historischen Kommission für Niedersachsen und Bremen* 218), Hannover 2004, S. 81.

der zur Verfügung stehenden Informationen und unter Berücksichtigung der jeweiligen Perspektive auf die Vergangenheit rückprojiziert, eine Arbeits- und Sichtweise, die er bei den Geschichtsschreibern der Renaissance vermisste. So weist er in der Einleitung zu den *Scriptores rerum Brunsvicensium* nochmals eindrücklich daraufhin, dass vom Historiker Beweise gefordert würden.

3. Historische Quellen und Quellenkritik

Der Zugang zur Vergangenheit kann nie direkt erfolgen, sondern ist nur durch die zur Verfügung stehende Überlieferung annäherungsweise möglich und bleibt in jedem Fall lückenhaft, da ein historisches Geschehen in all seinen Zusammenhängen weder in den Einzelheiten seines Ablaufs noch in seinen vorherigen Intentionen zu rekonstruieren ist. In ihrer Eigenschaft als Vermittler von Vergangenem sind Quellen jedoch zunächst einmal nur Fakten und Tatsachenbestände und haben isoliert betrachtet keinen Beweischarakter. Diesen erfahren sie erst durch Interpretation, Vergleich und Kritik, i.e. Beurteilung durch den Historiker.

Während heute die Unterteilung in Text-, Sach-, Bild- oder audiovisuelle Quellen üblich ist, nahm Leibniz eine geschichtsphilosophische Differenzierung vor, bei der er zwischen einer *historia arcana* und einer *historia publica* unterschied.[13] In seiner Edition völkerrechtlich-historischer Dokumente, dem *Codex juris diplomaticus*,[14] entstanden in den Jahren 1693–1700, erläutert Leibniz in der ausführlichen Einleitung u.a. die „Gesetze der Geschichtsschreibung". Diesen Gesetzen zufolge äußert sich Geschichte zum einen als Phänomen, das aber nicht erkennen lässt, wie z.B. eine Entscheidung zustande gekommen ist, sondern das letztlich nur ein Ergebnis präsentiert. Die tatsächlichen Ursachen, die zu diesem Ergebnis geführt haben, sind daher nicht nachvollziehbar, daher auch nicht historiographisch fixierbar, ebenso wenig wie Alternativen, andere Meinungen, Kompromisse etc., die zur Debatte gestanden haben können. Zum anderen äußert sich Geschichte auch auf einer „geheimen" Ebene, die auf die zugrundeliegenden Wirkursachen zielt, die möglicherweise selbst den Entscheidungsträgern nicht unbedingt bewusst gewesen sein müssen, die aber weitreichende Konsequenzen für den historischen Prozess haben oder ihn in eine bestimmte Richtung lenken können, wie

---

[13] Horst Eckert: *G. W. Leibniz' Scriptores rerum brunsvicensium. Entstehung und historiographische Bedeutung*, Frankfurt a. M. 1971, S. 3.
[14] Babin/van den Heuvel: *Gottfried Wilhelm Leibniz*, S. 148f.

beispielsweise Launenhaftigkeit, Reaktionen auf Beleidigungen oder weibliche Reize als psychologische Komponenten. Nicht immer müssen es große Ereignisse sein, die den Lauf der Geschichte bestimmen. Leibniz erkannte, dass häufig aus unsichtbaren, psychologisch begründeten Motivationen heraus historische Entscheidungen getroffen werden und dass einer später als heroisch eingeschätzten Tat sogar niedere Beweggründe zugrunde gelegen haben können.[15]

Leibniz war sich der Diskrepanz zwischen öffentlicher und geheimer Geschichte bewusst und er suchte daher nach einer Möglichkeit, „den Aussagewert der einzelnen Quellen nach einer Regel festzulegen."[16] Da die Wahrheit einer Quellenaussage nicht auf eine Identität zurückzuführen war, wollte Leibniz das Abwägen der Gründe für oder gegen die wahre Aussage in einem stufenweisen Prozess, „des degrés de probabilité"[17], mit Hilfe der Logik herausarbeiten. Analog zum juristischen Prozessverfahren wären dabei die fünf folgenden Stufen zu berücksichtigen: 1. Die Notorietät, also die Offenkundigkeit, derer es keiner weiteren Beweise bedürfte. 2. Der vollständige Beweis. 3. Die Präsumption,[18] die einen höheren Grad an Wahrscheinlichkeit besitzt als die Konjektur. Sie kann für wahr erachtet werden, solange keine besseren Gründe das Gegenteil bewiesen haben. 4. Die Konjektur,[19] das Hinzufügen externer Kenntnisse, die von geringer Wahrscheinlichkeit ist und die gegen andere Konjekturen abgewogen werden muss. 5. Schließlich wären noch als zu berücksichtigende Hinweise die Indizien zu nennen.

Leibniz erhoffte sich durch eine solche Vorgehensweise der zu seiner Zeit weitverbreiteten historischen Skepsis bzw. dem historischen Pyrrhonis-

---

[15] Vgl. ebd., S. 148f.
[16] Eckert: *G. W. Leibniz' Scriptores*, S. 3.
[17] Ebd., S. 4.
[18] Ebd. – Zur Leibniz'schen Definition von Präsumption und Konjektur vgl. auch: Oliver R. Scholz: „Ius, Hermeneutica iuris und Hermeneutica generalis. – Verbindungen zwischen allgemeiner Hermeneutik und Methodenlehre des Rechts im 17. und 18. Jahrhundert", in: Jan Schröder (Hrsg.): *Entwicklung der Methodenlehre in Rechtswissenschaften und Philosophie vom 16. bis zum 18. Jahrhundert. Beiträge zu einem interdisziplinären Symposion in Tübingen, 18.–20. April 1996* (= Contubernium. Tübinger Beiträge zur Universitäts- und Wissenschaftsgeschichte 46), Stuttgart 1998, S. 94f.
[19] Der Begriff der Konjektur stammt aus dem Bereich der philologisch-kritischen Textbearbeitung und wurde in seinem Wahrscheinlichkeitscharakter maßgeblich von italienischen Renaissance-Philologen Francesco Robortello (1516–1567) geprägt. Vgl. dazu Klara Vanek: *Ars corrigendi in der frühen Neuzeit. Studien zur Geschichte der Textkritik* (= Historia Hermeneutica Series Studia 4), Berlin/New York 2007, S. 251 und 301.

mus, der die Möglichkeit einer wahren Geschichtsschreibung gänzlich verneinte, methodisch entgegenwirken zu können. Eine auf Präsumptionen, Konjekturen und Indizien gestützte, kritische Sichtung historischer Quellen erforderte eine differenzierte Ausdrucksweise, die Leibniz sowohl in seinen *Scriptores* als auch seinen *Annales* praktiziert, wo folgende abwägende Wendungen immer wieder zu finden sind: valde verisimile est […], credibile est […], quantum judico […], videtur […], pro certo habendum est […] – um nur einige zu nennen.[20] Bei Leibniz ist die Geschichte somit nicht mehr Hilfswissenschaft für die Jurisprudenz, sondern umgekehrt: das juristische Prozessverfahren liefert der Geschichte das „know-how" der Beweisführung.

4. Die Welfengeschichte und die Suche nach dem historischen Beweis

Während seiner Forschungsreise nach Italien entdeckt Leibniz im Februar 1690 im Kloster Vangadizza (heute Kommune Badia Polesine) die Gräber der Welfin Kunigunde und ihres Gemahls, des Markgrafen Alberto Azzo II. (gest. 1097),[21] aus der Familie D'Este, deren Sohn Welf IV. von 1070 bis 1101 Herzog von Bayern war. Leibniz konnte also Kunigunde als Stammmutter des neuen Welfengeschlechts bestätigen. Bereits im April 1688 war Leibniz im Klosterarchiv von St. Ulrich und Afra in Augsburg auf das entscheidende Dokument gestoßen, aus dem die Verbindung der Welfen mit den D'Este deutlich hervorging.[22] Leibniz gelang hier ein „Mehrfachbeweis":[23] Die schriftliche Überlieferung konnte durch eine Sachquelle bestätigt werden.

Doch nicht der chronologische Ablauf dieses sich letztlich selbst auferlegten, nicht enden wollenden Mammutprojekts soll hier thematisiert werden, sondern vielmehr die dem Opus zugrundeliegende, methodische Intention und Konzeption, wie sie sich in der Anfangsphase von Leibniz' genealogischen Am-

---

[20] Eckert: *G. W. Leibniz' Scriptores*, S. 4f. – Vgl. Conze: „Leibniz als Historiker", S. 21.
[21] André Robinet: *G. W. Leibniz Iter Italicum (Mars 1689–Mars 1690). La dynamique de la République des Lettres. Nombreux textes inédits* (= Accademia Toscana di Scienze e Lettere La Colombaria 90), Florenz 1988, S. 385ff.
[22] A I, 5, 119. – Vgl. auch Kurt Müller/Gisela Krönert (Bearb.): *Leben und Werk von G. W. Leibniz. Eine Chronologie*, Frankfurt a. M. 1969, S. 88. – Die Handschrift befindet sich heute in der Bayerischen Staatsbibliothek Sign. Clm 4352.
[23] Alois Schmid: „Die Herkunft der Welfen in der bayerischen Landeshistoriographie des 17. Jahrhunderts und bei Gottfried Wilhelm Leibniz", in: Herbert Breger/Friedrich Niewöhner (Hrsg.): *Leibniz und Niedersachsen. Tagung anläßlich des 350. Geburtstages von G. W. Leibniz* (= *Studia Leibnitiana Sonderhefte* 28), Wolfenbüttel 1996, S. 138.

bitionen zeigte. Und diese beginnen keineswegs erst mit der offiziellen Auftragserteilung durch Herzog Ernst August zu Braunschweig-Lüneburg im Jahre 1685, sondern reichen zurück in Leibniz' Mainzer Zeit. Am Beispiel einer kurzen Analyse zweier Briefe an den Benediktinermönch Gabriel Bucelin und von dem Sekretär und Bibliothekar Ludwigs XIV., Henri Justel, soll Leibniz' durchaus zielgerichtete und systematisch angelegte Arbeitsweise mit den sich daraus ergebenen Folgeproblemen demonstriert werden.

5. Erste Korrespondenz mit Gabriel Bucelin und Henri Justel

Bei seiner Suche nach den Vorfahren der Welfen aus dem Hause der Familie D'Este war der Weingartener Benediktinermönch und Historiograph Gabriel Bucelin (1599–1681)[24] für Leibniz ein wichtiger Ansprechpartner. Aufgrund seiner umfangreichen historischen Sammlungen und Studien dürfte Bucelin zu seiner Zeit einer der besten Kenner genealogischer Zusammenhänge gewesen sein. Entsprechend intensiv waren seine Kontakte zu allen bedeutenden Familien, mit denen er in regem persönlichen und schriftlichen Kontakt stand. Die Tatsache, dass er von vielen Seiten immer wieder gedrängt wurde, die Ergebnisse seiner Forschungen möglichst bald zu veröffentlichen,[25] zeigt das große Interesse und Bedürfnis der adligen Familien jener Zeit an einer historisch begründeten Präsentation der eigenen Dynastie.

Neben zahlreichen zeitgleich verfassten Arbeiten u. a. über die Geschichte des Benediktinerordens konnte Bucelin in den Jahren 1655 bis 1678 seine genealogischen Forschungen in den vier Bänden seiner Germania Topo-chrono-stemmato-graphica sacra et profana [...][26] vorlegen. Den Bänden wurden jeweils Widmungen vorangestellt; so dem zweiten Band (erschienen 1662) eine acht Seiten umfassende Dedikation an die Herzöge zu Braunschweig-Lüneburg, namentlich an die vier Söhnen Georgs von Calenberg: Christian Ludwig, Georg Wilhelm, Johann Friedrich und Ernst August zu Braunschweig-Lüneburg.

Als ein besonderer Gönner und Förderer von Bucelins Arbeiten erwies sich der Mainzer Kurfürst und Erzbischof Johann Philipp von Schönborn, dem

---

[24] A I, 3, 635: dort irrtümlich 1691 als Todesjahr angegeben.
[25] Claudia Maria Neesen: *Gabriel Bucelin OSB (1599–1681). Leben und historiographisches Werk*, Ostfildern 2003, S.165.
[26] Ebd., S. 393ff.

das Werk vorgelegt wurde, und der im Juni 1653 die Druckgenehmigung erteilte.[27] Mit dem Kurfürsten verband Bucelin eine enge Bekanntschaft, ebenso mit dessen Minister Johann Christian von Boineburg und weiterhin mit dem zum Katholizismus konvertierten Herzog Johann Friedrich zu Braunschweig-Lüneburg sowie mit dessen Bruder Ernst August, damals noch Fürstbischof zu Osnabrück. Unschwer zu erkennen ist, dass es sich hier um einen Personenkreis handelt, mit dem es auch Leibniz noch zu tun haben sollte.

Ob Leibniz bereits in jungen Jahren, d.h. während seiner Tätigkeit bei Schönborn und Boineburg mit dem Benediktiner aus dem welfischen Hauskloster Weingarten persönlich in Kontakt trat, lässt sich nicht nachweisen. Fest steht jedoch, dass er Ende 1679 oder Anfang 1680 mit dem damals schon hochbetagten Bucelin wegen genealogischer Fragen zur Welfenfamilie korrespondierte und dass ihn bereits zu diesem Zeitpunkt gerade der neuralgische Punkt der gesamten Welfengeschichte beschäftigte: weniger die in der mittelalterlichen Chronistik bereits bekannte Heiratsverbindung der Welfin Kunigunde mit dem italienischen Markgrafen Alberto Azzo II., die beide als Stammeltern der neuen welfischen Linie gelten, sondern vielmehr die Frage nach der Herkunft des genannten Azzo.

Bucelins Antwortschreiben[28] vom 8. März 1680 ist zu entnehmen, dass die von Leibniz an ihn gerichtete Anfrage zu den väterlichen Vorfahren des *Azzo Atestinus* schon eine geraume Zeit zurückliegt, wahrscheinlich noch aus dem Jahre 1679, oder eventuell früher stammen muss, denn Bucelin entschuldigt sich für sein verspätetes Antwortschreiben. Bezüglich der genannten Frage verweist er Leibniz auf Band eins und zwei seiner *Germania*, in denen die „sichersten Beweise"[29] zu finden seien. Er selber habe nachweisen können, dass Giambattista [Giovan Battista] Pigna[30] „ohne auf eine Autorität gestützt, das meiste nach seinem Gutdünken geschrieben"[31] habe und zusammen mit

---

[27] Ebd., S. 165.
[28] A I, 1, N. 278, 359f.
[29] Ebd.
[30] Giovan Battista Pigna, eigentlich: Giovan Battista Nicolucci (1529–1575) war ein italienischer Dichter und Gelehrter; am Hofe der Este in Ferrara war er der Erzieher Alfonsos II., dem Sohn Ercoles II. D'Este und seiner Gemahlin Renata (Renée) von Frankreich. Vgl. Salvatore Ritrovato: Art.: „Nicolucci, Giovan Battista (detto il Pigna)", in: *Dizionario Biografico degli Italiani,* Bd. 78, Rom 2013. auch: http://www.treccani.it/enciclopedia/giovan-battista-nicolucci_(Dizionario-Biografico)/.
[31] A I, 1, N. 278, 359f.

dem von ihm hochgeschätzten Kaspar Schoppe³² habe er die „schwerwiegenden Fehler des Pigna und der anderen Schriftsteller herausgefunden"³³; weiterhin betont er nochmals die Korrektheit seiner Studien.

Leibniz' Antwort, bzw. das undatierte Konzept der Antwort, befindet sich auf der zweiten Seite von Bucelins Brief. Da auch Leibniz sich entschuldigt, erst nach Erledigung diverser anderer Dinge, nun endlich Zeit für eine Erwiderung gefunden zu haben, kann man als Abfassungsdatum eventuell Juni 1681 annehmen.³⁴ Zwischenzeitlich war Leibniz jedoch offensichtlich Bucelins Rat gefolgt und hatte die empfohlenen Bände der *Germania* durchgesehen, habe aber, so schreibt er, nicht gefunden, was er suche, denn:

> „Du siehst mich nämlich vor allem auf der Suche nach dem Ursprung des Markgrafen Hugo von Tuszien, den du ganz deutlich auf Karl den Großen zurückführst. Aber in Übernahme der Meinung neuerer Autoren nimmst du mehr an, als dass du beweist, dass dieser Azzo Atestinus, Ehemann der Welfin Kunigunde, Sohn des Markgrafen von Tuszien gewesen ist. Wenn man dies doch durch die Autorität alter Schriftsteller und Urkunden bestätigen könnte. Allerdings behauptet der nicht zu verachtende Scipione Ammirato³⁵, dass Hugo ohne Kinder gestorben sei. Pigna und andere Parteigänger des Arduinus³⁶ wollen dagegen, dass der heilige Heinrich³⁷ folgte und dass er von Heinrich aus dessen Botmäßig-

---

[32] Caspar Schoppe (1576–1649), Philologe und Jesuit, ursprünglich Protestant, konvertierte er 1597 zum Katholizismus und wurde zum entschiedenen Verfechter der Gegenreformation. – Vgl. dazu Klaus Jaitner: Art.: „Kaspar Schoppe", in: *Neue Deutsche Biographie (NDB)*, Bd. 23, Berlin 2007, S. 475–478. – Schoppe war seit 1610 mehrfach im Kloster Weingarten, das ihm von 1630–1632 als Wohnstätte diente. Während dieser Zeit schlossen er und Bucelin eine „aufrichtige Freundschaft." Vgl. Neesen: *Gabriel Bucelin OSB*, S. 64ff.
[33] A I, 1, N. 278, 359f.
[34] A I, 3, N. 415, 487f.
[35] Scipione Ammirato d. Ä. (1531–1601) war Historiograph am Hofe Cosimos I. von Medici, Großherzog der Toskana, der ihn mit der Niederschrift der Geschichte von Florenz beauftragte. – Vgl. Roberto De Mattei: Art.: „Ammirato, Scipione", in: *Dizionario Biografico degli Italiani*, Bd. 3, Rom 1961. Vgl. http://www.treccani.it/enciclopedia/scipione-ammirato (Dizionario_Biografico)/.
[36] Arduin von Ivrea (um 955–1015) war von 1001–1015 Markgraf von Ivrea, nach dem Tode Kaiser Ottos III. ließ er sich im Jahre 1002 zum König von Italien wählen, unterlag aber 1004 militärisch dem römisch-deutschen König Heinrich II., der zum König von Italien gekrönt wurde. – Vgl. Livia Fasola: Art.: „Arduin von Ivrea", in: *Lexikon des Mittelalters*, Bd. 1, München/Zürich 1980, Sp. 915f.
[37] Heinrich II. (973–1024), Sohn des bayerischen Herzogs Heinrich des Zänkers, war 995–1004 und 1009–1017 Herzog von Bayern, 1002–1024 König des ostfränkischen Reichs, 1004–1024 König von Italien und 1014–1024 römisch-deutscher Kaiser. Im Jahre 1146 wurde er von Papst

> keit [...] abzog. Aber eine gewisse alte Chronik aus Pisa besagt, dass er gestorben ist, bevor Heinrich Kaiser wurde, was sich auch mit der Erzählung von Sigonius[38] beißt, wonach es nicht jener ehrenwerte Hugo ist, wenn Azzo einen Vater mit diesem Namen hat, sondern ein anderer von den Markgrafen von Tuszien. Deshalb tu mir den Gefallen und zeige mir an, wenn du ein sicheres Argument über den Vater des Azzo hast, denn das ist das einzige, was ich suche und worum ich schon in den früheren Briefen gebeten habe, obwohl du dies wohl durch andere Beschäftigungen nicht ausreichend bemerkt hast. Wenn aber Schoppe (deine Briefe erinnern mich an ihn) irgendwo bewiesen hat, was ich wünsche, dann zeige mir bitte den Ort, aber *deine* Begründungen will ich lieber haben. Wenn du aber diesen Knoten losmachst, verkündige ich, dass nur du uns den wahren Ursprung des Estensischen Geschlechts aus allen abgelehnten Fabeln eröffnet hast. [...]"[39]

Zu einer weiteren Korrespondenz zu diesem Thema dürfte es kaum noch gekommen sein, denn der Benediktinerpater verstarb am 9. Juni 1681.

Parallel zu Leibniz' Anfragen an Gabriel Bucelin richtete er entsprechende Briefe auch nach Frankreich an den Bibliothekar und Sekretär Ludwig XIV., den Hugenotten Henri Justel (1620–1693). Nach der Aufhebung des Edikts von Nantes im Jahre 1685, das den Hugenotten bis dahin freie Religionsausübung gestattet hatte, emigrierte Justel nach England, wo er am Hofe Wilhelms III. die Stellung des königlichen Hofbibliothekars bekleidete und engen Kontakt zu den Mitgliedern der Royal Society unterhielt.[40]

Neben zahlreichen Berichten über diverse Experimente, philosophische Themen sowie Kuriositäten aus ganz Europa geht es in der Korrespondenz mit Leibniz auch immer wieder um die Suche nach den Vorfahren des Hauses Braunschweig-Lüneburg. In seinem Brief vom 15. April 1680[41] (damals noch aus Paris) verweist Justel auf die schwierige und unzuverlässige Quellenlage, die die Suche erschwert und zu Spekulationen Anlass gibt:

Eugen III. heiliggesprochen. – Vgl. Stefan Weinfurter: „Heinrich II", in: Bernd Schneidmüller/Stefan Weinfurter (Hrsg.): *Die deutschen Herrscher des Mittelalters. Historische Portraits von Heinrich I. bis Maximilian I*, München 2003, S. 97–118.

[38] Carlo Sigonio (1524–1584), der italienische Historiker verfasste 1574 seine umfangreiche Geschichte Italiens von 500–1200 *De regno Italianae*. Vgl. Giulio Bertoni: Art.: „Sigonio", in: *Enciclopedia Italiana*, 1963. Vgl. auch: http://www.treccani.it/enciclopedia/sigonio_ (Enciclopedia-Italiana)/.

[39] Ebd. – Übersetzung des Briefes A. v. B.

[40] Vgl. Frank Thomas Marzials: „Justel, Henri", in: *Dictionary of National Biography (DNB)*, Bd. 30, London 1892, S. 231f.

[41] A I, 3, N. 297, 372f.

„[…] parce que uous n'auez aucun Historien du temps, ny aucune charte veritable qui vous aprenne une chose aussi cachée que celle la. Ie ne scai pas mesme si Messrs les Ducs de Lunebourg uiennent de la Maison d'Este. il suffit qu'ils sont d'une tres grande Maison. Les origines des Maisons sont pour la pluspart fabuleuses a cause de leurs incertitude."[42]

Einen Tipp hat Justel dennoch für Leibniz: Der Genealoge du Fautray,[43] der sich sein ganzes Leben mit genealogischen Dingen beschäftigt habe, führe den Ursprung der Welfen auf die Herzöge von Lucca zurück:

„Il les faict uenir des Ducs de Lucque aussi bien que la Comtesse Mathilde, qui a fait tant de bruit dans le monde. Il a appris beaucoup de choses d'un liure qui a pour *titre Memorie di Matilda la gran'Contessa con l'antica serie degli antenati da Francesco Maria Fiorentini in Lucca 1642.*"

Das Buch sei lesenswert, allerdings inzwischen schwer zu bekommen. Falls es Leibniz von Nutzen sei, wolle Justel sich um ein Exemplar bemühen.[44] Gleichzeitig deutet Justel jedoch ein Problem an, das sich grundsätzlich bei der Suche nach gesicherten historischen Kenntnissen stellt: das Verschweigen der Informationsquelle. So schreibt Justel:

„Ce Mr. Du Fautray est persuadé qu'il n'y a que luy qui ait deterré la Maison de Brunswic et qui en sache la veritable origine qu'il n'a pas uoulu me dire."[45]

Auch in einem weiteren Brief von Justel an Leibniz vom 12. Juli 1680[46] geht es nochmals, wenn auch nur in zwei Sätzen, um dieses Buch von Fiorentini: „Il croit que Sigefroy Comte de Lucques estoit pere d'Azzo."[47] Leibniz hat es sich allem Anschein nach sich daraufhin besorgen lassen, denn ein Exemplar, versehen mit Leibniz' Marginalien, befindet sich heute in der Gottfried Wilhelm Leibniz Bibliothek in Hannover.[48] Leibniz verfolgte also jeden Hinweis.

---

[42] Ebd., 372.
[43] Wahrscheinlich handelt es sich um den Parlamentsrat der Normandie, Michel du Fautray. Vgl. *Mémoires de la Société de l'Histoire de Paris de de L'Île-De-France*, Paris 1882.
[44] A I, 3, N. 297 mit Anm. 1: Die Tatsache, dass der Buchtitel im Brief unterstrichen ist, zeigt, dass Leibniz an dem Buch interessiert war.
[45] A I, 3, N. 297, 297.
[46] A I, 3, N. 331, 409.
[47] Ebd.
[48] Francesco Maria Fiorentini: *Memorie Di Matilda La Gran Contessa Propvgnacolo Della Chiesa Con Le Particolari Notitie Della Sva Vita E Con L'Antica Serie Degli Antenanti*, Lucca 1642. Das Buch mit der Signatur Leibn. Marg. 195 trägt den Besitzvermerk: Ex Libris Francisci de Podio Nunc Martinj Manfredj sowie die Widmung: Al[…] so Franco Poggi.

Er konnte nicht wissen, dass er in diesem Fall auf der falschen Fährte war. Wie sich später herausstellen sollte, war Alberto Azzo I. der Vater Alberto Azzos II., der gesuchte Hugo der Onkel von Letzterem.[49] Leibniz hatte dies bereits selber in Erwägung gezogen.

Leibniz' hermeneutisch-empirische Vorgehensweise wird hier erkennbar: Nach dem eingehenden Studium der vorhandenen historiographischen und genealogischen Werke richtet er gezielte Fragen an einen möglichen Expertenkreis, auch auf die Gefahr hin, zwar gut gemeinte, aber auch unvollständige Hinweise zu bekommen oder auf eine falsche Fährte gelenkt zu werden. Am Beispiel dieser ausgewählten Briefe wird weiterhin deutlich, welchen Schwierigkeiten Leibniz sich gegenübersah: Bei aller Hochachtung vor der genealogischen Forschungsleistung von Gabriel Bucelin musste er feststellen, dass bloße Datenkompilation nicht zu Beweisen führte, wie er sie sich erhoffte. Andererseits ließ sich angesichts der bei ihm eingehenden und von ihm selber gesammelten Informationsflut nicht durchgängig ein historisches Beweisverfahren, wie er es hypothetisch angelegt hatte, durchführen, bedeutete doch schon allein das rein praktische Informationsmanagement eine für eine einzelne Person kaum zu bewältigende Aufgabe, zumal sich ständig neue forscherische Nebenschauplätze eröffneten wie beispielsweise seine Abhandlung zur angeblichen Päpstin Johanna.[50] In Zeiten fehlender bibliographischer Nachschlagewerke oder systematisch geführter Bibliothekskataloge sowie nicht vorhandener archivischer Findmittel in den ohnehin nicht öffentlichen, sondern immer noch geheimen Archiven war Leibniz' Ausgangposition schwierig genug. Dennoch setzte Leibniz zweifellos Maßstäbe in der historischen Forschung, bei der neben der juristischen Vorgehensweise und Gabriel Bucelins systematische Sammlertätigkeit auch Aristoteles' empirisch-vergleichende Überlegungen Vorbild gewesen sein dürften.

Wenn man sich vergegenwärtigt, dass Leibniz allein in seinen Scriptores 202 Quellentexte (Annalen, Chroniken, Exzerpte und kopiale Überlieferungen Viten etc.) zusammenstellte und damit überhaupt erstmals die mittelalterliche Überlieferung textkritisch sichtete und erfasste, so leistete er zwar

---

[49] Roberto Ricci: *La marca della Liguria orientale e gli Obertenghi (945–1056). Una storia complessa e una storiografia problematica,* Spoleto 2007, S. 147.
[50] Vgl. dazu Wilhelm Herse: „Leibniz und die Päpstin Johanna", in: Georgi Schischkoff (Hrsg.): *Beiträge zur Leibniz-Forschung,* Reutlingen 1947, S. 153–158.

nicht seinem Dienstherrn, dafür aber nachfolgenden Historikergenerationen eine unschätzbar wertvolle Basisarbeit für künftige Forschungen.[51]

6. Von Leibniz über Chladenius und Gadamer in die Gegenwart

Dass das überwiegende Interesse immer noch dem Mathematiker, Techniker und Philosophen und weniger dem Historiker Leibniz, gilt, mag daran liegen, dass Leibniz auf diesem Fachgebiet weder ein geschichtswissenschaftlich-theoretisches Werk noch ein abgeschlossenes Ergebnis vorweisen konnte. Die von ihm postulierte geschichtswissenschaftliche Methodik liegt vielmehr in seiner umfangreichen Korrespondenz verborgen und äußert sich in seinen historiographischen Fragmenten eher als „work in progress".

Auf nachvollziehbare Weise sind bei Leibniz' Vorgehen aber diejenigen Arbeitsschritte erkennbar, die heute als standardmäßig in jeder Einführung zum wissenschaftlichen Arbeiten genannt werden: 1. Sichtung und Bewertung des vorhandenen Materials und der Literatur, 2. Sammeln aller zur Verfügung stehenden Quellen und Auffinden neuer Quellen, 3. kritische Bewertung von Schrift- und Sachquellen, 4. Präsentation von Ergebnissen oder Teilergebnissen.[52] Erklärtes Ziel der so entwickelten Methodologie der Historie ist die Steigerung der Objektivität bei der Bewertung von Geschehnissen in der Vergangenheit und ihrer Wirkung und Bedeutung für die Gegenwart.

Dem Universalgenie Leibniz scheint auch in Bezug auf die Geschichtswissenschaft einmal mehr lediglich der Status des genialen Vordenkers zuzukommen. Den Ruhm, die Geschichte zur Wissenschaft erhoben zu haben, teilen sich im 19. Jahrhundert Gelehrte wie Leopold von Ranke (1795–1886) und Carl Gustav Droysen (1808–1884)[53] oder Theodor Mommsen (1817–

---

[51] Für den Ranke-Schüler Georg Waitz (1813–1886) und andere Herausgeber der *Jahrbücher des Deutschen Reiches* galten Leibniz' Arbeiten durchaus als Leitfaden für die eigene Editionstätigkeit. Vgl. dazu Martina Hartmann: „„die Arbeit seines Lebens [...] dem Gedächtnisse entschwunden". Leibniz' Annales Imperii Occidentis Brunsvicenses und ihre Edition durch Georg Heinrich Pertz (1843–1846)", in: Nora Gädeke (Hrsg.): *Leibniz als Sammler und Herausgeber historischer Quellen* (= *Wolfenbütteler Forschungen* 129), Wiesbaden 2012, S. 217.
[52] Vgl. Schmid: „Die Herkunft der Welfen", S. 139f.
[53] Im Sinne eines forschenden Verstehens brachte Droysen die Hermeneutik in die Geschichtswissenschaft mit ein und plädierte dabei für eine Kombination von analytischer und hermeneutischer Verfahrensweise in der Historik, um sich einer objektiv-historischen Wahrheit weitestgehend zu nähern. Vgl. Christian Georg Schuppe: *Der andere Droysen. Neue Aspekte seiner Theorie der Geschichtswissenschaft,* Stuttgart 1998, S. 71f.

1903). Eine konkrete Bezugnahme der Genannten auf Leibniz ist nicht erkennbar.[54]

Es gibt also kaum Verbindungslinien, die direkt von Leibniz' historisch-kritischem Ansatz zur wissenschaftlichen Geschichtsforschung der Neuzeit und Gegenwart führen. Eine solche Linie ist lediglich erkennbar über die geschichtsphilosophischen Überlegungen des Erlanger Professor, Theologen und Historiker Johann Martin Chladenius (1710–1759), der in seinem Werk *Allgemeine Geschichtswissenschaft*[55] aus dem Jahre 1752 die hermeneutische Methode bei der Deutung von historischen Quellen miteinbezieht und sich dabei nachdrücklich auf Leibniz und den aus der Optik entlehnten Begriff des Sehepunkts, des *point de vue*, bezieht. Chladenius war der Ansicht, dass Parteilichkeit keineswegs im Gegensatz zu wissenschaftlicher Erkenntnis stehen müsste, im Gegenteil, „die Einsicht in die historische Perspektivität sei vielmehr eine ihrer Bedingungen."[56]

In der *Allgemeinen Geschichtswissenschaft* heißt es dazu in Kapitel 5, das überschrieben ist „Vom Zuschauer und Sehepunckte", dort unter § 12:

> „Der Sehepunckt ist der innerliche und aeusserliche Zustand eines Zuschauers, in so ferne daraus eine gewisse und besondere Art, die vorkommenden Dinge anzuschauen und zu betrachten fluesset. Ein Begriff, der mit den allerwichtigsten in der gantzen Philosophie im gleichen Paare gehet, den man aber noch zur Zeit zu Nutzen anzuwenden noch nicht gewohnt ist, ausser daß der Herr von Leibnitz hie und da denselben selbst in der Metaphysik und Psychologie gebraucht hat. In der historischen Erkentniß aber kommt fast alles darauf an."[57]

---

[54] Hartmann: „„die Arbeit seines Lebens", S. 217.
[55] Johann Martin Chladenius: *Allgemeine Geschichtswissenschaft. Neudr. der Ausgabe von 1752* (= Klassische Studien zur sozialwissenschaftlichen Theorie, Weltanschauungslehre und Wissenschaftsforschung 3), Wien u.a. 1985.
[56] Horst Walter Blanke: Art.: „Chladenius", in: Rüdiger vom Bruch/Rainer A. Müller (Hrsg.): Historikerlexikon. Von der Antike bis zur Gegenwart, München ²2002, S. 56.
[57] Chladenius: *Allgemeine Geschichtswissenschaft*, S. 100 f. – Vgl. auch: John Stanley: „Leibniz's Contribution to the Development of Hermeneutics", in: Hubertus Busche (Hrsg.): *Departure for Modern Europe. A Handbook of Early Modern Philosophie (1400–1700)*, Hamburg 2011, S. 777: „[…] Chladenius – also much like Leibniz – wants to use the concept of a perspective to explain how different persons observing the same event can come up with rather different accounts. […] It is interesting to note here that it is especially Leibniz' notion of 'point-of-view' that serves as a lead-in to the issue of how the background of the observer affects his or her perception, […]."

Bereits zehn Jahre zuvor schrieb Chladenius in seiner *Einleitung zur Auslegung vernünftiger Reden und Schriften* in dem Kapitel „Von der Auslegung der historischen Bücher:"

> „Das Wort, Sehe=Punckt, ist vermuthlich von Leibnizen zuerst in seinem allgemeinen Verstande genommen worden, da es sonsten nur in der Optick vorkam. […]§ 310. Aus dem Begriff des Sehe=Puncts folgt, daß Personen, die eine Sache aus verschiedenen Sehe=Puncten ansehen, auch verschiedene Vorstellungen von der Sache haben müssen; […]"[58]

Die Hermeneutik als Methode des stufenweisen Verstehens verband Chladenius mit dem von Leibniz vertretenen Kausalitätsprinzip, wonach alles einen Grund hat, wenn man es von seinem jeweiligen Blickwinkel oder Standpunkt aus betrachtet. Dabei wäre weniger die aus der eigenen Perspektive abgeleitete Wahrheitsaussage des Erkannten von Bedeutung, sondern vielmehr die Einbeziehung der Perspektive eines anderen Betrachters.[59] Jean Grondin bemerkt an dieser Stelle, dass bei der Berücksichtigung der Perspektive bei Leibniz eine universale Gerechtigkeitserwartung des Verstehens vorliegt, „die im Prinzip bereit ist, alles zu billigen, was sie liest, für alles einen Grund zu vermuten, auch wenn er uns unerschöpflich bleiben mag."[60] In dieser Hinsicht bezieht wiederum Hans Georg Gadamer Leibniz „als Denker der prinzipiellen Berechtigung einer jeden Perspektive" und „Modell für die hermeneutische Vernunft"[61] in sein Denken ein und hebt damit gleichzeitig die Aktualität von Leibniz hervor:

> „Ich würde sagen, es gibt eigentlich kein so hermeneutisches Vorbild, das ich in der Geschichte der Philosophie kenne, als Leibniz, der den inneren Zusammenhang und das gegenseitige Aufeinanderangewiesensein wechselnder Standpunkte und wechselnder Perspektiven letzten Endes für die Struktur der Wahrheit selber gehalten hat. […] Unter Hermeneutik verstehe ich die Fähigkeit, einem anderen zuzuhören in der Meinung, er könnte Recht haben. […] Denn heute geht es ja doch letzten Endes um eine Weltzivilisation, in der sich

---

[58] Johann Martin Chladenius: *Einleitung zur richtigen Auslegung vernünftiger Reden und Schriften*, Leipzig 1742 (Neudr. Düsseldorf 1969), S. 188f.
[59] Jean Grondin: „Das Leibnizsche Moment in der Hermeneutik", in: Manfred Beetz/Giuseppe Cacciatore (Hrsg.): *Die Hermeneutik im Zeitalter der Aufklärung* (= *Collegium Hermeneuticum. Deutsch-italienische Studien zur Kulturwissenschaft und Philosophie* 3), Köln u.a. 2000, S. 5f.
[60] Ebd., S. 9.
[61] Ebd., S. 15.

in aller Verschiedenheit der Herkunft und der Geschichte doch eine gemeinsame Solidarität bilden muss, wenn wir überhaupt überleben wollen. Wenn wir nicht lernen, was ein so umfassender, versöhnender Geist wie Leibniz gewesen ist, werden wir wohl die großen Krisen, denen wir entgegengehen, nicht meistern können. Also es wird darauf ankommen, eine solche universale Einigungskraft in großen Persönlichkeiten, wie Leibniz eine war, als Vorbild zu ehren, wenn wir mit unseren Menschheitsaufgaben von heute fertig werden wollen."[62]

Seit der Mitte des 20. Jahrhunderts wurden in der Geschichtswissenschaft unterschiedliche Theorien und Forschungsansätze entwickelt, die die Vergangenheit in ihren kausalen, gesellschaftspolitischen Zusammenhängen neu zu definieren und zu positionieren versuchten. Am Beginn des 21. Jahrhunderts ist die historische Forschung nun gekennzeichnet durch eine große Bandbreite unterschiedlicher Forschungsfelder und durch einen mehrfachen Perspektivwechsel: vom Historischen Materialismus über die Strukturgeschichte, Gesellschaftsgeschichte, Global History bis hin zur Historischen Anthropologie unter Einschluss von Mentalitäts-, Gender- und Alltagsgeschichte, um nur einige Positionen zu nennen.[63] Dieser Prozess hat sich zunächst einmal ohne erkennbaren Einfluss von Leibniz entwickelt, doch wäre die Beschäftigung mit Leibniz' historisch-methodischer Arbeitsweise in Kombination mit seiner Fähigkeit, eigene und fremde Sicht- und Handlungsweisen perspektivisch-distanziert zu betrachten, in jedem Fall dazu geeignet, die historische Urteilskompetenz in den genannten Forschungsbereichen zu fördern. Und dies wäre eine wesentliche Voraussetzung dafür, Geschichte im Sinne des niederländischen Kulturhistorikers Johan Huizinga (1872–1945) zu begreifen, nämlich als „die geistige Form, in der eine Kultur sich Rechenschaft über die Vergangenheit ablegt."[64]

---

[62] Grondin: „Das Leibnizsche Moment", S. 15f.
[63] v. Boetticher: *Wissenschaftliches Arbeiten*, S. 17ff.
[64] Christoph Strupp: *Johan Huizinga. Geschichtswissenschaft als Kulturgeschichte,* Göttingen 2000, S. 100, Anm. 239.

La critique leibnizienne de la définition cartésienne du mouvement

Laurence Bouquiaux (Liège)

Au cours de son œuvre, Leibniz a formulé à l'encontre de la conception cartésienne du mouvement une série de critiques dont la juxtaposition peut sembler problématique. Dans le §18 du *Discours de Métaphysique*,[1] Leibniz écrit que le mouvement défini comme un changement de place n'est pas « une chose entièrement réelle », et que si l'on s'en tient à cette définition – qui est, selon lui, l'essentiel de la définition cartésienne – il n'est pas possible de déterminer à quel corps le mouvement ou le repos doit être attribué. En revanche, si l'on prend en considération « la force ou cause prochaine des changements [de place] » on peut, toujours selon le *Discours*, connaître à qui le mouvement appartient. C'est le recours à la force qui permet de désigner le corps qui est véritablement en mouvement.[2] Dans les *Animadversiones* de 1692, Leibniz commente dans le même sens la définition du mouvement que Descartes formule dans le §25 de la deuxième partie des *Principes* :

> « [...] s'il n'y a rien dans le mouvement que ce changement réciproque, il n'y a aucune raison dans la nature qui puisse nous obliger à attribuer le mouvement plutôt à un objet qu'aux autres. Alors la conséquence s'impose, qu'il n'y a pas de mouvement réel. Pour pouvoir dire qu'un objet est en mouvement, nous ne demanderons donc pas seulement qu'il change de position par rapport aux autres, mais encore qu'il y ait en ce corps même une cause du changement, une force, une action [...] .»[3]

S'en tenir au seul mouvement au sens où le comprend Descartes, comme changement de situation ou de voisinage, mènerait en quelque sorte à une concep-

---

[1] A VI, 4 B, 1559.
[2] On retrouve ce thème dans une multitude de textes. Voir par exemple *Lettre à Arnauld du 30 avril 1687* : « [...] le mouvement en tant qu'il n'est qu'une modification de l'étendue et changement de voisinage enveloppe quelque chose d'imaginaire, en sorte qu'on ne saurait déterminer à quel sujet il appartient parmi ceux qui changent, si on n'a recours à la force qui est cause du mouvement. » (A II, 2, 187). Ou encore *Specimen inventorum* : « Idem dicendum est de Motu, nam uti Locus, ita et Motus in solo respectu consistunt, quod recte agnovit Cartesius, neque ulla datur ratio determinandi exacte quantum cuique subjecto absoluti motus sit assignandum. At vis motrix sive potentia agendi reale est quiddam, discernique in corporibus potest.» (A VI, 4 B, 1622).
[3] GP IV, 369, traduction de Paul Schrecker in: Gottfried Wilhelm Leibniz : *Opuscules philosophiques choisis*, Paris 1978, p. 41.

tion trop relativiste. Dans le *Specimen dynamicum*, cependant, Leibniz reproche à Descartes de ne pas avoir compris les implications relativistes de sa propre définition du mouvement. Descartes serait en quelque sorte trop peu relativiste. Il aurait très justement reconnu que le mouvement est quelque chose de relatif en le définissant comme le transport du voisinage d'un corps au voisinage d'un autre corps, mais il aurait ensuite oublié sa définition et aurait, à tort, formulé des lois du mouvement qui ne respectent pas le principe de relativité.[4]

Les textes évoqués ci-dessus ont bien sûr tous quelque chose de commun, ils affirment qu'il faut distinguer la force, qui est quelque chose de réel, et le mouvement qui « a quelque chose de l'être de raison » et qui n'est réel qu'en tant qu'il suppose la force, mais ils ne semblent pas s'accorder quant à la possibilité de déterminer, au niveau des phénomènes, quels corps sont véritablement en mouvement. Pour expliquer cette divergence entre les textes, certains commentateurs comme Daniel Garber[5] ont suggéré que la manière dont Leibniz comprend le principe de relativité a évolué entre 1686 et 1695. Jusqu'à la fin des années 1680, Leibniz n'aurait pas considéré que les lois de la physique doivent être telles qu'il est impossible d'attribuer le mouvement à tel corps plutôt qu'à tel autre. Ce n'est que par la suite qu'il aurait développé une conception véritablement relativiste du mouvement et adopté un principe d'équivalence des hypothèses strict. Il aurait ainsi découvert la relativité mais perdu le monde, en ce sens qu'il aurait introduit une rupture entre le monde physique, monde d'apparences soumis au principe de relativité, et la réalité métaphysique, où les notions de repos et de mouvement vrais continueraient à avoir un sens, mais un sens désormais inaccessible à l'observation.

Je voudrais reprendre ici cette question, en suivant comme fil conducteur les critiques que Leibniz adresse à la conception cartésienne du mouvement et montrer que si, à partir de la fin des années 1680, Leibniz fait en effet un usage de plus en plus important du principe de relativité – ou comme il

---

[4] GM VI, 247. Sur ce point, Leibniz a parfaitement raison : les lois du choc formulées par Descartes prévoient dans certains cas un résultat différent selon que l'on considère que tel ou tel corps est en repos ou en mouvement.
[5] Daniel Garber : « How Leibniz found Relativity, and lost the World », conférence, Dibner Institute for the History of Science (M.I.T.), December, 1994. Je remercie Daniel Garber de m'avoir généreusement communiqué le texte de cette conférence qui a largement inspiré mes propres développements. Paul Lodge considère, lui aussi, que la manière dont Leibniz conçoit la relativité du mouvement a évolué dans les années 1680, mais il donne de cette évolution une interprétation différente. Voir Paul Lodge : « Leibniz on Relativity and the Motion of Bodies » in : *Philosophical Topics* 31/1–2, Modern Philosophy (Spring/Fall 2003), pp. 277–308.

l'appelle, du principe de l'équivalence des hypothèses –, ce principe était présent, même si c'est de manière problématique, dès les années 1670 et que, par ailleurs contrairement à ce qu'une compréhension contemporaine du principe de relativité pourrait nous laisser penser, Leibniz ne conclura pas de ce principe qu'il n'y a aucune différence entre un corps en repos et en corps en mouvement. Quoi qu'il en soit de ses nombreuses déclarations sur le caractère purement relatif de l'espace et du mouvement, Leibniz considérera, jusqu'à la fin de sa vie qu'il y a, comme il l'écrira encore en 1715, à Clarke

> « de la différence entre un mouvement absolu véritable d'un corps et un simple changement relatif de la situation par rapport à un autre corps. »[6]

Malgré le principe de l'équivalence des hypothèses, Leibniz ne renoncera pas à chercher des arguments en faveur d'une distinction entre mouvement vrai et simple changement relatif de situation. Pour le dire en des termes quelque peu anachroniques, cela l'amènera à considérer que, si tous les référentiels sont acceptables en ce sens que l'observation ne donnera jamais tort à celui qui aurait choisi de considérer tel ou tel corps comme en repos, il y a néanmoins des référentiels qui permettent de mieux faire apparaître ce qu'est le mouvement véritable – c'est le cas, nous le verrons ci-dessous, du référentiel du centre de gravité d'un système. Pour Leibniz, un corps en mouvement est intrinsèquement différent d'un corps au repos et le mouvement doit avoir une véritable « réalité », qu'il convient de fonder d'une manière ou d'une autre, et peut-être pas seulement au niveau métaphysique.[7]

Avant de commencer le parcours que je me propose de retracer ici, il convient de s'arrêter sur le caractère relativiste (ou non) du mouvement selon Descartes. Leibniz considère que la définition cartésienne, comme changement de *situs*, ou transport du voisinage de quelque corps dans le voisinage d'un autre – c'est en ces termes qu'il reprend la définition cartésienne – est

---

[6] GP VII, 404.

[7] Un argument essentiel à l'appui de cette thèse, que je n'envisagerai pas ici mais que je signale rapidement, est le fait que Leibniz distingue nettement la force passive, cette paresse par laquelle un corps résiste au mouvement, qu'il associe à la matière, et la force active par laquelle un corps persévère dans son mouvement, qu'il associe à la forme. Si l'on adopte le principe de relativité, il est évident que l'on doit au contraire considérer que cette distinction n'a aucun sens et que c'est par la même *vis insita* qu'un corps que nous considérons comme au repos résiste au mouvement que l'on cherche à lui communiquer et qu'un corps en mouvement rectiligne uniforme (mru) tend à persévérer dans son mru malgré les obstacles qu'il peut rencontrer.

relativiste, parce que comme le dit Descartes lui même[8] le transport est réciproque, en sorte que si deux corps A et B s'éloignent l'un de l'autre, on peut tout aussi bien considérer que A s'éloigne de B au repos, que considérer que B s'éloigne de A au repos, ou encore que A et B sont tous deux en mouvement. Cette interprétation relativiste du mouvement cartésien est largement répandue parmi les commentateurs. Le livre de Garber, *Descartes' Metaphysical Physics*[9] apporte cependant des arguments décisifs à l'encontre de cette thèse. Je ne reprendrai pas ici les développements de Garber, mais il me semble incontestable que, lorsque Descartes entreprend dans le fameux §25 de la deuxième partie des *Principes* de définir « ce que c'est que le mouvement selon la vérité », il propose en réalité une définition qui empêche d'envisager que le même corps, au même moment, peut être considéré comme en mouvement ou comme au repos, ce que supposerait précisément une conception relativiste du mouvement. En affirmant que le mouvement est

> « le transport d'une partie de la matière, ou d'un corps, du voisinage de ceux qui le touchent immédiatement, et que nous considérons comme en repos, dans le voisinage de quelques autres, »[10]

Descartes désigne en réalité le référentiel privilégié, unique, dans lequel il convient de juger du mouvement ou du repos du corps, à savoir le voisinage du corps, c'est-à-dire les corps qui le touchent immédiatement. Ainsi, le marin assis sur le bateau est vraiment en repos, parce qu'il est en repos par rapport à son voisinage, et la terre est vraiment en repos dans le tourbillon qui l'emporte. La définition cartésienne cherche à déterminer de manière univoque le mouvement d'un corps. Dans le §28 de cette même 2ème partie des *Principes*, Descartes précise d'ailleurs que c'est parce qu'elle permet de n'attribuer à un corps qu'un mouvement déterminé qu'il a adopté cette définition.

À certains égards, on pourrait donc considérer que Descartes introduit, comme Newton, un mouvement « vrai », un mouvement « absolu » dans les corps. Les deux auteurs diffèrent cependant sur un point essentiel : pour Newton, le référentiel par rapport auquel il convient de déterminer le mouvement vrai des corps – l'espace absolu – est le même pour tous les corps, alors que pour Descartes, le référentiel par rapport auquel il convient de déterminer le

---

[8] *Principes de la philosophie*, 2ème partie, § 29.
[9] Daniel Garber : *Descartes' Metaphysical Physics*, Chicago 1992.
[10] René Descartes : *Principes de la philosophie,* 2ème partie, § 25.

mouvement d'un corps dépend de ce corps ; cela a pour conséquence que plusieurs corps en repos peuvent néanmoins être en mouvement l'un par rapport à l'autre. Newton qui, dans le fameux *scolie* du début des *Principia mathematica,* s'en prend à Descartes sans le nommer, ne s'y est pas trompé. La manière dont il comprend la définition cartésienne est toute différente de celle dont Leibniz l'interprète. Pour Newton, le propos de Descartes est bien de définir un mouvement et un repos « vrai », mais Newton estime que sa manière de le faire est inadéquate. Le célèbre argument du seau est destiné à montrer que le mouvement qui est physiquement signifiant – celui qui a des effets, celui qui fait grimper l'eau sur les parois – n'est pas le mouvement « selon la vérité » de Descartes, le mouvement par rapport au voisinage.[11] Lorsqu'on lâche un seau suspendu à une corde tordue et que le seau, dans un premier temps, tourne sur lui-même sans avoir encore entraîné l'eau, la surface de celle-ci reste plane, quoiqu'elle soit en mouvement par rapport à son voisinage (le seau); ce n'est qu'à partir du moment où l'eau, entraînée par la rotation du seau, est en mouvement par rapport à l'espace absolu qu'elle tend à s'élever sur les parois du seau. Le mouvement par rapport au voisinage ne produit aucun effet, c'est le mouvement par rapport à l'espace absolu qui en produit et c'est donc lui qui est le mouvement vrai.

La conception cartésienne du mouvement n'est pas aussi relativiste que Leibniz ne semble le penser. Il y a pour Descartes des corps qui sont « vraiment en repos » et d'autres qui sont « vraiment en mouvement » et, contrairement à ce que lui reproche Leibniz, Descartes ne serait donc pas incohérent lorsqu'il formule des règles du choc incompatibles avec le principe d'équivalence des hypothèses. Un corps en repos sur le sol où il est posé est « vraiment en repos » et il n'est pas inconcevable qu'il ne réagisse pas à un choc de la même manière que s'il était « vraiment » en mouvement. Cela dit, même si le reproche adressé à Descartes d'avoir « oublié » sa définition est injustifié, on ne peut qu'être impressionné par la lucidité de Leibniz, qui semble ici avoir parfaitement compris – après Huygens, il est vrai – que le mouvement est purement relatif et que, par conséquent, rien, dans les phénomènes, ne doit permettre d'attribuer le repos à tel corps plutôt qu'à tel autre.

Les choses ne sont cependant pas aussi simples parce que, comme je l'ai rappelé au début de cet article, Leibniz affirme d'autre part que, si l'on prend en compte la force qui cause le mouvement, il est possible d'attribuer le mouvement à un corps plutôt qu'à un autre. À partir de là, deux cas sont

---

[11] Je reprends ici l'interprétation de Ori Belkind : « Leibniz and Newton on Space », in : *Foundations of Science* 18 (2013), pp. 467–497.

envisageables: ou bien la force qui fonde le mouvement vrai est accessible à l'observation, ou bien elle ne l'est pas. Si elle ne l'est pas, Leibniz se trouve dans une situation qui, *mutatis mutandis*, ressemble à celle de Newton : de même que Newton pose l'existence d'un mouvement absolu inaccessible à l'observation – et, pour fonder ce mouvement, d'un espace absolu tout aussi inaccessible empiriquement –, Leibniz aurait posé l'existence d'un mouvement vrai inaccessible à l'observation – et, pour fonder ce mouvement, d'une force tout aussi inaccessible empiriquement. Un positiviste pourrait, bien sûr, reprocher à Leibniz, comme Mach l'a fait à Newton, d'introduire en physique d'oiseuses entités métaphysiques qui ne devraient pas y avoir droit de cité, mais la position leibnizienne n'est cependant pas intenable. Si, en revanche, la force qui fonde le mouvement est accessible à l'observation, la position de Leibniz semble plus problématique, parce qu'il est impossible de concilier l'observabilité de la force avec l'équivalence des hypothèses. Or, certains textes encouragent à considérer que l'on peut non seulement observer mais même mesurer cette force (qui vaudrait mv^2).

Si l'on ne veut pas considérer que Leibniz est incohérent, il est tentant d'explorer la proposition mentionnée ci-dessus, selon laquelle Leibniz n'aurait pas soutenu simultanément mais successivement les deux thèses incompatibles que sont l'observabilité de la force et l'équivalence des hypothèses.

Certains textes de la fin des années 1670, indiquent, comme l'ont montré Garber et Lodge, que Leibniz ne désespérait pas à cette époque de trouver le moyen de repérer les corps véritablement en mouvement. Cependant, il y a aussi des textes de la même époque dans lesquels on trouve déjà une formulation du principe de l'équivalence des hypothèses. À la fin des années 1670, Leibniz affirme déjà, comme il le fera par la suite, que le mouvement pris « en lui-même », simple changement de *situs,* est purement relatif, mais aussi qu'un corps qui est vraiment en mouvement a en lui la cause de ce changement de *situs*. Et il ajoute qu'un corps véritablement en mouvement est capable de produire un effet.[12] On pourrait alléguer plusieurs textes de cette époque dans lesquels Leibniz reprend ainsi la définition cartésienne du mouvement comme changement de *situs* par rapport au voisinage, mais aussi les préoccupations de Descartes quant à la manière d'attribuer un mouvement déterminé à chaque corps. Certains textes sont très relativistes, d'autres moins, mais la position de

---

[12] Newton affirmera, lui aussi, dans son fameux *scolie* que les mouvements relatifs et les mouvements absolus se distinguent par leurs causes et par leurs effets, mais il donne à ces termes un sens différent. Par exemple, la *vis impressa*, cause du mouvement vrai selon Newton n'est évidemment pas la force intrinsèque que possède, selon Leibniz, un corps en mouvement.

Leibniz est, en général, après avoir constaté le caractère relatif du mouvement, d'estimer qu'on ne peut pas en rester là et qu'il faut chercher malgré tout des raisons d'attribuer le mouvement à un corps plutôt qu'à un autre – au bateau plutôt qu'au port parce qu'on voit le vent gonfler la voile et les rames frapper la mer, aux marcheurs plutôt qu'à la ville parce qu'ils jugent que ce sont eux qui marchent et qu'ils sentent leur fatigue, etc.[13] Même s'il conclut que les tentatives pour attribuer le mouvement vrai à tel ou tel corps sont finalement vouées à l'échec, Leibniz ne se satisfait pas de cette interprétation relativiste. Il résiste au principe de l'équivalence des hypothèses. C'est, sans doute, une des raisons pour lesquelles, lorsqu'il entreprend de formuler les lois du choc dans le *De corporum concursu*,[14] il ne reprend pas la solution parfaitement satisfaisante de Huygens, qu'il connaît pourtant, et dont les textes de 1677 publiés par Michel Fichant dans *La réforme de la dynamique* montrent qu'il la maîtrise parfaitement. La solution de Huygens repose, avec la célèbre méthode du bateau, sur une compréhension approfondie du principe de relativité. Leibniz, quant à lui, va poser le problème en des termes qui évoquent la conception, pourtant bien moins élégante, de Descartes et distinguer des cas – la collision frontale, le cas où un corps en choque un autre au repos, le cas où un corps en rattrape un autre plus lent – dont celui qui a compris le principe de relativité voit immédiatement qu'ils sont en réalité tous le même cas.

L'un des textes de 1677 publié par M. Fichant[15] manifeste de manière particulièrement claire cette résistance de Leibniz au principe de relativité. Dans ce document, Leibniz envisage le cas d'un corps C qui se déplace sur un bateau, avec une vitesse égale et opposée à celle du bateau. La question posée est de savoir si *absolute loquendo*, il faut attribuer un mouvement au corps en question. On pourrait, bien sûr, être tenté de considérer que ce corps est au repos, puisqu'il recule avec la même vitesse que celle avec laquelle le bateau avance, mais ce serait, selon Leibniz une erreur : le corps a en réalité « une double puissance » et, bien loin d'être au repos, il se meut plutôt deux fois, de deux mouvements contraires. Pour prouver cela, Leibniz va imaginer un dispositif qui mettra en évidence que le corps C peut agir deux fois sur un corps immobile sur la rive: une première fois du fait de la vitesse qu'il a en commun avec le bateau et une seconde fois du fait de la vitesse qu'il a par rapport au bateau. Le corps pourrait donc exercer une double action du fait de son

---

[13] *Principia mechanica* (1676?), A VI, 3, 101–110, ici 104.
[14] *De corporum concursu* (1678), publié et traduit par Michel Fichant in : Gottfried Wilhelm Leibniz: *La réforme de la dynamique,* Paris 1994.
[15] Ibid., pp. 375f..

(double) mouvement. Le dispositif consiste à imaginer que l'on a fixé sur le bateau un ressort que le corps en mouvement va tendre avant de s'immobiliser. Une fois le corps C en repos sur le bateau, il sera comme une partie du bateau, dont il augmentera dès lors la puissance (puisqu'il augmente sa masse), en sorte que si l'on imagine que le bateau choque un autre corps immobile de même masse et lui transmet dès lors toute sa force, la force du corps C comptera dans le bilan (le corps que le bateau pourra mettre en mouvement aura pour masse celle du bateau + celle du corps C). Le corps agira ainsi, du fait de son mouvement commun avec le bateau, une première fois sur un corps immobile par rapport à la rive.[16] Si on libère ensuite le ressort (auquel est toujours attaché le corps C), le corps pourra exercer à nouveau sa puissance sur un corps immobile par rapport à la rive. Et Leibniz conclut que le corps C aura finalement agi deux fois sur un corps immobile par rapport à la rive. Il pense ainsi pouvoir affirmer que *absolute loquendo*, le corps se meut et même doublement, par rapport à la rive.

Ce passage témoigne d'une conception du mouvement tout à fait non-relativiste, qui interdit clairement de considérer qu'un même corps peut être considéré comme en repos ou comme en mouvement selon le référentiel dans lequel on se place. Le corps qu'envisage Leibniz a en lui *absolute loquendo* un mouvement, et même un double mouvement. Ce corps n'est pas dans le même état qu'un corps qui serait tout simplement posé sur la rive, même s'il est apparemment en repos par rapport à ce corps. Le corps en mouvement sur le bateau possède une puissance, il peut produire des effets, ce que le corps en repos sur la rive est incapable de faire. Leibniz pense qu'en observant les effets des interactions entre les corps, il est possible de déterminer l'état de mouvement ou de repos de ces corps. Le corps C 'est *absolute loquendo* en mouvement par rapport à la rive, et celui qui le considérerait comme au repos se tromperait; l'observation du double effet que peut produire le corps lui donnerait tort. Le principe d'équivalence des hypothèses n'est pas d'application.

Les premiers des textes que les éditeurs de l'Académie ont rassemblés sous le titre *Specimina de motus causa et de corporum qualitatibus*[17] méritent également de retenir l'attention. Ces textes ont été commentés de manière tout

---

[16] Leibniz ne voit pas qu'en tirant sur le ressort attaché au bateau, le corps en question a en réalité diminué la vitesse, et donc la puissance, du bateau.
[17] A VI, 4 C, 2010–2019. Les éditeurs de l'Académie datent cet ensemble de 1678–1681 (?).

à fait éclairante par Paul Lodge[18] et par D. Garber.[19] Leibniz y propose à nouveau des exemples de situations dans lesquelles on est en droit d'affirmer qu'un corps est en mouvement: s'il y avait dans la terre une certaine intelligence, ou s'il y avait dans le fluide qui entoure la terre quelque chose qui soit la conséquence du mouvement de la terre, et qu'il n'y ait rien de tel pour le soleil, on pourrait affirmer que c'est la terre et non le soleil qui se meut.[20] Si l'on s'en tient au seul changement de lieu, c'est-à-dire au mouvement mathématique, écrit encore Leibniz, on ne peut dire quel corps est en mouvement. Mais si on prend en compte les causes physiques, on peut voir plus facilement à qui attribuer le mouvement. Pour illustrer cela, Leibniz considère aussi l'exemple suivant[21]: soit trois corps, a et b en repos l'un par rapport à l'autre et c, en mouvement par rapport aux deux premiers. Si on ne considère que les changements de position, on peut tout aussi bien considérer que a et b sont en repos et que c se meut, ou que c'est en repos et que a et b se meuvent ; même s'il est plus simple de considérer qu'un corps se meut plutôt que deux, les deux hypothèses sont acceptables, et il en irait de même quel que soit le nombre de corps présents. En revanche, si l'on ajoute un quatrième corps, d, que c va choquer, on passe, selon Leibniz, de la simple considération mathématique d'un changement de lieu à la physique, à la communication d'un mouvement, et cela permet d'affirmer qu'il faut attribuer une certaine action à c.[22] Contrairement à ce que Leibniz dira par la suite, il semble donc bien considérer ici que les chocs entre les corps permettent de déterminer quel corps est en mouvement. Leibniz prend encore l'exemple de l'homme qui marche sur le pont du bateau, avec une vitesse égale et opposée à celle du bateau, en sorte qu'il ne change pas de position par rapport à la rive. Il convient, selon Leibniz, de dire que cet homme est en mouvement, parce qu'il se fatigue, et parce qu'il est capable de pousser ou de tirer quelque chose du fait de son mouvement.[23] Avoir en soi une puissance d'agir et pouvoir produire des effets sont des critères de mouvement. Dans la suite du texte,[24] Leibniz s'en prend à nouveau

---

[18] Lodge : « Leibniz on Relativity ».
[19] Daniel Garber : « How Leibniz Found Relativity » ; id : *Leibniz: Body, Substance, Monad*, Oxford 2009, pp.111–115.
[20] A VI, 4 C, 2011.
[21] Ibid., 2017f.
[22] Leibniz ne prend pas en considération le fait que le choc que l'on observe entre c et d pourrait s'expliquer en supposant que c'est d plutôt que c qui est en mouvement.
[23] A VI, 4 C, 2018f.
[24] Ibid., 2019.

explicitement à la conception cartésienne. Il estime que c'est à tort que Descartes considère que la terre est en repos parce qu'elle est emportée par un tourbillon: elle ne l'est pas davantage que les poutres emportées par des fleuves, dont personne ne doute qu'elles se meuvent, et parfois avec une force telle qu'elles endommagent les ponts. On retrouve, à nouveau, l'idée que si l'on constate qu'un corps produit des effets, on doit considérer qu'il agit, et qu'il possède dès lors un mouvement. Le recours aux causes physiques et l'observation des effets peuvent, au moins dans certains cas, permettre d'attribuer le mouvement à un corps plutôt qu'à un autre.

Les considérations développées dans les *Specimina de motus causa* vont cependant tout à fait à l'encontre de ce que Leibniz dit dans un autre texte de la même époque publié par Fichant qui le date des années 1678–1679.[25] On trouve en effet dans ce texte une formulation tout à fait précise du principe de l'équivalence des hypothèses, selon laquelle, si l'on considère un ensemble de corps, il est impossible de discerner où se trouve le mouvement « que ce soit avant ou après le concours ». La collision, contrairement à ce que suggérait le texte précédent, ne permettrait donc pas de désigner le corps en mouvement. Leibniz précise que, si l'on a une collision entre deux corps,

> « il est nécessaire que rien de différent n'arrive du fait du choc, dans n'importe lequel des deux qu'on suppose le mouvement ou le repos, ou un mouvement distribué entre eux de façon quelconque, pourvu qu'en résulte l'approche et l'éloignement en question. »[26]

Comme ce sera le cas plus tard dans le *Specimen dynamicum*, Leibniz exige ici que les lois de la physique respectent le principe de relativité. Quelles que soient les observations que l'on peut faire, elles ne contrediront jamais l'affirmation que tel ou tel corps est en repos. Pour le dire en d'autres termes, il n'y a pas de référentiel privilégié; aucune observation ne nous empêchera jamais de considérer que le bateau plutôt que la rive est en repos. Dans la dernière partie de la *Dynamica*, Leibniz affirmera de manière tout à fait explicite que ni les collisions[27] ni les mouvements de rotation[28] ne peuvent rompre le principe de relativité. En ce qui concerne les collisions, à tout le moins, le texte que nous venons de citer l'affirmait déjà plus de dix ans plus tôt.

---

[25] Leibniz : *La réforme de la dynamique*, pp. 410–413.
[26] Ibid., p. 413.
[27] *Dynamica* ; GM VI, 500.
[28] Ibid.; GM VI, 507.

Cela dit, il est incontestable qu'à la fin des années 1680, les textes qui affirment l'équivalence des hypothèses se multiplient, notamment à l'époque du voyage en Italie, lorsque Leibniz s'efforce de convaincre Rome de renoncer à la censure contre Copernic en arguant que l'hypothèse géocentrique et l'hypothèse héliocentrique sont toutes deux recevables.[29] Leibniz a désormais compris que la capacité de produire un effet, de pousser un corps, de le briser ou de l'élever à une certaine hauteur, n'est pas la preuve d'un mouvement absolu, mais seulement la manifestation d'un mouvement relatif.[30] Comme il l'écrira à Huygens en juin 1694, dans une lettre très souvent cité, les phénomènes ne peuvent fournir (ni même aux anges) une raison infaillible pour déterminer le sujet du mouvement.[31]

Quoiqu'il ait adopté le principe l'équivalence des hypothèses, Leibniz continue cependant à penser, comme il le dit dans la même lettre à Huygens de juin 1694, que chaque corps a bien un certain degré de mouvement, ou de force. La force mouvante des corps est quelque chose de réel, et elle a un *subjectum*, même si l'observation ne nous donne pas les moyens de désigner ce *subjectum*.[32] De même, dans les *Animadversiones* de 1692, lorsqu'il commente à nouveau le § 25 de la deuxième partie des *Principes*, Leibniz le fait d'une manière qui évoque plutôt la position peu relativiste des années précédant le *Discours de Métaphysique* qu'une adhésion nette au principe de l'équivalence des hypothèses : il affirme que l'on ne peut pas se contenter de faire du mouvement un simple changement de voisinage, parce qu'alors, il n'y aura « aucune raison dans la nature qui puisse nous obliger à attribuer le mouvement plutôt à un objet qu'aux autres »[33]. Même dans le *Specimen dynamicum*, où il affirme explicitement qu'il faut formuler des lois du mouvement qui, contrairement à celles de Descartes, préservent la nature relative du mouvement, il ajoute que « la force est quelque chose de tout à fait réel dans les substances créées. »[34]

---

[29] Leibniz ajoute néanmoins que l'hypothèse la plus vraie est la plus simple ou la plus intelligible, ce qui est une manière de marquer sa préférence pour Copernic. Je n'envisagerai pas ici ce critère de la simplicité, qui est pourtant un autre moyen de déterminer à quel(s) corps il convient d'attribuer le repos ou le mouvement.
[30] Voir par exemple le texte *De praestantia systematis copernicani* (1689), A VI, 4 C, 2070, dans lequel Leibniz reprend l'exemple d'un corps qui se déplace sur un bateau avec une vitesse égale et opposée à celle du bateau, exemple auquel il donne une interprétation toute différente de celle qu'il en donnait dans le texte de 1677 évoqué ci-dessus.
[31] Christiaan Huygens : *Œuvres complètes,* tome X, Den Haag, 1905, p. 645.
[32] Ibid.
[33] GP IV, 369.
[34] GM VI, 247.

À partir des années 1690, Leibniz considère sans doute que chaque corps a en lui une force d'agir déterminée, mais que cette force d'agir n'est pas accessible à l'observation et que, même si elle l'était, elle ne permettrait pas de faire de la physique, puisqu'elle ne permettrait pas de définir un référentiel unique dans lequel chaque corps aurait une vitesse conforme à cette force – comme c'est le cas pour Descartes, et contrairement à ce que l'on a chez Newton où il existe un référentiel dans lequel tous les corps pourraient avoir comme vitesse leur vitesse vraie, absolue. Ainsi, pour Leibniz, celui qui est assis dans un bateau est en repos vrai, il n'a pas de force d'agir, il ne se fatigue pas, mais celui qui est assis sur la rive est également en repos vrai, et l'on ne peut manifestement pas trouver un référentiel unique dans lequel ils seraient tous deux en repos. Cette notion de force ou de puissance d'agir est dès lors le plus souvent inutilisable pour une physique qui entreprend de décrire les interactions entre les corps. Celui qui veut faire de la physique doit trouver un référentiel unique dans lequel il déterminera les vitesses de tous les corps, vitesses qui ne pourront pas être toutes le reflet de la force ou de la puissance d'agir des corps au sens où l'entend Leibniz. Leibniz continuera jusqu'à la fin de sa vie à penser qu'un corps déterminé est vraiment en repos ou vraiment en mouvement, et que, comme il l'écrit par exemple dans le §13 du *de ipsa natura*,[35] un corps en mouvement est différent d'un corps en repos. Il reconnaîtra cependant qu'une description des phénomènes qui n'attribue pas aux corps leur mouvement ou leur repos véritable peut être, pour le physicien, parfaitement acceptable.[36]

Ce qu'il y a de remarquable, mais aussi de problématique, chez Leibniz, c'est que, s'il distingue ainsi nettement le niveau physique, observable, et le niveau métaphysique qui le fonde sans être lui-même accessible à l'observation, il ne renoncera cependant pas à chercher dans la physique même des images aussi fidèles que possible de la réalité métaphysique. Peut-être faut-il voir dans les développements que Leibniz consacre à l'action le meilleur exemple de cette volonté.[37] Je voudrais, pour terminer, évoquer rapidement un

---

[35] GP IV, 513.
[36] Cette position est aussi, *mutatis mutandis*, celle de la physique de Newton: les mouvements absolus des corps sont inaccessibles à l'observation, et l'on est donc dans l'impossibilité d'attribuer aux corps leurs mouvements véritables, mais cela n'empêche pas de faire de la physique.
[37] C'est ce que suggère Anne-Lise Rey : le modèle physique qui convient le mieux à la métaphysique de Leibniz, celui qui permet de la rendre intelligible, ce n'est pas la physique de la force, qui s'épuise en produisant son effet, mais la physique de l'action, avec son effet formel et son action immanente. Voir Rey : « L'ambivalence de l'action », in : *Leibniz-De Volder: Correspondance*, éd. par Anne-Lise Rey et Michael Fichant, Paris 2016.

autre cas où la physique peut, selon Leibniz, nous permettre de comprendre quelque chose de la réalité métaphysique : la description d'un choc entre deux corps dans le référentiel de leur centre de gravité. L'équivalence des hypothèses implique que l'on peut choisir de décrire ce choc en considérant que tel corps ou tel autre est en repos et donc que tel corps agit et que tel autre pâtit (ou l'inverse), ou encore que les deux corps sont en mouvement. Pour Leibniz, il existe néanmoins un référentiel qui révèle mieux que les autres la vérité de cette rencontre : le référentiel du centre de gravité. Dans ce référentiel, on le sait, chacun des corps rejaillit avec sa vitesse initiale – les corps rebondissent sur le centre de gravité –, en sorte qu'on ne peut plus dire qu'un corps agit tandis que l'autre pâtit, mais qu'il devient manifeste qu'un corps n'agit jamais que par sa propre force, ce qui est tout à fait conforme aux thèses métaphysiques de Leibniz. Il ne serait pas impossible de soutenir que, pour Leibniz, les mouvements vrais des corps impliqués dans un choc, ce sont, par excellence, les mouvements des corps dans le référentiel du centre de gravité parce que c'est par rapport à ce système qu'est exprimée dans le monde de la physique cette vérité métaphysique que les choses n'agissent jamais que par elles-mêmes et sur elles-mêmes, sans que l'on ait besoin, comme le dit le *Specimen dynamicum* de supposer aucun influx de l'une vers l'autre.[38] Leibniz l'affirme par exemple dans le *Specimen inventorum* (1688). Après avoir établi que « dans la rigueur métaphysique, toutes les opérations des substances, actions et passions, sont spontanées », il poursuit :

> « Tout cela est à ce point vrai qu'en physique aussi, à examiner la chose de près, il apparaît que l'*impetus* n'est point transféré d'un corps à un autre, mais que chacun est mû par la force qui est en lui, qui est seulement déterminée à l'occasion d'un autre ou respectivement à lui. Et déjà des esprits distingués ont reconnu que la cause de l'impulsion qui éloigne un corps d'un autre est le ressort même du corps, qui le fait rebondir loin de l'autre. [...] Mais pour comprendre cela correctement, il faut distinguer le mouvement propre de chaque corps, qui produit le choc, du mouvement commun : qui peut toujours être conçu avant le choc, et se conserve toujours après lui, tandis que le mouvement propre, qui seul fait obstacle à l'autre n'a d'effet dans le corps de l'autre que par le ressort de celui-ci. »[39]

---

[38] GM VI, 251.
[39] *Specimen inventorum* ; A VI, 4 B, 1620f., traduction de Christiane Frémont in Leibniz : *Discours de métaphysique et autres textes*, Paris 2001. La distinction entre le mouvement propre de chaque corps, qui est son mouvement par rapport au centre de gravité du système, et le mouvement commun, qui est le mouvement du centre de gravité du système, est précisée dans la dernière partie de la *Dynamica*. Voir en particulier la proposition 11, GM VI, 495.

Même si l'on peut décrire une collision dans n'importe quel référentiel, c'est dans le référentiel du centre de gravité que l'on aperçoit qu'un corps ne s'éloigne jamais que par son propre ressort.

The Material Perspective in Leibniz through the *Sympnoia panta*

Manuel Higueras Cabrera (Granada)

1. Introduction

One of the most controversial Leibnizian theses appears in paragraph 7 of the Monadology: *Monads have no windows at all.*[1] This statement could be erroneously interpreted as Leibniz's fall into *solipsism.*[2] Nothing could come in or go out of a monad since its development and deployment comes from the interior of itself. With no doors or windows, the monad seems to remain isolated within its inner richness. The whole becoming, change and alterations that occur in each of the monads are contained in its interior, folded up, awaiting the moment of its deployment.

Paragraph 18 extends this thesis with the application of the concept of αὐτάρκεια to the monad.[3] The monad is self-sufficient in its development; it is itself its own source of change and movement. In this sense, Leibniz had the key concept ready at least from his correspondence with Arnauld and it is none other than *notio complete*.[4] However, the essential aspect of atomicity of the real comes from further back, perhaps from the beginning of his lifework as a thinker. On the basis of the motives that lead Leibniz to escape from the atom (material), one can get a better understanding of his shift towards the monad (formal atom).

From this idea, a key element emerges in the already mature Leibnizian ontology, that is, if the atom is formal, the possible interactions among those *elementa* must also be of a formal nature.

In parallel with his thesis of the atomicity of the real, the philosopher of Hannover sets out that of the ligation of everything with everything. And this ligation is woven through another of the key concepts of the German thinker, that of expression. Through this concept it is likely to reach an ideal interaction between substances, since the influence between one and the other would only

---

[1] *Monadology* § 7; GP VI, 607.
[2] Alain Renaut tries to find in the monadological theory the main source of the whole modern individualism. See Alain Renaut: *L'ère de l'individu*, Paris 1989.
[3] Cf. *Monadology* § 18; GP VI, 609.
[4] Gottfried Wilhelm Leibniz: *Philosophischer Briefwechsel*, vol. 1: *Der Briefwechsel mit Antoine Arnauld*, frz.-dt., ed. and transl. by. Reinhard Finster, Hamburg 1997, p. 89); A VI, 4 B, 1541.

occur ideally. Leibnizian philosophy seemed to remain, then, framed as idealism.

In paragraph 61, though, Leibniz opens a way of interaction and ligation between compounds. In this sense, compounds or material bodies are also linked with each other. And at this ontic level the influence is no longer ideal, but material and corporal. Quoting Hippocrates, Leibniz characterises this other type of influence and ligation, as συμπνοια παντα.

In first place we will analyse how this atomized reality or this atomicity of the real is characterised. From that point we will try to get to understand the meaning of the ontologic priority of the individual-atomic within the monadologic system.

The following step will be an attempt to understand how this aspect of essential individuality agrees with the ligation of everything with everything. And this, not by as much from the point of view of the concept of expression, as from the interaction between material bodies, which appears in paragraph 61 of the text Leibniz wrote 302 years ago.

2. Atomicity of the Monad

In which sense is it stated that monads have no windows? We have already pointed out in the introductory paragraph that this assertion can be interpreted as a sort of "monadic solipsism" in which each monad would act in a complete independent way.

However, a new strand of research that can result in a more fruitful outcome can be taken. It seems that Leibniz's intention was not to isolate the monad in its interior, however rich this is. We may interpret the statement (that is, "monads have no windows at all") as an attempt to establish the ontologic priority of the atomic individual. The Leibnizian monad, at least from a structural point of view, is not like the isolated Cartesian self. If a monad had an opening to the outside, the ontologic priority would come from the outside; the sense of it would be made up from this something which is outside the monad and gets into it. What Leibniz intents to do with the monad is something different, and to be so, the constitution of sense must sprout from the interior. To be the foundation of the real, monads must be *authentic atoms*.[5]

---

[5] Great part of the meaning "authentic atoms" consists in being immaterial. This necessity is better understood if we consider the metaphysical reason as the main argument Leibniz has

The sense in which Leibniz understands the concept "atom" here is not exactly that of indivisible. If we move to paragraph 18, Leibniz himself can help us better understand why he refers to monads as atoms of nature:

> "because they have a certain degree of perfection within themselves (ἔχουσι τὸ ἐντελες) and a sufficiency (αὐτάρκεια) that converts them in a source of their internal actions and, so to speak, in incorporeal automata."[6]

They are atoms, not because they are indivisible (which they are and hence they are incorporeal, as we will see later), but because they are independent in the sense of *autarchic automata*. They operate in an autonomous way and they provide their own laws to themselves. The primarily distinctive trait of the monad-atom would not exactly be its closure, but the *autopoiesis* exclusively from the interior.

In addition, in order to be the real atoms of nature they must be, of course, atomic, but to be "true", they cannot be of a material nature, they must form a different ontic level.

We do not mean that Leibniz defends a sort of atomism, which would imply to say that the reality is made up of atoms and for the philosopher of Hannover it is made up of monads. What we intend to point out is that Leibnizian monads possess a component of fundamental atomicity. This component of atomicity is developed mainly in the concept of *notio completa*, which is defended by Leibniz, at least, from his correspondence with Arnauld.

3. Systematicity in the Monadology

Throughout his actual monadologic period (what is often called his system of maturity) Leibniz has already fitted the minds together within his conception of material bodies. We have already seen how from a very young age he was not convinced of atomism and how little by little he developed his own ontology.

However, if we think of Leibniz's path across atomism as a search of the ultimate units that make up the real, the resulting ontology has to be one

---

against atomism (material atomism). See Manuel Higueras: "Critique of atomism from Aristotle to Leibniz", in: Juan A. Nicolás/Niels Öffenberger (eds.): *Beiträge zu Leibniz' Rezeption der Aristotelischen Logik und Metaphysik*, Hildesheim/Zürich/New York 2016, pp. 333–350.
[6] *Monadology* § 18; GP VI, 609f.

in which primacy falls on these units. Consequently, the accent of the resulting ontology falls on the individual-atomic.[7]

Does this mean that Leibniz's philosophy is an atomism that ends up conceiving the individuals as closed and self-sufficient elements? We do not think it is, or at least it does not have to be so. In this regard, the fundamental contribution of the philosopher of Hannover would be to have put in value the individual in relation with the constitution of the real, but not falling in an individualism that entails the danger of solipsism. The structure of the monad as a true unit permits to consider individuals as independent entities and at the same time a fundamental relationship between everything that exists (System). The importance of this monadic structure in history is even greater if we take into account that it is presented as a sole approach. The German philosopher conceives this compatibility out of the incommensurability of both poles: individual and the System. That is to say, compatibility cannot be solved as a movement from both antithetical poles in a synthesis.[8] In that case, Dumont would be right and

> "Leibniz would not then represent a model, from the point of view of the investigation of a conciliation between both principles rather than to the extent that he would have been able to register and preserve its deep incompatibility."[9]

However, from a different point of view, compatibility would turn out to be total if we think of it out of the concept of *integration*. Not in the sense of integration of the individual in the system; that would be a form of commensurability. Rather on the contrary, the system is integrated within the individual. Would this not be a way to end up with the system, by subjugating it to the individual? By no means, the individual represents the system in full in its interior, it consists itself of its representation. Then, does the individual subsume the system? Of course not, representation is always *in perspective*, thus the individual component being preserved as fundamental, as a priority.

Everything is linked together by means of the internal representation of the entire universe that the monad keeps in its interior. The monad, as a living mirror, expresses the other monads in its interior. A few years before his death,

---

[7] We can call it individual-monadic. We have chosen the expression "atomic" to emphasise the sense of independence that we have talked about in the first part.
[8] That would be the movement in Hegel's philosophy with the absolute spirit.
[9] Quoted in Renaut: *L'ère de l'individu*, p. 112.

Leibniz states this connection of everything with everything by means of the internal expression:

> "Everything is connected and as each body acts upon every other body, according to the distance, and is itself affected in turn by reaction, it follows that each body is a living mirror or provided with internal activity, representative of the universe according to its point of view and as regulated as the universe itself."[10]

The main reason why Leibniz rejects atomism is not the materiality of atoms. Leibniz is not an anti-materialist who rejects all inclusion of matter at ontological level or who relegates it to a mere worthless phantasmagorical phenomenon (ontologic or epistemological). On the contrary, the material aspect is essential, both at individual level (monads are necessarily incorporated) and at the level of the system that the individuals form. We will try to show how this double aspect of the system appears in the Monadology through the concept of *simpnoia panta* of paragraph 61.

3.1. Gnoseo-Ideal Systematicity

It is true, indeed, that monads have no windows. But it is also true that they do not need them, they themselves are a huge window to its interior. From this window towards its interior the monad gains access to the entire universe, although it does it in its own and individual perspective, as we have already seen.[11]

It is true, as pointed out by Hubertus Busche, that with this concept of expression and the absence of windows (*Fernsterlosigkeit*), the type of influence or relationship that Leibniz wants to allow is exclusively ideal, excluding the other type of influence, the one that is usually called real, physical.[12] Our philosopher makes it explicitly clear in Monadology § 51: "in simple substances the influence of a monad upon another is only ideal."[13]

---

[10] Gottfried Wilhelm Leibniz: *Principes de la nature et de la grace fondés en raison. Principes de la philosophie ou Monadologie*, ed. by André Robinet, Paris 1954, 31.
[11] The difference that Leibniz points out between God and monads is not the object of knowledge, but the way of this knowledge. That is, the specificity of the monads, in contrast to God, is that they are always a perspective: "It is not for the object, but for the modification of the knowledge that monads are limited". *Monadology* § 60; GP VI, 617.
[12] See Hubertus Busche: "Übernatürlichkeit und Fensterlosigkeit der Monaden", in: G. W. Leibniz: *Monadologie* (= *Klassiker Auslegen* 34), Berlin 2009, p. 57.
[13] *Monadology* § 51; GP VI, 615.

The only interaction envisaged between monads is produced at the level of representations.

The monad, characterised by *perceptio* and moved by *appetitus*, goes from one representation to another. That is to say, the network of monads know one another under the form of *representation*. This concept of representation implies that the individual perspective regarded as a priority is already in the very hinge post in which knowledge starts.

We want to refer to this type of systematicity in the Monadology as *gnoseo-ideal* mainly due to the fact that the influence between monads that Leibniz describes is ideal and it is framed within the knowledge of the world. But also, because the individuals (monads) are systematised from its cognizant perspective (individual) and do so ideally. This is the reason why it is especially important to see how Leibniz comes to his conception of formal atom through the critique of the material atom.

What we find in his famous metaphor of the mirror is the ontologic priority of the perspective. Consequently, what God regulates and arranges are perspectives. However, both the constitution of the perspectives of the monad and the regulation of perspectives constitute a systematization which is crossed necessarily and fundamentally by the ligation of everything with everything.

At this level, that of monads, is where we can fall into the trap of accusing the German philosopher of dropping into solipsism. Glenn A. Hartz, for instance, calls it *solipsistic level*.[14] The reason is obvious; at the level of monad only the monad and God would exist (and this last one because otherwise I would not have a sufficient reason). The motives that Hartz has so as to use the word solipsism are entirely justified since he is distinguishing different ontologic levels within Leibnizian thought and making an effort of conceptual clarity to avoid confusions.

Strictly speaking, however, there is no solipsism in the monad. There exist other monads apart from the monad itself; the motive, once again, is in the principle of a sufficient reason, set in the principle of perfection and richness of creation: it stands to reason that not only I exist in the universe when many other things, and more perfect than I myself, could exist.[15] A world full of monads would be infinitely more perfect than one world which had only one. Thus, God would have no reason to create that sort of *monoworld*. Consequently, there exist other monads in the world, apart from mine, and what I

---

[14] See Glenn A. Hartz: *Leibniz's Final System*, New York 2007, pp. 9–12.
[15] See A VI, 4 B, 1396.

know of the universe is but the aforesaid monads. It is my individual perspective upon them what constitutes me and what I consist of as a monad.

The possible solipsism of the monad becomes void out of the very formal structure of the monad itself. The monad, as we have just observed, consists of being perspective. This *being perspective* can be understood not only as a way of giving ontologic priority to the individual-atomic, but it also opens the monad to a certain type of exteriority, that of totality. It is perspective of the other monads and this respectivity places the individual essence of the monad in a position of total dependence on the rest of the monadic universe. Actually, when Leibniz says that a monad cannot be altered in its interior *from the outside*, he says this as something obvious and that goes without saying. And it is true that it is something obvious, but only when we go deep into the concept of monad as formal atom, that is, with the characteristics of *notio completa* (each monad already contains in its interior the totality of its past, present and future traits) of *perspectivism* (each monad possesses in its interior the totality of the world in perspective) and of immaterial.

The monad is perspective, but it is perspective of the whole and therefore it is also pure exteriority. In this sense, there is no room for the critique of solipsism on Leibnizian Monadology.

3.2. Physical-Corporal Systematicity

However, there is a feature of the monad we cannot forget: it is necessarily incorporated. And between bodies this physical influence does exist, in fact, to the extent that "compound symbolise the simple", all bodies are linked and

> "that way each body is affected not only by those which are in contact with, and in some way it feels what it happens to them, but also, through them, it feels the ones that they touch the first ones with which it is immediately in contact."[16]

Leibniz characterises this type of relationship of all bodies with all bodies, quoting Hippocrates, as *Sympnoia panta* (*everything is in concordance, accordance*).

---

[16] *Monadology* § 61; GP VI, 617.

In another text from 1716, 300 years ago, Leibniz makes reference to Hippocrates and *Sympnoia panta*: "the universe is *Sympnoia panta*, as – according to Hippocrates – in the human body."[17]

The material world works just like our body, in unison and interacting one part with the others all the time. Because of this, *who everything knows* could understand the whole universe even in the smallest chunk of matter, thanks to the *harmony of things*, that works concurrently to what we can call the *harmony of minds*.

This phrase belongs to a discussion about Hippocrates and his thought. Here appears the question about how a substance only could perish by annihilation and Leibniz takes the words from Hippocrates: "A living being couldn't die unless that the whole universe would die." And the philosopher of Hannover point out "taken literally, I cannot fin words more appropriate to express my opinion."[18]

So interrelated are the livings than if one perishes, everything would perish with him.

As a quick conclusion, the Leibnizian philosophy is far away from any kind of solipsism and any idealism incapable of explain the material reality. On the contrary, from the *Sympnoia panta* the interaction between bodies is essential, constant and universal. Almost literally too, Leibniz could endorse the celebrated words of the poet John Donne:

> No man is an island,
> Entire of itself,
> Every man is a piece of the continent,
> A part of the main.
> If a clod be washed away by the sea,
> Europe is the less.
> As well as if a promontory were.
> As well as if a manor of thy friend's
> Or of thine own were:
> Any man's death diminishes me,
> Because I am involved in mankind,
> And therefore never send to know for whom the bell tolls;
> It tolls for thee.[19]

---

[17] Ibid., 627.
[18] Ibid., 624.
[19] John Donne: *Meditation* XVII.

Spinoza and Leibniz on Chimaeras and Other Unthinkable Things

J. Thomas Cook (Winter Park, FL)

In 1669, knowing very little of Spinoza, Leibniz numbered him among the Cartesians who had summarized the works of their master, but not added significantly to his discoveries.[1] When the *Tractatus Theologico-politicus* appeared (anonymously) in late 1669 or early 1670, Leibniz read it very soon and expressed respect for the unknown author and consternation at the work's intolerable lack of restraint.[2] By the spring of 1671 he knows for sure the identity of the author and thus knows that Spinoza is not just another unoriginal Cartesian. Presumably he then looked more attentively at the one other published work that was available at the time,[3] and in October of that year (1671) he wrote directly to Spinoza, explicitly addressing questions of optics, but hoping to instigate a more wide-ranging correspondence. In the mid-seventies he went to great lengths to find out what this reclusive Jew was thinking – pumping Tschirnhaus and Steno for information, copying out letters from Spinoza to Oldenburg, and going to visit the man himself in the Hague. By the time of these visits in late 1676 he had gained a pretty thorough understanding of Spinoza's position, and when the *Opera Posthuma* appeared in 1678 he

---

[1] A II, 1, 15 – translated: G. W. Leibniz: *Philosophical Papers and Letters*, ed. by Leroy E. Loemker, Dordrecht 1976, p. 94. Cited and discussed in E. M. Curley: "Homo Audax: Leibniz, Oldenburg and the Tractatus Theologico-politicus", in: Ingrid Marchlewitz/Albert Heinekamp (eds.): *Leibniz' Auseinandersetzung mit Vorgängern und Zeitgenossen (= Studia Leibnitiana, Supplementa XXVII)*, Stuttgart 1990, S. 277f.

[2] Goldenbaum's discovery of marginalia in Leibniz's hand in the Boineburg copy of the *Tractatus Theologico-politicus* settles the question of whether Leibniz read the work with care soon after its publication. She argues (with Rüdiger Otto: *Studia zur Spinozarezeption in Deutschland im 18. Jahrhundert (= Europäische Hochschulschriften, Reihe 23, Theologie*, p. 451), Frankfurt a. M. 1994. and with Curley: "Homo Audax") that he did so sometime in the early fall of 1670. See Ursula Goldenbaum: "Die *Commentatiuncula de judice* als Leibnizens erste philosophische Auseinandersetzung mit Spinoza" in: Martin Fontius/Hartmut Rudolph/Gary Smith (eds.): *Labora Diligenter: Potsdamer Arbeitstagung zur Leibnizforschung vom 4. bis 6. Juli 1996 (= Studia Leibnitiana, Sonderhefte 29)*, Stuttgart 1999, especially pp. 95–97. The phrase "intolerably unrestrained" comes from Leibniz's letter to Thomasius (A II, 1, 66), cited by all three of these scholars.

[3] The only work then published under Spinoza's name was the geometrical demonstration of Descartes' Principles (*PPC*) from 1663. The body of this work is a presentation of Descartes' ideas, but the preface by Ludwig Meyer and the Appendix entitled *Cogitata Metaphysica* reveal more of Spinoza's own views.

read them eagerly. We know that he was intrigued and also repelled by Spinoza's ideas – and that the interest as well as the repulsion were in part a result of his recognition that the subterranean similarities between their views ran too close for comfort.[4]

It is difficult to trace in any detail the development of specific ideas as Leibniz worked his way through various issues in this period. But I think that in some cases we can learn something about how his views fit together and how they might have arisen by looking at them in light of positions held by another thinker with whom he was in intensive (if sporadic) intellectual interaction. In this paper I will try to illustrate this claim by looking at a constellation of views developed during this period of encounter with Spinoza. I will use, as a conceptual thread, the chimaera.

The chimaera is a creature often sighted in the bestiary of early modern philosophy. The original of the species was a fire-breathing monster of Greek mythology with a lion's head, a goat's body and a serpent's tail. His later descendants are a less dramatic, but more diverse lot – they often figure prominently in discussions among metaphysicians of the 17th century.

Often the term "chimaera" was used to refer to a "mere wild fancy" as the *OED* puts it. In more careful writing the usage usually referred to something not only unreal, but having an incongruous composition as did the fabled monster. In the course of the 17th century the term began to take on a more specific technical meaning, referring to those things (if "things" is the right word) whose very nature or essence involves a contradiction. In this carefully defined sense, the chimaera provides an interesting angle of approach for a juxtaposition of Spinoza and Leibniz, for it lives at the place where logic, cognition, modality and metaphysics come together.

1. Spinoza on the Unthinkable

In *Ethics* 2P7 Spinoza makes the famous claim that the order and connection of ideas is the same as the order and connection of things. Certain things, in

---

[4] This is an area that has been well-studied over a long period of time. See Ludwig Stein: *Leibniz und Spinoza*, Berlin 1890 and Georges Friedman: *Leibniz et Spinoza*, Paris 1946. In addition see Curley: "Homo Audax", Goldenbaum: "Die *Commentatiuncula*", Mark Kulstad: "Leibniz, Spinoza and Tschirnhaus: Metaphysics a Trois, 1675–1676", in: Olli Koistinen/John Biro (eds.): *Spinoza: Metaphysical Themes*, Oxford 2002, Mogens Lærke: *Leibniz lecteur de Spinoza. La genèse d'une opposition complexe*, Paris 2008.

so far as they cannot exist in extended reality, can also not be the objects (*ideata*) of ideas. If the order of things does not include a certain item, neither will the order of thinking include the idea thereof.

This is Spinoza's mature statement, but we find in his earlier works signs of his wrestling with the relationship between what can be and what can be thought. In the *Cogitata Metaphysica*, published in 1663, and in the *Tractatus de Intellectus Emendatione* – an unfinished work first published after his death, but written much earlier – we find him addressing these themes. Let us follow for a moment the presentation of the issues as they appear in these early works.

There are certain things which, by their very nature, cannot exist. Better: there are certain verbal descriptions which, as a matter of logic, cannot be instantiated. In the *Cogitata Metaphysica* Spinoza refers to these as chimaeras; a square circle is his favorite example. Spinoza holds that just as such a putative essence could not be instantiated as an extended thing, nor can it be instantiated in thought – there cannot be an idea of it. We cannot conceive of such a thing. We cannot even imagine such a thing.[5]

So too with other putative items and states of affairs which are, for similar reasons of internal contradiction, impossible. If their chimaeric verbal descriptions cannot be instantiated, there cannot be ideas of them, and we cannot conceive or imagine them. This is plausible enough when the topic of conversation is square circles, or indeed anything from the realm of, say, logic or mathematics. But logic and mathematics are special cases in that one might hold that necessity and impossibility exhaust the modal alternatives in these fields.

Spinoza is notoriously quick to use geometrical examples to explain things that seem to us far removed from geometry. And it is pretty clear that he thinks that necessity and impossibility are the only real modal alternatives *tout court*.[6] Still, within the restrictions imposed by his views on modality, he does distinguish between those things that are impossible due to their own self-contradictory essences (i.e. chimaeras) and those that are impossible by virtue of the fact that their existence does not follow in the causal order of

---

[5] *Cogitata Metaphysica* I, 241. Parenthetical page references are in standard form for the Gebhardt edition. For the *Tractatus de Intellectus Emendatione* and *Ethics* I am using Curley's translations throughout. E. M Curley (ed. and trans.): *The Collected Works of Spinoza*, Vol. I, Princeton 1985.

[6] This issue will of course be at the focus of Leibniz's disagreement with Spinoza (see section 4 below).

nature. The cases are different, metaphysically, and that difference seems to be marked by a psychological difference.[7] In the case of a chimaera, as noted above, not only can we not conceive of the thing, but we cannot even imagine it. In the cases of those things whose essences are not internally self-contradictory but which are impossible due to the absence of the causes requisite for their existence, it seems as if we *are* capable of imagining them even though their existence is, strictly speaking, impossible.

If, as Spinoza directly says, those things that do not exist as a result of the absence of their causal antecedents are just as impossible as those which do not exist because of their self-contradictory essences, why would we be able to imagine the one, but not the other? The answer, in these early works, seems to be that in the case of the chimaera the impossibility is hard to miss. You think "round," you think "square," and you can't think them together. The impossibility is obvious. In the case of those things whose impossibility is a causal matter, only an in-depth knowledge of the causal order would reveal the impossibility. The upshot would seem to be that to the extent that we understand the causal order we would be unable to imagine those things that are in fact causally impossible. And if indeed what is false for Spinoza is impossible, it would seem that if we knew enough, we would be unable to imagine what is false. But empirically/experientially this seems like an odd view.

This is actually a deep and interesting problem in Spinoza's thought – and one that I am not sure he ever fully resolved to his satisfaction. The *Tractatus de Intellectus Emendatione* devotes a number of pages to the issue of how (and whether) we can feign that which is contrary to what we know to be true.[8] As we might expect, Spinoza begins here with things whose essences either preclude or necessitate their existence, and argues that we cannot feign what we know to be false or impossible in cases such as these.[9] The transition from clearly chimaeric cases of this sort – that deal with what we would call purely conceptual truths – to more empirical matters comes easily to Spinoza. Within one sentence he goes from our inability to feign God's non-existence to our inability to feign "an elephant that passes through the eye of a needle." One might object that we can feign an elephant passing through the eye of a needle – indeed, perhaps my reader conjured up a mental image of just such a thing when she read these words. But I think that Spinoza would hold that given the fact that elephants are huge and the eyes of needles are tiny, your putative

---

[7] *Tractatus de Intellectus Emendatione*, II, 19.
[8] Ibid., 19–25.
[9] Ibid., 20, 8–14.

mental image of an elephant passing through the eye of a needle is either not an image of an elephant or not an image of a needle. We can say the words. We can conjure up images of two things and feign that they are conjoined. We can put the words together; but according to Spinoza we cannot feign something that we know to be impossible.

In the *Cogitata Metaphysica* Spinoza directly claims that an elephant passing through the eye of a needle is more like a chimaera – more like an internally inconsistent description of an individual that cannot be instantiated – than like something whose non-existence is a result of the lack of a cause. His treatment of this is interesting, I think. He is discussing the fact that there are some things whose essences we can clearly and distinctly conceive, but which do not, cannot and will not exist because the causal conditions for their existence are not fulfilled. And he says,

> "[…] if we were to conceive the entire order of nature, we should find that many of these things […] could in no way exist. For we should find that the existence of such things in nature is just as much impossible as we now see it to be impossible that an elephant should pass through the eye of a needle, although we can clearly perceive the nature of both of these. Hence the existence of those things would be only a chimaera, which we could neither imagine nor understand."[10]

In general, Spinoza's discussion in the *Tractatus de Intellectus Emendatione* supports the view that understanding and feigning are at odds

> "[…] [T]he less men know nature, the more easily they can feign many things, such as, that trees speak, that men are changed in a moment into stones and springs." An important summary statement: "From this it follows that if there is a God, or something omniscient, he can feign nothing at all […]."[11]

Back to Leibniz – As we noted above, in the second half of 1670's Leibniz was thinking about logic and modality as he struggled with difficult doctrines of traditional theology. He was developing revolutionary ideas in mathematics as he sought to avoid a necessitarian metaphysical view. As he worked through these issues he was well aware of the danger of inadvertently falling into self-contradiction – of putting words together and thinking that one is thinking about something, when in fact that putative something is chimaeric. This concern appears with some frequency in the writings of this period, quite

---

[10] *Cogitata Metaphysica*, Chap. 3.
[11] *Tractatus de Intellectus Emendatione*, II, 20, 8.

often in connection with the name or the ideas of Spinoza. We will focus on three distinct areas. In the first of these, the two philosophers are in agreement. In the second and third, however, their differences clearly emerge. I hope that the juxtaposition of these thinkers, using chimaeras as a connecting conceptual thread, may highlight the roots of their divergence at the deepest levels of their thought.

2. The Ontological Argument

Leibniz was a proponent of the ontological proof of the existence of God. But he thought that previous thinkers had been lacking, for they left out a crucial step. As Leibniz tells it (for example, in the *Discourse on Metaphysics*),

> "They say that I must have an idea of God or a perfect being, since I think of such a being, and one cannot think without an idea."[12]

This is the step with which Leibniz takes issue, for the fact that we "think of" something does not mean that we have an idea of it. Leibniz points out cases in which we "think of" something (better: we think that we are thinking of something), but in fact are thinking of "impossible chimaeras," and hence have no idea at all. For example, the phrase "the greatest number" sounds intelligible, but in fact we can have no idea of the greatest number, for such an idea is self-contradictory – an impossible chimaera.

Of course if an idea is self-contradictory, it cannot serve as a premise for a useful argument. Thus, if the ontological proof is to succeed, it must be shown that God or the most perfect being is not a chimaera. Leibniz sought to show just that in 1676 in a passage that we know under the title "Quod Ens Perfectissimum existit." The proof itself is interesting, but we will not go into it here. More important for our purposes is the note at the end of the proof: "I showed this argument to Mr. Spinoza when I was at The Hague, and he thought it to be sound."[13]

We do not know as much as we would like to about the content of the face-to-face discussions between these two philosophers, so it is helpful to

---

[12] Gottfried Wilhelm Leibniz: *Philosophical Essays*, ed. and transl. by Roger Ariew and Dan Garber, Indianapolis 1989, p. 56.
[13] Gottfried Wilhelm Leibniz: *De Summa Rerum: Metaphysical Papers, 1675–1676*, ed. and trans. by G. H. R. Parkinson, New Haven 1992, p. 103.

know that they spent time on the question of whether the *ens perfectissimum* is a chimaera. I do not find this surprising, for by focusing on the "most perfect being" Leibniz could secure some agreement from Spinoza, for after all, two great rationalists were discussing, at a highly abstract level, the "god of the philosophers." But their agreement about the non-chimaerical character of the *ens perfectissimum* conceals vast disagreement at other levels. For of course Leibniz embraced not only the God of the philosophers, but also the Christian God of Scripture. And he had reason to know that Spinoza considered this God chimaerical in the extreme.

3. The Mysteries, Parrots and Chimaeras

Leibniz recognized the Mysteries as definitive of the Christian faith. In order to defend that faith he had to defend the Mysteries and the Christians' belief in those Mysteries. This is of course inherently difficult since the Mysteries are, in their very nature, not amenable to rational analysis. As Goldenbaum has shown in interesting detail[14], Leibniz had at least three strategies for defending the Mysteries against the attacks of various critics. Of greatest interest to us here is one of these strategies, a direct response to a challenge posed by Spinoza's *Tractatus Theologico-politicus*.

As mentioned above, Leibniz was impressed with the erudition of the *Tractatus Theologico-politicus* and with the author's extensive knowledge of the Hebrew language. Leibniz was sensitive to the fact that due to linguistic and historical factors we might not always have a clear understanding of the meaning of the terms in which the articles of faith are expressed. In the case of the Mysteries the difficulty is even greater due to the inherently mysterious character of the claims themselves. How are we to embrace these articles in faith if we manifestly do not understand them? How can we believe them if we do not know what we are believing?

---

[14] See especially Ursula. Goldenbaum: "Leibniz's Three Strategies for Defending Christian Mysteries", in: *American Catholic Philosophical Quarterly* 76 (Fall 2002). Goldenbaum acknowledges the work of M. Dascal for its in-depth consideration of the epistemological difficulties of the mysteries. See Marcelo. Dascal: "Reason and the Mysteries of Faith: Leibniz on the Meaning of Religious Discourse", in: Id.: *Leibniz: Language, Signs and Thought – A Collection of Essays,* Amsterdam 1987.

In the *Tractatus Theologico-politicus* Spinoza is very direct in his critique of the attempt by theologians to take passages in scripture that we cannot understand and to elevate them into divine Mysteries.

> "Now if anyone says that, while there is no need to understand God's attributes, there is a plain duty to believe them straightforwardly without proof, he is plainly talking nonsense [...] [W]hen they merely repeat what they have heard of such matters, this is no more relevant to, or indicative of their mind than the words of a parrot or a puppet [*automaton*] speaking without meaning or sense."[15]

The young Leibniz was definitely troubled by this line of argument. Soon after reading the *Tractatus* he composed a paper in which he addresses these issues in some detail.[16] In this context he says:

> "Since one has to have faith not in the words but in their meanings, it is not enough for us to believe that the person who uttered the sentence "this is my body" told the truth unless we know also what he said. However we do not know what he said if we have only the words and ignore their meaning."[17]

But of course Leibniz is in a bind here, for especially with regard to the Mysteries we cannot have a clear understanding of what the words mean. Leibniz pronounces this a "very hard problem" (*durissimus nodus*). Lest his reader be left with the impression that one can believe the words articulating the Mystery without having any idea of just what one is believing, Leibniz takes up Spinoza's challenge in the next paragraph (without mentioning Spinoza's name):

> "However, the mind should not be exposed barely [nude] to the words like a parrot. It should rather perceive some meaning, albeit general and confused or – so to speak – disjunctive, as is the perception by a peasant or any other common person of every theoretical matter."[18]

---

[15] *Tractatus Theologico-politicus* Chapter 13 from Shirley's translation, quoted in Goldenbaum: "Leibniz's Three Strategies."
[16] *Commentatiuncula de Judice controversiarum*. The following passages come from Dascal's translations (Dascal: "Reason and the Mysteries of Faith").
[17] Dascal (trans.): *Commentatiuncula* #9–13, in: Dascal: "Reason and the Mysteries of Faith," p. 99.
[18] Dascal (trans.): *Commentatiuncula #22*, in: Dascal: "Reason and the Mysteries of Faith," p. 103.

So when we hear or speak the words that articulate the mysteries of the faith, we can have a "general and confused or – so to speak – disjunctive" sense of what is meant by the words. And that is sufficient for us to believe in the truth of the words – even though we do not understand clearly what the words mean. After all, Leibniz says,

> "[…] the faith of the majority of Christians consists in and has always consisted in the approval [approbatio] of propositions that are not understood."[19]

But it is hard to believe that Leibniz was really satisfied by this line of argument. He wants to deny that we are like a parrot, because the parrot has the words with no thought or idea at all. Leibniz is suggesting that with regard to the Christian mysteries we have the words and also some not-very-clearly perceived notions about the meaning of those words. In this sense it might seem that we are one step up from the parrot, but we are uncomfortably close to the position of those who speak of the greatest number or the fastest motion. How do we know that we are not just putting words together and thinking that they have some significance – when in fact they are chimaeras, mere words which seem to express meaningful content only because we have not analyzed or understood the meanings of the terms?

Spinoza holds that when we do not understand some claim about the divine, we should admit that we do not understand and withhold judgment on the truth or falsity of the claim. For example, when writing about "the things certain Churches say about Christ" he says: "[…] I freely confess that I do not understand them."[20] In the *Tractatus Theologico-politicus* Spinoza does not tell the reader exactly what doctrines he fails to understand. However, at the end of a later letter to Oldenburg (Letter 73), he reveals which doctrines he has in mind. In response to a question from Oldenburg about his views on Christ, Spinoza mentions the doctrine of the Incarnation – the view that in Christ God assumed a human nature. He says:

> "Indeed, to confess the truth, [those who teach this] seem to me to speak no less absurdly than someone would who said to me that a circle had taken on the nature of a square […]."[21]

---

[19] Dascal (trans.): *Commentatiuncula #30*, in: Dascal: "Reason and the Mysteries of Faith," p. 103.
[20] Baruch Spinoza: *Theological-Political Treatise*, ed. and transl. by Samuel Shirley, Indianapolis ²2001, p. 14.
[21] Id.: *The Letters*, ed. and transl. by Samuel Shirley, Indianapolis 1995, p. 333 (G IV, 309).

In short, Spinoza holds that the basic tenet of Christianity – God-made-man in Christ – is a chimaera. By implication he claims that this doctrine cannot be an intelligible object of thought – indeed, that one who speaks in this way puts words together but expresses no idea at all.[22]

When Leibniz wrote the *Commentatiuncula*, Letter 73 had not been written. But from his reading of the *Cogitata Metaphysica* and the *Tractatus Theologico-politicus* he might have guessed that Spinoza would hold certain of the Mysteries to be among those chimaeric notions that cannot be meaningfully thought (and that thus, by extension, cannot be believed). By the time they met in The Hague in 1676, Leibniz knew much more about Spinoza's systematic views and had made a copy of Letter 73. Presumably the in-person discussions between these two remained at the level of the ontological argument, but even as Leibniz read aloud his proof of the intelligibility of the *ens perfectissimum* he knew that Spinoza thought certain of his Christian religious convictions to be unthinkable.

4. Contingency, Impossibility and the Unthinkable

In a passage written in the late 1680's Leibniz tells us that he was once very close to the precipice of a full-blown necessitarian view:

> "When I considered that nothing happens by chance or by accident [...], that fortune distinguished from fate is an empty name, and that no thing exists unless its own particular conditions (*requisitis*) are present (conditions from whose joint presence it follows, in turn, that the thing exists), I was very close to the view of those who think that everything is absolutely necessary [...]."[23]

If we look at the view that he says he was "close to" we see a view very close to Spinoza's. In Chapter 3 of the *Cogitata Metaphysica*, entitled "Concerning What is Necessary, Impossible, Possible and Contingent" – the same chapter that includes the account of chimaeras discussed above – Spinoza embraces in no uncertain terms a view according to which indeed "everything is absolutely necessary."

---

[22] Curley's discussion of this exchange (and of Leibniz's response) is especially helpful. Cf. Curley: "Homo Audax".
[23] G. W. Leibniz: *Philosophical Essays*, p. 94.

It seems that the time that Leibniz was most "close to" this view was in the late 1660's. In a famous letter to Wedderkopf from 1670 we find him embracing remarkably necessitarian views.

> "But," he tells us (again looking back from the late 1680's), "the consideration of possibles, which are not, were not and will not be, brought me back from this precipice. For if there are certain possibles that never exist, then the things that exist, at any rate, are not always necessary, for otherwise it would be impossible for others to exist in their place, and thus everything that never exists would be impossible."[24]

Sometime in the early 1670's Leibniz developed his account of possibles that (he thinks) provides him with room for contingency in the rationally ordered universe.

I have suggested that after discovering the identity of the author of the *Tractatus Theologico-politicus* in early 1671, Leibniz would have looked back with greater care at the *Cogitata Metaphysica* – the one other available published work of Spinoza. There he would have discovered a defense of necessitarianism and a hard-nosed claim that our belief in contingency and possibility are a result only of our ignorance. I think that Leibniz saw Spinoza's position as rationally appealing, but ultimately unacceptable for moral and religious reasons. Still we can see Spinoza's discussion as suggesting a framework within which Leibniz could develop his counter-argument.

Spinoza and Leibniz agree that some things are necessary or impossible simply by virtue of their own essences. There is no disagreement here.

Then there are those things (most things) whose essences neither entail existence nor involve a contradiction. We can conceive their essences clearly and distinctly without existence. But both Leibniz and Spinoza agree that we must look beyond the individual to the rest of the world, for it may be that the existence of the individual in question is ruled out, not by any internal contradiction within its own essence, but by its incompatibility with other existent things. Our philosophers agree on this point as well.

When Spinoza looks beyond the individual thing's essence in order to ascertain whether that individual is necessary or impossible, he looks to the rest of the causal order. If the causal prerequisites are present, then the existence of the thing in question is a necessary consequence of the fulfillment of those causal conditions and the thing exists necessarily. If the causes are not present, the existence of the thing is impossible. And if the existence of the

---

[24] Ibid.

thing is impossible, only our ignorance of the causal order could lead us to think it possible.

In Spinoza's discussion thus far the order of nature has been, so to speak, the last word. Nothing has been said as yet about the divine author and creator of that great causal order. One might think that contingency could be reintroduced by considering the whole order of nature to be contingent upon the decrees of its creator. Then the existence of individual things in nature would be only conditionally necessary – conditional upon God's having created just this natural order with just these laws. Since there are other natural orders that God might have created, this one is not absolutely necessary.

This is of course exactly the move that Leibniz makes. He grants that the rest of nature can preclude or necessitate the existence of an individual thing (via the laws of nature and the constraints of compossibility), but holds that there are many internally consistent complete orders of nature – many possible worlds. Since these are internally consistent, they are in themselves possible, but in fact only one of them will be actualized. Still these unactualized worlds are not internally self-contradictory – not chimaeras.

Spinoza does not want to countenance this view of things. This is not surprising to those of us who are familiar with his mature metaphysics, for we know that in the end he does not envision God as a creator separate from and prior to His creation. In the context of the *Cogitata Metaphysica*, though, he speaks in more traditional terms about the creator and his divine decrees. But he avoids introducing contingency into the order of things by arguing that God's decree could not have been other than it was:

> "[...] since in God there is no inconstancy or change, he must have decreed from eternity that he would produce those things which he now produces...Nor can we say that those things are contingent because God could have decreed otherwise. For since in eternity there is no when, nor before, nor after, nor any other affection of time, it follows that God never existed before those decrees so that he could decree otherwise."[25]

In this way Spinoza avoids introducing contingency at the level of God's choice.

Leibniz maintains that the fact that God exercises choice in the creation preserves contingency. The possible worlds remain possible so long as God's choice is treated as if it were indeterminate. But of course ultimately Leibniz

---

[25] *Cogitata Metaphysica* I 243.

grants that God's choice is not indeterminate, for God's nature is not indeterminate. God's nature is good and he will thus choose the good. But with the granting of this point Leibniz's position threatens to collapse again into Spinoza's necessitarian view. We find this issue in the famous letter to Wedderkopf in May of 1671,[26] and we find him still struggling with this question in the early 1680's in the following passage:

> "[...] things remain possible, even if God does not choose them. Indeed, even if God does not will something to exist, it is still possible for it to exist, since, by its nature it could exist if God were to will it to exist. "But God cannot will it to exist." I concede this, yet, such a thing remains possible in its nature, even if it is not possible with respect to the divine will, since we have defined as in its nature possible anything that, in itself, implies no contradiction, even though its coexistence with God can in some way be said to imply a contradiction.[27]

The final sentence in this passage provides the proponent of Spinozistic necessitarianism with powerful support against Leibniz. Given that God's existence is necessary, if something's "coexistence with God can in some way be said to imply a contradiction," that thing's existence would seem to be impossible. A few years later, in recounting his correspondence with Arnauld, Leibniz notes,

> "[...] Arnauld testifies that he is strongly led to think that these purely possible substances are only chimaeras. I do not wish to dispute this, but I hope that, in spite of this, he will grant me what I need."[28]

Conclusion

Using the chimaera as a conceptual thread I have tried to show that in three specific areas Leibniz was influenced by Spinoza's thought and that he developed his thinking in dialogue and in juxtaposition with the latter's positions. I do not claim that Leibniz was a Spinozist – on the contrary, in many ways his views are quite opposed to those of Spinoza. But the influence of Spinoza is perhaps most evident precisely there where their ways of thinking diverge.

---

[26] Adams has an excellent discussion of this letter and its necessitarian implications. Robert M. Adams: *Leibniz: Determinist, Theist, Idealist*, Oxford 1994, p. 10.
[27] G. W. Leibniz: *Philosophical Essays*, pp. 20f.
[28] Ibid., p. 75.

Leibniz did not believe that Christians reciting the creed were professing belief in chimaeras and thus speaking, like parrots, without any idea attached to their words. But he saw that the Christian mysteries border on chimaeric unintelligibility and that this is a troubling issue that needs to be addressed. Leibniz did not believe that possible worlds and a benevolent God had the same epistemological and ontological status as round squares, but he saw this as an important problem to which he had to respond.[29]

---

[29] An earlier version of this paper was published (in Turkish) as Sebahattin Çevikbaş: "Spinoza Ve Leibniz' in Kaymera ve Diğer Akıl Almaz Şeyler Hakkındaki Fikirleri", in: *Felsefe Tartışmaları* 48 (2013).

On the Leibnizian Principle of Continuity[*]

Sorin Costreie (Bucharest)

The main purpose of this article is the examination of the fundamental role played by the principle of continuity in founding the relationship between metaphysics, mathematics and physics. In particular, I intend to explore the possible solution to the following paradox in Leibniz: on the one hand, he considers mathematical truths as analytic and necessary and, on the other hand, he considers mathematical objects such as figures in geometry, numbers in arithmetic and infinitesimals in mathematical analysis as ideal fictional entities. One could thus wonder how some fictional entities could be regulated by necessary laws. Pârvu suggests an approach that may solve this paradox:

> "The presence of the law of continuity in nature allows for the introduction of continuous geometrical dimensions, which could take the smallest possible values – thus becoming smaller than any given dimension. […] The principle of continuity represents that *fundamentum in re* of fictions such as the infinitesimal and the imaginary numbers."[1]

This is an important suggestion that emerges from the fact that the solution to the paradox should be found during the examination of the metaphysical function of the principle of continuity in the Leibnizian system. What is this principle then and how can it offer the solution to the problem raised above? In the preface to his *Essays on Theodicy*, Leibniz is explicit about this:

> "There are two famous labyrinths where our reason very often goes astray: one concerns the great question of the Free and the Necessary, above all in the production and the origin of Evil; the other consists in the discussion of continuity and of the indivisibles which appear to be the elements thereof, and where the consideration of the infinite must enter in. The first perplexes almost all the human race, the other exercises philosophers only."[2]

---

[*] This article is part of the research project PN-II-RU-TE-2014-4-2522 (*Philosophy between Mathematical Method and Experiment: The Berlin Academy*) funded by UEFISCDI.
[1] Ilie Pârvu: *Infinitul (The Infinite)*, Bucharest 2000, p. 103.
[2] Gottfried Wilhelm Leibniz: *Essays on Theodicy: On Divine Goodness, Human Freedom and the Origin of Evil,* hereafter Leibniz: *Theodicy*, ed. with an Introd. by Austin Farrer, transl. by E. M. Huggard from C. J. Gerhardt's Edition of the *Collected Philosophical Works, 1875–90*, Bibliobazaar 1985, "Preface", p. 55

The trial of the second labyrinth is a fundamental one since somewhere else[3] Leibniz would maintain that "nobody could found a truly solid metaphysics unless he had passed through this labyrinth." What is then, more precisely, this *labyrinth of the continuum*?

A continuous quantity is something ideal that is applied to the possibles and the actuals in as much as they are possible. Thus, on the one hand, a continuum involves indeterminate parts but, on the other hand, there is nothing indefinite in the actuals, in which any division that can be done is actually done. The actuals are composed as a number is composed of units, the ideals are composed as a number is composed of fractions; the parts are actual in a real whole, but they are not actual in an ideal one. We nevertheless fail to differentiate the ideal and the real substances when we look for actual parts in the order of the possibles and for indeterminate parts in conglomerates of actuals. We are thus caught within the labyrinth of the continuum and in unexplainable contradictions.[4]

In other words, for Leibniz, there are both real and ideal entities in the realm of existence. The real entities are discrete and composed – for them the parts preceding the whole; the ideal entities are continuous and unitary – for them the whole preceding the parts.[5] One should note that these real entities are the physical bodies, the "actuals" Leibniz referred to, and not the monads or the individual substances, which are unitary and, as such, not composed, themselves being part of the composition of the universe as fundamental atoms of the real world. The labyrinth of the continuum thus creates the following paradox: *any finite part of matter is infinitely decomposable*. The problem is clearly observed by Johann Bernoulli, who, in a letter from August 1698, writes to Leibniz: 'You admit that any part of matter is actually divided into

---

[3] GM VII, 326.
[4] GP III, 123; GP II, 282 (my translation).
[5] In his correspondence with Volder, Leibniz writes: 'In reality, matter is not continuous, but discrete, actually infinitely divided, – although no assignable portion of space lacks matter. In its turn, space as well as time, is not substantial, but ideal and consists of possibilities, that is in the order of the coexistents in as much as they are possible. Thus, there are no divisions in it besides those determined by our spirit and the part is posterior to the whole. On the contrary, in the real things, the units are anterior to the set they form and the sets only exist through their units. (The same is applicable in relation to changes, which, in reality, are not continuous.)' Gottfried Wilhelm Leibniz: *Opere Filosofice (Philosophical Works)*, vol. 1, transl. Constantin Floru, introductory study Dan Bădărău, Bucharest 1972, p. 418.

an infinity of parts, but, by that, you reject the fact that any of these parts can be infinitely small.'[6]

I have already presented elsewhere[7] one Leibnizian solution to the problem of *finite matter that is infinitely decomposable*. Only briefly here, Leibniz's solution was to offer a mathematical model (*spheres within spheres*) that could explain the plenitude of the universe due to the fact that there is an infinite countless number of *worlds within worlds*: the universe we know is one of the infinite universes that infinitely coexist one within the other. The mathematical model thus offers intelligibility to the world and makes it comprehensible for our finite minds. Coming back to our initial problem (*necessary laws for fictional objects*), the question here is whether one could find a similar mathematical solution for that. The answer is affirmative and the solution is indeed very similar to the one mentioned above – in as much as mathematics continues to be considered here the link that gives intelligibility to the connection between the world of metaphysical objects (the monads) and the world of physical objects (the material substances). In the case of the *infinitely decomposable matter*, the mathematical model is given by the fact that among three tangent spheres there is always a fourth one that is tangent to the initial spheres and this continues *ad infinitum*. Here one could continue to speculate on the fundamental aspect in mathematics of making the world intelligible while noticing that this fictional character of the mathematical objects does not also involve the property of being arbitrary. All entities comply with the same fundamental laws, the solution being to detect the metaphysical law that could entail constraints for the mathematical objects so that they become compatible and applicable to the physical world. The ideal candidate in this case is obviously the *continuity*.

The principle or *the law of continuity* can be found in Leibniz in a multitude of forms and contexts. The common set phrase would be that "nature makes no leaps" (*natura non saltum facit*).[8] The technical formula would be offered by the fact that 'a singularity extends over a sequence of ordinal points until it touches the vicinity of other singularity.' The crucial importance of the principle of continuity is ensured by the fact that it is a 'principle of general

---

[6] GM III, 529 (my translation).
[7] Valentin-Sorin Costreie: "Leibniz on Void and Matter", in: Dana Jalobeanu/Peter Anstey (eds.): *Vanishing Matter and the Laws of Motion. Descartes and Beyond*, London 2011.
[8] GP V, 49.

order,"⁹ by that being meant that it has not only a limited, local applicability, but also a general one, as one of the fundamental principles that found the universe in its entirety. The principle of the continuum is a fundamental one that makes nature intelligible and harmonious. This is explicitly asserted in Leibniz's correspondence with Varignon, a French mathematician 'converted' to the Leibnizian infinitesimal calculus:

> "[T]his principle (of continuity) is general and valid not only in geometry, but also in physics. [...] the universality of this principle in geometry has recently made me think that he cannot but occur in physics as well: because, in order to have regulation and order in nature, it is obviously necessary that the physical be in constant harmony with the geometrical; and this harmony would be contradicted if the physical were suddenly interrupted where geometry required continuity. In my view, on the basis of metaphysical foundations, everything is connected in the Universe, so that the present always contains the future within itself and no state of facts can be naturally explained otherwise but through the state that immediately preceded it. If this is denied, then the world would have gaps and that would contradict the wider principle of sufficient reason; such gaps would also compel us to make use of miracles or of pure hazard in explaining the phenomena."[10]

For Leibniz, the fundamental principle of the construction of his metaphysical system is the principle of sufficient reason (*nihil sine ratione*). As one can note in the quotation above, by rejecting the continuity of the world one would deny this fundamental principle – something that would be absolutely impossible for Leibniz. Lack of continuity would suppose the existence of gaps in the chain of existence, that is of inconceivable metaphysical gaps. These metaphysical gaps would imply the existence of vacuum, a fact that would contradict yet another two fundamental Leibnizian principles – the *vacuum* is denied both by the principle of plenitude (the entire universe is a *plenum*) and by the principle of identity (everything is identical only with itself).[11]

Being such a fundamental, universally applicable principle, it can also be used as a test or criterion for accepting or rejecting a theory. In view of the

---

[9] James E. McGuire: "'Labyrinthus continui': Leibniz on Substance, Activity, and Matter" (1976), in: Roger Stuart Woolhouse (ed.): *Gottfried Wilhelm Leibniz. Critical Assessments, Bd. III – Philosophy of Science, Logic, and Language,* London 1994, p. 289.
[10] Leibniz: *Opere Filosofice,* vol. 1, pp. 56f.
[11] In a portion of vacuum or of material void there can be conceived two identical portions, something that would contradict this fundamental principle, which is actually composed of two sub-principles: the principle of the identity of the undiscernibles and the principle of the undiscernibility of the identical.

principle of the continuum, Leibniz attacked and rejected Descartes' and Newton's physics. In the case of Descartes, the problem was constituted by the fact that we need infinitely divisible matter in order not to have gaps in the flow of the fluids – atomism was thus rejected.[12] In the case of Newton, the problem was the conceiving of gravitation as a force that acts at a distance, portions void of matter being thus necessary in an absolute space.[13]

This principle (continuity) has its origin in the *infinite* and is absolutely necessary in geometry, but it also acts in physics due to the supreme wisdom, the source of all things, who acts like a perfect geometrician, observing a harmony in which nothing else can be added. For that reason this principle is necessary as a test or criterion by which the errors of a wrong opinion can be directly and outwardly noticed even before a minute internal examination can be initiated. It can be formulated as follows:

> "When the difference between two instances of a given or supposed sequence can be diminished until it becomes smaller than any given quantity, the corresponding difference in what is looked for or in the results has also to be diminished; otherwise it becomes smaller than any other quantity. Or, in common terms, when two instances or data are continuously getting nearer each other so that at least one tends to become the other, it is necessary for their consequences or results (or for what is looked for) to undergo the same course of action. [Datis ordinatis etiam quaesita sunt ordinate.]"[14]

The principle, as we have already seen, is a general, metaphysical and thus universally applicable one. The inspiration behind this principle seems to come nevertheless from mathematics and two arguments can be presented in support of this assertion. The first is the mode in which continuity is conceived and formulated in the mathematical terms of quantity, point, sequence [...]. The second argument is historical – in the sense that Leibniz was the first to formulate this principle after he was required to clearly explain the metaphysical foundations on which his infinitesimal calculus was based. One should also add here that the idea of continuity was not a Leibnizian invention, but was borrowed from Aristotle.[15] Conceiving continuity in mathematical terms

---

[12] For details, see R. Arthur: "Leibniz on Continuity", in: *PSA: Proceedings of the Biennial Meeting of the Philosophy of Science Association* I (1996), pp. 107–115.
[13] For details, see Costreie: "Leibniz on Void".
[14] GP III, 52f. (my translation)
[15] Aristotle defined *continuity* as related to *contiguity* and the *infinite*; for details, see Gottfried Wilhelm Leibniz: *The Labyrinth of the Continuum. Writings on the Continuum Problem, 1672–1686*, ed. by R. T. Arthur, Yale 2001 and Adrian William Moore: *The Infinite*, London 1990.

and imposing it as a fundamental and universal metaphysical law seems to have been nevertheless Leibniz's true contribution.[16]

I admit that time, extension, movement and, generally, the continuum, in the manner they are discussed in mathematics, are only ideal things – that is, things that express possibilities, as numbers themselves do. [...] And, even if there are neither perfectly uniform changes, as the idea that mathematics gives us on movement requires, nor exact actual figures, as the ones described in geometry, actual phenomena of nature are nevertheless thus regulated and should be thus ordered that nothing could be found in them that may go against the law of continuity (which I introduced and which I first mentioned in Mr. Bayle's periodical, "News from the Republic of Letters") and against all the other exact rules of the mathematicians. On the contrary, things can only become intelligible through these rules, which are the only capable, together with those of harmony and perfection, procured by true metaphysics, of introducing us to the reasons and the views of the creator of all things. But the great number of infinite compositions makes us indeed finally lose our way and we are thus forced, in applying the rules of metaphysics and mathematics, to stop at physics; however, these applications never delude us.[17]

On the other hand, the fact that this metaphysical principle could be of mathematical inspiration should not surprise us since Leibniz himself confessed to the Marquees of l'Hospital, in a letter from 27 December 1694, that: 'all his metaphysics was mathematics.'[18] The principle itself, metaphysically speaking, cannot be used at all in pure mathematics or in the explanation of any specific natural phenomenon. In fact, such metaphysical considerations do nothing but 'obscure' the thought of the mathematician, who may want, in fact, only to demonstrate some theorem or another. Leibniz himself clearly maintained that one should not make mathematical analysis dependent on metaphysical controversies.[19] This becomes obvious in his correspondence with Arnauld:

---

[16] For a more detailed discussion regarding the evolution of the concept of continuity in the work of Leibniz, see Samuel Levey: "Matter and Two Concepts of Continuity in Leibniz", in: *Philosophical Studies* 94 (1999), pp. 81–118 and Timothy Crockett: "Continuity in Leibniz's Mature Metaphysics", in: *Philosophical Studies* 94 (1999), pp. 119–138.
[17] Leibniz: *Opere Filosofice,* vol. 1, p. 359..
[18] GP II, 255–262.
[19] GM IV, 91.

> "[I]t could even be said that there was no determined and precise figure in the bodies because of the actual subdivision of the parts. However, it is of no use to mention the unity, the notion or the substantial form of the bodies when particular phenomena of nature are to be explained. Likewise, it is of no use for geometricians to explain the difficulties raised by the *compositio continui* when they look for the solution of some problem or another."[20]

In mathematics, it is important to show that the infinitesimals are well founded and rigorously defined entities. An error in this case is infinitesimally small and thus inexistent.

> "[I] showed that it is enough for mathematicians, for the rigour of their demonstrations, to change the infinitely small dimensions with sufficiently small ones in order to prove that the error is smaller than any dimension that an adversary may try to establish and that, consequently, there is no assignable error so that, even if the exact small infinites, which express the limit of the decrease of the assignable values, would only be something like imaginary roots, they would not affect the infinitesimal calculus – of the differences and of the summations – that I proposed and that excellent mathematicians cultivated in such a useful manner; mistakes can only be made within this calculus when it is not understood or because of lack of attention because it contains its own demonstration in itself."[21]

The problem is to find out how to successfully apply the infinitesimal calculus in physics since we have there, as we have already seen, discrete quantities that, *prima facie*, do not comply with the law of continuity. The problem is difficult and requires an immediate solution. This solution will appear again under the metaphysical pressure of a fundamental principle: that of the predetermined universal harmony. There is a structural agreement between the two worlds, which are thus comprehensively coordinated. The main point of this continuous coordination is the double placement of the monads and of the natural phenomena in time. Time is itself ideal, entering the evolution of the universe as an order of successions. Any change has to be a continuous change. The universe evolves continuously and its movement is possible due to the universal principle of continuity, which regulates both the ontological realm of the monads and the phenomenal realm of the material substances. The link between them is, in this case, the mathematical continuity of the two realms itself – a continuity that is metaphysically supported by the Creator through the principle of predetermined harmony. Continuity is a necessary

---

[20] Leibniz: *Opere Filosofice*, vol. 1, p. 215.
[21] Ibid., p. 360.

requisitum, a *sine qua non* condition for temporality, movement, becoming. [...] It is interesting that we also find continuity in biology, linguistics or epistemology.

But, given the fact that the law of continuity requires that, when the essential determinations of a finite get nearer those of another finite, all the properties of the first also get gradually nearer the properties of the other finite, it necessarily happens that all the realms of the natural beings form a sole chain, in which different classes are connected as the rings of a chain are – so tightly connected among themselves that it is impossible for our senses or imagination to establish a fixed point in which one or another starts or ends; the inflexion and the direction reversal areas have to be blurred and they have to present features that can be reported in various neighbouring species.[22]

Languages, in general, as the oldest monuments of the people, which pre-date writing and the arts, are the best indicators of descendance and migration. For this reason, well-devised etymologies would deserve constant interest; but one should compare the languages of many peoples and should avoid too many leaps from one nation to a far remote one unless good reason can be found for that, a case in which intermediary peoples should always be considered as possible guarantees. In general, one should not count too much on etymologies unless numerous concomitant pieces of evidence can be found.[23]

Nothing can be done out of a sudden and one of my basic and best verified axioms is that *nature makes no leaps*:

> "[...] And all these things make us understand that noticeable perceptions are gradually born out of those that are too small to be noticed. To think otherwise means not to understand the immense subtlety of the things that contain the actual infinite always and everywhere."[24]

This last passage is very interesting and shows how Leibniz was considering the link between consciousness and perception. The idea is that, besides our

---

[22] Ibid., p. 58. It is already self-evident that, through such passages, Leibniz turns out to be a great precursor of Darwin – one who conceived all beings as related and situated on a gradual variation scale.

[23] Gottfried Wilhelm Leibniz: *Noi eseuri asupra intelectului omenesc* (= G. W. Leibniz: *New Essays on the Human Intellect*), transl. by Marius Tianu, introductory study by Mircea Flonta, Bucharest 2003 (hereafter Leibniz: *New Essays*), III (cap. 2, §1), p. 198.

[24] Leibniz: *New Essays*, pp. 7f.

conscious perceptions, we also have unconscious ones,[25] the difference between the two being one of degree. The difference between the conscious and the unconscious is given by a specific degree of continuous perceptual discrimination – something different from what we find in psychoanalysis, for instance, were we only consider different and insurmountable levels. It is important to observe that this continuous transition does not only mean a shift from one point to another, but also a shift from one state to another.

To sum up, the idea of this article was provided by a Leibnizian problem: how the ideal objects of mathematics can be regulated by necessary laws. The solution, as we have seen, is provided by the principle of continuity, which is the link and the guarantee of the (mathematical) connection between the metaphysical realm of individual substances (the monads) and the physical realm of the material substances (the physical bodies). This is possible due to the infinite goodness of the Creator, who conceived the two realms as being placed in an eternal universal harmony, which was predetermined before the creation of the world. The intelligibility of this harmonious world is provided by mathematics, the mathematical analysis offering the possibility of understanding the world in its becoming. But for this to be understood, dozens or even hundreds of years of debate and controversy had to pass since Leibniz's century was not yet ready for that:

The principle of continuity is thus beyond doubt for me and it could serve to establish numerous important truths of the true philosophy – the philosophy that, rising above the senses and the imagination, looks for the origin of the phenomena in the intellectual realms. I like to believe that I possess a few of the ideas belonging to this philosophy, but our century is not ready to receive them.[26]

---

[25] For details, see Larry M. Jorgensen: "The Principle of Continuity and Leibniz's Theory of Consciousness", in: *Journal of the History of Philosophy* 47/2 (2009), pp. 223–248.
[26] Leibniz: *Opere Filosofice*, vol. 1, p. 59.

Perspectivisme et Monadologie

Martine de Gaudemar (Paris)

Cet exposé (i) fait profit d'une lecture collective de la *Monadologie* effectuée au sein du Centre d'Études leibniziennes, où mon travail a porté plus particulièrement sur la redéfinition des esprits issue des nouveaux concepts de « machine de la nature » et de « monade dominante. »[1] Prolongeant un travail publié en 2005 par la revue *XVIIème siècle*[2] sous le titre « Perspectivisme et Relativisme chez Leibniz, » il se demande en quoi la constitution monadologique des êtres renouvelle la question du perspectivisme. Il constitue en même temps (ii) une première ébauche d'une étude comparative des perspectivismes leibnizien et amazonien, en vue d'un colloque sur la place de Leibniz dans l'anthropologie contemporaine. La notion de *perspectivisme* étant largement utilisée par l'anthropologie dans une référence souvent implicite et non travaillée à Leibniz, il faut éclairer ces notions.

Si la *perspective* construit une image de l'objet en fonction du point de vue de l'observateur, on appelle *perspectivistes* des philosophies qui articulent la représentation de la réalité à des « points de vue » particuliers voire singuliers. Le réel est à l'horizon d'une démarche exprimant une situation particulière. Il peut même être considéré comme l'objet d'une construction qu'on peut disqualifier comme subjective, voire dénoncer comme arbitraire : le perspectivisme est alors assimilé à un constructivisme sceptique.

Or la caractérisation de *perspectivisme* semble convenir particulièrement bien à la métaphysique de Leibniz qui pose l'être comme multiple, fait de substances individuelles qui sont autant de « points de vue » différents, à considérer un par un. C'est ce que la littérature anglophone appelle la *mirroring thesis*, thèse clairement énoncée dans le *Discours de Métaphysique*, art. XIV. Y aurait-il un changement notable dû à l'abandon de la notion de substance individuelle au profit d'une constitution monadologique de tout être ?

J'avais examiné en 2005 comment la thèse perspectiviste, corollaire immédiat de la théorie de la notion complète,[3] était une thèse non-relativiste, du

---

[1] Voir les différentes présentations aux congrès-Leibniz de Grenade (2014), de Paris (2014) et de Lyon (2016).
[2] Martine de Gaudemar : « Perspectivisme et relativisme chez Leibniz », in : *XVIIème siècle* 1/N° 226 (2005), pp. 111–134.
[3] Stefano di Bella: *The Science of the Individual : Leibniz's Ontology of Individual Substance*, Dordrecht 2005, p. 348 : « In the typical texts of eighties, he introduces the *mirroring thesis* as a quasi-immediate corollary to the complete concept theory. »

point de vue de la connaissance comme du point de vue de la conduite. Il faut aujourd'hui faire un pas de plus, dès lors que a) la théorie de la notion complète semble abandonnée ou au moins reléguée à l'arrière plan de la spéculation leibnizienne, et que b) la théorie des monades produit une nouvelle constitution de la nature, tant individuelle que commune. Ces deux nouveautés imposent de reprendre la question à nouveaux frais.

1. Avant la Monadologie

Mon article de 2005 s'appuyait d'abord sur les professions de foi leibniziennes autour de la conjugaison de l'unité et de la variation, puis sur la différence de statut entre les vérités de fait et les vérités de raison universelles inscrites en nous sous forme de virtualités. »

1. Les déclarations d'universelle similitude dans le fond, mais variée à l'infini à travers les manières et les degrés de perfection, sont résumées dans les énoncés populaires tels que « C'est partout comme ici, et toujours et partout comme chez nous. » L'universel de la variation ordonnée est inséparable de la thèse ontologique (*mirroring thesis*), selon laquelle l'univers est composé de substances individuelles qui sont autant de vues différentes prises par Dieu sur l'univers (DM XIV). Tous les phénomènes gardent un certain ordre, car les vues différentes forment entre elles un « système général des phénomènes. » En conséquence, ce perspectivisme ne conduit pas à dire que les perceptions et représentations sont subjectives et arbitraires, même si elles sont considérées comme « choses mentales. »[4]
2. L'article poursuivait avec la distinction des vérités de fait, *consciences* ou expériences immédiates, toutes différentes puisqu'exprimant des point des vues différents sur l'univers, et des vérités de raison, immuables, universelles, qui sont le point fixe sur lequel tout roule.[5] Ce point fixe permet d'accorder la variété des points de vue. La géométrie et la logique sont les mêmes pour toutes les substances individuelles, et fondent un accord possible entre des êtres raisonnables capables d'enchaîner des définitions, d'établir des liens de principe à conséquence, et de produire des connexions universellement valides. Les esprits retrouvent donc par leurs

---

[4] À Antoine Arnauld, 30 avril 1687 ; GP II, 91 ; A II, 2 N. 42.
[5] À l'Electrice Sophie, 1696 ; Grua, 379.

moyens cognitifs propres les connexions entre phénomènes et apparences que la thèse métaphysique d'un Dieu origine des substances individuelles permettait d'escompter. Le relativisme peut alors être pragmatiquement dénoncé[6] :

> « Au reste, il est vrai aussi que, pourvu que les phénomènes soient bien liés, il importe peu qu'on les appelle songes ou non, puisque l'expérience montre qu'on ne se trompe point dans les mesures qu'on prend sur les phénomènes, lorsqu'elles sont prises selon les vérités de raison. »

L'horizon d'universalité est toujours fermement dessiné. Le consensus vient pragmatiquement consacrer une possibilité de convergence fondée *a priori* sur l'universalité des vérités de raison.

L'affaire est plus délicate en matière de conduite morale. On peut légitimement se demander si les décisions et les analyses qui les précèdent ne sont pas dépendantes de la situation qu'elles concernent et du point de vue respectif de ceux qui y sont engagés : comment s'accorder sur une proposition de morale ou une décision collective quand on est juge ou accusé, ami ou ennemi, agresseur ou victime, propriétaire ou homme d'état ? L'analyse du précepte de « prendre la place d'autrui, » dépendant de la capacité réflexive, montrait qu'on peut ordonner la diversité des cas selon un ordre de variation, en faisant apparaître une structure intelligible rendant raison des différences observées entre les « points de vue. » Plus encore, on peut dans le leibnizianisme établir des critères pour hiérarchiser les préférables et démêler les cas perplexes.

La question est donc à présent de savoir si l'élaboration monadologique remet en cause ou transforme ce perspectivisme leibnizien.

Solidaire de la notion d' « organique » ou d'organicité,[7] la thèse monadologique conduit à reconsidérer (i) tant les rapports de l'âme et du corps que (ii) l'entr'expression des créatures, c'est-à-dire le rapport expressif de toutes les parties de la matière, ou « rapport général de toutes

---

[6] *Nouveaux Essais*, IV, 2, § 14 ; A VI, 6, 375.. Je souligne.
[7] Plusieurs auteurs l'ont reconnu. Par exemple Donald Rutherford : *Leibniz and the Rational Order of Nature*, Cambridge 1995, ch. 9: « Dynamics, Matter and Organisms », 229 : « Panorganicism emerges as an essential part of Leibniz's account of the harmonious order realized within the best of possible worlds. It is necessary to emphasize, however, that this doctrine is fully consistent with the theory of monads. According to the panorganicist picture, there is no part of matter that is not endowed with life : Either it is itself the body of an animated creature, or it is a collection of such creatures, each of whose bodies is in turn composed of smaller organic creatures. »

choses. » La thèse monadologique enveloppe un nouveau regard de Leibniz sur l'univers entier. Je l'examinerai sous quatre aspects, dont les deux premiers (phénoménisme et relativisme) sont étroitement solidaires.
3. La thèse monadologique semble *contribuer* à l'interprétation *phénoméniste* courante.
4. La thèse monadologique semble *aggraver* un *relativisme* de la multiplicité des points de vue. Ces deux premiers aspects sont le plus souvent associés, comme si le relativisme était la conséquence du phénoménisme.
5. La thèse monadologique induit un remaniement des rapports de l'âme et du corps : le *dualisme* de type cartésien s'en trouve *évincé*.
6. La thèse monadologique *souligne* la *continuité* et la communauté de nature entre les êtres vivants, les humains et les non-humains ne pouvant être séparés que par un degré de perfection (le degré de la raison). Tous les individus procèdent en effet de monades percevantes qui, grâce à une *monade dominante*, sont en connexion avec toutes les monades composant les autres individus du monde. En résulte ce qu'on peut appeler un *maillage monadique* de l'univers. Cet apport leibnizien complique le perspectivisme en ouvrant une infinité de niveaux de perception, laissant dans l'inconnu les mondes perçus par les monades subordonnées et emboîtées que nous, esprits, ne pouvons percevoir.

2. Monadologie et renouvellement du perspectivisme

1. Phénoménalisme La thèse monadologique semble d'abord apporter de l'eau au moulin de la lecture phénoméniste des textes leibniziens postérieurs aux années 90 (et pour certains aux années 1700), avec ses risques de subjectivisme et de relativisme, la réalité s'évanouissant ou perdant toute consistance en faveur des perceptions des différentes monades. Robert M. Adams et D. Garber ont défendu cette lecture de manière nuancée, sans accréditer la lecture relativiste.

R. M. Adams[8] a souligné le statut d'apparences que la thèse monadologique confère à des agrégats corporels dont l'unité est mentale ou relative à la perception d'un sujet immatériel. Mais il souligne également la localisation des monades à travers l'emplacement de leur corps organique, emplacement qui *fait* leur point de vue, ce qui ancre les monades dans un monde. Adams

---

[8] Robert Merrihew Adams : *Leibniz – Determinist, Theist, Idealist*, New York/Oxford, pp. 200 et 229.

retrouve donc les affirmations leibniziennes du *Système nouveau* art. 13, selon laquelle le corps *fait* le point de vue de l'âme, et de *Monadologie* art. 62, selon laquelle l'âme représente tout l'univers en représentant le corps qui lui appartient d'une manière particulière. Il en infère que le consensus perceptif ou la congruence des apparences témoignent que toutes les monades perçoivent bien le même univers, ce qui conjure le risque de relativisme.

D. Garber limite la lecture phénoméniste aux années postérieures à 1700. Son interprétation repose sur le caractère « soul-like » ou « mind-like » de toutes les monades. Sans nier leurs connexions avec des corps organiques, il en réduit toutefois l'importance. Il souligne le caractère d'apparences phénoménales d'un monde dont la réalité est d'abord celle d'être objet de perception. Garber prend les perceptions de ces *minds* au sens le plus large, qui comprend non seulement les perceptions des esprits, créatures capables de conversation, mais celles des âmes des substances corporelles, et même les perceptions d'esprits concevables qui pourraient être sans connexions avec les nôtres, tels les esprits angéliques. Garber conclut prudemment que Leibniz n'a pas élaboré (*worked out*) sa position dans le détail : on manque d'éléments décisifs pour dire s'il s'agit d'un phénoménalisme de l'esprit humain, ou de l'esprit au sens le plus large, incluant toutes les âmes.[9]

Or cette précision est importante pour comparer le perspectivisme leibnizien avec le perspectivisme amérindien étudié par Ed. Viveiros de Castro, et dont Philippe Descola tient le plus grand compte dans son examen des métaphysiques occidentales ou multinaturalistes.[10] Plus exigeant que le perspectivisme leibnizien, le perspectivisme amérindien spécifie un monde habité par différentes espèces de sujets ou personnes, qui se considèrent comme humaines, et considèrent les autres comme non-humaines ou humaines selon qu'elles se mettent à leur place et en adoptent le point de vue. Il fait reposer les identités sur des situations respectives susceptibles d'inversion, l'ami devenant ennemi, le chasseur devenant chassé, et pouvant alors être considéré comme non-humain sauf adoption de la place d'autrui. Les amazoniens voient certains animaux, leurs partenaires, par exemple jaguars ou aigles, comme des personnes douées de subjectivité, qui les considèrent eux-mêmes comme des proies animales, et veulent boire leur sang comme nous voulons boire de la bière. Les points de vue échangeables sont respectifs, ils ont lieu dans des relations mouvantes où les places s'échangent, les perspectives différant selon

---

[9] Daniel Garber : *Leibniz – Body, Substance, Monad*, Oxford 2009, « Leibnizian Phenomenalism », pp. 283sq. Garber parle alors d'*extended mind phenomenalism*.
[10] Philippe Descola : *Par-delà Nature et Culture*, Paris 2005, pp. 629–634.

les corps en relation. Ces corps sont définis non pas simplement comme des anatomies, mais comme des systèmes d'*habitus* ou des faisceaux de capacités d'être affectés, autrement dit ils sont ethno-biologiques. La continuité des esprits ou personnes annule donc en grande partie les différences de capacités biophysiques, puisqu'un même type de pensée habite ces différentes corporéités.

Le perspectivisme leibnizien, tout en défendant une véritable continuité de nature entre les organismes et les subjectivités percevantes, est assez éloigné du perspectivisme amérindien. Leibniz se contente d'installer les natures des humains et des autres créatures sur une échelle graduée qui ne peut être inversée, comme en témoigne le traitement des métamorphoses possibles d'êtres humains en bêtes,[11] et le critère décisif de la communication pour définir l'esprit (la fille de roi se fait reconnaître en parlant à ses proches). Il n'y a pas de symétrie susceptible d'inversion entre humains et non humains ; il s'agit seulement de reconnaître certaines indéterminations ou incertitudes de fait qui rendent la frontière entre humains et non humains difficile à tracer, et le jugement malaisé sur les cas perplexes. Un possible déplacement du curseur sur l'échelle graduée n'empêche pas une distinction de principe incontournable entre l'animal raisonnable et l'animal non raisonnable. Ce qui justifie le traitement célèbre du « baptême conditionnel » pour un être trouvé dans les bois et ayant une figure un peu différente des figures humaines habituelles, exemple que Locke et Leibniz traitent différemment, l'un de manière sceptique, l'autre de manière confiante.[12]

En première approche, on dira que le perspectivisme leibnizien réserve aux esprits la pensée et le jugement, quand le perspectivisme amazonien étend cette capacité à tous les vivants partageant un monde avec les humains, avec lesquels ils ne diffèrent que par leurs organes (ce qui minimise le poids différentiel de la physicalité, puisqu'ils ont l'agentivité et la subjectivité en commun). Leibniz maintient une rigoureuse correspondance entre capacités organiques et capacités mentales, ce qui ne se vérifie pas dans un perspectivisme animiste. Mais aucun des deux perspectivismes n'est vraiment concerné par le phénoménisme.

2. Relativisme Aucun des perspectivismes n'est prêt à tirer de conséquence sceptique du phénoménisme supposé. Ce n'est un obstacle ni pour la connaissance ni pour l'action.

---

[11] Voir dans les *Nouveaux Essais*, II, 27, § 9, la fille de roi transformée en perroquet, qui reste la fille de ses parents même si elle n'est plus « humaine », puisque l'humanité enveloppe une certaine corporéité et figure.

[12] Martine de Gaudemar : *De la puissance au sujet*, Paris 1994/2002, pp. 151sq.

— Du côté de Leibniz, la possibilité de la connaissance est garantie par la congruence et le consensus, et cela suffit. Depuis le *De modo distinguendi phaenomena realia ab imaginariis* des années moyennes de 1683-1686, Leibniz a souligné la vanité de se prononcer sur la réalité objective des agrégats corporels (« peu importe qu'on les appelle songes ou non »). La confiance dans la possibilité de construire un géométral qui rende compte des variations de perspectives est suffisante pour affirmer qu'il y a une connaissance commune à tous les esprits. Ils sont capables d'appréhender des règles qui commandent aux fictions aussi bien qu'aux phénomènes réels, et sont valides dans les mondes possibles comme dans le monde créé : cette congruence donne au monde partagé une réalité incontestable. L'assurance ontologique est donc forte dans le leibnizianisme.

— De son côté, le perspectivisme amazonien donne précisément pour tâche à l'anthropologue de décrire les pratiques et les positions relatives qui s'y échangent : elles sont la réalité même et non un obstacle à sa découverte. Si un relativisme est évoqué, il sert à dénier au « naturalisme » occidental la prétention à être le seul schème ontologique valide, mais en aucun cas à déprécier quelque schème épistémologique que ce soit. Il s'agit plutôt de rapporter toute thèse, et toute identité, au système d'options ontologiques et épistémologiques qui organise le monde que l'on décrit, comme tout jugement est à rapporter à une situation et à un enjeu. Ce perspectivisme est explicitement relationniste plutôt que relativiste.

3. Complication Peu concerné par le phénoménisme et le relativisme, le perspectivisme leibnizien est (i) *compliqué* par la construction monadologique, car celle-ci descend au-dessous du niveau des corps visibles qui forment les individualités organiques de notre monde. Le perspectivisme joue à plusieurs étages de la réalité. Les individualités organiques procèdent en effet des efforts conjugués d'une multitude de monades elles-mêmes percevantes, qui expriment chacune un point de vue singulier. Cette construction emboîtée (ii) *facilite l'éviction* de la forme cartésienne du dualisme âme-corps. Le problème qu'elle laisse sans solution (iii) est celui des mondes perçus par les monades subordonnées emboîtées par leurs corps organiques dans les corps des individus visibles sur la scène du monde créé. Toutes ces monades partagent-elles un même monde ? Afin de démêler cette complication, je l'envisagerai sous ces trois aspects.

i) **Maillage monadique et monade dominante** Il faut noter deux conditions de l'activité expressive propre à toutes les monades : le maillage monadique de l'univers, et l'activité d'une monade dominante.

1. Sous-jacent au grouillement organique apparent (*Monadologie* 69), on trouve un maillage de tout l'univers par des monades s'exprimant dans des corps organiques, avec lesquels elles tissent les individualités organiques que nous nommons humains ou bêtes, mais aussi les milieux intermédiaires remplis de corps organiques inapparents (*Monadologie* 68). Ce maillage assure, en même temps que l'inséparabilité de tout ce que nous appelions âme et corps (tout corps organique est lui-même tissé de monades), la connexion de tous les individus qui font un monde : cette connexion n'est autre que l' « ordre général. » Le maillage monadique fait de la matière une réalité vivante (puisque toutes les monades sont des centres de force d'agir et de pâtir qui animent les corps organiques), et il donne un contenu à la notion d'ordre général. Il met donc au premier plan l'entr'expression de toutes les parties de la matière pleines d'organique ou d'organisme.[13] Comme le musicien de la lettre à Arnauld d'avril 1687 doit prendre en compte le rapport entre les chœurs pour comprendre ce qu'il fait dans son propre chœur, de même la pensée, dans l'élaboration monadologique, est reliée à travers son expression spontanée et ses petites perceptions à l'interconnexion, condition pour que chaque partie de la matière se ressente de ce qui se passe dans les autres (*Monadologie* 61). L'organicité devient l'opérateur de l'entr'expression de toutes choses entre elles,[14] et par conséquent de la pensée réfléchissante qui la reprend en un *cogito* où l'être affecté est la condition d'un *Je pense* : « Je suis affecté de beaucoup de manières. » Le dualisme de type cartésien s'en trouve frappé d'obsolescence, voué à mouliner du vide, faute des connexions que l'organicité apporte aux monades[15]. Le maillage monadique met en lumière le fondamental rapport au monde depuis lequel il peut y avoir perception et pensée : c'est depuis le monde que l'individu est pensant et pensable.

---

[13] *Du rapport général de toutes choses*, A VI, 4 B, 1615 : « Le rapport général et exact de toutes choses entre elles prouve que toutes les parties de la matière sont pleines d'organisme. »
[14] Comme l'a bien formulé Jeanne Roland : *Leibniz et l'individualité organique*, Paris 2009, p. 259.
[15] Voir À l'Electrice Sophie, 1706 ; GP VII, 567.

2. Leibniz a recours à un nouveau concept, celui de *monade dominante*, pour rendre compte de l'unification de l'être affecté dans un organisme percevant et sentant. La monade dominante prend en charge le *point de vue* de l'unité. J'en propose une lecture musicale : elle vient concentrer en un accord et ainsi exprimer, à chaque moment de la ligne musicale qu'est la trajectoire d'un être individuel, d'une part les rapports internes entre monades subordonnées, et d'autre part les rapports, si l'on veut externes, aux monades d'où résultent les autres machines de la nature qui peuvent l'affecter au titre du corps organique qu'une monade résume et concentre. La pensée comme opération est un accord à la fois momentané (comme un accord de dominante), et poursuivi de manière ininterrompue dans une mélodie polyphonique qui a ses transitions et ses renversements. La monade dominante exprime à tout moment les rapports entre monades sous la forme d'un sentiment plus ou moins clair ou confus, sentiment qui est le commencement de la pensée. Rappelons en effet que ce ne sont pas seulement les hommes mais aussi les vers et même tous les êtres vivants, qui ont une monade dominante exprimant les impressions sous la forme d'un accord, et donc une pensée embryonnaire.[16] Le concept de *monade dominante* prend en effet le relais de l'âme, et en assume les fonctions dans un ensemble. À la manière d'un chef d'orchestre, elle n'est pas l'auteur de la partition et donc des accords inter ou intra-monadiques, mais elle coordonne les interprètes. Cette comparaison musicale éclaire l'activité de la monade dominante : sans donner leurs notes aux monades subordonnées, elle compose leurs mouvements, et dégage de leurs notes une tonalité dominante à ce moment précis, qui correspond au « point de vue ». La monade dominante est bien le principe de synthèse d'une machine de la nature, tout en consacrant la nature profondément relationnelle de la composition organique, inscrite dans un réseau de relations qui lui donne ses conditions d'existence.

C'est ainsi que la monade dominante fait l'entéléchie d'un corps organique dont elle ne saurait être séparée, en donnant la tonalité de l'ensemble à chaque moment où elle fait entendre un accord. Le *point de vue* se déploie donc dans

---

[16] À Des Bosses, in : Christiane Frémont : *L'Être et la relation avec Trente-Sept Lettres de Leibniz au R. P. des Bosses*, Paris 1981. 16 juin 1712 : « Un ver peut être une partie de mon corps, et sous ma monade dominante ; il peut à son tour comprendre dans son corps d'autres animalcules sous sa monade dominante ».

une ligne mélodique rythmée par des accords qui synthétisent ponctuellement l'ensemble des opérations de l'organisme vivant. Et comme il n'y a pas de musique sans notes, sans instruments ni musiciens, il n'y a pas de pensée-expression sans machine organique. On aboutit à des machines naturelles sentantes et pensantes, ou des subjectivités incorporées.[17]

Le vocabulaire dualiste nous égare. Mais il semble garder une certaine pertinence dans le cas particulier des esprits, ce qui pose problème.

(ii) La pensée-expression A l'époque de la théorie de la notion complète et des substances individuelles-miroirs de l'univers, Leibniz avait déjà commencé à emprunter le chemin détourné des perceptions confuses pour faire comprendre la connexion entre des âmes qui n'interagissent pas entre elles.[18] Les âmes se rencontrent dans leurs perceptions, du fait qu'elles expriment l'état de l'univers suivant le rapport des autres corps au leur, ce qui implique que cet état de l'univers est bien le même sous divers points de vue. De telles perceptions doivent contenir quelque sentiment confus, car chaque corps reçoit l'impression de tous les autres du fait que tous les corps sympathisent.[19] L'expression montre l'interconnexion et la correspondance des êtres et de leurs phénomènes. Même si Dieu était encore requis directement comme cause de la correspondance des phénomènes, c'était déjà un ordre général qui permettait de penser médiatement cette causalité.

Leibniz n'a cessé de perfectionner cette notion d'un ordre général médiateur. D'abord coexistant avec la causalité divine, il devient la manière dont cette causalité s'exerce. Dans la *Monadologie*, l'ordre général s'exprime dans les corps organiques qui, en recevant l'impression de tous les autres, sont la condition de l'expression perceptive et pensante des monades. L'accent est mis sur cette activité spontanée présente dans tous les êtres, activité toujours sensible à elle-même, qu'on peut appeler « pensée » ou « expression » sans qu'il soit nécessaire de requérir un dédoublement réflexif qui demande un traitement à part en ce qu'il n'appartient qu'aux esprits.

---

[17] Ce pourquoi l'expression d' « organic minds » ou « organic souls », employée par Andreas Blank : « Twin-Consciousness and the identity of Indescernibles »,in: François Duchesneau/Jérémie Griard (éds.) : *Leibniz selon les Nouveaux Essais sur l'entendement humain*, Montréal/Paris 2006, pp. 189–202, me paraît heureuse, correspondant à l'expression des PNG 4 : « quand une monade a des organes si ajustés que [...]. »

[18] Hide Ishiguro: *Leibniz's Philosophy of Logic and Language*, Cambridge 1990. Soulignant l'importance des prédicats relationnels, elle voyait bien que cela éloignait Leibniz de tout solipsisme.

[19] *Discours de Métaphysique* XXXIII, trad. et ed. par Daniel Garber et Roger Ariew, 36 ; A VI, 4 B, 1581.

En faisant du rapport au maillage monadique la condition de la pensée-expression, Leibniz corrode et assouplit l'opposition de l'âme[20] et du corps. Il est vrai que le sujet de l'expression percevante et pensante est difficile à déterminer : est-ce la monade dominante, dans la mesure où elle prend en charge le « point de vue » ? Est-ce le corps entier animé et conçu comme une machine de la nature, puisque le point de vue que l'âme constitue en exprimant son corps ne peut être situé, comme l'âme ou monade dominante, que dans l'ensemble du corps ? Que veut dire Leibniz quand il dit « nous », ou « notre âme », « notre corps » sinon la substance vivante tout entière ?

Mon hypothèse est que Leibniz a longtemps cheminé, voire erré dans ses formulations quand il répondait aux objections sur des terrains augustiniens ou cartésiens qui ne convenaient pas à sa conceptualité, comme dans sa métaphore des deux horloges, inadaptée en ce qu'elle oublie le monde, théâtre des accords, et qu'elle suppose des entités substantielles. Mais il a toujours maintenu le fil directeur de la médiation expressive, sans laquelle il n'y a ni perception ni pensée. S'interposant entre les deux supposées entités de l'âme et du corps, l'expression *sous le point de vue d'un corps affecté* par tous les changements de l'univers vient donner un contenu à la notion de *point de vue* singulier. L'élaboration monadologique accomplit un dispositif conceptuel déjà présent à la fin de la correspondance avec Arnauld.

On en avait un avant-goût dans l'image des bandes de musiciens que Leibniz utilise dans sa lettre du 30 avril 1687, à condition de la lire au-delà d'une simple explication insatisfaisante de l'union de l'âme et du corps. Il faut être attentif au détail :

- son point de départ n'est pas duel mais pluriel : Plusieurs différentes bandes de musiciens. Cette multiplicité annonce le dispositif monadologique, où les corps vivants comme machines de la nature procèdent des efforts conjugués d'une multitude de monades toutes différentes.
- le musicien appartient à une bande ou un chœur, il n'est ni dans une extériorité ni en surplomb. En voulant mettre en rapport sa perception avec ce que font l'une ou l'autre des bandes de musiciens, il incarne l'activité

---

[20] Id., Avril 1709 : « Je ne pense pas […] qu'il convienne de considérer les âmes comme étant dans des points. Peut-être pourrait-on dire qu'elles ne sont en un lieu que par une opération, suivant l'ancien système de l'influx, ou plutôt (suivant le nouveau système de l'harmonie pré-établie) qu'elles sont en un lieu par une correspondance et qu'ainsi elles sont dans la totalité du corps qu'elles animent. »

de pensée immanente à une multiplicité organisée. Celle-ci, réfléchissant sur elle-même, cherche à attribuer l'opération expressive spontanée à un sujet. Or ce sujet n'est pas simple mais composé : le musicien s'aperçoit qu'il peut inférer d'une partition à une autre, attribuer indifféremment les mouvements qu'il fait ou qu'il voit faire à l'une ou l'autre bande. Parler en termes d'âme ou en termes de corps est équivalent[21] : l'important est l'accord préexistant. Les musiciens n'ont pas à travailler pour s'accorder.
La leçon de cette image anticipe donc l'élaboration monadologique, qui, au-delà de l'opposition dualiste, va revenir à la multiplicité des chœurs ou bandes de musiciens, et conférer l'activité coordinatrice à une monade dominante immanente à un chœur, multiplicité organisée.

La comparaison musicale enveloppe virtuellement la notion de compositions organiques expressives. Tout se passe comme si une même mélodie était interprétée par des lignes musicales différentes, sur différentes portées, certaines plus simples ou sommaires, d'autres chargées d'ornements ou d'improvisations, mais toutes accordées comme dans une partition d'orchestre.

Leibniz a donc suggéré dès la fin de la correspondance avec Arnaud, à travers le musicien-pensant son expression, une correspondance d'instances plutôt qu'une union de deux entités substantielles. En figurant un accord de multiplicités constituantes, l'image musicale est proche d'une conception monadologique.[22]

Les concepts monadologiques éclairent en effet et fortifient ces suggestions. Le corps à travers lequel une âme pouvait exprimer l'univers devient une « machine de la nature », résultant des activités d'une infinité de monades qui en sont les réquisits. Cette machine sentante, qui perçoit confusément les autres corps-machines, est affectée par tout ce qui a lieu dans l'univers.[23] L'unité de la monade dominante et du corps organique devient la substance vivante. La machine expressive, percevante et pensante, devient le vrai sujet

---

[21] *Monadologie* Art. 81 : « Ce système fait que les corps agissent comme si (par impossible) il n'y avait point d'Ames ; et que les Ames agissent comme s'il n'y avait point de corps ; et que tous deux agissent comme si l'un influait sur l'autre. »
[22] Art 78 : Ces principes m'ont donné moyen d'expliquer naturellement l'union, ou bien la conformité de l'Ame et du corps organique.
[23] Voir aussi à Arnauld, 9 octobre 1687 ; A II, 2, N. 58 ; GP II, 111sq., *Philosophical Papers and Letters*, ed. by Leroy Loemker, V.1, 520sq. : « A tous les mouvements de notre corps répondent certaines perceptions ou pensées plus ou moins confuses de notre âme, donc l'âme aura aussi quelque pensée de tous les mouvements de l'univers, et selon moi toute notre âme ou substance en aura quelque perception ou expression. » Et *Monadologie*, 61.

de la pensée-expression, qui se dépasse en réflexion dans certaines conditions déterminées.

(iii) Problèmes en suspens Reste un problème non résolu par le concept de *monade dominante* qui fait l'entéléchie ou l'âme d'un corps vivant : les capacités architectoniques des âmes raisonnables qui font le privilège des esprits semblent difficiles à dériver des représentations qu'un organisme se fait spontanément et naturellement de l'univers qui l'affecte. Certes, il faut un individu sentant à travers son corps organique pour faire l'expérience de la conformité entre ce qu'on appelle âme et corps, nécessaire pour que ce corps fasse le *point de vue* de l'âme, ou encore que l'âme constitue ce *point de vue* en exprimant son corps. Mais cette condition nécessaire n'est pas suffisante ; il y faut ajouter des capacités logiques particulières, que Leibniz n'a jamais prêtées à d'autres vivants, même si ses formules sont prudentes[24] :

> Les bêtes, autant qu'on en peut juger, manquent de cette réflexion qui nous fait penser à nous-mêmes.

Même inscrites en « nous », esprits, à titre de virtualités ou instincts de la raison, elles semblent irréductibles aux capacités d'un organisme vivant, puisqu'elles demandent une « élévation » des monades destinées au devenir humain « au degré de la Raison » (*Monadologie*, 82). La puissance rationnelle des esprits, sans rompre la continuité établie par Leibniz entre humains et non humains, justifie leurs privilèges.

Nous sommes alors placés devant une alternative. Il faut choisir entre deux options explicatives : une option naturaliste et une option métaphysique. Entendons *naturalisme* au sens où Descola en fait le schème ontologique adopté par l'Occident depuis la coupure galiléo-cartésienne entre physique et métaphysique comme condition de la connaissance scientifique. Une option *métaphysique*, au contraire, admet des notions allant au-delà des lois ou régularités de l'univers physique, à la façon des ontologies animiste et totémique que recense Descola.

— Une explication purement naturaliste de la présence active de virtualités rationnelles en nous consisterait à l'imputer à l'organisation corporelle.

---

[24] *Considérations sur les principes de vie* ; GP VI, 542.

La réflexivité pourrait être fondée dans une structure plissée de l'organisme, comparable au *nested model* évoqué par Nachtomy.[25] On pourrait découvrir dans la structure du corps entier, sa complication en pliures et niveaux, la condition organique des schémas d'inférence, des formes de connexion qui nous permettent de raisonner et de tirer des conséquences de certaines assertions ou observations.
– Mais ces privilèges rationnels, condition de la réflexion, pourraient être issus de la société établie par un Dieu partageant avec les esprits, pour ainsi dire gracieusement, les vérités logiques. Une telle explication, qui dépasse l'explication scientifique, n'invalide pas pour autant de futures explications naturalistes, puisque « les choses conduisent à la grâce par les voies mêmes de la nature » (*Monadologie* 88), et qu'une explication naturelle est toujours préférable à un recours au miracle. On se retrouve devant un problème analogue à celui que Leibniz ne tranche pas lorsqu'il s'agit d'expliquer l'élévation des âmes sensitives au degré de la raison, lors de la conception d'un être humain (*Monadologie* 82).

3. Pour conclure

Soulignons trois aspects du renouvellement monadologique du perspectivisme leibnizien.

1. Dualisme Leibniz a réorienté une philosophie bloquée par le dualisme cartésien, en ouvrant une issue grâce à l'hypothèse d'une unité de la pensée avec les capacités d'un être vivant, la monade dominante actualisant les virtualités expressives des corps ou machines de la nature. Le vocabulaire dualiste de l'âme et du corps semble dépassé puisque le corps organique est lui-même composé ou tissé de monades. Au schème dualiste succèdent des machines naturelles sentantes et même pensantes, des subjectivités incorporées. Le vocabulaire dualiste ne semble pertinent que pour les esprits dans leurs moments réfléchissants, quand ils reprennent leur activité sentante et pensante spontanée et irréfléchie, comme si cette reprise dépassait les capacités organiques. Mais il convient d'être prudent car il pourrait y avoir des capacités organiques encore insoupçonnées.

---

[25] Ohad Nachtomy/Ayelet Shavit/Justin H. Smith : « Leibnizian Organisms, Nested Individuals, and Units of Selection », in : *Theory of Biosciences* 12/2 (2002), pp. 205–230.

2. Solipsisme L'élaboration monadologique nous sauve également d'un solipsisme qui menaçait non seulement les cartésiens, mais la philosophie d'une substance individuelle considérée comme un monde à part. L'organicité, comme opérateur du « rapport général de toutes choses » qui s'entr'expriment, inscrit toute individualité dans le monde des monades connectées. L'individu ne pense que depuis un monde dans lequel il est inscrit. Comme Leibniz n'abandonne pas la notion de *point de vue*, nous sommes dans une version perfectionnée de la *mirroring thesis*, combinée avec ce que Rutherford appelle le « panorganicisme. »[26]
3. Problèmes Le statut de la pensée réfléchissante privilège des seuls esprits reste problématique et peu travaillé. En s'élargissant aux autres points de vue, elle peut établir des connexions et énoncer des règles jusqu'à découvrir les sciences suivant lesquelles Dieu a réglé les choses, imitant dans son petit monde ce que Dieu fait dans le grand. Les capacités architectoniques des esprits font donc signe vers un dépassement du point de vue individuel vers des points de vue de communautés particulières, voire à l'humanité entière. Hiérarchisables, ces perspectives font objection à un perspectivisme de l'inversion infinie, voire absolue des points de vue. Mais ces capacités architectoniques semblent irréductibles à l'expression d'un organisme, si compliqué soit-il. La comparaison avec les perspectivismes de type animiste s'en trouve malaisée, ceux-ci dotant tous les vivants des mêmes capacités mentales alors que leurs corps organiques ont des capacités très dissemblables. Le perspectivisme amérindien ou amazonien diffère donc du perspectivisme leibnizien en étendant à tous les vivants l'aptitude à faire des inférences et à prendre la place d'autrui, sans s'appuyer sur la correspondance leibnizienne entre capacités organiques et capacités mentales.

Pour faire droit à la rationalité que partagent les esprits chez Leibniz, et qui interdit tout subjectivisme et tout relativisme, je propose de parler d'une double nature organique et logique des esprits. Cela donne une tonalité très particulière, *sui generis,* au perspectivisme leibnizien. Il est tempéré par l'universalisme des vérités rationnelles, qui permet aux esprits de partager un même monde et d'élargir leur point de vue individuel. Partageons nous pour autant un même monde avec tous les êtres vivants, perceptibles ou imperceptibles? La question reste posée.

---

[26] Voir supra note 7.

Can We Unify Theories of the Origin of Finite Things in Leibniz's *De Summa Rerum*?

Shohei Edamura (Kanazawa)

Introduction

The authors of two recent works, focused upon the discussions in *De Summa Rerum* (hereafter DSR) of 1675–76,[1] have argued that Leibniz once introduced a monistic metaphysics, according to which God is the only substance. Robert M. Adams takes note of *That a Perfect Thing is Possible* from DSR, in which Leibniz asserted "[i]t can easily be demonstrated that all things are distinguished, not as substances (i.e., radically) but as modes."[2] In commenting on this passage, Adams has argued that Leibniz had come to a "monistic conclusion."[3] By referring to the same passage, Mogens Lærke also suggests that Leibniz held a quasi-Spinozistic system of metaphysics at that time.[4] Here some readers of their works might be tempted to conclude that when Leibniz wrote DSR he held a stable system of metaphysics, in which we can find many claims to which he was explicitly committed, and one of the claims is that there is only one substance, namely God. But it is not clear whether we can appropriately interpret DSR as presenting a unified system, given that DSR is a collection of relatively short articles, which was first named so in the Academy Edition. If Leibniz had written DSR as a single work, which is obviously not the case, we would be more confident in taking it to present a solid system

---

[1] The following abbreviations will be used: *De Summa Rerum*, trans. and ed. by G. H. R. Parkinson, New Haven 1992 (DSR); B. Spinoza: *Ethics*, cited by book and axiom (A), definition (D), or proposition (P), followed by a page number from *A Spinoza Reader: The Ethics and Other Works*, ed. and trans. by Edwin Curley, Princeton 1994 (Ethics); G. W. Leibniz: *Philosophical Papers and Letters*, trans. and ed. by L. E. Loemker, Dordrecht ²1969 (L).
[2] A VI, 3, 573 = DSR, 93. See Robert M. Adams: *Leibniz: Determinist, Theist, Idealist*, New York 1994, p. 129. Against Adams, Christia Mercer argues that Leibniz did not have "pantheistic" tendencies in 1676. She argues that Leibniz was committed to the Platonistic view that every finite thing emanated from God, and nonetheless it is not external to him. According to her, even if Leibniz believed that every finite thing is within God, it does not mean that he was a pantheist. See Christia Mercer: *Leibniz's Metaphysics: Its Origins and Development*, New York 2001, p. 454. But whether Leibniz was a "pantheist" or "platonist" in 1676, it is still meaningful to provide a clear explanation for the origin of finite things on the basis of DSR.
[3] Adams: *Leibniz: Determinist*, p. 129.
[4] More precisely, Lærke uses the term "quasi-spinozisme" or "système quasi-spinoziste." See Mogens Lærke: *Leibniz lecteur de Spinoza*, Paris 2008, p. 444 and p. 507f.

of metaphysics. While Mark Kulstad considers Adams' reading of the passage as showing a monistic inclination,[5] he also notices that in DSR there are actually three distinct theories concerning the origin of finite things:

> "It is my belief that this idea of relating a single attribute to all others to give rise to the infinite variety of the world is one of several at least nominally different Leibnizian answers to be the question of how the variety of the world arises from the forms or attributes of God present in the *De Summa Rerum*, and that answering this question is one of the driving forces of the *De Summa Rerum*. [...] What we will do in this section is to start by developing some details of the answer that we have already encountered in connection with the correspondence between Tschirnhaus and Spinoza (an answer which, for reasons that will become clearer later, we will label the 'pure relations theory'). The sort of numerical analogy just mentioned will be central in this. Then we will raise some questions about details that will lead us to what appears to be a related but distinct answer to the question of the origin of things (which we shall label the 'subjects theory'). Finally we will turn to an answer which, in at least in one of its formulations, seems the furthest removed from the idea on origins suggested in Tschirnhaus's letter to Spinoza of June 23, 1676. (We shall label this final approach the 'matter theory.')"[6]

And following Kulstad, Lærke argues that concerning the origin of finite things, we can find the following explanations in DSR: (1) the explanation only referring to the essence of God; (2) the explanation referring to a conjugation of simple forms; (3) the explanation that combines a subject with forms; (4) the explanation that adds the matter to forms.[7] As Kulstad and Lærke do, I notice several passages in DSR that seem to present different explanations on how finite things are produced. As we have seen, since DSR is a collection of short articles, it might be the case that Leibniz tried to write down different hypotheses. Here we have an interpretative problem. That is, if we take DSR as presenting incoherent hypotheses, then we may not be able to ascribe a stable view to Leibniz based on DSR, since in that case it seems that Leibniz was not seriously committed to what he wrote. Thus, for instance, it may be

---

[5] Kulstad notes that according to Adams, as well as his own reading of DSR, "Leibniz did not have a traditional view of creation," and he "adopted at least temporarily a Spinozistic and pantheistic view of the things of this world as modes of God rather than as distinct substance." See Mark Kulstad: "Leibniz's De Summa Rerum. The Origin of the Variety of Things, in Connection with the Spinoza-Tschirnhaus Correspondence," in: Frédéric Nef/Dominique Berlioz (eds.): *L'actualité de Leibniz: les deux labyrinth* (= *Studia Leibnitiana*, Supplementa 34), Stuttgart 1999, pp. 69–85.
[6] Ibid., p. 77f.
[7] Lærke: *Leibniz lecteur*, p. 518.

hard to ascribe what Lærke calls the "quasi-Spinozistic system" to Leibniz on the basis of DSR. But as Lærke does, I assume that DSR will look even more attractive if it presents an early version of Leibniz's system. In this paper, I attempt to present possible readings of some important passages in DSR, so that we can take three of seemingly distinct theories as fitting together.[8]

1. Kulstad's Distinction of Three Theories on the Origin of Finite Things

1.1 Pure Relations Theory

Kulstad cites a passage from *On Simple Forms* in which Leibniz wrote:

> "There is the same variety in any kind of world, and this is nothing other than the same essence related in various ways, as if you were to look at the same town from various places; or, if you relate the essence of the number 6 to the number 3, it will be 3 x 2 or 3 + 3, but if you relate it to the number 4 it will be 6/4 = 3/2, or 6 = 4 x 3/2."[9]

In this passage, Leibniz explains how "various things" are brought about by the same essence of things, which consists in an infinite number of simple forms of God. In *On Simple Forms*, Leibniz previously wrote that "there are infinitely various things," and the "infinite variety can result only from an infinite cause, that is, from various forms."[10] On the basis of this fact, Leibniz argued that "simple forms are infinitely many."[11] In another article *On Forms, or the Attributes of God* of DSR, Leibniz stated that "[a]n attribute of God is any simple form,"[12] which implies that any simple form must belong to God as his attribute.[13] Leibniz added that "the essence of God consists in the fact that

---

[8] Here I cannot provide an argument to unify all of the four explanations proposed by Lærke, since I focus upon the original three theories suggested by Kulstad. But I believe that my discussions might be helpful for understanding the relationship of Lærke's four explanations.
[9] A VI, 3, 522 = DSR, 83; Kulstad: "Leibniz's De Summa Rerum", p. 78.
[10] A VI, 3, 522 = DSR, 83.
[11] Ibid.
[12] A VI, 3, 514 = DSR, 69.
[13] In *On Forms, or the Attributes of God*, Leibniz used "form" and "attribute" as synonyms, as we can guess from the very title. For instance, he wrote that "[i]t is a wonderful fact that a subject is different from forms or attributes" (A VI, 3, 514 = DSR, 69).

he is the subject of all compatible attributes."[14] Thus, Leibniz thinks that God has an infinite number of simple forms or attributes, and the whole set of the simple forms is considered as the essence of God. The number 6 in the passage of *On Simple Forms* is a metaphor of God's essence or the whole set of all the simple forms, while according to Kulstad, the number 3 is associated with one of the simple forms or attributes.[15] The passage seems to suggest how various things are produced by introducing some simple form related to the set of all the forms. For Kulstad, given the analogy of the passage, "nothing else is needed for the origin of things other than the relation of attributes, taken singly, to all attributes taken together."[16] Thus the theory introduced in the passage of *On Simple Forms* is called the "pure relations theory."

1.2 Subjects Theory

Kulstad states that

> "[s]ome passages of the *De Summa Rerum* suggest relations involved in the origin of things extending beyond those of the pure relations theory, that is, relations which have as 'relata' entities distinct from the forms or attributes of God."[17]

Here Kulstad quotes the following passage:

> "Things are not produced by the mere combination of forms in God, but along with a subject also. The subject itself, or God, together with his ubiquity, gives the immeasurable, and this immeasurable combined with other subjects bring it about that all possible modes, or things, follow in it. The various results of forms, combined with a subject, bring it about the particulars result."[18]

According to the subjects theory, various things require the subject, or the holder of all the simple forms. The theory seems to suggest that relations of forms are not enough for producing various things, and these various things must be related to the subject or God, in addition to the set of all the forms.

---

[14] Ibid.
[15] Kulstad: "Leibniz's De Summa Rerum", p. 79.
[16] Ibid., p. 80.
[17] Ibid.
[18] A VI, 3, 523 = DSR, 85.

Another distinct feature of the passage of the subjects theory is that the expression "other subjects" is used. Kulstad takes note of this expression as the following:

> "The key question raised by the passage, for present purposes, is whether Leibniz's statement, "this unmeasurable combined with other subjects brings it about that all possible modes, or things, follow in it", ([Kulstad's] emphasis) means that relations to these "other subjects", whatever they might be, is part of what is intended by Leibniz here in accounting for the origin of things from forms or attributes, so that this account would be different from the pure relations theory, which involves, as we have presented it, relations among forms or attributes alone."[19]

Certainly, the "subjects theory" is named after this expression of "other subjects," and the expression also made Kulstad consider Adams' "insightful comments" on the passage of the subjects theory.[20] Adams notes the expression "subjects," saying that Leibniz may have oscillated between monistic and pluralistic options of metaphysics.[21] Adams suggests that Leibniz was trying to establish a stable system of metaphysics, introducing different ideas to see how they fit together. Consequently, two components, which seemingly have tensions with respect to each other, show up in the same passage. On the one hand, Leibniz suggests that all finite things are modifications, and God is the only substance. Here finite things and God clearly belong to different categories. On the other hand, Leibniz also suggests that finite things are subjects that can be related to a greater subject, namely God. Finite things, together with God, are taken to be subjects, and to this extent they are in the same status.

1.3 Matter Theory

Kulstad lastly offers the matter theory, and it is introduced on the basis of the following passage:
> "However, it is true that there cannot exist any modifications, either in space or in the mind, except with the help of matter, whose nature it is to combine the two. But matter being given, then there exist modifications in the mind and in that which is extended."[22]

---

[19] Kulstad: "Leibniz's De Summa Rerum", p. 81.
[20] Ibid.
[21] Adams: *Leibniz: Determinist*, p. 130.
[22] A VI, 3, 514 = DSR, 75.

At a first glance, the matter theory is different from the subjects theory. The matter theory requires matter in addition to simple forms, whereas according to the subjects theory, finite things seem to need subjects and simple forms. Kulstad introduces Leibniz's theory of imperfection in explaining the ontological status of matter that is discussed in the quoted passage. Kulstad states that according to Leibniz's later view (especially, I think, one proposed in *Discourse on Metaphysics* and letters to Arnauld),[23] "possible finite substances have complete concepts involving limited versions of the unlimited perfections of God."[24] Since "only God is entirely free" of imperfection, any created substance has some imperfection, and hence it is limited in power, knowledge, and moral perfection. This imperfection is called "matter." Although Kulstad is careful enough to avoid arguing that we can interpret DSR on the basis of later texts, he still argues that the matter theory fits "tolerably well" with it.[25] Indeed, finite things in the framework of DSR are limited in some aspects. For instance, an extended body is limited in that it has a specific shape and size. It cannot have an infinite extension, and thus limited in some area. Likewise, the human mind is limited in perceptions in the sense that it cannot have completely distinct perceptions. Thus the human mind is also characterized by limitation, which is called matter. Leibniz suggested that matter is necessary for human minds to have specific perceptions such as sensations of various colors.[26] Here sensations seem to be taken as perceptions that are not completely distinct. More generally, finite things are embodies as individuals through some limitations introduced by matter.

One thing to note is that "matter" shows up in many places of DSR, and the contexts are different. Considering how it is used, I interpret that Leibniz had two different concepts of matter when he wrote DSR. The first concept is close to that of primary matter in the late period.[27] It means a limited aspect of some concrete thing, and it does not independently exist as such. Likewise, the second is similar to the late concept of secondary matter. It means a concrete extended body rather than an abstracted aspect of something. For in-

---

[23] The doctrine of complete individual concept is introduced in the section 13 of *Discourse on Metaphysics* (L, 310f.). Leibniz also discussed the original imperfection of a human being in the section 30 (L, 321–323).
[24] Kulstad: "Leibniz's De Summa Rerum", p. 83.
[25] Ibid., p. 83.
[26] A VI, 3, 518 = DSR, 77.
[27] GP II, 252; also see Adams: *Leibniz: Determinist*, p. 265.

stance, Leibniz thought about the case in which "certain bodies are put together into an arch" which is "full of a more subtle matter."[28] Also, Leibniz argued that "one mind has a more special relation to another portion of matter."[29] Here he mentions the visible and concrete organic body of a mind. Now obviously, the matter theory is based upon the first concept of matter.

2. Attempts to Unify Theories

So far I have attempted to introduce Kulstad's important distinction of three theories that can be found in DSR. But I now want to argue that three theories can perhaps be consistent. Here I do not attempt to refute Kulstad and Lærke, since in fact, both of them do not deny the possibility of seeing the theories as consistent: "Conceivably," Kulstad states,

> "Leibniz did not mean that the matter theory is distinct from the pure relation theory, or perhaps not even from the subjects theory."[30]

Also, he suggests that Leibniz's three explanations of how various things arises from forms or attributes of God are "at least nominally different."[31] This expression suggests that these answers might not be utterly different in a way that they are incoherent to each other. Similarly, Lærke states that his "diverse explanations are not exclusive to each other."[32] Hence my attempt to see a possible consistency of the three theories, I think, is not against what they maintain.

2.1 Unifying the Pure Relation and Subjects Theories

The two passages to support the pure relations and subjects theories are, in fact, both from *On Simple Forms*. In the very same article, Leibniz wrote that

> "[t]hings are not produced by the mere combination of forms in God, but along which a subject also," and he also wrote that "[t]here is the same variety in any

---

[28] A VI, 3, 585 = DSR, 101.
[29] A VI, 3, 394 = DSR, 47.
[30] Kulstad: "Leibniz's De Summa Rerum", p. 80.
[31] Ibid., p. 84.
[32] "[c]es explications diverses ne sont pas exclusives les unes des autres [...]", Lærke: *Leibniz lecteur*, p. 518.

kind of world, and this is nothing other than the same essence related in various ways."[33]

Moreover, these two passages are mutually close in the article.[34] Although if the passages are from different articles in DSR, then Leibniz might have written down inconsistent hypotheses in them, it is hard to believe that Leibniz intentionally wrote inconsistent hypotheses in mutually close passages of the same article.

But for what reason can we take the subjects theory to be consistent with the pure relations theory? Here I suggest the distinction of "possible" and "actual" modifications in the framework of DSR. Although Leibniz did not use these terms,[35] I think we can reasonably introduce this distinction following his discussions in DSR. Possible modifications do not exist in the actual world, but they are conceived as such by the perfect intellect of God. In contrast, actual modifications do exist in this world, and they exist as results of God's power and will that produce them in accordance with possible modifications. In *On the Secret of Sublime* of DSR, Leibniz wrote that God is not "nature, fate, fortune, necessity, the world," but he is "a certain substance, a person, a mind."[36] Also, in *On the Truths, the Mind, God, and the Universe* of DSR, Leibniz explicitly wrote that a finite mind is "created by God," and it exists and remains "by the will of God."[37] In these passages, Leibniz suggested that God is a person who has a will to create finite things that he conceives. Moreover, at the beginning of *On the Secret of Sublime* from DSR, he wrote that "something exists, and all possibles cannot exist."[38] Leibniz obviously did not hold that all possible things exist, as Spinoza did. We can understand that according to Leibniz of DSR, God chooses some possible things out of others to actualize. Hence we can conceive of the distinction between actual things created by God, on the one hand, and possible things that are not actualized by him, on the other.

To be sure, since DSR is a collection of articles, we need to be careful when we interpret one of them on the basis of another. But at least, even in *On the Simple Forms*, in which we found the passages of the pure relation and

---

[33] A VI, 3, 523 = DSR, 83–85.
[34] I only find seven lines of words between two passages in the translation of G. H. R. Parkinson.
[35] Leibniz only used the expression "possible mode" in the passage of the subjects theory.
[36] A VI, 3, 475 = DSR, 27.
[37] A VI, 3, 512 = DSR, 65–67.
[38] A VI, 3, 472 = DSR, 21.

subjects theories, Leibniz suggested that there are many possible worlds, since he wrote that "if it is a law in our world that the same quantity of motion is always preserved, there can be another universe in which there are also other laws."[39] Here Leibniz argued that this actual world has a specific law of motion, but it does not hold in another possible world or universe. Leibniz also suggested that different possible worlds are given through relations of many simple forms in *On Simple Forms*, since he wrote that

> "[t]here is the same variety in any kind of world, and this is nothing other than the same essence related in various ways."[40]

Although Leibniz did not use "possible modification" in this article, we can understand that he there distinguished a part of the actual world from a part of some merely possible world.

Now given my distinction between actual and possible modifications, I suggest that according to the passage of the subjects theory, possible modifications are given through relations of the form of extension to the other forms, and these possible modifications are actualized by God's power and will to create them. I think in the passage of the subjects theory Leibniz took "the immeasurable" as the form of extension, and he seems to discuss combinations of the extension with other forms or attributes. In the passage of the subjects theory, Leibniz stated that

> "[t]he subject itself, or God, together with his ubiquity, gives the immeasurable, and this immeasurable combined with other subjects bring it about that all possible modes, or things, follow in it."[41]

By paying special attention to the immeasurable, Lærke argues that Leibniz assumes that the immeasurable is nothing but the attribute of absolute extension. In *On the Origin of Things from Forms* of DSR, Leibniz seems to assume that "the immeasurable [*immensum*]," "absolute extension [*extensum absolutum*]," and "the expanded [*expansum*]" refer to an indivisible foundation of the space.[42] "Absolute extension" is contrasted with the space in the sense that the space has a quantitative extension, while absolute extension does not.[43]

---

[39] A VI, 3, 522 = DSR, 83.
[40] A VI, 3, 523 = DSR, 83.
[41] A VI, 3, 523 = DSR, 85.
[42] A VI, 3, 519 = DSR, 77–79 and Lærke: *Leibniz lecteur*, p. 470.
[43] A VI, 3, 519 = DSR, 77–79.

Also, the space is composed of parts and changes, whereas the absolute extension is not composed and changed.[44] Now if the immeasurable is understood to be the attribute of extension, which I found fairly convincing, then it seems that it is God having the form of extension,[45] not God as a subject, is needed for producing possible modifications. Here relations of the extension to "other subjects" seem to be sufficient for bringing about possible modifications.

But the subjects theory still seems to be distinct from the pure relations theory, since it seems that "other subjects," in addition to combinations of simple forms, are needed to produce particular modifications. As we have seen, Adams suggests that "other subjects" in the passage of the subjects theory are subjects of finite things, and each subject underlies some finite individual. Against Adams, I follow Lærke's interpretation of the passage, according to which "other subjects" do not refer to subjects that are really distinct from God. In response to Adams' interpretation, Lærke argues that another reading of the passage is possible. For Lærke, although "the passage is very obscure and it allows diverse interpretations," Adams' reading is not the only possible interpretation on the basis of the texts, and it is not "perhaps the most coherent" among possible readings.[46] Lærke goes on to argue that Adams' interpretation has a problem, that is, his interpretation introduces another category in Leibniz's ontology of DSR, a "fourth ontological category" that is different from God, simple forms, and things.[47] "Subjects" need to be distinct from things, since they are requirements of producing things. It seems that a subject is embodied as a thing by having some properties through relations. But it is difficult to find evidence to show that Leibniz introduced this fourth category in other texts. To avoid this interpretation problem, Lærke proposes to take a subject to be God insofar as having some simple attribute:

> "Therefore it is the subject itself or God, *insofar as having absolute extension*, that has to be related to other subjects. This restriction allows us to understand the expression "the other subjects" differently from what Adams understood.

---

[44] Ibid., p. 470f. and cf. A VI, 3, 391.
[45] Kulstad pays more attention to the distinction of "ubiquity" and "the immeasurable," and states that the former is "a term Leibniz uses for one of the forms or attributes of God," and the latter is "a term Leibniz uses to refer to God insofar as God has the attribute of ubiquity." See Kulstad: "Leibniz's De Summa Rerum", p. 81.
[46] Lærke: *Leibniz lecteur*, p. 532.
[47] Ibid.

[...] Thus the "other subjects" are, for instance, "God insofar as having absolute thought," or "God insofar as such and such attribute."[48]

According to Lærke's reading, Leibniz did not introduce a plurality of really distinct subjects in the passage of the subjects theory. By using the term "subjects," Leibniz eventually referred to the only subject God. In this reading, God is taken as different subjects, insofar as he has many distinct attributes. God as having extension, for instance, is conceptually distinct from God as having thought. I think Lærke's interpretation is worth considering, given that in the passage of the subjects theory Leibniz declared that things are produced "along with a subject," and that "various results of forms" are "combined with a subject." It seems that Leibniz means to emphasize that one subject is needed. If we assume that Leibniz suddenly declared that many subjects are required for producing modifications, his statement seems to be out of the context of the whole passage.

It is still true that Lærke also assumes that the subjects theory is distinct from the pure relations theory. Why? Since according to the subjects theory, God as the subject of forms (especially that of extension) is required, in addition to many forms or attributes to produce modifications. But I interpret the passage of the subjects theory as implying that possible modifications are actualized by God as the subject having the power to produce things. I especially take note of the statement that "[t]he various results of forms, combined with a subject, bring it about the particulars result." Here it seems that various results are distinguished from particulars. What is the difference between them? In my reading, "particulars" are concrete and actual particular things which exist in the actual world. "Various results" are, I think, possible finite things before created by God, who grasps what finite things are by "mere combination" of forms, especially utilizing the form of extension. Then he creates finite things as they are, by utilizing his power, and actualize them. In my reading, God is needed as a subject when possible modifications are actualized. As the pure relations theory implies, possible modifications are given as possibles through mere combinations of forms. But this does not mean that God as a subject is not needed for actualizing them. In my interpretation, God as

---

[48] "C'est donc le sujet lui-même ou Dieu, *en tant qu'étendue absolue*, qui doit être rapporté aux autres sujets. Cette restriction nous permet de comprendre l'expression 'les autres sujets' différemment que ne le fait Adams. [...] Donc que les 'autres sujets' sont, par example, "Dieu en tant que pensée absolue" ou 'Dieu en tant que tel ou tel attribut'" [ibid., p. 534].

having power and will is needed for producing actual modifications. I understand the pure relations theory as asserting that possible, not actual, modifications are given through relations of forms, which seems to be consistent with an implication of the passage of the subjects theory that possible modifications are given by relations of the form of extension to the other forms. To be sure, my interpretation has a weak point: Leibniz did not give an explicit expression for how God exercises his will. Leibniz merely suggested that particular things are produced when "various results of forms" are "combined with a subject." This is obviously not the best expression for how God activated the will. Still, I don't think it is impossible to read the passage as consistent with my interpretation.

2.2 Unifying the Matter Theory with the Others

The passage of the matter theory is from *On the Origin of Things from Forms*, while that of the pure relations theory is from *On Simple Forms*. They don't belong to the same article. But in fact, we can find a passage from *On the Origin of Things from Forms*, in which Leibniz gave a suggestion that is remarkably similar to what he said in the passage of the pure relations theory:[49]

> "It seems to me that the origin of things from God is of the same kind as the origin of properties from an essence; just as $6 = 1 + 1 + 1 + 1 + 1 + 1$, therefore $6 = 3 + 3, = 3 \times 2, = 4 + 2$, etc. Nor may one doubt that the one expression differs from the other, for in one way we think of the number 3 or the number 2 expressly, and in another way we do not; but it is certain that the number 3 is not thought of by someone who thinks of six units at the same time."[50]

Here Leibniz asserted that many distinct properties arise from one essence, which is fairly close to a claim of the passage of the pure relations theory that variety is "nothing other than the same essence related in various ways." Given that the passage of the matter theory is also from *On the Origin of Things from Forms*, it is difficult to see how Leibniz intentionally wrote inconsistent hypotheses in the very same article. It seems to me that Leibniz was trying to show a consistent picture of metaphysics in the article, and thus it is worthwhile to attempt to read the passages of the two theories as mutually

---

[49] Lærke also takes the passage from *On the Origin of Things from Forms* as supporting the pure relations theory. See ibid., p. 523.
[50] A VI, 3, 518f. = DSR, 77.

consistent. Therefore it may be a mistake to suppose that the matter theory obviously contradicts the pure relations theory.

But how can the matter theory be coherent with the pure relations theory? Here I take note of Leibniz's statement that "change and matter, i.e., modifications, are what result from all other forms taken together."[51] Previously, Leibniz noted that "[p]erception and situation are simple forms," suggesting that by the term "form" he meant simple form or attribute. Leibniz seems clearly to endorse the idea that matter results from relations of simple forms. I also take note of the passage in which Leibniz suggests that negative affections are given by many simple forms or attributes. Although Leibniz did not use the term "matter," I think it provides a clue to understand how matter is given in the framework of DSR:

> "Every purely affirmative attribute is infinite; or, it is as great as it can be, or contains all the things that belong to its genus. There are necessarily several affirmative primary attributes; for if there were only one, only one thing could be understood. It seems that negative affections can arise only from a plurality of affirmative attributes-for example, thought and extension. For as it is impossible for something extended to be thought without variety, it follows that certain modes of extension are necessary, and that all those which have been, are, or will be can be thought by one being. From this the origin and necessity of modification is evident."[52]

So, Leibniz suggests that thought can be negated by extension, and vice versa. It seems that a thinking thing can have a negative affection of "non-extended." And Leibniz seems to suggest that modes or modifications of extension are embodied with negative affections that are given by a plurality of affirmative attributes. Also, Leibniz suggests that a mind needs matter to have specific perceptions, such as a sensation of red color.[53] Since matter consists in relations, this claim seems to suggest that specific perceptions are given by relations of simple forms, and in my reading, they are brought about by negative affections given by many simple forms. For instance, a perception of red color seems to be distinguished from that of blue color since the former has some property originated from some simple form(s), while the latter does not.

Hereby I think that matter or limitation is introduced through relations of forms or attributes. In other words, one attribute can be limited by other attributes. If so, the matter theory could be explained in terms of relations of

---

[51] A VI, 3, 522 = DSR, 83.
[52] A VI, 3, 573f. = DSR, 93.
[53] A VI, 3, 518 = DSR, 77

attributes. The view that one attribute is limited by other attributes is utterly inconsistent with Spinoza's metaphysics, according to which each attribute is independent of any other attribute. But I think that Leibniz's view in DSR is at most "quasi-Spinozistic," if we are to use Lærke's term, and that it is entirely possible that Leibniz did not accept some of Spinoza's claims.[54]

---

[54] As we have seen, Leibniz wrote that God is not "nature, fate, fortune, necessity, the world", but he is "a certain substance, a person, a mind" (A VI, 3, 475 = DSR, 27). Here Leibniz seems to keep a distance from Spinoza's pantheistic view that everything necessarily follows from God. Also, Leibniz explicitly criticized Spinoza in DSR, saying that an individual mind does not extinguish with its body (A VI, 3, 510 = DSR, 61; cf. *Ethics* 5P23).

Leibniz on Compossibility and the Unity of Space and Time

Michael Futch (Tulsa, OK)

In this paper, I will offer a brief exploration of three of the four fundamental ordering relations of all possible worlds: space, time, and, what I will argue is more (even most) fundamental, compossibility. Along with the relation of *commercio*, which I will set to the side entirely, these relations obtain among any and all substances (or at least the phenomena they represent) that can be conceived as existing within the same world. They are, indeed, constitutive of the *worldliness* of a world's substances, i.e. what it means for substances to exist in the same world is for them to be compossible with and spatially and temporally related to each other. I will have a little more to say about this briefly, but will mostly take it as an assumed background for the focus of the paper. That focus is how Leibniz conceived the relation among these relations, and more specifically which of these relations – compossibility, space, and time – he understood to be more ontologically fundamental and analytically prior to the others. Against the cosmological interpretation, I will suggest, though will certainly not try to prove in any strong sense, that compossibility is analytically basic with respect to space and time, and that an understanding of what Leibniz intends by "compossibility" cannot therefore be explained in terms of the spatial and temporal relatedness of compossible substances. I will also argue that the cosmological interpretation is not a sufficiently strong understanding of compossibility for establishing the unity of space and time.

A qualifying remark before I proceed. Leibniz's comments on compossibility span almost the entirety of his oeuvre. And with good reason: the notion of compossibility is crucial to the overarching architectonic of Leibniz's philosophy, and in particular his attempts to stave off the philosophical *bête noir* of Spinozism. And yet, this centrality notwithstanding, his recurring remarks about compossibility, individually and in aggregate, amount to little more than telegraphic adumbrations. Not only that, but they are often difficult to reconcile with each other, and can support divergent construals. This shouldn't be surprising, for Leibniz himself famously says that

> "it is as yet unknown to men whence arises the incompossibility of different things, or of how different essences can conflict with each other, since all purely positive terms seem to be compatible with each other."[1]

---

[1] GP VII, 194.

In short, one searches in vain for a unified and consistent account of compossibility across the Leibnizian corpus. So my thesis comes to this: there are strands in Leibniz's philosophy, not always seamlessly interwoven with the overall tapestry of his thought, that militate in favor of some conceptions of compossibility and against others, and to the extent that different conceptions are in the foreground and others in the background, his grounds for denying the plurality of distinct spatiotemporal frameworks are considerably weakened.

That space and time are orders of connection of all possible worlds is a recurring theme in Leibniz's writings. In a 1687 letter to Arnauld, Leibniz writes that for substances to harmonize with each other they must represent the same spatiotemporal phenomena:

> "[...] all substances must have a harmony and connection which links them together, and must express in themselves the same universe. [...] Otherwise, the phenomena of different minds would not harmonize with each other, and there would be as many systems as substances [...] The whole concept we have of time and space is based upon this harmony."[2]

And ten years later in response to Bayle, Leibniz avers that were God to create substances representing different spatiotemporal phenomena, he would have "made as many worlds without connection [...] as there are substances."[3] In these passages Leibniz promulgates the tenet that if two or more substances each represent different phenomenal events then they express in themselves different universes: there are as "many worlds" as "there are substances." On the other hand, the perceptions of diverse substances are connected if and only if they are harmonious with one another, and they are harmonious with one another if and only if they express within themselves the same universe. Thus, for substances to be connected, they must express the same phenomena and the same spatio-temporal system. That substances in the same world must represent the same spatio-temporal phenomena is affirmed in an earlier essay, where Leibniz explains that space

> "[...] is that which brings it about that several perceptions cohere with each other at the same time [...] Therefore, the idea of space is recognized by this: namely, it is that by which we separate the place and, as it were, the world of dreams from our own [...] And it follows further, on the assumption that there

---

[2] Ibid., II, 115.
[3] Ibid., V, 519.

are minds having perceptions not congruent with ours, that there can be an infinity of other spaces and other worlds such that there is no distance between them and ours [...] Whoever asks whether there could be another world and another space is just asking if there are other minds having no communication with ours."[4]

The world as represented in my dreams and the world as represented in my waking states are worlds with distinct spaces, Leibniz argues, because the representations of these worlds are incongruent with one another. They are incongruent with one another because they represent different phenomena, representations of phenomena not cohering with one another. If two minds perceive events in principle unobservable to the other mind, they perceive two different systems, or, as Leibniz says, they perceive a numerically distinct and consequently discernible spatial array.

Other texts make this point, but for purposes of brevity I will assume that a substance must represent phenomena that are spatially and temporally related to the phenomena represented by another substance in order for those two substances to be part of the same world. And of course, those two substances must also be compossible. The question arises: what does it mean for substances to be compossible, and how is their compossibility related to the temporal and spatial connectedness of the phenomena they represent?

One understanding of the relation among compossibility, space, and time, and one that contrasts sharply with the view that I will be addressing, is succinctly summarized in Nicholas Rescher's statement that "substances are located in different spaces *because* they contradict one another."[5] At least two claims are being advanced here. First, in the natural order of reasons, compossibility is prior to space (and time, we might add) in a way that the compossibility of substances determines their spatial and temporal relatedness. Or rather, their compossibility with each other determines *whether* they are spatially and temporally related. It is because of their compossibility or incompossibility that we can or cannot conceive substances as being spatially and temporally connected, not vice-versa. Second, compossibility is to be understood as logical compatibility (logical compatibility among their complete concepts, according to Benson Mates).

Contrary to the claims of some, one can easily cull passages that support the second part of this claim. Leibniz variously writes that

---

[4] A VI, 3, 511f.
[5] Nicholas Rescher: *Leibniz's Metaphysics of Nature*, Dordrecht 2013, p. 99.

> "Compossible is what, with another thing, implies no contradiction,"[6] or, again, "there are as many possible worlds as there are series of things that can be posited without implying a contradiction."[7]

More support, both textual and architectonic, can be found in Leibniz's view that possible worlds, and not just possible substances, have their own concepts:

> "I shall add that I conceive that there was an infinite number of possible ways of creating the world [...] and that each possible world depends upon certain of God's principal plans or ends [...] that is to say upon [...] [the] laws of the general order of that possible universe to which they are suited and whose concept they determine."[8]

On the assumption that something is possible if and only if its concept contains no contradiction, it would not be unreasonable to conclude from this that the possibility of worlds, just like the possibility of abstract or concrete beings, depends on the principle of contradiction: possible worlds have concepts that contain no contradiction. Furthermore, it is a well-known tenet of Leibniz's philosophy that "all truths that concern possibles [...] rest on the principle of contradiction."[9] A world *qua* possible is one whose concept does not contain a latent or patent logical contradiction. The idea, to quote Catherine Wilson (who is critical of this view) is that we get

> "possible worlds from a set of pre-existing possible substances that are able to coexist because they are compossible."[10]

An alternative understanding of compossibility, space, and time – the "cosmological interpretation" – has recently been ably defended by Rutherford and Messina in their article "Leibniz on Compossibility."[11] Variations of this can

---

[6] Grua, 325.
[7] Ibid., 390.
[8] *The Leibniz-Arnauld Correspondence*, ed. and trans. by H. T. Mason, p. 57.
[9] G. W. Leibniz: *Philosophical Essays,* ed. by R. Ariew and D. Garber, Indianapolis 1989, p. 19.
[10] Catherine Wilson: "Response to Ohad Nachtomy's 'Individuals, Worlds, and Relations: A Discussion of Catherine Wilson's "Plenitude and Compossibility"'", in: *Leibniz Review* 11 (2001), pp. 125–129, here p. 125.
[11] Donald Rutherford/James Messina: "Leibniz on Compossibility", in: *Philosophy Compass* 4/6 (December 2009), pp. 962–977.

be found in Catherine Wilson's "Plenitude and Compossibility in Leibniz,"[12] as well as Koistinen's and Repo's "Compossibility and Being in the Same World,"[13] but I will focus on the first article. According to the cosmological interpretation, compossibility is to be explained in terms of whether or not God can conceive of two or more substances as existing in the same world. If such substances can be so conceived, they are ipso facto compossible, and if they cannot be so conceived, they are thereby incompossible. Notice that this makes the notion of a world, or membership in the same world, primary vis-à-vis that of compossibility. As Rutherford and Messina put it, "The notion of a world is conceptually prior to the notion of compossibility."[14] Hence, we cannot determine if two substances are compossible unless we can first determine if they can belong to the same world. Further, since we are using the idea of a world to define "compossibility", we cannot partition substances into possible worlds based on the fact that they are compossible with each other. Such a procedure would be blatantly circular: our partitioning of substances into worlds would presuppose precisely what it is trying to explain, their compossibility. Possible problems lurk here, but I will postpone them for now.

Given this understanding of compossibility, we might well wonder what it is about substances that enables God to conceive of them as existing in the same world. What constitutes the worldliness of substances that is used to explain their compossibility? The cosmological interpretation has a ready reply to this question: substances can be conceived as existing in the same world if and only if they stand in appropriate temporal and spatial relations to one another. Write Rutherford and Messina:

> "According to the cosmological interpretation, substances can be conceived as belonging to the same world, within which they are lawfully connected, only if they are related according to the orders of space and time."[15]

Substances being compossible just is the phenomena they represent being spatially and temporally related; absent that spatial and temporal relatedness, the substances are incompossible. Moreover, in the logical ordering of relations, space and time are conceptually prior to compossibility. Consequently, com-

---

[12] Catherine Wilson: "Plenitude and Compossibility", in: *Leibniz Review* 10 (2000), pp. 1–20.
[13] Olli Koistinen/Arto Repo: "Compossibility and Being in the Same World in Leibniz's Metaphysics", in: *Studia Leibnitiana* 31 (1999), pp. 196–214.
[14] Rutherford/Messina: "Leibniz on Compossibility", p. 969.
[15] Ibid., p. 971.

possibility considerations cannot be drawn upon to determine which substances are or can be spatially and temporally related to each other, for it is substances (or the phenomena they represent) being spatially and temporally related to each other in a possible world that accounts for their compossibility. It is not as though substances are (logically) first compossible and then, from that, spatially and temporally related (as Rescher maintains); it is precisely that spatial and temporal relatedness that constitutes their compossibility. Thus, to be compossible is to be connected in the sense specified in the first section of this talk: compossibility and harmony come to the same thing, on this reading. All and only those substances that represent the same spatiotemporal phenomena are part of the same world, and that is what makes them compossible.

The cosmological interpretation can find support in a certain way of reading select texts. For example, in a letter from 1714, Leibniz rejects his correspondent's assertion that to know if something is possible "[…] it is necessary to know its connection with the rest of the universe," though goes on to add that knowing that its connection with the rest of the universe would be necessary in order to know if something is compossible with the universe, "for surely there would be no place for it without such connections."[16] The romance story between the shepherd and shepherdess is possible in its own right because it contains within itself nothing contradictory, but it is possible relative to the actual world – it is *compossible* with the world's history – only if it is appropriately connected to it, only if, as Leibniz says, there is a "place" for it, where that place is partly its standing in spatial and temporal connections to other existents. This lack of connections is what accounts for its incompossibility. Similarly, "On the Ultimate Origination of Things" analogizes the assembly of possible worlds to a board game where the objective is to leave no empty spaces:

> "time, place, or in a word, the receptivity or capacity of the world can be taken for the cost [to place something] […]. And so, assuming that at some time being is to prevail over nonbeing […] it follows that there would be as much as there possibly can be, given the capacity of time and space (that is, the capacity of the order of possible existence)."[17]

Adopting a literal reading of this analogy yields the conclusion that space and time delimit the range of what things possible in themselves are compossible

---

[16] GP III, 572.
[17] Ibid., VII, 303f.

with each other: for two or more things to be jointly actualizable, they must fit into the spatial and temporal structure of a possible world in the right way. Indeed, a possible world is a possible world because of the right spatiotemporal fit, so to speak, of its possible substances.

[I will note that this is not the only way to read these texts: even if it is true that all and only compossible substances are spatially and temporally related to each, it doesn't follow that this is the defining characteristic of their compossibility.]

And then there is the tantalizing passage from Section 14 of the *Discourse on Metaphysics* where Leibniz says all sorts of things that he shouldn't say, including the statement that

> "the result of each view of the universe, as seen from a certain position, is a substance which expresses the universe in conformity with this view."

According to Catherine Wilson, this shows not only that worldhood is prior to compossibility (against the combinatorial and compossibility-checking models of world making), but even prior to substances. I can't make heads or tails of Leibniz's remarks here, and they flatly contradict what he says elsewhere (the *Theodicy*, among other texts),[18] so I'll note them only to pass by in silence.

Other texts are less favorable to the cosmological interpretation, and point to a very different understanding of the logical ordering of compossibility, space, and time. We have seen above that it is a consequence of this interpretation that spatial and temporal relations are logically and conceptually prior to the relation of compossibility since the latter is analyzed in terms of the former. As Leibniz might say, space and time, and with them the notion of a world, are prior by nature to compossibility. It can reasonably be objected, however, that this reverses the order of definition usually on offer by Leibniz. For instance, Leibniz writes, in the very same letter to Bourget referenced above, that

---

[18] "The wisdom of God, not content with embracing all possibles, penetrates them, compares them [...] to estimate their degrees of perfection and imperfection. [...] By this means the divine Wisdom distributes all the possibles it had already contemplated separately, into so many universal systems." (*Theodicy*, Section 225). Here, Leibniz makes clear that possible worlds are formed by God first understanding the possible connections of possible substances, thus making the complete concepts of substances explanatorily prior to possible worlds.

> "since there are different combinations of possibilities, some of them better than others, there are many possible universes, each collection of compossibles making up one of them."[19]

This appears to accord explanatory priority to the notion of compossibility: *since* there are different possible combinations of compossibles, there are different possible universes; it is the different combinations of compossibles that give rise to different worlds, not different worlds partitioning possible substances into compossible classes. Put differently, a possible universe is a collection of compossibles, rather than a collection of substances being compossible because they can be understood to exist within the same possible universe. Along these same lines, Leibniz avers that "Space, just as a common time, is taken to be nothing more than a certain order of compossibles."[20] This, too, is most naturally read as partially defining space and time in terms of compossibility, as orders constituted by compossibles. But if that is right, then the spatial and temporal relatedness of substances cannot enter into the analysis of their compossibility, for that would be to introduce into the *analysans* precisely what is being analyzed.

The preceding statements are not just occasional remarks shorn of firm footing in Leibniz's philosophy, but are instead interwoven into a deeper metaphysical substructure that points in the direction of making spatial and temporal relatedness derivative of the relation of compossibility. This comes into view most clearly in a series of studies dating from Leibniz's middle period. Leibniz writes:

> "All of our concepts perhaps are comprehended in these few: there are the most general realities, such as possibility, positive, complete, and absolute, and the contraries of these, such as impossibility, negative, incomplete, limited. From these come being and non-being, subject and attribute, and God and creatures. There is also *variety*, whence comes sameness and difference and one and many; *consequence*, and those things which come between consequences; and *order* and those things which come between the prior and posterior (by nature, that is). From order and consequence taken together arises cause and effect. From them, in turn, comes *change* [*Mutatio*] [...]."[21]

Leibniz's proposal holds out the promise of laying bare the fundamental ingredients of all concepts, of offering a complete resolution of any concept that will analyze it into adequate component notions, any one of which must be an

---

[19] GP III, 572.
[20] GP VII, 467.
[21] A VI, 4 A, 398.

instance of the above categories. Thus, these categories and the notions contained in them are exhaustive of the possible kinds of elements of any concept. Equally importantly, Leibniz provides an ordering of the categories themselves. There is a succession among the categories of consequence, order, causation, and change such that each presupposes the preceding category. One cannot, for instance, provide an analysis of change without invoking the categories of order and consequence.

In all of these studies, relations of compatibility, incompatibility, opposition and connection are conceptually prior, in the ordering of the categories, to spatial and temporal relations. Glimmerings of this can be seen in the above passage, where Leibniz situates change – *mutatio* – at the very end of categories, after variety, consequence, order, and cause and effect. Consequence is itself a genus of relations, the species of which include "incompatibility" and "inconnegability." These relations of opposition and connection are the ingredients that enter into change, and as several other similar studies make plainly evident, time is itself grounded on *mutatio*, thus making it conceptually derivative of the logically prior categories. Writes Leibniz:

> "From order and consequence taken together come cause and effect, and then from them comes change, and then time and temporally prior and posterior."[22]
> Or again, "time is a continuous order of existence *according to change*."[23]

The conceptually derivative nature of temporal relatedness comes out more clearly still in Leibniz's myriad definitions of "temporally prior" and "temporally posterior," which unfailingly utilize what Leibniz dubs relations of consequence and order, and especially the relations of natural priority and cause and effect. These definitions are too numerous to catalogue entirely in this talk, but a representative statement would include the following:

> "Things are simultaneous if one is absolutely the condition of the other. But if one is the condition of the other with an intervening change, then one is prior, the other posterior. That is understood to be prior which is simultaneous with the cause, and posterior which is simultaneous with the effect. Or, prior is understood to be that which is simpler or which is a requisite of the other."[24]

---

[22] Ibid.,399.
[23] C, 479 (emphasis added).
[24] A VI, 4 A, 628. Still more: "Also prior or posterior to another thing [...] is whatever is simultaneous with a thing incompatible with the other thing. So that if A is simultaneous with B, and B and C are incompatible, and C is, then A will be prior or posterior by time to C" (ibid., 390).

To avoid confusion, it is no part of my argument to characterize the kind of incompatibility involved in the analysis of change and time as logical in nature, so I'm not defending the so-called analytic understanding compossibility (though I think that some version of it is right). My co-panelist Stefano has cautioned against reading these relations as "properly logical ones," suggesting that the Leibnizian square of opposition involves ontological relationships that are "true to a large extent on extra-logical grounds."[25] I think that that's correct, all the more so since they are typically cashed out in terms of implication of existence and non-existence among things. In any case, it would be question-begging in the extreme against the cosmological interpretation to assume that the relevant notion of incompatibility is of a strictly logical character. Even if we do not construe compatibility or compossibility along narrowly logical lines, however, it remains true that many of Leibniz's writings identify compossibility as a kind of compatibility and incompossibility as a kind of incompatibility: "But since some things are incompatible with each other, it follows that not all possibles are able to exist."[26] This, from the *Resume of Metaphysics*, or the following from the *De Summa Rerum*: "Whatever can exist, and is compatible with others, exists."[27] Surely any reading of Leibniz must grant that incompossibility is a kind of incompatibility, however one understands that compatibility – logically or ontologically. And Leibniz explicitly says as much, identifying compossibility as one of the relations falling into the category of consequence, which, as we've seen above, is prior to change and temporal relations.[28] To the extent that Leibniz places the relations of compossibility and incompossibility in this category, he cannot draw on the logically posterior relations of time to define them. Strikingly, at no point in these studies does Leibniz provide an explication of compossibility that draws upon any class of relations logically subsequent to relations of consequence, whereas compossibility is at least sometimes identified as a relation of consequence.

Insofar as one is focusing on the ontological architecture envisioned in these texts, there is a strong, albeit not definitive, case to be made that relations

---

[25] Stefano Di Bella: *The Science of the Individual: Leibniz's Ontology of Individual Substance*, Dordrecht 2005, pp. 240f.
[26] C, 534.
[27] A VI, 3, 582.
[28] Ibid., 600.

of compossibility and incompossibility are prior in the order of nature to spatial and temporal relations. While acknowledging that Leibniz's texts as a whole do not speak with a single voice on how to understand compossibility, I would suggest that these studies are not easily reconciled with the central claim of the cosmological interpretation, namely, that the notion of worldhood – of being spatially and temporally connected – is conceptually prior to that of compossibility, and that compossibility is to be partially analyzed using spatial and temporal relations.

One other possible objection that can be leveled at the cosmological interpretation is that it does not have the "right" implications for the unity of space and time, or at least not the implications that it wants. Put as a question, does the above view of compossibility rule out the metaphysical possibility of a plurality of distinct spatial and temporal frameworks, where a thing in one framework is connected to all things in that framework but to nothing in other frameworks? Rutherford and Messina suggest that it does –

> "the cosmological interpretation is intended to provide an account of compossibility sufficiently strong to ground a response to Spinoza"[29]

– though some commentators have recently argued that it doesn't. I think that the latter is closer to the mark for the following reasons. If compossibility does indeed come to nothing more than substances being spatially and temporally connected, then there is nothing in Leibniz's philosophy to rule out on *compossibility* grounds the logical or, more weakly, metaphysical possibility of many such sets of substances. It is certainly true that on the basis of the cosmological interpretation, we can infer that there are no *worlds* with spatially or temporally unconnected substances, but this is merely because the foregoing interpretation tells us only under what conditions substances can exist in the same world, not what substances can exist full stop. The cosmological interpretation specifies the conditions under which substances can be conceived as being part of the same world, but it doesn't show *that* or explain *why* multiple non-harmonizing sets of substances cannot be actualized; it simply shows that the set of all of those sets (or the set of any two or more sets) does not itself constitute a world, at least not in the relevant sense of the term. Take two sets of substances – S1{A, B, C, D} and S2{E, F, G, H} – such that all the substances in S1 have mutually-harmonizing perceptions, and all the substances in S2 have mutually-harmonizing perceptions, and no substance in S1

---

[29] Rutherford/Messina: "Leibniz on Compossibility", p. 969.

has perceptions harmonizing with any substance in S2 (and, by the symmetry of harmony, vice-versa). At most, the cosmological interpretation shows that a third set – S3{A, B, C, D, E, F, G, H} – doesn't count as a world in the strict sense, but it doesn't preclude the creation of multiple worlds – say, S1 and S2 – each with substances spatially and temporally connected to substances in their world but to no substance in a different world. Even if we grant with the cosmological interpretation that God cannot create a world with temporally and spatially disconnected substances, we cannot on that basis rule out the creation of many unconnected worlds of appropriately intra-mundanely connected substances. Indeed, Rutherford and Messina appear to concede that the cosmological interpretation is perfectly consistent with multiple worlds:

> "God could decide not to create a world, choosing instead to create one or more separate substances, which lacked the unity of a world."[30]

But the extent to which God makes such a choice must be a function of something other than those substances being incompossible. If spatially and temporally unconnected worlds cannot be brought about by God, it cannot simply be because their substances are incompossible with those in other worlds (on this theory of compossibility).

Let me very quickly and even more dogmatically conclude where I began: Leibniz's theories of compossibility seem themselves to be too disunified to provide a consistent basis for establishing the metaphysically necessary unity of space and time. Indeed, with the possible exception of a variant of the analytic understanding of compossibility (something akin to Margaret Wilson's reading), it isn't clear that any theory of compossibility by itself suffices for that purpose. Leibniz might have other arguments to that effect – Cover and Hawthorne suggest that all substances are per se compossible and that it is only with the addition of *morally* necessary laws of harmony that they become incompossible – but these are perhaps too weak to establish the metaphysical necessity of unified of space and time. If so, there are possible worlds in a more extended and attenuated sense of the term – a world being the totality of every created thing – that are not worlds in the narrower sense of the term, systems of spatially and temporally related substances.

---

[30] Ibid., p. 973.

Leibniz in Early Twentieth-Century Spanish Philosophy: d' Ors, Ortega y Gasset, and Zubiri

Mattia Geretto (Venice)

1. Introduction

It is no exaggeration to say that Leibniz held a prominent position in late nineteenth and early twentieth century Spanish philosophy, fostered by major and minor Spanish intellectuals who addressed Leibniz's thought and thus contributed independently to the "Leibniz Renaissance" that gradually took hold in Europe, especially after the eminent works by Couturat and Russell were published.

Leibniz was a key reference point for Spanish intellectuals, as can be seen in the theory of "*correlacionismo*" by Ángel Amor Ruibal (1869–1930), the *dim perceptions* of consciousness in the works of Antonio Machado (1875–1939), poet and philosopher, the appeal of *virtual innatism* in early works by Unamuno (1864–1936), the reworking of the principles of *contradiction* and *sufficient reason* by Eugenio d'Ors (1881–1954), an exploration of the *idea of principle* by José Ortega y Gasset (1883–1955), and a reconsideration of the concept of *monads* by Xavier Zubiri (1898–1983). However, Leibniz also heavily influenced foremost European philosophers such as Lotze in Germany, Renouvier in France, Varisco in Italy, and MacTaggart and Whitehead in England, to name but a few.

The importance of Leibniz in the works of the writers mentioned above could well be explored in single monographs for each author, as critical essays on this topic are few and far between, not to mention at times completely absent, but not all can be addressed here. Hence, considering that various thinkers could be dealt with in future projects, I shall limit my considerations to three intellectuals: d'Ors, Ortega y Gasset, and Zubiri. I will attempt to highlight (1) elements of Leibniz's thought interpreted by these authors and (2) and how Leibniz's ideas were reworked by them.

2. Eugenio d'Ors

Although a leading figure in his time, to date Eugenio d'Ors Rovira is still one of the least known Spanish philosophers. This may be due to his political activities or his tormented academic career which frequently drove him away from home. His thought resists easy categorization according to traditional philosophical canon, as he was a theorist gifted with a rare aesthetic sensitivity who wished to restore the integrality of a person as an individual who "works and plays" ("el hombre que trabaja y que juega").[1] He was undoubtedly an original thinker, especially concerning his original use of language, which even led him to develop a brilliant composition style "in five hundred words" in which he distilled topics such as the "history of the world", the "history of philosophy", "hygiene" and "angelology", within the framework of five hundred words. This particular use of terminology is also an indication of the central role that aesthetic considerations played in his thought, to the extent that he is most remembered for his essay *Du Baroque*,[2] or for his popular and frequently reprinted *Tres horas en el Museo del Prado*.[3] Actually, his most ambitious theoretical work that in turn is drawn from the renowned *Glosari* is *El Secreto de la Filosofía* (1947), a work in which we find some important sections that reveal his deep knowledge of Leibniz's works. For example, in reference to the *Nouveaux Essais*, he reflects on the fact that the "early Leibniz" considered mere illusion an extra-logical reasoning to make a discovery, whereas he acknowledged the "leap" that the scholar makes in a given moment in order to reach the light of truth. (Note that d'Ors refers to the author of the *Nouveaux Essais* as "early Leibniz").[4]

---

[1] We find this famous expression for the first time in *Religio est libertas* (1908); it will be used again, in a very suggestive way, also in his most important theoretical book *El Secreto de la Filosofía*: "Del existir – en la especie del existir humano – decía el príncipe Hamlet: 'Estamos tejidos con la misma trama que nuestros sueños': es una fórmula que, antes y después, y para preservación de ilusiones, ha sido muchas veces adoptada por la Filosofía, más particularmente por la filosofía oriental u orientalizante. A este nihilismo del hombre contemplativo, puede y debe el hombre activo, el hombre que trabaja y que juega, responder: 'Son nuestros sueños los que están engendrados de la misma substancia auténtica que nosotros': o sea que, más bien que decir: 'La vida es sueño', hay que decir: 'El sueño es vida'." Cf. Eugeni d'Ors: *El Secreto de la Filosofía. Doce lecciones, tres diálogos y, en apéndice, "La filosofía en quinientas palabras". Con 28 ilustraciones*. Estudio introductorio de J. Ferrater Mora, Madrid 1998, pp. 217f. (see also p. 156). (All translations from Spanish are mine).
[2] Cf. id.: *Du Baroque*, Paris 1935.
[3] Cf. id.: *Tres horas en el Museo del Prado. Itinerario estético seguido de los Avisos al visitante de las exposiciones de pintura con Prólogo a la undécima edición y Nota Preliminar: a la décima ilusión [sic]*, Madrid 1951. In 2004 the publishing house Tecnos (Madrid) printed the 28th edition.
[4] "El primer Leibniz juzgaba, en su racionalismo, que esta preparación extralógica al feliz hallazgo es pura ilusión, pero reconocía el hecho del *salto*, que, en un determinado momento, da el sabio para alcanzar la luz de la verdad. 'Es verdad, dice, que muchas veces un ejemplo, hallado casualmente, sirve de medio al hombre de intendimiento para dar con una verdad general. Pero todavía le cuesta, encima de esto, el incontrarla... Algunos han creído que Arquímedes ha encontrado la cuadratura de la parábola pesando en un trozo de madera cortada en forma parabólica, y que esta experiencia particular le hizo encontrar la verdad general. Pero

The presence of Leibniz in d'Ors' philosophy may be detected also in the terminology that he adopted. Indeed, friends and disciples of d'Ors who edited Petit Vocabulaire de Philosophie Orsienne included a separate text for the entry "Monadologie", which is defined in the following way:

> "Pour réduire la vie de l'esprit à ses éléments derniers ou 'monades', E. d'O. ne se contente pas, comme Leibniz, de lui attribuer deux facultés, la représentative et l'active, le principe d'intelligence et le principe de volonté; mais il juge nécessaire de reconnaître un troisième élément irréductible, la disposition figurative, qui contient le principe de personnalité. Cet élément n'envisage pas le passé comme la représentation, ni le futur comme la volonté, mais, immédiatement, l'éternel, ce qui se trouve situé hors du temps: la présence de l'Ange."[5]

(In this case, the key meaning of the term "Ange" is related to the "superconscious", our divine and universal part). However, d'Ors may also be likened to Leibniz in some other respects when considering further important "elective affinities", such as the courageous striving towards conciseness, the use and great weight given to the principle of analogy as a fundamental principle in the process of acquiring knowledge, as well as the subtle use of irony. However, what is strikingly evident is the original reinterpretation by d'Ors of the Principle of Contradiction and the Principle of Sufficient Reason which become respectively Principle of Figuration ("principio de figuración") and Principle of Required Function ("principio de función exigida"). As regards the latter, in the Petit Vocabulaire de Philosophie Orsienne we can find the following brief description:

> "Dans la dialectique d'E. d'O. ce principe se substitue au principe de 'raison suffisante' de la logique rationaliste. Il supprime, dans le lien entre deux événements, les exigences de prélation causale et d'équivalence quantitative. Il se formule ainsi: 'Rien n'arrive qu'en fonction de quelque chose', ou en d'autre termes: 'Tout phénomène est un épiphénomène.'"[6]

In *El Secreto de la Filosofía* d'Ors dwells on the importance of defining the Principle of Sufficient Reason as undertaken by Leibniz, who for this reason

---

quienes conocen la penetración de ese grande hombre ven claramente que no necesitaba recurrir a esto'." Cf. id.: *El Secreto de la Filosofía*, pp. 199–200. The reference to *Nouveaux Essais* is located in A VI, 6, 416.

[5] Cf. *Petit Vocabulaire de Philosophie Orsienne*, "Les Nouvelles Lettres Françaises", I, n. 2, Paris 1937, pp. 1–10. The term *"Monadologie"* is located on p. 8; the authors of this *Petit Vocabulaire* are the following: P. H. Michel, J. Ferrater Mora, A. de Acevedo, M. M. Machet and C. Rodríguez Pintos.

[6] Cf. ibid., p. 7.

is defined as a "Keplerian reformer of philosophy."[7] Moreover, d'Ors recognizes a precedent in Leibniz as regards the doctrine according to which there is no final birth or death, but only a constant metamorphosis. It is a doctrine that he integrates with what he terms "relative constance", which he applies to the historical field.[8] Finally, we should also remember that, in one of his writings dated 1943, d'Ors comments on Leibniz's thought as follows:

> "Par la hauteur de sa pensée et l'étendue universelle de sa science; par son savoir encyclopedique; par le mérite d'une sensibilité égale devant les problèmes spéculatifs les plus sublimes et devant les questions pratiques les plus immédiates; par sa vocation d'unité dans le connaissance, Leibniz renferme en lui la leçon que de la philosophie allemande peut attendre l'Europe que naît."[9]

3. José Ortega y Gasset

Ortega is undoubtedly the most "fervent" out of the group of "Spanish Leibnizians" under consideration, also because unlike the other thinkers he explored Leibniz's philosophy dedicating to him some specific works. Hence, he will be examined in greater depth here compared to the other philosophers.

Various terms have been applied to Ortega's philosophy, but perhaps the most concise and appropriate term could be what critics have dubbed as "ratio-vitalism", an expression that reconciles the need to come to terms with the external world that is part of a person's existential "circumstance", and the ethical imperative to carry out a project of existence to achieve self-fulfilment according to a reason or logos. Hence, Ortega refutes abstract "rationalism", but at the same time recognizes the importance of reason in order to realize one's "destiny" in the social, cultural, and political context, in other words throughout history. What had already been stressed in Meditaciones del Quijote (1914), a work that sets out nascent aspects of Ortega's philosophy that would be developed later on, is precisely the decisive and illuminating nature of reason within life. Reason "cannot" and "must not" seek to substitute life, as life is not only thought. However, without reason "we possess nothing in

---

[7] Cf. d'Ors: *El Secreto de la Filosofía*, p. 272.
[8] Cf. ibid., pp. 275f.
[9] Cf. *Dictionnaire philosophique portatif. L'Europe et la Philosophie allemande*, "Le Courrier de Genève" – "Le Courrier littéraire. Supplément hebdomadaire", n. 44, 1943, p. 3.

its totality."[10] The light of reason, thought and concept thus becomes an "imperative" within life: "Clarity is not life, but is the fullness of life."[11] The reason why Ortega was attracted to Leibniz may be found in the "clarity" of his philosophy. From the Meditaciones del Quijote onwards Ortega considered Leibniz difficult – together with Kant and Hegel representing "Germanic" thought as opposed to "Mediterranean" thought –, but at the same time as "clear as a spring morning."[12] In his short article, La metafísica y Leibniz (1925), Ortega is even more full of praise for Leibniz. He views Leibniz's philosophy as "the clearest in the whole world", almost a twist of fate, seeing that such great thinking should have appeared far earlier in classical antiquity, in the period of Plato and Aristotle and not during the height of the Baroque era, a period considered by some as "leaning towards what is confused and chaotic." Plato and Aristotle are hardly clear, when comparing them to Leibniz, to the extent that they could even be termed "Baroque" themselves.[13] According to Ortega, it is precisely this crystal clear writing that enabled Leibniz to set out his philosophical system in such a compact manner. Referring of course to Monadology, Ortega asserts that it is

> "the only total exposition of Leibniz's system [...] a small book of few pages, epitomized in ninety diamond-like theses, each of which is transparent and at the same time irradiates an ethereal light."

---

[10] "La razón no puede, no tiene que aspirar a sustituir la vida. [...] No todo es pensamiento, pero sin él no poseemos nada con plenitud." Cf. José Ortega y Gasset: "Meditaciones del Quijote", § 10, in: Id.: *Obras completas*, vol. I: *1902–1906*, Madrid 1993, pp. 353f.
[11] "Claridad no es vida, pero es la plenitud de la vida". Cf. Ortega, ibid., § 12, p. 358.
[12] "Leibniz o Kant o Hegel son difíciles, pero son claros como una mañana de primavera [...]". Cf. ibid., § 7, p. 345.
[13] "¿No es una burlesca coincidencia que el pensamiento más claro del planeta haya florecido en la cima del barroquismo que, según se dice, representa la simpatía hacia lo confuso y caótico? Ha habido aquí evidentemente un desliz del poder que dirige la historia. Guillermo Pacidio (Got[t]fried Wilhelm) debía haber nacido hacia el año 400 (a. de J. C.) en Atenas, que es a lo que parece el lugar común de la claridad y de la sencillez. Mas, por equivocación, nació de casta eslava en Leipzig, a la altura de 1646. Este desliz de la Providencia nos invita a corregir el nuestro y a hablar con menos certidumbre de la claridad helénica. Porque no tiene duda: Fidias será un escultor divinamente claro; pero Platón y Aristóteles no son, como pensadores, ejemplos de claridad. [...] No significa esto que los dos maestros de Grecia me parezcan el superlativo de la oscuridad; pero sí que comparados con Leibniz serían ellos los enormemente barrocos, y éste es el clásico, suponiendo que lo clásico sea lo claro y sencillo, cosa que me parece demasiado clara y sencilla para ser verdad." Cf. id.: "La metafísica y Leibniz", in: Id.: *Obras completas*, vol. III: *1917–1928*, Madrid 1994, pp. 431f.

The Spanish philosopher also considers Monadology as the work of the human mind more similar to a "clockwork apparatus."[14] The famous Leibnizian work is further defined as "pocket metaphysics", a quality which for Ortega pertains to all "good metaphysics". This claim prompts Ortega to explain what he means by "metaphysics", thus also providing a further interpretation of Leibniz's Monadology. It is worth citing the whole sentence here:

> "Why is good metaphysics pocket-sized? Because it should not consist of more or less incentivizing, plausible tirades that need lengthy explanations, but rather of razor-sharp definitions and arguments, sheer dialectical nerve, triple mental extracts that are then collected together into a short list. Metaphysics should be a vademecum."[15]

However, the work in which Ortega should have compared his ideas to those of Leibniz may be found in his monograph of 1947 entitled La idea de principio en Leibniz y la evolución de la teoria deductiva, which was never completed.[16] Truth to tell, the work draws on Leibniz and then takes "a wide detour"("amplísimo rodeo"– cf. § 2, sub finem), ranging from antiquity to modern thought and a polemic discussion on Heidegger concerning the question of "Being" (cf., § 29). The starting point concerns the topic of principles, and according to Ortega Leibniz is precisely the "man of principles par excellence" for the following four basic reasons:

---

[14] "El único sistema filosófico que ha podido ser expuesto íntegramente en unas pocas páginas as el de Leibniz. Esto indica, por lo pronto, que su autor ha pensado sus pensamientos con una claridad sin par. La *Monadología*, única exposición total del sistema leibniziano, es, en efecto, un librito de pocas páginas, un epítome de noventa tesis, cada una de las cuales, como un diamante, se transparenta y a la vez irradia en torno una luz etérea. Yo no conozco obra de la mente humana que más se parezca a un aparato de relojería." Ibid., p. 431.

[15] "¿Por qué la buena metafísica es de bolsillo? Porque debe componerse, no de tiradas verbales, más o menos incitativas, plausibles que necesitan estirarse en un amplio volumen, sino de definiciones y argumentos buídos, puro nervio dialéctico, triple extracto mental que se aloja holgado en un breve repertorio. La metafísica debe ser *vademecum.*" Ibid., p. 432. Another short article where Ortega deals briefly with Leibniz is "La resurrección de la mónada" (1925) – cf. id.: Obras completas, vol. III, pp. 339–343. After a wide-ranging speech that carries a bold analogy between features of contemporary physics and some aspects of contemporary literature, Ortega, finally, put forwards the following description of the Leibnizian monad: "Entre la función separada de la sustancia, propia al pensamiento moderno, y la sustancia inactiva, mera potencia abstracta que el aristotelismo enseñó a la Edad Media, cabe una excelente posición intermedia. La sustancia como fuerza; por tanto, como germen de acción. Ahora bien, esto es la mónada de Leibniz." Ibid., p. 343.

[16] Cf. id.: "La idea de principio en Leibniz y la evolución de la teoria deductiva", in: Id.: *Obras completas*, vol. VIII: *1958–1959*, Madrid 1994.

"[…] first, [Leibniz] is the philosopher that used the greatest number of principles sensu stricto, that is to say maximally general. Second, he is the philosopher that introduced the greatest number of new principles in philosophical theory. Third, in his writings he constantly refers to one or the other of these principles […]. Fourth, because, […] according to Leibniz knowledge depends on the principles in a more important – and more paradoxical – way than what had been conjectured before him."[17]

Ortega listed ten of these principles:

1. Principle of Principles.
2. Principle of Identity.
3. Principle of Non-Contradiction.
4. Principle of Sufficient Reason.
5. Principle of Uniformity, or Principle of Harlequin.
6. Principle of Identity of Indiscernibles, or Principle of Differentiation.
7. Principle of Continuity.
8. Principle of the Best, or of Convenience.
9. Principle of Equilibrium, or Law of Justice (Principle of Symmetry in current Mathematics).
10. Principle of Least Action or of Most Perfect Forms.[18]

However, the Spanish philosopher immediately added three reservations which would thoroughly scale down Leibniz's "Principlism." First of all, Ortega observes that Leibniz is not consistently rigorous in his proposal of his principles, whereas he is so when defining his other concepts. Ortega continues with the reflection that it seems as though Leibniz plays with his principles, he is fond of them but he does not respect them! The second problem that Ortega poses concerns the fact that Leibniz

---

[17] "[…] Primero, [Leibniz] es el filósofo que ha empleado mayor número de principios *sensu stricto*, es decir, máximamente generales. Segundo, es el filósofo que ha introducido en la teoría filosófica mayor número de principios nuevos. Tercero, le vemos en sus escritos aducir constantemente uno u otro de esos principios […]. Cuarto, porque, […], el conocimiento depende de los principios, para Leibniz, en un sentido más grave – y más paradójico – de cuanto antes de él se había supuesto." Cf. id.: "La idea de principio en Leibniz", § 1, p. 64.
[18] "1.°El principio de los principios./ 2.°Principio de identidad./ 3.°Principio de contradicción./ 4.°Principio de la razón suficiente./ 5.°Principio de la uniformidad o principio de Arlequín./ 6.°Principio de la identidad de los indiscernibles, o principio de la diferenciación./ 7.°Principio de continuidad./ 8.°Principio de lo mejor o de la conveniencia./ 9.°Principio del equilibrio o ley de justicia (principio de simetría en la actual matemática)./ 10.°Principio del mínimo esfuerzo o de las formas óptimas." Cf. ibid., § 1, pp. 64f.

"never seriously bothers to organize his grouping of principles into a hierarchy, by subordinating and coordinating them."

Lastly, Ortega comments that Leibniz stresses the fact that principles must be demonstrated, while a principle is such precisely because it provides the basis on which each demonstration is accomplished. All of these observations puzzle Ortega, to the extent that in a provocative manner he even takes back what he stated at the beginning:

"Does all this not mean that Leibniz refuted principles and was the least principlist among all philosophers?"[19]

This is why he takes a "wide detour", starting by analyzing the essence of the principle and continuing with two classic philosophical issues – the "dioscuros" as he terms them – namely "Thinking" and "Being". Thus, Ortega may have meant to end his analysis by getting to the heart of Leibniz's discourse on "Being", but, as we mentioned above, he did not manage to complete his study, and so the only comment we have on the relation between Leibniz and Being is that "To be more precise, neither Descartes nor Leibniz questioned themselves about Being, but about something very different."[20] However, the meaning of this criticism is not further explained in La idea de principio en Leibniz. If we wish to have a work that fully explored Leibniz with conclusive comments, we must refer to the paper that Ortega delivered in San Sebastián in 1947 to inaugurate the Nineteenth Congress of the Spanish Association for the Advancement of Science on "Del optimismo en Leibniz."[21]

---

[19] "Primera: Leibniz suele encontrar para enunciar sus principios fórmulas llenas de gracia, de eficacia verbal; pero el hecho de que emplee diversas para un mismo principio, y que casi nunca los términos sean rigorosos, cuando en el resto de sus conceptos lo es en tan alto grado, produce en el studioso de su obra una inquietud peculiarísima, cuya primera – y claro está, informal, pero sincera – expresión sería esta: Leibniz juega con los principios, los quiere; pero no los respeta. Segunda: siendo para Leibniz lo constitutivo del conocimiento el orden en los pensamientos, no se ocupó nunca en serio de ordenar el convoluto de sus principios jerarquizándolos, subordinándolos, coordinándolos [...]. Tercera, y de mayor sustancia: Leibniz insiste una y otra vez en que es conveniente y es preciso probar o intentar probar los principios. Ahora bien; solía entenderse por principio lo que ni puede ni necesita ser probado, sino que es precisamente lo que hace posible bajo sí toda prueba. ¿No significa todo esto que Leibniz desdeñaba los principios y que ha sido, entre todos los filósofos, el menos principialista?" Cf. ibid., § 1, p. 65.
[20] "Pero también vamos a ver que Descartes y Leibniz no se preguntan tampoco, hablando precisamente, por el Ser, sino por algo no poco diferente" – cf. ibid., § 29, p. 272.
[21] The conference has been published as "First Appendix" to La idea de principio en Leibniz – cf. id.: "Del optimismo en Leibniz", in: Id.: Obras completas, vol. VIII, pp. 325–351.

We shall now turn to this paper. The conference opened with a celebration of Leibniz as "one of the most extraordinary minds offered for the future of Europe,"[22] and after pointing out that the term "eclectic" was inadequate to define Leibniz's philosophy, he went straight to the heart of his thesis by illustrating his "doctrine of optimism". What is the most fascinating part is the way in which Ortega illustrated this doctrine, because he takes into consideration another key Leibnizian theory, namely that of possibilities or rather existence of possibilities. The presentation of the doctrine includes considerations that highlight aspects of Ortega's own philosophy, as in the following example, where Ortega reflects on the "I" and his "circumstance":

> "A person must understand what concerns him/her. What concerns him/her is the effective situation, what is commonly termed as reality, the thing that exists, the world in which we live. […] However, not only do we have to deal with reality, but we also have to deal with possibility at the same time. […] the presence of mere possibility is more determining for a person than reality itself which imprisons him/her. These possibilities intrude between us and the real world. Leibniz was the first to understand that a person has no direct or immediate contact with reality compared to a stone, for example. Our relation to reality is utterly strange: it consists in a constant advance towards it from outside, from the possibilities."[23]

Ortega goes on to elucidate the ontology of the possible, considered a characteristic of Leibniz's metaphysics. We later learn that it is precisely "ontology" in relation to optimism and pessimism that is the core of his lecture.[24]

---

[22] "No era bueno que esta Asociación dejase de consagrar alguna de sus manifestaciones al recuerdo de una de las mentes más poderosas con que ha sido regalado el destino europeo". cf. id.: "Del optimismo en Leibniz", p. 325. Worth considering is also the next sentence in the text: "Se ha dicho muchas veces, y no sin fundamento, que si Aristóteles fue el intelecto de más universal capacidad en el mundo antiguo, lo es Leibniz en el modern."
[23] "El hombre necesita comprender lo que le importa. Lo que le importa es su situación efectiva, lo que solemos llamar la realidad, lo existente, el mundo en que estamos. […] Pero no solo tenemos que habérnoslas con la realidad, sino que nos encontramos también, y a la vez, con posibilidades. Por ejemplo, pensamos que *podía* muy bien no haber realidad ninguna, que *podía* muy bien no existir nada. Pensamos, asimismo, que *podía* existir un mundo real distinto del que existe. Sobre el fondo de esas posibilidades la realidad del mundo pierde su firmeza, se hace cuestionable, se convierte en enigma. ¿Por qué hay algo y no simplemente nada? ¿Por qué el algo que hay es este y no otro? Come se ve, la presencia de meras posibilidades es más decisiva para el hombre que la realidad misma en que está prisionero. Ellas se interponen entre nosotros y el mundo real. Leibniz fue quien primero vio claramente que el hombre no está en la realidad de modo directo o inmediato como lo está la piedra." Cf. ibid., p. 329.
[24] "He aquí, señores, el tema sobre el cual hubiera yo querido hablar a los presentes: qué significan, últimamente, el optimismo y el pesimismo en ontología […]." Cf. ibid., pp. 342f.

We gain the impression that the analysis of Leibniz's modal metaphysics – let us remember that Ortega acknowledges that "Leibniz's ontology was the only one to focus on the modality of being"[25] –, is precisely the missing complement to his book, La idea de principio en Leibniz, that is to say the material that should have been included to complete the final part of his monograph. Indeed, a substantial part of his considerations focuses on the theme of Being and Creation, through striking intuitions and thought-provoking reflections, among which I shall indicate the following points:

1. An assessment of the Monadology asserts the insidious and deceptive nature of his propositions (anticipating critical historiographers);[26]
2. there are some interesting reflections on the Theodicy concerning a sort of implicit Manichaeism in God;[27]
3. there is the proposal for a new intellectual discipline that he terms "empirical disteleology" ["disteleología empírica"];[28]
4. he justifies the plural expression of "possible worlds" on the basis of the intrinsically dissociative character of possibility.[29]

Finally, if we wish to sum up the "Leibnizian echoes" in Ortega's philosophy, undoubtedly there is a constant search for clarity in his discussion or the presence of a subtle modal framework also in Ortega's metaphysics (see the theme

---

[25] "El ángulo tal vez más importante y fértil según el cual debería estudiarse a Leibniz es el análisis de la estructura que tiene su ontología […]. La ontología de Leibniz ha sido la única centrada en la modalidad del ser." Cf. ibid., p. 344.

[26] "Téngase en cuenta, que las fórmulas de la *Monadología*, si bien son con frecuencia las más impresionantes, son en muchos casos las más infieles al auténtico pensamiento del autor." Cf. ibid., p. 334.

[27] "La lectura de la *Teodicea* nos deja flotando en la mente esta consecuencia: de tal modo es malo el ser que ni Dios mismo ha podido contrarrestar plenamente su maldad y ha tenido que pactar con ella para evitar un mal mayor […]. Lleva a fórmulas que equivalen a algo así como un maniqueísmo interior a Dios." Cf. ibid., p. 343.

[28] "[…] al presentarnos el sistema optimista de Leibniz un panorama del ser en que aparece como constitutivo de este una dimensión de maldad, de imperfección, nos hace caer en la cuenta de que falta hasta ahora entre las disciplinas intelectuales una *disteleología* empírica que debería investigar, definir y analizar la imperfección de la Naturaleza. Solo esta contrapartida frente al inveterado teleologismo del pensamiento puede volver a ajustar la mente del hombre a su destino." Cf. ibid., pp. 343f.

[29] "El plural con que aparece en Leibniz siempre la idea de "mundo posible" no es accidental sino que procede inevitablemente del carácter disociativo propio de la posibilidad." Cf. ibid., p. 346.

of the "possible" represented by the image of the "wood" in its first appearance in Meditaciones del Quijote).[30] However, the most evident influence of Leibniz may be found in his "perspectivism". Armando Savignano argues that "perspectivism" is an aspect of Ortega's philosophy that would never be challenged by Ortega,[31] and this is undoubtedly significant if we consider that this doctrine had been clearly outlined as early as 1916, in Verdad y perspectiva. In Ortega's perspectivism we clearly perceive not only the immovable presence of the individual point of view, but also the innate perspectival nature of reality itself. In certain respects, this doctrine matches perfectly what Leibniz outlines in the renowned § 57 of the Monadology.[32]

4. Xavier Zubiri

Zubiri is a philosopher who developed an original form of "realism", whose evolution was initially inspired by Ortega (his doctoral adviser) and was later influenced by Husserl and Heidegger.

The first thing that strikes us when comparing Zubiri with Leibniz is his attempt to reformulate what he terms the "monadic nature" of monads. In his work entitled Sobre el Hombre we find the following observation:

> "Leibniz believed that each monad reflected from its own point of view all the other monads, and that monads were reclusive in character. However, I maintain that the monadic character is completely the opposite: the only possibility for others to exist for me lies in familiarity with otherness and what is monadic in me is the character of otherness as otherness, which as such is a possibilitating power of my own reality."[33]

---

[30] Cf. id.: "Meditaciones del Quijote", § 1, pp. 330f.
[31] Cf. Armando Savignano: *Panorama della filosofia spagnola del Novecento*, Geneva/Milano 2005, p. 159.
[32] Cf. *Monadology*, § 57; GP VI, 616.
[33] "Leibniz pensó que cada mónada refleja desde su punto de vista el resto de las mónadas, y que el carácter monádico está en la reclusión. Pero yo considero que el carácter monádico es todo lo contrario: la única posibilidad de que los demás existan para mí está en la habitud de alteridad, y lo que en mí hay de mónada es el carácter de alteridad como alteridad, que como tal es un poder posibilitante de mi propria realidad." Cf. Xavier Zubiri: *Sobre el Hombre*, Madrid 1998, pp. 322f. I would like to point out that the "reclusive" character of monads was precisely what Leibniz had sought to avoid at all costs, also uttering a famous witticism: "Interim Monades non existunt solitariae. Sunt Monades, non Monachae" (cf. Leibniz [1698]: Grua, 395). Hence, Zubiri interprets reclusion as the consequence of the fact that monads are defined by Leibniz as lacking "doors" and "windows", completely ignoring all the implications of the metaphysical doctrine of pre-established harmony.

In this case, Zubiri's reformulation of the "monadic character" of monads was intended to provide the theoretical basis for an important political concept, namely the concept of "social body":

> "When I accept or refuse such power, establishing my own life and self-determination, I make myself other for the others, and the power and possibility that stem from my life unceasingly flow back again into the social body, which thanks to them, changes intrinsically as a result of what each man does. Since the social body has no substance in itself, its variations possess a special character: all men in a society constitute a social body in a supportive manner, but they constitute it throughout all their personal experiences, and within the context of history."[34]

The subject of "social body" thus brings us to the subject of history, on which we should remember Zubiri's early reflections in his crucial book, Naturaleza, Historia, Dios (1944), which has been reprinted frequently. Here Zubiri introduces a concept in which history is likened to an act of "quasi-creation" that a person can perform. Indeed, a person does not affirm him/herself simply through a series of actions, but accomplishes new possibilities of actions for humanity. Moreover, in order to express this exceptional capacity for action in a person, Zubiri borrows Leibniz's expression "petit Dieu", which is to be found in Leibniz's Monadology when referring to "rational souls" or "spirits", which are defined precisely as "little gods."[35]

Zubiri often turns to Leibniz when seeking to identify the creator of a doctrine that he intends to challenge or to point out flaws. For example, he is critical of the concept of mathematical objects regarded as metaxú ("μεταξύ"),

---

[34] "Cuando acepto o rechazo ese poder, haciendo mi propria vida y autodeterminación, me convierto en otro para los demás, y el poder y posibilidad que dimanan de mi vida refluye inexorablemente sobre el cuerpo social, con lo cual éste va cambiando constitutivamente por lo que cada hombre hace. Porque el cuerpo social no tiene sustantividad, sus cambios tienen un carácter especial: todos los ombre de una sociedad constituyen solidariamente un cuerpo social, pero lo constituyen a lo largo de todas sus vicisitudes, lo constituyen a lo largo de la historia." Cf. Zubiri: *Sobre el Hombre*, p. 323.

[35] "La historia no es un simple hacer, ni es tampoco un mero 'estar pudiendo': es, en rigor, 'hacer un poder'. La razón del acontecer nos sumerge en el abismo ontológico de una realidad, la humana, fuente no sólo de sus actos, sino de sus posibilidades mismas. Ello es lo que hace del hombre, en frase de Leibniz, un petit Dieu." Cf. id.: *Naturaleza, Historia, Dios*, Madrid 1994, p. 380 (cf. *Monadology*, § 83; GP VI, 621).

namely "a sort of intermediary between pure ideas and physical reality". According to Zubiri such an idea is unacceptable, because he argues that there is only one reality, which is physical reality.[36]

Another criticism associated with this is the idea of mathematical entities considered as ideal objects ("objetos ideales"). Zubiri argues that what is considered as an "ideal object" is rather the simple idea of an object, which, however, remains separate from the idea. The idea of an object cannot be converted into an "ideal object", and he believes this is one of the greatest sophisms of Rationalism, "from Plato to Leibniz."[37] Other examples of this kind concern the criticism of the concept of the infinite "notes" that are characteristic of individuals, in *Sobre la esencia* (1962);[38] or else when he questions the identity of "substantive being" and "copulative being" in *Inteligencia y logos* (1982).[39]

---

[36] "De ahí que, a mi modo de ver, son filosóficamente indefendibles dos ideas muy clásicas en la historia de la filosofía. Una de ellas, que viene desde los tiempos de Platón y que ha rodado de formas muy distintas por toda la historia de la filosofía todavía hasta los tiempos de Kant, consiste en decir que los objetos matemáticos son un *metaxú* (μεταξύ), una especie de intermediario entre las puras ideas y la realidad sensible. ¡Ah!, esto de ninguna manera. Realidad no hay más que una: la realidad física." Cf. id.: *Espacio. Tiempo. Materia*, Madrid 1996, p. 80. See also id.: *Sobre el Hombre*, pp. 652f. (however, we should certainly not go seeking trivial materialism in Zubiri).

[37] "Lo que se llama el objeto ideal sería más bien la idea de un objeto. Pero esto es distinto. No se puede convertir la idea de un objeto en objeto ideal. Ha sido uno de los grandes sofismas de todo el razionalismo – desde los tempo de Platón hasta Leibniz – a lo largo de la historia de la filosofía. A mi modo de ver, absolutamente inaceptable." Cf. id.: *Espacio. Tiempo. Materia*, pp. 80f.

[38] "Algunos escolásticos y Leibniz pensaron por el contrario que todo individuo tiene infinitas notas. Pero esto es imposible. Lo que sucede es que han confundido las notas físicas con los predicados objetivos." Cf. id.: *Sobre la esencia*, Madrid 1998, p. 366.

[39] "El indiscernimiento platónico se toma en positiva identidad entre el ser real y el ser copulativo en la filosofía moderna. En esta identidad se puede partir del ser real, y entonces el ser copulativo tiene estructura que le impone la estructura del ser real: fue la filosofía de *Leibniz*. Lo real es una sustancia 'una' (mónada), cuya unidad consiste en *vis* de unidad de unión y separación de los 'detalles' que constituyen aquella unidad monádica de lo real. El juicio predicativo es la forma intelectiva de esta estructura monádica de lo real: por esto es por lo que el juicio es complexión o copulación. El 'es' copulativo es la intelección adecuada de lo que es la realidad en sí misma. Visto desde la intelección: la intelección tanto conceptiva como afirmativa es una intelección de lo que es la realidad en sí misma. Es lo que se llama 'racionalismo'. Esto es imposible. La afirmación no es complexión como pretendía ya Aristóteles y repite hasta la saciedad Leibniz. [...] Platón, Leibniz, Hegel son la puesta en marcha de la identidad entre ser real y ser copulativo. La entificación de lo real y la logificación de la intelección, son los dos fundamentos de la filosofía clásica, que no por azar han conducido sea al racionalismo ontologista, sea al idealismo. Pero esto es insostenible." Cf. id.: *Inteligencia y logos*, Madrid 1982, pp. 380ff.

Hence, out of the three philosophers under study here Zubiri seems to be the most critical of Leibniz , but this does not alter the fact that he preferred to investigate Leibniz when setting out his vision of the world, rather than someone else. It is no coincidence that Leibniz is focused on once again in his last essay Inteligencia y razón (1983), part of the trilogy entitled Inteligencia sentiente, where the more complex points of his "realism" need to be elucidated. Also in this case Zubiri's criticism of Leibniz enables him to introduce concepts that constitute his own vision of what is "real", such as the concepts of "intellective actualitas of the real", "respectivity" and "openness."[40]

---

[40] Cf. id.: *Inteligencia y razon*, Madrid 1983, pp. 76f., and pp. 279ff. (about the Leibnizian distinction between *truths of reasoning* and *truths of fact*).

Gottfried Wilhelm Leibniz' Naturrecht im Kontext der frühneuzeitlichen Autonomisierung der Ethik

Holger Glinka (Berlin)

„Sapienter IC^{ti} Romani Legibus indefinibilia remittunt toties ad Arbitrium boni Viri, qvemadmodum Aristoteles in Ethicis omnia regulis non comprehendenda ad arbitrium prudentis, ὡς ἂν ὁ φρόνιμος ὁρίσειε."[1]

1. Eine Ethik

Das angezeigte Thema ist problemgeschichtlich[2] zu erörtern.[3] In ihrem Bestreben nach Manifestation eines autonomen wissenschaftlichen Ressorts im

---

[1] Vgl. *Aristotelis Ethica Nicomachea*. Recognovit brevique adnotatione critica instruxit I. Bywater. Oxonii e typographeo clarendoniano 1979 (= *Scriptorum classicorum bibliotheca oxoniensis*) 1107a1f. – „Weise waren die römischen Rechtsgelehrten, als sie dasjenige, was durch die Gesetze nicht näher bestimmbar ist, jeweils dem freien Ermessen eines guten Menschen überließen; ebenso wie Aristoteles in seiner Ethik alles, was in Regeln nicht miterfaßbar ist, dem freien Ermessen eines einsichtigen Menschen anheimstellte, ‚wie es der Kluge bestimmen würde'". – Vgl. Gottfried Wilhelm Leibniz: *Entwürfe zu den ‚Elementen des Naturrechts' (1669–1671)*, in: Ders.: *Frühe Schriften zum Naturrecht*, Hamburg 2003, S. 300f.

[2] „*Philosophiegeschichtlich* […] bedingt Leibnizens Lehre […] die Idee einer Disziplin, die die philosophischen Probleme in der Mannigfaltigkeit ihrer zeitlichen Erscheinungsformen nur in Rücksicht auf die Gemeinsamkeit ihres sachlichen Bestandes und diesen sachlichen Bestand wieder nur als Ausdruck der Vielgestaltigkeit seiner zeitlichen Erscheinungsformen zu ergreifen vermag. Es ist der einer besonderen Aufgabe angepaßte Gedanke der Kontinuität, der kritische Begriff einer *Problemgeschichte* der Philosophie; die Forderung, daß in jeder philosophischen Frage jede andere virtuell enthalten sei, daß die Philosophie die ganze Fülle ihrer Aufgaben an jeder ihrer geschichtlichen Besonderungen zu bewähren habe." – Vgl. Richard Hönigswald: *G. W. Leibniz. Ein Beitrag zur Frage seiner problemgeschichtlichen Stellung* (= *Philosophie und Geschichte. Eine Sammlung vor Vorträgen und Schriften als dem Gebiet der Philosophie und Geschichte* 19), Tübingen 1928, S. 51. – Den Begriff „Problemgeschichte" prägt Windelband; er bezeichnet sein *Lehrbuch der Geschichte der Philosophie,* das erstmals 1892 erscheint, als „Geschichte der Probleme und der zu ihrer Lösung erzeugten Begriffe". – Siehe: Wilhelm Windelband: *Lehrbuch der Geschichte der Philosophie*, mit einem Schlusskapitel *Die Philosophie im 20. Jahrhundert* und einer Übersicht über den Stand der philosophiegeschichtlichen Forschung hrsg. v. Heinz Heimsoeth, Tübingen ^{15}1957, S. V. bzw. S. III. – Siehe auch: Ernst Cassirer: *Das Erkenntnisproblem in der Philosophie und Wissenschaft der neueren Zeit*, 4 Bde., Darmstadt 1974, hier: Erster Band. – Bzw.: Nicolai Hartmann: „Zur Methode der Philosophiegeschichte", in: *Kant-Studien* 15 (1910), S. 459–485. – Unter Beibehaltung der Idee der Problemgeschichte weiterentwickelt in: Ders.: *Der philosophische Gedanke und seine Geschichte*, aus den Abhandlungen der Preußischen Akademie der Wissenschaften. Jahrgang 1936, Phil.-hist. Klasse, Nr. 5, Berlin 1936.

[3] Vgl. den „Problemgeschichtliche[n] Überblick" von Alexander Hollerbach: „Das christliche Naturrecht im Zusammenhang des allgemeinen Naturrechtsdenkens", in: Franz Böckle/Ernst-

Dienste geglückter Lebensführung befördert die Ethik seit der griechischen Antike in entscheidenden Momenten ihrer Ausdifferenzierung die Verabschiedung von Formen theonomer Versicherungen[4] – eine Entwicklung, auf deren Resultate nicht erst Gottfried Wilhelm Leibniz, sondern auch schon Denker wie Thomas Hobbes, Baruch de Spinoza oder Pierre Bayle jeweils reagieren (und hierin entschiedener als Leibniz). Aufgeworfen wird das Problem der Ethik im alten Griechenland durch die Fragestellungen der Sophisten: Wie seien die Sitten (ἔθοι) in der Polis zu rechtfertigen? Sind sie naturgegeben oder von Göttern oder sogar Menschen eingesetzt? Schon die Sophisten eint die Überzeugung, dass das Recht und die Moralgesetze nicht von Göttern stammen, sondern jeweils Resultate bilden von Übereinkünften zwischen Menschen, d. h. gewissermaßen Formen sittlicher Verabredungen darstellen. Im Gegensatz zur Schule Platons halten die Sophisten die Begriffe ‚gut' und ‚böse' für relative: Wer das Gute kenne – und so argumentiert noch Sokrates –, strebe auch danach, es zu verwirklichen, und die im Orakel von Delphi geforderte Selbsterkenntnis (γνῶθι σεαυτόν)[5] gilt als einzige Quelle wahrhaft verbindlichen Wissens. Wissen wiederum sei der Ursprung wahrhafter Tugend; aber auch für Platon bilden Wissen (Theorie[6]) und Handeln (Praxis) noch eine untrennbare Einheit – eine Doktrin, die Leibniz' Begriff der Wissenschaft, verstanden als Idee der Praxis, zu bewahren sucht.

Die Aufdeckung eines natürlichen, sprich allgemein-menschlichen Anteils der Vernunft – ein Projekt, dem sich Leibniz ausdrücklich verschreibt – hat die Notwendigkeit einer Begründung des Mensch-Seins aus sich selbst heraus zur Konsequenz. Dieser Anspruch auf wissende Selbstverwirklichung: *Autonomie*, hat ein neuartiges technisch-herstellendes Verhältnis zur Welt,

---

Wolfgang Böckenförde (Hrsg.): *Naturrecht in der Kritik*, Mainz 1973, S. 9–38. – Otto Veit: „Der geistesgeschichtliche Standort des Naturrechts", in: Werner Maihofer (Hrsg.): *Naturrecht oder Rechtspositivismus?* (= *Wege der Forschung* XVI) Darmstadt 1966, S. 33–51.

[4] Das antike Rechtsverständnis, in welchem der Begriff Nomos im Zentrum steht, charakterisiert Rolf Grawert wie folgt: „Aus der ursprünglich theonomen Bedeutung einer Ethos, Recht, Sitte und Satzung umgreifenden Gesamtordnung der Polis schichtet sich mit den Sophisten im 5. Jahrhundert v. Chr. in einem Säkularisierungsprozess das zeitbedingt positiv gestaltbare Gesetz von den ewigen Ordnungsprinzipien ab [...]." – Siehe Rolf Grawert: Art.: „Gesetz", in: Otto Brunner/Werner Conze/Reinhardt Koselleck (Hrsg.): *Geschichtliche Grundbegriffe*. Historisches Lexikon zur politisch-sozialen Sprache in Deutschland, Bd. 2, Stuttgart 1975, S. 863–922, hier S. 864.

[5] Zum historisch-systematischen Prius des Konzepts der Selbsterkenntnis vor demjenigen des Selbstbewusstseins siehe: Joachim Ritter †/Karlfried Gründer/Gottfried Gabriel (Hrsg.): *Historisches Wörterbuch der Philosophie*, völlig neubearbeitete Ausgabe des „Wörterbuchs der philosophischen Begriffe" v. Rudolf Eisler, Basel 1995, S. 406–413.

[6] Es sei in Erinnerung gerufen, dass θεωρία oder θεωρεῖν den griechischen Wurzeln dieser Begriffe nach bedeutet, „einem Schauspiel beizuwohnen".

mit einem Wort: eine neue Form von Wissenschaft zur Konsequenz. Ein bedeutsamer Beitrag Leibnizens hierzu besteht in seiner *Lehre vom auf sich selbst reflektierenden geistigen Punkt*, welcher das Prinzip bezeichnet, das sein projektiertes Erkenntnissystem trägt: Von hier aus sollen sämtliche Bereiche der das Wissen überhaupt betreffenden Kenntnisse aufeinander bezogen sein. Leibniz' Geist-Begriff, ein Spiegel göttlicher Harmonie („sphaera intellectus"[7]), wird veranschaulicht als Wirkungsfeld des menschlichen Geistes im Zentrum eines Pentagramms verstanden als Bild der psycho-physischen[8] Natur des Menschen: Als Allerheiligstes im Tempel des menschlichen Leibes ortet Leibniz diesen Punkt zwar im Gehirn, für empirisch nachweisbar hält er ihn gleichwohl nicht. Mit dem Herborner Universalgelehrten Johann Heinrich Alsted, der in seiner *Encyclopaedia* (1630) die Wissenschaften insgesamt – und insbesondere die reformierte Theologie seiner Zeit – zu einem komplexen System zusammenfügt, bleibt eine solche Idee unversehrter Ganzheit des Wissens lange Zeit lebendig und erreicht mit Georg Wilhelm Friedrich Hegels *Enzyklopädie der philosophischen Wissenschaften im Grundrisse*, die in letzter von insgesamt drei Auflagen 1830 erscheint, ihre in philosophiegeschichtlicher Sicht letzte Gestalt.[9]

Wie Ernst Cassirer und in Fortsetzung Hans Blumenberg zeigen, resultiert aus der Begegnung von Philosophie, Religion und frühneuzeitlicher Naturwissenschaft ein umfassend modifizierter Erkenntnisbegriff, der eine Individualisierungstendenz im Naturrechtsdenken verursacht, die vielfältige Auswirkungen auf die politischen, wirtschaftlichen und nicht zuletzt religiösen bzw. klerikalen Lebensverhältnisse europäischer Gesellschaften zeitigt. Die reale politische Gefährdung indes, die mit der Dynamik *individualistischer* Autonomiebestrebungen einhergeht, erfordert – wie sich bald zeigt – einen hohen Analyseaufwand besonders für diejenigen, die Einheitskonzepte für den Bereich des praktischen Lebens zu begründen suchen, wie z. B. für Thomas Hobbes oder auch für Leibniz, der ja nicht nur in seinen Schriften zum Naturrecht – das er von seinen Vorgängern wissenschaftlich noch längst

---

[7] Zudem gilt: „*Scientia* exercitium intellectus." – Vgl. *Elemente des Naturrechts*, in: *Frühe Schriften zum Naturrecht*, S. 193.
[8] Vgl. ebd., S. 298: „[...] effecit tamen DEUS addito aethere seu spiritu universali, ut omnia in corporis, ut in mentibus evenirent." („[...] so hat es doch GOTT durch Hinzufügung des Äthers, d.h. des allumfassenden Spiritus, so eingerichtet, daß im Körper der Geschöpfe alles genauso wie in ihrem Geist abläuft.")
[9] „Bei Leibniz ist Enzyklopädie die Topographie des offenen Weltprozesses, bei Hegel die Applikation der begrifflichen Schematik des Weltprozesses auf eine geschlossen konzipierte Wirklichkeit. Hier begegnen uns grundverschiedene Typen des Enzyklopädischen [...]." – Vgl. Hans Heinz Holz: *Leibniz*, Stuttgart 1958, S. 96.

nicht erschöpfend abgehandelt sieht[10] –, sondern auch in seiner *Théodicée* praktische Fragen des menschlichen Zusammenlebens erörtert.[11] Leibniz' beabsichtigte Optimierung der bisherigen juristischen Methode bedeutet einen Beitrag zur näheren Verhältnisbestimmung von individualistischem Naturrecht und Ethik, wenn er fragt:

> „Warum hat man nicht Personen [...] nach der Ethik aufgeteilt: [...] z.B. in Taube, Stumme und Blinde, Zwitter und Normale, Männer und Frauen, Kinder, Jugendliche und Erwachsene, Reiche und Arme, Adelige und Staatsdiener, Bauern und Fahrende, Häretiker und Schismatiker usw. [...]."[12]

2. Weltliche vs. himmlische Herrschaft

2.1 Mittelalter

Im Übergang vom Mittelalter in die Neuzeit spielt der Einfluss der aristotelischen Ethik und zwar insbesondere die dort vertretene Lehre von der nach Gemeinschaft strebenden Natur des Menschen, eine tragende Rolle im Blick auf die Verhältnisbestimmung von weltlicher und himmlischer Herrschaft. Wolfgang Stürner führt aus:

> „Wir treffen vor allem auf die aristotelische, von der Stoa aufgenommene und neubegründete Vorstellung vom Staat als einem Produkt des natürlichen menschlichen Strebens, vom Zusammenwirken im herrschaftlich strukturierten Staatsganzen als der Lebensform, auf die hin die menschliche Natur angelegt ist, in der sich die natürliche Entwicklung vollendet."[13]

---

[10] Vgl. Leibniz an Hermann Conring, 13./23. Januar 1670, S. 323–337, in: *Frühe Schriften zum Naturrecht*, hier S. 327; A II, 1, N. 15.
[11] Vgl. *Essais de Théodicée sur la Bonté de Dieu, la Liberté de l'Homme et l'Origine du Mal*, Amsterdam 1710. – Vgl. hierzu näher: Adelheid Thönes: *Die philosophischen Lehren in Leibnizens Théodicée* (= Abhandlungen zur Philosophie und ihrer Geschichte 28), Halle a. d. Saale 1908, S. 37–60.
[12] „[...] cur non subdivisit personas [...] ex [...] Ethicis, v.g. Personas in surdos, mutos, coecos, hermaphroditos, perfectos, viros, foeminas, impuberes, minores, adultos, divites, pauperes, nobiles, magistratus, rusticos, peregrinos, haereticos, schismaticos etc. [...]." – Vgl. „Neue Methode, Jurisprudenz zu lernen und zu lehren", in: *Frühe Schriften zum Naturrecht*, S. 39; A VI, 1, N. 10.
[13] Wolfgang Stürner: *Peccatum und potestas. Der Sündenfall und die Entstehung der herrscherlichen Gewalt im mittelalterlichen Staatsdenken* (= Beiträge zur Geschichte und Quellenkunde des Mittelalters 11), Sigmaringen 1987, S. 36; vgl. auch S. 189, S. 192f., S. 195f., S. 200, S. 204, S. 207f.

Stürner erbringt den Nachweis, wie die im Mittelalter verbreiteten Modelle zur Erklärung von Herrschaft fast durchweg eine ursächliche Verbindung zwischen menschlichem „peccatum" und dem Auftreten der herrscherlichen „potestas" zur Voraussetzung haben. Im Vordergrund steht dabei zunächst die Auffassung, die Obrigkeit sei von Gott für den Kampf gegen das Böse, zur Sicherung der ausschließlich lebensbewahrenden Ordnung auf Erden geschaffen worden; im Spätmittelalter urteilt ähnlich etwa Wilhelm von Ockham;[14] noch Friedrich der Große (1712–1786) konstatiert eine solche herrscherliche Stellung. Die gegensätzliche Position hat in voller Schärfe Papst Gregor VII. (zwischen 1025 und 1030–1085) formuliert:[15] Die Herrschaft könne als eine die Ordnung Gottes pervertierende Erfindung der zum Satan Abgefallenen („damnates") nur eine *positive* Bedeutung nach ihrer völligen *Unterwerfung unter Kirche und Papst* gewinnen. Wenn sich Theologen und Kanonisten der folgenden Jahrhunderte Gregors schroff ablehnenden Ansatz auch meist nicht vollgültig zu Eigen machen, so folgen sie ihm doch darin, dass sie aus menschlicher Sündhaftigkeit und kirchlichem Erlösungsmonopol die wesensmäßige Unterordnung des Herrschers unter Kirche und Papst ableiten. Das Faktum irdischer Macht erscheint so als ein Ergebnis, welches aus der biblischen Erzählung vom Sündenfall resultiert.[16] Demgemäß stellt sich die Frage nach dem Grund der Staatsgewalt – eine solche sieht Leibniz mit Bezug auf Hobbes legitimiert[17] –: Ist sie ein von Gott gegebenes Instrument zur Rettung der sündigen Menschheit vor der Selbstzerstörung oder eine Erfindung der von Gott abgefallenen Menschen zur Unterjochung von ihresgleichen? Je nach Standpunkt ergeben sich gravierende Konsequenzen für die politische Praxis: Müssen sich die Regenten Kirche und Papst unterordnen, um eine positive Bedeutung in Gottes Weltordnung zu erlangen – oder verkörpern sie darin eine *unabhängige* Einrichtung mit unverzichtbaren *eigenen* Aufgaben?

---

[14] Vgl. Ockhams Ausführungen im Kontext seiner Kommentierung der *Römerbrief*-Deutung des Augustinus: „[…] ita imperator est dominus in temporalibus omnium immediatus, ita ut in his, que spectant ad regnum mortalium, magis sit obediendum imperatori quam cuicunque domino inferiori […]." – Vgl. *Guillelmi de Ockham Opera politica*, Bd. VIII, hrsg. v. John Kilcullen/John Scott/Jan Ballweg/Volker Leppin, Oxford 2011, Dialogus Part II, ii, c. 20.
[15] 1075 lässt Gregor VII. 27 Leitsätze, den „Dictatus Papae", aufzeichnen, in denen er u.a. die Vorrangstellung der geistlichen Gewalt gegenüber weltlichen Machthabern betont.
[16] Für nicht wenige Autoren des philosophischen Mittelalters – so z. B. Irenäus von Lyon, Tertullian, Origines, Laktanz, Chrysostomus und Augustinus – zieht die Abkehr des Menschen von Gott schwerwiegende Folgen für das Zusammenleben innerhalb einer politischen Gemeinschaft nach sich; sie formulieren grundlegende Positionen, auf die sich die Staatsdenker der Folgezeit stützen können.
[17] Vgl. *Frühe Schriften zum Naturrecht*, S. 421, Anm. 74.

Leibniz gibt die zweite Antwort, wie nicht zuletzt seiner Polemik gegen das seit dem klassischen Altertum diskutierte „Sophisma" der sogenannten „faulen Vernunft" zu entnehmen ist – ein Phänomen, welches vordringlich auch die fatalistischen Gruppen der Christenheit seiner Zeit betreffe, so Leibniz.[18] Ungeachtet seiner Lehre von der prästabilierten Harmonie hält Leibniz theologischen Determinismus und persönliche Verantwortlichkeit für miteinander verträglich: Wenn Notwendigkeit nicht als *absolute* Notwendigkeit definiert werde, sondern die Möglichkeit *hypothetischer* Notwendigkeit eingeräumt werde, dann sei *freies* Entscheiden über das eigene Handeln möglich.[19] Wenn Freiheit nicht als Eigenmächtigkeit, sondern als freies Denken und Meinen verstanden werde, dann sei auch im Rahmen der prästabilierten Harmonie Platz für die Freiheit des Menschen. Wenn schließlich die Vorherbestimmung nicht als Beschließen einer zukünftigen Tatsache, sondern als Erkennen und Vorhersehen eines Zustandes oder einer Handlung aufgefasst werde, sei die Determination durch Gott möglicherweise mit verantwortlichem Handeln vereinbar. Von den drei Wurzeln der Freiheit: *Zufälligkeit, Spontaneität* und *Einsicht*, bleibt aber für den Menschen wenigstens die Spontaneität fraglich. Und auch die „wahre Wurzel der Freiheit":[20] nämlich die *Einsicht*, kann dem Menschen nur eingeschränkt zuerkannt werden, hat doch ausnahmslos Gott einen unendlichen Verstand,[21] während der Mensch lediglich in sehr geringem Maße die Folgen seines Handelns bedenken und deswegen eigentlich nie eine Entscheidung treffen kann, zu deren *Folgen* er sich bewusst und frei *entschlossen* hat. Einleuchtend dagegen erscheint Leibniz' Verständnis von zufälligen

---

[18] Vgl. Gottfried Wilhelm Leibniz: *Versuche in der Theodicée über die Güte Gottes, die Freiheit des Menschen und den Ursprung des Übels*, in: Ders.: *Philosophische Werke*, Bd. 4, übers. u. mit Anm. versehen v. Artur Buchenau, Hamburg 1996, S. 9–18 (Vorrede). – Dieses Argument erfährt noch einen Widerhall („[…] denn was ist fauler, als sich bei einer jeden Naturbegebenheit auf den Willen GOttes zu berufen, ohne zu überlegen, ob der vorhabende Fall auch ein Gegenstand des göttlichen Willens habe sein können?") bei: Gotthold Ephraim Lessing/Moses Mendelssohn: *Pope als Metaphysiker!*, in: Ders.: *Werke*, 3. Bd.: *Frühe kritische Schriften*, Bearbeiter dieses Bandes Karl S. Guthke, München 1972, S. 631–670, hier S. 634.
[19] Vgl. Ulrich Steinvorth: *Freiheitstheorien in der Philosophie der Neuzeit*, Darmstadt ²1994, S. 112f.
[20] Concha Roldán: „Ist es möglich, nach der Leibnizschen Freiheitslehre eine Ethik zu begründen?", in: *Tradition und Aktualität*, Vorträge des V. Internationalen Leibniz-Kongresses, Hannover 1988, S. 811–818, hier S. 815.
[21] „Die Rezeption aristotelischer Theorien über tätigen und leidenden Verstand führt in der Hochscholastik zum Vordringen von *intellectus* […]. An derartigen Unberechenbarkeiten ändert sich in der Neuzeit nicht viel. Man stimmt überein in der Annahme höherer und niederer geistiger Vermögen, aber ihre Benennung und Abgrenzung ist kontrovers und mannigfaltig." – Vgl. Rainer Specht: „Zur Vernunft des Rationalismus", in: Herbert Schnädelbach (Hrsg.): *Rationalität. Philosophische Beiträge*, Frankfurt a. M. 1984, S. 70–93, hier S. 71f.

Handlungen – dass nämlich absolute logische Notwendigkeit *nicht* gegeben ist – durch die von ihm vorausgesetzten Begriffe von Notwendigkeit und Vorherbestimmung. So werden Fatalismus und ‚faules Sophisma' ausgeschlossen: „Indessen soll man immer für die Wahrheit zeugen und einer Lehre nichts vorwerfen, was nicht aus ihr folgt."[22]

2.2 Frühe Neuzeit

Hat während des gesamten Mittelalters die religiöse Sinngebung weltlicher Macht Bestand, setzt sich im Zuge aufgeklärten Denkens zunehmend die *naturrechtliche* Begründung von Herrschaft durch. Wie gesehen wird in diesem Sinne seit dem 13. Jahrhundert verstärkt aristotelisches Gedankengut erörtert, wobei nun ein neuer Aspekt an Gewicht gewinnt: Nach dem Vorbild antiker Theorien werden fortan Staat und Herrschaft als Ergebnis des *natürlichen* menschlichen Strebens nach einem das Glück befriedigenden Dasein aufgefasst.[23] Diese Neuausrichtung halte ich für maßgeblich mit Blick auf Beantwortungsversuche der Frage, wie es dazu komme, dass der bislang untersuchte enge Kausalnexus zwischen der Sündhaftigkeit des Menschen und seiner Unterwerfung unter die Staatsgewalt sich allmählich zu lockern beginne. So kommt mit Leibnizens Lehre vom Optimismus nicht zuletzt die Überzeugung zum Ausdruck, dieser Optimismus sei für den Menschen vonnöten, um sein – diesseitiges – Leben überhaupt bewältigen zu können. Zwar habe Gott die Welt erschaffen – aber so, dass den Menschen die Freiheit bleibt, diese zu verbessern: Die Welt *ist und bleibt* die „beste aller möglichen" v.a. dann, wenn die Menschen sie hienieden immer wieder zu einer solchen *machen*, sie also als (eine) solche zu bewahren suchen. Möglichkeit impliziert für Leibniz stets auch Machbarkeit: *Möglich* ist das, was *wirklich* werden kann.[24]

Nach Rolf Grawert bezeichnet das Wort „Gesetz" sogar noch im modernen Sprachgebrauch einen „im Sakralbereich zu verortenden Ursprung als

---

[22] Leibniz: *Versuche in der Theodicée*, S. 133.
[23] Entsprechend dem Grundsatz seiner *Théodicée*, Gottes Güte führe notwendig dazu, das Beste (= das im höchsten Maße Gute; vgl. ders.: „Elemente des Naturrechts", in: *Frühe Schriften zum Naturrecht*, S. 313) zu wählen (vgl. ders.: *Versuche in der Theodicée*, S. 96), heißt es in Leibnizens *Elementen des Naturrechts*: „Glück ist der Bestzustand einer Person." („*Felicitas est status personae optimus*.") – Vgl. *Frühe Schriften zum Naturrecht*, S. 246f., S. 313.
[24] Vgl. Hans Burkhardt: „Modaltheorie und Modallogik in der Scholastik und bei Leibniz", in: *Anuario. Filosofico* 16/1 (1983), S. 273–291, hier S 279f. (mit Blick auf *Elementa juris naturalis*), S. 280–286 (bezogen auf den Topos aller möglichen Welten).

einer Explikation der göttlichen Weltordnung bis zu der Bedeutung einer falsifizierbaren Hypothese in den modernen Naturwissenschaften".[25] Diese zwei strikt voneinander zu unterscheidenden Bereiche: das Gebot eines Gesetzgebers – das Rechtsgesetz – bzw. eine beobachtbare Regelmäßigkeit in der Natur – das Naturgesetz –, lassen die Ambiguität des Gesetzesbegriffs dieser Zeit erkennen. Diese Mehrdeutigkeit ist das Ergebnis einer komplizierten problemgeschichtlichen Entwicklung in der frühen Neuzeit. Aufschlussreich ist in diesem Zusammenhang, dass Leibniz im Kontext der Darstellung der Elemente und Quellen des reinen Rechts (*ius solum*) nicht nur über das Gesetz, sondern auch schon über den Begriff der Regel nachdenkt.[26] Gleichwohl befördern diese Überlegungen keineswegs die seit Mitte des 17. Jahrhunderts zu konstatierende Tendenz der Aushöhlung des positiven Rechtsgesetzes, die eine wichtige Voraussetzung für die Vertreibung Gottes sowohl aus dem rechtlich-moralischen als auch dem physikalischen Naturgesetz bedeutet. Denn Leibniz kennt in Bezug auf das Theonomie-Prinzip keine ‚Ausnahme von der Regel', vermag doch göttliches Schöpfungsrecht durch keinerlei übergeordnetes Recht gebeugt zu werden. Als entschiedener Befürworter maßgeblicher Einflussnahme von Philosophen auf Politik,[27] Gesellschaft und Wirtschaft versteht er unter menschlicher, sprich politischer Herrschaft die Realisierung des fürstlichen Willens, durch einen Machtspruch Rechtsgesetze zu erlassen. Dies beinhaltet für Leibniz jedoch keineswegs, dass solche Gesetze die dem Recht notwendig innewohnende Gerechtigkeit tatsächlich zum Ausdruck bringen: Macht und Recht unterhalten kein interdependentes Verhältnis, sind also nicht schlicht Ausdruck der Staatsraison. Auch wenn Leibniz selbst zeitlebens keine philosophische Staatslehre systematisch ausarbeitet,[28] empfiehlt er, Philosophen sowie Staatenlenker sollten sich nicht nur mit Fragen der Ethik und Staatskunst befassen, sondern sich auch – als Naturwissenschaftler und Naturphilosophen gleichsam – ein Verständnis von Naturzusammenhängen aneignen.

---

[25] Siehe: Grawert: Art.: „Gesetz", S. 863–922, hier S. 863. – Dieses Verständnis teilt Leibniz. – Vgl. „Verteidigungsrede auf die Streitkräfte des allerchristlichsten Königs gegen die Christen", in: Gottfried Wilhelm Leibniz: *Politische Schriften I*, hrsg. u. eingel. v. Hans Heinz Holz, Frankfurt a. M. 1966, S. 161–191, hier S. 167–170.
[26] Vgl. „Neue Methode, Jurisprudenz zu lernen und zu lehren", in: *Frühe Schriften zum Naturrecht*, S. 63ff.
[27] Zur Verbindung von Ethik und Politik bei Aristoteles vgl. *Ethica Nicomachea*, 1094a27–b7 u.ö.
[28] Leibniz' Ideal eines an der *iustia universalis* ausgerichteten Gottstaats rekonstruiert verständig: Klaus Luig: „Die Wurzeln des aufgeklärten Naturrechts bei Leibniz", in: Otto Dann/Diethelm Klippel (Hrsg.): *Naturrecht – Spätaufklärung – Revolution.* (= Studien zum achtzehnten Jahrhundert, Herausgegeben von der Deutschen Gesellschaft für die Erforschung des achtzehnten Jahrhunderts 16), Hamburg 1995, S. 61–79.

Vor diesem Hintergrund ist es bezeichnend, dass Leibniz gleich das erste Angebot (1667) einer Professur für Jurisprudenz in Altdorf ausschlägt,[29] gerade weil er schon als junger Mann die Nähe zur politischen Macht, als Berater nämlich, sucht. Sein Credo: Was vernünftig ist, ist auch politisch richtig. Demgemäß mögen rationale Einsichten Kaiser und Könige davon Abstand nehmen lassen, militärische Siege auf den Schlachtfeldern Europas erringen zu wollen (anempfohlen quasi schon gemäß *ius strictum* i.S. des Grundsatzes *neminem laedere* als Ausdruck der *iustitia commutativa*). In einem Brief an Hermann Conring – für Leibniz eine große, ihn zudem persönlich fördernde rechtgelehrte Autorität – wird das Verhältnis von Ethik und Politik wie folgt bestimmt:

„Scientia autem juris naturae, de qva Grotius, Hobbes, Feldenus, Pufendorfius, Ethica est, de justo, eoqve ut Grotius vocat strictè dicto; scientia Nomothetica de condendis Legibus, Politica est, de Utili, sed in commune, seu de aeqvo, vel ut Grotius vocat jure laxè dicto (ad qvod in me est obligatio, sed in altero non est actio seu ius exigendi)."[30]

Zwar vollzieht sich in Mitteleuropa die frühneuzeitliche Restitution der ‚Ethik', die seit Aristoteles als Titel der entsprechenden philosophischen Disziplin, will sie Wissenschaft sein, fungiert,[31] unter ständigem Rekurs auf die in den gelehrten Diskussionen zentralen Lehrbestände christlicher Moraltheologie (und nicht zuletzt der auf sie bezogenen Dogmengeschichte); doch als theoretische Disziplin erhebt die Ethik die Praxis als solche zum Objekt:[32] Es

---

[29] *Leben und Werk von Gottfried Wilhelm Leibniz. Eine Chronik.* Bearbeitet v. Kurt Müller und Gisela Krönert. (= *Veröffentlichungen des Leibniz-Archivs*, hrsg. von der Niedersächsischen Landesbibliothek 2), Frankfurt a. M. 1969, S. 10.
[30] „Die Wissenschaft vom Naturrecht allerdings, von der Grotius, Hobbes, von Felden und Pufendorf gehandelt haben, heißt Ethik. Sie handelt vom Gerechten, und zwar, wie Grotius sagt, im strengen Sinne des Wortes. Die gesetzgebende Wissenschaft, die von der Aufstellung der Gesetze handelt, heißt Politik; und sie betrifft das Nützliche, aber im Sinne des Gemeinwohls, d. h. sie betrifft dasjenige, was billig ist, oder, wie Grotuis sagt, das Recht im weiteren Sinne (dasjenige, wozu zwar meinerseits eine Verpflichtung besteht, wozu aber bei einem anderen kein Recht auf einen Prozeß bzw. kein Recht auf Erzwingung besteht)." – Vgl. Leibniz an Hermann Conring, 13./23. Januar 1670, in: *Frühe Schriften zum Naturrecht*, S. 324f.; A II, 1, N. 15.
[31] Ebbersmeyer erinnert daran, daß die „‚Verwissenschaftlichung' der Ethik […] eng mit der Rezeption der *Nikomachischen Ethik* […] sowie mit dem Aufstieg und der Etablierung des aristotelischen Wissenschaftsbegriffs in fast allen Disziplinen im 13. Jahrhundert" zusammenhänge. – Siehe: Sabrina Ebbersmeyer: *Homo agens. Studien zur Genese und Struktur frühhumanistischer Moralphilosophie* (= *Quellen und Studien zur Philosophie* 95) Berlin/New York 2010, S. 23.
[32] Ludwig Siep konstatiert mit Blick auf den Jenaer Hegel eine „Erneuerung der praktischen Philosophie", die auf eine „Kritik des Naturrechts und Rehabilitierung der klassischen politischen Philosophie" in dessen *Naturrechtsaufsatz* (1802/03) hinauslaufe. – Siehe: Ludwig Siep: *Anerkennung als Prinzip der praktischen Philosophie*, Freiburg/München 1979, S. 146 bzw.

gehe nicht mehr – lediglich ‚theoretisch' – um die Frage, was Tugend sei, sondern zunehmend um das tugendhafte *Leben* des Einzelwesens in der Polis. Daher auch erkennt Aristoteles, den Leibniz ausdrücklich zu den großen Naturrechtslehrern rechnet,[33] in der *eudaimonía* (εὐδαιμονία) das höchste Gut (vgl. Buch I der *Ethika Nikomacheia*). Dieser Gedanke kehrt wieder in Gestalt der ‚Handlungstheorie' Leibnizens, die das Kernstück eines an der Differenz Gerechtigkeit – Ungerechtigkeit orientierten Moralitätsbegriffs ausmacht. Auch schon in seinem Thomasius-Kommentar *Das Leib-Seele-Pentagon und die moralische Sphäre des Verstandes* kündigt Leibniz – selbst Sohn eines Professors für Morallehre – an, er suche die „Moralität [...] der Aristotelischen Ethik, nämlich die der Geisteshaltung und des Glückes",[34] einer Prüfung zu unterziehen.[35] Zum Ergebnis hat diese Prüfung einen Ausgleich von stoischem Gleichmut und christlichem Vertrauen auf die unerschütterliche Güte göttlicher Vorsehung. Wenn Leibniz freilich Glückseligkeit bestimmt als *Zustand* beständiger Freude, welche – ähnlich wie bei Platon – die Seele an ihrer eigenen Vollkommenheit, Kraft, Harmonie und Freiheit empfinde, liegt hiermit ein fundamentaler Unterschied zur aristotelischen Ethik vor, gemäss welcher Glückseligkeit „eine Art von tugendgemäßer *Tätigkeit* der Seele"[36] bedeutet. Leibniz setzt hingegen auf ein *theoretisches* Vermögen, nämlich den verordnenden Verstand:

> „Welcher allezeit thut was der verstand ihm anweiset, der kan stets im gemüth sich vergnüget befinden. Denn entweder er erlanget das worumb er nach anleitung des Verstandes sich bemühet, und dieweil es ihm also nach wundsch ergehet, kan er nicht anders als vergnügt sich befinden; oder es gehet ihm *contrar*, und hier kan er nicht minder vergnügt seyn, bedenckend daß er dennoch gethan, was ihm seyn gewißen zu thun erinnert, und weil es dennoch wieder seinen wundsch ergangen, siehet er leichtlich, daß es Gott (ohne deßen zulaßen nichts geschehen kan) also beliebet."[37]

3. Leibniz zum Verhältnis von Naturrechtslehre und Jurisprudenz

---

S. 156. – Siehe ebenso: Manfred Riedel (Hrsg.): *Die Rehabilitierung der Praktischen Philosophie*, 2 Bde., Freiburg i. Brsg. 1972–73.

[33] „Neue Methode, Jurisprudenz zu lernen und zu lehren", in: *Frühe Schriften zum Naturrecht*, S. 75 („Naturrecht und Nomothetik").

[34] „Ego habitum, aut obiectum, et sic moralitatem non justitiae et Ethicae qvasi ejus, sed Ethicae qvasi Aristotelicae habitus et beatitudinis expendo." – Vgl. *Frühe Schriften zum Naturrecht*, S. 12.

[35] Vgl. Hubertus Busche: „Das Leib-Seele-Pentagon und die Kombinatorik attraktiver Vorstellungen – Ein folgenreiches Konzept der Leibnizschen Frühphilosophie", in: *ZphF* 46 (1992), S. 489–507; ders.: *Leibniz' Weg ins perspektivische Universum. Eine Harmonie im Zeitalter der Berechnung*, Hamburg 1997, S. 489–507.

[36] *Aristotelis Ethica Nicomachea*, 1099 b 26: εἴρηται γὰρ ψυχῆς ἐνέργεια κατ' ἀρετὴν ποιά τις. (Hervorh. im dt. Zitat von H. G.) – Vgl. ebd., 1102 a 5–6.

[37] A VI, 3, S. 650.

Der frühneuzeitliche Naturrechtsgedanke befestigt die gesellschaftlich etablierte Ständehierarchie zunächst einmal *juristisch* – und nicht schon moralisch. Michael Stolleis untersucht diese Ablösungsbewegung des Politisch-Rechtlichen vom Moralischen: Die Gesetzeskodifikationen der frühen Neuzeit seien darauf aus, faktische Rechtsfälle vor moralischen, d. h. persönlich motivierten Urteilsfindungen – beispielsweise im Höfischen, d. h. Majestätischen, oder Klerikalen – zu bewahren.[38] Hier setzt auch der junge Leibniz an, agiert er doch in dem Interesse, das Naturrecht in der Jurisprudenz, die er in einen göttlichen, menschlichen und bürgerlichen Teil untergliedert sieht,[39] heimisch zu machen.[40] In diesem Zusammenhang richtungsweisend ist Leibnizens „*Umbesetzung*",[41] in Rechtsfragen die Jurisprudenz an Stelle der Theologie zur Zentralwissenschaft aufrücken zu lassen. *Einerseits* steht Leibniz hierin in der Tradition des römischen Rechts, dessen abstrakt definierte, kodifizierte Form die Ausbildung der *iuris prudentia* befördert;[42] in der griechischen Antike sind anders – so würden wir sie heute nennen – Rechtsphilosophien erdacht worden (vgl. Platons Alterswerk *Nomoi*[43]). *Andererseits* steht Leibniz aber noch in der zu seiner Zeit zunehmend verblassenden Tradition, die göttliche Schöpfung als Rechtsordnung dieses Schöpfers zu deuten.[44] Einen solchen Anspruch, diese zu bewahren, vertritt zu Leibniz' Zeit vor allen Dingen Francisco Suárez mit seinem zehnbändigen rechtsphilosophischen Mammutwerk *Tractatus de legibus ac Deo legislatore* (1612ff.). Die Gesetze, so Suárez, seien der Weg zu Gott; habe dieser die Welt einmal geschaffen, so

---

[38] Vgl. Michael Stolleis: *Staat und Staatsräson in der frühen Neuzeit. Studien zur Geschichte des öffentlichen Rechts*, Frankfurt a. M. 1990. – Stolleis' Beobachtung bestätigen beispielsweise auch Niklas Luhmanns Untersuchungen zum System des Rechts.
[39] *Frühe Schriften zum Naturrecht*, S. 47.
[40] *Frühe Schriften zum Naturrecht*, S. XXVII (Einleitung Busche). – Insofern ist Erik Wolfs Ansicht, erst mit Chr. Thomasius gebe es ein „juristisches" Naturrecht, welches nunmehr auch lehrmäßig vom „philosophischen" und „theologischen" getrennt werde, zu präzisieren. – Vgl. Erik Wolf: *Große Rechtsdenker der deutschen Geistesgeschichte*, Tübingen 1963, S. 374.
[41] Vgl. den Unterschied von „*Umsetzung*" und „*Umbesetzung*" nach: Hans Blumenberg: *Die Legitimität der Neuzeit*, Frankfurt a. M. ²1988, S. 75.
[42] Vor diesem Hintergrund kann Leibniz das Recht als eine Wissenschaft verstehen, deren Grund der Beweis ausmacht und dessen Prinzip wiederum die Definition von Worten wie z. B. Recht („Ius"), Gerechtes („Iustum") oder Gerechtigkeit („Iustitia") bedeutet. – Vgl. „Universale Gerechtigkeit als Liebe zu allen", in: *Frühe Schriften zum Naturrecht*, S. 215–243, hier S. 222. – „Deinde nemo est qvi justitiam à prudentia disjungere audeat […]." – Ebd., S. 224.
[43] Vgl. Gunther Eigler (Hrsg.): *Platon: Werke in acht Bänden*, Bd. 8, Teile 1 und 2, Darmstadt ²1990. (Abdruck der kritischen Ausgabe von Édouard des Places und Auguste Diès; Übersetzung von Klaus Schöpsdau)
[44] Vgl. *Frühe Schriften zum Naturrecht*, S. LV–LVII (Einleitung Busche).

habe er auch ihr Gesetzgeber werden müssen.[45] Weil die Theologie Gott als Gesetzgeber anerkenne, beziehe der Gesetzestheoretiker Suárez hieraus seinerseits die Legitimation, diesen Wesenszug Gottes *per rationem* zu ergründen.[46] Verstehen wollen heißt hier auch rechtfertigen wollen – Theodizee. Die Theologie deutet Gott als universalen Gesetzgeber – anders als die Philosophie, die Gott unmittelbar als Erstursache oder Kraft in der Zweitursache wirkend begreift.[47] Suárez betont, die Ausleger des kanonischen Rechts[48] würden ihrer Sache nur gerecht, „wenn sie die heiligen Vorschriften von einer höheren Zielsetzung und Vernunft aus [der übernatürlichen Ordnung nämlich, H. G.] berücksichtigen und auslegen";[49] die Theologie jedoch betrachte alles insgesamt um willen einer noch einmal höheren Zweckorientierung, denn sie untersuche sogar das *Naturrecht* unter der Voraussetzung, es unterstehe einer übernatürlichen Ordnung und empfange so eine stärkere Kraft als es sich selbst zu geben vermag.[50] Auch wenn Leibniz sich nicht expressis verbis auf ihn bezieht, folgt er Suárez doch darin, Gott als letzten Grund des Naturrechts – verstanden als Summe der Sitten – anzusetzen.[51]

Nichtsdestoweniger korrespondiert damit Leibnizens Gefolgschaft der Lehren des Ulpian, wenn es heißt, die Rechtswissenschaft betreffe neben der „Kenntnis von den göttlichen und menschlichen Dingen" ebenso die Rechtsweisheit (*sapientia iuris*),[52] sprich ein weltliches Geschäft.[53] Demgemäß ist

---

[45] *R. P. Francisci Suarez e Societate Jesu. Opera Omnia.* Editio nova, a Carolo Berton, Tomus quintus. Parisiis MDCCCLVI. Lib. II, c. 6, n. 23.
[46] Zur Gotteserkenntnis nach Suárez cf. noch immer: Josef Leiwesmeier: *Die Gotteslehre bei Franz Suarez* (= *Geschichtliche Forschungen zur Philosophie der Neuzeit* 6) Paderborn 1938.
[47] Vgl. zuletzt: Stephan Schmid: *Finalursachen in der frühen Neuzeit* (= *Quellen und Studien zur Philosophie* 99) Berlin/New York 2011, S. 115–121.
[48] Francisco Suarez: *De legibus ac Deo legislatore.* VI u. VII. – In: *Edicion critica bilingüe,* hrsg. v. Luciano Pereña, Pedro P. Suñer/Vidal Abril/César Villanueva/Eleuterio Elorduy, 8 Bde. (= *Corpus hispanorum de pace.* Editado bajo la direccion de Luciano Pereña, Bd. XI–XVII; XXI u. XXII), Madrid 1971–1978.
[49] Francisco Suárez: *Abhandlung über die Gesetze und Gott den Gesetzgeber,* übers., hrsg. u. mit einem Anhang versehen v. Norbert Brieskorn, Freiburg/Berlin 2002, S. 20.
[50] „Juris ergo canonici interpretes, per se ac ex proprio instituto, superiori fine et ratione sacros canones considerant ac interpretantur. Theologia vero sub altiori ratione hæc omnia complecitur; nam jus ipsum naturale considerat, ut supernaturali ordini supponitur, et ab illo firmitatem majorem accipit; leges vero civiles solum, vel ut de earum honestate ac rectitudine per altiores regulas dijudicet, vel ut obligationes conscientiæ quæ ex illis oriuntur juxta principia fidei declaret; […]." – Suárez: *De legibus.* Prooemium, X / Pereña, I, 6.
[51] Leibniz: *Neue Methode, Jurisprudenz zu lernen und zu lehren,* S. 83.
[52] Cf. *Frühe Schriften zum Naturrecht,* S. LV (Einleitung Busche).
[53] Locus classicus: „Iuris prudentia est divinarum atque humanarum rerum notitia, iusti atque iniusti scientia." – Vgl. Domitius Ulpianus: *Ulpian primo libro reg.* Digesen 1,1,10,2.

Leibniz' Programm zur *Neuen Methode, Jurisprudenz zu lernen und zu lehren* (1667) zu entnehmen, dass „die Lehre von der Heiligen Schrift und vom Wort Gottes der Lehre *von den Gesetzen und ihrer Auslegung*"[54] entspricht. Im zweiten Teil der dort angestellten Überlegungen, der, wie Leibniz sagt, „speziell ist und sich allein auf die Jurisprudenz beschränkt", gibt es wiederum einen dritten Teil, der mit dem „Naturrecht" und der „Nomothetik" quasi die Perspektive der ‚zwei Augen des Richters' einnimmt. Hier heißt es gleich zu Beginn, in § 69:

> „So haben wir endlich das Meer der exegetischen Jurisprudenz durchmessen. Doch scheinen wir an die Meerenge von Gibraltar gelangt zu sein, wo sich der Durchgang zum Mittelmeer zum Ozean auftut. Die polemische [d. h. materiale oder positive, H .G.] Jurisprudenz nämlich ergießt sich derart ins Unendliche, daß sie sich nicht erschöpfen läßt. Denn täglich tauchen neue Fälle auf. Indessen muß sich der Rechtsgelehrte die Arbeit machen, zumindest die bekannten Regionen zu durchqueren, d. h. die bereits durchsegelten Fälle zu sichten und zu entscheiden. Wenn er vom Sturm an die neuen Gestade geworfen wird, d. h. auf neue Fälle stößt, so wird er mit Hilfe eines Kompasses, nämlich des Naturrechts, leicht hindurchfinden."[55]

4. Weder Säkularisierung noch Resakralisierung

Die Leerstelle, welche die Austreibung des Theonomie-Grundsatzes aus dem Rechtsbegriff der frühen Neuzeit hinterlässt, wird nach meinem Verständnis der Naturrechtsdebatten dieser Zeit mit divergierenden Moral-Konzepten neu besetzt.[56] Es liegt die Vermutung nahe, dass die philosophische Potenz des Moralbegriffs nicht aus der Alternative zu dem vermeintlich untilgbaren Gegensatz von Naturrecht und positivem Recht erwächst, sondern vielmehr der

---

[54] Cf. *Frühe Schriften zum Naturrecht*, S. 31
[55] „Ita tandem Jurisprudentiae Exegeticae pelagus emensi sumus; sed videmur nobis ad fretum Gaditanum pervenisse, ubi ex mediterraneo mari in Oceanum transitus panditur. *Jurisprudentia* enim *Polemica* ita in infinitum diffusa est, ut exhauriri non possit, novi enim quotidie casus emergunt. Intereà danda Jurisconsulto opera est, ut cognitas saltem regiones lustret, id est, casus jam ventilatos colligat et decidat; ita cùm ad nova littora tempestate deferetur, id est, in novos casus incidet; ope magnetis, id est, Juris naturalis facilè se explicabit." – Vgl. „Neue Methode, Jurisprudenz zu lehren", in: *Frühe Schriften zum Naturrecht*, S. 70.
[56] Vgl. Holger Glinka: *Zur Genese autonomer Moral. Eine Problemgeschichte des Verhältnisses von Naturrecht und Religion in der frühen Neuzeit und der Aufklärung*, Hamburg 2012, S. 1–10.

naturrechtlichen Gerechtigkeitsformel „Recht aus Moral"[57] je schon innewohnt – eine These, der Leibnizens Lehre einer umfassenden Gerechtigkeit (*iustitia universalis*) als Inbegriff sämtlicher (realisierter) Tugenden entspräche; die wissenschaftliche Verhandlung des Ganzen fällt in das Ressort der Jurisprudenz.[58] Hiermit korrespondiert Leibniz' Definition der Freiheit: „*Freiheit* ist die Übereinstimmung der moralischen, d. h. der von einem guten Menschen verantwortbaren Möglichkeit mit der natürlichen Möglichkeit."[59] Tatsächlich steht auch die Frage, wie eine von theonomen Merkmalen befreite Moralphilosophie möglich sei, in direktem Zusammenhang mit dem in der frühen Neuzeit gemachten Lösungsvorschlag, die Vernunft sei je schon einer naturhaft gegebenen Rechtssphäre – und damit einer Form der Praxis – übereignet.

Allerdings kritisiert Leibniz die zu seiner Zeit längst vorherrschende Säkularisierung (oder Entsakralisierung) des Naturrechts.[60] So entpuppt sich z. B. die in Leibnizens *Elementen des Naturrechts* eröffnete Alternative „Gerechtigkeit mit und ohne Gott"[61] als eine nur scheinbare, wie seine dort geführte Kritik an Grotius beweist: Dessen Hypothese einer unabhängig von Gott in Geltung befindlichen Gerechtigkeit kontert Leibniz, indem er Gerechtes im allgemeinen ohne den Lohn Gottes, sprich ein Leben nach dem Tod, *nicht* für möglich hält. Aber er versucht nicht wie Descartes (vgl. dessen *Meditationes de prima philosophia*), die Atheisten – die „Aufrührer" („rebelles"), wie Leibniz sagt – zu bekämpfen, sondern beabsichtigt vielmehr eine „Apologie der christlichen Lehre und Kirche" (1668/69).[62] Dessen ungeachtet konzipiert Leibniz eine Naturrechtslehre, die gleichermaßen für nicht religiös orientierte Personen geeignet sein möge. Dies markiert einen deutlichen Unterschied zu Descartes. Leibniz akzeptiert also nicht nur die Schwierigkeiten, denen die religiöse Weltanschauung in seiner Zeit ausgesetzt ist, sondern er anerkennt sie auch – zieht aber die Konsequenz, nach neuen Möglichkeiten,

---

[57] Siehe z. B.: Otto Veit: „Der geistesgeschichtliche Standort des Naturrechts", in: Werner Maihofer (Hrsg.): *Naturrecht oder Rechtspositivismus? Wege der Forschung*, Bd. 16, Darmstadt 1966, S. 40.
[58] „IURISPRUDENTIA est scientia justi, seu scientia libertatis et officiorum, seu scientia juris, proposito aliqvo casu seu facto." – Vgl. „Elemente des Natur*rechts*", in: *Frühe Schriften zum Naturrecht*, S. 248f.
[59] „*Liberatas* est potentiae moralis seu cadentis in virum bonum congruitas cum naturali." Vgl. ebd., S. 250f.
[60] Vgl. auch ebd. S. XVI (Einleitung Busche).
[61] Vgl. ebd., S. 91–97; vgl. das Gedankenexperiment „[…] si qvem sublato DEO […]." – ebd., S. 304.
[62] Vgl. ebd., S. XXXIX (Einleitung Busche).

das christliche Weltbild mit wissenschaftlichen Mitteln darzustellen, zu suchen. Dementsprechend verfolgt er schon früh, wie Hartmut Busche zu Recht betont, sowohl kontroverstheologische – sprich das Trennende betonende – als auch unionstheologische – also das einende betonende – Interessen.[63]

So sucht Leibniz auch – quasi im Gefolge Spinozas – die naturphilosophische Dimension der im Naturrecht vorausgesetzten Freiheitslehre aufzudecken. Zur Erinnerung: Zwischen dem 18. und 28. November 1676, als Leibniz über Holland in die Heimat unterwegs ist, kommt es zu mehrmaligen Besuchen des 14 Jahre jüngeren Leibniz bei dem von seiner Krankheit bereits schwer gezeichneten Spinoza, vier Monate vor dessen Tod. Man tauscht sich nicht über religionskritische Fragen aus, sondern führt „mehrere lange Gespräche über [Spinozas, H. G.] ‚Ethik', Descartes' Bewegungstheorie, die characteristica universalis und das Gottesproblem"; Leibniz legt Spinoza auch den Text *Quod Ens perfectissimum existit,* „für Spinoza in seiner Gegenwart geschrieben", zur Prüfung vor; zudem ist Spinozas Briefwechsel mit Oldenburg Thema.[64] Das bedeutet, es geht auch um *das* Zentralproblem ihrer beider Metaphysik und Naturtheologie, sprich um das Verhältnis von Geist und Körper. Leibniz beabsichtigt aber einen „universellen Nachweis der Vereinbarkeit der christlichen Glaubensgeheimnisse mit der mechanis[tis]chen Naturerklärung".[65] Kondylis analysiert diese „Priorität des Weltanschaulichen bei Leibniz", d.h. seine christliche Religiosität, vor dem Hintergrund der systematischen Konzipierung seiner Metaphysik, wie sie in der Auseinandersetzung mit den Philosophien des Descartes und Spinoza entsteht.[66]

---

[63] Ebd. – Vgl. aber: Paul Hazard: *Die Krise des europäischen Denkens. La Crise de la Conscience Européenne. 1680–1715,* aus dem Franz. übertragen v. Harriet Wegener, Hamburg 1939, S. 258–280 („Leibniz und das Mißlingen einer Einigung der Kirchen").
[64] Siehe: *Leben und Werk von Gottfried Wilhelm Leibniz. Eine Chronik,* S. 46.
[65] Vgl. *Frühe Schriften zum Naturrecht,* S. XL, Anm. 105 (Einleitung Busche); vgl. auch ebd., S. XLVIII.
[66] Panajotis Kondylis: *Die Aufklärung im Rahmen des neuzeitlichen Rationalismus,* München 1986, S. 580–594.

Es hat sich gezeigt, dass die sogenannte „praktische Philosophie" nicht erst bei Kant,[67] sondern schon in der griechischen Philosophie[68] systematisch, d. h. die Unversehrtheit der Idee einheitlichen Wissens versichernd, verortet ist. Ihre problematische Signatur umgreift die Begriffe Naturrecht (das Juristen und Theologen der frühen Neuzeit als rechtlich-moralisches Naturgesetz verstehen[69]), Gesetz, Recht, Tugend, Vernunftrecht und Moral. Deutlich geworden ist zudem, dass die Frage nach dem frühneuzeitlichen Naturrecht interdisziplinäre Antworten erfordert. So auch bei Leibniz, der das Naturrecht in den Anwendungsgebieten der Rechtswissenschaft, deren internationale Quellengeschichte er schon in seiner Jugend erforscht,[70] zu orten sucht, in seinem Denken *summa summarum* aber die Interferenz zum Austrag kommen lässt von *Philosophie* und *christlicher Theologie* (Theodizee, Trinitätsspekulation), *Naturwissenschaften* (der mechanistisch begriffene menschliche Geist, nicht die Materie, ist der Grund von allem), *Mathematik* (die Ausarbeitung der Differentialrechnung sowie die Idee zu einer binären Rechenmaschine [1679]

---

[67] Kant identifiziert „reine praktische Gesetze" als Produkte der reinen Vernunft mit moralischen Gesetzen: „mithin gehören diese allein zum praktischen Gebrauche der reinen Vernunft, und erlauben einen Kanon." – Siehe: Immanuel Kant: *Kritik der reinen Vernunft*, in: *Kants Werke*, Bd. III: *Kritik der reinen Vernunft*, Akademie-Textausgabe, unveränderter photomechanischer Abdruck des Textes der von der preußischen Akademie der Wissenschaften 1902 begonnenen Ausgabe von Kants gesammelten Schriften, ²1787, Berlin 1968, B 828. – Kant nennt die wahre Sittlichkeit des Handelns im Gegensatz zur bloßen Gesetzlichkeit (Legalität) Moralität; insofern bedeutet seine praktische Philosophie für die Geschichte des Gesetzesbegriffs einen Endpunkt. Seine Vorlesungen über Naturrecht stehen in der problemgeschichtlichen Linie Achenwall-Pütter: „§ 12 Actio voluntatis dicitur, *actio libera* seu *moralis*, et lex actionis liberae, quatenus rationi est conformis, vocatur *lex moralis*. Voluntas itaque agit perpetuo secundum legem voluntatis; non vero semper secundum legem moralem. § 13 Scientia legum moralium, seu scientia de dirigendis secundum rationem actionibus liberis, dicitur *Philosophia practica*." (§ 12 Eine Handlung des Willens wird *freie* oder *moralische Handlung* genannt, und das Gesetz der freien Handlung, soweit es mit der Vernunft übereinstimmt, heißt *moralisches Gesetz*. Der Wille handelt daher fortwährend gemäß dem Gesetz des Willens, nicht aber immer gemäß dem moralischen Gesetz. § 13 Die Wissenschaft der moralischen Gesetze, oder die Wissenschaft, freie Handlungen vernunftgemäß zu bestimmen, heißt *praktische Philosophie*.") – Vgl. Gottfried Achenwall/Johann Stephan Pütter: *Anfangsgründe des Naturrechts (Elementa iuris naturae)* (= Bibliothek des deutschen Staatsdenkens 5), hrsg. v. Jan Schröder, Frankfurt a. M./Leipzig 1995, S. 18f.
[68] Nach Diogenes Laertius unterscheidet Platon die Wissenschaften in praktische, poietische und theoretische. – Siehe: Diogenes Laertius: *Leben und Meinungen berühmter Philosophen*, 2 Bde, übers. aus dem Griechischen v. Otto Apelt, Berlin 1955, III, 84. – Aristoteles folgt darin Platon. – Siehe: *Aristoteles: Metaphysik*, in der Übers. v. Friedrich Bassenge, Berlin 1990, Buch E, 1. 1025b 25.
[69] Siehe: Jan Schröder: „Gesetz und Naturgesetz in der frühen Neuzeit", in: *Akademie der Wissenschaften und der Literatur*, Stuttgart 2004, S. 7–11.
[70] Vgl. *Codex iuris gentium diplomaticus* (1693); A IV, 5, N. 7.

begründen die These, Denken sei Rechnen[71] [weil so Lösungen gefunden werden]), *Logik* (auf der Basis von Analyse und Synthese lassen sich wenige Prinzipien, aus denen alles zu verstehen ist, gewinnen), *Geschichtswissenschaft* (kritische Quellenforschung) und *Philologie* (Universalsprache; Sprachgeschichte des Deutschen). Leibniz wird von der Überzeugung geleitet, in die Harmonie, die unter den verschiedenen Wissensbereichen herrscht, einzudringen und damit Universalität und Individualität zu vermitteln.[72] Diesem Anspruch folgt auch sein Idealbegriff ‚gründlicher Kenntnis',

> „was ein Ding wirken bzw. aushalten kann; und zwar bald für sich genommen, bald in Verbindung mit anderen Dingen. (Dies ist die wahrhaft praktische Kenntnis. Denn ein Lehrsatz dient ja der Lösung eines Problems; Wissenschaft wird getrieben um des Handelns willen.) Hieraus folgt, daß niemand auch nur von einer einzigen Sache gründliche Kenntnis haben kann, wenn er nicht außerordentlich weise ist, d. h. den Gesamtzusammenhang der Dinge gründlich kennt."[73]

Leibniz wirkt mit bei der vom Kurfürsten Friedrich III. von Brandenburg-Preußen (1688–1701) gegründeten Preußischen (oder Berliner) Akademie der Schönen Künste (1696) sowie der Societät der Scienzien (1700) (deren erster Präsident er wird).[74] Ulrich Im Hof bemerkt hierzu:

---

[71] Leibniz ist der Überzeugung, dass, wer Gott näher kommen wolle, rechnen, also die Sprache Gottes sprechen müsse. Im Christentum spielt die Zahl 7 eine wichtige Rolle insofern, als Gott, der alles aus Nichts erschafft, am siebenten Tage ruht (*Gen* 2,2). Im dualen Binärcode stellt sich die Zahl 7 als „1 1 1" dar – für Leibniz ein Hinweis auf die christliche Trinität.

[72] „Unter solchen Umständen setzt Leibniz sich das Ziel, die Aufgabe des Aristoteles wieder aufzunehmen und die Einheit und Harmonie der Dinge, die der menschliche Geist scheinbar nicht mehr begreifen kann und vielleicht nicht mehr zugeben will, wieder aufzunehmen." – Vgl. Paul Hazard: *La Crise de la Conscience Européenne 1680–1715*, Paris 1935; dt. Übersetzung: *Die Krise des europäischen Geistes 1680–1715*, aus dem Frz. übertr. v. Harriet Wegener, Hamburg 1939, S. 262.

[73] „*Pernoscere* est nosse qvid res agere aut pati possit. Scilicet tum per se, tum cum aliis combinata. Haec vera notitia practica est. Theorema enim est propter problema, Scientia propter operationem. Hinc seqvitur neminem posse unius rei esse pernoscentem, nisi idem sit sapientissimus, seu pernoscens universalis." Vgl. „Elemente des Naturrechts", in: *Frühe Schriften zum Naturrecht*, S. 315ff.

[74] Siehe: Adolf von Harnack (Hrsg.): *Geschichte der Königlich Preußischen Akademie der Wissenschaften zu Berlin*, im Auftrage der Akademie bearbeitet v. Adolf von Harnack, Berlin 1900 (ND Hildesheim 1970) – Zum weiteren Kontext dieser Institution vgl. Wolfgang Reinhard: *Geschichte der Staatsgewalt. Eine vergleichende Verfassungsgeschichte Europas von den Anfängen bis zur Gegenwart*, München ²2000, S. 399–401.

> „Endlich erhielt der Philosoph die Gelegenheit, seine so oft formulierten Akademiegedanken in Wirklichkeit umzusetzen, jenes dreifache Ziel der Ausbreitung einer offenen christlichen Weltanschauung durch die Wissenschaft, der Pflege und Beförderung der Wissenschaften und von *Ruhm, Wohlfahrt und Aufnahme der deutschen Nation, Gelehrsamkeit und Sprache.* Insbesondere ging es ihm um die *utilitas,* den Praxisbezug der Wissenschaften."[75]

So ziert das Wappen der Berliner Akademie bis zum heutigen Tage der Wahlspruch „Theoria cum Praxi" (anders als beispielsweise das Pariser oder Londoner). Vorliegende Ausführungen haben nicht zuletzt diesen Willen zur Praxis, zur (wissenschafts-)politischen Gestaltung ins Licht zu rücken gesucht, vergrößert sich doch im Deutschland dieser Zeit deren (philosophische) Strahlkraft kontinuierlich. Zur historisch nächsten Entfaltung kommt im sogenannten Zeitalter der Aufklärung besagte Tendenz in Gestalt der praktischen Philosophie des Empiristen Christian Thomasius, der als Anwalt und Dozent in Leipzig das Naturrecht nach Grotius und Samuel Pufendorf vertritt.[76] Thomasius – weniger Leibniz – trägt sodann Entscheidendes bei zur Begründung und begrifflichen Ausbuchstabierung der der Ethik innewohnenden Differenz von Moral und Recht.[77]

---

[75] Siehe: Ulrich Im Hof: *Das Europa der Aufklärung.* (= *Europa bauen,* hrsg. v. Jacques Le Goff), München 1993, S. 98. – Zur religionspolitischen Einordnung der Gründung großer nationaler Akademien vgl. Werner Schneiders: *Hoffnung auf Vernunft. Aufklärungsphilosophie in Deutschland,* Hamburg 1990, S. 33

[76] Aspekte, welche der Erhellung der gegenseitigen Missachtung Leibniz' und Chr. Thomasius' dienlich sind, bringt bei: Hans Poser: „Leibniz' Kritik an Christian Thomasius. Anmerkungen zu IV,6 N. 44", in: Friedrich Beiderbeck/Stephan Waldhoff (Hrsg.): *Pluralität der Perspektiven und Einheit der Wahrheit im Werk von G. W. Leibniz. Beiträge zu seinem philosophischen, theologischen und politischen Denken,* Berlin 2011, S. 15–20. – Zur übergreifenden Verortung von Leibniz und Thomasius vgl. Werner Schneiders: *Die wahre Aufklärung. Zum Selbstverständnis des deutschen Aufklärung,* Freiburg/München 1974, S. 14.

[77] Vgl. Max Fleischmann: *Christian Thomasius,* Halle a. d. S. 1931, S. 59f. – Werner Schneiders: *Naturrecht und Liebesethik. Zur Geschichte der praktischen Philosophie im Hinblick auf Christian Thomasius,* Hildesheim/New York 1971, S. 12, S. 273–281, insb. S. 300–346 (auch als Ausblick). – Vgl. ebenso: S. Martin Kühnel: *Das politische Denken von Christian Thomasius. Staat Gesellschaft, Bürger* (= *Beiträge zur politischen Wissenschaft* 120), Berlin 2001, S. 58–65.

Leibniz on Time and Duration

Geoffrey Gorham (Saint Paul, MN)

1. Introduction

This paper examines one aspect of Leibniz's philosophy of time which, despite its rich historical lineage, has been somewhat underplayed in recent treatments of his metaphysics and philosophy of science. In a number of works explicating his mature metaphysics of space and time, Leibniz emphasizes the distinction between space and time, on the one hand – where

> "space is only the order of existing for possibles existing simultaneously, just as time is the order of existing for possibles that exist successively" – and extension and duration, on the other – where "extension is the extension *of* something, just as we say a multitude or duration is a multitude of something or a duration of something."[1]

I will first consider the origins of this distinction in sources important to Leibniz. I will next attempt to isolate the most important aspects of the distinction. Leibniz, perhaps more than any other early modern metaphysician, tended to analyze space and time analogously while giving the lion's share of attention to the former. I will attempt to show that this methodology, however fruitful in the abstract realm of space and time, is more problematic in the concrete realm of extension and duration.

2. Historical Background

It is worth reviewing briefly the origin of the time/duration distinction in sources Leibniz knew and drew upon. In scholastic thought, duration is a generic notion common to God and created beings in so far as they persist in being. Aquinas writes that whereas God's eternal duration lacks any succession or 'before and after' created things endure successively: "the divine Being is simultaneously

---

[1] To De Volder June 30, 1704; Gottfried Wilhelm Leibniz: *Philosophical Papers and Letters*, ed. by L. E. Loemker, Dordrecht 1989, p. 536 (further as L); Id.: *Philosophical Essays,* ed. by R. Ariew and D. Garber, Indianapolis 1989, p. 179 (further as AG).

without succession; but with the world it is otherwise."[2] Created beings are in "time itself, which is successive."[3] Somewhat more systematically, Suarez explains,

> "Duration can be divided first of all between permanent and successive. Permanent duration is said to be wholly simultaneous without successive parts; successive duration is not permanent but rather one part always succeeds another."[4]

For both Aquinas and Suarez, successive duration is closely associated with motion, in line with the canonical Aristotelian formula: "time is the measure of motion with respect to before and after"[5] (although Suarez and other late scholastics admit an 'imaginary time' with successive structure prior to the creation of the world).

While retaining the duration/time distinction, Descartes transforms it in two important respects. First, he makes all duration intrinsically successive, even the duration of God and of rest:

> "the duration which we find to be involved in movement is certainly no different from the duration involved in things which do not move."[6]

After commenting to Burman that "we can divide his duration into an infinite number of parts, even though God himself is not therefore divisible" Burman objected that God's "eternity is all at once and once and for all."[7] Descartes' reply is curt: "that is inconceivable."[8] But although he extends successive duration to all things, Descartes does not separate it from things themselves, as Newton would later do. Rather,

---

[2] St. Thomas Aquinas: *Summa Theologica*, in : *Great Books of the Western World*, vols. 19 and 20, transl. by Fathers of the English Dominican Province Chicago, Encyclopedia Britannica 1952, 1, 46, 2 (further ST).
[3] ST 1, 10, 1.
[4] Francisco Suarez: *Disputationes Metaphysicae (1866)*, in: *Opera Omnia,* ed. by Carolo Berton, Paris, 50, 5, 1 (further MD).
[5] 220a24; Aristotle: *Complete Works*, 2. vols., ed. by Jonathan Barnes, Princeton 1971, I 373 (further ACM).
[6] René Descartes: *Oeuvres De Descartes*, 11 vols., edited by Charles Adam and Paul Tannery. Paris 1983, 8A 27 (further AT); Id.: *The Philosophical Writings Of Descartes*, 2 vols., translated by John Cottingham/Robert Stoothoff and Dugald Murdoch, Cambridge 1988, 1 212 (further CSM).
[7] simul et semel. AT 5 148
[8] hoc concipi non potest. Ibid.

"since a substance cannot cease to endure without also ceasing to be, the distinction between a substance and its duration is merely a conceptual one."[9]

And hence he dismisses Henry More's postulation of 'intermundane' duration: "it involves a contradiction to conceive of any duration intervening between the destruction of an earlier world and the creation of a new one."[10] For Descartes, empty time is as contradictory as empty space. Second, Descartes reserve the label 'time' for conventional measure of duration (clock time). In order to measure this duration common to all things,

"we compare their duration with the greatest and most regular motions, which give rise to years and days, and call this duration 'time'."[11]

But we must not conflate duration itself, which is intrinsic to all things, with its temporal measure, which is an intellectual abstraction:

"when time is distinguished from duration taken in the general sense (*duratione generaliter*) and called the measure of movement, it is simply a mode of thought."[12]

So duration is real, successive and intrinsic to substance; time is ideal, abstract and dependent on the human intellect.[13]

The young Spinoza follows Descartes closely in his conception of time. In the 1663 *Cogitata Metaphysica* he defines duration as

"the attribute under which we conceive the existence of created things insofar as they persevere in their actuality."[14]

So conceived, he notes, duration is

---

[9] AT 8A 39; CSM 1 214.
[10] AT 5 343; CSMK 3 373.
[11] AT 8A 27; CSM 1 212.
[12] Ibid.
[13] See Geoffrey Gorham: "Descartes on Time and Duration", in: *Early Science and Medicine* 12 (2007), pp. 28–54.
[14] Baruch de Spinoza: *The Principles of Cartesian Philosophy and Metaphysical Thoughts*, transl. by S. Shirley, Introd. and Notes by S. Barone and L. Rice, Indianapolis 1998, 104 (further S); Id.: *Opera,* vols. I–IV, ed. by C. Gebhardt, Heidelberg 1925, 1, 244 (further G).

"distinct only in reason from the total existence of a thing" since "as much as you take away from the duration of thing so much necessarily you take away from its existence."[15]

So Spinoza likewise agrees with Descartes that duration (and time)

"ceases when created things cease to exist and begins when created things begin to exist."[16] As for time, "in order that duration my be determined, we compare it with other things that have a fixed and determinate motion, and this comparison is called time."[17]

Such clock time, he emphasizes, "is not an affection of things [...] but rather a mode of thinking that we use to explicate duration."[18] The same distinction between concrete duration and abstract time is found in the contemporaneous Letter 12 'On the Infinite':

"when we conceive quantity abstracted from substance, and separate duration from the way it flows from eternal things, we can determine them as we please, there arises time and measure."[19]

Such division is the source of Zeno-like paradoxes of infinity:

"when someone has conceived Duration abstractly, and by confusing it with time begun to divide it into parts, he will never be able to understand how an hour can pass."[20]

Similarly, in the *Ethics*, duration is defined as "an indefinite continuation of existing"[21] while time is the conventional measure, derived from periodic motions, by which the imagination compares the durations of things:

"we imagine time from the fact that we imagine some bodies to move more slowly than others, or more quickly, or with the same speed."[22]

---

[15] S 104ff; G 1, 244.
[16] S 129; G 1, 169.
[17] S 105; G 1, 244.
[18] Ibid.
[19] GP IV, 56, 15–19; C 203.
[20] GP IV 58, 5–7; *The Collected Works of Spinoza*, vol. I, ed. by E. Curley, Princeton 1985, 203.
[21] 2Def5; *The Collected Works of Spinoza*, vol. I, 447.
[22] 2P44schol; *The Collected Works of Spinoza*, vol. I, 480. See further Geoffrey Gorham: "Spinoza on the Ideality of Time", in: *Idealistic Studies* 43 (2014), pp. 27–40.

Finally, Thomas Hobbes famously called space in abstraction from bodies: "the phantasm of a thing existing thing simply insofar as it exists."[23] Leibniz himself invokes Hobbes' doctrine in support of his own.[24] It is less often noticed that Hobbes also admitted a real space: "the extension of a body, which is the same as its magnitude."[25] This "real space", Hobbes insists, "does not depend on our thought, as imaginary space does."[26] Time is likewise conceived as imaginary "the phantasm of before and after in motion."[27] But although he does not specifically articulate a corresponding "real time", his physics seems to require it – presumably it is the intrinsic succession of motion itself (apart from its measure).[28]

3. Leibniz on Space/Time vs. Extension/Duration

From Leibniz's brief comments scattered across a number of late works, a few salient features of the Space/Time vs. Extension/Duration distinction emerge:[29]

3.1 Extension and Duration Fill Space and Time:

In the *New Essays* (1704), Leibniz comments on Locke's claim

> "by this idea of solidity, the extension of body is distinguished from the extension of space."[30]

---

[23] Thomas Hobbes: *Elementorum Philosophiae, Sectio Prima: De Corpore,* ed. by K. Schuhmann, Paris 1999, 2.7.2 and 3.15.1 (further *De Corpore*); Id.: *Opera philosophica quae latine scripsit omnia*, 5 vols., ed. by W. Molesworth, London 1845, i, 83 and i, 176 (further OL); id.: *English Works*, 11 vols., ed. by W. Molesworth, London 1839–1845, i, 94 and i, 204 (further EW).
[24] L 583.
[25] *De Corpore* 2.8.4; OL i, 93; EW i, 105.
[26] Ibid.
[27] *De Corpore* 2.7.3; OL i, 84; EW i, 94.
[28] See further Geoffrey Gorham: "Hobbes on the Reality of Time", in: *Hobbes Studies* 27 (2014), pp. 80–103.
[29] My reconstruction here is similar, in certain respects, to Glenn Hartz and Jan Cover's reconstruction of the phenomenal/ideal distinction, though I focus more directly on time and duration: "Space and Time in the Leibnizian Metaphysics", in: *Nous* 22 (1988), p. 493–519 and p. 504–506.
[30] John Locke: *An Essay Concerning Human Understanding*, ed. by P. H. Nidditch, Oxford 1975, II, iv, 5: 126, (further Essay).

Leibniz insists "there is no need to postulate two extensions, one abstract (for space) and the other concrete (for body)."[31] He compares this to number: to conceive of three apples is not to conceive of the three-ness of the apples as distinct from the number. But neither are the apples nothing but their number, nor a body nothing but its extension as the Cartesians hold. Body is rather the concrete instantiation of abstract space. He further observes that the "concrete one is as it is only by virtue of the abstract one."[32] His point is not that space somehow produces extension but that a body has motion or situation in relation to the abstract orderings of space and time. We can even speak of a body filling a vacuum just as a couple might anticipate a third child though they only have two.

But how do concrete bodies "fill" abstract space and time?[33] For Cartesians, the questions is trivial: corporeal extension fills space because it *is* space. Similarly, duration is a universal attribute, not really or modally distinct from things themselves as noted above. Similarly, a substance fills time simply by persisting: "we should regard the duration of a thing as simply a mode under which we conceive the thing insofar as it continues to exist."[34] But although Richard Arthur is surely right to note the Cartesian source of the Leibnizian distinction between concrete duration and abstract time,[35] the Cartesian theories of extension and duration are ill-suited to Leibniz's late metaphysics of body. This comes out clearly in Leibniz' rejection of the Cartesian theory of extension and duration as *attributes*. Although he explicitly designates extension and duration as "attributes of things",[36] Leibniz rejects the Cartesian conception of attributes, as he explains to De Volder:

> "I do not at all approve of the doctrine of attributes which people are formulating today: as if one simple absolute predicate, which they call and attribute, constituted a substance."[37]

---

[31] Gottfried Wilhelm Leibniz: *New Essays on the Human Understanding*, ed.by P. Remnant and J. Bennett, Cambridge 1996, 127 (further NE).
[32] Ibid.
[33] Ibid; see also Letter 5, 27; L 700.
[34] AT 8A 26; CSM 1 211.
[35] Richard Arthur: "Leibniz's Theory of Time", in: *Leibniz's Natural Philosophy*, ed. by K. Okruhlik and J. R. Brown, Dordrecht 1985, p. 281
[36] AG 261.
[37] June 20, 1703; L 528.

His attack on the Cartesian theory of attributes is part and parcel of his campaign against the Cartesian theory of corporeal substance. But given his strong extension/duration parallelism –

> "duration, time and the enduring thing are in relation to one another in proportional to the relations among extension, place and the placed thing"[38] –

he must also reject the Cartesian account of duration as simple persistence of substance.

Although I cannot go into this complex issue in detail, it is worth considering whether Leibniz's alternative speculations about the nature and origin of extension can be applied easily to duration. In the 1702 anti-Cartesian tract *On Body and Force*, Leibniz explains that extension is a "simultaneous repetition" or, more specifically, the "extension of resistance, diffused through body" while duration is a "successive repetition" of some sort.[39] He does not explain more fully how resistance is diffused nor how succession constitutes duration, since his main concern is to confute the Cartesian doctrine that extension is the whole essence of body. And in the 1712/15 dialogue between Philarete and Ariste he stresses that duration and extension do not "stand alone" but are rather the durations/extensions *of* something, just as "in milk there is an extension or diffusion of whiteness."[40] He tells us that extension is the diffusion of antitype[41] but neglects to explain what sort of diffusion duration is, though he is clear that it is the concrete, temporal analogue of extension: "extension is to space as duration is to time."[42]

This alternative to the Cartesian picture of extension is developed more fully in the long exchange with De Volder. On De Volder's theory of 'mathematical body' – basically Cartesian *res extensa* – Leibniz comments:

> "If you regard this mathematical body as space, it must be correlated with time; if as extension, it must be correlated with duration". But "as the physical body is to space so the status or series of things is to time"; he says both "add to" space and time."[43]

---

[38] June 23, 1699; L 519.
[39] AG 251.
[40] Ibid.
[41] AG 262; L 622.
[42] AG 261; L 621.
[43] June 30, 1704; L 536.

What extension adds is a

> "simultaneous repetition or diffusion of some particular nature or, what amounts to the same thing, a multitude of things of this same nature which exist together with some order between them."[44]

This multitude of things are the simple substances: "extended things involve a plurality of things with position, but things which are simple."[45] The correlated notion of duration arises from

> "the law of the series" which "involves all of the future states of that which we conceive to be the same – that is the very fact I say which constitutes the enduring substance."[46]

While there is much obscurity in this account, it seems to apply equally well (or ill) to extension and duration. The extension of corporeal substance derives from the simultaneous order of simple substances manifesting the force of resistance and its duration derives from the successive states of simple substances following the law of the series.

In the exchange with Des Bosses, Leibniz introduces a new, controversial tool to explain corporeal substance. He conceives of extension in a fairly traditional way: "the extension of a body seems to be nothing but the continuation of matter through parts external to each other (*partes extra partes*), or diffusion."[47] But since it is fair to ask about the simple substances or monads:

> "by what compact can they make an extended being when they are not themselves extended?" He says it "seems further necessary to resort to something unifying which can be called absolute accidental extension."[48]

Without this *viniculum substaniale*

> "all bodies along with all their qualities would be nothing but well-founded phenomena, like the rainbow or an image in a mirror."[49]

---

[44] Ibid.
[45] June 20, 1703; L 531.
[46] L 535.
[47] February 5, 1712; L 600; see also L 601.
[48] L 602.
[49] L 600. Cf., L 603. For detailed discussion see Brandon Look: "Leibniz and the Substance of the Viniculum Substantiale", in: *Journal of the History of Philosophy* 38 (2000), pp. 203–220.

Leibniz says almost nothing about how *viniculum substaniale* accounts for real or concrete duration. This is unsurprising since it is designed specifically to account for the unity of corporeal substance; still, it is hard to see how such a unity characterizes duration and succession. Perhaps a substantial bond is needed to account for the unity of my body at this time; but how does it help to account for the successive duration of my body? We could, of course, call on the appetitions of monads, combined with their mutual perceptions and harmony – and indeed Leibniz assures us that the substantial chain "corresponds accurately in the course of nature to the affections of the monads, that is, to their perceptions and appetite"[50] – but then we will have abandoned a strictly symmetrical treatment of extension and duration.

3.2 Space and Time are ideal; Extension and Duration are real

I am sympathetic with the view that space and time are ideal, above all, in virtue of being *abstract*.[51] On this view, we should expect that extension and duration are real, above all, in virtue of being *concrete*. This is what Leibniz tells Clarke:

> "The parts of time and space considered in themselves, are ideal things and therefore they perfectly resemble one another, like two abstract units. But it is not so with two concrete ones, or two real times, or two spaces filled up, that is, truly actual."[52]

To say that extension and motion are concrete, and hence real, simply means they inhere in actually existing bodies, whereas space and time are merely the possible orders of co-existence and succession among bodies. Thus, Leibniz has Philarete observe on his behalf:

> "extension is to space as duration is to time. Duration and extension are attributes of things (*attributs des choses*), but time and space are taken to be outside of things (*hors des choses*) and serve to measure them."[53]

And because extension and duration are inherent, but space and time are not:

---

[50] L 608.
[51] Arthur: "Leibniz's Theory of Time".
[52] Letter 5, 27; AG 334; L 700.
[53] AG 261.

> "Things keep their extension but they do not keep their space. Everything has its own extension, its own duration, but it has not its own time and does not keep its own space."[54]

The space-time parallelism evinced in this passage is typical of Leibniz.[55] But even within the Clarke correspondence he also declares: "From extension to duration, *non valet consequential*."[56] Leibniz might have more carefully heeded his own warning. Presumably, things keep their extension but give up their space when they move. But things do not 'move' in time by transferring their duration out of temporal place. Although my very same extension can fill distinct spaces, my very same duration occupies only a single time (even if I time travel). Still, there is a sense in which even my concrete duration could have filled a different time. Leibniz concedes this about the duration of the universe as a whole: "absolutely speaking, one can conceive that a universe began earlier than it did."[57] He says

> "one might conceive something added to the beginning, so one might also suppose something taken off towards the end."[58]

I can conceive that I was born a week earlier, and will die a year earlier, and in this sense my counterpart has the same duration but a different time. If we stick to this world, however, the duration and time of something do not come apart in the ways its extension and space routinely do. As Leibniz says,

> "God created things at what time he pleased, for this depends on the things he resolved to create. But things being once resolves, together with their relations, there no longer remains any choice."[59]

It is worth noting one other asymmetry regarding the reality of extension and duration. Against Clarke's assertion of the eternity of time, Leibniz observes

---

[54] Letter 5 46; AG 337; L 703.
[55] "the analogy between time and space will easily make it appear that the one is as merely ideal as the other" (Letter 5, 49; AG 340).
[56] Letter 5, 74: AG 54; L 711.
[57] Letter 5, 56; AG 342; L 707.
[58] Ibid.
[59] Letter 5, 56; AG 342; L 708.

> "whatever exists of time and duration, being successive, perishes continually and how can a thing exist eternally which (to speak exactly) does not exist at all?"[60]

He draws the conclusion that time "can only be an ideal thing" and furthermore "the analogy between time and space will easily make it evident that one is as merely ideal as the other."[61] Richard Arthur rightly points out that the fleeting nature of duration clearly does not extend to extension.[62] A more problematic implication of the argument is that time and duration are equally ideal, undercutting the supposed reality of the latter. However, Leibniz makes it clear that his concern about time is not so much the that it is fleeting but that it is reduces to points or instants: "nothing of time does ever exist but instants, and an instant is not even itself a part of time."[63] He does not allege this about duration or the time 'filled' by an enduring thing: on the contrary he says:

> "if in saying that a thing is eternal is meant only that the thing endures eternally, I have no objection."[64]

So on this point, space and time are asymmetrical, but the crucial symmetry between real extension and duration is maintained.

3.3 Space and Time are Homogeneous and Infinitely Divisible; Extension and Duration are Heterogeneous and Reducible to Parts

Leibniz holds that

> "space is something absolutely uniform and without the things placed in it, one point in space absolutely does not differ in anything from another point in space" and "the case is the same with respect to time."[65]

And we have already noted his observation that

> "the parts of time and space considered in themselves, are ideal things and therefore they perfectly resemble one another, like two abstract units. But it is not so

---

[60] Letter 5, 49; L 705.
[61] Ibid.
[62] Arthur: "Leibniz's Theory of Time", p. 282f.
[63] Letter 5, 49; L 705.
[64] Ibid.
[65] Letter 3, 5f; AG 325; L 682f.

with two concrete ones."⁶⁶ So "I deny that there are any two parts of water perfectly alike, or any two other bodies perfectly indiscernible from one another."⁶⁷

And he tells De Volder that, unlike the parts of space abstractly considered, e.g. geometrical objects, "in nature there cannot be two bodies at the same time perfectly similar and equal."⁶⁸ Later in this careful exchange Leibniz insists that whereas "continuous quantity is something ideal", pertaining strictly to possibles, "in actual things nothing is indefinite" [...] they are "composed as a number is composed of unities."⁶⁹ The continuity of space/time vs. the aggregate structure of extension/duration is also noted in letter to Princess Sophie:

> "although matter consists of a numberless collection of simple substances, and although duration along with motion likewise consists in a mass of momentary instants, it must nevertheless be said that space is not at all composed of points not time of instants."⁷⁰

Although it is plausible that the parts of concrete extension or matter satisfy the principle of the identity of indiscernibles, thus distinguishing concrete extension from ideal space, it is far from clear that the principle extends to the parts of duration. In his concise but path-breaking treatment of time and duration, Descartes does not go so far as to postulate duration independent of substance; like Leibniz, he rejected empty time as much as empty space. However, he insisted in opposition to the long Aristotelian tradition that made time the number of motion that

> "the duration which we find to be involved in movement is certainly no different from the duration involved in things which do not move."⁷¹

Leibniz seems to be with Aristotle in ruling out changeless duration. But, for the sorts of reasons given by Descartes – we do not reckon the duration of something strictly by the changes it undergoes – it is implausible to deny concrete duration to unchanging things. Leibniz insists that, unlike the parts of abstract time and space, the parts of concrete duration and extension do not

---

[66] Letter 5, 27: AG 334.
[67] Letter 5, 25; AG 334; Cf., Letter 5, 21f.
[68] June 20 1703; AG 175.
[69] January 19, 1706; AG 185.
[70] 1705; GP VII, 562.
[71] AT 8A 27; CSM 1 212.

"perfectly resemble one another."[72] Similarly, he tells De Volder that "nothing is permanent in things except the law itself which involves a continuous succession."[73] But the insistence that all duration in bodies involves change seems to be motivated only by a dogmatic attachment to the analogy between extension and duration.

In the exchange with Clarke he insists that the same arguments which rule out an extramundane spatial vacuum also exclude a local or intramundane vacuum: "for they differ only as greater or less."[74] But it is not clear that the corresponding temporal vacua differ only in this way. An extramundane temporal vacuum is an abstract time before the world began (or between worlds), which Leibniz confutes repeatedly in the exchange with Clarke. An intradmundane temporal void is the cessation of change of the world for some finite duration, like the "freezer world" of Sidney Shoemaker's thought experiment.[75] Certain of Leibniz' arguments against extramundane time might be as effective against mere freezes, for example, there would be no sufficient reason or even distinction among freezes of different lengths.[76] But others seem not to apply. Thus, Leibniz says

> "extension must be the affection of something extended. But if that space is empty, it will be an attribute without a subject, an extension without something extended."[77]

But a frozen world, unlike time before creation, does not posit an enduring nothing.[78]

---

[72] Letter 5, 27; AG 334.
[73] January 21, 1704; L 534.
[74] Letter 4, 7: AG 328; see also Letter 5, 33.
[75] Sidney Shoemaker: "Time Without Change", in: *Journal of Philosophy* 66 (1969), pp. 363–381.
[76] Letter 5, 55; AG 341.
[77] Letter 4, 9; AG 328.
[78] So I think Futch rightly emphasizes the importance of such considerations in Leibniz's case for reductionism about space and time. Michael Futch: *Leibniz's Metaphysics of Time and Space*, New York 2008, p. 43f. I do not agree they extend as forcefully to concrete duration. Futch emphasizes Leibniz' remark that "if space is an affection or property of the things which is in space, the space will sometimes be the affection of one body, sometimes of another body [...] but this is a strange property or affection which passes from one subject to another." (L 5, 39) This does not apply to duration or extension since, as we have noted, "Things keep their extension but they do not keep their space. Everything has its own extension, its own duration, but it has not its own time and does not keep its own space." (Letter 5, 46; AG 337).

Nothing that Leibniz maintains that any vacuum violate the principle of sufficient reason, since there would be no reason to prefer one ratio of matter to void than another,[79] Michael Futch has suggested in passing that the same applies to local temporal vacuum: "one would be unable to provide sufficient reason for one particular ration of change to empty time."[80] I'm not sure the case is parallel, especially if we allow the world to endure through a local freeze, since it seems God might have reason to prefer a 'day of rest' for the world vs. a week of rest. In any case, the application of Leibniz' argument to time would seem to entail that there is never any rest or stasis, but only maximal change, in the material world.[81]

There is a final asymmetry between local spatial vs. temporal vacua, which Leibniz himself notices in another context. But this asymmetry favors intramundane spatial voids as compared with freezer-worlds. In the *New Essays* he notes this difference: "If there were a local vacuum within extension we could "determinate its size" by the surrounding bodies.

> "But if there were a vacuum in time, i.e. a duration without a change, it would be impossible to determine its length."[82]

Since it is one-dimensional, a limited changeless duration is less 'accessible' empirically than a local void;[83] but it is more intelligible ontologically since it does not lack a subject.[84]

4. Conclusion

Leibniz' commitment to parallelism in the abstract realm of space and time falters in the concrete realm of extension and duration.

---

[79] Letter 4, 46; AG 332.
[80] Futch: *Leibniz's Metaphysics*, p. 51.
[81] I'm not sure whether this is a principle Leibniz can live with. He does say that "exactly speaking there is not any one body that is perfectly and entirely at rest." (Letter 5, 53; AG 341) But the target here is absolute rest.
[82] Letter 4, 46; AG 332.
[83] Futch makes a similar point about this passage in his compelling case against the possibility of Leibnizian vacuums, in: *Leibniz's Metaphysics*, p. 49.
[84] Clarke pressed Leibniz that mere order or succession does not seem to determine quantity of time (Clarke letter 4, 41; L 695). Leibniz responded that in "if the time is greater there will be more successive and similar states interposed there will be fewer" (L 5 105; L 715). A similar suggestion is made in the *Initia Rerum* around the same time (L 666f.). But as Arthur has observed this account is sketchy and far less detailed than the parallel account of spatial quantity. Richard Arthur: *Leibniz*, Cambridge UK 2014, p. 164.

Calculus Ratiocinator:
Aspects of Leibniz' Contribution to the Origins of Symbolic Logic

Natascha Gruver (Berkeley/Vienna)

1. Introduction

In my paper I'd like to explore Leibniz' contribution to the development of concept logic and symbolic logic, both corner stones of modern logic as they expanded the frame of Aristotelian syllogism. The history of modern logic, i.e. the development of propositional logic and predicate logic pre-dates to the 19th century, when its founding fathers, notably Gottlob Frege and George Boole developed algebraic solutions for syllogistic propositions. As for nowadays assessment of the history of logic it is regarded uncontested that Leibniz' extensive, yet fragmented studies on logic, prepared to a large part the ground for modern logic, in particular for concept and relation logic.

Leibniz, the mathematician-philosopher, occupied himself many years with the problem of how a 'calculation with concepts' by means of a formalization of subject-predicate relations could be conducted. Leibniz' rudimentarily developed concept logic (Begriffslogik) aimed to replace the Aristotelian syllogistic framework with a mathematical that operated with addition, subtraction and multiplication in order to express subject-predicate relations. Leibniz' ambitious idea sketched out in numerous fragments was realized about two hundred years later by George Boole who gained the merits for mathematizing syllogistic logic.

The aim of my paper is to explore the early modern origin of symbolic logic with some examples of Leibniz' fragments on logic. I will outline the larger philosophical-historical context that drove Leibniz' motivation for his efforts to develop a formal calculus. In the last sections I will briefly discuss some differences between Leibniz (early modern) logic and modern, 19th/20th century logic. A wider philosophical approach also needs to take into account Leibniz' views on knowledge and knowledge systems and the entangled relation between logic, epistemology and metaphysics within Leibniz' philosophy. Leibniz dealt with problems of identity and substitution and questions regarding synthetic and analytic methods of inference. Logical questions had been occupying already the young Leibniz, documented in his earliest pieces, the *Disputatio metaphysica de Principio Individui* of 1663[1] and the dissertation *De arte combinatoria* of 1669.[2] Numerous studies in logic, dating up until 1686 and after, followed. However, Leibniz' logical fragments remained largely unnoticed until the turn of the 20th century, when Louis Couturat first published a collection of these fragments.[3] Due to the sparse publication during Leibniz' lifetime (given the volume of his writings), and perhaps also due to the first editions of Leibniz' manuscripts by Erdmann, Dutens and Gerhard,[4] Leibniz became primarily established as a metaphysician within the collective memory of philosophy, while within the collective memory of mathematics Leibniz become renown as the inventor of the infinitesimal and differential calculus and binary arithmetic. But after Couturats editions, followed by two influential receptions by B. Russell[5] and E. Cassirer,[6] new light was shed on Leibniz, the logician. This reception and emphasis on Leibniz' studies in logic flourished especially within the discourses of analytic philosophy. In combination with the explicitly anti-metaphysical program of positivism and logical empiricism the multi-facetted and visionary framework of Leibniz' philosophy slipped out of the picture.

In contrast to this I will argue in my paper for the importance of taking into account the inseparable, entangled relationship between logic and metaphysics that Leibniz establishes throughout his work, from his earliest pieces to his last ones. I pursue the theses that Leibniz' views on logic – and the task thereof – illuminates our understanding of his metaphysics and vice versa: that his metaphysical principals inform and complement his axioms in logic.

2. *Characteristica Universalis and Calculus Ratiocinator*

Leibniz' project of a *characteristica universalis* aimed to formalize propositions, and thus knowledge content, by means of assigning what he called a

---

[1] A VI, 1, N 1.
[2] Ibid., 163.
[3] Louis Couturat: *La Logique de Leibniz*, Paris 1901, and id.: *Opuscules et Fragments Inédits de Leibniz*, Paris 1903, republished Hildesheim 1966.
[4] Gottfried Wilhelm Leibniz: *Opera omnia, nunc primum collecta*, ed. by Ludwig Dutens, T. 1–6, Genevae 1768; C. I. Gerhardt. (ed.): *Leibnizens mathematische Schriften*, Vol. 1–7, Berlin 1849–1863; id.: *Die philosophischen Schriften von Leibniz*, vol. 1–7, Berlin 1875–1890.
[5] Bertrand Russell: *A Critical Exposition of the Philosophy of Leibniz*, Cambridge 1900, tries a reconstruction of Leibniz' metaphysics.
[6] Ernst Cassirer: *Leibniz' System in seinen wissenschaftlichen Grundlagen*, Marburg 1902, is an interpretion from a neo-Kantian perspective.

'universal character' (a number, letter or symbol) to a thing, a concept, or a proposition. Once proper characters were assigned, certain calculations could be performed in order to derive the truth or falsehood of a proposition. Leibniz' vision was to calculate with symbols or 'characteristic numbers' as in mathematical operations such as addition, subtraction, multiplication. This approach, to express concepts (the subject-predicate relation that defines a concept) formally, required the development of a logical calculation: the *calculus ratiocinator*. Numerous fragments, compiled for example in Couturat, give impressive evidence of Leibniz' ongoing effort to develop symbolic calculi. However, both characteristica universalis and calculus ratiocinator do not stand for themselves alone. Both form crucial elements within Leibniz larger project of a *scientia generalis* – a universal science – an analytically constructed, encompassing and overarching system of knowledge; an encyclopedia of science that represented reality in the systematic of rational thought.[7] Together the characteristica universalis as an 'alphabet of human thought' and *calculus ratiocinator* formed the *ars inveniendi*, the art or method to securely derive new knowledge and propositions from the given (as in mathematics).

Already Descartes had spread the concept of a 'mathesis universalis', the idea to apply mathematical analysis in philosophy,[8] but did never attempted to spell out a formal method. Also Leibniz' project was never completed – too profound and complex were the difficulties he encountered. But "by his construction of these calculi, Leibniz proved that it is possible to operate with concepts in a purely formal way."[9]

2.1 Early Modern Encyclopedia and 'Philosophical Language'

As stated before, I propose an understanding of the *characteristica universalis* and the *calculus ratiocinator* as elements of Leibniz' visionary project of a

---

[7] Vgl. Hans Heinz Holz: "Leibniz' Wissenschaftskonzeption zwischen den Enzyklopädien Alsteds und Hegels", in: Id.: *Das Lebenswerk eines Universalgelehrten*, ed. by Jörg Zimmer, Darmstadt 2013, p. 201.
[8] Rene Descartes proposed an analytic method in his piece *Regulae ad directionem ingenii. Rules for the Direction of the Natural Intelligence* (1628). For a contemporary account see Volker Peckhaus: *Logik, Mathesis universalis und allgemeine Wissenschaft. Leibniz und die Wiederentdeckung der formale in Logik im 19. Jahrhundert*, Berlin 1997.
[9] Jürgen Mittelstrass: "The Philosopher's Conception of Mathesis Universalis from Descartes to Leibniz", in: *Annals of Science* 36/6 (1979), p. 593.

scientia generalis – a 'universal science'. This project was inspired by early modern encyclopedia as the first comprehensive collections of knowledge in Western culture. As the first encyclopedia count Alsteds *Encyclopaedia Cursus Philosophici*, the *Ars magna sciendi* of polymath Athanasius Kircher, and the *Idea totius Enyclopaediae mathematico-philosophicae* of Erhard Weigel.[10]

But Leibniz aspired to archive more than a mere collection and aggregation of knowledge. He was looking for a systematic classification for all sorts of knowledge, and he was looking for the intrinsic, ontological relation between things and concepts, notably the species-kind relation, formalized as a thing A being part of B (like a dog being a mammal). Leibniz view was that the species-kind relation is an intrinsic and thus an analytic relation that can be expressed in an analytic subject-predicate proposition.

Following this approach the idea of formalizing "dog is a mammal" into AB expressing a containment relation is a small one. Leibniz was convinced, that all intrinsic relations that constitute the *very definition* of a thing or a concept (as in dog: being a mammal or a human: being a rational mammal) can be formalized and depicted symbolically with the use of letters, numbers and signs. A system of all of these analytic propositions (aka knowledge content), expressing the ontological structure of things in reality, would be the scientia generalis Leibniz envisioned. Thus the scientia generalis exceeded the summative character of the encyclopedia project as it sought to establish a systematic relation between all sorts and areas of knowledge.

The fragments I will discuss briefly in section 3 demonstrate Leibniz' efforts to formalize the S-P relation (e.g. species, kind) with the mathematical operations of addition, subtraction and multiplication. With these operations Leibniz tried to express containment relations, such as A=B or A=nonB or nonA=B etc. to mention only the simplest. Related to the containment problem are the problem of transitivity (if A=B, C=A, then C=B) and of substitution (AB=CB) and identity (AB=BA).

I argued before that Leibniz did not pursue logic for an end in itself, but that his efforts have been fueled by the goal to develop a formalism to express ontological relations, inherent in concepts. The outcome of his efforts was revolutionary as he expanded the syllogistic framework and laid groundwork for concept and relation logic about two hundred years later to come.

---

[10] Johann Heinrich Alsted (1588–1638): *Encyclopaedia Cursus Philosophici* (1630) in seven Volumes, Athanasius Kircher (1602–1680): *Ars magna sciendi sive combinatoria* (1669), and Erhard Weigel (1625–1699): *Idea totius Enyclopaediae mathematico-philosophicae* (1671).

Next to the encyclopedia, so-called 'philosophical language' schemes, circulating during Leibniz' time have been another mayor influence for Leibniz. Ideas of a 'philosophical language' were formulated as early as in 1360, in Ramon Lullus' *Ars Magna* and *Ars brevis*.[11] An influential contemporary source had been the 'philosophical languages'[12] of John Wilkins and George Dalgarno. Wilkins had in fact succeeded to develop an abstract 'character' language that allowed the translation from one language into another. Wilkins 'philosophical language' was primarily aimed to facilitate international communication among merchants, travelers and to replace the elitist Latin as the lingua franca among scholars. Leibniz had studied these systems[13] and together with the encyclopedia and matheis universalis he amalgamated them into his own ambitious *scientia generalis* plan.

3. Fragments on Concept Logic and Symbolic Logic

In this section I will sketch out briefly how Leibniz intended to develop a calculus ratiocinator, a calculation with terms. His numerous fragments on logic throughout the years (from about 1679–1686 and onwards) proof an ongoing effort to invent a mathematical form of logic. From these fragments[14] I found the piece *Elementa Calculi* (Elements of a Calculus) most useful, as in this piece Leibniz provides clear guidelines on how to find and to assign characteristic numbers to concepts that would further allow their calculation. While the characters and symbols ascribed to a concept (or thing) are chosen arbitrarily, the structure and relationship between these characters representing a concept (or thing) is not. The relationship of the numbers or characters

---

[11] Ramon Lull (1232–1315): in his *Ars Magna* (1305) or *Ars Generalis Ultima* (The Ultimate General Art).
[12] John Wilkins (1614–1672), an English philosopher and polymath conducted the project of a philosophical language, in his *An Essay towards a Real Character and a Philosophical Language*, London 1688. George Dalgarno (1626–1687) was a Scottish scholar, dealing with linguistic problems. He was interested in developing a sign language for the deaf and mute. He was a collaborator of Wilkins. Dalgarno published his *Ars Signorum vulgo Character Universalis et Lingua Philosophica* already in 1661.
[13] See Leibniz' notes and excerpts in A VI, 4 B.
[14] Other notable pieces are for example *Fundamenta Calculi Logici* (foundations of a logical calculus), *Specimen Calculi Coincidentium* (specimen of a calculus of the coinciced), or 118 in A VI, 4 B. 595ff: *De formis syllogismorum Mathematice definiendis* (ca. 1682), published Gottfried Wilhelm Leibniz: *Grundlagen des logischen Kalküls*, ed. by Franz Schupp, Hamburg 2000.

has to represent the relationship of the things in reality. This raises the problem of the sign-system and its relation to the domain of real concept and things.

3.1 Elementa Calculi – Finding the Characteristic Number

Some of the key aspects Leibniz is dealing with in his fragments on logical calculi are problems of identity, containment, coincidence and substitution. The task was to define arithmetical conditions for determining if a syllogistic interference is logically valid. The basic idea is the following: a term C that is composed of the concepts A and B is assigned the product of the numbers assigned to its components A and B, thus C's characteristic number would be the product of (AxB). The fragment *Elementa Calculi* is one of a rare in which Leibniz provides comprehensive guidelines on how to assign characteristic numbers to concepts in order to represent their analytic / ontological relation:

> "(1) *Terminus* est subjectum vel praedicatum propositionis categoricae [...].
> (2) *Propositiones* hic intelligo categoricas, [...].
> (3) Cuilibet Termino assignetur suus *numerus characteristicus* [...].
> (4) *Regula inveniendi numerous characteristicos* aptos haec unica est [...]."[15]

(1–2): Leibniz defines a *term* as the subject or predicate of a categorial proposition, and intends to operate with categorial propositions solely, as they form the basis from which others (e.g. the modal, the hypothetical, the disjunctive etc.) can be derived and formed. A categorial proposition would be a simple statement like „A is B" or „A is not B". Considering the quantity: all A, B; some, or at least one A, B, expresses if a proposition is universal or particulate. (3) Alphabetic or numeral terms ('characters') are assigned, suitable for calculation. (4) The only guideline for assigning these characters is: if a term C consists of the components A, B then the characteristic number of C must be the product of the characteristic number of its multipliers A and B, such as C=AxB, in the Leibniz notation: C=AB.

Leibniz gives an example: if the definition of *man* is a *rational animal*, with animal=2, rational r=3, the characteristic number of man would be $m= 2 \times 3 = 6$. Analogous: the number of metal a assigned 3, the heaviest metal b assigned 5, the characteristic number of gold s would be $ab=15$. Note that

---

[15] "Elementa Calculi", in: G. W. Leibniz: *Schriften zur Logik und zur philosophischen Grundlegung von Mathematik und Naturwissenschaft* (= *Philosophische Schriften* 4), ed. by Herbert Herring, Frankfurt am Main 1996, p. 70.

Leibniz uses primary numbers, as their factorization always delivers natural numbers. Where numerals (prime numbers) cannot be assigned, letters are used, for example to list the predicate components of a subject, analogously with the use of symbols (a, b, x, y, etc.) in algebra and geometry.

In point (6) of *Elementa Calculi* Leibniz optimistically states that this procedure, outlined in (1–4), is sufficient to formally capture and express *all* the things in the world. At this point we need to make clear, what kind of concepts or things Leibniz had in mind: only those of which a definition can be given distinctly. This criterion thus concerns only analytic subject-predicate relations (as in human: rational animal). It does not concern contingent, synthetic subject-predicate relations (as in red haired human, blue eyed dog etc.). Subject to formalization are thus only ontologically intrinsic, or analytic components of a thing or concept that constitutes its very definition (as in human: the rational animal).

After having defined 'term', 'proposition', etc., and addressed the problem of assigning characteristic numbers to single/simple concepts in *Elementa Calculi*, Leibniz takes up the problem of finding characteristic numbers to determine the validity of syllogistic interference in the *General Inquiries*,[16] where "Leibniz attempts to make use of divisibility properties to correlate the characteristic numbers with the syllogisms."[17]

3.2 Transformation of Syllogistic Logic

The first step of a transformation of syllogistic logic into a framework of concept and relation logic consists in the reformulation of universal affirmative or universal negative proposition with formalized (symbolic) subject-predicate expressions. Leibniz consistently supposes the analytic *praedicatum inesse subjecto* principle. Working with this principle, syllogistic figures (consisting of two premises and one conclusion) can be expressed with algebraic or set theoretical containment relations, operating with addition, subtraction, and multiplication.

---

[16] Gottfried Wilhelm Leibniz: "Generales Inquisitiones de Analysi Notionum et Veritatum (1686)", in: Leibniz: *Allgemeine Untersuchungen über die Analyse der Begriffe und Wahrheiten*, ed. by Franz Schupp, Hamburg 1982.
[17] Bradley Bassler: "Leibniz on Intension, Extension, and the Representation of Syllogistic Inference", in: *Synthese* 116/2 (1998), pp. 117–139.

Using this method, Leibniz succeeded in transforming universal affirmative and universal negative propositions, but struggled with expressing the particulate affirmative and negative propositions[18]. Those could not be so easily formalized. What was necessary in order to do so was the use of quantifiers (total and existential quantifiers), introduced about two hundred years later by Frege.[19] The use of quantifiers gave way to modern predicate logic, greatly improving proposition and concept logic.

First, a single proposition i.e. its subject-predicate relation is notated: for example A=B, or B=C. The problem of syllogistic interference emerges as soon as two propositions are combined, in order to derive a third: if A=B, and B=C, then A=C. As mentioned above, within the framework of Leibniz' calculi, the symbols A, B, C and so forth can be used only to express universal affirmative (for all x: ϵA) or universal negative (for all x: -ϵA) concepts. Leibniz was unable to find formal solutions for particular propositions as some x: ϵA, or some x:-ϵA, and their related syllogism.

A universal affirmative proposition (UA), as for example: all humans are mortal, Suzie is human, ergo Suzie is mortal, would read in its conceptual notation as:

AB, CA | CB. Regarding notation, Leibniz introduces operators such as the ∞ sign or the non (-) sign to express conjunctions, sums, containment and identity relations. The definition of *identity* or *coincidence* of concepts is expressed with the relation of *containment*: A∞B: if AϵB and BϵA. The concept of identity can be axiomatized by the law of reflexivity in conjunction with the rule of substitution per *salva veritate*. The piece *Specimen Calculi Coincidentium*[20] for example provides a famous definition for the substitution principle: *"Eadem vel Coincidentia sunt quea sibi ubique substitui possunt salva veritate. Diversa quae non possunt"*, and I translate freely: the same or coincident are those, that can be substituted everywhere, while maintaining the truth (A∞B if A=B and A=B). Different are those, where this is not possible. Reflexivity and transitivity relations are expressed as: AϵA; AϵB et BϵC, ergo → AϵC.

---

[18] See for example, "Der Plus-Minus-Calculi", in: Leibniz: *Die Grundlagen des logischen Kalküls*, p. XLVII.
[19] Gottlob Frege introduced existential and total quantifiers in *Begriffsschrift* (1879).
[20] "*Specimen Calculi Coincidentium*", 2. Aug. 1690, in: Leibniz: *Die Grundlagen des logischen Kalküls*, p.116ff.

In the scope of this paper I have presented only the basic elements of Leibniz' concept and combinatory relation logic. I sum up with some primary aspects of the transformation of syllogistic logic into symbolic concept logic:

1. axiomatization of the theory of syllogism; the reduction of the syllogisms to basic laws from which other syllogisms can be derived
2. The use of symbols for denoting concepts and/or propositions; introduction of characteristic numbers, for calculating the syllogism
3. The use of graphical representation, tables and linear diagrams, e.g. Euler-circles to depict syllogistic figures.[21]

3.3 Classification of Identities and Truths

For these basic elements presented above to work, an analytic subject-predicate relation must be assumed. Consistently, Leibniz uses concepts only in their intentional meaning and proposes formalization only for analytic judgments and propositions. Analytic truths are given by definition of the subject (thing, concept), or are derived by deductive reasoning in logic and mathematics (*Vernunftwahrheiten* or rational truths). The truth status of definitions or propositions in logic and mathematics is not derived from experience, as it is in truths of matter (*Tatsachenwahrheiten*). Truths of matter, derived from perception, observation, experience are contingent and synthetic regarding their subject-predicate relation (a red haired human, a blue eyed dog observed), because the predicates red haired/blue eyed, etc. do not constitute and are thus not part of the analytic necessary and ontologically inherent definition of human (or dog, respectively). While for the definition of 'dog' the predicate 'mammal' and the definition of 'human' the predicates 'rational' and 'mammal' constitute ontologically necessary predicates, hence an analytic S-P relation, the negation of an analytic S-P relation would lead into a contradiction. In contrast to this, synthetic predicates such as red, brown, blue haired etc. merely contribute to, or expand the concept of its subject, and their negation is not contradictory.

The problem of analytic/synthetic truths raises the question of how to distinguish analytic and synthetic predicates and propositions? We might find

---

[21] Vgl. Wolfgang Lenzen: "Leibniz Innovations in the Theory of the Syllogism", in: *"Für unser Glück oder das Glück anderer", Vorträge des X. Internationalen Leibniz-Kongresses*, vol. 5, Hildesheim 2016, p. 578ff.

no difficulties in identifying statements like "the circumference of a circle C=2r.π", or "a triangle consists of three sides" as analytic propositions and statements like "this circle is red", "this triangle green" as synthetic propositions.

But how to classify a proposition such as 'Caesar crosses the Rubicon' or 'Judas, the betrayer of Jesus'? At this point Leibniz reveals a remarkable view that leads us straight into his metaphysics (a realm I cannot touch in this paper): while for us humans, the predicate "crosses the Rubicon" obviously seems to be arbitrary, contingent, an event that happened to happen in Caesars life, Leibniz' stance is, that from gods point of view the S-P relation is analytic too. Since god (as the *totality* of *all* possible S-P relations) *per definition* already knew that Caesar would cross the Rubicon, that Judas will betray Jesus and that Adam will sin. This states no less as that the predicates 'crosses the Rubicon' 'betrays Jesus' and 'sins' are analytical, thus ontological constituents of the definition of 'Caesar', 'Judas', and 'Adam' respectively. The view that empirical truths – from the perspective of humans limited knowledge – are in fact analytical truths from the standpoint of gods overarching wisdom has far-reaching consequences as it translates right into Leibniz' metaphysics of determinism and the concept of pre-established harmony.

Leibniz classifies propositions into three categories and axioms regarding their derivation of truth:[22]

1. simple concepts: axiom of identity
2. eternal truths, rational truths: logical and mathematical principles, the concept of god, for humans derivable from simple identities
3. empirical, contingent truths: humans derive it from experience and observation; derivable from identities for god.

This classification correspond three major epistemological principles or axioms:

1. for simple identities: the principle of identity
2. for eternal and rational truths: the axiom of contradiction (e.g. for propositions in mathematics and logic)
3. for contingent truths: the principle of cause, the axiom of sufficient reason (causality and continuity) for propositions in natural science and natural philosophy.

---

[22] Bogumil Jasinowski: *Die Analytische Urteilslehre Leibnizens in ihrem Verhältnis zu seiner Metaphysik*, Wien 1918.

4. Calculus Ratiocinator – Reception and Interpretation

The predominant view of today's analytic philosophy and logic is that the calculus ratiocinator was a precursor and an anticipation of mathematical logic that was later successfully accomplished by G. Boole. This view focuses primarily on Leibniz' efforts to develop a concept logic that operated with symbols, numbers and signs. Consequently, the transformation of propositions into symbolic notation has expanded the structure of syllogistic logic (two premises, one conclusion), as symbolic concept and relation logic is able to operate with numerous propositions.

Notable successors of Leibniz' plan to 'calculate with concepts' have been above-mentioned George Boole[23] *Laws of Thought* and Gottlob Freges *Begriffsschrift* of 1879 that was specifically intended as a formula language, modeled after and in the footsteps of the *calculus ratiocinator*.

I have also expressed my doubt that Leibniz conducted logic as a mere end in itself, and that his only goal had been to overcome the Aristotelian syllogism. While proponents of analytic philosophy, e.g. Hartley Rogers[24] or Norbert Wiener[25] focus exclusively on the logical, mathematical or computational aspect of Leibniz' work, I suggest a reading that takes into consideration his far-reaching vision and the entangled complexity of Leibniz philosophy that interlocks logic, ontology and metaphysics. Surely, Leibniz was a logician, among so many other things, but it would be one-sided to view Leibniz as either a logician/mathematician or a metaphysician. Both *characteristica universalis* and *calculus ratiocinator,* and hence his efforts in logic are inseparable from the *scientia generalis* project – an enterprise that was aimed for the public god and the service of mankind.[26]

---

[23] George Boole (1815–1864) founded algebraic logic in: *An Investigation of the Laws of Thought on Which are Founded the Mathematical Theories of Logic and Probabilities*. Boole's goal was to go beyond Aristotle's logic by 1) providing it with mathematical foundations and equations, 2) extending the set of propositions, and 3) expanding the range of applications, from propositions having only two terms to propositions with arbitrarily many.
[24] Hartley Rogers, Jr.: "Example in Mathematical Logic", in: *The American Mathematical Monthly* 70/9 (1963), pp. 929–945.
[25] Norbert Wiener: "Time, communication, and the nervous system", in: *Teleological mechanisms. Annals of the N.Y. Acad. Sci.* 50/4 (1948), pp. 197–219.
[26] For an account on the scientia generalis project see Natascha Gruver/Cornelius Zehetner: "*Ad felicitatem publicam*: Leibniz' 'Scientia Generalis' – Momente einer Wissenschaftskonzeption und deren gegenwärtige Relevanz", in this Volume.

Ad felicitatem publicam:
Leibniz' „Scientia Generalis" – Momente einer Wissenschaftskonzeption und deren gegenwärtige Relevanz

Natascha Gruver / Cornelius Zehetner (Wien)

1. Einführung

„Unter Generalwissenschaft verstehe ich die Wissenschaft, die die Prinzipien aller anderen enthält, zudem die Art und Weise, die Prinzipien so zu gebrauchen, dass jeder auch nur mittelmäßig Begabte, sobald er zu irgendwelchen besonderen [Dingen] herabsteigt, durch leichtes Nachdenken und ein bisschen Erfahrung sogar das Schwierigste verstehen und die schönsten Wahrheiten wie die nützlichsten Praktiken – so weit es dem Menschen aus den Gegebenheiten möglich ist – herausfinden kann. Sie muss also zum einen die Art des richtigen Denkens behandeln, d. h. des Herausfindens, des Urteilens, des Beherrschens der Affekte, des Behaltens und des Erinnerns, zum anderen aber die Elemente der ganzen Enzyklopädie und die Untersuchung des höchsten Guts, dessentwegen jedes Nachdenken erst in Angriff genommen wird; denn Weisheit ist nichts anderes als die Wissenschaft vom Glück."[1]

Unser Beitrag hat sich zur Aufgabe gestellt, Leibniz' Konzepte zu einer „scientia generalis" (im Folgenden: SG), einer Universalwissenschaft zum Wohle der Menschen und der Menschheit, im Kurzen darzustellen und einige Facetten dieses faszinierend-utopischen, aber unvollendet gebliebenen Projekts zu diskutieren. Wir vertreten die These, dass sich am Projekt der *SG* Leibniz' umfassendes Verständnis von Philosophie und deren Aufgabe im Reigen der Einzelwissenschaften zeigt; auch was Philosophie in der Praxis, d. h. für die Gesellschaft und deren Gemeinwohl zu leisten hat. Es wird sich zeigen: Leibniz spannt in der SG einen maximalen thematischen Bogen, der alle Lebens- und Wissensbereiche umfasst. Methodologisch betrifft dieses Projekt folgende Bereiche und Fragestellungen:

1. wissenschaftsphilosophische Fragen, z. B. wie sich verschiedene Wissenschaftstypen wie Formal-, Natur-, Gesellschafts- und Geisteswissenschaften voneinander abgrenzen und in ein System bringen lassen.
2. wie das Verhältnis von Wissenschaft und Gesellschaft zu gestalten sei und die Aufgabe der Wissenschaften öffentliches Wohl (*felicitas publica*)

---

[1] Gottfried Wilhelm Leibniz: *Definitio Brevis Scientiae Generalis* (1683/85), nach A VI, 4 A, 532, N.127); Übersetzung C. Z.

zu befördern. Damit verbunden ist auch die Frage der Beteiligung der akademischen und öffentlichen Gemeinschaft am SG-Projekt. Leibniz' frühe Vision einer *societas philadelphica* führte schließlich zur Gründung der Akademien der Wissenschaften. Und schließlich
3. wie das Verhältnis und Zusammenspiel von Logik und Metaphysik innerhalb von Leibniz' Philosophie zu denken ist: Fundiert Logik die Metaphysik oder umgekehrt?

Diese weitreichenden Fragestellungen können im Rahmen dieses Beitrags freilich nur angesprochen werden. Daher wollen wir uns im Folgenden drei Aspekte dieses umfang- und facettenreichen Projektes widmen und diese ein wenig beleuchten. Zum Ersten den philosophiehistorischen Kontext: Die ersten frühneuzeitlichen Enzyklopädien als Sammlungen von Wissen werfen Fragen nach deren Ordnung und Systematik auf. Die jüngsten Enzyklopädien, welche zu Leibniz' Zeiten vorlagen, stammen von J. H. Alsted, A. Kircher und J. Comenius. Zweitens formal-logische Aspekte, welche den methodischen Zugang bzw. Plan beschreiben, eine Systematik von Wissensbeständen bewerkstelligen. Leibniz hatte eine durchgehende Formalisierung und Symbolisierung der enzyklopädischen Wissensbestände vor Augen gehabt. Zu diesem Zwecke galt es eine *characteristica universalis* sowie einen *calculus ratiocinator* zu ‚erfinden' bzw. zu entwickeln. Einerseits originäre Pläne, doch greift Leibniz hier auf zu seiner Zeit bereits zirkulierende Konzepte zurück: auf Ramon Lullus' *Ars Magna* und die *lingua philosophica* von George Dalgarno und John Wilkins. Drittens beleuchten wir die Frage nach der Rolle von Metaphysik und ihrem Stellenwert innerhalb der SG. Damit verbunden ist letztendlich auch die Frage nach Leibniz' Auffassung von Philosophie generell – als *prima philosophia*, welche Logik, Metaphysik sowie die Einzelwissenschaften als „zweite Philosophien" umfasst und miteinander in Beziehung stellt. Inwiefern hier ein systematisches Konzept in Leibniz' Philosophie zu erkennen ist, wo Leibniz ja nicht so wie z. B. Hegel als Systemphilosoph gesehen wird, wäre zu diskutieren. Dennoch ist bei all den fragmentarisch, skizzenhaft und lückenhaft gebliebenen Ansätzen zu erkennen, dass bei Leibniz alle Stränge rational zusammengeführt und zusammengedacht werden (ohne jedoch in einer konzisen Systemphilosophie zu münden).

2. Scientia generalis im Kontext: Encyclopaedia, Lingua Philosophica

Wir wollen uns zunächst in aller Kürze einigen historischen Vorläufern, welche Leibniz als Inspirationsquelle dienten, widmen. Damit wird das SG-Projekt in einen umfassenderen Rahmen kontextualisiert. Ersichtlich wird daraus, dass Leibniz in seiner Konzeption mehrere Aspekte aufgegriffen und verbunden hat, und dass seine Originalität nicht so sehr in der SG-Idee als solcher liegt – denn diese kursierte bereits und lag etwa in Form einer ‚Pansophia' vor[2] –, sondern in welcher Weise Leibniz zeitgenössische innovative Ideen zusammenführte und in seiner einzigartigen SG-Konzeption synthetisierte.

Als früher, mittelalterlicher Vorläufer wäre zu aller erst Ramon Lull (Raimundus Lullus, 1232–1316) mit seiner *Ars Magna* oder „Lullischen Kunst" zu nennen, die wohl als erste Fassung der Idee gilt, Logik und deduktives Schließen zur Systematisierung von Wissen einzusetzen. Mittels mechanisch verbundener Tafeln und Scheiben, welche Begriffe und Operationen enthalten, sollte es möglich sein, Aussagen logisch stringent abzuleiten. Die Grundidee bestand darin, die Vielfalt der Aussagen und Begriffe auf Grundbegriffe zurückzuführen. Zu diesen zählten z. B. quaestiones, subjecta, principia absoluta, principia relativa, virtutes, vitia. Als frühneuzeitliche Inspirationsquellen sind zu nennen Athanasius Kircher (1602–1680) mit seiner *Ars magna sciendi*, sehr wichtig auch Johann Heinrich Alsteds (1588–1638) *Encyclopaedia Cursus Philosophici* (1630) in sieben Bänden oder Erhard Weigels (1625–1699) *Idea totius Enyclopaediae mathematico-philosophicae* (1671).

Leibniz wollte sich jedoch mit einer lexikalisch-summativen Enzyklopädie der Wissenschaften nicht zufrieden geben. Für Leibniz stellte sich die Frage nach dem systematischen Zusammenhang von Wissen auch als ontologische. Eine derart *nicht-summative*, sondern *systematische* Enzyklopädie der Wissenschaften gründet, wie Leibniz erkannte, in einer geordneten Verknüpfung der Begriffe. Eine Enzyklopädie der Wissenschaften wäre für Leibniz daher eine Abbildung der Wirklichkeit in der Systematik des Denkens, welche Seiendes und Seins-Verhältnisse in einen Gesamtzusammenhang stellt. Ein System solcher Begriffe würde in einem zusammenhängenden Kontinuum stehen, und nicht bloß ein Aggregat (Sammelsurium) von Begriffen sein.

Dies wirft freilich die Frage auf, nach welchen (Ordnungs-)Prinzipien eine derartige Enzyklopädie aufzubauen sei. Und Leibniz hat sich in der Tat diesem Problem in zahlreichen Fragmenten, in denen er Begriffstafeln entwirft und aufstellt, gewidmet (siehe u.v.a. etwa die umfangreiche *Table de définitions* von 1702–04 und als kleines Beispiel unseren Auszug unten im

---

[2] Siehe z. B. Johann Amos Comenius: *Prodromus pansophiae*, Oxford 1637.

4. Abschnitt).³ Doch der Leitfaden, den Leibniz im Auge gehabt zu haben scheint, ist das Prinzip der „harmonia universalis" – die Universalharmonie aller Dinge. Dieser Leitfaden kann als Ausgangsaxiom für Leibniz' Wissenschaftsverständnis als auch für die Wissenschaften im Dienste des öffentlichen Nutzens betrachtet werden.

Neben den Enzyklopädikern und der Wissenschaftsphilosophie etwa Francis Bacons (1561–1626) mit seiner *Instauratio magna* und dem *Novum Organum* sind als dritter wesentlicher Einfluss die frühneuzeitlichen Projekte zu einer Idealsprache, Formalsprache oder „lingua philosophica" zu nennen. Im 17. Jahrhundert hatten in England die Universalgelehrten George Dalgarno mit *Ars Signorum vulgo Character Universalis Et Lingua Philosophica* (London 1661) sowie John Wilkins mit *Essay towards a Real Character and a Philosophical Language* (London 1668) wichtige Originalarbeiten vorgelegt.

George Dalgarno (1626–1687), Mitarbeiter von Wilkins bis 1659, befasste sich mit linguistischen Problemen und war darum bemüht, eine Zeichensprache für Taubstumme zu entwickeln. Wilkins wiederum war daran interessiert, eine internationale, d. h. in jede Sprache übersetzbare Formelsprache zu entwerfen, welche das Latein als lingua franca ablösen sollte – im aufstrebenden Handel mit zunehmender Internationalisierung sicher ein relevantes und innovatives Bestreben. Entsprechend war Wilkins ‚philosophical language' keine Gelehrtensprache, sondern für Händler, Reisende, Buchhalter, Diplomaten usw. gedacht.

Leibniz hat die Systeme von Dalgarno und Wilkins aufgegriffen⁴ und sich von ihnen Inspiration geholt. In innovativer und originärer Weise kombiniert Leibniz die frühneuzeitlichen Konzepte und Projekte – encyclopaedia, pansophia, gesellschaftliche instauratio magna, lingua philosophica und mathesis universalis zu Elementen seines eigenen, umfangreichen *scientia generalis*-Plans. Als weitere wesentliche Quelle für Leibniz' SG muss der Bereich

---

³ *Table de définitions*; C, 437–509. Auf die erheblichen philologischen Probleme einer Zusammenstellung der Textzeugnisse der SG einzugehen ist hier nicht der Ort. So bietet GP VII eine kleine Zusammenstellung, A bringt die Fülle von Texten en Detail (wohl weit über tausend Seiten), jedoch in chronologischer, nicht systematischer, wenngleich akzentuierter Anordnung (die SG beansprucht in Reihe VI im bislang jüngsten 4. Band eine eigene Rubrik), was eine Synopsis der relevanten Textzeugnisse aus allen Rubriken bzw. auch Bänden der diversen anderen Reihen nicht ersparen kann.
⁴ Vgl. u.a. die Exzerpte in A VI, 4 B, 1005–1012.

der *juristischen Logik* veranschlagt werden, worauf wir im Rahmen dieses Beitrags jedoch nicht näher eingehen können.[5]

3. characteristica universalis – calculus ratiocinator – ars inveniendi

In welcher Weise hatte nun Leibniz die Umsetzung des ambitionierten SG-Projekts als nicht-summative, sondern systematische Erfassung von Wissensbeständen vor Augen gehabt? Als formale Elemente der SG sollen die von Leibniz zu entwickelnde *characteristica universalis* und der *calculus ratiocinator* den logisch-ontologischen Zusammenhang von Begriffen erschließbar und formal darstellbar machen. Jedoch geht es Leibniz nicht nur um eine systematische Erfassung von Begriffen, Dingen, Wissen und der Darstellung ihres strukturellen (analytischen) Zusammenhangs. Leibniz möchte mit seinem Formalismus auch die Deduktion, d. h. die sichere Herleitung von neuen Begriffen, Wissensinhalten und Zusammenhängen aus bereits bestehenden ermöglichen: Leibniz' *ars inviendi* als Kunst des ‚Rechnens mit Begriffen', aber auch um neue Erkenntnisse zu gewinnen, orientiert sich an den präzisen Methoden der Deduktionen in der Mathematik.

Als formales Grundproblem der SG ergibt sich daher die Frage, in welcher Weise diese Formalisierung geleistet werden kann. Insbesondere geht es um Begriffe in ihrer Subjekt-Prädikat Relation, wobei es Leibniz ausschließlich um den analytischen S-P Zusammenhang geht, d. h. welches Prädikat (welche Prädikate) einem Begriff (Subjekt) analytisch, d. h. essentiell, d. h. aber auch: ontologisch zukommen. Diese analytische S-P Relation liefert die allgemeingültige, notwendige Definition des Begriffs: z. B. Def. „Mensch = vernunftbegabtes Lebewesen" bzw. „lebendiges Vernunftbegabtes"; (S, a, b) mit Subjekt (Mensch) und den Prädikaten (vernunftbegabt, Lebewesen, bzw. umgekehrt). Kontingente, d. h. synthetische Prädikate (z. B. rothaarig, blauäugig) fließen in die Definition nicht ein. Leibniz zielt darauf ab, mit einer deduktiven Darstellung und Verknüpfung von Begriffen und Aussagen (d. h. S-P Verhältnissen) ein Ordnungssystem für gegenwärtige und zukünftige Wissensbestände einrichten zu können.

---

[5] So etwa Jakob Thomasius' *Philosophia practica* (1661) mit ihren Tabellen und Definitionen. Vgl. hierzu und allgemein zur erheblichen Bedeutung der Juristik für Leibniz' Philosophie Hubertus Busche: „Einleitung" in: Gottfried Wilhelm Leibniz: *Frühe Schriften zum Naturrecht*, hrsg. v. Hubertus Busche, Hamburg 2003, XI–CXII.

Dem zugrunde liegt Leibniz' Auffassung, dass die analytische S-P Relation eines Begriffs, genauer gesagt der *Definition,* welche diesen Begriff konstituiert, formal, d. h. symbolisch (mittels Zahl oder Zeichen) darstellbar sei. Jedem Begriff käme demnach eine ‚charakteristische Zahl' (zusammengesetzt aus den Zahlwerten seiner Prädikate) zu. Ein System derart formalisierter Begriffe wäre die *characteristica universalis.* Die Relationen der Dinge (Substanzen, Subjekte) in der Wirklichkeit werden auf diese Weise in ein Zahl/Zeichen-System übertragen, aus dem neue Aussagen (S-P Relationen) her leitbar sind. Dies führt Leibniz unweigerlich in die Gefilde der syllogistischen Logik und in begriffslogische Überlegungen und Konzeptionen.

Leibniz hat mit seiner *characteristica universalis* die Arbeiten von Wilkins und Dalgarno, d. h. die ‚philosophical language', eine formal-logische Sprache, die mit Zahlen, Zeichen und Symbolen operiert, aufgegriffen und weiterentwickelt. Die Idee einer *mathesis universalis*[6] konkretisiert Leibniz im *calculus ratiocinator*, ein Kalkül, das die „Rechnung" mit Begriffen und Aussagen ermöglichen sollte. Ein derartiges System würde deutlich den Rahmen der aristotelischen Syllogismen sprengen, bzw. über diesen hinausgehen. Und genau dies hatte Leibniz auch vor Augen und sich zum Ziel gesetzt.[7] Dieses Vorhaben führte ihn zur Entwicklung von ersten begriffslogischen, relationslogischen und kombinatorischen Operationen, denn Leibniz ersetzt die syllogistische Operation mit Begriffen und Aussagen durch logisch-mathematische Operationen mit Zahlen und Buchstaben, d. h. allgemein mit Symbolen. Nach dem Prinzip *praedicata insunt subjecto,* oder *inesse praedicati in subjecto,* hat die analytische Einheit, welche es zu explizieren gilt, die Erkenntnisleistung grundzulegen: Die analytische ‚inesse'-Relation ist somit ontologisch höchst relevant, da in ihr die ontologische Struktur der Wirklichkeit und die Verhältnisse der Außenwelt ausgesagt werden sollen. Ob allerdings, wenn

---

[6] Vgl. zum mathesis-Begriff z.B. Erhard Weigels oben genannte *Idea Totius Encyclopaediae [...],* Jena 1671 oder *Philosophia mathematica, theologia naturalis solida, per singulas scientias continuata universæ Artis Inveniendi prima stamina complectens,* Jena 1693. Bereits bei René Descartes angedacht, allerdings nicht systematisch ausgearbeitet ist der Gedanke einer mathesis universalis, einer Universalmathematik, welche die deduktive Methode der Logik zur Erkenntnisgewinnung propagiert.

[7] Siehe hierzu seine zahlreichen Fragmente zur Logik, welche ein eindrucksvolles Zeugnis seiner Bemühungen geben. Es ist allerdings wichtig nicht aus den Augen zu verlieren, dass Leibniz die Studien zur Logik nicht nur zum Selbstzweck betrieben hat, sondern dass seine Bestrebungen, ein begriffs- und relationenlogisches Kalkül zu entwickeln, vor dem Hintergrund des SG-Projekts zu sehen und zu bewerten sind. Vgl. Luis Couturat: *La Logique de Leibniz,* Paris1901, und die von ihm hrsg. *Opuscules et Fragments Inédits de Leibniz,* Paris 1903.

das Subjekt dieser Sätze ontologisch keine *Monade*, sondern das synthetisch-relationale „substantielle Band [...] der im Subjekt enthaltenen Prädikate" und somit eine *zusammengesetzte Substanz* ist, die analytische Einheit nicht gesprengt wird, hat Leibniz bis zuletzt als ungelöstes Problem hinterlassen[8] (hierzu auch im folgenden Abschnitt 4).

Das Problem der Repräsentation von Begriffen und Verhältnissen (letztendlich von Wirklichkeit) wird virulent und durchzieht die Fragmente von Anfang bis zum Ende. Die Zuweisung der Zeichen oder Charaktere ist willkürlich, aber ihr Zusammenhang ist es nicht; vielmehr muss der analytische Zusammenhang der Zahlen und Zeichen (als *characteristica universalis*) die ontologische Struktur der Begriffe in der Wirklichkeit aussagen, sodass eine „Abbildung" der Wirklichkeit eine systematische Struktur des Denkens erfordert.

4. Scientia Generalis und Erste Philosophie

Welche Stelle nimmt die SG im System der Philosophie von Leibniz ein? Und umgekehrt: Inwiefern ist Philosophie ein Teil der SG?

Unter dem Leibniz'schen System der Philosophie bzw. seiner Ersten Philosophie lassen sich formal – sehr vorsichtig und allgemein formuliert – bestimmte theoretische (metaphysische und logische) Grundsätze in Verbindung mit praktischer Zielsetzung verstehen. Abgesehen von dem in permanenter Entwicklung befindlichen Instrumentarium an Grundbegriffen (Definitionen) wie Seiendes, Substanz, Abstrakta/Konkreta, Perzeption, Appetition, formal: *notiones*, *conceptus*, sind dies der Satz des Widerspruchs bzw. der Identität, das Prinzip der Identität des Nichtunterscheidbaren/-unterschiedenen (*p. identitatis indiscernibilium*) und das Prinzip des zureichenden Grundes (*p. rationis sufficientis*). Leibniz selbst thematisiert kaum einen akkuraten Allgemeinbegriff vom philosophischen „System" als solchem – vergleicht man es etwa mit Kant oder Hegel –, sondern spricht in der Regel speziell von „seinem" neuen System der prästabilierten universalen Harmonie, also einem besonderen Aspekt metaphysischer Welt-Konzeption. Dennoch ist das praktische Ziel der Glückseligkeit mit naturaler und spiritueller Komponente, gesellschaftlich wie individuell, impliziter Teil des Leibniz'schen Systems. Den

---

[8] Siehe Cornelius Zehetner: „Vinculum substantiale: der Briefwechsel zwischen Leibniz und Des Bosses. Einleitung", in: Gottfried Wilhelm Leibniz: *Der Briefwechsel mit Bartholomäus Des Bosses*, hrsg. v. Cornelius Zehetner, Hamburg 2007, S. XLIVff.

philosophischen Rahmen bildet buchstäblich die Weisheit, also *sophia*, als „Wissenschaft vom Glück."[9]

Was die vielfältigen Wissenschaften betrifft, so verlangt Leibniz zunächst, um empirische Fakten (verités de fait) zu erkennen/gewinnen und sie aus ihrer blinden Kontingenz herauszuholen, über die bloße Tatsachenfeststellung hinaus auch Hypothesenbildung mit einer Wahrscheinlichkeitslogik.[10] So erhält die apriorische Analytizität des Wissens (praedicata insunt subjecto) eine Dynamik, deren Grund nach Leibniz in der ontologischen Dynamik der Substanzen als perzipierender und strebender Wesen liegt, die auch die Vorläufigkeit, zugleich Optimierbarkeit, allen Wissens fundiert. Was übrigens bei Kant eine Leerstelle in der Schematik der Urteile bildet (analytisch-apriori, synthetisch-aposteriori und synthetisch-apriori), erscheint hier als analytisch-aposteriori,[11] im Sinn einer je „vollkommeneren" Bestimmung eines Sachverhalts. Nur in dieser eigentümlichen Dynamik können auch die *ars combinatoria* und die Erfindungskunst der *ars inveniendi* konkrete Resultate erzielen.

Einerseits also liefert die SG einen begrifflich-strukturellen Ordnungsrahmen und umfassenden Raster von Definitionen, andererseits liefert sie ein dynamisches Verfahren, um überhaupt Erfahrung und empirische Erkenntnis zustande kommen zu lassen. Oder anders gesagt: Wissenschaft könne auch funktionieren, wenn die Erkenntnis bzw. der jeweilige Erkenntnisstand vom Ideal des vollkommenen Begriffs noch um einiges entfernt ist.

Was nun die Wissenschaftsfundierung qua Erkenntnistheorie anbelangt, so entwickelt Leibniz eine Verzahnung von Logik und Substanzontologie etwa in den *Nouveaux Essais* im 3. Buch, Kap. 6 („Von den Namen der Substanzen"), indem er die Beziehung von Wort und Ding durchdiskutiert. Er erkennt hinsichtlich des Problems gewissermaßen der ‚natural kinds' so etwas

---

[9] Diese definitorische Formel verwendet Leibniz etwa in *Nouveaux Essais* III, Kap. 10, § 3 Gottfried Wilhelm Leibniz: *Philosophische Schriften* 3, Bd. 3.2, hrsg. u. übers. von Wolf v. Engelhardt/Hans Heinz Holz, Frankfurt a. M. 1996, S. 182; *Table de définitions [1702-04]*, C, 496; *Discussion avec Gabriel Wagner [1698]*, Grua, 397; *Paraenesis de scientia generali [1688]*, A VI, 4 A, 975; *De vera hominis perfectione [1684/85]*, A VI, 4 A, 583, u.v.a.
[10] Vgl. u.a. *Nouveaux Essais* IV; zur Relevanz des Wahrscheinlichkeitsprinzips für die Geschichtswissenschaften vgl. „Geschichtsforschung als Wahrscheinlichkeitslogik. Aus den *Nouveaux Essays sur l'entendement humain* (1703/1704)", in: Gottfried Wilhelm Leibniz: *Schriften und Briefe zur Geschichte*, hrsg. v. Malte-Ludolf Babin/Gerd van den Heuvel, Hannover 2004, S. 101.
[11] Zur „Analyse a posteriori" der Begriffe vgl. *De Definitionibus characterisandis et propositionibus demonstrandis* von 1688, A VI, 4, 924.

wie wesentliche (vs. unwesentliche) Spezies von Individuen (§ 1, S. 83f.) an, jedoch:

> „Man wird niemals die letzten logischen Spezies finden [...], und niemals sind sich zwei wirkliche oder vollständige Individuen derselben Spezies vollkommen gleich."[12]

Somit führt das Prinzip der Identität des Nichtunterscheidbaren zu einem ontologischen Überschuss über die logische Klassifizierung, ohne diesen Überschuss als irrationalen Rest à la Nominalismus dahingestellt sein zu lassen. Vielmehr pointiert Leibniz die Möglichkeit von *Realdefinitionen*, also Definitionen, durch die die Verursachung eines Dings oder Sachverhalts als möglich demonstriert wird. Von anderer Seite schlägt wiederum das Prinzip der Kompossibilität auf die (zugrunde gelegte, vorauszusetzende) ontologische Struktur ansonsten bloß logischer (nominaler) Definitionen durch, dass also alle jemals und künftig realisierten Dinge, die nach unendlich-möglichen Spezies und substantiellen Formen strukturiert sind, in einer gemeinsamen, vergangen-gegenwärtig-zukünftigen Welt in „Harmonie" existieren können und auch existieren.[13] Es hänge, so Leibniz,

> „oft von uns ab, Kombinationen von Eigenschaften herzustellen, um auch die substantiellen Wesen vor aller Erfahrung zu definieren, sobald man diese Eigenschaften hinreichend versteht, um über die Möglichkeit ihrer Kombination zu urteilen"[14]

– wie etwa bei der Züchtung und Benennung neuer Obstsorten. Allerdings geht Leibniz in den *Nouveaux Essais* bei dem Problem, wie Dinge als „Substanzen" zu gruppieren und voneinander zu unterscheiden seien, nicht auf den andernorts eingeführten Unterschied zwischen Substanzen und Substantiaten ein, der darauf abzielt, die Welt gleichsam in ontologischen Schattierungen und Zwischenstufen (Halb-Seiende, Halb-Substanzen, Halb-Akzidentien) zu artikulieren.[15] Somit sind Technik, Konstruktion, generell Pragmatik bei Leibniz ein Indiz für den ontologischen Gehalt der Welt; der ontologische Gehalt drückt sich in Handlungen aus – „Die Substanz ist das der Tätigkeit fähige

---

[12] *Nouveaux Essais* III, Kap. 6, § 1, S. 85 (Übersetzung geringfügig modifiziert, C. Z.)
[13] Vgl. u.a. die *24 Sätze* (o.T.) in GP VII, 289 f., sowie *Nouveaux Essais* III, Kap. 6, § 13, S. 89f.
[14] *Nouveaux Essais* III, Kap. 6, § 28, S. 129f.
[15] Vgl. besonders Leibniz: *Briefwechsel mit Bartholomäus Des Bosses*, hier S. 336f. (Beilage zum 19.5.1715).

Wesen (Être capable d'Action),"[16] konstituiert durch Perzeption und Appetition. Dies evoziert die durchgängige Machbarkeit als Kennzeichen des Seienden, zumal Existenzsetzung letztlich eine Aktion des Willens, nicht des Verstandes sei.

Andererseits leitet Leibniz aus der „Unvollkommenheit" der Sprache[17] – dass also die Wörter und Termini den vollkommenen ontologischen Gehalt der Dinge als Substanzen verfehlen – das Postulat einer *characteristica universalis* ab (siehe oben Abschnitt 3): Welche ontologischen Probleme hilft diese nun zu lösen bzw. zu vermeiden? Nützlichkeit für die Kombinatorik (das synthetische Moment) kontrastiert hier mit der *Aporie* der Analytik: *Wie* die *characteristica* in ihrem abstrakten logischen Formalismus die *realen*, nicht bloß nominellen ontologischen Elemente der Welt freizulegen, und bloßer Zeichengebrauch die ontologische Dynamik von Ursache/Existenz zu erreichen vermag. Man müsse sich, um Fehler im wissenschaftlichen Verfahren zu vermeiden, möglichst von Abstraktionen fernhalten.[18]

So befinden sich die Definitionsketten und Ansätze zu Enzyklopädien bei Leibniz im logisch-ontologischen Schwebezustand: Begnügt er sich in frühen Überlegungen noch mit einer „Parallele" zwischen Dingen und Wörtern – „Vocabula rebus parallela sunt (sic satis). Parallelorum eadem cognitio,"[19] – so erfährt danach das Problem der Affinität von Denken und Sein zusehends eine Artikulation in zwei Strängen: Einerseits der bekannten Monadologie, die Leibniz ihrerseits aber einer Revision, nämlich der Theorie des *vinculum substantiale* als nicht-monadischer Substanz, unterzieht; andererseits der *SG*, insofern diese durch Analyse die Elemente der Welt sichtbar machen, die letzten Dinge/Sachverhalte – Begriffe – Prinzipien gleichsam als Atome zutage fördern soll. Allerdings ist „Welt" bei Leibniz bestimmt als Komplexion aller Dinge, aller „Serien" (Zustandsreihen) und Relationen – insofern einerseits kein Ganzes, sondern unendliches Ensemble unendlicher Reihen, andererseits als die *eine* Welt zu identifizieren. In Bezug auf die *Repräsentation*, die in ihrer ontologisch-systematischen Funktion die Grenzen des Wissbaren und der Wissenschaft aufzeigt – denn jede Monade (Einzelsubstanz), so Leibniz, repräsentiere zwar kraft prästabilierter Harmonie die ganze Welt in ihrer unendlichen Differenziertheit, doch eben deshalb könne sie von endlichen Wesen

---

[16] *Principes de la Nature et de la Grace [...]*, § 1.
[17] Vgl. *Nouveaux Essais* III, Kap. 8.
[18] Vgl. *De Definitionibus characterisandis et propositionibus demonstrandis*, A VI, 4 A, 924.
[19] *Aus und zu der Appendix Practica von J. J. Becher (1669?)*; A VI, 2, 390.

(ergo auch Wissenschaftlerinnen und Wissenschaftlern) nicht vollkommen erkannt werden, ebenso wenig wie die ganze unendliche Welt[20] – stellt sich aber eine doppelte Frage: Erstens nach der *Vollständigkeit* der wissenschaftlichen Repräsentation, zweitens nach der *Kommunizierbarkeit* der vollständigen Repräsentation; ist doch gemäß Leibniz' Metaphysik jede Monade (deren charakteristische Perzeptionsreihen und Perspektiven-Abfolgen) nicht-kommunizierbar, insofern sie kein Außen besitze, sondern alles eben schon in sich habe, sodass die *SG* so etwas wie die von der Nichtkommunizierbarkeit befreite Repräsentation der Welt darstellte; wie ist aber eine Repräsentation der Welt ohne Ontologie möglich? So war Leibniz wohl auch von daher veranlasst, die Monadenontologie (Nichtkommunizierbarkeit der Monaden) in Richtung einer außermonadischen, relationalen, kommunikativen Substanzmetaphysik zu modifizieren.[21] Insgesamt steuert Leibniz daher mit der Verbindung von Logik, Natur- und Gesellschaftsontologie die Möglichkeit an, einen gemeinsamen Vernunftraum für Natur-, Gesellschafts- und Geisteswissenschaften in praktischer Relevanz, eben die SG, einzurichten.

Was sind nun die metaphysisch-ontologischen Konstituenten der praktischen Zielsetzung der SG, nämlich der Glückseligkeit? Am Beispiel eines Ausschnitts aus einer Leibniz'schen Definitionskette soll das enzyklopädisch-definitorische Verfahren der Generalwissenschaft aufgezeigt werden – hier abgekürzt und paraphrasiert:

> „Glückseligkeit (felicitas) ist dauerhafte Freude
> Freude ist die Vorstellung von Lüsten (opinio voluptatum)
> Lust ist die Empfindung (sensus) von Vollkommenheit
> Vollkommenheit ist Zuwachs an Vermögen (potentiae incrementum
> Vermögen ist die Quantität der Wirkung,"[22]

womit eine lückenlose Transformation ethisch-psychologischer Konzepte in logische bzw. – aristotelisch betrachtet – metaphysische Kategorien erfolgt (Quantitätskategorie und Kausalität als ontologische Bestimmungsstücke gemäß der traditionellen Schulphilosophie) und ein durchgängiger Konnex diverser wissenschaftlich erfassbarer Phänomene vorgestellt ist.

Letztlich aber stellt Leibniz gerade in seinen Panoramen der SG wohl nicht den Anspruch, mit der auf Definitionen beruhenden Enzyklopädik die

---

[20] Vgl. u.a. Leibniz im *Briefwechsel mit Bartholomäus Des Bosses*, S. 187 (4.8.1710).
[21] Vgl. den *Briefwechsel mit Des Bosses*.
[22] *Aphorismi de felicitate, sapientia, caritate, justitia [1678/79]*; A VI, 4 C, hier 2793f.

unendliche Welt ‚abzubilden', sondern vielmehr eine pragmatische Annäherung an den ontologisch postulierten „vollkommenen Begriff" der substantiellen Weltelemente zu ermöglichen: vorläufige, aber zunehmend differenzierte und verlässliche Erkenntnisse über die Generationenabfolgen hinweg zu gewinnen und hierfür ein denk-ökonomisches und methodisches wie technisches Instrumentarium, einschließlich der *characteristica universalis*, zur Verfügung zu stellen. So prägt eine bestimmte Spannung zwischen Abbreviatur (Abstrakta, Symbolismus, Charakteristik-Notation) und vollem Begriff, der letztlich nicht nur das Einzelding, sondern die Welt erfasse, weil das Einzelding (Substanz) die ganze Welt repräsentiere, der SG den immanenten Charakter der Vorläufigkeit auf.

Entsprechend umfassend setzt Leibniz die SG programmatisch in einen geschichtlich-gesellschaftlichen Großzusammenhang. Zahlreich sind die Notizen, literarischen Entwürfe, Tabellen, Listen, Werbeschriften, belletristischen Einkleidungen (Wilhelm Pacidius, Insula Utopica) schon seit den späten 1660er Jahren, zahlreich auch die visionären Prognosen und Panoramen der Wissenschaftsentwicklung, neben seinen Akademieplänen und -Gründungen – sie bilden einen Großteil seines nachgelassenen Schrifttums überhaupt.

5. Zusammenfassung – Schluss

Hinsichtlich der Aktualität der Leibniz'schen SG sei auf das Schlusskapitel der *Nouveaux Essais* (IV, 21) verwiesen: Leibniz hebt einerseits die traditionellen Grenzen und Einteilungen der Wissenschaften auf (Logik, Ethik, Physik) und ersetzt sie durch eine Alternative, nach der die jeweils vorliegenden (ausgeforschten, feststehenden oder vorläufigen) Wahrheiten (Tatsachen- und Vernunftwahrheiten) vielfältig verbunden werden können: Es gibt dabei sachlich keine fixe Hierarchie oder sonstige starre systematische Anordnung der Wissensbestände, sondern durchgängige, wechselnde Funktionszusammenhänge: Der Gesundheitszustand einer bestimmten Persönlichkeit hat beispielsweise historische, medizinische, politische Relevanz, und wechselseitige Subsumtionen sind möglich. Andererseits schlägt Leibniz zur besseren Handhabung des Wissensbetriebes eine alternative Einteilung der gesamten Erkenntnisbereiche nach vier verschiedenen Methoden vor, die einander ergänzen: 1. die synthetisch-theoretische, als Natur erfassende, beherrschende und formende, 2. die analytisch-praktische, letztlich an der Glückseligkeit orientierte, 3. die registrierend-logische (auf ein „Repertorium", gleichsam ein unendliches Schlagwortverzeichnis mit Definitionen und Verweisen hinarbeitende), und schließlich 4. die soziopolitische („bürgerliche") Einteilung, etwa nach Institutionen oder Berufen. Trotz aller angesprochenen Schwierigkeiten, die Affinität von logischen und ontologischen Strukturen einsichtig zu begründen, ist der Gewinn der Leibniz'schen Konzeption demnach ein extensiver Wissenschaftsbegriff, von formallogischen und ontologischen Prinzipien bis zu Fachkenntnissen in manuellen Tätigkeiten, der eine bestimmte Art von *Einheitswissenschaft* vorzeichnet, diese aber zugleich allen Arten von Reduktionismus – den „einäugigen Zyklopen der Wissenschaft", wie Kant sagte, ebenso wie dezisionistischen PopulistInnen und OpportunistInnen – entgegen setzt.

Die Frage einer *scientia generalis* als System des Wissens wie auch als „Wissenschaft von der Glückseligkeit" stellt sich in der gegenwärtigen Wissens- und Informationsgesellschaft erneut, vielleicht sogar mehr denn je. Die Fragmentierung und Hochspezialisierung (siehe ZyklopInnen) scheint in einer geordneten Verknüpfung der Begriffe und Sachverhalte, als Abbildung der Wirklichkeit, in der Systematik des Denkens zu gründen, und lässt doch eine zersplitterte, fragmentierte ‚vereinzelte' Wirklichkeitswüste hinter sich. Keine Rede von *harmonia universalis* – ist dieser Gedanke für heutige Generationen überhaupt noch nachvollziehbar, intelligibel? Sind Wissens- und Informationsgesellschaft in ganzheitlicher Systematik heute undenkbar, unmöglich – oder erst recht möglich angesichts der digitalen Technik? Umso wichtiger mag es sein, den Gedanken der *harmonia universalis* wenigstens wieder in Erinnerung zu rufen und gegenüber der bloßen „Vernetzung" einzumahnen.

Konkret ist für die Disziplin der Philosophie die Frage nach dem Verhältnis von Logik und Metaphysik erneut zu stellen, nach deren großen Entzweiung im 20. Jahrhundert. Angesichts dieser folgenreichen Trennung wäre es Aufgabe einer Philosophie des 21. Jahrhunderts, Logik und Metaphysik wieder zusammen zu denken, und dies im Rahmen einer Vereinbarung von Logik, *scientia generalis* und Erster Philosophie in humaner, anthropologischer Zielsetzung.

Wie die Leibniz'sche Konzeption von Wissenschaft, die von einer institutionellen, staatlichen Umsetzung „von oben" und einem entsprechenden Ausbau riesiger Apparate, Netze und Maschinerien ausgeht, aus dem mittlerweile überbordenden Zauberlehrlingssyndrom unserer Lebenswelten doch wieder herausgedreht und einer souveränen gesellschaftlichen Handhabung unterstellt werden kann – dies kritisch zu bedenken stünde allerdings auf einem weiteren Blatt heutiger philosophischer Agenda.

Leibniz's View on Time in the Light of His General Views on the Nature of Mathematics. Reading Emily Grosholz's "Leibniz's Mathematical and Philosophical Analysis of Time"[1]

Julia Jankowska (Warsaw)

1. The Question of the Direction of Time in Leibniz's Metaphysics

Although this view can be ascribed already to Aristotle,[2] in the history of the philosophy of time it is Leibniz who is remembered mainly as a representative of relationism. For Aristotle, what really existed were change and movement. He identified time neither with change, nor with movement, but according to him time depended on both. For him, time was an objective measure of change, a way of measuring certain changes by a comparison with other changes – for example with cyclical processes occurring in nature.[3] Time is for Aristotle "[…] not movement, but only movement in so far as it admits enumeration"[4] and, just as time depends on movement, movement also depends on time: "[…] we measure the movement by the time and vice versa."[5]

Newton did not accept the consequences of the relationist notion of movement. He assumed that absolute time and space exist independently of any movement, and defined absolute movement relying on them. Leibniz, in his letters to Clarke, rejected Newton's position and defended the claim that time and space do not exist as separate beings. He considered that the only sensible way of speaking about time is to view it just as a way of how things are ordered. He wrote in his third letter to Clarke:

> "[…] I have said more than once that I hold space to be something merely relative, as time is; that I hold it to be an order of co-existences as time is an order of successions."[6]

---

[1] This is an extended version of the paper "Leibniz i kierunek czasu" which is to appear in Polish in the journal *Przegląd Filozoficzny. Nowa Seria* 4 (2016).
[2] Adrian Bardon: *A Brief History of the Philosophy of Time*, New York 2013, pp. 12–14.
[3] Ibid., p. 14.
[4] Aristotle: *The Complete Works of Aristotle. The Revised Oxford Translation. One Volume Digital Version*, transl. by J. Barnes, Princeton, NJ 1984, p. 821.
[5] Ibid., p. 825.
[6] "The Controversy between Leibniz and Clarke", in: *Philosophical Papers and Letters*, transl. by L. E. Loemker, Chicago 1956, pp. 1095–1169, here p. 1108.

In the present article, I focus on the question whether, and if so, in what sense, time in Leibniz's philosophy can be considered to have a direction. Emily R. Grosholz, in her article "Leibniz's Mathematical and Philosophical Analysis of Time,"[7] defends the claim that time in Leibniz does have a direction, and, moreover, that for Leibniz the world is "strongly asymmetric."[8] This article is a brief polemic with the thesis defended by Grosholz. In its first section, I will examine the roles of, and relationships between, mathematics, metaphysical principles, and collecting empirical data, as Grosholz sees them in her account of what was the proper scientific method according to Leibniz. In the second section, I will present her thesis about the strong uni-directionality of time in Leibniz and explain how she derives it, in accordance with what she considers the proper scientific method (as discussed in the first section), from the metaphysical principles. In this part I will also propose an alternative account of the problem of reality of time and of the problem of it having or not having a direction in Leibniz. Finally, in the last section I will conclude with a general evaluation of Grosholz's argumentation, proposing an alternative approach to the topic, one inspired by an account of truth and ideas in Leibniz presented by Massimo Mugnai in his article "Leibniz and Gödel."[9]

2. Leibniz's View on the Nature of Mathematics and on Its Role in Cognition

Grosholz, relying on the *Tentamen Anagogicum*, examines time in Leibniz in the context of broader considerations concerning what, in his view, constitutes the proper method "[…] in the human search for wisdom […]."[10] In the *Tentamen*, Leibniz firmly opposed materialism, writing that although geometric notions which concern sizes and shapes and their transformations are sufficient to describe movement, the very content of the laws of movement – i.e., why they state what they state – cannot be explained by appealing only to pure mathematics.[11] According to him, such an explanation is, however, possible if one refers to metaphysical principles. Grosholz is of the view that the example

---

[7] Emily R. Grosholz: "Leibniz's Mathematical and Philosophical Analysis of Time", in: Norma B. Goethe/Philipp Beeley/David Rabouin (eds.): *G.W. Leibniz, Interrelations between Mathematics and Philosophy*, Dordrecht 2015, pp. 75–88.
[8] Ibid., pp. 85f.
[9] Massimo Mugnai: "Leibniz and Gödel", in: Gabriella Crocco/Eva-Maria Engelen (eds.): *Kurt Gödel. Philosopher-Scientist*, Aix-en-Provence 2016, pp. 401–416.
[10] Grosholz: "Leibniz's Mathematical", p. 75.
[11] "Tentamen Anagogicum", in: *Philosophical Papers*, pp. 777–788, here p. 779.

of the Leibnizian account of time allows one to understand particularly well the relationships which, according to Leibniz, should exist between mathematical reasoning, metaphysics, and collecting empirical data, because time provides a concrete object of scientific investigation while at the same time being the most abstract of any such objects – because of its independence from any specific content. As Grosholz puts it:

> "Of all the parameters involved in mechanics, time is the least tied to any specific content, even though it presents a determinate topic for scientific investigation."[12]

By writing that time is a "determinate topic for scientific investigation", she suggests that time is a kind of object that we can identify relatively well. By writing that time is "the least tied to any specific content", she seems to suggest in turn that time itself is not a concrete being (and this fits Leibniz's conviction that only monads are real concrete beings) but something that needs external content, and therefore an abstract notion or maybe even a theoretical, rather than real, being. The conviction that time is easier to identify than other abstract notions may reflect the conviction that time has an exceptionally strong metaphysical grounding, but it may also be the case that it simply means that time can be easily grasped in mathematical models.

Referring to a text originating from the same year as the *Discourse on Metaphysics*, namely the *Projet et Essais pour arriver à quelque certitude pour finir une bonne partie des disputes et pour avancer l'art d'inventer*,[13] Grosholz points out next that the special role of mathematics in our cognition of the world results from the fact that mathematical objects are highly determined. It is thanks to this determinacy that, when we represent the world in the language of mathematics, we can perform calculations and draw formal inferences in cases in which this was previously impossible. We can thus observe that mathematics is similar to time, because mathematical notions are, like the notion of time, determined to a greater extent than other abstract notions. This, as was the case with respect to time, may or may not be the result of their having an exceptionally strong metaphysical grounding.

It is worth adding here that Leibniz suggests in the text of the *Projet* that performing calculations and drawing formal inferences is facilitated when we are representing the world in the language of mathematics not only due to

---

[12] Grosholz: "Leibniz's Mathematical", p. 76.
[13] "Projet et Essais pour arriver à quelque certitude pour finir une bonne partie des disputes et pour avancer l'art d'inventer", in: C, pp. 175–182.

the fact that in such a case instead of vague notions we are dealing with notions which are sharp, and which correspond to the objects of precise definitions, but also due to the very narrowing of the scope of the problem considered when we confine ourselves to a mathematical model. This gives us practical benefits, because the more topics one thinks about, the easier it is to make a mistake, and the other way round: the smaller the amount of material processed, the smaller the risk of an error.[14] Also, thinking with symbols makes it easy to see where a possible mistake could have been made.[15] In other texts, Leibniz points out the benefits following from mechanical calculation: when dealing with symbols, we do not encumber our imagination and memory with thoughts relating to complex notions. Thanks to this we should be able to focus more easily on correctly handling symbols, which is the essence of any calculus. This idea can be traced back already to the "Dissertation on the Art of Combinations", where Leibniz develops a program of replacing metaphysical notions by numbers.[16] What is also interesting is that the symbols involved are nothing more than material objects (for example signs on paper or sounds). Therefore, one may say that all reasoning is reduced to the manipulation of physical objects, although, as Massimo Mugnai points out, the relations holding between the notions these symbols stand for are grounded metaphysically in the eternal realm of possibilities existing in God's mind but not chosen or created by him.[17]

Grosholz on her part claims that, for Leibniz, all kinds of cognition have to combine both an empirical aspect, consisting of collecting and sorting the data, and a mathematical one which connects the sensual presentations with mathematical notions, where the latter are precise counterparts of the former. Mathematical notions make a theoretical analysis possible, because they can be subject to deductive reasoning which leads to certain or at least probable conclusions.[18] As a comment to that I would like to note that Leibniz not only in the *Projet*, but already in the year 1666 when he wrote the *Dissertatio*, believed in the universal applicability of mathematics,[19] and that in the *Projet* he

---

[14] Cf. „Projet", p. 176.
[15] Ibid.
[16] „Dissertation on the Art of Combinations", in: *Philosophical Papers*, pp. 117–133; A VI, 1, N. 8. Later Leibniz will even come to the conclusion that thinking without symbols is not possible at all. Cf. Mugnai: „Leibniz and Gödel", pp. 407f.
[17] Cf. ibid., pp. 398–403 and p. 405.
[18] Grosholz: "Leibniz's Mathematical", p. 77; Leibniz: "Projet", p. 176.
[19] „Dissertation on the Art of Combinations" (Selections), in: *Philosophical Papers*, pp. 117–133; A VI, 1, N. 8.

even writes that although it would be optimal to combine clarity and an ordered structure of reasoning with its certainty,

> "[...] if one cannot achieve both at the same time, it is better to be precise at the cost of order than to preserve order at the cost of truth," [20]

because when one gives up the exactness one loses also the truth. Therefore, while exactness is, according to the *Projet*, the most important virtue of reasoning, this is not only because it makes deductive reasoning at all possible, but also because it protects us from the error of unconsciously endorsing contradictory claims: whereas it is possible to reason deductively about vague notions and arrive at contradictory conclusions, having determinate notions at our disposal we can avoid endorsing contradictions.

At the same time Leibniz thought mathematics to be a finite representation of reality, which itself contained for him infinity and was continuous. This aspect of Leibniz's philosophy, one which is obsolete from the point of view of contemporary mathematics, is discussed by Witold Marciszewski, who nevertheless considers Leibniz's philosophical system to be independent from his mathematics.[21] For Grosholz, the incongruence between finite mathematics and an infinite and continuous world is additional evidence corroborating mathematics' inability (in the eyes of Leibniz) to deliver a final description of the world: the great benefits brought by mathematics to cognition shouldn't lead – as follows from the *Tentamen*, and as she points out – to us endorsing a materialist picture of world, which picture, while it admittedly fits well to mathematical modeling, nevertheless is false, because it contradicts metaphysical principles. This is, hence, a deficiency of mathematics.

It is not clear, however, what exactly the logical character of the relationship between metaphysical principles and mathematics is for Grosholz. She writes that a materialist picture of the world should be rejected because it violates metaphysical principles, but at the same time the very reason for endorsing any metaphysical principles at all seems to be for her the insufficiency

---

[20] "Projet", p. 180, translation from French by Julia Jankowska.
[21] Witold Marciszewski: "Leibniz's Mathematical and Philosophical Approaches to Actual Infinity. A case of cultural resistance", in: *Studies in Logic, Grammar and Rhetoric* 4/17 (2001) *Language, Mind and Mathematics*, reprint of the text to be found originally in: Hans Poser/Christian Asmuth/Ursula Goldenbaum/Wenchao Li (eds.): *VII. Internationaler Leibniz-Kongreß. Nihil sine ratione. Mensch, Natur und Technik im Wirken von G. W. Leibniz. Berlin, 10.-14. September 2001*, vol. II, Hannover 2002.

of mathematics. We are guessing that an additional reason must be the explanatory insufficiency of other, competing metaphysical principles, such as the materialist assumption. But, after all, materialism on the one hand, and the very set of Leibnizian metaphysical principles on the other hand, don't seem to form an exhaustive list of possible metaphysical views.[22]

In any case, it is clear that, in her paper, Grosholz does not analyze these kinds of problems, but bases her analysis on the assumption that, according to Leibniz, mathematics alone is not enough. It must be made complete by including metaphysics, and especially the principle of sufficient reason and principle of the best, which together govern the world.[23] She thinks that it is from these principles that Leibniz derives the, well-known to the reader of the *Monadology*, claim that the world is endowed with feeling and striving for perfection, which express the Creator and the world's intelligibility.[24] This striving for perfection imposes a uni-directionality and strong asymmetry of time.

But is at least Grosholz's inference of one metaphysical fact (of such and not other nature of time) from another one (of the holding of the principles of sufficient reason and principle of the best) convincing? I would like to analyze here (without questioning the primacy of concrete metaphysical principles in Leibniz's philosophy) whether it is not too far-fetched to base a conclusion about (radical) asymmetry of time in Leibniz on monads striving for perfection.

3. Deriving the Thesis about the Uni-Directionality of Time in Leibniz from Metaphysical Principles

To do so, I propose first to have a closer look at Grosholz's description of the fruitful cooperation between mathematics and metaphysics that takes place in cognition, which according to her we can observe particularly well on the example of time. On her account, the cooperation mentioned is a complex one.

---

[22] Moreover, from some Leibnizian statements it is even not so clear whether these views are mutually exclusive – Leibniz sometimes writes as if they were just two perspectives of looking at the same, i.e., alternative and not competing descriptions.
[23] Cf. *Monadology*, in: *Philosophical Papers*, pp. 1044–1061, here p. 1049.
[24] Grosholz: "Leibniz's Mathematical", p. 75, cf. for example the following excerpt from the *Monadology*: „All simple substances or created monads might be given the name of entelechies, for they have in them a certain perfection [...]. There is in them a certain sufficiency [...] which makes them the sources of their internal actions and, so to speak, incorporeal automata" (Leibniz: *Monadology*, in: *Philosophical Papers*, p. 1047) It also follows from the points 14, 15, and 19 of the *Monadology* that all monads are endowed with feeling in a general sense.

Thanks to the world's intelligibility – which is another metaphysical assumption, following reportedly from the principle of the best – mathematics is applicable to the world. For Grosholz – who relies again on the text of the *Tentamen* – scientific investigation as such should consist precisely in moving back and forth between, on the one hand, intuitively classified empirical data, and, on the other hand, a classification following from the application of a mathematical conceptual framework.[25] Empirical research should form an initial source of tentative definitions, thanks to which one can, in a second step, construct relevant mathematical models of things. Such models are nevertheless only provisional, and the definitions that had been posited can be amended as the existing body of knowledge is subject to expansion;[26] expansion which (as we understand Grosholz) may be due, firstly, to the appearance of new empirical data, and secondly, to discoveries made by applying mathematics.

Moreover, metaphysical assumptions impose constraints on possible mathematical models, as can be seen on the example of the models of time proposed by Leibniz.[27] In a letter to Louis Bourget, written in August 1715, i.e., shortly before Leibniz started to correspond with Clarke, Leibniz presents three possible representations of time: as two parallel straight lines, as a straight line and a hyperbole parallel to it, and as two half-lines with a common initial point.[28] These three representations are supposed to stand for three worlds respectively: Firstly, a world in which time has no beginning; such a world is equally perfect in each moment (parallel straight lines). Secondly, a world which has no beginning but which continuously becomes more perfect (a straight line and a hyperbole). Thirdly, a world which becomes ever more perfect but has a beginning (half-lines with a common initial point). According to Leibniz, each of these models is equally good. He writes to Bourget: „I do not yet see any way of demonstrating which of these we should choose by pure reason."[29]

Grosholz, summarizing Leibniz's account of the proper scientific method, which, to repeat, according to him, should combine empirical data, mathematical reasoning and reference to metaphysical principles, concludes that if pure reason which she interprets as mathematics alone, i.e., a science of

---

[25] Grosholz: "Leibniz's Mathematical", p. 78.
[26] Ibid.
[27] Ibid., pp. 83–85.
[28] Letters to Louis Bourget, in: *Philosophical Papers*, pp. 1074–1081, here p. 1080.
[29] Ibid., p. 1081.

necessities, gives no answer to the question which of these models is the right one, and if from its perspective all three models seem to represent the world equally well, then an answer ought to be sought by appealing to what we know about the created, contingent world governed by the principle of sufficient reason.[30] Moreover, according to her, from the principle of sufficient reason it follows that everything strives for perfection, hence the right model is either the second, or the third one. As she writes:

> "This is the best of all possible worlds because it is continually becoming more perfect [...],"[31] and „[...] creation is a continuous temporal process."[32]

We have to note that here Grosholz combines two motives of Leibniz's philosophy – the fact that, according to him, monads themselves are the source of change, and his idea of the best of possible worlds. She writes:

> "[...] since all of his monads are body-souls, everything that exists is provided with a developed or rudimentary intentionality, that drives it forward in time. The strong asymmetry observed in the organic, sentient world is guaranteed for everything that exists."[33]

Thanks to such an interpretative step not only does she obtain an answer to the question which model of time best fits Leibniz's philosophical system, i.e., an answer that Leibniz himself did not possess, as explicitly stated by him in his letter to Bourget, but in addition she seems to be indirectly suggesting a pleasantly sounding understanding of the theodicy: it doesn't matter that the world in which we live doesn't look like the most perfect of possible worlds; what matters is that it becomes ever more perfect over time. I think that this interpretative step is unjustified. The constant and universal movement in monads and the striving for perfection present in them can be understood differently. To see this, one should come back to the history of philosophy of time – to which Grosholz appeals as well.

On the one hand, Descartes defined movement as follows:

---

[30] Cf. points 31–36 of the *Monadology*, in: *Philosophical Papers*, pp. 1049f.
[31] Grosholz: "Leibniz's Mathematical", p. 81.
[32] Ibid.
[33] Ibid., p. 86.

"[…] motion is the transfer of one piece of matter, or one body, from the vicinity of the other bodies, which are in immediate contact with it, and which are regarded as being at rest, to the vicinity of other bodies."[34]

A consequence of such a definition is a radically relativist account of movement:

"Motion, in the ordinary sense of the term, is simply *the action by which a body travels from one place to another*. By 'motion' I mean local motion; for my thought encompasses no other kind, and hence I do not think that any other kind should be imagined to exist in nature. Now I pointed out above that the same thing can be said to be changing and not changing its place at the same time; and similarly the same thing can be said to be moving and not moving. For example, a man sitting on board a shop which is leaving port considers himself to be moving relative to the shore which he regards as fixed; but he does not think of himself as moving relative to the ship, since his position is unchanged relative to its parts."[35]

On the other hand, Newton postulated the existence of absolute time and space, which would provide a reference frame, making it possible to describe movement in an unequivocal way. Absolute time and space also provided an explanation of Newton's famous experiment concerning the behavior of water in a rotating bucket, which was better than those provided by other competing theories.

Grosholz believes that Leibniz came up with a solution which avoided Descartes' radical relativism by relying on the metaphysical principle of perfection of the world and on the conviction that a constantly moving world can only be the most perfect one if it becomes ever more perfect over time. She interprets the active force and the striving for perfection present in the world not as a simple source of movement and information (which, in Leibniz's philosophy, are basically the same thing, since both can be reduced to the clarity of a monad's perceptions), but as a source of movement which at each point in time immediately and directly contributes to an increase of the world's perfection. She takes this for granted and either considers it obvious (which it is not), or thinks that it is a reasonable assumption to be made within the framework of Leibnizian philosophy, if one wants to save at least a bit of objectivity of time in his account of it, so that it doesn't collapse into the radical relativism of Descartes.

---

[34] René Descartes: *The Philosophical Writings of Descartes*, transl. by J. Cottingham/R. Stoothoff/Dugald Murdoch, New York 1985, pp. 232f.
[35] Ibid., p. 232.

Now, one may ask what we do know about time in Leibniz if we reject the assumption that in the most perfect possible world perfection constantly, necessarily increases. To what extent will time then remain real? Leibniz argued that absolute time and space are against the principle of sufficient reason, because, if they existed, it would be impossible to explain why God created the world at a particular point and not in a different one, or – respectively – earlier or later. He did not reject the reality of change though; he believed, however, that change has to be defined without reference to absolute time and space. If one accepts that the source of change lies in the monads themselves, and additionally that everything in the world is in constant movement, then there is no need to deny the objectivity of movement. It is this incessant movement of everything, this constant change, that constitutes time, time which is nothing more than the order in which subsequent states of the world follow each other, just like space is the order in which monads in particular states coexist. To be sure, for Leibniz the world has some structure, and the structure that it in fact has is partly time structure, i.e. a structure identical with the structure of what we normally call "time"; but for Leibniz this structure is in fact built on the different degrees of clarity of perceptions, their similarity, our interpretation of causal relations, and, perhaps, some specific experiences of the relations between certain perceptions that could explain our impression of the time flow. Nevertheless, on the metaphysical level, in Leibniz we do not go beyond the Parmenidean claim that the impression that time flows is nothing but a result of our specific and narrow perspective.[36] Leibniz avoids radical relativism not by positing a uni-directionality of time resulting from the world constantly becoming more perfect but by his thesis about the pre-established harmony which guarantees the world's structure, including its time structure, is intersubjective in the sense that it is the same in each monad, although seen from different perspectives. If time for Leibniz is reducible to relations between monads, or perceptions of one monad, is it in the end just a manner in which data are ordered by the mind? In my view that is not the case, and time, for Leibniz, is something existing in the world; this follows from his conception

---

[36] With respect to Parmenides cf. Bardon: *A Brief History*, p. 21.

of the pre-established harmony, according to which the content of a substance's, i.e. a monad's, perceptions,[37] notwithstanding its full causal independence from any other created substances, nevertheless changes in full harmony with the rest of the world.

A direction of time could, in turn, be established at most by appealing to the clarity of perceptions or any other aspect of reality that would be asymmetrical with respect to the time order: for example this clarity being lower in the case of the future than of the past. The practical consequences of the past being known and the future being unknown are also probably an effect of the metaphysical design of the world chosen by God as the best possible one, and may contribute to our perception of time flow and of time having a direction.[38] But what is most important is that although prima facie time as such in Leibniz can be reduced to the mental contents of the created monads, because basically everything in the created world can be reduced to them (and everything in both the created and the un-created world can be reduced to the mental content of the created and un-created monads if we assume that God is also a monad, just not a created one), nevertheless in a narrower sense time cannot be reduced to what would be normally called the mental content of monads, that is, to the conscious mental content of created monads. At best, time can be thus reduced to the content of the mind of God. In contrast, the direction of time can be reduced to the conscious contents of the minds of the created monads.

4. Conclusion

To me, the reasoning of Grosholz in her paper is not entirely convincing because of some circularity of explanation present in it: Grosholz argues that mathematics and metaphysics should be complementary to each other because of the deficiencies of mathematics; but I simply don't see a good reason for believing in metaphysical principles on the basis that mathematics is deficient. I am no more convinced by her deriving the strong asymmetry of time in Leibniz from the fact that the monads themselves are the source of change, and from the idea that the world is continuously becoming more perfect.

---

[37] Given that the monads are always „sources of their internal actions" (cf. the excerpt quoted in the footnote 24) and that each created monad „[...] is said to act outwardly insofar as it has perfection and to suffer from another insofar as it is imperfect." (*Monadology*, in: *Philosophical Papers*, p. 1050).

[38] Cf. points 26–28 of the *Monadology*.

Grosholz also does not comment on an aspect of the Leibnizian account of mathematics which is important in this context: the idea of symbolical thinking, as well as the fact that according to Leibniz, having determinate notions at our disposal, we can not only subject them to deductive thinking (for which having symbols is enough, and the symbols can stand for as vague and misleadingly overlapping ideas as we wish) but also avoid contradictions.

Mugnai combines these two motives in an interesting way, offering an account of truth and ideas being, for Leibniz, grounded metaphysically in God's mind, and reflected via the pre-established harmony. He writes:

> "[...] Leibniz seems to attribute to language a kind of pictorial power, i.e. a natural power of representing the main features of the things, or state of affairs, about which one is speaking. The picture, however, will not necessarily be the same in different languages: usually, in different languages we will have different descriptions and representations of the same things or state of affairs. But, according to Leibniz, it is precisely *because* two different systems of characters represent the same thing, that they may be correlated and 'communicate' between them."[39]

According to Mugnai, truths and ideas are, in Leibniz's philosophy, metaphysically grounded, and so is the adequacy of languages that express these truths and ideas, as well as their mutual relations, although the structure of the realm of truths and ideas is not reflected in the languages in a literal way. It is rather the deep structure of these languages that reflects the structure of truths and ideas. This general rule applies to all truths, including mathematical truths, but not only them.

Therefore, since time is in Leibniz "an order of successions,"[40] truths concerning the time-ordering of things are not different to other truths, and time's metaphysical grounding would lead to truths concerning time expressing eternal truths in God's mind. If we accept such an account of time in Leibniz, we no longer need to argue that it has, in a strong sense, a specific direction, in order to avoid the conclusion that time in the light of his philosophy is a mere illusion.

---

[39] Mugnai: „Leibniz and Gödel", p. 405.
[40] Cf. "The Controversy between Leibniz and Clarke."

The Problem of Scientific Demonstration in Early Writings of Leibniz (1667–1672)

Ryoko Konno (Paris)

Introduction

This paper will consider the criteria of science in the thought of the young Leibniz, focusing on his early writings (1667–1672) before his period in Paris. Around 1670, at the time of his two treatises on physics, the *Hypothesis physica nova* (*New Hypothesis of Physics*) and the *Theoria motus abstracti* (*Theory of Abstract Motion*), he also formulated his theory of knowledge, which is presented in the *Dissertatio praeliminaris de veris principiis et vera ratione philosophandi contra pseudophilosophos, libri IV* (*Preface to an Edition of Marius Nizolius*). Here we are confronted with the following difficulties. First, Leibniz seems not to have elaborated any methods capable of suitably describing motion as such. In the *Theory of Abstract Motion*, motion is treated as a trace, like a segment in geometry, although he refers to the *conatus* in the description of the continuity of motion. Thus, it is not clear whether the object of physics is distinguished from that of geometry. Second, in this period, his physics has a strong theological connotation. Further, the sciences are in general framed within the perspective of God as the "ultimate reason of things."[1] In this context, physics is supposed to contribute to the demonstration of the existence of God and the mind.

Even so, it is worth noting that Leibniz struggles to show the autonomy of physics. He confesses that "hitherto, [the theory of motion] has not yet been constituted in scientific form."[2] Then what is such a form that would satisfy the criteria of science? If physics is strictly autonomous from other sciences, on what basis is this possible? Again, what is the theoretical specificity of physics for Leibniz? As for the question of form, the elemental theory of movement is, for him, demonstrative. However, this does not mean that he dissolves the specificity of physics into logical arguments.

In the first section of this presentation, we will examine Leibniz's description of natural phenomena in his early writings on theology, especially in the *Confessio naturae contra atheistas* (*Confession of Nature against the Atheists*) (1668). We will articulate three types of arguments contained in the

---

[1] A II, 1, 131.
[2] "[…] nondum hactenus in scientiae formam constituta […]" (ibid.).

first part of this work, which will show us in which aspect Leibniz treats natural phenomena. In the second section, we will examine the reason why Leibniz considered mechanical principles, namely *magnitude*, *shape* [*figura*], and *motion*, to be valid for the explication of natural phenomena, focusing on a letter to Jakob Thomasius that dates back to April 1669. After these analyses, in the third section, for our conclusion, we will show how Leibniz revised these discussions in his writings on physics. We will mainly discuss his preparatory works for the *Theory of Abstract Motion*.

1. Natural Phenomena in the Theological Writings of Leibniz

1.1 Leibniz's Writings on the Demonstration of God's Existence

Following the consultation between 1668 and 1669 with the first counselor of the electorate of Mainz, Baron Johann Christian von Boineburg, Leibniz elaborates a grand plan for the restoration of the unity of the churches[3] in the *Catholic Demonstrations* (*Demonstrationes catholicae*) (1668–1669(?)). This work was not completed, but we have a sketch of it, showing that it was to contain four parts: 1) a demonstration of the existence of God, 2) a demonstration of the immortality and immateriality of the soul, 3) a demonstration of the mystery of the Christian faith, 4) a demonstration of the authority of the Catholic church and the Scriptures. Beyond this plan, in the ensuing years Leibniz wrote a series of treatises on theological matters such as the refutation of atheism, the possibility of the sacraments of the Incarnation, a defense of the Trinity, the possibility of divine grace, and the way to judge religious controversies.

Concerning the existence of God, Leibniz lists four types of demonstration, according to the principles on which that demonstration is based: 1) the demonstration based on the principle that there is nothing that occurs without a reason, 2) the demonstration based on the principle that motion cannot take place without continuous creation, 3) the demonstration based on the principle that there is no origin of motion in bodies, and 4) the demonstration based on the principle that there is no origin of solidity [*consistentia*] in bodies.[4]

---

[3] Yvon Belaval: *Leibniz: initiation à sa philosophie*, Paris ⁶2005 [1st ed., 1969], p. 69.
[4] A VI, 1, 494, translation from *Leibniz on God and Religion*, ed. by Lloyd Strickland, London 2016, p. 22 modified.

The importance of theological reflection has been restated by interpreters of Leibniz,[5] but our task here is not to recreate his entire argument. However, it is worth following the main line of his demonstration of God's existence, because it may show on what basis and to what extent Leibniz thought natural phenomena are to be explained. In the first part of the *Confession of Nature against the Atheists*, entitled "That corporeal phenomena cannot be explained without an incorporeal principle, that is God,"[6] Leibniz determines his strategy and the aim of his demonstration. Addressing himself to the "corpuscular philosophers" of his age, he maintains that

> "[...] in explaining corporeal phenomena, we must not unnecessarily resort to God or to any other incorporeal thing, form, or quality, [...] but as far as possible, everything should be derived from the nature of body and its primary qualities: magnitude, shape, and motion."[7]

Here Leibniz strategically takes as a premise of the demonstration the explication of nature by the principles of mechanistic philosophy. He agrees with the mechanical philosophers that natural phenomena are accounted for by the concepts of magnitude, shape, and motion, but he disagrees with them, because mechanical principles themselves cannot defend their validity. Then on what basis does Leibniz make nature *confess* the limit of mechanical principles?

1.2 Leibniz's Strategies: Three Types of Arguments for Describing the Natural Phenomena

In the *Confession of Nature*, the explication of natural phenomena contains two kinds of arguments. On the one hand, based on the definition of a body,

---

[5] Jean Baruzi: *Leibniz et l'organisation religieuse de la terre, d'après des documents inédits*, Paris 1907; Ursula Goldenbaum: "Transubstantiation, Physics and Philosophy at the Time of the *Catholic Demonstrations*" in: Stuart Brown (ed.): *The Young Leibniz and His Philosophy (1646–76)*, Dordrecht 1999, p. 79–102; Maria Rosa Antognazza: *Leibniz on the Trinity and the Incarnation: Reason and Revelation in the Seventeenth Century*, New Haven/London 2008.
[6] "Quod ratio Phænomenorum Corporalium reddi non possit, sine incorporeo Principio, id est DEO" (A VI, 1, 489, translation from Gottfried Wilhelm Leibniz: *Philosophical Papers and Letters*, ed. by Leroy Earl Loemker, Dordrecht ²1969, p. 109).
[7] "[...] in reddendis corporalium Phænomenorum rationibus neque ad Deum, neque aliam quamcunque rem, formaque aut qualitatem incorporalem sine necessitate confugiendum esse [...] sed omnia quod ejus fieri possit, ex natura corporis, primisque ejus qualitatibus: Magnitudine, Figura et Motu deducenda esse" (A VI, 1, 490, Loemker, p. 110 modified).

which consists of "space" and "existence-in [*inexistentia*]", Leibniz explains the magnitude, shape, and motion of a body. Magnitude and shape are treated as an issue of the determination of a body in space. Motion is treated as an issue of the mobility of body in space. On the other hand, as to the substantiality of body, Leibniz explains its consistency on the basis of its properties. Thus, the *Confession of Nature* contains, in a broad sense, three types of arguments for describing natural phenomena. We will briefly characterize them.

1. The argument concerning the determination of a body in a spatial order:
   For Leibniz, the determination of a body in a spatial order is explained in terms of its border, because a body is considered to have the same magnitude and shape as the space which it fills. However, the reason why a body has a such-and-such shape rather than a different one cannot be explained from the nature of bodies themselves. Leibniz gives two possible causes: from eternity and from the motion of another body. As for eternity, it cannot explain the cause of a shape as such. As for the determination by the motion of another body, even if it is accepted, this explanation has an infinite regress.

2. The argument concerning the mobility of a body:
   Leibniz derives the mobility of a body from the concept of "existence-in." He maintains that because a body is not in the same place as it was previously, it is considered to have changed the space where it is. Thus one can consider that a body is moved "because motion is the change of space."[8] He stresses that one cannot derive actual motion as such from the nature of body. Therefore, the reason for motion cannot be found in the body itself. Leibniz gives the same possible causes as above, but he denies them for the same reasons.

3. The argument concerning the consistency of a body in terms of its properties:
   Leibniz explains the consistency of a body in terms of its properties, namely resistance, reflection, and cohesion. Even if one supposes that shapes that combine with each other in a body explain the cohesion and substantiality of a body, this analysis regresses infinitely. Then, if one

---

[8] "Motus enim est mutatio spatii" (A VI, 1, 491).

supposes certain indivisible corpuscles, which are supposed to be "atoms," as the last step in analyzing bodies, one can find no reason for cohesion and of indivisibility.

In this context, we may summarize the scope and the limits of mechanical principles: for Leibniz, mechanical principles are capable of explaining natural phenomena from the perspective of the description in spatial order, insofar as the mobility and divisibility of body are admitted. In this respect, mechanical principles are supposed to function operationally. However, they cannot explain the reasons why a body has a certain magnitude and a certain shape in nature, the reason why an actual motion is given, or the reason why a body has substantiality, because these reasons are not found in the body itself. Thus, for Leibniz, it is not mechanical principles but the principle of reason that accomplishes the explication of nature. Therefore, he postulates the existence of an incorporeal principle, namely God.

Despite these limitations, if mechanical principles are supposed to explain natural phenomena to a certain extent, on what basis does Leibniz validate them? Moreover, if the domain of natural phenomena is not merely a premise of Leibniz's theological arguments for the demonstration of God's existence, on what basis is the autonomy of natural phenomena characterized? To find the answers to these questions, we will examine one of his letters to Jakob Thomasius.

2. Leibniz's Account of Mechanical Principles

2.1 Leibniz's Letter to Jakob Thomasius (20./30. April 1669)

At the same period as the *Catholic Demonstrations*, Leibniz was confronted with the rise of the *new physics,* represented by the mechanical philosophy of Cartesians. In a letter of April 1669 to his professor Jakob Thomasius, Leibniz presents his ambition to reconcile Aristotelian hylomorphism and contemporary philosophy. He considers the two philosophies to be not opposed but rather compatible with each other. At the beginning of the letter, Leibniz defines Cartesians as those who followed the principles of Descartes, distinguishing them from those who just *paraphrased* the doctrine of Descartes. He declared,

"I am nothing but a Cartesian."⁹ He agreed with them that "nothing is to be explained in bodies except by means of magnitude, shape and motion."¹⁰

However, the extent of Leibniz's definition is broad. It is not clear in what sense his interpretation of mechanical principles can be said to be Cartesian. In fact, it has been noted by several commentators that Leibniz did not deeply understand the philosophy of Descartes at that time.¹¹ If in spite of this, he in a certain sense follows the philosophy of Descartes, in what sense is this possible? To clarify his position, it seems worth mentioning his own principle for reconciling the two philosophies:

> "[...] the clearer and more intelligible of two possible hypotheses must always be chosen, and without any doubt this is the hypothesis of the moderns, which conceives no incorporeal entities within bodies, but assumes nothing beyond magnitude, shape and motion."¹²

His engagement with Cartesian principles is to be considered as a choice of hypothesis, insofar as its scope is delimited to the explication of corporeal phenomena. In this respect, on what basis is his choice validated? In this letter, Leibniz's position seems ambiguous, because he presents, on the one hand, a reductionist view that natural phenomena are explained solely by mechanical principles. On the other hand, he seems to hold to a certain type of physical reality for bodies that is not proved by those principles. He repeatedly mentions the concept of *antitypia*, which is supposed to be the nature of a body in terms of sensitive cognition.

Here it is also worth mentioning Leibniz's criterion of *clarity* in this period. He discusses this concept in a semantic context. As it is presented in the *Preface to an Edition of Marius Nizolius,* clarity is an epistemic state of the subject which is obtained when all of the meanings of the words contained

---

⁹ "[...] me fateor nihil minus quam Cartesianum esse" (A II, 1, 25; A VI, 2, 434, Loemker, p. 94 modified).

¹⁰ "[...] nihil explicandum in corporibus, nisi per magnitudinem, figuram et motum" (ibid., Loemker, p. 94, modified).

¹¹ Francisque Bouillier: *Histoire de la philosophie cartésienne*, vol. 2, Paris 1868, [reprint, Genève 1970], p. 408ff.: *Leibniz-Thomasius, Correspondance (1663–1672)*, transl. by Richard Bodéüs, Paris 1993, commentary, p.168.

¹² "[...] ex duabus tamen possibilibus Hypothesibus semper eligenda est clarior et intelligibilior, qualis haud dubie est hypothesis recentiorum, quae nulla entia incorporalia in mediis corporibus sibi fingit, sed praeter magnitudinem, figuram et motum assumit nihil" (A II, 1, 26; A VI, 2, 435; Loemker, p. 95 modified).

in a speech are known.[13] In this condition, clarity comes, in a broad sense, from the word itself or the context of the speech. Concerning the former, this is supposed to have three sources: 1) the origin of the word, 2) the usage of the word, namely the meaning that is shared with speakers of the same language, and 3) the formal meaning, namely the meaning that is abstracted from many instances of usage. Concerning the latter, as far as speech is concerned with its subject, such speech is considered to be clear. However, when the vocabulary contained in speech is well defined in advance, speech is considered to avoid obscurity. Furthermore, Leibniz continues:

> "Once chosen, however, the meaning must be reduced to a definition (for a definition is nothing but the expressed meaning of the word or more briefly, the meaning signified)."[14]

Therefore, for Leibniz in this period, a basis for clarity is found in elucidating the meaning of word in accordance with popular ordinary language. He declared that "whatever cannot be explained in popular terms is nothing [...] unless it can be known by immediate sense experience."[15]

This is not to deny that Leibniz employs technical terms in certain domains. For the definition of a shapes in geometry, he stresses that the elements of the definition are to be resolved until they are expressed in popular terms, because concepts in geometry do not necessarily correspond to popular usage, and he considers that judgment to be more reliable that proceeds by the elucidation of technical terms with popular ones. Regarding objects that are neither accessible to the senses nor discussed frequently in common usage, especially the objects of mathematics, physics, and mechanics, technical terms are needed. Thus, for Leibniz in this period, the clarity of the term is founded on its meaning in ordinary language, but he distinguishes its application from its theoretical basis.

In the remainder of this paper, we will examine Leibniz's approach to showing mechanical principles as clear and intelligible and the reasons why his choice is valid.

---

[13] A VI, 2, 408f.
[14] "Electa autem semel significatio si locus fert redigenda in definitionem (definitio enim nihil aliud est, quam significatio verbis expressa; seu brevius, significatio significata) [...]" (A VI, 2, 411; Loemker, p. 123 modified).
[15] "[...] quicquid terminis popularibus explicari non potest, nisi immediato sensu constet [...] esse nullum [...]" (A VI, 2, 414; Loemker, p. 124).

2.2. Mechanical Principles as Explicative Principles of Natural Phenomena

First, Leibniz discusses the determination of body, reducing matter to mass and form to shape. According to him, prime matter is nothing but "the mass itself, in which there is nothing but extension, and antitypy or impenetrability."[16] This is considered to have an indefinite quantity and no boundaries but is supposed to be divided into parts when motion is introduced. For him, this is the shape of a body. Then he asks about the origin of division, whether or not mass was created separately by emptiness, because it is also possible to explain the origin of the boundary of each body by introducing gaps in space. However, he denies this possibility, because the annihilation of certain parts in matter is for him a question of the supernatural. He says stubbornly: "I do not speak of it."[17] Thus he delimits the context where he explains natural phenomena. Hence, as the origin of the discontinuity of natural phenomena, he postulates motion. Therefore, for him, the form of a body, assimilated to its shape, originates from motion.

As regards motion, although Leibniz admits the Aristotelian concept that nature is the principle of motion and rest,[18] he does not think that a body moves itself spontaneously, because a body does not move until something extrinsic moves it. For him, the form of a body is considered a cause of motion, but not the primary one. For example, in the case of a collision of spheres on a plane, he explains motion with two principles, in terms of activity and passivity in a motion. He classifies the body that gives the impulsion as the "principle of impressed motion," and on the other hand, the shape of body that is given the impulsion as the "principle of the received motion." We can see here that the form, that is, the shape, plays a role for him in transmitting motion. He insists that

> "I admit therefore that form is the principle of motion within its own body, and that body is itself the principle of motion in another body. But the first principle of motion is the primary form, which is really abstracted from matter, namely mind, which is at the same time the efficient cause. [...] Therefore it is not absurd that of the substantial forms only mind should be designated as the first

---

[16] "[...] ipsa Massa in qua nihil aliud quam extensio et ἀντιτυπία, seu impenetrabilitas" (A II, 1, 26; A VI, 2, 435; Loemker, p. 95).
[17] "[...] nam de annihilatione certarum partium as vacuitates in materia procurandas, quia supra natura est, non loquor" (A II, 1, 27; A VI, 2, 436; Loemker, p. 96).
[18] Aristotle: *Physica*, III, 1, 200 b 12.

principle of motion, all the others receiving their motion from mind. [...] and it is by this argument that he [Aristotle] ascends to the prime mover."[19]

This confirms that Leibniz deprives the body of its autonomy of mobility. When he says, following Aristotle,[20] that the object of physics is the movable body, this means that physics is the science of *moved* bodies.[21] Here he rigidly delimitates the domain of natural phenomena. In light of this geometrized conception of body, his reductionist view can be seen to validate his choice of mechanical principles.

Despite this view, one may find his explication limited. Even if Leibniz generalizes the case of collision to a certain extent, we may not consider this explication as a model representing motion in natural phenomena. This is because, first, a model that only divides the moment of collision instead of explaining the process does not articulate causality in motion, and second, such a model gives no explication that allows the classification of different cases.

2.3 Constructive Principles of Body

Although Leibniz employs a reductionist view, he seems to defend the physical reality of body in the context in which he looks for the qualities that tell of the nature of body. He presents the view that the materiality derived from physical experience is indispensable for designating the concept of body. He examines sensible qualities in the following three steps: 1) to seek a quality that could be common to all bodies, first he lists color, smell, taste and sound, but these are rejected as not constituting the nature of body. Air, for example, is considered to be a body although it lacks all of these qualities. 2) He considers tactile qualities like heat, humidity, dryness, and cold, and he also rejects them for not being constitutive of body, because they can be absent individually as cold is absent from fire. In addition to this, Leibniz takes other tactile qualities, such as smoothness, lightness, and tenacity, to arise from other constitutive

---

[19] "Forma igitur est principium motus in suo corpore et corpus ipsum est principium motus in alio corpore fateor; sed primum principium motus est prima et realiter a materia abstracta forma (quae simul est efficiens) nempe Mens. [...] Absurdum ergo non est, unicam ex formis substantialibus mentem principium motus primum dici, caeteras a mente motum habere. Et hoc argumento adscendit ad primum motorem" (A II, 1, 32; A VI, 2, 440; Loemker, p. 99).
[20] Aristotle: *Metaphysica*, E, 1, 1026 a 12.
[21] This point has been already stressed by Bodéüs. Cf. Bodéüs: "Commentary", in: *Leibniz-Thomasius, Correspondance*, p.194–198.

qualities. 3) Finally, Leibniz settles on the quality of density or antitypy, assumed to coexist with the extension of body, as applicable solely to the body:

> "[…] therefore, men find that the nature of body consists in two things: extension and antitypy together. The former we derive from sight, the latter from touch, and by the combination of both senses we usually ascertain that things are not phantasms."[22]

Between the argument for sensible qualities at the level of the species of body and the argument at the level of the kind of body, Leibniz slips from an inquiry into constructive principles to an inquiry into the criterion for judging the existence of body. He seems to use a concept derived from sensible perception and physical experience in the argument for the definition of body:

> "The nature of body therefore evidently is constituted by extension and antitypy, since there is nothing in things without a cause, and nothing ought to be supposed in bodies whose cause cannot be explained from their constitutive principles. And this cause cannot be explained by these principles unless they are well defined. Therefore we can assume nothing in bodies which does not follow from the definition of extension and antitypy."[23]

It should be noted first that Leibniz accounts for causality in natural phenomena in terms of the constituents of the objects. That is to say that the generation of the object is, for him, essential to achieving the explication of natural phenomena. Secondly, it is not the data as such, but it is the definitions of the constituents that are allowed to explain the natural phenomena, even though these constituents are rooted in sensible perception and physical experience.

---

[22] "[...] In duobus igitur homines [...] naturam corporis collocant, in extensione et ἀντιτυπία simul sumtis, illam sumunt a visu, hanc a tactu, unde et ex conjunctione utriusque sensus certificari de rebus solemus, quod non sint phantasmata"; (A II, 1, 36; A VI, 2, 443; Loemker, p. 101). In another letter to Thomasius (16/26 February 1666), Leibniz mentions the concept of phantasm in the context in which he maintains that the colour is the impression on the sensory organ and is not the quality which is supposed to be inside the body, along the same line as Hobbes does in the *De corpore*, chap. 5, 6 (A II, 1, 7). The point of their argument is that the appearance of body is varied according to the distance to the object or its surroundings. A refined formulation is found in Leibniz's later text: "Phantasms are forms of sensible things without their matter [Phantasmata sunt formae rerum sensibilium sine materia]." (A VI, 4, 2911).

[23] "Ex his patet, naturam Corporis constitui per Extensionem et Antitypiam, cumque nihil sit in rebus sine causa, nihil etiam poni debet in corporibus, cujus causa reddi non possit ex primis eorum constitutivis. Jam causa ex iis reddi non potest, nisi per eorum definitiones. Nihil igitur ponendum est in corporibus, quod non ex definitione Extensionis et Antitypiae fluat" (A II, 1, 36; A VI, 2, 443; Loemker, p. 101f. modified).

In these conditions, the definition should be understood as an instrument for inference in physics.[24] Therefore, one may read this paragraph as an insight into the means of the construction of the objects that Leibniz puts forward in the part on general problem of his *Theory of Abstract Motion*:

> "The construction is threefold: geometrical, that is, imaginary but exact; mechanical, that is, real but not exact; and physical, that is, real and exact. [...] The construction of physics [contains the means] whereby nature can produce things, that is to say the means that bodies produce by themselves."[25]

Although definition is not a mechanical principle, it underlies the mechanical explication of natural phenomena in the sense that it allows the explanation of the generative process of object in physics. Therefore, definition is also taken to validate the choice of mechanical principles.

It is also worth mentioning that his conception of definition in physics contains essentially sensible and empirical elements. In this sense, this paragraph should not be read as an evidence of disorder, but rather as his basic insight in the *New Hypothesis of Physics,* namely a *Theory of Concrete Motion*. The density of a body is taken as an essential element that allows the explanation of the variety of structures of bodies and the reason for gravity.

3. Conclusion

Looking at his approaches, we may say that the theoretical specificities of Leibniz's physics lie in the delimitation of the domain of natural phenomena by mechanical principles and in the explication of the generative process of objects by definition. Leibniz's originality is to be found especially in the second point, due to which we cannot consider him to be a Cartesian. It is important to stress that definition plays a prominent role in his reasoning in physics, because even his theory of *conatus*, which is the key concept in the *Theory of Abstract Motion*, is elaborated by means of the definition.

For the conclusion, it seems appropriate to briefly present how Leibniz revised the arguments on the geometrized body and the explication of natural

---

[24] To compare Leibniz's aspect for the definition with that of Descartes, see Yvon Belaval: *Leibniz. Critique de Descartes*, Paris 1960, [reprint Paris 2003], p. 169ff.

[25] "Triplex constructio est: Geometrica, id est imaginaria, sed exacta; Mechanica, id est realis, sed non exacta; et Physica, id est realis et exacta [...] Physica eos quibus natura res efficere potest, id est quos corpora producunt seipsis" (A VI, 2, 270).

phenomena based on the definition in his writings on physics. We will remark the salient points in his preparatory work for the *Theory of Abstract Motion*.

First, in the *Rationibus motus* (*On the Reasonings of Motion*), which was written just after the letter to Thomasius we discussed above, Leibniz articulated his argument on the principle of impressed–received motion in the following points. 1) He focuses on the moment of collision, classifying typical cases with geometrical descriptions. In this treatise, as elements for determining motion after impact, he mentions the difference in the width (*latitudo*) and the length (*longitudo*) of the bodies concerned (§15–18) and the angle of collision (§28–31). 2) he treats the transmission of motion as the unity of the bodies concerned. He insists that "when a moved body strikes a resting body, from both bodies, one body made."[26] "For the reason of the varied shapes of the bodies in collision, an astonishing variety of shapes of a [unified] body occur from the collision."[27]

Second, Leibniz divided the methods of physics into two parts according to their cognitive function, that is, the method of reason and that of sense. The former is a certain type of analysis, which cannot be captured by fact or by sense and requires demonstration by reason. According to him, the proposition that no matter how tiny it is and how weakly it moves, a body gives an impulsion to a bigger one, is to be demonstrated by reason,[28] namely by the "definition of the terms."[29] An analysis of motion on a micro scale is integrated into the scope of definition.

Third, these views on the unification of bodies and on the micro-scale analysis of motion are furthermore refined in the following second draft. According to him, the first principles of motion are concerned with the following issues: 1) whether or not a body stops; 2) whether a body is made up of one or several bodies; 3) whether a body touches the others; and 4) how different bodies touch each other at a point, on a line, or on a surface. Nevertheless, the senses cannot explore these issues. One may say that arguments about the interactions of motion are pursued alongside the argument on the unification of bodies. In the course of this discussion, Leibniz first mentions the concept of

---

[26] The *Rationibus Motus*, §19 "Si corpus motum impingit in quiescens, ex utroque corpore fit unum" (A VI, 2, 162).

[27] Ibid., §20 "Pro variis figuris concurrentium corporum mira oritur varietas figurarum corporis unius ex concursu orientis" (ibid.).

[28] Ibid., §3 "rationis longe alia demonstratio est, nimirum quiescens quantumcunque impelli a moto quantulocunque, etiam motu quantulocunque" (A VI, 2, 159).

[29] Ibid., §5 "[...] terminorum definitionibus [...]" (A VI, 2, 160).

conatus in the fourth draft. The *conatus* functions here as mediating motion: "*Conatus* is the beginning, the limit and the medium of motion."[30] With this textual evidence, we can note the evolving nature of Leibniz's concept of definition in physics. We cannot treat his confrontation with Hobbes here, which is critical for the elaboration of his concept of *conatus*. However, we can say without doubt that his concept of definition prepares the "basic, abstract, and purely rational"[31] part of his theory of motion.

---

[30] "Conatus est initium, finis ac medium motus" (A VI, 2, 171).
[31] "[...] Partem Phoronomicae Elementalem, abstractam, mere rationalem [...]" (A VI, 2, 274).

The End of Melancholy.
Deleuze and Benjamin on Leibniz and the Baroque

Mogens Lærke (Lyon)

In the central chapter of *Différence et répétition* (1968), devoted to the critique of the so-called "regimes of representation", Gilles Deleuze places Leibniz along with Hegel in the group of particularly loathsome philosophers who instead of overcoming representation had made it infinite.[1] This is also the Leibniz we encounter in the conclusion of *Spinoza et le problème de l'expression* (1968), where Deleuze, while acknowledging that Leibniz's philosophy takes part in the "hidden history" of expression, still reproaches him for having subjected expression to determinate symbolization and finality:

> "Expression according to Leibniz will never be separated from a symbolization whose principle is always finality or final accord."[2]

Elsewhere, he even suggests that there is something totalitarian and repressive about Leibniz:

> "He is the philosopher of order; moreover, of order and police, in all the senses of the word 'police'. And in the original meaning of the word 'police' in particular, e.g. the ordered organization of the city. He only thinks in terms of order. In that sense he is extremely reactionary; he is the friend of order."[3]

Nonetheless, Deleuze also asserts, with formulas not devoid of Nietzschean pathos, that "in Leibniz, there is even more depth, more orgiasm and bacchanalian delirium, in the sense that the ground has greater initiative"[4] and that

> "the ground rumbles with more power in Leibniz, [...] the drunkenness and dizziness are not so feigned, the obscurity better grasped, and more truly close to the Dionysian shores."[5]

---

[1] Gilles Deleuze: *Différence et répétition*, Paris 1968, pp. 71, 62f., 119, 338ff. Unless otherwise indicated, translations are my own.
[2] Id.: *Spinoza et le problème de l'expression*, Paris 1968, p. 212, 306–310.
[3] Id.: Lecture on Leibniz, 15.04.1980. Deleuze's lectures, including English translations can be found on http://www.webdeleuze.com. In the following, I will simply refer to them by their date. Unless otherwise indicated, translations are my own.
[4] Id.: *Différence et repetition*, p. 70.
[5] Ibid., p. 340.

And when summing up his relations to the "classical philosophers" in the preface to the English edition of *Spinoza et le pro-blème de l'expression*, Deleuze admits that, while he mainly considers himself to be a Spinozist, "I owe a lot to Leibniz."[6] In the earlier work, especially *Différence et répétition* and *Logique du sens*, Deleuze's use of Leibniz mostly turns around the notion of "compossibility."[7] Later, however, this relatively narrow appropriation gave way to a much broader and overall more positive engagement with Leibniz's philosophy. This can be observed in the lectures given at Paris VIII-St. Denis throughout the eighties, but most importantly, of course, in *Le Pli. Leibniz et le Baroque* from 1988.[8]

In *Le Pli*, Leibniz is depicted not so much as a "friend of order" as a deeply creative philosopher.[9] Indeed, while most of Deleuze's assessments of Leibniz's philosophy remain ambiguous, there is a clear development in *Le Pli* towards a more positive evaluation. This, unsurprisingly, was a consequence of Deleuze's discovery of the two central notions figuring in the title of the book, namely, the philosophical concept of the *fold* and the aesthetic and epochal category of the *Baroque*. I have elsewhere attempted to reconstruct the basic construction of the concept of the fold and show how it captures a striking number of the basic metaphysical intuitions behind Deleuze's monadological metaphysics.[10] In this contribution, I would like to consider how the notion of the Baroque contributed to this reevaluation of Leibniz's philosophy in *Le Pli*.[11] I believe this can best be done by comparing Deleuze's reading with a previous attempt at associating Leibniz with the Baroque.[12] Deleuze was not the first to make the connection. For example, in his interesting book *La Logique chez Leibniz. Essai sur le rationalisme baroque* from

---

[6] Id.: "Preface", in: *Spinoza: Expressionism in Philosophy*, transl. by M. Joughin, New York 1990, p. 11.
[7] See id.: *Différence et répétition*, pp. 68, 338f.; and id.: *Logique du sens*, Paris 1969, pp. 133–141 and pp. 198–203.
[8] Id.: *Le Pli. Leibniz et le Baroque*, Paris 1988.
[9] See ibid., pp. 168f., and p. 189. See also id.: *Pourparlers*, Paris 1991, p. 211.
[10] See Mogens Lærke: "Four Figures of Folding: Deleuze on Leibniz's Monadological Metaphysics", in: *British Journal for the History of philosophy* 23/6 (2015), pp. 1192–1213.
[11] See id.: "Four Things Deleuze Learned from Leibniz", in: Niamh McDonnell/Sjoerd van Tuinen (eds.): *Deleuze and the Fold: A Critical Reader*, Basingstoke 2009, pp. 25–45. Some aspects of the present paper are also treated in this article.
[12] Deleuze: *Le Pli*, p. 173.

1973, Herbert Knecht already argues that "one must always return to the Baroque to understand Leibniz's thought."[13] Here, however, I will consider Deleuze's reading of Leibniz and the Baroque in relation to an even earlier and considerably more famous predecessor, namely Walter Benjamin who, in his *Ursprung des deutschen Trauerspiels*, similarly pointed to Leibniz as the Baroque philosopher *par excellence*.[14]

Benjamin's reading of the Baroque is most evidently present in Deleuze's argument in *Le Pli* in his appropriation of the concept of "allegory":

> "Walter Benjamin made decisive progress in the understanding of the Baroque when he showed that the allegory was not some failed symbol, an abstract personification, but a power of figuration completely different from the symbol [...]."[15]

Breaking with his critique of Leibniz as a philosopher steeped in symbolization in the texts from the late sixties, Deleuze thus insists in *Le Pli* that

> "one must see Leibniz's philosophy as an allegory of the world, and no longer in the old way as the symbol of a cosmos."[16]

This seems to amount to a fairly straightforward endorsement of Benjamin's conception of the Baroque. However, when we turn to the lectures on Leibniz that Deleuze gave while writing *Le Pli*, his remarks about Benjamin are strikingly evasive. Thus, in lecture from 1987, Deleuze even self-consciously admits

---

[13] See Herbert Knecht: *La Logique chez Lebniz. Essai sur le rationalisme baroque*, Lausanne 1981, pp. 34, 335, 340, 352. Deleuze refers to Knecht, but in quite critical terms: "[...] those who have compared Leibniz and the Baroque have often done that in the name of a concept which was too broad, such as Knecht with his 'coincidence of opposites'" (Deleuze: *Le Pli*, p. 47). He seems mainly to disapprove of the dialectics that informs Knecht's vision of the Baroque. Knecht argues for example that "the baroque man, who certainly is conscious of the contradictory aspects of his situation and of the world in which he lives, accepts the multiplicity of his state by integrating it on a higher level in a conception of the unitary whole where the antagonisms are conciliated" (Knecht: *La Logique chez Lebniz*, p. 14, I translate; see also id., p. 16 and p. 339). Deleuze fails to recognize other substantial proximities between his own analysis and Knecht's, especially with respect to the *optimism* of the Baroque and the fact that they refuse to consider the philosophical paradigm of the Baroque as a precursor to modernistic theories of subjectivity, but both situate it firmly within a classical, theological paradigm (see id., p. 16 and p. 341).
[14] See Walter Benjamin: *Ursprung des deutschen Trauerspiels*, Frankfurt a. M. 1972, transl. as *The Origin of German Tragic Drama*, transl. by J. Osborne, London 1977.
[15] Deleuze: *Le Pli*, p. 170. See also Deleuze: Lecture on Leibniz, 20.01.1987.
[16] Id.: *Le Pli*, p. 174.

that he "can't really get into [Benjamin's] text."[17] As I will argue in the following, this laconic remark reflects a kind of double standard in Deleuze's approach to Benjamin. Benjamin's way of associating Leibniz to the baroque mindset allows Deleuze to bring out the creative aspects of Leibniz's way of thinking, its essential relation to a non-circular form of infinity, its affirmation of an open-ended production of meaning, its incessant creation of concepts.[18] However, at the same time, and now in opposition to Benjamin for whom the Baroque was inseparable from the experience of a world turning to ruin and of "mourning" (*Trauer*) without tragic redemption, Deleuze also associates the Baroque with Leibnizian optimism and the titillating emotion of "delight" (*laetitia*). While taking over central figures of Benjamin's interpretation of the baroque "way of seeing", Deleuze thus proposes an entirely different *evaluation* of the Baroque. Hence, at the same time, he uses Benjamin's association of Leibniz and the Baroque in *Ursprung des deutschen Trauerspiels* in a positive way to reassess his own reading of Leibniz while also, in a more negative key, using Leibniz to transform Benjamin's image of the Baroque, turning its form of expression into a joyful one.

* * *

According to Benjamin's account in *Ursprung des deutschen Trauerspiels*, an allegory is an emblem or trope containing elements of infinite iteration, deferral of meaning and difference, as opposed to a symbol which is based on determinate reference, recognition and identity. As Leibniz puts it in a text that neither Benjamin nor Deleuze seem to know, allegory is a kind of "continuous metaphor" (*metaphora continuata*).[19] Benjamin presents allegory as the preferred trope in the Baroque to the extent that it helps conveying the idea of a world from which God has withdrawn and that provides not clear image of divine providence. Instead, the quintessential baroque experience is that of a fragmented, hopelessly ruined world that

---

[17] Id.: Lecture on Leibniz, 20.01.1987.
[18] See id.: *Pourparlers*, p. 211.
[19] Gottfried Wilhelm Leibniz: Epistolae tres D. B. Spinoza ad D. Oldenburgium, October 1676 [?], A VI, 3, 366: "Haec a mortius resurrectio, utique non nisi metaphorica sit, aut si mavis allegorica (Allegoria enim metaphora continuata est) […]."

"[piles] up fragments ceaselessly, without any strict idea of a goal [...] in the unremitting expectation of a miracle."[20]

On Benjamin's reading, the baroque world of mourning (*Trauer*) is thus allegorical in the sense that it is engaged in

"a successively progressing, dramatically mobile, dynamic representation of ideas which has acquired the very fluidity of time."[21]

Allegory incarnates indefinite deferral of proper meaning, or the absence of the kind of original, ultimate reference that Benjamin, in another context, refers to by the notion of "authenticity."[22] While never attaining such authenticity, the baroque man instead fills up his world with diversions without determinate content or value: "Allegory goes away empty-handed."[23] Benjamin construes the baroque experience taking departure in a modernistic conception of an absent eschatology. It is construed around a patent sense of lack. The way he conveys the "allegorical way of seeing" is thus never liberated from the idea of constitutive negativity.[24] Even though we are denied escape, the eschatological motive is still prominent in the form of an insurmountable absence. We thus get caught up in "the supposed infinity of a world without hope" and "taken up entirely with the hopelessness of the earthly condition."[25] Now, allegory is a "form of experience", an "allegorical way of seeing."[26] By this, we should understand a form in which nature presents itself to our experience. It is the way that we subjectively shape the world that is presented to us, the world as *Darstellung*.[27] Benjamin thus mainly considers the Baroque

---

[20] Benjamin: *Ursprung*, p. 198, transl. p. 178. See also id., p. 150, transl. p. 139: "For those who looked deeper saw the scene of their existence as a rubbish heap of partial, inauthentic actions."
[21] Ibid., p. 182, transl. p. 165.
[22] See Walter Benjamin: "L'œuvre d'art à l'époque de sa reproduction méchanisée", in: *Zeitschrift für Sozialforschung* 5 (1936), pp. 40–68.
[23] Benjamin: *Ursprung*, p. 264, transl. p. 233.
[24] See ibid., p. 56, transl. p. 66: "[T]he Baroque knows no eschatology and for that very reason it has no mechanism by which it gathers all earthly things in together and exalts them before consigning them to their end."
[25] Ibid., p. 264, transl. p. 232, and p. 75, transl. p. 81.
[26] Ibid., p. 183, transl. p. 166.
[27] Ibid., p. 188, transl. p. 170: "From the point of view of the baroque, nature serves the purpose of expressing its meaning [*Ausdruck ihrer Bedeutung*], it is the emblematic representation [*Darstellung*] of its sense, and as an allegorical representation it remains irremediably different from its historical realization."

as a subjective form, in terms of intentionality, insofar as the nature that expresses itself in allegory is presumed to be essentially linked to the expressing subject, as the authentic nature of that subject. For example, in the context of his analysis of evil, Benjamin explains that the "allegorical form" is a "subjective phenomenon": allegories "point to the absolutely subjective pensiveness, to which alone they owe their existence" and they are "related to the depths of the subjective."[28] Benjamin's argument is, as should be evident, governed by the post-Kantian notion idea that self-representation, or what Benjamin describes as the *Sich-Darstellendes*, is the method of truth.[29] But insofar as such "authentic" self-representation seems to elude us permanently, the baroque form of experience corresponds to the expression of unfulfilled subjectivity, lack of self-determination, and a sense of arbitrariness. In this way, writes Benjamin, "the triumph of subjectivity and the onset of an arbitrary rule over things, is the origin of all allegorical contemplation."[30]

* * *

Deleuze's approach to the Baroque can be understood as an attempt to dissociate it from Benjamin's abyssal sense of self-loss and turn the allegory of the world into an affirmation of divine infinity. Leibniz plays an absolutely central role in this attempt, insofar as he formulates the "perspectivist" doctrine that will allow Deleuze to turn the Baroque experience away from the self towards God.

Perspectivism is a doctrine according to which truth is dependent on the viewpoint. Deleuze puts considerable effort into dissociating it from relativism: "Perspectivism does not mean that everyone has his own truths, it means that the viewpoint will be the condition of the manifestation of truth."[31] This is first of all an effort to forestall any notion that the ground of subjective experience is itself subjective. In Benjamin, the world of the baroque *Trauerspiel* is the world as perceived by the subject: mourning is the inner expression of its own constitutive melancholy. Experience is an expression of how

---

[28] Ibid., p. 265, transl. p. 233. Objective truth, on the contrary, is "an intentionless state of being [*intentionsloses Sein*], made up of ideas [...]. Truth is the death of intention [*Wahrheit ist der Tod der Intention*]" (ibid., p. 17, transl. p. 36).
[29] Ibid., p. 10, transl. pp. 28f.
[30] Ibid., p. 265, transl. p. 233.
[31] Deleuze: Lecture on Leibniz, 16.12.1986.

the world is perceived *in* the subject. Similarly, in Leibniz, the world of experience is essentially an inner one, to the extent that all our perceptions are spontaneously produced by ourselves as active substances. As Leibniz puts it in the *Système nouveau*,

> "God originally created the soul [...] in such a way that everything must arise for it from its own depths, through a perfect spontaneity relative to itself."[32]

Like in Benjamin, all experience is essentially an experience of ourselves, of the world that we create for ourselves in perception. In Leibniz, however, this world may very well reflect only our own viewpoint, but, contrary to Benjamin, the viewpoint itself does not originate in us, or it is not an intention. It is a perspective on the world that has been allotted to each of us by God. Leibniz's theory of viewpoints is well-known. Hence, according to Leibniz,

> "every substance represents the whole universe exactly and in its own way, from a certain point of view, and makes the perceptions or expressions of external things occur in the soul at a given time [...]."[33]

All monads express the same infinite world, but they do not express it in the same way, because they do not express it from the same perspective but each from their determinate, individual point of view.[34] According to Deleuze, this "theory of viewpoints introduces what one must indeed call a perspectivism in philosophy."[35] It does, however, involve no relativism or subject-dependence of truth:

> "We call it [i.e. the subject] a view point to the extent that it represents a variation or an inflection. Thus is the foundation of perspectivism. It does not mean some dependence in relation to some given defined subject. On the contrary, the subject is that which comes to the viewpoint, or rather which inhabits the viewpoint."[36]

---

[32] Gottfried Wilhelm Leibniz: *Système nouveau de la nature*, 1695, GP IV, 484, transl. in: G. W. Leibniz: *Philosophical Essays*, ed. and transl. Roger Ariew and Daniel Garber, Indianapolis/Cambridge 1989, p. 143.
[33] Ibid.
[34] Deleuze: *Logique du sens*, p. 133.
[35] Id.: Lecture on Leibniz, 16.12.1986.
[36] Id.: *Le Pli*, p. 27.

This formulation is Deleuze's way of expressing the fact that, in Leibniz, the world is *preestablished*. God first conceives the world he wishes to create in his mind and only subsequently does he create the individual substances or monads that will actualize this world in and through their perceptive activity. As Deleuze already put the point very early, in *Différence et répétition*,

> "the world, as the common term expressed by all the monads, is pre-existent in relation to its expressions [...]. God has not created Adam the sinner, but first the world in which Adam sins."[37]

In other words, since each individual substance takes up a situation in the world that has been assigned to it and that its individual experience of the world is entirely determined by this situation, the individual does not express a subjective intention through its experience, but an objective perspective, i.e. a world or series of events *for which* it was created. Our experience of the world is thus necessarily ordered according to the objective element of divine harmony: subjective expression is "in perfect conformity relative to external things."[38]

In this way, perspectivism is presented as an alternative to the post-Kantian phenomenology that underlies Benjamin's account of the Baroque. To say it very briefly, perspectives replace intentions. This is what is at stake when Deleuze repeatedly insists that the world is *in* the monads, but the monads are *for* the world:

> "There is antecedence [of the world] in relation to the monads, even though a world does not exist outside the monads which express it [...]."[39]

The essence of truth is not *self*-representation, but the representation of the *divine* order that each soul is folded into. Subjects are destined to live in the same world, insofar as they "come to" the world that they each express from their individual perspective, as "a circle of convergence where all the *viewpoints* are distributed."[40] Now, this "distribution" is necessarily harmonious and reflects divine providence. In this way, insofar as it is created to express a world it was made *for*, the subject does not express *lack of self-determination*, but

---

[37] Id.: *Différence et répétition*, p. 68.
[38] Gottfried Wilhelm Leibniz: *Système nouveau de la nature*, 1695, GP IV, 484, transl. in: Leibniz: *Philosophical Essays*, p. 143.
[39] Deleuze: *Le Pli*, p. 81.
[40] Id.: *Différence et répétition*, p. 351.

quite on the contrary the *omnipresence of infinite divine determination*: the soul only expresses the world it was created to express, in perfect harmony with all the other souls.

* * *

We have seen how Deleuze turns the baroque allegory of the world away from the problem of self-representation towards the contemplation of the divine. Let us now move to another, but very closely related, aspect of allegory in both Benjamin's and Deleuze's understanding, namely the way in which it includes infinity or is a "continuous" metaphor as Leibniz put it. For Deleuze, "classical" or pre-Kantian modern thought generally upholds a certain uncomplicated relation to infinity. Deleuze often quotes a text by Maurice Merleau-Ponty where the latter characterizes the philosophers of the classical age by their "innocent way of beginning in the infinite."[41] Indeed, according to Deleuze,

> "classical thought may be recognized by its way of thinking the infinite [...]. The classical thinking is certainly not a serene, dominant thinking: it constantly loses itself in the infinite [...]."[42]

This same innocence with regard to infinity also applies to the Baroque: "The Baroque trait is the fold going to infinity."[43] Indeed, for Deleuze, in this respect, "the Classical and the Baroque are two poles of the same enterprise."[44] The Baroque is thus, in reality, unconcerned by the distinctly modernistic problems of constitutive finite subjectivity that underlies most of Benjamin's reasoning.[45] Along the same lines, Deleuze suggests that Leibniz can provide and anti-dote to a post-Kantian modernity much too preoccupied with finitude:

> "[...] what could it mean to be Leibnizian today? One has to take seriously one of the Kantian revolutions that Kant left aside, notably that the infinite is truly the act of finitude insofar as it overcomes itself. Kant had left that aside because he was content with a reduction of the infinite to the indefinite. To return to a

---

[41] Lecture on Leibniz, 22.04.1980.
[42] Gilles Deleuze: *Foucault*, Paris 1986, p. 131.
[43] Id.: *Le Pli*, p. 5.
[44] Id.: Lecture on Leibniz, 20.05.1980.
[45] Ibid.

strong conception of the infinite, but in the manner of the Classics, one has to show that the infinite is an infinite in the strong sense [...] doing that means returning to Leibniz, but on a basis different from Leibniz's."[46]

One of the central places where Leibniz's philosophy thus "loses itself in the infinite" is in its conception of individuality: "Leibniz will tell us: the individual envelops the infinite."[47] Now, in his efforts to understand the relations between ideas and history, Walter Benjamin already pointed to Leibniz's monadological conception of the individual as a place where the Baroque cosmos and Leibniz's philosophy converge:

> "The idea is the monad. The being that enters into it, with its past and present history, brings [...] an indistinct abbreviation of the rest of the world of ideas, just us [...] every single monad contains, in an indistinct way, all the others. The idea is the monad – the pre-established representation of phenomena resides within it, as in their objective interpretation [...]. The idea is the monad – that means briefly: every idea contains the image of the world."[48]

Benjamin's reading of Leibniz is, of course, somewhat creative.[49] In Leibniz, monads are souls or soul-like substances that *have* ideas, they *are* not ideas.[50] Moreover, the notion of monads "containing" other monads is, at best, puzzling. Nonetheless, one can sense the idea that Benjamin is trying to convey, namely that the representation of ideas in the world has become inextricably entangled in the infinite. Allegory expresses the way in which the subject finds itself submerged in both the infinity of the world and the infinity of itself much in the same way as in Pascal man finds himself suspended helplessly between two infinities. Benjamin speaks of it in terms of "melancholic immersion."[51]

---

[46] Id., Lecture on Leibniz, 22.04.1980.
[47] Deleuze: Lecture on Leibniz, 16.12.1986.
[48] Benjamin: *Ursprung*, p. 32, transl. pp. 47f. (translation modified).
[49] For a deeply insightful study of the contemporary background for Benjamin's reading of Leibniz, see Paula L. Schwebel: "Intensive Infinity: Walter Benjamin's Reception of Leibniz and its Sources", in: *Modern Language Notes* 127/3 (2012), pp. 589–610.
[50] See Gottfried Wilhelm Leibniz: *Ad Ethicam B. D. S.*, 1678, A VI, 4 B, 1713: "Ideae non agunt, mens agit". See also id., J.-G. Wachteri de recondita hebraeorum philosophia, 1709 (?), ed. by Philip Beeley: "Leibniz on Wachter's Elucidarius cabalisticus", in: *The Leibniz Review* 12 (2002), p. 9: "Ani-ma non est idea, sed fons innumerabilium idearum."
[51] See Benjamin: *Ursprung*, p. 264, transl. pp. 232–233: "And this is the essence of melancholy immersion: that its ultimate objects, in which it believes it can most fully secure for itself that which is vile, turn into allegories, and that these allegories fill out and deny the void in which they are represented, just as, ultimately, the intention does not faithfully rest in the contemplation of bones, but faithlessly leaps forward to the idea of resurrection."

In Leibniz, the most striking sign of infinity in the individual soul is the feeling of *uneasiness* that Leibniz describes in the preface of the *Nouveaux essais*, pointing to what Deleuze describes as a "differential unconsciousness" of minute perceptions.[52] According to this theory, following Leibniz's formulation in *Principes de la nature et de la grâce*,

> "each soul knows the infinite – knows all – but confusedly [...]. Confused perceptions are the result of impressions that the whole universe makes upon us."[53]

The notion of uneasiness captures two aspects of how the soul the world presents itself to us in perception. First, on a purely descriptive level, it shows how all souls relate directly to their differential unconscious, their perceptive depths, through a feeling of *dizziness*. As Deleuze writes,

> "dizziness is an example that recurs constantly in Leibniz's work. I get dizzy, I faint, and a flow of minute unconscious perceptions arrives: a buzz in my head."[54]

For example, according to *La Monadologie*,

> "we experience within ourselves a state in which we remember nothing and have no distinct perceptions; this is similar to when we faint or when we are overwhelmed by a deep, dreamless sleep [...] when there is a great multitude of small perceptions in which nothing is distinct, we are stupefied. This is similar to when we continually spin in the same direction several times in succession, from which arises a dizziness that can make us faint and does not allow us to distinguish anything."[55]

Incidentally, Benjamin also stresses dizziness as a distinctly Baroque feeling, even though he formulates the point in a dialectical way by referring it to spiritual contradictions rather than, like Deleuze, to a differential unconscious:

> "That characteristic feeling of dizziness [*Schwindelgefühl*] which is induced by the spectacle of the spiritual contradictions of this epoch is a recurrent feature in the improvised attempts to capture its meaning."[56]

---

[52] On the differential unconscious, see Deleuze: *Différence et répétition*, pp. 214 and 275f. and *Le Pli*, pp. 114–117.
[53] Gottfried Wilhelm Leibniz: *Principes de la nature et de la grâce*, 1714, § 13, GP VI, 604, transl. in: *Philosophical Essays*, p. 211.
[54] Deleuze: Lecture on Leibniz, 29.04.1980.
[55] Gottfried Wilhelm Leibniz: *La Monadologie*, §§ 20–21, GP VI, 610, transl. in: *Philosophical Essays*, pp. 215f. See also Deleuze: *Le Pli*, p. 17.
[56] Benjamin: *Ursprung*, pp. 43f. and p. 56.

Second, on a more normative level, uneasiness can also be construed as a form of *anxiety*. In this respect, it corresponds to the experience of evil: perceptions of apparently unjust events constantly swell up from our perceptive depths and obscure minute appetitions incline us to act in ways that we know are morally reprehensible. And insofar as we do not fully grasp the reasons for these inclinations, insofar as we cannot be retrieve them fully from the obscure infinity of our soul's perceptive life, we come to fear that there are no such reasons. It could thus seem that the theory of uneasiness and minute perceptions is correlated with an experience of self-loss not unlike the one that also underlies Benjamin's image of the Baroque. Leibniz, however, does not proceed at this juncture to complain about the absurdity of the world or the wretchedness of man. In this respect, the allegorical story recounted by Leibniz towards the end of the *Essais de Théodicée* about Sextus Tarquinus complaining to Jupiter about his assigned historical destiny as a wretched rapist.[57] Leibniz's Sextus strongly evokes Benjamin's "melancholy man:"[58] he regrets his lack of self-determination, his incapacity to control his individual inclinations and to seize the deeper principle governing his own actions. However, Leibniz's implied reply to Sextus, which captures the very essence of optimism, is that, instead of regretting the lack of autonomy or self-determination, he should make an affirmation of his state of divine determinedness, not passively, like the quietists, but actively, by living up to what occurs to him, affirming it as divine will.[59] Leibniz calls this disposition the *fatum christianum*:

> "It is as if one said to man: perform your duty and be content with what will happen, and not only because you cannot resist divine providence or the nature of things [...] but also because you are dealing with a good master. And this is what one can call a *fatum christianum.*"[60]

The sense of unfulfilled subjectivity – i.e. our experience of lacking autonomy – must thus serve to make an affirmation of divine providence. This is the lesson that Jupiter will teach Sextus when showing him a vision of all the possible worlds in the form of a pyramid of rooms, where the room at the summit represents the actual, chosen world, where Sextus performs his disgraceful deed for the sake of this best possible world.

---

[57] See Gottfried Wilhelm Leibniz: *Essais de Théodicée*, 1710, §§ 413–417, GP VI, 661–665.
[58] See Benjamin: *Ursprung*, pp. 154f., transl. pp. 142f.
[59] See Gottfried Wilhelm Leibniz: *Discours de métaphysique*, 1686, art. IV, A VI, 4 B, 1535f. transl. in: *Philosophical Essays*, p. 38.
[60] See id.: *Essais de Théodicée*, 1710, Preface, GP VI, 31.

In a sense, then, Leibniz describes the exact same Baroque experience as Benjamin will do later, but he recommends adopting an entirely different moral and emotional attitude towards it. He encourages us to affirm it and embrace it with confidence in divine providence. This leads to the third aspect of uneasiness, after dizziness and anxiety, namely the kind of positive appropriation of the differential unconscious that Leibniz himself describes in terms a "law of delight" (*lex laetitiae*) that applies whenever we grasp order *in* the apparent disorder of our world of experience:

> "[…] the most distinguished masters of composition often mix dissonances with consonances in order to arouse the listener, and pierce him, as it were, so that, anxious about what is to happen, the listener might feel all the more pleasure when order is soon restored […], just as we delight on the spectacle of rope-walkers or sword dancing for their very ability to incite fear, or just as we ourselves laughingly toss children, as if we are about to throw them off […]. Pleasure does not derive from uniformity, for uniformity brings forth disgust and makes us dull, not happy: this very principle is a law of delight [*laetitiae lex*]."[61]

In Leibniz's theory of uneasiness, we find thus an epistemology driven by the pleasure that our general dizziness affords us when we occasionally manage to extract a clear idea from it. But, more importantly, we find a moral psychology concerned with the joy that anxiety can yield when it is finally dispelled. This moral psychology is constructed around the *lex laetitiae* which, then, expresses the nature of Baroque harmony as a "dissonant accord."[62] As opposed to Benjamin's world of mourning, such "delight" is, I think, exactly the promise of what Deleuze describes as the "strange" optimism of Leibnizian philosophy that, for him, heralds the end of melancholy.[63]

---

[61] Gottfried Wilhelm Leibniz: *De rerum originatione radicali*, 1697, GP VII, 307, transl. in: *Philosophical Essays*, p. 153.
[62] Deleuze: *Le Pli*, p. 179.
[63] Ibid., p. 92.

Leibniz' Diskussion mit Baudelot über den Pariser Nautenpfeiler
oder
Wie weit trägt die Sprache als Quelle der Geschichtsschreibung?

Stefan Luckscheiter (Potsdam)

Bekanntlich[1] hegte Leibniz – wie viele seiner Zeitgenossen[2] – die Hoffnung, die Erforschung der Sprachen könne die Herkunft und Verwandtschaft der Völker erhellen und so Aufschluss über diejenigen frühen Zeiten verschaffen, für die schriftliche und archäologische Quellen fehlen. Ich will im Folgenden anhand einiger Aspekte einer Auseinandersetzung, die Leibniz in den Jahren 1711 und 1712 führte,[3] darstellen, wie er diese Theorie von der Sprache als Geschichtsquelle in die Praxis umzusetzen versuchte.

Am 16. März 1711[4] wurde bei Grabungen in Notre Dame von Paris der sogenannte Pariser Nautenpfeiler gefunden,[5] und im April wurden an der Académie Royale des Inscriptions et Médailles zwei Vorträge über dieses gallische Monument aus der ersten Hälfte des ersten Jahrhunderts gehalten: Der

---

[1] Vgl. zum Beispiel G. Bonfante: „A Contribution to the History of Celtology", in: *Celtica*, Vol. III, 1956, S. 17–34, hier S. 25–30; Hans Aarsleff: „The Study and Use of Etymology in Leibniz", in: *Akten des Internationalen Leibniz-Kongresses* (= *Studia Leibnitiana*, Supplementa 3), Wiesbaden 1969, S. 173–189, hier S. 175 und S. 185; Stephan Waldhoff: „Leibniz sprachwissenschaftliche und polyhistorisch-antiquarische Forschungen im Rahmen seines *Opus historicum*. Mit einem Blick auf die *Collectanea Etymologica*", in: Wenchao Li (Hrsg.): *Einheit der Vernunft und Vielfalt der Sprachen. Beiträge zu Leibniz' Sprachforschung und Zeichentheorie* (= *Studia Leibnitiana*, Supplementa 38), Stuttgart 2014, S. 269–311, hier zum Beispiel S. 310.
[2] Wenn Leibniz über die Sprache sagt: „nullum est certius cognationis gentium argumentum" („Brevis Disquisitio, utros incolarum Germaniae citerioris aut Scandicae ex alteris initio profectos verisimilius sit judicandum", in: Joachim Friedrich Feller: *Monumenta varia inedita variisque linguis conscripta*, Trimestre tertium, Jena 1714, S. 132–141, hier S. 134), dann zitiert er damit fast wörtlich William Camden, der geschrieben hatte, die Sprache sei „certissimum originis gentium argumentum" (William Camden: *Britannia*, Frankfurt 1590, S. 16), oder Olivier de Wrée, bei dem es heißt: „Gentium originis nullum certius argumentum est lingua" (Olivier de Wrée: *Historiae comitum Flandriae libri prodromi duo. Quid comes? Quid Flandria?* Bd. 1, Brügge 1650, S. 237); vgl. John Considine: *Dictionaries in Early Modern Europe. Lexicography and the Making of Heritage*, Cambridge u.a. 2008, S. 109; Toon van Hal: „Sprachen, die Geschichte schreiben. Zu Leibniz' sprachhistorischem Forschungsprogramm und dessen Nachwirkung", in: Li (Hrsg.): *Einheit der Vernunft*, S. 177–204, besonders S. 180–182.
[3] Darstellungen dieser Diskussion finden sich auch in Johann Georg Eckharts Vorrede zu Leibniz' *Collectanea etymologica*, Hannover 1717, S. 13–30; Daniel Droixhe: *L'étymon des dieux. Mythologie gauloise, archéologie et linguistique à l'âge classique*, Genf 2002, S. 200–207.
[4] Droixhe: *L'étymon des dieux*, S. 7.
[5] Vgl. *Corpus Inscriptionum Latinarum* XIII, 1,1, 3026.

erste war von Charles-César Baudelot de Dairval, der zweite von Philibert Bernard Moreau de Mautour. Beide Texte erschienen bis August im Druck, und da sie noch im selben Monat im *Journal des sçavants* rezensiert wurden,[6] dürfte Leibniz schon bald über den Fund und den Stand der Diskussion unterrichtet gewesen sein.

Noch vor Oktober erhielt er – über Elisabeth Charlotte von der Pfalz und Sophie – Baudelots Buch,[7] dem ein Stich beilag, den er (oder sein postumer Herausgeber Johann Georg Eckhart) später für die *Collectanea etymologica* nachbilden lassen sollte[8] und auf dem die in den Pfeiler gehauenen Inschriften und Basreliefs abgebildet waren, die – neben Jupiter, Vulcanus und anderen römischen Gottheiten – unbekannte Gestalten zeigen wie zum Beispiel „Tarvos trigaranus": einen Stier, auf dem drei Kraniche sitzen,[9] und eine männliche Gestalt mit Hörnern: „Cernunnos".[10]

1. Cernunnos

Baudelot hatte versucht, diesen Götternamen mit Hilfe des zeitgenössischen Bretonischen zu deuten, das – wie schon damals bekannt war[11] – der Sprache der antiken Gallier nahe stand. Er war der Ansicht, „Cernunnos" sei aus zwei Wörtern zusammengesetzt, nämlich aus „cer" und aus „nunnos", wobei das

---

[6] Charles-César Baudelot de Dairval: *Description des bas-reliefs anciens trouvez depuis peu dans l'Eglise Cathedrale de Paris*, Paris 1711 (Rezension in: *Journal des sçavants*, 24. August 1711, S. 529–534); Philibert Bernard Moreau de Mautour: *Observations sur des monuments d'antiquité trouvez dans l'Eglise Cathedrale de Paris*, Paris 1711 (Rezension in: *Journal des sçavants*, 17. August 1711, S. 513–518). Baudelot hatte seinen Vortrag am 4. April gehalten, Moreau einige Tage später (vgl. *Journal des sçavants*, 17. August 1711, S. 513).
[7] Vgl. *Collectanea etymologica*, pars I, S. 7f.
[8] Vgl. Eckharts Vorrede zu den *Collectanea etymologica*, S. 13; in den meisten Exemplaren der *Collectanea* fehlt dieser Stich; eine entsprechende Abbildung liegt Eckharts *De origine Germanorum*, Göttingen 1750, bei.
[9] Vgl. den Eintrag „Tarw" im „Glossarii Celtici specimen" (*Collectanea etymologica*, pars I, S. 81–146, hier S. 142).
[10] Moderne Deutungen dieses Gottes finden sich zum Beispiel in: Helmut Birkhan: *Kelten. Versuch einer Gesamtdarstellung ihrer Kultur*, Wien ²1997, S. 694–701; Michael Altjohann: „Cernunnos-Darstellungen in den gallischen und germanischen Provinzen", in: Peter Noelke (Hrsg.): *Romanisation und Resistenz in Plastik, Architektur und Inschriften der Provinzen des Imperium Romanum. Neue Funde und Forschungen*, Mainz 2003, S. 67–80.
[11] Vgl. etwa Bertrand d'Argentré: *L'histoire de Bretagne*, Paris 1588, Bl. 26ʳ; Julien Maunoir: *Le sacré college de Jusus divisé en cinq classes*, Quimper 1659, S. 10 und S. 13–16; Daniel Droixhe: *La linguistique et l'appel de l'histoire (1600–1800)*, Genf 1978, S. 128.

eine „Land" oder „gut" bedeute, das andere „Herr" oder „Vater". „Cernunnos" sei also zu übersetzen als „guter Vater" oder „Herr des Landes". Daraus und aus den Hörnern des Gottes folgerte Baudelot, Cernunnos[12] müsse Pan sein.[13] Er hatte auch darauf hingewiesen, dass „Cern" „Horn" bedeute, meinte aber, dieses Wort könne nicht Element des Namens sein, denn dann wäre das zweite Element „unnos" und ein solches Wort gebe es nicht. Moreau dagegen hatte (wie auch der Rezensent des *Journal des sçavants* referierte) den Namen schlicht mit „der Gehörnte" übersetzt und geschrieben, es sei möglicherweise ein Gott der Seine.[14]

Obwohl Leibniz beide Deutungen gekannt haben dürfte, erwähnte er sie nicht in seinem Schreiben an Sophie vom 1. Oktober 1711,[15] mit dem er auf die Übersendung von Baudelots Buch reagierte. Er behauptete vielmehr, Cernunnos sei offenkundig Bacchus. Das erste Argument für diese *interpretatio Romana* fand er darin, dass auch Bacchus Hörner zugeschrieben worden seien; das zweite – mit dem er sich für die Übersetzung als „der Gehörnte" entschied – in dem alten süddeutschen Namen des Februars „Hornung":

„Ce nom du mois venoit apparemment de l'usage des Celtes, qui se reposant en hyver, jouissoient alors de leurs travaux, et beuvant plus qu'à l'ordinaire, faisoient honneur à Bacchus, et celebroient sa fête."[16]

Die „Kelten", so meint er also, dürften den Februar dem Bacchus geweiht haben, und da dieser Monat auch „Hornung" hieß, sei davon auszugehen, dass Cernunnos, der „Gehörnte", kein anderer als eben Bacchus war.

Dieselbe Ansicht findet sich in dem erst 1717 in den *Collectanea etymologica* publizierten *Glossarii Celtici specimen*, das aus Auszügen aus Marcus

---

[12] Bei dem Bild handelt es sich um einen Ausschnitt aus der Tafel XII zu § 57 in: Johann Georg Eckhart: *De origine Germanorum*, Göttingen 1750, S. 124.
[13] Baudelot de Dairval: *Description des bas-reliefs anciens*, S. 34–37.
[14] *Journal des sçavants*, 17. August 1711, S. 518.
[15] Die Abfertigung befindet sich in: Paris *Bibliotheque Nationale de France* NAF 22082 Bl. 47–50; zuerst gedruckt wurde der Brief in *Collectanea etymologica*, pars I, S. 75–81.
[16] *Collectanea etymologica*, pars I, S. 80.

Zuërius Boxhorns *Antiquae linguae Britannicae lexicon Britannico-Latinum*[17] und (als solchen nicht kenntlich gemachten) Ergänzungen und Bemerkungen von Leibniz besteht.[18] Es heißt dort unter dem Lemma „CERN, cornu" unter anderem: „Kernunnos (Hornung) Celtis, Deus cornutus, Bacchus."[19]

Sophie leitete Leibniz' Brief an Elisabeth Charlotte weiter und diese gab ihn Baudelot, der seinerseits mit einer weiteren Denkschrift antwortete. In dieser Auseinandersetzung, in der insgesamt sechs Denkschriften ausgetauscht werden sollten, stellte Baudelot unter anderem Leibniz' Deutung des „Cernunnos" stark in Frage.

In seiner ersten Denkschrift, der „Reponse à quelques remarques de Monsieur Leibniz sur la description des monuments trouvéz en 1711. dans Nostre Dame,"[20] schrieb Baudelot, der Gott könne keinesfalls Bacchus sein, denn erstens sehe er mit seinen Hörnern und dem Bart nicht so aus; zweitens sei durch Caesar bezeugt, dass die Gallier es damals ablehnten, Wein zu trinken, und keinen Wein anbauten;[21] und drittens verehrten sie, wieder laut Caesar,[22] nur Pluto, Merkur, Apollo, Mars, Jupiter und Minerva.

Leibniz' Erklärung des Namens „Hornung" hingegen gefiel auch Baudelot. Er versuchte aber, sie zu seinen Gunsten zu wenden: Die Römer hätten nicht das Fest des Bacchus, so sagt er, wohl aber das des Pan im Februar gefeiert, und dementsprechend sei zu vermuten, dass der Name „Hornung" von diesem Gott herkomme. Indem er dies als weiteres Argument dafür verwendete, Cernunnos sei Pan, schloss er sich stillschweigend der Übersetzung dieses Namens als „der Gehörnte" an.

---

[17] Mit eigener Paginierung in: Marcus Zuërius van Boxhorn: *Originum Gallicarum liber*, Amsterdam 1654. Boxhorns *Lexicon* wiederum beruht auf John Davies' *Dictionarium duplex*, London 1632.
[18] In den Eintrag zu „Cern" hat Leibniz aus seiner Vorlage nur die Information übernommen, dass „corn" auch bei den Bretonen „Horn" bedeute, denn bei Boxhorn steht nur: „Corn: cornu, sic Arm[oricis]" (Boxhorn: *Antiquae linguae Britannicae lexicon Britannico-Latinum*, S. 18). Leibniz hat also auch – in Übereinstimmung mit der Inschrift des Nautenpfeilers und mit dem von Baudelot zitierten, aber als Element von „Cernunnos" nicht anerkannten Wort – aus Boxhorns „corn" „cern" gemacht.
[19] *Collectanea etymologica*, pars I, S. 81–146, hier S. 104; vgl. auch Leibniz' Schreiben an Gisbert Cuper vom 15. September 1711 (in den Transkriptionen zur Akademieausgabe, Reihe I, 1711, S. 255 [http://www.gwlb.de/Leibniz/Leibnizarchiv/Veroeffentlichungen/ Transkriptionen1711.pdf, eingesehen im September 2016]) und vom 30. Dezember 1711 (LBr 187 Bl. 161, hier Bl. 161ᵛ).
[20] Hannover *GWLB* LK – MOW Baudelot 10 (ehemals LBr 36) Bl. 13–24; die Ausführungen über Cernunnos auf Bl. 23–24.
[21] Caesar: *De bello Gallico*, II,15.
[22] Ebd., VI, 17.

In seiner Entgegnung gab Leibniz (anstatt darauf aufmerksam zu machen, dass Pan auf Caesars Götterliste genauso wenig auftaucht wie Bacchus) Baudelot zu bedenken, dass auf Caesar offensichtlich kein Verlass sei, denn die übrigen Inschriften des Nautenpfeilers zeigten ja, dass die Gallier auch andere Gottheiten verehrten. Er lobte Baudelots Hinweis darauf, dass die Gallier damals noch keinen Wein anbauten, als gewichtigen Einwand, fügte allerdings hinzu, die Reichen könnten dennoch Wein getrunken und die einfachen Leute Bacchus unter Zuhilfenahme von Bier geehrt haben. Da er auch Baudelots Hinweis, dass das Fest des Pan im Februar gefeiert wurde, als triftiges Argument anerkannte, schrieb er abschließend (und nachdem er unter anderem auch Gisbert Cuper um seine Meinung gebeten hatte): [23]

> „Je ne decideray point absolument si Kernunnos ou Hornung Dieu des Gaulois et des Germains, a eté Bacchus, ou Pan, ou un melange des deux (comme Hecate etoit un melange de la Lune de Diane et de Proserpine) ou s'il a eté selon le soubçon de l'illustre M. Cuper, quelque dieu des chasseurs ou autre divinité inconnue; [24] car il y a de l'apparence que les divinités Celtiques avoient quelque rapport à celles des Grecs, et des Latins, mais qui n'etoit pas tousjours exact [...]."[25]

Nach der Diskussion mit Baudelot war sich Leibniz also nicht mehr so sicher, dass Cernunnos Bacchus sein müsse, wie zuvor. Dass dies im *Glossarii Celtici specimen* dennoch wie eine unbezweifelbare Tatsache behauptet wird, mag daran liegen, dass sich die *Collectanea* während der Auseinandersetzung mit Baudelot, die sich bis in den Sommer 1712 erstreckte, schon im Druck befanden.[26]

---

[23] Vgl. Leibniz' Schreiben vom 30. Dezember 1711 (LBr 187 Bl. 161).
[24] Gisbert Cuper hatte am 1. März 1712 geschrieben: „Cum autem cornua ramosa sint, suspicabar nonnunquam cervi cornua nobis representari, et ita potuisse hunc deum a Celtis illorum animalium venationi fuisse praepositum, et referri debere inter deos montium et nemorum." (LBr 187 Bl. 164–169, hier Bl. 166ʳ.)
[25] Paris *Bibliotheque Nationale de France* NAF 22082 Bl. 61–62, hier Bl. 62.
[26] Leibniz schrieb am 8. April 1712 an Gisbert Cuper: „Excuduntur nunc quaedam mea ad rem etymologicam, sed maxime Germanicam, pertinentia, sub nomine Apparatus." (Christoph Gottlieb von Murr: *Neues Journal zur Litteratur und Kunstgeschichte*, 1. Theil, Leipzig 1798, S. 317; den Titel „Apparatus" nennt auch der Katalog der Leipziger Herbstmesse: „Specimen apparatus ad Etymologicam praesertim Teutonicam" [*Catalogus universalis*, 1711 Herbst, Bl. Gᵛ]). Dementsprechend schrieb Eckhart 1717, Leibniz habe das Werk noch selbst zum Druck gegeben, aber die Wienreise (ab Ende 1712) und anderes hätten das Erscheinen verzögert (*Collectanea etymologica*, Vorrede, S. 5f.); und in einem Brief, der nicht nach 1714 entstanden sein kann, heißt es, das Werk sei bereits vor zwei Jahren gedruckt worden (Hannover *GWLB* LBr 411 Bl. 387, zitiert nach Waldhoff: „Leibniz' sprachwissenschaftliche", S. 300f. mit Fn. 151

Baudelot dagegen war bis zuletzt der Überzeugung, dass Cernunnos Pan sei. Sein Resümee der Debatte lautet:[27]

> „La teste cornue de nos monuments n'étant pas d'un Bacchus ne pouvoit estre par consequent que d'un Dieu connu dans le pays, et dont le culte fut en quelque façon conforme aux moeurs des peuples où l'on en trouve la figure. Pan étoit le Dieu des bois, de la chasse, du menage de campagne, toutes choses qui conviennent à la maniere de vivre des anciens Gaulois. L'air de teste enfin, tel qu'on le remarque dans nos bas-reliefs, est du consentement de tous les anciens celuy du Dieu Pan, je l'ay démontré [...]."

Leibniz und Baudelot hatten bei ihrem Versuch, etwas über den unbekannten Gott zu erfahren, keine andere Wahl, als ihn mit den bekannten römischen Gottheiten zu vergleichen, denn gallische Quellen gab es nicht. Ihr Wille, die Identität des Gottes trotz dieses Mangels zu ermitteln, verführte sie allerdings zu einer Unterstellung, die diesen Vergleich erst sinnvoll machte: Nämlich die Ansicht, die römischen und gallischen Götter seien entweder dieselben gewesen oder hätten zumindest in enger Beziehung miteinander gestanden – eine Ansicht, die Leibniz allerdings (nach Rücksprache mit Cuper und nach den Einwänden Baudelots) mit der Erwägung, Cernunnos könnte auch ein ganz unbekannter Gott gewesen sein, vorsichtig relativierte.

Auch bei der Interpretation des Namens „Cernunnos" zog Leibniz, weil Quellen aus dem näheren kulturellen Umkreis des Nautenpfeilers fehlten, Vergleichsmaterial aus einem sehr weiten Umkreis heran: das Wort „cern" oder „corn" aus der Bretagne, Wales oder Cornwall und das Wort „Hornung" aus Süddeutschland. Er wusste, dass Ähnlichkeiten zwischen Wörtern aus

---

und 153). Tatsächlich besteht die Ausgabe von 1717 zum Großteil aus schon zu Leibniz' Lebzeiten gedruckten Partien. Das geht aus dem unter der Signatur Leibn. Marg. 10 in der Hannoveraner *GWLB* aufbewahrten Buch hervor: ein Exemplar der *Collectanea*, in dem zwar Titelblatt, Stiche, die „Unvorgreifflichen Gedancken, betreffend die Ausübung und Verbesserung der Teutschen Sprache" und Eckharts Vorrede fehlen, das aber eigenhändige Marginalien von Leibniz enthält und nicht nur denselben Zeilenfall und Seitenumbruch aufweist wie der 1717 von Eckhart herausgegebene Druck, sondern auch dieselben Druckfehler. Auf S. 66 in pars I fehlt auch hier wie bei den meisten von mir eingesehenen Exemplaren die Seitenzahl (die aber im Exemplar der Staatsbibliothek Berlin mit der Signatur V 5250a vorhanden ist). Dieses Exemplar zeigt auch, auf welchem Stand Leibniz die Arbeit an seinem Werk abbrach: Er hat darin einige wenige Korrekturen (wohl für eine Corrigenda-Liste), vor allem aber Stichpunkte für ein noch zu erstellendes Register eingetragen. Eckhart hat dem 1717 wahrscheinlich schon fünf Jahre alten Druck also nur die genannten Stücke hinzugefügt; auf ein Register hat er verzichtet.

[27] Paris *Bibliotheque Nationale de France* NAF 22082 Bl. 57–60, hier Bl. 59r.

Sprachen, die zu weit voneinander entfernt sind, nicht aussagekräftig sind.[28] Aber seiner Ansicht nach war das zeitgenössische Keltisch nicht nur mit dem antiken Gallischen verwandt, sondern auch mit dem Deutschen.[29] Er schrieb in seiner Entgegnung auf Baudelots „Reponse", die keltischen Sprachen und das Deutsche „s'approchent fort, et ont un grand nombre de mots communs"; man könne sogar davon ausgehen, dass sie sich früher noch näherstanden und dass die Sprache der Gallier und die der Germanen zunächst nur zwei Dialekte ein und derselben Sprache (des „Keltischen" nämlich[30]) gewesen seien.[31] Auch Baudelot war dieser Ansicht,[32] die im Übrigen nicht neu war.[33]

2. Stammbäume und Wanderungen

In einer anderen Frage aber, für die sich beide sehr interessierten, konnten sie sich nicht einig werden: Stammten die Gallier von den Germanen ab oder waren vielmehr die Germanen Nachfahren der Gallier? Da sich beide Gelehrte offensichtlich einen Prestigegewinn für ihre eigene Nation von einer Verlängerung deren Stammbaums in die Vergangenheit hinein erhofften, vertraten sie jeweils die Meinung, die ihrem eigenen Land die Priorität einräumte. Da

---

[28] Vgl. G. W. Leibniz, *Nouveaux Essais*, liv. III, chap. 2, § 1;A VI, 6, 285, Z. 12–17; vgl. auch Aarsleff: „The Study and Use of Etymology in Leibniz", S. 185f.
[29] Diese These von der frühen nahen Verwandtschaft des Germanischen und des Keltischen ermöglicht auch erst das Vorhaben, das Leibniz mit dem „Glossarii Celtici specimen" verfolgte, in dem er versuchte, durch einen Vergleich deutscher Ausdrücke mit den von Boxhorn angeführten kymrischen oder bretonischen Wörtern die Wurzeln der deutschen Wörter zu finden: „Unde multae se aperiunt Origines, alias futurae ignotae, dum passim radices aut harum indices voces Celticae, apud Teutonicas gentes amissae aut obscuratae, apud Gallorum veterum reliquias, Cambros vel ut ipsi se vocant Cumros (haud scio an non Cimbros) id est Walliae et Cornu Walliae habitatores; et apud Aremoricos Britanniae minoris incolas conservatae sunt, extantioresque conspiciuntur." (*Collectanea etymologica*, pars I, S. 81f.)
[30] Vgl. Gottfried Wilhelm Leibniz: *Nouveaux Essais*, liv. III, chap. 2, § 1 (A VI, 6, 280, Z. 15–20).
[31] Paris *Bibliotheque Nationale de France* NAF 22082 Bl. 51–56, hier Bl. 52ʳ.
[32] „Reponse au 2.e ecrit de M.r Leibniz" (Hannover *GWLB* LK – MOW Baudelot 10 [ehemals LBr 36] Bl. 25–36, hier Bl. 28ᵛ).
[33] Vgl. zum Beispiel Wolfgang Lazius: *De gentium aliquot migrationibus, sedibus fixis, reliquiis, linguarumque initiis et immutationibus ac dialectis, libri XII*, Frankfurt 1600, S. 130; Philipp Clüver: *De Germania antiqua libri tres*, Leiden 1631, S. 39–43; Daniel Georg Morhof: *Unterricht von der Teutschen Sprache und Poesie*, Kiel 1682, S. 31; Droixhe: *La linguistique et l'appel de l'histoire*, S. 126–142; Toon van Hal: „From Alauda to Zythus. The Emergence and Uses of Old-Gaulish Word Lists in Early Modern Publications", in: *Keltische Forschungen* 6 (2013–14), S. 219–277, hier insbesondere S. 265.

es aber unmöglich war, die Entwicklung beider Sprachen über einen langen Zeitraum lange vor Christi Geburt nachzuverfolgen, und da auch andere Quellen fehlten, agierten beide Gelehrte hier in völligem Dunkel; und nur ihrem nationalen Interesse dürfte es zu verdanken sein, dass sie ihre Positionen dennoch mit großem Nachdruck verteidigten.

In seinem Brief an Sophie hatte Leibniz geschrieben:[34]

> „Il y a plus d'apparence, que la langue et la nation Gauloise soient venues des Germains; si nous admettons que les peuples d'Europe sont venus de l'Orient, et si nous considerons, que les plus anciennes migrations ont été faites par terre, les hommes ayant sû marcher, avant qu'ils ont appris à naviger."

Man kann Leibniz vielleicht zugestehen, die Völker, die in der Antike im heutigen Frankreich lebten, oder ihre (wie weit auch immer entfernten) Vorfahren seien dorthin über Deutschland gekommen; aber daraus zu folgern, die damaligen Bewohner Frankreichs stammten von den damaligen Bewohnern Deutschlands ab, bleibt gewagt. Denn selbst wenn man Leibniz des Weiteren zugestehen wollte, dass Europa in schöner Gleichmäßigkeit von Osten nach Westen besiedelt wurde, gäbe es noch zwei Möglichkeiten: Entweder haben die Völker sich gewissermaßen mittels Ausläufern ausgebreitet, indem sie Länder besiedelten, die etwas weiter westlich lagen als ihre Herkunftsorte und von dort aus dann nach einiger Zeit Siedlungen noch weiter nach Westen sandten. Oder sie sind – Wellen gleich – nacheinander aus dem Osten gekommen und die jeweils nachrückenden drängten die schon früher angekommenen weiter nach Westen. Verlief die Besiedlung dem ersten Typ gemäß, so sind die weiter westlich lebenden Völker die jüngeren, verlief sie dem zweiten Typ gemäß, so müssen sie im Gegenteil die älteren sein.

Zur Zeit der Auseinandersetzung mit Baudelot vertrat Leibniz eine Kombination beider Vorstellungen. Er schrieb, die Sprache der Gallier hätte sich von der der Germanen entfernt, denn

> „le mêlage de quelque autre peuple, qui habitoit peutêtre dans les Gaules, avant que les peuples Germaniques y sont entré; a fait la difference."[35]

---

[34] *Collectanea etymologica*, pars I, S. 76 f.
[35] Paris *Bibliotheque Nationale de France* NAF 22082 Bl. 51–56, hier Bl. 52.

Er geht also offenbar davon aus, dass Frankreich zunächst von einem unbekannten Volksstamm (nämlich, so seine Vermutung, den Vorfahren der Basken[36]), der schon sehr früh aus dem Osten gekommen war, besiedelt worden sei, dass die gemeinsamen Vorfahren der Germanen und Gallier später zunächst Deutschland besiedelten und dass einige von ihnen wieder später von dort aus als Kolonisten nach Frankreich vordrangen, wo sie sich mit den früheren Einwohnern vermischten und so zu den Galliern wurden.

    Einen Grund dafür, warum er beide Modelle ausgerechnet in dieser Weise kombiniert, gibt er nicht an. Zwar wäre wohl die Behauptung, die Basken stammten (als deren Ausläufer) von den Galliern ab, der offenkundigen Fremdheit des Baskischen wegen schwer zu vertreten. Angesichts des völligen Fehlens von Beweismaterial hätte sich aber auch durchgängig das Wellen-Modell anwenden und die Ansicht vertreten lassen, die am weitesten im Westen lebenden Basken seien die ältesten Bewohner Europas, die etwas weiter östlich lebenden Gallier seien etwas jünger und die am weitesten östlich lebenden Germanen am jüngsten. Tatsächlich war Leibniz selbst noch einige Jahre früher dieser Meinung gewesen.[37]

---

[36] „J'entends les Gaulois Belgiques et Celtiques, et j'excepte les Aquitains, dont selon Strabon l'origine etoit toute differente, et commune avec les Espagnols: ce qui me fait conjecturer qu'ils habitoient dans les Gaules avant l'irruption des Celtes venus de la Germanie: et que la langue Basque ou Vasconne si differente de la Gauloise est un reste de celle de ces peuples, comme la Bretonne des bas Bretons est un reste de la Gauloise." (Paris *Bibliotheque Nationale de France* NAF 22082 Bl. 61–62, hier Bl. 62r.)

[37] 1692 hatte er geschrieben: „La Germanie et particulierement nostre pays proche de l'ocean a esté habité par les Cimmeriens avant les Germains. Les Cimmeriens, Gaulois, Galates ou Celtes estoient à peu pres un meme peuple et remplissoient les pays depuis le milieu de l'Allemagne jusqu'au delà des Pirenees. Il est voicy qu'ils avoient beaucoup de ressemblance avec les Germains à l'egard de la langue aussi bien que des moeurs. Les Cimmeriens habitoient proche de la mer noire lors que les Germains estoient encor plus reculés vers le Levant, et il est à croire que la cognation extraordinaire qu'il y a entre la langue Allemande et la Persienne vient de ces temps eloignés. Les Cimmeriens pressés par les Germains allerent dans ces pays occidentaux jusqu'au oceans Britannique; et furent tousjours talonnés de ces mêmes Germains qui ont esté suivis à leur tour depuis par les Huns et par les Wendes ou Sarmates, et ceuxcy encor plus recemment par les Tartares, derniers habitans de la mer noire, dont les Cimmeriens ou Cimbres sont sortis les premiers qu'on sçache." (Hannover *GWLB* Ms XII 713q 1 Bl. 141–143, hier Bl. 141ʳ; die Datierung dieser Notiz ergibt sich daraus, dass auf denselben Blättern auch eine Vorarbeit zur „Histoire de Bronsvic" [Gottfried Wilhelm Leibniz: *Schriften und Briefe zur Geschichte*, hrsg. v. Malte-Ludolf Babin u. Gerd van den Heuvel, Hannover 2004, Nr. 50, S. 838–874] zu findet ist.) Und in einer anderen Notiz sagt er, folgende Völker seien nacheinander aus Skythien nach Europa eingewandert: „Celtae, Cimmerii, Germani, Slavini, Hunni, Avares, Hungari, Bulg.[,] Cumani […], Tartari. Ex his Celtae, Cimmerii, Germani, Sclavini, Sarmatae nostras terras attigere, imo et Hunni" („Notitia rerum terrae Brunsvicensis et Estensis antequam

Seine Argumentation hat aber vor allem den Schwachpunkt, dass sie sich durch die bloße Weigerung, von einem zwar rationalen, aber eben ohne empirische Belege konstruierten Modell auf die Wirklichkeit zu schließen, zurückweisen lässt. Es fiel Baudelot denn auch nicht schwer, sie durch den schlichten Hinweis darauf zu entkräften, dass die Völker auf dem Kontinent oft hin und her gewandert sein können.[38]

3. Tuisto, Namensgeber der Deutschen und Stammvater der Gallier

Nach diesem Misserfolg brachte Leibniz ein weiteres Argument ins Spiel,[39] das von Caesar überlieferte Zeugnis der Gallier selbst: „Galli se omnes ab Dite patre prognatos praedicant idque ab druidibus proditum dicunt."[40] In Wahrheit, so Leibniz, haben die Gallier hier freilich nicht Dis pater[41] gemeint, sondern einen Tuisto, der nach Tacitus ein Heroe oder Gott der Germanen war.[42] Da er außerdem der Namensgeber der „Teutschen" sei,[43] dürfe aus den beiden Zitaten geschlossen werden, dass die Gallier der Ansicht waren, von den Germanen abzustammen.

Romani in Germaniam intrarunt"; *GWLB* Ms XXIII 181, 2, 1b Bl. 26–27; gedr. in: Stefan Luckscheiter: „Leibniz' Schriften zur Sprachforschung", in: Li [Hrsg.]: *Einheit der Vernunft*, S. 317–432, hier S. 412). Vgl. auch James William Johnson: „The Scythian: His Rise and Fall", in: Journal of the History of Ideas Vol. XX, (April 1959), S. 250–257; Colin Kidd: *British Identities Before Nationalism*, Cambridge 1999, S. 189.
[38] „Combien de peuples ont esté chassez par d'autres, et combien y a t-il eu de colonies differentes de nations, et de langues, pour ainsy dire, apres les premiers établissements, et à la place des anciens peuples." („Reponse à quelques remarques de Monsieur Leibniz sur la description des monuments trouvez en 1711. dans Nostre Dame"; Hannover *GWLB* LK – MOW Baudelot 10 [ehemals LBr 36] Bl. 13–24, hier Bl. 15ᵛ.)
[39] Paris *Bibliotheque Nationale de France* NAF 22082 Bl. 51–56, hier Bl. 53.
[40] Caesar: *De bello Gallico*, VI,18.
[41] Ein anderer Name für Pluto.
[42] „Celebrant carminibus antiquis [...] Tuistonem deum terra editum" (Tacitus, *Germania*, 2).
[43] Auch im „Glossarii Celtici specimen" heißt es: „Teutates, Deus quidam apud Celtas, teste Lucano. Videtur esse idem cum Tuiscone vel Theodone, a quo dicti Theotisci, Tudesci." (*Collectanea etymologica*, pars I, S. 143.)

Diese Argumentation stammte nicht von Leibniz selbst, sondern von Otto Sperling (den er Baudelot gegenüber allerdings mit keinem Wort erwähnte[44]), und sie war schon über zehn Jahre alt.[45] Aber auch damit hatte Leibniz keinen Erfolg: Baudelot war zwar gern bereit, anzuerkennen, dass Caesar sich geirrt habe und dass die Gallier in Wahrheit der Ansicht waren, von Tuisto abzustammen; sogar dass derselbe der Namensgeber der Deutschen sei, gab er zu. Aber er hielt Leibniz entgegen, Tuisto sei schon viel früher ein Gott der Gallier gewesen. Die Gallier stammten also keineswegs von Tuisto und den Deutschen ab, sondern hatten vielmehr den Tuisto-Kult erst nach Deutschland gebracht.[46]

Leibniz hatte dem nichts entgegenzusetzen außer der recht defensiven Frage:[47]

> „Tuiscon (appellé Teutates par Lucain) est un Heros Germanique selon Tacite; et les Germains ont gardé de luy jusqu'à nos jours leur nom propre Teutsche, que jamais autre nation n'a porté. Or M. Baudelot soûscrit à ma conjecture, que les Gaulois chez Cesar se disant descendus à Dite patre, vouloient dire qu'ils etoient descendus de ce Tiet, Teut, Teutates ou Tuiscon: n'avois je donc point sujet d'inferer des expressions de ces deux grands auteurs que les Gaulois se croyoient descendus des Teutons ou Germains?"

Baudelot dagegen erklärte:[48]

> „A l'egard de Tuiscon qui de la confession de Mr. Leibniz est le méme que Teutates, il n'y a pas d'appar[ence] d'en faire un Heros purement Germain, quoyque [les] peuples de cette nation ayent conservé jusqu'à present [le] nom Teutch, aprez avoir prouvé comme j'ay fait que les Germains l'avoient eu des Celtes leurs auteurs. Si donc je souscris à la remarque de Mr. Leibniz sur [l'en]droit de Cesar, dont il releve la meprise, cela ne justifie aucunement que les Celtes proprements dits soient desse[ndus] des Germains, puisque c'est le contraire[.] Je n'en diray [pas] davantage, j'ay ce me semble donné dans mes 2

---

[44] Auch in seinem Schreiben an Gisbert Cuper vom 30. Dezember 1711 führt er diese Argumentation aus, ohne auf Sperling zu verweisen (LBr 187 Bl. 161).
[45] Otto Sperling: „De origine veterum Gallorum a Dite", in: *Nova literaria maris Balthici et Septentrionis*, Juni 1699, S. 174–181. Leibniz hatte auf diesen Text mit einigen kritischen, vor allem aber lobenden Bemerkungen reagiert („G. G. L. ad Dnn. collectores Novorum literariorum maris Balthici", in: *Nova literaria maris Balthici et Septentrionis*, August 1699, S. 245–248).
[46] „Reponse au 2.ᵉ ecrit de M.ʳ Leibniz" (Hannover *GWLB* LK – MOW Baudelot 10 (ehemals LBr 36) Bl. 25-36, hier Bl. 30ᵛ).
[47] Paris *Bibliotheque Nationale de France* NAF 22082 Bl. 61–62, hier Bl. 61ᵛ – Bl. 62ʳ.
[48] „Reponse sommaire au 3ᵉ escrit de Mʳ Leibniz au sujet des Bas-reliefs de N. D." (Paris *Bibliotheque Nationale de France* NAF 22082 Bl. 57–60, hier Bl. 57ᵛ – Bl. 58ʳ).

reponses une preuve complete de la verité de mon sentiment, et je m'étonne comment Mr. Leibniz aussy plein de raison que de lumiere revient à la charge sur ce sujet avec aussy peu de fondement[.]"

4. Resümee

In der Vorrede zu den *Collectanea Etymologica* schrieb Eckhart über Leibniz' Diskussion mit Baudelot:

„[…] sed cum ostenderet, se in antiquitatibus Celticis non adeo esse versatum, et ad aliena dilaberetur, Leibnitius, melioribus occupatus, disputationem abrupit."[49]

Auch Baudelot war der Ansicht, sich in den keltischen Altertümern besser auszukennen als Leibniz: In einem die Debatte abschließenden Text, der nur für Elisabeth Charlotte bestimmt gewesen und Leibniz nicht erreicht haben dürfte, schrieb er:[50]

„Aprez les éclaircissements que j'ay donné sur cette matiere et les reponses precises à quelques unes de ses propositions un peu trop hazardées, comme on l'a veu, j'ay lieu de croire que l'avantage de la dispute me demeure […]."

Tatsächlich stammt nichts von dem, was an Richtigem oder jedenfalls Wahrscheinlichem aus dieser Debatte hier referiert wurde, von Leibniz: weder die Deutung von „Cernunnos" mit Hilfe des Wortes „cern", noch die Erkenntnis, dass das Bretonische als keltische Sprache eng mit dem alten Gallischen verwandt ist. Alles hingegen, was Leibniz selbst beigesteuert hat, erwies sich als irrig oder wurde jedenfalls von der späteren Forschung nicht mehr ernsthaft in Betracht gezogen: Cernunnos ist nicht Bacchus, „Hornung" hat mit dem gehörnten Gott nichts zu tun, und Europa wurde nicht gleichmäßig von Ost nach West besiedelt.[51]

Wer ihm jedoch den Versuch zu verzeihen bereit ist, sich mit den Federn Sperlings, der ausschließlich mit der freien Assoziation von Eigennamen

---

[49] *Collectanea etymologica*, Vorrede, S. 14.
[50] „Reponse sommaire au 3ᵉ escrit de Mʳ Leibniz au sujet des Bas-reliefs de N. D." (Paris *Bibliotheque Nationale de France* NAF 22082 Bl. 57–60, hier Bl. 57ʳ).
[51] Natürlich dürften auch die meisten Thesen Baudelots nicht haltbar sein.

operierte, zu schmücken, wird, denke ich, dennoch sagen müssen, dass Leibniz Baudelot intellektuell überlegen war. Denn nicht nur zog er als der bessere Quellenkritiker zum Beispiel wenigstens die Möglichkeit in Betracht, Cernunnos könnte ein allein den Galliern eigener Gott gewesen sein – und alle Spekulation über seine Identität mit römischen Göttern hinfällig;[52] als der größere Empiriker stützte er auch die These von der Verwandtschaft des Keltischen und Germanischen mit einem im *Glossarii Celtici specimen* dokumentierten, umfassenden Vergleich beider Sprachen, während Baudelot sich nur auf ältere Literatur berief.[53]

Des Weiteren erfand er als bedeutender Philosoph ein bemerkenswerte Art, sich aus der Verlegenheit zu helfen, dass es schlicht keine Quellen gab, die Licht auf die Abstammungsverhältnisse zwischen Galliern und Germanen hätten werfen können: Indem er daraus, dass es einsichtig wäre, wenn Europa regelmäßig von Ost nach West besiedelt worden wäre, den Schluss zog, dass es auch so vonstattengegangen sein dürfte, ließ er die Stimmigkeit der Rekonstruktion selbst zum Argument für ihre Richtigkeit werden; er hat damit ein Verfahren gefunden, den Geschichtsverlauf zu rekonstruieren, das auf empirische Belege fast ganz verzichten und dennoch argumentative Kraft für sich beanspruchen durfte, ein Verfahren, das genauso von Vertrauen in die Vernunft wie von Skepsis gegenüber der Aussagekraft roher Fakten geprägt ist.[54]

Vor Baudelot, der seine Ansichten mit großer Überzeugung vortrug, zeichnet Leibniz aber vor allem das Wissen aus, dass seine Behauptungen nur tastende Vermutungen waren und dass sie weiter diskutiert und durch Fakten und Argumente untermauert werden mussten, bevor sie als wissenschaftliche Erkenntnisse gelten durften.[55] Eine Passage der *Collectanea etymologica* –

---

[52] Vgl. die oben, bei Fn 24, zitierte Stelle aus Paris *Bibliotheque Nationale de France* NAF 22082 Bl. 62.
[53] Er schrieb: „Et méme il est bien vray-semblable, comme le remarque Volfgangus Lazius, Alleman luy méme, que l'ancienne langue Germanique étoit la méme que celle des Celtes." (Hannover *GWLB* LK – MOW Baudelot 10 [ehemals LBr 36] Bl. 13–24, hier Bl. 15ᵛ.)
[54] Daniel Droixhe würde diese Methode gewiss zu denjenigen seiner Eigenheiten zählen, mit denen Leibniz dazu beitrug, „l'âge philosophique" in die Länge zu ziehen und „l'avènement du positivisme" hinauszuzögern (Droixhe: *La linguistique et l'appel de l'histoire*, S. 136).
[55] Vgl. Aarsleff: „The Study and Use of Etymology in Leibniz", S. 183f.

deren Anlage als große Materialsammlung auch dieses Bewusstsein zum Ausdruck bringt[56] – zeugt von ironischer Distanz und Nachsichtigkeit des Gelehrten gegenüber einer Wissenschaft, der es noch an Seriosität mangelte:[57]

> „Nempe ubi confusio est, quidvis ex quovis non difficulter facias, praesertim imaginatione, quod concinnitati deest, supplente ... Non despero tamen, posse majore industria et judicio aliquid erui certius; neque ideo quenquam deterreo, atque etiam conjecturas audaciores non ferendas tantum arbitror, sed et laudandas, ubi ingenium acumenque habent. Nam ut saepe juvat fortuna audaciam, fieri potest, ut superveniat aliquando nova lux, quae perficiat coepta. Ex tot quae ineuntur itineribus, credibile est, aliquod rectum esse. Itaque condonandum est nonnihil affectui eorum, qui patriae suae ornamenta aut inveniunt aut faciunt in abdita antiquitate."

Dass Leibniz der bessere Historiker war, zeigt sich genau darin, dass Baudelot sich als Gewinner der Debatte fühlen konnte.

---

[56] Vgl. Droixhe: *La linguistique et l'appel de l'histoire*, S. 136: „L'exigence d'une collecte des faits à la fois aussi large (historiquement, géographiquement et socialement) et détaillée que possible paraît constituer l'élément le plus solide de l'étymologie leibnizienne."

[57] *Collectanea etymologica*, pars I, S. 71. Renate Elisabeth Buerner vertrat in ihrer Ph.D. Thesis: *G. W. Leibniz' Collectanea etymologica: Ein Beitrag zur Geschichte der Etymologie* von 1971 (die ich leider nicht einsehen konnte) die Ansicht: „It is this understandig of the historical growth of language, his method of empirically collecting material and systematically comparing it, his criticism and his moderation that make him an early representative of the historico-comparative method" (*Dissertation Abstracts International*; *The Humanities and Social Sciences*, August 1971, vol. 32, n. 2, 956-A.)

Leibniz's Language Tools, Practices, and Strategies: Notes on *De Docendis Linguis*

Cristina Marras (Rome)

To address the main issues of the panel *The Language of Leibniz*,[1] I will follow as a pretext a manuscript entitled *De Docendis Linguis*. Leibniz wrote this short text in Latin in 1678, it is unedited and is not included in the *Akademie Ausgabe*. The text addresses methods and tools to teach Latin to German students. The *Vorausedition* classifies it under 'method' or 'didactic' in the preprint of the current volumes in Series 6.4, and the Leibniz handwritings catalogue classifies it under 'philology'. Scholars have not yet deeply explored these fields of Leibniz's theory and their reflection on languages and language's use; therefore, a closer look at them could contribute to reconstructing the complexity of the philosopher's work. Furthermore, I chose this manuscript, which I am currently preparing for publication, also because like most of Leibniz's work, it contains some key issues concerning language that relate to his own life. In presenting the text, I will thus select some conceptual issues crucial to explaining Leibniz's attitude towards the use of language and some strategies in writing and communication.[2]

---

[1] "Die Sprache von Leibniz". The panel is proposed by the *Sodalitas Leibnitiana* and is organized by me, and the colleague Margherita Palumbo. The speakers contributing to the discussion, beside my self, are Stefano Gensini, Michael Kempe, and Roberto Palaia. In the panel the language of Leibniz is discussed in a broader sense and from different perspectives. On the one hand, the attention focuses on Leibniz's language - in a constant clash between tradition and innovation - in different areas or disciplines of his thought, the language of his writings, Leibniz's contribution to the formation and development of philosophical and scientific encyclopaedia of modernity (e.g. neologisms, loanwords, translations), finally, his philosophy of language and linguistics. On the other hand, Leibniz presents a refined ability to linguistically adapt to different contexts, conversational floors or individual callers, thanks to his linguistic competences and the strategic use of argumentative, rhetorical and linguistic structures that do not directly belong to his horizon; a linguistic ability that does not preclude the application of practices of dissimulation and camouflage, diplomatic talks, particularly efficient and remarkable in correspondence.

[2] I have to admit that I am always attracted by those texts considered by the Leibniz's reception marginal to his master works.

1. De Docendis Linguis

The *Ritter Katalog* classifies *De Docendis Linguis* under the number 46720. In the catalogue of Leibniz's handwritings, it is under the signature LH V, 1, Bl. 3–4, 4.[3] That may be the reason why this text will belong to *Series* 5 of the *Akademie-Ausgabe*. Leibniz, in fact, devoted some of his years of work (namely from 1676 to 1683) to these topics. It is readable and does not present many corrections, amendments, or revisions. The margin contains only one note.[4]

How does this short and 'marginal' text in Leibniz's life and work concern language? The organisation of Leibniz's *Nachlass* is always controversial. It contains papers, fragments, essays, and thousands of letters. Most of them are still in the process of publication. However, scholars follow at least three main methodological approaches for the publication of Leibniz's work:

1. Those who follow a rigorous historical method and a chronological order;
2. Those that interpret Leibniz's thought as developing from a 'young' philosophy to a more 'mature' philosophy (this approach offers a limited view of the multidisciplinarity of Leibniz in a compact framework); and
3. Those who believe that the only way to capture and show the multidisciplinarity of Leibniz's philosophy is to follow a thematic order.
4. Regardless of the approach, it is actually difficult to have a real multidisciplinary point of view that encompasses all schools. Such a point of view should be able to discuss specific and central concepts in Leibniz's philosophy without losing sight of its complexity.[5] According to Leibniz, there is a complex interconnected multiplicity of different methods. Together, these constitute the 'trajectory'. In turn, the trajectory is an ensemble of 'destinations' and functions. In the spirit of Leibniz, there is usually a *via media*, which is the approach I will follow in this paper.

---

[3] See the online Ritterkatalogue at:http://ritter.bbaw.de/ritter/Suche/suche_datensaetze?ort = &jahr1=&jahr2=&absender=&adressat=&INCIPIT=&Titel=&SIGN_oL=LH+5%2C+1&sort=Titel&SUBMIT=Suche.

[4] For the transcription of the text, I am indebted to the colleagues of the Leibniz Forschungsstelle in Münster, particularly to Prof. Heinrich Schepers and Dr. Herma Kliege-Biller and Lucia Oliveri. My special thanks go to the Prof. Stephan Meier-Oeser for the thoughtful hospitality.

[5] On the relation between the notions of unity and multiplicity in Leibniz's thought, see Herbert Breger/Jürgen Herbst/Sven Erdner (eds.): *Einheit in der Vielheit VIII. Internationaler Leibniz-Kongress*, 3 vols., Hannover 2006.

We can consider *De Docendis Linguis*[6] to be a text of a 'young' Leibniz. He wrote it after his stay in Paris and his visit to the Royal Society, ten years before the *Nova Methodus pro Maximis et Minimis* (1684) and the *Discours de Métaphysique* (1686).

The text's core focus is on how to teach Latin to German students. It also addresses how to translate German into Latin and vice versa. The relation between Latin and German is not a neutral topic in Leibniz's work. Nonetheless, this text covers many of the issues concerning languages that engaged Leibniz all his life. These issues include the use of languages, their relation with classical philosophy, the dispute about neo-Latin, the importance of etymology, the principles of communication, and recommendations for teaching. Considering all these aspects, a chronological classification cannot adequately represent the richness and the interrelation of topics present in Leibniz's works over time.

At first sight, the manuscript shows that Leibniz gives some teaching recommendations to ensure students can learn Latin easily without getting bored: "ut puer sine tedio et facile discat intelligere linguam latinam."[7] We can mention here at least four of them:

1. Retracing the Latin roots of words and the structure of sentences, which shows the importance of etymology and syntax;
2. The use of catalogues of famous quotations to comprise a repertoire of quotes and examples;
3. Differentiating the use of the Latin from any other language when talking about metaphysics; and
4. The pleasure of learning a language.

This presents a pedagogical and didactic point of view. However, as Leibniz said, the text includes several important points on his views on language and language use. The next section discusses this 'toolkit'.

---

[6] This text relates to Leibniz's other texts that share the same concerns, as for example *Didactica* of 1678–1679, A VI, 4 A, N. 223; *Methodus docendi una popularis altera scientifica perfectior*, of 1683, A VI, 4 A, N. 139; *De modo docendi ludimagistrorum*, Middle of 1685 (?), A VI, 4 A, 145; *Schenckelii Methodus Latinam Linguam Discendi et Ars Memoriae* ,1680–1682 ?, A, VI, 4 B, N. 232.
[7] Quotations without bibliographical references are from the manuscript.

2. The Toolkit

In the manuscript, Leibniz argues for teaching language in two ways:

> "Duobus modis docere possumus linguam, uno, ex ipsis rebus nullo respectu ad linguam quam discipulus jam tenet; altero ex lingua que jam ipsi nota est, discriminibus tantum annotates."[8]

1. Focusing on words but completely ignoring the language the student speaks or knows; or
2. Focusing on the 'entire' language, that is, to start with the language the student knows. Clearly, we are talking here about an analytic and a synthetic method.
3. Those who want to be good language teachers will get the best advantage if they compare the languages they are teaching with their own language or with some other language they already know. Leibniz in this way acquainted students and teachers with the multilingualism in which they were involved at that time. In so doing, he set up a comparative method in studying languages:

> "Qui egregium linguarum Magister esse volet, ei opus erit plurium linguarum quas docere volet suos (+ et quascit discipulos suos uti) comparationem instituisse."

To teach Latin in Germany, it will be enough to compare accurately the two languages, Latin and German:

> "Sed si quis latinam linguam in Germania tantum docere velit eum suffecerit Germanicam linguam latinae diligenter comparavisse." This can be done with the help of grammars, dictionaries, and lexicons: "Si volumus Latinam ex Germanica docere condatur breviculum latinae grammaticae et lexici adiuvetur. Hoc Lexicon contineat voces maximè necessarias, et utiles."[9]

---

[8] This incipit occurs with slight changes in *Methodus docendi una popularis altera scientific perfectior* (1683–1686), A VI, 4 A, where Leibniz said: "[…] in nominandis rebus servari posso ordo duplex, unus aptus ad usum, ut quam primum disceret cum nostris hominibus conversari, alter aptus ad accuratam rerum cognitionem cum verbis comparandam."

[9] *Lamb. Th. Schenckelii Methodus, sive declaratio quomodo Latina lingua sex mensium spatio ab adolescentibus octodecim aut plurium annorum magnum desiderium et diligentiam afferentibus possit addisci.1 His subjungitur brevis tractatus de utilitatibus et effectibus artis memoriae summa dignis admiratione. Elogia de eadem doctorum hominum. Item Apologia in eos*

2.1 Grammars

As Giorgio Tonelli noted in his *Short-Title List of Subject Dictionaries [...]*:

> "the connection of dictionaries with doctrinal trends contemporary to them, and their influence on the diffusion of thought should be a basic field in the history of ideas."[10]

Leibniz mentions some of the most important grammars as a basis for comparing languages and analysing sources:

> "Cui rei duo erunt utiles libri Grammatici; scilicet Vossii Aristarchus et Schottelii, lingua Germanica. Deinde quo facilius de omnibus discriminibus judicet, conferet versiones latinas cum fontibus germanicis; aut contra versiones germanicas cum fontibus latinis."[11]

From this apparently simple quotation emerges an important point in Leibniz's philosophy of language. Notably, the linguistic work of Leibniz differs in many respects from that of 16th- and 17th-century scholars.[12] Unlike many of his contemporaries, Leibniz implicitly assumes that language has a cognitive ability. This emerges to overcome the mnemonic function of signs. Signs have therefore a constitutive and substitutive function for our thought, Marcelo Dascal calls this a 'psychotechnic' function.[13] Leibniz's concern is to build a system of signs, symbols, and words. This relates to his project of a universal language for the progress of humanities and science. Moreover, it

---

qui librum Schenckelii de arte memoriae male edidere. Argentorati impensis Eberhardi Zezneri 1619, 80. Libellus est 124 paginarum in 80).

[10] Giorgio Tonelli: *Short-Title List of Subject Dictionaries in the Sixteenth, Seventeenth, and Eighteenth Centuries as Aids to the History of Ideas*, Extended Edition, Revised and Annotated by Eugenio Canone/Margherita Palumbo, Firenze 2006, p. 77.

[11] *Gerardi Ioannis Vossii Aristarchus, sive de arte grammatica libri septem. Quibus censura in grammaticos praecipue veteres exercetur; caussae linguae Latinae eruuntur; scriptores Romani illustrantur, vel emendantur. Editio secunda, pluribus locis aucta.* Amstelaedami, ex officina Ioannis Blaeu, 1662, and J. G. Schottell: *Ausführliche Arbeit von der teutschen Haubt-Sprache*, Braunschweig 1663.

[12] See for example John Wilkins: *Essays toward a Real Character and a Philsophical Language*, 1668; Georg Dalgarno: *Ars signorum*, 1661, an accurate analysis is in: Paolo Rossi: *Clavis Universalis. Arti della memoria e logica combinatoria da Lullo a Leibniz*, Firenze 1983, and in Jacob Maat: *Philosophical languages in the seventeenth century: Dalgarno, Wilkins, Leibniz*, Amsterdam, Institute for logic, language and computation 1999, Dissertation series.

[13] Marcelo Dascal: *La sémiologie de Leibniz*, Paris 1978.

concerns the study of natural languages connected to his political, theological, and academic aims.

Leibniz's project is ambitious. It encompasses languages analysis, analysis of language structures, norms, and meanings. Within these activities, the study of grammar becomes strategic. As we know, the term 'grammar' occurs in Leibniz with two different definitions: natural grammar and rational grammar. The first relates to natural historical languages, whereas the second to artificial languages. In particular, the latter relates to the rational, universal language, albeit the rational grammar born from a process of simplifying Latin grammar. The *characteristica universalis* also arose from an accurate analysis and comparison of the different natural historical language grammars:

> "celuy qui écriroit une Grammaire Universelle feroit bien de passer de l'essence des langues à leur existence et de comparer les Grammaires de plusieurs langues"

said Leibniz in the *Nouveaux Essais*.[14]

2.2 Lexicons and Dictionaries

Leibniz stresses the importance of the use of lexicons. For example, he mentions the "Lexicum illud Schikalianum more etymologicis ex Germanico", and he pointed out that: "Hoc Lexicon contineat voces maxime necessarias, et utiles."

A rigorous analysis of a word's meaning can be useful in understanding its intellectual operations.[15] In this sense, the study of linguistic meanings intrinsically relates to tropes and the philosophical analysis of language. For example, the study of metaphor is a bridge between cognitive-epistemological and rhetoric-argumentative levels,[16] an area that certainly requires further investigation and thought.

---

[14] Chap. III, § 5, A VI, 6, 301.
[15] On the function of signs, see Stephan Meier-Oeser: *Die Spur des Zeichens: Das Zeichen und seine Funktion in der Philosophie des Mittelalters und der frühen Neuzeit*, Berlin 1997.
[16] I have demonstrated this in my previously works, see for example Cristina Marras: *Metaphora translata voce. Prospettive metaforiche nella filosofia di Leibniz*, Firenze 2010. On this point see also Francesco Piro: "Are the canals of tropes' navigable?", in: Klaus D. Dutz/Stefano Gensini (eds.): *Im Spiegel des Verstandes. Studien zur Leibniz*, Münster 1996, pp. 137–160; Giovanna Varani: *Leibniz e la topica aristotelica*, Milano 1995. Leibniz mentions tropes both as figures of discourse and as essential instruments for linguistic creativity

In addition, the comparison within languages and lexicons enables us to see the contribution of exchanges, tracings, and borrowings of words in building the philosophical lexicon of modern thought. The philosophical vocabulary established between the 17th and 18th centuries, along with related conceptual fields, forms a sort of 'intelligibility grid' of the reality that conditioned the history of intellectual modern thought. Leibniz is aware that it is difficult to transfer conceptualisation from one language to another. It is also difficult to make it accessible in the original language.

Leibniz's addresses these issues specifically in the *Prefatio Nizolii* and the *Nova Methodus*. This also has echoes in the manuscript presented here. In the *De Docendis Linguis*, Leibniz in fact does not avoid referring to the importance of translations.[17] Translation involves moving from one linguistic context to another. Yet it also attributes new meanings to old or sedimented lexemes. In other words, it accepts the traditional 'meaning' but at the same time inserts it into new contexts.

According to Leibniz, we do not have to limit ourselves to the resources of natural languages. We also should expand upon the entire set of terminology that previous philosophers used and borrow terms from different knowledge domains.[18] Leibniz indicates the terminological method as being

---

from the *Nova methodus* (1667) till the *Epistolica de historia etymologica dissertation* (1712); for example: *Nova methodus,* A VI, 1, 278, 339; *Dissertatio praeliminaris* A VI, 2, 10, 413, 418; *Epistolica* § 40.

[17] *Dissertatio praeliminaris de instituto operis atque optima philosophi dictione* al *De veris princippis et vera ratione philosophandi contra pseudophilosophos,* is one of the most significant works of Leibniz in which his articulated semiology is intrinsically interconnected to the language reform in philosophy. See Cristina Marras: "Che lingua parla la filosofia? brevi riflessioni tra Nizolio e Leibniz", in: Cristina Marras/Annalisa Schino (eds.): *Linguaggio, filosofia, fisiologia nell'età moderna*, Atti del convegno, Roma 23.–25. Jan. 2014, Roma, "ILIESI digitale. Ricerche filosofiche e lessicali", vol. 1, ILIESI-CNR, Sept. 2015, http://www.iliesi.cnr.it/pubblicazioni/Ricerche-01-Marras_Schino.pdf; Cristina Marras/Giovanna Varani: "The Rennaissance debate, about rhetoric and dialectics in Leibniz's Prefatio to Nizoli", in: *Studi Filosofici XXVII* – 2004, Napoli 2004, pp. 183–216.

[18] Systematic works dedicated to Leibniz's lexicon are still missing. Some reflections are in Martine de Gaudemar: *Le vocabulaire de Leibniz*, Paris 2001. A project aiming to build a lexicon of Leibniz's metalanguage is in Cristina Marras: *Materiali per un lessico critico-linguistico di G. W. Leibniz*, Cagliari 1994–1995, dissertation thesis.

the means for the progress of science[19] and the transmission of culture (*translatio studiorum*).[20]

Leibniz was very critical of the Aristotelian tradition. However, he indubitably belongs with those scholars who profit from the ancient or medieval lexicons built upon the Arabs' translation of Aristotle and his comments on Greek texts and Hellenistic tradition. For Leibniz in fact Aristotle doesn't have any responsibility *vis-à-vis* the absurdities used by the scholasticism that "polluted his philosophy."[21]

The lexicons and terminology to which Leibniz refers contain a rich vocabulary of ancient and modern terms, neologisms, and translations. The text often stresses the importance of ancient terms and the problems emerging once a scholar copes with their translations: "optime discimus linguas per parallelismus cum linguis nobis notis."

The *De Docendis Linguis* reflects the 16th- and 17th-century attitudes on coping with different linguistic registers. Scholars, especially scientists,

---

[19] For the concept of *translatio studiorum* see Tullio Gregory: "Translatio studiorum", in: *Quaderni di storia*, 70, luglio-dicembre 2009, Bari 2009, pp. 1–39, and *Translatio Linguarum. Traduzioni e storia della cultura*, Firenze 2016. For the *Monadologie* and its translations, see the work of Antonio Lamarra/Roberto Palaia/Pietro Pimpinella: *Le prime traduzioni della Monadologia di Leibniz (1720–1721). Introduzione storico-critica, sinossi dei testi, concordanze contrastive,* Firenze 2001. In particular, see Roberto Palaia/Pietro Pimpinella: *Linguaggio e terminologia filosofica nelle prime traduzioni della Monadologie*, pp. 119–141. It would be interesting to work on a comparison between the 'writing' of Leibniz and that of some of his contemporaries as for example the work on alloglossia in Leibniz and Spinoza in Mogens Lærke: *The problem of Alloglossia. Leibniz on Spinoza's innovative use of philosophical language*, in: *British Journal for the History of Philosophy* 17/5 (2009), pp. 939–953. More in general, some reflections between lexicography and philosophy are in André Robinet: *Lexicographie et caractéristique universelle*, in: G. Abel/H-J. Engfer/C. Hubig (eds): *Neuzeitliches Denken. Festschrift für Hans Poser zum 65. Geburtstag*, Berlin 2002, pp. 169f.; and Leibniz as lexicographer discussed in John Considine: "Leibniz and Lexicography", in: M. Mooijaart/M. van der Wal (eds.), *Yesterday's Words. Contemporary, Current and Future Lexicography*, Cambridge 2008, pp. 41–52, and by the same author, "Leibniz as lexicographer?", in: Gerda Hassler (ed.): *History of Linguistics 2008. Selected papers from the Eleventh International Conference on the History of the Language Sciences (ICHoLS XI), Potsdam, 28th August –2nd September 2008*, Amsterdam/Philadelphia 2011, pp. 217–224. A discussion on Leibniz's contribution to lexicography between 17th and 18th century is for example in Ulla Birgegård: *Johan Gabriel Sparwenfeld and the Lexicon Slavonicum: his contribution to 17th century Slavonic lexicography*, Uppsala 1985, and in Rolf Schneider: *Der Einfluß von Justus Georg Schottelius auf die deutschsprachige Lexikographie des 17./18. Jahrhunderts*, Frankfurt a. M. 1995.

[20] We do not have to forget that Leibniz knows very well Daniel Georg Morhof (1639–1691) and his *Polyhistor, sive de auctorum notitia et rerum commentarii* (Lübeck, 1688, not completed till 1707), a kind of encyclopaedia of the knowledge and learning of his time, where he could find precious indications for all the available lexicons.

[21] *Preface*, p. 85.

had to deal not only with the need for a new terminology, or a more adequate one, but also with the possibility of using their 'national languages' for writing science and philosophy.

Analysing and comparing these different registers can contribute to a confrontation between a consolidated language (that of the tradition) and a modern one that in some cases is a 'national *common* language'. Leibniz did not explore this aspect in detail. Yet it is certainly present in this manuscript, in particular with the reference to German language. A topic thus emerges here that will be central in the writing after 1686: This writing focuses on the political and social role of national languages, particularly German.

Moreover, from this emerges another important classical issue: the relationship between language and metaphysics.

> "Regulae constitunt in solis convenientiis et discriminibus latini et Germanici sermonis. Ita opus non erit onerare juventutem Metaphysicis contemplationibus, et vocabulis abstractis; quas sibi nobisque intelligere videntur cum praesentes sumus, et exempla damus, at cum primum terga vertimus (si sic dicere licet non inepto Germanismo, den rucken gewendet haben) ipsi per se hoerent, neque regulas applicare novunt."

More precisely, this concerns the language of metaphysics:

> "Sententia Grammatica brevis, ostendendus, que flexiones constructionesque Latinas, quibus Germanicis exprimendae sint et contra; ita nullis opus erit regulis metaphisicis."

Two contenders are involved: Latin and German. Leibniz also extensively addresses this dispute in the *Prefatio Nizolii* and recalls it in the *Ermahnung an die Teutsche* and *Unvorgreiffliche Gedanken*. This dispute concerns several political issues and writings.

The promotion of the use of German contributed to a discussion that had been taking place since the 15th century. It concerned the use of Latin and the legitimacy of using national languages in science. Leibniz took a position against the 'supremacy' of a language as Latin in favour of a 'national' language, in his case German:

> "[...] in Germania inter alias causas, ideo fiior est scholastica philosophia, quod sero, et ne nunc quidem satis, Germanice philosophari coeptum est."[22]

---

[22] *Prefatio Nizolii*, A VI, 2, 144.

This issue is significant not only for social and intellectual life but also for political programmes. Germany at the time lacked a common cultural (and political) capital. For Leibniz, time and language were mature for philosophising in German, not only in metaphysics but also in science.

2.3 Historiolas and Sentence Catalogues

In addition to the lexicons and grammars in use at the time, the study of Latin should start with classical books, fairy tales, and everything that can facilitate the study of the language. In addition, sentence catalogues and short histories called *historiolas* are important in this respect.

> "Adsit lexicon in quo omnes voces usitatae Latinas et Germanicas reddantur et contra ut puer sine tedio et facile discat intelligere linguam latinam, incipiat legere librum Latinum, cujus argumentum ei jam tam notum est hunc de verbo ad verbum poterit reddere Germanice, ut de Evangelia sacra sunt Novi Testamenti quaedam, aut fabulas Esopi; aut historiolas quales sunt in acerra philologica."[23]

A short discussion on a side aspect of learning is relevant here. This is actually a strategic point in communication and writing. It concerns the use of 'formulas' or catchphrases, generally considered forms and discursive functions on the periphery of an utterance. As an alternative, I would like to propose approaching these forms from the point of view of analysing discourse. This proposal would consider formulas and sentences as linguistic mediators. In fact, formulas, catchphrases, and proverbs have a role in theoretical elaboration and in philosophical inter-discourse. As Leibniz states:

> "Utile erit condere historiolas quasdam orationesque vertendas, quas ingredientur omnia discrimina Latinae et Germanicae etymologicae et syntaxis, hae pueris pro modulo erunt, et semper in exemplum poterunt citari. Imo utilius erit exhiberit Catalogum sententiarum egregiarum, in quibus reperiantur plereque et voces utiliores ex constructiones communes, in quibus differt sermo Latinas ad Germanicas."

---

[23] Peter Lauremberg: *Acerra Philologica. Das ist/ Dritte hundert=außerlesener/ nützlicher/ lustiger/ und denckwürdiger Historien und Discursen, zusammen gebracht auß den berühmsten Griechischen und Lateinischen Scribenten [...] Hallervord*, Rostock 1637.

How do formulas work? What do they do? They are structural as well as instrumental elements of philosophical discourse.[24] Leibniz noted this[25] in the *Disputatio Inauguralis de Casibus Perplexis in Jure*.[26] In this work, he addresses one of the most difficult issues in legal theory and practice, the so-called 'hard case'. In the exploration of *casus perplexus,* Leibniz points to metaphors such as the Gordian knot, squaring of the circle, and the blind intestine. In addition, he refers to proverbs such as "for a hard knot a hard wedge" and applies all the language resources.

Formulas work on least at three levels:

1. The structural level: they connect ordinary discourse, the universe of lore, with the tangle of philosophical discourse;
2. The organisational level: they condense a particular theory in a emblematic formulation, and at the same time they become general values presenting themselves as being part of a shared wisdom to universal values; and
3. The conceptual level: they participate in the effectiveness of philosophical words and concepts, working as 'ambassadors', as watchwords, passwords see for example the expressions: *monads* without doors and windows, or *tabula rasa*.
4. These three levels relate to three crucial roles that formulas play in the structure of philosophical discourse:
5. In the elaboration of text (like the metaphors of the labyrinth that became a *leitmotiv*) which at the same time elaborates crucial aspects of Leibniz's philosophical and mathematical theory;
6. In philosophical fecundity: detached from the text itself, the formula relates to the entire net of references, as in Voltaire's 'best of all possible words' from *Candide* (which become a popularised expression); and
7. As a way of transmitting and crystallising text (monads without doors and windows).

It is important to recognise the role of formulas in discourse. It is also important to understand the role they play in the constitution of a philosophical

---

[24] To elaborate this short paragraph I benefit from the work of Frédéric Cossutta/Francine Cicuriel (eds.): *Les formules philosphique. Détachement, circulation, recontextualisation,* Lambert/Lucas 2014, which I largely used here.
[25] Marcelo Dascal: *Leibniz: What Kind of Rationalist,* Dordrecht 2014, p. 47.
[26] A VI, 1, 233–256.

work, in discursive practices and, last but not least, in the reception of a work. In this respect, I propose to approach philosophy throughout philosophical discourse. I also propose to approach linguistic activities that inscribe textuality in philosophy's social and institutional context. Philosophical concepts relate to their inter-discursive and institutional discourse. However, this doesn't mean that philosophy finds its ultimate explication in this. More precisely, in this way philosophy negotiates the possibility of its enunciations in relation to the scenes that establish.[27]

3. Conclusion

This analysis went beyond Leibniz's manuscript to stress how Leibniz was aware not only of the constitutive function of signs but also[28] of the way philosophy constitutes its own vocabulary. He seizes the categories that spoken and national languages offer. Furthermore, he elaborates upon traditions and doctrines. There are choices in language (Latin, French, or German), words (a technical or a common vocabulary), and the kind of language (abstract, universal, formal, and ordinary). These are all fundamental to emancipate philosophy from the constraints of its schools. This should apply especially in Germany where according to Leibniz Scholastics is particularly rooted in the schools.

A technical vocabulary complements a daily life vocabulary, and it is certainly not devoid of consequences concerning the delicate equilibrium between transparency and opacity in language and philosophy.

For Leibniz, philosophers actually have to use the multiplicity of meanings and words in ordinary language. They need to make an effort not only in comprehending the words or in coping with the obscurity of a style, but in understanding the form of philosophical discourse. Teachers and students are particularly aware of this concept, especially when they have to translate and delve into the secrets of a new language.

---

[27] See Dominique Maingueneau: "Le discours philosophique comme institution discursive", in: *Langage*, n. 119, 1995, p. 40–62.
[28] One of Leibniz's definition of sign is for example: "signum est quod nunc sentimus et alioquin cum aliquo connexum esse ex priore experientia nostra vel aliena judicamus" (A VI, 2, 500).

Leibniz captures and stresses a tension between innovators in philosophy (those who invent new words and expressions that create obscurity and ambiguity) and those using ordinary language. In this sense, Leibniz appears as someone who makes a concrete and clear use of language. Terminological and stylistic choices echo conscious and strategic choices.[29]

There is still room for dedicated investigations on the relation between so-called public and private writings, between dissimulation and transparency and we should avoid the idea of a 'double Leibniz', a distinction between a secret and a public figure. Let us stress instead the profile of a diplomat, a politician, a philosopher, a scholar, and a teacher aware of his interlocutors and contexts. He is aware of his audience, all those who make a strategic and appropriate use of language and all of its argumentative resources.[30]

The *De Docendis Linguis,* although apparently marginal, adds another small piece to the complex frame of Leibniz's thought and to his 'projects'. No portion is too small as to be valueless in the construction and transmission of knowledge. Certainly, language teaching, pedagogical methods, and an attention to language and terminology are part of it. At the beginning of the manuscript, Leibniz said:

> "Prior difficilior est sed ad progressum in scientiis faciendum utilior, posterior compendiosior, et suffectura illi, qui porro operam Scientiis daturus non est, linguam quemadmodum in usu est didicisse consertus."

The relation between Latin and German central to *De Docendis Linguis* is a part of Leibniz's 'nationalist' discourse in the *Republique des Lettres*. Teaching and learning a language, a foreign language, are the bricks for building a common scientific discourse, first in Latin, then in German. This is the scientific *koine* of the multilingual Europe of the 17th century, where wisdom is nothing else than the science of happiness (*scientia felicitatis*) as he said in the *Definitio brevis scientiae generalis,* 1683–1685.[31]

---

[29] The notion of style stile in Leibniz certainly deserves deep investigations, a contribution to this topic is in Marras: "Che lingua parla la filosofia?"; see also Paul Rateau: "Art et fiction chez Leibniz", in: *Les Cahiers Philosophiques de Strasbourg* 18 (2004), pp.117–148.

[30] An original contribution in this sense is that of Roberto Palaia: "Zwischen Autobiographie und Selbstrezension", in: *Anonymität Pseudonymität Camouflage. Leibniz und der Gelehrtenhabitus*, Akten der internationalen Tagung Hannover, 15.–16. November 2013, Berlin 2016. An accurate analysis of argumentative strategies along with a collection of polemical texts is in Marcelo Dascal: *G. W. Leibniz. The Art of Controversies*, Dordrecht 2008.

[31] A VI, 4 A, 532.

The Role of *'ius strictum'* in the Legal Philosophy of Leibniz

Stephan Meder (Hannover)

1. Introduction

Gottfried Wilhelm Leibniz, in his numerous writings, fragments and letters, formulated a universal jurisprudence that became known by such terms as *'Dreistufenlehre'* [the three divisions of law] or *'Naturrechtstrilogie'* [the trilogy of natural law].[1] It was based on a combination of three elements – or more precisely, on the three highest legal norms (*praecepta iuris*) which were defined in classical Roman jurisprudence as *'honeste vivere'* (live honestly), *'neminem laedere'* (injure no one) and *'suum cuique tribuere'* (to give each his due).[2] Leibniz built on this division but chose a different order. He placed the principle of *'neminem laedere'* on the first level and viewed it as separate from the other two *'praecepta'*, i.e. *'suum cuique tribuere'* and *'honeste vivere'*, which he classed as being on the two next higher levels.

The fact that this order was indeed original – that it seems to have had no precursors or successors – is due to the complex meaning attributed by Leibniz to the concept of *'ius strictum'*.[3] In Leibniz' view, 'strict law' (*ius*

---

[1] Gottfried Wilhelm Leibniz: *Nova methodus discendae docendaeque Jurisprudentiae* (1667), in: A VI, 1, 259–364, 343–345 (§§ 73–75); letter to Hermann Conring dated 13th/23rd January 1670, in: A II, 1, 44–50; letter to Hermann Conring dated 9th/19th April 1670, in: A II, 1, 67–70; Praefatio to the Codex Juris Gentium Diplomaticus (1693), in: A IV, 5, 48–79; *Méditation sur la notion commune de la justice* (1703), in: Georg Mollat (ed.): *Rechtsphilosophisches aus Leibnizens ungedruckten Schriften*, 1885, pp. 56–81. Amongst the abundant literature on Leibniz' three divisions of law, most of which, however, are sketchy overviews, two works by Hubertus Busche stand out: *Leibniz' Weg ins perspektivische Universum. Eine Harmonie im Zeitalter der Berechnung*, Hamburg 1997, pp. 297–403; id.: "Leibniz' Lehre von den drei Stufen des Naturrechts", in: Wenchao Li (ed.): *"Das Recht kann nicht ungerecht sein." Beiträge zu Leibniz' Philosophie der Gerechtigkeit*, Stuttgart 2015, pp. 29–53.
[2] Ulpian in D. 1.1.10; Inst. 1.1.3 (in this order).
[3] For more on this see Chapter V. On the controversial question as to whether Leibniz' three divisions of law were strictly drawn from his own ideas, see the references in the introduction by Hubertus Busche, in: Gottfried Wilhelm Leibniz: *Frühe Schriften zum Naturrecht*, ed. by Hubertus Busche, Hamburg 2003, pp. XI–CXII, LXVIII. Ulpian's division has often been discussed in the literature, amongst others, by such diverse writers as Kant and Savigny. Their views can be seen as exemplifying the variety of interpretations that have been put forward for the concept of *'praecepta iuris'*. Savigny dealt with them in the appendix of his "system" because this "classification" was no longer used by "the current writers": *System des heutigen*

strictum) embodies law in the actual sense. It is governed by the instruction to injure no one (*neminem laedere*) and its task is to ensure security and peace. The next higher level, equity (*aequitas*), on the other hand, only imparts law 'in the wider sense of the word'. It applies to losses or gains that are not always actionable or legally enforceable by the persons concerned.[4] The precept here is

> "to be of service to all, however, only to the extent that it is agreeable to the individual or that they deserve it, because it is not possible, after all, to favour everyone to the same degree" (*suum cuique tribuere*).

Piety (*pietas*) sits enthroned on the third and highest level and commands us to lead a righteous and honourable life (*honeste vivere*).

Leibniz also connects these levels or grades with another trichotomy, namely with Aristotle's famous concept of justice, which is based on a division between corrective justice (*iustitia commutativa*), distributive justice (*iustitia distributiva*) and universal justice (*iustitia universalis*).[5] In this case Leibniz sees corrective justice (*iustitia commutativa*) as being on the same level as strict law, whilst he places distributive justice (*iustitia distributiva*) and universal justice (*iustitia universalis*) on the next higher levels.[6]

Moreover, Leibniz debates '*ius strictum*' in association with the sources of positive law. Here, the grades of natural law appear in bipartite form. '*Ius strictum*' stands for the 'formal' side of the law, whilst '*aequitas*' and '*pietas*' encompass its material elements. They are situated on the boundary between law and morality and those who break their rules cannot always be prosecuted by worldly courts. '*Aequitas*' and '*pietas*', if anything, belong within the realm of public law, whilst '*ius strictum*' is mainly private law. Leibniz, with his 'dual' breakdown of the sources disagrees with those authors who restrict their teaching on the sources of law to '*ius strictum*' and are thus willing only to accept a single, i.e. a formal structure of law. The subdivision into strict and

---

römischen Rechts, Vol. I, ed. by Friedrich Carl von Savigny, Berlin 1840, pp. 407–410. A critical appraisal of Kant's reception of the '*praecepta iuris*' was published 2012 by Philipp-Alexander Hirsch: *Kants Einleitung in die Rechtslehre* von 1784. For Immanuel Kant's concept of law see the Lecture of Ethics "Mrongovius II" and the Lecture on Natural Law "Feyerabend" from 1784 as well as from 1797 *Die Metaphysik der Sitten*, ed. by Hans Ebeling, Stuttgart 2012, pp. 58–62 passim.

[4] E.g. *Nova Methodus*, § 74 (pp. 343 and 344); "Praefatio" to the *Codex Juris Gentium Diplomaticus*, p. 62 (Leibniz cites 'gratitude' and 'mercy' as examples of non-enforceable 'rights').

[5] Aristotle: *Nicomachean Ethics*, Book V, Chapters 1–8.

[6] See references in fn. 1 (particularly the letter to Conring dated 13th/23rd January 1670, p. 47).

unstrict law is still relevant today. Jurisprudence continues to differentiate between 'formal' and 'material' elements.[7] Leibniz manages, with his concept of '*ius strictum*' to combine the old and new in a harmonious way. As will be shown here, the core of his concept constitutes a reception and further development of structures that were already laid out in Roman law.

2. '*Ius strictum*' in Roman Law

Whilst the term '*ius strictum*' does not appear in the '*praecepta iuris*', it did originate in Roman law. Its meaning, however, went through several changes over the course of its lengthy development from the Law of the Twelve Tables (5th century BC) to the dissolution of the western Roman Empire (5th century AD). In short, a distinction can be made between the '*ius strictum*' of ancient (pre-classical) Rome and the '*ius strictum*' of classical (or post-classical) Rome.

2.1 The '*ius strictum*' of Ancient Rome

Like other early legal systems, ancient Roman law was also characterised by structural orality. '*Ius strictum*' then was a question of the formal structure of justice. We may assume that there can be no law in an oral culture without any degree of formalism. Where written records did not exist or were the exception, society commemorated its past by means of rituals, gestures and incan-

---

[7] For more on this see Chapters IV and VII. One must draw on a bipartite system of sources in order to subsume '*aequitas*' and '*pietas*' under the same material union. Leibniz' division between '*iustitia particularis*' and '*iustitia universalis*' opens up an alternative approach to the concept of 'dualism'. According to this approach the former (*aequitas*) is divided into formal (*ius strictum*) and material law (*ius aequum*), whilst the latter (*pietas*) is separated from law and restricted to the area of conscience, inner jurisdiction and ethics, e.g. *Tentamina quaedam ad novum codicem legum condendum* (1680?), in: A VI, 4 C, 2862–2871, 2864: "est autem justitia particularis duplex *commutativa* et *distributive*"; *Méditation sur la notion commune de la justice*, pp. 75f.; more detailed statements in Busche: "Leibniz' Weg", pp. 309f., 319: on '*iustitia particularis*'; pp. 304, 331: '*pietas*' motivated by religious compensation mechanisms. A straight line leads from '*pietas*' to § 89 of *Monadology*, cf. Matthias Armgardt: "Die Monadologie als Vollendung der Rechtstheorie von G. W. Leibniz", in: Michael Kempe (ed.): *Leibniz' letztes Lebensjahr – Unbekanntes zu einem bekannten Universalgenie*, Hanover 2016, pp. 343–353, here pp. 351–353.

tations. This mainly depended on the frequent repetition and memorable nature of the rituals thanks to their short and formulaic sayings or thoughts that were easy to memorise. Legal rites outwardly visible by formulae or gestures had a decisive impact on the legal act in that any slip of the tongue when uttering the prescribed incantation or any wrong pose or gesture could lead to the loss of one's legal position (*qui cadit a syllaba, cadit a causa*). The adversary, meanwhile, was watching for every mistake and every stutter or hesitation, or any relaxation of one's posture. In ancient law it was often not even the role of the courts to retrospectively ascertain what had actually occurred. The idea was rather to let the law proclaim and put itself into practice. In order for this to work, it was sufficient to have a knowledge of the forms and formulae – not unlike the knowledge of rituals and liturgy in the religious sphere.

That is why, in the early period of the Roman empire, the correct use of an incantation could force a debtor to pay up, even in cases where the creditor had not actually given the loan or delivered the goods in the first instance.[8] The court case itself could also be a source of injustice because both parties had to plead their rights using precisely defined incantations. The 2nd century AD Roman jurist Gaius, in his '*Institutes*', debated the problems associated with legal systems based on structural orality. He showed that classical Roman jurisprudence found it necessary to dilute the old '*ius strictum*' in order to eliminate injustices that were linked with the formal strictness of the ancient law.[9]

2.2 'Ius strictum' and 'ius gentium' in the Classical and Post-Classical Periods

'Ius strictum' overlapped with the old 'ius civile', which had always encompassed the area of the legal order that applied to Roman citizens only. The joint aspect from which the rapidly increasing links between 'ius civile', which was characterised by structural orality, and the more recent legal layers

---

[8] Cf. Stephan Meder: *Rechtsgeschichte. Eine Einführung*, Köln/Weimar/Wien ⁵2014, pp. 30, 62, 132.
[9] Gaius: *Institutiones*, ed. by Emil Seckel/Bernhard Kübler, ⁷Leipzig 1935, e.g. III, 18–25 (here, Gaius speaks of '*iniquitates*', i.e. 'inequities' of strict law); see also Gaius IV, 11. Other sources are cited by Hermann Gottlieb Heumann/Emil Seckel: *Handlexikon zu den Quellen des römischen Rechts*, Jena ¹¹1907, p. 558 (*strictus*); Alfred Manigk: Art.: "Ius strictum", in: *Paulys Realencyclopädie der classischen Altertumswissenschaft*, vol. X, 2, Stuttgart 1919, Sp. 1301.

of 'ius honorarium' and 'ius gentium' can be viewed, is the reduction of formalities.[10] 'Ius gentium' can be seen as a type of 'natural law' (ius naturale) within Roman law – as a time-transcending law that is based on natural reason (naturalis ratio) and, irrespective of the civil rights of the parties involved, should apply to all human beings. Gaius described 'ius gentium' as follows:

> "All peoples who are ruled by laws and customs partly make use of their own laws, and partly have recourse to those which are common to all men; for what every people establishes as law for itself is peculiar to itself, and is called the Civil Law, as being that peculiar to the state; and what natural reason establishes among all men and is observed by all peoples alike, is called the Law of Nations, as being the law which all nations employ. Therefore the Roman people partly make use of their own law, and partly avail themselves of that common to all men."[11]

The triumph of *'ius gentium'*, therefore, established the rule of an (at least) bipartite system of law. Whilst the law was still strictly interpreted, it was now possible to adapt *'ius civile'* if its application led to results that fell foul of *'naturalis ratio'*.[12] Apart from *'ius gentium'* and *'ius honorarium'*, a variety of terms have been used for this second source of law, including *'ius aequum'* (equity), *'humanitas'* (humanity) and *'bona fides'*. The details are not relevant for the purposes of this article. Suffice it to say that Roman law over time took on a 'dualistic' structure, whereby *'ius civile'* mainly protected self-serving interests whilst *'ius aequum'* could also be used to accommodate third-party interests and take into consideration the community.[13]

---

[10] On the terminology see Meder: *Rechtsgeschichte*, pp. 62–68.
[11] Gaius: *Institutiones*, I, 1.
[12] See the examples in D. 23.2.67.1; C. 3.42.8 (and the references in fn. 9 and Chapter V 2).
[13] For more on this see Okko Behrends: Struktur und Wert. Zum institutionellen und prinzipiellen Denken im geltenden Recht (1990), in: id.: *Institut und Prinzip. Siedlungsgeschichtliche Grundlagen, philosophische Einflüsse und das Fortwirken der beiden republikanischen Konzeptionen in den kaiserzeitlichen Rechtsschulen*, vol. I, Göttingen 2004, pp. 55–89, here 56–60; id.: Gesetz und Sprache. Das römische Gesetz unter dem Einfluß der hellenistischen Philosophie (1995), in: *Institut und Prinzip*, pp. 91–224, here 151–155; id. (ed.): *Rudolf von Jhering. Ist die Jurisprudenz eine Wissenschaft? Jherings Wiener Antrittsvorlesung vom 16. Oktober 1868. Aus dem Nachlaß herausgegeben und mit einer Einführung, Erläuterungen sowie einer wissenschaftsgeschichtlichen Einordnung versehen*, Göttingen ²2009, pp. 196–202. See also id.: Überlegungen zum Vertrag zugunsten Dritter im römischen Privatrecht, in: *Institut und Prinzip*, vol. II, pp. 839–878.

3. Excursus: How the Historical School of Jurisprudence Interpreted the Dualistic Nature of the Sources of Roman Law

The founder of the German Historical School of Jurisprudence, Friedrich Carl von Savigny, differentiated in his teaching on the sources of law between a 'pure' principle of law, which creates formal competences, and a 'mixed' principle of law, by virtue of which material aspects can also come into play. In accordance with advanced Roman jurisprudence he claimed that law could not exist without structural formalism (*ius strictum*), but that this formalism required a corrective, which was called '*aequitas*', '*naturalis ratio*' or 'the nature of things'.[14] These "two elements of the law are" quite often "at odds, and fight and restrict each other, only to come together in a higher union perhaps at a later point in time."[15] In this conflict between formal and material elements, Savigny thus saw a basic precondition for all areas of the law. He stated further that there was no all-inclusive answer as to how this conflict could be resolved in a 'higher union'. This was a question that each era would have to find its own answer to and this would prove more difficult for some than for others.

Savigny thus opposes the 'modern' understanding of state which strives to monopolise justice within its laws. It is based on the notion of a social contract, which seeks to justify the liquidation of any non-state-derived normative system such as that defined by customary law, by associations or by science. Entering into a social contract has the purpose of founding a legal system by agreeing to confer undivided power to a single sovereign. The same narrative served as a basis for the legal and political philosophies of such different proponents of natural law as Hobbes, Pufendorf, Thomasius, Rousseau and Kant. The political philosophies developed by these authors were based on a number of premises, only the most important of which shall be mentioned here. Humankind originally lived in a natural state and the legal system was an artificial construct created on the basis of the social contract; any law developed outside of the state must be classified as 'non-law' and aspects of equity must be ignored, even in cases where a decision runs contrary to the "obvious

---

[14] Savigny: *System I*, pp. 54–56, 55.
[15] Ibid., p. 54f. See also Alfred Manigk: *Savigny und der Modernismus im Recht*, Berlin 1914, pp. 14, 150; Behrends: *Struktur und Wert*, pp. 58–60.

claims" of justice because a judge must not base his decisions on 'undetermined conditions'.[16] Savigny refuted these theories. In his work on the legal philosophy of enlightened absolutism he stressed that the law already existed prior to the conclusion of the social contract. Moreover, he criticised the voluntarist attitude of the 'modern' doctrine of legal sources and made a fundamental distinction between legislation and law. Despite the fact that it had seemed to have been overcome, etatism based on theories surrounding the sources of law gained new momentum with the foundation of the German Empire in 1870/71. The authors of the German civil code once again began to doubt the legal potency of non-state sources and to push them into the role of mere interpretative tools. It was not without reason then that towards the end of the 19th century Gierke made these resigned remarks:

> "Therefore, the teachings of the masters of historical jurisprudence have had no impact on the German lawmaker. Whilst the *scientific* achievements of the Historical School cannot be undone, it has become obsolete in *life*. The legislative powers have taken up exactly where they once left off, at a time when new insight into the nature and development of the law, which had emanated from Germany, called on them to take stock."[17]

For the time being, we may state that the Historical School of Jurisprudence was opposed to constitutional positivism, which had come to power as a result of the teachings on enlightened absolutism. 'Modern' etatism seeks to monopolise justice within state laws. It attempts to overcome the dualist nature of classical Roman jurisprudence by recognising only *one* legal framework, i.e. formal statutory law (*ius strictum*). Leibniz was among the opponents of the one-sidedness of a legalism that is expressed by the notion of an omnipotent lawmaker. His objections against the legal philosophy of Hobbes culminated in the statement that he (Hobbes) had "only considered the strict law."[18]

---

[16] On this and on the following statements see the references cited in Stephan Meder: *Doppelte Körper im Recht. Traditionen des Pluralismus zwischen staatlicher Einheit und transnationaler Vielheit*, Tübingen 2015, pp. 99, 131, 137–190 (and Chapter IV).
[17] Otto von Gierke: *Der Entwurf eines bürgerlichen Gesetzbuches und das deutsche Recht*, Leipzig 1889, p. 122 (italics in the original text).
[18] Leibniz: *Méditation sur la notion commune de la justice*, pp. 76–78.

4. Leibniz' 'ius strictum' as an Element of the Doctrine of Legal Sources

As suggested at the beginning of this contribution, Leibniz discusses the term *'ius strictum'* in two different contexts: as an element of the sources of statutory law on one hand and as a level in his three-part division of natural law on the other. Due to the 'dual' or 'bipartite' structure of the doctrine of legal sources, it is essential to include the material elements when studying *'ius strictum'* in addition to its formal side.[19] Leibniz discusses the peculiarities that separate statutory law from natural law by using the teaching of jurisprudence as an example. He says that while the different grades of natural law can be "precisely taught" without "mentioning current law", the same is not possible "in reverse."[20] Positive law, therefore, lacks the independence that characterises natural law and the former cannot be taught without mentioning the latter. This approach was compatible with advanced Roman jurisprudence which, besides *'ius civile'* also took into account *'ius gentium'*, *'ius aequum'* and *'naturalis ratio'*. According to Leibniz, Hobbes' failing was to consider only 'strict law', i.e. the formal structure of the law of the land. In Leibniz' opinion this type of strict law could also be viewed as 'volitional law' (*ius voluntarium*), which should be seen as separate from a law that is based on rational thought.[21]

As a positive law, strict law draws its effectiveness from those who have the "highest power" (*summam potestatem*) "within a state system."[22] This refers to the notion of personal power which found a new basis of legitimisation in the 'modern' idea of sovereignty developed in the 16th century. Bodin already recognised that the main feature of a sovereign was his ability to prescribe laws and to change them at will, that they were "dependant solely on the will of the holder of sovereignty", who could thus "bind all his subjects."[23]

---

[19] Letter to Conring dated 9th/19th April 1670, pp. 68, 69 ('dual' or 'bipartite' in the sense that *'ius strictum'* is juxtaposed with *'aequitas'* on one hand and *'pietas'* on the other).
[20] Letter to Conring dated 9th/19th April 1670, p. 68. On the function of 'reversal' in Leibniz' teaching on natural law see Busche: *Leibniz' Weg ins perspektivische Universum*, p. 395.
[21] Leibniz: *Praefatio to the Codex Juris Gentium Diplomaticus*, pp. 63, 64.
[22] Ibid., pp. 63, 64. This also applies to non-state sources such as custom and autonomy, whose validity had to be confirmed by an act of volition on the part of the sovereign, cf. Stephan Meder: *Ius non scriptum. Traditionen privater Rechtsetzung*, Tübingen ²2009, pp. 63–66.
[23] Jean Bodin: *Sechs Bücher über den Staat*, ed. by Peter Cornelius Mayer-Tasch, Munich 1981, I 8 (p. 216) as well as I 10 (p. 292) and I 8 (p. 223).

Similar statements were made by such diverse representatives of secular natural law as Hobbes, Pufendorf, Rousseau and Kant.[24] Leibniz, on the other hand, questioned how far law and justice were dependant on the will of the sovereign, i.e. on his power. He assumed in this context that the proponents of the 'modern' notion of the state viewed the law as an arbitrary command issued by a ruler to his subjects to abide by the law.

As a positive law strict law is based on power which, according to Leibniz, is ambivalent in character. Power can be a valuable asset if "it is linked with wisdom and goodwill."[25] It is therefore entirely possible that the laws that spring forth from power correspond with natural law, which is based on reason. However, power often lacks wisdom and benevolence. It runs the risk of putting volition above reason. The consequence is that "very bad laws are passed and enforced."[26] Leibniz argues against authors like Hobbes who construe the concept of law from the phenomenon of power and who wish to make the law conditional on power. In Leibniz' view this is an error that leads to the sources of law becoming restricted. Citing the dangers linked with voluntarism he cautions against restricting the law to legislation and against eliminating natural law. Where power reigns, it converts "law into a fact", which can significantly differ from a higher justice. One must make a distinction between law to mean *lex* and law to mean *ius*; they must not be confused because only law as in *lex*, and not law as in *ius*, which is based on God, can be unjust.[27]

Leibniz, therefore, had good reason to argue against Hobbes by accusing him of focusing only on 'strict law'. The objection was based on the claim that Hobbes was dispensing of the central condition of all law, i.e. the conflict between the formal and material elements, in such a way that only *one* legal structure would remain. Leibniz' criticism against the monistic view of the

---

[24] For a more detailed discussion see Meder: *Doppelte Körper im Recht*, pp. 127f.
[25] Leibniz: *Méditation sur la notion commune de la justice*, pp. 62, 63; for more on this see Hartmut Schiedermair: *Das Phänomen der Macht und die Idee des Rechts bei Gottfried Wilhelm Leibniz*, Wiesbaden 1970.
[26] Leibniz: *Méditation sur la notion commune de la justice*, p. 61.
[27] Ibid., pp. 61–63; *Nova Methodus*, § 70 (pp. 341f.). The governing thought for Leibniz' distinction between '*quaestio iuris*' and '*quaestio facti*' is that there can be no recourse to any of the higher levels of legitimacy as long as the argument is made only from the viewpoint of positive private law. See also Peter König: "Das System des Rechts und die Lehre von den Fiktionen bei Leibniz", in: Jan Schröder (ed.): *Entwicklung der Methodenlehre in Rechtswissenschaft und Philosophie vom 16. bis 18. Jahrhundert*, Stuttgart 1998, pp. 137–161, here 145–152 (in Leibniz' view, statements like "*auctoritas, non veritas facit legem*" or "*stat pro ratione voluntas*" are maxims "*d'un tyran*").

legal sources is of fundamental significance; it goes way beyond Hobbes's thinking and is directed at the entire 'modern' theory of the state. Bodin had already favoured the command of the sovereign over the concept of equity: "A legal prohibition is stronger than even the obvious claims of equity."[28] As suggested above, Kant also viewed equity as a "right without force" because "a judge cannot base his rulings on undetermined conditions."[29] Leibniz was critical of this notion because in his view such teaching resulted in a purely negative concept of justice. He claimed that authors like Hobbes and many others, who limited themselves to a restricted notion of justice whilst ignoring the concept of equity, ran the risk of allowing the highest law to become the highest violation of law (*summum jus summa est injuria*).[30]

The interim finding for now is that as well as being a grade of natural law, '*ius strictum*' can also be a source of positive law. Drawing on the 'dualism' that characterised advanced Roman jurisprudence, Leibniz formulated a bipartite doctrine of legal sources. He therefore considered it to be impossible to teach "current law" independent of natural law.[31] According to Leibniz, Hobbes was wrong to believe that one could dispense of the bipartite structure of the doctrine of legal sources by focusing solely on strict law whilst uncoupling formal law from its material elements. Whilst positive law must remain linked with natural law, the latter can in fact be taught in isolation[32] because it is entirely independent of '*ius voluntarium*', i.e. from the commands of the highest statutory power. This is significant particularly with regard to '*ius strictum*' and its relationship with the other two grades, which shall now be discussed in more detail.

---

[28] Bodin: *Sechs Bücher über den Staat*, I 8 (p. 231).
[29] Immanuel Kant: *Metaphysik der Sitten* (1797), in: *Werksausgabe*, vol. VIII, Berlin ¹⁰1993, pp. 341f. (Einleitung § E).
[30] Leibniz: *Méditation sur la notion commune de la justice*, pp. 76–78.
[31] Letter to Conring dated 9th/19th April 1670, p. 68 (see above). See also Busche: *Leibniz' Lehre von den drei Stufen des Naturrechts*, pp. 29–53, 37 (the bipartite structure of Leibniz' doctrine of legal sources characterised as a '*second-order*' principle).
[32] Letter to Conring dated 9th/19th April 1670, p. 68 (because here the link is a precondition within the three grades).

5. Leibniz' 'ius strictum' Within the Grades of Natural Law

Leibniz dealt with the norms of '*ius strictum*' as a natural law in various writings.[33] The crucial point here was not the will of the sovereign but the general precept of '*neminem laedere*'. The notion that one must not injure anyone, in his view, was a rule of actual, 'pure law' (*iuris meri*).[34] At times he also termed '*ius* strictum' as a law of ownership (*ius proprietatis*). The term 'ownership' must be understood in a rather broad sense, since it encompasses both the law of property and the inalienable basic rights to freedom and equality as well as the right to life and physical integrity, to name but a few. In principle, 'ownership' as '*ius proprietatis*' is equivalent to the precept of '*neminem laedere*', or in Leibniz' own words: "*ius proprietas cuius est neminem laedere.*"[35]

5.1 The Relationship Between 'ius strictum' on One Hand and 'aequitas' and 'pietas' on the Other

The concepts of ownership and the ban on injuring anyone, however, have yet another meaning with regard to the structure of law. In Leibniz' view, '*ius strictum*' in essence is private law, whilst '*aequitas*' and '*pietas*' rather belong to the sphere of public law.[36] In accordance with advanced Roman law Leibniz therefore makes a distinction between the individual parts of '*ius strictum*' and the 'collective' aims of the other two levels or grades. That is why he also characterises the principle that governs '*ius strictum*' as '*utilitas propria*'.[37] This notion is also in accord with the perspective of advanced Roman law, in which private law as '*ius strictum*' protects an individual's self-interests.[38]

---

[33] E.g. *Nova Methodus*, § 73 (p. 343); *Praefatio to the Codex Juris Gentium Diplomaticus*, pp. 61–64; *Méditation sur la notion commune de la justice*, pp. 74–81.

[34] *Praefatio* (fn. 1), pp. 61f. The terminological parallels between Leibniz and Savigny, who also uses the word 'pure' in this context, are remarkable (see the references in Chapter II 3).

[35] Leibniz: *Tentamina quaedam ad novum codicem legum condendum*, p. 2867.

[36] Ibid., p. 2865 (where '*iustitia particularis*', for instance, is referred to as '*commutativa in privato, distributiva in publico*'). See also *Praefatio*, pp. 61–64 ("within the state, equity is governed by political laws which ensure that the subjects are happy"); *Méditation sur la notion commune de la justice*, pp. 75f.; Busche: *Leibniz' Lehre von den drei Stufen des Naturrechts*, p. 37.

[37] Leibniz: De legum rationibus inquirendis (1678/79?), in: A VI, 4 C, 2775–2780, 2778.

[38] Behrends: *Struktur und Wert*, p. 56; id.: *Überlegungen zum Vertrag zugunsten Dritter im römischen Privatrecht*, pp. 848, 852, 857, 859 (as distinct from the *bona fides* principle); Busche: *Leibniz' Lehre von den drei Stufen des Naturrechts*, p. 37. One should take into account

According to Leibniz formal law has a fundamental impact on the order of law and its removal would plunge any human community into pure chaos. As opposed to Hobbes and other proponents of a statutory positivism, however, Leibniz is of the opinion that formal law should be accompanied by a material principle in order to ensure that a legal system also has adequate regard for third-party interests.

The central role that Leibniz attaches to '*ius strictum*' raises the question as to its relationship with the other two grades. The opinion that '*ius strictum*' is placed at the lowest level is widely held and the proponents of this view can partially invoke Leibniz' teaching.[39] Upon closer inspection, however, it becomes clear that with regard to private rights the higher levels or grades of jurisprudence, i.e. *aequitas* and *pietas* also come into play.[40]

The topic of private property shall serve here as an example for Leibniz' view on how the three legal precepts work together. The viewpoint from which he discusses the problems that arise from legitimising the concept of property is defined by his perception of the ideal state. However, the opinions on how this perception should be interpreted diverge considerably and include labels such as 'communism', 'virtuous state', 'Christian natural law', 'philosophy of charitable justice' and 'decided liberalism'.[41] This divergence arises from the fact that Leibniz gave different opinions when discussing the legitimisation of private property in different contexts. He felt that in an ideal state

---

here that 'self-interest' and 'benefit' in Leibniz' writings have special meaning because he views them as being linked with honour and respectability; for more on this see Busche: *Leibniz' Weg ins perspektivische Universum*, pp. 299–303.

[39] Hans-Peter Schneider: *Justitia universalis. Quellenstudien zur Geschichte des "Christlichen Naturrechts" bei Gottfried Wilhelm Leibniz*, Frankfurt a. M. 1967, p. 409; Klaus Luig: "Leibniz als Dogmatiker des Privatrechts", in: Okko Behrends (ed.): *Römisches Recht in der europäischen Tradition*, Ebelsbach 1985, pp. 213–256, here 213 (both with further references).

[40] As mentioned above, these material elements belong in the realm of public law inasmuch as they have a redistributive impact and apply to society in general. The phenomenon here, however, refers to the realm of private law where, in the words of Savigny, not only 'pure' elements but also 'mixed' elements can arise in the shape of statutory purposes. (*System I*, fn. 3, pp. 54–56). Structures of this kind are not limited to private law but also exist in criminal and public law, where formal elements can also be accompanied and corrected by material elements.

[41] Cf. Werner Schneiders: "Respublica optima", in: *Studia Leibnitiana* 9 (1977), pp. 1–26, 16, 22f. (communism, virtuous state); Schneider: *Justitia Universalis*, p. 333 (Christian natural law); Luig: *Leibniz als Dogmatiker des Privatrecht*, p. 256 (charitable justice); Gerhard Otte: "Leibniz und die juristische Methode", in: *ZNR* 5 (1983), pp. 1–21, here 21 (decided liberalism).

all goods should be common property, as is the case in monastic communities.⁴² In reality, however, everyone must "have their own sphere", which they can "properly take care of". Competition, according to Leibniz, is beneficial: "If everything belonged to everyone, it would be neglected by all." He does concede that there are exceptions to this general rule, for instance in tax law. However, intrusions into the right of ownership are only rarely acceptable and must be well-founded.⁴³

Strict law, therefore, puts boundaries on the concept of the Christian welfare state or charitable justice. It is not permitted "to dispossess the rich of their property to placate the poor",⁴⁴ since at the level of 'ius strictum' all humankind must be seen "as equal." All are treated as if they had the same ability to pursue their affairs in an autonomous and autocratic manner: "Differences between people may not have an impact here."⁴⁵ In order to explain the concept of 'abstract' equality, Leibniz refers to the Greek philosopher Xenophon, who recounted the following story of a conflict between two boys:

> "Kyros had been elected judge in a dispute between two boys. The stronger of the two had forced the other to swap his clothes because he had decided that the other's garment would better suit his stature and vice versa. Kyros had ruled in favour of the robber but his educator had suggested that the point was not whom the toga suited best but to whom it belonged."⁴⁶

---

⁴² Leibniz: *Méditation sur la notion commune de la justice*, p. 81; for more on this see Patrick Riley: *Leibniz' Universal Jurisprudence. Justice as the Charity of the Wise*, Cambridge 1996, pp. 202–205.
⁴³ Leibniz: *Méditation sur la notion commune de la justice*, pp. 80f.
⁴⁴ Ibid., pp. 80f.
⁴⁵ Leibniz: *Praefatio*, p. 62. Almost 200 years later, Georg Friedrich Puchta got to the heart of the matter of legal equality from the point of view of 'abstraction': "How much abstraction is required to see a man [who is poverty-stricken due to sickness and through no fault of his own] and a rich man, who takes up capital in order to speculate, thereby adding thousands more to his already existing thousands, and to view these as equal, as indeed they are from a legal standpoint." Nevertheless, according to Leibniz, the principle of equality does not exclude the recognition of aspects of imparity. This matter shall be revisited below (V. 2).
⁴⁶ Leibniz: *Praefatio*, p. 62 (cf. Hugo Grotius: *De jure belli ac pacis*, 1625, lib. 1, cap. 1, § VIII). Leibniz' interpretation of this tale can also be seen as a criticism of utilitarianism. Based on the utilitarian felicific calculus, there is no reason why individuals should lay claim to goods in cases where others would derive more benefit from them ("whom the toga suits better"). In the absence of a 'bulwark' such as '*ius strictum*' (VIII.1), individuals cannot be recognised as separate entities nor can their (subjective) rights be seen as boundaries (for a criticism of utilitarian principles see John Rawls: *A theory of justice*, Oxford 1971, revised edition 2000, pp. 19–24). It is no more possible to draw such boundaries from the platform of the *Innentheorie* (internal theory) (VIII.2), which is ultimately where its ideological susceptibility lies.

Under the premises of '*ius strictum*' it is therefore completely irrelevant to whom the garment is best suited. "Differences between people" or the "standing of a person" must not be taken into account when "exchanging goods".[47] Only in exceptional cases is it permissible to deviate from '*iustitia commutativa*', for instance, "when a higher legal right carries weight."[48] How can this preference for strict law (*iustitia commutativa*) vis-à-vis equity (*iustitia distributiva*) be explained? Do property law and contract law, as branches of '*ius strictum*' not belong on the lowest level? Leibniz appears to be pre-empting objections by stating that the principle of equity demands that "strict law must be adhered to."[49] However, the fact that positive law is sometimes forced to take a back seat to the principle of equity raises the question as to whether this statement could perhaps amount to a *petitio principii*. In any case, the various grades of the law must not be separated at all costs; they overlap and interact in a variety of ways.

The interaction between the three grades also becomes evident in cases where 'higher' principles impose restrictions on '*ius strictum*'. One example that was controversially discussed in the 17th century was the question of whether the right to property should also extend to one's children. Hobbes and some of his contemporaries clearly answered in the affirmative. Whilst Leibniz did not dispute the fact that parents have power over their children, he believed that the concept of property was "too far-reaching" if it was used in reference to children. In Leibniz' view, children – contrary to "horses or dogs" – had the right as "intelligent and rational souls to be naturally and inalienably free."[50] For the same reason, there could be no right to ownership of slaves.

---

[47] Leibniz: *Praefatio*, p. 62.

[48] Ibid., p. 62 (the fact that such 'weight' must also be taken into account in other areas such as contract law will be revisited in the next paragraph). The background to this is the current debate on 'balancing' (e.g. Robert Alexy: "On Balancing and Subsumption. A Structural Comparison", in: Ratio Iuris 16/4 (2003), pp. 433–449). Under the premises of a 'dual' structure, however, this can be done within the realms of private law itself, whilst conduct values today must often be brought to bear by way of an (albeit controversial) interpretation of the constitution. The foundations of Leibniz' philosophy of law in the study of Roman law can thus also be used to make an argument in support of recent calls for the regaining of 'autonomy' in private law and relief for constitutional jurisdiction (see also fn. 40).

[49] *Nova Methodus*, § 74 (pp. 343, 344); for similar statements see *Praefatio*, p. 62 (where he claims that it is equity itself that prompts us to apply *ius strictum* in business dealings); on the question of competition between the different levels see also *Méditation sur la notion commune de la justice*, pp. 80, 81 (priority of the right to property over aspects of reasonableness).

[50] Leibniz: *Méditation sur la notion commune de la justice*, pp. 78, 79.

The principles of equity demanded "that one must care for the welfare of others in the same way as one would expect them to care for oneself."[51] He also cited the principle of charity (*caritas*), "to promote the happiness of others."[52]

Such restrictions to the concept of property by equity (*aequitas*) are checked once more at the highest level (*pietas*) and the result is confirmed: God created man in His own likeness. That is why in his empire "slaves have the same right of citizenship as their masters."[53] The concept of property therefore goes beyond the level of *ius strictum*. Its contents and boundaries can only be identified by paying regard to *aequitas* and *pietas*. Mutatis mutandis this also applies to other private rights. Because Leibniz does not show how some of the conflicts between the precepts should be resolved, Adolf Trendelenburg presumed that "if equity means distributive justice, it requires the usual as a measure of the differences in the unusual."[54] There is substantial evidence to suggest that Leibniz was guided by the principle of rule (*ius strictum*) and exception (*aequitas*) when determining the relationship between the formal and material elements of law. This hypothesis shall now be examined in greater detail.

5.2 The Principle of Rule and Exception as a Basis upon Which to Determine the Relationship Between the Formal and Material Elements of Law

As shown above, Leibniz attached fundamental importance to '*ius strictum*' as part of the order of law. In contrast to the proponents of statutory positivism, however, he believed that formal law should be accompanied by material prin-

---

[51] Leibniz: *Méditation sur la notion commune de la justice*, pp. 79, 80. The background to this is a negative version of the 'Golden Rule' ("do not do unto others as you would not have them do unto you"), which Leibniz repeatedly referred to in other contexts, see e.g. *Nova Methodus*, § 74 (pp. 343, 344). For a conflicting understanding of the 'Golden Rule' put forward by Pufendorf, Thomasius or Kant see Hans-Ulrich Hoche: Art.: "Regel, goldene", in: *Historisches Wörterbuch der Philosophie*, vol. 8, Darmstadt 1992, Sp. 450–464, here 554f.
[52] Leibniz: *Méditation sur la notion commune de la justice*, pp. 79, 80. In this case he was referring to *caritas* as a subset of equity (*angustiore vocis sensu caritas*), Praefatio, p. 61, which must not be confused with '*caritas sapientis*' not discussed here.
[53] Leibniz: *Méditation sur la notion commune de la justice*, pp. 78, 79; see also Schiedermair: *Das Phänomen der Macht*, pp. 114f.
[54] Adolf Trendelenburg: "Das Verhältniss des Allgemeinen zum Besondern in Leibnizens philosophischer Betrachtung und dessen Naturrecht", in: *Historische Beiträge zur Philosophie*, vol. 2, Berlin 1855, pp. 233–256, here 241–250, 247, 249.

ciples. In his thinking, '*aequitas*' and '*pietas*' were the 'higher' or more perfect (*perfectior*) levels or grades, which 'in cases of dispute' could override '*ius strictum*'.[55] This means that Leibniz placed the grades of natural law in a hierarchical order. What consequences can be drawn from this for the application of law? Should in Leibniz' view the 'higher' and 'more perfect' grades have been given the lead in legal decisions? This question can be answered in the negative, and the reasons are as follows:

Liberty, equality, property, physical integrity and peace are all among the basic principles of human interaction and communal living. They are values that are safeguarded by '*ius strictum*' and are confirmed and reinforced on both 'higher' levels. At first glance, it is therefore very difficult to discern any differences between the three grades. They are only brought to the fore when a legal decision based on '*ius strictum*' comes into conflict with either '*aequitas*' or '*pietas*'. How can this conflict be resolved? How can a higher level or grade assert itself over a lower one? Leibniz uses 'equality' as an example to illustrate his beliefs. He stresses that it is not only strict law but also equity that dictates that we must "start from the assumption that all men are equal", unless (*nisi*) a higher legal right has such a strong impact that deviation from the principle of equality appears justified.[56] A similar wording can be found in his drafts for the second edition of *Nova Methodus*. In them Leibniz first of all repeated the emphatic basic principle that "equity itself" demands that we "adhere to strict law."[57] The planned second edition included a clarification in the form of a reservation: "unless there is an obstacle" (*si nil obstet*).[58]

It was thus the old pattern of 'rule and exception' which is still accepted today and which Leibniz used to determine the relationship between the different levels or grades. The principle initially states that the legal system is based on a dual structure, within which the 'rule' belongs within the realm of '*ius strictum*' and the exception within the spheres of '*aequitas*' and '*pietas*'. There is no general answer to the question whether it should be the formal or material elements that take precedence. We may, however, assume that the presumption of appropriateness speaks in favour of implementing the 'rule' ('*ius strictum*') as opposed to the exception. This presumption absolves those who wish to invoke strict law because there is no need to deduce or justify the

---

[55] Leibniz: *Nova Methodus*, § 73 (p. 343); *Praefatio*, pp. 61–64.
[56] Leibniz: *Praefatio*, p. 62.
[57] Leibniz: *Nova Methodus*, § 74 , (pp. 343, 344).
[58] Ibid., (p. 344, l. 26).

values upon which it stands for each new case. There are, however, situations where the application of strict law would lead to injustice (*summum jus summa est injuria*).[59] In such cases, those who feel obliged to mitigate the severity of '*ius strictum*' must offer plausible reasons why they believe that deviation is appropriate in a particular case. The consequence of the assumption is therefore that those who wish to dismiss it carry a particular burden of argument. If '*ius strictum*' did not have its own weight or priority, any detailed reasoning would become redundant in cases where it was put aside. The burden of argument thus makes it more difficult to dispense with '*ius strictum*' and the consequence is that it is binding to some degree, even in cases where it has been breached for reasons of equity.

The interaction between '*ius strictum*' on one hand and '*aequitas*' (or '*pietas*') on the other can be defined more precisely by saying that the severity of formal law is mitigated in certain circumstances and that it is restricted in its administration or enforcement whilst still continuing to exist. Strict law is rather static, in Leibniz' words "it derives from the definition of the terms".[60] Today we would speak of the 'subsumption' of the circumstances under the facts of a case.[61] The advantages of '*ius strictum*' are apparent and have often been stressed: it gives clarity, security and predictability to the law. Unstrict law, on the other hand, is characterised by increased dynamics and as a consequence by a certain lack of definition.[62] This does not mean that it cannot be given somewhat more definition by typifying it and in fact it often finds its way into legislation via general clauses or indefinite legal terms. The values it represents, however, have an open impact, i.e. they must be put in concrete terms. They cannot be used indiscriminately but have to be adapted to a particular situation with due regard being paid to all aspects of each individual case.[63]

---

[59] Leibniz: *Méditation sur la notion commune de la justice*, pp. 76–78.
[60] E.g. *Nova Methodus*, § 73, (p. 343).
[61] See e.g. Ulfrid Neumann: "Subsumtion als regelorientierte Fallentscheidung", in: Gottfried Gabriel/Rolf Gröschner (ed.): *Subsumtion. Schlüsselbegriff der Juristischen Methodenlehre*, Tübingen 2012, pp. 311–334.
[62] In his "Elemente des Naturrechts" (A VI, 1, 431–485) Leibniz made an attempt at developing criteria that would help jurists to decide cases where aspects of equity played a special role. However, he concluded that such aspects could only be legally posited to a limited degree. To define equity as a norm, he felt, was "*difficillimè generaliter*" (Elemente, p. 455), for more detail see Busche: *Leibniz' Weg ins perspektivische Universum*, pp. 310, 340–346.
[63] We now use terms such as 'complexity' or 'boundaries of subsumption' when we discuss this situation-based dilution of the law, cf. Neumann: *Subsumtion als regelorientierte*

5.3 Implementation and Enforcement of 'ius strictum'

Next, Leibniz attempts to measure the weight of *'ius strictum'* and of *'aequitas'* against each other even more precisely by raising the question of the ways in which the material elements can be put into practice.[64] Here he uses contract law and picks the principle of contract compliance as an example. Using sentences like 'a contract is a contract' or *'pacta sunt servanda'* the legal system puts words to the principle that each partner is strictly bound to the declaration of his will.[65] Only under this precondition is it possible for an area, within which large parts of society move about freely, with private autonomy and in a self-regulatory manner, to achieve the necessary structural security and stability. This does not mean, however, that material aspects, which are targeted at ensuring a certain degree of consideration in a society's legal dealings, should not be taken into account.

Leibniz discusses the topic based on cases where one party hopes to gain an advantage over the other by means of a 'deceitful' (*subtiles*) contract or 'contract refinement': those who seek to dispense of their duties in this manner, "owe me something nonetheless."[66] The only problem is to find a way for the outsmarted creditor to enforce his rights which are solely based on the principle of equity. He has no inherent 'right to prosecution' because a claim

---

Fallentscheidung, pp. 329–332. Of course, it once again becomes apparent that, due to its 'fixedness on rules' modern methodological teaching can only have limited regard for the material side of the law (p. 329). Whilst the process of 'subsumption' has great importance for *'ius strictum'*, it cannot be applied to principles such as 'good faith', *'aequitas'* or similar behavioural values. Another question is whether and how far 'legal doctrine', though very important in private law, can be covered by the 'rule' concept that is widely used in legal theory.

[64] *Nova Methodus*, § 74 (p. 344).

[65] The fact that Leibniz, in accordance with Roman jurisprudence, was opposed to the notion that so-called '*pacta nuda*' were legally binding, can be disregarded in this context, see Stephan Meder: "Gottfried Wilhelm Leibniz: Reform des Privatrechts auf Grundlage historischen Naturrechts", in: *ZEuP* 2016, pp. 687–707.

[66] *Nova Methodus*, § 74 (p. 344). Leibniz discusses the same subject in even more detail in his 'Elemente des Naturrechts': "It is an unjust action to create a disadvantage for someone else in order to gain advantage for oneself" (for instance by using unclear or non-transparent wording). According to Leibniz' system of three levels or grades, aspects of imparity can therefore indeed be brought to bear. However, the self-damaging disposition of one's own rights is also a distinct possibility in Leibniz' view and this is still widely recognised in accordance with the principle of contractual freedom, see further references in Busche: *Leibniz' Weg ins perspektivische Universum*, pp. 311, 316.

such as that can only be brought in accordance with '*ius strictum*'. Nevertheless, based on the principle of distributive justice, those who have acted deceitfully, are obliged to give him something (*suum cuique tribuere*).[67]

Leibniz does not discuss in detail, which of the aspects of equity could be used to justify breaking with '*ius strictum*' in this case. He is more interested in the question of how the outsmarted creditor can enforce his rights. The obvious solution is to refer to the 'law' (*lex*).[68] In Leibniz' conviction, material elements of law can also by typified and given a structure by the lawmakers. Examples from present-day law include the protection of a buyer who has acted in good faith against an owner's claim for surrender of property in property law, the differentiation of the duty of care in the law of torts or the general principle of strict liability.[69]

Equity, however, can only be posited to a limited degree because the weight of its demands is often dependent on the situation in question and on the circumstances of the individual case. There must therefore be other ways and means beyond legislation by which it can be incorporated into the legal order. Leibniz speaks in pointed but also erratic terms of a 'superior being' (*superior*), who is able, particularly by means of objection (*exceptio*), to help the material elements to establish their position. Who is this 'superior being'? Hubertus Busche offers the following explanation:

---

[67] *Nova Methodus*, § 74 (p. 344).
[68] Ibid., § 74 (p. 344).
[69] On Leibniz' attempts to generalise material elements to such a degree that they can be incorporated into legislation see fn. 62. Modern consumer rights have also developed out of the aspects of 'good faith': the appeal to '*ius strictum*' ('a contract is a contract') must be curtailed in cases where an overly powerful contractual partner has created a disproportionate disadvantage (e.g. § 307 of the German Civil Code). However, this legislative structure must not result in the model of independent freedom being replaced by 'bound' freedom or the sovereign by an inferior individual (see below, Chapter VIII). Incidentally, the structures that develop from the material side of the law can develop their own formalism. Modern consumer rights, for instance, have become a source of new formal requirements. One example is an increase in the rights of revocation, which can be exercised without providing an explanation. Because these rights are often abused, the question increasingly being raised is whether the legal system should be allowed to make an exception to the 'exception' (in the sense of a lack of worthiness of protection and a return to '*ius strictum*' in the area of private autonomy). The fundamental problem, i.e. the question as to whether some of these new phenomena (standard terms and conditions) are even contracts or perhaps, rather, just norms, cannot be discussed here.

"Aspects of equity cannot be claimed from below but only granted from above. The 'superior being' is a person authorised by the state."[70]

To this entirely fitting interpretation of the linguistically difficult statement of the young Leibniz, which in German translation loses its meaning, one might add that the 'superior being' would have been the Roman judicial magistrate – the *praetor*.[71] During a particular period of advanced Roman law, this 'judicial magistrate' was charged with enforcing material elements, for instance the concept of *bona fides* or the prohibition of *dolus*, in such a way that the formal law would be left intact but its implementation was slightly moderated.[72] However, because humankind, according to Leibniz, lives in a constant flow of time, and the past, present and future are thus in a continuum and closely intertwined, we may assume that the term 'superior being' could also refer to a modern-day judge.[73]

The fact remains: Leibniz' concept of '*ius strictum*' largely harmonises with that of the 'dualism' that had developed in Roman law on the basis of the rule and exception pattern. How closely Leibniz identified with Roman jurisprudence is clear, particularly from his recourse to a 'superior being' and the function of this person to enable the material elements of the law to prevail by granting an opportunity to object (*exceptio*). Whilst '*ius strictum*' may be placed on the lowest level of natural law, this hierarchy must not be misunderstood to mean that Leibniz wished to give the lead to '*aequitas*' (or '*pietas*'). The opposite was in fact the case: based on the rule and exception

---

[70] Editor's remarks on *Nova Methodus*, in: Gottfried Wilhelm Leibniz: *Frühe Schriften zum Naturrecht*, p. 430. On questions of the legal implementation and enforceability of equity rules see also Busche: *Leibniz' Weg ins perspektivische Universum*, pp. 318–320, 322, 345.

[71] E.g. D.44.4.1.1 (by allowing the respondent to file an objection, the praetor grants him an opportunity to defend himself and this prevents the claimant from using the severity of strict law to his own advantage).

[72] Behrends: *Struktur und Wert*, pp. 57f.; id.: "Das Werk Otto Lenels und die Kontinuität der romanistischen Fragestellungen. Zugleich ein Beitrag zur grundsätzlichen Überwindung der interpolationistischen Methode", in: *Index: quaderni camerti di studi romanistici : organo del Gruppo di Ricerca sulla Diffusione del Diritto Romano* 19 (1991), pp. 271–309, 272f.

[73] In any case, the premises upon which Leibniz' political philosophy was based, granted judges much greater power than for instance Bodin, Hobbes, Pufendorf, Rousseau or Kant would have had. The fact that Leibniz gave judges a comparatively large scope of action, has justifiably been stressed by several authors, cf., amongst others, Luig: *Leibniz als Dogmatiker des Privatrechts*, pp. 255f. Ronald Dworkin's concept of the Judge Hercules, however, would not have found Leibniz' approval because of the danger of arbitrary judgements. This is supported by his varied attempts at structuring and typecasting those elements of the law that modern legal theory tends to label 'principles'.

pattern, '*ius strictum*' is presumed to be appropriate. This presumption can only be refuted by making a concerted effort to build an argument to prove that reasons for equity exist.

6. The Subsidiary Character of Natural Law in the Contemporary System of the Sources of Law

Besides the levels of natural law, Leibniz distinguished yet another set of three levels pertaining to positive law. This was to create a structure for the multitude of sources of law that existed in the Holy Roman Empire in Leibniz' time. The division started on the lowest level with municipal law (*ius municipale*). If a case could not be solved on the basis of municipal law, imperial law was to be invoked and where that did not result in a ruling, "Roman law" was to "be applied" on the third level.[74] This list, however, was by no means complete. Written law was to be accompanied by unwritten law.[75] Leibniz made no mention of the ranking of these two groups of sources. We may, however, assume that he would – in accordance with contemporary teaching – have placed (unwritten) customary law on the lowest and written law on the 'higher' levels.[76] In this division, even the 'lower' level can claim a certain primacy. However, because customary, municipal or Imperial law often showed a lack of usable rules, legal practice still often reverted back to Roman law, even as late as the 17th century.

Leibniz' description of the levels of positive law was largely congruent with the core ideas of the medieval theory of statutes, which regulated the relationship between competing sources of law. The ranking in medieval

---

[74] Leibniz repeatedly discussed the subject, however, in by far the greatest detail in his letter to Conring dated 9th/19th April 1670, p. 68.

[75] Leibniz, letter to Conring dated 9th/19th April 1670, p. 68 (it was implied here that unwritten law and the 'lower' levels of law (special law) had the same 'dual' structure as outlined above with respect to written law).

[76] In Leibniz' view – and indeed the prevailing view at the time – Roman law, i.e., *ius commune*, would have been a 'written' law, cf. e.g. his letter to Louis Ferrand dated 31st January 1672, in: A I, 1, pp. 180f., 181 ("core of Roman laws"); letter to Conring dated 9th/19th April 1670, p. 69 ("forest of Roman laws"). Whilst Conring had raised new questions with regard to the validity of *ius commune* by exposing the Lothar legend (Meder: *Rechtsgeschichte*, pp. 244, 252), more time would pass before this would have any consequences for the theory of legal sources and the *ius commune* would be classified as an (unwritten) customary law. For more detail see Stephan Meder: *Ius non scriptum. Traditionen privater Rechtsetzung*, Tübingen ²2009, pp. 130–132.

thinking adhered to the following formula: the statute overruled the law of the region, the law of the region overruled Imperial law and Imperial law overruled common law (*ius commune*). Besides special laws such as customary or statutory law, the more common law (*ius commune*) therefore was only of subsidiary importance: Roman law could only be applied where there were no norms available from more immediate sources.[77] It was possible, of course, that none of these sources contained a ruling for a judge to follow. This prompted Leibniz, in a letter to Conring, to raise the following question:

> "What if the law is silent with regard to a particular case, and it neither expressly deals with it nor allows us to draw a conclusion from it? Then, I believe, you cannot deny that the judge must still make a ruling outside of the constitution as it were, like an elected referee (*arbiter*) must declare his verdict between two who are not linked by means of a community of civil law."[78]

This is where Leibniz introduced natural law.[79] In his view, a judge could make a ruling on the basis of natural law if there was no solution to be found in the structure of the sources of positive law. However, he added that in that case a judge must first refer back to natural law "in the strict sense."[80] This caveat appears logical because natural law in this situation takes up the role of positive law which must be the 'rule' and thus '*ius strictum*', even just for reasons of legal certainty. On the other hand, aspects of equity must not be excluded as a matter of principle because of a subsidiary application of natural law. This follows from the fact, which has already been discussed, that Leibniz was opposed to a monadic legal structure and because the individual levels of natural law collaborate in such a way that they cannot be completely separated.

---

[77] See e.g. Reiner Schulze: Art.: "Statutarrecht", in: *Handwörterbuch zur Deutschen Rechtsgeschichte*, vol. IV, Berlin 1990, Sp. 1922–1926; Peter Oestmann: *Rechtsvielfalt vor Gericht. Rechtsanwendung und Partikularrecht im Alten Reich*, Frankfurt a. M. 2002, pp. 108–138 (this thought has survived up to the present in the rule of competing laws *lex specialis derogat legi generali*).
[78] Letter to Conring dated 9th/19th April 1670, p. 68.
[79] Of course, Leibniz was not the first party to appeal to 'nature' or to 'natural law' in court, cf. Oestmann: *Rechtsvielfalt vor Gericht*, pp. 108, 135–138. By incorporating natural law into his legal philosophy, however, he gave it a new scope that was both comprehensive and part of a system.
[80] Letter to Conring dated 9th/19th April 1670, p. 68 (with mention of the general precept of '*neminem laedere*' as a 'basic norm', see also the remarks in the preceding paragraph).

7. The Current Discussions on the Ongoing 'Materialisation' of the Law

"From a formal to a material rationality!" is a maxim that has been amongst the most-discussed theses in the theory, history and legal doctrine of private law for several decades.[81] The starting point was and still is the thoughts voiced by Franz Wieacker on the differences between the 'liberal' private law of the 19th and the 'social model' of the 20th century. Wieacker's core idea was put into words by the famous and still cited statement that the administration of justice under the aegis of the German Imperial court had

> "transformed the formal ethics of liberty, which formed the basic roots of the German order of private law, back into a material ethical construct of social responsibility"; "'transformed *back*' because it had returned, largely subconsciously, to the ethical principles of the earlier European common and natural law."[82]

Wieacker's statement therefore dealt with the same 'basic roots' of natural law that have been discussed here in the context of Leibniz' concept of '*ius strictum*'. In Wieacker's view, the Pandectists, with their "formal ethics of liberty" had turned their backs on these basic roots in the 19th century whilst the 20th century had returned to them. The following paragraphs will analyse this thesis in detail.

7.1 'Liberal' Private law in the 19th and 'Social' Private Law in the 20th and 21st Centuries?

The proponents of the materialisation thesis ('Materialisierungsthese') usually draw on the example of contract law when describing the contrast between formal and material law. They claim that the authors of the German Civil Code, had their sights firmly set on the abstract principle of equality, which

---

[81] See the references in Claus-Wilhelm Canaris: "Wandlungen des Schuldvertragsrechts – Tendenzen zu seiner 'Materialisierung'", in: *AcP* 200 (2000), pp. 273–364; Gerhard Wagner: Materialisierung des Schuldrechts unter dem Einfluss von Verfassungsrecht und Europarecht – Was bleibt von der Privatautonomie?, in: Uwe Blaurock/Günter Hager (ed.): *Obligationenrecht im 21. Jahrhundert*, Baden-Baden 2010, pp. 13–84; Günter Hager: *Strukturen des Privatrechts in Europa. Eine rechtsvergleichende Studie*, Tübingen 2012, pp. 3–23; Marietta Auer: *Der privatrechtliche Diskurs der Moderne*, Tübingen 2014, to name but a few.

[82] Franz Wieacker: "Das Sozialmodell der klassischen Privatrechtsgesetzbücher und die Entwicklung der modernen Gesellschaft (1953)", in: id.: *Industriegesellschaft und Privatrechtsordnung*, Frankfurt a. M. 1974, pp. 9–35, here 24 (italics in the original).

simply meant that all legal subjects had the same ability and willingness to look after their affairs in an autonomous and autocratic manner. This vision of bourgeois liberalism would have suited the society of merchants and property owners that prevailed at the time with its concept of unbridled selfishness, whose only control mechanism was free competition between all market participants. Since living conditions had fundamentally changed in the 20th century, however, it was no longer possible to hold on to the abstract model of equality and the notion of an equilibrium between contractual partners. It had been shown that the consumer, who had only a limited income at his disposal, was hardly in a position, in view of the crushing superior force of the producer, to have any kind of impact on the contents of contractual agreements. In recognition of the general economic inferiority of the consumer it was necessary to replace formal private law with an independent material contract law that accounted for the social reality.[83]

However, 'materialisation' means not only that personal responsibility is supplanted or even replaced by "a material ethical construct of social responsibility" (Wieacker), it also means that the law is influenced by values, morals or politics. In the past number of decades, private law has developed its own vocabulary for this, including 'protection of the weak', 'social connections', 'structural inequality' or 'information deprivation'. As a consequence, the 'materialisation' claim in private law is also linked with the question of its autonomy. Two arguments can be made against the materialisation thesis. Whilst the first targets its historical premises, the second comes in the shape of a counter-thesis, which claims that private law will remain formal and will attempt to protect itself as much as possible from infringement by public law, ethics, values or politics.

---

[83] Similar features can be found in the law of torts. Here, the increasing encroachment of aspects of 'legal capacity' in the sense of 'objective responsibility' and 'strict liability' on the classical principle of fault is perceived as a displacement of '*iustitia commutativa*' by '*iustitia distributiva*', as a 'promulgation' or, indeed, a 'materialisation' of private law, see e.g. Hager: *Strukturen des Privatrechts in Europa*, pp. 18–23; Stephan Meder: *Schuld, Zufall, Risiko. Untersuchungen struktureller Probleme privatrechtlicher Zurechnung*, Frankfurt a. M. 1993.

7.3 'Retransformation' of a Social Model? A Lopsided View of the History of Private Law

There are at least two reasons for questioning the historical prerequisites of the 'materialisation thesis' ('Materialisierungsthese'). Firstly, 'classical' private law was never just 'formal' and secondly, it does not appear very plausible that the 17th and 18th century 'tradition of natural law' above others would have been the breeding ground for an "ethicization of juristic thinking" or an "orientation towards the social functions of an exchange of services."[84] The detailed study of the leading protagonists of secular natural law does not support this statement. In the wake of the constitutional positivism of a Jean Bodin, natural law thinkers as diverse as Hobbes, Pufendorf or Kant were not even willing to give the general aspect of equity (*aequitas*) a worthy position in the legal system. The prevailing view was that an omnipotent lawmaker would be able to settle all legal questions that could possibly arise within a state and that material elements such as values, ethics or equity would have to take a backseat in cases of conflict between 'the law' and 'justice'.[85] Leibniz was the only scholar to criticise Hobbes' legal philosophy because secular natural law only took into account '*ius strictum*', in other words formal law. Leibniz was an exception among the scholars of natural law and there is no evidence to suggest that Wieacker intended to refer to his legal philosophy.[86]

It is also incorrect, or at least misleading, to describe the 19th century as an era in which the formal ethics of private law experienced its heyday. Whilst one may concur with Wieacker's suggestion that the society of entrepreneurs that existed in the early period of capitalism

---

[84] Wieacker: *Das Sozialmodell der klassischen Privatrechtsgesetzbücher*, p. 25 (the term 'natural law' has a variety of meanings and should be defined more precisely. As mentioned above, the term was already used in Antiquity. Wieacker, however, did not have '*ius gentium*' or '*naturalis ratio*' of classical Roman jurisprudence in mind, but historical natural law that is part of the law of reason).

[85] See on this and the following remarks the references cited in Chapter IV. Similar arguments in: Hans Welzel: *Naturrecht und materiale Gerechtigkeit*, Göttingen ⁴1990, p. 122.

[86] Wieacker's *History of Private Law in Europe* (Oxford 1995), only mentions Leibniz in passing as one of many natural law thinkers (p. 210). Wieacker views Leibniz' legal philosophy as an "idealistic rationalist variation" of the "voluntarist course of the law of reason (Hobbes, Thomasius)". Recent research, which has begun to tease out the fundamental differences between Leibniz and Hobbes (or Thomasius), has probably shown that this interpretation is not, in fact, justified. On Leibniz' criticism of the voluntarist perspective see, amongst others, Armgardt: "Die Rechtstheorie von Leibniz im Licht seiner Kritik an Hobbes und Pufendorf", pp. 13–27, 15–20.

"as a pioneering society was particularly reliant on the freedom to conclude contracts, invest capital and inherit",[87]

this did not prompt the Historical School of Jurisprudence to promote a one-sided legal principle that was limited to formal responsibilities, self-interests and the pursuit of profit. The opposite is in fact the case: Savigny stressed that '*ius strictum*' required a corrective which was discussed in Roman jurisprudence under headings such as '*ius gentium*', '*naturalis ratio*' or '*ius aequum*'.[88] This also has consequences for the much-discussed role played by public law within private law.

The prevailing view to this day is that 19th century thinking was based on a simple dichotomy, where the notion of unconditional (formal) freedom in private law was confronted more or less loosely with the enforcement of ethics and morality in public law.[89] Some have even claimed that 19th century legal thinkers, under the spell of German idealism, exaggerated the differences between private and public law and created an "a priori" division that was "lacking in legal experience."[90] It could easily be demonstrated that Savigny did not support such idealised divisions. He was as opposed to the decoupling of the public and private legal spheres as to the separation of formal and material elements. He would, rather, have seen 'public momentum' as a structural feature in its own right, which could occur anywhere and at any time in private law. Therefore, Savigny dealt with '*ius publicum*' early-on in the 'general section' of his eight-volume "System of current Roman law", in a paragraph on the legal sources of private law.[91]

---

[87] Wieacker: *Das Sozialmodell der klassischen Privatrechtsgesetzbücher*, p. 14.
[88] See references in Chapter II 3.
[89] Michael Stolleis: "Öffentliches Recht und Privatrecht im Prozeß der Entstehung des modernen Staates", in: Wolfgang Hoffmann-Riem/Eberhard Schmidt-Aßmann (ed.): *Öffentliches Recht und Privatrecht als wechselseitige Auffangordnungen*, Baden-Baden 1996, pp. 41–61, here 57; Moritz Renner: *Zwingendes transnationales Recht. Zur Struktur der Wirtschaftsverfassung jenseits des Staates*, Baden-Baden 2011, p. 18.
[90] Sten Gagnér: "Über Voraussetzungen einer Verwendung der Sprachformel 'Öffentliches Recht und Privatrecht' im kanonistischen Bereich", in: *Deutsche Landesreferate zum VII. Internationalen Kongreß für Rechtsvergleichung in Uppsala 1966*, Berlin 1967, pp. 23–57, here 27, 29–36.
[91] Savigny: *System I*, pp. 57–66 (further references in Chapter II.3). Leibniz had similarly viewed the elements concerning the benefit of others and communal solidarity as belonging to the sphere of public law (see references in Chapter V.1).

Another notion that is not very convincing is the characterisation of the German Civil Code as the "much younger child of classical liberalism."[92] Whilst it is true that its authors rejected material regulatory tools such as '*iustum pretium*', '*laesio enormis*' and '*clausula rebus sic stantibus*',[93] this failing cannot simply be laid at the Pandectists' door. It should be remembered that it was the Pandectist Bernhard Windscheid, who argued that the German Civil Code should contain the ideas of the school which viewed jurisprudence as a '*clausula* rule', a 'precondition for' or 'disruption to the basis of a transaction'. As Leibniz and Savigny before him, Windscheid believed that antagonism between formal and material elements was one of the essential aspects of law. If a state legislator feels he can ignore the 'dual' structure of the law, he must not be surprised if the excluded elements find other ways of being reintroduced:

> "There is no doubt that legal certainty is actively promoted if the silent assumption, i.e. that which is implied on the basis of the circumstances, is excluded. A high price must, however, be paid for this benefit, and the price is that the judge may be prevented from implementing that which he believes to be just. This is the old battle between the formalistic and the material-based application of the law! Incidentally, rulings of this kind are very interesting. They allow us to catch a glimpse of how customary law comes into being. The judge makes his ruling not because he has found guidance in the rules of the law that he must apply but because he cannot help it. In his ruling he expresses the law that resides within him and he is convinced that he is doing the right thing. If he is not the only one to proceed in this manner and if other judges feel compelled to do the same, customary law has already taken shape."[94]

It would not take long for Windscheid's prophecies to be fulfilled. As is well known, the old *clausula* rule experienced a wondrous renaissance as a customary law soon after the German Civil Code came into force. The fact that Windscheid lost his battle for the 'basis of the transaction' ('Geschäftsgrundlage') therefore is not so much a consequence of the formalism promoted by the Pandectists or by the Historical School of Jurisprudence as it is evidence of a crisis that had already begun at the time the German Civil Code was being created: the founding of the German Empire in the final third of the 19th century encouraged a 'new' etatism, which only accepted *one* legal

---

[92] Wieacker: *Das Sozialmodell der klassischen Privatrechtsgesetzbücher*, p. 22.
[93] Ibid., p. 15.
[94] Die Voraussetzung (1892), in: *Gesammelte Reden und Abhandlungen*, ed. by Paul Oertmann, Leipzig 1904, pp. 375–409, 408f.

order, i.e. that of the sovereign state as the sole bearer of the power to make decisions.[95]

However, the claim that the German Civil Code was committed to the 'positivist' ideal of completeness and strict law-abidance must nevertheless be rejected.[96] The 'dualism' of form and value that is characteristic of Roman law found its way into the German Civil Code and its administration, amongst other things, via general clauses such as 'good faith' and 'public policy'. This can also be seen in the fact that the editor of the German Civil Code, Gottlieb Planck, paid close attention to the antagonism between formal and material elements. Planck's attempt at introducing material aspects into a great variety of subareas of private law has been discussed in detail elsewhere.[97] Many other issues were left unresolved by the authors of the Civil Code on the grounds that science and jurisprudence would find the right solutions.[98] 'Less is more' was their maxim, formulated virtually in complete opposition to the 'positivist' ideal of completeness and strict law-abidance.[99]

---

[95] See above (II 3, fn. 17) for the critical remarks made by Gierke in respect of not just the German branch but the entire Historical School of Jurisprudence. One example that illustrates this is a statement made by the editor of the general section of the German Civil Code, Albert Gebhard, who – despite criticism of the natural law codifications voiced by the Historical School – no longer wished to exclude the possibility that "those legislations that are based on the absolute authority of the legal will of the state" could serve as models for the German Civil Code, Albert Gebhard: "Entwurf eines bürgerlichen Gesetzbuches für das Deutsche Reich", in: Werner Schubert (ed.): *Die Vorlagen der Redaktoren für die erste Kommission zur Ausarbeitung des Entwurfs eines bürgerlichen Gesetzbuches, Allgemeiner Teil*, part 1, Berlin 1981, pp. 1, 80f. (however, this opinion did not prevail).

[96] Wieacker: *A History of Private Law in Europe*, p. 409; Roger Berkowitz: *The Gift of Science. Leibniz and the Modern Legal Tradition*, New York 2005.

[97] Stephan Meder: *Gottlieb Planck und die Kunst der Gesetzgebung*, Göttingen 2010, pp. 29–36, 77–99. As an aside it may be worth mentioning that Planck, in a dispute with Gierke over the protection of the weak in the German Civil Code also referred to the rule-exception pattern, loc. cit., pp. 29–32 (if Wieacker's statements concerning the German Civil Code were correct, such a dispute should not in fact have arisen).

[98] See, amongst others, Horst Heinrich Jakobs: *Wissenschaft und Gesetzgebung im bürgerlichen Recht nach der Rechtsquellenlehre des 19. Jahrhunderts*, Paderborn 1983, p. 140 ("The task" of the authors of the Civil Code could "only be understood in view of its limitations: the task of creating a code of law which is aware of a field of science running alongside it that is capable of putting it in order and which therefore assumes that the appropriate expertise to understand it exists").

[99] Wieacker's description of the German Civil Code is much more suited to the natural law codifications (which were in fact intent on completeness) and in particular the Prussian Land Law, which were seen by many Pandectists as an off-putting example of an excessively positivist perspective, see for instance the references in Meder: *Rechtsgeschichte*, p. 342.

By juxtaposing the school of formal Pandectists with material natural law, Wieacker gave a lopsided view of the history of private law. It is not even necessary to bring to mind the foundations of the Pandectist school in Roman law. The political philosophy at its core also allows it to use plain language: by adding a corrective to '*ius strictum*', Savigny and Windscheid took an irreconcilably opposite view to the teaching of Kant, Pufendorf, Hobbes or Bodin.[100] The fact that most natural law thinkers felt compelled to banish material elements from law as much as possible can be explained quite simply: the 'dual' structure of the legal sources would bestow on the discipline of jurisprudence a degree of authority to decide and powers to create that would simply be incompatible with the concept of sovereignty promoted by constitutional positivism.[101]

8. Continued: The Current Relevance of Leibniz' Bipartite Doctrine of Legal Sources

The current relevance of Leibniz' legal philosophy is rooted in precisely this fact, i.e. that he had no problem with granting the discipline of jurisprudence such powers to create. At their core, his grades of natural law were compatible both with the 'dualism' of Roman law and with Savigny's division into pure and mixed legal principles. Leibniz' philosophy provides a simple way of explaining why the dual nature of the sources is an inherent attribute of the law and why private law still strives to be formal in the 21st century. The reason, once again, can be found in his teaching on '*ius strictum*' which vouches for the inalienable rights to freedom and competence. According to Leibniz any legal entity has a right to basic independent freedom, to act autonomously and to enter into contracts of his own free will and, as long as he remains within the realms of the law, he can do this even if these contracts are detrimental to

---

[100] See also the references in Chapter II 3. Canaris believed that Kant's concept of law also had a 'material' variant, "Wandlungen des Schuldvertragsrechts", pp. 282, 287. He did not, however, offer proof, and it would, in fact, be difficult to furnish, cf. Meder: *Doppelte Körper im Recht*, pp. 130–133: equation of law and justice, interpretation according to the letter of the law, 'assertive judicial power', banishment of evaluation aspects from juridical decision-making.
[101] The notion that the background to the formalistic nature of Kant's concept of law can be found in political philosophy was convincingly shown in a series of contributions by Ingeborg Maus: cf. e.g. *Zur Aufklärung der Demokratietheorie. Rechts- und demokratietheoretische Überlegungen im Anschluß an Kant*, Frankfurt a. M. 1992; id.: *Über Volkssouveränität. Elemente einer Demokratietheorie*, Berlin 2011.

him, to others or to the general public.[102] This broad understanding of freedom, which is orientated towards self-interest, however, is retracted in a second step when the legal system refers back to correctives or counter-principles in order to take into account the interests of third parties and the community at large.

8.1 'Ius strictum' as a Bulwark Against the Political Usurpation of Private Law

Is such a paradoxical process really necessary? Would it not be more appropriate to renounce the idea of an unconditional self-determination from the beginning? The latter question was in fact examined by the proponents of the materialisation thesis and answered in the affirmative.[103] It leads back to the old controversial question whether the system of private law bestows independent and in that sense 'absolute' power on the bearer of subjective rights. Gierke, as early as 1873, had rejected the idea that the principles of freedom and equality could grant absolute legal power to the individual will. In his opinion

> "it is counter to any deeper insight into the essence of things to lay down the principle of equality, only to rescind it by formulating a hundred exceptions. Either the principle is correct and the exceptions run counter to the principle and call for removal or the exceptions are justified, which renders the principle an empty and harmful abstraction."[104]

---

[102] The subject leads us to a question that has previously been raised by modern neurosciences, as to whether free will actually exists or whether everything we as human beings think or do is not perhaps fully determined by prior internal or external events. Recently, Wolfgang Prinz convincingly showed that the concept of 'free will' can still be retained in the field of jurisprudence, "Selbstverantwortung aus Sicht der Kognitionswissenschaften", in: Karl Riesenhuber (ed.): *Das Prinzip der Selbstverantwortung. Grundlagen und Bedeutung im heutigen Privatrecht*, Tübingen 2012, pp. 73–91; see also Viktor J. Vanberg: Freiheit und Verantwortung – Neurowissenschaftliche Erkenntnisse und ordnungsökonomische Folgerungen, in: Ibid., pp. 45–72. Leibniz also defended the possible existence of free will against determinist objections, see, amongst others, Tilman-Anselm Ramelow: Art.: "Wille", in: *Historisches Wörterbuch der Philosophie*, vol. 12, Darmstadt 2004, Sp. 778.

[103] See e.g. Wagner: *Materialisierung des Schuldrechts unter dem Einfluss von Verfassungsrecht und Europarecht*, pp. 81–84.

[104] Otto von Gierke: *Das deutsche Genossenschaftsrecht, vol. II: Geschichte des deutschen Körperschaftsbegriffs*, Berlin 1873, p. 35. The concept of purpose and interests formulated by Rudolf von Jhering points in a similar direction, but cannot be dealt with further here.

Gierke took umbrage at the 'separation' of rule and exception and the "features of the absolute", which he identified as the basic principles of Roman legal thinking. According to him, "German" law does not have the concept of "an absolute and unconnected will", but "assumes that all wills are dependent on each other". Therefore, the law is not a "system of competences" but a "system of competences and duties". The German subject

> "from the start is only subject in relation to other subjects and it is an important feature of the concept that the will it represents is bound and limited within itself".

Every will, according to Gierke, is "dominant and at the same time dominated, as appropriate to the German personality."[105] In 1889 he once again raised the subject in his famous work on "The social task of private law": whilst it is the "most holy task" of the system of private law to recognise "free will", "freedom of contract" cannot mean "arbitrary freedom" but "only reasonable freedom that is at the same time boundedness". He went on to say that

> "little is achieved simply by guaranteeing the inalienability of the formal right to freedom" and one must also "work towards the material protection of the social classes that are threatened by contractual freedom."[106]

Of course, the fact that "the guaranteed inalienability of the formal right to freedom" must not be the end of the matter was also one of the premises of the tradition that Gierke felt compelled to counter with his "Germanic legal thinking". Based on a 'dual' structure of the system of private law it is, in fact, possible to take into account any lack of information when a will is formed or any peculiarities when concrete negotiations are conducted. Only in this case the starting point is not the bound but the sovereign individual, the independent power or Juvenal's much-discussed adage *"pro ratione stat voluntas."*

The assumption here is that the contract, as an instrument of successful self-determination, is a vessel of legitimacy and dignity. This, however, can be disproved by norms that set limits to contractual freedom.[107] Because they

---

[105] Gierke: *Genossenschaftsrecht II*, p. 36.
[106] Otto von Gierke: *Die soziale Aufgabe des Privatrechts*, Berlin 1889, pp. 22 and 23. See also id.: *Deutsches Privatrecht, vol. I: Allgemeiner Teil und Personenrecht*, Berlin 1895, §§ 27 and 28 (pp. 251–256).
[107] E.g. §§ 134, 138, 242, 307, 826 of the German Civil Code. In view of the many abstract legal concepts in the German Civil Code and the extensions added by science, judicial practice or customary law, it goes without saying that this list is by no means complete.

are promulgated by a state lawmaker, such norms can be classified as 'written' law. However, and this distinguishes them from many other rules in the German Civil Code, they cannot simply be subsumed under. They are not '*ius strictum*' and as such not part of the formal but of the material side of private law. 'Good faith', 'public policy', 'hardship', 'appropriateness', 'reasonableness' or 'equity' are, as Leibniz rightly noted, on a different 'level' of the legal system and, because they can be structured only to a limited degree by a lawmaker, border on being 'unwritten' law. They are open to changes in values and can act as vehicles for aspects of public law or state purposes to enter into the system of private law.[108] However, this does not mean that a case is made for forcing a benefit on citizens or for incapacitating them by imposing ideological precepts. The assumption remains that the parties have acted as autonomous individuals. This, however, can be refuted, for instance, by arguing that there was a lack of actual prerequisites of self-determination when the contract was concluded. The priority of freedom is not shattered but confirmed if the legal system offers protection where self-determination is threatened or not possible.

The system of private law can also offer 'material protection' as mentioned by Gierke by preventing a person from exercising their basic right to power. Gierke feels that it is a contradiction for the legal system to grant absolute powers only to subsequently curtail them. He would like strict law and the limitations of its application to converge side by side as equal elements of an inseparable union. By calling for this he removes the priority of freedom and merges the pairing of rule and exception into a single open balance, a simple reconciliation of interests. He dismantles the bulwark that was erected by the assumption of full self-determination against political usurpation and breaks the resistance created by the requisite of its refutation. As a consequence, 'freedom' runs the risk of losing its standards: whoever is interpreting the law can introduce the 'values' they deem 'reasonable' into the concept of freedom, only to draw them back out as an argument. In this case, the rule-exception pattern has been replaced by a *petitio principii*.

---

[108] It has already been shown that both Leibniz and Savigny viewed considerations of the community as parts of the system of private law (cf. Chapters II.3 and V.1).

8.2 "Pro Ratione Stat Voluntas" Versus "Pro Voluntate Stat Ratio"

Gierke's notion that every law has its immanent limits has proved extremely influential. It led to the formulation of the controversial '*Innentheorie*' (internal theory) after the German Civil Code came into force.[109] The fact that proponents of the materialisation thesis are today once again invoking Gierke is tantamount to reviving this "idcology-prone theory" (Neuner).[110] They once again strive to move on from the paradoxes of the individual that acts with

---

[109] See Hans-Peter Haferkamp, in: *Historisch-kritischer Kommentar zum BGB*, vol. II, 1: Schuldrecht, Allgemeiner Teil, Tübingen 2007, § 242 marg. no. 53f.; Behrends: *Struktur und Wert*, pp. 84–87. In the National Socialist period the subject was discussed mainly in the context of 'forfeiture', cf. e.g. Wolfgang Siebert: "Die neueste grundsätzliche Entscheidung des Reichsgerichts über die Verwirkung", in: *JW* (1937), pp. 2495f. ("German-law approach" to contracts whose "organisational task within the overall system" followed on from the "idea of community in legal relations between comrades ("Volksgenossen")" which was determined by heteronomy). See also Karl Larenz: "Der Vertrag als Gestaltungsmittel der völkischen Ordnung", in: *Vertrag und Unrecht, 1. Teil: Vertrag und Vertragsbruch*, Hamburg 1937, pp. 31–36 (criticism of the formalistic legal approach taken by liberalism; the contract as an "organisational opportunity" which had a particular purpose "to begin with" and was characterised by the "racial order"); Franz Wieacker: "Der Stand der Rechtserneuerung auf dem Gebiete des bürgerlichen Rechts", in: Karl August Eckhardt (ed.): *Deutsche Rechtswissenschaft* (1937), pp. 3–27, 15 and 23 (criticism of the "liberal individualistic social theory" ("liberal-individualistische Gesellschaftstheorie") from which the "legal subject had emerged with a power of volition it had been granted for its own sake"). The '*Innentheorie*' (internal theory) still had many supporters even after the Second World War, see the references in Hans Carl Nipperdey, in: Ludwig Enneccerus: *Allgemeiner Teil des Bürgerlichen Rechts*, Tübingen [15]1960, § 239, p. 1442 ("German legal thought"). Critically Jörg Neuner: *Allgemeiner Teil des bürgerlichen Rechts*, Munich [10]2012, § 20 marg. no. 70 (with appropriate reference to the risks inherent in dissolving the rule-exception pattern).

[110] This is largely going unnoticed by the prevailing textbook and commentary literature, insofar as it still views subjective (absolute) law as an independent sovereign law, e.g. Bernd Rüthers, Astrid Stadler: *Allgemeiner Teil des BGB*, [18]2014, §§ 4 and 5; Burkhard Boemke/Bernhard Ulrici: *BGB Allgemeiner Teil*, Munich [2]2014, § 17 marg. no. 12; Karl Otto Scherner: *BGB-Allgemeiner Teil*, Munich 1995, p. 21 (with reference to Savigny); Staudinger/Honsell, Berlin 2013, Einl. zum BGB marg. no. 163 (the "basic ideas" of the Pandectist school have "not yet been abandoned"). Contrary Reinhard Bork: *Allgemeiner Teil des Bürgerlichen Gesetzbuchs*, Tübingen [4]2016, who, based on the '*Innentheorie*' (internal theory) (§ 10 marg. no. 343) takes as a starting point a "uniform structure" which dissolves "the difference between absolute and relative rights" (§ 9 marg. no. 288). See also Palandt/Grüneberg, *BGB*, Munich [75]2016, § 242 R marg. no. 38; Erman/Hohloch: *BGB*, Köln [14]2014, § 242 marg. no. 101 f.; *Münchener Kommentar*, Schubert, BGB, München [7]2016, § 242 marg. no. 84 (with reference to Siebert); BGH *NJW-RR* 2005, pp. 619–621, here 620; BAG *BB* 2009, pp. 2655f., here 2655. Those who call for a dissolution of the difference between absolute and relative rights, should of course discuss the question of the consequences this would have for the organisation of civil law in respect of the laws of obligations and property. Should this difference also be abolished?

sovereignty and turn their attention to the "real" and only "partially" free individual who is "governed" by the collective and "who finds rational self-determination difficult."[111] It thus appears obvious to interpret the most recent 'changes in the law of obligations' as a process of replacing formal law with the new paradigm of materialisation.

Against this background I would like to call to mind the advantages of a bipartite structure of the sources of law and of a dualism of formal and material law: only on the basis of an ethical concept of individual freedom can the parties be prevented from

> "being subjected to an economic calculus either for their own good, which is determined by heteronomy and paternalism, or for the good of the greater public, which is also determined by heteronomy."[112]

Moreover, history teaches us that if '*ius strictum*' was abandoned, private law would be completely at the mercy of infringements by politics, ethics or values.[113] Finally, it is conducive to methodological transparency when corrections of '*ius strictum*' or violations of private autonomy generate an increased demand for legitimisation.[114] This demand results from the fact that the principles of freedom and self-interest differ in many ways from those of solidarity and third-party interests. 'Materialisation' as such is hardly capable of creating fast rules. Its limitations are undetermined, open and flowing, and the suffix '*-ation*' merely proposes that the future of private law will consist of a liquidation of the formal structure and a dissolution of the rule-exception pattern. In that case, the proponents of the materialisation thesis, like the constitutional positivists, would only recognize a single legal structure. This structure, however, speaking in support of Leibniz and in opposition to Hobbes, would not be limited to '*ius strictum*' but would amount to an 'equitable jurisprudence'

---

[111] Wagner: *Materialisierung des Schuldrechts*, pp. 81–84 (with reference to Gierke's 'social task of private law').

[112] Ulrich Huber: "Eigenschaftsirrtum und Kauf", in: *AcP* 209 (2009), pp. 143–163, 163 (by way of summing up the teaching on private autonomy as conveyed by Werner Flume based on the tradition of the study of Roman law).

[113] One example worth mentioning here is the disposal of subjective law and the construction of limitations within the right to freedom in the National Socialist period. Whilst the call for an abolishment of absolute rights did not prevail and § 903, for instance, was retained in the German Civil Code, the carrying out of seizures shows that the legal position of the owner was *de facto* removed by a heteronomous alleged 'notion of public welfare'. It is also worth remembering the consequences of the abolishment of the principle of abstract equality in the 1930s, for more see Meder: *Rechtsgeschichte*, pp. 411–417.

[114] Cf. Neuner: "Das Prinzip der Selbstverantwortung im Sozialstaat", pp. 187–203, 189.

that is open to all kinds of values and that is determined by heteronomy. This is perhaps one of the reasons why the proponents of the materialisation thesis tend to forgo the independence of both '*ius strictum*' and the legal form in favour of purpose and interest protection. In view of the events of the 20th century, however, this 'modern' or even 'postmodern' type of one-sidedness must appear much more dangerous than the insistence on a formal ethics of freedom.

Therefore, pitting the formal against the material elements cannot be the objective. It should, rather, be our goal to ascertain the present-day relationship between the elements of formal and material law, which always have and still continue to compete in one way or another in every legal system. Leibniz did not stop at recognising formal freedom and personal responsibility as principles. His legal philosophy went further by asking when and under what circumstances the severities of '*ius strictum*' should be mitigated by 'social' considerations. Freedom and personal responsibility should still be the rule and breaches should be the exception and as such require legitimisation. As a consequence, the suffix '*-ation*' would have to be interpreted to mean that material elements play a different and certainly bigger role today than they did one-hundred (German Civil Code), two-hundred (Savigny) or three-hundred years ago (Leibniz). This would simply confirm the notion that each era must find its own answer to the question of the relationship between formal and material elements. With his concept of '*ius strictum*' Leibniz succeeded in providing one such answer. While we search for a solution that is appropriate to our era, this could save us today from the errors of '*pro voluntate stat ratio*'.

9. Summary

The prevailing opinion in current private law research is that the 19th century Pandectist school reached the pinnacle of a formal liberal ethics of freedom and that one of its features was that one was not obliged, for instance with regard to contract law, to consider the actual preconditions for self-determination.[115] This is correct insofar as formal law starts out from the concept of a

---

[115] The critics and proponents of the materialisation thesis largely agree on this, see, amongst others, Michael Martinek: "Das Prinzip der Selbstverantwortung im Vertrags- und Verbraucherrecht", in: *Das Prinzip der Selbstverantwortung*, pp. 247–276, 252 on one hand and Wagner: *Materialisierung des Schuldrechts*, p. 82 on the other.

sovereign individual and accords this individual independent power. Statements like "a contract is a contract" or "*pacta sunt servanda*" belong in this formal realm of the law, in the area of '*ius strictum*', whose correctness is assumed. However, this by no means proves that the Pandectists suppressed the material elements of the law. Using Savigny's doctrine of legal sources as an example, it has been shown that the Historical School of Jurisprudence saw aspects of public law or statutory purposes as parts of the system of private law. The assumption of the correctness of formal law can be disproved on the basis of such aspects or purposes. The parallel with Leibniz is that he too worked on the presumption, in accordance with advanced Roman jurisprudence, of a bipartite nature of the sources of law. Leibniz was opposed to secular natural law and specifically to the legal philosophy of Hobbes, whom he otherwise held in the highest esteem, but who was in fact only willing to take into account '*ius strictum*' and thus formal law. If there was indeed a pinnacle of the formal ethics of freedom, it was reached by 17th and 18th century secular law, which was rejected by Leibniz and Savigny.

The fundamental differences are particularly evident in the endeavour of secular natural law to displace equity from the system of private law as much as possible, since a judge, in the words of Kant and of the authors of the Prussian Land Law, must not base his rulings on undetermined conditions.[116] The founding of the Historical School of Jurisprudence, which dominated the discipline in 19th century Germany, was in fact triggered by opposition against this approach. The call for a 'dual' structure of the sources of law, legal sovereignty of jurisprudence as a discipline and criticism of the monopolisation of the law by statutory positivism were elements of the battle against a traditional trajectory which had put too great an emphasis on the formal character of the law.

The polarisation of the formal school of Pandectists and material natural law paints a lopsided picture of the history of private law, which still characterises academic debate to this day. It is time to take a renewed stand for the formal structure of law. However, this is only possible if the false alternatives between 'formal' and 'material' are overcome. It must be our goal to strike a new balance between these elements. The current relevance of Leibniz' concept of '*ius strictum*' lies in the fact that he placed its conflict and relationship with unstrict law at the heart of his legal thinking.

---

[116] A direct line can be drawn from this to the so-called 'prohibition of commentary' and the '*référé législativ*', whose function was to protect the sovereign's legal order against academic intervention, amongst other things (for more detail see Meder: *Rechtsgeschichte*, pp. 115, 281).

Raummetaphorik in Sprache, Denken und Realität.
Leibniz über Präpositionen

Stephan Meier-Oeser (Münster)

Wenn es um das Thema von Sprache und Denken sowie um Leibniz' Konzeption des Verhältnisses von beidem geht, sind in der Regel die *Unvorgreifflichen Gedancken, betreffend die Ausübung und Verbesserung der Teutschen Sprache* nicht weit, enthält doch dieser von Leibniz zwischen 1697 und Ende 1712 ausgearbeitete und 1717 posthum von Eckhardt veröffentlichte Text[1] die wohl bekanntesten und mit Abstand am häufigsten gedruckten und übersetzten[2] Ausführungen von Leibniz zur kognitiven Funktion von Sprache. Nach der Einschätzung von Karl Otto Apel handelt es sich bei hierbei um die bis dahin „eindringlichste und folgenreichste Analyse der Sprachgebundenheit des menschlichen Denkens."[3] Diese Einschätzung – die hier zunächst kritisch hinterfragt werden soll – gründet in dem Umstand, dass Leibniz diese Schrift, die er bekanntlich mit der plakativen und späterhin vielzitierten Charakterisierung der Sprache als „Spiegel des Verstandes" eröffnet,[4] mit der Bemerkung einleitet, dass der Sprache neben und zusätzlich zu ihrer kommunikativen Funktion auch eine wichtige kognitive Funktion zukommt, da wir, wie er sagt, „Zeichen nöthig haben, nicht nur unsere Meinung andern anzudeuten, sondern auch unsern Gedancken selbst zu helffen."[5] Bekanntlich erläutert Leibniz dies durch den prägnanten funktionalen Vergleich der Worte mit „Wechsel-Zetteln", „Marcken" (also Spielmarken) oder „Rechen-pfennigen". Er schreibt:

> „[…] gleich wie man in grossen Handels-Stäten, auch im Spiel und sonsten, nicht allezeit Gelt zehlet, sondern sich an dessen stat der Zettel oder Marcken, bis zur letzten Abrechnung oder Zahlung bedienet; also thut auch der Verstand mit den Bildnissen der dinge, zu mahl wenn er viel zu dencken hat, das er nemlich Zeichen dafur brauchet, damit er nicht nötig habe, die Sache jedesmahl, so offte

---

[1] G. W. Leibniz: „Unvorgreifflichen Gedancken, betreffend die Ausübung und Verbesserung der Teutschen Sprache" [= Gedancken], in: *Collectanea etymologica, illustrationi linguarum, veteris Celticae, Germanicae, Gallicae, aliarumque inservientia*, hrsg.v. J. G. Eckhardt, Hannover 1717, S. 255–314; im Folgenden zitiert nach A IV, 6 N. 79.
[2] Vgl. A IV, 6, 528f.
[3] Karl Otto Apel: *Die Idee der Sprache in der Tradition des Humanismus von Dante bis Vico*, Bonn 1963, S. 305.
[4] A IV, 6, 532.
[5] Ebd., 533.

> sie vorkomt, von neuen zu bedencken. Daher wenn er sie einmal wol gefasset, begnügt er sich hernach offt, nicht nur in eusserlichen Reden, sondern auch in den Gedancken und innerlichen selbst-Gespräch, das wort an die Stelle der Sache zu setzen. [...] Also wenn man im Reden, und auch selbst im Gedencken, kein Wort sprechen wolte, ohne sich ein eigentliches Bildniss von dessen [534] bedeutung zu machen, würde man überaus langsahm sprechen, oder vielmehr verstummen müssen, auch den Lauff der Gedancken nothwendig hemmen; also in reden und dencken nicht weit kommen. Daher braucht man offt die wort als zifern, oder als Rechen-pfennige an stat der Bildnisse und Sachen, bis man stufen weise zum Facit schreitet, und beym Vernunfft-Schlus zur Sache selbst gelanget."[6]

Zunächst fällt an dieser Passage auf, dass Leibniz hier, offenbar mit Bedacht, mehrere traditionelle, zu seiner Zeit noch weithin geläufige Topoi der älteren Erkenntnistheorie aufgreift: Zum einen den seit der Antike gebräuchlichen Topos der Beschreibung des Denkens als „innere Rede" (*lógos endiáthetos, locutio interna, oratio mentalis*)[7] oder, wie es hier heißt, als ein „innerliches Selbst-Gespräch". Zum anderen die von ihm sonst nirgends in dieser Form verwendete traditionelle Charakterisierung der geistigen Begriffe (*conceptus* bzw. *notiones*) als Ähnlichkeiten (*similitudines*), Bilder (*imagines*) bzw. „Bildnisse der dinge". Er rekurriert damit auf jene beiden paradigmatischen Modelle von Sprache und Bild, die die Beschreibung des Denkens oder der kognitiven Repräsentation von der Antike bis in die gegenwärtig im Rahmen der *Philosophy of Mind* geführte Debatte zwischen den Propositionalisten und den Piktorialisten prägen.[8]

Unter Verwendung dieser traditionellen Topoi beschreibt Leibniz die kognitive Instrumentalisierung der sprachlichen Zeichen hier als eine Prozedur, bei der, in Analogie zur Substitution des Geldes durch Wechsel oder Spielmarken, der Verstand die Bildnisse der Dinge (d. h. die Sachbegriffe oder, in scholastischer Terminologie, die *conceptus rei*) – für eine gewisse Zeit und unter bestimmten Voraussetzungen – durch Worte (bzw. Wortvorstellungen, *conceptus vocis*) ersetzt, so dass er „in den Gedancken und innerlichen

---

[6] Ebd., 533f.
[7] Vgl. Stephan Meier-Oeser: „Wort, inneres / Rede, innere", in: Joachim Ritter/Karlfried Gründer/Gottfried Gabriel (Hrsg.): *Historisches Wörterbuch der Philosophie*, Bd. 12, Basel 2004, Sp. 1037–1050; Ders.: „Mental Language and Mental Representation in Late Scholastic Logic", in: Russell L. Friedman/Sten Ebbesen (Hrsg.): *John Buridan and Beyond. Topics in Language Sciences 1300–1700* (= The Royal Danish Academy of Sciences and Letters, Historisk-filosofiske Meddelelser 89), Kopenhagen 2004, S. 237–265.
[8] Vgl. Stephan Meier-Oeser: „Sprache und Bilder im Geist. Skizzen zu einem philosophischen Langzeitprojekt", in: *Philosophisches Jahrbuch der Görres-Gesellschaft* 111 (2004), S. 312–342.

selbst-Gespräch" an die Stelle der kognitiv anspruchsvolleren mentalen Bilder, die als mehr oder weniger genaue und ausführliche Repräsentation der Sache deren wesentliche Merkmale zum Ausdruck bringen, die wesentlich leichter zu ‚handhabenden' Wörter treten lässt. Damit beschreibt er die kognitive Instrumentalisierung der Wörter allerdings als eine Prozedur, die für das Denken insofern nicht zwingend notwendig zu sein scheint, als sie – wie es heißt – „nicht allezeit" angewendet wird, sondern nur „offt", und die allein schon deshalb nicht erkenntniskonstitutiv sein kann, weil sie nur unter der Voraussetzung funktioniert, dass das, was die Wörter temporär ersetzen sollen, nämlich die Begriffe oder Bilder der Dinge, bereits „einmal wol gefasset" sind. Die Funktion der Sprache bestünde – so, wie sie hier beschrieben wird – also nur in einer temporären Ersetzung, die dem Verstand beim Vollzug des rationalen Diskurses gewissermaßen eine intermediäre Erleichterung des gedanklichen Marschgepäcks gewährleistet. Ebenso nämlich, wie der Wechsel oder die Spielmarken am Ende, d. h. bei der „letzten Abrechnung oder Zahlung" wieder gegen bare Münze eingetauscht werden, läuft auch der hier beschriebene Gebrauch der Wörter letztlich darauf hinaus, dass der Verstand am Schluss, bzw. „beym Vernunfft-Schluss" – die Sprache wiederum hinter sich lassend – „zur Sache selbst gelanget".

Angesichts dieses Befundes ist wohl der erwähnten Einschätzung von Apel zu widersprechen und festzuhalten, dass es sich bei der betrachteten Passage weder um die „folgenreichste" noch um die „eindringlichste" Analyse der Sprachgebundenheit des menschlichen Denkens handelt, die sich im späten 17. und frühen 18. Jahrhundert finden lässt.[9] Einerseits gibt es nämlich in der Tradition der Konzeption des Denkens als „innere Rede" eine Reihe von Autoren, die in der Betonung der „Sprachgebundenheit des Denkens" bereits weiter gegangen sind als es hier der Fall ist; denn (spätestens) seit dem 14. Jahrhundert (William Crathorn) wird unter Hinweis auf die prinzipielle Unmöglichkeit der Existenz allgemeiner Bilder die Auffassung vertreten, dass das abstrakte Denken, bzw. das Denken abstrakter Gegenstände sich ausschließlich in Form von sprachlichen Repräsentationen (*conceptus vocis*) vollzieht.[10] Diese Auffassung hat in der frühen Neuzeit zahlreiche Vertreter gefunden. So betont

---

[9] Für eine angemessene Bewertung dieser Ausführungen wäre natürlich zu berücksichtigen, dass der Skopus dieser Schrift eben nicht die detaillierte Analyse der kognitiven Funktion von Sprache ist, sondern dass es sich um eine populär gehaltene Propagandaschrift zugunsten der Einrichtung einer staatlichen Institution zur Beförderung der deutschen Sprache handelt.
[10] Zu William Crathorn vgl. Stefan Meier-Oeser: „Sprache und Bilder im Geist", in: *Philosophisches Jahrbuch der Görres-Gesellschaft*, 111 Heft 2 (2004), S. 312–342, hier S. 327.

etwa – um nur Autoren aus der Zeit um 1690 zu nennen – der neapolitanische Coelestiner Bernardo de Rojas, dass es viele abstrakte Gegenstände des Denkens gibt (wie etwa die „spiritualia, virtutes, vitia, scientiae [...] veritas, unitas, bonitas"), von denen wir keine mentalen Bilder haben und die wir daher allein mittels einer sprachlichen „cognitio enuntiativa" erkennen können.[11] Auch nach Richard Burthogge, der seinen 1694 veröffentlichten *Essay upon Reason and the Nature of Spirit* Locke gewidmet hat, basiert die Verstandeserkenntnis, die sich auf das nicht in Form von Bildern repräsentierbare Allgemeine bezieht, wesensmäßig auf der kognitiven Funktion Wörtern, wenn er betont: „the Understanding hath not of its own, (as the Imagination hath) any proper Images, any Figures of the things it converses with", so dass gilt: „The only Images it [sc. the Understanding] has [...] of all things [...] that are purely intelligible and mental, are the Words that signify them". Der Verstand operiert also lediglich mit aus Wörtern bestehenden Definitionen von Wörtern.[12] Noch weiter geht zu jener Zeit Christian Thomasius, wenn er nicht nur die Operationen des Verstandes sondern auch die ontogenetische Ausbildung der Ratio selbst als durch die soziale Vermittlung von Sprache oder Rede begründet darstellt, indem er deutlich macht,[13] dass der Mensch nur insofern vernünftig ist, als er denken kann, sein Denken sich aber nur in Form einer inneren Rede vollzieht, die wiederum seine soziale Existenz innerhalb einer Sprechergemeinschaft zur Voraussetzung hat:

---

[11] Bernardo de Rojas: *De formarum generatione contra atomistas opusculum*, Neapel 1694, S. 470f.: „[...] constat, plura esse obiecta, quae nec per se immediate, nec ad modum aliorum cognoscantur a nobis cognitione obiectiva, seu repraesentativa, sed tantum per mentalem enunciationem percipiuntur, atque per intellectualem discursum proferuntur, et probantur, et demonstrantur. [...] Est enim contemplatio quaedam repraesentatio rei secundum propriam et immediatam ipsius quidditatem, ita ut per contemplationem ipsa rei propria imago, seu, ut alii dicunt, idolum et idea in mente appareat; constat autem multarum rerum nullam in mente nostra imaginem, nullumque idolum apparere; et hujusmodi sunt etiam spiritualia, virtutes, vitia, scientiae, imo [471] ipsa veritas, unitas, bonitas, quae sunt attributa entis; haec igitur omnia, et alia plurima enunciativa tantum cognitione attingimus [...]. Nec propterea cognitio, quam enunciativam vocavimus, minoris certitudinis est, quam cognitio obiectiva, quae sensuum ministerio, aut per immediatas obiecti species habetur. Imo certior saepius, atque evidentior est illa, quam ista."
[12] Richard Burthogge: *An Essay upon Reason and the Nature of Spirit*, London 1694, S. 27.
[13] Vgl. hierzu Stephan Meier-Oeser: „Das Ende der Metapher von der ‚inneren Rede'. Zum Verhältnis von Sprache und Denken in der deutschen Frühaufklärung", in: Hans Erich Bödecker (Hrsg.): *Strukturen der deutschen Frühaufklärung 1680–1720* (= *Veröffentlichungen des Max-Planck-Instituts für Geschichte*) Göttingen 2008, S. 195–223.

"Die Gedancken sind eine innerliche Rede. [...] Diese innerliche Rede praesupponiret eine äusserliche. [...] wo wolte er [sc. der Mensch] also innerlich mit sich reden, wenn nicht andere Menschen, mit denen er in Gesellschafft lebet, durch ihre äusserliche Rede seine innerliche anzündeten?"[14]

Diese knappen, die Komplexität der historische Situation stark verkürzenden Hinweise sollen lediglich deutlich machen, dass die These von der grundlegenden Bedeutung der Sprache für das Denken – anders als es die geläufige Rede von der an den Namen Herder und Humboldt festgemachten sog. „kopernikanischen Wende der Sprachphilosophie" nahelegt – auch schon zur Zeit von Leibniz keine ungewöhnliche Auffassung darstellte und von vielen Autoren in einer Deutlichkeit vertreten wurde, die weit über die eher vage gehaltenen Formulierung der *Unvorgreifflichen Gedancken* hinausgeht.

Andererseits hat aber auch Leibniz selbst in zahlreichen Texten die Angewiesenheit des Denkens auf Sprache (oder allgemeiner: auf Zeichengebrauch) deutlich prägnanter artikuliert als in den *Unvorgreifflichen Gedancken*; so etwa, wenn er erklärt, dass all unser schlussfolgerndes Denken nichts andere ist, als eine Verknüpfung und Ersetzung von Zeichen („Omnis Ratiocinatio nostra nihil aliud est quam characterum connexio, et substitutio")[15] oder betont, dass ein Denken zwar ohne Wörter möglich ist, nicht jedoch ohne jegliche andere Zeichen („cogitationes fieri possunt sine vocabulis […] at non sine aliis signis").[16] Leibniz' Äußerungen in diese Richtung sind bekannt und in der einschlägigen Forschungsliteratur ausführlich dokumentiert; sie brauchen hier daher nicht wiederholt zu werden.

Fest steht in jedem Fall, dass das Œuvre von Leibniz durchaus Schriften enthält, die sich als vielversprechende oder sogar als die aussichtsreichsten Kandidaten für die Auszeichnung als *folgenreichste* und *eindringlichste* Analyse der kognitiven Funktion von Sprache nahelegen: nämlich zum einen die *Meditationes de cognitione, veritate et ideis*, als – wie sich leicht nachweisen lässt – Kandidat für die *folgenreichste* Analyse und zum anderen – wie ich zeigen möchte – die *Nouveaux Essais* als Kandidat für die *eindringlichste* Analyse des Zusammenhanges von Sprache und Denken.

---

[14] Christian Thomasius: *Einleitung zur Sittenlehre*, Halle 1692 (ND Hildesheim 1968), S. 89f.; ebd., S. 25f.: „Ohne andere Menschen wäre der Mensch höchst elende [...] die Gedancken bestehen aus einer innerlichen Rede, die innerliche Rede entsteht von einer äußerlichen." Vgl., ders.: *Institutiones jurisprudentiae divinae*, Frankfurt 1688, S. 135: „Ratio absque sermone non est, sermonis extra societatem nullus est usus, nec ratio citra societatem se exserit."
[15] „De modis combinandi characteres" (1688–99); A VI, 4, 922.
[16] „Dialogus", August 1677; A VI, 4, 22.

Das systematische Zentrum der 1684 veröffentlichten *Meditationes de cognitione* bildet die von Leibniz eingeführte Unterscheidung von *cognitio intuitiva* (der unmittelbaren intellektuellen Erfassung eines Gegenstandes) und *cognitio symbolica* (der Erkenntnis des Gegenstandes im Medium beliebiger Zeichen). Leibniz wendet sich damit explizit gegen die von Descartes vertreten, metaphysisch im Dualismus von Geist und Körper begründete Trennung der ‚pura intellectio' von aller Sinnlichkeit und Imagination. Demgegenüber erklärt Leibniz, dass eine *cognitio intuitiva* (die der *pura intellectio* Descartes entspricht) dem Menschen (wenn überhaupt) nur bei sehr wenigen, allereinfachsten Konzepten möglich ist, alles andere aber nicht anders als im Modus der zeichenbasierten *cognitio symbolica* erkannt wird. Das Leibniz'sche Konzept der symbolischen Erkenntnis hat, besonders durch ihre Aufnahme und Verbreitung durch Christian Wolff im 18. Jahrhundert eine keineswegs nur auf den Wolffianismus beschränkte Rezeption erfahren und avanciert zu *dem* zentralen Lehrstück der Erkenntnistheorie dieser Zeit,[17] dessen massive Wirksamkeit sich bis ins späte 19. Jahrhundert verfolgen lässt. Es ist vor allem auf die Wirksamkeit der Leibniz'schen Theorie der symbolischen Erkenntnis zurückzuführen, dass es bereits um die Mitte des 18. Jahrhunderts die vorherrschen Auffassung ist, dass, wie Johann Heinrich Lambert sagt, „all unsere allgemeine oder abstrakte Erkenntnis […] durchaus symbolisch" ist,[18] bzw., wie bereits Georg Bernhard Bilfinger konstatiert: „omnis cognitio universalis symbolica est, symbola autem communia voces sunt […]."[19]

Wenn die *Meditationes* nicht zugleich auch ein Anwärter auf den Titel der *eindringlichsten* Analyse sind, so deshalb, weil in ihnen die Fundierung der Erkenntnistheorie in der Leibniz'schen Metaphysik (die sich ja zu jener Zeit gerade erst formiert) bzw. die metaphysischen Implikationen der Erkenntnistheorie noch nicht entfaltet dargelegt werden. Jedenfalls nicht so explizit und deutlich, wie in späteren Texten, wo es als unmittelbare gnoseologische Konsequenz der prästabilierten Harmonie von Seele und Körper beschrieben wird, dass abstrakte Gedanken stets mit sinnlichen Zeichen verbunden sind[20] und

---

[17] Zur *cognitio symbolica* bei Wolff und im Wolffianismus vgl. Matteo Favaretti Camposampiero: *Conoscenza simbolica*, in: Christian Wolff: *Gesammelte Werke*, hrsg. v. Jean Ecole, III. Abt. Bd. 19, Hildesheim/Zürich/New York 2009.
[18] Johann Heinrich Lambert: *Neues Organon*, Bd. 2, Leipzig 1764, S. 12f.
[19] Georg Bernhard Bilfinger: *Praecepta logica*, Jena 1742, S. 87.
[20] Vgl. „Nouveaux Essais" I, 1, § 5; A VI, 6, 77: „[…] c'est par une admirable Oeconomie de la nature, que nous ne saurions avoir des pensées abstraites, qui n'ayent point besoin de quelque chose de sensible, quand ce ne seroit que des caracteres tels que sont les figures des lettres et

dementsprechend gilt: „Il n'y a jamais un entendement si pur qu'il ne soit point accompagné de quelque imagination."[21] Die Notwendigkeit der sinnlichen Anteile sogar am abstraktesten Denken ist in dieser Perspektive geradezu die conditio sine qua non der prästabilierten Harmonie von Körper und Seele: „si les traces sensibles n'etoient point requises, l'harmonie preétablie entre l'ame et le corps [...] n'auroit point de lieu."[22]

Hatte Descartes in der sechsten Meditation seinen Intuitionismus anhand der Figur des Tausendecks (*chiliogon*) zu beweisen versucht, indem er darauf hinwies, dass sich eine solche Figur zwar nicht imaginieren, durch eine ‚intellectio pura' jedoch genauso präzis erkennen lasse, wie ein Dreieck,[23] so sieht Locke im *Essay concerning Human Understanding* seine empiristische Erkenntnistheorie durch das sprachgeschichtliche Faktum bestätigt, dass es ein in allen Sprachen beobachtbares Phänomen, das die Termini von Gegenständen, die nicht unter die Sinne fallen ursprünglich aus sinnlichen Ideen entstanden sind.[24] D. h.: „obvious sensible ideas are transferred to more abstruse significations". Locke belegt diese These anhand einiger Namen für kognitive Operationen (*imagine, apprehend, comprehend, conceive*), epistemische Einstellungen (*adhere, disgust*), seelische Zustände (*disturbance, tranquillity*) und immaterielle Wesen, wenn er bemerkt: „Spirit, in its primary signification, is breath: Angel a messenger."[25] Was Locke damit deutlich machen will, ist die Tatsache, dass große Teile gerade auch unserer philosophischen Begrifflichkeit metaphorische Konzepte sind, durch die ein ursprünglich sinnlicher Gehalt auf den Bereich abstrakter Erkenntnis übertragen wurde.

---

les sons, quoiqu'il n'y ait aucune connexion necessaire entre tels caracteres arbitraires, et telles pensées."
[21] „Extrait du Dictionnaire de M. Bayle article Rorarius [...] avec mes remarques", GP IV, 541.
[22] Ebd.
[23] Vgl. René Descartes: *Meditationes de prima philosophia* VI, 2, in: *Œuvres de Descartes*, Bd. VII, hrsg. v. Charles Adam/Paul Tannery, Paris 1897–1910, S. 72f. Genau hiergegen wendet sich Leibniz mit dem Konzept der *cognitio symbolica*, indem er deutlich macht, dass Descartes' vermeintliche Erkenntnis des Tausendecks nicht (qua *pura intellectio*) den Wesensbegriff desselben erfasst, sondern vielmehr lediglich (qua *cognitio symbolica*) das Zeichen ‚Tausendeck'– das jedoch, als bekanntes und in seine Teilbedeutungen analysierbares Zeichen, genau jene Erkenntnis generiert, die Descartes einer – nach Leibniz metaphysisch unmöglichen – *pura intellectio* zuschreibt. Vgl. „Meditationes de cognitione, veritate, et ideis"; A VI, 4, 587.
[24] John Locke: *An Essay concerning Human Understanding* III, 1, 5, hrsg. v. Peter H. Nidditch, Oxford 1975 [= *Essay*], S. 403.
[25] Ebd.

Wenn Leibniz, der in den *Nouveaux Essais* die gesamte Passage nahezu wörtlich aus Costes französischen Übersetzung des *Essay* übernimmt, an dieser Stelle nicht näher auf die angeführten Beispiele eingeht, so gewiss nicht deshalb, weil er, wie Hans Aarsleff unterstellt hat,[26] in der Herleitung der beiden metaphysischen Termini „Engel" (*angelus*) und „Geist" (*spiritus*) aus den sinnlichen Erfahrungsbegriffen „Bote" und „Hauch" eine „dangerous impiety" gesehen hätte, welche ihn „schockiert und verstört" („shocked and disturbed") hat.[27] Vielmehr hat er, was die grundlegende Struktur des Denkens und deren Bezug zur Sprache betrifft, Wichtigeres zu sagen; denn der von Locke angesprochene Gedanke ist Leibniz seit langem bestens vertraut. Die These vom sinnlichen Ursprung der Bezeichnung intelligibler Gegenstände ist bei ihm bereits sehr früh nachweisbar.[28] 1698 hat er sie in Johannes Claubergs *Ars Etymologica Teutonum* wiedergefunden;[29] und in der Zwischenzeit intensiv weiterentwickelt.

Lockes Bemerkungen zum sinnlichen Ursprung der abstrakten Ideen werden daher nicht einfach zurückgewiesen. Vielmehr werden sie in einer subtilen Argumentationsbewegung zugleich erweitert und substanziiert, um dann – wie sich weiter unten zeigen wird – in eine Richtung gelenkt zu werden, die von der Intention Lockes signifikant abweicht: Leibniz unterstreicht durchaus die Wichtigkeit, jene Analogie der sinnlichen und unsinnlichen

---

[26] Vgl. Hans Aarsleff: „Leibniz on Locke on Language", in: *Philosophical Quarterly* 1 (1964), S. 165–188, hier 187.
[27] Zum einen charakterisiert er (bzw. Theophile) Lockes Feststellung, dass die Termini der Theologie, Moral und Metaphysik ursprünglich von ‚handfesten' sinnlichen Dinge hergenommen sind („que les termes de Théologie, de Morale et de Métaphysique sont pris originairement des choses grossières") ausdrücklich als ‚Wahrheit' („cette vérité"), und zum anderen hat Leibniz selbst in der *Epistolaris de Historia Etymologica Dissertatio* (1712) das Beispiel der sinnlichen Herkunft des Geistbegriffs – und zwar viel ausführlicher als Locke – dargelegt. Vgl. „Epistolaris de Historia Etymologica Dissertatio", hrsg. v. Stefano Gensini, in: Ders.: *Il naturale e il simbolico. Saggio su Leibniz*, Rom 1991, S. 229: „Rerum autem naturalium, sensibilium, crebrius occurrentium appellationes priores fuêre quam rariorum, artificialium, moralium et metaphysicarum. Itaque pneûma spiritus, anima, quae nunc vocabula res incorporeas significant, originarie denotant flatum: unde translata sunt ad alias res invisibiles, et tamen activas, quales sunt animae et spiritus. Et Germanicum Geist eodem modo originarie significat spiritum corporeum, qui a liquoribus inter fermentandum emittitur […]."
[28] Vgl. *Disputatio de Casibus perplexis in Jure* (1661), A VI, 1, 236: „A corporalibus ad incorporalia frequenti Metaphora translata voce, Nodus pro omni intricato sumitur."
[29] Vgl. Johannes Clauberg: *Ars Etymologica Teutonum e Philosophiae fontibus derivata*, Duisburg 1663, S. 9: „A sensibilibus ad intelligibilia quamplurima vocabula sunt traducta." Leibniz hat diese Schrift in seine *Collectanea etymologica* aufgenommen; dort S. 187–252.

Dinge zu betrachten, die als Fundament der Tropen gedient hat („de considerer cette analogie des choses sensibles et insensibles qui a servi de fondement aux tropes"), eine Analogie, die sich insbesondere dann besser verstehen lässt, betrachtete man

> „l'usage des prepositions, comme *à, avec, de, devant, en, hors, par, pour, sur, vers*, qui sont toutes prises du lieu, de la distance, et du mouvement, et transferées depuis à toute sorte de changemens, ordres, suites, différences, convenances."[30]

Derartige Bedeutungsübertragungen sind im allgemeinen und philosophischen Sprachgebrauch quasi omnipräsent und z. B. wirksam, wenn man die Akzidentien als etwas betrachtet, das ‚in' dem Gegenstand ist, oder sagt, dass man ‚über' etwas nachdenkt – ungefähr so, wie ein Handwerker sich über das von ihm zu bearbeitendes Stück Holz beugt.[31]

Mit seinem Insistieren auf der erkenntnistheoretischen Relevanz der Betrachtung der *particulae* (*particules*) und insbesondere der Präpositionen (*prepositions*), von denen er behauptet: „nichts ist geeigneter, die verschiedenen Formen des Verstandes erkennen zu lassen", geht Leibniz weit über Lockes generelle Bemerkungen hinaus; denn damit ist im Grunde gesagt, dass nicht nur das Wörterbuch des Denkens, sondern ebenso auch die Grammatik desselben – und damit das menschliche Denken insgesamt – von metaphorischen Transposition durchzogen ist. Die Präpositionen korrespondieren nämlich zum einen den grammatischen Kasus, und sind zum anderen oftmals in die Nomina eingefaltet (envelopée) und gleichsam aufgesogen (absorbée), während andere Präpositionen in den Flexionsformen der Verben versteckt sind.[32]

---

[30] „Nouveaux Essais"; A VI, 6, 277. Hervorhebungen von Leibniz, in A allerdings in Form von Sperrungen.

[31] Vgl. ebd., 278: „[…] les accidens sont considerés […] comme *dans* le sujet, *sunt in subjecto, inhaerent subjecto*. La particule *sur* aussi est appliquée à l'objet, on dit qu'on est *sur* cette matiere, à peu prés comme un ouvrier est sur le bois […]."

[32] Vgl. ebd., A VI, 6, 330: „Il est très vrai que la Doctrine des particules est importante, et je voudrois qu'on entrât dans un plus grand detail là dessus. Car rien ne seroit plus propre à faire connoitre les diverses formes de l'entendement. […] les cas repondent aux prepositions, et souvent la preposition y est enveloppée dans le nom, et comme absorbée, et d'autres particules sont cachées dans les flexions des verbes." Zur besonderen Bedeutung der *Particulae* in der Sprachphilosophie von Leibniz vgl. Marcelo Dascal: „Leibniz on Particles. Linguistic Form and Comparatism", in: Lia Formigari/Tullio De Mauro (Hrsg.): *Leibniz, Humboldt and the Origins of Comparativism* (= *Studies in the History of the Language Sciences* 49), Amsterdam/Philadelphia 1990, S. 31–60; Massimo Mugnai: „‚Voces constituunt materiam, particulae formam orationis': osservazioni sulla filosofia del linguaggio leibniziana", in: *Lingua e stile* 25 (1990), S. 337–350; Stefano Gensini: „‚De Linguis in Universum': on Leibniz's ideas on languages; five

Zugleich kann Leibniz, anders als Locke, die interne Logik dieser Transpositionen näher bestimmen. Dabei bringt er auch mit dieser Konstatierung der zentralen Bedeutung der raummetaphorischen Transpositionen eine Thematik zu Sprache, die ihn bereits lange Zeit intensiv beschäftigt hatte. Die früheste Notiz über die metaphorische Bedeutungserweiterung der Präpositionen findet sich in den wohl aus der Mitte der 60er Jahre stammenden Marginalien in seinem Handexemplar von Bisterfelds *Philosophiae primae Seminarium*.[33] Später kommt er bei seinen grammatischen Sprachanalysen immer wieder auf dieses Thema zurück, wobei die Tendenz einer zunehmenden Betonung sowohl der Weite als auch der kognitiven Bedeutung des Phänomens der metaphorischen Übertragungen sichtbar wird. Während Leibniz zunächst (um 1679) nur allgemein konstatiert, dass die Präpositionen durch die Verhältnisse zwischen den Dingen gestützt sind und neben Ort und Zeit auch vielfältige andere Arten von Relationen bezeichnen,[34] betont er um 1685 den tropischen Charakter der meisten Präpositionen, wenn er feststellt, dass

> „alle Präpositionen im eigentlichen Sinn ein Ortsverhältnis bezeichnen, im übertragenen Sinn jedes beliebige andere Verhältnis" („Omnes praepositiones proprie significant relationem Loci, translate aliam relationem quamcunque").[35]

---

essays", Münster 2000, S. 85, 212f.; Jap Maat: *Philosophical Language in the Seventeenth Century: Dalgarno, Wilkins, Leibniz*, Dordrecht/Boston/London 2004, S. 378–381. Auf die grundlegende kognitive Funktion speziell der Präpositionen ist erstmals eingehend hingewiesen worden von Lucia Oliveri: „Logische und semantische Funktionen der Präpositionen in Leibniz' Sprachphilosophie", in: Wenchao Li (Hrsg): *Einheit der Vernunft und Vielfalt der Sprachen. Beiträge zu Leibniz' Sprachforschung und Zeichentheorie*, Stuttgart 2014, S. 55–82.

[33] „Notae ad Joh. Henr. Bisterfeldium"; A VI, 1, 153: „Praepositiones [...] rerum habitudines, statum motumve, exprimunt; et petuntur ex circulo situs corporei." Wenn Leibniz auch die 1661 unter dem Titel *Bisterfeldius redivivus* erschienene Sammlung von Bisterfeldtexten rezipiert hat, konnte er dort auch den expliziten Hinweis darauf finden, dass die Präpositionen im übertragenen Sinn allgemein die Ordnung (*ordo*) und den Zusammenhang (*connexio*) der Dinge, sowie, ganz allgemein, den „processum Metaphysicum, qui in omni omnino operatione occurrit" zum Ausdruck bringen. Vgl. Johann Heinrich Bisterfeld: „Parallelismus Analyseos Grammaticae et Logicae", in: *Bisterfeldius redivivus: Seu Operum Joh. Henrici Bisterfeldii [...] Tomus primus*, Den Haag 1661, S. 224.

[34] „Characteristica verbalis" [Mai bis Juni 1679 (?)]; A VI, 4, 336: „Praepositiones igitur nituntur relationibus rerum, quae significant locum, tempus, locum et tempus simul ut locum praeteritum, locum futurum (terminum a quo et ad quem), Causam (id est efficientem vel finalem), Materiam, Convenientiam, Oppositionem, Exceptionem, separationem; permutationem (seu mutuam separationem et adjunctionem), Unionem."

[35] „Omnes praepositiones proprie significant relationem loci" [Herbst 1685 (?)]; A VI, 4, 645.

Wenig später spricht Leibniz in diesem Zusammenhang noch ausdrücklicher von der metaphorischen Übertragung aus dem Bereich sichtbarer Dinge auf den Bereich der res invisibiles;[36] und gegen 1688 heißt es dann in *De lingua philosophica*, seiner reifsten Schrift zur grammatischen Sprachanalyse, dass hinsichtlich der Präpositionen

> „in allen gebräuchlichen Sprachen zu beobachten ist, dass sie ursprünglich den Bezug zu einem Ort bezeichnen und von dort aus durch eine gewisse tropische Wendung auf gewisse metaphysische, weniger der Imagination unterworfene Begriffe übertragen worden sind."

Was jedoch, wie Leibniz betont, insofern kein Wunder ist, als

> „die Menschen stets bestrebt sind, auch diejenigen Dinge, die sie sich nicht bildlich vorstellen können, durch der Imagination unterworfene Gegenstände zu erklären".[37]

Mein Vorschlag, Leibniz' Bemerkungen über die Präpositionen in den *Nouveaux Essais* als die ‚eindringlichsten' Analyse des Zusammenhangs von Sprache und Denken zu betrachten, ist nicht dadurch begründet, dass sie in sprachtheoretisch-linguistischer Hinsicht besonders detailliert ausgeführt wären. Das sind sie sicherlich nicht – und sollen es auch gar nicht sein. Ebenso nämlich, wie Lockes Bemerkungen über den sinnlichen Ursprung der abstrakten Begriffe nicht als linguistische oder sprachgeschichtliche Ausführungen gemeint sind, sondern in erkenntnistheoretischer Perspektive stehen, geht es hier auch Leibniz bei seiner Betrachtung der Präpositionen letzten Endes nicht um Sprachgeschichte oder Etymologie, sondern vielmehr um Sprachanalyse zum Zweck der Erkenntniskritik, die – und daraus resultiert das besondere Maß der ‚Eindringlichkeit' – in ihren Konsequenzen tief in den Bereich der Metaphysik hineinreicht.

---

[36] „Analysis particularum" [Herbst bis Winter 1685/86 (?)]; A VI, 4, 647: „Mirum autem non est homines in praepositionibus formandis loci tantum rationem habuisse, quia initio res tantum sensibiles sive corporales spectarunt; quibus proprias voces postea per tropos ad res invisibiles transtulerunt."
[37] Vgl., „De lingua philosophica" [Ende 1687 bis Ende 1688 (?)]; A VI, 4, 890: „Circa praepositiones observandum videtur omnes in nostris linguis usitatis originarie significare respectum ad situm, et inde transferri tropo quodam ad notiones quasdam metaphysicas minus imaginationi subjectas. Quod mirum non est, quia homines etiam ea quae imaginari non possunt per res imaginationi subjectas explicare conantur."

Dabei vollzieht Leibniz, trotz der scheinbaren Zustimmung zu und Weiterentwicklung von Lockes Thesen, eine subtile Inversion der Argumentation Lockes: Während Locke mit seinem Hinweis auf den tropischen Charakter der abstrakten Begriffe zeigen möchte, dass sich auch die vermeintlich abstrakten Gegenstände unseres Denkens letztlich auf sinnliche Phänomene reduzieren lassen, will Leibniz natürlich nicht darauf hinaus, dass alle Arten von Relationen letztlich auf räumliche reduzierbar sind. Im Gegenteil: Der Hinweis auf die metaphorisch-metaphysische Verwendung von Termini, die eigentlich räumliche Verhältnisse bezeichnen, soll vielmehr zu Bewusstsein bringen, dass das, was sich uns in Form räumlicher Verhältnisse darstellt und was wir, wie alle Sprachen zeigen, offenbar nicht anders als in Form räumlicher Verhältnisse ausdrücken oder denken können, in letzter, metaphysischer Instanz, keineswegs räumliche Verhältnis sein müssen – oder mehr noch: keineswegs räumliche Verhältnisse sind. Zwar können wir es kaum vermeiden, in räumlichen Kategorien (i.e. Metaphern) zu denken, und noch weniger können wir umhin, unsere Gedanken in dieser Form auszudrücken, selbst dann, wenn sie – eigentlich – unangemessen sind. Es ist jedoch möglich – und notwendig –, sich dieser Übertragungen bewusst zu sein, um den nicht-räumlichen Sinn nicht mit der räumlichen Bedeutung zu verwechseln.

Die Relevanz, die diese Ausführungen gerade auch für ein angemessenes Verständnis der metaphysischen Texte von Leibniz hat, ist offenkundig angesichts des massiven Gebrauchs, den er bei der Darstellung seiner Metaphysik von räumlichen Termini und Bildern macht. Denn angesichts der Tatsache, dass Monaden oder im strengen metaphysischen Sinn verstandene reale Substanzen unausgedehnte Entitäten sind, müssen Leibniz' Ausführungen zur Metaphysik, wenn man sie beim Wort nimmt, als voll von Kategorienfehlern erscheinen. So etwa, wenn er die Individualität der Monaden durch ihren je eigenen „point de vue" erklärt, oder die Struktur der Welt dadurch beschreibt, dass an jedem ihrer Punkte „mundi in mundis in infinitum" sind; ebenso, wenn er von „zusammengesetzten" Substanzen spricht, deren Einheit jeweils in einer „monade central" gründet. Gerade weil durch derartige Redeweisen durchgängig räumliche Vorstellungen erzeugt werden, ist es wichtig, den fiktionalen Charakter von Räumlichkeit und räumlichen Verhältnisse im Blick zu haben. Gilt doch, wie er gegenüber Des Bosses betont:

> „[…] es gibt keine räumliche Nähe oder Distanz zwischen den Monaden, und zu sagen, dass die Monaden in einem Punkt zusammengeballt oder im Raum verteilt sind, heißt sich gewisser Fiktionen unseres Geistes zu bedienen, wenn wir uns vorstellen wollen, was sich nur vom Verstand einsehen lässt." („[…]

> nec ulla est monadum propinquitas aut distantia spatialis vel absoluta, dicereque, esse in puncto conglobatas, aut in spatio disseminatas, est quibusdam fictionibus animi nostri uti, dum imaginari libenter vellemus, quae tantum intelligi possunt."[38]

Und doch gilt nach Leibniz eben auch, dass jene Einsicht des Verstandes, die eben keine „pure intellectio" im Sinne Descartes sein kann, gemäß der untrennbaren Verbindung von Intellekt und Imagination, bzw. gemäß der prästabilierten Harmonie von Geist und ‚Körper' sich niemals von der Sprache oder den Zeichen im Allgemeinen ablösen kann. In welchem Maße Leibniz' Ausführungen zum (quasi unvermeidbar) metaphorischen Charakter der gängigen metaphysischen Terminologie – die er zwar am Beispiel der Präpositionen näher darstellt, die aber keineswegs nur diese Wortklasse allein betrifft – auch für seine eigenen philosophischen Schriften gelten, wird deutlich, wenn man etwa eine prominente Passage der *Principes de la Nature* (§ 3) nimmt und all jene Wörter markiert (bzw. einklammert), die hier entweder explizit räumliche Verhältnisse benennen (*centre, composée, environné, centrale, dans, centre, hors*) oder doch implizit bzw. transumptiv (*substance, distinguée, par, infinité, constituant, suivant, affections, represente*):

> „[...] chaque [substance] simple ou Monade [distinguée], qui fait le [centre] d'une [substance] [composée] (comme [par] exemple, d'un animal) et le principe de son Unicité, est [environnée] d'une Masse [composée] [par] une [infinité] d'autres Monades, qui [constituent] le corps propre de cette Monade [centrale], [suivant] les [affections] duquel elle [represente], comme [dans] une maniere de [centre], les choses qui sont [hors] d'elle."[39]

Es ist leicht zu sehen, dass Leibniz' Hinweise in den *Nouveaux Essais* auf eine ebenso verbreitete wie fundamentale Funktion von Sprachelementen verweisen, die, wie insbesondere die Präpositionen und jene zahlreichen Verben und Nomina, deren Bedeutung durch die ‚Absorption'[40] von Präpositionen bestimmt wird, in unmittelbarer Bedeutung extensionale oder räumliche Verhältnisse bezeichnen, im übertragenen Sinn jedoch alle möglichen Arten von Verhältnissen.

Mit diesen Andeutungen geht es Leibniz jedoch, wie gesagt, nicht primär um Sprache, sondern um das, was sich in ihr zeigt. Die Tatsache, dass wir

---

[38] An des Bosses, 16. 6. 1712; GP II, 450f.
[39] *Principes de la Nature et de la Grace, fondés en raison* (1714); GP VI, 598f.
[40] Vgl. Anm. 32.

die meisten, wenn nicht sogar sämtliche Arten der zwischen Dingen oder Konzepten bestehenden Verhältnisse nicht anders denken (können), als unter – zumeist unbewusster – Instrumentalisierung von Vorstellungen räumlich-extensionaler Verhältnisse, rührt nicht daher, dass uns dies kontingenterweise durch die Sprache vorgegeben ist. Es ist vielmehr das erkenntnismetaphysische Prinzip der prästabilierten Harmonie von Intellekt und Imagination, dass sich in der Sprache *zeigt*, es hat jedoch nicht seinen *Grund* in der Sprache. Die Prozedur der Übertragung – des μεταφέρειν – ist uns so unvermeidbar, dass auch die Benennung derselben, nämlich „transpositio", nichts Anderes als eine solche Transposition ist. Was Leibniz hiermit andeutet, ist vielmehr so etwas wie eine den zumeist raummetaphorischen Ausdrücken zugrundeliegende ‚verborgenen Kunst in der Tiefe der menschlichen Seele', eine Prozedur, die – in kantischer Terminologie ausgedrückt – irgendwo zwischen schematischer und symbolischer Hypotypose liegt oder auch (vielleicht sogar eher noch) beide umfasst.

Die sprachlichen Transpositionen basieren auf durch die prästabilierte Harmonie vorgegebenen kognitiven Transpositionen, die funktional mit einer weiteren Transposition verbunden sind (weshalb auch im Titel meines Beitrag von „Raummetaphorik in Sprache, Denken und *Realität*" die Rede ist): Die phänomenale Welt, d. h. jene traditionell als *mundus aspectabilis* beschriebene Welt, die den Raum der menschlichen Erfahrungen und Aktionen, mithin den Raum unserer lebensweltlichen Realität bildet, ist nach Leibniz selbst in letzter Instanz nur eine sinnliche Transposition – und damit gleichsam eine Metapher – der ihr zugrundeliegenden metaphysischen Realität, in der es nichts anderes gibt als unausgedehnte Monaden und deren interne Bestimmungsmomente von *perception* und *appetition*.

Von der „Cité de Dieu" zum „weltbürgerlichen Ganzen".
Zu Glückseligkeit, Kulturarbeit und Moral bei Leibniz und Kant

Anselm Model (Freiburg im Breisgau)

Zwei hervorragende Gestalten der Philosophie stehen am Anfang und Ende derjenigen geschichtlichen Epoche, die man in Deutschland die „Aufklärung" nennt. Im Beginn ragt *Gottfried Wilhelm Leibniz* (1646–1716) hervor. Er hat der Aufklärung des achtzehnten Jahrhunderts wesentliche Impulse und Gedanken vermittelt. Nach *Immanuel Kant* (1724–1804) verklingt das Jahrhundert der Aufklärung in Deutschland. Sein kritischer Idealismus wird als eine Aufklärung der Aufklärung selbst verstanden.

Kant wurde von Zeitgenossen als ein Zerstörer derjenigen Metaphysik erachtet, die, auf Leibniz'sche Gedanken und Prinzipien sich berufend, das aufklärerische Denken Deutschlands im achtzehnten Jahrhundert dominierte.

Nachfolgend soll versucht werden, die Ansicht vom Zerstörer Kants zu relativieren. Dies kann hier nur skizzenhaft geschehen. Dies soll besonders an der ausgereiftesten Schrift Kants, an der *Kritik der Urteilskraft* gezeigt werden, an der Art, wie Kant sich in diesem Werk auf Leibniz und auf dessen Vorstellung von der „Cité de Dieu" und auf das „Reich der Gnaden" bezieht. Dabei sollen insbesondere die Ausgänge der *Kritik der Urteilskraft* und der *Monadologie* verglichen werden.

1.

Beide Denker, Leibniz und Kant, haben zur Zeit ihrer vollen geistigen Reife vermocht, ihr Gedankensystem jeweils in den soeben genannten Schriften zusammenfassend darzustellen.

Das Äußere beider Schriften spiegelt die unterschiedlichen Lebens- und Berufssituationen beider Autoren wieder. Der vielseitig tätige Diplomat und Hofrat Leibniz fasst seine Philosophie 1714 in der *Monadologie* thesenhaft zusammen, wobei die Zahl der Thesen zwischen 90 und 93 gering variiert sowohl auf den vorhandenen Manuskripten als auch in den gedruckten Wiedergaben zur Zeit Kants.

Kant als langjähriger Hochschuldozent vermochte seine letzte zusammenfassende Schrift 1790 in der umfangreichen 482 Seiten zählenden *Kritik der Urteilskraft* niederzulegen. In der *Kritik der Urteilskraft* dominiert eine schulmäßige Gliederung mit Vorrede, Einleitung, zwei Teilen mit Unterteilungen in

Analytik und Dialektik und endet mit einer Methodenlehre, die auch als Anhang bezeichnet ist. Daneben ist allerdings diskret eine weitere Gliederung sichtbar. Kant nummeriert, der *Monadologie* entsprechend, über beide Teile der *Kritik der Urteilkraft* durchlaufend 91 Paragraphen.

Zur Zeit der Abfassung der *Kritik der Urteilskraft* stand Kant unter starkem Druck von Seiten der Leibniz-Wolff'schen Schule. Er empfahl in einer Streitschrift gegen Eberhard damals (1790) seinen Kritikern, seine Kritik der reinen Vernunft als eine Apologie für Leibniz zu lesen.

Kant verweist u.a. als Rechtfertigung seiner Nähe zu Leibniz am Ende dieser Streitschrift die Leser auf die *Kritik der Urteilskraft*, die im Erscheinen begriffen sei. Der kundige mit Leibniz *Monadologie* vertraute Leser konnte dann bereits aus dem Inhalt und Aufbau der *Kritik der Urteilskraft*, besonders mit dem zweiten Teil, der *Kritik der teleologischen Urteilskraft*, und mit der Gleichzahl der Paragraphen der *Kritik der Urteilskraft* mit der Thesenzahl der *Monadologie* entnehmen, dass Kant hier eine Nähe zu Leibniz und seine Verbundenheit mit Leibniz auszudrücken wünschte.

Auch verweist Kant am Ende der genannten Streitschrift ausdrücklich darauf hin, dass und in welcher Weise er den Leibniz'schen Gedanke der Harmonie des moralischen Reichs der Gnade mit dem Reiche der Natur in seine praktische Philosophie aufgenommen habe.

Am Ende des zweiten Teiles der *Kritik der Urteilskraft*, in der *Methodologie*, führt Kant den Leser zu zentralen Themen seiner Ethik, zu Kulturarbeit, Glückswürdigkeit, zum ethischen Grundgesetz und zur Ethikotheologie. Die *Kritik der teleologischen Urteilskraft* enthält in der *Methodenlehre* so die abschließende und differenzierteste Darstellung der praktischen Philosophie Kants.

Obgleich Kant in der *Kritik der Urteilskraft* Leibniz nicht mehr eigens nennt, ist doch implizit aus dem Inhalt erkennbar, dass Kant am Ende der *Kritik der Urteilskraft* sich erneut auf Leibniz und dessen Vorstellung der „Cité de Dieu" und des Reiches der Gnade bezieht.

Die Ethik hatte Kant bereits 1781 ausdrücklich mit Leibniz und mit dessen Vorstellung vom Reich der Gnade verknüpft. 1790 erneuert nun Kant diese Verbindung zu Leibniz, direkt in der der *Streitschrift gegen Eberhard* und ohne Leibniz eigens nochmals zu nennen in der *Kritik der Urteilskraft*.

Schauen wir darauf zurück!

2.

Im ersten Entwurf einer kritischen Ethik, den Kant an der zur *Kritik der Urteilskraft* entsprechenden Stelle, in der *Methodenlehre* der *Kritik der reinen Vernunft* 1781 verortete, hat Kant explizit die Verbindung seiner Ethik zu Leibniz gezogen. Er verband dort seinen ethischen Grundgedanken, dass die Glückswürdigkeit der Glücksseligkeit vorauszugehen habe, mit der Leibniz'schen Idee des Reiches der Gnade:

> „Leibniz nannte die Welt, sofern man darin nur auf die vernünftigen Wesen und ihren Zusammenhang nach moralischen Gesetzen unter der Regierung des höchsten Guts acht hat, das *Reich der Gnaden* und unterschied es vom *Reich der Natur,* da sie zwar unter moralischen Gesetzen stehen, aber keine anderen Erfolge ihres Verhaltens erwarten, als nach dem Laufe der Natur unserer Sinnenwelt. Sich also im Reiche der Gnaden zu sehen, wo alle Glückseligkeit auf uns wartet, außer sofern wir unsern Anteil an derselben durch die Unwürdigkeit, glücklich zu sein, nicht selbst einschränken, ist eine praktisch notwendige Idee der Vernunft."[1]

Wenden wir uns zur Kritik der Urteilskraft.

Aufbau und die Themenzusammenstellung der *Kritik der Urteilkraft* haben manchen Interpreten irritiert. Duktus, Logik und Stringenz des Aufbaus der *Kritik der Urteilskraft* werden einsichtig, wenn diese Schrift wahrgenommen wird als eine Kantische Parallele zur *Monadologie* von Leibniz.

Zwar stand diese Parallelität wohl Kant noch nicht bei der ursprünglichen Planung des Werkes vor Augen, ihm haben aber später allem Anschein nach bei der Ausarbeitung der *Kritik der teleologischen Urteilskraft* Inhalt und Aufbau der *Monadologie* als Leitfaden gedient.

Aus Äußerungen Kants selbst in seinen Werken und Briefen, aus Inhalt und logischem Aufbau des Werkes und aus der Terminologie und deren Vorkommen im Werk besteht die Möglichkeit, eine Geschichte der Werkentstehung zu rekonstruieren.

Als Kant 1781 die *Kritik der reinen Vernunft* veröffentlichte, glaubt er zunächst im Großen und Ganzen das gesamte kritische Geschäft mit diesem Werk bereits vollendet zu haben. Zwei weitere Kritiken waren damals nicht geplant. Eine Kritik der praktischen Philosophie lag in Grundzügen bereits im *Kanon* der *Kritik der reinen Vernunft* behandelt vor. Eine Kritik der Ästhetik im Sinne einer Kritik des Geschmackes hielt er damals nicht für möglich.

---

[1] KrV A 812.

Schließlich veröffentlichte Kant dann doch in den darauffolgenden Jahren im Zuge der Auseinandersetzung mit den Gegnern, eine weitere, die zweite Kritik, die *Kritik der praktischen Vernunft* (1788). Im Verlauf der Ausarbeitung der zweiten Kritik wiederum scheint Kant auf die Möglichkeit gestoßen zu sein, entgegen seiner früheren Annahme auch die Gemeingültigkeit des Geschmacksurteils transzendental begründen zu können. Wohl im Bedenken der Rolle des moralischen Gefühls in der *Methodenlehre* der *Kritik der praktischen Vernunft* scheint ihm diese Einsicht aufgegangen zu sein.

Bei der dritten *Kritik* erarbeitete Kant zunächst die Kritik des Geschmacks als eine Kritik des Schönen und Erhabenen. Erst im Zuge der detaillierten Ausarbeitung dieser Kritik des Geschmacks scheint Kant den Begriff der reflektierenden Urteilskraft gebildet zu haben. Reflektierende Urteilskraft kennzeichnet als fixierter Terminus und Begriff die höchste differenzierte Stufe der Reflexion auf die Möglichkeiten und Grenzen der Vernunftleistungen, die Kant mit *Kritik der Urteilskraft* erreichte.

Wahrscheinlich bildete Kant den feststehenden Terminus und Begriff der reflektierenden Urteilskraft bei der Ausarbeitung der *Dialektik* des Schönen, als sein Blick auf das Verhältnis des Geschmacksurteils zur „*Vernunft*" im engeren Sinne sich richtete, während im zuvor abgehandelten Teil der *Analytik* das Verhältnis des Geschmacksurteils über das Schöne zum „*Verstand*" zu betrachten war.

Der einmal gebildete Begriff der reflektierenden Urteilskraft eignete sich dann dazu, bereits beschriebene Funktionen der Vernunft im engeren Sinne aufzunehmen. Es sind dies die im theoretischen Bereich bisher als „*regulativer Gebrauch der Ideen*" beschriebenen und die im praktischen Bereich der Vernunft als „*Postulate*" erklärten. Vernunft im engeren Sinne konnte so von Kant eindeutiger von traditionellen spekulativen Aufgaben befreit und etwaige Missverständnisse eindeutiger ausgeräumt werden. Die in „reflektierend" anklingende optische Metaphorik war zudem geeignet, schon sprachlich an den Leibniz'schen Substanzbegriff, an die damit verknüpften Spekulationen und an das eingängige Bild des lebendigen Spiegels zu erinnern. Mit dem Begriff der reflektierenden Urteilkraft konnte Kant zudem die *Kritik der teleologischen Urteilskraft*, deren Thematik bereits 1781 die *Kritik der reinen Vernunft* im Anhang zur transzendentalen Dialektik ansprach, an die Geschmackskritik, an die *Kritik der ästhetischen Urteilskraft* anbinden und damit die *Kritik der Urteilskraft* insgesamt mit der Zahl von 91 Paragraphen – wie bereits genannt – äußerlich der *Monadologie* anpassen. Der Begriff der reflektierenden Urteilskraft krönt die letzte Kritik Kants und blieb dieser Schrift vorbehalten. Kant selbst hat diesen Begriff später in seinen dogmatischen Schriften nicht mehr verwendet.[2]

Dem philosophischen Terminus „Reflexion" liegt als Bild der optische Strahlungs- und Brechungsprozesse zugrunde. Indem Leibniz seinen philosophischen Grundbegriff „Monade" als einen „lebendigen Spiegel" charakterisierte, erhielten die Spiegelmetaphorik und der davon ausgehende Begriff der „Spekulation" neue Sag- und Strahlkraft. Spiegel und Spiegeln avancierten zu den wichtigsten Metaphern nicht nur im philosophischen Denken des achtzehnten Jahrhunderts.

Die Monaden entstehen nach Leibniz sozusagen durch ununterbrochenes Blitzen der Gottheit von Augenblick zu Augenblick derart, dass ihnen eine relative Selbstgenügsamkeit (Autarkie) zukommt. Als relativ selbständige Substanzen ist ihnen ein inneres aktives Prinzip der Darstellung (Repräsentation) und der kontinuierlichen Veränderung ihrer Perzeptionen eigen, so dass es unangemessen wäre, sie als bloß passive, tote Spiegel zu charakterisieren. Als lebendige Spiegel des Universums bringen sie ihren eigenen Standpunkt und ihre spezifische Perspektive in die Betrachtung der Sachverhalte ein und vermehren so die Vielfalt der Welt.

Gott hat nach Leibniz die beste aller möglichen Welten nach dem Maßstab von Angemessenheit (Convenance) und Vollkommenheit (Perfection) geschaffen; darin liegt die Rechtfertigung dieser Welt: Vollkommen ist diejenige Ordnung, wo die größte Mannigfaltigkeit mit dem geringsten Aufwand erzielt wird. Dieser Maßstab der Vollkommenheit gilt sowohl für die Naturordnung als solche als auch für die Übereinstimmung des physischen Reiches der Natur mit dem moralischen Reiche der Gnade. Leibniz, der ein mit dem Gleichheitsgedanken verbundenes Ideal proportionierter Gerechtigkeit im Rechtsdenken vertritt, denkt Gerechtigkeit auch im eschatologischen Sinne nach im Prinzip mathematisierbaren Maßstäben von Angemessenheit und Vollkommenheit: Die Zuteilung von Strafe und Belohnung (das Maß an Glückseligkeit) für böses und tugendhaftes Verhalten kann danach kraft der Naturordnung maschinenmäßig erfolgen.[3]

Beide Leibniz'sche Kriterien, das der Vollkommenheit und das der Angemessenheit, wird Kant in der *Kritik der Urteilskraft* aufgreifen sowohl als Prinzipien der Naturordnung als auch im eschatologischen Sinn. Er verbindet

---

[2] Kant spricht lediglich einmal in begrifflicher Anlehnung an „reflektierende Urteilskraft" in „Die Religion innerhalb der Grenzen der bloßen Vernunft von „reflektierenden Glauben" in Gegenüberstellung zu einem „dogmatischen Glauben." AA VI, 52.
[3] *Monadologie*, § 89.

diese jedoch mit der menschlichen Vernunft und deren transzendentalen Leistungen. Das eschatologische Moment erscheint in der „Ethikotheologie", mit der Kant *die Kritik der Urteilskraft* ausklingen lässt.

Auch Kant denkt in der *Kritik der Urteilskraft*, wie zuvor in der *Kritik der praktischen Vernunft,* Gott weniger als den neutestamentlichen Gott der Liebe, sondern als einen zwar gütigen, aber unerbittlich nach dem Maßstab des Sittengesetzes richtenden Gott und bestimmt Gott als Garant für die Erfüllbarkeit des Gegenstandes des Sittengesetzes, „des höchsten Gutes" (die Erlangung von Glückseligkeit gemäß der Glückswürdigkeit).

In der *Monadologie* erörterte Leibniz ab These 61 das Verhältnis der einfachen Monaden zur zusammengesetzten Materie, insbesondere der Seelenmonaden zu den ihnen zugehörigen Körpern, ferner das Beziehungsgefüge der organischen Körper als solcher.

Diese Erörterungen mündeten in die Fragen nach dem Verhältnis des Menschen zu Gott (ab These 83) und nach dem Zusammenhang des Reiches der Natur mit dem Reiche der Gnade.

Entsprechend setzt die *Kritik der teleologischen Urteilskraft* Kants mit dem Paragraphen 61 ein, mündet ab § 83 in die Erörterung des letzten Zweckes der Natur und des Endzweckes und schließt mit Ausführungen zur Theologie, insbesondere zur Ethikotheologie.

Wenn Leibniz in der *Monadologie* (83) „Geister", insbesondere die Menschen als „Abbilder der Gottheit" auffasste, die in der Lage sind, „in Proben eigener Systemkunst das Universum nachzubilden", dann wird Kant im § 83 der *Kritik der Urteilskraft* Art, Bedingungen und Zweck geschichtlich-kultureller Aufbauleistungen des Menschen beschreiben.

Dass Kant in der *Kritik der Urteilskraft* seine Philosophie der Kultur und Geschichte (wenn auch nur kurz) erneut darlegt, liegt in der Stringenz dieses an Leibniz angelehnten Aufbaus der Schrift. Darüber hinaus gab es Kant Gelegenheit, in seine Geschichtsphilosophie, wo er bislang mit dem Vernunftbegriff allgemein operierte, den neuen Begriff der reflektierenden Urteilskraft einzuführen, der den Status seiner Geschichtsphilosophie als ein bloß reflektierendes, regulatorisch-heuristisches Denken deutlicher und unmissverständlicher kennzeichnet als zuvor. Ziel der Geschichte kann nach Kant für den vernünftigen Menschen nicht die „Glückseligkeit" sein, deren Bestimmung empirisch nicht greifbar wird. Sollen Freiheit, Humanität und Sinn in der geschichtlichen Entwicklung verwirklicht werden, dann kann nach Kant nur „Kultur" als leitendes Ziel gelten.

Leibniz nannte in These 87 der *Monadologie* das „moralische Reich der Gnade", Kant überschreibt den § 87 der *Kritik der Urteilskraft* mit „Von dem moralischen Beweise des Daseins Gottes."

Leibniz beendete die *Monadologie* in § 90 mit dem Begriff des „Glückes" (bonheur), Kant verweist im Schlusssatz des letzten Paragraphen der *Kritik der Urteilskraft* (§ 91) auf die „Hoffnung" und endigt die darauf folgende Anmerkung mit einer deutlichen Anspielung auf Leibniz' großes metaphysisches Prinzip, auf den Satz vom zureichenden Grunde.

Bei all diesen Übereinstimmungen der Thematik in der *Monadologie* und der *Kritik der teleologischen Urteilskraft* fallen inhaltliche Differenzen zwischen Kant und Leibniz nicht weniger ins Auge. Einige seien genannt: Für Kant ist der Organismus „ein Fremdling" in der Natur.[4]

Wenn Leibniz in der Zusammenschau von Reich der Natur und Reich der Gnade betont, „dass es unmöglich ist, die Welt besser zu machen als sie ist"[5], dann vertritt Kant einen vorsichtigen Fortschrittsglauben. In materialer Hinsicht verpflichtet die Kantische Ethik die Menschen, zum Besten der Welt beizutragen.

Kant lehnt alle fünf traditionellen Gottesbeweise, die auf der Basis der theoretischen spekulativen Vernunft geführt werden ab und schließt damit auch die beiden Gottesbeweise ein, die Leibniz a priori und a posteriori geführt in der *Monadologie* für zureichend hält.[6]

Kant lässt nur einen auf das moralische Gesetz gegründeten Gottesbeweis gelten, mit dem erst seine Ethik volle Stringenz erhält. Sein in der *Kritik der praktischen Vernunft* vorgestelltes moralisches Argument erneuert und erweitert Kant in der *Kritik der Urteilskraft*, insofern er dieses unter Einbringung des neuen systematischen Begriffs der reflektierenden Urteilskraft verfeinert: Kant kann jetzt innerhalb des Beweises zwei Schlussschritte unterscheiden.[7]

Wenn Leibniz allen Monaden, allen unkörperlichen Automaten, eine Art Selbstgenügsamkeit zugesprochen hatte, dann radikalisiert und überträgt Kant diesen Gedanken der Autarkie auf die reine praktische Vernunft, insbesondere auf die Ethik.

---

[4] KU, § 72, AA V 390.
[5] *Monadologie*, § 90.
[6] *Monadologie*, §§ 37–40, § 45.
[7] § 88, AA V 455.

Die Moral – wie Kant 1793 in seiner Schrift *Die Religion innerhalb der Grenzen der bloßen Vernunft* rekapitulieren wird – ist vermöge der reinen praktischen Vernunft „sich selbst genug."[8]

Es sei rückblickend zusammengefasst: Kant, der zur Zeit der Abfassung der *Kritik der Urteilskraft* wünscht als ein Apologet für Leibniz gewertet zu werden, zeigt eine Verbundenheit zu Leibniz und ein Interesse an dessen Philosophie bereits äußerlich an der Gestaltung der *Kritik der Urteilskraft*. Dies wird implizit insofern sichtbar, als Kant die Thematik der *Kritik der teleologischen Urteilskraft* und der *Methodenlehre* fortlaufend am Leitfaden der *Monadologie* entwickelt und insgesamt – neben seiner gewohnten Gliederung – die gesamte *Kritik der Urteilskraft* mit der Thesenzahl der *Monadologie* durchnummeriert. Mit dem zentralen methodischen Begriff des Werkes, mit dem der „reflektierenden Urteilskraft", erinnert Kant an die Leibnische Metaphorik vom lebendigen Spiegel. Kant, der mit der qualitativen Unterscheidung von Sinnlichkeit und Verstand und der Begrenzung der Verstandesleistungen auf den Sinnesbereich weitergehende theoretische Leistungen der Vernunft ablehnt, überträgt solche für ihn sinnvolle und notwendige Momente der Vernunft zuletzt in der *Kritik der Urteilskraft* auf den Begriff der „bloß" reflektierenden Urteilskraft. Es sind dies vorzüglich Themen derjenigen rationalen Theologie, die sich in ihren Grundlagen auf Leibniz beruft: der Glaube an Gott, an die Unsterblichkeit der Seele und die Hoffnung auf ewige Glückseligkeit. Kant sieht diese Ideen an das Faktum der Freiheit gebunden. In Form eines solchen "reflektierenden Glaubens" bleibt bei Kant Leibniz' Gedanke des „Reiches der Gnade" und mit diesem die Tradition des augustinischen Leitbildes der „Cité de Dieu" lebendig.

---

[8] AA VI 3.

Das andere „Beste". Leibniz und das allgemeine Wohl

Keisuke Nagatsuna (Tokio)

Der Titel dieser Referierung heißt „das andere Beste". Es zeigt den Begriff des gemeinen Besten oder allgemeinen Besten bei Gottfried Wilhelm Leibniz. Wir können denken, dass dieser Begriff synonym mit dem Begriff des allgemeinen Wohls, des Gemeinwohls oder der gemeinen Wohlfahrt ist.

Wir wissen, dass Leibniz sagt:

„S'il n'y avait pas le meilleur (optimum) parmi tous les mondes possibles, Dieu n' en aurait produit aucun."[1]

Diese von Gott geschaffene wirkliche Welt sei also die „beste" unter den möglichen Welten. Aber der Begriff des „Besten" in dieser Referierung, der synonym mit dem Begriff des allgemeinen Wohls ist, wird im politischen Kontext gebraucht. Es ist klar, dass wir das „Beste" im politischen Sinn von dem „Besten" im metaphysischen Sinn unterscheiden sollen. Aber diese zwei „Besten" verbinden sich in der Lehre vom allgemeinen Wohls bei Leibniz, die z. B. in seiner Schrift *Grundriss eines Bedenkens von Aufrichtung einer Societät in Deutschland zu Aufnehmen der Künste und Wissenschaften* (1671?) gefunden wird. Dort spielt der Begriff der Technik eine wichtige Rolle. Ich möchte diesen Punkt später feststellen.

Die hauptsächliche Absicht dieser Referierung ist, die grundlegende Struktur der Lehre vom allgemeinen Wohl bei Leibniz festzustellen. Aber ich möchte auch die gegenwärtige Bedeutung oder Aktualität der Leibniz'schen Lehre vom allgemeinen Wohl zeigen.

1. Das allgemeine Wohl als der Zweck der Territorialstaaten

Die Modernisierung der deutschen Territorialstaaten, die das Heilige Römische Reich Deutscher Nation aufbauten, erschien in der Form der Entwicklung von Wohlfahrtsstaaten. Die Lehren vom allgemeinen Wohl oder die Polizeiwissenschaften der damaligen Staatsdenker, z. B. Johann Oldendorp (1488?–1667), Melchior von Osse (1506/7–1557), Georg Obrecht (1547–1612), und

---

[1] *Essais de Théodicée*, premiere partie, § 8; GP VI, 107.

Veit Ludwig von Seckendorff (1626–1692) haben die gedanklichen Grundlagen zu dieser Tendenz gegeben. Nach ihnen ist der Zweck des Staats, das allgemeine Wohl zu schaffen. Also können wir sagen, dass der Hauptzweck der von 16. bis 18. Jahrhundert auf Deutsch geschriebenen Literatur mit dem Begriff des allgemeinen Wohls gezeigt wurde. Und man hat den Begriff des gemeinen Besten als Synonym mit dem Begriff des allgemeinen Wohls gebraucht.

Auch Leibniz diskutiert über das allgemeine Wohl und also das gemeine Beste als seinen Schlüsselbegriff seiner Staatslehre. In seiner Schrift *Vom Naturrecht* (1690–1697?) sagt Leibniz:

> „Die Gerechtigkeit ist eine gemeinschaftliche Tugend, oder eine Tugend, so die Gemeinschaft erhält. Die Gemeinschaft ist eine Vereinigung verschiedener Menschen, aus einem gemeinen Absehen. [...] Die vollkommenste Gemeinschaft ist, deren Absehen ist die allgemeine und höchste Glückseligkeit. [...] Die fünfte natürliche Gemeinschaft ist die bürgerliche Gemeinschaft [...]. Ihr Absehen ist zeitliche Wohlfahrt."[2]

Wie dies, Leibniz hält deutlich die Wohlfahrt oder das allgemeine Wohl für den Zweck des Staats.

2. Caritas als eine Grundlage des allgemeinen Wohls

Eine Voraussetzung des allgemeinen Wohls als des Zwecks des Staats stammt bei Leibniz deutlich aus dem Christentum, weil man ihre theoretische Grundlage in der christlichen Idee der ‚caritas' suchen kann, die sich mit der altgriechischen Gerechtigkeitslehre und der altrömischen Naturrechtslehre verbindet.

Aber das meint nicht, dass das allgemeine Wohl bei Leibniz auf die mittelalterliche Wohltätigkeit und Almosen als die Arbeit der Kirchen oder der Klöster reduziert wird. In der Frühneuzeit wurde diesen Tätigkeiten allgemein die neue Stelle als besondere Abteilungen der vom Staat bestimmten allgemeinen Wohlfahrtspolitik gegeben (z. B. Gesundheitsversorgung der Bevölkerung). Ich meine, dass diese Tendenz auch auf Leibniz zutrifft. Zwar ist es möglich, dass Leibniz die Traditionen seit dem Mittelalter nachschlägt und sie in einigen Fällen als Modell seines Begriffs des allgemeinen Wohls gebraucht. Aber ich meine dies: Wann Leibniz jedoch die ‚caritas' als die ‚benevolentia

---

[2] Gottschalk E. Guhrauer (Hrsg.): *Leibniz's deutsche Schriften*, Bd. 1, Berlin 1838, S. 414–416.

universalis' oder die ‚benevolentia' als ‚amandi sive diligendi habitus' definiert,[3] sind die Nuancen der tugendhaftigen Tätigkeiten für das Heil der eigenen Seele, die die Idee der ‚caritas' traditionell besessen hatte, hier nicht so deutlich. Dass Leibniz die Idee der ‚caritas' auf die Grundlage seiner Lehre des allgemeinen Wohls stellt, meint die Kundgabe seiner Überzeugung, die Liebe zu anderen Menschen zu brauchen, um das Glück in der ganzen Gemeinschaft zu verwirklichen.

In dem Vorwort seiner Schrift *Codex juris gentium diplomaticus* (1693) nimmt Leibniz die aristotelische Lehre an, die die Gerechtigkeit in drei Stufen einteilt:

> „Ex hoc jam fonte fluit jus naturae, cujus tres sunt gradus: jus strictum in justitia commutativa, aequitas […] in Justitia distributive, denique pietas […] in Justitia universali: unde neminem laedere, suum cuique tribuere, honeste […] vivere, totidem generalissima et pervulgata juris praecepta nascuntur […]."[4]

Nach Leibniz ist „jus strictum" ein Gesetz, das auf alle Menschen gleich angewendet wird. Wenn man es verletzt, entsteht im nationalen Verhältnis das Recht des Prozesses und im internationalen Verhältnis das Recht des Kriegs. Also können wir sagen, dass wegen dieses Gesetzes Ordnung und Frieden gesichert werden. Aber was hier realisiert wird, ist nicht das Glück selbst, sondern nur seine Bedingungen. Aber ‚aequitas' berücksichtigt die Unterschiede zwischen jeden Personen und wird das Prinzip der Entscheidungen ihrer Belohnung und Bestrafung. Leibniz nennt ‚aequitas' auch ‚caritas' im engeren Sinn.[5] Diese ‚caritas' sei das grundlegende Prinzip nicht nur der Moral, sondern auch der Politik. Nach diesem Prinzip sollen die Politiker das allgemeine Wohl des Volks berücksichtigen. In der Stufe der ‚pietas' erreicht die ‚caritas' über den Kreis der Menschen das ganze Universum als ‚civitas Dei'. Auch hier ist der Zweck des Staates das Wohl. Aber der Zweck der bürgerlichen Gesellschaften ist das zeitliche Wohl, wie gesagt. Der Zweck der ‚civitas Dei', die der universale Staat sei, ist das ewige Wohl. Also wird die letztliche Vollendung des allgemeinen Wohls im universalen Staat gesucht. Auf jeden Fall funktioniert die Idee der ‚caritas' als die theoretische Grundlage für die Lehre vom allgemeinen Wohl.

---

[3] GP III, 387.
[4] Ebd.
[5] Ebd.

3. Die Verbindung von zwei „Besten"

Wie wird ‚caritas' zum Ausdruck gebracht? Im *Grundriss* setzt Leibniz ‚caritas' mit ‚amor Dei' gleich. Nach Leibniz ist ‚amor Dei':

> „nicht nur obenhin, sondern practicè wollen, das ist alles thun was in unsern Krefften ist umb wahr, und würcklich zu machen, daß auch wir ihn eüserst lieben. Die würckligkeit der Liebe besteht darinn, daß wir thun was den Gebliebten lieb ist."[6]

Daraus wird dieser Schluss gezogen:

> „Hieraus folgt unwiedertreiblich, daß Caritas, daß Amor Dei super omnia, und die wahre Contritio, [...] nichts anders sey als amare bonum publicum, et harmoniam universalem; vel qvod idem est gloriam Dei et intelligere, et qvantum in se est facere majorem, denn zwischen Cörper und Schatten, Person und bild, radio directo et reflexo, in dem daß was jene in der That, diese in den Seelen ist derer die ihn kennen."[7]

Leibniz identifiziert weiter die Ehre Gottes mit dem gemeinen Nutzen. Seine Inhalte sind z. B. Ernährung, Erleichterung, Kommodität, Unterweisung und Erleuchtung der Nebenmenschen, Entdeckung, Durchsuchung und Verbesserung der Kreaturen.[8]

Leibniz gründet diese Diskussion auf dem Zweck der göttlichen Kreation. Leibniz sagt:

> „Denn Gott zu keinem andern End die vernünfftigen Creaturen geschaffen, als daß sie auch einem Spiegel dieneten, darinn seine unendtliche Harmoni auff unendtliche weise in etwas vervielfältiget würde."[9]

Dann sagt Leibniz, dass die ‚amor Dei' oder die ‚caritas' durch diese doppelten Arbeiten realisiert wird: einerseits die Fassung der Schönheit Gottes und der universalen Harmonie nach der Fähigkeit jedes Verstandes und ihre Reflexion auf andere, andererseits die Beförderung und Vermehrung ihrer Hervorleuchterung nach der Proportion jeden Vermögens.[10]

---

[6] A IV, 1, 531.
[7] Ebd., 532.
[8] Ebd.
[9] Ebd.
[10] Ebd.

Nach Leibniz kann man Verstand und Vermögen im Fall der vernünftigen Kreaturen auf drei Weisen gebrauchen: Erstens, mit guten Worten handeln wie Oratorien und Priester. Zweitens, mit guten Andenken handeln wie die natürlichen Philosophen, die Naturwissenschaftler heißen. Drittens, mit guten Werken handeln wie die moralischen Philosophen oder Politiker. Diese guten Werke nennt Leibniz auch caritas efficax.[11]

Also wird das Leibniz'sche allgemeine Wohl, dessen theoretische Grundlage die ‚caritas' ist, bei den Tätigkeiten der moralischen Philosophen und Politiker realisiert. Sie bemühen sich nicht nur den Glanz göttlicher Herrlichkeit in der Natur zu finden, sondern auch ihn durch Imitation nachzuahmen[12].

Mit den guten Werken der moralischen Philosophen und Politiker wird das allgemeine Wohl realisiert. Das meint, dass die Beförderung und Vermehrung der Ehre Gottes durchgeführt werden. Leibniz erklärt das weiter:

> „[...] dardurch mehr gutes zu gemeinen und sonderlich des Menschlichen geschlechts, nutzen, als dem zum besten alle sichtbare Creaturen, in welche wir zu würcken macht haben, geordnet, geschaffet werde."[13]

Hier verknüpft sich das Beste im metaphysischen Sinn mit dem Besten als dem allgemeinen Wohl, weil man traditionell auch den Begriff des gemeinen Nutzens synonym mit dem Begriff des allgemeinen Wohls, also des gemeinen Besten gebraucht hat.

Das Beste im metaphysischen Sinn verdoppelt sich im Besten als dem allgemeinen Wohl. Ich meine, dass dieser Ausdruck sehr interessant ist. Der allwissende Gott hat das Volumen der Güter in allen möglichen Welten überblickt und eine Welt, die meist Güter enthält, als die beste Welt ausgewählt und geschaffet. Wenn es so ist, ist es möglich, mehr Güter als etwas, was Gott vorherbestimmt hat, in dieser Welt zu realisieren? Wenn man die Allwissenheit Gottes strikt versteht, ist es unmöglich. Aber, ich meine, Leibniz möchte die gesellschaftliche Bedeutung der menschlichen Freiheit und die Praxis für das allgemeine Wohl betonen, selbst wenn die Allwissenheit Gottes schwach zu werden scheint.

---

[11] Ebd., 533.
[12] Ebd., 535f.
[13] Ebd.

4. Die positive Verwendung der Technik

Bei Leibniz hat das gute Werk zu dem guten Wort und dem guten Andenken den Primat. Aber man darf nicht die positive Bedeutung des guten Andenkens übersehen, weil es als die Voraussetzung für das gute Werk funktioniert.

Nach Leibniz ist die Arbeit der natürlichen Philosophen, die Ehre Gottes mit dem Verstand aufzufassen und zu spiegeln. Es ist sehr interessant, dass diese Meinung mit anderen Worten ausgedrückt wird:

> „Als [natürliche] Philosophi aber verehren Gott die jenigen, so eine neüe Harmoni in der Natur und Kunst entdecken, und seine Allmacht und Weisheit sichtbarlich zu spüren machen."[14]

Ob durch Experiment oder durch Theorema, sei alle entdeckte Wahrheit selbst ein neuerfundener Spiegel der Schönheit Gottes. Also, die Kosten für die Vervollkommnung der Naturkündigung und der realen Künste beruhen auf der andächtigsten Causa und sollen als die Stiftung zur Ehre Gottes angesehen werden.[15] Das ist der Inhalt des guten Andenkens.

Wie gesagt, die moralischen Philosophen haben den Primat gegenüber den natürlichen Philosophen. Aber was die moralischen Philosophen aktuell tun, ist nicht anders als die Anwendung des Wunders der Natur und der Kunst auf die Praxis. Dieses Wunder ist von den natürlichen Philosophen entdeckt worden.[16]

Also ist es unmöglich, ohne die Vermehrung der Kenntnisse über die Natur und die Vorbereitung der Technik das allgemeine Wohl zu realisieren. Deshalb steht in dem Kern der Leibniz'schen Lehre vom allgemeinen Wohl ein Gesichtspunkt, Technik als ein Mittel für die Realisierung des allgemeinen Wohls positiv zu gebrauchen. Wir können mit Hans Heinz Holz sagen:

> „Leibniz war wohl einer der ersten, der sich die Bedeutung der Technologie für den ökonomischen Gesamtprozeß und für den gesellschaftlichen Fortschritt bewußt machte und der daraus praktisch-organisatorisch Folgerungen zog."[17]

---

[14] Ebd., 534.
[15] Ebd., 535.
[16] Ebd., 536.
[17] Hans Heinz Holz: „Einleitung", in: Gottfried Wilhelm Leibniz: *Politische Schriften*, Bd. II. Frankfurt a. M. 1967, S. 6.

Wie bei Francis Bacon, so verbindet sich auch bei Leibniz die Hoffnung auf entscheidende wissenschaftliche und technische Fortschritte mit der Hoffnung auf grundsächliche gesellschaftspolitische Entwicklungen.

5. Die Bedingungen der Technik

Wie dies, Leibniz bewertet positiv die Technik. Aber in diesen Leibniz'schen Diskussionen kann man auch die Bedingungen der Technik herauslesen. Hier markieren sich die aktuellen Bedeutungen von der Leibniz'schen Lehre des allgemeinen Wohls.

Erstens, die Entscheidung, ob man die Idee einer Technik in die Praxis umsetzen soll, wird von den moralischen Philosophen und Politikern getroffen. Auch wenn die natürlichen Philosophen irgendeine Technik neu gefunden haben, wenn die moralischen Philosophen und Politiker ihre Bedeutung zum allgemeinen Wohl nicht anerkennen, wird diese Technik nicht realisiert. Das ist eine interessante Diskussion über die Beziehung zwischen der Technik und der Gesellschaft. Bleibt die Technik nur im Bereich der modernen naturwissenschaftlichen und ingenieurwissenschaftlichen Kenntnisse? Vielleicht denkt Leibniz, dass es nötig ist, die Möglichkeiten einer Technik mit den Kenntnissen der Geistes- und Sozialwissenschaften zu erwägen.

Zweitens, wenn die Vollendung des allgemeinen Wohls in ‚Civitas Die' realisiert wird, darf die Technik nicht das sein, was den Nutzen einer bestimmten Person oder dem Staat dient. Beruhend auf der Ansicht über den Nutzen eines universalen Staates soll man sie gebrauchen. Diese Diskussion ist auch als die Ansicht über den Zweck der Technik interpretierbar. Wird er nur aus der Nützlichkeit für die Menschen bestimmt? Vieleicht denkt Leibniz, dass der Zweck der Technik auch aus etwas bestimmt wird, was über den Menschen ist.

Drittens, die Technik muss in der Harmonie mit der Natur stehen. Die Natur ist das Vorbild der Technik. Also wird die Technik als das angenommen, was die Natur unterstützt. Die Technik darf nicht das sein, was die Natur beherrscht. In diesem Punkt spricht Leibniz gegen Bacon und Descartes. Leibniz versteht die Natur oder die ganze Welt als eine große Maschine. Im System Leibnizens, wenn man sie strikt phänomenal annimmt, erscheint die Maschine der Natur nur als das mechanische Ding. Aber für Leibniz ist die Natur auch das Aggregat der Organismen, die aus den Seelen und den Leibern besteht.

Hier erscheint die Natur als etwas, was eine teleologische Struktur hat. Und auch die Technik wird teleologisch konzipiert. Wenn es so ist, könnte man irgendeinen Faktor für die harmonische Verbindung der Natur mit der Technik in der Teleologie suchen.

Leibniz and the Political Theology of the Chinese

Eric S. Nelson (Hong Kong)

1. Introduction[1]

Gottfried Wilhelm Leibniz (1646–1716) was born during the chaotic era of the concluding years of the Thirty Years' War. The political and religious conflicts of his epoch that devastated central Europe have been used to explain his sensibility that aimed at philosophical, political, and religious accommodation and reconciliation. Leibniz's polymathic synthesizing efforts at reconciling diverse elements have led interpreters to highlight different tendencies in his project. Leibniz practical thought has been portrayed as conservative and as reformist, as oriented toward conserving the threatened past and toward furthering the development of enlightenment, modernity, and progress that threatened that heritage.[2] Rather than representing or embodying a disjunction between the ancients and the moderns, in which Leibniz must be categorized as belonging to either one camp or the other, Leibniz would be more appropriately interpreted as both a conservative and reformer. He simultaneously hearkens back to the pre-modern wisdom of the ancients while pursuing a modernizing philosophical and practical project.

This complex configuration of the "simultaneity" of tradition and reform is characteristic not only of Leibniz's practical philosophy. It also arguably describes an intellectual figure, and the tradition associated with his name, which fascinated Leibniz and other early Enlightenment intellectuals.[3] These include – with different degrees of enthusiasm – Leibniz, Wolff, Bilfinger, Diderot, and Voltaire. The figure of Confucius (Kongzi 孔子) has seen multiple incompatible interpretive avatars in modern Western thought from a superstitious pagan and simplistic moralist to a reactionary founder of Oriental

---

[1] Note that this chapter incorporates elements from and relies in part on the interpretation of Leibniz's political philosophy summarized in Eric S. Nelson: "Leibniz, Gottfried Wilhelm (1646–1716)", in: Michael Gibbons (ed.): *The Encyclopedia of Political Thought*, Oxford 2015, pp. 2098–2100.
[2] These two perspectives are respectively agued in Patrick Riley: *Leibniz' Universal Jurisprudence: Justice as the Charity of the Wise*, Cambridge 1996; and Roger Berkowitz: *The Gift of Science: Leibniz and the Modern Legal Tradition*, Cambridge 2005.
[3] On Confucius and China in the Enlightenment, see Walter W. Davis: "China, the Confucian ideal, and the European Age of Enlightenment," in: *Journal of the History of Ideas* 44/4 (1983), pp. 523–554; Simon Kow: *China in Early Enlightenment Political Thought*, Abingdon 2017.

despotism to a figure of enlightened morally oriented political rule guided by tradition and reform insofar as both embody ethical ideals. Unlike Bayle, Montesquieu, and Malebranche, or later Herder, Kant, and Hegel, Leibniz's reception of Confucian China belongs to the more positive appropriation of Chinese thought and culture.[4] Leibniz's engagement on behalf of Chinese and Confucian ethics and politics resonates with his own ethical and political thought.

Leibniz was able through the circuitous transmission of Chinese thought from East to West through the Jesuit missionaries and others to develop his own analysis of its significance. He detected affinities between his own thought and that of an alien and distant Chinese cultural and intellectual tradition. This sentiment is not completely inappropriate. The early Ruist 儒家 (Confucian) thinkers were born into a period of war and its quest for stability – whether it is rooted in the moral nature of human beings (Mengzi 孟子) or externally imposed through effort by a strict and rigorous moral-political order (Xunzi 荀子) – has been interpreted as a response to the reality of conflict and instability.

Leibniz described his endeavors as preserving and redeeming the wisdom of the ancients – which had fallen into disrepute after the development of the new sciences, mathematics, and philosophy – in accord with the innovations in knowledge and practice of the present. The dispute between the ancients and the moderns in modern European philosophy, which Leibniz attempted to resolve, is repeated in modern European reception of Chinese philosophy and religion. The legitimacy of contemporary Chinese thought and culture is not only evaluated according to internal Western standards but also according to the Western – in particular the Jesuit – reconstruction of the wisdom of the ancient Chinese that attempted to identify and contrast it with Jewish and Greek wisdom.

In this context, Confucius is perceived to be concurrently an inheritor of the past and an Enlightened reformer of the present for his early Enlightenment advocates. Confucius has been characterized as both a traditionalist and an innovator: a scholar who projects an innovative ethical model into the past to morally educate and reform the crisis-ridden present or who looks at the past in order to reform and renew the present.

One paradox of interpreting Leibniz's and the early Enlightenment's reception of Confucian political thought is the problem of Enlightened

---

[4] Wenchao Li/Hans Poser: "Leibniz's Positive View of China," in: *Journal of Chinese Philosophy* 33/1 (2006), pp. 17–33.

absolutism. Leibniz was a persistent opponent of political absolutism, including Enlightened absolutism, in his writings concerning political philosophy and current European politics. He explicitly and repeatedly advocated the plurality and mediation of powers, defending the Holy Roman empire against its absolutist critics such as – in the German setting – Samuel Pufendorf who Leibniz dismissed as a "man who is a small jurist and a very small philosopher."[5] However, early modern European enthusiasm for Chinese political thought and culture is often considered a correlate not of the mediation of powers promoted by Leibniz but of Enlightened despotism that legitimated the modern centralized absolutist monarchies that Leibniz opposed.

The model of benevolent enlightened kingship rooted in natural theology (in Leibniz's language) and practical philosophy (in Wolff's language) unfolded in the interpretation of China in Leibniz, Wolff, and Voltaire would in the later Enlightenment – in thinkers such as Kant, Herder, and Hegel – become a model of the abuses of absolute power and the obedience of the *ancien régime* as much as the "Orient." The Western idea of China as a regime embodying the "Oriental despotism" of "total power" harkens back to earlier thinkers such as Montesquieu, who contended that the Chinese conflated law and custom (i.e., the political and the social) and was governed by a despotic unitary regime akin to ancient Sparta, while being shaped during the long eighteenth-century by disputes over the appropriate relationship between politics and religion and enlightened kingship and popular self-determination.[6] This problem can be resolved in the case of Leibniz by properly understanding both the plurality of powers and the function of an enlightened ruler.

2. Against Oriental Despotism: The Political Theology of the Chinese in the Novissima Sinica

Leibniz's attention to the Chinese moral and political system as a potentially superior model that can instruct and help reform the way of life and

---

[5] "Vir parum jurisconsultus, minime philosophus." Dutens VI, 3, 261. Citation from Marcelo Dascal: *The Practice of Reason: Leibniz and his Controversies*, Philadelphia 2010, p. 250.
[6] "One must not be astonished if the legislators of Lacedaemonia and those of China confused laws, mores, and manners; this is because mores represent laws, and manners represent mores" (Charles de Montesquieu: *The Spirit of the Laws*, Cambridge 1989, p. 317). Montesquieu also claimed in the *Spirit of the Laws* that there were an "infinite number of people in Japan and China" because they subsisted primarily on oily fish. (Ibid., p. 435.)

institutions of the West is expressed in his *Novissima Sinica* (*Latest News from China*, 1697). In this early sustained discussion of China, which thematized the distance and complementary of the two extremes of the Eurasian continent, Leibniz stressed how civil precepts and laws, as well as the hedge of customs and the network of obligations in the subsequent passage, are coordinated to achieve the best possible equilibrium of society:

> "But who would have believed that there is on earth a people who, though we are in our view so very advanced in every branch of behavior, still surpass us in comprehending the precepts of civil life? Yet now we find this to be so among the Chinese, as we learn to know them better. And so if we are their equals in the industrial arts, and ahead of them in contemplative sciences, certainly they surpass us (though it is almost shameful to confess this) in practical philosophy, that is, in the precepts of ethics and politics adapted to the present life and use of mortals. Indeed, it is difficult to describe how beautifully all the laws of the Chinese, in contrast to those of other peoples, are directed to the achievement of public tranquility and the establishment of social order, so that men shall be disrupted in their relations as little as possible."[7]

How is such a harmonious adaptive equilibrium possible? On the one hand, human relations are left to themselves with less intervention and interference in them than in Europe. On the other hand, this self-ordering is possible because of a deeply-ingrained system of interconnected customs, duties, and feelings of duty and respect that form a functional whole. Leibniz described in the next passage of the *Novissima* how to Europeans, who are

> "not enough accustomed to act by reason and rule, these [practices] smack of servitude; yet among [the Chinese], where these duties are made natural by use, they are observed gladly."[8]

The Chinese, Leibniz claimed, have achieved a higher social niveau in which obedience and reverence have become the practiced norms of society and negative social affects, such as "hatred, wrath, or excitement," have been tempered and brought under control.[9]

The deployment on words such as obedience in these passages might suggest the idea of a despotic subordination of inferiors to superiors, of the

---

[7] Gottfried Wilhelm Leibniz: *Writings on China*, transl. by Daniel J. Cook and Henry Rosemont, Jr., La Salle 1994, p. 45: *Novissima Sinica* § 3; A IV, 6, N. 61.
[8] Ibid.
[9] Ibid.

weak to the powerful, the young to the old, and females to males. Herder would near the end of the eighteenth-century in his *Ideas for a Philosophy of the History of Humanity* (1784), contrasting European freedoms with Oriental oppression, interpret such facets of Chinese social life as an unnatural and static order of unreflective childlike obedience to despotic power.[10]

It is noteworthy that Leibniz has an alternative conception that does not rely, as Herder and Hegel would, on the opposition of the natural and the artifical and the pre-reflective customary and merely reflexive with the self-consciously reflective. He is not describing the imposition of an artificial external Leviathan-like power onto the powerless undifferentiated equal masses in which only one, namely, the Emperor, is free as Hegel would assert in the *Lectures on the Philosophy of History*.[11] In this construction of an image of total power: "everything derives solely from the emperor."[12] The interpretations of Herder and Hegel would play a significant part in the evolution of the Oriental despotism thesis that has dominated modern Western thinking about China and became a Western influence on modern Chinese anti-democratic thinking.

Leibniz focuses on the customary and rational self-regulating character of – a no doubt idealized portrayal – Chinese society. The *Novissima* suggests the moral self-organization and, what could be well described as, the autonomy that characterizes a proper equilibrium and harmony in which the parts coordinate through internal (e.g., customs, habits, and dispositions) as well as external (e.g., laws) reasons and mechanisms. The coordination of Chinese society is a practical exemplar of the harmonious balance and mediation of different powers in Leibniz in contrast with Hegel's portrait of the arbitrary, bureaucratic, and unjust imposition of domination from above.[13]

Leibniz's understanding of Chinese society is of a morally and normatively guided self-ordering system in which tranquility and order are achieved through the activities and participation of members of society with their own social agency and roles. Social participation in roles reaches its high-point in the Emperor who is not above or external to Chinese moral-political life:

---

[10] Johann Gottfried Herder: *Ideen zur Philosophie der Geschichte der Menschheit. Werke in zehn Bänden*, Frankfurt 1985, pp. 436f.
[11] Georg Wilhelm Friedrich Hegel: *Lectures on the Philosophy of World History*, vol. 1, Oxford 2011, pp. 226–232.
[12] Ibid., p. 230.
[13] Ibid., p. 232.

"Who indeed does not marvel at the monarch of such an empire? His grandeur almost exceeds human stature, and he is held by some to be a mortal god. His very nod is obeyed. Yet he is educated according to custom in virtue and wisdom and rules his subjects with an extraordinary respect for the laws and with a reverence for the advice of wise men. Endowed with such eminence he seems fit indeed to judge. Nor is it easy to find anything worthier of note than the fact that this greatest of kings, who possesses such complete authority in his own day, anxiously fears posterity and is in greater dread of the judgment of history, than other kings are of representatives of estates and parliaments. Therefore he carefully seeks to avoid actions which might cast a reflection upon his reputation when recorded by the chroniclers of his reign and placed in files and secret archives."[14]

The Chinese emperor has powers akin to an earthly god, and an authority and height that demands his command be obeyed. He can set masses of humans into motion. This description could be used to support the idea of the Oriental despot, who has unlimited arbitrary power over all and duties and responsibilities to none, as seen in Hegel's claim that in the Orient "only one is free."[15] Despite his own emphasis in his practical philosophy on the self-organization of the community in ethical life and the political system of the state, Hegel did not recognize the moral self-organization of the community and the mediation of powers at play in Chinese society. Hegel interprets Chinese life as dominated by external despotic and bureaucratic powers, and Western (in particular, German) social life as the achievement of freedom.

Leibniz, however, focuses on the delimited role of the Chinese monarch and how this role shapes and limits political power: his account gives the ruler both power and responsibility for the use of that power in a way that corelates with Confucian moral-political philosophy. In this conception, the ruler ought to be educated in virtue, wisdom, and respect for the laws and act in view of them; that is to say, reign according to the good instead of an arbitrary voluntarist will and pure power. The ruler is evaluated by the internalized standards maintained in Confucian practical philosophy, fears the judgment of the sages and history, and thus appropriately (according to the Confucian notion of *yi* 義) fulfills his role and mandate.

---

[14] Leibniz: *Writings on China*, p. 47: *Novissima Sinica* § 6; A IV, 6, N. 61; On this passage and Leibniz's particular enthusiasm for the Kangxi (康熙) Emperor (r. 1661–1722), compare Franklin Perkins: *Leibniz and China: A Commerce of Light,* Cambridge 2004, p. 128.
[15] Hegel: *Lectures on the Philosophy of World History*, p. 87.

Leibniz asks his readers to construe the ritual reverence for Confucius, the monarch, and the ancestors to be primarily political rather than religious.[16] Leibniz's description of the Chinese political system accords with his own political philosophy and, as we will see later, his political theology that can identify Chinese moral principles with natural theology while distinguishing between civil-political and religious cults. These two claims distance the essence – if not the present reality – of Chinese political theology from charges of paganism as well as irreligious atheism, materialism, and Spinozism.[17]

The Chinese monarch has more power, no doubt, than the ruler of the Holy Roman Empire; both, however, are given roles and responsibilities. These are limited by the customary and rationally justified sense and scope of that role. The Chinese ruler is accordingly not the pure despot of the Oriental despotism thesis in Leibniz's description.This thesis found inspiration in Montesquieu and gained prominence over the Enlightenment period as European attitudes toward China became increasingly more negative.

Leibniz had his own account of political despotism and we can distinguish what actual despotic power looked like for him. He portrayed Louis XIV of France as despotic in his polemical political writings and rejected political absolutism in his critiques of Pufendorf and Hobbes. Pufendorf commented about the Chinese:

> "The Readiness of the Chinese to obey their King blindly, does but confirm his Tyranny and encrease their Misery. For those, who depend on the Will of one Man, subject to a Thousand Passions, whose, Fancies can be restrain'd by no Law, can be sure of Nothing."[18]

But, conspicuously, the Chinese ruler was not a tyrant like the French sun-king in Leibniz's Chinese writings. There were elements, such as the description of authority and command, which could be employed in line with the Oriental despotism thesis. The title of this section is anachronistic. The

---

[16] Leibniz: *Writings on China*, p. 59: *De cultu Confucii civili* § 3; A IV, 8, N. 70.
[17] Leibniz repeatedly opposed atheistic and materialist interpretations of Chinese thought, at least in its ancient and essential form, maintaining in his correspondence with Des Bosses that these interpretations: "were so far from succeeding in this that, instead, all the contrary propositions seem to me most probable. In fact, the ancient Chinese more than the philosophers of Greece seem to have come near to the truth, and they seem to have taught that matter itself is the production of God." Leibniz to Des Bosses, 13 January 1716; Gottfried Wilhelm Leibniz: *The Leibniz–Des Bosses Correspondence*, transl., ed., and with an introd. by Brandon C. Look and Donald Rutherford, New Haven 2007, p. 359.
[18] Samuel Pufendorf: *Law of Nature and Nations*, London 1716, p. 285.

Western conception of Oriental despotism had earlier incarnations in thinkers such as Montesquieu and Pufendorf developed into its full modern form that encompassed West, South, and East Asia in distinction from Europe after Leibniz.[19]

Leibniz offered, in contrast to Montesquieu and Pufendorf, an alternative arguably more nuanced interpretation of the roles of appropriate authority and responsibility in Chinese practical life that recognized the interconnections between power and responsibility. The Confucian statement from the *Analects* (*Lunyu* 論語) 12.19 that "as the wind blows, the grass must bend" (cao shang zhi feng bi yan 草上之風必偃) is ambiguous: it is a statement of the exemplary influence of moral governance that could be construed as the assertion of power. These two possibilities of a morally guided politics and a regime of absolute power are evident in modern European interpretations of Chinese moral-political life.

3. Leibniz as a Political Thinker

To understand the connections between Leibniz's political philosophy and his interpretation of the practical philosophy of the Chinese, we need to contextualize his political philosophy and its relationship with his understanding of China.

Leibniz's political philosophy has been underappreciated in the reception of his thought. The young Leibniz studied law and then spent his adult life in the diplomatic and political service of nobility and royalty, particularly the House of Hanover that assumed the British crown a few years before his death. He is most familiar for his writings on metaphysics, mathematics, and logic to such an extent that there are Leibniz scholars who maintain that "there is no explicit political philosophy in Leibniz."[20] Leibniz's

---

[19] An early contrast between European freedom and "Oriental despotism" in German thought, which has sources in Greek conceptions of the Persians and more recently in Montesquieu's portrait of Muslim and Eastern empires, was made by Johann Georg Meusel in his 1776 work *Der Geschichtforscher*, Partes 3–4, p. 239. On the role of Herder's interpretation of China and its relation to Montesquieu and Hegel, see Günter Zöller: "'[D]er Name Confucius ist mir ein grosser Name.' Herders politisch-geschichtsphilosophische China-Deutung zwischen Montesquieu und Hegel," in: Dieter Hüning/Gideon Stiening/Violetta Stolz (eds.): *Herder und die klassische Deutsche Philosophie*, Stuttgart 2016, pp. 25–49.

[20] See Philip Wiener's remark in his introduction to Gottfried Wilhelm Leibniz: *Selections*, New York 1951, p. xlviii.

wide-ranging political correspondence and writings concerned the foundations of law, local and international political affairs and social problems, and moral and political philosophy.

The youthful Leibniz's practical interests and reformist inclinations led him to decline an academic career in the university and into the service of the archbishop and elector of Mainz.[21] From his service in Mainz to Hanover, Leibniz was an advocate of legal reforms, the reconciliation of conflicting Catholic and Protestant parties within the empire and Europe, and the practical defense and theoretical justification of the Holy Roman Empire with its loose federation of non-identical diverse overlapping and intersecting powers.[22] This diversity of powers included intellectually informed advisors, like himself, who might be compared with the administratively active Confucian literati. This plurality of distinct overlapping spheres and centers of powers was condemned as "irregular" and "monstrous" (*monstro simile*) by Pufendorf and justified by Leibniz as a check on absolute power. In a series of polemical (sometimes witty) writings, Leibniz challenged the internal centralization and the external expansionism of the absolutist French monarch, who he called the "Most Christian War-God," Louis XIV.[23]

Leibniz criticized the vision of absolute unified sovereignty maintained by Hobbes and Pufendorf in his more theoretically oriented political writings. Leibniz had ambivalent views throughout his career of early modern thinkers of sovereign power such as Hobbes and Pufendorf. Leibniz recognized the strengths of Hobbes' rationalizing method even as he critiqued it for reviving Thrasymachus's position in Plato's *Republic* that justice is the interest of the stronger power and upholding a political-theological voluntarism that reduced the justice and goodness of God to an arbitrary political despotism motivated by fear that is unworthy of the dignity of the divine. God cannot be forced to choose the good, but does so through rational freedom.[24]

---

[21] See Maria Rosa Antognazza: *Leibniz: An Intellectual Biography*, Cambridge 2009, p. 79.
[22] Patrick Riley: "Three 17th century German Theorists of Federalism: Althusius, Hugo and Leibniz," in: *Publius* 6/3 (1976), pp. 7–41.
[23] Gottfried Wilhelm Leibniz: *Political Writings*, transl. and ed. by Patrick Riley, Cambridge 1988, pp. 121–145.
[24] Compare Gottfried Wilhelm Leibniz: *Theodicy: Essays on the Goodness of God, the Freedom of Man, and the Origin of Evil*, transl. into English by E. M. Huggard, La Salle 1985, p. 59; "Our end is to banish from men the false ideas that represent God to them as an absolute prince employing a despotic power, unfitted to be loved and unworthy of being loved. These notions are the more evil in relation to God inasmuch as the essence of piety is not only to fear him but also to love him above all things."

Recent interpreters of Leibniz have accentuated either: (1) his backward looking traditionalism in striving for a morally oriented and religiously informed legal and political philosophy (Riley) or (2) his progressive modernism in applying the paradigm of the new mathematical sciences to law and politics so that, despite his own intentions, he becomes a primary source for the reduction of legal thinking to the positivistic scientific model of legal scientism and positivism (Berkowitz). Both of these readings capture significant dimensions of his thought; but they are inadequate to the extent that Leibniz is neither a pure traditional natural law theorist nor modernizing positivist. Leibniz's efforts – beginning with his early juridical works – endeavor to preserve by reforming traditional conceptions of ethics, law, and politics through their modernistic rationalization. Leibniz's practical philosophy encompasses and remains beholden to Pauline Christian, Roman legal, Reformation Aristotelian, and classical Platonic sources, amongst others. It is this synthetic configuration of the ancient and the modern that shapes Leibniz's encounter with Chinese culture.

4. Ethical Ideals and Political Realities

Leibniz interprets his conception of reason to be embodied in Enlightened political systems such as Chinese society.[25] His idea of reason is practical and political-theological; it encompasses normative reasoning about ends guides instrumental rational calculations about means. There is less of a bifurcation between the ethical-normative and the prudential-instrumental in Leibniz's practical philosophy than found in Kant's moral thinking.[26] This emphasis on continuity between degrees of variation is evident beginning with Leibniz's early legal writings that analyze how positive civil law stems from natural law that offers both grounds of justification and norms that guide social-political reform and renewal. The language of roman legal thinking and Pauline Christian charity cannot merely serve as a conservative rhetoric for Leibniz; they were sources of his project of enlightened reform and social policy through the use and extension of reason.

---

[25] Leibniz: *Writings on China*, p. 45: *Novissima Sinica* § 6.
[26] On the prudential and instrumental in Kant's practical philosophy, see Eric S Nelson: "Moral and Political Prudence in Kant," in: *International Philosophical Quarterly* 44/3 (2004), pp. 305–319.

Leibniz applied his practical conception of reason, with all the presuppositions that this has for him, to the implicit rationality at work in Chinese practical philosophy in the "Discourse on the Natural Theology of the Chinese" (1715–1716). It is interesting to note the difference between Leibniz and Nicolas Malebranche. Both thinkers upheld the idea of the universal character and scope of reason that all peoples share, such that a Christian philosopher could rationally convince a Chinese philosopher through argumentation in Malebranche's *Dialogue Between a Christian Philosopher and a Chinese Philosopher on the Existence and Nature of God* (1708), while they differed on the issue of the legitimacy of Chinese thought.[27] Leibniz's stress on the continuity between diverse levels of thinking and charity in interpretation marks one crucial difference. Another difference is Leibniz's description of Chinese philosophy in light of Western categories of reason and a natural theology that unites the religious and the political:

> "What we call the light of reason in man, they call commandment and law of Heaven. What we call the inner satisfaction of obeying justice and our fear of acting contrary to it, all this is called by the Chinese (and by us as well) inspirations sent by the Xangti [Shangdi 上帝] (that is, by the true God). To offend Heaven is to act against reason, to ask pardon of Heaven is to reform oneself and to make a sincere return in word and deed in the submission one owes to this very law of reason. For me I find all this quite excellent and quite in accord with *natural theology*. Far from finding any distorted understanding here, I believe that it is only by strained interpretations and by interpolations that one could find anything to criticize on this point. It is pure Christianity, insofar as it renews the natural law inscribed in our hearts – except for what revelation and grace add to it to improve our nature."[28]

The practical and political achievements of the Chinese, which Leibniz suggests can be an example and model to reform the practical and political life of the Occident, is interconnected with the purity of the insights of Chinese natural theology that only needs Christian revelation to perfect itself. In this sense, we can describe Leibniz's interpretation as "political-theological". It

---

[27] Nicolas Malebranche: *Dialogue between a Christian philosopher and a Chinese philosopher on the existence and nature of God*, Washington, D.C. 1980. Malebranche also retained the Medieval idea of "natural reason" in humanity. He maintained that the Chinese have the same capacity for reason and impulse toward happiness as Europeans, and therefore can be converted to Christianity through rational philosophical argumentation. On the relation between these two interpretations of China, compare Gregory M. Reihman: "Malebranche's Influence on Leibniz's *Writings on China*," in: *Philosophy East and West* 65/3 (2015), pp. 846–868.
[28] Leibniz: *Writings on China*, p. 104: *Discours sur la théologie naturelle des Chinois* § 31.

depends on a rationalized and moralized account of Christianity and the relation between religion and politics.

The interdependence of the religious and political spheres is not accidental nor merely an instrumental concern for Leibniz in his political and Chinese writings. Politics is thought in relationship to political theology, political and religious principles express one another, and pragmatic political concerns of general well-being in these texts. Based on his pragmatic understanding of political affairs, Leibniz recommended that we "imagine things at their worst in politics" while "imagining things at their best in morality."[29] Leibniz applies this maxim and pragmatic concern in his list of areas where Europe surpasses China. Passivism – which he associates with the overly "Christian" attitude of the Chinese in this passage – permits evil to flourish and the good to be undone:

> [The Chinese] "also yield to us in military science, not so much out of ignorance as by deliberation. For they despise everything which creates or nourishes ferocity in men, and almost in emulation of the higher teachings of Christ (and not, as some wrongly suggest, because of anxiety), they are averse to war. They would be wise indeed if they were alone in the world. But as things are, it comes back to this, that even the good must cultivate the arts of war, so that the evil may not gain power over everything."[30]

The Chinese have to this extent failed in Leibniz's estimation to properly mediate the higher religious and lower prudential teachings necessary for maintaining social-political life. Granted that Leibniz might appear to be committed to thinking of the political through the dualistic extremes of a pragmatic and calculative self-interested realism and an idealistic image of altruistic charity for others inspired by Saint Paul and Saint Augustine, he emphasized their political theological mutuality and the moral direction of political policy and action in his writings and correspondence. Leibniz articulated the possibility of reconciling the ethical and the prudential in an ethically oriented politics in his portrayals of justice as the charity of the wise (*caritas sapientis*), as a philosophically enlightened love (*agapê*), and as a universal benevolence informed by prudence so that mere power and evil will not win.[31] This mediation of morality and knowledge is the basis for his applied utilitarian "science

---

[29] Id.: *Political Writings*, p. 81.
[30] Id.: *Writings on China*, p. 45: *Novissima Sinica* § 2.
[31] Leibniz appeals to Paul's conception of love while reintegrating it with knowledge in contrast with Paul's skeptical remark that: "Knowledge puffs up; love builds up" (*Gnôsis phusioi, agapê*

of felicity" (*scientia felicitates*) that ought to orient and guide enlightened morally oriented pragmatic policies. The Chinese political system guided by Confucian literati provided an exemplary model of a philosophically oriented politics.

Leibniz supported limited monarchy, arguing for the diversity of powers as a way to restrict abuses of authority. This political stance appears to be in conflict with the image of the Enlightened despot. Accordingly, as we saw above, Leibniz deploys his own political sensibility to define and limit the potentially excessive power of the Chinese monarch. One essential limit is the perspective and judgment of the Confucian literati intellectuals who mediate the Emperor's power through the administration of scholar-bureaucrats. The literati form a sort of critical public that can philosophically and pragmatically guide the polity. Notions of publicity and accountability are constitutive of Leibniz's interpretation of political authority, and these elements are not lacking in his account of the responsibility and scope of the Chinese monarch and its Confucian literati "philosophical" administrators.

5. Leibniz's Platonic Confucianism

Leibniz maintained the priority of the wise in governing (the philosophical monarch) and the role of divine providence in human affairs, both of which have in his interpretation Chinese political-theological correlates: the sage-king (*shengren* 聖人) and "will of heaven" (*tianzhi* 天志).[32] From his Platonizing perspective, Leibniz rejected John Locke's social contract theory, including the principle of equal natural rights, and appealed to providence in order to justify obedience to de facto regimes in his interpretation of William Sherlock's *Case of Allegiance*.[33] Leibniz's position here has its Chinese correlates

---

oikodomei). 1 *Corinthians*, 8:1. Leibniz describes his ideal of charity and how piety is only possible in charity in the *Theodicy*: "Our charity is humble and full of moderation, it presumes not to domineer; attentive alike to our own faults and to the talents of others, we are inclined to criticize our own actions and to excuse and vindicate those of others. We must work out our own perfection and do wrong to no man. There is no piety where there is not charity; and without being kindly and beneficent one cannot show sincere religion" (Leibniz: *Theodicy*, p. 52).

[32] I want to express my thanks to Axel Rüdiger for pointing out the importance of the Utopian elements in Leibniz's interpretation of China and earlier European thinkers who noted affinities between the Confucian sage ruler and the Platonic philosopher-king, including Michel de Montaigne, Georg Hornius, and Isaac Vossius.

[33] This text has been consequently construed as "Hobbesian," despite its different providential rationale for accepting the existing regime as legitimate.

in the Confucian interpretation and hierarchical ranking of social and familial roles and "heaven's will" as expressing the moral and natural order of the world. Leibniz's interpretation of the idea of a Confucian sage-ruler is informed by his prudentially mediated Platonic-Pauline conception of benevolent political wisdom as much as by actual Chinese moral and political sources.

In contrast to Kant's radical differentiation of pure practical reason (ethics) and pragmatic prudence, Leibniz upheld the eudaemonist dimension of the political that aims at general well-being. He articulated the bonds between one's own self-interested happiness and the happiness of others, as ends for their own sake, in addition to the general good and common welfare of society, humanity, and God's creation. This line of argumentation led him to assert the continuity between human justice and divine justice (theodicy), agreeing with Plato in the *Meno* that the divine – rationally and spontaneously – follows the good rather than the good being posited through the will.[34]

Leibniz maintained the acceptance of de facto authority while rejecting conflating such authority with the principle of justice. He argued against both legal positivism, which conflates actual force and positive laws with justice, as well as voluntarism, which prioritizes the capricious arbitrary will and coercive power of worldly kings and God. Legal positivism and practical voluntarism reduce the political to the relativism of the rightness of power[35]; and they undermine possibilities of criticism and complaint that are the prerequisites of enlightened reform.[36] Belief in the primacy of the will and coercive power independent of reasons necessarily undermines goodness and justice.[37] Freedom is constitutive of morality, and freedom naturally and rationally tends toward that which is best: the good. Leibniz concluded in a Platonic vein that even God's will – and hence correspondingly the Chinese idea of the will of heaven – must follow the good that is the object of divine understanding and, furthermore, that there is a "common conception of justice" (i.e., the good) that orients both humans and God.[38] God and heaven are not irrational

---

[34] Leibniz: *Political Writings*, p. 45; compare Gaston Grua: *Jurisprudence Universelle et Théodicée selon Leibniz*, New York 1985.
[35] On the relationship between power and right in Leibniz, compare Hartmut Schiedermair: *Das Phänomen der Macht und die Idee des Rechts bei Gottfried Wilhelm Leibniz*, Wiesbaden 1970.
[36] Leibniz: *Political Writings*, pp. 47f.
[37] Id.: *Theodicy*, p. 59.
[38] Ibid.; id.: *Political Writings*, pp. 45–64.

powers; they key aspects of the rational order of nature and of rational knowledge of that order.³⁹

In the Chinese context, the common principle of justice extends between heaven, humans, and earth. The Platonic priority of the good is visible for Leibniz in the Neo-Confucian account of patterning principle, form, or coherence (*li* 理). *Li* was one of the candidates for a Chinese correlate to the Christian idea of God in the discussions of the Jesuits and Leibniz. Leibniz glosses *li* as "spirit." Leibniz's reading of *li* is Platonic. He takes patterning principle (*li*) to be the good. He understands the principle of *li* to assert the priority and unity (theoretical and practical) of reason. This approach was mediated by the early Jesuit reception of Neo-Confucianism that was shaped by its more rationalist form (*lixue* 理学) associated with Zhu Xi 朱熹.

Leibniz adopts an eclectic Platonic strategy in his discussion of *li* in *Annotationes de Cultur Religioneque Sinensium* ("Remarks on Chinese Rites and Religion") in 1708, noting how: "From the *li*, taken in itself, emanates justice, wisdom and the other virtues [...]."⁴⁰ Whereas the normative world originates in *li* in itself, the material world stems from modified *li* linked and intermixed with *qi* 氣. *Li* in and of itself, defined as harmony and justice, is essentially rational and normative. *Li* is imperfectly realized and expressed in the rational order of the natural world. In the Neo-Confucian framework, and ultimately in the end for Leibniz who emphasizes gradations of continuity in contrast to Kant's strategy of conceptual separation, the categories of the normative and the political cannot be separated from the categories of the cosmological and the theological.

According to Leibniz, the universe challenges us with questions of its harmony and justice. These questions echo and have their correlates in Chinese traditions as well. Leibniz's nominal definition of justice is: "a constant will to act in such a way that no one has reason to complain."⁴¹ This point is clarified in his account of the degrees of justice that ascend from the legal to the ethical and then to the religious, which emerged in his earlier interpretations of the Roman legal tradition and Pauline charity.⁴² Leibniz differentiated three practical spheres: (1) the *legal* is the minimal negative duty to harm no

---

³⁹ A careful and comprehensive account of the rational order of nature in Leibniz can be found in Donald Rutherford: *Leibniz and the Rational Order of Nature*, Cambridge 1998.
⁴⁰ Leibniz: *Writings on China*, p. 67: *Annotationes de Cultur Religioneque Sinensium* § 1.
⁴¹ Id.: *Political Writings*, p. 53.
⁴² Hans-Peter Schneider: *Justitia universalis Quellenstudien zur Geschichte des "Christlichen Naturrechts" bei Gottfried Wilhelm Leibniz*, Frankfurt a. M. 1967.

one (the "strict right" of commutative justice based in self-interest); (2) the *ethical* is the positive duty to "give each his due" and act with charity for the sake of others (the equity or distributive justice oriented by concern for others and general welfare); and (3) the *religious* is to live honestly or piously for its own sake (the universal justice and divine republic of God and humans).[43]

Leibniz commented in the *Theodicy*:

> "The true God is always the same: natural religion itself demands that he be essentially as good and wise as he is powerful. It is scarcely more contrary to reason and piety to say that God acts without cognition, than to maintain that he has cognition which does not find the eternal rules of goodness and of justice among its objects, or again to say that he has a will such as heeds not these rules."[44]

Leibniz's conception of justice is best indicated in pure or philosophically interpreted Christianity. Yet, as natural theology, Leibniz finds the inspiration of "the true God" at work in Chinese moral and political practices and ideas, which as natural (political) theology express a form of "pure Christianity" or the 'charity of the wise.'[45] Confucian benevolence (*ren* 仁) is an expression of the compassion of the philosopher habitualized and institutionalized in social-political life.

6. Conclusion

Leibniz often appears to rediscover, as in a reflection, his own conception of ethics and political theology in his response to Chinese practical philosophy. He no doubt at times dreamed of converting the Chinese to his own philosophical vision of pure natural theology rather than the impure Christianity that dominated European society and that the missionaries sought to transmit to China. It remains an open question to what extent Leibniz's encounter with China modified his thinking though it cannot be said to have radically altered it.

Leibniz's ethical principle of charity was adopted into an interpretive strategy of normatively oriented charity that is noticeable in the way he wishes

---

[43] Leibniz: *Political Writings*, pp. 171f.
[44] Id.: *Theodicy*, p. 238.
[45] Id.: *Writings on China*, p. 104: *Discours sur la théologie naturelle des Chinois* § 31.

his readers to interpret Chinese sources.[46] He points towards ways of uncovering the rationality in Chinese discourse despite its distance and foreignness to Europeans. Leibniz's attempt to articulate the intrinsic meaningfulness and rationality of other perspectives in his approach to China remains fairly remarkable in the primarily Eurocentric history of modern Western philosophy. It continues to be suggestive for contemporary intercultural thinking although it is an insufficient hermeneutical model for it.[47]

Leibniz's theoretical and practical, ideal and pragmatic, political thinking are not discontinuous; they converged in his humanistic and cosmopolitan vision that is reflected in his diverse practical and theoretical efforts at peace and reconciliation between distinct and conflicting forms of life and philosophical perspectives. A number of his writings in practical philosophy and his diplomatic and intellectual correspondence concerned tolerance, compromise, and coming to an agreement across political, religious, scientific, and cultural disputes and distances from the Holy Roman Empire and Europe to Peter the Great's Russia and the far East.[48] Leibniz's writings concerning China exemplify, as this chapter has illustrated, these broader concerns.

---

[46] I develop this account of the hermeneutical character of Leibniz's interpretation of China further in Eric S. Nelson: "Leibniz and China: Religion, Hermeneutics, and Enlightenment," in: *Religion in the Age of Enlightenment* 1 (2009), pp. 277–300.

[47] On intercultural hermeneutics and the history of the European reception of Chinese philosophy, see id.: *Chinese and Buddhist Philosophy in early Twentieth-Century German Thought*, London 2017.

[48] See Nelson: "Leibniz and China" and Eric S. Nelson: "The Yijing and Philosophy: From Leibniz to Derrida," in: *Journal of Chinese Philosophy* 38/3 (2011), pp. 377–396.

The Language of the Last Leibniz: *Monadologie* vs. *Principes*

Roberto Palaia (Rome)

In the present paper I will be focusing on the *Monadologie* and the *Principes de la nature et de la grâce*. I will examine the two texts and their language, in order to compare the different styles and forms of expressions which the author used in view of the different readerships – and different degrees of understanding – which the two works presupposed. I will set out to challenge the historiographical thesis that the *Monadologie* belongs to a series of texts reflecting a 'secret' Leibnizian philosophy, one quite distinct from the philosophy which may be inferred from his published texts. I will therefore attempt to evaluate whether it is correct to draw such a clear-cut distinction in terms of content between published and unpublished works, and hence whether it is really the case that the real Leibnizian philosophy can only be known by focusing on his unpublished texts.

Scholars have long been faced with the problem of accounting for the vast range of unpublished texts that Leibniz produced over the course of his life, and for the striking disproportion between these works and those he actually published. The need to reconstruct genuine Leibnizian philosophy – the philosophy which Leibniz must have conceived, yet without ever setting down in writing – has been a mixed blessing for scholars. The need to address this point has proven a very fruitful concern, which inspired many 20th-century interpretations of Leibnizian philosophy. To this day, Bertrand Russel's words may be seen to provide a precise definition of the whole issue:

> "he had a good philosophy which (after Arnauld's criticisms) he kept to himself and a bad philosophy which he published with a view to fame and money. In this he showed his usual acumen: his bad philosophy was admired for its bad qualities, and his good philosophy, which was known only to the editors of his manuscripts, was regarded by them as worthless, and left unpublished."[1]

---

[1] Bertrand Russel: *A Critical Exposition of The Philosophy of Leibniz*, London ²ᵃ1949, "Preface to the Second Edition", p. vi. Moreover, should be emphasized the importance of the unpublished works for understanding Leibniz's reflection; Leibniz wrote: „Qui me non nisi editis novit, non novit", Letter to Placcius, 21. February 1696; Dutens VI, 1, 65; A II, 3, 139.

The dichotomy between published texts, illustrating 'simpler' theses, and more complex reflections remains a prominent feature of Leibnizian literature.²

Scholars have expressed different, if not downright opposite, opinions as to the value of the *Principes* and *Monadologie*. The *Monadologie* has been presented as a "schematic notebook, designed to provide a blueprint for a focus on Leibnizian philosophy."³ More recently, Bertrand Irrgang has distinguished the *Monadologie* from the *Principes* based on the terminology it employs, a specialist philosophical jargon, whereas the *Principes* – in his words – provide "an overall view of the principles of the system, expounded by means of a simpler terminology."⁴

The common yet at the same time different destiny of the two texts reflects the context of their composition and the choice of titles. The enduring historiographical misunderstanding whereby one work has often been mistaken for the other is well known, so I will only refer here to André Robinet's critical investigations and to further, more recent studies for a historical reconstruction of this history.⁵ Be that as it may, Leibniz records the drafting of the two texts in the correspondence from his last sojourn in Vienna, in the spring and summer of 1714. Leibniz mentions the two short pieces of writing in several exchanges with Rémond: in a letter written in June, Leibniz informs his correspondent that he is behind with his writing of the *Monadologie* – "the explanation about monads which [...] has grown in my hands" – and apologises for failing to send Rémond a summary of the main topics he is planning to discuss in the text. Later, in a letter dated August the 26th, Leibniz encloses "a short exposition which I composed here for Prince Eugene about my philosophy", which is to say the *Principes de la Nature et de la grâce*.⁶ By combining this information with the evidence from the manuscripts of the two

---

² "The existence of two treatments of the same topic, of similar size and scope, intended for the same broad lay readership, and written during the same period raises the obvious question of why Leibniz should simultaneously have composed two such similar works." Cf. Maria Rosa Antognazza: *Leibniz: An Intellectual Biography*, New York 2015, p. 501.
³ "Di questi due brevi scritti (*Principes* and *Monadology*) il migliore è senza dubbio il primo [...] il secondo scritto è invece una sorta di brogliaccio schematico, destinato a fornire il canovaccio per un poema sulla filosofia leibniziana", cf. V. Mathieu: *Introduzione a Leibniz*, Bari 1976, p.74.
⁴ Cf. Bertrand Irrgang: "*Principes de la nature et de la grâce fondés en raison*", in: F. Volpi/J. Nida-Rümelin (eds.): *Lexicon der philosophischen Werke*, Stuttgart 1988, p. 581.
⁵ Cf. Gottfried Wilhelm Leibniz: *Principes de la nature et de la grâce fondés en raison. Principes de la philosophie ou Monadologie*, ed. by A. Robinet, Paris 1954.
⁶ Gottfried Wilhelm Leibniz, Letter to Remond, 26. August 1715; GP III, 624.

works, we may conclude that the two texts were drafted almost simultaneously in Vienna in the summer of 1714. The *Principes* were completed in early July and then sent to Eugene of Savoy, before being forwarded to Rémond in August. The *Monadologie*, which remained fully unpublished, was instead written in Vienna during and after the completion of the *Principes*. Only the last draft of the *Monadologie* was produced in Hannover, after Leibniz's return to the city in mid-September.

The correspondence with Rémond is among the sources which best help define the target readership of the two texts. In the opening section of the letter dated August the 26th, and enclosing a copy of the *Principes*, Leibniz explicates the argumentative strategy he has adopted to spread his ideas:

> "In the journal of Leipzig, I adapted myself to the language of the School; in the others I adapted myself rather to the style of the Cartesians; and in this latest piece I try to express myself in a manner that can be understood by those who are not yet too well accustomed to the style of either."[7]

In the case of the *Principes*, then, it is quite clear that Leibniz sought to express himself in a non-specialist language, which could be understood even by readers unfamiliar with the technical jargon of the School and of Cartesianism. Leibniz, then, does not refer to the possibility of reserving some of his writings for those capable of understanding them; on the contrary, he seeks to make his philosophy accessible to all possible interlocutors.

As regards the *Monadologie,* it is possible to infer its intended readership from the occasion which led to the composition of the work. In a letter dated the 5th of May 1714, Rémond mentions some presentation of philosophy in verse. In his replies, Leibniz variously alludes to his intention of developing a succinct presentation of his philosophy. Compared to the *Principes,* the *Monadologie* lent Leibniz' philosophical notions a more assertive form, based on the use of a paratactic style and on formal rigour. Whatever Leibniz's initial motives may have been, the final text displayed a markedly rigorous style, with a sharp argumentative focus. It is more plausible to assume that the rigid structure of the work was one of the reasons why its publication was repeatedly put off, than to posit a desire on Leibniz's part to conceal content which he regarded as either dangerous or difficult to understand. In order to concretely evaluate the similarities and differences between the two texts, I

---

[7] Ibid.

will compare the frequency of terms and argumentative structures used to illustrate the topics of the two works.

A formal comparison between the texts reveals both divergences and affinities: the *Monadologie* is approximately 6000 words long and is divided into 90 paragraphs; as already noted, the style is chiefly paratactic and subordinate clauses are very rare, with the partial exception of the last two paragraphs, where the style becomes freer and more articulate. The topics presented in the *Monodologie* encapsulate the key elements of Leibnizian philosophy, and the 90 paragraphs may roughly be divided into thematically coherent groups: paragraphs 1–27 define the monad, its modes of perception and knowledge, and memory; paragraphs 28–37 draw a distinction between human beings and animals, identify the two principles of contradiction and of sufficient reason, and the two kinds of truth deriving from them; paragraphs 38–48 are devoted to God the creator and to the principle of the best; paragraphs 49–60 describe the relations between monads, the best of all possible worlds, and universal harmony; paragraphs 61–80 define organisms and distinguish artificial machines from divine ones, while also illustrating the concepts of metamorphosis and pre-established harmony; finally, paragraphs 81–90 draw a distinction between ordinary souls and rational souls, and describe God the architect and lawgiver, and his kingdom.

The text of the *Principes* is around 3500 words long and is divided into 18 paragraphs which may thematically be grouped as follows: paragraphs 1–2 are devoted to simple and composite monads, their capacity to perceive and desire, and the relations between them; paragraphs 3–4 discuss nature, harmony, perceptions and apperceptions, and men and animals; paragraph 5 describes memory and necessary and eternal truths; paragraph 6 explores the topics of life, death, and metamorphosis; paragraphs 7–8 are devoted to the principle of sufficient reason; paragraphs 9–11 focus on God; paragraphs 12–13 on the constitution of the best of all possible worlds; paragraphs 14–16 describe the soul, God, the City of God, and pre-established harmony; finally, paragraphs 17–18 discuss the love of God and future happiness.

So while an analysis of the structure of the texts reveals considerable differences in terms of length and arrangement, their treatment of topics is more homogeneous than what might seem to be the case at first: they both set out from a definition of the simplest elements in order to then move on to analyse man, nature and finally God as the architect and lawgiver of his city. The language used in the *Principes* is more fluid and simple, and closer to the Cartesian philosophical tastes of the period, particularly when it comes to the definition of bodies and composite substances.

In his texts, Leibniz frequently refers to or quotes other authors, both in support of his claims and to refute opposite positions. Whereas in the *Monadologie* Leibniz refers to various authors in order to clarify his arguments, in the *Principes* such references are rare. The first example comes from paragraph 4, where Leibniz criticises the Cartesians for having misunderstood the notion of *petit perception*; the polemic here almost perfectly matches, in both form and content, the one expressed in paragraph 14 of the *Monadologie*.[8] The second case is that of Leibniz's anti-Stoic polemic in the *Principes* (§18), where the author sets the strained patience of the Stoics in contrast with the serenity stemming from the love of God, which provides a foretaste of the happiness to come.[9] As regards the *Monadologie*, it is worth noting the reference made in paragraphs 16 and 59 to the *Rorarius* entry of Bayle's *Dictionnaire*, one of the main polemical targets of the text.[10]

What plays a considerable role in relation to the argumentative structure of Leibniz's texts is the use of metaphors, understood not as mere embellishments, but as a means for assertion enabling a clear understanding of conceptually more complex passages. In this context, it is significant that a greater use of metaphors is made precisely in the *Monadologie*: language is here used to illustrate the most difficult passages of the German philosopher's thought in the most rigorous possible way.

The metaphors in question are featured in passages where the author switches from a strictly analytical and descriptive register to a more figurative

---

[8] "C'est aussi ce qui a fait croire aux mêmes Cartesiens, que les seuls Esprits sont des Monades, qu'il n'y a point d'Ame des Bêtes, et encore moins d'autres principes de Vie", Leibniz: *Principes*, ed. by A. Robinet, p. 37; „Et c'est en quoi les Cartesiens ont fort manqué, aïant compté pour rien les perceptions dont on ne s'appercoit pas. C'est aussi ce qui les a fait croire, que les seuls Esprits etoient des Monades, et qu'il n'y avoit point d'Ames des Bêtes ny d'autres Entelechies; et qu'ils ont confondu avec le vulgaire un long étourdissement avec une mort à la rigueur, ce qui les a fait encor donner dans le prejugé scholastique des ames entièrement separées et a même confirmé les esprits mal tournés dans l'opinion de la mortalité des ames." Id.: *Monadologie*, ed. by A. Robinet, p. 77.
[9] "[…] non pas comme chez les Stoiciens, resolus à une patience par force, mais par un contentement present qui nous assûre même un bonheur futur […]", Id.: *Principes*, p. 63.
[10] In *Monadologie* Leibniz refers to Descartes also in paragraphs 46 and 80; in the first case Descartes is mentioned, together with theologian Pierre Poiret, as an example to deny the arbitrariness of the eternal truths; in the second case Leibniz stresses the inadequacy of the Cartesian conservation law of momentum. In Monadology he quotes also Ermolao Barbaro, about the use the term *perfectihabies* as a synonym of *entelechies* or *substances* (§ 48), and Hippocrates (§ 61) regarding συμπνοια παντα, expression used by Leibniz in various works, but not in the *Principes*.

and evocative one. I will not attempt to define just what is meant by metaphor here, as this would sidetrack my argument.

In the *Principes* we find two instances of the use of a metaphor, in paragraphs 5 and 13. In the first case, in order to present the role of memory as connected to perception, Leibniz puts forward the example of a dog that, upon seeing a stick, remembers the punishment previously inflicted on him. This argument is the same as the one Leibniz resorts to in paragraph 26 of the *Monadologie*, where the relation between perception and memory is presented along much the same lines. The second instance of the use of a metaphor in the *Principes* is the comparison drawn between confused perceptions and the perception of the roaring of the sea, where it is impossible to make out the sound of individual waves. The German philosopher had already employed this metaphor in a 1702 letter to Sophia Charlotte and, before that, in his *Discours de Metaphysique* in 1684.[11]

Analysing the terms used in the two texts and comparing their frequencies yields very interesting results in relation to Leibniz's vocabulary. A table of frequencies for the words used in the two texts produces two almost identical lists of the most common terms: *âme* is the most frequent word in both texts – it appears 41 times in the *Monadologie* and 24 in the *Principes*; the second most frequent term is *Dieu*, which occurs respectively 39 and 21 times. These terms are then followed by other ones such as *substance*, *monade*, *simple* and *perception*, which again have much the same frequency across the two works. It is reasonable to conclude, then, that Leibniz used a homogeneous vocabulary in drafting the two texts. Indeed, even when we consider the definitions provided for these key words, no significant discrepancies are to be found in terms of content.

Certainly, this does not answer the question of Leibniz's almost obsessive caution in publishing the *Monadologie*, which was only issued in a German and then Latin translation after his death; however, what it *does* suggest is the need to adopt a less radical perspective on the German philosopher's alleged desire to conceal some of his philosophical convictions. Considering that the two works were drafted almost simultaneously, Leibniz may be seen to display a striking capacity to adapt his own style to suit different readers. Leibniz did not so much strive to conceal content which he regarded as best

---

[11] Cf. *Discours de metaphyique*, § xxxiii; A VI, 4 B, 1582; GP IV, 459. "C'est ainsi qu'on entend le bruit des vagues de la mer, qu'on n'entendroit pourtant pas, si on n'avoit point quelque petite perception de chaque vague." See *Leibniz an die Königin Sophie Charlotte*; GP VI, 515; A I, 24, N. 410.

left unpublished, as vary his style to ensure the widest possible circulation of his philosophy.

Besides, the research of recent years – which has been made possible precisely by the colossal work undertaken with the *Akademie Ausgabe* of Leibniz's unpublished texts – has taught us to analyse Leibniz's philosophy not as a fossilized set of doctrines, but as a range of findings which he discussed, corrected and rethought throughout his life, and only partly published.

A comparative analysis of the two texts, then, reveals not so much a desire on Leibniz's part to conceal certain aspects of his thought, as an eagerness to adapt the form in which such thought was expressed, so as to ensure its broader diffusion in the European cultural milieu. In his choices, the German philosopher actually proved to be more in tune with the 'public' perception of philosophy which was destined to become prevalent in the 18th century than with the mystical and sectarian inclinations of the philosophers of the previous century.

Leibniz in Rom

Roberto Palaia (Rom)

Der Aufenthalt in Rom von März bis Oktober 1689 ist aus mindestens zwei Gründen für die Beziehung zwischen Leibniz und der kulturellen und politischen Welt Europas bedeutsam:
- Der Zeitraum, in dem sich Leibniz in Rom aufhielt, entspricht den Jahren, in denen sich sein philosophisches Denken organischer darstellt und seine Überlegungen erhalten, die aus diesen Jahren erhalten sind, sind die für ihn charakteristischen Inhalte;
- Rom ist Ende des 17. Jahrhunderts noch eines der bedeutendsten europäischen Kulturzentren; auch wenn die größte Glanzzeit des päpstlichen Hofes schon am Untergehen war, traf Leibniz in Rom wertvolle Gesprächspartner zu diversen philosophischen und wissenschaftlichen Themen seines Interessengebiets an.

Diese zwei Aspekte lassen sich auch in Bezug setzen zu zwei unterschiedlichen Beobachtungsstandpunkten, von denen aus das Thema angegangen werden kann: a) einerseits aus der Perspektive von Leibniz, also ausgehend von den Errungenschaften, zu denen er um die 1690er Jahre gelangt war; b) andererseits kann das Thema auch aus der Perspektive der Stadt Rom behandelt werden. Wie im Fall von Leibniz, hat Rom auch während des Religionskriegs gegen die Reformierten, wichtige Vertreter jener deutschen Welt aufgenommen, die es – im Verständnis des römischen Klerus – wiederzuerobern galt.

1. Leibniz in Rom: Themen und Diskussionen

Die Reise Leibniz' in den Süden und nach Italien erfolgte in den Jahren, in denen er organischere und hochentwickelte, philosophische und wissenschaftliche Reflexionen verschriftlichte. Auch aus linguistischer Sicht nahm Leibniz in diesem Zeitabschnitt viele Neuigkeiten in seine Lexik auf, wie die Begriffe Dynamik und Monade.[1] Zu den Schwerpunkten, die ihn während seines Aufenthalts in Rom stärker beschäftigten, zählten die endgültige Begründung der

---

[1] „La dénomination de 'dynamique', toujours en usage dans la nomenclature des sciences, et principalement de la physique, doit son invention et son premier emploi à Leibniz; elle est caractérisée à l'origine par le caractère singulier, idiosyncrasique en quelque sorte de sa signification

Voraussetzungen der Dynamik, der Versuch, im römischen Umfeld die Prinzipien der kopernikanischen Kosmologie zu rehabilitieren gegen die aristotelisch-ptolemäische Weltsicht, die noch als Anachronismus von der offiziellen Lehre der Kirche vertreten wurde, sowie schließlich die Diskussion zur Einführung des gregorianischen statt des julianischen Kalenders auch in den reformierten Ländern. Diese Fragestellungen, die auf verschiedene konstitutive Aspekte der späteren Reflexionen des deutschen Philosophen verweisen, waren mit Diskussionen im Kulturraum Roms verbunden; diese Diskussionen wurden jahrzehntelang von unterschiedlichen kulturellen Gruppierungen geführt, wie zum Beispiel von einer jesuitischen Gruppe, die sich mit Clavius' Lehren auseinandersetzte, oder auch von anderen Zirkeln oft innerhalb oder am Rande der päpstlichen Kurie: In diesem Kontext stellte der Entwurf der Leibniz'schen Dynamik eine besonders ansprechende Position dar, insbesondere für diejenigen mathematischen und wissenschaftlichen Kreise in Rom, die sich der stets wachsenden Verbreitung der Prinzipien kartesischer Physik auch im katholischem Umfeld entgegenstellen wollten.[2] Der Versuch, Kopernikus zu rehabilitieren traf in Rom auf besonders interessierte Beobachter; viele hielten es für günstig, das biblische Diktat mit den Daten der experimentellen Studien zu versöhnen.[3] Im Thema des Kalenders manifestierte sich letztlich aus Sicht der Kirche der universale Stellenwert der eigenen Vorgaben zur Berechnung der Zeit, angefangen von der genauen Berechnung der österlichen Feiertage.

2. Die wichtigsten Briefwechsel

André Robinets Studie über die Italienreise von Leibniz ist bis heute das Standardwerk für diese Themen.[4] Um die dreißig Personen frequentierten damals

---

leibnizienne", vgl. M. Fichant: „Les dualités de la dynamique leibnizienne", in : *Lexicon Philosophicum International Journal for the History of Texts and Ideas* 4 (2016), s. insbesondere Seiten 12–16, http://lexicon.cnr.it.
[2] In diesem Zusammenhang sind die Studien über die Verbreitung des Kartesianismus in den jesuitischen Kollegs und in anderen religiösen Orden zu beachten. Vgl. U. Baldini: *Legem impone subactis. Studi su filosofia e scienza dei gesuiti in Italia 1540–1632*, Roma 1992.
[3] Um die Rolle gespielt von der Clavius-Argumentationen gegen Kopernikus vgl. E. Knobloch: „Sur la vie et l'œuvre de Christophore Clavius (1538–1612)", in: *Revue d'histoire des sciences*, tome 41, n. 3–4 (1988), pp. 331–356.
[4] André Robinet: *G. W. Leibniz Iter Italicum (Mars 1689–Mars1690)*, Firenze 1988.

die Physisch-Mathematische Akademie von Ciampini; es ist der Gelehrtenkreis, den Leibniz während seines Aufenthalts in Rom bei Weitem am häufigsten aufsuchte. Es waren allerdings vor allem zwei Personen, die für eine gewisse Zeit eine bedeutende Korrespondenz mit dem deutschen Philosophen führten: Giovanni Giustino Ciampini, die Seele der physisch-mathematischen Akademie und Francesco Bianchini, einer der herausragendsten jungen in Rom wirkenden Wissenschaftler im Ausgang des 17. Jahrhunderts.

Wie Erik Amburger, Herausgeber der sich der Zeit der Italienreise widmenden Akademie Ausgabe des Leibniz'schen Briefwechsels, anmerkt, hilft die Analyse des Briefverkehrs nur sehr beschränkt bei der Rekonstruktion der Debatten und Reflexionen, die Leibniz während seines Romaufenthalts beschäftigten;[5] die persönlichen Begegnungen, der Kontakt mit dem reichen kulturellen Leben in Rom werden nur bruchstückhaft im oftmals rein formellen Briefverkehr sichtbar; auch in Fällen, in denen man erwartet, interessante Nachrichten zu entdecken, gibt es stattdessen häufig nur höflich-formelle, wenn nicht sogar belanglose Schriftstücke, wie im Fall von Alessandro Melani, Ansprechperson des Herzogs von Hannover beim Papst.[6] Vor diesem Hintergrund sticht die Korrespondenz mit Ciampini heraus, der Seele jener physisch-mathematischen Akademie, in der Leibniz verschiedenen Quellen zufolge diverse Themen diskutiert hatte, die ihn in jenen Jahren intensiv beschäftigt hatten. Diese Themen wurden Gegenstand des *Phoronamus*, eines Werkes, das Leibniz während des römischen Aufenthalt erstellte und das der deutsche Denker eben genau Ciampini und allen Freunden der physisch-mathematischen Akademie widmete.[7]

Der Briefwechsel mit Giovanni Giustino Ciampini beginnt im Jahr 1689, während des Romaufenthalts, und dauert bis 1695 an. Aus den Briefen gehen Informationen zu den verschiedenen Diskussionsthemen hervor; es handelt sich zumeist um Themen allgemeiner Bildung oder, sehr oft, um extrem spezifische Fragestellungen. Ein Beispiel: Auf dem Rückweg aus Florenz

---

[5] „[...] der Briefwechsel während der Italienreise [...] nicht entfernt ausreicht, um den Reiseweg und vor allem die Erlebnisse in Italien zu rekonstruieren", E. Amburger: „Einleitung"; A I, 5, XLI.
[6] Alessandro Melani, berühmter Komponist vieler Oratorien und Kirchenmusik, war der herzogliche Agent der Braunschweiger in Rom.
[7] „Les prmiers paragraphes de ce cet écrit constituent un véritable 'journal' des interventions de Leibniz devant les membres de l'Accademia, qui nous révèlent en même temps ce qui s'y passe dans ces années dont l'histoire n'a pas été écrite", André Robinet: „G. W. Leibniz: Phoranomus seu de potentia et legibus naturae", in: *Physis Rivista internazionale di storia della scienza* XXVIII (1991), S. 431.

versandte Leibniz am 10. Dezember 1689 einen Brief; darin zögert Leibniz nicht, seinen römischen Freund darum zu bitten, eine Inschrift genau zu datieren und befragte ihn dadurch in Bezug auf die richtige Interpretation der Datierung, die eine der drängendsten Gründe für die gregorianische Kalenderreform war; diese trat in den reformierten Ländern in den Jahren darauf in Kraft.

Der Briefwechsel mit Francesco Bianchini besteht aus sieben Briefen von Leibniz und drei des römischen Briefpartners; es finden sich darin viele wissenschaftliche Themen, die den deutschen Denker in jenen Jahren bewegten; Bianchini, ein Wissenschaftler für den Leibniz Wertschätzung und Lob ausdrückte, war der einzige römische Briefpartner, mit dem der deutsche Philosoph bis fast zu seinem Lebensende in Kontakt blieb. Leibniz lernte Bianchini wahrscheinlich in den Versammlungen der physisch mathematischen Akademie von Ciampini kennen, die regelmäßig jede Woche abends stattfanden. Bianchini lernte den deutschen Philosophen mit weniger als dreißig Jahren kennen. Geboren in Verona im Jahr 1662 vertiefte er dort das Studium der Physik und der Astronomie. Im Jahr 1684 zog er, protegiert von Kardinal Ottoboni (der unter dem Namen Alexander VIII. 1689 Papst werden wird) nach Rom und wurde dort Doktor in *utroque iure*, auch wenn er nie die mathematischen und astronomischen Studien aufgab. Genau diese Breite an Interessen hatte er mit dem deutschen Philosoph gemein, der stets schmeichelnd über ihn sprach, ihn als großen Astronom bezeichnete und versuchte, ihn bei dem Versuch einzubinden, den Kopernikanismus am päpstlichen Hof zu rehabilitieren.[8]

Der Briefverkehr zwischen Leibniz und Bianchini entwickelte sich in drei bestimmten Phasen: Die erste um das Jahr 1690, während der Rückkehr nach Deutschland gleich nach dem römischen Aufenthalt, als Leibniz sich in einigen Briefen auf das römische Umfeld und die in der Accademia von Ciampini diskutierten Themen bezog; die zweite in den Jahren um die Jahrhundertwende mit dem Hauptthema des gregorianischen Kalenders, der 1700 in den reformierten Ländern in Kraft trat; in der letzten Phase, während des ersten Jahrzehnts des 18. Jahrhunderts, sind uns die letzten Briefe der Korrespondenz überliefert. Sie sind vor allem antiquarischen oder geschichtlichen Fragestellungen gewidmet.

---

[8] Um Francesco Bianchini s. S. Rotta: „Francesco Bianchini" in: *Dizionario Biografico degli Italiani* Bd. 10, Roma 1968; V. Kockel/B. Sölch (Hrsg.): *Francesco Bianchini (1662–1729) und die europäische gelehrte Welt um 1700*, Berlin 2005; L. Ciancio und G. B. Romagnani: *Unità del sapere molteplicità dei saperi. Francesco Bianchini (1662–1728) tra natura, storia e religione*, Verona 2010.

3. Von Deutschland nach Italien

Leibniz brach für seine lange Reise Richtung Süddeutschland, Österreich und Italien im November 1687 auf und beendete sie erst fast drei Jahre später im Juni 1690. Er unternahm die Reise, so schrieb Arnauld,

> „par ordre de mon Prince, servant pour des recherches historiques [...] à justifier la commune origine des S^{mes} Maisons de Brunsvic et d'Este."[9]

Die lange Leibniz'sche Reise war auch eine bedeutende Wegstrecke, auf der er Persönlichkeiten aus Politik und Kultur aus halb Europa traf und die ihm eine besondere Perspektive auf die europäische Kultur und Politik Ende des 17. Jahrhunderts bot.

Leibniz besuchte die Höfe im südlichen Deutschland zwischen Ende 1687 und Frühling 1688. Nachdem er Würzburg, Nürnberg, Sulzbach und Regensburg aufgesucht hatte, kam Leibniz am 30. März nach München und einen Monat später nach Wien; dort hielt er sich ungefähr 9 Monate lang auf. Kurz vor seinem Aufbruch nach Italien Mitte Februar, gab Bischof Rojas y Spinola, ein Unterstützer der Wiedervereinigung der Kirchen, Leibniz ein Referenzschreiben für den Kardinal Decio Azzolini mit;[10] dieser war nicht nur mächtiger Vertreter der römischen Kurie und des Staatssekretariats, sondern auch Freund und Förderer Cristina von Schweden. Er stellte eine sehr gewichtige Persönlichkeit am päpstlichen Hof dar und betrieb eine Politik der vorsichtigen Öffnung gegenüber versöhnlicheren Positionen in Bezug auf die Reformierten; er war zudem Mäzen der Künstler und Intellektuellen. Mit dem Referenzschreiben in der Tasche setzte Leibniz seine Reise nach Triest, Verona, Ferrara, Bologna und Loreto fort und kam schließlich am 14. April in Rom an.

In diesen Jahren feierte die Stadt den Triumph der Gegenreformation; noch frisch war die Erinnerung an den denkwürdigen Einzug in Rom 1655 der Königin Cristina von Schweden, reformierte, zum Katholizismus konvertierte Herrscherin und vielsagendes Symbol der diplomatischen Wirksamkeit der Aktivitäten der Gesellschaft Jesu. Um ihre Gestalt herum und in ihrem Palast, Sitz der Accademie dei Lincei, versammelte sich ein Intellektuellenzirkel, der bald darauf die Accademia dell'Arcadia bilden sollte. Das 17. Jahrhundert war

---

[9] Leibniz an Arnauld, 23. März 1690; GP II, 134 und A II, 2 N. 78.
[10] Vgl. Robinet: *G. W. Leibniz. Iter Italicum*, S. 13.

für Rom noch ein Jahrhundert, vielleicht das letzte, mit einem gewissen kulturellen Eifer: Zu Beginn des Jahrhunderts hatte sich die Accademia dei Lincei gebildet, die vatikanische Bibliothek verzeichnete einen Zuwachs von ungefähr 3500 Kodizes und 5000 Bücher aus der palatinischen Bibliothek, unter dem Pontifikat von Alexander VIII. wurde die Bibliothek von Cristina aus Schweden erworben.[11]

Der Zeitraum jedoch, in dem sich Leibniz in der ewigen Stadt aufhielt, war auch ein Moment des schnellen und substantiellen Wandels von Gleichgewichten, die das römische Leben in den Jahren zuvor bestimmt hatten. Fünf Tage nach der Ankunft von Leibniz, starb Cristina von Schweden, die circa dreißig Jahre lang die wahre Protagonistin des römischen Kulturlebens war. Nach weniger als zwei Monaten, am 8. Juni, starb Kardinal Azzolini, Staatssekretär, Freund und Förderer Cristina von Schweden. Durch sein Ableben veränderte sich deutlich das Gleichgewicht innerhalb der Kurie genauso wie dasjenige innerhalb des Konklaves, das bald darauf einberufen wurde, da auch Innozenz XI. am 12. August desselben Jahres starb. Innerhalb von vier Monaten entschwanden somit drei Protagonisten der kulturellen und politischen Bühne Roms und es entwickelte sich ein neues Gleichgewicht, das Konformisten und Traditionalisten begünstigte.[12]

Der Aufenthalt Leibniz', die Diskussionen, die er mit berühmten römischen Wissenschaftlern und Politikern führte, spielten sich in einem Kontext ab, der sicherlich die Absichten des deutschen Philosophen entscheidend beeinflusste: Das Wohlwollen, mit dem Leibniz in die römischen kulturellen Zirkel eingebunden wurde, hatte im deutschen Philosophen die Hoffnung und die Illusion genährt, es zu schaffen, die Vernunft der Wissenschaft geltend zu machen, um die kopernikanischen Hypothesen zu rehabilitieren, die Prinzipien der neuen Physik durchzusetzen und die Versöhnung zwischen den Überzeugungen der reformierten Kirchen und denjenigen der Kirche in Rom zu begünstigen, um so ein politisches und kulturelles Gleichgewicht in einem von

---

[11] Über Cristina di Svezia vgl. G. Platania (Hrsg.): *Roma e Cristina di Svezia. Una irrequieta sovrana*, Viterbo 2016; A. Partini: *Cristina di Svezia e il suo cenacolo alchemico*, Roma 2010; S. Åkerman: *Queen Christina of Sweden and her Circle: the Transformation of a Philosophical Libertine*, Leiden 1991; A. Clericuzio/M. Conforti: „Christina's Patronage of Italian Science: A Study of Her Academies and of the Dedicatory Epistles to the Queen", in: M. Beretta/T. Frangsmyr (Hrsg.): *Sidereus Nuncius and Stella Polaris. The Scientific Relations Between Italy and Sweden in Early Modern History*, Canton, MA 1997, S. 25–36.

[12] Ueber die Kulturkreisen in Rom in XVII. Jahrhundert, s. M. Petrocchi: *Roma nel Seicento*, Bologna, Il Mulino 1970; auch U. Baldini: „L'attività scientifica nel primo Settecento", in: G. Micheli (Hrsg.): *Storia d'Italia. Annali 3: Scienza e Tecnica nella cultura e nella società dal Rinascimento a oggi*, Torino 1980, S. 482–485.

Brüderkriegen verwüsteten Europa zu errichten. Von römischer Seite existierte vielleicht die Hoffnung, durch eine mögliche Konversion eines der einflussreichsten Denker des Kontinents einen neuen Sieg zu erringen; zudem könnte er es ermöglichen, mit seiner Philosophie eine Alternative für die kartesianischen Doktrinen anzubieten, die sich immer weiter auch in katholischem Umfeld verbreiteten; so war die Hoffnung, die triumphierende Machtdemonstration zu wiederholen, die die Konversion der Prinzessin Cristina aus Schweden für alle anderen Europäischen Staaten bedeutet hatte. Der veränderte geschichtliche Kontext jedoch führte zur vollständigen Auflösung der Voraussetzungen, in denen die Begegnung zwischen Leibniz und der ewigen Stadt entstanden war.

Es ist erschütternd zu bemerken, wie schnell Rom und das Papsttum in den letzten Jahren des 17. Jahrhunderts nebensächlich werden, in einem europäischen Gleichgewicht, in dem Rom und das Papsttum gänzlich unbedeutend geworden ist: Der Wille der Kirche, durch das repressive Instrument der Inquisition am Ende des Jahrhunderts die eigene hegemoniale Rolle stärken zu wollen, wird sich als fataler Fehler erweisen:[13]

> „es wäre mir schon längst wunderlich vorgekommen, daß man zwischen den Irrtümern und Lastern einen Unterschied gemacht habe und daß der Geist der katholischen Religion gegen die Lehren, welche mit ihren Kirchensatzungen nicht übereinkommen, mehr eifere als gegen das unordentliche Leben."[14]

Leibniz war Zeuge des Übergangs vom innovationsorientierten Papst Innozenz XI. zur Wahl von Alexander VIII. (dem Venezianer Piero Ottoboni), der sich als Wärter einer sehr geschlossenen Orthodoxie erwies; weil er den Anfragen des französischen Königs Ludwig XIV. nachkommen wollte und gleichzeitig Kaiser Leopold I. nicht vor den Kopf stoßen wollte, untergrub er definitiv die Rolle und das Prestige der Kirche auf dem europäischen Kontinent. Unter seinem Pontifikat trat die Offensive gegen die Quietisten ein, mit

---

[13] Vgl. C. Donati: „La Chiesa di Roma tra antico regime e riforme ecclesiastiche", in: *Storia d'Italia* (= *Annali* 9), Torino 1986, S. 733.
[14] „[...] j'avois toujours trouvé fort étrange la différence que l'on fait entre les erreurs et les vices, et de voir l'esprit de la Religion Catholique bien plus contraire aux Dogmes qui ne s'accomodent pas à ses Décision, qu'à la vie déréiglée." P. Bayle: *Pensées diverses, écrites à un docteur de Sorbonne, a l'occasion de la cométe qui parut au mois de décembre 1680*, Rotterdam 1683, § CXCIX, S. 618; dt. Uebrs. *Verschiedene einem Doktor der Sorbonne mitgeteilte Gedanken über den Kometen, der im Monat Dezember 1680 erschienen ist*, Leipzig 1975, http://www.zeno.org/Lesesaal/N/9781484030677?page=298.

der Verurteilung des Werks *Guìa Espiritual* von Miguel de Molinos (ein vorsichtig gewürdigter Text von Innozenz XI.) aufgrund eines besonderen Dekrets des Heiligen Amtes gegen die sogenannte ‚philosophische Sünde', das schon 20 Jahre zuvor zur Verurteilung der kartesianischen Philosophie geführt hatte.[15]

4. Rückkehr in die Heimat

Zurück am Hannoverschen Hof gewannen auch die Probleme des päpstlichen Hofes für den deutschen Philosophen immer mehr an Distanz und verblassten; aus dem Norden Deutschlands betrachtet erschienen sie wenig bedeutsam, sowohl von den diskutierten Inhalten (wie zum Beispiel dass nur noch von den Römern als Problem wahrgenommene, von allen anderen als selbstverständlich angesehene kopernikanische Modell und die Voraussetzungen der galileischen und kartesianischen Physik); als auch die tatsächlich unzeitgemäß erscheinende Möglichkeit einer Versöhnung der Kirchen (nachdem die Entscheidungen des neuen Papstes allen Perspektiven für versöhnende Schritte die Türen geschlossen hatten).

Nicht aus Zufall war das letzte, mit den römischen Gesprächspartnern diskutierte Thema der Wechsel zum gregorianischen Kalender; bei dieser Fragestellung opponierten die reformierten Staaten sehr stark, da sie sich nicht der ‚römischen' Entscheidung anpassen wollten; der Kalender wurde schließlich nach vielen Jahrzehnten des Zögerns akzeptiert. In Deutschland, wie in der Mehrheit der nicht katholischen Staaten, trat der neue Kalender zwischen 1699 und 1700 in Kraft und von diesem Zeitpunkt an ging auch die Korrespondenz zwischen Leibniz und den römischen Gesprächspartnern zurück; in den Briefen der letzten Lebensjahre des deutschen Philosophen gibt es keine Spur dieser Gesprächspartner mit Ausnahme von einigen kurzen Schreiben an Bianchini.

In einigen Briefen von Leibniz auf dem Rückweg, nachdem er den römischen Aufenthalt hinter sich gelassen hatte, kann man insgesamt den Sinn

---

[15] Donec corrigantur. Dec. 20. November 1663, in: *Index Librorum Prohibitorum*, Romæ, M.CC.LVIII. (1758), p. 46. Für die Zensuren der cartesianischen Werke vgl. J.-R. Armogathe/V. Carraud: „La première condamnation des Œuvres de Descartes, d'après des documents inédits aux Archives du Saint-Office", in: *Nouvelles de la République des Lettres* II (2001), S. 103–137; s. auch C. Carella: „Le Meditationes cartesiane ‚Amstelodami 1709' e la condanna del 1720" in: *Nouvelles de la République des Lettres* I (2008), S. 111–120.

des römischen Aufenthalts herauslesen. In der ersten Woche im März 1690 unterbrach Leibniz seinen venezianischen Aufenthalt, um die Orte aufzusuchen, die dem Haus der Este gehörten, wie zum Beispiel Monselice oder die Abtei der Kamaldulenser in Santa Maria delle Carceri, die der Papst Alexander VIII. den Venezianern abgetreten hatte. Nachdem er in die Lagunenstadt zurückgekehrt war, schrieb Leibniz am 22. März 1690 einen Brief an Albrecht Philipp von dem Busche, dem Hannoveraner Finanzminister, indem er ihn darüber informierte, im Klosterarchiv „des preuves indubitables, concernant les deux S^{me} maisons de Brunsvic et de Modena ont connexion ensable" gefunden zu haben.[16] Dem heutigen Leser liefern die Dokumente, viel mehr als einen definitiven Beweis der Verbindungen zwischen den deutschen und italienischen Adelsgeschlechtern, das Zeugnis der Methode historischer Forschung, die Leibniz auch in seinem Brief (auf Italienisch!) dem Herzog Francesco II. von Modena aus Anlass seiner Ankunft in der Stadt am 1. Januar 1690 aufgezeigte/empfahl:

> „[…] das beste dessen, was man sich erhoffen kann für mein Vorhaben in Italien, muss man in diesen Blättern finden, wo die Archive Licht bringen bis in die tiefste Vergangenheit der Este."[17]

Und im Folgenden erläutert er die moderne historiographische Methode, die auf der Grundlage von Zeugnissen arbeitet, und die er von den Geschichten unterscheidet, die zwar formschön, aber ohne objektive Überprüfung geschrieben sind:

> „[…] Pigna [es handelt sich hier um den Humanisten und Historiker Giovanni Battista Pigna, der im 16. Jahrhundert in Ferrara tätig war] hat seine Historie, wunderschön im Ausdruck und wegen der edlen Worte, aber im Übrigen konform mit der Art des Schreibens aus seinem Jahrhundert verfasst, wo es noch nicht üblich war, Urkunden, Begründungen und ähnliche, nicht gemeine Einzelheiten zu veröffentlichen, die unser Jahrhundert verlangt um Schmuck zu bieten und Grundlage der Historie."[18]

---

[16] Vgl., A I, 5, 550.
[17] „[…] il migliore di quello che si può sperar in Italia per il disegno mio, si deve trovar in queste Carte, dove gli archivi contengono lumi delle più remote antichità estensi"; A I, 5, 499.
[18] Vgl. ebd.

All diese Themen nimmt Leibniz in der letzten Phase seines Venedigaufenthalts vor dem definitiven Aufbruch nach Österreich und Deutschland in einem Brief an den Hofkanzler von Modena Camillo Marchesini wieder auf.[19]

Leibniz verließ Venedig direkt nach Ostern; am Gründonnerstag bereitete er sich für die bald bevorstehende Rückreise vor und zog zugleich auch Bilanz in Bezug auf seinen langen Italienaufenthalt; zwei wichtige Briefe schrieb er an diesem Donnerstag, 23. März 1690, und verschickte sie in einem einzigen Umschlag an seinen Freund und Förderer Ernst von Hessen-Rheinfels: der erste Brief war an Antoine Arnauld gerichtet, der letzte Brief übrigens an den französischen Jansenisten; der zweite war direkt an Hessen-Rheinfels adressiert. Die beiden Schreiben zusammen ergeben ein präzises Bild von Leibniz' eigener Evaluierung seiner langen Italienreise.

Leibniz erinnert im Brief an Arnauld das Interesse und die Wertschätzung, die ihm während seines Aufenthalts in Rom entgegengekommen waren und die ungewöhnlich offenen Meinungen, die er unerwartet in der Stadt des Papstes vorgefunden hatte. Im zweiten Teil des Briefes berührt der Autor die wichtigsten Themen seiner eigenen philosophischen und wissenschaftlichen Ausarbeitungen, die er während seines römischen Aufenthalts diskutiert und vertieft hatte: Der Körper ist nichts anderes als eine Ansammlung von einfachen Substanzen, die Vereinigung der Seele mit dem Körper besteht aus deren perfekter, reziproker Übereinstimmung. Jene schrittweise Virtualisierung der Beziehung zwischen Körper und Seele, charakteristisch für das Spätwerk des deutschen Philosophen, scheint noch fern.

Die Betrachtungen über das Leben in Rom erhalten ganz andere Schattierungen in dem Brief an Hessen-Rheinfels, in dem sich Leibniz in einem visionären und ironischen Ton ausdrückt: Es beeindruckt die Klarheit, mit der der deutsche Philosoph die Veränderungen analysiert, die sich in Rom beim Übergang vom Papsttum von Innozenz XI. zu dem von Alexander VIII. ereignen und die enttäuschten Erwartungen in letzterem, der sich selbst auch als Förderer/Beschützer der meisten in der ewigen Stadt anwesenden Intellektuellen darstellte.[20]

---

[19] Siehe Marchesini-Briefe von 24. Februar und 22. März 1690, vgl. ebd., 533, 551 und folgende.
[20] Alexander VIII. (d.h. Piero Ottoboni) war der Beschützer der Accademia dei Lincei gewesen; Francesco Bianchini, einer der bedeutendsten Wissenschaftler in Rom und Leibniz-Korrespondent, war lange einer der engsten Mitarbeiter des Papstes.

„La Cour de Roma – schreibt Leibniz – s'est changée entierment pendant que j'y estois par la mort du Pape, et par la succession d'un sujet dont les maximes sont toutes opposèes."[21]

Leibniz war sich der Rolle wohl bewusst, die der Papst in der Krise Ende des 17. Jahrhunderts hätte einnehmen können, genauso wie auch der verlorenen Gelegenheiten, um wieder ein für den christlichen Glauben günstigeres Klima in Europa zu schaffen; während seines Aufenthalts erschienen ihm Rom und der päpstliche Hof als äußerst ausgezeichnetes Heer im Dienste der Wissenschaft und des Fortschritts im Namen des Glaubens, mit den verschiedenen religiösen Orden als Legionen.

„Pour moy je voudrois que les moines fussent conservès mais bien employés. Et si j'estois Pape je voudrois distribuer entre eux les recherches de la Verité qui servent à la gloire de Dieu, et les oeuvres de la Charité qui servent au salut et bien des hommes."[22]

Das Gefühl der Frustration jedoch und die unausweichliche Enttäuschung in den Absichten und nur wenige Jahre zuvor gereiften Hoffnungen in Hinblick auf die Möglichkeit, die Trennungen und Spannungen zu überwinden, die den europäischen Kontinent in Unruhe hielten, tritt deutlich am Ende des Briefes an seinen Freund ans Licht:

„[…] je me demeure d'accord, que ce ne sont que des idées divertissantes. Mais aussy c'est de quoy nous avons bien besoin à present dans ces temps malheureux."[23]

Leibniz überschritt die Grenze am Brenner an den letzten Tagen im März, schrieb am 30. März aus Innsbruck einen Brief an Magliabechi und erinnerte an seine italienischen Freunde, von denen er „stete Erinnerung mit mir [sich] nach Deutschland trage", und er erinnerte an die bedeutenden Hinweise über die verwandtschaftlichen Verbindungen zwischen den Häusern der Este und Braunschweigs, die er entdeckt hatte.[24]

Im Juni 1690 kehrte Leibniz schließlich nach Hannover und zu den täglichen Geschäften des Hoflebens zurück. Eine Antwort von Hessen-Rheinfels

---

[21] Leibniz an Hessen-Rheinfels, Venedig, 23 März 1690; A I, 5, 556.
[22] Ebd., 557.
[23] Ebd., 558.
[24] „Memoriam duraturam mecum in Germaniam ferre". Leibniz an Magliabechi, 30 April 1690; ebd., 563.

auf den direkt nach seiner Rückkehr verfassten Brief, führte ihn zur Sprödigkeit der religiösen Wortgefechte Europas zurück, die – nach Wiederaufnahme der Verfolgungen der Jansenisten – seinen Freund Arnauld zur Flucht nach Holland gezwungen hatten: „J'ay appris avec beaucoup de douleur que Mr Arnauld est si mal traité par cex qui le devroient cherir."[25] Von den Hoffnungen und der Illusion der Versöhnung in Rom blieben nur noch die Enttäuschung und eine ferne Erinnerung.

---

[25] Leibniz an Hessen-Rheinfels, Ende Juni 1690; ebd., 590.

Francesco Bianchini und die römische Kalenderkongregation

Margherita Palumbo (Rom)

Bekanntlich kam Leibniz im Mai 1689 in Rom an.[1] In der Stadt, in der die Kopernikanische Lehre im Jahre 1616 verdammt worden war und 1634 der *Dialogo dei due massimi sistemi* in den *Index librorum prohibitorum* aufgenommen worden war, fand er mathematische Akademien, schöne Galerien und Bibliotheken, Naturaliensammlungen, gelehrte Zeitschriften und lebhafte Gesprächspartner, darunter den jungen Veroneser Francesco Bianchini, der in jener Zeit ein protegé des Kardinals Pietro Ottoboni war.[2]

Trotz der oben genannten Verdammung des Heliozentrismus war in Rom das Interesse an Astronomie und allgemein an Sternbeobachtungen so weit verbreitet, dass es die Ebene der Gelehrten überschritt. Leibniz konnte Paläste besuchen, in denen vermögende Adelige und Prälaten Sonnenuhren, Observatorien und Fresken als Lob der Astronomie herstellen lassen hatten: die gemalte Loge in der Residenz des Marquise Mariano Patrizi und die Sonnenuhrgalerie im Palazzo Spada seien hier als treffende Beispiele einer Verbindung zwischen Kunstpatronage und Visualisierung des astronomischen Wissens genannt.[3]

Ab 1698 blickte Leibniz wieder mit Nachdruck auf Rom: nicht nur wegen der gleichzeitige Wiederaufnahme der Religionsgespräche, sondern auch wegen der möglichen Einführung des gregorianischen Kalenders in den protestantischen Territorien des Reiches, eine heikle Frage nicht nur auf rein wissenschaftlicher Ebene. Immerhin bot sie Leibniz die Gelegenheit zur Wiederaufnahme des brieflichen Austausches mit Bianchini. Kurz nach seiner Abreise aus der päpstlichen Stadt war Leibniz in Korrespondenz mit dem Italiener getreten, allerdings brach der Austausch schon im September 1690 ab. In

---

[1] Für Leibniz' Aufenthalt in Rom, vgl. André Robinet: *G. W. Leibniz Iter Italicum (Mars 1689–Mars 1690). La dynamique de la République des Lettres* (= Accademia toscana di scienze e lettere „La Colombaria". Studi 90), Florenz 1988.
[2] Zu Francesco Bianchini vgl. Valentin Kockel/Brigitte Solch (Hrsg.): *Francesco Bianchini, 1662–1729 und die europäische gelehrte Welt um 1700* (= Colloquia Augustana 21), Berlin 2005; Brigitte Solch: *Francesco Bianchini (1662–1729) und die Anfänge öffentlicher Museen in Rom* (= Kunstwissenschaftliche Studien 134), München 2007; Luca Ciancio/Gian Paolo Romagnani (Hrsg.): *Unità del sapere molteplicità dei saperi. Francesco Bianchini (1662–1729) tra natura, storia e religione*, Verona 2010.
[3] Zu diesem Punkt vgl. Ulrike Feist: *Sonne, Mond und Venus. Visualisierungen astronomischen Wissens im frühneuzeitlichen Rom* (= Actus et Imago 10), Berlin 2013.

seinem ersten Brief an Bianchini vom 18. März 1690 aus Venedig hatte Leibniz hierbei gewünscht, dass „in Te si vacat novum spero Tychonem vel Hevelium aliquando habebimus,"[4] und inzwischen hatte sich sein Korrespondent einen Namen als Wissenschaftler und Antiquar in ganz Europa gemacht.

Am 24. September 1699 hatte das *Corpus evangelicorum* des Regensburger Reichstages zum 1. März 1700 eine Kalenderreform vorgesehen, welche die seit 1583 bestehende zehntägige Zeitdifferenz zwischen den katholischen und evangelischen Reichsterritorien beenden sollte. Die Frage wurde heftig in zeitgenössischen Korrespondenzen diskutiert, zahlreiche Flugblätter wurden gedruckt und viele Petitionen an den Reichstag adressiert.[5] Die Frage war an sich sehr relevant und so waren es die politischen und konfessionellen Implikationen.

Die Protestanten wollten bzw. konnten den Gregorianischen Kalender nicht ohne weiteres übernehmen. Genau wie im 16. Jahrhundert war es immerhin eine Frage von Macht und Primat, oder – wie in einigen Pamphleten zu lesen ist – von *Directorium*, und so wurde es auch von beiden Seiten – Katholiken wie Protestanten – wahrgenommen.

Von den Regensburger Debatten über die Kalenderkorrekturen schrieb Leibniz an Jacob Hendrik Hildebrand, dem schwedischen Gesandten in Wien und bemerkte, dass die deutschen Fürsten auf jeden Fall eine „maniere qui garde le *decorum*" finden sollten,[6] selbst wenn der Gregorianische *Almanac* der bessere sei und vieles erleichtere. Vorsicht sei deshalb angebracht, die Berechnung müssten gründlich geprüft werden und regelmäßige Kontrolle stattfinden, weil „on n'est pas asseuré, que le calcul Gregorien répondra tousjours au ciel."[7] Darüber hinaus, „il y a des disputes dans l'Eglise Romaine même sur le temps de la Pâque qu'il faudroit examiner."[8] Die Diskussion hatte die Grenzen des Reiches schnell überschritten und zahlreiche Spuren der Debatten sowie der *Conclusa* haben sich bis in die Korrespondenz der Päpstlichen Segreteria di Stato mit Wien hinterlassen. Die Römische Kurie war selbstverständlich unter Druck, besonders nachdem Frankreich Stellung dazu bezogen hatte; auf Befehl Ludwigs XIV., nahm der berühmte Astronom und Erschaffer

---

[4] Leibniz an Bianchini, Venedig, 18. März 1690, A III, 4, N. 244, 481.
[5] Dazu vgl. Edith Koller: *Strittige Zeiten. Kalenderreformen im Alten Reich 1582–1700* (= Pluralisierung und Autorität 41), Berlin/Boston 2014.
[6] Leibniz an Jacob Hendrik Hildebrand, [Hannover, 12. Juni 1699]; A I, 17, N. 162, 253.
[7] Ebd.
[8] Ebd.

der Meridianenlinie in San Petronio in Bologna, Gian Domenico Cassini Kontakt mit Rom auf. Im Mai 1700 schrieb Cassini an einige Kardinäle und schickte Denkschriften und Berechnungen und im Vatikanischen Geheimarchiv befinden sich beispielsweise Briefe von Cassini über die fehlerhaften Berechnungen des Jesuiten Cristoforo Clavio und eine handschriftliche Kopie seiner *Tabula paschalis iuxta decretum Gregorii XIII supputata* im Nachlass des mächtigen Kardinals Gaspare Carpegna.[9]

In diesem Rahmen bemüht sich Leibniz sehr intensiv – und tatsächlich intensiver als andere protestantische Gelehrte – darum, die katholische Seite zu einer erneuten Reform des Gregorianischen Kalenders zu bewegen.[10] Deshalb schrieb er auch nach zehnjährigem beidseitigem Schweigen am 5. März 1700 an Bianchini und verlangte – im vollen Bewusstsein ob der heiklen Frage – die Kalenderreform *caute et sine strepitu* zu behandeln.[11] Diese Diskretion veranlasste sicherlich auch Bianchini dazu, sich vorsichtig zu verhalten und seine Briefe an Leibniz an einen Italiener und Katholiken, an den Abt Giuseppe Guidi zu adressieren. Oder, „si quid aliud mihi destinare velis, quod cursori publico non conveniat" konnte er Bianchini als Vermittlung den Wiener Georg Ludwig von Offeln, in jener Zeit in Rom, nennen.[12]

Am 27. September 1700 starb Innocenz XII., und am 23. November wurde der Kardinal Gianfrancesco Albani als Clemens XI. gewählt. Anfang September des nächsten Jahres setzte der neue Papst eine Kommission zur Überprüfung der Genauigkeit des Gregorianischen Kalenders bezüglich der Berechnung der beweglichen Feste, vor allem des Osterfests ein und verlangte eventuelle Verbesserungen. Von der Einrichtung dieser Kongregation berichtetendie deutschen Gazetten, wie die *Historischen Remarques*, am 1. November, und später im Dezember 1701 der *Monatliche Staats-Spiegel*:

---

[9] Vgl. z. B. *Città del Vaticano, Archivio Segreto Vaticano, Fondo Carpegna, Varia*, Bd. 87, N. 6. und N. 7.
[10] Zu Leibniz' Rolle in dieser Auseinandersetzung vgl. Peter Aufgebauer: „Zwischen Astronomie und Politik: Gottfried Wilhelm Leibniz und der ‚Verbesserte Kalender' der deutschen Protestanten", in: *Niedersächsisches Jahrbuch* 81 (2009), S. 385–404; Charlotte Wahl: „ad harmoniam quae voluntaria et deliberata habeatur." Zu Leibniz' Bemühungen um eine interkonfessionelle Kalenderreform", in: Wenchao Li (Hrsg.): *„Für unser Glück oder das Glück anderer". Vorträge des X. Internationalen Leibniz-Kongresses*, Bd. IV, Hildesheim 2016, S. 549–561.
[11] Leibniz an Francesco Bianchini, Hannover, 5. März 1700, A III, 8, N. 134, 161, „Haec ego tibi fiducia prudentiae Tuae; satis enim intelligis rem caute et sine strepitu esse tractandam."
[12] Ebd.

"Ihro Päpst. Heil. haben ein Collegium von 12. Mathematicis angeordnet, um den Gregorianisce Calen. verbessern, und wie solches am besten zu bewircken, deren und anderer Gelehrten Gutachten zu vornehmen. Die Cardinale Pamphilius und Norris sind die Vornehmsten in solchem Collegio, und der Päpstliche Cammerer Bianchini vertrit dabey die Stelle eines Secretarii."[13]

Die Zahl der Mitglieder dieses *Collegium* – die Congregatio Calendarii – stieg kurz danach auf fünfzehn an. Die Kalenderkongregation stand unter der Leitung des Kardinals Enrico Noris, der zwei weitere Kardinäle – Benedetto Pamphili und Tommaso Maria Ferrari – zur Seite hatte. Der Präfekt Enrico Noris, den Leibniz in Rom sehr geschätzt hatte, wurde geleitet von einem tiefen Interesse für die *Sacra Chronologia*, immerhin hatte er schon 1691 das Werk *De Paschalis Latinorum cyclo* veröffentlicht.[14] Die übrigen Mitglieder waren Theologen, Gelehrte, Mathematiker und Astronomen: Lorenzo Zaccagni, Bibliothekar oder *primus custos* der Vaticana, der Benediktiner Giovanni Battista de Miro, zweiter Bibliothekar in der Vaticana, Domenico Quarteroni, Professor für Mathematik am Archiginnasio der Sapienza, Vitale Giordani, der berühmte Autor des *Euclide restituto*,[15] der Jesuit Antonio Baldigiani, Professor für Mathematik und Moraltheologie im Collegio Romano, sein Ordensbruder Francesco Eschinardi, der Verfasser eines *Cursus physicomathematicus* von 1689.[16] Der Abt Filippo Della Torre, künftiger Bishof von Adria und in jener Zeit Auditor und Bibliothekar des Kardinals Giuseppe Renato Imperiali, der Augustiner Guillaume Bonjour, der genau 1701 das Werk *Calendarium Romanum chronologorum causa constructum* in Rom veröffentlicht[17] und im Vorwort eine Geschichte des Kalenderwesens skizziert und die *accuratio* und *certitudo*, des Gregorianischen Kalender sehr gelobt hatte. Außerdem Francesco de Rossi, Pfarrer der Kirche S. Salvatore a Ponte Rotto in Trastevere, der Jurist und Astronomie-Amateur Flaminio Mezzavacca aus Bologna, und der junge Giacomo Filippo Maraldi, Cassinis Neffe. Als letztes Mitglied

---

[13] *Monatliche Staats-Spiegel*, Dezember 1701, S. 98.
[14] Enrico Noris: *Annus et epochae Syromacedonum in vetustis urbium Syriae nummis praesertim mediceis expositae additis Fastis consularibus anonymi omnium optimis. Accesserunt nuper dissertationes De paschali Latinorum cyclo annorum LXXXIV. Ac Ravennate annorum XCV*, Florentiae 1691.
[15] Vitale Giordani: *Euclide restituto overo Gli antichi elementi geometrici ristaurati, e facilitati*, Roma 1680.
[16] Francesco Eschinardi: *Cursus physicomathematicus [...] Pars prima. De cosmographia. Tomus primus continens duplicem tractatum. Primum de sphaera. Secundum de astronomia*, Romae 1689.
[17] Guillaume Bonjour: *Calendarium Romanum chronologorum causa constructum cum gemino epactarum dispositu, ad novilunia civilia*, Romae 1701.

ist nun Francesco Bianchini zu nennen, der zum Sekretär der Kongregation ernannt wurde. Bianchini war ein *protegé* von Papst Clemens XI sowie von Enrico Noris. Kurz nach der Wahl von Papst Albani wurde er zu dessen *cameriere di onore* ernannt. Die Übernahme des Sekretariats der Kalenderkongregation markiert den Höhepunkt in seinem von päpstlicher Patronage bestimmten Werdegang und gilt als entscheidender Schritt in seiner Karriere und für sein internationales Renommee als Astronom.

Die personelle Zusammensetzung und die deklarierten Ziele der Kalenderkongregation waren – zumindest auf dem Papier – vielversprechend. Einige Mitglieder waren Leibniz noch aus seiner Zeit in Rom wohl bekannt. Durch seinen Neffen hatte Cassini bereits im Oktober 1701 eine Zusammenfassung der verschiedenen Gründe für die Korrektur des Kalenders nach Rom kommen lassen.[18] Und auch Leibniz sandte dem Präfekten Noris und dem Sekretär Bianchini Berechnungen und Überlegungen von Mathematikern und Astronomen, wie Samuel Reyher und Joachim Tiede.[19] Zudem schaltete sich im März 1702 auch Christoph Schrader ein, der erwog, wie „in diesem Sinne […] die Berliner Akademie auch beitragen" konnte.[20] Anscheinend waren die Voraussetzungen für eine erfolgreiche – sogar interkonfessionelle – Kooperation unter Wissenschaftlern da.

1702 konstruierte Bianchini eine Meridianlinie in der von Michelangelo in den früheren Diokletiansthermen errichteten Kirche S. Maria degli Angeli in Rom. Das Instrument wurde zu Ehren von Papst Clemens XI. als *Linea Clementina* bezeichnet und Giacomo Filippo Maraldi, der Neffe Cassinis, assistierte Bianchini bei den Berechnungen. Die offizielle Darstellung dieses Pracht-Instruments fand in Anwesenheit des Papstes am 6. Oktober statt: das Sonnenlicht fällt auf die verlaufende Meridianlinie zur Mittagszeit durch ein kleines Loch in dem an der Wand angebrachten Papstwappen.[21] Es wurde eine

---

[18] Vgl. z. B. Cassinis Brief an Bianchini, Paris, 3. Oktober 1701, Rom, Biblioteca Vallicelliana (= Vallicelliana), ms. U 16, Bl. 435r. „Ho ristretti in un foglio i motivi della correzzione, che le sara communicata dal Signor Maraldi che lo metteva in netto havendolo fatto scrivere in fretta all'aviso datomi della prossima congregazione, a cui potrebbe servire se lo stimava opportuno". Über Bianchinis Nachlass in der Vallicelliana vgl. Ugo Baldini: „La rete di corrispondenza astronomica di Francesco Bianchini: un'analisi del fondo Vallicelliano", in: Luca Ciancio/Gian Paolo Romagnani (Hrsg.): *Unità de sapere molteplicità dei saperi*, 2010, S. 75–99.
[19] Vgl. Leibniz' Briefe an Joachim Tiede, Hannover, 16. November 1701; A III, 8, N. 311 und an Bianchini, Hannover, 27. Dezember 1701; ebd., N. 319.
[20] Christoph Schrader an Leibniz, Regensburg, 20. März 1702; A I, 20, N. 482, 845.
[21] Für eine Beschreibung der Meridianlinie in S. Maria degli Angeli, vgl. Bianchinis Bericht vom 6. Dezember 1701, Vallicelliana, ms. U 20, Bl. 12–14. Vgl. auch John L. Heilbron: *The*

Gedenkmünze mit dem Profilportrait Clemens' XI. geprägt und 1703 veröffentlichte Bianchini sein *De nummo et gnomone Clementino* mit der Beschreibung dieses wunderbaren Instruments, das in sich Astronomie, heilige NG: heilige oder sakrale Chronologie und römischen Kalender vereinige.[22]

Die Ergebnisse der Beobachtungen wichen allerdings nicht weit genug von den im Gregorianischen Kalender definierten Größen ab, um die Osterberechnung tatsächlich verändern zu müssen. Bianchini bevorzugte die zyklische Bestimmung des Ostertermins, die er allerdings verbessern wollte und zu diesem Zweck einen neuen 1184-jährigen Zyklus vorschlug, der jedoch nicht angenommen wurde. Die Kalenderkongregation brach die Arbeiten kurz und recht unerwartet nach dem Tode des Kardinals Noris im Februar 1704 ab. Ein Schlussbericht wurde nicht verfasst und merkwürdigerweise hat die Tätigkeit dieser römischen Kongregation auch keine Spuren im Vatikanischen Geheimarchiv hinterlassen. Weder sind Aktenkonvolute nachweisbar, noch die von der Kalenderkongregation verfassten und bei ihr eingehenden Relationen, Gutachten, Berichte und Berechnungen systematisch erhalten. Es scheint, dass sich die Kalenderkongregation im Bau einer schönen Marmor-Meridianlinie mit Papstwappen erschöpft hatte.

Danach wurde in Rom nicht mehr über den Kalender diskutiert und auch die Briefe zwischen Leibniz und Bianchini wurden immer seltener. 1705 bedankte er sich bei seinem Korrespondenten für das Geschenk des *De kalendario et cyclo Caesaris* von 1703.[23] Bianchini schrieb noch im September 1707,[24] während Leibniz' letzter Brief auf den 17. Januar 1713 datiert ist. Leibniz teilte aus Wien mit, dass er eine neue *machina astronomica* gesehen hätte, die „Gregoriano etiam calendario subsidia vel supplementa" anbieten

---

Sun in the Church. Cathedrals as Solar Observatories, Cambridge, MA/London 1999, S. 144–175; Ettore Curi: „Francesco Bianchini e la meridiana di Santa Maria degli Angeli", in: *Atti e memorie dell'Accademia di Agricoltura, Scienze e Lettere di Verona* 181.2004/05 (2009), S. 435–450.
[22] Francesco Bianchini: *De kalendario et cyclo Caesaris ac De paschali canone s. Hippolyti martyris dissertationes duae [...] His accessit enarratio per epistolam ad amicum De nummo et gnomone Clementino*, Romae 1703.
[23] Leibniz an Bianchini, 28. Dezember 1705, in: Enrico Celani (Hrsg.): „L'epistolario di Monsignor Francesco Bianchini Veronese. Memoria ed indici", in: *Archivio Veneto* N.S. 18 (1888), S. 182f.
[24] Bianchini an Leibniz, Rom, 1. September 1707, in: Johann Georg Heinrich Feder (Hrsg.): *Commercii epistolici Leibnitiani typis nondum vulgati selecta specimina*, Hannover 1805, S. 335–341.

könne.²⁵ Eine Antwort von Bianchini kam nie. Der Italiener war auf seiner Reise nach Frankreich und England. Im April 1713 schrieb Leibniz noch an Johann Bernoulli und bat ihn um Neuigkeiten über Bianchini – „mihi olim Amicus, praeclarus in Astronomia et Antiquitate."²⁶ Spätere Nachrichten von Pierre Varignon vom Juli 1715 haben Leibniz sicherlich befremdet:

> „Bianchini ne nous a dit rien du dessein que le pape Innocent XII et en suite celui d'a present avaient eu de faire faire une revision du calendrier gregorien; on y a travaille quelque temps à Rome dans une Congregation dont etait M Maraldi qui se trouvait pour lors en ce pays-la [...] mais le but est demeuré sans etre achevé et sans qu'on sache pourquoi, à ce qu a dit M. Maraldi."²⁷

1703 – eben zu der Zeit, als Bianchini seinen Prachtband über die *Linea Clementina* veröffentlicht hatte – erschien in den *Mémoires de Trévoux* ein Brief des Mathematikers und damaligen Mitglieds der Ciampini Academia Physico-Mathematica, Francesco Serra, der gelegentlich für die Kalender-Kongregation als Berater gearbeitet hatte.²⁸ Er kritisiert gründlich die Haltung des *Collegium*, und besonders die von Bianchini, an der man den päpstlichen Willen habe ablesen können. Clemens XI. wollte nur Berechnungen überprüfen und keinesfalls eine Revolution des Kalenderwesens einführen. Serra erwähnt auch Streitigkeiten und Zwiespalt innerhalb der Kongregation.

1704 widersprach Bianchini zwar Serras Kritik und Verdächtigungen in seinem *Considerazioni teoriche e pratiche intorno al trasporto della Colonna di Antonino Pio*,²⁹ doch die Dokumentation in seinem Nachlass in der Biblioteca Vallicelliana in Rom sowie in der Biblioteca Capitolare in Verona strafen ihn Lügen.

In Deutschland war die Diskussion um die Kalenderreform eine interkonfessionelle und auch an der Kurie wurde sie als solche unter Berücksichtigung aller davon ausgehenden Gefahren wahrgenommen. In seinem *Entwurff der Conciliation des alten und neuen Calender-Styli* des Jahres 1699

---

²⁵ Leibniz an Bianchini, Wien, 17. Januar 1713, in: Enrico Celani (Hrsg.): *L'epistolario di Monsignor Francesco Bianchini*, S.185f.
²⁶ Leibniz an Johann Bernoulli, 26. April 1713; GM III, 906.
²⁷ Pierre Varignon an Leibniz, 20. Juli 1715; GM IV, 201.
²⁸ „Extrait d'une Lettre de M. François Serra, l'un des Consulteurs de la Congregation du Calendrier, à M. Bianchini Secretaire de la même Congregation: du seize Avril 1703", in: *Mémoires pour l'Histoire des Sciences & des Beaux Arts. Août 1703*, Trévoux-Paris 1703, S. 1511–1514.
²⁹ Francesco Bianchini: *Considerazioni teoriche e pratiche intorno al trasporto della Colonna di Antonino Pio collocata in Monte Citorio*, Roma 1704.

präsentierte Erhard Weigel seinen Plan für eine überkonfessionelle Astronomie und sprach von einem Neu-Conciliation-Kalender. Voraussetzung einer überkonfessionellen Astronomie ist, nach Weigels Absicht, die Gründung eines Collegiums von evangelischen und katholischen Mathematikern, die kollegialerweise astronomische Beobachtungen durchführen sollten.[30] Kalenderreform galt notwendigerweise – wie Leibniz im Dezember 1699 an Anton Ulrich schrieb – als „Matiere demymathematique",[31] d. h. als eine Frage die „en meme temps sur les canons de l'Eglise et sur les dogmes de l'Astronomie" zu regeln sei.[32] Für die Kurie war die Kalenderreform erst recht eine *Matiere demymathematique*, immerhin handelt es sich um ein milieu, in dem *Conciliatio* ein sehr verdächtiges Wort war, wie der Verlauf der Religionskolloquien in Leibniz' Zeit deutlich belegt.

Wie schon angedeutet, waren die Mitglieder der Kalender-Kongregation ausgezeichnete Mathematiker, Astronomen, Experten in Chronologie, Kirchengeschichte, usw. Es gibt aber einen andere Aspekt zu beachten: die meisten von ihnen waren zugleich – mit verschiedenen Rang, Aufgaben und Verantwortungen – Mitglieder einer anderen und viel wichtigeren Kongregation der römischen Kurie: des Heiligen Offiziums. Tommaso Maria Ferrari und Enrico Noris waren beide Kardinal-Inquisitoren. Das Heilige Offizium konnte, selbst indirekt, nicht bei der Klärung einer heiklen Frage fehlen. Immerhin bedeutete diese Materie, die im Wesentlichen als *demimathematique* wahrgenommen wurde, vor dem Hintergrund der interkonfessionellen Lösungsansätze in Deutschland, dass man bei der Behandlung dieses Problems im Umkehrschluss Verkehr mit Häretikern zu pflegen hatte.

Als Zensoren im Dienste des Heiligen Offizium sowie der Indexkongregation waren auch andere Mitglieder der Kalenderkongregation tätig, wie z. B. Lorenzo Zaccagni, Giovanni Battista de Miro, Domenico Quarteroni. Und eine lange zensorische und sogar intransigente Tätigkeit ist auch für Francesco Bianchini dokumentiert. Keine Überraschung: Das gelehrte Milieu hat in Rom nicht zufällig einen Doppelstatus gehabt und zugleich eine doppelte Funktion ausgeübt: die Bemerkung betrifft auch andere Wissenschaftler

---

[30] Erhard Weigel: *Entwurff der Conciliation des alten und neuen Calender-Styli, Welcher gestalt solche im Novembr. Ao. 1699. anzustellen ist [...] Nebst einer kurtzen hierzu diensamen Instruction*, Regenburg 1699. Vgl. dazu Katharina Habermann: „Die Kalenderreform von 1700 in persönlichen Korrespondenzen und publizistischer Debatte", in: Li (Hrsg.): „*Für unser Glück*", Bd. IV, S. 535–547.
[31] Leibniz an Herzog Anton Ulrich, Wolfenbüttel, 17. (27.) Dezember 1699; A I 17, N. 120, 125.
[32] Ebd., S. 124.

und Gelehrte, die Leibniz bereits 1689 getroffen hatte: z. B. Giovanni Giustino Ciampini, Raffaele Fabretti, Giambattista del Palagio, Giovanni Pastrizio.

Wenn das Vatikanische Geheimarchiv in Bezug auf die kurze Lebensdauer der Kalenderkongregation anscheinend schweigt, sind hingegen einige Hinweise im Archiv des Heiligen Offiziums noch aufbewahrt: es handelt sich um knappe Bemerkungen über laufende Diskussionen und vor allem Aufrufe zur Vorsicht. In diesen Zusammenhang sind auch zahlreiche Belege in Bianchinis Nachlass in der Biblioteca Vallicelliana zu finden. Es handelt sich um Briefe und Berichte, die die sogenannte *destruttori del calendario Gregoriano*, d. h. die Vernichter des Gregorianischen Kalender betreffen. Dieser Ausdruck ist einem Zettel zu finden, der von dem Mathematiker Domenico Quarteroni geschrieben wurde. Unter diesen *destruttori* kann man auch Leibniz nennen, „Direttore della Accademia di Brandenburgo, Consigliero di Anover, et Accademico Reale di Parigi."[33] Immerhin wird er in einem Bericht eines anderen Faszikels des Nachlasses in der Vallicelliana als „uno die più scaltri e maliziosi luterani, che si possa trovare."[34] Der Bericht wurde von Giusto Fontanini für Francesco Bianchini geschrieben und ist auf den 9. Februar 1703 datiert, zeitgleich mit dem Zensurverfahren gegen die von Leibniz 1696 herausgebrachte und, – wie Fontanini schreibt – die ‚scandalosissima' *Historia arcana sive de vita Alexandri VI Papae*, das mit der Indizierung des Werkes endete.[35] Es ist also kein Zufall, dass hier die *Historia arcana* als Beweis für Leibniz' Unehrlichkeit und für seine Neigung zum Vertrauensmissbrauch angeführt wurde. Schließlich habe Leibniz nur deshalb bestimmte Urkunden ediert, um die Päpste niederträchtig anzugreifen. Der Bericht wollte natürlich Leibniz als Gesprächspartner in der Diskussion über das Kalenderwesen diskreditieren. Man konnte weitere Briefe und Gutachten von Quarteroni im Bianchini Nachlass nachweisen, in denen der Mathematiker sich über die der von den sogenannten *scismatici* geführten Diskussionen über die Kalenderreform äußerte, Diskussionen in denen – laut seinen Worten – der Gregorianische Kalender so dargestellt wird, „come se fosse stato fatto dalla gente piu

---

[33] Domenico Quarteroni an Bianchini, Rom, 9. Februar 1703, Vallicelliana, ms. U 25, Bl. 127v.
[34] Vgl. dazu Robinet: *G. W. Leibniz Iter Italicum*, S. 59–61.
[35] *Specimen historiae arcanae sive Anecdotae de vita Alexandri VI. Papae seu Excerpta ex Diario Johannis Burchardi Argentinensis, Capellae Alexandri Sexti Papae Clerici Ceremoniarum Magistri. Edente G. G. L.*, Hannoverae 1696. Dazu vgl. Margherita Palumbo: „Sed quis locus orbis nobis plura dare posset et meliore, quam Roma? Die Römische Kurie und Leibniz' Editionen", in: Nora Gädeke (Hrsg.): *Leibniz als Sammler und Herausgeber historischer Quellen* (= *Wolfenbütteler Forschungen* 129), Wiesbaden 2012, S. 155–187.

sciocca e ignorante che vi fosse in quel tempo."³⁶ Die Diskussion über den Gregorianischen Kalender und die Ansprüche einer Kalenderreform

> „non havea altra origine che dagli infami raggiri degli heretici di Germania, i quali hanno gia stampato un nuovo Calendario intitulato Leopoldiano contrario al Gregoriano, e non potendo questo havere esecutione appresso i catolici di Germania havendo essi già accettao il Gregoriano, pretendono adesso gli Eretici che il Pontefice dica che il Gregoriano sia erroneo a cio che possano con giustizia fare accettare da tutto lo imperio il Leopoldiano gia accettato dalla Germania Eretica. Ecco dove va a terminar tutto lo studio che si fa adesso in Roma per destrugere il Calendario Pontificio."³⁷

Man vermutet darin einen der möglichen – vielleicht sogar den wichtigsten – Grund für die Auseinandersetzungen, die letztlich zum Abbruch der Kongregationsarbeit und zur Entscheidung gegen die Verbesserung – von Quarteroni als eine *rivoluzione* oder *distruzione* bezeichnet³⁸ – des Gregorianischen Kalenders geführt hatten.

In einem Brief vom Dezember 1701 am Andrew Fountaine teilte Leibniz *in aurem* mit, er habe Bianchini und Noris von der im selben Jahr stattgefundenen Veröffentlichung von Joachim Tiedes *Cyclus lunae-solaris* geschrieben,

> „le Cycle le plus exact pour le nombre des années, qu'on ait connu jusqu'icy, et dont on se devroit servir asseurement, si on ne veut pas *inventa fruge glandibus vesci*."³⁹

Die Nachricht wollte selbstverständlich kollaborativ sein, weil die Anwendung dieses *cyclus*

> „seroit glorieux au pape moderne, car il feroit quelque chose de fort beau qui luy seroit dû et marqueroit un grand respect pour la verité, et seroit suivi par tout apparemment."⁴⁰

In Rom mussten diese Worte und Vorschläge hingegen vor allem als gefährliche und großspurige Forderung nach einer interkonfessionellen Astronomie klingen und die in Bianchinis Nachlass aufbewahrte Dokumentation belegt

---

³⁶ Vallicelliana, ms. U 18, Bl. 147r.
³⁷ Ebd.
³⁸ Ebd.
³⁹ Leibniz an Andrew Fountaine, Berlin, 27. Dezember 1701; A I, 20, N. 396, 685f.
⁴⁰ Ebd., 686.

diese Hypothese. Nicht zufälligerweise sind die in der Biblioteca Vallicelliana aufbewahrten Berichte von Quarteroni nach zwei Briefen von Samuel Reyher am Kardinal Enrico Noris und einem Brief von Leibniz an Bianchini vom 8. März 1702 eingebunden, in dem Leibniz die Berechnungen nicht nur von Reyher, sondern auch von Joachim Tiede als die beste zur Verfügung vorlegt, und deren Anwendung vorschlägt.[41] Genau wie in seinem Brief an Fountaine. Nur wird der Anspruch *inventa fruge glandibus vesci* selbstverständlich ausgelassen.

Quarteroni hatte seine Berichte im Auftrag vom Papst Clemens XI. verfasst. Wie er schreibt, wollte der Papst die Meinung von römischen Mathematikern, über die aus Deutschland angekommenen Berechnungen und Vorschläge. Quarteronis Schlussfolge sind sehr negativ. Die *Heretici della Germania* haben jetzt ihre Erben in Rom gefunden, im evidenten Bezug auf scharfe Auseinandersetzungen innerhalb derselben Kalenderkongregation.

Unsere Feinde – schreibt noch Quarteroni, der laut der neulich gefundenen Dokumente als echter Leiter der Fraktion gegen die Kalenderreform zu bezeichnen ist –

„non cessano di fare computi, di osservare Eclissi, Equinozi, Pleniluni, ed altre cose non mai pratticate prima da Santi padri nel formare i Cicli Paschali."[42]

Daher, sollten der Papst und die Kardinäle die Manöver der Häretiker, sowie die Unterstützung ihrer Erben in Rom definitiv beenden und den universellen und absoluten Primat – auch im Kalenderwesen – der Römische Kirche wieder zu klarzustellen. Darüber hinaus – fügt Quarteroni in einem Brief an Bianchini vom Jahre 1703 hinzu – „Sua Santità ha dato piu volte segni di dispiacere per aver fatto la Congregazione del Calendari."[43] Aus Bologna sollte im Oktober 1703 der schon angesprochene Flaminio Mezzavacca – Mitglied der Kongregation – an Kardinal Benedetto Pamphili schreiben, dass wegen der internen Differenzen über „ricerche da Libri, e da parte lontana", d. h. fremde Bücher und Berechnungen, die päpstliche Absicht, ein universelles Kalender-Gesetz festzusetzen, nie befriedigt nie umgesetzt wird.[44] Die Kalenderkongregation brach die Arbeiten kurz nach dem Tode des Kardinals Noris im Februar 1704 definitiv ab.

---

[41] Vgl.Vallicelliana, ms. U 25, Bl. 119r–124v.
[42] Ebd., ms. U 18, Bl. 147r.
[43] Quarteroni an Bianchini, [1703], ebd., ms. U 15, Index, *sub. lit.* Q (ohne Blattzählung).
[44] Flaminio Mezzavacca an Benedetto Pamphili, Bologna, 4. Oktober 1703, ebd., ms. U 25, Bl. 129v–130r.

Nur im Laufe der Jahre sollte Leibniz verstehen, und lernen: wie mühsam, schwierig und oft vergeblich die Kommunikation mit Rom – auch auf der Ebene der Gelehrsamkeit – sein konnte. Sein langer Brief vom Jahre 1704 an Papst Clemens XI. – ein echtes *Manifesto* von Leibniz' Überzeugung der interkonfessionellen Bedeutung der gelehrten Kommunikation, in dem auch Bianchinis Meridianlinie genannt ist[45] – wurde genau so wenig beantwortet wie Bianchinis klare Antworten jemals nach Hannover gelangten. Immerhin war er ein Gelehrter, der zugleich die Werke von Jean Mabillon, Benedetto Bacchini und das *Dictionnaire* von Pierre Bayle streng zensuriert hatte.[46]

Im Jahre 1704, nach dem Tode vom Kardinal Noris und dem Ende der Kalenderkongregation, sollte Bianchini wieder zur Frage der Kalenderreform zurückkehren. Im Auftrag des Heiligen Offiziums verfasste er ein Gutachten über einige in Venedig gedruckte Büchlein über Kalender. In diesem Zusammenhang erklärt Bianchini die Aufgaben und Ziele der damaligen Kalenderkongregation: Die Kongregation sollte nicht die Substanz des „Calendario ottimamente ordinato da Gregorio XIII" ändern, sondern nur die Erfindungen und Manöver der Häretiker zurückstoßen:

> „togliere ogni ansa alli Eretici di inventare nuovi regolamenti per la Pasqua, che paressero piu conformi alle leggi del Sac. Concilio Niceno, come si seppe che tentavano, e come tentano tuttavia."[47]

Als Ludovico Antonio Muratori 1704 Bianchini fragte, ob er die Rolle der wissenschaftlichen Eminenz und Garant einer künftigen, konfessionslosen und politisch unabhängigen Accademia Letteraria Italiana bekleiden wolle, sagte ihm Bianchini ab: im Namen der kulturellen Zentralität und des Primats der römischen Kirche.[48]

---

[45] Vgl. Leibniz an Benedict Andreas Caspar de Nomis für Papst Klemens XI., Hannover, [8] Mai 1704, A I, 23, N. 248, 351–354; bes. 352, „Nec decepta est spes nostra, multa enim et jam egisse intelligo, et moliri adhuc Summum Pontificem quibus recta studia adjuventur. Linea Meridiana metallo ducta, cura perficiendi computi temporis viris egregiis mandata, aliaque multa id genus jam memorantur."
[46] Über Bianchini Tätigkeit als Zensor im Dienst der Indexkongregation vgl. Marco Cavarzere: *La prassi della censura nell'Italia del Seicento. Tra repressione e mediazione* (= Tribunali della Fede 92), Roma 2011, S. 135–171.
[47] Vallicelliana, ms. U 25, Bl. 42r–v.
[48] Vgl. Bianchini an Ludovico Antonio Muratori, Rom, 7. Februar 1705, in: Gian Francesco Soli Muratori: *Vita del proposto Lodovico Antonio Muratori già Bibliotecario del Serenissimo Sig. Duca di Modena*, Venezia 1756, S. 246–251.

Leibniz and minutiae

Enrico Pasini (Turin)

> Noi siamo gente avvezza
> alle piccole cose,
> umili e silenziose.
> (Puccini: *Madama Butterfly*, first act)

Indeed there are passages in Leibniz's oeuvre, both published and unpublished, where he speaks of small things – things that are minute in the sense of tiny and difficult to observe – as mere trifles: f.i. he laments many a time that old-school minor logicians often present applications of their methods only to *minutias*, and thus flatter themselves on trivial results.

Such are *minutiae* if understood as objects that may be considered insignificant, at least in comparison to more dignified subjects of reflexion: in Leibniz's words, "minuta [...] ac sterilia."[1] While there are innumerable small things the knowledge of which can be separately pursued with some usefulness, all this will remain meaningless at large, in the absence of a *Scientia generalis*:

> "et licet infinitae rerum minutiae utcunque utiles aliquo modo et certorum hominum indagationi transcribendae, seponi possint a caeteris, omnino tamen ad sapientiam opus est *Scientiae generalis*."[2]

While it is true that, in the meantime, particular knowledge of minute things may be of great use in politics, economics, warfare, and medicine

> ("Interdum enim quae minuta videri possent, in re politica atque oeconomica, in re militari, in Medicina maximae utilitatis fuere"[3]),

in the end, one would say, the moral of these passages is rather the old *de minimis non curat praetor*.

Yet, be they the *magnarum rerum tenuis notitia* that, at the beginning of the *Protogea*, is said to be precious;[4] or the infinite minimal differences

---

[1] A VI, 4 A, 459.
[2] *Paraenesis de scientia generali*, 1688; A VI, 4 A, 979f.
[3] A VI, 4 A, 138.
[4] *Protogaea*, ed. by C. L. Scheid, Göttingen 1749, p. 12: "Magnarum rerum etiam tenuis notitia in pretio habetur. Itaque ab antiquissimo nostri tractus statu orsuro dicendum est aliquid *de prima*

between possible individuals and worlds, or the small perceptions that together form the murmur of waves and the roar of waterfalls; or the minute circumstances of which the inventories would be a most serviceable complement to the *scientia generalis* for use in politics, economics and medicine, it must be said that indeed *de minimis multum curat Leibnitius*.

1. Erudition and Epistemology

As a matter of course, it is not Leibniz who will despise erudition. If Seneca had written: "Nam etiam quod discere supervacaneum est, prodest cognoscere,"[5] Leibniz would surely like to learn absolutely everything possible, and he is evidently proud of the immensity of his erudition, of his command of historical notions, of his partiality to those 'small books' containing practical and particular knowledge, of his interest for the secrets and the techniques of artisans and engineers, and maybe of his vast collection of recipes for pomades and herbal remedies.

He openly states his appreciation of punctilious historical knowledge in a letter to Placcius of 1690:

> "Gaudeo quod Cryptonymorum detegendorum consilium urges, insigni haud dubie rei litterariae accessione; cujus pars non contemnenda consistit in notitia scriptorum. Scio esse qui omnem illam curiositatem inutilem judicent, quasi rerum non scriptorum, habenda sit ratio. Sed hi non vident in tanta multitudine rerum cognoscendarum, ingentis compendii esse, aliorum frui laboribus. Itaque necessaria librorum notitia est, libros autem plerumque commendat autor, facileque intelligitur, quod ab insigni viro scriptum est utiliter legi."[6]

---

facie terrarum, et soli natura contentisque." ("Even a slight notion of great things is of value. Therefore, those who would trace our region back to its beginnings must also say something about the original appearance of the earth, and about the nature of the soil and what it contains", *Protogaea*, ed. by C. Cohen and A. Wakefield, Chicago/London 2008, p. 3).

[5] Seneca: *De benef.* VI, 1 ("there is some advantage in discovering even what is not worth learning", *Moral Essays*, vol. 3, ed. by J. W. Basore, Cambridge MA 1970–1979, p. 365).

[6] A II, 2, 342. "I rejoice when you call for collaboration in detecting cryptonims: this would surely be an enhancement of literary studies, a part of which, and one not to be despised, consists in knowledge of the authors. I know that some deem useless such inquiries, as if we should have regard to things and not to writers. But they do not perceive that in such vastness of things to be known, to be able to use the work of others is a great help. So it is necessary to have some notion of books, and many books stand out due to their author, since it is useful to read what is written by illustrious men." Collaboration had been asked by Placcius in his *Invitatio amica ad*

This attitude is also particularly apparent in epistemology – a domain which admittedly has somewhat more philosophical import – as it is shown by Leibniz's comparison of analysis' attention to particulars, with the craftiness of miniaturists. It is found in the famous passage where Leibniz says that analytical minds are rather myopic, whereas combinatory minds seem more presbyopic:

> "Caput praemittendum de differentia Methodi Analyticae et Combinatoriae, et de differentia ingenii Analytici et ingenii combinatorii. In analysi magis opus attentione ad pauca, sed valde acri, in combinatoria opus respectu ad multa simul, itaque simile est discrimen atque inter *pictores rerum minutissimarum* et statuarios. Analytici magis Myopes; Combinatorii magis similes presbitis."[7]

He clearly has in mind the way an uncorrected eye will have either to get very near to its object, or to look from a distance, in reason of those very defects. It may be remarked that the condition attributed to analysis was known to him by experience, because of his own shortsightedness, that made him constantly be analytic at short distance, and fail to recognize people in the street; whilst, of combinatoric presbyopia, he had at the time only third-person knowledge. He would eventually suffer from both and quit the use of this simile.

2. Minutiae minutissimae

As I said, in the same passage he also compares analysis and combinatorics respectively to miniature and sculpture. Now Leibniz applies to God different metaphors: he characterizes him chiefly as an architect, as a gardener, as a geometer, sometimes as a lute player, once as a novel writer, but never as a miniaturist. Yet, in particular, it is in the machines of nature that only the most perfect being can have created that, truly and essentially, no *minutiae* are negligible:

Antonium Magliabecchi, aliosque illustres [...] super symbolis promissis partim et destinatis ad anonymos et pseudonymos detectos et detegendos, Hamburg 1689.
[7] A VI, 4 A, 425f. (my emphasis). "I must premise a chapter concerning the difference between the analytical and the combinatory method, and the difference between analytical and combinatory minds. In analysis it is suitable to pay attention to fewer things, but with more precision, whereas combinatorics considers many things together; thus the difference between them is similar to that between miniature painting and sculpture. Analytical mind are rather shortsighted, while combinatory ones are rather presbyopic."

> "L'organisme est essentiel à la matière, mais à la matière arrangée par une sagesse souveriane. Et c'est pour cela aussi que je définis l'Organisme, ou la Machine naturelle, que c'est une machine dont chaque partie est machine, et par conséquent que la subtilité de son artifice va à l'infini, *rien n'étant assez petit pour être négligé*, au lieu que les parties de nos machines artificielles ne sont point des machines. C'est là la différence de la Nature et de l'Art, que nos modernes n'avaient pas assez considérée."[8]

This clearly differentiates natural *minutiae* from infinitesimals, which, as it is well known, are negligible – by institution, in a way, if not by nature. This brings me to the first main question I should like to consider in this paper. Is there a dimension that can be referred to, at least locally to a certain domain, as the standard, so to say, for *minutiae*?

In Leibniz's examples of *petites perceptions*, f.i., we mostly encounter accessible entities of finite, determinate dimensions: we are not able to distinguish the noise of each single wave, but the wave has perceptible existence; we are not able to tell blue grains apart from yellow grains in a green powdery mixture,[9] but it would in principle be possible to separate them patiently with ordinary means, albeit with extraordinary patience.

When we consider the ambient noise in a room, there is no perception of the movements of microscopic beings that seems to directly account for our overall apperception of that noise: even fluttering eyelashes, although they

---

[8] To Lady Masham, 1704; GP III, 356 (my emphasis). "The organism is essential to matter, but only to matter arranged by a sovereign wisdom. That is why I define the Organism, or the Natural Machine, as a machine each part of which is a machine, and where, as a consequence, the subtlety of the artifice goes ad infinitum, since nothing is so small that it be neglected; whereas the parts of our artificial machines are not machines. This is the difference between Nature and Art, that has been overlooked by our Moderns."

[9] See the *Meditationes de cognitione, veritate, et ideis* of 1684: "Caeterum cum colores aut odores percipimus, utique nullam aliam habemus quam figurarum, et motuum perceptionem, sed tam multiplicium et exiguorum, ut mens nostra singulis distincte considerandis in hoc praesenti suo statu non sufficiat, et proinde non animadvertat perceptionem suam ex solis figurarum et motuum minutissimorum perceptionibus compositam esse, quemadmodum confusis flavi et caerulei pulvisculis viridem colorem percipiendo, nil nisi flavum et caeruleum *minutissime* mixta sentimus, licet non animadvertentes et potius novum aliquod ens nobis fingentes" (A VI, 4 A, 592; my emphasis). "Furthermore, when we perceive colors or smells, we certainly have no perception other than that of shapes and of motions, though so very numerous and so very small that our mind cannot distinctly consider each individual one in this, its present state, and thus does not notice that its perception is composed of perceptions of minute shapes and motions alone, just as when we perceive the color green in a mixture of yellow and blue powder, we sense only yellow and blue finely mixed, even though we do not notice this, but rather fashion some new thing for ourselves" (Ariew/Garber, 27).

may move the heart of some – allow me some ciliary association – supercilious character of a romantic novel, would not look like the typical "small" contribution to ordinary perceptions. Much less the noise of the cilia of unicellular beings seems to be envisaged by Leibniz, although they surely are not, in terms of natural philosophy, "assez petit[es] pour être négligé[es]."

In fact, many years before, Leibniz had written in the *De affectibus* [D], that an overall reduction to the confused perception of things too small in comparison with ordinary perceptions characterizes all states of stupor:

> "Cum res ea multa nobis confuse exhibet, id est minuta nimis quam ut cum caeteris rebus quas cogitamus comparari possint, attoniti videmur; et talis est status in ebrietate, in morbo, imo ut credibile est, etiam in morte."[10]

Such problems of scale can easily be extended: waves, drops, vibrations of parts that produce elasticity, and imperceptible movements that produce the "artificial" appearance of solidity in perception, might well all be bunched together under the viewpoint of universal monadic perception – but also not, if we consider the domain of natural discourse and science.

It can thus be surmised that there really is a level of "impending" *minutiae* – and I use this expression only provisionally, being in lack of a better connotation – that directly and strongly count for us in a way that sub-minimal notions of our own pancreas, or of living creatures on far-away worlds, do not. Even Leibniz's own attempt at a "twin-earth argument" in the *New Essays* seems to confirm it:

> "[I]l se peut que dans un autre lieu de l'univers ou dans un autre temps, il se trouve un globe qui ne différé point sensiblement de ce globe de la terre où nous habitons, et que chacun des hommes qui l'habitent, ne differe point sensiblement de chacun de nous qui luy repond. [...] Au reste parlant de ce qui se peut naturellement, les deux globes semblables et les deux ames semblables des deux globes ne le demeureroient que pour un temps. Car puisqu'il y a une diversité individuelle, il faut que cette difference consiste au moins dans les constitutions insensibles, qui se doivent développer dans la suite des temps."[11]

---

[10] A VI, 4 B, 1425. "When something presents us with many confused things, that is, with things exceedingly small, such to be incomparable with the other things that we conceive of, we appear to be stupefied. And such is the one's state in drunkenness, illness, and, plausibly, even in death."
[11] *New Essays* II, 27, § 29; A VI, 6, 245f. "[I]n another region of the universe or at some other time there may be a sphere in no way sensibly different from this sphere of earth on which we live, and inhabited by men each of whom differs sensibly in no way from his counterpart among us. [...] I will add that if we are speaking of what can naturally occur, the two similar spheres

3. Platyhelminthes and Drops of Wax

I shall conclude this paper discussing the importance of *minutiae* in the thought of Leibniz from the point of view of moral philosophy, the very domain where they can be deemed to be properly effectual. Even they might be the most important of all things. As Nietzsche would put it in the work he wrote in my home town just a few weeks before going insane, like most philosophers who come to live there are known to have done:

> "diese kleinen Dinge [...] sind über alle Begriffe hinaus wichtiger als Alles, was man bisher wichtig nahm."[12]

We shall see that in at least two important ways, admittedly very different from what Nietzsche had in mind in this page of his, *minutiae* really play a crucial role in the ethical balance of Leibniz's universe.

A very good example of such effectual *minutiae* is that famous single drop of wax that day after day, in the *New Essays*, counterbalances the weakness of the will, or the constant effect of the *petits aiguillons du desir* that the power of reason alone, and even of moral instinct, is not able to counter. The most fascinating example, in fact, of the practical measures that Leibniz's anti-stoic moral reason can adopt, is that of the Jesuit general who was given to drinking heavily when he was a member of fashionable society and, when he was considering withdrawing from the world, retrenched gradually to almost nothing, by each day letting a drop of wax fall into the cup which he was wont to empty:

> "Un voyage entrepris tout exprés guérira un amant, une retraite nous tirera des compagnies qui entretiennent dans quelque mauvaise inclination. François de Borgia General des Jesuites qui a esté enfin canonisé, estant accoutumé à boire largement, lorsqu'il estoit homme du grand monde; se réduisit peu à peu au

---

and the two similar souls on them could remain similar only for a time. Since they would be numerically different, there would have to be a difference at least in their insensible constitutions, and the latter must unfold in the fullness of time." (Remnant/Bennett, *ad loc.*).

[12] Friedrich Nietzsche: *Ecce homo. Eine Besprechung*, in: *Werke. Kritische Gesamtausgabe*, VI/3, ed. by G. Colli and M. Montinari, Berlin/New York 1969, p. 294. "These small things [...] are inconceivably more important than everything one has taken to be important so far" (*On the Geneaology of Morals and Ecce Homo*, ed. by W. Kaufmann and R.J. Hollingdale, New York 1967, p. 256).

petit pied, lorsqu'il pensa à la retraite, en faisant tomber chaque jour une goutte de cire dans le bocal qu'il avoit accoustumé de vuider."[13]

The other example, that is also especially interesting for the theme of this Congress, is that of the simplest and microscopic living beings that, in the *Theodicy*, contribute to the positive balance of happiness even in this disgraced corner of the universe.

The overall line of argumentation of the *Theodicy* concerning the problem of evil, and of the balance that the creator must needs have held between virtue and vice, misery and happiness, in this world, is clearly summarized at §222:

> "[…] ces volontés antecedentes ne font qu'une partie de toutes les volontés antecedentes de Dieu prises ensemble, dont le resultat fait la volonté consequente, ou que le decret de créer le meilleur: et c'est par ce decret que l'amour de la vertu et de la felicité des creatures raisonnables, qui est indefini de soy et va aussi loin qu'il se peut, reçoit quelques petites limitations, à cause de l'égard qu'il faut avoir au bien en general. C'est ainsi qu'il faut entendre que Dieu aime souverainement la vertu et hait souverainement le vice, et que néantmoins quelque vice doit être permis."[14]

A lovely expression: *quelques petites limitations*. What shall we do of such small limitations? They are very apparent in this corner of the universe, and Leibniz is perfectly aware of this. A famous answer of his to this problem is the following:

---

[13] *New Essays* II, 21, § 31; A VI, 6, 187. "A lover will be cured by a voyage undertaken just for that purpose; a period of seclusion will stop us from keeping company with people who confirm some bad disposition in us. Francisco Borgia, the General of the Jesuits, who has at last been canonized, was given to drinking heavily when he was a member of fashionable society; when he was considering withdrawing from the world, he retrenched gradually to almost nothing, by each day letting a drop of wax fall into the flagon which he was accustomed to drinking dry" (Remnant/Bennett, *ad loc.*).

[14] *Théod.*, § 222; GP VI, 250f. "These acts of antecedent will make up only a portion of all the antecedent will of God taken together, whose result forms the consequent will, or the decree to create the best. Through this decree it is that love for virtue and for the happiness of rational creatures, which is undefined in itself and goes as far as is possible, receives some slight limitations, on account of the heed that must be paid to good in general. Thus one must understand that God loves virtue supremely and hates vice supremely, and that nevertheless some vice is to be permitted" (Haggard, *ad loc.*).

> "je crois qu'effectivement, à le bien prendre, il y a incomparablement plus de bien moral que de mal moral dans les Creatures raisonnables, dont nous ne connoissons qu'un tres petit nombre."[15]

In the line of Huygens' *Cosmotheoros*, of Fontenelle's *Entretiens sur la pluralité des mondes*, and of an argument that was quasi a commonplace of Cartesian theodicies,[16] Leibniz envisages here a universal moral balance that is squared by rational creatures of better morality living on faraway stars.

> "Et quoyqu'il y ait apparemment en quelques endroits de l'univers des animaux raisonnables plus parfaits que l'homme, l'on peut dire que Dieu a eu raison de créer toute sorte d'especes, les unes plus parfaites que les autres. Il n'est peutêtre point impossible qu'il y ait quelque part une espece d'animaux fort ressemblans à l'homme, qui soyent plus parfaits que nous. Il se peut même que le genre humain parvienne avec le temps à une plus grande perfection, que celle que nous pouvons nous imaginer presentement. Ainsi les loix da mouvement n'empêchent point que l'homme ne soit plus parfait: mais la place que Dieu a assignée à l'homme dans l'espace et dans le temps, borne les perfections qu'il a pu recevoir."[17]

But this is the poorest of consolations. Should we be content with living in the worst possible place of the albeit best possible world?

There are two strategies deployed by Leibniz in this respect. One is the special mission that we have to show to the universe that even from its moral bottom some good can eventually arise; and of course that is why we have been given a Saviour.

The other one entails again a reasoning about a balance, but not a moral one. It is the local balance of "good" (*du bien*). In the second section of the *Abregé de la controverse reduite à des Argumens en forme*, we read the following (Baylean) objection:

---

[15] *Théod.*, § 219; GP VI, 249. "I think that in reality, properly speaking, there is incomparably more moral good than moral evil in rational creatures; and of these we have knowledge of but few" (Haggard, *ad loc.*).

[16] See Sergio Landucci: *La teodicea nell'età cartesiana*, Napoli 1986.

[17] *Théod.*, §341; GP VI, 317. "And although there be apparently in some places in the universe rational animals more perfect than man, one may say that God was right to create every kind of species, some more perfect than others. It is perhaps not impossible that there be somewhere a species of animals much resembling man and more perfect than we are. It may be even that the human race will attain in time to a greater perfection than that which we can now envisage. Thus the laws of motions do not prevent man from being more perfect: but the place God has assigned to man in space and in time limits the perfections he was able to receive" (Haggard, *ad loc.*).

> "S'il y a plus de mal que de bien dans les Creatures intelligentes, il y a plus de mal que de bien dans tout l'ouvrage de Dieu.
> Or il y a plus de mal que de bien dans les creatures intelligentes.
> Donc, il y a plus de mal quo de bien dans tout l'ouvrage de Dieu."[18]

If there is more evil than good in intelligent creatures, there is more evil than good in all God's work. Now there *is* more evil than good in intelligent creatures, therefore there is more evil than good in all God's work. Leibniz's answer to this quite powerful objection is this:

> "[…] à la Majeure, on ne l'accorde point, parce que cette pretendue consequence de la partie au tout, des creatures intelligentes à toutes les creatures, suppose tacitement et sans preuve, que les creatures destituées de raison ne peuvent point entrer en comparaison et en ligne de compte avec celles qui en ont. Mais pourquoy ne se pourroit il pas que le surplus du bien dans les creatures non intelligentes, qui remplissent le monde, recompensât et surpassât même incomparablement le surplus du mal dans les creatures raisonnables? Il est vray que le prix des dernieres est plus grand, mais en recompense les autres sont en plus grand nombre sans comparaison; et il se peut que la proportion du nombre et de la quantité surpasse celle du prix et de la qualité."[19]

As for the major, Leibniz says, he does not admit it because

> "this supposed inference from the part to the whole, from intelligent creatures to all creatures, assumes tacitly and without proof that creatures devoid of reason cannot be compared or taken into account with those that have reason."

But, he adds,

> "why might not the surplus of good in the non-intelligent creatures that fill the world compensate for and even exceed incomparably the surplus of evil in rational creatures? It is true that the value of the latter is greater; but by way of compensation the others are incomparably greater in number; and it may be that the proportion of number and quantity surpasses that of value and quality."[20]

To be so innumerable, indeed, the unreasonable creatures *must* comprehend *legions* of significantly smaller beings; but let us not resort to the evocation of the Lord of the Flies, since it is quite clear that, when Leibniz thinks of innumerable living creatures, he has in mind his ponds full of fishes, each part of which is like a minute pond with fishes, and so on *ad imminutissimum*.

---

[18] GP VI, 377. See Haggard, *ad loc.*, for the translation.
[19] Ibid., 378.
[20] Ibid.

4. Conclusion

This fascinating and, at the same time, disturbing theme – that the well being of monads is assured by the overall happiness of Platyhelminthes – would deserve to be studied more in deep, and it may deserve to be mentioned that the inherent happiness of unreasonable creatures has conspicuously been deemed by Alexander von Humboldt a "seliger Gedanke der Leibnizschen Philosophie"[21], that is to say, a 'blissful notion' of Leibnizian philosophy.

But what we have read both from the *Theodicy* and from the other various Leibnizian sources that have been extracted here, can suffice to our purpose: it seems to me that, in the end, we are positively allowed to say that suitably-sized *minutiae* play an irrenounceable role in Leibniz's ethics and in making real, as the refrain of this Congress goes, our happiness as well as the happiness of the others – *felicitatem nostram alienamve*.

---

[21] Alexander von Humboldt: Letter to his brother Wilhelm, Febr. 25 1789: "Eben komme ich von einem einsamen Spaziergange aus dem Tiergarten zurück [...] So ganz im Genuß der reinsten, unschuldigsten Freude, von Tausenden von Geschöpfen umringt, die sich (seliger Gedanke der Leibnizschen Philosophie!) ihres Daseins freuen, [...] Solche Betrachtungen, lieber Bruder, versetzen einen immer in eine süße Schwermut!" (In: *Gesammelte Werke*, vol. 12, Stuttgart 1807, p. 190).

Malebranche dans le *Discours de métaphysique* : à propos des notions de Dieu et de perfection.

Paul Rateau (Paris)

Dans *Malebranche et Leibniz. Relations personnelles*,[1] André Robinet reprend l'hypothèse, déjà avancée par Martial Guéroult, suivant laquelle «°Leibniz avait sous les yeux le *Traité de la Nature et de la Grâce* quand il composait le *Discours de métaphysique.* »[2] Il estime que «°dans sa structure et dans sa phraséologie, le *Discours* est le fruit d'une compilation du *Traité*.°» Pour le prouver, il dresse un tableau mettant en regard des séquences du *Traité* et du *Discours*, et soutient que «°quatre séries d'articles°» du texte de Leibniz «°suivent pas à pas quatre séries correspondantes°» de l'ouvrage de Malebranche. C'est ainsi par exemple que l'article 1 du *Discours* – sur lequel va porter cette communication – correspondrait aux articles 11, 12 et 13 de la «°Première Partie°» du «°Premier Discours » du *Traité*.[3] L'affinité entre les deux textes, que révèle ce tableau comparatif, ne résiderait pas seulement, selon Robinet, dans la structure et dans le plan adopté, comme si Leibniz avait simplement trouvé dans le *Traité* l'ordre d'exposition de ses propres thèses. Pour le commentateur,

> «°il [Leibniz] aborde les problèmes métaphysiques dans les termes et dans les perspectives que vient d'imposer la querelle des vraies et des fausses idées, issue de la publication du *Traité de la Nature et de la Grâce*. La métaphysique de Malebranche, telle qu'elle se présente dans les articles du *Traité*, est le canevas général, la cause informatrice qui permet à Leibniz d'édifier la première expression de son système. Cette systématisation est alors dépendante dans ses thèses, dans ses problèmes, dans son langage, des pensées développées dans l'œuvre et dans la polémique de Malebranche.°»[4]

L'objet de cette contribution n'est pas de remettre en cause l'hypothèse d'une lecture attentive du *Traité de la Nature et de la Grâce* par Leibniz, ni même de contester une certaine ressemblance structurelle entre les deux textes – quoique l'inspiration soit très libre, à voir combien le *Discours de métaphysique* s'écarte de l'ordre choisi par Malebranche, au point d'adopter le plus

---

[1] *Malebranche et Leibniz. Relations personnelles*, éd. par André Robinet, Paris 1955.
[2] Ibid., p. 139.
[3] Cf. ibid., p. 140.
[4] Ibid., p. 142.

souvent un cheminement propre, au lieu de le suivre «°pas à pas.°» Ce qui rend finalement les rapprochements très ponctuels.⁵ Il s'agit plutôt ici de montrer, à partir de l'examen de l'article 1, où sont introduites les notions de Dieu, de perfection, et une certaine conception de l'action divine, en quoi l'œuvre leibnizienne, dans son langage et dans ses thèses, se révèle dès cette époque indépendante de la métaphysique malebranchiste.

1. L'Être absolument parfait

Le *Discours de métaphysique* commence par la considération de «°la notion de Dieu [la plus receue et] la plus significative que nous ayons°.»⁶ Le terme de *notion* est souvent pris par Leibniz comme synonyme d'idée.⁷ Mais à l'article 27, le philosophe opère une importante distinction entre les idées, «°expressions qui sont dans nostre ame, soit qu'on les conçoive ou non,°» et les notions ou concepts, expressions «°qu'on conçoit ou forme.°»⁸ La notion est une idée, mais toute idée n'est pas une notion. L'idée est cette qualité que possède l'âme de se représenter quelque nature, forme ou essence (comme l'énonce l'article 26). Avoir l'idée d'une chose signifie donc avoir la faculté d'y penser, que nous y pensions actuellement ou non. Cette faculté, qui est toujours en nous, n'est pas la simple puissance de penser à cette chose, comme à n'importe quelle autre – autrement dit elle ne désigne pas la simple capacité de penser en général –, mais une *disposition* à y penser, car elle repose sur l'existence en nous de l'expression de cette chose.⁹ L'idée devient *notion* ou *concept* dès lors qu'elle n'est pas seulement connue virtuellement (sans que nous y pensions effectivement) mais actuellement, c'est-à-dire à partir du moment où nous nous tournons vers elle et y faisons attention – conformément au sens premier de *notio*, qui vient du verbe latin *noscere*, signifiant l'action d'apprendre à connaître, de prendre connaissance. La notion de Dieu est ainsi son idée en nous, en tant que nous la contemplons, l'exprimons par un terme

---

⁵ Outre que le *Discours* ne suit pas le plan exact du *Traité*, certains de ses articles ne sont pas du tout mentionnés dans le tableau proposé par Robinet (c'est-à-dire n'ont pas leur correspond exact dans le texte de Malebranche) : IV, VIII à XVI, XIX à XXIX, XXXII à XXXVII. Soit 27 articles sur les 37 que comptent le *Discours* !
⁶ *Discours de métaphysique* ; A VI, 4 B, 1531.
⁷ Cf. par exemple A VI, 4 A, 40 ; A VI, 4 A, 288.
⁸ A VI, 4 B, 1572.
⁹ Cf. *Quid sit idea?* ; A VI, 4 B, 1370.

déterminé (Dieu), sommes capables d'en donner une définition et d'en faire l'analyse.

Il est à noter que Leibniz ne part pas d'une démonstration de l'existence de Dieu, mais de sa notion la plus communément admise par les philosophes et les théologiens.[10] Celle-ci n'est autre que celle que chacun trouve en lui-même, sans avoir besoin de la Révélation pour cela. Elle n'est donc tirée ni des Écritures, ni d'un prétendu consentement universel des hommes, qui serait une opinion couramment partagée, mais constitue bien ce qu'il faut appeler une *notion commune*[11] puisqu'elle est inscrite originairement dans nos âmes et, comme le diront les *Nouveaux Essais*, que «°nous ne faisons qu'y prendre garde.°»[12] Cette notion est encore dite «°la plus significative°» – et c'est pourquoi elle doit retenir l'attention et servir de point de départ à la réflexion – car elle fait entendre beaucoup, et, pour qui se donne la peine d'examiner ce qu'elle renferme, conduit à des considérations dont on n'a pas mesuré jusqu'à présent toute la fécondité et toutes les implications.

La définition retenue par Leibniz – « Dieu est un estre absolument parfait » – est seulement *nominale*, et non réelle, puisqu'elle ne montre pas la possibilité de son objet et par là même son existence.[13] Elle ressemble assez à celle que donne Malebranche dans le *Traité de la Nature et de la Grâce*. On notera même que tout le début du premier article du *Discours de métaphysique* est très proche du texte de l'oratorien, qui déclarait se fonder sur «°l'idée qu'ont tous les hommes de l'Être infiniment parfait°»[14] et tirait de cette idée les mêmes attributs relevés par Leibniz (à l'article 1) : la sagesse et la puissance.

> «°Cette idée de l'Être infiniment parfait, renferme deux attributs absolument nécessaires pour créer le monde ; une sagesse qui n'a point de bornes, et une puissance à qui rien n'est capable de résister.°»[15]

---

[10] Leibniz a d'abord écrit puis barré : «°L'idée de Dieu la plus ancienne et la plus receue°» (A VI, 4 B, 1531).
[11] Dans les *Elementa rationis*, Leibniz range l'Être, la substance, l'un, le possible, le nécessaire, la cause, l'ordre, la durée, parmi les notions communes que nous pouvons saisir par l'esprit et non par les sens (A VI, 4 A, 723–724).
[12] *Nouveaux Essais*, II, 23, § 33 ; A VI, 6, 225. Voir aussi ibid., I, 1, §§ 2–4, p. 76.
[13] Tel est en effet le «privilège» de Dieu qu'il suffit de prouver qu'il est possible pour démontrer qu'il existe nécessairement (cf. *Discours de métaphysique* § 23).
[14] *Traité de la Nature et de la Grâce*, 1er Discours, 1ère Partie, article 11. Cette idée qui « nous représente le vrai Dieu» doit être distinguée de la représentation que s'en font «°la plupart des hommes.°» Voir aussi le *Troisième Éclaircissement* au *Traité*, article 1 : «°Par ce terme *Dieu*, j'entends un Être infiniment parfait.°»
[15] Ibid., 1er Discours, 1ère Partie, article 12.

Leibniz se distingue cependant ici de Malebranche sur deux points.

a) Certes, les deux auteurs s'appuient sur l'idée de Dieu fournie par la lumière naturelle. Mais, alors que Leibniz commence son *Discours* par elle, Malebranche fait précéder l'examen de celle-ci de remarques sur la fin poursuivie par Dieu en créant le monde : «°Dieu ne pouvant agir que pour sa gloire, et ne la pouvant trouver qu'en lui-même, n'a pu aussi avoir d'autre dessein dans la création du monde, que l'établissement de son Église,°»[16] Église dont Jésus-Christ est le chef.[17] Ce qui fait de l'Incarnation du Fils la voie par laquelle Dieu accomplit son dessein glorieux. Par conséquent, Malebranche inscrit explicitement sa réflexion philosophique dans le cadre de la théologie révélée, même s'il prend soin de congédier le langage anthropologique et imagé de l'Écriture lorsqu'il s'agit de «°parler de Dieu avec quelque exactitude°,» comme aux articles 11 et 12. La philosophie sert chez lui un projet apologétique centré sur la figure du Christ médiateur, instrument de sanctification du monde et de l'homme, et artisan véritable de la Gloire divine. Leibniz, lui, ne part pas de la Révélation, mais finira par elle, en l'évoquant dans le dernier article du *Discours* (article 37). Il s'en tient strictement à la théologie naturelle et à ce que la notion de Dieu permet, à elle seule, de dire sur sa nature et sur la manière dont il agit.

b) Leibniz parle d'un être *absolument* parfait – formulation qui semble avoir sa préférence également dans d'autres textes[18] –, quand Malebranche évoque un être *infiniment* parfait. Cette différence est significative, car elle révèle comment chacun des deux philosophes conçoit la perfection et la manière dont l'Être suprême la possède. L'absolu renvoie à deux caractéristiques principales. D'une part, l'*indépendance* : est absolu ce qui est et est conçu par soi et non par autre chose (par la relation à autre chose qui lui serait concomitante ou plus fondamentale). D'autre part, l'achèvement, la *perfection* : est absolu ce qui est entièrement, complètement, ce qui est tout à fait réalisé ou actualisé. Affirmer que Dieu est un être *absolument* parfait est donc affirmer qu'il est *parfaitement parfait*, c'est redoubler la perfection, comme le suggère la suite de l'article 1, en posant que Dieu possède toutes les perfections, et qu'il les possède chacune au plus haut degré, à savoir de manière entière, complète et totale. Dieu n'est pas seulement *parfait*, mais *parfaitement parfait*, c'est-à-dire *perfectissimum* – expression employée par Leibniz dans un texte

---

[16] Ibid., article 1.
[17] Ibid., article 2.
[18] Jusque dans la *Monadologie* § 41.

célèbre de 1676,¹⁹ et qu'il faut traduire par «°tout parfait°» plutôt que par «°le plus parfait°», puisqu'il s'agit d'un superlatif absolu et non relatif.

L'infini, auquel Malebranche fait quant à lui référence, renvoie à deux caractéristiques différentes. D'une part, il signifie l'absence de limites et de bornes et, à ce titre, il est ce qui dépasse toute représentation, toute idée et par là même est incompréhensible. D'autre part, de façon cette fois plus positive et par opposition à l'*indéfini*, il désigne depuis Descartes «°une chose réelle, qui est incomparablement plus grande que toutes celles qui ont quelque fin.°»²⁰ C'est en ce sens que, pour Malebranche, Dieu est l'infini même, «°l'infini en toutes manières°», le seul être «°qui puisse contenir la réalité infiniment infinie que je vois quand je pense à l'être […].°»²¹ Affirmer que Dieu est un être infiniment parfait revient donc à affirmer qu'il est *infiniment infini*, c'est-à-dire à redoubler l'infinité (et même à la tripler²²), puisque Dieu n'est pas seulement celui qui possède toutes les perfections sans aucune limite ni restriction, mais celui qui les possède encore à un degré incomparable et d'une manière incommensurable avec ce qui existe et avec ce que nous pouvons connaître dans l'ordre du fini.

Une différence majeure apparaît là avec Leibniz, une différence que celui-ci a peut-être voulu marquer en choisissant le terme *absolument* plutôt qu'*infiniment* (parfait) – s'il avait effectivement sous les yeux le *Traité de la Nature et de la Grâce*. Malebranche introduit une discontinuité entre fini et infini. L'infini, tel qu'il le conçoit (comme équivalent à Dieu ou à «°l'être sans restriction°»), ne diffère pas seulement du fini en degré – du plus au moins – mais *en nature*. Sa propriété essentielle est

«°d'être en même temps un et toutes choses, composé, pour ainsi dire, d'une infinité de perfections différentes, et tellement simple, qu'en lui chaque perfection renferme toutes les autres sans aucune distinction réelle.°»

Et lorsque Dieu communique ses perfections aux créatures, il ne les leur communique pas

«°telles qu'elles sont dans sa substance, mais telle que sa substance les représente, et que la limitation des créatures le peut porter.°»²³

---

¹⁹ *Quod Ens perfectissimum existit* ; A VI, 3, 575–579.
²⁰ À Clerselier (23 avril 1649) ; AT V, 356.
²¹ *Entretiens sur la métaphysique et sur la religion*, II, article 3.
²² Malebranche dit en effet de Dieu qu'il est « l'infini infiniment infini » (ibid.).
²³ Ibid., II, article 6. Suit l'exemple de l'étendue intelligible.

Or il est clair que Leibniz ne saurait admettre cette indistinction des perfections – il souligne au contraire à l'article 1 du *Discours* leur pluralité et leurs différences[24] –, ni l'équivocité, ou tout du moins le rapport analogique qui s'introduit entre l'infini et le fini. Il soulignera au contraire dans la *Théodicée* que

> «°Les perfections de Dieu sont celles de nos ames, mais il les possede sans bornes : il est un Ocean, dont nous n'avons receu que des gouttes : il y a en nous quelque puissance, quelque connoissance, quelque bonté, mais elles sont tout entieres en Dieu.°»[25]

Le rapport est ici celui de la partie au tout (de la goutte d'eau à l'océan), ou de l'incomplet au complet (de la connaissance particulière au savoir total) : nous sommes dans l'ordre de l'homogène, de sorte que les perfections de Dieu ne sont que nos perfections portées au maximum, considérées sans limite ni restriction. Alors que Malebranche insiste sur l'écart ontologique avec le fini et fait de Dieu l'infini incompréhensible comme tel, Leibniz réduit cet écart à une différence de degré et considère Dieu comme l'absolu, c'est-à-dire comme l'être entièrement réel, positif et en acte, ne comportant aucune négation ni limitation.[26] Pour ce dernier, Dieu ne peut donc être identifié à l'infini qu'au sens où

> «°le vray infini à la rigueur n'est que dans l'*absolu* qui est anterieur à toute composition, et n'est point formé par l'addition des parties.°»[27]

Cet absolu est premier et le fini est obtenu en le modifiant ou en le bornant. Ainsi la perfection divine n'est pas sans commune mesure et sans comparaison

---

[24] « […] il y a dans la nature plusieurs perfections toutes differentes […] » (A VI, 4 B, 1531). C'est d'ailleurs leur hétérogénéité qui rend insuffisante et même problématique la démonstration cartésienne de l'existence de Dieu (cf. article 23). Voir aussi A II, 1, 489 : « Idem ergo est de Ente perfectissimo, nam plures perfectiones non sunt homogeneae, nam plures perfectiones non constituunt unum quoddam, etsi in communi perfectionis nomine conveniant. »
[25] Préface, GP VI, 27.
[26] A VI, 4 A, 401 : «°*Deus* est Ens absolutum, seu positivum sine omni negatione nisi ejus quod jam negationem involvit.°» A VI, 4 A, 560 : «°*Absoluta* [substantia realis] quae pure positiva est, et omnem realitatem, vel Actum vel Entelechiam involvit […]. Absoluta est Deus, limitata est creatura, ut ego.°» Voir aussi Grua, 11–12.
[27] *Nouveaux Essais*, II, 17, § 1 ; A VI, 6, 157. Les attributs de Dieu ne sont autre chose que des «°absolus. °» Ainsi l'idée de l'absolu rapportée à l'espace est l'idée d'immensité de Dieu (cf. ibid., § 3, p. 158), comme l'idée de l'absolu rapportée au temps est celle de l'éternité (§ 16, p. 159). Pour Leibniz, Dieu est l'infini au sens de l'infini *hypercatégorématique*, distinct de l'infini catégorématique et de l'infini syncatégorématique; cf. À des Bosses (1er septembre 1706) ; GP II, 314–315.

avec celle des créatures, mais bien du même genre qu'elle. Reste alors à déterminer cette notion commune de perfection, ou plus exactement à distinguer ce qui est une perfection de ce qui ne l'est pas – tâche que Malebranche n'a pas besoin d'accomplir, dès lors que, pour lui, *parfait* signifie tout simplement infini et qu'il n'y a pas de notion de perfection qui puisse réellement valoir de manière absolument univoque pour Dieu *et* pour les créatures.

2. Les trois sens de la perfection

En réalité, Leibniz ne livre pas à l'article 1 du *Discours* de définition de la perfection, comme il semble pourtant l'annoncer («°Il faut connaître aussi ce que c'est que perfection°»). Il évoque seulement une «marque assez seure» permettant de la reconnaître et, ainsi, de faire le partage entre ce qui est une perfection et ce qui ne l'est pas. Cela ne revient pas à dire ce qu'elle est, mais à indiquer qu'elle est l'objet d'une connaissance *distincte*, selon la terminologie employée à l'article 24, qui reprend celle des *Meditationes de Cognitione, Veritate, et Ideis* (1684). En effet, je connais *distinctement* une chose, quand je suis capable non seulement de la distinguer d'autres – ce qui fait que j'en ai une idée *claire* – mais encore d'en énumérer les caractéristiques distinctives et suffisantes, c'est-à-dire lorsque je peux en donner une définition au moins *nominale* – sauf dans le cas des notions primitives, qui sont à elles-mêmes leur propre marque, sont indécomposables et comprises immédiatement par soi.[28]

> «°Et telle est, écrit Leibniz, la connoissance d'un essayeur, qui discerne le vray or du faux par le moyen de certaines épreuves ou marques qui font la definition de l'or °»[29]

L'essayeur sait reconnaître l'or des autres métaux en utilisant des procédures de contrôle spécifiques et en réalisant certaines expériences pour l'affiner. C'est de cette manière *claire et distincte* que nous connaissons le nombre, la grandeur, la figure mais aussi la plupart des affections et des passions de l'âme.

Or la perfection – à l'instar de l'*être*, de l'*existant* ou du *moi* – est une notion primitive, simple, par conséquent inanalysable, irréductible en notions

---

[28] Cf. *Meditationes de Cognitione, Veritate, et Ideis* ; A VI, 4 A, 586–587.
[29] *Discours de métaphysique* § 24 ; A VI, 4 B, 1568.

plus fondamentales : «°Les perfections, ou formes simples, ou qualités absolues positives, sont indéfinissables ou irrésolubles.°»[30] À ce titre, et au sens strict, la perfection n'est donc pas susceptible d'une définition nominale, mais peut être reconnue au moyen du contrôle suivant (équivalent métaphysique du test expérimental réalisé par l'essayeur sur l'or) : est perfection toute forme, qualité ou nature capable d'être portée sans contradiction au maximum. Au contraire, n'est pas authentiquement une perfection, toute forme, qualité ou nature qui ne peut atteindre ce maximum, ou pour laquelle poser un maximum est contradictoire. Avant d'en venir au résultat de cette épreuve, on notera que dans certains textes Leibniz, à défaut de *définir* la perfection – puisqu'elle est proprement indéfinissable (*indefinibilis*) –, explique ce qu'il entend par ce terme. Dans l'opuscule *Quod Ens perfectissimum existit* (1676), il écrit par exemple : «°J'appelle *perfection* toute qualité simple qui est positive et absolue, c'est-à-dire qui exprime sans aucune limite tout ce qu'elle exprime.°»[31] Dans un autre fragment, contemporain du *Discours* :

> «°La perfection est la réalité pure ou ce qui est positif et absolu dans les essences. L'imperfection consiste au contraire dans la limitation.°»[32]

La perfection est ainsi identifiée à la réalité elle-même, prise absolument, sans négation ni limite, dans sa positivité, c'est-à-dire encore dans sa pure affirmation.

Pourquoi Leibniz ne mentionne-t-il pas cette équivalence entre perfection et réalité? Parce que ce n'est pas ce sens général de la perfection qui est visé à l'article 1 du *Discours*. Il n'y avait donc pas lieu de l'évoquer explicitement ici. Il n'est en effet d'aucun secours, puisqu'il ne fournit aucun critère permettant de distinguer ce qui est perfection de ce qui ne l'est pas. Au contraire, suivant cette acception générale, toute réalité, c'est-à-dire toute chose (*res*) prise dans ce qu'elle contient de positif, en ce qu'elle renferme véritablement de l'être, peut être déclarée à bon droit *perfection*. Et il n'y a aucun

---

[30] A VI, 3, 575 ; 577.
[31] A VI, 3, 578. On aurait tort d'interpréter cette déclaration comme une *définition* de la perfection, sinon au sens général où définir est expliquer un mot ou signifier exactement une idée (voir par exemple A VI, 2, 411 ; 454 ; 479). Car une définition, en son acception technique, consiste à résoudre une notion en ses réquisits ; cf. *À Conring*, 19/29 mars 1678, A II, 1, 602 ; A VI, 4 B, 1644 : «°Omnes autem reliquae veritates reducuntur ad primas ope definitionum, seu per resolutionem notionum, in qua consistit *probatio a priori* […].°»
[32] *Notationes Generales* ; A VI, 4 A, 556. Voir aussi *Théodicée*, § 33.

moyen de distinguer parmi les natures, entre le nombre, la figure, le mouvement, et la puissance, la connaissance, etc. Par conséquent, un autre sens doit être envisagé. La perfection pour Leibniz n'est pas seulement synonyme de la réalité pure ou de l'être positif, elle est encore la *mesure* de cette réalité ou de cet être. Elle est en effet

> «°le degré ou la quantité de réalité ou d'essence, comme l'*intensité* est le degré de la qualité, et la *force* le degré de l'action [...].°»[33]

L'introduction de degrés dans la perfection permet de considérer comme «°plus parfait°» (*perfectius*) «°ce qui possède plus de *réalité* ou d'entité positive.°»[34]

Apparaît ici, après le premier sens, général et absolu, un deuxième sens, quantitatif et relatif : la perfection est l'estimation de la perfection possédée (entendue au premier sens du terme). Un troisième sens – celui qui prévaut à l'article 1 – peut dès lors être dégagé, car il suppose les deux premiers : la perfection est la perfection (au premier sens) en tant qu'elle peut être possédée au suprême degré, c'est-à-dire le plus parfaitement possible (suivant cette fois le deuxième sens). Une perfection, selon cette troisième acception, est une réalité susceptible d'atteindre une limite supérieure maximale – limite qu'il ne faut pas comprendre comme une borne mettant fin arbitrairement à toute progression possible, mais comme la limite qui indique la perfection acquise totalement, entièrement réalisée dans le sujet. Dieu n'est l'être tout parfait (*perfectissimum*) que parce qu'il possède toutes les perfections de cette manière parfaite (*perfectissime*), c'est-à-dire maximale.

On distinguera alors les deux expressions suivantes, souvent employées par Leibniz : *degrés de perfection* et *degrés dans la perfection*. Il y a des *degrés de perfection* dans la mesure où tout être contient plus ou moins de réalité et devient plus parfait par l'obtention de plus d'«entité positive» (perfection au deuxième sens).[35] La perfection consiste ici dans la quantité de réalité acquise. Il y a des *degrés dans la perfection* (prise au troisième sens), dans la mesure où une perfection authentique peut être possédée par un sujet à des

---

[33] À Eckhard (été 1677) ; A II, 1, 543. Voir aussi *De rerum originatione radicali* ; GP VII, 303 ; C, 474 : «°*Perfectio* est magnitudo realitatis°» ; *Monadologie* § 41.
[34] A VI, 4 A, 867.
[35] C'est en ce sens que Leibniz considère que la charité «°doit estre reglée par la justice selon les *degrés de perfection* qui se peuvent trouver ou introduire dans les objects°» (À Madame de Brinon, 9./19. Mai 1691 ; Klopp I, 7, 111. Nous soulignons).

degrés divers : une créature est plus ou moins puissante, plus ou moins savante, mais Dieu l'est entièrement et au dernier degré. La perfection désigne là un attribut *et* la manière dont cet attribut est possédé.

Le critère qui permet d'établir ce troisième sens de la perfection est indirect. L'épreuve du passage au maximum conduit à reconnaître la science et la puissance comme de véritables perfections et d'écarter, comme ne pouvant prétendre à ce titre, le nombre, la figure et, à l'article 23, le mouvement – notions, il faut le souligner, qui sont centrales dans la physique cartésienne pour penser l'étendue.

3. De la perfection de l'action divine à la perfection du monde

À la différence du nombre, de la figure et du mouvement, «°la plus grande science°» et la «°toute-puissance°» sont possibles, c'est-à-dire non contradictoires. Elles sont donc bien des perfections. Cependant, en les attribuant à Dieu, Leibniz ne démontre pas qu'elles sont compatibles dans le même sujet, défini comme l'Être absolument parfait. Il semble plutôt *supposer* qu'elles le sont. Or l'article 23 nous apprendra que la preuve *a priori* de l'existence de Dieu donnée par Descartes[36] est insuffisante car imparfaite, en ce que, justement, elle ne montre pas que la réunion de toutes les perfections, élevées chacune au suprême degré, dans un seul sujet est possible. En l'absence d'une définition *réelle* de Dieu, rien ne garantit que son idée ne soit pas celle d'une chimère. Certes, nous l'avons dit, ce premier article du *Discours* ne vise pas à démontrer l'existence de Dieu, puisqu'il se contente de considérer la notion que nous en avons. Cependant il y prépare : d'une part, en montrant que chaque perfection retenue – omniscience et omnipotence – n'enveloppe pas, prise à part, de contradiction interne inaperçue ; d'autre part, en choisissant ces perfections-là plutôt que d'autres (la justice, l'immensité, l'éternité, etc.), c'est-à-dire des perfections dont la compatibilité est incontestable, puisqu'elles sont complémentaires et toutes deux requises pour qu'il y ait *création* – comme l'avait déjà vu Malebranche.[37]

---

[36] Cf. *Méditation cinquième* et l'article 14 de la «°Première partie°» des *Principes de la philosophie*.
[37] Cf. *Traité de la Nature et de la Grâce*, 1er Discours, 1ère Partie, article 12 : «°La sagesse de Dieu lui découvre une infinité d'idées de différents ouvrages, et toutes les voies possibles d'exécuter ses desseins : et sa puissance le rend tellement maître de toutes choses, et tellement indépendant du secours de quoi que ce soit, qu'il suffit qu'il veuille, afin que ses volontés soient exécutées.°»

Les deux perfections citées peuvent ainsi être mises en rapport immédiatement, sans justification ni preuve explicite de leur accord possible. De la possession conjointe de la sagesse suprême et de la toute-puissance, il suit alors que

> «°Dieu [...] agit de la maniere la plus parfaite, non seulement au sens metaphysique, mais encor moralement parlant, ce qu'on peut exprimer ainsi à nostre égard, que plus on sera éclairé et informé des ouvrages de Dieu, plus on sera disposé à les trouver excellens et entierement satisfaisants à tout ce qu'on auroit pû souhaiter.°»

Deux remarques s'imposent sur cette conclusion de l'article 1, qui sert en même temps d'introduction aux articles suivants (2 à 7).

1. On observe d'abord le passage subreptice opéré par Leibniz de la perfection de l'*action* divine à la perfection de l'*ouvrage* créé, c'est-à-dire de la considération du mode d'agir (les voies divines) à la considération de l'œuvre produite (l'effet obtenu par l'emploi de ces voies). Ce passage pourrait sembler injustifié et même illégitime, car de la façon dont Dieu agit (forcément la plus parfaite, car la plus digne de lui), à l'excellence du monde créé la conséquence n'est pas forcément nécessaire. Il faut même rejeter une telle conséquence pour Malebranche, qui soutient que le monde aurait pu être créé meilleur, quoiqu'il aurait fallu pour cela des voies plus compliquées[38] – thèse que Leibniz contestera à l'article 3. À la différence de l'oratorien (mais aussi de Thomas d'Aquin,[39]) Leibniz refuse en effet de séparer les voies (parfaites) par lesquelles Dieu crée et gouverne l'univers, de l'univers lui-même et de l'appréciation qu'on en doit faire. Pour lui, les voies font partie intégrante de l'ouvrage, les moyens sont eux-mêmes des fins et les lois d'un monde ne sont pas séparables du monde qu'elles règlent.[40] Ainsi l'évaluation de la perfection de

---

[38] Cf. ibid., article 14.
[39] Cf. *De potentia*, qu. 3, a. 16, ad 17 : «°L'univers produit par Dieu est le meilleur (*optimum*) au regard de ce qui existe, non cependant au regard de ce que Dieu peut faire. » Pour Thomas, il faut admettre conjointement ces deux vérités : que «°quelle que soit une chose donnée, Dieu peut toujours en faire une meilleure, » et, pourtant, que «°Dieu ne peut pas faire mieux qu'il ne fait ; car il ne peut rien faire avec plus de sagesse et de bonté°» (*Somme théologique*, Ia pars, qu. 25, a. 6, p. 1).
[40] Cf. *Théodicée*, § 78, § 208 ; Grua, 492 : «°Je croy qu'il faut comprendre les voyes mêmes dans l'ouurage, car les moyens que Dieu choisit sont eux-mêmes des fins autant qu'il se peut, afin qu'il se produise le plus de bien qu'il est possible.°» Voir aussi la lettre de Leibniz à Malebranche de janvier 1712, dans : *Malebranche et Leibniz. Relations personnelles*, p. 418.

l'univers doit comprendre indissociablement la manière divine d'agir (son mode opératoire) et le résultat de l'action même (les effets).
2. On remarque ensuite que la perfection de l'action divine doit se comprendre aussi bien au sens *métaphysique* qu'au sens *moral*. Ce qui revient à conférer une nouvelle acception à la perfection (une quatrième). La perfection de l'œuvre de Dieu ne consiste pas seulement dans les voies choisies pour créer le monde – voies à la fois les plus simples, les plus générales et les plus fécondes en effets – et dans le choix de la série de choses qui contient le plus de réalité possible (perfection *métaphysique*). Elle consiste encore dans la bonté de ce monde (sa perfection *morale*) et dans les lois de la justice par lesquelles Dieu le gouverne, de sorte qu'aucun crime n'y restera impuni ni aucune vertu sans récompense, en cette vie ou dans l'autre. La perfection n'est pas uniquement dans la quantité d'être, d'essence réalisée et dans la manière dont cette quantité est effectivement produite (les voies employées), elle est aussi dans la quantité de bien accompli et dans la manière dont ce bien est donné et distribué (selon la justice). Après la puissance et la sagesse, c'est alors un autre attribut de Dieu qui est mis en lumière : la *bonté*. Et ce sont deux qualités différentes de la Divinité qui apparaissent. Le même Dieu qui, comme architecte et ouvrier, est l'auteur du monde physique, de l'ordre naturel le plus parfait est, comme monarque, le chef de «la plus parfaite republique composée de tous les esprits», dont le dessein principal est le bonheur de ses sujets.[41] Comme l'écrira Leibniz en 1697 dans le *De rerum originatione radicali*°:

> «°[…] il faut savoir […] non seulement que le monde est le plus parfait physiquement, ou si l'on préfère métaphysiquement, c'est-à-dire qu'est réalisée la série de choses dans laquelle se montre la plus grande quantité de réalité en acte, mais aussi qu'il est le plus parfait moralement, parce que la perfection morale est en effet une perfection physique pour les esprits mêmes. D'où il suit que le monde est non seulement une machine très admirable, mais encore, en tant qu'il est constitué d'esprits, la meilleure République, dans laquelle les esprits reçoivent la plus grande quantité de félicité ou de bonheur, qui fait leur perfection physique.°»[42]

Un dernier sens de la perfection se dessine alors : celui que la correspondance avec Wolff mettra en avant, en faisant consister la perfection dans l'*harmonie*. Cette harmonie est à comprendre en un double sens (ontologique et épistémique) et à un double niveau (universel et particulier). Elle est «°l'accord ou

---

[41] Voir le titre de l'article 36.
[42] GP VII, 306.

l'identité dans la variété°» et l'expression de l'ordre le plus intelligible, par le caractère remarquable des propriétés que l'on peut y observer (*observabilitas*). Le monde le plus parfait est le plus harmonieux, c'est-à-dire celui où se manifeste le plus de régularité et s'offre à la raison le plus de matière à des considérations générales (*gradum considerabilitatis*). Au niveau particulier, la perfection se mesure aux «propriétés harmoniques» que possède chaque substance, et à sa capacité à s'accorder avec la plus grande variété de choses.[43]

Quel que soit son degré de connaissance du *Traité de la Nature et de la Grâce*, Leibniz élabore, dès le *Discours de métaphysique*, un lexique et des thèses philosophiques qui lui sont propres. En dépit de formulations apparemment voisines, il est clair que la notion de Dieu qu'il définit à l'article 1 diffère de celle proposée par Malebranche. La perfection est susceptible d'une pluralité de sens, dont cet article se fait l'écho et offre un critère de reconnaissance original, sans équivalent dans l'œuvre de l'oratorien. Là même où les deux auteurs semblent se rejoindre – la détermination des deux principaux attributs divins que sont la sagesse et la puissance, à l'origine de la création du monde –, deux conceptions opposées du rapport voies/effets et, par suite, de l'œuvre divine se font jour. En distinguant la manière dont Dieu gouverne le monde (par les lois simples et générales) du monde lui-même et de l'évaluation de sa bonté, Malebranche s'engage dans une «théodicée» qui justifie l'imperfection de la création par la perfection du mode opératoire divin. En affirmant la solidarité des moyens et des fins, Leibniz s'oblige, quant à lui, à une justification du mal qui le met sur la voie de la thèse du meilleur des mondes possibles.[44]

---

[43] Cf. À Wolff (lettre non datée), dans : *Briefwechsel zwischen Leibniz und Christian Wolff*, éd. par C. I. Gerhardt, Halle, 1860, p. 161 ; À Wolff (18. Mai 1715), p. 170, p. 171 et p. 172. Sur ce sens de la perfection, voir notre ouvrage *Leibniz et le meilleur des mondes possibles*, Paris 2015, pp. 97sq.

[44] Pour une comparaison entre Leibniz et Malebranche en matière de «°théodicée°», voir notre article : «°La question du mal chez Malebranche et Leibniz: théosophie *vs.* Théodicée°», dans : Antoine Grandjean (éd.) : *Théodicées*, Hildesheim/Zürich/New York 2010, pp. 95–115.

"La place d'autruy". Perspectivism and Justice in Leibniz

Mariangela Priarolo (Siena)

Introduction

Perspectivism is usually – and rightly – associated with Friedrich Nietzsche. As we read for instance in On the Genealogy of Morality,

> "There is *only* a perspectival seeing, *only* a perspectival 'knowing'; the *more* affects we are able to put into words about a thing, the *more* eyes, various eyes we are able to use for the same thing, the more complete will be our 'concept' of the thing, our 'objectivity'."[1]

According to some interpretations of Nietzsche, perspectivism is based on the idea that it is impossible to reach a universal truth, independent from the subjects, because there is no truth-in-itself to reach.[2] In this sense, Nietzsche's perspectivism goes hand in hand with the denial of any metaphysical truth. However, a different approach to perspectivism can be found in other thinkers who directly or indirectly questioned Nietzsche's conception. One example is José Ortega y Gasset, who, in 1916, dedicated the introduction to his review "El Espectador" ("The Spectator") to the relationship between truth and perspectivism.[3] According to Ortega y Gasset, perspectivism is different from both skepticism and rationalism, which in his view are more similar than one might think. In fact, skepticism and rationalism would share the same premise: they actually consider the individual points of view *false*. For this reason and because one of its tenets is that only individual points of view exist, skepticism is obliged to reject the existence of the truth. On the other hand, rationalism believes that the truth is attainable, but expels the subject from the knowledge, which can thus be reached only through an extra-individual access. In regard to these theories, perspectivism agrees with skepticism that truth can be grasped only by the individual points of view, but shares with rationalism the

---

[1] Friedrich Nietzsche: *On the Genealogy of Morality*, Third Essay, § 12, ed. by Keith Ansell-Pearson, transl. by Carol Diethe, Cambridge 2006, p. 87.
[2] But see on this Chiara Piazzesi: *Perspectivisme et éthique de la connaissance chez Nietzsche*, forthcoming.
[3] See José Ortega y Gasset: "Verdad y Perspectiva", in: *El espectador*, Madrid 1998, pp. 45–55.

belief in the existence of the truth. Therefore according to perspectivism individual points of view are *true* and, moreover, are the only ways to the truth. But if the truth is attainable only through the individual points of view, it follows that in order to reach a more complete truth human beings necessarily have to cooperate. As a consequence, according to Ortega y Gasset, perspectivism is not only an epistemological theory, but also implies an ethical commitment: the obligation to work together, leaving aside every form particularism.[4]

Ortega y Gasset thought that one of the forerunners of his theoretical framework was Leibniz, whose *Monadology*, particularly article 57,[5] would perfectly describe perspectivism. In effect, Leibniz's life is characterized by the pleas to work together for the unity of knowledge. In this sense, nothing is more distant from Leibniz than Descartes' idea of a self-subsistent subject, working alone in his "stove-heated room (*poêle*)" and thinking that "the works of one man" are the most perfect, as we read in the second part of the *Discourse on the Method*.[6] Nonetheless, it is well known that Leibniz's monads "have no windows, through which anything could come in or go out",[7] and that each monad is radically different from the others and that "*must be different*"[8]. But if so, how is it possible for different beings to find a way to understand each other in order to cooperate?

In the following pages I will try to give an answer to this question by analyzing Leibniz's notion of justice as "the charity of the wise". In the first part I will briefly recall the principal elements of this notion. In the second part I will show how it is actually possible according to Leibniz's main tenets to be just, i.e. to reach the place of others. In the conclusion I will suggest that, contrarily to Ortega y Gasset's opinion, Leibniz thinks that from an ethical point of view perspectivism must be overtaken.

---

[4] "como las riberas independientes se aúnan en la gruesa vena del río, compongamos el torrente de lo real", Ortega y Gasset: "Verdad y Perspectiva", p. 52.
[5] "Et comme une même ville regardée de diffèrents côtés paraît tout autre et est comme multipliée perspectivement, il arrive de même, que par la multitude infinie des substances simples, il y a comme autant de différent univers, qui ne sont pourtant que les perspectives d'un seul selon les différent points de vue de chaque Monade"; GP VI, 616.
[6] *Oeuvres de Descartes*, ed. by Charles Adam and Paul Tannery, Paris 1964–1974, 11 vols., vol. VI, p. 11.
[7] *Monadologie*, § 7; GP VI, 607; English translation in: Gottfried Wilhelm Leibniz: *Philosophical Texts*, transl. and ed. by Richard S. Woolhouse and Richard Francks, Oxford 1988, p. 268.
[8] "il faut que chaque monade soit differente de chaque autre", *Monadologie*, § 9, GP VI, 608 my emphasis; Leibniz: *Philosophical Texts*, p. 269.

1. Justice and Perspectivism

Leibniz's definition of justice is well known: justice is "the charity of the wise". As the scholars have pointed out, the first appearance of this definition is in a letter to Johann Friedrich in 1677.[9] However, in Leibniz's writings we can find the most occurences of this term from the beginning of the 1690s, which however Leibniz stated in public only in 1693, in the preface to the *Codex Iuris Gentium*. The *Codex* was a collection of acts and treaties, occasioned by the battles of the Duke of Hannover for the Electorate – which was obtained by the House of Hannover in December 1692. The aim of the *Codex* was to clairify the grounds of the international law through the exposition of several documents concerning the European states from the end of the eleventh century until the seventeenth century. That because of Leibniz's essential thesis according to which phenomena express their metaphysical reasons. As we read in the second paragraph of the *Codex*, for instance,

> "from what is obvious one divines what is hidden, and phenomena are observed in order to discover the reasons for that which appears."[10]

In this sense the history of the states, of their formation, of the conquering, more or less bloody, of new territories does not only reveal the signs of their actual future, but also suggests the main principles of the natural law on which the international law is, or better, *has to be* grounded. The gap between what the international law is and what it has to be depends also on the ignorance regarding what the principles of the right actually are. As Leibniz observed in the central paragraphs of the preface to the *Codex*,

> "The doctrine of right (*juris*) [...] presents an immense field for human study. But the notions of right and of justice (*juris et justitiae*), even after having been treated by so many illustrious authors, have not been made sufficiently clear."[11]

---

[9] More precisely, on the 9th May 1677. See A I, 2, 23. On Leibniz's definition of justice the literature is wide. See at least Gaston Grua: *La justice humaine selon Leibniz*, Paris 1956 and Patrick Riley: *Leibniz' universal jurisprudence: Justice as the charity of the wise*, Cambridge 1996

[10] A IV, 5, 52; translation in: *The Political Writings of Leibniz* ed. by Patrick Riley, Cambridge 1972, p. 167.

[11] A IV, 5, 60; *The Political Writings of Leibniz*, p. 170 (slightly modified).

According to Leibniz, right (*jus*) is "a kind of moral possibility (*potentia moralis*)"[12], a definition that can be already found in the *Nova methodus discendae et docendaeque jurisprudentiae* (1667).[13] Since moral is "that which is equivalent to natural to a good man", therefore right is therefore the quality of all good actions, or, conversely, the frame in which the actions of good men take place. In other words, according to Leibniz the field of the right, the *jus naturalis*, corresponds to the field of morality, so that every possible good action from the *social* point of view is also a right action from the *moral* point of view. In this sense, Leibniz refuted Machiavelli's separation between the moral dimension and the political dimension of life, as well as the autonomy of the political sphere. As is well known, this separation concerns not only Machiavelli's thought but also Hobbes' and Pufendorf's, which are the target of several critics of Leibniz and particularly of Leibniz's widest writing on justice, the *Meditation on the Common Concept of Justice* (1702–1703).[14]

The first part of the *Meditation* precisely addresses the refusal of Hobbes's conception of justice as a consequence of the will of the sovereign:

"It is agreed – Leibniz wrote – that whatever God wills is good and just. But there remains the question whether it is good and just because God wills it or whether God wills it because it is good and just: in other words, whether justice and goodness are arbitrary or whether they belong to the necessary and eternal truths about the nature of things, as do numbers and proportions."[15]

Leibniz's answer stressed the danger in considering justice and goodness arbitrary, a danger that can be summarized in one word: tyranny. Leibniz's reasoning which we can also find in the *Observations on the Principles of Pufendorf*, written in the same period of the *Meditation on the Common Concept of Justice* (1706), was as follows: if we state that justice is arbitrary and, as a result, the foundation of laws is just the command of a superior as Pufendorf thinks, therefore

---

[12] A IV, 5, 61.

[13] A VI, 1, 301 (§ 14): "Moralitas autem, seu Justitita vel Injustitia actionis oritur ex qualitate personae agentis in ordine ad actionem, ex actionibus praecedentibus orta, quae dicitur: qualitas moralis. Ut autem Qualitas realis in ordine ad actionem duplex est: Potentia agendi, et necessitas agendi; ita potentia moralis dicitur Jus, necessitas moralis dicitur Obligatio."

[14] See on this Ian Hunter: *Rival Enlightenments. Civil and Metaphysical Philosophy in Early Modern Germany*, Cambridge 2011.

[15] *The Political Writings of Leibniz*, p. 45.

> "there will be no duty when there is no superior to compel its observance; nor will there be any duties for those who do not have a superior. And since, according to the author [=Pufendorf], duty and acts prescribed by justice coincide [...] it follows that all law is prescribed by a superior. [...]. Now, then, will he who is invested with the supreme power do nothing against justice if he proceeds tyrannically against his subjects, torments them, and kills them under torture; who makes war without a cause?"[16]

If all obligations are derived only by a command, Leibniz continues, then international law, along with every pact and covenant, are impossible, because there is no common superior and therefore no common obligation. But if this is so, Pufendorf's argument proves too much

> "namely that men cannot set up any superior for themselves by consent and agreement: which is contrary to what [even] Hobbes admit."[17]

As a consequence, according to Leibniz, Hobbes' and Pufendorf's conception of justice as arbitrary ends up denying the main tenets of Hobbes' and Pufendorf's political doctrine, i.e., contractualism, a clear sign of the inconsistency of such a view. On the contrary, both justice and goodness, far from being arbitrary, have the same ontological and epistemological status of mathematical truths:

> "justice follows certain rules of equality and of proportion [which are] no less founded in the immutable nature of things, and in divine ideas, than are the principles of arithmetic and of geometry."[18]

As Leibniz clarifies in the *Meditation*, justice is absolute, i.e., independent from God's decrees, and is the same for God and men, although there is an obvious difference of degree between divine and human (just) actions.[19] Hence, those who think that justice is arbitrary, depending on the will of a superior, confound right and law and attribute to the first the feature of the second. In this sense, Leibniz observes,

---

[16] Dutens IV, 3, 279; *The Political Writings of Leibniz*, p. 70.
[17] Ibid.
[18] Dutens IV, 3, 280; *The Political Writings of Leibniz*. p. 71.
[19] Cf., Ibid., p. 48

"[r]ight cannot be unjust, it is a contradiction; but law can be. For it is power which gives and maintains law; and if this power lacks wisdom or good will, it can give and maintain quite evil laws."[20]

Far from being arbitrary, justice has an intelligible notion, a formal reason or a definition from which all its properties *in principle* can be derived. According to this definition, "Justice is nothing else than that which conforms to wisdom and goodness joined together."[21] Justice is then a virtue that joins both the intellectual and the practical side of the human beings: it joins the intellectual side because wisdom is a property of the understanding, but also the practical side because goodness pertains to the will. According to this view, justice is not only an intellectual concept, but a real way of being, or in Leibniz's words a *habitus*, "the habit of loving in accordance with wisdom."[22]

The thesis that justice is a *habitus*, which is present in Leibniz's writings since the *Elementa juris naturalis* (1670–1671),[23] is pivotal for understanding the difference between his definition of justice and the definitions given by the authors he refers to, namely Grotius, Hobbes and Pufendorf. As in the juridical tradition, for Leibniz justice concerns the relationships between the individuals, but not *externally*, as something that regulates the quarrels among people "giving to each his due". This function is, of course, also present in Leibniz but represents a lower degree of the right, i.e., the second degree of right.[24] The universal concept of justice, which coincides with Leibniz's third degree of right "piety" and with the third precept "honeste vivere", prescribes something more, i.e., to do something positive to the others. In this sense, as Leibniz explains, justice is nothing but the golden rule, "the rule of reason and of our Master", i.e. "*quod tibi non vis fieri, aut quod tibi vis fieri, neque aliis facito aut negate.*"[25] From this definition, we understand that according to Leibniz the golden rule has to be read in a positive way, as a rule

---

[20] Ibid., p. 50.
[21] Ibid., p. 50.
[22] "Happiness" (1694–1698?) in Grua, 581ff. and now also in A VI, 5, Internetausgabe, n. 1302, English translation in: *The Shorter Leibniz Texts. A collection of New Translations*, ed. by Lloyd Strickland, London 2006, p. 167.
[23] "Justitita est habitus (seu status confirmatus viri boni)"; A VI, 1, 480.
[24] See for instance *Nova methodus discendae docendae jurisprudentiae*; A VI, 1, 290 and ff. On the three degrees of right see Christopher Johns: *The Science of Right in Leibniz' Moral and Political Philosophy*, London/New York 2013, pp. 12 and ff.
[25] Georg Mollat: *Rechtsphilosophisches aus Leibnizens ungedruckten Schriften*, Leipzig 1885, pp. 41–70, here 58; *The Political Writings of Leibniz*, p. 56. On Leibniz's golden rule see Mo-

that command us to do something and not only to abstain from doing something. In order to avoid injustice – for instance, because we do something that we think is good for the others despite the others' real desires – we have to put ourselves "in the place of another". Only in this way will we "have the true point for judging what is just or not."[26]

The aim of justice is then precisely to leave our point of view and take the perspective of others. But how is it possible to be just and therefore to deplace ourselves if, as we mentioned, we are monads, i.e., self-subsistent individuals with no windows? We will address this question in the next part.

2. Different Points of View

> "[E]ach substance is like a separate world, independent of every other thing except God. So all our phenomena, that is to say everything which can ever happen to us, can only be consequences of our being."[27]

With these words in the *Discourse on Metaphysics* Leibniz summarized the definition of individual substance as something that has a complete notion in the mind of God. Since the substance is completely determined, everything that will happen to it is already inscribed in its notion, so that she who had a complete knowledge of this notion would know *a priori* if the individual described by the notion would do this or that (§ 8). However this independence does not imply the isolation of the substance in regard to the others. As Leibniz explained to Gabriel Wagner, a materialistic philosopher who corresponded with him for about four months between December 1697 and March 1698,[28] "Monads do not exist in isolation. They are monads, not nuns [*Sunt monadae, non monachae*]."[29] On the contrary: because substances constitute the world

---

gens Lærke: "The golden rule: Aspects of Leibniz's method for religious controversy", in: Marcelo Dascal (ed.): *The Practice of Reason. Leibniz and His Controversies*, Amsterdam/Philadelphia 2010, pp. 297–319.
[26] Mollat: *Rechtsphilosophisches aus Leibnizens ungedruckten Schriften*, p. 58; *The Political Writings of Leibniz*, p. 56. On the "place of the other" see Naaman Zauderer: "The Place of the Other in Leibniz's Rationalism", in: *Gottfried Wilhelm Leibniz: What Kind of Rationalist*, ed. by Marcelo Dascal, Dordrecht 2008, pp. 315–327.
[27] *Discours de Metaphysique*, § 14; A VI, 4, 1550; *Philosophical Texts*, p. 66.
[28] See Daniel Garber: "Monads on My Mind", in: Adrian Nita (ed.): *Leibniz's Metaphysics and Adoption of Substantial Forms: Between Continuity and Transformation*, Dordrecht 2015, pp. 161–176, in part. pp. 169–172.
[29] A II 3 704.

and in every possible world "all things are connected"[30], in every substance there are the "traces of everything that happens in the universe."[31] This is precisely the ground of Leibniz's perspectivism. As we read in article 9 of the *Discourse on Metaphysics*,

> "each substance is like a whole world, and like a mirror of God, or indeed of the whole universe, which each one expresses in its own fashion – rather as the same town is differently represented according to the different situations of the person who looks at it."[32]

The same argument is present in the *Monadology*, articles 56 and 57:

> "§ 56 [...] this *interconnection* or this adapting of all created things to each one, and of each one to all the others, means that each simple substance has relationships which express all the others, and that it is therefore a perpetual living mirror of the universe.
> § 57. And just as the same town when seen from different sides will seem quite different, and is as it were multiplied perspectively, the same things happens here: because of the infinite multitude of simple substances it is as if there were as many different universes; but they are all perspectives on the same one, according to the different *point of view* of each monad."[33]

The independence and self-subsistence of every monad in regard to others goes hand in hand with the interconnection among all the monads in the universe, an interconnection that is the *pre-established harmony* founded in God's *ars combinatoria* decribed by Leibniz especially in the *Système nouveau* of 1695. Every monad is then at the same time autonomous and integrated in a system of relationships which it grasps only in part from its specific point of view. This "grasping" is nothing but perceiving, the main activity of each monad. As Leibniz explains in article 60 of the *Monadology*, "a monad is representative in its nature"[34], and as a consequence it perceives the whole universe, albeit in a confused way. The difference among the monads lies precisely in the degree of distinction of their perceptions, so that we pass from

---

[30] *Essais de Théodicée*, I, § 9; GP VI, 107.
[31] *Discours de Metaphysique*, § 8; A VI 4, 1541; Leibniz: *Philosophical Texts*, p. 60.
[32] A VI, 4, 1542; Leibniz: *Philosophical Texts*, p. 61.
[33] GP VI, 616; Leibniz: *Philosophical Texts*, p. 275.
[34] *Monadologie*, § 60; GP VI, 617; Leibniz: *Philosophical Texts*, p. 276.

the "completely naked monad"[35] which lies in a condition of "permanent stupor"[36] to the monad that has only distinct thoughts, i.e., God.[37] Therefore, according to Leibniz the universe is a net of monads with varying degree of awareness of what they perceive, with each of them representing the same object but in different ways:

> "They all [the monads] reach confusedly to infinity, to everything; but they are limited and differentiated by their level of distinct perception."[38]

This description, however, seems to portray a status of the universe that we can call its "starting point". In fact, since the monads are by nature active – they perceive and move endlessly from one perception to another – the degree of their perceptions, as well as their perceptions, changes through time.[39] This means that although the point of view from which the monad looks at itself and at the world around it remains the same, the content of the perceptions varies. The variation can depend on an external cause (for instance, the sound of a glass broken by my cat walking on the table which makes me aware of that part of my house and of my life) or on the monad itself (I wonder what my cat is doing and look at her until she breaks the glass) which according to Leibniz is free. As Leibniz stressed in the *Theodicy*, the freedom of the monad is grounded in its spontaneity, that is, in having the principle of its action in itself.

> "§ 290 [...] spontaneity [...] belongs to us in so far as we have within us the source of our actions, as Aristotle rightly conceived [...]."[40]

---

[35] § 24; GP VI, 611; Leibniz: *Philosophical Texts*, p. 271.
[36] Ibid.
[37] See also *Principes de la nature et de la grâce*, § 13: "Chaque Ame connoit l'infini, connoit tout, mais confusement; comme en me promenant sur le rivage de la mer, et entendant le grand bruit qu'elle fait, j'entends les bruits particulier de chaque vague dont le bruit total est composé, mais sans les discerner; nos perceptions confuses sont le resultat des impressions que tout l'univers fait sur nous. Il en est de même de chaque Monade. Dieu seul a une connoissance distincte de tout, car il en est la source"; GP VI, 604.
[38] § 60; GP VI, 617; Leibniz: *Philosophical Texts*, p. 276.
[39] On this see for instance the short text *De mundi perfectione continuo augente* (1689–1690?); A VI, 4 B, 1642.
[40] *Essais de Théodicée*, III, § 290, 291; GP VI, 288, English translation in: Gottfried Wilhelm Leibniz: *Theodicy. Essays on the Goodness of God, the Freedom of Man and the Origin of Evil*, ed. and with an introd. by Austin Farrer, transl. by E. M. Huggard, Charleston 2007, p. 307.

In the case of the monads of a "higher degree", i.e., the monads that are aware of themselves, the spontaneity allows them to dominate their own actions:

> "§ 291 [...] true spontaneity is common to us and all simple substances, and that in the intelligent or free substance this becomes a mastery over its actions."[41]

For Leibniz, this mastery seems to correspond mainly to an increase in the monads' awareness, which gives rise to an extension of the knowledge of ourselves and of the world. In fact, the wider our knowledge, the more powerful we are:

> "§ 289 Our knowledge is of two kinds, distinct or confused. Distinct knowledge, or *intelligence*, occurs in the actual use of reason; but the senses supply us with confused thoughts. And we may say that we are immune from bondage in so far as we act with a distinct knowledge, but we are the slaves of passion in so far as our perceptions are confused."[42]

Our freedom is thus strictly tied with the awareness of what we do, of our actions and as much as possible of the consequences of our actions.

Now, according to Leibniz all our actions are driven by what appears to be good to us:

> "[...] I do not require the will always follow the judgement of the understanding, because I distinguish this judgement from the motives that spring from insensible perceptions and inclination. But I hold that the will always follows the most advantageous representation, whether distinct or confused, of the good or the evil resulting from reasons, passions and inclinations [...]."[43]

Therefore, the extension of our distinct perceptions also implies an extension of the understanding of what real good is. As a consequence, the increase of our distinct perceptions also implies an increase of our capacity to act well. In this sense, as Leibniz wrote in the *Meditation on Justice*,

---

[41] *Essais de Théodicée*, III, § 290, 291; GP VI, 288; *Theodicy,* transl. by E.M. Huggard, p. 307.
[42] *Essais de Théodicée*, III, § 289; GP VI, 289; *Theodicy,* transl. by E. M. Huggard, p. 306
[43] *Remarques sur le livre de l'origine du mal, publié depuis peu en Angleterre*, GP VI, 413; *Theodicy,* transl. by E. M. Huggard, p. 420.

> "Wisdom, which is the knowledge of our own good, brings us to justice, that is to a reasonable advancement of the good of others."[44]

By improving our awareness and our knowledge of ourselves, of the world, and of those necessary truths whose knowledge distinguishes the reasonable souls from the bare monads,[45] we can thus reach that wisdom that turns on our practical dimension, leading us to justice. In fact, although Leibniz claimed that the act of will does not derive automatically from an intellectual judgement,[46] the expansion of the conscious knowledge increases our perfection and gives us a feeling of pleasure. As we read in a writing on happiness of the end of the 1690s,

> "Happiness is a lasting state of joy [...]. Joy is the total pleasure which results from everything the soul feels at once [...]. Pleasure is the feeling of some perfection, and this pefection that causes pleasure can be found not only in us, but also elsewhere. For when we notice it, this very knowledge excites some perfection in us, because the representation of the perfection is also a perfection. This is why it is hood to familiarize oneself with objects that have many perfections. And we must avoid the hate and envy which prevent us from taking pleasure in these objects."[47]

This means, firstly, that knowledge produces in us some changes in both the intellectual and the affective sphere, and, secondly, that it connects us with the others in both spheres. In this sense, Leibniz defines wisdom as "the science of happiness", i.e., the knowledge of what is needed to reach that lasting state

---

[44] See *Meditation sur la notion commune de la justice*, Mollat, p. 59; *The Political Writings of Leibniz*, p. 57.
[45] See *Monadologie*: "§ 29 [...] la connoissance des verités necessaires et eternelles est ce qui nous distingue des simples animaux et nous fait avoir la *Raison* et les sciences, en nous éelevant à la connoissance de nous mêmes et de Dieu. Et c'est ce qu'on appelle en nous Ame raisonnable, ou *Esprit*. § 30 C'est aussi par la connoissance des verités necessaires et par leur abstractions, que nous sommes éelevés aux *Actes reflexifs*, qui nous font penser à ce qui s'appelle *Moy*, et à considerer que cecy ou cela est en Nous: et c'est ainsi, qu'en pensant à nous, nous pensons à l'Etre, à la substance, au simple et au composé, à l'immateriel et à Dieu même, en concevant que ce qui est borné en nous, est en luy sans bornes. Et ces Actes Reflexifs fournissent les objetct principaux de nos raisonnemens"; GP VI, 612.
[46] See the passage from Gottfried Wilhelm Leibniz: *Remarques sur le livre de l'origine du mal*, 1710 quoted *supra* in the main text.
[47] See for instance the writing on *Happiness* quoted above, *The Shorter Leibniz Texts*, p. 169. On happiness see Donald Rutheford: *Leibniz and the Rational Order of Nature*, Cambridge 1998, pp. 46 and ff.

of joy that corresponds to happiness.[48] However, as Leibniz stated in the *Elementa juris naturalis*, "No one can easily be happy in the midst of miserable people."[49] As a consequence, to be just – that is, to do to the others what we would like others to do to us – is not only desirable from the point of view of goodness, but also from an egoistic point of view. The bridge that can join the natural egoism with the (less natural) altruism is the central element of justice, a particular condition of the soul: love.

As we read for instance in the *Elementa verae pietatis* (1677–1678?),

> "Love is to be delighted by the happiness of someone, or to experience pleasure from the happiness of another. I define this as true love."[50]

This definition of love will remain until the last writings, in which Leibniz uses it also to argue against quietism, one of the most important philosophical controversies of the time.[51] Since, as we mentioned, happiness arises from the sentiment of perfection, the one who loves finds pleasure in the perfections of the beloved. Therefore, love connects the lover and the beloved, whose well-being produces egoistic pleasure in the lover.

From this description it looks like the feeling of pleasure for the perfections of others follows as a consequence of love: that is, love is the condition for feeling delighted by the beloved. In this sense, it is because Mary loves Anna that Mary feels pleasure for the perfections of Anna. In another context, however, Leibniz states something different. As he writes precisely in the *Meditation on the Common Concept of justice*,

> "One cannot know God as one ought without loving him above all things, and one cannot love him without willing what he wills. His perfections are infinite and cannot end, and this is why the pleasure which consists in the feeling of his perfections is the greatest and most durable which can exist. That is, the greatest happiness, which causes one to love him, causes one to be happy and virtuous at the same time."[52]

---

[48] Ibid.
[49] A VI 1, 460. English translation in Gottfried Wilhelm Leibniz: *Philosophical Papers and Letters. A Selection*, ed. by Leroy Loemker, Dordrecht 1989, p. 132.
[50] A VI, 4 B, 1357; *The Shorter Leibniz Texts*, p. 189.
[51] See on this the letter to Nicaise, 19th August 1697; A II, 3, N. 140 (Online Edition 8129): "l'amour est cet acte ou estat actif de l'ame qui nous fait trouver nostre plaisir dans la felicité ou satisfaction d'autruy. Cette definition, comme j'ay marqué dés lors, est capable de resoudre l'enigme de l'amour desinteressé, et le distingue des liaisons d'interest ou de débauche."
[52] *The Political Writings of Leibniz*, p. 59.

In the case of God, therefore, the knowledge of his perfections causes that specific act of the soul which is love for god, and in addition produces in us the virtue of loving others as God loves them. In other words, by knowing God, the infinite being, we love him and become able to love others.[53] But how can we know God and make God known to other people? Certainly not through books on religion or by means of preachers, which "far from removing doubts, rise them",[54] Leibniz wrote in a letter to Thomas Burnett. On the contrary,

> "I would like that in order to make known the wisdom of God one tries with physics and mathematics, through revealing always more the marvels of nature."[55]

In this sense, Leibniz observes in the *Meditation on Justice*, the progress of the knowledge of truth would also influence the public good

> "which is strongly interested in the augmentation of the treasure of human knowledge."[56]

But in order to do that we must not only cooperate but above of all set aside that spirit of sectarianism that prevents us from seeing the truth in different

---

[53] See also Letter on Christian Thomasius to the abbot of Boccum: "Je ne suis pas dans son sentiment lorsqu'il fait l'amour anterieur à la lumiere. [Je crois que nous avons de la lumiere et de l'intelligence en tant que nous sommes passif et recevons en nous l'action de Dieu, mais nous sommes agissans en tant que nous agissons envers les autres creatures, car nous ne scaurions agir sur Dieu, ainsi nostre union avec Dieu ne peur estre que passive de nostre costé]. Nous ne pouvons estre unis avec Dieu que passivement à son egard car nous ne scaurions agir sur luy, et nous devons recevoir son action en nous [mais cette lumiere faisant naistre en nous un effort pour agir sur nous et sur les autres choses conformement à cette lumière, cet effort d'un esprit eclairé qui va à exprimer le bien est l'amour], pour agir par apres conformement à son esprit, tant sur nous que sur les autres choses. Ainsi la lumiere est notre passion, l'amour est le plaisir qui en resulte, et qui consiste dans une action sur nous mêmes, dont provient un effort d'agir encor sur les autres pour contribuer au bien en tant qu'il depend de nous", Grua 87. On the love of God as "the fountain of true justice", see Stuart Brown: "Leibniz's Moral Philosophy", in: Nicholas Jolley: *The Cambridge Companion to Leibniz*, Cambridge 1995, pp. 423 and ff.
[54] Leibniz to Thomas Burnett s.d. s.l.; GP III, 279.
[55] Ibid.
[56] *The Political Writings of Leibniz*, p. 53.

opinions.[57] This (bad) attitude depends, again, mostly on our unconscious beliefs, on our personal history, and on our particular point of view on the universe. As a consequence, in order to attain that knowledge of God that teaches us to leave our particular point of view and reach "the place of others", we first have to become aware of the limits of our being a particular point of view on the universe. In other words, to open our minds and take the point of view of others, we must first acknowledge that we are just a point of view on the universe. The new point of view that we adopt will thus be that "appropriate place [...] to make us to discover thoughts, which would otherwise not occur."[58]

Conclusions

"We are not [...] born for ourselves, but for the good of society, as are parts for the whole."[59]

Written around 1686, the same year as the *Discourse on Metaphysics*, these words express Leibniz' thought regarding the main reason that explains the moral and the political obligation we have with respect to other people. "We are not born for ourselves", and therefore we cannot close ourselves in our egoism; instead we must move toward the others. However, it is also true that despite our being "parts" we are nonetheless "wholes", every monad being "a separate world."[60] For this reason a form of perspectivism, not to say *egocentrism*, is unavoidable, because each of us experiences, and cannot help but

---

[57] See for instance Gottfried Wilhelm Leibniz: *Eclaircissement des difficultés que Monsieur Bayle a trouvées dans le systeme nouveau de l'union de l'ame et du corps*: "lorsqu'on entre dans le fonds des choses, on remarque plus de la raison qu'on ne croyoit dans la plupart des sectes des philosophes. Le peu de realité substantielle des choses sensibles des Sceptiques; la reduction de tout aux harmonies ou nombres, idées et percetions des Pythagoristes et Platoniciens; l'un et même un tout de Parménide et de Plotin, sans aucun Spinozisme; la connexion Stoïcienne, compatible avec la spontaneité des autres; la philosophie vitale des Cabalistes et Hermetiques, qui mettent du sentiment par tout, les formes et les entelechies d'Aristote et des Scholastiques; et cependant l'explication mecanique de tous les phenomenes particuliers selon Democrite et les modernes, etc. se retrouvent reunies comme dans un centre de perspective, d'où l'object (embrouillé en regardant de tout autre endroit) fait voir sa regularité et la convenance de ses parties: on a manqué le plus par un esprit de Secte, en se bornant par la rejection des autres"; GP III, 523f.
[58] *La place d'autruy*, 1679?;Grua, 701; A IV, 3 N. 137. English translation in Gottfried Wilhelm Leibniz: *The Art of Controversies*, transl. and ed., with an introductory essay and notes by Marcelo Dascal, with Quintín Racionero and Adelino Cardoso, Dordrecht 2006, p. 165.
[59] *Sur la generosité* (1686–1687?); A VI, 4 C, 2722; *The Shorter Leibniz Texts*, p. 159.
[60] *Discours de Metaphysique*, § 14.

experience, the world from a specific perspective. This is the consequence of Leibniz's basic perspectivism, a perspectivism that we can call *metaphysical perspectivism*, and which Leibniz described in the article 57 of the *Monadology* mentioned above. According to this, as we have seen, each individual is a certain view of God on the world and contributes to constituting reality. Additionally, we can also identify two other kinds of perspectivism. The first is *perceptual perspectivism*, which follows directly from the metaphysical perspectivism, i.e., the idea according to which every individual perceives the world from her point of view, and since these perceptions are mostly confused or unconscious, she has a very limited understanding of what happens. The second form of perspectivism can be defined as *ethical perspectivism*. This perspectivism is the one prescribed by the notion of justice and invites us to change our perspective, to decenter ourselves and reach the place of others. However, it is important to note that by reaching this place we are not only obtaining a new perspective or a new point of view. As Leibniz explains in the *Meditation on Justice*, while commenting on the objection one can make against the golden rule, i.e., "that a criminal can claim, by virtue of this maxim, a pardon from the sovereign judge, because the judge would wish the same thing if he were in a similar position"[61]:

> "The reply is easy: the judge must put himself not only in the place of the criminal, but also in that of others, who are interested that the crime be punished. And the balance of good (in which the lesser evil is included) must determine it [the case]."[62]

Hence, to reach the place of others does not mean to reach another specific point of view, but on the contrary *to leave* any specific point of view. In this sense the only point of view that seems really desirable is the point of view of God, that is, a global view of the world that would reveal all its perfection and harmony:

> "[…] those who examine the interior of things – Leibniz writes to Sophie Charlotte – find everything so well ordered there that they would not be able to doubt that the universe is governed by a sovereign intelligence, in an order so perfect, that, if one understood it in detail, one would not only believe but would even see that nothing better could be wished for. […] and just as what we see now is only a very small portion of the infinite universe, and as our present life is only

---

[61] *The Political Writings of Leibniz*, p. 56.
[62] Ibid.

a small fragment of what must happen to us, we should not be surprised if the full beauty of things is not initially discovered there; but we will enter into it more and more, and it is for precisely this reason that it is necessary that we change our situation."[63]

This implies that, contrary to what Ortega y Gasset thought, Leibniz cannot be seen as a forerunner of perspectivism, at least in Ortega y Gasset's meaning of perspectivism, because in his philosophy, and even more in his ethics, the aim of ethical perspectivism is to make the metaphysical and perceptual perspectivism *disappear*. For this reason, it seems that Leibniz can be hardly separated from rationalism, that is, from the thesis that the truth exists as independent of the subjects and therefore must be grasped as much as possible independently from the singular points of view. However, Leibniz's rationalism, far from being a rejection of the truth of the different perspectives on the world as Ortega y Gasset stated, invites us to give to all these perspectives a real value.

---

[63] Leibniz to Sophie Charlotte, 9/19 May 1697; A I, 14, 196, English translation in: *Leibniz and the Two Sophies: the Philosophical Correspondence*, ed. and transl. by Lloyd Strickland, Toronto 2011, p. 160.

Leibniz' Akademiepläne als europäisches Projekt

Hartmut Rudolph (Hannover)

Es sind zwei große Projekte, die der junge Leibniz im Dienst des Mainzer Kurfürsten Erzbischofs und Reichserzkanzlers Johann Philipp von Schönborn entwirft und die beide einen Großteil seines Wirkens bis in seine letzten Lebenstage hinein ausfüllen werden, zum einen die Einigung der gespaltenen Christenheit und zum anderen die Gründung gelehrter Gesellschaften oder wie sie später genannt werden, Akademien der Wissenschaften. Beide Projekte werden in ihrer Bedeutung nicht erfasst, wenn man sie losgelöst betrachtet von der Metaphysik, der Wissenschaftslehre, der Rechtsphilosophie und der politischen Philosophie und Ethik; und sie werden der Leibniz'schen Intention nach nicht begriffen, wenn man sie lediglich zu Pflichtarbeiten eines höfischen Bediensteten oder zu Unternehmungen, fixen Ideen eines – dazu nicht sonderlich erfolgreichen – barocken Projektemachers degradiert.

In der hier gebotenen Kürze sei stattdessen thesen- und stichwortartig auf gewisse Elemente hingewiesen, in denen jene Zusammenhänge sichtbar werden, an denen aber vor allem geprüft werden soll, inwiefern das Leibniz'sche Akademienprogramm ein europäisches Projekt genannt werden kann. Doch seien zuvor in sieben Punkten einige gemeinsame Kennzeichen der Leibniz'schen Projekte angeführt.

1. Schon in den Entwürfen der Mainzer Zeit (1668–1672) fordert Leibniz, dass die Wissenschaften und somit auch die gelehrten Gesellschaften nicht bloß der Befriedigung der *curiositas* dienen dürfen, sondern sich durch *utilitas*, durch den Nutzen für die gesamte Menschheit (nicht nur für Europa also) auszeichnen.
2. Worin die Nützlichkeit, die *utilitas*, besteht, definiert Leibniz schon in einer seiner ersten Entwürfe 1669, *Societas philadelphica*, mit folgendem Dreischritt:

> „Das für jeden Nützlichste ist dasjenige, was Gott am angenehmsten ist", sodann „Gott ist aber dasjenige am angenehmsten, was die Perfection des Universums herbeiführt" und schließlich „Zur perfection des Universums führt alles das, was der Perfection der Menschheit dient. Denn in der sensiblen Welt gibt es nichts Vollkommeneres als den Menschen."[1]

---

[1] A IV, 1, 552f. (Übers. H. R.).

Das Nützliche, so der Sinn dieser Deduktion, ist das, was der Vervollkommnung der Menschheit dient, die Leibniz dann in allen späteren Sozietätsprojekten mit der *gloria dei* gleichsetzen wird. Das bedeutet: Seine Akademiepläne betreffen nicht irgendeinen Teilbereich staatlichen Handelns, wie z. B. die Fischzucht, den Ackerbau oder das Theaterwesen, sondern sind gesamtgesellschaftlich und global ausgerichtet.

3. Das aber heißt: Seine Akademiepläne sieht Leibniz als Bestandteil dessen, was er im *Discours de métaphysique* und in der *Monadologie* als das universelle Wirken des göttlichen Monarchen an der größtmöglichen Glückseligkeit beschreibt.[2] Der universelle Monarch wirkt durch die Geister, die eine Art Gemeinschaft mit Gott eingehen und ihn, den Architekten des Universums, in architektonischen Probemustern als kleine Gottheiten imitieren.[3]

4. Das Ziel größtmöglicher Glückseligkeit klingt unerreichbar, ist aber alles andere als utopisch gemeint, sondern äußerst nüchtern: Schon im *Grundriß eines Bedenckens von auffrichtung einer Societät in Teütschland zu auffnehmen der Künste und Wißenschaften* (1671) distanziert sich Leibniz explizit von allen Utopien, auch denen Bacons und Campanellas, mit nahezu denselben Worten wie in einer Schrift aus den 1680er Jahren und schlägt stattdessen vor:

> „ein ieder [thue] das seine in seiner Sphaera activatis [...], Maßen vielleicht Mittel zu finden, die dem ansehen nach gering, auch von nicht großen Kosten, und dennoch zu gemeinem Nuzen, zu aufnehmen des Vaterlandes, zu vieler Menschen unterhalt und conservation, zur ehre Gottes und entdeckung seiner Wunder, große Würckung haben köndten."

Das genau ist die Aufgabe der Politiker,

> „der Moralistae, als P o l i t i c i , als Rectores Rerum publicarum". Sie sollen sich bemühen, „nicht allein den glanz Göttlicher Herrligkeit in der Natur zu finden, sondern auch durch imitation (schon hier also ein Gedanke der *Monadologie*) nachzuahmen",

---

[2] *Discours de métaphysique* XXXV; A VI, 4, 1587 und *Monadologie* ch. 86–90; Gottfried Wilhelm Leibniz: *Discours de métaphysique suivi de Monadologie et autres textes*, hrsg. v. Michel Fichant, Paris 2004, S. 242–244.

[3] „Les Esprits sont encore des images de la Divinité même [...] capables de connaître le Système de l'univers et d'en imiter quelque chose par des échatillons architectoniques"; *Monadologie* ch. 83; S. 242.

[...] die vollkommenste Art, Gottes Ehre zu suchen in der Arbeit an der Vervollkommnung der Menschheit.[4] Dieser antiutopische Zug, diese Beschränkung auf das in einer gegebenen Situation mit den vorhandenen Kräften Machbare ist ein grundlegender Zug in Leibniz' politischem Wirken. Man erkennt es auch daran, dass Leibniz schon in Mainz, sodann in allen folgenden Projektentwürfen und Memoranden detaillierte Finanzierungsvorschläge vorgetragen hat. Dass zu seinen Lebzeiten außer der Berliner Akademie der Wissenschaften kein weiteres Projekt realisiert werden konnte, liegt nicht an einem Mangel praktischer Umsetzbarkeit, es liegt auch nicht, etwa im Fall Sachsens, Habsburgs und Russlands, an mangelnder Überzeugung der jeweiligen Herrscher, sondern es liegt an unvorhergesehenen Kriegsverläufen. Mir liegt besonders an diesem Punkt, weil m. E. zu leichtfertig in der Forschung vom utopischen Denken bei Leibniz oder vom Utopiker Leibniz gesprochen wird. Hier wird etwas Entscheidendes übersehen: Leibniz glaubt und beabsichtigt nicht, mit seinen Projekten, mit seiner Arbeit die Vervollkommnung der Menschheit erreichen zu können. Es geht ihm nur um das Ziel, das télos, das der Schöpfung innewohnt und innewohnen muss, weil der Schöpfer und universelle Monarch in seiner Gerechtigkeit und Güte vollkommen ist. Leibniz will nur, dass unser Wirken, dass die Politik, die Wissenschaften so geplant und realisiert werden, dass sie sich im Sinne einer asymptotischen Kurve diesem Ziel annähern, einem Ziel, das jedoch erst im Unendlichen vollends verwirklicht und erreicht werden wird. In großer Nüchternheit hat Leibniz mehrmals Paulus zitiert: beständig dranbleiben, „opportune et importune" (2. Timotheus 4,2), „nach Kräften zu arbeiten, aber eben entsprechend dem eigene Vermögen, und den Rest Gott zu überlassen."[5]

5. Diesem Ziel entsprechend weist Leibniz der Akademie zwei Aufgaben zu: Die Sammlung des der Menschheit verfügbaren Wissens und dessen Verbesserung und Vermehrung „ad publicam felicitatem", wie er 1686 Guilelmus Pacidius[6] sagen lässt.

---

[4] A IV, 1, 535.
[5] 1685 an Ernst von Hessen-Rheinfels; A I, 4, 353; ähnlich am 22. November (2. Dezember) 1692 an Lorenz Hertel; A I, 8, 96.
[6] *Plus ultra sive initia et specimina SCIENTIAE GENERALIS de instauratione et augmentis scientiarum, ac de perficienda mente, rerumque inventionibus ad publicam felicitatem* (1686); A VI, 4, 674.

6. Die Royal Society of London, die Leibniz als Mitglied, wie er betont, gewissermaßen von innen her kennt, und die trotz ihrer nur zehn Jahre währenden Arbeit doch berühmte Accademia del Cimento in Florenz waren deshalb nur in begrenztem Maße als Vorbilder geeignet: Zwar verfügen sie über hervorragende Gelehrte, die jedoch ihre Wissenschaft eher „in curiosis" betreiben, die aber den gesellschaftlichen Nutzen, nämlich die Vermehrung der „Bequemlichkeit des menschlichen Lebens und der Ernährung der Untertanen", unbeachtet ließen.[7] Am ehesten war Leibniz noch bereit, der *Académie des sciences* in Paris einen solchen Nutzen zuzugestehen, sie sei jedoch, so beklagt er, durch Kriege in ihrer Arbeit eingeschränkt und erfülle deshalb nicht die an eine Akademie zu knüpfenden Erwartungen.
7. Die *utilitas* oder gar *felicitas publica* als Ziel für die Berliner und sodann für alle weiteren Akademien machen es erforderlich, alle Zweige der Wissenschaft, der Medizin, nicht zuletzt die Effektivierung der land- und forstwirtschaftlichen Produktion, des Handwerks, des Handels, der Finanzwirtschaft, der Erziehung der Jugend, des Militär-, Versicherungs- und Gesundheitswesens, zunehmend der gesamten Staatsverwaltung zum Aufgabengebiet der Akademien zu zählen. Fast könnte man, wie Ines Böger es im Blick auf die von Leibniz projektierte sächsische Akademie sagt, angesichts einer solchen Aufgabenfülle von einer „fürstlich-staatlichen Zentralanstalt" sprechen, die, „ausgestattet mit weitreichenden Kompetenzen, das Leben im Kurfürstentum wesentlich mitgestalten sollte."[8]

All dies soll der *utilitas publica*, der Verbesserung der Lebensbedingungen der Bewohner des jeweiligen Territoriums dienen. Was macht aber Leibniz' Pläne und Entwürfe für Reich, für Hannover, Berlin, Dresden, Wien und Russland zu einem ganz Europa betreffenden Projekt?
1. Leibniz denkt bei der Bestellung der Mitglieder der jeweiligen Akademien europäisch, das heißt, er möchte die Besten aus einem Land mit den besten der gesamten Republik der Geister zusammenbringen. Wie seine Korrespondenz zeigt, deckt dies zum mindesten die am höchsten entwickelten Länder Europas ab.

---

[7] *Denkschrift zur Einrichtung einer Sozietät* (1700); A IV, 8, 407 und 410.
[8] Ines Böger: *„Ein seculum [...] da man zu Societäten Lust hat." Darstellung und Analyse der Leibnizschen Sozietätspläne vor dem Hintergrund der europäischen Akademiebewegung im 17. und frühen 18. Jahrhundert*, München ²2002, S. 423.

2. Leibniz plant die Akademien nicht unter dem Gesichtspunkt der Verbesserung der Lebensverhältnisse der Untertanen, der allgemeinen Wohlfahrt und des Reichtums in einem Herrschaftsgebiet zu Lasten und auf Kosten eines anderen. Er will, vor allem im Falle Preußens, Habsburgs und Russlands, vielmehr, den in Ländern wie Frankreich, England oder den Niederlanden konstatierten höheren Lebensstandard, die dort erlangte größere ökonomische Effizienz und höhere Entfaltung der Wissenschaften für die Verbesserung der Lebensverhältnisse in den bislang unterentwickelten Herrschaftsgebieten nutzbar machen. Hier gilt also voll das Motto des Leibniz-Kongresses 2016: *Ad felicitatem nostram alienamve.*
3. Selbst unter den ungünstigen Bedingungen des Aufbaus der Berliner Sozietät konnten bis 1714 bereits Gelehrte aus acht nicht-deutschen Ländern gewonnen werden.
4. Zu den Aufgaben der Berliner Sozietät zählen auch solche, die nicht auf Preußen beschränkt sind, sondern nur als europäische Projekte realisiert werden können, nämlich der Aufbau einer protestantischen Mission als eines weiteren Instruments, die beiden Lichter der Menschheit in Europa und China einander anzuzünden, und die Förderung der Wissenschaften und Bildung in Russland.
5. Leibniz weitet in seinen Entwürfen für die Berliner Sozietät den Blick auf andere Völker, in Sonderheit auf China. Schon 1688 hatte er in einem Memorandum für Kaiser Leopold I. sein Projekt der *Characteristica universalis* erläutert und daran angeschlossen:

> „Diese Sprache köndte Ecclesiae et rei christianae treflich dienen sonderlich pro Missionariis in Oriente, weilen die Chinesen, Japonesen, und andere orientalische Nationen, die ohne dem so vortrefflich gedächtnüß haben, sie gleichsam spielend und mit hochster begierde lernen, dadurch aber nicht nur auß der communication, sondern auch ex ipsa natura linguae zu dem liecht des glaubens und der christlichen Wißenschafften gefuhret würden."[9]

In den *Novissima sinica* (1697/1699)[10] und schließlich in den Berliner Akademieplänen von 1700 plädiert er dann aber dafür, mit Hilfe des russischen Zaren eine protestantische Mission nach Osten auf den Weg zu bringen, wofür der brandenburgische Kurfürst wie kein anderer ausgerüstet sei. Eine Voraussetzung dafür sieht Leibniz nun in der Überwindung

---

[9] *Ausführliche Aufzeichnung für den Vortrag bei Kaiser Leopold I.* (1688); A IV, 4, 62.
[10] A IV, 6, N. 61.

der innerprotestantischen Streitigkeiten, so dass die Aufnahme des wahren Christentums sowohl „bei uns" als auch den anderen Völkern befördert werde. Dieses vorrangige Werk müsse zusammen mit dem Wachstum „realer" (d. h. auf die Lebensverhältnisse der Menschen ausgerichteter) Wissenschaften und der „Vermehrung des allgemeinen Nutzens" zu einem „funiculum triplex indissolubile" zusammengebunden werden.[11]

6. Noch deutlicher wird die europäische Dimension der Leibniz'schen Akademiepläne teilweise schon vor, besonders jedoch nach der Gründung der Berliner Sozietät an der Synchronizität seiner auf Sachsen, Habsburg und Russland zielenden Initiativen sichtbar. Um mit letzterem anzufangen: 1695, wahrscheinlich aber durch Adam A. Kochansky schon seit 1692, verfügt er über Nachrichten, dass der junge Zar Peter I. sein bis dahin weithin als barbarisch geltendes Land den kultivierteren Sitten Europas zuführen will.[12] Anfang August 1697 konkretisieren sich Leibniz' Bemühungen, an diesem Werk mitzuwirken und zu dessen Erfolg beizutragen. Die Teilnahme an einer Zusammenkunft der Kurfürstin mit dem Zaren blieb Leibniz verwehrt, so reiste er der Delegation nach, um seine Gedanken zumindest einer dem Zaren näherstehenden Person vortragen zu können. Zu dieser Gelegenheit hatte er eine Denkschrift in französischer und deutscher Sprache angefertigt, die bereits wesentliche Punkte der über ein Jahrzehnt später konkretisierten Akademiepläne für Russland enthält.[13] Mehr noch als bei den bisher beschriebenen Projekten sah Leibniz in Peter I offenkundig eine geniale Herrscherpersönlichkeit, deren Reformpläne nicht nur für dessen eigenes Reich, sondern für die gesamte Christenheit von Bedeutung werden könnte. Verglichen mit den für Deutschland entworfenen Akademieprojekten liegen die meisten für den Zaren eher im Bereich des Präliminaren. Die russische *tabula rasa* bedürfe vor-

---

[11] *Denkschrift*, 411.
[12] Entwurf eines Briefes vom 18. Juli 1695 an Johann Reyer; A I, 11, N. 408. – Vgl. Stefan Luckscheiter: „Auskünfte für und von Leibniz über Zar Peter I. und die russische Gesandtschaft", in: Wenchao Li (Hrsg.): *Komma und Kathedrale. Tradition, Bedeutung und Herausforderung der Leibniz-Edition*, Berlin 2012, S. 293–299, hier S. 296f. und Regina Stuber: „Leibniz' Bemühungen um Rußland: eine Annäherung, in: Leibniz' letztes Lebensjahr", in: Michael Kempe (Hrsg.): *1716 – Leibniz' letztes Lebensjahr. Unbekanntes zu einem bekannten Universalgelehrten*, Bd. 2, Hannover 2016, S. 203–239. – Grundlegend für den gesamten Abschnitt bleibt W. Guerrier: *Leibniz in seinen Beziehungen zu Russland und Peter dem Grossen. Eine geschichtliche Darstellung dieses Verhältnisses nebst den darauf bezüglichen Briefen und Denkschriften*, Hildesheim 1873.
[13] *Sur l'avancement des sciences et des arts en Russie* (1697); A IV, 6 N. 40.

bereitender Maßnahmen, damit die Wissenschaften zum Nutzen des Landes und seines Herrschers wirken können. An erster Stelle steht die Einrichtung eines „Établissement General pour les Sciences et Arts". Dieses sollte mit ausgewählten Gelehrten besetzt werden, die über ein möglichst großes Korrespondentennetz und breite Kenntnisse verfügen. Sodann schlägt er eine Liberalisierung der Gesetze vor, damit ausländische Gelehrte in das Land kommen. Man solle sie dort großzügig behandeln, damit sie weitere nachziehen. Sodann erklärt er die Notwendigkeit von Bibliotheken, Buchdruckereien, Raritätenkabinetten, botanischen Gärten und zoologischen Sammlungen, damit das Wissen der Menschheit zur Verfügung stehe. Er schlägt eine Liberalisierung der Reisemöglichkeiten vor, eine Verbesserung der Transportmöglichkeiten, damit das im Ausland vorhandene Wissen, die dortigen Fähigkeiten und Vorzüge (möglichst frei von den dort auch vorhandenen Lastern) nach Russland importiert werden können. Ein Bildungswesen müsse aufgebaut werden, Schulen und Akademien, um der Jugend Tugenden und Wissenschaften beizubringen. Schulbücher seien zu drucken und sie (die Jugend) solle Geschichte, Mathematik, die alten Sprachen, vor allem Latein, aber auch Deutsch erlernen. Des weiteren empfiehlt Leibniz die geographische Erschließung des Landes in allen Bereichen der Wissenschaften und schließlich die Förderung von Landwirtschaft, Manufakturen, den Ausbau der Verkehrswege, die Trockenlegung von Sümpfen etc. Dieser Versuch der Kontaktaufnahme zu einem der Ratgeber des Zaren blieb ohne Erfolg. Auch die Kontakte zu mehreren ausländischen Wissenschaftlern in Russland, darunter Heinrich van Huyssen, von 1702 bis 1705 Erzieher des Zarewitsch, und Nicolaas Witsen,[14] brachten Leibniz zunächst nicht weiter. Während seines kurzen Aufenthaltes in Dresden Anfang 1704 hatte Leibniz nicht nur wegen seines Plans einer sächsischen Akademie Kontakt zu dem russischen Bevollmächtigten Johann Reinhold von Patkul aufgenommen, sondern ihm auch ein Memorandum zugehen lassen, das *Specimen Einiger Puncten, darinnen Moscau denen Scienzen beförderlich seyn könnte*.[15] Manches von diesen den Präliminarbereich betref-

---

[14] Hierzu und zu weiteren Ansprechpartnern vgl. vor allem Guerrier: *Leibniz in seinen Beziehungen*. Huyssen wurde 1710 als erstes in Russland tätiges Mitglied in die Berliner Sozietät aufgenommen.
[15] A I, 23, N. 49.

fenden Vorschlägen für Russland ist in die Arbeitsprogramme der Berliner Sozietät aufgenommen worden. Konkrete Schritte zur Realisierung werden Leibniz aber erst seit 1708 und vor allem 1712 möglich. Das Jahr 1704 belegt die Synchronizität am besten. In diesem Jahr greift Leibniz die 1688 in Wien vorgetragene Idee in einem Memorandum für den Schwager des Kaisers, Kurfürst Johann Wilhelm von der Pfalz, erneut auf,[16] im selben Jahr also, als er auch vorbereitende Schritte auf Russland und Sachsen hin unternahm. Zu Sachsen sei nur stichwortartig dies erwähnt: Ende Januar 1704 reiste Leibniz für wenige Tage inkognito nach Dresden, um bei mehreren Personen zu antichambrieren, die Einfluss am Hofe besaßen. Dabei ging es besonders um das Akademieprojekt. Im weiteren Verlauf des Jahres schickte er seinen Mitarbeiter Johann Georg Eckhart mit einer Instruktion und Empfehlungsschreiben für Jakob Heinrich von Flemming und Carlo Maurizio Vota nach Sachsen,[17] um sein Projekt in Gang zu bringen, von dem er Männer am Hof überzeugen konnte, die über einen großen Einfluss auf August den Starken verfügten. Dies mag an Hinweisen genügen.

7. Denn noch stärker als jene Beobachtungen vermag ein weiterer Punkt die europäische Dimension der Leibniz'schen Akademiepläne zu veranschaulichen. Es ist Leibniz' Person selbst, die Selbsteinschätzung seiner Persönlichkeit, seines Gelehrtentums, seiner bedeutenden Rolle und Vernetzung in der europäischen Gelehrtenrepublik. Das, was ihm in Berlin gelungen war, nämlich die Präsidentschaft in der Sozietät zu erwerben, hat er aktiv und offen auch in Sachsen, Wien und Russland angestrebt – nicht ohne darauf hinzuweisen, welchen Vorteil ein Präsident Leibniz, der zudem auch Mitglied in den Königlichen Sozietäten in Paris und London war, nicht nur für die jeweilige Akademie, sondern auch für die jeweils anderen besäße, welcher Gewinn in der Koordination der Arbeit in sämtlichen Akademien liege. Auch die Tatsache, dass er sich mit seinen Akademieplänen an die mächtigsten Fürsten wandte,[18] zu denen er Zugang besaß, und dass er 1695 deshalb eine sich ihm bietende Möglichkeit

---

[16] Vgl. Josef Bergmann: „Leibnizens Memoriale an den Kurfürstin Johann Wilhelm von der Pfalz", in: *Sitzungsberichte der philosophisch-historischen Classe* 16 (1855), S. 3–23.
[17] A I, 23, N. 113, 114 und 116.
[18] Vgl. zu diesem Gesichtspunkt die überzeugende Darlegung von Rüdiger Otto: „Leibniz' Projekt einer Sächsischen Akademie im Kontext seiner Bemühungen um die Gründung gelehrter Gesellschaften", in: Detlef Döring/Kurt Nowak(Hrsg.): *Gelehrte Gesellschaften im mitteldeutschen Raum (1650-1820): Abhandlungen der Sächsischen Akademie der Wissenschaften zu Leipzig. Phil.-hist. Klasse*, Bd. 76, Heft 2, Stuttgart/Leipzig 2000, S. 73–79.

in Hessen-Kassel ausschlug, bestätigt diesen Anspruch. Nur die Residenz eines der großen Fürstenhäuser erschien ihm für solche Institutionen geeignet, wenn denn diese tatsächlich die von Leibniz davon erhofften globalen Früchte erbringen sollte, die im Blick auf die herausragende Rolle der Wissenschaften für die Vervollkommnung der Menschheit eben nur in Europa gezüchtet und geerntet werden konnten. Sein Bemühen um die Präsidentschaft in den einzelnen Akademien gründet wie gesagt in seiner Selbsteinschätzung. Es mangelte ihm schlicht an der nötigen Dummheit, die ihn hätte daran hindern können, sich seiner herausragenden Genialität als Gelehrter und Kommunikator in der Republik der Geister bewusst zu werden. Leibniz sieht deshalb seine Lebenszeit als eine besondere Chance zur Erfüllung einer solchen globalen Aufgabe an – deshalb 1679, 1694, 1695, 1704, 1712 auch sein Drängen, ihn unverzüglich an die Arbeit gehen zu lassen, die Projekte schnellstens zu verwirklichen. Die Menschheit werde hunderte von Jahren brauchen, um das zu erreichen, was jetzt in zehn Jahren möglich sei.[19] Und der Grund für diesen *kairos*, auf den Leibniz mehrfach mit Nachdruck hingewiesen hat, liegt darin, dass er seine Person als einen Schlüssel für die Verwirklichung seiner europäischen Akademiepläne ansah, dem für ihn entscheidenden Schritt auf dem Weg zur Vervollkommnung der Menschheit.

---

[19] Vgl. Leibniz am 24. Februar 1695 (nicht abgesendeter Entwurf) an Johann Sebastian Haes: „Je suis persuadé, que si on s'y prenoit comme il faut, nous ferions en dix ans des choses plus importantes pour accroistre le tresor de nos connoissances, qu'on ne fera sans cela en quelques siecles"; A III, 6, 304; vgl. hierzu auch Otto: „Leibniz' Projekt", S. 59, Anm. 43 – dort weitere Fundstellen.

Leibniz' Begriff der „Justitia". Mit Schwerpunkt auf der „aequitas"

Kiyoshi Sakai (Tokio)

Einleitung

Bekanntlich legt Leibniz über die Tradition des „jus naturale" hinaus seine eigene These von dessen drei Stufen vor, d. h. jus strictum („Neminem laedere"), aequitas („Suum cuique tribuere"), und pietas („Honeste vivere"). Diese drei Stufen bezeichnet er jeweils als „justitia commutativa", „justitia distributiva" und „justitia universalis". Unter diesen drei Stufen nimmt „jus strictum" die unterste, gründliche Stelle ein, worauf die andere zwei Stufen beruhen; dagegen nimmt „pietas" die oberste Stelle ein. Die zweite (aequitas) sowie die dritte Stufe (pietas) beinhalten jeweils ihre vorangehenden Vorstufen. Diese „Drei-Stufen-These" stellt er schon in einer seiner frühesten Schriften *Nova methodus discendae docendaeque jurisprudentiae*, 1667, II-§73–75 dar. Seitdem hat Leibniz in den im jeweiligen Zeitabschnitt wichtigen Schriften wie in *Elementa juris naturalis,* 1669–70(?), *Codex juris gentium diplomaticus. Praefatio,* 1693 oder in *Meditations sur la notion commune de justice,*1703(?) immer wieder die drei Stufen der Justitia erläutert.

Zunächst müssen wir zweierlei beachten: Erstens, das jus strictum hatte ein wesentliches Moment der Hobbes'schen Theorie der Gerechtigkeit ausgemacht und dieser Vorrang des jus strictum bei Hobbes war schon damals weit erkannt. Gerechtigkeit bejaht Hobbes' Voluntarismus zufolge auch eine willkürliche Entscheidung. Sie lässt sich in der folgenden Maxime zusammenfassen: Nur wenn man keinen anderen verletzt und von keinem anderen verletzt wird, wird somit der Inhalt der Gerechtigkeit erfüllt. Dies führt zur Denkart, dass jeder seine uneingeschränkten, fundamentalen Rechte auf das Leben, den Körper, das Eigentum, die Meinungsfreiheit usw. nur aufrechterhält, wenn er die Rechte anderer nicht verletzt. Hierzu findet man in John Stuart Mills *On Liberty,* 1859 eine kanonische Formulierung. Dies ist nichts anderes als der Ansatz für den modernen Liberalismus,[1] d. h. die leitende Ideologie der heutigen Globalisierung. Zweitens, die Theorie der Gerechtigkeit seit der Neuzeit bis in die Gegenwart konzentriert sich tendenziell auf das jus strictum. Aber

---

[1] Auch der seit den 1990er Jahren bis heute oft erwähnte Neo-Liberalismus, Libertarianismus oder Marktfundamentalismus entspringen nach der Ansicht des Verfassers im Grunde dieser Erklärung von Mill.

Leibniz hält es wegen dessen bloß formalen Charakter für ungenügend als Inhalt des Gerechtigkeitsbegriffs. Auch die Billigkeit (aequitas) könnte gewissermaßen einen quantitativen Charakter haben.[2] Leibniz setzt deswegen die Frömmigkeit an die oberste Stelle und findet darin eine universale Gerechtigkeit. Man könnte hierzu sagen, dass Leibniz schon Kants Moralphilosophie vorwegnimmt, insofern als Kant den hinter der Handlung steckenden Egoismus oder den utilitaristischen Gedanken kritisiert und somit nur in seinem „kategorischen Imperativ" des reinen Willens die wahre „Moralität" findet.[3]

Im Vorliegenden möchte ich die Billigkeit untersuchen, die von Leibniz zwischen das jus strictum und die Frömmigkeit gesetzt ist, aber einen eigentümlichen Charakter von Leibniz' Gerechtigkeitstheorie am besten zeigt.

1. Aequitas (Billigkeit). Nova methodus, II. §74

Leibniz definiert am Anfang des §74 des zweiten Teiles der *Nova methodus*:

> „Die Billigkeit oder Ausgewogenheit, d.h. die Verhältnismäßigkeit oder Proportionen zwischen zwei oder mehreren Rechtsansprüchen, besteht in deren Harmonie oder Kongruenz."[4]

Anschließend zeigt er, Aristoteles und Grotius folgend, konkrete Beispiele der Billigkeitsgebote: Sie gebieten, dass ich gegen den, der mich verletzt hat, keinen mörderischen Krieg führe, sondern ihn zum Schadensersatz veranlasse; dass Schiedsrichter zugelassen werden; die „Goldene Regel" eingehalten werde; dass nicht so sehr Unklugheit als vielmehr Arglist und Tücke bestraft werden; dass hinterlistige Verträge entkräftet werden; dass man den Geschädigten helfen solle.

Hier können wir drei Punkte beachten: Erstens, Leibniz fügt hinzu, „Im Übrigen gebietet die Billigkeit selbst, das strenge Recht zu beachten. Hierhin

---

[2] Wie etwa, wenn eine Partei vor der Wahl verspricht, allen Bürger über fünfundsechzig Jahren, egal mit welchem Einkommen oder in welcher Lebenskondition, als sogenanntes „zeitweiliges Schmerzensgeld" jeweils 300 Euro zu bezahlen.
[3] Hans Poser: *Leibniz und die Ethik der deutschen Aufklärung*, Vortrag gehalten am 17.02.2007 an der Gakushuin-Universität Tokio.
[4] A VI, 1, 343f. Deutsche Übersetzung in: Gottfried Wilhelm Leibniz: *Frühe Schriften zum Naturrecht*, hrsg. v. Hubertus Busche, Hamburg 2003, S. 81.

gehören Hobbes' Anforderungen zum Frieden."⁵ Zweitens, die Billigkeit garantiert das Recht im weitesten Sinne (Grotius). Drittens, die Billigkeit gibt einem den kurzen Weg zum Erwerb des Rechtes, aber dem anderen eine volle Verpflichtung. (Das erklärt Leibniz mit dem Beispiel eines Mannes, welcher sich durch hinterlistige Vertragsraffinessen einer Schuld dem anderen gegenüber entzogen hat).⁶

Aristoteles erläutert in seiner *Nikomachischen Ethik*, Bd. 5, Kap. 10 über die Billigkeit und die Gerechtigkeit, wie folgt:

> „Ausgewogene Gesinnung (‚ἐπιείκεια') ist gerecht, und überlegener, wenn sie mit einem bloß einfachen (und somit möglichen) Gerechten verglichen wird (1137b20). Ein Mann mit Billigkeit (‚ἐπιεικής') heißt nicht derjenige, der ‚streng' im sozusagen schlechten Sinne der Gerechtigkeit folgt, sondern derjenige, „der sich möglichst weniger Sachen in Anspruch nimmt, auch wenn das Gesetz auf seiner Seite steht." (1138a)

Aristoteles unterscheidet außerdem die distributive Gerechtigkeit auch von der beschränkenden (Anfang 2. Kap.) und bemerkt, dass die distributive Gerechtigkeit gerade die Gemeinschaft („κοινωνία") voraussetzt. Sie ist also eine Gerechtigkeit, welche das Kriterium gibt, um damit unter den Gemeinschaftsangehörigen etwas zur Gemeinschaft Gehöriges zu verteilen. Wenn man denkt, dass es so lange die Gerechtigkeit gibt, als eine Gemeinschaft bestehen bleibt (Bd. 8, Kap. 9), lässt sich sagen, dass die distributive Gerechtigkeit die fundamentalste ist.

Es sei im §74 des zweiten Teils der *Nova methodus* noch angemerkt, dass Leibniz die Notwendigkeit eines Schiedsrichters (arbitrium) (d. i. des Staats!) vertritt, um das Goldene Gesetz verwenden zu können; dass Leibniz nicht einen Vertrag durch Fahrlässigkeit oder Unwissenheit, sondern gerade einen durch den bösen Willen abgeschlossenen Vertrag für ungültig erklärt (Kants

---

⁵ „De caetero Jus strictum observari ipsa aequitas jubet. Huc pertinent Hobbii dispositiones ad pacem" (A VI, 1, 344).
⁶ Ebd. Hier bemerkt Stephanie Ertz, dass Leibniz mit den Bedingungen der Verwirklichung des Billigkeitsbegriffs sich einsetzt, um dann zum Ergebnis zu kommen, dass die Billigkeit noch innerhalb von Grotius' Gebrauch, rein zum Bereich der Gesetzlichkeit oder wenigstens zu deren Herrschaft gehöre, während er in den *Elementa jus naturalis* die Billigkeit noch in die Staatstheorie erweitern wird. Vgl. Stephanie Ertz: „Pietas, Aequitas. Caritas: Einige Bemerkungen zur Terminologie und historischen (Übergangs-)Stellung von Leibniz' Naturrecht", in: Wenchao Li (Hrsg.): „*Das Recht kann nicht ungerecht sein*" ... – *Beiträge zu Leibniz' Philosophie der Gerechtigkeit* (= Studia Leibnitiana Sonderhefte 44), Stuttgart 2015, S. 69–108, hier S. 97, Z. 5 v. u.

Begriff der Moralität im Gegensatz zur Legalität!). Darüber hinaus gibt die Billigkeit einem das Recht, aber dem anderen die Pflicht, sie kann also bei verschiedenen, d. h. nicht bloß quantitativen, sondern auch juristischen, moralischen und politischen Verhältnissen die Ausgewogenheit bedeuten. Die Billigkeit bedeutet also für Leibniz keineswegs eine bloß formal quantitative Verbreitung, die sich aber in der heutigen, leider populistischen Politik nicht selten beobachten ließe.

2. Aequitas, die nicht nur einzelne Menschen betrifft
(Elementa juris naturalis)

In den *Elementa juris naturalis* (die im auf die *Nova Methodus* gleich folgenden Zeitraum niedergeschrieben wurden) greift Leibniz, Stefanie Ertz zufolge, den Billigkeitsbegriff etwas tiefer auf als die undeutlichen Termini, die in der christlichen Naturrechtslehre gebraucht worden waren.[7] Der Versuch der *Elementa juris naturalis* besteht darin, die Billigkeit auf einen autonomen Ursprung der „obligatio civilis" (Schuldverhältnis beim Bürgerrecht) zu erhöhen und damit das Souveränitätsrecht des Staates zu begründen, und zwar als einen unmittelbar naturrechtlichen Geltungsvorrang des Staats.

Was in den *Elementa* thematisiert wird, ist das Verhältnis zwischen dem öffentlichen Nutzen und dem privaten Nutzen, d. h. die Harmonie zwischen der universalen und der partikularen Gerechtigkeit, während diese in der vorangehenden *Nova methodus* noch bloß hierarchisch dargestellt worden war. Leibniz definiert in den *Elementa* die Billigkeit gerade als ein größtes Prinzip, in dem die partikulare und die allgemeine Gerechtigkeit im menschlichen Bereich übereinstimmen. Dafür scheint aber die „Pietas" gewisser weise in den Hintergrund zurückgezogen, und somit zu einer Erscheinungsform für die allgemeine Gerechtigkeit geworden zu sein.

Ertz urteilt, dass in den *Elementa* gerade die Koordinaten festgelegt worden seien, nach denen die allgemeine Gerechtigkeit später der „caritas sapientis" gleichgesetzt wird. Im Mittelpunkt einer Rechtsanthropologie in den *Elementa* stehe, wenn wir eingehender beobachten, das Interesse des Individuums, für sich ein ständiges Wachstum des Glücks sowie der Güter zu verlangen, während der Vorrang des strengen Rechts in der *Nova methodus* noch bloß formal (als Verbot) gezeigt worden war. Der Vorrang des strengen

---

[7] Vgl. ebd., S. 94f.

Rechts wird also vermittels einer „eudaimonischen" Lesart noch verstärkt. Um sich von der Hobbesschen Theorie des Naturzustandes abzukehren, wird der in den Prolegomena von Grotius' *De jure belli ac pacis* verteidigte, skeptische Standpunkt verstärkt. Und diese Leibniz'sche Abkehr von Hobbes wird dadurch im ersten Blick paradoxerweise gesprochen. Auch dem Eigennutz wird in den *Elementa* der Status eines naturrechtlichen Prinzips zugewiesen. „Felicitas est status personae optimus." In eine Hierarchie der Gerechtigkeit in *Nova methodus* hatte Leibniz den Eigennutz einfach in den Kommunen gemeinsamen Nutzen subsumiert.[8]

Leibniz' Billigkeitsbegriff richtet sich gegen den von Grotius. Bei Grotius war noch kein Schuldverhältnis im Sinne eines ausgewogenen, beiderseitigen Verhältnisses gedacht worden. In Vergleich zu Grotius, bei dem die Aristotelische „epikeia" noch stark war, wird Leibniz' Billigkeitsbegriff erweitert, so dass dieser mehr die Pflicht des Individuums bedeutet. Diese Differenz zwischen Grotius und Leibniz liegt vielleicht daran, dass es hier bei Leibniz nicht bloß um die aequitas im herkömmlichen Diskurs, sondern auch um die Billigkeit geht, wobei bereits eine staatstheoretische Perspektive herangezogen ist. Deswegen wäre es zu kurzschlüssig, wenn man Leibniz als einen Vorläufer des modernen Utilitarismus betrachten wollte.

Leibniz sagt: „Aequitas est prudentia in dispensatione bonis malisque."[9] Die Pflicht des Bürgers besteht darin, die staatsökonomischen Vernunftprinzipien möglichst zu eigen zu machen und zu gebrauchen. Die Billigkeit bei Leibniz verbindet sich mit der „obligatio" als Schuldverhältnis.[10] Fernerhin gebraucht Leibniz, so Ertz, ein Experimentsmodell von „Vir bonus", der aber seinerseits einen Doppelcharakter trägt: Leibniz legt einerseits mit seiner Kritik an Grotius die Carneadesche Maxime vor: Wer nicht aus seinem Eigennutz handeln will, ist dumm oder nicht fähig zu überleben.[11] Aber andererseits versucht Leibniz, so Ertz,[12] anhand dieser zu einer subjektiven Allgemeinheit erhobenen Carneadischen Maxime als Handlungsbegriff den Gegensatz im Naturrecht zwischen jus strictum und aequitas zu lösen.

---

[8] Vgl. ebd., S. 96, Z. 4.
[9] *Elementa juris naturalis*; A VI, 1, 465, Z. 16f.
[10] Vgl. Ertz: „Pietas, Aequitas", S. 98.
[11] A VI, 1, 431.
[12] Vgl. Ertz: „Pietas, Aequitas", S. 98.

> „Justum [...] est proportionale inter amorem mei et proximi. Aequum est publicum utile quosque privatim tolerabile est."[13]

3. Aequitas in der Praefatio Codicis juris gentium diplomatici 1693

In der Praefatio seines Codex juris gentium diplomaticus versucht Leibniz nochmals klarzustellen, dass die Billigkeit keine bloß quantitative Verteilung bedeutet. An dieser Stelle bezeichnet er die Billigkeit deutlich als „caritas."[14] Überdem verstärkt er die Formulierung der Billigkeit, derart, dass sie vom bisher gebrauchten Gebot, „suum cuicumque tribuere", noch auf ein anderes Gebot, „cunctus prodesse" (zum Nutzen aller anderen etwas Gutes tun) erhoben wird. Dies bedeutet aber keine bloße formale Erweiterung des Begriffsinhalts, sondern es soll dabei berücksichtigt werden, „der für jeden angemessene Grad" oder „der Grad, sofern jeder es tun kann." Hiermit sind die distributive Gerechtigkeit und deren Rechtsbestimmungen gemeint. Leibniz fordert auf, dass hier die politischen Gesetze herangezogen werden. Wer nur die facultas besitzt, gewinnt noch die possibilitas, er kümmert sich damit auch um die Glückseligkeit der Untertanen.

Beim strengen Recht spielt der Unterschied unter den einzelnen Individuen keine Rolle. Bei der Billigkeit wird dagegen nach verschiedenen Verdiensten, Privilegien, Belohnungen, Bestrafungen etc. gefragt. Leibniz zitiert hierzu aus Xenophons Κύρου παιδεία (I, 17) die Episode von Kyros und den zwei Knaben, die sich um das Kleid stritten.[15] Das Billigkeitsgebot, „suum cuique tribuere", könnte zwar eine Verschiedenheit unter den Individuen beinhalten, z. B. wie Größe oder Form des Körpers. Aber der Rücksicht auf solche Individualitäten muss das strenge Recht vorausgesetzt werden. Das Gebot, „suum cuique tribuere" muss nach Leibniz prinzipiell (besonders beim Handelsgeschäft) ebenso von der Gleichheit der Menschen ausgehen, wie es beim „jus strictum" geschieht.

> „Das sogenannte Ansehen der Person (acceptio personarum) aber darf sich nicht im Vertauschen fremder Güter äussern, vielmehr hat es seinen Ort, wenn wir unser eigenes oder aber öffentliches Gut verteilen."[16]

---

[13] A VI, 1, 455, Z. 12–14.
[14] A IV, 5, 61f.
[15] Ebd., 62.
[16] Ebd., 62, Z. 24f. Deutsche Übersetzung: Malte-Ludolf Babin/Gerd van den Heuvel (Hrsg.): *Gottfried Wilhelm Leibniz. Schriften und Briefe zur Geschichte,* Hannover 2004, S. 171.

Es lässt sich zwar bemerken, dass Leibniz auf die Billigkeit als Zuteilungsprinzip einen in sich gedoppelten Gesichtspunkt, d. h. „aequalitas" und „acceptio personarum,"[17] miteinbezieht. Er denkt jedoch, dass bei der Handlung prinzipiell eine „Gleichheit" vorausgesetzt wird. Die Billigkeit nennt er das mittlere Gebot, um sie somit über dem untersten Gebot, d. i. dem strengen Recht zu legen. Die Antreibung des heutigen Liberalismus (bzw. Neoliberalismus) zusammen mit der Globalisierungsideologie bringt in der Realität die folgende Wirkung mit sich: Durch ein absichtliches oder unabsichtliches Missverständnis tendiert man heute, mittels einer Reihe der „Bestimmungslinderungen" oder im Namen der „Sparpolitik" die eigentlich zum Menschenrecht gehörende Gleichheit der Menschen zu vernachlässigen bzw. zu ignorieren (wie der stärkere Knabe den anderen gezwungen hatte, mit ihm das Kleid zu tauschen, was die Episode aus Xenophons Κύρου παιδεία zeigt), oder umgekehrt, hinter dem Gleichheitsprinzip die Billigkeit als solche abzuschaffen (Abkürzung der sozialen Wohlfahrt?). Gerade durch diese doppelte Verdrehung des Billigkeitsbegriffs ergibt sich in der Gesellschaft eine immer größere Kluft zwischen Armen und Reichen.

Leibniz gebraucht mehr als die Hälfte der Seiten[18] im §12 der *Praefatio Codicis* („Die drei Stufen des Naturrechts und vom jus gentium")[19], um den Lesern die Billigkeit zu erklären. Nach der Erwähnung des Abschnitts aus Κύρου παιδεία sagt Leibniz:

> „Die Billigkeit selbst legt es uns ja nahe, in Geschäften das Recht im engeren Sinne anzuwenden, d. h. von der Gleichheit der Menschen auszugehen, sofern dann nicht die Erwägung eines höheren (Rechts)gutes ins Gewicht fällt und vom Gleichheitsgrundsatz abzuweichen veranlasst."[20]

Der sogenannte Respekt für die (individuelle) Person darf nicht zum Austausch der Güter anderer verwendet werden. Er wird vielmehr berücksichtigt, wenn wir unseren eigenen oder die gemeinsamen Güter austauschen. „Namque ipsa aequitas nobis in negotiis jus strictum, id est hominum aequalitatem commendat."[21]

---

[17] Ein ursprünglich biblischer Begriff, vgl. 2. Chronik 19,7; Babin/van den Heuvel: *Gottfried Wilhelm Leibniz*.
[18] A IV, 5, 61f.
[19] Die Paragraphenteilung mit jeweiligen Titeln ist der Ausgabe von Dutens IV–III, 287 entnommen.
[20] A IV, 5, 62, Z. 22, Babin/van den Heuvel: *Gottfried Wilhelm Leibniz*.
[21] A IV, 5, 62, Z. 22.

Die Billigkeit besteht Hubertus Busche zufolge im Verhältnis unter den konkurrierenden Rechtsansprüchen.[22] Der rechtmäßige Anspruch auf die Billigkeit ist darum keineswegs eine aufzwingbare Facultas, sondern dieser Anspruch sei eine bloße Geeignetheit. Die Pflicht der Billigkeit kann sich nur innerhalb des beschränkten Rahmens positiv und rechtlich geltend machen. Wie weitgehend dieser Geltungsbereich der Billigkeit ist, lässt sich durch ihre folgenden Unterarten zeigen: Erstens, die Billigkeit bzw. Ausgewogenheit in der Güterverteilung, die auf der Balance zwischen Gütern und Verdiensten verwirklicht wird und zwar in einer volkswirtschaftlichen Sicht.[23] Zweitens, die Billigkeit hat auch mit dem Schadensersatz zu tun. Die Billigkeit im Strafrecht: Die Ausgewogenheit zwischen dem Grad des Vergehens und der Schwere der Straftat soll berücksichtigt werden; Bosheit oder Betrug müssen mehr bestraft werden als reine Unwissenheit. Drittens, die Billigkeit im Vertragsrecht. Soziale gegenseitige Hilfe unter den Bürgern unterscheidet sich gemäß ihrer Notwendigkeit oder Dringlichkeit, und zwar in folgenden Stufen:
1. Verhütung des Elends, des Unglücks und der Armut
2. Verhinderung des bloßen Schadens und des Nachteils
3. Gewinnung des Vorteils oder des Nutzens
4. Reserve: Aufgrund des Billigkeitsprinzips bin ich verpflichtet, anderen zu helfen, wenn meine eigene Not leicht ist.[24]

Was ist dann die soziale Unbilligkeit? Sie heißt, anderen gegenüber den Anspruch zu haben, die Schwierigkeiten anderer zu beseitigen, auch wenn man seinen eigenen Nutzen dabei verliert. Solches Gebot darf insofern nicht gegeben werden, als beide nicht wahre Freunde, nicht eines sind.[25] Zusammengefasst: Die Billigkeit kann nicht durch die Staatsgewalt erzwungen werden. Die Billigkeit ist ein System, welches den Rechten der rational begründeten Ansprüche analog ist. Recht und Pflicht von der Billigkeit betreffen bei Leibniz in erster Linie nicht ein „bonum private", sondern das „bonum commune".

---

[22] Hubertus Busche: „Leibniz' Lehre von den drei Stufen des Naturrechts", in: Li (Hrsg.): „Das Recht kann nicht ungerecht sein", S. 37f.
[23] Die Billigkeit ist die ihren höchsten Grad erreichende Ausgewogenheit der Güter unter vielen Menschen und zwar ohne die ganze Produktion zu reduzieren. Von daher ist die Billigkeit nur ungenügend zu realisieren, wenn man sie nur an die (quantitative) Proportion zurückführen will; sie ist kurzum nicht anders als die Tugend vom „Goldenen Mittelweg" (*Elementa juris naturalis*, 2; A VI, 1, 454, Z. 27–30).
[24] Ebd.
[25] Ebd., 433, Z. 19–23.

Die Billigkeit ist weder das Gebot der Unterlassung noch das Verbot des Schadens, sondern sie enthält das Verbot der Unterlassung oder das Gebot der Beihilfe. Die so verstandenen, praktizierten Rechten und Pflichten gehören der „Justitia distributiva". Sie lassen sich mit jener Ulpianischen Rechtsbestimmung („suum cuique tribuere") zusammenfassen.[26]

In den *Nova Methodus* hatte sich Leibniz, wie beim strengen Recht, auch bezüglich der Billigkeit bemüht, konkrete Anwendungsregeln und inhaltliche Bestimmungen zu zeigen. Er sagte aber, „Für die Billigkeit kann man nur mit Schwierigkeit eine allgemeine Definition vorlegen." Damit sucht er aber nicht in der Theologie die Normen der Billigkeit."[27]

4. Leibniz' Begriff der „proprietas" (Eigentum)
„Meditations sur la notion commune de justice" (1703?)

In den Fragmenten „De tribus juris praeceptis sive gradibus" (1677–78?)[28] gibt Leibniz die folgende Definition:

„Atque haec Justitia distributiva vocatur, quam tum privati in rebus propriis, tum societas in (rebus) communibus dispensandis exercent."

Es wird die distributive Gerechtigkeit nicht nur vom privaten Eigentum bzw. von dessen Austausch unter den Individuen bestimmt. Wichtig ist hier, dass der Besitz der Güter nicht nur für die Individuen, sondern auch für die Gemeinschaft anerkannt wird, und dass die Gerechtigkeit in erster Linie offensichtlich als eine distributive betrachtet wird.

In den *Meditations sur la notion commune de justice* (1703?) wird das dreistufige Naturrecht wieder einmal thematisiert, wobei Leibniz aber die Billigkeit noch eingehender erläutert. Er erklärt es für nötig, dass jeder seine „possesions" bewahrt. Als Grund dafür nennt er die folgenden drei Punkte. Erstens, wenn das private Eigentum nicht anerkannt werden sollte, dann würde das dadurch entstandene Chaos noch mehr Übel verursachen. Hier erwähnt Leibniz wieder die bereits zitierte Episode aus Xenophons „Kurou Paideia" und sagt, man dürfe nicht den Reichen ihr Eigentum wegnehmen, um

---

[26] *Nova Methodus*, späterer Zusatz zu §74 des II. Teils; ebd., 344, Z. 31: „Ad hunc juris gradum *justitia distributiva* pertinent et praeceptum quod jubet: *Suum cuique tribuere*."
[27] A VI, 1, 455, Z. 32; Busche: „Leibniz' Lehre", S. 38f.
[28] Grua II, 607.

dieses den Armen zu geben; man dürfe ebenso nicht von demjenigen, der ein Kleid von nicht passender Größe trägt, dieses Kleid wegnehmen, um es dann einem anderen, dem das besser passen könnte, zu geben. Zweitens, da der Staat sich um die Einzelnen nicht so eingehend bzw. im Detail kümmern kann wie die Familie es tut, zu der sie jeweils gehören, so soll jeder für sich versuchen, in seinem eigenen Bereich das Eigentum zu verwalten und zu vermehren. Drittens, wenn alles mit anderen gemeinsam besessen würde, könnte kein Wettbewerb geschehen. Allerdings: Zugunsten eines größeren Gemeinwohls oder einer öffentlichen Sicherheit muss man manchmal akzeptieren, dass das Recht auf das Eigentum aus diesen gewissenweise politischen Gründen beschränkt wird.

Leibniz lässt also nicht nur dem Privatmenschen, sondern auch der Gemeinschaft bzw. Gesellschaft den Begriff der „proprietas" und das Eigentumsrecht. Er sieht aber zugleich eine Gefahr, wenn der Mitbesitz zu weit gehen würde und dadurch den Gesellschaftsmitgliedern das Wettbewerbsprinzip geraubt würde, was dann zu einer Stockung der Gemeinschaft führen könnte. Ein Beispiel für die ideale Verbindung bzw. Koexistenz von Mit-Besitz und Wettbewerbsprinzip findet er beim Jesuitenorden, sofern er diesen als eine wissenschaftliche Institution betrachtet. Er wird sie in seinen Entwürfen zur Sozietät der Wissenschaften zu verkörpern versuchen. Das Eigentumsrecht gehört jedem, ohne jeglichen Unterschied der einzelnen Personen. In diesem Eigentumsrecht ist das strenge Recht bereits vorausgesetzt. Aufgrund des Verbots „Neminem laedere" besteht die Billigkeit („suum cuique tribuere") qua distributive Gerechtigkeit sowohl für jeden einzelnen Menschen als auch für die ganze Gemeinschaft. Die Billigkeit unter den Einzelnen bezieht sich auf den „Austausch"; die Billigkeit zwischen der Gemeinschaft und den dazu gehörenden Individuen bezieht sich auf die „Zuteilung".

Was der Theorie des Eigentumsrechts bei Leibniz deutlich gegenübersteht, ist John Lockes Theorie des Eigentumsrechts. Locke verteidigt das private Eigentum („property") als ein unantastbares Recht jedes Menschen, in der Weise, wie der Körper und das Leben dem Individuum gehören. Der klassische Text von Locke zum Thema des Eigentumsrechts („property") ist *Two Treatises of Government*, 1689, II–5. Locke behauptet dort: Derjenige, der in einem Naturzustand seine Arbeit investiert und damit den Boden kultiviert, Obst oder Getreide anpflanzt oder Tiere züchtet, um damit den Boden als Ganzes mit Effekt gebraucht zu haben, darf für sich ohne Genehmigung anderer diesen Boden einschließen und monopolisieren. So fällt dieser ohne Zeitbegrenzung in seinen Privatbesitz. Mit diesem Argument versucht Locke, abgesehen davon, ob er sich der Konsequenz seiner Theorie von „property" genügend bewusst war oder nicht, die Tatsache zu rechtfertigen, dass die aus England eingewanderten Weißen mit Gewalt die Ureinwohner=Indianer beseitigten.²⁹ Locke zögert nicht, den Geltungsbereich des Eigentumsrechts des Individuums bis zum Grundstück zu erweitern. Sein Blick diesbezüglich richtet sich gerade nicht auf einen gemeinsamen Besitz der Erde, sondern ganz und gar auf das private Eigentum und dessen Sicherstellung. Ein ursprünglich (seit der Urzeit) nur unkultiviert gelassener (besser: nur so aussehender) Boden soll jetzt ausschließlich denjenigen gehören, die nachher gekommen sind, und ihre Arbeit und ihren Fleiß investiert haben. Dagegen müssten die Ureinwohner=Indianer beseitigt werden, wenn sie trotzdem den von den eingewanderten Weißen kultivierten Boden zu betreten versuchen sollten. Als sein Patron 1672 „Lord Chansellor" wurde, trat Locke mit ihm in die Politik ein. Locke diente von 1673 bis 1674 als Vorstand (Secretary) des für Handel und Kolonie zuständigen Komitees (Board of Trade and Plantations) und beschäftigte sich mit dem Projekt oder mit der Direktion der Kolonie in Nordamerika. Er hatte 1669 beim Entwurf der „Carolina-Verfassung" mitgewirkt, und zwar gerade zu einem Artikel über die Berechtigung des Sklaven-Systems. Lockes Theorie des Eigentumsrechts war nichts anders als ein (ideologischer) Motor zugunsten der Kolonialisierung des weit erstreckten Bodens durch die weißen Siedler. Abgesehen davon, wieweit Locke selbst an die Kolonialisierung im heutigen Sinne dachte, kann man sagen, dass Locke mindestens als Folge seiner These des Eigentumsrechts sicherlich dazu beigetragen hat.³⁰

Bei seiner Definition des Eigentumsrechts ist Lockes Interesse ganz anderes als das von Leibniz. Wie wir V–27 seiner *Two Treatises on Government*, 1689 entnehmen, erläutert Locke wie folgt: Gott hat die Welt als das der Menschheit Gemeinsame gegeben; in einem Naturzustand besteht noch keine private Herrschaft über den Boden, aus der gemäß alle anderen ausgeschlossen werden müssten. Wenn es sich so verhält, in welcher Weise sind gewisse Menschen darauf gekommen, für einen bestimmten Gegenstand (hier: den Boden) das private Eigentumsrecht zu beanspruchen und zwar ohne einen expliziten Vertrag geschlossen zu haben? Lockes Antwort auf diese Fragen ist mit einem Wort gesagt, „Arbeit": Gerade durch die Arbeit erklärt man die bisher

---

²⁹ Hierzu ist 2009 eine bahnbrechende Untersuchung veröffentlicht worden: Eimitsu Miura: *Jon Rokku to amerika senjumin. Jiyuushugi to shokuminchi sihai (John Locke und die Koloniepolitik)*, Tokio 2009.
³⁰ Vgl. ebd., S. 178ff.

lange unangetastet gebliebene Natur ohne Zustimmung[31] anderer für sein Eigentum, um dann das herkömmliche gemeinsame Eigentumsrecht aller für den selben Boden auszuschließen:[32]

Lockes Denkschema lässt sich also folgendermaßen zusammenfassen: (a) Der Mensch hat von Gott die Vernunft geschenkt bekommen, um damit die Natur benutzen und sein Leben komfortabel machen zu können. (b) Mit diesem Zweck investiert er in seine Arbeit (mit Fleiß, Schweiß, Zeit). (c) Demzufolge ergibt sich ihm ein Eigentumsrecht ohne jegliche Zustimmung von anderen (egal von wem, d. h. auch wenn es um die Ureinwohner geht, die seit der Urzeit ihren Anspruch auf den betreffenden Boden gehabt hatten). (d) Aufgrund dieses einmal erlangten und erklärten Eigentumsrechts darf man alle anderen, die da hineinzukommen versuchen mit Gewalt ausschließen.

Kurzum: Locke geht es darum, zu begründen, dass das Eigentumsrecht durch die investierte Arbeit bestehe und das dadurch entstandene Eigentumsrecht einen ausschließenden und zugleich unverletzbaren Anspruch gewinne. In diesem Argument findet sich weder die distributive Gerechtigkeit noch die Billigkeit („suum cuique tribuere"). Der Schwerpunkt ist oben deutlich auf (c) und (d) gelegt, wobei es am Gesichtspunkt des „öffentlichen Wohls" oder der Gemeinschaft überhaupt fehlt. Dagegen betrachtet Leibniz das private Eigentumsrecht als „unnötig", er behauptet vielmehr das verbindliche „Gemeinschaftsrecht" (als „jus strictum communitatis").[33] Denn Leibniz ist davon überzeugt: Wenn ein bester Staat (= der Vernunftstaat) da wäre, müsste das darin angeordnete, innere System vollkommen mit dem Naturrecht übereinstimmen und müsste das Interesse der Bürger daher vollkommen auf dem „bonum commune" gründen.[34]

Bei Leibniz ist die Gerechtigkeit nichts anderes als Erhaltung der bürgerlichen Gesellschaft. Leibniz betrachtet die „Gerechtigkeit im Grunde immer in enger Verbindung mit der „societas, Gesellschaft". Er unterstreicht: „Justitia distributiva est virtus qua quod commune est societatis ita in socios

---

[31] John Locke: *Two Treatises on Government,* Bd. II, 1689, 5, 28.
[32] Ebd., 5, 27.
[33] „In einem besten Staat (Idealstaat) würde also das strenge Recht des Eigentumsrechtes abgeschafft und es würde dafür ein „strenges Recht des gemeinsamen Besitzes" eingeführt. Es gäbe keinen Privatmann, der über das Eigentumsrecht oder das gemeinsame Eigentumsrecht der Güter unsicher wäre, noch einen Richter, der sich wegen seiner Gesetz-Interpretationen oder der Verteilung der gemeinsamen Güter fraglich fühlte." (Grua II, 607).
[34] Michael Stolleis (Hrsg.): *Staatsdenker im 17. und 18. Jahrhundert. Reichspublizistik, Politik, Naturrecht,* Frankfurt a. M. ²1987.

distribuitur ne qua sit causa querelae."[35] Anders gesagt, erst wenn das der Gesellschaft gehörige Gut neu zugeteilt und in diesem Sinne von allen Bürgern besessen wird, kann man von „Gerechtigkeit" sprechen. Die drei Stufen der Gerechtigkeit werden jeweils auch universalis, distributiva, particularis genannt. Diese dritte Stufe kann auch „commutativa" heißen und sie entspricht dem strengen Recht („Neminem laedere"). Und dass diese dritte ebenso als „particularis" bezeichnet wird, bezieht sich auf den Gebrauch eines sozialen Guts, wobei unter den Bürgern noch eine gewisse Gleichheit (aequalitas) vor dem Recht erhalten werden soll.

Es sei noch Leibniz' kritische Reaktion gegen Lockes *Two Treatises of Government* angemerkt. Locke betont, dass kein Herrscher die Freiheit und das Eigentum der Bevölkerung verletzen darf. Locke kommt es ausschließlich auf ein Gesichertsein des privaten Eigentums an. Im Kontrast zu Locke kommt es Leibniz auf die (gute, kluge) Herrschaft als solche an. Leibniz meint nicht, dass man im „natürlichen Zustand" die Herrschaft eines Klügeren absolut passiv akzeptiert hätte. Denn, wenn der Herrscher korrumpiert wäre, dann ginge die Bevölkerung von ihm weg. Der Herrscher verpflichtet sich, eine akzeptablere Ordnung herzustellen und diese der Bevölkerung anzubieten. Kurz: Während Lockes Absicht darin liegt, das Recht zu begründen, mit dem das private Eigentum keinem in der Bevölkerung geraubt werden darf, wendet sich Leibniz eher demjenigen Recht zu, mit dem der Herrscher herrschen oder die Bevölkerung beherrscht werden soll.[36]

In der Politischen Philosophie Lockes als Theorie der Gerechtigkeit spielt das Billigkeitsprinzip im Leibniz'schen Sinne fast keine Rolle. Es ist auch anzumerken, dass eine der fruchtbaren Folgen des Leibniz'schen Aequitasbegriffs darin liegt, dass er aufgrund des stärkeren Rechts der vernunftbegabten Seele, d.i. aufgrund des Rechts Gottes, gegen den Missbrauch des Sklavenrechts expressis verbis Stellung nimmt. In seinen „Meditations sur la notion commune de justice" betont Leibniz, dass unter Gott alle Herren Mitbürger ihre Sklaven sind. Es ist beachtenswert, dass Leibniz hierzu seinen Begriff des einzuschränkenden Eigentumsrechts heranzieht. Der Körper eines

---

[35] A VI, 4 C, 2907, Z. 18f. („Ex *Elementis* Feldenii excerpta et subinde immutata"[1677?]).
[36] Vgl. Stefan Luckscheiter: „Leibniz' Kritik an Lockes Two Treatises of Government", in: *VIII. Internationaler Leibniz-Kongress. Einheit in der Vielheit. Vorträge Teil 1 u. 2. Hannover, 24. bis 29. Juli 2006*, 1. Teil, hrsg. v. Herbert Breger, Jürgen Herbst und Sven Erdner, Hannover 2006, S. 532–537, hier S. 534f.

Menschen ist das Eigentum seiner Seele und er kann ihr nicht weggenommen werden, solange er lebt. Er schließt also:

> „Or l'usufruit a ses bornes, – on le doit exercer salva re –, de sorte que ce droit ne peut point aller jusqu'a render un esclave mechant ou malheures."[37]

Schluss

Die Billigkeit versucht Leibniz nicht als eine bloß quantitative, formale Zuteilung, sondern einschließlich der beiden Begriffe, d. h. vom strengen Recht sowie von der Angemessenheit („convenance"), als einen realen Begriff zu definieren. Er hält für die Begründung der Billigkeit auch ein gewissermaßen sinnliches Moment wie Liebe („amor") für unentbehrlich, um dann die „caritas sapientis" und „la place d'autruy" mit einzubeziehen. In der Gegenwart, in der Zeit des Liberalismus bzw. Neoliberalismus, ist die ganze Diskussion um die Gerechtigkeit, so scheint es mir, auf die Debatte um das strenge Recht reduziert worden. Ist der Verfasser der Einzige, der in der heutigen gesellschaftlichen Lage nicht wenig besorgt ist, dass im Schatten der heutigen, globalisierten Welt die Kluft zwischen Armen und Reichen immer wachsen würde?

---

[37] Gottfried Wilhelm Leibniz: „Meditations sur la notion commune de justice"(1703?), in: René Sève (Hrsg.): *G. W. Leibniz: Le droit de la raison*, Paris 1994, S. 134. Vgl. Gottfried Wilhelm Leibniz: *Gedanken über die Gerechtigkeit* (= *Hefte der Leibniz-Stiftungsprofessur* 27), hrsg. von Wenchao Li, Hannover 2014, S. 48ff.; Vgl. auch die Edition der Schrift durch Stefan Luckscheiter, in: Li (Hrsg.): *„Das Recht kann nicht ungerecht sein"*, S. 177.

Erudition, Rhetoric and Scientific Hypothesis.
Some Remarks on the Structure of Leibniz's *Protogaea*

Federico Silvestri (Milan)

In this paper I will present some remarks on Leibniz's *Protogaea* which have resulted by the preliminary work of an ongoing project on the making of a new critical edition and the first Italian translation. I will start with some observation on the manuscripts, which suggest how much our reading of the text has been shaped by Scheidt editorial work for the *editio princeps* to then turn to some remarks on the order underlying Leibniz's *Protogaea* which, in my opinion is better understood when analysed not much in the linear development of its topics, but in the creative equilibrium among some of its structural elements: the style in its most general sense (rhetorical construction of the test, as well as the use of erudition) and the status of scientific hypothesis in natural history. This two elements can be easily connected with the two main *raison d'etre* for this work. The *Protogaea* is in fact at the same time a scientific treatise and the preface to an historical work which had apologetic and political aims, among others.

1. Manuscript Sources of Leibniz's Protogaea.

There are today three manuscripts of the *Protogaea* all of them conserved under the signature LH ms XXIII at the Leibniz Archiv in Hannover. The first[1] is a draft written by Leibniz, which testifies a laborious composition, with a very accurate choice of words and stylistic expression as well as some changes in content. The second[2] (hereafter *a2*) is a copy by unknown hand with corrections by Leibniz that testifies another level of intervention on the text, which represent the last changes that can be attributed to Leibniz beyond doubt, as I will soon try to justify. Finally, the third manuscript (hereafter *b*), classified under the signature LH ms XXIII b is a copy made by unknown hand and revised by Eckhart. Editors of the latest edition[3] had therefore rightly

---

[1] LH XXIIIa, ff. 11-26.
[2] LH XXIIIa, ff. 29-64.
[3] I am referring to: Gottfried Wilhelm Leibniz: *Protogaea*, in: Id.: *Werke* I, ed. by W. E. Peuckert, Stuttgart 1949; id.: *Protogaea. De l'aspect primittive de la terre [...]*, ed by J. M. Barrande, Toulouse 1993; id.: *Protogaea*, ed. by A. Wakefield and C. Cohen, London/Chicago 2008.

decided to base their work on what they refer to as *a* manuscript, by that meaning *a2*.

The *b* manuscript is the only one that shows paragraph numbering and titles. The paragraph numbering in *b* has been added later, probably at the same time as other corrections made by Eckhart, basically following the paragraph indent of the manuscript, as it is testified by the fact that when the Latin numbers become quite long they harshly fit into the paragraph indent. This indenting correspond quite faithfully to the one in *a2*, where paragraphs are marked either by indent or by the use of the two vertical bars. There are however some differences: what in *b* appears as paragraph XV is not so marked in *a2*.[4]

At this state of my research I have no evidence of Leibniz's intervention on the *b* manuscripts. Moreover, other marks on the manuscript suggest that it was intended as a copy for the printer, which lead to the possibility that the manuscript itself is contemporary to Eckhart's correction and might therefore even had been composed, and not just corrected, after Leibniz's death for Eckhart's editorial purposes. Nonetheless, one could cast doubt on this strongest conclusion. Eckhart's intervention may have been done on an existing manuscript, maybe even contemporary to *a2*, or a new manuscript may have been copied later when Eckhart was Leibniz's secretary: considering that plates for the pictures in the *Protogaea* had been prepared by Seelander probably during Leibniz last year of life, a renewed interest in the text might have led to the composition of a new manuscript. While I'm hoping for the possibility of some objective dating, I would like to stress that *b* is surely a source of the *editio princeps*,[5] but at the same time it has not gone unchanged. The concordance of the paragraph's titles and the presence of *b*'s paragraph XV in the *editio princeps* prove its derivation from *b* yet there are relevant differences in the structure, which show at least another passage before printing (which, by the way, is made even more probable by the very presence of *b* among

---

Quotation from Leibniz's *Protogaea* in the following section will be taken from this last edition; in following footnotes, this two last editions are distinguished by years of publishing, while Peuckert is cited as *Werke*. The fact that the 1949 edition is based on *a2* may not be, after all, a matter of choice: see *infra*, n. 9. Peuckert's edition is the only one that do not numbers paragraphs or reports their title, but just indent them, basically following *a2*.

[4] See respectively LH XXIIIa, 40r and LH XXIIIb 30r.

[5] Gottfried Wilhelm Leibniz: *Summi polyhistoris Godefridi Gilielmi Leibnitii Protogaea. Sive De Prima facie telluris*, ed. by C. L. Scheidt, Göttingen 1749.

Leibniz's paper today) so that Scheidt has probably provided his own indication for printing somewhere else. First, the division in paragraphs is different: paragraphs XXIX and XXXII in Scheidt's edition are not paragraphs in the manuscripts, while Scheidt does not have a paragraph corresponding to *b*'s number XXXIII, which is indented in *a2* as well.[6] Second, in the *editio princeps* pictures are put together at the end, while marks and insertions of pictures in *b* seems to indicate the will to include them where the relevant text is. A final, more important, point is that some discordances between Scheidt edition and the *a2* manuscript, which in modern edition appears as variant testified by *b* do not appear there.[7] There is also at least one passage that some modern editors consider as *b*'s variant, which can be found in *a2* too, albeit later added.[8] Eckhart revised copy is therefore much closer to *a2* manuscript than it has been supposed. I then think, at this stage of my research, that it is highly plausible that the differences between the manuscripts and the *editio princeps* should be considered as the result of insertions made by Scheidt.[9]

---

[6] It has to be noticed that in *a2* the beginning of what is paragraph XXIX in the *editio princeps* (and in subsequent edition) comes after a crossed section, so that it appears indented. This may be the reason why it is indented in Peuckert's edition (Leibniz: *Werke*, p. 94) which is based (probably solely, see *infra* n. 9) on *a2*. This may then suggest that *a2* has been consulted by Scheidt. Something similar could have occurred in the case of Scheidt's paragraph XXXII; the relevant text begin in a new line in *a2*: albeit to me it seems not to be indented, it is in Peuckert's edition (ibid., p.102). What correspond to b's paragraph XXXIII is indented also by Peuckert (ibid., p. 124).

[7] Most of the variant in the *editio princeps* may appear as mere stylistic changes with no theoretical relevance. There is however at least one important exception: in paragraph VI, when discussing the aquatic origin of terrestrial animals, Leibniz states that this theory is in contrast with the Holy Scriptures: "Sed pugnat ista cum sacris Scriptoribus, a quibus discedere religio est." In Scheidt's *editio princeps* there is something more, that regards the hypothesis itself: "Sed praeterquam quod ista cum Sacris Scriptoribus, a quibus discedere religio est, pugnent, hypothesis ipsa in se spectata immensis difficultatibus laborat" (p. 10). In both the French and the English (p. 14 and 26 respectively) edition this sentence appear as grounded in *b*, where it is not present (see LH XXIIIb, 17v.) The fact that at least in the following years Leibniz had maintained a similar thesis increases the relevance of this insertion.

[8] The passage is at the end of *editio princeps*' paragraph XXXVIII "Circa Gartoviam, illustriss. Bernstorfi i, Ducis Cellensis Status Ministri, oppidum,frequentius succinum in paludosa ibi regione fodientibus occcurit, et varia inde parata, ac inter caetera vasculum satis amplum ipse ego saepicule admiratus sum." The passage, omitted by Peuckert (Leibniz: *Werke*, p. 140) has later been presented as a variant of *b* (see Leibniz: *Protogea*, 1993, p. 138 and id.: *Protogaea*, 2008, p. 114). It is a different ending (instead of "satis [...] sum": "satis amplum admiratus est Eccardus.") both in *a2* (LH XXIII a, 59r) and *b* (LH XXIII b, 62v).

[9] Against this thesis one may rely on a lost manuscript which existed until the Second world war, and was apparently in *b*'s folder. This version has been accepted by Barrande, as well as Cohen and Wakefield ("Though the A manuscript [the basis for our translation] has survived,

Notwithstanding our differences in the reconstruction of the history of the texts, I think that Cohen and Wakefield remarks, that

> "the structure of the 1749 Latin edition of *Protogaea-* and all subsequent editions of the work- owed much to the editorial work of Leibniz's successors, Eckhart and Scheidt",[10]

is correct. In my view, Scheidt's intervention had a greater impact on the text then Eckhart's: the new texts taken from Lackmund that Cohen and Wakefield attribute to Eckhart's intervention might have been materially inserted following his instructions, but it nonetheless respects Leibniz's own indication in *a2*. On the other hand, I think there is no evidence to attribute to Scheidt the heading and numbering of paragraphs, as Cohen and Wakefield do, which may after all be due to Eckhart's intervention. As said, the paragraphing of *b* is quite close to *a2* indenting. This said however, I once again agree on the fact "the result with its discrete sections and chapter headings somewhat masked the fragmentary and disconnected flavour of the original manuscript,"[11] for the internal structure provided to the text, may result in an overestimation of the autonomy of *a2*'s textual blocks.[12]

Scheidt's editorial work has shaped the way in which Leibniz's text had been read on various other level. First, by making textual insertion, which until 1949 edition where considered part of the text and are still presented as if they were grounded in manuscripts; and by making the *Protogaea* a self-standing

---

the original B manuscript was lost during World War II, and all that remains of it is Eckhart's revision", "Introduction", in: Leibniz: *Protogaea*, 2008, p. XL). To my knowledge it has been first mentioned in Leibniz: *Werke*, pp.175f., where the *Protogaea* is published with Engelhardt's German translation. Though further research on this issue may be needed, I would like to stress that, by know, I have no evidence that while mentioning a lost manuscript Engelhardt is referring to something different than *b* itself, which may indeed have been lost for some period after the war. The description of the *Protogaea* manuscripts made by Bodemann in his catalogue of Leibniz manuscripts, shortly resumed by Engelhardt, fits well with what is today conserved at the Leibniz Archive. Daniel Garber: *De ortu et antiquissimis fontis protogaea leibnizianae dissertatio: observation, explanation and natural philosophy*, in J. A. Nicolas/S. Toledo (eds.): *Leibniz y las sciencias empiricas*, Granada 2011, p. 166 assumes the same, though apparently thinking that Eckhart's revised copy is still lost.

[10] "Introduction" in: Leibniz: *Protogaea*, 2008, p. XL.
[11] Ibid.
[12] It has to be pointed out, however, that in the *editio princeps*, headings appear only on the right margin of pages as they do in *b*, so that they might be seen as tools for indexing more then real titles.

text. First, as it has already been observed by Daniel Garber,[13] by giving it a title it was probably not supposed to have, for in no occasion Leibniz refers to it as in such terms, while when speaking of *Protogaea* he always refers to the article appeared that title in the *Acta eruditorum* and which he did try to spread among scholars, while apparently keeping well secured in his locket what is now called *Protogaea*. In doing so Scheidt had focused the attention on the ancient history of the planet, somehow underestimating other topics, such as the focus on natural history of Lower Saxony which, by the way, is central in the heading of *b*: *De ortu et antiquissimo statu rerum naturalium in regionibus Brunsvico-Luneburgensibus Dissertatio*.

Second, by making it an autonomous text simply by publishing it alone. A decision that should not be blamed, obviously, but kept in mind when analysing the *Protogaea* which was meant to be a preface or introductory chapter to a much broader work, the history of Braunschweig. As a result we then have a self standing text structure organized on blocks whose textual autonomy appears sometimes arbitrary (e.g. the division of the discussion on fossils) or is at least puzzling.

Yet subtracting these elements and try to have an edition closer to the original seems not very helpful in defining an underlying order to the *Protogaea*, for what we are left with is a text with no title, maybe no chapters, and in which the very choice of topics appears difficult to reconcile with a specific plan of the work. The somehow fragmentary character of the text is amplified by the elevate number of anecdotes, curiosities, digression that it presents, making somehow puzzling not just the succession but also the internal structure of paragraphs.

In Garber's account the fragmentary and disconnected character of the *Protogaea* is, at least partially, due to the fact that it combines two rather different types of work: a geological project that can be traced back to Leibniz's early years and a mineralogical study with practical aims that was inspired mainly by the time spent in the Harz. It is the decision to combine this two aspects in the preface to his historical work that brings some "confusion" to the work.[14]

---

[13] Cf. Daniel Garber: *De ortu et antiquissimis fontis*, pp. 165–167. As Garber notices, *b*'s heading echoes a book by Conring: *De antiquissimo statu Helmestadii et viciniae coniecturae*, Helmstedt 1665.
[14] Ibid., pp. 182f. and *passim*.

I think however that there are two, non conflicting ways of finding an underlying unity to the *Protogaea*, that may help in finding an equilibrium by the different strands of research by which it admittedly derives.

2. Rhetorical Construction of the Text

The first one is its rhetorical construction both local and global, so to say.

As a preface to an erudite and politically committed work, in writing the *Protogaea*, Leibniz paid a great attention to the style of writing, as even a quick look at the manuscripts testifies. Among the changes in the second draft one can find many stylistic corrections. He uniforms the usage of infinite past in main proposition and adds examples of a rhetorical figure extensively used within the whole *Protogaea*, a form of lexical *variatio*, where two synonyms are used together (a very leibnizian figure, by the way: more than baroque redundancy it exemplifies Leibniz concepts of harmony as *varietas identitate compensata*). The complex rhetorical construction which honestly I have only started analysing, is often used to underline central scientific and epistemological issue. An interesting example of list is used with polemical aims against those who sees figures in stones, to underlines how various and unregulated imagination can be, if compared to the rigorous observation of the structure of material things:

> "Neque enim animalia tantum, et plantas, partesque eorum in saxis vident, sed et historias fabulasque Christum et Mosen, in crusta Bumannianae specus; Apollinem cum Musis in Achate Pyrrhi; Papam et Lutherum, in Islebiensi petra; et solem cum luna stellisque in marmore."[15]

Metaphors and comparison taken from classical world are often used to mark the scientific relevance of some passages. When talking about a petrified fish, Leibniz writes that it looks like he was found "flexo corpore, ore aperto, quasi sic deprehensus vivus gorgonia vi obriguisset."[16] Here the power of the Gorgon is used to amplify the image of the sudden death of a *real* fish; as obvious

---

[15] Leibniz: *Protogaea*, 2008, p. 72.
[16] Ibid., p. 44. Both *a2* and *b* clearly report "gorgonia", though it probably should be read as "gorgonea": "gorgonia" is in fact the nominative case for "coral". At least since XV. century another adjective began to be used: *gorgonicus:* the first attestation I could find is in Vives' commentary to Augustine's *De civitate dei* (Augustine: *Opera: De Civitate Dei Libros XXII*, vol. V, Basileae 1569, p. 1038); it has been used also by Walter Charleton, in the title of his

as the comparison may be, it is enriched by the adjectivation of *Gorgon*, which though attested is, to my knowledge, quite rare. In other case classical references, though still quite transparent, lays on more complex background. In an important passage where Leibniz grounds the use of hypothesis based on human technique, Leibniz writes

> "nec refert eandemne rem Daedalus aliquis Vulcanius in furno inveniat, an lapicida ex terrae visceribus proferat in lucem"[17]

to state an equivalence between products of nature and products of art.

The complex of constructions of the text provide also an equilibrium among the various aims, scientific, historical and political of the *Protogaea*. The two main scientific issues the earlier history of the earth and the nature of fossils occupies a bit more then the first half of the text. In both cases the discussion of the general problem is followed by the local examples of the phenomena. The second part has a more complicated form: after the description of Luneburg's *glossopetrae*, Leibniz moves to the description of some relevant phenomena of the region such as cave, or types of amber which can be found there, to turn again to local examples of changes made by water in the region. This last point allows him to move to the region of the Este at one time anticipating the main result of his historical work (the Este's and Braunschweig's families relationship) and discussing a very relevant scientific problem (the origin of Modena's springs), that was about to become the argument of a sharp scientific controversy in Italy, sometimes referred to as the "fountain war". The discussion of springs reintroduces the question of the various layer of the earth, which allows the connection with the first part for in layers of earth we found the confirmation and means of improvement of the general hypothesis of the history of the world. So Leibniz comes once again to the nature of Lower Saxony, describing layer of earth near Göttingen and finished

---

Spiritus gorgonicus, vi sua saxipara exutus; sive De causis, Lugd, Batav 1650. If I am correct, Leibniz chooses to rely on the classical term.

[17] Leibniz: *Protogaea*, 2008, p. 26. Though Dedalus and Hephaestus are often seen as similar figures, so much that, for instance, they are both indicated as makers of Talos in different versions of the myth, explicitly juxtaposing Dedalus and Vulcan is not, again, to my knowledge, very common. There are however some possible sources. Aristotle in his *Politics* mentions both as creators of the types of automata which would made slavery superfluous. Leibniz may also rely on a passage of the (disputed) platonic dialogue *Alcibiades I*, where Socrates ironically replying to Alcibiades' pride of his descending from Zeus, draws his own genealogy, putting together the two names among his ancestors, probably for their common activity activity as sculptors and craftsmen.

describing the layer of earth in a pit in Amsterdam, which is used to briefly recap how the present aspects of the earth has been shaped by repeated flood and catastrophes.

3. Scientific Hypothesis: The Method of Natural History

The equilibrium built by this stylistic characteristic may look a bit extrinsic to the various aims and topics of the *Protogaea*. As I said before, there is however another way of reading the structure of the *Protogaea*, following the method Leibniz uses for natural history. In this way, one of the stylistic characteristic of the text, the impressive erudition, will reveal a much more intrinsic role.

The *Protogaea* is very rich of what might look like curiosities, unrelated information and digressions taken from an impressive amount of sources that goes from apodemic books, chronicles, books of natural history as well as from popular knowledge and human technique. The information that the *Protogaea* provides can be seen as a direct consequence what is stated right at its beginning as sort of justification of the work:

> "Magnarum rerum etiam tenuis notitia in pretio habetur. Itaque ab antquissimo nostri tractus statu orsuro dicendum est aliquid de prima facie terrarum, et soli natura contentisque. Nam editissimmum Germaniae inferioris locum tenemus, maximeque metallis foecundum; et domi nobis insignes conjecturae, et velut radii nascuntur publicae lucis, unde ad caeteras regiones aestimatio procedat. Quodsi minus assequimur destinata, saltem exemplo profi ciemus: Nam ubi in suo quisque curiositatem conferet, facilius origines communes noscentur."[18]

This is more than a rhetoric justification: not only it fits with Leibniz's encyclopedic projects and ideas on collective works in science, but shred some light on the method that pertains to the topics that are going to follow. Collecting and communicating local data is a preliminary work for having a more structured version of the new science called natural geography which means both a structural description of places and a causal explanation of their present appearance, that in turns imply an analysis of the historical development of the natural world that should bring to a stage where the transformation analysed regard the whole world. Local descriptions, information on the nature of plants, animals and fossils, memories of the previous look of a place or of the

---

[18] Leibniz: *Protogaea*, 2008, p. 2.

effects of local catastrophes are data for scientific hypothesis. As we shall see, some of this data can have also another role, by now, I'd like to stress that so conceived the method of natural history has lot in common with Human and Holy history. All types of history starts from what Leibniz calls *monumenta* or *vestigia*; traces or memories of the past in order to reconstruct their genesis. In natural history the look of the earth at present time or as it has been described at some times constitute such a trace. As Leibniz puts it in the very end of the *Protogaea*, nature has here the role of histories or chronicles.

When it comes to how the causal hypothesis should be built, however, natural history gains its autonomy from various types of history, an autonomy that can be seen in the set of constraints that Leibniz elaborate for describing legitimate hypothesis, which are mainly based on specific versions of some of his metaphysical principles.

Leibniz approach to natural history is in the path traced by Stensen, that has described what he thought was an "universal problem" in his *De solido*, which Leibniz probably read in 1678:

> "dato corpore certa natura praedito et juxta leges naturae producto, in ipso corpore argumenta invenire locum et modum productionis degentia."[19]

Leibniz can be seen as generalizing this problem in a double sense: by considering that in principle it can be extended to all natural phenomena and also to a complete state of the Earth, which is considered itself as a natural phenomena. At the same time, there should be some restrictions, which can be considered on one hand as relying on what *one* body is and on the other on a logical difference between place and the causal process:

> "Bien des gens amassent des Cabinets où il y a des mineraux, mais à moins que d'avoir desobservations exactes, du lieu d'où elles ont este´ tirées et de toutes les circomstances, ces collections donnent plus de plaisir aux yeux, que les lumieres à la raison. Car une plante ou un animal est un tout achevé, au lieu que les Mineraux sont ordinairement des pieces detaché es, qu'on ne scauroit bien considerer que dans leur tout."[20]

A derivation of means of production can be done by considering the whole mineral as inserted in a place, which should be regarded as one of the condition of the causal development, therefor itself contains traces of the way a

---

[19] Niels Stensen: *De solido intra solidum naturaliter contento: dissertationis prodromus*, Florentiae 1669, pp. 5f.
[20] Leibniz to S. Foucher, 1687; A II, 2, 205.

mineral was produced. The resulting approach is well founded in Leibniz's metaphysics: the nature of the place is among the *requisita,* logical conditions, of natural phenomena, therefore included in their sufficient reason, that makes them what they are and not something else, while the method of productions can be seen as the whole sufficient reason, and therefore being the main object of explanation. By this, both internal and external elements should be considered as containing information of the causal process. The famous leibnizian statements, "le present est plein de l'avenir, et chargé du passé,"[21] taken in a very literal sense by which relevant information on the past are included in the way the present is, is the main grounding for this historical method. It is in this frame, that analysis of layers of earth represent the main tool for reconstructing the nature of earth in its causal and temporal development. As Evaristo Munoz has suggested, the various analysis of layers of the earth developed by Leibniz provides a sedimentological explanation which encompasses the purely geometrical descriptions made by, for instance, Ramazzini, so that geology becomes at the same time a geographical and historical science.[22] Though Leibniz did not provide, at least by what we know now, any time-scale for his geological works, it seems to me that the analysis of layers developed is indeed "historical" from Leibniz's point of view, for it provides sketches of concrete instances of the relations of "priority of nature", which is a key notion for defining time directions in the historical development of the world.

One of the ideas that drives Stensen's *De Solido* is that similar shapes and structures require similar causes (the place of production being one of such causes). A similar idea of some sort of causal homogeneity is in the background of one of the structural elements of Leibniz method: analogy. As he writes to Thevenot this is the mean to know nature: *naturam cognosci per analogiam.*[23] Within the *Protogaea* Leibniz uses two different types of analogies: description of local phenomena (such as falls of mountains, effect caused by extraordinary strong winds, raising of new island and seeking of old ones, changes in places of rivers, local flood and so on) where we can register the effects of natural forces and try to generalize and amplify their effects in order to have descriptions of possible global changes and probably the most important, an analogy with human technique. This last analogy introduces the

---

[21] *Nouveaux Essais [...]*; A VI, 6, 55.
[22] Cf. Evaristo Alberto Munoz: "Leibniz y las ciencias de la terra", in: Juan A. Nicolás/Sergio Toledo (eds.): *Leibniz y las sciencias empiricas*, Granada 2011, p. 143.
[23] Cf. Leibniz to Thevenot; A I, 7, 354.

first, well known constraint to any hypothesis: explanation should be mechanical, the only type of explanation that makes changes in phenomena intelligible. As Leibniz states in the *Protogaea*, nature is like an artifice: there is a causal homogeneity between technique and nature: they both use the same means and follow the same laws. If we know a way to produce a phenomenon there is no need to find complicate explanation, for we already have one. By this we then have a possible cause or at least, given that products of art and of nature are usually not exactly the same we have a possible scheme of mechanical generation. An interesting example is in the discussion on the nature of fossils, where Leibniz uses a comparison with the art of making insects shaped jewels in order to a show that a similar mechanical process can produce the shape of an animal within a stone.

Yet there is more: in Leibniz's eyes hypothesis can have stronger status than just a possible cause and he tries to make not just the similarity but also the differences between *ars* and nature, local and global changes fit into the scheme in two interrelated ways. In the already mentioned letter to Thevenot he proceeds mentioning his principle of continuity when it is possible to find a series, (order or progression) resulting from various analogy or comparison. There we have a mark of the truth of our hypothesis. Some of the analogies of the *Protogaea* fit, in principle, this requisite: the main example is the comparison between our furnaces and the effect of fire at the beginning of history: they are different, but the effects can in principle be inserted in a series that can be related to changes in degrees and duration of heat, that is quantitative changes in the cause. Yet the *Protogaea* follows another way, focusing on others central Leibnizian concepts: harmony and the distinction between God's power and his wisdom. This theme appears once again in relation with human technique, but it fits well (and maybe even more) for the comparison between local and global phenomena. The variety of possible causes is grounded in God's Power, however his wisdom assures that the he has chosen the most harmonically way to obtains his goals, varying the effect while maintaining constant causes.[24] In both cases, direct or indirect observation stands as a prove for an hypothesis not just as singular empirical confirmation, with all the logical difficulties implied, but rather as ways of proving that the hypothesis fits what we know about some key features of the abstract structure of the world order.

---

[24] "Nam etsi ejusdem rei plures causas in potestate habeat ditissimus rerum parens, amat tamen et constantiam in varietate." Leibniz: *Protogaea*, 2008, p. 26.

The Leibnizian idea of order is then in the background of the *Protogaea* and of natural history, defining its method and justifying its tools. This concept of order can be seen at stake in one of the central issues of the *Protogaea*, the proof of organic origin of fossils. Leibniz praises Agostino Scilla's rigorous description of the structure of stone-fish relating them to existing fishes, while others, Kircher for instance, had let their imagination flow and have searched hidden messages in rock and stones. In doing so they try to justify the apparent disorder represented by petrified animals by seeking hidden divine messages and signs of his particular will. In Leibniz's eye fossils (as well as catastrophes) may be considered signs, though they are better defined as traces, but not of singular specific divine messages, but rather of a causal history. There is no disorder in natural phenomena, so there is no need to search for hidden meanings or specific justifications, because anything in nature happens according to the laws which expresses the set of architectonic principles that rules the world order and subsequently our scientific hypothesis.

This concept of order and the method that it justifies is what in my opinion rules the complicated dialectic between global and local phenomena in the *Protogaea* and at least partially helps in understanding the many digressions it reveals. Leibniz is well known for having developed fascinating and powerful philosophical metaphors: to some extent the rhetorical construction of the text, as well at least some of his rhetorical instruments may be seen as a complex metaphor for the method of natural history and some of its underlying metaphysical principles.

The Pharmaceutical Preparations in Leibniz' Manuscripts: Presentation and Comments

Sebastian W. Stork (Berlin)

The manuscripts in the Corpus Leibnitianum on medical topics are quite numerous, but have not found much attention so far. Efforts to enhance the knowledge on these activities of Leibniz have found a rather large portion of said manuscripts to be descriptions of pharmaceutical preparations. As can be derived from their number, this topic was obviously of substantial concern to Leibniz. Thus some initial observations on the texts of this nature are reported.

1. Formal Features

The first observation is the heterogeneous appearance of these manuscripts. They vary strongly in sheet-size, extent of the description and hands of writers. Some appear as notes of different lengths within other texts, some are independent texts continuing over several pages.

Although a description of a (partial) corpus does best start with a reliable survey, any assessment of an exact number and catalogue for the pharmaceutical preparations is futile. This is not only due to limited knowledge about this part of Leibniz' manuscripts, but also due to the characteristics of these texts. Many notes do refer to pharmaceutical preparations and practices. But formally they are not independent texts, and materially they are too short for any useful information about constitution and application of the mentioned preparation. An example is the note: "Pillen aus [Silber] vor serum und hydropem (pills from silver for serum and dropsy."[1] This is a pharmaceutical text, describing a pharmaceutical preparation and its application. But it misses the formal requirements of an instruction about a pharmaceutical preparation, and its shortness does not allow any implementation into therapeutical practice. It is thus a matter of arbitrary discretion to count such notes among the number of pharmaceutical preparations or not.

The pharmaceutical preparations are also markedly heterogeneous in material characteristics. They stem from a wide range of different sources. They are copied from printed sources like pharmacopoeia or from collections

---

[1] LH IV 8, 22 Bl. 73v, cf. A VIII, 1, 15.

of manuscripts, an unknown number has been supplied by various individuals. The time of the origin of the prescriptions has still to be determined, but examples are known from antiquity as from sources contemporary to Leibniz.

2. Two Examples

2.1 Formal Characteristics

The first example[2] serves to demonstrate the short notes on pharmaceutical preparations. This note is part of the *Observata Philosophica*. For his visit to London during spring 1673 Leibniz had subdivided a folio-sized sheet into several areas and assigned those to different fields of observation. In the section headed "Medica" he scribbled names of medical authors and their works for further reading, examples for particular cures, and notes on pharmaceutical preparations. The text of one of these notes can be given in full: "Paronychia folio rutaceo simplici infusione cerevisiae (beer) curat das kings evil" and may be englished as: 'Paronychia folio rutaceo by a simple extraction of beer cures the king's evil'.

The other example[3] is presently known as the most elaborate text on a pharmaceutical preparation. It is written by another hand, the language is French. The header reads: "Memoire sur le Faldtranck [!] au decoction vulneraire ou Panacée Helvetique donné par Monsieur Dapples Docteur en Medicine". The almost seven pages of explanations are structured into 14 sections. The first section gives the names of the herbs involved, the third describes the intended effects as "attenuer le sang, empécher les obstructions, and accelerer la circulation". The fourth section gives the advices to employ herbs grown and picked at high altitude. Section 6 states four varieties or degrees of the decoction. Notable is the fourth degree, that is achieved by preparing an alcoholic extraction from the herbs and distilling it. The final product contains the lipophilic substances, the most likely candidats for physiologically active substances, in rather concentrated fashion. This indicates the decoction vuneraire as remnant of the medicine practised by monasteries throughout medieval times, based on herbs and charity. Section 7 assigns the decoction and its "degrés" or "fortes" to particular illnesses such as apoplexie or phrenesie. The following sections list more indications of this remedy,

---

[2] LH IV, 8, 22f., 73v; edited in A VIII, 1, 15.
[3] LH III, 5f., 134–137.

among them "dysenterie, passion nephretique, les menstrües, ulceres, fievres, and maladies externes." The last section collects some specifications about the administration, distinguishing between applications in refrigerated or heated state. The only contribution of Leibniz is a note in the upper left corner on the first page, stating: "1709 communiqué par M. Bouquet chirurgien de l'Electeur à Hanover."

2.2 Material Characteristics

Of the first example the materials employed begin with Paronychia folio rutaceo. This is a small ground-covering plant, also known as rue-leaved Whitlow grass and today classified as species of the genus Saxifraga. It combines a ring of green leaves close to the ground with a central single flower. It is home to the temperate areas of the northern hemisphere. Thus, this plant is readily available to the general population. Leibniz probably meant to write 'infuso' instead of 'infusione'. 'Infusio' is the act of pouring a liquid into any flask. 'Infusum' is the term for a liquid preparation by a most often aqueous extraction of plants or parts thereof. The king's evil is an illness with the symptoms of bulbous tumours in the neck and the lower jaw of the patient. The name of this condition derives from the opinion, that a touch by the recently annointed king (of England or France) is competent of curing this condition.

The name 'Saxifraga' may be read already as a therapeutical classification, since it refers to the assumption, that this plant is capable of fragmentation kidney stones. Another explanation sees the origin of this name in the (assumed) capability of breaking stones on the ground during growing. Although beer is a rather well known liquid and drink, there are so many varieties of it, that a specification is helpful or required. Even if the use of beer is only to assure an extraction in a slightly acidic and alcoholic aqueous phase by heat, the ratio of plant to liquid and the time and temperature of extraction as all other specifications concerning quantities are missing.

Since Leibniz indicates Boyle as his source for this preparation (the U concluding this note is an abbreviation for Boyle, Usefulness), the original can be quoted for comparison. Under the heading: "A cure for the king's-evil", the description of the preparation reads:

> "300. Take a handful of Paronychia folio rutaceo, called rue-whitlow-grass, and boil it, every morning, in a quart of small beer; strain it, and drink it for ordinary

drink. It wastes the peccant humour, appeases the pain, discusses the unbroken tumours, and heals the broken ones."[4]

The information absent from Leibniz' note is present in the original. Small beer is a beer low in wort and thus in alcohol. It was stored and consumed without filtering after the brewing process, thus it was high in calories. Little and cheap ingredients and simple preparation-procedure allowed an affordable price, making small beer a widely consumed drink. Thus, both components of this pharmaceutical preparation were readily available. During its preparation the boiling removes the alcohol and carbon dioxide, expedites the hydrolysis of the solid remains in the small beer, and the straining frees the final product from all de-appetising parts. There is no contemporary information about the extent and results of the treatment by this pharmaceutical. The plant appears in several herbal-books, and this pharmaceutical preparation is printed in other collections. While this points at some use, no exact information is available, nor any reports about the consequences in patients.

The description as given by Boyle lists the expected effects as relieve of pain, discussion of the unbroken tumours and healing of the broken ones. Broken tumours refers to the fact, that often on top of the bulbous exostoses the skin splits or a discharge of puss occurs. Discussion of a tumour is in modern terms the reduction of its size. The description of the effects describes this preparation as competent to end the affliction. This information is not copied by Leibniz, but it may be the reason for his interest.

The description of the decoction vulneraire states (f. 134r) the names of the herbs employed as pirola, sanicula, virga aurea, vincapervinca, and pes leonis. Pirola is a small evergreen plant, growing in temperate to arctic areas of the northern hemisphere. Since its growth occurs in a clustered pattern, it is not ubiquitous available. Sanicula plants consist of a circle of leaves close to the ground, and in the centre several stalks up to 60 cm tall bearing flowers and small fruit. It is commonly found throughout all of Europe. Its use for medical purposes is attested by several sources starting in the 15th century. The plant was to be picked preferably during summer and all parts of it were to be processed. It was applied by way of pulver, tea or ointment. Drinking its extract was assumed to heal wounds, and to end all maladies of the digestion tract. Virga aurea is home to temperate regions of Europe. At the time of Leibniz it has been considered an astringent and styptic herb. Vincapervinca (vinca maior, greater periwinkle) at the time of Leibniz was probably restricted to the

---

[4] Robert Boyle: *Philosophical Works of Boyle*, London 1725, p. 647.

western Mediterranean basin. It is a plant with vines spreading along the ground, best noticed by its flowers of five purple coloured and diamond shaped leaves. Its use as medicinal herb is otherwise almost unknown, only in the regions of its natural occurrence it was used as antitumoral, anti-inflammatory, analgesic and astringent agent. 'Pes leonis' or 'leontopodium' refers to the many members of the plant genus Asteraceae, better known by their German name Edelweiß. The medicinal use of this plant is limited to the Alpine species and area. At least one plant from the genus edelweiss is included in several editions of the Dioskurides.[5]

All other information besides the herb-names is missing. There are no specifications concerning the amount of herbs in relation to water volume, no ratios of herbs relative to each other, no description of the procedure of preparation. This is in stark contrast to the several pages stating the maladies, which allegedly are addressed by this decoction. It is also substantially less information than that given by other sources describing the use of the single herbs.

The pattern of information given and not given in this prescription is identical to the pattern describing another remedy of the time named 'aurum potabile'. This was produced by the pharmacy of the Franckesche Waisenhaus in Halle, and was shipped probably worldwide. The printed description intended to make this remedy and its alleged medical benefits known to the general public, thus advertising a prepared, ready to use pharmaceutical. It is not a procedure for apothecaries to prepare this remedy. In analogy, Leibniz did receive not a pharmaceutical-preparation, but a description of a pharmaceutical preparation for people without medical knowledge.

Bouquet's biography before his post at the court in Braunschweig is not known. Thus it remains unknown, whether he brought this preparation with him from France, or whether it is of German origin. The language of the description, and the incorrect spelling of Feldtrunck indicate a French origin of this copy, the employment of vincapervinca for medicinal purposes points at a Mediterranean origin. The name Dapples can not be correlated to a particular area. Thus, at present the origin of this preparation remains unknown.

Applying the biochemical and pharmaceutical knowledge of today, the Saxifraga plants are not known to contain any physiologically active sub-

---

[5] Barabara Orelli-Messerli: "Von der Exotik des Edelweiss'", in: *Zur Regionalität der Keramik des Mittelalters und der Neuzeit. Beiträge des 26. Internationalen Hafnerei-Symposiums, Soest 5.10.-9.10.1993*, ed. by Eberhard Grunsky and Bendix Trier, Bonn 1995, pp. 93–100.

stances. Today the king's evil is known to be caused by an infection with mycobacteria. There is no antibacterial potency known from Saxifraga plants. Thus, in general and in particular against a disease caused by infection the extract in the short note is not a helpful remedy at all.

In the decoction vulneraire pirola does contain a glycoside named Aucubin, that is known to have some antibacterial and health sustaining effects, but is also toxic in large doses. For sanicula a recent testing[6] did not find observable physiological effects. The virga aurea is today named Solidago virgaurea. Its diuretic effect has been confirmed and the molecular basis is known for its diuretic, and several other physiological effects. But none of them is capable of the therapeutic benefits listed in the memoire. The alpine variety of the edelweiss-family has developed molecular protection-mechanisms against the intense uv-radiation at high altitudes. These provide some anti-inflammatory potency, but significant antibacterial properties could not be observed. Extracts of edelweiß are used as food additive, but they are not effective as therapeutic agents. In summary, these two examples of pharmaceuticals recorded by Leibniz have either no therapeutic effect at all, or cause at most a minor and non-specific stimulation of the general metabolism.

It is noteworthy, that these two preparations do not contain any metal as active agent, in contrast to the preparation[7] that Leibniz was given to cure an inflammation in his leg. Preparations employing heavy metals are all strongly disturbing the metabolism of the patient and often actually life-threatening. While the two pharmaceutical preparations presented here are no help, at least they do not threaten the life of the patient.

In general for Leibniz and his era the experiences of patients with pharmaceuticals are not well known. This is due to the small number of sources and their characteristics. Most physicians did keep records of the pharmaceuticals that they did prescribe to patients, but they did most often not monitor the effects on the patients, or did so by following observables, that are not sufficient for a differential diagnosis and a subsequent case history of therapeutic activities. Reports by patients taking medicaments are small in number, and not very specific about the pharmaceuticals administered nor about the consequences. Already the small number of accounts by patients narrating the course of pharmaceutical treatments points at a traumatic character of such

---

[6] Sylvia Vogl et al.: "Ethnopharmacological In Vitro Studies on Austria's Folk Medicine – An Unexplored Lore In Vitro Anti-Inflammatory Activities of 71 Austrian Traditional Herbal Drugs", in: *Journal of Ethnopharmacology* 149/3 (2013), pp. 750–771.
[7] LH III, 5f., 128.

experiences. The information available most often does not allow to reconstruct illness and treatment in comprehensive medical and pharmaceutical terms.

3. Pharmaceutical Paradigm

Boyle's description of the preparation acting against the king's evil does not only supply the necessary information about ingredients, preparation-procedure and details of application. It also contains an explanation of the mode of action. The preparation wastes the peccant humour. In modern terms, the remedy is said to remove or correct the liquid that is causing the swellings. The liquid is not identified at all, the humour might be read as tumour, and there is no distinction whether humour refers to a physical liquid in the body or the metaphorical humor of the humoralpathologic paradigm. This aetiology is too inarticulate to describe and correlate cause and consequence, but it is an effort to inform physician and patient.

The advice concerning the decoction vulneraire to prefer specimens grown at high altitude and harvested during periods of hot weather, is accompanied by an extensive motivation. This preference is based on the intense sunlight, enhanced by reflections from the snow, that agitates terrestrial salt and the plant alike, thus producing herbs rich in sel nitreux, which attenuates the blood, causing the ascribed therapeutic effects. This explanation of physiological action is based on physical materials, their properties and the quantification of a transfer process.

Leibniz does not respond to these incentives. His extract of Boyle's description focuses on the materials and the indication. His note is a praxis-centred, albeit incomplete, extraction of the prescription. There is no response to the memoire and its explanation of the therapeutic properties of the involved herbs.

The use of pharmaceutical preparations is based on experience. A patient with particular symptoms receives a certain pharmaceutical preparation and in consequence his appearance does or does not turn to the state associated with healthiness. But such an accumulation of experience puts strong limits on the use of pharmaceuticals. The accumulated experience is based on chance observations, often contains unwanted results like the death of the patient. At least it is always incomplete. Since humans and their illnesses are complex, equally variable are their responses to therapeutic measures. All experience has to be modified before its use. Thus, to apply pharmaceutical experience to another patient, a model of the action of pharmaceuticals is necessary. Since Leibniz was not a practising physician, but trained and well versed in discussing theories, he was well prepared to design and discuss suggestions for a model of the actions of pharmaceuticals. But so far, there is no indication known that Leibniz has reflected on and presented any model of the effect of pharmaceuticals.

A few fragments, that may be contributions to a discussion or development of a therapeutically paradigm are reported here. Pharmaceutical preparations are classified into groups, and the groups assigned to particular illnesses. There is a distinction between amara et acida, the former acting against fevers, the latter agains pestilence. Specific criteria for categorisation of substances and their assignment are not given.

So far, only one explanation of the mode of action of a pharmaceutical preparation is known. LH III, 5f., 131 is a small piece of paper, containing a note describing a preparation, and an addition by Leibniz. The preparation reads:

> "D. simp. diaeth. / f. Fernel. [Unze]ij / in vitr. s. / suo nomine, and the addition by Leibniz reads: antinephrit. quia lubricat vias, ut sine incommodo exeat sal [tartarum]" (last word uncertain).

The pharmaceutical acts by lubricating the paths by which a stone in the kidney can leave the body. Leibniz declares the preparation to act by a plain change of mechanical properties of parts. This single example is insufficient to decide, whether this mechanical explanation is due to the characteristics of this particular malcondition, or whether it is an indication of a more fundamental feature of Leibniz' medical thinking. Today the body is recognised as a complex mix of (complex) molecules. Pharmaceuticals are described as specific molecules interacting with specific molecules in the body. For Leibniz, describing matter as continuous, to think in molecules is unlikely, if not impossible. It is more probable, that Leibniz explains pharmaceuticals by transfer of qualities, as he does in this example. But so far, there is no sufficient support for any hypothesis.

The words most frequently associated with Leibniz are probably infinitesimal calculus, vis viva, theodicy, and monads. This list needs to be expanded by an extent, but fragmented work on medical topics, which did not help to relieve the complete lack of medical and pharmaceutical competence at his time.

Natürliche Theologie und Philosophia perennis.
Leibniz' Interpretation der alten und modernen chinesischen Philosophie in der Abhandlung Niccolò Longobardis S.J.

Rita Widmaier (Essen)

Leibniz' These im Vorwort[1] der *Novissima Sinica*: Die Europäer könnten von den „in den Regeln eines noch kultivierteren Lebens"[2] erzogenen Chinesen die „Anwendung und Praxis einer Natürlichen Theologie" lernen,[3] richtete sich *nicht* gegen die christliche Religion oder deren Kleriker und Sekten,[4] sondern gegen den durch Uneinigkeit und Kriege „ins Unermessliche wachsenden" moralischen Verfall in Europa.[5] Die Europäer sollten es nach Leibniz besser wissen: „Nur von der himmlischen Gnade und der christlichen Lehre" dürfe man wohl jene „wahre tugendhafte Lebensführung" erwarten, die selbst die Chinesen „noch nicht ganz erreicht" hätten.[6] Die sich aufdrängende Frage, was den Chinesen dazu noch fehle, beantwortet Leibniz rund zwölf Jahre später „mit einem Wort" in einem Brief an die Kurfürstin Sophie:

> „Man muss das Gute tun und *glauben*, dass Gott es tut. Das wäre die Vereinigung der natürlichen und der offenbarten Religion, *wenigstens in der Praxis*", wie er betont, um dann erläuternd hinzuzufügen: „Denn die Mysterien betreffen viel mehr die *Erkenntnis*."[7]

---

[1] Vgl. A IV, 6 N. 61, 393–409.
[2] Vgl. *Nov. Sin.* (= Gottfried Wilhelm Leibniz: *Novissima Sinica (1697). Das Neueste von China*, mit ergänzenden Dokumenten hrsg., übers. u. erl. v. Heinz-Günter Nesselrath und Hermann Reinbothe, Nachdruck der Ausgabe von 1979, mit einem Vorwort, aktualisiertem Literaturverzeichnis u. Register v. Gregor Paul/Adolf Grünert, München 2010), § 3, S. 11.
[3] Vgl. ebd., § 10, S. 19.
[4] Vgl. René-Henri de Crux de Monceaux an Leibniz vom 4. (14.) Oktober 1697: „Votre pensée de faire venir des Missionnaires, pour apprendre la Religion naturelle, aux sectes de l'Europe, m'a extremement plù! Quel Bonheur! Si sans aller si loin, les Ecclesiastiques des 3. Religions daignoient s'humaniser d'avantage!" Leibniz antwortete demselben am 8. (18.) Oktober 1697: „La grande et veritable religion porte à procurer du bien. Si cette religion avoit beaucoup de sectateurs en Europe, [...] nous n'aurions point besoin de faire venir des missionnaires Chinois pour nous apprendre la religion naturelle." Vgl. A I, 14 N. 330, 563, bzw. N. 354, 608f.
[5] Vgl. *Nov. Sin.*, § 10, S. 19.
[6] Vgl. ebd.
[7] Vgl. Leibniz' Brief vom April 1709: „En un Mot, il faut faire le bien et croire que Dieu le fait. Voilà la reunion de la Religion naturelle et la religion revelée, au moins dans la pratique. Car les mysteres regardent plustôt la connoissance." Vgl. Klopp, I, 9, 300–305, hier 302 (Hervorheb. R. W.).

Offensichtlich konnten die Chinesen bei der Anwendung und Praxis der Natürlichen Theologie ohne die offenbarte Religion an Gott nicht glauben. Könnten sie aber, ungeachtet dieser Tatsache, von Gott theoretisch schon gewusst oder wenigstens geahnt haben? Schon im Vorwort der *Novissima Sinica* versichert Leibniz, dass die modernen und die zeitgenössischen Chinesen – die von den Jesuitenmissionaren und allemal von deren Gegnern für Atheisten gehalten wurden – gerade in dieser Hinsicht von den Europäern lernen könnten, nämlich in den theoretischen Wissenschaften, der Logik und der „Erste[n] Philosophie, durch die wir zu der Erkenntnis auch unstofflicher Dinge gelangen konnten."[8]

Bereits Matteo Ricci S.J. (1552–1610), der Begründer der alten Jesuitenmission in China, hatte bei seiner Interpretation der kanonischen Bücher Chinas festgestellt, dass viele Stellen darin – etwa über die Einheit Gottes und die Unsterblichkeit der Seele – mit der christlichen Religion übereinstimmten. Dabei hielt er sich an jene Zeitgenossen unter den chinesischen Gelehrten, die nach einer Rückkehr des Denkens zur Reinheit des ursprünglichen Konfuzianismus strebten.[9] Im Unterschied zu den modernen Gelehrten hätten demnach die alten Chinesen unter dem – *vor* dem mosaischen Gesetz und der christlichen Offenbarung geltenden – „natürlichen Gesetz"[10] nichts anderes als „den Himmel und die Erde und deren Herrn" verehrt.[11] Ricci bezeichnet diese alten Autoren als „natürliche Philosophen" und vergleicht sie mit Platon und Aristoteles; da er in ihren Texten überdies primär die *nicht*-religiösen, nämlich ethisch-sozialen Werte erkennt, interpretiert er auch die Riten des Konfuzius- und Ahnenkults als rein weltliche Praxis.[12] Mit der These von dem natürlichen Wissen der alten Philosophen in China knüpfte Ricci an die Lehre von den frühen Theologen (*prisci theologi*) an, die als *Philosophia perennis* zwar erst durch das Werk Agostino Steucos (1422–1513) ihren Namen erhielt, aber der Sache nach schon in der Spätantike existiert hatte.[13]

---

[8] Vgl. *Nov. Sin.*, §§ 2 u. 9, S. 9 bzw. 17.
[9] Vgl. Paul A. Rule: *K'ung-tzu or Confucius? The Jesuit interpretation of Confucianism*, Sydney/London/Boston 1986, S. 29.
[10] S. dazu Caudia von Collani: „Philippe Couplet's Missionary Attitude towards the Chinese in Confucius Sinarum Philosophus", in: *Philippe Couplet, S.J. (1623–1693). The Man Who Brought China to Europe*, Nettetal 1990, S. 37–54, hier S. 47f.
[11] Vgl. Rule: *K'ung-tzu or Confucius?*, S. 30.
[12] Vgl. ebd., S. 29.
[13] Bereits Philon von Alexandria (13 v.–45/50 n. Chr.) hatte die Weisheit der Patriarchen im *Alten Testament* mit der Metaphysik der griechischen Philosophen verglichen, um so die biblischen Offenbarungen für die gebildeten Griechen seiner Zeit attraktiv zu machen. Die Exegeten des frühen Christentums übernahmen diese Methode, um die *figürlich* oder auch *allegorisch* im

Das darin enthaltene, das europäische Weltbild erschütternde Problem, *wie* die Personen und Fakten der biblischen Erzählung mit den Personen und Fakten der konfuzianischen Überlieferung in Einklang zu bringen wären, sollte die Chinamission im sogenannten Ritenstreit erst nach Riccis Tod auf die Zerreißprobe stellen. Schon sein unmittelbarer Nachfolger, Niccolò Longobardi (1565–1655), bezweifelte Riccis Interpretation und setzte sich in seiner 1623 verfassten Abhandlung[14] intensiv mit einer dreifachen Frage auseinander: Ob die chinesischen Philosophen einen wahren Begriff von Gott, von den Geistern und von der rationalen Seele besessen hätten. Auf der Grundlage der kanonischen Werke Chinas gelangte dieser Pater zu dem Schluss, dass nicht nur die modernen, sondern – entgegen Riccis Lehre – auch schon die

---

Alten Testament angeblich bereits vorgebildete Wahrheit mit der offenbarten, eigentlichen Wahrheit im *Neuen Testament* zu erweisen. Diese figürliche oder allegorische Interpretation unterscheidet sich von der typologischen Auslegung dadurch, dass in der letzteren die universale Menschheits- und Heilsgeschichte eine grundlegende und bedeutsame Rolle spielt: Hier werden Personen und Ereignisse in der Überlieferung nichtchristlicher Texte als Vorgebildetes oder als Antitypisches gegenüber dem Vorbild und Typos im Neuen Testament betrachtet, so dass die ‚eigentliche Wahrheit' jener Textzeugnisse in der biblischen Erzählung ‚aufgeht'. Weniger riskant bezüglich des autochthonen Weltbildes anderer Völker ist die schon von den Vätern der Alten Kirche in den ersten vier Jahrhunderten entwickelte Lehre von den *prisci theologi*, die in der Renaissance zu voller Blüte kommen sollte (und die in Verbindung mit der typologischen Methode von dem Figuristen Joachim Bouvet S.J. und dessen Anhängern im Hinblick auf die chinesische Historiographie und Geistesgeschichte erneut praktiziert wurde). Hier wird den Weisen aller Völker eine natürliche, unmittelbar von Gott offenbarte Erkenntnis zugebilligt. Vgl. zum Thema Claudia von Collani: *P. Joachim Bouvet S.J. Sein Leben und sein Werk*, Nettetal, 1985, S. 1–9; Daniel Pickering Walker: *The Ancient Theology. Studies in Christian Platonism from the Fifteenth to the Eighteenth Century*, London, 1972, S. 1–40; Martin Mulsow (Hrsg.): *Das Ende des Hermetismus. Historische Kritik und neue Naturphilosophie in der Spätrenaissance*, Tübingen 2002.

[14] Vgl. Niccolò Longobardi: *Traité* (=Niccolò Longobardi: „*Traité sur quelques points de la religion des Chinois*", in: Gottfried Wilhelm Leibniz: *Discours sur la théologie naturelle des Chinois*, im Anhang, S. 113–146. Dort auch Sainte Marie: *Traité* (=Antoine de Sainte Marie: „*Traité sur quelques points importans de la Mission de la Chine*"); Nicolas Malebranche: „*Entretien d'un Philosophe Chrétien et d'un Philosophe Chinois sur l'Existence et la Nature de Dieu*"; Leibniz' *Marginalien zu den Texten von Longobardi und de Sainte Marie*; *Rezensionen aus dem Journal des Sçavans*; Leibniz' „*Annotationes de cultu religioneque Sinensium*", hrsg. [mit einem Faksimile des Manuskripts, Bl. 1–32] u. mit Anm. versehen von Wenchao Li/ Hans Poser, Frankfurt am Main 2002)); Gottfried Wilhem Leibniz: *Lettre* (= Gottfried Wilhelm Leibniz: „*Lettre sur la philosophie Chinoise à Nicolas de Remond*", in: Ders.: *Zwei Briefe über das binäre Zahlensystem und die chinesische Philosophie*, aus dem Urtext neu ediert, übers. u. komm. v. Renate Loosen/Franz Vonessen, Stuttgart 1968, S. 27–132; vgl. zur Geschichte des *Traité* Collani: *The Treatise on Chinese Religions* (= Claudia von Collani: „The Treatise on Chinese Religions (1623) of N. Longobardi, S.J.", in: *Sino-Western Cultural Relations Journal* XVII (1995), S. 29–37.

alten Chinesen Atheisten und Materialisten gewesen wären.[15] Nach seiner Auffassung kannten die Chinesen keine von der Materie losgelöste Substanz, und da ihnen keine Offenbarung zuteilgeworden war, glaubten sie folglich auch an keine Schöpfung aus dem Nichts.[16]

Leibniz sollte sich erst gegen Ende seines Lebens in seinem unvollendeten *Discours*, dem nicht abgesandten letzten Brief an Nicolas Remond vom März 1716, mit der *théologie naturelle des Chinois* auseinandersetzen.[17] Dabei stützte er sich insbesondere auf die erwähnte Abhandlung Longobardis, indem er die dort zitierten kanonischen Bücher Chinas als wesentliche Zeugen seinem eigenen Urteil zugrunde legte: Danach hätten nicht nur die alten Chinesen des ursprünglichen Konfuzianismus eine Natürliche Theologie besessen,[18] sondern ebenso auch die modernen Chinesen des Song(Neo)-Konfuzianismus. Damit widerspricht Leibniz jedoch sowohl dem, was Ricci und seine Freunde, die Jesuitenmissionare, in dem mehr als hundert Jahre andauernden Ritenstreit[19] stets beteuert, als auch dem, was alle Gegner der Jesuitenmission

---

[15] Vgl. Longobardi: *Traité*, S. 141.
[16] Vgl. ebd., S. 129.
[17] Vgl. dazu Rita Widmaier: „Die Rolle der Dyadik in Leibniz' letztem Brief an Remond", in: *Studia Leibnitiana* (2016), in Vorbereitung.
[18] Diese scheinen sich nach Leibniz sogar „über die griechischen Philosophen hinaus der Wahrheit angenähert und gelehrt zu haben, dass die Materie selbst eine Schöpfung Gottes sei". Vgl. Leibniz an Barthélemy Des Bosses vom 13. Januar 1716, in: GP II, 508: „Quin Sinenses veteres ultra Graeciae Philosophos veritati accessisse et docuisse videntur, materiam ipsam esse productionem Dei."
[19] Da die Literatur zum chinesischen Ritenstreit überaus umfangreich ist, verweise ich hier nur auf J. Brucker, Art. „Chinois (Rites)", in: *Dictionnaire de théologie catholique*, T. 2, 2, 1932, Sp. 2364–2391; George Minamiki: *The Chinese Rites Controversy from Its Beginning to Modern Times*, Chicago 1985; *The Chinese Rites Controversy. Its History and Meaning*, ed. by David E. Mungello, Nettetal 1994. In diesem Streit ging es um die Fragen, ob der chinesische Name für Gott überhaupt zulässig sei, da er der wahren (christlichen) Bedeutung nicht entspreche, und ob die chinesischen Riten gegenüber Konfuzius und den Ahnen nicht reiner Götzendienst und Aberglauben und demnach chinesischen Christen zu verbieten wären. Matteo Ricci S.J. hatte diese Fragen für die alten, jedoch nicht für die modernen und die zeitgenössischen Chinesen positiv beantwortet. Danach wiesen die in den kanonischen Büchern Chinas von den Philosophen verwendeten Namen *tian* („Himmel") und *shangdi* („Herrscher in der Höhe") auf die Kenntnis des wahren Gottesbegriffes hin, die chinesischen Riten dagegen wären nicht religiös, vielmehr eine rein zivile, staatsbürgerlich-ethische Form des Kults. Leibniz gehörte stets zu den Anhängern dieser Interpretation. Vgl. seine kleine Abhandlung *De cultu Confucii civili*, Beilage eines Briefes an Antoine Verjus S.J. vom 18. Januar 1700; *China-Korrespondenz* (= Gottfried Wilhelm Leibniz: *Der Briefwechsel mit den Jesuiten in China (1689–1714)*, hrsg. u. mit einer Einl. vers. v. Rita Widmaier, Textherst. u. Übers. v. Malte-Ludolf Babin, Hamburg 2006), Nr. 35, S. 248–257, und ebenso seine Haltung in dem in Kürze erscheinenden Folgeband

immer hartnäckig geleugnet hatten.²⁰

Im Folgenden wird zu fragen sein, wie Leibniz zu diesem erstaunlichen Ergebnis gelangte und welche Theorie er ins Auge fasste, um in der Überlieferung der kanonischen Bücher Chinas das Vorhandensein einer Natürlichen Theologie zu begründen. Vor dem Hintergrund seines lebenslangen Projekts einer *Scientia generalis* ist dafür zunächst die systematische und methodologische Beziehung zwischen der Natürlichen Theologie und der *Philosophia perennis* zu erörtern. Anschließend ist zu klären, auf welche zusätzlichen Quellen, neben Longobardi, sich Leibniz bei seiner Interpretation aller Wahrscheinlichkeit nach ebenfalls bezogen hat.

1. Die wissenschaftstheoretische und methodologische Beziehung zwischen Natürlicher Theologie und Philosophia perennis[21]

Der Begriff der Natürlichen Theologie taucht früh in Leibniz' Plänen zu seinem lebenslangen Projekt einer *Scientia generalis* auf. Nach dem Beispiel der aristotelischen „Ersten Philosophie"[22] sollte diese Prinzipien-Wissenschaft[23]

Briefe über China (1694–1716), Leibniz' Korrespondenz mit Barthélemy Des Bosses S.J. und anderen Mitgliedern des Ordens, Hamburg, in Vorbereitung.

[20] Diese Tatsache betont auch Meynard: *Vortrag* (= Thierry Meynard: „Leibniz as the first proponent in Europe of Neo-Confucianism", Vortrag, den er uns dankenswerter Weise zur Verfügung stellte, gehalten auf der Tagung *G. W. Leibniz und die europäische Begegnung mit China – 300 Jahre Discours sur la théologie naturelle des Chinois am 30.–31. Oktober 2015*, veranstaltet von der Leibniz-Universität Hannover; erscheint in: *Studia Leibnitiana*, Sonderheft, im Druck), S. 1–13, vgl. ebenfalls Lundbaek: *Notes* (= Knud Lundbaek: „Notes sur l'image du Néo-Confucianisme dans la littérature européenne du XVIIe à la fin du XIXe siècle", in: *Appréciation par l'Europe de la tradition Chinoise à partir du XVIIe Siècle. Actes du IIIe Colloque international de Sinologie*, Chantilly 1980, Paris 1983), S.131–176, hier S. 144: „Notre lecteur du *Confucius Sinarum Philosophus* et de Longobardi en 1701 se souvient du contraste existant entre les anciens et les modernes, net dans l'un , repoussé dans l'autre. Il s'étonnera que Leibniz, en s'accordant avec Longobardi – il n'y a pas de grande différence entre les anciens et les modernes – arrive à la conclusion opposée."

[21] Vgl. zum Folgenden auch die ausführlichere Darstellung in den ersten beiden Kapiteln meines Vortrages „Leibniz' natürliche Theologie und eine „gewisse" Philosophia perennis", in Bd. II, S. 580–596, dort S. 582–589.

[22] Vgl. ebd., S. 583f. mit Anm. 10 u. 11. in seinem Vortrag.

[23] Vgl. *Definitio brevis scientiae generalis* [Sommer 1683 bis Anfang 1685 (?)]; *A* VI, 4 Teil A, N. 127, 532: „Scientiam Generalem intelligo, quae caeterarum omnium principia continet, modumque principiis ita utendi, ut quisque mediocri licet ingenio praeditus ubi ad specialia quaecunque descenderit, facili meditatione et brevi experientia, difficillima etiam intelligere, et pulcherimas veritates, utilissimasque praxes, quantum ex datis homini possibile est, invenire

drei einander bedingende Hauptteile behandeln:[24] Erstens eine Enzyklopädie der Wissenschaften,[25] in der als systematisch geordnetem Inventar aller rational erfassbaren Disziplinen auch deren materialer Gehalt erkennbar wäre; zweitens ein Instrument des Denkens,[26] das in der Sprache einer universalen Zeichenkunst das menschliche Denken abbildete; sowie drittens einen rationalen Kalkül oder „eine Kunst, leicht und unfehlbar vernünftig zu überlegen", um zu erfinden und zu urteilen.[27]

Die Natürliche Theologie ist als theoretische Wissenschaft „von den unkörperlichen Substanzen" im System der Enzyklopädie eingeordnet;[28] dabei ist der Letzteren eine praktische Enzyklopädie unterzuordnen, die „nämlich über den Nutzen der Wissenschaften zur Glückseligkeit oder über das rechte Handeln" Auskunft gäbe.[29] Unter wissenschaftstheoretischem Aspekt ist darum jede Wissenschaft unter einem theoretischen und einem praktischen *Prinzip* zu betrachten, dem theoretischen – vom Wesen der Dinge auf Grund ihrer wirkenden Ursache – und dem praktischen – vom Nutzen der Dinge und

---

possit." („Ich verstehe unter *Scientia generalis* die Wissenschaft, welche die Prinzipien aller übrigen Wissenschaften umfasst, und die Art, diese Prinzipien so zu gebrauchen, dass jeder, mag er auch nur mäßig begabt sein, wenn er sich auf eine beliebige Einzelfrage einlässt, durch leichtes Nachdenken und kurze Übung auch Schwierigstes begreifen und die schönsten Wahrheiten sowie die nützlichsten Anwendungen, soweit es dem Menschen gegeben ist, finden kann.").

[24] Vgl. ebd.: „Tractare ergo debet tum de modo bene cogitandi, hoc est inveniendi, judicandi, affectus regendi, retinendi ac reminiscendi, tum vero de totius Encyclopaediae Elementis, et Summi Boni investigatione, cujus causa omnis meditatio suscipitur, est enim nihil aliud sapientia, quam scientia felicitatis." („Gegenstand [der *Scientia generalis*] sind also zum einen die Art des rechten Denkens, das heißt des Erfindens, des Urteilens, des Beherrschens, Zügelns und Bedenkens der Affekte, zum andern die Bestandteile des ganzen Kreises der Wissenschaften und die Erforschung des Höchsten Gutes, das jedem Nachdenken zugrundeliegt, denn die Weisheit ist nichts anderes als die Wissenschaft von der Glückseligkeit.")

[25] Vgl. *Ma Characteristique demande une Encyclopedie nouvelle* [März bis April 1697 (?)]; A VI, 4 Teil A, N. 52, 161.

[26] Vgl. *De Organo sive arte magna cogitandi* [März bis April 1679 (?)]; A VI, 4 Teil A, N. 50, 156–160.

[27] Vgl. *Calculus ratiocinator seu artificium facile et infallibiliter ratiocinandi. Res hactenus ignorata* [Frühjahr bis Sommer 1679 (?)]; A VI, 4 A, N. 68, 274.

[28] Vgl. *Consilium de Encyclopedia nova conscribenda methodo inventoria*, 15. (25.) Juni 1679; A VI, 4 A, N. 81, 343 und 349.

[29] Vgl. ebd. S. 349: „Huic Encyclopaediae subjicienda est Practica, nempe de Usu scientiarum ad felicitatem, sive de agendis, considerando scilicet, quod nos ipsi homines sumus".

den Mitteln zur Erreichung des Guten und Vermeidung des Bösen auf Grund ihrer Endursache.[30]

Der Leibniz'schen Wahrheitstheorie zufolge hat dieser wissenschaftstheoretische Aspekt Konsequenzen für die Wahrheit der Aussagen in diesen Wissenschaften: Bei den Sätzen der Vernunft (Definitionen, Axiomen und Theoremen) der „wahren" und der „Natürlichen Theologie" handelt es sich um die ewigen Wahrheiten (der Vernunft), deren Wahrheit metaphysisch gewiss ist. Da hier identische Wahrheiten zu beweisen sind, sind für diese Aussagen die syllogistische Logik und das Prinzip des Widerspruchs oder der Identität gültig. Bei den historischen Texten (Behauptungen, Meinungen, Glaubensüberzeugungen) der Natürlichen Theologie handelt es sich dagegen um wahrscheinliche (probable) Wahrheiten (der Erfahrung und Gaubensgewissheit), deren Wahrheit zwar moralisch gewiss, aber nur wahrscheinlich ist. Es sind zufällige Wahrheiten, bei denen nach dem „Prinzip des genügenden Grundes" eine Logik der Wahrscheinlichkeit anzuwenden ist.[31] Glaubenssätze wie Mysterien und Wunder, die nach Leibniz jedoch nichts Widersinniges enthalten dürfen, betreffen zwar die Erkenntnis; sie sind jedoch, da sie „die Vernunft übersteigen", unmöglich je zu beweisen oder zu widerlegen. Sie können deshalb, so Leibniz, ohne Rücksicht auf Einwände behauptet werden.[32]

Da es sich bei den historischen Aussagen der Natürlichen Theologie nur um „Wahrscheinlichkeiten" handelt, müssen dieserart Texte allerdings interpretiert werden. Obzwar „die Kunst, nach wahrscheinlichen Gründen zu urteilen, [noch] nicht ausreichend entwickelt" sei, wie Leibniz zugesteht, müssten sich nämlich die Gründe für deren „Glaubwürdigkeit" vor der Vernunft rechtfertigen lassen. An diesem Punkt weist er ausdrücklich auf die Autoren

---

[30] Vgl. *De systemate scientiarum*, [Nicht vor Juli 1695]; A IV, 6 N. 75, 501, und *C*: „*Philosophia est complexus* [...]", 524–529, hier 524f., 527.
[31] Vgl. *Origo veritatum contingentium ex processu in infinitum ad exemplum Proportionum inter quantitates incommensurabiles*, in: *C*, S. 1f. Zum Thema vgl. Rita Widmaier: *Modallogik versus Probabilitätslogik: Logik der Tatsachenwahrheiten bei G. W. Leibniz und Martino Martini bei den virulenten Fragen im Ritenstreit*, in: *Martino Martini. Man of Dialogue*, hrsg. v. L. M. Paternicò [u.a.], Trento 2016, S.183–197, hier S. 192–195.
[32] Vgl. *Essais de Theodicée*, Discours de la conformité de la Foi avec la raison, §§ 23, 26, 28; GP VI, 64–67, hier 65f.: „C'est une autre question, si nous sommes tousjours obligés d'examiner les objections qu'on nous peut faire, et de conserver quelque doute sur nostre sentiment [...]. J'oserois dire que non, car autrement on ne viendroit jamais à la certitude, et nostre conclusion seroit tousjours provisionelle."

„mehrerer guter Schriften über die Wahrheit der Religion" hin, – an erster Stelle auf den bereits oben genannten Agostino Steuco.[33]

Steuco bezeichnet in seinem Werk *De Philosophia perenni* das Ziel, die Methode und den Begriff dieser Philosophie als das Bestreben, die Spuren religiöser und philosophischer Wahrheit in allen Jahrhunderten und bei allen Völkern aufzufinden und mit der christlichen Wahrheit zu vergleichen und dieser nachzubilden. Um zu zeigen, dass es nur *eine* „himmlische Religion" gibt, die „seit den Anfängen der Menschheit immer dieselbe gewesen ist,"[34] bezieht sich der Autor auf die ältesten Theologen: die griechischen Philosophen, besonders Platon und Aristoteles, auf Philon von Alexandria, die Neuplatoniker, die alten Kirchenväter und die Renaissance-Philosophen, besonders Marsilio Ficino und Giovanni Pico della Mirandola.[35] Unter den inhaltlich und zeitlich fixierten Rahmenbedingungen der Theologie konzipiert Steuco den Begriff der *Philosophia perennis* zweifellos „mit der erklärten philosophischen Absicht", „die Theologie zu stützen."[36]

Für den Missionsorden der Gesellschaft Jesu war die *Philosophia perennis* von Anbeginn die Grundlage der Metaphysik, und auch Leibniz[37] wird – „konservativ interpretiert"[38] – zu Recht als einer der letzten Anhänger dieser Philosophie bezeichnet.[39] Für Leibniz bedeutet dies im Jahre 1700 beispielsweise, „alles zum Guten auszulegen, wie Ricci, der den „Kirchenvätern folgte,

---

[33] Vgl. *Theodicée*, Discours, § 29; GP VI, 67.
[34] Vgl. *De Philosophia perenni*, Lugduni, 1540, Bl. 3 r.
[35] Dazu s. Theobald Freudenberger: *Augustinus Steuchus aus Gubbio*, [...] *sein literarisches Lebenswerk*, Münster in Westfalen 1935, S. 347–363.
[36] Vgl. zur Definition Wilhelm Schmidt-Biggemann: *Philosophia perennis: Historische Umrisse abendländischer Spiritualität in Antike, Mittelalter und früher Neuzeit*, Frankfurt a. M. 1998, S. 49.
[37] Leibniz erwähnt Steuco schon in den 1660er Jahren, vgl. A VI, 1, 532; in den 1680er Jahren, vgl. A VI, 4 A, 435; A VI, 4 Teil C, 2307; *Theodicée*, Discours, § 29; GP VI, 67).
[38] Vgl. Wilhelm Schmidt-Biggemann: „Leibniz konservativ interpretiert: Der letzte Vertreter der Philosophia perennis", in: *Leibniz und Europa. VI. Internationaler Leibniz-Kongreß, Vorträge*. I. Teil. Hannover, 1994, S. 265–282, bes. S. 277–282, vgl. zum Thema auch Frances A. Yates: *The Art of Memory*, London 1966, Kap. 17.; Walker: *The Ancient Theology*, Kap. 6.; Charles B. Schmidt: „Perennial Philosophy: From Agostino Steuco to Leibniz", in: *Journal of the History of Ideas*, 27 (1966), S. 505–532.
[39] Alle China betreffenden Schriften und Briefen bestätigen dies, vgl. besonders *Nov. Sin.*, §§ 11, 19; *De cultu Confucii civili*, Beilage für Verjus vom 18. Januar 1700; *China-Korrespondenz*, S. 248–257, und Leibniz' Beilage für Des Bosses vom 12. August 1709; GP II, 379f.

die Platon und andere Philosophen im christlichen Sinn" interpretierten. „Sollten wir nicht das Recht haben, das von den Schlacken der Irrtümer gereinigte Gold ihrer Lehren zu bewahren?"⁴⁰ Auch im Jahre 1709 erscheint es ihm

> „möglich, die Substanz der alten chinesischen Theologie zu bewahren, [später] hinzugefügte Irrtümer auszumerzen und die großen Wahrheiten der christlichen Religion hinzuzufügen;"⁴¹ er beabsichtigt aber nun zu untersuchen, „was mehr den Philosophen angeht, d.h. die Natürliche Theologie betrifft."⁴²

Er vergleiche gern seine „Lehre mit denen der Alten und anderer fähiger Männer", heißt es im Jahre 1714, sei doch „die Wahrheit verbreiteter als man denkt."⁴³ Diesen Schritt gewissermaßen vorbereitend, hielt Leibniz noch im selben Jahr einen Vortrag in Wien über den Fortschritt der Erkenntnis bezüglich der Natürlichen Theologie in der Geschichte der Menschheit,⁴⁴ nämlich der Erkenntnis von Gott und der Unsterblichkeit der Seele.⁴⁵

Offensichtlich galt Leibniz' Interesse *nicht* der frühen Geschichte Chinas und den Anfängen dieser Nation, um diese dann mit der universalen Menschheits- und Heilsgeschichte der Bibel in Einklang zu bringen,⁴⁶ sondern

---

⁴⁰ Dabei scheint Leibniz die Deutung der uralten Charaktere des *Yijing* durch Bouvet „nach Maßgabe der wahren Weisheit" durchaus nicht verächtlich, ebenso wenig hält er es für abwegig, wenn Ricci die alten Schriften Chinas besser deutete, als die Chinesen es zu tun vermögen; könnten doch heute auch die christlichen Gelehrten weit besser als die Juden selbst die ältesten Bücher der Hebräer auslegen (vgl. *De cultu Confucii civili*, S. 252f.).
⁴¹ Vgl. die Beilage für Des Bosses; GP II, 383: „Itaque quantum hactenus intelligo putem salva substantia veteris Sinensium Theologiae excludi errores addititios, adjungi magnas Christianae religionis veritates posse."
⁴² Vgl. ebd., S. 382: „Illud examinare malim, quod magis ad philosophum (id est ad Theologiam naturalem) pertinet [...]."
⁴³ Leibniz an Nicolas Remond vom 26. August 1714; GP III, 624.
⁴⁴ Vgl. LH XXXIX 19, Bl. 54–61; Konzept Bl. 54–57, seit 1945 Kriegsverlust; Bl. 58–61, verbesserte Reinschrift, gedr.: in: Patrick Riley: „An Unpublished Lecture by Leibniz on the Greeks as Founders of Rational Theology: Its Relation to ‚Universal Jurisprudence'", in: *Journal of the History of Philosophy* 14 (1976), S. 205–216, hier S. 214.
⁴⁵ Vgl. ebd., S. 214: „Unum esse Deum rerum omnium autorem et gubernatorem; Animas autem humanas non morte extingui, sed post hanc vitam ad aliam pervenire in qua praemia accipiant, aut poenas luant hujus vitae bene vel male actae."
⁴⁶ In Bezug auf das Alter der Welt hütete sich Leibniz, sich auf die Diskussionen über die biblische Chronologie einzulassen (vgl. *China-Korrespondenz*, Einleitung, S. CVI–CXXXIII), und verwarf sowohl den Versuch christlicher Autoren (wie Daniel Huet: *Demonstratio evangelica ad Serenissimum Delphinum*, Paris 1679, und Paul Beurrier: *Speculum christianae religionis in triplici lege naturali, mosaica et evangelica*, Paris 1663), die ganze heidnische Mythologie von der jüdischen Religion abzuleiten – „als ob die anderen Völker ihren Aberglauben nicht selbst erfunden haben könnten" – (vgl. Leibniz' Brief an Ezechiel Spanheim vom 7. Mai

auf das in der Geschichte überlieferte Wissen über die Natürliche Theologie. Im Rahmen der *Scientia generalis* bedeutete dies für deren Geschichte nicht nur methodologisch die Dominanz des Prinzips vom „genügenden Grunde" gegenüber dem Prinzip des Widerspruchs und ebenso der Wahrscheinlichkeitslogik gegenüber der syllogistischen Logik, sondern zugleich auch die Anwendung einer vergleichenden und interpretierenden Methode (der *Philosophia perennis*) auf einen ganz bestimmten Bereich in der frühen Menschheitsgeschichte, d.h. auf die Erkenntnisgeschichte der Disziplin von den unkörperlichen Substanzen.

War es denkbar, dass die kanonischen Bücher Chinas, die von der Weisheit seiner Philosophen und dem hohen Alter seiner Geschichte Zeugnis ablegten und in China wie die Bibel in Europa verehrt wurden, in das logische, eher unhistorische Konzept der *Scientia generalis* integriert werden konnten? Leibniz scheint im November 1697 diese Möglichkeit in Betracht zu ziehen. Er möchte mehr Information über die chinesische Geschichte erhalten, wobei er zunächst die Notwendigkeit einer „Art kritischen Untersuchung" hervorhebt, „um zu prüfen, wieweit man auf die historischen Bücher der Chinesen bauen kann und soll."[47] Im August 1705 heißt es dagegen ausdrücklich:

> „Vor allem aber wird es erforderlich sein, diese Bücher so auszulegen, dass sie mit der Natürlichen Theologie zumindest nicht in Widerspruch stehen, ja diese vielmehr bestätigen."[48]

In diesem Zusammenhang ist Leibniz' Urteil über das 1687 von Philippe Couplet und seinen Mitbrüdern herausgegebene Prachtwerk des *Confucius Sinarum Philosophus*[49] zu beachten, das lautet:

1697; A I, 14 N. 94, 160) – , als auch den Figurismus Bouvets, der die Frühe Geschichte Chinas als eine Erfindung interpretieren wollte (vgl. Joachim Bouvet an Leibniz vom 8. November 1702; *China-Korrespondenz*, Nr. 47, S. 387).

[47] Vgl. Leibniz' Brief an Joachim Bouvet vom 2. (12.) November 1697; *China-Korrespondenz*, Nr. 18, S. 138f.: „Quant à l'Histoire je trouve qu'il faudroit avant toute chose une espece de Critique pour examiner fort distinctement, quel fonds on peut et doit faire sur les livres Historiques des Chinois." Zum Thema s. auch das Sachregister s. v. „Geschichte/ Historiographie".

[48] Im vorangehenden Satz heißt es sogar. „Il sera tres utile de trouver dans les livres classiques des Chinois quelque chose qui ait du rapport à Nostre religion [,] comme il y a un passage de Platon, qui semble faire esperer un Messie au genre humain. Mais il sera sur tout necessaire d'expliquer ces livres en sorte qu'ils ne choquent point au moins la Theologie naturelle, et qu'ils la confirment plustost." Vgl. Leibniz an Bouvet vom 18. August 1705, ebd., Nr. 57, S. 486f.

[49] *Confucius Sinarum Philosophus* (= *Confucius Sinarum Philosophus, sive Scientia Sinensis latine exposita*. Studio et opera Prosperi Intorcetta, Christiani Herdtrich, Francisci Rougemont,

„P. Couplet von Ihrem Orden […] hat uns einen gewissen Vorgeschmack gegeben von der originalen chinesischen Geschichte, doch hat er unseren Durst mehr angeregt, als ihn zu stillen."[50]

Hatte Leibniz wirklich nur die dort angehängte *Tabula Chronologica* von 1686 gelesen[51] – und *nicht* auch die *Proëmialis Declaratio*, welche die Jesuitenmissionare ihrem gemeinschaftlichen Übersetzungswerk vorangestellt haben?[52]

Im Folgenden wird darauf zurückzukommen sein. Dabei steht im Blickpunkt, nicht *wie* Leibniz die *Philosophia perennis* als Theorie einer Interpretation auf den *Traité* Longobardis praktisch anwendet, sondern die Frage, *warum* er sich dabei auch gegen die Interpretation Riccis in Bezug auf die modernen chinesischen Philosophen gewendet hat.

Philippi Couplet, Patrum Societatis Jesu. […]. (Auf S. IX–CXIV die *Operis origo et scopus* […] *Proëmialis Declaratio*). Adjecta est *Tabula Chronologica Sinicae Monarchiae ab hujus Exordio ad haec usque Tempora*. Parisiis 1687).
[50] Vgl. Leibniz an den nach China zurückreisenden Jesuitenmissionar Claudio Filippo Grimaldi vom 21. März 1692; *China-Korrespondenz*, Nr. 7, S. 38f.
[51] Vgl. Leibniz' Brief an Daniel Larroque, 2. Hälfte September 1693; A I, 9 N. 385, 574. Dort heißt es: „Le P. Couplet ayant cité M. Thevenot et M. l'Abbé Renaudot comme temoins d'un passage d'un Persan ou Arabe qui confirme le monument Chrestien dans la Chine que le P. Kircher a publié, M. l'Abbé Renaudot nous en pourroit eclaircir." (Die Stelle findet sich in der *Tabula Chronologica Monarchiae Sinicae juxta cyclos annorum LX. Ab anno post Christum primo, usque ad annum praesentis Saeculi 1683* [= TC]. Auctore R.P. Philippo Couplet Belgâ, Soc. Jesu, Sinensis Missionis in Urbe Procuratore. Nunc primum in lucem prodit e Bibliotheca Regia. Parisiis 1686, cum privilegio Regis; *Praefatio*, S. I–XX; Text S. 1–20; TC [zweite *Titelseite* und zweite *Praefatio*], S. 36–106, hier S. 56: „[…] Certum videtur eos ipsos fuisse, quos lapideum in provinciâ *Xen si* monumentum effossum anno 1625. aetati nostrae prodidit, disertè referens et annum eundem, et imaginem S. Crucis, et legis Christianae compendium charactere Sinico, et nomina 72. praeconum Syriacis litteris insculpta lapidi. De hoc consule Kircheri Sinam illustratam, et vetus Manuscriptum Arabicum quod asservatur in Regiâ Galliarum Bibliothecâ, ubi disertè scribitur circa idem tempus missos esse Evangelii praecones in Sinam à Catholico Patriarcha Indiae et Sinae, qui in Urbe *Mossue* degebat.").
[52] Es fragt sich nämlich, woher Leibniz im Vorwort der *Novissima Sinica* den selbstbewussten Vergleich der Chinesen mit anderen Völkern kennt, der lautet: „Tametsi autem illi nos monoculos crediderint, habemus tamen alium adhuc oculum nondum satis ipsis cognitum, primam scilicet Philosophiam, per quam ad rerum incorporalium etiam notitiam admissi sumus." Auch die Jesuitenpatres in Peking verwenden diesen Vergleich (*ideoma*) in der *Proëmialis Declaratio* ihres *Confucius Sinarum Philosophus*, S. XI. Nach der (fraglichen) Datierung von Leibniz' Schrift *Contemplatio de historia literaria statuque praesenti eruditionis* ins Frühjahr 1682; A VI, 4 A, N. 1142, 457, hätte dieser sich jedoch aus einer bisher noch unbekannten Quelle schon früher auf diesen Vergleich bezogen.

2. Die Rolle der „Proëmialis declaratio" im Confucius Sinarum Philosophus in Leibniz' Interpretation der chinesischen Philosophie

1. Tatsächlich muss die negative Ansicht Longobardis Leibniz seit längerer Zeit beunruhigt haben.[53] Dieser Kritiker im eigenen Orden hielt nicht nur die modernen, sondern auch die alten chinesischen Philosophen für Atheisten[54] und berief sich dafür ebenso wie Ricci auf die authentischen chinesischen Klassiker. Um zu verstehen, weshalb Leibniz erst in seinem Discours 1716 zu einer eigenen festen Ansicht gelangen konnte, muss an dieser Stelle auf die Rezeptionsgeschichte des Textes von Longobardi kurz eingegangen werden.

Longobardis Bericht war 1623 aus einer Art *brainstorming* innerhalb des Ordens hervorgegangen. Die Aufgabe lautete, in den chinesischen Büchern diejenigen Stellen zu finden, in denen von Gott, den Geistern und der rationalen Seele die Rede ist, um dann zu prüfen, ob diese mit der bisherigen Auslegung der Missionare vereinbar waren. Das heikle Ergebnis, zu dem Longobardi

---

[53] Vgl. *De cultu Confucii civili*, S. 250f. Fraglich ist allerdings, was Leibniz im Jahr 1700 von Longobardi schon kannte. Er konnte bis dahin wohl dessen *Traité* auszugsweise im 6. Teil der *Morale pratique des Jesuites*, 1692, gelesen haben, den Antoine Arnauld anonym unter dem Titel *Histoire des differens entre les Missionaires* herausgegeben hatte. Longobardis *Traité* wird dort im *Inventaire*, S. VII, aufgeführt und im 3. Kapitel besprochen. Möglich ist aber auch, dass Leibniz den *Traité* aus dem Werk *Tractados Históricos, politicos, ethicos, y religiosos de la Monarchia de China, Madrid 1676*, des Dominikaners Domingo Fernandez Navarrete kannte, in dem die Abhandlung in spanischer Übersetzung enthalten ist. Ursprünglich hatte Longobardi 1623 seine Abhandlung auf Portugiesisch verfasst (für den damaligen portugiesischen Visitator Franciso Vieiro S.J., 1555–1619); sie wurde später, wenn nicht von ihm selbst, von dem Franziskaner Antonio Caballero de Santa Maria (franz. Antoine de Sainte Marie) ins Lateinische übertragen. Auch dieser hatte 1668 als Kritiker der Interpretation Riccis eine Abhandlung geschrieben, die dann zusammen mit dem *Traité* Longobardis auf Französisch vom Seminar der *Missions Etrangères* als Buch unter dem Titel *Anciens Traitez de divers auteurs sur les ceremonies de la Chine*, Paris 1701, herausgegeben wurde. – Die Rezensionen der beiden Abhandlungen im *Journal des Savans* von 1701 las Leibniz höchstwahrscheinlich im selben Jahr und später erneut im Jahre 1709 (vgl. Leibniz' Beilage für Des Bosses; GP II, 380), bevor ihm das Buch im Jahre 1715 von Nicolas Remond zugesandt wurde. Vgl. Remond an Leibniz vom 4. September 1715; GP III, 651.

[54] Aufgrund ihrer Prinzipien hätten sie „keinerlei Begriff von unkörperlichen Dingen", weshalb ihnen „Gott, die Engel und die Seele unbekannt" wären; sie „glaubten, dass die Entstehung der Welt und der Dinge „auf einem Zufall beruhe" und dass die Seelen der Toten in „die Leere des ersten Ursprungs zurückkehren"; so jedenfalls Leibniz' Résumé 1709 in der Beilage für Des Bosses; GP II, 380.

schließlich gelangte, war aus naheliegenden Gründen nicht zur Veröffentlichung bestimmt[55] und schon gar nicht in Europa. Als dies dann doch 1679 in den *Tractados* des Dominikaners Navarrete geschah – nachdem der Text aus dem Lateinischen ins Spanische übersetzt worden war – wurde in Europa kaum Notiz von dieser Publikation genommen. Als dagegen der *Confucius Sinarum philosophus* 1687 von Couplet in Paris herauskam, war dieses Jahrhundertwerk der Jesuiten von vielen, darunter Leibniz,[56] schon lange ungeduldig erwartet worden. Die Patres erwähnten in ihrer einführenden Erklärung (*Proëmialis declaratio*) Longobardi (der 1655 gestorben war) allerdings mit keinem Wort, obwohl dessen Abhandlung auf diese „Erklärung" zweifellos Einfluss hatte, wenn nicht prägend für sie war.[57] Erst auf dem Höhepunkt des Ritenstreits, als die Gegner der Jesuiten 1701 in Paris die *Traités* von Longobardi und de Santa Maria in französischer Übersetzung veröffentlichten und das Buch anschließend im *Journal des Savans* besprochen wurde, erregten diese Abhandlungen allgemeine Aufmerksamkeit. Da Leibniz jedoch nur deren Rezensionen gelesen hatte,[58] musste ihm die eigentliche Brisanz dieser Neuerscheinung so lange verborgen bleiben, bis er das Buch 1715 selbst vor Augen hatte.

Tatsächlich erfährt das europäische Publikum durch Longobardi zum ersten Mal von der *Metaphysik des Song/Neo-Konfuzianismus*, indem es zugleich auf die philologischen und interpretatorischen Probleme in den von zeitgenössischen Gelehrten anerkannten kanonischen Büchern Chinas hingewiesen wird. Für die Europäer waren allerdings Longobardis Ausführungen nicht leicht zu verstehen, waren diese doch unklar, verwirrend und sogar irreführend: Unklar und verwirrend, da er diese Bücher in vier Arten (*quatre sortes*)[59] einteilte und aus dem *Xingli daquan shu*, der überaus wichtigen, von Kaiser Yongle im Jahre 1415 herausgegebenen Anthologie des Song/Neo-Konfuzianismus, zwei Bücher machte, die er der zweiten bzw. dritten Art zuteilte (s. unten). Irreführend und folgenreicher war die Datierung des Werkes, das nach Longobardi vor 2500 (*deux mille cinq cent*) Jahren entstanden sein sollte (und Leibniz zu dem Versuch anleiten sollte, das Datum auf dem rechten Rand seines Exemplars zu verifizieren, indem er es mit den Angaben bei Santa

---

[55] Im Orden der Gesellschaft wurde über das Problem bis 1635 diskutiert und sogar beschlossen, Longobardis kritische Abhandlung zu vernichten; vgl. Meynard: *Vortrag*, § 2, S. 4.
[56] Vgl. Leibniz an Daniel Papebroch vom Februar (?) 1687, A I, 4 N. 517, 622.
[57] Vgl. Lundbaek: *Notes*, S. 135.
[58] Er berichtet darüber in der Beilage seines Briefes an Des Bosses; GP II, 380.
[59] Vgl. Longobardi: *Traité*, S. 117f., hier S. 117.

Maria verglich).⁶⁰ Tatsächlich ist die Falschdatierung jedoch nicht Longobardi anzulasten, sondern geht auf einen Übertragungsfehler bei der Übersetzung der Abhandlung aus der lateinischen Version in die spanische zurück.⁶¹

Doch nicht diese Fehlschreibung allein, sondern primär Longobardis allgemeine Sicht auf die chinesische Geistesgeschichte – er sah im Atheismus der Modernen „nur ein Echo" des Atheismus der Alten⁶² – verwischte die tatsächlich bestehenden, beträchtlichen Unterschiede der Hauptbegriffe im alten und neuen Konfuzianismus. Dabei beurteilte er jedoch den Atheismus der alten Chinesen nach denselben scholastischen Prinzipien, nach denen auch Ricci den Atheismus der Modernen interpretiert hatte. Der entscheidende Unterschied zwischen Longobardis und Riccis Interpretationen bestand aber darin, dass Longobardi die Notwendigkeit einsah, die Kommentarliteratur der modernen Gelehrten zu berücksichtigen, wollte man denn von den zeitgenössischen Gelehrten anerkannt werden. Es beeindruckte ihn offenbar, dass alle Interpreten in den „wesentlichen und grundlegenden Punkten ihrer Lehre übereinstimmen", denn er erkannte, dass man um dieser Übereinstimmung willen „so viel Aufhebens" um die Kommentare machte.⁶³

2. Als Leibniz seinen *Discours* über die Natürliche Theologie der Chinesen schrieb, tat er dies in der festen Absicht, Longobardi zu widerlegen⁶⁴ und in der Gewissheit, dafür die ‚wahre' Philosophie und mit seiner Interpretationstheorie eine moralisch ‚sichere' Wahrheit zu besitzen.⁶⁵ Bevor darauf am Ende zurückzukommen ist, stellen sich einige Fragen, die sich in einer einzigen zusammenfassen lassen:⁶⁶ Wie war es möglich, dass sich Leibniz nur

---

⁶⁰ Vgl. ebd., S. 117; dazu auch Leibniz: *Discours*, (Gottfried Wilhelm Leibniz: *Discours sur la théologie naturelle des Chinois*, hrsg. u. mit Anm. versehen v. Wenchao Li/Hans Poser, Frankfurt a. M. 2002), S. 70 und die Erläuterungen zu Z. 6.
⁶¹ Vgl. dazu Meynard: *Vortrag*, § 2, S. 4. Danach übersetzte Longobardi selbst sein portugiesisches Manuskript ins Lateinische, vgl. ebd., § 2.
⁶² Vgl. Longobardi: *Traité*, Section seizième, S. 141.
⁶³ Vgl. ebd., Section première, S. 117: „De-là vient qu'à la Chine on fait un si grand cas des Commentaires , et qu'on n'admet point les compositions que font sur le Texte ceux qui subissent l'examen pour recevoir les degrez, à moins que ces sortes de compositions ne soient conformes au Commentaire."
⁶⁴ Vgl. Leibniz an Des Bosses vom 13. Januar 1716; GP II, 508.
⁶⁵ Schon 1714 hatte Leibniz in seinem Wiener Vortrag das menschheitliche Ursprungswissen von Gott erkenntnismäßig wie folgt begründet: „Theologia naturalis est, quae ex seminibus veritatis menti a Deo Autore inditis enascitur ad caeterarum scientiarum instar." (Vgl. Riley: „Unpublished Lecture", S. 214.)
⁶⁶ Diese Tatsache hat immer höchstes Erstaunen ausgelöst. Vgl. David E. Mungello: *Leibniz and Confucianism. The Search for Accord*, Honolulu 1977, The Question of Influence, S. 13–17; ders.:

auf die eine, für eingeweihte und sachkundige Leser vor langer Zeit geschriebene Abhandlung des Jesuitenpaters Longobardi stützte und dabei eine schlüssige und aus moderner Sicht weitgehend richtige Interpretation der neokonfuzianischen Philosophie lieferte? Im Einzelnen:

Erstens: Warum stützte sich Leibniz primär auf Longobardi?

Zweitens: Wie konnte sich Leibniz in seiner Interpretation mit geradezu schlafwandlerischer Sicherheit über die verwirrenden Angaben Longobardis hinwegsetzen und dessen Behauptung vom Atheismus und Materialismus der Chinesen in ihr Gegenteil verkehren?

Drittens: Wie konnte er überhaupt von einer „Natürlichen Theologie" der Chinesen sprechen?

Viertens: Warum erwähnt Leibniz mit keinem Wort den *Confucius Sinarum* der Jesuiten, das ihm – viel jüngeren Datums als Longobardis *Traité* – in der *Proëmialis declaratio* doch manches hätte verständlich machen können?

Meine These soll hier vorweggenommen werden: Leibniz hat die *Proëmialis Declaratio* gründlich gelesen, und zwar (nach einer ersten Lektüre in den Jahren nach 1687) zum zweiten Mal, als er Longobardis Abhandlung studierte. Er wurde durch diese Lektüre vom Monotheismus auch der Neueren Philosophen überzeugt, denn er erkannte in der Metaphysik des Song/Neo-Konfuzianismus nicht nur die *Potenz und Grundlage* für die Entwicklung einer Natürlichen Theologie in China, sondern auch die *Ähnlichkeit* dieser Metaphysik mit seiner eigenen Metaphysik der Substanzen. Dabei war er vollkommen ehrlich in seinem Urteil bezüglich des Monotheismus der Alten und der Neueren Philosophen Chinas. Aus Rücksicht auf die Missionspolitik der Gesellschaft Jesu mochte Leibniz aber nicht zugeben, dass er sich auf die im Sinne Riccis argumentierenden Darlegungen der Patres in der *Proëmialis Declaratio* stützte und dennoch zu einem anderen Ergebnis als Ricci gelangte. Im begrenzten Rahmen dieses Vortrages kann ich meine These nicht so ausführlich untermauern, wie es möglich und wünschenswert wäre; ich werde mich deshalb auf die Beantwortung der vier oben genannten Fragen beschränken.

Die 1. Frage, warum sich Leibniz primär auf Longobardi stützte, hat er selbst bereits in seinem *Discours* beantwortet: Gerade weil der Jesuit Longobardi Textstellen aus den kanonischen Schriften Chinas in der Absicht benutzt

---

„Leibniz's Interpretation of Neo-Confucianism", in: *Philosophy East and West* (1971), S. 1–22, hier S. 1–5, 20–22; Lundbaek: *Notes*, S. 131–176, hier S. 144–147.

habe, die modernen Chinesen als Atheisten zu erweisen, sei dieser, wie Leibniz meint, unverdächtig, diese Quellen im Sinne einer gegenteiligen Deutung begünstigt zu haben. Leibniz hält deshalb seine eigene, „vernünftige Deutung" für „recht gesichert" und einer schmeichlerischen Darstellung ebenfalls kaum verdächtig.[67]

Zur zweiten Frage: Wie konnte sich Leibniz seiner eigenen Interpretation so sicher sein, dass er sich über Longobardis Angaben hinwegsetzte? Diese waren hinsichtlich der kanonischen Bücher Chinas[68] besonders irreführend und bezüglich deren Entstehungszeit sogar fehlerhaft, soweit es sich um

---

[67] Vgl. Leibniz: *Lettre*, § 3, S. 44: Interpretiert habe Longobardi „dans un petit ouvrage imprimé (mais non entier) plusieurs passages des auteurs classiques Chinois, mais dans le dessein de les refuter, ce qui le rend d'autant moins suspect de les avoir favorisés [...]." Deshalb glaubt Leibniz, „que ce que j'en tirerois pour donner un sens raisonnable aux dogmes autorisés, seroit plus seur et moins sujet à être soubçonné de flatterie."

[68] Vgl. Longobardis Angaben zu den kanonischen Büchern in seinem *Traité*, Section première, S. 117f., 144, und Santa Maria: *Traité*, S. 160 (vgl. auch die entsprechenden Anmerkungen der Herausgeber). Dabei handelt es sich *erstens* um die *Wu jing*, d.i. die „Fünf Schriften" (*Shi*. Buch der „Lieder"; *Shu*. Buch der „Geschichte"; *Li*. Buch der „Sitte"; *Yi*. Buch der „Wandlungen"; *Chunqiu*. „Frühlings- und Herbstannalen"), die vermutlich von Konfuzius ediert wurden und im traditionellen China die Grundlage der Erziehung und Bildung darstellten. – Dazu gehören *zweitens* die *Si shu*, d. i. die „Vier Bücher" (*Lunyu*. „Gespräche des Konfuzius"; *Mengzi*. „Menzius"; *Daxue*. „Die Große Wissenschaft"; *Zhongyong*. „Lehre von Maß und Mitte"). Die „Vier Bücher" wurden in der Song-Zeit (960–1276) von den Song-oder Neokonfuzianern interpretiert und von dem epochemachenden Philosophen Zhu Xi (1130–1200) zusammengestellt und ediert; sie bildeten die Grundlage klassischer Bildung in China und blieben als kanonische Texte im Examenssystem für die Staatsbeamten von entscheidender Bedeutung bis ins 20. Jahrhundert. – Zum Wissenskanon der chinesischen Gelehrten gehörte drittens das *Xingli daquan shu*, eine Anthologie neokonfuzianischer Philosophen, die im Auftrag des Kaisers Yongle (reg. 1403–1424) von 42 Gelehrten unter der Leitung von Hu Guang (1370–1418) in 70 Kapiteln (*juan*) zusammengestellt und im Jahre 1415 vollendet worden war. Seiner Struktur nach setzt sich das Werk aus zwei Teilen zusammen. Beim ersten Teil (*juan* 1–25) handelt es sich um vollständige Abhandlungen von neun Autoren der Song-Zeit (Zhou Dunyi, Zhu Xi etc.); der zweite Teil (26–70 *juan*) ist ein Sammelsurium unterschiedlichster Sachgruppen von ca. 120 verschiedenen Verfassern. Longobardi bezieht sich auf zwei Teile des *Xingli daquan shu*, die von ihm *Sing-Li* bzw. *Ta-Ziven* genannt werden. Es ist denkbar, dass Longobardis Exemplar in zwei Hälften geteilt und auf dem Außenumschlag jeweils mit *Xingli* (*Singli*) bzw. mit *Daquan* (*Taciven*) beschriftet war (so die Vermutung von Prof. Dr. Martin Gimm, dem an dieser Stelle gedankt sei). Tatsächlich bleibt jedoch unklar, was Longobardi unter dem *Taciven* verstanden hat. (Vgl. dazu auch Mungello: *Leibniz and Confucianism*, S. 163, Anm. 16). Etwa fünfzig Jahre später bezogen sich die Autoren der *Proëmialis declaratio* ebenfalls auf das *Xingli daquan shu*, und zwar am häufigsten auf das 26. Kapitel, das wie das Gesamtwerk den Titel *Xingli* trägt. Vgl. Lundbaek: *The Image* (= Knut Lundbaek: „The Image of Neo-Confucianism in Confucius Sinarum Philosophus", in: *Journal of the History of Ideas* 44 (1983), S. 19–30), S. 22 mit Anm. 7. – Viertens gehörte zum Wissenskanon wahrscheinlich auch das *Zizhi tongjian waiji*, kurz *Tongjian waiji* aus der Sung-Zeit (960–1279) – eine Fortsetzung von Sima Guang's

das Werk *Xingli daquan shu* handelt. Leibniz konnte es besser wissen, als seine Randbemerkungen in Longobardis *Traité* vermuten lassen, denn in der *Proëmialis Declaratio*[69] zum *Confucius Sinarum Philosophus* wird deutlich und klar darüber berichtet.[70]

Hier heben die Patres hervor, dass die Autoren des *Sim li ta çiven* (*Xingli daquan*), das heißt „Pandekten der Naturphilosophie", die Überlieferung, nach der es 600 und mehr Interpreten der kanonischen Bücher gegeben hätte, der Lüge (*mendacium*) verdächtigen. Mehr als zwanzig wären es nicht gewesen.[71] Sie stellen fest, dass das folgende Zeitalter der Ming-Dynastie diesen neuen Deutern der kanonischen Bücher Chinas „wie Lehrern (*magistri*)" gefolgt wäre. Doch in Wirklichkeit hätten diese Lehrer mit ihren Kommentaren vieles darin „verdunkelt und entweiht."[72] Von ihnen habe dieser Schandfleck (*labes*) seinen Ausgang bis in das gegenwärtige Zeitalter genommen, „sehen wir" doch, wie es heißt, „dass nicht wenige aus den Reihen der Literaten Mühe auf jene neuen Kommentare verwenden."[73] Die Patres wissen, dass die Häupter dieser Neoteriker unter den Herrschern der im Jahre 960 n. Chr. beginnenden Song-Dynastie lebten, dass es sich bei diesen Häuptern um „Cheu, Cham und die zwei Brüder Chim çi genannt" handele, „die ungefähr

---

Universalgeschichte *Zizhi tongjian* –, das von dem Historiker Liu Shu (1032–1078) zusammengestellt worden war.

[69] Der Titel der *Proëmialis Declaratio*, Teil 1 [S. IX–LIII] lautet: *Ursprung und Absicht/Ziel des Werkes sowie der chinesischen Bücher, der Interpreten/Deuter, der Schulen und der sogenannten natürlichen Philosophie* (*Operis origo et scopus nec-non Sinensium librorum, interpretum, sectarum, et philosophiae, quam naturalem vocant*); Teil 2 [S. LIIII–CXIII] trägt den Titel: *Es wird erklärt, welches sowohl stoffliche als auch wirkende Prinzip der Dinge sowohl die alten als auch die neueren Chinesen eingeführt haben* (*Explicatur quod principium rerum tam materiale quàm efficiens constituerint Sinae tam Priscsi quam Moderni.*) – Die Patres versichern hier, dass es sich bei dem, was sie dem Leser darbieten, im Unterschied zu den Neueren (*Neoterici*) um den Kern der alten Philosophie handele, wie Ricci ihn in den alten klassischen Texten erkannt hatte. Was sie allerdings in ihrer *Proëmialis Declaratio* tatsächlich bieten, ist laut Knud Lundbaek „the first picture of Neo-Confucianism"; vgl. *The Image*, S. 20.
[70] Auf Grund der in Paris eingesehenen Druckvorlage vermutet Lundbaek, dass Couplet 1687 primär der Herausgeber des Werkes war, dass mindestens der 1. Teil der *Proëmialis Declaratio* 1667 während des Exils der Patres in Kanton geschrieben wurde und dass die Übersetzungen selbst in den 1660er Jahren abgeschlossen waren und dabei auf Arbeiten der Patres aus rund einem Jahrhundert zurückgegriffen wurde. Vgl. *Notes*, S. 135.
[71] Vgl. *Proëmialis Declaratio*, S. XXII: „Mendacii tamen suspectam faciunt hanc famam qui operis *Sim li ta çi ven* , dicti, hoc est, naturalis Philosophiae pandectae, Auctores sunt; […]".
[72] Vgl. ebd., S. XXXIV.
[73] Vgl. ebd., S. XXXVII.

im Jahre 1070 schrieben", und dass „ihnen Chu çi, auch Chu hi genannt, folgte, der im Jahre 1200 n. Chr. starb."[74]

Als Quelle, aus der die Neuerer (*Neoterici Interpretes*) die Art der neuen Lehre schöpften, identifizieren die Missionare das Buch *Ye kim* (*Yijing*), das Fohi (Fuxi) „ganz wie einen zweiten Gordischen Knoten" der Nachwelt zur Erklärung zurückgelassen habe.[75] Nachdem sie die zwei teils durchgehenden, teils unterbrochenen Grund-Linien des Werkes, deren Kombination zu den acht Trigrammen und deren neuerliche Vervielfältigung zu den 64 Hexagrammen beschrieben haben, kommen die Patres auf das *Xingli daquan* „oder [das Buch] über die Natur" zurück, das sich „insbesondere auf das materielle Prinzip der Dinge" beziehe, welches die Neoteriker *Tai kie* (*taiji*) nennen.[76] Wie Zhu Xi zugebe, käme dieser Terminus nirgendwo in den kanonischen Bücher Chinas vor; vielmehr stützten die Neoteriker sich auf die Autorität eines einzigen Buches: der Appendix (*Dazhuan*), *Hi çi* (*Xici*) genannt, die Konfuzius dem von ihm interpretierten „Buch der Wandlungen" hinzugefügt habe.[77] Den zentralen Passus zitieren und übersetzen die Patres hier wie folgt:

---

[74] Vgl. ebd., S. XXXIV–XXXVI. Es handelt sich um die Neokonfuzianer *Cheu*, d.i. Zhou Dunyi (1017–1073), *Cham*, d.i. Zhang Zai (1020–1077), die zwei Brüder *Chim*, d. i. Cheng Yi (1033–1077) und Cheng Hao (1032–1085) sowie *Chu çu*, d.i. Zhu Xi (1130–1200). Vgl. zu diesen Alfred Forke: *Geschichte der neueren chinesischen Philosophie*, Hamburg ²1964, S. 45v55, bzw. S. 56–69, bzw. S. 69–104, bzw. S. 164–202.

[75] Vgl. *Proëmialis Declaratio*, § 6, S. XXXVIII.

[76] Vgl. ebd., S. LV.

[77] Seit der Beschäftigung des Konfuzius (551–479) und seiner Schüler mit dem *Yijing* entstanden sieben Kommentare zu diesem Klassiker. Sie werden als die *Zehn Flügel* bezeichnet, da drei der Kommentare aus zwei Abteilungen bestehen. Auch der berühmteste Kommentar, der *Dazhuan* (die „Große Abhandlung") oder *Xici* (die „Abhandlung zu den angefügten Urteilen") besteht aus zwei Teilen. Vgl. Helmut Schmidt-Glintzer: *Geschichte der chinesischen Literatur von den Anfängen bis zur Gegenwart*, München ²1999, S. 60f. – Über die Verfasserschaft des *Dazhuan* ist viel diskutiert worden. Richard Wilhem (I *Ging. Buch der Wandlungen*, erstes und zweites Buch, aus dem Chin. verdt. und erl., Düsseldorf/ Köln 1923, Bd 2, S. 211) ist der Ansicht, dass der *Dazhuan* (*Da Dschuang*) oder *Xici* (*Hi Tsi*) nicht von Konfuzius stammt. Auch Alfred Forke (*Geschichte der alten chinesischen Philosophie*, Hamburg 1964, S. 10) versichert, „daß wir kaum fehlgehen, wenn wir alle ,10 Flügel' als aus der Schule des Konfuzius hervorgegangen betrachten", und verweist dafür auch auf James Legge. Er vermutet, dass der *Dazhuan* vielleicht aus derselben Zeit stamme wie die erste Schöpfungstheorie des Daoisten Liezi (um 440–ca. 370 v. Chr.), der von der Existenz der acht Trigramme auf das absolute Ursprungsprinzip *taiji* zurückgeht. Der Daoist Huainan Zi (ca 179–122 v. Chr.) stimme mit Liezi überein, bezeichne aber statt des *taiji* das *dao* als „die Große Einheit oder die Monade". An diese Naturphilosophie habe der Neokonfuzianismus der Song-Philosophien angeknüpft (vgl. Alfred Forke: *Die Gedankenwelt des chinesischen Kulturkreises*, München/Berlin 1927, S. 89f.).

„Der Wandel enthält die Große Achse oder den Wendepunkt (*taiji*); dieser erzeugte die zwei Kräfte, das Vollkommene und das Unvollkommene, wie den Himmel und die Erde. Die zwei Kräfte erzeugten die vier Bilder, die vier Bilder erzeugten die acht schwebenden Figuren."[78]

„Was aber auch immer die Neoteriker über dieses ihr Prinzip der Dinge" sagen, hätten diese „sich selbst ausgedacht", versichern die Patres.[79] Dabei redeten sie über das *taiji* als etwas für den menschlichen Geist Unaussagbares, als etwas Geistiges, als eine Macht, die zu untersuchen „wir nicht imstande sind", und als etwas, das „auszudrücken es kein Wort gebe."[80] Sie sagten, dass das *taiji* begriffen werden müsse als etwas zunächst „Unbewegliches und Ruhiges"; das aber, sowie es sich bewege, das *yang* oder das Vollkommene erzeuge, und sowie es wieder ruhe das *yin* oder das weniger Vollkommene hervorbringe. Sie verglichen dies mit einem nachdenkenden Menschen, der irgendwelche Gedanken wälze und dann ausspreche, worüber er nachgedacht habe.[81] Sie veranschaulichten das *taiji* auch anhand eines Quantums Quecksilber, das unbeweglich in einer Kapsel verborgen sei; würde diese dann aber geöffnet, flösse das Quecksilber heraus und verteilte sich wie in tausend Strahlen, die in Materie und Form mit dem Quecksilber identisch sind.[82] Es sei ganz

---

[78] Vgl. *Proëmialis Declaratio*, S. LV: „Mutatio continet magnum axem seu cardinem: Hic produxit duas virtutes, puta perfectum et imperfectum ut coelum et terram. Duae virtutes produxerunt quatuor imagines, quatuor imagines produxerunt octo figuras pendulas." Wilhelm übersetzt: „Darum gibt es in den Wandlungen den großen Uranfang. Dieser erzeugt die zwei Grundkräfte. Die zwei Grundkräfte erzeugen die vier Bilder. Die vier Bilder erzeugen die acht Zeichen." Vgl. *I Ging*, 2. Buch: *Da Dschuan/Die Grosse Abhandlung* (auch Hi Tsï Dschuan, Kommentar zu den beigefügten Urteilen, genannt), Bd 1, S. 243, § 5. – In der *Proëmialis Declaratio*, § 3, S. XXIV, berichten die Patres u. d. T. „Kurze Nachricht zur Schule des Philosophen Li lao Kiun (Lao Zi), die sie in China Daoisten nennen" [*Brevis notitia sectae Li lao Kiun, quos in Sinis Tao su vocant*] über die Bücher des Lao Zi: „Wo er aber über die Erzeugung der Dinge spricht, bringt er unter anderen diesen Satz hervor, den die Anhänger wie das edelste Axiom seiner Philosophie unablässig herleiern (*decantant*), nämlich: Dao [....], das Gesetz oder die Vernunft hat das Eine erzeugt, das Eine hat die Zwei erzeugt, die Zwei haben die Drei erzeugt und die Drei haben alles erzeugt". Vgl. *Laotse Tao te King. Das Buch des Alten vom Sinn und Leben*, aus dem Chin. verdt. u. erl. v. Richard Wilhelm, Jena 1921, S. 47, Nr. 43.
[79] Vgl. *Proëmialis Declaratio*, 2. Teil, § 1, S. LV: „Quidquid afferunt […] de suo illo rerum principio totum scilicet effinxerunt ipsi."
[80] Vgl. ebd., S. LV: „Tametsi porrò dicant quod *Tai Kie* sit humanis ingeniis inexplicabile quid, quod spirituale quid, quod potentia quam investigare non possimus, neque esse nomen quo queat exprimi."
[81] Vgl. ebd., S. LVI.
[82] Vgl. ebd.

erstaunlich, wundern sich die Missionare, was diese Kommentatoren ihrem *taiji* an Fähigkeiten und Eigenschaften zusprächen: So wäre es

> „ein erstes und aus sich selbst Hervorgegangenes, ein Höchstes, Subtilstes, Reinstes, Schönstes, die wahre Mitte, die höchste Vollkommenheit und das Gute, Vorbild und Idee aller Dinge, ohne Anfang und Ende". „Wenn sie nur konsequent wären", so die Patres, „würde der Leser kaum zweifeln, dass sie immer wieder von der wahren und damit ersten und höchsten Gottheit (*supremum Numen*) sprächen."[83]

> „Dass sie jedoch mit unseren Philosophen [unter dem *taiji*] die bloße erste Materie verstehen", so behaupten die Patres im Rahmen ihrer scholastischen Begrifflichkeit, werde dadurch bestätigt, „dass sie ihr *taiji* mit einem anderen Namen *li* nennen."[84]

Dieses Wort bedeute aber offenbar bei den Chinesen nichts Anderes als bei den Römern *ratio* („Beschaffenheit"). Für „umso wahrscheinlicher" halten es deshalb die Missionare, dass die Neoteriker

> „so wie sie richtig unter dem *taiji* die erste Materie verstehen, so auch unter dem *li* die Beschaffenheit oder konstitutive und von anderen unterscheidende Form der Dinge."[85]

Jedenfalls sind sie fest davon überzeugt: Wo die Neoteriker mit vielen Worten

> „über ihr *li* und *taiji* diskutieren, [...] scheinen sie kaum merklich in den Atheismus herabzugleiten, weil sie ja jedes wirkende übernatürliche Prinzip ausschließen; und wie sehr sie auch immer wieder vom Sinn und der Materie zu abstrahieren scheinen, bleiben sie tatsächlich doch [ganz] der Materie verhaftet."[86]

Obgleich hier die Patres die kanonischen Werke Chinas ganz wie Matteo Ricci in aristotelisch-scholastischer Begrifflichkeit interpretieren, indem sie den darin erkennbaren Monotheismus bei den Alten mit dem materiellen Ursprungsprinzip der Neoteriker kontrastieren, äußern sie sich doch an manchen Stellen höchst verwundert und positiv über die Philosophie der Letzteren: „Man

---

[83] Vgl. ebd.
[84] Vgl. ebd., S. LVI–LVII.
[85] Vgl. ebd., S. LVII.
[86] Vgl. ebd.

glaubt", heißt es, „immer wieder einen Platon oder andere, keineswegs abwegig über Gott denkende Philosophen zu hören."[87]

Leibniz muss die vergleichende Beschreibung des *taiji* und des *li* bei den Neoterikern in der Darstellung der Jesuitenpatres zutiefst verwundert, ja sie muss ihn, wegen der offenbaren Nähe zur neuplatonischen Philosophie und seiner eigenen Metaphysik,[88] zugleich sogar unmittelbar angesprochen haben. Musste er nicht ehrlicherweise in seinem *Discours* zu einem ganz anderen Urteil kommen als Longobardi, aber auch als die Autoren des *Confucius Sinarum Philosophus*? Doch auch unter dem christlich-philosophischen Aspekt einer „gewissen Philosophia perennis,"[89] scheint es nichts anderes als durchaus konsequent zu sein, dass für Leibniz die Unterscheidung zwischen den Texten der alten Konfuzianer und jenen der Neokonfuzianer ziemlich bedeutungslos war. Für ihn war ja die Erkenntnisgeschichte der Natürlichen Theologie nicht auf die biblische Geschichte beschränkt.

Ich komme damit zur dritten Frage: Wie konnte Leibniz überhaupt von einer „Natürlichen Theologie der Chinesen" sprechen? Meine Antwort ist kurz: Leibniz brauchte sich dafür nur an die Buchtitel der Neoteriker zu halten, welche die Missionare als „Pandekten der Naturphilosophie" oder als „Über die Natur" wiedergegeben haben.[90] Im Licht seiner wissenschaftstheoretisch fundierten *Philosophia perennis* war jedoch diese Philosophie für ihn unmissverständlich mit einer Natürlichen Theologie identisch.

Für die vierte und letzte Frage komme ich auf meine These zurück: Leibniz hat den *Confucius Sinarum Philosophus* gelesen; dessen Lektüre überzeugte ihn vom Monotheismus einer Natürlichen Theologie der alten *und* der modernen Chinesen; mit Rücksicht auf die Missionspolitik seiner Freunde in der Gesellschaft Jesu hat er sich jedoch weder auf dieses Werk bezogen noch auf die 1711 erschienene Übersetzung der „Sechs klassischen Bücher

---

[87] Vgl. ebd, S. LVIII: „Platones subinde aliquos audire te credas, aliosve Philosophos haudquaquam malè sentientes de Deo."
[88] Vgl. Rita Widmaier: *„Leibniz, Plotin und die Weltseele"*, in: *Natur und Subjekt*. IX. Internationaler Leibniz-Kongress, Vorträge, 3. Teil hrsg. v. Herbert Breger/Jürgen Herbst/Sven Erdner, Hannover 2011, S. 1189–1201.
[89] Leibniz würde gern seine eigene Lehre mit den Lehren der Alten vergleichen, heißt es in seinem Brief an Remond vom 26. August 1714: „ce seroit en effect *perennis quaedam philosophia*"; vgl. GP III, 625.
[90] Vgl. zur genauen Erklärung der Bedeutung des Ausdrucks *Xingli*, Forke: *Geschichte der neueren chinesischen Philosophie*, S. 212.

des chinesischen Reiches" des Jesuitenmissionars François Noël.[91] Beide Bücher sind aber im Altbestand der G. W. Leibniz Bibliothek vorhanden. Wer sonst, wenn nicht Leibniz, sollte sich zu jener Zeit für China so brennend interessiert haben, dass er diese Werke sofort beschaffte?

3. Rückblick: Leibniz' ‚wahre' Philosophie und moralisch ‚sichere' Wahrheit

Leibniz war – abgesehen von seinen durch die Lektüre der *Proëmialis Declaratio* gewonnenen Einsichten – der festen Überzeugung, dass alle Philosophen in China von der Vergangenheit bis in die Gegenwart immer Monotheisten gewesen wären. Was unterschied ihn dabei sowohl von Ricci als auch von Longobardi? Im Rückblick zeigt sich, dass es ihm im Unterschied zu den beiden Letzteren nicht nur um die Übereinstimmung der chinesischen Überlieferung mit dem Christentum ging, sondern um eine Geschichte der Natürlichen Theologie, in der unter dem Aspekt des Monotheismus ein gewisser *Fortschritt* der Erkenntnis festzustellen ist.[92] Anders als in der traditionellen *Philosophia perennis* ist dieser Fortschritt weder zeitlich (von Mose bis zur Ankunft des Messias) noch heilsgeschichtlich (auf das *Alte* und *Neue Testament*) beschränkt.[93] Im Rahmen seiner *Scientia generalis* umfasst dieser Fortschritt neben der Gotteserkenntnis in der Anfangsgeschichte der Menschheit zugleich auch alle

---

[91] *Sinensis imperii libri classici sex, nimirum Adultorum Schola, Immutabile Medium, Liber Sententiarum, Mencius, Filialis Observantia, Parvulorum Schola. E Sinico idiomate in Latinum traducti a P. Francisco Noël, Societatis Jesu missionario*, Pragae 1711. Noël übersetzte darin außer den drei ersten der klassischen „Vier Bücher" (wie die Übersetzer im *Confucius Sinarum Philosophus*) auch das vierte, den *Mengzi*, sowie das *Xiaojing* („Buch der Kindlichen Ehrfurcht"), das zum Kanon der konfuzianischen Klassiker gehörte, und das *Xiaoxue* (Buch der Jungen), das Pflichtlektüre war. Vgl. Christian Wolff: *Oratio de Sinarum philosophia practica, Rede über die praktische Philosophie der Chinesen*, übers., eingel. u. hrsg. v. Michael Albrecht, Hamburg 1985, Einleitung, §§ 7–8.
[92] Vgl. zum Thema Jules Delvaille: *Essai sur l'histoire de l'idée de progrès jusqu'à la fin du XVIIIe siècle*, Paris 1910.
[93] In den Grundzügen stimmt Leibniz zwar mit einem der bekannten Anhänger der Philosophia perennis, Pierre Daniel Huet, Bischof von Avranches, überein. Doch seine Kritik an dessen *Demonstratio Evangelica ad serenissimum Delphinum*, Parisiis 1676, ist in einem Brief an Ezechiel Spanheim vom 7. Mai 1697 (A I, 14 N. 94, 159) ablesbar: „Et quoyque Mons. D'Avranche ait employé une grande erudition en ce qu'il dit sur ce sujet dans sa demonstration Evangelique, il me paroit neantmoins que la broderie vaut mieux que l'etoffe, et que la solidité manque bien souvent à ces scavantes et ingenieuses conjectures dont il se sert pour rapporter tout à Moise […]".

Wissenschaften von der Natur und dem Menschen, deren Tatsachen und Geschehnisse es nicht nur zu erforschen,[94] sondern auch zu interpretieren gilt. Bei der Interpretation der Natur und Menschheitsgeschichte müsse jedoch „das Ziel der Philosophie sein", wie Leibniz betont, die Weisheit Gottes erkennen zu lassen; und diesem Ziel hätten sowohl die Mathematik und Physik[95] als auch die Geschichte zu dienen,[96] während die *Philosophia perennis* die Theorie der Interpretation bereitstelle.

Ein zweiter Unterscheidungspunkt ist besonders hervorzuheben: Im Unterschied zu den Anhängern der traditionellen *Philosophia perennis*, welche die historischen Überlieferungen des vor- und nichtchristlichen Altertums als Vorwissen neutestamentlicher Glaubenssätze interpretieren, betrachtet Leibniz jene „Spuren" einer Natürlichen Theologie in der Überlieferung der „Alten" als historisches Tatsachenmaterial, das vernunftgemäß erklärt werden muss. Einerseits hatte er nämlich seit längerem erkannt, dass man den Glauben an Gott in den Überlieferungen der Heiden nicht beweisen, vielmehr voraussetzen und als möglich erklären müsse;[97] andererseits sah er ebenfalls klar, dass bei der Untersuchung historischer Tatsachen, nicht die syllogistische Logik, sondern eine Wahrscheinlichkeitslogik anzuwenden sei. Hier kam es Leibniz darauf an, sich *nicht* auf die größte Zahl der Meinungen oder die besten Autoritäten zu stützen, bewies ihm doch der Fall des Kopernikus, dass die

---

[94] Dabei verlangte Leibniz in den Naturwissenschaften Aktualität: So werde er keinen Autor akzeptieren, der den Blutkreislauf verwirft (vgl. Leibniz an Burnett of Kemney vom 18. Juli 1701; A I, 20 N. 185, 282).

[95] Vgl. ebd., S. 287: „Je voudrois qu'on s'attachât à faire connoistre la sagesse de Dieu par la physique et mathematique, en decouvrant de plus en plus les merveilles de la nature. C'est là le vray moyen de convaincre les profanes et doit estre le but de la Philosophie."

[96] Vgl. *Contemplatio de Historia Literaria*; A VI, 4 Teil A, N. 114₂, 460–465, u. 468: „Historia enim servit ad pietatem et ex ea veritas religionis nostrae demonstrari potest, quod hic nonnihil adumbratur."

[97] Vgl. Leibniz an Friedrich Wilhelm Bierling, März 1713 (GP VII, 511): „*Itaque si Deus nobis non indidit principia, unde immortalitatem nosceremus, inanis est Theologia naturalis, nec quicquam contra atheismum practicum valet*; et licebat hominibus esse atheis ante revelationem, neque enim in hac vita se vindicat divinitas. Non est necesse ad animae immortalitatem tuendam, ut sit substantia separata, potest enim semper induta manere subtili corpore, quale ego etiam angelis tribuo." (Hervorhebung R.W.) („Wenn Gott uns also nicht die Grundbegriffe eingegeben hat, die uns die Erkenntnis der Unsterblichkeit erlauben, dann ist die Natürliche Theologie Schall und Rauch, vermag nichts gegen den praktischen Atheismus, und es war den Menschen vor der Offenbarung erlaubt, Atheisten zu sein, denn die Gottheit rächt sich nicht in diesem Leben. Soll die Unsterblichkeit der Seele gewahrt bleiben, muss sie nicht notwendig eine abgetrennte Substanz sein, denn sie kann immer in einen subtilen Leib gehüllt bleiben, wie ich selbst ihn auch den Engeln zuschreibe.").

auf Beobachtungen und mathematische Berechnungen gestützte Meinung eines Einzelnen manchmal „unvergleichlich wahrscheinlicher" sei als die der übrigen Menschheit.[98]

Die Erkenntnis, dass die Logik der Wahrscheinlichkeit nicht nur auf historische Fakten und Meinungen, sondern auch auf mathematische Entdeckungen angewandt werden könne, lieferte Leibniz nicht zuletzt der Briefwechsel mit dem Figuristen Joachim Bouvet. Dieser Jesuitenmissionar hatte die Isomorphie der Leibniz'schen Dyadik mit den 64 Hexagrammen des *Yijing* entdeckt, als deren Autor traditionell Fuxi, der legendäre Gründer und erste Weise Chinas betrachtet wurde.[99] Da Leibniz aber die Dyadik zugleich als unmittelbar einleuchtende Analogie zur Schöpfung (*creatio ex nihilo*) betrachtete,[100] erschien es im Rahmen der Wahrscheinlichkeitslogik durchaus denkbar, dass auch die ältesten Chinesen schon eine Ahnung oder gar Erkenntnis von Gott gehabt hätten. Denn nicht nur den Israeliten wäre der Begriff eines einzigen Gottes bekannt gewesen, heißt es in seinem Wiener Vortrag, „soweit wir es erraten können, billigten ihn auch die ältesten chinesischen Weisen."

> Denn „Fuxi, der vor mehr als 3000 Jahren bei den Chinesen zugleich herrschte und sich der Philosophie widmete", habe „alle Zahlen unter Verwendung von nur zwei Zeichen" geschrieben, „deren eine die Einheit, die andere das Nichts bezeichnet, um so erkennen zu lassen, dass Gott alles aus dem Nichts herausgeführt hat."[101]

Leibniz hielt diese Analogie aus dem Bereich der Mathematik nicht nur für eine plausible *Erklärung* der Schöpfung, sondern auch für den methodisch

---

[98] Vgl. *Nouveaux Essais* IV, 2, § 14; A VI, 6, 372f.: „Mais le probable ou le vraisemblable est plus etendu: il faut le tirer de la nature des choses; et l'opinion des personnes, dont l'autorité est de poid, est une des choses, qui peuvent contribuer à rendre une opinion vraisemblable, mais ce n'est pas ce qui acheve toute la verisimilitude. Et lorsque Copernic etoit presque seul de son opinion, elle etoit tousjours incomparablement plus vraisemblable que celle de tout le reste du genre humain."
[99] Für den Figuristen bedeutete dies die Identität beider Systeme; vgl. Bouvets Brief an Leibniz vom 4. November 1701; *China-Korrespondenz*, Nr. 44, hier S. 334f.
[100] Vgl. Leibniz an Herzog Rudolf August vom 2. (12.) Januar 1697; A I, 13 N. 75, S. 116–121. Zum Thema vgl. Hanz J. Zacher: *Die Hauptschriften zur Dyadik von G.W. Leibniz. Ein Beitrag zur Geschichte des binären Zahlensystems*, Frankfurt a. M. 1973, §§ 6 u. 8.
[101] Vgl. Riley: „An Unpublished Lecture", S. 214: „Hinc Fohius qui ante ter mille et amplius annos apud eos simul regnavit et philosophatus est, ut significaret omnia à Deo esse de nihilo educta, Numeros omnes scripsit adhibitis duabus tantùm notis, una significante unitatem, altera significante nihilum."

kürzesten Weg, diese gänzlich jenseits der Erfahrung und über dem Verstand liegende Tatsache einsichtig zu machen. Ein anderer, systematischer Weg bedeutete für ihn nichts anderes als die Darlegung seines eigenen metaphysischen Systems der Substanzen. Dabei betrachtete Leibniz sein System nicht nur als eine „Natürliche Theologie"[102] oder eine „Religion der Vernunft", sondern auch als eine Grundlage der Offenbarung selbst, ohne welche diese Letztere „immer übel ausgedeutet" werde.[103] Folgerichtig bildet dieses System auch im Vergleich der alten chinesischen mit der antiken griechischen Philosophie in seinem *Discours sur la Théologie naturelle des Chinois* das *Tertium comparationis*.[104]

Fragen wir zuletzt, was Leibniz veranlasste, sich in seinem Urteil über die Natürliche Theologie der Chinesen sowohl von Ricci als auch von Longobardi zu distanzieren. Allem Anschein nach ging er davon aus, dass, würde die Überlieferung des alten und des modernen Konfuzianismus nach den wissenschaftstheoretischen und methodologischen Richtlinien seiner *Scientia generalis* zunächst als eine Natürliche Theologie interpretiert, die Bekehrung Chinas zum Christentum gewissermaßen leichtes Spiel wäre.[105] Leibniz versprach sich damit offensichtlich Unabhängigkeit von jenem Problem, das

---

[102] Brief an Joachim Bouvet vom 18. Juli 1704; *China-Korrespondenz*, Nr. 53, S. 456f. Im Rahmen seiner *Scientia generalis* hofft hier Leibniz, sein „System der Monaden oder einfachen Substanzen zu beweisen, die alles begründen und die, ohne voneinander abhängig zu sein, sich zueinander fügen kraft der Harmonie, die ihr gemeinsamer Schöpfer in ihren Naturen im Voraus festgelegt hat. [...] Dieses System bringt eine sehr reichhaltige Philosophie hervor und eine *Natürliche Theologie*, wie man sie sich nur wünschen kann." (Hervorhebung R.W.).
[103] Vgl. Leibniz an Kurfürstin Sophie, April 1709; Klopp, I, 9, 300: „On envoye des Missionnaires jusqu'à la Chine pour prescher la religion Chrestienne [...] il nous faudroit des Missionnaires de la Raison en Europe, pour prescher la Religion naturelle, sur laquelle la Revelation même est fondeée, et sans laquelle la Revelation sera tousjours mal prise. La Religion de la Raison est eternelle, et Dieu l'a gravée dans nos coeurs."
[104] Die Ähnlichkeit seines Systems mit der Natürlichen Theologie der Chinesen ist öfter diskutiert worden; vgl. dazu Lundbaek: *Notes*, S. 144–148; Mungello: *„Leibniz's interpretation of Neo-Confucianism*, S. 1–22. Es wurde darüber hinaus vermutet, dass Leibniz in seinem Denken vom der neokonfuzianischen Philosophie abhängig war oder doch beeinflusst (s. Joseph Needham: *Science and Civilisation in China*, Bd. 2, Cambridge 1956, S. 496–505; Arthur Zempliner: „Gedanken über die erste deutsche Übersetzung von Leibniz' Abhandlung über die chinesische Philosophie", in: *Studia Leibnitiana* 2 (1970), S.223–231). Es bleibt jedoch mit Mungello (*Leibniz and Confucianism*, S. 13–17, 99) festzustellen, dass die Grundlinien der Leibnizschen Philosophie schon lange vor der Veröffentlichung des großen Übersetzungswerks *Confucius Sinarum Philosophus*, 1687, feststanden und großenteils ausgearbeitet waren.
[105] So kündigt Leibniz in einem Brief an Antoine Verjus vom 2. (12.) Dezember 1697 an, dass mit dem „neuen philosophischen Kalkül seiner *spécieuse universelle*" (sonst auch *ars charac-*

nicht nur Ricci und Longobardi, sondern *alle* Missionare betraf: Diese hatten einer so hochentwickelten und selbstbewussten Kulturnation wie der chinesischen nämlich überzeugend zu erklären, weshalb sie gekommen waren und weshalb ihre Lehre nicht nur zum Nutzen, sondern auch zur Glückseligkeit der Chinesen beitragen werde. Seitdem sich die Mitglieder des Ordens in China als Gelehrte aus dem Westen darstellten, war es jedoch die Gretchenfrage, wie sich das Evangelium mit dem Konfuzianismus in Einklang bringen lasse. Während Ricci gerade mit dem Atheismus und Materialismus des zeitgenössischen Neokonfuzianismus sein Dasein in China rechtfertigte und die Notwendigkeit, seine Lehre zu verbreiten, war das schon seinem Nachfolger nicht mehr möglich. Longobardi befand sich in einem Dilemma: Hätte er die spirituelle Substanz und Nähe des Neokonfuzianismus zu einer Natürlichen Theologie erkannt und offen zugegeben, musste in den Augen seiner ‚gelehrten Kollegen im Osten' die neue Lehre und deren Verbreitung gänzlich überflüssig erscheinen. Hielt er dagegen sowohl den alten als auch den neuen Konfuzianismus kompromisslos für atheistisch und materialistisch (was geschah) und deshalb die Verbreitung des Christentums für notwendig, so nahmen ihn im besten Fall die Gelehrten und einflussreichen Chinesen nicht ernst und sein Orden hielt ihn sogar für abtrünnig. Leibniz suchte das eine und das andere zu vermeiden: Er interpretierte den Neokonfuzianismus ‚vernünftig' im Sinne Riccis als eine Natürliche Theologie. Dabei verglich er die Autorität der modernen Interpreten des *Xingli dachuan shu*, dessen neuzeitliche Entstehung ihm sichtlich nicht verborgen war,[106] mit der Autorität der „arabischen und scholastischen" Kommentatoren des Aristoteles, deren Wert er hier wie dort gegenüber dem „wahren Sinn der alten Texte" für geringer hielt. In dieser missiologischen Kontroverse innerhalb des Ordens nahm Leibniz folgerichtig den Standpunkt Riccis ein, denn auf der Grundlage der *Philosophia perennis* lag allemal die *tiefere*, wenn auch nicht die deutlichere Wahrheit der Texte bei denen, die an Alter der ursprünglichen Wahrheit am nächsten waren.[107]

---

teristica universalis) ein „wunderbares Hilfsmittel" geschaffen würde, um selbst „fernsten Völkern", wie den Chinesen, die „wichtigsten und abstraktesten Wahrheiten der Natürlichen Theologie nahezubringen. *Auf diese Wahrheiten ist die offenbarte Religion [des Christentums] gleichsam aufgepfropft*". Vgl. *China-Korrespondenz*, Nr. 17, S. 132f. (Hervorhebung R.W.).
[106] Leibniz erklärt hier: Wenn den Angaben des Paters de Sainte Marie zufolge die Schriften des „Taciven Singli" erst vor 300 Jahren kompiliert worden seien, so dass man sie „comme modernes" betrachten könne, dann hätten sie – geht es um den wahren Sinn – weniger Autorität als der ursprüngliche Text. Vgl. Leibniz: *Lettre*, § 38, S. 89f., hier S. 90.
[107] Vgl. auch ebd., § 1, S. 39f.

Sartres und Leibnizens Sicht auf Freiheit und Faktizität[*]

Rainer E. Zimmermann (München/Cambridge)

1.

Das erste Kapitel im vierten Teil von Sartres frühem Hauptwerk *Das Sein und das Nichts* beginnt mit einer Diskussion des Freiheitsbegriffs, der als Bedingung allen Handelns betrachtet wird, bevor Sartre das Verhältnis von Freiheit und Faktizität in Sicht nimmt, welches geeignet ist, seinerseits den Situationsbegriff zu begründen. Es ist kein Zufall, dass Sartre den Freiheitsbegriff im Abgleich mit dem Ansatz Leibnizens einführt, der freilich weiter auf die moderne Philosophie ausstrahlt, insofern er sich zum einen auf den früheren Ansatz Spinozas abstützt, zum anderen aber auf die Philosophie Schellings vorausweist. Dieser Zusammenhang soll im Vorliegenden kurz erläutert werden. Um auch die weitere Entwicklung Sartres hin auf eine marxistische Philosophie in Rechnung zu stellen, werden zudem die konkreten Randbedingungen der Freiheit im Rahmen seiner späteren sozialistischen Ethik thematisiert.

2.

Wir beginnen zunächst mit dem Verhältnis Sartres zu Leibniz, müssen zu diesem Zweck aber kurz auf den Sartre'schen Ansatz in einigem Detail rekurrieren, der seinerseits vor allem auf Schelling zurückgreift: Passend hierzu hat Michael Blamauer auf sehr anschauliche Weise darauf hingewiesen, dass es evidentes Wissen von einer objektiv gegebenen Welt Schelling zufolge nur im Rekurs auf ein *erstes Wovonher* dieses Wissens geben kann, denn Wissen ist als *Wissen von* immer synthetisch, deshalb bedingt und prinzipiell bezweifelbar.[1] In der frühzeitig bereits von Manfred Frank[2] erhellten Sichtweise ergibt sich recht

---

[*] Beitrag zu Sektion: Leibniz, Marx und der Marxismus.
[1] Michael Blamauer: *Subjektivität und ihr Platz in der Natur. Untersuchung zu Schellings Versuch einer naturphilosophischen Grundlegung des Bewußtseins*, Stuttgart 2006, S. 56. (par.) In diesem Abschnitt folge ich im Wesentlichen meinem Aufsatz: „Diskursive Aberration als Grundlage des Gelingens", in: Hans Feger/Manuela Hackel (Hrsg.): *Existenzphilosophie und Ethik*, Berlin/Boston 2014, S. 355–368.
[2] Nach wie vor unerreicht Manfred Frank: *Der unendliche Mangel an Sein. Schellings Hegelkritik und die Anfänge der Marxschen Dialektik*, München ²1992.

zwanglos in einer nachkantisch mit Fichte ansetzenden und bei Schelling entscheidend weitergeführten Neuentwicklung, dass

> „die Jemeinigkeit des Wissens [...] sich [daher] als irreduzibles Moment objektiver Gegebenheit erwiesen [hat]. Die objektiven Tatsachen sind somit wesentlich auf meine faktische Existenz angewiesen, insofern *diese* sich als grundlegende Bedingung des Erscheinens *jener* gezeigt hat. Darum ist die Überlegung legitim, ob nicht zwischen der Faktizität meiner selbst und der Faktizität einer gegenständlich gegebenen Welt ein unmittelbarer Zusammenhang besteht. Das könnte allerdings nur gezeigt werden, wenn die Faktizität der wechselweisen Erscheinungsbedingtheit von subjektiver Perspektive und objektiver Dingwelt auf die Faktizität meiner *originären Selbstgegebenheit* rückbegründet wird. Dieses originäre Selbstgegebensein ist das Selbstbewußtsein. In ihm bin ich mir ursprünglich selbsterschlossen."[3]

Allein schon wegen des Anhebens der Reflexionsbewegung von jener Jemeinigkeit her,[4] ist somit das unmittelbare *Objekt der Transzendentalphilosophie* immer bereits das Subjektive, und die *Aufgabe der Transzendentalphilosophie* liegt mithin in der Freilegung seiner konstitutiven Strukturen für eine gegenständliche Welt, die für sein subjektives Sich-Wissen zugleich notwendige Bedingung seiner selbst ist. Das heißt, das Objekt der Analyse ist die Subjektivität selbst, das schlechthin Nicht-Objektive.[5] Die Frage ist dann aber, wie ein schlechthin Nicht-Objektives zum Objekt transzendentaler Reflexion werden könne:

> „Die ganze Philosophie geht aus", schreibt Schelling, „und muß ausgehen von einem Princip, das als das absolut Identische schlechthin nichtobjektiv ist. Wie soll nun aber dieses Nichtobjektive doch zum Bewußtseyn hervorgerufen und verstanden werden, was nothwendig ist, wenn es Bedingung des Verstehens der ganzen Philosophie ist?"[6]

Schellings Antwort wird lauten: Indem sich das Subjektive in einem stetigen Akt selbst zum Objekt macht und so ein identisches Wissen produziert, in welchem es sich selbst (als Wissen) mit sich selbst (als Gewusstem) identifiziert. Diese Identifizierung ist wiederum nur möglich, weil es im Wesen der Subjektivität liegt, schon vor jeglichem identifizierenden Akt *sich selbst* erschlossen,

---

[3] Blamauer: *Subjektivität und ihr Platz*.
[4] Vgl., Rainer E. Zimmermann: *System des transzendentalen Materialismus*, Paderborn 2004.
[5] Blamauer: *Subjektivität und ihr Platz*.
[6] Friedrich Wilhelm Joseph von Schelling: *Sämmtliche Werke*, Bd. 3, 1799/1800, hrsg. v. Karl Friedrich August Schelling, Stuttgart/Augsburg 1858, S. 624f.

mit *sich selbst* vertraut zu sein.[7] Ob aber das Selbstbewusstsein noch etwas Erklärbares ist oder nicht, das heißt, ob es außerhalb seiner noch etwas gibt, von woher es verstanden werden kann, ist (zumindest zu jener Zeit bei Schelling) eine sinnlose Frage, da unser Wissen hier an eine Grenze stößt, die es nicht aufheben kann.[8] (Die Sartre'schen Konnotationen – und im Übrigen auch die Bloch'schen – sind hier schon mehr als deutlich.)

Ich habe zudem vor längerem in meinem ersten Schelling-Buch[9] bereits ausführlicher auf jene Zusammenhänge zwischen Schelling einerseits und Sartre und Bloch andererseits verwiesen, die sich vor allem aus der *Freiheitskonzeption* bei Schelling ableiten lassen: In seinen mittleren und späteren Schriften nämlich rekurriert Schelling neuerlich auf seinen frühen Freiheitsbegriff, der im Grunde das Selbstbewusstsein immer schon qualifiziert. Freilich fasst er nunmehr die kontextuelle Einbettung der Freiheit systematischer, insofern sie ihm nicht nur als rein abstrakter Grund des Absoluten selbst (und insofern auch als Abgrund oder Ungrund) gilt, sondern auch mit *praktischer* Freiheit verflochten wird, indem sie nicht mehr bloße Überwindung von Abhängigkeit ist, wie noch bei Fichte, sondern eher als Vereinigung von Gegensätzen verstanden wird. Sie zielt also mehr auf eine alle Gegensätze übergreifende Einheit, nicht allein auf das Für-sich-sein eines Subjektes.[10] So bleibt Schelling letztlich seinem ganzheitlichen Ansatz treu: Denn theoretische wie praktische Philosophie verbinden sich miteinander zu einer Gesamtsystematik, die Einsichten über den Grund des Philosophierens und den Grund des konkreten Weltwerdens gleichermaßen vermitteln soll, so, wie sie ebenfalls Aussagen über die Welt als Natur wie auch über die Welt als Kultur zu ermöglichen angelegt ist.[11]

Von diesem Bogen hat Sartre allerdings nur die *eine* Hälfte ernsthaft in Betracht gezogen, offenbar seinen eigenen Grundsätzen durchaus entgegen handelnd und dadurch vielleicht eine wichtige Komponente seines Denkens, die bereits in seiner Epoche angelegt war, zu Unrecht unberücksichtigt lassend. Denn wie Jörg Villwock in der Einleitung zu seinem Buch *Signaturen des erdkolonialen Zeitalters* zu Recht (und durchaus Sartresch, aber auch Heideggersch) vermerkt:

---

[7] Blamauer: *Subjektivität und ihr Platz*.
[8] Ebd., S. 57 (par.).
[9] Rainer E. Zimmermann: *Die Rekonstruktion von Raum, Zeit und Materie. Moderne Implikationen Schellingscher Naturphilosophie*, Frankfurt a. M. 1998.
[10] Dazu führt Erhellendes aus Dieter Henrich: *Der Grund im Bewußtsein. Untersuchungen zu Hölderlins Denken*, Stuttgart 1992.
[11] Zimmermann: *Die Rekonstruktion von Raum*, S. 219 (par.).

„[…] Dasein heißt in sich über sich hinaus mit einer Epoche vermittelt sein und in einem Epochen*verständnis* existieren. Wir nennen das die Säkularität des bewußten Daseins. Ihre Lichtung ist je verschieden, sie hängt vom Bezug ab, nicht von / schulmäßiger Lehre, die hier eher behindert, weil sie *die Unwissenheit als Grund von Wissenschaft* nicht anerkennen will und die produktive Verwirrung nicht aufkommen läßt, aus der heraus allein der seinshaltige und seinlassende Blick hervorzugehen vermag, der Blick, in dem das Dasein sich vorweg ist, der vorspringende Blick, der das Sehen vor dem Sehen, das Wissen vor dem Wissen vermittelt."[12]

Manfred Frank hatte in diesem Zusammenhang gezeigt, dass es eine charakteristische Weise der Exteriorisierung des Individuums gibt, die man allgemein als ihren *Stil* bezeichnen kann, der auch bezogen auf eine Person als das irreduzibel Nicht-Allgemeine eines Textes verstanden werden kann, welcher im Rahmen eines Kon-Textes gedeutet werden muss. Und es gibt dabei eine Dialektik zwischen dem Sagbaren und dem Unsagbaren, zwischen der Ordnung der Zeichen und der Anarchie des Individuums, das sich ihrer bedient.[13] *Der zu verstehende Sinn gründet mithin nicht in einem Kontinuum aus lauter Sinn seinesgleichen, sondern in einem selbst nicht Sinnhaften. Die unmittelbare Durchsichtigkeit des Sinns ist schon im Ursprung getrübt;* und wenn man ihn als das Sagbare bezeichnen wollte, so müsste man seinen Ursprung allerdings das Schweigen nennen, wie z. B. Mallarmé es tut. Einerseits ist die Bestimmtheit des Gedankens ‚Ich' (d. h. sein Begriff) an die Differenz wenigstens zweier gegeneinander abgehobener Ausdrücke gebunden (Du denkst ‚Ich' und insofern alles andere nicht, also nicht ‚Nicht-Ich'). Andererseits muss diese Aufspaltung durch unmittelbare Anschauung ihrer Nicht-Geschiedenheit auch wieder unterlaufen werden, sonst ist eben das Andere nicht mehr dasselbe wie das Eine, und die unabdingbare Identität des Gedankens ‚Ich' wäre verfehlt. Zur Bedingung der Möglichkeit des Ich wird also seine Verausgabung an das Andere, und deshalb ist das Subjekt, wie schon Schleiermacher wusste, immer in der Krise.

Im Grunde kann man eine situative Bestimmung des sozialen Systems auf seine elementare Konstituentin, nämlich auf die Person, beziehen, indem man in der terminologischen Tradition der antiken (und damit im europäischen Kulturraum erstmaligen) Polis-Theorie die innere Krise des Individuums inmitten der Spannung zwischen seinen Polen von Ich (Je) und Selbst

---

[12] Jörg Villwock: *Signaturen des erdkolonialen Zeitalters. Physik und Philosophie – Mythologie und Erotik*, Aachen 2008, xxvi sq. (2. H.v.m.).
[13] Manfred Frank: *Das individuelle Allgemeine*, Frankfurt a. M. 1977, S. 297f. und S. 317f. (zum Beispiel).

(Moi) als *stásis* kennzeichnet, bezogen also auf ein Individuum, das zwischen präreflexivem und reflexivem Cogito eher verloren ist als zureichend positioniert, und die äußere Krise des Individuums inmitten anderer Individuen, die somit ihrer Anlage gemäß wesentlich aus dem kommunikativen Diskurs der verschiedenen Selbste entstammt, als *pólemos*. Mit anderen Worten: Der konstitutive Konflikt der Person selbst, dem jene Lücke zugrunde liegt, welche die Zustände des Cogitos in Ansich und Fürsich auftrennt, bewirkt recht eigentlich seine eigene Fortsetzung hinaus in jenen kommunikativen Konflikt, der die Wechselwirkung der Individuen auf dem Grund ihrer sozialen Vermitteltheit immer schon bestimmt. Wie es bei Frank heißt:

„Indem sich an der Faktizität unverfüglicher Selbstvermittlung des Subjektes Macht bricht, kommt es nicht länger in Frage als Ort, von dem her in monologisch verfahrender Deduktion über das objektiv Seiende historischer Welt geurteilt werden kann. Die Evidenz seiner Erkenntnisse muß sich vielmehr an intersubjektiver Kommunikation bewähren."[14]

Eben deshalb gibt es auch keine Denkgemeinschaft, die ihren dialektischen Konsens nicht in der Grammatik eines Sprachsystems niederlegte. Jede sprachliche Äußerung ist insofern – ganz gemäß Schleiermacher – wir würden heute sagen: durch Sprachsystem und Sprechweise formatiert. Oder anders: Sofern überhaupt gedacht wird, ist die Gesamtheit der Sprache als Differenzierungssystem immer schon vorausgesetzt. Es ist aber das Individuum, als im Wortsinne *poetisch* (nämlich: neuen Sinn produzierendes) Handelndes, welches aktiv zu differenzieren hat. Eben von diesem Aspekt aus gilt es, Kommunikation als Instrument der permanenten Vermittlung zu begreifen – oder wie Manfred Frank die berühmte Eingangspassage aus dem *Idiot der Familie* interpretiert:

„Man sollte den Menschen ein *einzelnes Allgemeines* nennen: Durch seine Epochenzugehörigkeit totalisiert (einem im Heideggerschen Sinne Bewandtnis-Ganzen eingefügt), ist er eben damit als ein Allgemeines definiert (universalisiert), aber er retotalisiert sie (er zieht die Grenzen dieses Ganzen einer Epoche dadurch neu), indem er sich in ihr als Einzelheit (Singularität) reproduziert."[15]

---

[14] Manfred Frank: „Einleitung", in: Ders.: *Das Sagbare und das Unsagbare*. Frankfurt a. Main 1980, vgl.: n. 16.; vgl. auch: Ders.: *Das individuelle Allgemeine*, S. 84ff.
[15] Manfred Frank: „Das Individuum in der Rolle des Idioten. Die hermeneutische Konzeption des *Flaubert*", in: Traugott König (Hrsg.): *Sartres Flaubert lesen. Essays zu Der Idiot der Familie*, Reinbek 1980, S. 84–108, hier: S. 92. Vgl. auch Ders.: „Archäologie des Individuums", in: Ders.: *Das Sagbare und das Unsagbare*, erweiterte Neuausgabe, Frankfurt a. M. 1990, S. 256–333, hier: 265.

Der ganze Prozess findet auf diese Weise im Spannungsfeld zwischen Faktizität und Transzendenz statt: Zum einen kann man das bereits dem Terminus vom „Bewandtnis-Ganzen" entnehmen, denn von den Techniken des Kollektivs erwartet, die bereitstehen, eine (wie Frank sie nennt) *Sozialisationsdressur* durchzuführen, gibt es für jedes Individuum vorab keinerlei Möglichkeit, der Totalisierung durch die herrschende Struktur zu entkommen. Indem aber die Individuen sich auf dem Grunde der vorgegebenen Ordnung auf eine Weise neu hervorbringen, die von Seiten (jener) Struktur gar nicht vorherzusehen war, bereiten sie einen Umsturz dieser Ordnung vor. Zugleich werden jedoch (und das ist das andere) alle diese Individuen für sich von der Kontingenz ihrer Interpretation (und deren Folgen) bedrängt, denn in der Hauptsache leiden sie alle unter einem Mangel an Begründung. Wie Sartre in seinem Kierkegaard-Vortrag von 1964 sagt:

> „Der Mensch, diese nicht wieder heil zu machende Einzelheit, ist das Seiende, durch welches das Allgemeine zur Welt kommt [...] Das Gelebte [...] das sind die nicht-bedeutenden Unwägbarkeiten des Seins, sofern sie über sich hinaus auf einen Sinn verweisen, den sie nicht schon von Beginn hatten und den ich das einzelne Allgemeine nennen möchte."[16]

Wir wissen bereits: Auf diese Unwägbarkeit gründet sich ihrerseits die zelebrierte *Angst*. Im Gegensatz zu Heidegger freilich, bei welchem diese auf das nichtende Nichts bezogen wird, gilt sie bei Sartre der Existenz selbst, präziser dem Ekel vor der Existenz. Lütkehaus hat dazu formuliert:

> „[Bei Sartre] wird [die Ontologie mithin] negativ-ästhetisch. Oder auch nur psychopathologisch – es sei denn, der Ekel hätte einen ausweisbaren philosophischen Sinn. Und den soll er haben."[17]

So fängt ja Sartre auch an, in *Das Sein und das Nichts*:

> „Hinter den Dingen, da gibt es zwar nichts. Trotzdem sind die Dinge nicht ganz und gar, was sie scheinen."[18]

---

[16] Jean-Paul Sartre: „L'Universel singulier", in: *Situations IX*, Paris 1972, S. 152–190, hier S. 175. Vgl. auch ebd., S. 178f. Zudem Frank: *Das Sagbare und das Unsagbare*, S. 184.
[17] Ludger Lütkehaus: *Nichts.*, Frankfurt a. M. 2010, S. 433. (Mit Bezug auf Sartres „Ekel", S. 136ff. und *Das Sein und das Nichts* 597f. Ich zitiere hier ausschließlich nach der deutschsprachigen Neu-Übersetzung in der Ausgabe von Traugott König: *Das Sein und das Nichts*, Reinbek 1993, nehme aber an der Übersetzung von Zeit zu Zeit einige (dann auch bezeichnete) Modifikationen vor.
[18] Ebd., 434 (mit Bezug auf *Das Sein und das Nichts* 131).

Wenn also das Fazit lautet: „Nichts. Existiert."[19] dann ist damit nicht gemeint, es gäbe keine Möglichkeit der Befreiung aus der selbstverschuldeten Befangenheit. Nochmals Lütkehaus dazu:

> „Die Hölle, das sind die Anderen. Damit kann man zur Not leben. Die Hölle – es gibt nichts anderes: damit lebt und stirbt es sich ziemlich schlecht."[20]

Für Sartre heißt somit, die Frage nach dem Grund der Existenz stellen, die Existenz ausgerechnet mit dieser Frage weitertreiben.[21] Es geht also um eine permanente Dynamik, die sich selbst nicht einzuholen in der Lage ist. In diesem Sinne hat das Für-sich nicht bloß Fragen, es *ist* eine Frage:

> „Seine Realität ist rein interrogativ. Wenn es Fragen stellen kann, so deshalb, weil es selbst immer in Frage steht; sein Sein ist nie gegeben, sondern erfragt."[22]

Die Infragestellung des Seins ist in diesem Sinne das Nichts. Das hat Lütkehaus ganz richtig zusammengefasst. Und die Frage nach dem Grund des Seins verschiebt sich zu der nach dem Ursprung des Nichts.[23] Zugleich heißt es, dass die menschliche Realität der einzige Grund des Nichts innerhalb des Seins sei. Insbesondere ist das Für-sich als Seinsbewusstsein vom Sein durch nichts getrennt.[24] Das Für-sich wird letztlich aus dem Geist der Nichtung geboren.

> „Die abgründige Ambivalenz dieser auf den grundlosen Grund des Nichts gestellten Freiheit zeigt die Philosophie des menschlichen Selbstentwurfs."[25]

Wir müssen hier aber sorgfältig zwischen dem *Nichts* (rien) und dem *Nichtsein* (néant) unterscheiden (obwohl auch Sartre selbst diese Unterscheidung nicht immer allzu genau beachtet): Das Erste ist das, was nicht ist, aber sein kann, also das Mögliche (griechisch: mè ón); das Zweite ist das, was nicht ist, aber auch nicht sein kann, also das Unmögliche (griechisch: ouk ón). Das erste muss aber weiter differenziert werden: Denn es gibt das denkbare (mithin auch sagbare) Nichts und das undenkbare (mithin unsagbare) Nichts. Soll deshalb

---

[19] Ebd., 443.
[20] Ebd., 443.
[21] Ebd., 444. (par.) Man sehe hierzu im Vergleich Ernst Bloch: *Das Materialismus-Problem*, Frankfurt a. M. 1985, S. 450.
[22] Ebd., 449 (Mit Bezug auf *Das Sein und das Nichts* 1058).
[23] Ebd., 450.
[24] Ebd., 450f.
[25] Ebd., 452.

das Nichts der Grund von Allem sein, so kann es sich nur um das letztere, das
undenkbare Nichts handeln, das als Grund dann zugleich tatsächlich Ungrund
oder Abgrund ist. Und daher heißt es auch bei Lütkehaus, speziell auf Sartre
bezogen:

> „Das Sein des An-sich ist nicht nur unbegründet, es kennt überhaupt keinen
> Grund. Es ist, was es nun einmal ist, in seiner völligen, unableitbaren Kontingenz.
> Diese gilt auch für das Sein des Für-sichs; Sartre nennt sie seine Faktizität."[26]

Zugleich aber entfaltet sich parallel zur Faktizität die *Transzendenz*, deren
Konfrontation jedoch welthaft als Aktualität zu verstehen ist und ansonsten
von der Immanenz der Welt immer schon übergriffen wird (wie bereits bei
Spinoza): Mit anderen Worten, diese Begriffe bezeichnen lediglich das welthaft Zugängliche, nicht dessen Grund, der nicht unter dieselbe Terminologie
fallen kann. So ist der Mensch transzendent, weil er über jede Erfahrung hin-
ausreicht, die man mit ihm (welthaft-empirisch!) machen kann. Was vor allem
daran liegt, dass die Beziehung des Ego zu den Qualitäten wesentlich ein Verhältnis der poetischen Produktion ist, wie Sartre bereits frühzeitig anmerkt.[27]
Um sich daher in der Welt gehörig einzurichten, bedarf es einer angemessenen
Haltung diesem Konflikt von Faktizität und Transzendenz gegenüber. Und
das ist gerade die skandalöse Überforderung des konkret vorfindlichen Menschen, der er annähernd bestenfalls unter größter Reflexionsanstrengung nach-
zukommen imstande ist.

Thomas Flynn hat es auf den Punkt gebracht: Authentisch ist eine Existenz im Sinne Sartres dann, wenn sie die immanente Dualität zwischen Faktizität und Transzendenz in einer „schöpferischen Spannung" zu halten in der
Lage ist.

> „Die Unaufrichtigkeit [so nennt sie bei Flynn der Übersetzer Erik M. Vogt]
> flieht vor dieser Spannung (und ihrer *Angst*), indem sie entweder die Transzen-
> denz zur Faktizität kollabieren läßt oder die Faktizität zur Transzendenz ver-
> flüchtigt. Beide Versuche stellen eine Verleugnung unserer ontologischen Ver-
> fassung dar und sind aus diesem Grunde zum Scheitern verurteilt."[28]

---

[26] Ebd., 453.
[27] Jean Paul Sartre: *Transzendenz des Ego: Philosophische Essay 1931–1939,*. Reinbek, 1982, S. 71.
[28] Thomas R. Flynn: *Existenzialismus. Eine kurze Einführung*, Wien 2008, S. 189.

Die Lösung kann also 1. immer nur approximativ sein und 2. nur in einer ästhetischen Durchdringung der konkreten Ethik erreicht werden. Aber in beidem – also im sich auf den Weg begeben auf ein Ziel hin (Bloch hätte gesagt: unter der Invarianten der Richtung) und in der Invention einer ästhetisch begründeten (mithin innovativen) Lebensführung – also in diesen beiden Handlungsweisen, besteht bereits das, was Sartres *authentisches Verhalten* nennt. Und im Übrigen besteht darin – nicht ganz ohne historische Ironie – der Sartre'sche Rekurs auf das Freud'sche Unbewusste (das Sartre ja zuerst abgelehnt hatte), denn durch dieses authentische Verhalten gewinnt Lacans berühmte Freud-Paraphrase ihre Geltung: „Wo *Es* (mit keinem *das* oder anderem vergegenständlichenden Artikel versehenes Objekt) *war* (es ist ein Ort des Seins, um den es sich handelt, und an diesem Ort) *soll* (das ist ein Sollen im moralischen Sinne, welches sich da ankündigt, […]) *Ich* (je, das soll Ich, wie wenn man verkündete: ce suis-je, bevor man sagt: c'est moi) *werden* (das heißt, nicht vorkommen, survenir, noch selbst ankommen, advenir, sondern an den Tag des Ortes selbst kommen, venir au jour de ce lieu lui-même, insofern er der Ort des Seins ist). Es beginnt also alles immer noch mit dem antiken „Gnothi s'auton!" nur daß es jetzt auf Lacan'sche Art gewendet wird im Begriffspaar: me connaître = méconnaître. Und das Ego zerfällt in die zwei Pole: sujet véritable (Je) vs. sujet narcissique (Moi). Wie Lacan sagt: „Je pense où je ne suis pas, donc je suis où je ne pense pas." – denn ich befinde mich zwar auf dem Weg zum Ziel, bin mir dabei aber immer selbst voraus. Es kommt jedoch darauf an, das zu wissen.[29]

Wichtig ist hierbei, dass ein wechselseitiges *Verfehlen der Diskurse* immer schon angelegt ist, denn ich stelle meinen Weltbezug überhaupt erst her, indem ich mich zum anderen wie zu einem Objekt verhalte, gerade weil ich auf den Weltbezug abziele, *durch den Anderen hindurch*. Weil die Anderen zur selben Zeit das Gleiche tun, erhellt daraus, dass sich alle am je Anderen vorbei-verhalten und im Prinzip nur die eigene Konstitution betreiben. Wie Lacan später sagen wird (und wie Sartre wird letztlich bestätigen müssen), appelliere ich schon immer mittels meines Diskurses an den Anderen, indem ich seinen Diskurs zu meinen Gunsten besetze. Und eben dies tut der Andere entsprechend. Die Pointe dabei ist aber, dass gleichwohl ein konsensueller Diskurs möglich ist, der seine Stabilität gerade aus jenen Bereichen wechsel-

---

[29] Frank: *Das individuelle Allgemeine*, S. 79 (par.).

seitigen Verfehlens schöpft, die im Grunde den ganzen Diskurs zugleich redundant machen und recht eigentlich in einen poetischen Spielraum der Interpretation verwandeln.

Wir wussten es bereits von Schelling: Es geht im Grunde um eine Form der Selbstreferenz. Schon in den Kriegstagebüchern sagt Sartre:

> „So ist also der Sinn unserer Situation in jedem Augenblick gegeben durch die Möglichkeiten-Optionen, noematische Korrelate unseres Wollens, die uns in der Zukunft erwarten. Und sie sind es, die unsere Perspektiven motivieren und gestalten."[30]

Diese Möglichkeiten-Optionen erscheinen also „[...] am Horizont meiner Handlungen als ihr Sinn", und ich produziere indem ich handle. Gerade dieser Zirkel von Sinn und Handlung verweist auf die Selbstreferenz. Die reale Zukunft als Sinn meiner Gegenwart sind die Optionen.[31]

So hat Lacan letztlich Recht:

> „Das Unbewußte ist der Diskurs des Anderen."[32] „Gibt es", fragt Lacan, „ sich des Punktes, in dem man sich täuscht, zu vergewissern, ein besseres Mittel, als den anderen von der Wahrheit dessen zu überzeugen, was man vorbringt?"[33]

Das ist die Grundstruktur der Liebe: den anderen überzeugen, dass er das habe, was uns zu ergänzen vermag. Damit sichern wir uns zu, weiterhin verkennen zu können, was uns fehlt. Und das ist das grundsätzliche (Ver-)Fehlen bei Lacan:

> „[Diesem] begegnet das Subjekt im Anderen, in Form jener Einladung, die der Andere in seiner Rede an es ergehen läßt. In den Intervallen des Diskurses dieses Anderen entsteht dann für die [...] Erfahrung etwas, dessen radikaler Ausdruck in der Formel *Er sagt mir das, aber was will er?* zusammenzufassen wäre."[34]

---

[30] Jean-Paul Sartre: *Carnets de la drôle de guerre*. Septembre 1939 – Mars 1940, hrsg. v. Arlette Elkaïm-Sartre, Paris, 1983, 1995. Deutsche Ausgabe: Jean-Paul Sartre: *Tagebücher. November 1939 – März 1940*, aus d. Franz. von Eva Moldenhauert, Reinbek 1984. Hier *Carnets de la drôle de guerre* 56/61.
[31] *Carnets de la drôle de guerre* 58/64.
[32] Jacques Lacan: *Seminar. Die vier Grundbegriffe der Psychoanalyse*, übers. v. Norbert Haas, Olten/Freiburg 1980, 140.
[33] Ebd.
[34] Ebd., 225.

Der Diskurs rekurriert in seinem Verfehlen auf die Differenz. Die ethische Forderung besteht darin, dass ich die Differenz nicht nur zur Sprache bringe, sondern auch noch auf den Begriff. Nochmals der unvergleichliche Lacan:

> „Ich liebe Hammelragout. Das ist das gleiche, als wenn Sie sagen würden – *Ich liebe Frau Soundso*, nur mit dem Unterschied, daß Sie das zu ihr sagen, und das ändert alles."[35]

3.

Zum expliziten Verhältnis Sartres zur Philosophie Leibnizens hat ja bereits vor längerer Zeit Jürgen Herbst zureichend Erschöpfendes ausgeführt.[36] Vor allem kommt dabei zum Ausdruck, dass Sartre noch während seiner Studienzeit Leibniz zwar ausgiebig studiert, ihn dann aber nicht gerade zu einem seiner Favoriten erklärt hat. Unter systematischen Aspekten wird allerdings die Beschäftigung mit dem Freiheitsbegriff bei Leibniz durchaus relevant: Dazu schreibt Sartre in seinem frühen Hauptwerk *Das Sein und das Nichts*:

> „Es ist seltsam, daß man endlos über den Determinismus und den freien Willen hat diskutieren und Beispiele zugunsten der einen oder der anderen These hat anführen können, ohne vorher zu versuchen, die in der Idee des *Handelns* selbst enthaltenen Strukturen zu klären."[37] Und er konstatiert: „Zunächst muß man nämlich darauf hinweisen, daß ein Handeln grundsätzlich *intentional* ist."[38]

und weiter: […] daß Handeln als seine Bedingung notwendig die Erkenntnis eines objektiven Mangels impliziert.[39] Er fährt fort:

> „Das bedeutet, daß er [der Handelnde] Abstand gegenüber dem Leid gewonnen und eine zweifache Nichtung ausgeführt haben muß: einerseits muß er nämlich

---

[35] Ebd.
[36] Jürgen Herbst: „Leibniz und Sartre", in: *Tradition und Aktualität. V. Internationaler Leibniz-Kongreß Vorträge*. Bd. 2, Hannover 1988, S. 202–221.
[37] Jean-Paul Sartre: *L'Etre et le néant*, Paris 1943. – Ich zitiere hier wie auch schon im ersten Teil des vorliegenden Papiers ausschließlich nach der deutschsprachigen Neu-Übersetzung in der Ausgabe von Traugott König: *Das Sein und das Nichts*, Reinbek 1993, nehme aber an der Übersetzung von Zeit zu Zeit einige (dann auch bezeichnete) Modifikationen vor. Hier: *Das Sein und das Nichts* 753
[38] Ebd.
[39] *Das Sein und das Nichts* 754, par.

einen idealen Zustand als reines *gegenwärtiges* Nichtsein[40] setzen, andererseits muß er die augenblickliche Situation in Bezug auf diesen Zustand als / Nichtsein setzen."[41]

Somit heißt es schließlich:

„Daraus ergeben sich zwei wichtige Folgerungen: 1. kein faktischer Zustand […] kann von sich aus irgendeine Handlung motivieren. […] 2. kein faktischer Zustand kann das Bewußtsein dazu bestimmen, ihn als Negatität oder Mangel zu erfassen. […] Also hat jedes Handeln zur ausdrücklichen Bedingung nicht nur die Entdeckung eines Zustands als ‚Mangel an …', das heißt als Negatität, sondern auch – und zuvor – die Konstituierung des betrachteten Zustands als isoliertes System."[42]

Damit evoziert Sartre sein eigenes Entwurfsmodell:

„Für das Bewußtsein impliziert das die permanente Möglichkeit, mit seiner eigenen Vergangenheit zu brechen, sich von ihr loszureißen, um sie im Licht eines Nichtseienden[43] betrachten und ihr die Bedeutung verleihen zu können, die sie *hat* vom Entwurf eines Sinns aus, den *sie nicht hat*."[44]

Denn für Sartre hat die Freiheit tatsächlich kein Wesen. Er formuliert mit Verweis auf Heidegger:

„In ihr [der Freiheit] geht die Existenz der Essenz voraus und beherrscht sie. Die Freiheit macht sich zur Handlung […]"[45] Anders gesagt: „Die Freiheit ist genau das Nichtsein, das im Kern des Menschen *gewesen wird* [est été] und die menschliche-Realität zwingt, *sich zu machen* statt *zu sein*. Wir haben gesehen, daß sein für die menschliche-Realität *sich wählen* ist […]"[46]

In diesem Sinne konfrontiert Sartre seinen eigenen Ansatz mit jenem Leibnizens: Am Beispiel Adams listet Sartre die Hauptpunkte des Leibniz'schen Freiheitsverständnisses auf. Er formuliert:

---

[40] Meine eigene Modifikation hier und beim nächsten Mal statt „Nichts". („[…] il faudra qu'il pose un état de choses idéal comme pur néant *présent*, d'autre part il faudra qu'il pose la situation actuelle comme néant par rapport à cet état de choses." (Edition TEL, 1986, 489).
[41] *Das Sein und das Nichts* 756f.
[42] *Das Sein und das Nichts* 757.
[43] Hier eigene Übersetzung statt „Nicht-sein". (im Original: „non-être", op. cit., 490).
[44] *Das Sein und das Nichts* 758.
[45] *Das Sein und das Nichts* 761.
[46] *Das Sein und das Nichts* 765. Hier eigene Übersetzung: einmal „Nichtsein" (néant) statt „Nichts" und „wird gewesen" (est été) statt „wird geseint." (Op. cit., 495).

„Für Leibniz ist also die von der menschlichen-Realität erforderte Freiheit so etwas wie die Organisation dreier verschiedener Begriffe: frei ist, wer 1. sich rational dazu bestimmt, eine Handlung zu vollbringen, 2. so ist, daß diese Handlung durch die Natur dessen, der sie vollbracht hat, vollständig zu verstehen ist, 3. kontingent ist, das heißt in der Weise existiert, daß andere Individuen, die anläßlich der gleichen Situation andere Handlungen vollbringen, möglich gewesen wären."[47]

Er fährt fort:

„Aber wegen der notwendigen Verknüpfung der Möglichkeiten wäre eine andere Bewegung Adams nur für und durch einen anderen Adam möglich gewesen, und [dessen] Existenz [...] implizierte die einer anderen Welt. Wir erkennen mit Leibniz an, daß die Bewegung / Adams die ganze Person Adams engagiert und daß eine andere Bewegung im Licht und im Rahmen einer anderen Persönlichkeit Adams zu verstehen gewesen wäre. Leibniz fällt aber in einen der Freiheitsidee gänzlich entgegengesetzten Necessitarismus zurück, wenn er gerade die Formel von der Substanz Adams an den Anfang stellt als eine Prämisse, die Adams Handlung als eine ihrer partiellen Schlüsse herbeiführt, das heißt, wenn er die chronologische Ordnung darauf reduziert, lediglich ein symbolischer Ausdruck der logischen Ordnung zu sein. Daraus ergibt sich nämlich einerseits, daß die Handlung gerade durch das Wesen Adams strikt notwendig gemacht ist, und auch die Kontingenz, die nach Leibniz die Freiheit möglich macht, findet sich ganz und gar im Wesen Adams enthalten. Und dieses Wesen wird nicht von Adam selbst gewählt, sondern von Gott. [...] Folglich trägt er [Adam] keineswegs die Verantwortung für sein Sein [und insofern auch nicht für seine Handlung]. [...] Für uns dagegen ist Adam keineswegs durch ein Wesen definiert, denn das Wesen kommt bei der menschlichen-Realität nach der Existenz."[48]

Für Sartre drückt die Kontingenz Adams stattdessen die abgeschlossene Wahl aus, die er von sich selbst getroffen hat:

„Von da an ist aber das, was ihm seine Person anzeigt, zukünftig und nicht vergangen: er wählt, sich das, was er ist, durch die Zwecke lehren zu lassen, auf die hin er sich entwirft – das heißt durch die Totalität seiner / Vorlieben, Neigungen, Abneigungen usw., insofern es eine thematische Organisation und einen dieser Totalität inhärenten *Sinn* gibt."[49]

Die Person ist somit für Sartre in ihrer Einheit zu verstehen:

---

[47] *Das Sein und das Nichts* 810.
[48] *Das Sein und das Nichts* 810 sq.
[49] *Das Sein und das Nichts* 811 sq.

„Diese Einheit, die das Sein des betreffenden Menschen ist, ist *freie Vereinigung*. […] Die unreduzierbare Vereinigung, der wir begegnen müssen, die [z. B.] Flaubert *ist* und die uns zu enthüllen wir von den Biographen verlangen, ist also die Vereinigung eines *ursprünglichen Entwurfs*, eine Vereinigung, die sich als ein *nichtsubstantielles Absolutes* enthüllen muß. Deshalb müssen wir auf Unreduzierbares im Detail verzichten und dürfen, indem wir die Evidenz selbst zum Kriterium nehmen, in unserer Untersuchung nicht stehenbleiben, bevor es evident ist, daß wir weder weitergehen können noch müssen."[50]

4.

Die Abgrenzung Sartres gegen Leibniz dürfte klargeworden sein: Es geht ihm vor allem um die Abwesenheit eigener Verantwortung angesichts des Einwirkens durch den Herrn selbst. Auch, wenn Jürgen Herbst einst darauf hingewiesen hatte, dass Sartre hier offenbar den postaugustinischen Gottesbegriff bei Leibniz nicht korrekt in Rechnung gestellt hat (Hans Poser hat schon 1981 Einiges dazu ausgeführt)[51], kann man der Sartre'schen Kritik an Leibniz hier doch durchaus folgen, denn am Ende ist auch ein Gott, der nicht selbst eingreift und auf diese Weise einen Spielraum des Handelns offenlässt, ebenso wenig befriedigend wie ein Gott, der alles immer genau reguliert. Im Grunde steht hier Sartres Kritik am Idealismus im Hintergrund, obwohl er selbst auch seinen eigenen ethischen Ansatz im Nachgang zu *Das Sein und das Nichts* (wie in den erst posthum veröffentlichten *Cahiers pour une morale* deutlich zu sehen) als immer noch idealistisch kritisiert. In der Hauptsache ist der Kernpunkt Sartres zu jener frühen Zeit im Entwurf einer expliziten Differenzphilosophie zu sehen, welche darauf ausgeht, in der ethischen Anwendung (und das heißt letztlich: im freien Handeln) die Differenz des je Anderen als andere stehenzulassen und mit in Rechnung zu stellen. Darauf gründet das ganze Prinzip des Engagements: Praktisch geht es darum, die Bedingungen sicherzustellen, die es dem Anderen ermöglichen, sein Recht auf freies Handeln auszuüben – es geht aber eben nicht darum, an seiner Stelle zu handeln, das heißt, ihm seine eigenen Ziele zu entwenden (das wäre es, was die Identitätsphilosophie traditionell auszuführen unternimmt und in ihren Begriff von der Solidarität einfließen lässt). Die Konsequenz seiner Selbstkritik aber ist die Hinwendung zur marxistischen Theorie, und zwar insbesondere in Hinsicht auf *die gesellschaftlichen Randbedingungen des Handelns*. Das ist im Wesentlichen

---

[50] *Das Sein und das Nichts* 963.
[51] Herbst: „Leibniz und Sartre", S. 214f. nebst n. 62 zu Hans Posers Publikation.

das, was Sartre 1960 in der *Kritik der dialektischen Vernunft* und in deren Einleitung („Fragen zur Methode") umsetzt: Zwar bleibt der Ansatz einer Differenzethik bestehen, dieser wird aber nunmehr im Hinblick auf die praktischen Bedingungen befragt. Sartre formuliert:

> „Für uns ist der Mensch vor allem durch das Überschreiten einer Situation gekennzeichnet, durch das, was ihm aus dem zu machen gelingt, was man aus ihm gemacht hat, selbst wenn er sich niemals in seiner Vergegenständlichung erkennt. [...] selbst das rudimentärste Verhalten muß sich zugleich mit Bezug auf reale, vorliegende Faktoren, die es bedingen, und mit Bezug auf ein bestimmtes zukünftiges Objekt, das es entstehen zu lassen sucht, bestimmen. Das aber nennen wir *Entwurf*."[52]

Man sieht bereits, dass die existentielle Grundbestimmung des Menschen hier nicht nur als Differenz der Differenz angesetzt wird, sondern dass sich zugleich eine Wendung von den letzten Resten des Idealismus zum Materialismus vollzieht:

> „[...] die materiellen Verhältnisse seiner [des Menschen] Existenz umreißen das Feld seiner Möglichkeiten [...] [Dieses aber] bildet daher das Ziel, woraufhin der Handelnde seine objektive Situation überschreitet."[53] Und weiter: „Gerade im Überschreiten des Gegebenen auf das Feld des Möglichen hin und im Realisieren einer Möglichkeit von allen leistet das Individuum seine Objektivierung und seinen Beitrag zur Geschichte; denn sein Entwurf gewinnt alsdann eine Realität, die der Handelnde vielleicht gar nicht zu überschauen vermag und die durch die Konflikte, die sie offenbart und erzeugt, den Lauf des Geschehens beeinflußt."[54]

Sartre geht also davon aus, jenes Feld des Möglichen für eine gegebene Epoche zu bestimmen, und er sieht letztlich darin das methodologische Novum, welches darin besteht, dem wesentlich regressiven Vorgehen der marxistischen Geschichtsmethode eine progressive Komponente hinzuzufügen. Wir wissen, dass später der Entwurf in der Hauptsache von der Werkproduktion des Individuums bestimmt wird und die Berücksichtigung beider methodischen Komponenten, in ihrer Zusammenführung zu einer allumfassenden progressiv-regressiven Methode, die als universelle Biographieforschung inmitten

---

[52] Ich zitiere hier nach der deutschen Übersetzung von Herbert Schmitt, erschienen bei Rowohlt, Reinbek, unter dem Titel Jean-Paul Sartre: *Marxismus und Existentialismus. Versuch einer Methodik*, Reinbek 1983 (1964), S. 75.
[53] Ebd., S. 76.
[54] Ebd., S. 77.

eines gesellschaftlichen Kontextes unter anderem am Beispiel Flauberts detailliert angewendet wird, von Sartre als erste Approximation an einen künftigen, noch zu entwickelnden Marxismus verstanden wird. Damit vervollständigt er das Projekt einer marxistischen Ethik, die bis zu diesem Zeitpunkt eher als uneinheitlich und wesentlich unklar angesehen werden musste. Philip Kain hat bereits in einer interessanten Betrachtung von 1988 auf diesen Umstand hingewiesen.[55] Spätestens an dieser Stelle (also 1960) verabschiedet sich Sartre von der idealistischen Philosophie, die er auch dann nicht mehr aufnimmt, als Benny Lévy in jenem zelebrierten letzten Interview im „Nouvel Observateur" vom März 1980 ihm dies versucht nahezulegen.[56]

---

[55] Philip J. Kain: *Marx and Ethics*, Oxford 1988.
[56] *L'Espoir maintenant. Le nouvel observateur*, 10., 17., 24. März 1980.

Leibnizforschung im Spiegel von zehn Leibniz-Kongressen

Hans Poser (Berlin)

Der X. Internationale Leibniz-Kongress, von Wenchao Li und seinen Mitarbeitern überaus sorgfältig und facettenreich organisiert und mit dem tiefdringenden Vortrag von Heinrich Schepers gekrönt, verlangt eine Rückbesinnung auf den in fünf Jahrzehnten zurückgelegten Weg nicht nur im Blick auf die Leibnizforschung. Natürlich beruhen alle zehn Kongresse auf der Einsicht, dass es nicht einfach um das Werk eines Universalgenies geht und ging, sondern dass all unser Denken und Reflektieren seine Wurzeln in der Geschichte hat, die unsere Sprache, unser Denken und unsere Werte tradiert und geformt hat. So ist jede Rückbesinnung auf einen Großen zugleich ein Klärungsprozess unserer eigenen Sicht – für jeden Einzelnen gerade so wie für jede Gesellschaft. Darum mag ein ganz subjektiver Blick zurück erlaubt sein, der zugleich verdeutlichen soll, wie gegenwärtige Forschung auch bezogen ist auf die jeweilige historische Situation.

Ungefähr drei Jahre vor Leibniz' 250. Todestag begannen in der Niedersächsischen Landesbibliothek Hannover, der Bewahrerin des immer noch nur in kleinen Teilen ausgeschöpften Erbes der 200 000 Blätter Leibniz'scher Manuskripte, die Überlegungen, dieses Ereignis zum Anlass zu nehmen, einer allerersten internationalen Leibniz-Kongress zu planen. Die treibenden Kräfte waren Wilhelm Totok, der Leitende Bibliotheksdirektor, Kurt Müller als Leibniz-Editor und der Bonner Philosoph Gottfried Martin, dessen Leibniz-Buch 1960 erschienen war. Dazu kamen die Mitarbeiter des Leibniz-Archivs, zu denen bald schon Albert Heinekamp gehörte, der bei Martin über Leibniz promoviert hatte und später Leiter des Leibniz-Archivs und dessen Editionen werden sollte. Es galt, Leibnizforscher aus aller Welt zusammenzuführen. Die Ausgangslage war günstig: Kein anderer als die Landesbibliothek hätte deren Namen und Adressen nennen können, weil bei ihr nicht nur die Leibniz-Sekundärliteratur so vollständig wie möglich gesammelt wird, sondern vor allem, weil jeder ernsthafte Leibnizforscher schon einmal bei ihr einen Blick in die Manuskripte geworfen hatte: Im alten Bibliotheksgebäude, dessen Etagen zur besseren Durchlüftung mit eisernen Gittern in den Fußböden verbunden waren, stand nahe den Leibniz'schen Faszikeln ein Schreibpult, respektvoll „das Bodemannsche" genannt, weil Bodemann an ihm seine Katalogisierung vorgenommen haben soll. Daran anschließend befand sich ein weit ausladender Tisch, auf dem die erbetenen Manuskripte eingesehen werden durften. Öffnete man solch eine Mappe, lag obenauf eine Liste, in die sich der Leser einzutragen hatte – unter Namen wie „Grua" oder „Belaval" oder „Robinet", Namen, die dem kleinen Leibniz-Anfänger, dem TU-Assistenten Poser gewaltigen Respekt einflößten (leider sind Bögen heute entfernt, zum Schutz der Privatsphäre, wie es heißt). Dort lesend kam es dazu, dass jener Anfänger in manche dieser vorbereitenden Gespräche einbezogen wurde: Wir waren völlig sicher, dass die Planungen einem ganz großen Ziel dienten; so wurden Konzepte, Finanzierungsanträge, Raumplanungen entworfen. Die Stadt Hannover war voller Stolz bereit, ihre monumentale Stadthalle zur Verfügung zu stellen. Die Firma Bahlsen übernahm die Versendung der Einladungen – wobei ein Leibniz-Keks-Firmenstempel den Umschlag zierte, weshalb mancher Adressat zunächst glaubte, es mit einer Werbekampagne zu tun zu haben. Doch das Wunderbare war die Begeisterung, mit der alle Angeschriebenen reagierten und ihre Mitwirkung zusagten: so alles, was beispielsweise in der französischen Leibnizforschung Rang und Namen hatte, etwa Ivon Belaval, Pierre Costabel, Jaques Jalabert, Joseph Moreau… Was Wunder, dass es der kleine TU-Assistent angesichts dieser Namen für vermessen gehalten hätte, der Bitte Heinekamps zu folgen, aus der gerade entstehenden Dissertation auch einen Beitrag anzumelden. Stattdessen half er an anderer Stelle: Man konnte damals durchaus nicht erwarten, dass etwa englische Vorträge hörend verstanden werden würden; so machten wir uns daran, eingereichte Manuskripte auf Wachsmatrizen abzuschreiben oder gar zu übersetzen, um sie den Kongressbesuchern an die Hand zu geben; mir war es dabei zugefallen, als begeisterter Leser von Harry Parkinsons *Logic and Reality in Leibniz's Metaphysics* dessen Beitrag zu übersetzen.

Sie alle kamen – doch eine Besonderheit aller Leibniz-Kongresse war es, anders als bei anderen Tagungen und Kongressen üblich, keineswegs mit längst benannten Keynote Speakers zu werben und Attraktivität zu suggerieren, sondern das ‚Familientreffen' der Leibnizianer anzukündigen: Die jeweilige inhaltliche Struktur wurde aufgrund der durchgesehenen Anmeldungen vorgenommen. Diese überaus offenen Familientreffen waren und sind durch einen harmonischen Umgang auch dann gekennzeichnet, wenn recht unterschiedliche Sichtweisen zusammenkommen: Leibnizforschung verlangt Bescheidenheit und Achtung anderer Auslegungen angesichts der Überfülle des Nachlasses, der Weite des Horizonts des großen Denkers und des Leitgedankens, eine bessere Welt zu erstreben. Solche Friedfertigkeit ist nicht selbstverständlich – gibt es doch Tagungsbeispiele für These hier, Antithese da, wo an die Stelle der Synthese persönliche Gegnerschaft tritt.

Sie alle kamen – jene, die bislang eher einsam über Leibniz gearbeitet hatten, als auch jene, die in der Analyse ‚ihres' Philosophen Verbindungen zu

Leibniz ziehen wollten. So wurde der erste Kongress zu einer großen Plattform, die bislang isolierte Untersuchungen über alle Grenzen hinweg zusammenführte, Ansätze aufzeigte und vor allem die Fruchtbarkeit einer weiteren, tiefergehenden, die neu verfügbaren Texte der Edition aufzunehmenden Forschung deutlich werden ließ. Rückblickend und vom X. Kongress her gesehen, haben sich diese Hoffnungen mehr als bestätigt: Zwar war 1966 schon am Bild der französischen Forschung ablesbar, dass es neben metaphysischen Problemen auch logische und naturwissenschaftliche Ansätze zu verfolgen galt, doch selbst die metaphysische Seite erscheint heute dank weiterer Quellen und neuer Analysen viel differenzierter; so hat etwa die substantia corporea im Laufe der letzten Jahrzehnte vor allem dank der angloamerikanischen Forschung eine eigene Bedeutung gewonnen. Ebenso wurden logische und mathematische Fragestellungen in viel größerer Tiefe ausgelotet, die Untersuchungen zur Dynamica verheißen geradeso neue Einsichten wie die fortschreitende Analyse der Leibniz'schen Rechtstheorie. Während das alles wie eine bloße Aufarbeitung historischer Positionen erscheint, gilt es doch festzuhalten, dass diese Analysen zugleich Anlass geben, Gegenwartspositionen neu zu durchdenken, sei es in Gestalt neuer Monadologien, sei es in Neudeutungen komplexer Systeme oder der Quantenphysik: Leibniz' Gedankengut ist rundum lebendig.

Nun sind gerade die Leibniz-Kongresse keine isolierten Ereignisse im Wolkenkuckucksheim, sondern reale Geschehnisse in realen geschichtlichen Situationen. Dies gilt es näher zu beleuchten. Darum zurück zum ersten Kongress:

Sie alle kamen – die Großen aus Frankreich, aus der Bundesrepublik etwa Johann Christian Horn und Wolfgang Janke und Hans Georg Gadamer als damaliger Präsident der deutschen Philosophen, aus den USA Leroy Earl Loemker, Nicholas Rescher und Margret D. Wilson, doch auch aus Großbritannien und Italien, aus Finnland und Japan und vielen anderen Ländern. So ließe sich scheinbar unbeschwert fortfahren – aber 1961 war die Mauer gebaut, die DDR durch den ‚eisernen Vorhang' des Kalten Kriegs von der Bundesrepublik hermetisch abgeriegelt worden. Darum war es nicht selbstverständlich, dass auch Forscher wie beispielsweise Eduard Winter und Franz Schmidt aus der DDR, Anna Simonovitis aus Ungarn, Waldemar Voisé aus Polen und Pavlovič Juškevič aus der Sowjetunion teilnehmen konnten. Überdeutlich war zu spüren, dass es darum ging, im Leibniz'schen Geist Brücken zu schlagen. Dies spiegelte sich auch in der Gottfried-Wilhelm-Leibniz-Gesellschaft, gegründet im Zuge des Kongresses: Als internationale Organisation wollte sie allen Leibnizforschern aller Nationen eine Heimstatt sein. So hatte dieser Kongress auch in einem viel weiteren Sinne eine nationenübergreifende Bedeutung.

Zu Beginn des ersten Kongresses lagen 13 Bände der Akademie-Ausgabe von Leibniz' Schriften vor, davon 7 aus der Nachkriegsperiode. In der Folgezeit wurde die Frage aufgeworfen, ob man nicht die ganze Leibniz-Akademie-Ausgabe in den Westen verlagern solle; denn die großen Arbeitsstellen waren beginnend in den 50er Jahren von Ost-Berlin nach Münster und Hannover gewandert, dort war die Mehrzahl der neuen Bände erarbeitet worden, in Hannover lagen und liegen die Manuskripte – aber gedruckt und verlegt wurde die Akademie-Ausgabe in der DDR. Wäre das alles nicht ein Grund, die Gesamtkonzeption in die Bundesrepublik zu transferieren? Doch mit Nachdruck wurde dem widersprochen: Ich erinnere mich, wie Gottfried Martin betonte, gerade diese Akademie-Ausgabe sei die letzte wirklich funktionierende Brücke im wissenschaftlichen Bereich – sie dürfe unter keinen Umständen eingerissen werden.

Während der nachfolgenden Kongresse 1972, 1977, 1983 und 1988 entspannte oder ‚normalisierte' sich die Lage – die Berlinverträge sicherten den Bestand West-Berlins und dessen Zufahrtswege, die wechselseitigen Kontakte wurden durchaus möglich, wenngleich nicht immer einfach. Die ideologischen Hürden wurden bei Einladungen gen Osten etwa so umschifft: Leibniz ist der Vater des deutschen Idealismus, der wiederum ist der Vater des Marxismus; dann sollte einer, der über den Großvater arbeitet, doch willkommen sein. So wurde der V. Kongress 1988 – der letzte, den Albert Heinekamp organisierte – eröffnet auch mit einem von Juškevič übermitteltem Grußwort der Akademie der Wissenschaften der UdSSR und mit einem Grußwort des Präsidenten der Akademie der Wissenschaften der DDR; die DDR war mit einer eigenen ‚Delegation' beteiligt. Doch die eigentliche weltweit bedeutsame Verschiebung ereignete sich im Folgejahr und beruhte auf dem sogenannten Mauerfall, der in jener Nacht vom 9. November 1989 begann und sich über ein Jahr hinzog – in Berlin ließ sich das hautnah erleben. Die dauerhaften Umwälzungen waren bemerkenswert: Es gab nicht nur ein wiedervereinigtes Deutschland, sondern Strukturveränderungen im einstigen Ostblock. Deren Folge bestand auch in Einladungen nach Moskau, Warschau, Budapest und Bukarest, die ich selbst erlebte, Einladungen, die uns alle auf eine friedliche Welt hoffen ließen – ganz im Geiste der Leibniz'schen Geschichtsphilosophie: Wir sind es, die dank der Vernunft im Blick auf die beste aller möglichen Welten eine friedliche Welt zu verwirklichen vermögen; und daraus erwächst uns die Verpflichtung, alles zu tun, diesen Weg gemeinsam voranzutreiben.

Das war der Geist, der die Teilnehmer des VI. Internationalen Leibniz-Kongresses 1994 beflügelte; dazu hat auch Herbert Breger beigetragen, der ihn (wie später den VIII. und IX. Kongress) auf seine zurückhaltende Weise exzellent organisierte.

Der nachfolgende VII. Kongress war zur 200-jährigen Wiederkehr der Gründung der Leibnizschen Berliner Societät für das Jahr 2000 und in Berlin vorgesehen; doch da die Berlin-Brandenburgische Akademie der Wissenschaften aus eben diesem Anlass eine große Zahl von Veranstaltungen plante, beschloss die Leibniz-Gesellschaft eine Verschiebung auf das Folgejahr. So kam es, dass der zweite Berliner Kongresstag, der 11. September 2001, all jene Hoffnungen auf eine friedfertige Welt in Frage stellte: Tausende von Menschen wurden mit den Twin-Towers in New York in einem erschütternden Terrorakt ausgelöscht: Eine für uns alle unbegreifliche unmenschliche Tat! Auch wenn über nähere Umstände noch nichts bekannt war, stand die Frage im Raum: Sollte der Kongress abgebrochen werden? Doch in einer kleinen internationalen Gruppe entwarfen wir eine Resolution, die uns als Leibnizianer zugleich Verpflichtung sein sollte. Sie wurde in je einer deutschen, englischen und französischen Fassung verlesen und von allen Kongressteilnehmern angenommen, ja, mit äußerstem Nachdruck unterstützt. Wegen der Zustimmung, die ihr in der Folgezeit von allen Seiten zuteilwurde, sei sie hier wiederholt:

> „Resolution des VII. Internationalen Leibniz-Kongresses
> Die Teilnehmer des VII. Internationalen Leibniz-Kongresses sind aus 32 Ländern von fünf Kontinenten in Berlin zusammengekommen, um das geistige Erbe des großen Universalgelehrten für die Gegenwart fruchtbar zu machen. Sie sind zutiefst betroffen von den erschütternden terroristischen Anschlägen in den USA. Im Geiste von Leibniz wenden wir uns gegen jede Gestalt des Terrorismus, wo immer in der Welt. Im Geiste von Leibniz mahnen wir, seine fundamentalen Prinzipien des menschlichen Zusammenlebens zu achten: Neminem laedere! Suum cuique tribuere! Honeste vivere! (Niemandem schaden! Jedem das Seine zugestehen! Ehrenhaft leben!) Im Geiste von Leibniz fordern wir auf zu Toleranz und Besonnenheit um des Friedens willen – unabhängig von allen Sprachen und Nationen, allen Überzeugungen und Religionen: Toleranz besteht in der Kraft und Stärke, andere Auffassungen zu respektieren – nicht aber Intoleranz und Terrorismus zu dulden."[1163]

[1163] Hans Poser: „Malum, Ratio und Technodizee. Schlußwort zum VII. Internationalen Leibniz-Kongreß", in: Ders. (Hrsg.): *VII. Internationaler Leibniz-Kongreß. Nihil sine ratione. Mensch, Natur und Technik im Wirken von G. W. Leibniz: Der Regierende Bürgermeister von Berlin,* Nachtragsband, Hannover 2002, S. 112.

Doch damit war es nicht getan – ein amerikanischer Kollege konnte keinerlei Verbindung zu seiner Familie in Manhattan nahe dem Terrorort aufnehmen, waren doch alle Telefone gekappt, alle Transatlantikflüge eingestellt: Die Sorge war allgegenwärtig. Es gelang dem Kongressteam, für ihn einen Platz in der ersten Maschine zu sichern, die wieder nach New York flog, zu seiner glücklichen Familie ...

Heute, drei Kongresse später, sind alle Hoffnungen auf Toleranz, Friedfertigkeit und den Willen, eine harmonische Weltordnung zu verwirklichen, zerstoben: In vielen Teilen der Welt begegnen wir Verletzungen des Völkerrechts, der Annexion anderer Länder, putschendem Militär, der Aufkündigung von Friedensvereinbarungen, pseudoreligiös bemänteltem Terrorismus. Hat die Leibniz'sche Hoffnung auf Vernunft getrogen, muss Resignation die Folge sein? Gerade der X. Leibniz-Kongress belegt mit seinen Teilnehmern aus allen Kontinenten und der fruchtbaren Aufnahme und Weiterführung Leibniz'schen Denkens ganz im Gegenteil, dass wir vor der Verpflichtung stehen, nicht nur die Hoffnung nicht aufzugeben, sondern gestaltend überall auf dieser Erden einzutreten für das Motto dieses Kongresses „ad felicitatem nostram alienamve", für unser Glück und das der anderen – also für jene weise Fürsorge, die allem Dasein zu gelten hat, von den schlummernden Monaden bis hin zu jenen, die als freie Individuen in ihrem Handeln dem Prinzip des Besten zu folgen aufgerufen sind: Über die drei römischen Rechtsprinzipien der Resolution hinaus gilt es, die justitia als caritas sapientis zur Leitschnur werden zu lassen.

Corrigenda

Band I

S. 35, 2. Abs., Z. 10: *Statt* Kon-tinuität *lies* Kontinuität; Z. 12: *Statt* Handlungsmaxime *lies* Handlungsmaxime

S. 385–390, Druck nicht vollständig, streichen; siehe S. 539–551

Band II

S. 224–234, im Kolumnentitel: *Statt* Corey W. Dick *lies* Corey W. Dyck

S. 6, Z. 5: *Statt* Wittgensteins' *lies* Wittgensteins

S. 165, Titel, Z. 1; S. 169, Z. 6; S. 170, Zwischentitel; S. 173, Z. 9, 12; S. 174, Zwischentitel; S. 179, 2. Abs. v. unten, Z. 4; S. 180, Z. 7, Z. 23; S. 181, Z. 6: *Statt* Wittgensteins' *lies* Wittgensteins

Band III

S. 52, 54, 56, 58, im Kolumnentitel: *Statt* Vivianne del Castilho *lies* Vivianne de Castilho

S. 53/54: Umbruchfehler auf S. 53, *lies*: Thus, he is allowed to claim that: […] Dieu …

S. 565, 567, 569, im Kolumnentitel: *Statt* reconnaisance *lies* reconnaissance

Band IV

S. 153, 155, 157, 159, 161, im Kolumnentitel: *Statt* Zu Xis *lies* Zhu Xis

Alphabetisches Verzeichnis der Autorinnen und Autoren
(Bd. I–V)

Volodymyr Oleksijovyč Abaschnik (Charkow)
„Leibniz als Verteidiger des Christentums". Die Charkower
Universitätstheologie (1804–1920) über Leibniz
....II | 557–569

Laurynas Adomaitis (Vilnius)
Leibniz's Scientific Instrumentalism Hypothesis
....I | 119–130

Joseph Anderson (Mount Pleasant, MI)
The Limits of Divine Goodness: A Good God Can't
Do Just Anything
....IV | 569–575

Raphaële Andrault (Lyon)
Passion, action et union de l'âme et du corps. Leibniz face
à ses lecteurs cartésiens
....I | 197–209

Peter Antes (Hannover)
Leibnizens Stellung zu den nichtchristlichen Religionen und
seine Lehre vom Heil
....II | 571–580

Maria Rosa Antognazza (London)
God, Creatures, and Neoplatonism in Leibniz
.... III | 351–364

Annette Antoine (Hannover)
Leibniz – Poet und literarischer Inspirator
....I | 493–506

Roberto R. Aramayo (Madrid)
Kant, lecteur et interprète de Leibniz: à propos de l'harmonie
préétablie, la téléologie, Dieu et le destin
....II | 15–25

CHLOE ARMSTRONG (Appleton, WI)
How Strong Is Divine Moral Necessity?
.... IV | 553–567

ALBERTO ARTOSI (Bologna)
Defeasibility and God's Existence
.... II | 357–370

KLAUS BADUR (Garbsen)
Design and Construction of Leibniz's Proposed *Machina Deciphratoria*
.... V | 361–375

ANDREAS BÄHR (Berlin)
„Tibi […] pro fausto nominis omine […] athanasian precor":
Athanasius Kircher, Leibniz und die Macht der Eigennamen
.... IV | 15–30

DIMITRI BAYUK (Moscow)
On Leibniz' Classification of Science
.... I | 131–141

ALESSANDRO BECCHI (Firenze)
Leibniz' Harlequin and the Theater of Organic Bodies
.... II | 401–416

SEBASTIAN BENDER (Houston, TX)
Interpreting Leibniz's Modal Language
.... I | 439–449

CRISTIANO BONNEAU (João Pessoa)
Leibniz entre Voltaire et Rousseau – un débat sur la conception
du monde et du mal
.... I | 313–323
The Relationship Between Love and Reason in Leibniz
.... II | 349–356

AUDREY BOROWSKI (London)
"Diversitas identitate compensata" – Leibniz's Art of Harmonic Variation
.... IV | 453–464

MARTHA BRANDT BOLTON (New Brunswick, NJ)
The Continuity of Species, Concepts of Species Determined by Nature,
and Concepts with Indeterminate Boundaries in *Nouveaux Essais*
.... V | 89–101

GREGORY BROWN (Houston, TX)
Did Clarke Really Disavow Action at a Distance in the
Correspondence with Leibniz?
.... III | 491–500
Leibniz on Motivation and Obligation
.... II | 371–383

WALTER BÜHLER (Berlin)
Rechnen mit musikalischen Intervallen – die harmonischen Gleichungen
aus dem Briefwechsel von Leibniz mit Henfling (LBr 390)
.... V | 273–289

LUIS CAMACHO (Costa Rica)
Leibniz's Perspectives on Truth
.... III | 97–109

ADELINO CARDOSO (Lisboa)
L'Europe comme espace de reconnaissance réciproque.
L'exemple de la citoyenneté littéraire
.... III | 563–569
The Viewpoint of Passivity in the Leibnizian *Monadology*
.... III | 111–117

ROBERTO CASALES-GARCÍA (Mexico City)
A Moral Approach to Leibniz's Perspectivism and His Notion of Justice
.... III | 119–129

MENG CHEN (Xuzhou)
Zhu Xis kommentierte *Vier Bücher*, Noëls *Sinensis Imperii libri classici
sex* und Wolffs Rede über die praktische Philosophie der Chinesen
.... IV | 151–161

DANIEL COLLETTE (Tampa, FL)
Leibniz's and Pascal's Account of Double Infinity
.... IV | 387–397

DANIEL J. COOK (Brooklyn, NY)
Leibniz: From Ecumenism to Globalization
.... II | 541–555

ANTONELLA CORRADINI (Milano)
Das Leibniz'sche Argument der Einheit des Bewusstseins in
der gegenwärtigen Philosophie des Geistes
.... II | 215–222

JOÃO CORTESE (Paris)
When Two Points Coincide, or Are at an Infinitely Small Distance: Some Aspects of the Relation Between the Works of Leibniz, Pascal (and Desargues)
.... IV | 165–178

MARIÁ RAMON CUBELLS (Tarragona)
Le rôle de la correspondance: Leibniz et les perspectives de
ses correspondants
.... III | 59–72

NAOUM DAHER (Besançon)
D'une Esthétique Analytique vers une Ethique Architectonique
au service des Fondements de la Physique
.... I | 57–71

VINCENZO DE RISI (Berlin)
Leibniz on the Continuity of Space
.... V | 179–191

JAIME JUAN DE SALAS ORTUETA (Madrid)
"Political Practice" in Leibniz and His Pamphlets in the
War of the Spanish Succession
.... III | 503–510

VALERIE DEBUICHE (Aix-en-Provence)
L'optimisme dans la pensée de Leibniz à la lumière de sa géométrie
.... IV | 521–536

VIVIANNE DE CASTILHO MOREIRA (Curitiba)
The Distinction Between Propositions of Essence and
Propositions of Existence and Leibniz's Perspectivism
.... III | 49–58

THIBAULT DE MEYER (Bruxelles)
Une conception synergique de l'action. L'action, la perception
et l'appétition dans la *Monadologie*
.... IV | 359–373

JAIME DERENNE (Bruxelles)
Sagesse et vertu aux sources de la science de la félicité chez Leibniz
.... I | 599–615

STEFANO DI BELLA (Milan)
Leibniz on Nature, Concept and Change
.... IV | 313–321
Time, Contradiction and Change in Leibniz: Some Reflections
.... IV | 263–267

CHUN-YU DONG (Beijing)
Leibniz's View on the Optimal World
.... IV | 435–439

MENGDAN DONG (Beijing)
On Leibniz's View of Life
.... II | 417–429

ARTHUR DONY (Liège)
Leibniz et J. S. Bach
.... V | 315–327

ANTONINO DRAGO (Naples)
Leibniz *Vindicatus*. His Central Role in the History of Western Philosophy
.... I | 73–87

FRANÇOIS DUCHESNEAU (Montréal)
Louis Bourguet et les machines de la nature selon Leibniz
.... I | 247–259

RONALD DURÁN ALLIMANT (Valparaíso)
Spontaneity, Body and Organism in Leibniz
.... II | 449–461

COREY W. DYCK (London)
Leibniz's Wolffian Psychology
.... II | 223–235

SHOHEI EDAMURA (Kanazawa)
Can We Unify Theories of the Origin of Finite Things in
Leibniz's *De Summa Rerum*?
.... I | 393–406

SUSANNE EDEL (Frankfurt a. M.)
Strafe zwischen Recht und Gerechtigkeit. Aspekte der
praktischen Philosophie von Leibniz
.... II | 277–294

JONATHAN C. W. EDWARDS (London)
Leibniz and Telicity
.... I | 175–193

EMESE EGYED (Budapest)
De la défense vers l'argument. Lecteurs protestants de
Leibniz au XVIIIe siècle en Europe Orientale
.... III | 585–600

GIORGIO ERLE (Verona)
Allgemeines Wohl und feste Frömmigkeit
.... I | 653–664

MIGUEL ESCRIBANO CABEZA (Granada)
Perspektivismus und Physiologie in Leibniz' Vorstellung des Organismus
.... III | 155–165

OSCAR M. ESQUISABEL (Buenos Aires)
Perspectivism, Expression, and Logic in Leibniz. A Foundational Essay
.... III | 73–87

RITA FANARI (San Gavino Monreale)
Le rapport Leibniz-Fontenelle : examen de quelques lettres inédites
.... IV | 89–100

CLAIRE FAUVERGUE (Montpellier)
Leibniz et la définition de l'idée de point de vue de Fontenelle à Naigeon
.... I | 299–311
La réception de l'hypothèse leibnizienne de l'harmonie
préétablie au siècle des Lumières
.... I | 407–419

MATTEO FAVARETTI CAMPOSAMPIERO (Venice)
Perfection as Harmony: Leibniz's 1715 Doctrine and
Wolff's Teleological Reformulation
.... IV | 465–477

OLGA FEDOROVA (Moscow)
On Leibniz' Classification of Science
.... I | 131–141

DAVID FORMAN (Las Vegas, NV)
The *Apokatastasis* Essays in Context: Leibniz and Thomas Burnet
on the Kingdom of Grace and the Stoic/Platonic Revolutions
.... IV | 125–137

HUGO FRAGUITO (Lisboa)
Efficient and Final Causes: Two Perspectives on Nature
.... III | 167–176

KLAUS FUCHS-KITTOWSKI (Berlin)
Zu Grundgedanken von Gottfried Wilhelm Leibniz aus der Sicht der
Informationsverarbeitung und Informationsentstehung
.... V | 217–234

MARIA GRISELDA GAIADA (Buenos Aires)
Le *bivium* de Cudworth: l' « intellectualisme » de Leibniz vs.
le « volontarisme » de Suárez. Deux supposita dans l'âme raisonnable?
.... III | 231–248

GÁBOR GÁNGÓ (Budapest)
Der junge Leibniz als Osteuropa-Experte
.... III | 511–523

ÁNGEL GARRIDO (Madrid)
Leibniz and Many-Valued Logics
.... V | 609–622

MATTIA GERETTO (Venezia)
"I Think That in the Universe Nothing Is Truer Than Happiness,
and Nothing Happier or Sweeter Than Truth". On the Relationships
between Happiness, Truth and Generosity in Leibniz's Philosophy
.... I | 617–632

EDWARD W. GLOWIENKA (Helena, MT)
God as Monarch: On the Relationship between Natural Theology
and Natural Law
.... III | 377–387

URSULA GOLDENBAUM (Atlanta, GA)
Jacob Hermann and Leibniz's *Theodicy*
.... III | 389–399

JÜRGEN GOTTSCHALK (Hamburg)
Die Holzwirtschaft im hannoverschen Welfenterritorium –
Leibniz' blinder Fleck?!
.... V | 393–411
Leibniz als Systemdenker und Erfinder regeltechnischer Konstruktionen
.... V | 413–426

NINA GROMYKO (Moskau)
Das Problem des Wissens und der Wissenschaft in der Philosophie
von Leibniz und Fichte
.... II | 27–42

TAHAR BEN GUIZA (Tunis)
Leibniz et Louis XIV : *le Consilium Aegyptiacum*
.... I | 237–246

JING GUO (Beijing)
The Way to the Other: A Comparison Between Leibniz and Levinas
.... II | 203–213

PRZEMYSŁAW GUT (Lublin)
The Problem of Human Freedom in Leibniz's Philosophy
.... I | 589–598

RICARDO GUTIÉRREZ AGUILAR (Madrid)
Smoke and Mirrors: Reflection, Mechanism and Imitation in Leibniz
.... III | 571–582

HOLGER GUTSCHMIDT (Göttingen)
Notio Dei. Descartes' „Antwort" auf Leibniz' Kritik am
ontologischen Beweis
.... II | 609–617
Perspektivismus im Briefwechsel von Leibniz und Antoine Arnauld:
Projekt eines neuen Kommentars
.... III | 41–48

OLEG GUZEYEV (Donetsk)
Leibniz' Binary Medallion and the Key Coin
.... IV | 245–259

KATHARINA HABERMANN (Göttingen)
Die Kalenderreform von 1700 in persönlichen Korrespondenzen
und publizistischer Debatte
.... V | 535–547

KARL HAHN (Münster)
Die Freiheitsproblematik bei Leibniz und Fichte
.... IV | 45–59

TAKUYA HAYASHI (Paris)
Le statut ontologique des possibles chez Leibniz
.... IV | 415–425

HARTMUT HECHT (Berlin)
Emilie du Châtelets *Institutions physiques*, erklärt durch den
Discours sur le bonheur
....II | 507–521

ROBERT HEINDL (Gotha)
Antiquarianismus in einer Konstellation um Leibniz, Cuper und
La Croze zwischen 1708/09 – Das Beispiel Persepolis
.... V | 491–508

LAURA E. HERRERA CASTILLO (Hannover/Granada)
Ausdruck, Funktion, Symbol. G. W. Leibniz' Expressionsbegriff
und seine Rezeption bei E. Cassirer
.... III | 261–270

CELI HIRATA (São Paulo):
Universal Jurisprudence: Leibniz Against the Hobbesian Concept of Justice
....II | 295–304

HYUN HÖCHSMANN (Jersey City, NJ)
Leibniz and Confucius on the Common Good
....II | 385–398

WOLFGANG HOFKIRCHNER (Wien)
Relationality in Social Systems
.... V | 235–243

MAXIMILIAN HOLDT (Kiel)
Gott und Physik – Zur Bedeutung des Théodicée-Kapitels in
Émilie du Châtelets *Institutions de physique*
....II | 523–538

CHARLES JOSHUA HORN (Stevens Point, WI)
Leibniz and Impossible Ideas in the Divine Intellect
.... IV | 539–551

ALEKSANDRA HOROWSKA (Wrocław):
The Basic Assumptions and Characteristics of Jurisprudence
in Leibniz's *Nova Methodus Discendae Docendaeque Jurisprudentiae*
.... I | 551–561

HIROYUKI INAOKA (Kobe)
What Constitutes Space? The Development of Leibniz's Theory
of Constituting Space
.... III | 427–439

ALFONDO IOMMI ECHEVERRÍA (Viña del Mar)
Leibniz et l'origine des Nombres
.... IV | 179–182

GODOFREDO IOMMI AMUNATEGUI (Curauma Valparaíso)
Leibniz et l'origine des Nombres
.... IV | 179–182

DOUGLAS M. JESSEPH (Tampa, FL)
The Principle of Continuity: Origins, Applications, and Limitations
.... V | 193–205

JULIA JORATI (Columbus, OH)
Why Monads Need Appetites
.... V | 121–129

LARRY M. JORGENSEN (Saratoga Springs, NY)
Sensation, Reason, and Instinct in the *Nouveaux Essais*
.... V | 15–27

KLAUS ERICH KAEHLER (Köln)
Monade und gesellschaftliche Totalität in der *Ästhetischen Theorie*
Theodor W. Adornos
.... I | 361–373

TAE-YEOUN KEUM (Boston, MA)
An Enlightenment Fable: Leibniz and the Boundaries of Reason
.... II | 335–348

STEFAN KIRSCHNER (Hamburg)
„Der wind selbst fast allezeit drehn, wenn die hauptflugel nicht
im winde stehn" – Der „Leibniz-Regler", ein Mechanismus zur
automatischen Ausrichtung von Windmühlenflügeln
.... V | 427–447

SACHA ZILBER KONTIC (São Paulo)
Vision en Dieu, Vision par Dieu: Leibniz and Malebranche's
Theory of Ideas
.... II | 619–626

SEBASTIAN KÜHN (Hannover)
Streiten zu dritt. Über agonale Praktiken des Korrespondierens mit
und ohne Leibniz
.... V | 509–521

MARK KULSTAD (Houston, TX)
The Soul of the World in the Leibniz-Clarke Correspondence
.... III | 455–470

WOLFGANG KÜNNE (Hamburg)
Bolzano und Leibniz. Ein Vergleich ihrer Monadologien
.... IV | 61–79

TESSA MOURA LACERDA (São Paulo)
La place d'autrui: bonheur et amour chez Leibniz
.... I | 633–642

MOGENS LÆRKE (Lyon)
The End of Melancholy. Deleuze and Benjamin on Leibniz
and the Baroque
.... I | 385–390
Materialism and the Political Invention of Religion. Leibniz,
Hobbes and the Erudite Libertines
.... III | 415–426

ARNAUD LALANNE (Pessac)
La correspondance de Leibniz avec le milieu janséniste français
.... I | 261–272

RICHARD LAMBORN (St. Petersburg, FL)
The Use and Abuse of Gottfried Wilhelm Leibniz in *Accord Between Different Laws Which At First Seemed Incompatible*
.... II | 117–127

ANTONELLA LANG-BALESTRA (Zürich)
Perspektivismus im Briefwechsel von Leibniz und Antoine Arnauld: Projekt eines neuen Kommentars
.... III | 41–48

CHRISTIAN LEDUC (Montréal)
Maupertuis entre moindre action et force vive
.... I | 325–337

WOLFGANG LENZEN (Osnabrück)
Leibniz's Innovations in the Theory of the Syllogism
.... V | 579–594

VINCENT LEROUX (Paris)
Sur les jeux chez Leibniz
.... IV | 235–244

ALEXANDRA LEWENDOSKI (Berlin):
Le ‹ Sentire harmoniam › dans les lettres et écrits de Leibniz lors de son séjour à Paris
.... I | 273–283

TIANHUI LI (Beijing)
Remarks on Leibniz's Philosophy of Mind
.... IV | 375–386

WILFRIED LIEẞMANN (Göttingen)
Die Holzwirtschaft im hannoverschen Welfenterritorium – Leibniz' blinder Fleck?!
.... V | 393–411

NIKOLAUS LINDER (Göttingen)
Legal Science, Codification and Constituent Imagination
According to G. W. Leibniz
.... I | 563–571

JINGYUAN LIU (Baton Rouge, LA)
On the Organic Cosmology of Leibniz and Whitehead
.... II | 151–164

VLADIMIR LOBOVIKOV (Yekaterinburg)
Leibniz's Motto "Calculemus!" and its Significance for Developing
the Natural Law Theory as a Consistent System of Universal Values
Uniting All Possible Rational Persons
.... I | 541–550

PAUL LODGE (Oxford, UK)
'Whether any Material Being Thinks, or No': Leibniz's Critique
of Locke on Superaddition
.... V | 103–117

ANSGAR LYSSY (Munich)
'Theoria cum Praxi' Revisited – Leibniz on 'Dangerous' Philosophers
.... IV | 113–124

FERDINANDO LUIGI MARCOLUNGO (Verona)
Christian Wolff et l'idéal leibnizien d'une perfectibilité sans limites
.... II | 129–141

LUCIO MARE (Tampa, FL)
Leibniz' More Fundamental Ontology: From Overshadowed
Individuals to Metaphysical Atoms
.... IV | 269–283

EDGAR MARQUES (Rio de Janeiro)
Inkompossibilität und Perspektivismus bei Leibniz
.... III | 89–96

ALFREDO GERARDO MARTÍNEZ OJEDA (Naucalpan de Juárez)
The Independence of the Possibles Within the Mind of God
.... IV I 427–433

TSUYOSHI MATSUDA (Kobe)
Actual Time in Later Leibniz
.... III I 441–454
The Nature and Norms of Economy from the Leibnizian Point of View
.... I I 421–435

JEFFREY K. MCDONOUGH (Cambridge, MA)
Leibniz's Formal Theory of Contingency Extended
.... I I 451–466

CHRISTOPH-ERIC MECKE (Hannover)
Leibniz und seine Instrumentalisierung durch Juristen in der NS-Zeit
.... II I 305–318

STEPHAN MEDER (Hannover)
Leibniz' politische Philosophie aus postnationaler Perspektive:
Sein Souveränitätsverständnis zwischen neuzeitlicher Staatlichkeit
und pluraler Reichsidee
....II I 319–334

STEPHAN MEIER (Hannover)
Leibniz' Harmonien
.... V I 291–300

MARTA DE MENDONÇA (Lisboa)
Leibniz et le miracle de la liberté
.... III I 29–40

JORGE ALBERTO MOLINA (Santa Cruz do Sul)
Leibniz et la topique
.... III I 287–297

LÁSZLÓ MOLNÁR (Budapest)
Leibniz-Rezeption in Ungarn in der ersten Hälfte des XIX. Jahrhunderts.
Michael Petőcz und seine Erneuerung der „Monadologie"
.... III | 613–625

ANTONIO MORETTO (Verona)
Knutzens Bemerkungen über die „Leibnitianische Dyadica"
....II | 59–72

VITTORIO MORFINO (Milano)
Combinaison ou conjonction : Althusser entre Leibniz et Spinoza
....I | 375–384

SAMUEL MURRAY (Notre Dame, IN)
A Difficulty That Must Be Solved: Leibniz's Moral Psychology
....I | 643–652

PETER MYRDAL (Turku)
Appetite as Activity
.... V | 143–153

OHAD NACHTOMY (Ramat Gan):
"The Organism of Animals is a Mechanism That Presupposes
Divine Preformation" (Fifth Letter to Clarke)
.... III | 471–479

FRITZ NAGEL (Basel)
„Ingeniorum Phoenix" – Leibniz' wissenschaftshistorische Verortung
in den akademischen Reden von Jakob Hermann (1678–1733)
....IV | 209–220

GÜNTHER NEUMANN (München)
Martin Heideggers Gesamtinterpretation der Monadologie
....II | 183–202

HARDY NEUMANN (Valparaíso)
Leibniz' ontologischer Perspektivismus. Un point de vue
.... III | 249–260

JUAN A. NICOLÁS (Granada)
Der Leibniz'sche Weg zur Geschichtlichkeit der Vernunft
.... III | 15–28

ADRIAN NITA (Bucharest)
Leibniz's Quasi-Monism
.... IV | 441–452

PETER NITSCHKE (Vechta)
Die (föderale) Ordnungsvision von Leibniz für Europa
.... III | 541–549
Utopisches Denken bei Leibniz – ein Programm des Unendlichen
.... II | 265–276

JAMES G. O'HARA (Hannover/Hameln)
"ova vel semina ... foecundare". Sexual Reproduction in
Leibniz's Scientific Correspondence
.... II | 431–448

JOSEP OLESTI VILA (Gérone)
Vera politica et politique vulgaire chez Leibniz. Une affaire
de perspective?
.... III | 141–153

LUCIA OLIVERI (Münster)
Leibniz on the Cognitive Conditions for the Origins of Natural Languages
.... I | 467–478
Leibniz on the Role of Innate Ideas in Human Cognition
.... V | 37–48

OSVALDO OTTAVIANI (Pisa)
Leibniz's Argument against a Plurality of Worlds
.... IV | 399–413

JESÚS PADILLA GÁLVEZ (Toledo)
Zur Modaltheorie von Leibniz. Anmerkungen über
kontrafaktische Bedingungssätze
.... V | 629–642

MIGUEL PALOMO (Sevilla)
Paths of Reason. Descartes Between Leibniz and Huygens
.... III | 215–230

GIRIDHARI LAL PANDIT (Delhi)
Scenarios of Global Interconnectedness: Turning Leibniz's
Research Programme Around
.... I | 159–174

BOGUSŁAW PAŹ (Breslau)
Cogito und Intentionalität. Leibniz' Umdeutung des Grundprinzips
von Descartes
.... IV | 101–111

ARNAUD PELLETIER (Bruxelles)
Metaphysics, Experience, and Demonstration: the *a priori* and
a posteriori Ways of the *Monadology*
.... IV | 489–503

CONSTANZE PERES (Dresden)
A. G. Baumgartens *Ästhetik – Aesthetica* (2016): Eine Edition
im Horizont der Philosophie von Leibniz
....II | 99–115

RICARDO PEREZ MARTINEZ (México D. F.)
La perspective et le point de vue : une révision critique de la lecture
heideggerienne sur la représentation chez Leibniz
.... III | 299–307

ULYSSES PINHEIRO (Rio de Janeiro)
Leibniz on the Concepts of Archive, Memory and Sovereignty
.... III | 309–321

MAREK PIWOWARCZYK (Lublin)
A Leibnizian Inspiration: The Nomological Model of the
Subject-Properties Structure
.... IV | 301–311

DAVIDE POGGI (Vérone)
Le dialogue épistolaire entre Leibniz et Pierre Coste : la discussion
sur la liberté à l'occasion des corrections à la traduction française
de l'*Essai* de Locke
....I | 285–297

ALESSANDRO POLI (Macerata)
"Quod unicuique sit optimum, cunctis vero commune bonum".
A Physical Proof of Leibniz's Platonic Notion of Common Good
....I | 509–524

CARLOS PORTALES (Edinburgh)
Variety and Simplicity in Leibniz's Aesthetics
.... V | 257–272

SIEGMUND PROBST (Hannover)
Leibniz und Roberval
.... IV | 183–189

STEPHEN PURYEAR (Raleigh, NC)
Evil as Privation and Leibniz's Rejection of Empty Space
.... III | 481–489
Thought, Color, and Intelligibility in the *New Essays*
.... V | 49–57
Leibniz on the Nature of Phenomena
.... V | 169–177

ARMANDO ISAAC QUEZADA MEDINA (Guanajuato)
Substances and Monads. Leibniz and Husserl
.... III | 271–279

DAVID RABOUIN (Paris)
A Fresh Look at Leibniz' *Mathesis Universalis*
....IV | 505–519

FEDERICO RAFFO QUINTANA (Buenos Aires)
The Infinite in Leibniz's Parisian Writings, Amongst Mathematics
and Metaphysics
.... III | 201–213

NICOLAE RÂMBU (Jassy)
Schopenhauers Kritik an Leibniz
....II | 143–150

JÁNOS RATHMANN (Budapest)
Zur Rezeption der Leibniz'schen Physik und Philosophie in der
Donaumonarchie, dann in Österreich und Ungarn
.... III | 601–611

NICHOLAS RESCHER (Pittsburgh, PA)
Design and Construction of Leibniz's Proposed *Machina Deciphratoria*
.... V | 361–375

ANNE-LISE REY (Lille)
Les usages de principe de raison suffisante dans les
Institutions de Physique
.... I | 339–345

ULRICH RICHTER (Münster)
Der gesetzte Gott und das setzende Individuum als Ich.
G. W. Leibniz' Prinzip des zureichenden Grundes im Horizont
des Denkens Nikolaus von Kues', G. W. F. Hegels und I. Kants
....II | 641–654

RICARDO RODRÍGUEZ HURTADO (Granada)
From 1670 to 1680. The Concept of Perspective in Leibniz's Thought
.... III | 323–334

STASCHA ROHMER (Medellín)
Leibniz' Idee des Rechts. Ein europäisches Konzept
.... III | 525–532

MARKKU ROINILA (Helsinki)
The Battle of the Endeavors: Dynamics of the Mind and Deliberation
in *New Essays on Human Understanding*, Book II, XX–XXI
.... V | 73–87

CONCHA ROLDÁN (Madrid)
Leibniz und die Idee Europas
.... III | 551–562

ARPITA ROY (Göttingen)
Particle Physics and Anthropology in Leibniz's Problem of Orientation
.... I | 105–117

MARLEEN ROZEMOND (Toronto)
Teleology and Activity in Leibniz and Cudworth
.... V | 155–167

LEONARDO RUIZ GÓMEZ (México)
Spatial Expression: Leibniz's Perspectivism and the
Representation of Nature
.... III | 189–200

DONALD RUTHERFORD (San Diego, CA)
Leibniz and the "Religion of Reason"
.... III | 365–376

MANUEL SANCHEZ RODRIGUEZ (Granada)
Leibniz' Perspektivismus in den *Nouveaux Essais*
.... III | 335–347

MARCO SANTI (Berlin)
On Leibniz' Reappraisal of Material Atomism
.... I | 89–103

BRIGITTE SAOUMA (Montrouge)
Pierre Bayle critique de Lactance et de Basile de Césarée, dans
sa réfutation du manichéisme
.... II | 627–640

STEFANO SARACINO (Wien)
Wissen über Griechentum und Ostorthodoxie in Wilhelm Ernst
Tentzels *Monatlichen Unterredungen* (1689–1698)
.... IV | 31–43

SANDRA SCHAUB (Hannover)
Zeichen! – Von Leibniz' „characteristica universalis" zu Wittgensteins
Tractatus logico-philosophicus und den *Philosophischen
Untersuchungen*
....II | 165–181

STEPHAN SCHMID (Hamburg)
The Intrinsic Directedness of Leibnizian Forces
.... V | 131–141

CLEMENS SCHWAIGER (München)
Der Streit zwischen Michael Gottlieb Hansch und Christian Wolff
um die Aneignung des Leibniz'schen Erbes
....II | 87–97

CLAIRE SCHWARTZ (Nanterre)
Leibniz et le « groupe malebranchiste » : la réception du calcul
Infinitésimal
....I | 223–236

SERGIY SECUNDANT (Odessa)
Zum Begriff der praktischen Logik und der reinen Vernunft bei Leibniz
....II | 43–58

PHILIPPE SÉGUIN (Nancy)
Das höchste wissenschaftliche Gut: die Einheit. Von A. Boeckh zu
D. Hilbert, mit Leibniz' Hilfe
....I | 143–158

ADRIANNA SENCZYSZYN (Wrocław)
Epistemological Basics of Human Identity in G. W. Leibniz's
New Essays on Human Understanding
.... IV | 479–486

MICHEL SERFATI (Paris)
Leibniz contre Descartes : l'invention de la transcendance
mathématique. Les aventures d'une exceptionnelle création
....I | 211–222

IDAN SHIMONY (Tel Aviv)
Leibniz, the Young Kant, and Boscovich on the Relationality of Space
....II | 73–85
Locke and Leibniz on Freedom and Necessity
....I | 573–588

YEKUTIEL SHOHAM (Tel Aviv)
Locke and Leibniz on Freedom and Necessity
....I | 573–588

NORMAN SIEROKA (Zürich)
Retrospective Analogies: Contemporary Physics as a Means for
Understanding Leibniz's Metaphysics
....IV | 285–299

TOMÁŠ SIGMUND (Prague)
Dual Character of Information – On the Relationship between
Individual and General Aspect of Reality
.... V | 245–253

CAMILO SILVA (Aix-en-Provence)
Y a-t-il vraiment une théorie causale du temps chez Leibniz ?
....IV | 323–334

AMELIA-MARIA ȘOOȘ (Budapest)
The Conception of Human Nature by Leibniz
.... III | 627–636

VLADIMIR SOTIROV (Sofia)
Leibniz's 'Calculemus!': an Algebraic Scope
.... V | 623–628

ZEYNEP SOYSAL (Cambridge, MA)
Leibniz's Formal Theory of Contingency Extended
....I | 451–466

ALEXANDRU ȘTEFĂNESCU (Bucharest)
From Monads to Men: Leibniz and "Social Metaphysics"
....IV | 349–358

ERWIN STEIN (Hannover)
Design and Construction of Leibniz's Proposed *Machina Deciphratoria*
.... V | 361–375

LLOYD STRICKLAND (Manchester)
How Sincere was Leibniz's Religious Justification for War in the
Justa Dissertatio?
.... III | 401–412

REGINA STUBER (Hannover)
Die Kontakte zwischen Leibniz und Urbich: ein Wechselspiel zwischen
Diplomatie und wissenschaftlichen Projektplänen
.... IV | 139–150

DIETER SUISKY (Berlin)
Du Châtelet's Interpretation of Leibniz's Concepts of Space and Time
....II | 493–505

WEI SUN (Hannover)
Leibniz's Organism and the Contemporary Bioethics
....II | 463–478

WIESŁAW SZTUMSKI (Katowice)
Die Theorie des Gemeinwohls von Leibniz und das Konzept der
nachhaltigen Entwicklung (zwei Utopien)
.... I | 665–677

JENS THIEL (Münster/Berlin):
Versöhnung als „Vater aller Dinge". Benno Erdmann und das Leibniz-
Jubiläum 1916 an der Preußischen Akademie der Wissenschaften
....II | 237–249

HERVE TOUBOUL (Besançon)
Leibniz dans Marx : la force et l'individu
.... I | 349–360

JOSEPH TRULLINGER (Washington, DC)
A Short History of Divine Blessedness: From Leibniz to Kant
.... IV | 577–592

ACHIM TRUNK (Hannover)
Sechs Systeme: Leibniz und seine *signa ambigua*
.... IV | 191–207

WALTER TYDECKS (Bensheim)
Die kleinen Perzeptionen bei Leibniz und die Kontinuum-Hypothese
nach Gödel – Entwurf für eine dynamische Logik nach Leibniz
und Gödel
.... IV | 221–233

GIOVANNA VARANI (Porto)
Menschliches Unglück und Technik. Leibniz' Perspektiven im
Schatten der frühmodernen Blütezeit der Technik
.... V | 331–347

EVELYN VARGAS (La Plata)
Sophie's Choice. Leibniz and Toland on 'l'empire de la raison'
.... IV | 81–88
Defeasible Reasoning in the *Nouveaux Essais*
.... V | 29–36

CELSO VARGAS ELIZONDO (Granada)
Is It Possible to Understand (Represent) Leibniz's Physics
from Perspectivism?
.... III | 177–187

LUIS A. VELASCO GUZMÁN (Mexico D. F.)
On Possible Justice. Thoughts on Leibniz's *Portrait d'un Prince*
.... III | 131–139

EDITH VELÁZQUEZ HERNÁNDEZ (Guanajuato)
Mode and Monad: The Discussion on Individuals in Leibniz's and
Spinoza's Metaphysics
.... III | 281–286

BARBARA VENTAROLA (Berlin)
Polyperspektivismus und die Verteilung der Handlungsmacht.
Leibniz' Beitrag zur Ausbildung moderner Gesellschaftstheorien
....I | 525–539

PEDRO A. VIÑUELA (Logroño)
Perception, Presumption and Perspectivism in Leibniz
....IV | 335–348

LORENZO VITALE (Verona)
Music in Leibniz's Metaphysics
.... V | 301–313

HERIBERT VOLLMER (Hannover)
Leibniz and the Development of Modal Logic in the 20th Century
.... V | 595–608

CHARLOTTE WAHL (Hannover)
„ad harmoniam quae voluntaria et deliberata habeatur". Zu Leibniz'
Bemühungen um eine interkonfessionelle Kalenderreform
.... V | 549–561

STEPHAN WALDHOFF (Potsdam)
Die Historie im Kosmos des Wissens
....II | 253–264

THOMAS WALLNIG (Wien)
Amicus, patronus und TEI. Überlegungen zum Modellieren von
Beziehungen anhand von Grußformeln in Gelehrtenbriefen
.... V | 523–533

ARIANE WALSDORF (Hannover)
Von der Idee der ‚Lebendigen Rechenbank' zur Konstruktion der
Staffelwalze – Die erste Entwicklungsphase der Leibniz-
Rechenmaschine
.... V | 377–392

QI WANG (Beijing)
Rationalism in Leibniz's Linguistic Philosophy
....I | 479–491

JULIA WECKEND (Oxford, UK)
Leibniz and the Limits of Certainty in the Human Sciences
.... V | 59–72

FRIEDRICH-WILHELM WELLMER (Hannover)
Die Holzwirtschaft im hannoverschen Welfenterritorium –
Leibniz' blinder Fleck?!
.... V | 393–411

RITA WIDMAIER (Essen)
Leibniz' natürliche Theologie und eine „gewisse" *Philosophia perennis*
....II | 581–596

ULRICH FRITZ WODARZIK (Lampertheim)
Zur trinitarischen Sache Gottes – *Felicitas* zwischen Einheit und Vielheit
....II | 597–608

PIEDAD YUSTE (Madrid)
Leibniz and Many-Valued Logics
.... V | 609–622

CORNELIUS ZEHETNER (Wien)
Zukunft nach Leibniz
....I | 679–691

BAICHUN ZHANG (Beijing)
Analysis and Annotation of Leibniz's Questions and Grimaldi's Answers
.... V | 449–487

JINGRU ZHANG (Beijing)
The Essence and Characteristics of Leibniz's Project for
Universal Characters
.... V | 565–577

TAO ZHANG (Beijing)
Some Remarks on Leibniz's Thoughts on Technology
.... V | 349–359

XIUHUA ZHANG (Beijing)
On the Organic Cosmology of Leibniz and Whitehead
....II | 151–164

RAINER E. ZIMMERMANN (Munich/Cambridge)
Emergence of Organization. On the Co-Evolution of System and Structure
.... V | 209–216

JUDITH P. ZINSSER (Oxford, OH)
Emilie du Châtelet: Past, Present and Future
....II | 481–491

MAURO ZONTA (Roma)
Leibniziana Hebraica. Texts about Leibniz and His Thought in Hebrew
.... III | 533–540